The
Bournonville Tradition

Volume II

August Bournonville.
Miniature in pastels on ivory, painted by N. Arnold (mid-1870s). Private collection.

The
Bournonville Tradition

The first fifty years, 1829–1879

Volume II

*An annotated bibliography of the choreography and the music,
the chronology, the performing history, and the sources*

Compiled and annotated by

Knud Arne Jürgensen

DANCE BOOKS
CECIL COURT LONDON

The author and publishers wish to express their gratitude to
the CARLSBERG FOUNDATION for its contributions towards the research and publication costs
of this book, and to the ROYAL LIBRARY in Copenhagen for housing the project.

Published in 1997 by Dance Books Ltd
15 Cecil Court, London WC2N 4EZ

Vol. II:
ISBN 1 85273 056 0

Vols I & II:
ISBN 1 85273 075 7

A CIP catalogue record for this book is available from the British Library

Printed and bound in Great Britain by
The Bath Press, Avon, UK

Contents

Preface   *page* vii

Introduction   1

The Works (1821–1879)   5

Additional Sources   431

Select Bibliography   439

List of Names   440

Index of Works   451

Preface

The work of the bibliographer can be compared with that of a cartographer. Only when piecing the myriad isolated 'topographical' items of information together does a general 'map' emerge which can confidently be claimed to reflect the true shape and contents of the subject under attention. In the case of the ballet bibliographer this 'cartographic' approach is even more necessary, since we are dealing with what is perhaps the most ephemeral of all the theatrical art forms.

Consideration of the repertory of nineteenth-century ballet and its scores is essential to our understanding of European theatrical culture of the period. As with all other forms of art, not every ballet is a masterpiece. There are, however, many forgotten works that merit revival. Greater attention to the heritage of the last century will, therefore, do much to balance and focus our perspective on the choreographers, the composers, the artists and the social context that defined European ballet in the last century.

At present the bibliography of nineteenth-century choreography and ballet music is, to put it politely, inadequate. Many of the most important collections in this field are either uncatalogued or listed in inventories that are accessible only at the premises where the collection is preserved, and nearly always include only a minimal level of description, if not outright erroneous attributions. Most major dance encyclopaedias and ballet monographs focus mainly on the history of individual dancers and choreographers, while the standard music encyclopaedias are (with a few shining exceptions) sparse in their presentation of the actual source material available to document productions other than the twenty or so most popular ballets of last century.

One of the main reasons for the rather poor state of the ballet bibliography is that only a minimal fraction of the music scores for nineteenth-century ballet have as yet been published, although innumerable adapted piano scores of individual dances and minor divertissements were published while they were still being performed. These often highly abridged piano scores are, however, in general so different from the original musical contents that

they should be ranked only as secondary sources and regarded as of little more than archival interest.

The same can be said about the innumerable printed ballet scenarios of the past. Only rarely can the dramatic action contained in these scenarios be said to reflect fully what actually took place on the stage. These published scenarios, which were aimed at introducing the ballets' dramatic action, were mainly written in rather free and highly poetic style, or were intended simply as a token of memory and souvenir of a special performance for the audience.

In the last two decades or so an interest in historical knowledge about authenticity in nineteenth-century ballet has reached a wide public. There is, however, as always a danger that new 'authentic' dogmas of style and interpretation will come to replace the anachronistic dogmas of the late romantic ballet tradition. The search for historical authenticity should, therefore, never be regarded as a single hard and fast answer when approaching a work of art from the past, but as a means of obtaining the highest number of possibilities from which to make valid analytical observations and performing decisions.

In the case of the great nineteenth-century Danish choreographer, August Bournonville (1805–1879), this renewed and historically oriented approach has never been more prominent than today. A native Dane (although his father was French and his mother Swedish), Bournonville created numerous ballets during the Romantic period of the mid-nineteenth century. Almost a dozen of these have survived – rather more than the handful of Petipa ballets and divertissements today treasured by the Russians.

Since Bournonville's time the Danes have consolidated a continuous performance tradition of this repertory, mainly for domestic consumption, but in recent years an increasingly integrated part of the international standard ballet repertory. Moreover, during the last decades, the international ballet world has witnessed a large number of new productions of the old Danish ballet-master's works, some of which have been very faithful to the traditions of the Royal Danish Ballet, while others have been subject to thorough revisions. The range of opinion as to how the Bournonville ballets ought to be produced and staged today and in the future is thus broader than ever.

Through Bournonville's ballets, Danish ballet has been able to enrich the European and international dance world with a living ballet-historical cultural heritage which, in significance and scale, is remarkable in relation to the size of his native country.

The spread and 'internationalisation' of Bournonville's life work during the last forty years has focused mainly on the traditional handed-down repertory of twelve ballets and shorter divertissements which have survived more than 150 years, thanks to the Royal Danish Ballet's established performance tradition and loyalty to its creator. However, an extensive, and partially unexplored bulk of archival material also survives, and could be just as valuable as the surviving ballets in shedding light on important aspects of Bournonville's artistry. These sources deserve thorough analysis, not just because they provide the possibility of increasing our knowledge of Bournonville's choreography, but also because, by these means, a more balanced picture of Bournonville's creativity and the artistic diversity of his *œuvre* can be attained.

To achieve this I have chosen, with this second volume of *The Bournonville Tradition* (which accompanies the biographical first volume), to explore and to catalogue the extensive part of the Bournonville legacy which describes the choreographic and musical contents of his complete works: his full-length ballets, minor dances and divertissements, stagings of operas and plays, his projected ballets, and his other occasional works. Moreover, an analysis of the many musical borrowings and the later changes made in the scores during Bournonville's lifetime is included, together with excerpts from his diary (here given in their original language, serving primarily as source documentation). Bournonville's own comments on his works are thus reproduced here in their original languages (Danish and/or French) primarily because they have never been published before. The highly repetitive character of these notes (which mostly list and describe the run of daily rehearsals, etc.) can be understood relatively easily by readers not familiar with the Danish language. My aim in reproducing Bournonville's diary notes in their original versions is, therefore, mainly to let the choreographer speak to us directly, just as he did to himself while actually creating and staging his works.

Finally, a summary introduction to each work dealing with its creation and performing history in Bournonville's lifetime is added, together with a complete list of the original choreographic, musical, and other contemporary sources for each work that was created by him or under his personal supervision.

Bournonville himself included a list of his works in his published memoirs *My Theatre Life* (1878). It was complemented almost a century later by the Danish music antiquarian, Dan Fog, who in 1961 devoted a section specifically to Bournonville's works and the printed musical sources for them in his chronological catalogue of the ballets performed at Copenhagen's Royal Theatre between 1760 and 1958. Later, Patricia McAndrew and Allan Fridericia drew up two separate expanded lists of Bournonville's works, while in the most recent *International Dictionary of Ballet* (1993) Erik Aschengreen includes a similar compilation (*see* Select Bibliography).

Common to all of these contributions, however, is that none of them makes adequate reference to the primary sources, nor do they attempt to establish the exact chronology of the works, in particular Bournonville's stagings of operas and plays. From his unpublished handwritten lists of his works (*see* Additional Sources) and the original choreographic and musical sources, it is clear that Bournonville not only choreographed far more works than was initially thought, or were included by himself in his memoirs. Thus, for the many private theatres and public amusement parks that sprang up in the 1840s, with a repertory of operettas, vaudevilles, and comedies, he prepared a great number of individual dances, tableaux, and divertissements, although his name rarely mentioned on the posters.

The exact chronology and contents of these dances and his mises-en-scène for operas and plays are essential for obtaining a correct understanding of his artistic development and cumulative experience in his own creative field. An exact chronology of Bournonville's works thus reveals what occupied him professionally while he was creating some of his major ballets or stagings of operas and plays.

Furthermore, the chronology and the exact dating of his holographs and the composer's autographed manuscript musical sources help us to establish the genesis of each work and its later revisions, in this way giving scope for a study of how Bournonville worked when revising his own works.

Finally, a catalogue of Bournonville's complete

works in the form of an annotated bibliography of the choreography and the music, which gathers in one volume the original sources collected from several countries, could serve as an example and model for the necessary groundwork in preparing a useful bibliography of nineteenth-century ballet. It may also exemplify some of the key factors that characterise the difficulties of documenting and describing the written and iconographical resources. A bibliography of the art of dance must thus always be regarded not as representing the actual works, but rather as a key and supplement to them.

As is the case with all such publications, it has been necessary to take pragmatic decisions about the details of the entries and the extent of the supporting material. For the manuscripts themselves, basic descriptions only are given (such as pagination, paper size, writing material, etc.), but always with cross-references to other relevant manuscript sources, and with the dates of their use during Bournonville's lifetime.

To annotate comprehensively each single entry in a catalogue of this nature and size would have taken almost as many man-hours as went into its compilation. The annotations in this volume will, therefore, deal exclusively with the genesis of the work, its musical and choreographic contents, and its performing history during Bournonville's lifetime. These editorial guidelines are all presented in further detail in the following Introduction.

By collecting and compiling this diverse material consisting of Bournonville's writings on ballet, his manuscript scenarios, and his notes on specific ballets included in the music scores, it is my hope to enable the modern scholar to recreate imaginatively the ballets of this great choreographer. It also gives immediate access to, and allows him or her to compare modern performances with, Bournonville's own detailed comments on the same works. Ultimately, it may permit us to recreate, in authentic style and detail, some of the Bournonville works that have been presumed lost for so many years, but are still preserved in his diligent notes and manuscripts and in the musical scores.

KNUD ARNE JÜRGENSEN
Copenhagen
May 1996

Introduction

Works listed

The bibliography includes the following nine groups of works by August Bournonville:
1. Ballets
2. Divertissements, tableaux, intermezzi, mimical prologues and epilogues.
3. Individual rôles, *pas*, and dances.
4. Operas, operettas, singspiels, vaudevilles, plays, intermediums, ballades, romances, and recited prologues and epilogues.
5. Translations into Danish of French texts for operas, vaudevilles, and plays.
6. Dances and tableaux choreographed and taught for Royal festivities, court balls, and masked balls.
7. Drama lessons, social or theatrical dances choreographed for and taught at private lessons.
8. Organisation of and dances choreographed for major public and social events.
9. Unidentified and unverified works.

Each work is listed in chronological order under the date of its première, followed by all later restagings of it during Bournonville's lifetime. Projected and unperformed works are listed under the date on which they are first mentioned in Bournonville's diary and/or his letters.

The contents of each entry are structured in five sections as follows:
1. Date of the work (given in **bold**).
2. Title(s) of work (given in **bold** and *italics*), followed (for divertissements and individual *pas* and dances) by the names of the main interpreters. All titles are given in English, followed (in parentheses) by the Danish titles with which they were first performed in Denmark. The only exception from this rule are works that were originally premièred with titles in languages other than English or Danish. These works (mainly foreign operas and plays) are listed with their original titles, followed (in parentheses) by the Danish title with which they were first mounted by Bournonville. Works that were originally premièred in Swedish are, though, listed with English titles, followed (in parentheses) by their original Swedish

titles. After the title of each work follows the name and the place of the theatre at which it was mounted by Bournonville. When no place and name of a theatre is given it means that the work in question was performed at Copenhagen's Royal Theatre at The King's New Square.
3. A general commentary on the genesis of the work, its music and choreography, and the performing history during Bournonville's lifetime.
4. Excerpts from Bournonville's diary (in the original language) describing the creation, the rehearsals, and the première of the work.
5. An annotated compilation of all relevant source material dating from Bournonville's lifetime. The sources included here are delimited to four main groups of material:
   (a) Bournonville's holographs concerning the creation, the staging, and the contents of his works.
   (b) The manuscript and printed musical sources which served for the rehearsing and the performances of his works during his own lifetime.
   (c) All other relevant manuscript sources that were made under Bournonville's personal supervision and/or received his approval (e.g. costume drawings, sketches for the décor, etc.).
   (d) All relevant printed sources (e.g. posters containing descriptions of the dramatic action, printed ballet scenarios, opera libretti, and textbooks for plays).

For further source material of significance from Bournonville's lifetime *see* Additional Sources.

Authenticity of works

All works included by Bournonville in his published memoirs *My Theatre Life* and/or in his handwritten lists of his works (*see* Additional Sources) are considered as authentic. In those cases when a work is not explicitly listed with Bournonville's name on the poster for its first performance, or when a work is not mentioned at all by Bournonville in his published memoirs or in his handwritten lists of his works, it will be catalogued with the heading 'uncredited' (given in parentheses). An entry under this heading, therefore, does not mean that the work in question is to be considered 'doubtful' or 'falsely attributed', but that it was first presented without any official indication of Bournonville as its original choreographer and/or director. These works, which at first sight may appear as 'doubtful works', have thus proven through the discovery of Bournonville's autographed manuscripts or of other conclusive historical evidence to be unquestionably authentic. To determine the authenticity of all such 'uncredited' works I have, whenever possible, availed myself of written statements by Bournonville; in some cases I have been obliged to express a personal judgement.

The sources

The sources are divided into four categories according to the genre and contents of the material.

Autograph sources

This heading is used for all holographs by Bournonville which deal with the planning, creation, rehearsing, staging, and revision(s) of his works. In order to reflect the genesis of each work these manuscripts are, as far as is possible, listed in chronological order and placed in connection with the particular production or restaging for which they were originally made. All undated holographs are given a date and/or year [in brackets] based on statements in Bournonville's diaries and/or letters. The autograph sources are arranged (according to the contents of each holograph) into nine subdivisions:

1. *Manuscript scenario.* All manuscripts describing the programme and/or the dramatic action of a ballet.
2. *Manuscript libretto.* All manuscripts describing the programme and/or the dramatic action of operas and plays.
3. *Manuscript mise-en-scène.* All manuscripts describing the actual mise-en-scène of operas and plays.
4. *Musical instruction.* All manuscripts containing Bournonville's instructions to the music composer(s) about the musical organisation of a work.
5. *Choreographic note.* All manuscripts describing the choreographic contents of a work in terms of specific steps and/or the general choreographic development on stage.
6. *Mimic note.* All manuscripts describing the mimic

dramatic contents of a work in terms of exact pantomime phrases and/or general descriptions of the dramatic action.
7. *Production note.* All manuscripts dealing with Bournonville's general planning of the creation, casting and staging of a work.
8. *Recommendation note.* All manuscripts in which Bournonville recommends to the theatre management whether a work (mainly operas and plays) should be staged or not.
9. *Press notes.* All manuscripts or articles written for the press and dealing with the actual contents and staging of a work.

The registration and description of each Bournonville holograph is arranged within five paragraphs as follows:

1. A general description of the manuscript (genre and category of contents, type of manuscript, number of pages, and format(s) in centimetres).
2. The title(s) of the manuscript given exactly as written by Bournonville on the front cover and/or title page, including his underlining of words, later changes, and errors in writing and spelling.
3. An indication of whether the manuscript holds Bournonville's autographed signature and dating or not. When datings occur these are transcribed exactly as written by Bournonville. In the cases of undated holographs a suggested dating (based on indications found in Bournonville's diary and/or letters) is added [in brackets].
4. An indication of where the manuscript is preserved today. This paragraph begins with an open square bracket ([) followed by a library sigla and the call number for the manuscript.
5. Additional notes (when necessary) describing in further detail the dating of the manuscript and its contents.

Abbreviations employed:
cm, centimetres
Ms., manuscript
no., number
p./pp., page(s)
vol., volume

Musical sources

This heading is used for all manuscript and printed musical sources employed for Bournonville's works and/or stagings during his lifetime. In order to reflect the creative process of each work the manuscript musical sources have been listed, as far as is possible, in chronological order after their creation and placed in connection with the particular production for which they were made. To all undated manuscript and printed musical sources have been added a date and/or year [in brackets] based on statements found either in Bournonville's diaries or his letters, or (for printed scores) in the music publishers' catalogues. The manuscript musical sources have been arranged (according to the genre and contents of each manuscript) in four subdivisions:

1. *Musical drafts.* The music composer's drafts, followed by a brief description of the notes by Bournonville contained in them. In those cases when Bournonville choreographed and/or mounted parts of a work (e.g. dances in operas and plays) only the musical drafts for those sections for which he was responsible are listed here.

2. *Orchestral score.* The music composer's autographed full orchestral score and all contemporary manuscript and printed copies of it that served for performances given during Bournonville's lifetime.

3. *Répétiteur's copy.* The music composer's autographed répétiteur's copy and all contemporary manuscript copies of it, followed by a brief description of the autographed notes by Bournonville contained in them.

4. *Parts.* Each instrumental part is listed in the following order and with these abbreviations:

   vl princ, violino principale/solo violin

   vl I, violino primo/first violin

   vl II, violino secondo/second violin

   vla, viola/tenor (viola)

   vlc, violoncello/violoncel

   cb, contrabasso/double bass

   fl picc, flauto piccolo/octave flute (piccolo)

   fl gr, flauto grande/flute

   fl 1/2, flauto primo e secondo/first and second flute

   ob 1/2, oboe primo e secondo/first and second oboe

   cl. 1/2, clarinetto primo e secondo/first and second clarinet

   Acl, clarinetto alto/alt clarinet

   Bcl/cor bassetto, corno bassetto/bass clarinet

   fag 1/2, fagotto primo e secondo/first and second bassoon

   cor, corno/horn

   Tcor, flicorno tenore/bugle tenor

   clno, clarino

   tr, tromba/trumpet

cnt, cornetta/cornet

cnt a chiavi, cornetta a chiavi/keyed bugle

serp, serpentone/serpent

trb, trombone

Atrb, trombone alto/alto trombone

Ttrb, trombone tenore/tenor trombone

Btrb, trombone basso/bass trombone

oph, ophicleide/ophichléide

tuba, tuba/tuba

Btuba, tuba basso/bass tuba

timp, timpani/kettledrums

gr cassa, gran cassa/bass drum

cassa, cassa (tamburo militare)/side drum

tamb rul, tamburo rulante/tenor drum

tamb, tamburino/tambourine

piatti, piatto (cinelli)/cymbal

tri, triangolo/triangle

gong, tam-tam/gong

cast, castagnette/castanets (bone)

glock, soneria di campane/chime

bells, campana tabulare/cloches tabulaires

xyl, zilafone/xylophone

mand, mandolino/mandolin

guit, chitarra/guitar

arpa, arpa/harp

org, organo/organ

piano, pianoforte/piano

Notes:

1/2 indicates that the first and second voices for a given instrument are written and bound separately.

1–2 indicates that the first and second voices for a given instrument are written and/or bound together.

e indicates that two (or more) instruments are written and/or bound together.

The registration and description of each musical source is arranged within five paragraphs as follows:

1. A general description of the musical source (genre and category of contents, type of manuscript, number of pages, and format(s) in centimetres).

2. The title(s) of the musical source given exactly as written/printed on the front cover and/or title page, including the underlining of words, later changes, and errors in writing/printing and spelling.

3. An indication of whether the musical source carries Bournonville's and other's autographed signatures and datings, or not. When a dating occurs it is transcribed exactly as written/printed.

In cases of undated musical sources a suggested dating based on indications found in Bournonville's diary, his letters, or elsewhere has been added [in brackets].

4. An indication of where the musical source is preserved today. This paragraph begins with an open square bracket ([) followed by a library sigla and the call number for the musical source.

5. Additional notes (when deemed necessary) describing in further detail the dating of the musical source and its contents.

Abbreviations employed:
cm., centimetres
Ms., manuscript
no., number
p./pp., page(s)
s. a., sine anno
s. l., sine loco
vol., volume

When references to score numbers and page numbers are given in quotation marks (e.g. score no. '12', or pp. '125–136') it means that the numbers and pagination are quoted exactly as written/printed in the musical sources.

Other sources

This group of material includes all other printed, manuscript, and iconographic sources which do not derive from Bournonville's hand, but were made under his supervision and/or with his personal approval and are considered of particular interest for the study of the genesis and the performing history of his works in his lifetime. The material in this category is catalogued using the same rules as those employed for Bournonville's holographs and/or the manuscript and printed musical sources.

Printed sources

This heading is used exclusively for printed ballet scenarios, opera libretti, textbooks for plays, and programme-posters for works that were choreographed and/or mounted by Bournonville and contain a description of the dramatic action. The material in this category is catalogued using the same rules as those employed for the manuscript and printed musical sources.

Library sigla

AWn, Österreichische Nationalbibliothek (Musiksammlung), Augustinerstraße 1, A-1010 Wien, Austria.

AWth, Österreichische Theatermuseum, Lobkowitzplatz 2, A-1010 Wien, Austria.

DKKk, Det kongelige Bibliotek (Musikafd./Håndskriftafd./Danske afd.), Postboks 2149, DK-1016 København K, Denmark.

DKKr, Danmarks Radios Nodebibliotek, Islands Brygge 81, DK-2300, København S, Denmark.

DKKt, Teatermuseet, Christiansborg Ridebane 10, DK-1218 København K, Denmark.

DKKkt, Det kongelige Teater (Arkiv og bibliotek/Musikarkivet), Postboks 2185, DK-1017 København, Denmark.

FPc, Bibliothèque du Conservatoire national de musique (transferred to Bibliothèque Nationale), Département de la musique, 2, rue Louvois, F-75002 Paris, CEDEX 02, France.

FPo, Bibliothèque-Musée de l'Opéra, 8, Rue Scribe, F-75009 Paris, CEDEX 02, France.

GBLbm, The British Library, Music Department, The British Museum, Great Russell Street, London WC1B 3DG, Great Britain.

IMc, Biblioteca del Conservatorio 'Giuseppe Verdi', Via del Conservatorio 12, I-20122 Milano, Italy.

NBo, Bergen Offentlige Bibliotek, Griegsamlingen, Strømgaten 6, N-5015 Bergen, Norway.

NOum, Universitetsbiblioteket i Oslo, Norsk Musikksamling, Drammensveien 42, N-0255 Oslo 2, Norway.

PLKj, Biblioteka Jagiellonska, al. Slowackiego, Kraków, Poland.

RF-SPtob, Tsentral'naia muzykal'naia biblioteka gosudarstvennogo akademicheskogo teatra opery i baleta imeni Marinskij (Marinskij Library), Rossi Street, St Petersburg, Russian Federation.

SSdt, Drottningholms Teatermuseum, Filmhuset, Borgvägen, Box 27050, S-102 51 Stockholm, Sweden.

SSk, Kungliga BibliToteket, Humlegården, Box 5039, S-102 41 Stockholm, Sweden.

SSkma, Musikaliska Akademiens Bibliotek, Nybrokajen 11, Box 16326, S-103 26 Stockholm, Sweden.

SSkt, Kungliga Teaterns Musikbibliotek (Vinstocken), Box 160 94, S-103 22 Stockholm, Sweden.

SSm, Musikmuseet, Sibyllegatan 2, Box 16326, S-103 26 Stockholm, Sweden.

USNYp, New York Public Library, Dance Collection, Performing Arts Research Center, 111 Amsterdam Avenue, New York, New York 10023, USA.

The Works (1821–1879)

1821

13.2.1821
Habor and Signe (Habor og Signe). **Projected tragic ballet in four acts.**
This projected ballet is clearly inspired by A. Oehlenschläger's five-act tragedy *Hagbarth and Signe* (*Hagbarth og Signe*), first published in March 1815 and premièred at Copenhagen's Royal Theatre on 19.1.1816. Apart from condensing Oehlenschläger's two final acts into one, Bournonville closely follows the dramatic action of this tragic love story as set out by the poet. However, he also interpolated several scenes of his own invention. Among these the most significant is the long dream scene of the character *Alf* in Act III (scene 1). In this half-mimed, half- danced scene, three malevolent valkyries in a series of *tableaux vivants* predict the victory of *Habor* over *Alger* and *Alf*. They also indict the latter to seek revenge for this humiliation. The ballet was originally drafted by Bournonville in Copenhagen in 1821 and was thoroughly revised by him during his second sojourn in Paris some four years later. However, for unknown reasons it was never carried out. It bears clear witness to his great acquaintance with the main literary works of his time even at this very early stage of his choreographic career.

Autograph sources:

Manuscript scenario. Ms. Autograph. Black and brown ink. 1 vol. 22 pp. (18,6 × 12 cm)
Habor og Signe/tragisk Ballet i 4 Acter/af/Antoine Auguste Bournonville/1821. -
Signed and dated: 'Kbhvn d: 13 Februar 1821. forbedret og/ reenskrevet i Paris d: 24 Januar 1825./ + <u>See 4 Acts 3 Scene</u>/[…]/12 sept 1825. -'
[DKKk; NKS 3285 4° 1 A 4

1.4.1821
The Spring (Foraaret). **Projected mythological ballet in one act.**
This projected ballet represents the first in a series of four allegorical ballets that depicted the four seasons, and for which two more autographed scenarios have been traced (*see* 4.12.1823 and 13.5.1825). Together, they bear witness to Bournonville's early fascination with exploring the dramaturgical and choreographic potential of the genre of allegorical-mythological ballets, a spell that was never broken during his life-long career. The ballet was never carried out, although many years later Bournonville resumed work on a similar idea of presenting the four seasons in a cycle of four allegorical ballets. However, that second project differed in having the action of each ballet situated in four different nations (*see* 16.6.1846).

Autograph sources:

Manuscript scenario. Ms. Autograph. Brown ink. 1 vol. 10 pp. (20,5 × 17,5 and 19,7 × 15,9 cm)
Foraaret./Original mythologisk Ballet i 1 Act/componeret af:/ Antoine Auguste Bournonville
Signed and dated: 'd. 1.ste April 1821.'
[DKKk; NKS 3285 4° 1 A 3

1822

13.10.1822
The Prize (Gevinsten). **Projected comic ballet in two acts.**
No autographed scenario for this projected Bournonville ballet has yet been traced.

Autograph sources:

The third entry in Bournonville's handwritten catalogue 'Compositioner/af,/<u>Auguste Bournonville</u>' (*see* Additional Sources) reading: '3/Gevinsten comisk Ballet i 2 Acter/d. 13 October 1822.'
Signed and dated: 'd. 13 October 1822.'
[DKKk; NKS 3285 4° 1 B 6

1823

19.2.1823
Le Devin du village (Landsbÿe Spaamanden). **Projected idyllic ballet in one act.**
According to the title page on Bournonville's autographed scenario for this idyllic ballet, it was based on J.-J. Rousseau's one-act intermedium *Le Devin du village* (premièred at Fontainebleau on 18.10.1752, and first performed at the Paris Opéra on 1.3.1753, but from 2.5.1779 with a partially revised score by F.-C. Lefèbvre). Bournonville had attended several performances of Rousseau's intermedium during his sojourns in Paris in the 1820s. Moreover, on two later occasions he did incorporate Lefèbvre's music for this work into the scores for his own ballets in Copenhagen (*see* 13.10.1829 and 31.10.1875). His projected Copenhagen staging of this balletic version of *Le Devin du village* was for unknown reasons never carried out.

Autograph sources:

Manuscript scenario. Ms. Autograph. Brown ink. 1 vol. 10 pp. (19,5 × 12,4 and 19 × 11,7 cm)
Landsbye = Spaamanden/Idÿllisk Ballet i 1 Akt/Mimisk Omarbeidelse af J. J. Rousseau's Devin du village/comp: af/Antoine Auguste Bournonville/1823.
Signed and dated: 'Kjöbenhavn d 19 Febr 1823.'
[DKKk; NKS 3285 4° 1 A 5

1.11.1823
The Feast of the Muses (Musernes Fest). **Projected mimic prologue.**
According to Bournonville's autographed scenario for this projected mimic prologue, it was intended as a homage to Denmark's King Frederik VI on his fortieth birthday on 28.1.1824. Although it was never carried out, several elements from its plot seem to have been reused many years later by Bournonville in his one-act pantomimic prologue *The Fatherland's Muses* (*see* 20.3.1840), a work that was also created for a special Royal red-letter day.

Autograph sources:

Manuscript scenario. Ms. Autograph. Brown ink. 1 vol. 6 pp. (20,7 × 16,8 cm)
Musernes = Fest/<u>mimisk</u>/Prolog/componeret af,/Antoine Auguste Bournonville/1823.
Signed and dated: 'd. 1.ste November 1823.'
[DKKk; NKS 3285 4° 1 A 6

4.12.1823
The Summer (Sommeren). **Projected mythological ballet in one act.**
This projected ballet was clearly part of the projected series of four mythological ballets, which Bournonville had begun drafting two years earlier (*see* 1.4.1821) but never carried out.

Autograph sources:

Manuscript scenario. Ms. Autograph. Brown ink. 1 vol. 13 pp. (18,9 × 11,5 cm with minor variants)
Sommeren./mӯthologisk Ballet/i/1 Act./comp: af/Antoine Auguste Bournonville/1823.
Signed and dated: 'Kbhvn d 4 Decbr 1823'
[DKKk; NKS 3285 4° 1 A 10

1824

28.2.1824
The Troubadour (Troubadouren). **Projected divertissement.**
No autographed scenario for this projected Bournonville divertissement has yet been traced.

Autograph sources:

The seventh entry in Bournonville's handwritten catalogue 'Compositioner/af,/<u>Auguste Bournonville</u>' (*see* Additional Sources) reading: '7 Troubaduren. Divertissement/d 28 Febr 1824.'
Signed and dated: 'd 28 Febr 1824.'
[DKKk; NKS 3285 4° 1 B 6

20.9.1824
The Talisman (Talismanen).
Projected comic fairy-ballet in one act.
This projected fairy-ballet was conceived and written by Bournonville in Paris in 1824. It seems to have drawn inspiration from attending a (not yet identified) play, operetta, or vaudeville in the Parisian repertory. This theory is supported by the fact that the ballet's cast exclusively includes French names (*Victor, Lise, Nicolas, Blaise,* and *Fadot*). Moreover, the

plot, which centres on a small love-intrigue showing the success of *Victor* in conquering his beloved *Lise* through the help of a magic mirror that makes him invisible to everybody but her, its typically French in style. The ballet was for unknown reasons never carried out.

Autograph sources:

Manuscript scenario. Ms. Autograph. Brown ink. 1 vol. 11 pp. (18,6 × 12 cm with minor variants)
Talismanen/comisk Trӯlle – Ballet/i 1 Act/af,/Antoine Auguste Bournonville/1824.
Signed and dated: 'Paris d 20 september 1824.'
[DKKk; NKS 3285 4° 1 A 11

8.10.1824
The Night at Norderhov (Natten paa Norderhoug). **Projected mimical performance in two acts.**
This projected pantomimic ballet depicts a supposedly real-life incident that took place in the town of Norderhov in Ringerike (Norway) in 1716. During the attack on Norway of the army of King Carl XII, the Swedish forces were totally defeated at Norderhov thanks to the intervention of the daughter of the local priest, Anna Colbjørnsdatter. With her great charm and wisdom she succeeded in informing her compatriots of the exact military strength of the occupying Swedish army after having put it out of action by offering the soldiers unlimited amounts of alcoholic drink. The same historical incident was also described by A. Oehlenschläger in his poem *Norderhaugs Præstegaard*, part of his 1833 collection of poems, entitled *Norgesreisen*. Bournonville's projected ballet, which bears clear witness to his fine talent at this early stage in his career to arrange lively and dramatic ballet scenarios on historical themes, was for unknown reasons never carried out.

Autograph sources:

Manuscript scenario. Ms. Autograph. Brown ink. 1 vol. 14 pp. (18,2 × 11,9 cm)
Natten paa Norderhoug/Mimisk – Historisk Fremstilling i 2 Acter./af/Antoine August Bournonville/1824.
Signed and dated: 'Paris d 8. October 1824'
[DKKk; NKS 3285 4° 1 A 7

1825

24.1.1825
Polichinel without knowing it (Polichinel uden at vide af det). **Projected mimic farce in one act.**
This projected mimic farce was conceived and written during Bournonville's sojourn in Paris in 1825. It seems to have been inspired by attending a performance of F. A. Blache's pantomimic divertissement *Polichinel-vampire* (premièred at Théâtre de la Porte-Sainte-Martin on 27.5.1823). That work was created for the Paris début of the great French character dancer, C. E. Mazurier, who had won great fame for his interpretations of the rôle of *Polichinelle* in several ballets in the French provinces during the 1820s. Bournonville, who often attended Mazurier's performances in Paris, reported about

one of them in a letter to his father written on 9.10.1824 (now in DKKk, call no. NKS 3528 4°):

'j'y ai occasion d'admirer la souplesse & le legereté du fameux Mazurier qui à fait sa reputation dans le role de Polichinel Vampire Vous ne faites pas d'idee de son agileté il fait l'exercise militaire avec sa jambe qu'il manie comme un fusil & on peut le plier en deux comme un livre & à cela il joint un talent vraiment comique –'.

Although his own projected ballet was never carried out, Bournonville succeeded nearly forty years later in mounting a Polichinelle-dance in the style of Mazurier. It was part of his ballet-vaudeville in two tableaux *Pontemolle (An Artists' Party in Rome)* and was premièred on 11.4.1866.

Autograph sources:

Manuscript scenario. Ms. Autograph. Brown ink. 1 vol. 9 pp. (18 × 11,8 cm)
Polichinel/uden at vide af det -/Mimisk Farce i 1 Act/af,/Antoine Auguste Bournonville/1825.
Signed and dated: 'Paris d. 13 Januar 1825'
[DKKk; NKS 3285 4° 1 A 8

13.3.1825
The Autumn (Efteraaret). **Projected mythological ballet in one act.**
This projected ballet was clearly part of the projected series of four mythological ballets which Bournonville had begun drafting four years earlier (*see* 1.4.1821) but never carried out.

Autograph sources:

Manuscript scenario. Ms. Autograph. Brown ink. 1 vol. 14 pp. (18,4 × 12 cm)
Efteraaret/mÿthologisk Ballet i 1 Act -/af -/Antoine Auguste Bournonville/1825. -
Signed and dated: 'Paris d. 13 Martz 1825'
[DKKk; NKS 3285 4° 1 A 2

24.4.1825
Praxiteles. **Projected ballet in one act.**
In this projected ballet Bournonville depicts, in anecdotal form, the life and works of the great Greek sculptor, Praxiteles, at the time of his completion of his masterpiece, the statue of Venus. The ballet is an interesting example of Bournonville's interest from the very beginning of his career in transforming into choreographic and mimic forms the plasticity and classical beauty of the great works of art from ancient Greece, a theme that he frequently returned to in later ballets, for instance the neo-allegorical fantasy *The New Penelope, or The Spring Festival in Athens* (*see* 26.1.1847), or his Greek mythological ballet *Psyche* (*see* 7.5.1850). *Praxiteles* was for unknown reasons never carried out.

Autograph sources:

Manuscript scenario. Ms. Autograph. Brown ink. 5 pp. (24 × 10,7 and 18,5 × 11,9 cm)
Praxiteles
Unsigned and undated [c. April 1825]
[DKKk; NKS 3285 4° 1 A 9

According to Bournonville's handwritten catalogue 'Compositioner/af,/Auguste Bournonville' (*see* Additional Sources) this projected ballet is entitled and dated: 'Praxiteles Episode [changed to:] Ballet i 1 Act af [word(s) illegible]/d 24 April 1825'.

c. July 1825
[*Aladin*]. Untitled projected ballet in three acts (incomplete).
Bournonville's (untitled) autographed scenario for this projected ballet seems to date from the early months of 1825. According to its contents it appears to have been based on N. Isouard's similarly incompleted three-act fairy-opera *Aladin, ou La Lampe merveilleuse,* the music of which had been finished by A.-M. Benincori and F.-A. Habeneck and given its first performance at the Paris Opéra on 6.2.1822. On 8.6.1825 Bournonville attended a performance of Isouard's opera at the Paris Opéra, the first inspiration for his own projected ballet, which takes place in the exact same Arabian *Thousand and One Nights* sphere.

Moreover, on 5.4.1826 he made his second début performance at the Paris Opéra in 'Le pas de trois de Mr. Albert avec Mmes Noblet & Lacroix' from Isouard's *Aladin, ou La Lampe merveilleuse.* This dance was later described by him in a letter to his father (dated 11.4.1826, now in DKKk, call no. NKS 3528 4°) as: 'Ce Pas d'un genre noble & gracieux'.

Finally, for his third début performance in Paris, on 16.4.1826, Bournonville again appeared in this dance. It is therefore reasonable to assume that he may also have planned to use at least some of the dance music from Isouard's opera for his own projected ballet on this same plot. This assumption is further supported by the circumstance that Bournonville actually purchased a copy in Paris of the full orchestral score for the *Pas de trois* in Isouard's *Aladin, ou La Lampe merveilleuse* some time during the 1820s. Later he brought this score to Copenhagen and used it for the *Pas de cinq* which he incorporated in G. Pacini's three-act *dramma giocosa,* entitled *La Gioventù di Enrico V* (*see* 28.10.1831).

Bournonville's projected three-act ballet *Aladin* was never carried out.

Autograph sources:

Manuscript scenario (incomplete). Ms. Autograph. Brown ink. 15 pp. (18,4 × 12 cm)
1.ste Act./1 Scene./Skuepladsen forestiller en aaben Plads. I Baggrunden/sees Kongens Palads. En uanseelig Hÿtte der ligger forrest paa Pladsen er Aladins ringe/Bolig. Det er Morgen. -
Unsigned and undated [c. July 1825]
[DKKk; NKS 3285 4° 1 A 1
In Bournonville's handwritten catalogue 'Compositioner /af,/Auguste Bournonville' (*see* Additional Sources) an entry, reading 'Aladin', is inserted between the dates of 24.1.1825 (*Polichinel without knowing it*) and 13.3.1825 (*The Autumn*). However, it was cancelled by himself at a later stage.

1826

No works dating from this year have yet been traced.

1827

25.2.1827
Acclaim to the Graces (Gratziernes Hyldning). **Projected divertissement.**
This projected work represents Bournonville's first draft for his later allegorical divertissement of that name (premièred at Copenhagen's Royal Theatre on 1.9.1829, but clearly conceived and written during his Parisian sojourn in the late 1820s).

Autograph sources:

Manuscript scenario. Ms. Autograph. Brown ink. 4 pp. (18,5 × 12 cm)
Gratziernes [*sic*] Hÿldning./Divertissement/af Auguste Bournonville. -
Signed and dated: 'Paris ce 25 fevrier 1827.'
[DKKk; NKS 3285 4° 2 G-K

1828

No works dating from this year have yet been traced.

1829

18.4.1829
Five projected stagings of French ballets in Copenhagen.
According to a letter written in Paris by Bournonville to his father (now in DKKk, call no. NKS 3528 4°) he was on this day working on what he then described as:

'un projet de representations à Copenhague non seulement à la Direction, mais à tous ceux qui peuvent s'interresser à moi & à la danse'.

That project is most probably identical with that referred to in two (undated) autographed manuscripts in which he wrote a complete casting list of Danish dancers in six French ballets then current in the Paris Opéra repertory. They include the following five works:

(1) J. Aumer's and A. Gyrowetz's one-act ballet *Les Pages du Duc de Vendôme* (premièred on 18.10.1820).
(2) P. Gardel's and R. Kreutzer's three-act pantomimic ballet *Paul et Virginie* (premièred on 12.6.1806).
(3) P. Gardel's and R. Kreutzer's one-act ballet *La Servante justifiée* (premièred on 30.9.1818).
(4) L. Milon's and L.-L. Persuis' two-act pantomimic ballet *Nina, ou La Folle par amour* (premièred on 23.11.1813).
(5) Albert's (François Decombe) and F. Sor's three-act fairy-ballet *Cendrillon* (premièred on 3.3.1823).
(6) L. Milon's and R. Kreutzer's three-act pantomimic ballet *Clari, ou La Promesse de mariage* (premièred on 19.6.1820).

Only three of these six projected stagings were later on carried out by Bournonville in Copenhagen (*see* 3.9.1830, 29.10.1830, and 30.9.1834).

Autograph sources:

Production note. Ms. Autograph. Brown ink. 8 pp. of which one is blank (20 × 12.5 cm with minor variants)

Ballets de l'Opéra/propres/au/Repertoire du theatre royal Danois.
Unsigned and undated [c. early 1829]
[DKKk; NKS 3285, 4°, 1, B 5, læg 5)

Production note. Ms. Autograph. Brown ink. 4 pp. (18,1 × 11,8 cm)
Udkast til Besætningen/af/Les Pages du duc de Vendome./[...]/Cendrillon. -/[...]/La Servante justifiée/[...]/Clari./[...]/Nina
Unsigned and undated [c. early 1829]
[DKKk; NKS 3285, 4°, 1, B 5, læg 5 a)

1.9.1829
Pas de deux **(uncredited) performed by Bournonville and A. Krætzmer as an incorporated divertissement in N. Isouard's three-act comic opera** *Jeannot et Colin (Jeannot og Colin eller Fosterbrødrene).*
In a letter written in Paris by Bournonville to his father on 9.12.1829 this (uncredited) *Pas de deux* is described as a dance by the French choreographer, Albert (François Decombe). According to the same source (now in DKKk, call no. NKS 3528 4°) it had been performed earlier in Paris as an incorporated divertissement in D.-F.-E. Auber's five-act opera *La Muette de Portici* from 1828, and was set to music by M. E. Caraffa. However, in Bournonville's handwritten list of his works, written c.1837 (*see* Additional Sources), the same *Pas de deux* is described as being originally performed in J. Aumer's and F. Hérold's one-act pantomimic ballet, entitled *Lydie* (premièred at the Paris Opéra on 2.7.1828). This is confirmed by the répétiteur's copy for this ballet (now in FPo, call no. Mat. 19 [283 (19), pp. 115–128), in which Caraffa's music for this dance is included as the third number of the final divertissement, originally performed by M. Taglioni (as Lydie) and Albert (as Amyntas). Consequently, Albert's *Pas de deux* must have been incorporated in *La Muette de Portici* in Paris at some later stage.

Bournonville's 1829 Copenhagen version of this *Pas de deux* also seems to be identical with the so-called *A New Pas de deux composed by Mr. Dance Director Bournonville*, which he mounted some six years later for his two pupils, F. Hoppe and L. Grahn. They too performed it as an incorporated divertissement in Act I of *La Muette de Portici* (*see* 23.9.1834). This theory is supported by the following two sources:

(1) The poster for the first performance of Bournonville's 1829 *Pas de deux* in *Jeannot and Colin* which reads: 'I den til stykket hørende Dands dandser Hr. A. Bournonville en Pas de deux med Mad. Kretzner [*sic*]'
(2) A pencilled note (reading: 'Musikken af Caraffa') in the part for the first clarinet of what is named: *Pas de deux af Solodanser A. Bournonville af 'Jeannot og Colin' indlagt i 'Den Stumme i Portici'* (now in DKKk, call no. KTB 209).

The 1829 *Pas de deux* was performed only once in Isouard's opera. It is not possible from the printed orchestral score for Isouard's *Jeannot et Colin* (now in DKKk, call no. U 6 (KTA 188)) to establish where in this opera Bournonville's *Pas de deux* was performed. Finally, according to the rehearsal book of H. C. J. Fredstrup it is unclear exactly how many rehearsals of this dance were held by Bournonville in 1829.

Autograph sources:

Production note. Ms. Autograph. Brown ink. 1 p. (24,8 × 19,8 cm)
En nye Pas de deux/dandset af:/Hr August Bournonville og M.d. Krætzmer.

Unsigned and undated [1829]
[SSm; Daniel Fryklunds samling no. 114

Musical sources:

Orchestral score. Ms. Copy. Brown ink. 50 pp. (26,8 × 36,9 cm)
209/Partituret/til/Pas de deux/brugt i Jeannot & Collin/Brugt i
Den Stumme/[…]/Pas de deux af A: Bournonville brugt i Synges-
tykket Jeanot og Collin:
Unsigned and undated [1829]
[DKKk; MA ms 2603 (KTB 209)

Répétiteur's copy. Ms. Copy. Brown ink. 12 pp. (31,8 × 23,7 cm)
af Den Stumme i Portici/Pas de deux/Violino Rep:
Unsigned and undated [1829?]
[DKKk; MA ms 2700 (KTB 209)
This répétiteur's copy dates most probably from the first time Car-
affa's *Pas de deux* was performed by Bournonville and A. Krætzmer in
Copenhagen as an incorporated divertissement in N. Isouard's
comic opera *Jeannot et Colin*. Only at a later stage does it seem to have
become an integral part of the répétiteur's copy for Auber's *La
Muette de Portici* (*see* 23.9.1834).

Parts. Ms. Copy. 32 vol.
3 vl I, 3 vl II, 2 vla, 3 vlc e cb, fl picc, fl 1/2, ob 1/2, cl 1/2, fag 1/2, cor
1/2/3/4, clno 1/2, trb 1/2/3, timp 1/2, gr cassa.
Unsigned and undated [1829]
[DKKk; KTB 209
According to pencilled notes in the parts for the third and fourth
horn, and in the part for the second 'clarino' (trumpet) this dance
was also performed during Bournonville's guest performances at
Hamburg's Stadttheater on 20.7., 26.7., and 7.8.1843, and at Christiania's Theatre (Oslo) on 15.6.1852.

1.9.1829

Acclaim to the Graces, New Divertissement
(Gratiernes Hyldning, nyt Divertissement).

This divertissement marks Bournonville's choreographic
début at Copenhagen's Royal Theatre after his Parisian sojourn 1824–29. The scenario was conceived and written in
Paris two years before the Copenhagen première (*see* 25.2.
1827), at a time when Bournonville was in the midst of planning a new repertory for his return to Denmark. The divertissement (an allegorical work based on classical Greek mythology) is clearly inspired by Ch.-L. Didelot's two-act
anacreontic ballet *Flore et Zéphire* that dates from 1796 (London), but was given its Paris Opéra première on 12.12.1815.
In Paris this ballet was kept continuously in the repertory
until 8.3.1826. Bournonville had seen *Flore et Zéphire* for the
first time in Paris during the autumn of 1820, when the leading male rôle was performed by the great French dancer,
Albert (François Décombe), whom he so greatly admired
and wanted to take as a rôle model.

Moreover, from his father, Antoine Bournonville, he came
into possession of a copy of the ballet's original scenario,
which includes Didelot's autographed signature and was
most probably donated as a personal gift from the choreographer (*see* Printed sources). From this scenario it is evident
that Didelot's ballet served as Bournonville's most direct
source of inspiration for his own divertissement *Acclaim to the
Graces*. By omitting the more action-packed pantomime
scenes in Act I of Didelot's ballet (which depict the entertainment of *Zéphire* by the muses) Bournonville revised the
ballet into a shorter and far more danceable one-act divertissement, which shows the muses' acclaim of the three

Graces. They appear as a group of classical Greek marble stat-
ues which suddenly come alive and perform a series of
dances together with *Apollo*. The ballet's main choreographic idea, however, was of showing the drastic changes in
Zéphire's dance from his wild abandon towards a more pol-
ished academic style under the influence of the *Graces*.
Obeying the command of *Terpsichore*, *Zéphire* sacrifices his
wings to the *Graces* in order to become a worthy suitor of
Flore. With this sacrifice his dancing undergoes a drastic
change of style. In Bournonville's 1827 scenario (p. 3) this
choreographic transformation is described as follows:

'Berøvet sine Vinger maa nu Zephyr gjenvinde i Ynde og Smag, hvad
han har tabt i Flugt og Lethed […] Ikke meere disse voldsomme
Sving, denne vilde Flugt; Gratziernes Indflydelse er højst mærkelig,
Zephyrs Adræthed formes med Gratziernes Gave, han er Flora
værdig'.

From these notes it seems clear that Bournonville (who performed the rôle of *Zéphire* at the divertissement's première in
Copenhagen) explicitly wanted to show to his fellow citizens
his own personal artistic development as a dancer and artist
after the six years of study in Paris with the legendary French
teacher and dancer, Auguste Vestris.

The choreographic culmination of *Zéphire*'s dancing takes
place in the ballet's *Pas de trois* (score no. 3) which is performed by *Terpsichore*, *Flore*, and *Zéphire*. This dance is described in Bournonville's memoirs *My Theatre Life* (p. 66) as a
composition arranged especially for him by Vestris, while the
ballet in general was assessed by him as follows:

'This little composition […] contained in microcosm my whole artistic credo and a picture of my own existence as a dancer'.

Bournonville's autographed pencilled notes in the répétiteur's copy indicate the initials of three dancers who originally performed this *Pas de trois*. After the initials 'k' (for A.
Krætzmer), 'W' (for M. Werning) and 'B' (for Bournonville)
we also find the names of two other female dancers (written
with brown ink): 'Sophie' [Price] and [Julie] 'Rostock'. This
seems to indicate that Bournonville was working on a revival
of this dance many years later, since the careers of these ballerinas lay between 1849 and 1864. However, no traces have
yet been found in the annals of the Royal Theatre to indicate
that the 1829 *Pas de trois* from *Acclaim to the Graces* was ever
revived in Copenhagen, the reason for this probably being
that which Bournonville himself expressed in his memoirs
(p. 66):

'The *divertissement* itself soon vanished amid the furor created by the
ballet *The Sleepwalker*. No one asked for it again, but as a omen for my
own and the Ballet's destiny on the Danish stage, it was not without
a certain importance'.

The score, which is divided into four numbers, was (according to Bournonville's memoirs) based on musical excerpts
borrowed from earlier works by M. E. Caraffa, R. W. v. Gallenberg, and F. Sor. Their music was most probably purchased by Bournonville in Paris in 1829 and brought by him
to Copenhagen the same year. Of these musical borrowings
two numbers are identified as follows:

(1) Score no. 2 (a *Pas de quatre* danced by P. Larcher as *Apollo*, and with L. D. Haack, S. M. F. Stramboe, and S. C. Møller as *The three Graces*): The music for this dance proves to be by M. E. Caraffa. In France it was originally part of J. Aumer's and F. Hérold's one-act ballet *Lydie* (premièred at the Paris Opéra on 2.7.1828). According to the original répétiteur's copy for that ballet (now in FPo, call no. Mat. 19 [283 (19), pp. 99–110) it accompanied a dance which (according to pencilled in the part for the oboe) was named 'Pas de trois de Coulon' and performed by the French dancer, A. Coulon, and two (not yet identified) ballerinas. However, according to an earlier printed Italian piano score of the same music (now in IMc, call no. Noseda D 67–15, with the title 'Pas de deux/Nel Gran Ballo/ TELEMACO') and a manuscript copy of Caraffa's full orchestral score (entitled 'Pasdedú/Musica/Del Sig.r Cav:re D. Michele Carafa', also preserved in IMc, call no. Noseda D 48–4) this music was originally composed for and first performed at Naples' Teatro San Carlo as an incorporated divertissement in P. Gardel's ballet *Telemaco nell'Isola di Calipso* (premièred on 13.2.1813 and restaged at the same theatre on 30.5.1820).

(2) Score no. 3 (a *Pas de trois* danced by Bournonville as *Zéphire*, A. Krætzmer as *Terpsichore*, and M. Werning as *Flore*): The music for this dance is borowed from F. Sor's score to Albert's (François Decombe) ballet *Cendrillon* (premièred at the Paris Opéra on 3.3.1823). According to the original répétiteur's copy for this work (now in FPo, call no. Mat. 19 [63 (3), pp. 89–103) it originally served as accompaniment for a dance, named 'Pas de trois/Cendrillon/2.de Divertissm./Mr. Paul' and first performed by the French dancers, A. Paul, F. Bias, and C. H. Anatole. It was most probably the choreography of this dance that Vestris re-arranged for Bournonville's in Paris for his planned 1829 Copenhagen début.

It is not clear from the rehearsal book of H. C. J. Fredstrup exactly how many rehearsals were held of this divertissement between 4.8.1829 and its première. *Acclaim to the Graces* received 11 performances, the last of which was given on 22.9.1832. According to pencilled notes found in several of the parts the divertissement played for approximately 20 minutes.

Autograph sources:

Production note. Ms. Autograph. Brown ink. 1 p. (24,8 × 19,8 cm)
Gratziernes – Hyldning/Nyt Divertissement comp af Hr A: Bournonville./Personer.
Unsigned and undated [1829]
[SSm; Daniel Fryklunds samling no. 114

Musical sources:

Orchestral score. Ms. Copy. Brown ink. 1 vol. 168 pp. (27,3 × 38,7 cm)
Gratiernes Hўldning/Divertissement/af:/A: Bournonville:/Partitur.
Unsigned and undated [1829]
[DKKk; C II, 127 (KTB 168)

Répétiteur's copy. Ms. Copy. Brown ink. 1 vol. 46 pp. (32,2 × 23,7 cm)
B. 168/Gratiernes Hўldning. – /257A
Unsigned and undated [1829]
[DKKk; MA ms 2929 (KTB 168 (1))

Répétiteur's copy. Ms. Copy. Brown ink. 1 vol. 37 pp. (32 × 23,4 cm)
B 168/Repetiteur Parti/til/Divertissementet/[words smeared]/No. 1./257B
Unsigned and undated [1829]
[DKKk; MA ms 2930 (KTB 168 (2))

Parts. Ms. Copy. 32 vol.
3 vl I, 3 vl II, 2 vla, 4 vcl e cb, fl picc, fl 1/2, ob 1/2, cl 1/2, fag 1/2, cor 1/2/3/4, clno 1/2, trb 1/2, timp, gr cassa e piatti, tri.
Unsigned and undated [1829]
[DKKk; KTB 168

Printed sources:

Printed scenario. 1 vol. 23 pp. (18,1 × 11,8 cm)
Zéphire et Flore,/Ballet-Anacréontique/en deux actes/de la composition de M. Didelot. Paris, Roullet, 1815.
Signed (with brown ink) on p. 5: 'C[harles]: Didelot'
[DKKk; UÆ8-A1318 S-1977

21.9.1829
La Somnambule, ou l'Arrivée d'un nouveau seigneur (Søvngjængersken).

La Somnambule represents Bournonville's first staging of a full-length ballet. It was freely arranged from E. Scribe's, J. Aumer's, and F. Hérold's original work (premièred at the Paris Opéra on 19.9.1827) and was performed with Bournonville and A. Krætzmer in the leading rôles as *Edmond* and *Thérèse*. During his Parisian sojourn Bournonville had followed at close quarters the creation and the rehearsals of this ballet. Moreover, he himself danced in the *Contredanse* and the *Pas de six* of Act I at the ballet's Paris Opéra première. It was, therefore, only natural that his choice of the first full-length ballet to be mounted under his artistic direction in Copenhagen would fall on this work.

During his stay in Paris he personally copied the ballet répétiteur's copy into which he inserted numerous annotations describing, in fine detail, the mime and the dramatic action. Of this manuscript most of the notes for Act II and III are still preserved (*see* Musical sources) and represent one of the most important sources for the study of Aumer's original Paris version that has yet come to light. Furthermore, Bournonville's notes for this ballet reveals his great talent at this early stage in his career to make apt descriptions in written form of even highly complex pantomime scenes.

While he seems to have kept very close to Scribe's and Aumer's original mime and dramatic action, most of the dance divertissements in Act I (score nos. 5, 7, 7 B, 7 C, and 8) were choreographed anew and set to music that, in parts, seems to have been purchased by Bournonville in Paris in the late 1820s and brought with him to Copenhagen in 1829.

Of this incorporated music two numbers are identified as follows:

(1) Score no. 7 B (a *Pas de deux*, performed by *Edmond* and *Thérèse*): This dance employes music borrowed from J. Aumer's and A. Gyrowetz's one-act ballet *Les Pages du Duc de Vendôme* (premièred at the Paris Opéra on 18.10.1820). According to the original répétiteur's copy for this work (now in FPo, call no. Mat. 19 [194 (3), pp. 46–56) it there served as an accompaniment for a *Pas de trois* performed by the French dancers, A. Paul, C. H. Anatole, and F. Bias.

(2) Score no. 7 C (a *Pas de six*): The music for this dance seems to have been borrowed from J. Aumer's and R. W. v. Gallenberg three-act pantomimic ballet *Alfred le Grand* (premièred at the Paris Opéra on 18.9.1822). Thus, in the orchestral score for this ballet (now in FPo, call no. A 467a [I], pp. 495–524) Gallenberg's music is completely identical with that incorporated by Bournonville for the Act I *Pas de six* in his 1829 Copenhagen version of *La Somnambule, ou l'Arrivée d'un nouveau seigneur*. However, according to an even earlier printed Italian piano score (now in IMc, call no. Noseda Q 49–1) the

opening *Allegretto vivace* movement of Gallenberg's music was originally composed for Arm. Vestris' five-act pantomimic ballet *Macbeth* (premièred at Naples' Teatro San Carlo on 4.10.1818) in which it was performed as the finale of Act V (score no. 26).

According to a later letter to his father (dated 9.4.1830) Bournonville also performed in Aumer's original version of the Act I *Pas de six* (in Paris known as *Pas des villageois* or *Pas de trompette*) at Berlin's Hofoper on 4.4.1830. Moreover, he appeared in the same dance when *La Somnambule, ou l'Arrivée d'un nouveau seigneur* was restaged at the Paris Opéra on 4.7.1834. That performance represents the last time he ever danced in the French capital.

The continuing success of Bournonville's 1829 Copenhagen version of this ballet is clear from the fact that excerpts of it were included in nearly all the tours he made abroad with selected groups of dancers from Copenhagen's Royal Theatre. Thus at Stockholm's Royal Theatre (where Aumer's ballet had been premièred in 1835 in a production by A. Selinder) Bournonville played his own Copenhagen version of the rôle of *Edmond* on 14.6.1839 together with C. Fjeldsted as *Thérèse*. Moreover, during the following years he mounted four different versions of selected excerpts or abridged dance divertissements from this ballet which were performed at the following four theatres:

(1) Göteborg's Stora Theater (Segerlindska Theatern) on 10.7.1839.
(2) Christiania's Theatre (Oslo) on 14.8.1840.
(3) Hamburg's Stadttheater on 31.7.1843 where the ballet was entitled *Therese, die Nachtwandlerin* and performed five times with the French ballerina, Maria (Jacob), in the title rôle.
(4) Stockholm's Mindre Theatern on 16.6.1860.

In Copenhagen the *Pas de trois* from Act I (score no. 5) was given as a separate divertissement on 8.4. and 14.4.1848. Four years later a so-called *Scene* and *Pas de quatre* from the same ballet were mounted at Christiania's Theatre (Oslo) on 16.6.1852. Furthermore, on 29.9.1857 the entire ballet was performed for the first time at Copenhagen's Court Theatre, while a so-called *'Fragment of the ballet La Somnambule'* was given at Christiania's Theatre on 14.6.1865.

Similarly, the *Pas de deux* from Act I (score no. 7 B) was mounted as a separate divertissement at Copenhagen's Royal Theatre on 28.10.1860 for the début performance of Bournonville's English pupil, A. Healey, while the complete ballet was given there for her second début in the rôle of *Thérèse* on 3.11.1860.

La Somnambule, ou l'Arrivée d'un nouveau seigneur was restaged by Bournonville for the third and last time in Copenhagen on 2.10.1868 in a thoroughly revised version, and with several musical cuts in order to tighten the rather lengthy mime scenes. For this production many of the dances were completely rechoreographed.

Finally, on 17.2.1875 a divertissement version of excerpts from Act I was mounted by Bournonville for the début of his pupil, A. Flammé. It represents the last time he ever worked on *La Somnambule, ou l'Arrivée d'un nouveau seigneur*.

According to the rehearsal book of H. C. J. Fredstrup the ballet was given 18 rehearsals between 2.9. and 21.9.1829. The 1829 production received 113 performances the last of which was given on 2.12.1864. Several pencilled notes in the

parts for the 1829 version indicate that the ballet played for approximately 1 hour and 36 minutes (Act I: 34 minutes; Act II: 16 minutes; Act III: 27 minutes).

Musical sources:

Répétiteur's copy (fragment). Ms. Autograph (by Bournonville). Black and brown ink. 20 pp. (31,2 × 22,8 cm).
La Somnambule. – Scène de Thérèse – /2.me Acte.
Unsigned and undated [late 1820s]
[DKKk; NKS 3285 4° 9 læg 2
The numeorus autographed notes by Bournonville contained in this répétiteur's copy describe most of the ballet's dramatic action and the mime. They were most probably written during Bournonville's Parisian sojourn and at about the time of the 1827 Paris Opéra première of the ballet. This theory is supported by the French watermark ('Peloux') contained in this manuscript.

Orchestral score. Ms. Copy (pp. 123-126 are H. S. Paulli's autograph). Brown and black ink. 1 vol. 374 pp. (26,5 × 35,4 cm).
Partituret/til/Sövngiængersken/Ballet i 3 Akter
Unsigned and undated [c.1827–1829 and 1875]
[DKKk; C I, 259 f (KTB 287)
This copy was clearly made in Paris in the late 1820s since all titles and the names of the instruments are here given in French. Moreover, it contains a French watermark showing a standing lion holding a sword. The score also includes a few sections which are H. S. Paulli's autographs and contain the new music in Act I, which became interpolated much later in this ballet (most likely for the separate dance divertissement version of *La Somnambule, ou l'Arrivée d'un nouveau seigneur* that Bournonville mounted on 17.2.1875). Several sections of Hérold's original music are missing in this volume. They were most probably taken out of the score in connection with the last, revised restaging of the ballet by Bournonville's successor, E. Hansen on 27.10.1886 (*see* the following entry).

Orchestral score (fragments). Ms. Copy and autograph (by H. S. Paulli). Brown and black ink. 108 pp. (26 × 34 with minor variants)
[Without title]
Unsigned and undated [c.1827–1829 and 1875]
[DKKk; C I, 259 f (b) (KTB 287)
These fragments contain the music for those sections of the original score for Bournonville's *La Somnambule, ou l'Arrivée d'un nouveau seigneur* which were taken out of the score at a later stage (most likely in connection with the last Copenhagen restaging of this ballet, mounted by E. Hansen on 27.10.1886). They also include a section which is H. S. Paulli's autograph and contains those musical insertions in the Act I *Pas de six* (score no. 7 C) that had been interpolated in this dance on either 2.10.1868 or 17.2.1875. The fragments were originally part of the orchestral score in which they were inserted between what is now (Act I:) pp. 28–29, 80–81. 84–85, 90–91,102–103, 146–147, 158–159, (Act II:) pp. 21–211, and (Act III:) pp. 282–283, 296–297.

Répétiteur's copy. Ms. Copy. Brown and black ink. 1 vol. 72 pp. of which one is blank (32 × 24,6 cm)
Repetiteur Parti/til/Sövngiængersken/Ballet i 3 Akter
Unsigned and undated [1829]
[DKKk; MA ms 2984 (KTB 287 (1))
This répétiteur's copy contains Bournonville's autographed choreographic notes (written with brown ink) that describe in fine detail the steps of the brief *Pas de trois*, danced by *Edmond*, *Thérèse*, and *Gertrude* in Act I (score no. 5). According to the technical terms and the many stenochoreographic signs employed by Bournonville in these notes they seem to have been written in connection with a later (rechoreographed?) staging of *La Somnambule, ou l'Arrivée d'un nouveau seigneur* during the 1850s or 60s (most likely that given at the Court Theatre on 29.9.1857).

Parts. Ms. Copy. 38 vol.
5 vl I, 4 vl II, 2 vla, 4 vcl e cb, fl picc, fl 1/2, ob 1/2, cl 1/2, fag 1/2, cor 1/2/3/4, tr 1/2, trb 1/2/3, timp, tri, gr cassa, piatti, arpa.
Unsigned and undated [1829]
[DKKk; KTB 287]
These parts were used for all productions of *La Somnambule, ou l'Arrivée d'un nouveau seigneur* in Copenhagen between 1829 and 1886.

Printed sources:

Printed scenario. 1 vol. 20 pp. (18 × 10 cm)
Sövngjængersken./Ballet i tre Acter,/af Aumer,/indrettet for den danske Skueplads/af/A. Bournonville./Musiken arrangeret af Herold.
Kiöbenhavn, Jens Hostrup Schultz, 1829.
[DKKk; 17, – 171 8°

26.9.1829
Pas de deux (uncredited) performed by Bournonville and A. Krætzmer as an incorporated divertissement in P. Funck's *A Divertissement in Oriental Style (Et Divertissement i Orientalsk stiil).*

In Bournonville's handwritten lists of his works, written c.1837 and 1851 (*see* Additional Sources), this (uncredited) *Pas de deux* is named 'Pas de deux oriental'. In the same lists it is described as a dance based partly on another choreographer's work and originally entitled 'Pas de Paul'. Moreover, Bournonville also indicates that it was originally part of L. Milon's and R. Kreutzer's three-act pantomimic ballet *Clari, ou la Promesse de mariage* (premièred at the Paris Opéra on 19.6.1820), in which it was performed by the French dancer, A. Paul. However, in Kreutzer's original score for this ballet (now in FPo, call no. A 458 [II], pp. 305–353) the only dance which includes the name of 'Mr. Paul' is a divertissement that is musically completely different from that of Bournonville's 1829 'Pas de deux oriental'. This seems to indicate that the *Pas de deux* mounted by Bournonville in Copenhagen in 1829 may have been incorporated in *Clari, ou la Promesse de mariage* at a time between its 1820 première and 1829 (Milon's ballet was performed for the last time in Paris on 24.12.1830). Furthermore, the total absence of this music in FPo seems to indicate the Copenhagen score as the only complete musical source for this dance that has come to light so far.

In Copenhagen the *Pas de deux* was given as part of P. Funck's divertissement, the latter having originally been premièred on 16.5.1829 to a score by Joh. P. Thræn and with the title *Et nyt af Hr. Solodandser Funck componeret Divertissement i orientalsk Stiil; med Sang*. The poster for later 1829 performance of Funck's divertissement in which Bournonville's *Pas de deux* was included reads as follows: *Et Divertissement i orientalsk Stiil, componeret af Hr. Solodandser Funck, hvori Hr. A. Bournonville dandser en nye Pas de deux med Mad. Krætzmer*. The *Pas de deux* was given twice in Funck's divertissement, the last time on 12.10.1833.

However, according to pencilled notes in the orchestral score and in the répétiteur's copy for this dance (reading: 'Til Weteranen' and 'I Veteranen') Bournonville's 'Pas de deux oriental' was also incorporated, on 29.9.1837, in his one-act idyllic ballet *The Veteran or The Hospitable House* (*see* 29.1.1833). It was danced three times in that ballet by P. C. Johansson and C. Fjeldsted (the last time on 9.10.1837).

Moreover, in the same period the *Pas de deux* was (according to the repertory book of F. Hoppe) performed twice as a separate divertissement, on 27.4.1836 (by Hoppe and L. Grahn) and on 8.11.1839 (by Hoppe and A. Nielsen). Finally, Bournonville's 'Pas de deux oriental' was (again according to the repertory book of F. Hoppe) incorporated eight times in Act III of A. Oehlenschläger's dramatic five-act play *Aladdin, or The Magic Lantern* between 13.5.1839 and 25.11.1842. It was then performed by Hoppe and A. Nielsen and replaced Bournonville's original *Pas de quatre* in this play.

The 'Pas de deux oriental' is probably also identical with the (uncredited) *Pas de deux* that was given as an separate divertissement by F. Hoppe and A. Nielsen on 19.1.1841.

It is not clear from the rehearsal book of H. C. J. Fredstrup exactly how many rehearsals were held by Bournonville of this dance in 1829.

Musical sources:

Orchestral score. Ms. Copy. Black ink. 1 vol. 40 pp. (25,7 × 37 cm)
C/Partituret/til/Pas de deux/brugt i Hr Funk's Divertissement/Til Weteranen/[…]/Orientalsk Divertissement Danses af Hr Hoppe og Jf Nielsen/[…]/C/Pas de deux af: A: Bournonville: brugt i Hr Funck's Divertissement.
Unsigned and undated [1829]
[DKKk; MA ms 2602 (KTB 218)]

Répétiteur's copy. Ms. Copy. Black ink. 1 vol. 6 pp. (32,6 × 23 cm)
Pas de Deux/af Hr Bournonville/Orientalsk Divertissement./249/[…]/I Veteranen/Pas de deux. Repetiteur Part[ie]
Unsigned and undated [1829]
[DKKk; MA ms 2948 (KTB 218)]

Parts. Ms. Copy. 24 vol.
3 vl I, 3 vl II, 2 vla, 3 vlc e cb, fl 1/2, ob 1/2, cl 1/2, fag 1/2, cor 1/2, clno 1/2, timp.
Unsigned and undated [1829]
[DKKk; KTB 218]

13.10.1829
Soldier and Peasant (Soldat og Bonde).
This work is entitled 'Pantomisk Idyl' and represents the first truly original ballet by Bournonville. Its score was composed and pieced together by Ph. L. Keck, who incorporated music borrowed from several earlier works by M. E. Caraffa, F.-C. Lefèbvre, and F. Romani. This borrowed music, which most probably was brought from Paris to Copenhagen by Bournonville in 1829, is identified as follows:

(1) Score no. 7 (a *Pas de trois* performed by Bournonville as *Victor*, A. Krætzmer as *Lise*, and M. Werning as *Anna*): The music for this dance is entirely by Caraffa. It was originally part of P. Gardel's and R. Kreutzer's three-act pantomimic ballet *Paul et Virginie* (premièred at the Paris Opéra on 12.6.1806). This is clear from the orchestral score and the répétiteur's copy for this ballet (both now in FPo, call nos. A 405 [II], pp. 255–343, and Mat. 19 [197 (16), pp. 43–61) and according to which Caraffa's music originally accompanied a *Pas de trois* in Act I, performed by the French dancer, Albert (François Decombe), and two (not yet identified) ballerinas. According to the same sources Caraffa's dance was originally entitled 'Polacca a Rondo pour Mr. Albert/pas Mr. Albert/Paul et Virginie/par Caraffa'.
(2) Score no. 8 (a *Clog Dance* performed by the corps de ballet): In the 1838 répétiteur's copy for the Stockholm staging of *Soldier and Peasant* this dance is named by Bournonville as: 'Les domestiques en Sabots./(d'après Milon.'). The music for it was borrowed from F.-C.

Lefèbvre's score to the third, revised staging at the Paris Opéra on 2.5.1779 of J.-J. Rousseau's intermedium *Le Devin de Village* (originally performed at Fontainebleau on 18.10.1752). According to the French répétiteur's copy for that production (now in FPo, call no. Mat. 18 [86 (91)], pp. 44–49) the dance consisted then of 119 measures. Lefèbvre's music was later also incorporated in his score for L. Milon's one-act ballet *Lucas et Laurette* (premièred at the Paris Opéra on 13.6.1803). In the répétiteur's copy for that ballet (now in FPo, call no. Mat. 19 [153 (1), pp. 112–117] it is listed as score no. '21' and plays for only 75 bars.

Soldier and Peasant was mounted once outside Denmark, by Bournonville's Swedish pupil, P. C. Johansson, at Stockholm's Royal Theatre (Operahuset) on 22.1.1838, with the new title *The Homecoming (Hemkomsten)*. In Norway the ballet was staged by Bournonville in an abridged divertissement version at Christiania's Theatre (Oslo) on 12.8.1840. For this version a not yet traced scenario was (according to *Norsk Bokfortegnelse*, 1814–47, p. 23) published by J. Dahl in Christiania. *Soldier and Peasant* was restaged three more times by Bournonville in Copenhagen on 10.3.1848, 27.9.1850, and 13.3.1861, reaching a total of 71 performances at the Royal Theatre (the last of which was given on 27.4.1862). In Sweden an abridged dance divertissement version was mounted by Bournonville's pupil, S. Lund, at Stockholm's Royal Theatre (Davidsons Paviljong) on 23.4.1860. Finally, on 23.11. and 25.11.1865 the *Pas de trois* from *Soldier and Peasant* (score no. 7) was performed as an independent divertissement at Copenhagen's Royal Theatre by H. Scharff, E. Gade, and J. Petersen. This staging was mounted by L. Gade and seems to represent the last time that excerpts from this ballet were performed in Bournonville's lifetime (*see also* 29.11.1867).

According to the rehearsal book of H. C. J. Fredstrup the original 1829 version of *Soldier and Peasant* was given 11 rehearsals between 6.10. and 13.10.1829.

Musical sources:

Orchestral score. Ms. Copy. Brown ink. 1 vol. 146 pp. (26,6 × 37,8 cm)
Partituret/til/Soldat og Bonde/Pantomimisk Idyl
Unsigned and undated [1829]
[DKKk; C II, 115 (KTB 286)]

Répétiteur's copy. Ms. Copy. Brown ink. 1 vol. 38 pp. (32 × 23 cm)
Repetiteur Parti/til/Soldaten og Bonden/31B/1829
Unsigned and undated [1829]
[DKKk; MA ms 3021 (KTB 1026, but originally KTB 286)]
This répétiteur's copy contains Bournonville's autographed notes (written with brown ink) which describe the mime and most of the choreography for the *Pas de trois* (score no. 7). According to the initials of the dancers [Johanne] 'P'[etersen], [Harald] 'S'[charff], and [Juliette] 'Th'[orberg], his notes were clearly written for the last restaging of *Soldier and Peasant* in Copenhagen on 13.3.1861, since these dancers only performed in this work in 1861. A pencilled autographed note by Bournonville on p. 8 reads: 'gaaer over til Tyrolerne/Vals i G Dur, – derpaa Faust'. It refers to the later interpolation of nearly all of Keck's music for score no. 4 in Bournonville's and V. C. Holm's ballet epilogue *Farewell to the Old Theatre* (*see* 1.6.1874).

Parts. Ms. Copy. 34 vol.
3 vl I, 3 vl II, 2 vla, 4 vcl e cb, fl picc, fl 1/2, ob 1/2, cl 1/2, fag 1/2, cor 1/2/3/4, clno 1/2, trb 1/2/3, cnt, timp, gr cassa e piatti, tri.
Unsigned and undated [1829]
[DKKk; KTB 1026 (originally KTB 286)]

These parts were used for all productions of *Soldier and Peasant* mounted in Copenhagen between 1829 and 1861.

Printed sources:

Printed scenario. 1 vol. 8 pp. (18 × 10 cm)
Soldat og Bonde./Pantomimisk Idyl,/componeret af Hr. A. Bournonville,/Musiken componeret og ordnet/af/Hr. Capelmusicus Keck.
Kiöbenhavn, Jens Hostrup Schultz, 1829.
[DKKk; 17, – 172 8°]

25.10.1829

Philomele, Romance (uncredited) sung by Bournonville.

According to the poster for this day, Bournonville performed an uncredited romance named *Philomele*, to the accompaniment of the French flutist, J. Galliou. It was in all probability identical with A. M. Panseron's romance entitled *Philomêle* («Le patre vers la bergerie»). That romance was published at about the same time in Copenhagen by C. C. Lose, with text in both French and Danish («Alt Hyrden under Flöitens Toner»), a copy of which is now in DKKk, call no. U 204. Bournonville's performance of the romance was given as part of a special charity performance for J. Guillou.

29.10.1829

Princess Isabella, or Three Nights at the Court (*Prindsesse Isabella eller Tre Aftener ved Hoffet*).

The dances in J. L. Heiberg's three-act play (set to music composed and arranged by L. Zinck) were all choreographed and/or mounted by Bournonville. They were as follows:

(1) An (unnamed) *Dance* in Act II (score no. 4).
(2) A *Guarache* in Act II (score no. 5).
(3) A *Pas de deux* in Act II (score no. 7, performed by Bournonville and A. Krætzmer).
(4) A *Tarantella* in Act III (score no. 11).

On 22.12.1830 Bournonville incorporated the Act II *Pas de deux* in P. Funck's Copenhagen version of Ch.-L. Didelot's and F.-M.-A. Venua's two-act anacreontic ballet *Flore et Zéphire*, (created at the Paris Opéra on 12.12.1815 and first performed in Copenhagen on 4.11.1820 to a partially new score arranged by L. Zinck). Venua's music for this dance had also been employed in Austria by Arm. Vestris for his four-act fairy ballet *Die Fee und der Ritter* (premièred at Vienna's Kärnthnerthor Theater on 31.12.1823). This is clear from a printed piano score of Vestris's complete ballet, published by P. Mechetti around 1823–1824 (a copy is now in the Derra de Moroda Dance Archive in Salzburg, call no. M 144, pl. no. P. M. 1395, pp. 2–7/14–19). According to this score, Venua's music was performed in Vienna as a *Pas de trois* (or 'Terzett') in Act I, score no. 3 of *Die Fee und der Ritter* by the dancers P. Samengo, A. Millière and A. Perceval. The music in Mechetti's printed piano score (which also includes an additional *Allegro maestoso* variation of 22 bars in 4/4 time) is credited to F. Romani, but proves to be identical with Venua's *Pas de deux* in Didelot's *Flore et Zéphire* from eight years earlier. In Funck's production of Didelot's ballet, however, the original *Pas de deux* was not included, but it was always an integral part of this ballet in Paris, and became known there (according to Bournonville's handwritten lists of his works) as *Pas de deux de la rose*. It was originally performed by the French dancers, Albert (François Decombe) and G. Gosselin. They were replaced by J. Perrot and M. Taglioni at the last restaging of *Flore et Zéphire* in the French capital on 14.3.1831.

According to his diary, Bournonville saw Didelot's ballet for the first time in Paris on 4.10.1820. However, he probably did not purchase Venua's score for the *Pas de deux* before his second Parisian sojourn in the mid-1820s (*Flore et Zéphire* was given in its original version in Paris until 8.3.1826, and was restaged there on 14.3.1831 in a thoroughly revised version by Albert and J. Aumer).

In Copenhagen the *Pas de deux* was performed twice by Bournonville and Krætzmer in Funck's *Zephyr and Flora*, the last time on 4.1.1831. The dance also seems to have been given as a separate divertissement by Bournonville and L. Grahn on two later occasions on 7.11.1837 and 6.1.1838.

According to pencilled notes found in a later, separate set of parts for this dance (now in DKKk, call no. KTB 1052) the *Pas de deux* was also incorporated in three other Bournonville ballets as follows:

(1) on 27.6.1838 in Act I of Bournonville's four-act romantic ballet *Waldemar* (danced by P. Larcher and C. Fjeldsted).
(2) on 31.7.1840 in an abridged divertissement version of Bournonville's two-act ballet *La Sylphide*, mounted at Christiania's Theatre (Oslo) and performed by Bournonville (as James) and C. Fjeldsted (as The Sylph).
(3) on 8.12.1849 in Act II of Bournonville's three-act romantic ballet *Faust* (performed by W. Funck and J. Price as score no. '19').

Moreover, Venua's *Pas de deux* appears to have been incorporated in Bournonville's 1847 staging at Stockholm's Royal Theatre of his ballet *Faust* (see 9.6.1847). Finally, the dance also seems to have been given as a separate divertissement in Copenhagen at the Court Theatre on 27.12.1850, and in Norway at Christiania's Theatre (Oslo) on 29.6.1852.

On 20.1.1864 a new dance entitled *Souvenir de Taglioni, Pas de deux* was choreographed by Bournonville for his two English pupils, the sisters A. and C. Healey, and premièred as a separate divertissement at Stockholm's Royal Theatre (Dramatiska Theatern). According to the original répétiteur's copy for this dance (now in SSkma, call no. KT Dansmusik 107) it was a freely adapted version for two women of Bournonville's 1829 *Pas de deux* in *Princess Isabella, or Three Nights at the Court* that employed most of Venua's music mingled with excerpts from Bournonville's and H. S. Paulli's two-act ballet-vaudeville *The Conservatoire, or A Proposal of Marriage through the Newspaper* (see 6.5.1849). *Souvenir de Taglioni* was also performed by the Healey sisters at Copenhagen's Royal Theatre on 19.9.1864.

The music for the *Tarantella* in Act III of *Princess Isabella, or Three Nights at the Court* was originally part of A. Petit's and F. Sor's one-act pantomimic ballet *Le Sicilien ou l'Amour peintre* at its Paris Opéra première on 11.6.1827 (the ballet was originally created for Moscow in 1824 with the title *Alphonse et Leonore ou L'Amant peintre*). According to the original répétiteur's copy for the Paris production of *Le Sicilien* (now in FPo, call no. Mat. 19 [280 (12), pp. 39-44) this dance was incorporated in Sor's score by J. Schneitzhoeffer, who seem-

ingly wrote (or at least arranged) this popular Neapolitan dance tune for Petit's ballet. In Copenhagen Schneitzhoeffer's *Tarantella* was later also incorporated by Bournonville in his Danish production of P. Gardel's three-act pantomimic ballet *Paul et Virginie* (see 29.10.1830).

Bournonville also played the rôle of *Giovanni (Prince of Parma)* in Heiberg's play, a part which included the performance of several songs.

It is not clear from the rehearsal book of H. C. J. Fredstrup exactly how many rehearsals were held of *Princess Isabella, or Three Nights at the Court* in 1829. Because the play was created for a specific Royal red-letter day it was performed only once.

Musical sources:

Orchestral score. Ms. Copy. Brown ink. 1 vol. 256 pp. (27,2 × 38 cm)
L. Zinck/Prindsesse Isabella/Partitur/[…] Partituret/til/Prindsesse Isabelle [*sic*]
Unsigned and undated [1829]
[DKKk; C II, 125 (KTA 276)

Répétiteur's copy (incomplete). Ms. Copy. Brown ink. 30 pp. of which three are blank (34,1 × 24,2 cm)
Prindsesse Isabella./No. 5 Guarache Violino 1.mo Repetiteurpartie/[…]/No. [space left open]/[…]/No. 8/[…]/No. 9.
Unsigned and undated [1829]
[DKKk; MA ms 2682 (KTA 276)
This répétiteur's copy contains the music for score no. 5 (the *Guarache*), no. 7 (the *Pas de deux*), and nos. 8-9.

Répétiteur's copy (fragment). Ms. Copy. Brown ink. 4 pp. of which one is blank (34,1 × 24,2 cm)
No. [space left open] Tarentelle Violino 1.mo Rep.
Unsigned and undated [1829]
[DKKk; MA ms 2617 (KTA 276)
This répétiteur's copy contains the music for score no. 11 (the *Tarantella*).

Parts. Ms. Copy. 32 + 24 vol.
3 vl I, 3 vl II, 2 vla, 3 vlc e cb, fl 1/2, ob 1/2, cl 1/2, fag 1/2, cor 1/2/3/4, tr 1/2, trb 1/2/3, timp, gr cassa, tri, arpa. On stage (score nos. 2 and 9): fl picc, fl 1/2, cl 1/2/3/4/5/6/7, fag 1/2/3/4, cor 1/2/3/4, tr 1/2, trb, gr cassa, piatti, tri.
Unsigned and undated [1829]
[DKKk; KTA 276

Parts (*Pas de deux*, incomplete). Ms. Copy. 4 vol.
vl I, vl II, vla, vlc e cb.
Unsigned and undated [late 1820s or 1830s]
[DKKk; MA ms 2763 (4) (KTB 217?)
This (incomplete) sets of parts was most probably written for a later restaging of Venua's *Pas de deux* performed as a separate divertissement. His music is here written together with the music for another (not yet identified) dance named 'No. 1'.

1830

3.9.1830

Les Pages du Duc de Vendôme (Hertugen af Vendômes Pager).
The score for Bournonville's two-act Copenhagen production of J. Aumer's and A. Gyrowetz's one-act ballet *Les Pages du Duc de Vendôme* (premièred at the Paris Opéra on 18.10.1820, but orginally created for Vienna's Hofoper on 16.10.1815) follows closely the Paris version except for its new divi-

sion into two acts. Moreover, two of its dances were new, incorporated numbers that were set to music from the Paris Opéra ballet repertory and replaced Aumer's original dances. Bournonville's reasons for making these changes are described in his preface to the ballet's printed scenario as follows:

'Dandsen [...] er derimod ganske componeret af mig, tildels mere overensstemmende med Situationen og med mangehaande locale Omstændigheder. Den eneste Fortieneste jeg da vover at tilskrive mig, er [...] at have interesseret ved Dandsen paa de Steder, hvor den i selve Paris afskar eller kiølede Handlingen'.

During his first visit to the French capital in 1820 Bournonville attended several rehearsals of *Les Pages du Duc de Vendôme* at the Salle Favart. Moreover, on 17.7.1826 he made his first performance as a dancer under contract with the Paris Opéra in the *Pas de trois* from Act I of Aumer's ballet. He therefore would have known this work from close quarters, and may already at that time (*see also* 18.4.1829) have decided to mount *Les Pages du Duc de Vendôme* in Denmark as one of the first ballets after his expected appointment as ballet-master at Copenhagen's Royal Theatre.

For the same purpose he purchased a copy of Gyrowetz's répétiteur's copy in Paris, in which he inserted a complete description of the ballet's mime and dramatic action. This manuscript represents one of the most important sources for the study of Aumer's original Paris version of this ballet. It also bears witness to Bournonville's fine talent at this early stage of his career in making apt written descriptions of both pantomime and dramatic action.

While he clearly kept close to the original mime and dramatic action of Aumer's work, the two new dances he added to the ballet were as follows:

(1) A *Pas de trois* in Act I (score no. 9), performed by Bournonville as *Victor*, C. A. Bauer as *Elise*, and M. Werning (the elder) as *Rosine*.
(2) A *Bolero* in Act II (score no. 22), danced by Bournonville and C. A. Bauer together with the corps de ballet.

According to Bournonville's handwritten list of his works, written c.1837 (*see* Additional Sources) the Act I *Pas de trois* was set to music by R. W. v. Gallenberg. In the same list it is described as a dance originally choreographed by [Filippo] Taglioni. Gallenberg's music for the opening *Adagio* movement of this dance was many years later reused by H. S. Paulli in his score for Bournonville's so-called 'Pas de trois (Julius Price)', which was created for the débuts of his pupils, Julius Price and E. Garlieb, and performed by them and S. Price on 29.5.1854.

Moreover, according to an Italian printed piano score (now in IMc, call no. Noseda Q 49-1) the *Tarantelle* in Act I (score no. 10) of Bournonville's *Les Pages du Duc de Vendôme* was also composed by Gallenberg. It was originally part of Arm. Vestris' five-act pantomimic ballet *Macbeth* (premièred at Naples' Teatro San Carlo on 4.10.1818) in which it was performed as the finale of Act IV (score no. 22).

Finally, the music for the Act II *Bolero* was borrowed by Bournonville from D.-F.-E. Auber's five-act opera from 1828 *La Muette de Portici* in which it was part of the divertissement in Act I.

According to the rehearsal book of H. C. J. Fredstrup the ballet was given 49 rehearsals between 7.7. and 3.9.1830. *Les Pages du Duc de Vendôme* reached a total of 9 performances in Copenhagen, the last of which was given on 24.11.1831.

Musical sources:

Orchestral score. Ms. Copy. Brown and black ink. 2 vol. Act I: 462 pp, Act II: 320 pp. (29,7 × 23 cm with minor variants)
Vol. I: Partitur/200/til/Gyrowetz/Hertugen af Vendomes Pager/fra No. 1. til No. 16./[...]/Les Pages./Ballet en un [changed to:] deux Acte [*sic*]/I.r Partie
Vol. II: Partitur/200/til/Gyrowetz/Hertugen af Vendomes Pager/fra No. 16. til No. 23./[...] No. 16. 2.den Akt [erased]
Unsigned and undated [c.1830]
[DKKk; C I, 259 (KTB 200)
This score is clearly a French copy since most of the titles are here given in French. However, the music for Act I *Pas de trois* (score no. 9) and the Act II *Bolero* are later insertions. Of these the former contains a (not yet identified) watermark reading 'N M' (in italics).

Répétiteur's copy. Ms. Copy. Brown ink. 76 pp. (26,6 × 20,8 cm)
Partie de Ballet/Les Pages/du/Duc de Vendôme
Unsigned and undated [c.1830]
[DKKk; MA ms 2639 (KTB 200)
This répétiteur's copy is a French copy and was almost certainly brought to Copenhagen by Bournonville in 1830. It contains the complete music for score nos. 1–6, 8, 10–21, and 23 in Bournonville's Danish version. It also includes his autographed notes (written with black ink) which describe the mime and dramatic action throughout the ballet. The fact that nearly all the dance numbers are missing here indicates that Bournonville intended from the outset to mount this ballet with his own incorporated dances.

Répétiteur's copy. Ms. Copy. Brown ink. 1 vol. 88 pp. (33,2 × 23,8 cm)
Repetiteur Parti/til/Balletten/Hertugen af Vendomes Pager/Bournonville-Girowetz/302/1830/Sept:/[...]/Violino 1.mo Rep:/til/Balletten/Hertugen af Vendomes Pager
Unsigned and dated: '1830/Sept:'
[DKKk; MA ms 2940 (KTB 200)
This répétiteur's copy was used for all rehearsals of *Les Pages du Duc de Vendôme* in Copenhagen. It includes Bournonville's pencilled autographed notes which concern the musical cuts (totalling 176 bars) that he made at some later stage in score nos. 6, 7, 10, 15, 20, and 22. Moreover, his autographed notes written (with brown ink) in the music of the 'Finale' (score no. 23) describe the choreography of this dance in more general terms.

Parts. Ms. Copy. 36 vol.
3 vl I, 3 vl II, 2 vla, 3 vlc e cb, fl picc, fl 1/2, ob 1/2, cl 1/2, fag 1/2, cor 1/2/3/4, tr 1/2, cnt a chiavi, serp, trb 1/2/3, timp, gr cassa, piatti, tri, arpa.
Unsigned and undated [1830]
[DKKk; KTB 200
According to notes written in several of these parts the ballet played for a length of time indicated as between 60 minutes and 1 hour and 25 minutes.

Printed sources:

Printed scenario. 1 vol. 16 pp. (17,5 × 10,2 cm)
Hertugen af Vendômes Pager./Pantomimisk Ballet i 2 Acter/af/Aumer./Musik af Gyrowetz./Med nye componerede Dandse fremsat paa den danske Scene/af/A. Bournonville.
Kiöbenhavn, Jens Hostrup Schultz, 1830.
[DKKk; 17, – 171 8°

29.10.1830
Paul et Virginie (Paul og Virginie).
Bournonville had attended a performance of P. Gardel's and R. Kreutzer's three-act ballet *Paul et Virginie* at the Paris

Opéra on 26.12.1825 when his teacher, A. Vestris, played the rôle of *Dominique*. This performance made such an overwhelming impression on him that he seems to have decided at that time to mount this ballet later on in Copenhagen (*see also* 18.4.1829). Moreover, he himself performed in the ballet's dance divertissements at the Paris Opéra on several occasions in the late 1820s (Gardel's ballet was given for the last time in Paris on 31.10.1828). Together, these experiences seem to have urged Bournonville to copy the entire orchestral score in Paris sometime during the late 1829 or early 1830.

In Copenhagen his staging was kept closely to Gardel's original mime and dramatic action, while the dances were nearly all choreographed anew and set to music borrowed from the then current Paris Opéra repertory. These dances, which replaced Gardel's original divertissements, were as follows:

(1) A *Pas d'ensemble* in Act I (score no. 8), performed by five creoles.
(2) A *Pas de cinq* in Act I (score no. 9), performed by Bournonville (as *Paul*), A. Krætzmer (as *Virginie*), P. Larcher (as *Domingo*), F. Hoppe, and M. Werning.
(3) A *Tarantella* in Act III (score no. 24 A), performed by the corps de ballet.

According to the original répétiteur's copy for G. Spontini's three-act lyrical tragedy from 1807 *La Vestale* (now in FPo, call no. Mat. 19 [278 (334), pp. 53–59) the music for the *Pas d'ensemble* in Bournonville's *Paul et Virginie* was originally part of Spontini's work, in which it was performed as 'Ballet no. 3' in Act I to choreography by P. Gardel and with the title 'Pas de Tambourin'. Similarly, Bournonville's *Pas de trois* in Act I of *Paul et Virginie* was set to music borrowed from the current Paris Opéra repertory, namely A. Deshayes' and J. Schneitzhoeffer's three-act fairy-ballet *Zémire et Azor* (premièred on 20.10.1824). According to the orchestral score and the répétiteur's copy for this work (now in FPo, call nos. A 477 [I], pp. 93–167, and Mat. 19 [276 (1), pp. 15–31) it originally served as accompaniment for a dance in the first act, entitled 'Zémire et Azor/Pas de 4./ferdinand' and was performed by the French dancer, Ferdinand (stage name for Jean La Brunière de Médicis) and three (not yet identified) ballerinas.

Finally, the Act III *Tarentella* in Bournonville's *Paul et Virginie* was borrowed from an earlier work of his own, namely the *Tarentella* in J. L. Heiberg's three-act play *Princess Isabella, or Three Nights at the Court* (*see* 29.10.1829). The music for this dance, however, was originally part of A. Petit's and F. Sor's ballet *Le Sicilien ou l'Amour peintre* and had been incorporated by J. Schneitzhoeffer for the Paris première of this ballet on 11.6.1827.

A second, abridged version of Bournonville's Danish 1830 version of *Paul et Virginie* was arranged and mounted by him nearly 25 years later at the Court Theatre on 19.6.1854, and at the Royal Theatre on 21.1.1855. This production was later also mounted by his pupil, S. Lund, at Stockholm's Royal Theatre (Operahuset) on 7.2.1858.

The original Copenhagen version of *Paul et Virginie* received 6 performances, the last of which was given on 12.4. 1831. According to the rehearsal book of H. C. J. Fredstrup, 40 rehearsals were held of it between 5.9. and 29.10.1830.

Autograph sources:

Production note. Ms. Autograph. Brown ink. 2 pp. (25,8 × 21,4 cm)
Requisiter til Balletten/<u>Paul og Virginie.</u> /[…]/<u>2.den Akt.</u>/[…]/<u>3.die Akt.</u>
Unsigned and undated [1830]
[SSm; Daniel Fryklunds samling no. 141

Production note. Ms. Autograph (partially in another's hand). Brown ink and pencil. 4 pp. (25,8 × 21,4 cm)
Balletten Paul og Virginie/af/<u>Mr Gardel.</u>
Unsigned and undated [1830]
[SSm; Daniel Fryklunds samling no. 141

Musical sources:

Orchestral score. Ms. Autograph (by Bournonville) and copy. Black and brown ink. 1 vol. 264 pp. + insert 4 pp. (no. 24 A) (25,8 × 30 cm, 27 × 38 cm, and 26 × 24,8 cm with minor variants)
170/Partituret/til/R. Kreutzer/Balletten/Paul og Virginie/[…]/Paul & Virginie. -
Unsigned and undated [1830]
[DKKk; C I, 270 b (KTB 170)
This orchestral score is for the main part a copy made personally by Bournonville in Paris from Kreutzer's original French score, but also includes several later insertions from other French scores that most probably were purchased by Bournonville in Paris and brought by him to Copenhagen in the late 1820s and/or 1830. This theory is supported by the three French watermarks ('D & C Blauw', 'C WISE/ 1828', and 'BLACONS') also contained in this score. Bournonville's arrangement of this score bears witness to his great experience even at this early stage of his career in copying and arranging even full-length ballet scores.

Répétiteur's copy. Ms. Copy. Brown ink. 1 vol. 84 pp. (33 × 23,3 cm)
B 170/Paul og Virginie/Ballet./1830/Oct,./[…]/Violino 1.mo
Rp:/til/Balletten Paul & Virginie
Unsigned and dated: '1830/Oct,.'
[DKKk; MA ms 2932 (KTB 170 (1))
This répétiteur's copy contains Bournonville's autographed notes for the Act I *Pas de cinq* (written with brown ink) which indicate the initials of the dancers who performed each section of this dance. His other pencilled autographed notes (pp. 79–82) describe the dramatic action in the ballet's finale (score no. 26).

Répétiteur's copy (fragment). Ms. Copy. Brown ink. 1 p. (34,2 × 24 cm)
No. 24:A./Repetiteur Parti/Tarentelle
Unsigned and undated [1830]
[DKKk; MA ms 2735 (KTB 170)
This manuscript contains most of the music for the Act III *Tarentella* which was incorporated by Bournonville as score no. '24 A'.

Parts. Ms. Copy. 28 vol.
3 vl I, 3 vl II, 2 vla, 3 vlc e cb, fl 1/2, ob 1/2, cl 1/2, fag 1/2, cor 1/2, clno 1/2, trb 1/2/3, timp, gr cassa e piatti e tri.
Unsigned and undated [1830]
[DKKk; KTB 170

Other sources:

Painting by E. Lehmann. Oil on canvas (15,4 × 13,5 cm)
[Untitled]
Signed and dated: 'E. L. 1835.'
[DKKt; Balletafdelingen (permanent udstilling)
According to K. Neiiendam this painting shows the scene in Act II where *Paul* (Bournonville) and *Virginie* (A. Krætzmer), after being left alone in the wild, pray to God for their safe return home.

Printed sources:

Printed scenario. 1 vol. 18 pp. (17,9 × 10,3 cm)
Paul og Virginie./Pantomimisk Ballet i tre Akter/af/Gardel./Musiken af Kreutzer./Med nye componerede Dandse fremsat paa den danske Skueplads/af/August Bournonville.
Kiöbenhavn, Jens Hostrup Schultz, 1830.
[DKKk; 17, – 183 8°

22.12.1830
Pas de deux (uncredited) performed by Bournonville and A. Krætzmer in P. Funck's divertissement *Zephyr and Flora* (*Zephyr og Flora*).

This (uncredited) *Pas de deux* was originally performed in Copenhagen by Bournonville and Krætzmer as an incorporated divertissement in J. L. Heiberg's three-act play *Princess Isabella, or Three Nights at the Court* (*see* 29.10.1829). According to the original répétiteur's copy for P. Funck's *Zephyr and Flora* it was also incorporated this year by Bournonville in Funck's Danish version of Ch.-L. Didelot's and F.-M.-A. Venua's two-act anacreontic ballet *Flore et Zéphire* (first performed at the Paris Opéra on 12.12.1815, and staged in Copenhagen by Funck on 4.11.1820 to a new score composed and arranged by L. Zinck). In Funck's 1820 Copenhagen version of Didelot's ballet, Venua's original *Pas de deux* was not included, while in Paris it was part of the ballet's divertissement in Act II. This much is clear from a note written with red crayon in the original répétiteur's copy for Didelot's *Flore et Zéphire* (now in FPo, call no. Mat. 19 [120 (14), p. 168). It reads: '[No.] 6 Albert/pas a donner'. According to the same source this *Pas de deux* was originally performed by the French dancers, Albert (François Decombe) and C. H. Gosselin as the sixth and final number of the Act II divertissement. However, Venua's music for this dance is no longer preserved in the Paris orchestral score (now in FPo, call no. A 443 [III]). This seems to indicate that the Copenhagen score and set of parts are the only full orchestral version for Didelot's *Pas de deux* that has yet come to light.

In Copenhagen the *Pas de deux* was performed twice in *Zephyr and Flora*, the last time on 4.1.1831. It is not clear from the rehearsal book of H. C. J. Fredstrup exactly how many rehearsals of this dance were held by Bournonville in 1830.

Musical sources:

Orchestral score. Ms. Autograph (L. Zinck). Black ink. 1 vol. 84 pp. (25,5 × 35 cm)
Partitur/til/Divertissementet/Zephir og Flora/Hrr Funk Solo Dandser/Musiken af/Hrr L: Zinck/1820
Unsigned and dated (in the front cover): '1820'
[DKKk; C II, 125 b (KTB 161)
A pencilled note on p. '31v.' in this score (reading: 'Pas de deux') indicates the exact place where the (uncredited) *Pas de deux* was incorporated in P. Funck's divertissement, namely between score nos. 13 and 14. The score for this *Pas de deux* is today preserved only in the 1829 orchestral score for J. L. Heiberg's three-act play *Princess Isabella, or Three Nights at the Court* (now in DKKk, call no. C II, 125).

Répétiteur's copy. Ms. Copy. Black ink. 1 vol. 38 pp. (34,6 × 25 cm)
Repititeur=Partie:/til/Divertissementet/Zephÿr og Flora./[...]/No. 206/Violino Primo No. 1/Repetiteur Partie/til Zephÿr og Flora/Divertissement af Funk.
Unsigned and undated [1820]
[DKKk; MA ms 2926 (KTB 161)

This répétiteur's copy contains the music for the (uncredited) *Pas de deux* which was incorporated in P. Funck's divertissement on 22.12.1830 and replaced the original music there for score no. 13. This is clear from a pencilled note on p. 24 reading 'andet i Enden af Isabella faaes hos H. Bournonville'. It gives definitive proof that the music for this dance was actually borrowed from the score of J. L. Heiberg's three-act play *Princess Isabella, or Three Nights at the Court* (*see* 29.10.1829). Moreover, a pencilled autographed note by Bournonville on p. 25 (reading: 'No. 19. Faust') clearly indicates that it was he who decided also to incorporate this dance as score no. '19' in the much later restaging of his three-act romantic ballet *Faust* (*see* 8.12.1849).

Parts (*Zephyr and Flora*). Ms. Copy. 22 vol.
3 vl I, 3 vl II, 2 vla, 3 vlc e cb, fl 1/2, ob 1/2, cl 1/2, fag 1/2, cor 1/2, cor ingl.
Unsigned and undated [1820]
[DKKk; KTB 161
On the title-page of the part for the second violin (no. 3) a note reads 'Musikken deels af L. Zink'. It clearly indicates that the music for P. Funck's *Zephyr and Flora* was arranged by L. Zinck from F.-M.-A. Venua's original 1820 Paris version. Other notes in the set of parts for this work indicate that the entire divertissement played for a total of 25 minutes.

Parts (the *Pas de deux*). Ms. Copy. 21 vol.
3 vl I, 3 vl II, 2 vla, 3 vlc e cb, fl 1/2, ob 1/2, cl 1/2, fag 1/2, cor 1/2.
Unsigned and undated [c.1829–1830]
[DKKk; KTB 217
A note on the cover of the part for the first violin reads: 'ingen Partituur Blodt Reppetitørparti'. It seems to indicate that no separate orchestral score existed for this dance in 1830. Consequently, the *Pas de deux* must have been performed this year with the use of the earlier 1829 score for it, which is part of the full orchestral score for J. L. Heiberg's three-act play *Princess Isabella, or Three Nights at the Court* (now in DKKk, call no. C II, 125).

1831

23.4.1831
Victor's Wedding, or The Ancestral House (*Victors Bryllup eller Fædrene-Arnen*).

The music for this one-act ballet (a sequel to Bournonville's one-act pantomimic idyll *Soldier and Peasant* from 13.10.1829) was composed and arranged by Ph. L. Keck. In his score for no. 7 (a *Pas de trois* performed by Bournonville as Victor, A. Krætzmer as Lise, and M. Werning as Anna) Keck incorporated music by S. Mercadante. This is clear from a note (written with black ink) on p. 115 in the orchestral score indicating that this dance was originally entitled 'Passo a Tre Musica del Mercadante'.

Moreover, in the light of the information given on the title page of a printed Italian piano score that contains the exact same music as that for Bournonville's *Pas de trois* (now in IMc, call no. Noseda T 38-22), Mercadante's music was originally written for a ballet by the French choreographer, L. Henry, entitled *L'Arrivo del Gran Signore*, first performed at Naples' Teatro San Carlo on 4.11.1825. According to the same piano score this *Passo a tre* was originally danced by P. Samengo, A. Brugnoli, and E. Vaque-Moulin. Bournonville may have received a copy of this piano score from Henry in Paris, or he may have purchased it himself in the French capital during the late 1820s or early 1830. Later he may have brought it with him to Copenhagen, where Keck seems to have reorchestrated Mercadante's music in 1831.

Finally, 23 years later, H. S. Paulli reused most of the Coda movement from Mercadante's score in his music for yet another Bournonville *Pas de trois*, which was choreographed for the débuts of Jul. Price, and E. Garlieb and performed (together with S. Price) on 29.5.1854.

Among the other dances in *Victor's Wedding* were also a *Pas de quatre* (score no. 5, performed by P. Larcher, P. E. Funck, C. A. Bauer, and S. C. Møller) and a 'Contredands' (score no. 6), both of which were reused later on in other Bournonville's ballets. Thus, the music for the *Pas de quatre* became incorporated as score no. '9 B' in Act I of Bournonville's Copenhagen version of L. Milon's two-act pantomimic ballet *Nina, ou La Folle par amour* (*see* 30.9.1834), while the 'Contradands' was interpolated by him in Act II (between score nos. 21 and 22) of his three-act romantic ballet *Faust* when this work was restaged on 8.12.1849.

The music for the *Finale* in *Victor's Wedding* (score no. 16) seems to have been copied by Bournonville from a (not yet identified) French ballet score during his sojourn in Paris in the late 1829 or early 1830. This is clear from an unnamed répétiteur's copy which is clearly written in Bournonville's hand and contains the exact same music as that of the *Finale*. Consequently this music may prove to have been copied by Bournonville from a ballet score in the Paris Opéra repertory, although no secure identification of it has yet been found in FPo.

Finally, the music for the *Finale* was reused 7 years later by J. F. Fröhlich, who incorporated it in his score for Bournonville's divertissement *Hertha's Offering* (*see* 29.1.1838). In that work it accompanied a *Pas de deux* danced by Bournonville (as *Zephyr*) and L. Grahn (as *Hertha*).

Victor's Wedding reached a total of 20 performances in Copenhagen, the last of which was given on 23.4.1833. According to the rehearsal book of H. C. J. Fredstrup 35 rehearsals were held of it between 17.2. and 28.10.1831.

Musical sources:

Répétiteur's copy (fragment). Ms. Copy (made by Bournonville). Black ink. 4 pp. (30,3 × 22,5 cm)
All° Moderato
Unsigned and undated [c.1829–1830]
[DKKk; MA ms 2669 (KTB 279)
This (incomplete) répétiteur's copy is clearly written in Bournonville's hand. It was most probably copied from a French ballet score during his Parisian sojourn in late 1829 or early 1830. This theory is supported by the French watermark ('Peloux') contained in the répétiteur's copy.

Orchestral score. Ms. Copy. Black ink. 1 vol. 332 pp. (27 × 37,8 cm)
Partituret/til/Balletten/Victors Bryllup/Keck
Unsigned and undated [1831]
[DKKk; C II, 115 (KTB 279)

Répétiteur's copy (incomplete). Ms. Copy. Black ink. 1 vol. 54 pp. (33,1 × 23,2 cm)
B 279/Repetiteur Parti/Bournonville/til Musik: Keck/Balletten/Victors Bryllup/304/1831,/Maj
Unsigned and dated (on p. 54): 'd: 18.de April 1831.'
[DKKk; MA ms 2973 (KTB 279)
In this répétiteur's copy the music for score no. 5 and nearly all of no.

6 is missing. It was probably taken out of this volume when the *Pas de quatre* and the 'Contradands' became incorporated by Bournonville in his stagings of *Nina, ou La Folle par amour* (1834) and *Faust* (1849) respectively.

Parts. Ms. Copy. 32 + 9 vol.
2 vl I, 3 vl II, 2 vla, 3 vlc e cb, fl picc, fl 1/2, ob 1/2, cl 1/2, fag 1/2, cor 1/2/3/4, tr 1/2, trb 1/2/3, timp, gr cassa, tri, alarm bell. On stage: cor 1/2/3/4/5, tr 1/2, gr cassa, tri.
Unsigned and undated [1831]
[DKKk; KTB 279

Printed sources:

Printed scenario. 1 vol. 8 pp. (17,9 × 10,4 cm)
Victors Bryllup/eller/Fædrene=Arnen./Ballet i een Act af A. Bournonville. Musiken/componeret af Keck./(Fortsættelse af 'Soldat og Bonde').
Kjøbenhavn, Jens Hostrup Schultz, 1831.
[DKKk; 17, – 172 8°

28.10.1831
Pas de cinq performed by Bournonville, C. A. Bauer, M. Werning, M. Bentzen, and S. C. Møller in *La Gioventú di Enrico V (Henrik den Femtes Ungdom).*

In his handwritten list of his works, written c.1851 (*see* Additional Sources), Bournonville named this dance 'Pas de cinq Henry V'. According to a pencilled note written in the Copenhagen orchestral score for G. Pacini's *La Gioventù di Enrico V* (reading: 'NB Her imellem kommer Dandsen', now in DKKk, call no. C I, 293, vol. III, p. '98v.'), Bournonville's *Pas de cinq* was incorporated on this day as a divertissement in Act III (score no. 14) of Pacini's three-act *dramma giocoso* from 1820. The music for this dance, however, was borrowed from the score of N. Isouard's, A.-M. Benincori's and F.-A. Habeneck's three-act fairy-opera *Aladin, ou La Lampe merveilleuse* (premièred at the Paris Opéra on 6.2.1822). In this opera all the dance divertissements were originally created by the French choreographer, P. Gardel.

According to the original orchestral score and répétiteur's copy for Isouard's *Aladin, ou La Lampe merveilleuse* (now in FPo, call nos. A 465 [III], pp. 353–427, and Mat. 19 [34 (108), pp. 167–182) the exact same music, which Bournonville reused for his *Pas de cinq* in *La Gioventú di Enrico V* in Copenhagen, is entitled: 'La Lampe Pas de 3 Gallenberg 4.me et dernière Edition Mr. Paul &c.'. It clearly provides us with the name of the music composer, the Austrian R. W. v. Gallenberg. Moreover, according to the same sources Gallenberg's music originally served as accompaniment for a *Pas de trois* performed by the French dancer, A. Paul, and two (not yet identified) ballerinas. However, other notes in the same sources indicate that during the mid-1820s these dancers were replaced by three other artists, namely the French dancers Albert (François Decombe), L. Noblet, and E. Lacroix. Furthermore, Bournonville himself had chosen this dance for his second début performance at the Paris Opéra on 7.4.1826. This is clear from a letter written to his father a few days later on 11.4.1826:

'Mon second début etoit dans *La Lampe merveilleuse*. Le pas de trois de Mr Albert avec Mmes Noblet & Lacroix. Ce Pas d'un genre noble & gracieux, me fut encore plus favorable sous plusieurs rapports & ayant déjà pris l'habitude de la scène, il s'en suivit plus de confiance

& l'avis de tout le monde confirmé par les encouragemens du public etoit que j'avais encore mieux été que la première [*sic*] fois, & j'espère [*sic*] bien que mes autres quatre débuts iront en augmentant [*sic*]'.

It therefore seems most likely that he purchased Gallenberg's orchestral score for this *Pas de trois* in Paris some time during the late 1820s with the direct aim of bringing it with him to Copenhagen at a later stage. This most probably happened during the early months of 1830, since *Aladin, ou La Lampe merveilleuse* was given for the last time in Paris on 11.9.1830.

In Copenhagen the *Pas de cinq* in *La Gioventù di Enrico V* reached a total of 5 performances, the last of which took place on 20.12.1831. It is not clear from the rehearsal book of H. C. J. Fredstrup exactly how many rehearsals were held by Bournonville of this dance in 1831.

Many years after the *Pas de cinq* had gone out of the repertory the middle section of Gallenberg's *Allegretto Moderato* movement became incorporated by H. S. Paulli in his score for Bournonville's new 1854 *Pas de trois*, choreographed for the débuts of Jul. Price and E. Garlieb, and first performed by them and S. Price on 29.5.1854.

Musical sources:

Orchestral score. Ms. Copy. Brown ink. 1 vol. 68 pp. of which one is blank (29,1 × 22,2 cm)
E/[...]/La Lampe/Pas de trois. Mr Paul. Bournonvi[lle]/E
Unsigned and undated [c.1830]
[DKKk; MA ms 2654 (KTA 279)
This score is clearly a French copy and was most probably brought to Copenhagen by Bournonville in the early months of 1830. This theory is supported by the French watermark ('W' for Wise) contained in the score.

Répétiteur's copy. Ms. Copy. Brown ink. 1 vol. 12 pp. of which one is blank (32 × 24,9 cm)
A 279/Repetiteur Parti/til/Henrik den femtes Ungdom/214
Unsigned and undated [1831]
[DKKk; MA ms 3058 (KTA 279)
This répétiteur's copy contains Bournonville's pencilled autographed notes indicating the exact tempi for each section of the dance.

No set of parts has yet been traced for this dance except for that dating from the original 1822 Paris production of *Aladin, ou La Lampe merveilleuse* (now in FPo, call no. Mat. 19 [34 (1–148)).

1832

30.1.1832
***Pas de deux* performed by Bournonville and A. Krætzmer as an incorporated divertissement in F. Hérold's three-act singspiel *Zampa, ou La Fiancée de Marbre (Zampa eller Marmorbruden)*.**
In Bournonville's handwritten list of his works written c.1851 (*see* Additional Sources) this dance is named 'Pas de deux af Zampa'. According to a note written with red crayon in the printed orchestral score for Hérold's three-act comic opera from 1831, *Zampa, ou La Fiancée de Marbre* (now in DKKk, call no. U 6, p. 309), the *Pas de deux* was incorporated in the finale of Act II (score no. 10). The music for this dance,

which was originally part of the Paris Opéra repertory, had most probably been purchased in Paris and brought to Copenhagen by Bournonville in the early months of 1830.

In France it was originally an integral part of J. Aumer's and F. Hérold's restaging on 17.11.1828 of J. Dauberval's two-act pantomimic ballet *La Fille mal gardée* (first performed at the Grand Théâtre in Bordeaux on 1.7.1789). According to the orchestral score and the répétiteur's copy for their 1828 Paris production of Dauberval's ballet (now in FPo, call nos. Shelve 31, score numbered '487', pp. 357–432, and Mat. 19 [284 (38) pp. 81–95)), Hérold's music for this dance originally accompanied a *Pas de trois* in Act I, entitled 'Pas de trois de Mr Paul'. According to a pencilled note in the répétiteur's copy it was first danced by A. Paul, P. Montessu (as *Lise*), and M. Taglioni.

Bournonville's 1832 *Pas de deux* in *Zampa, ou La Fiancée de Marbre* was (according to the repertory book of F. Hoppe) later also mounted in Copenhagen as a separate divertissement on 17.9.1836 (then performed by Hoppe and L. Grahn). Moreover, on 29.1.1833 it was incorporated in Bournonville's one-act idyllic ballet *The Veteran, or The Ancestral House* in which (according to a pencilled note on p. '168v.' of the orchestral score for this work) it replaced some originally planned music for score no. 28. It was danced in that ballet by Bournonville (as *Colin*) and A. Krætzmer (as *Louison*). However, on 29.9.1837 the *Pas de deux* was again replaced in *The Veteran, or The Ancestral House* by another *Pas de deux*, namely Bournonville's so-called 'Pas de deux oriental' (*see* 26.9.1829) which this year was performed by Bournonville (as *Colin*) and R. Lund (as *Louison*).

The original 1832 *Pas de deux* was only given 3 times within Hérold's *Zampa, ou La Fiancée de Marbre* (the last time on 15.2.1832). It is not clear from the rehearsal book of H. C. J. Fredstrup exactly how many rehearsals were given of this dance in 1832.

Musical sources:

Orchestral score. Ms. Copy. Black ink. 1 vol. 46 pp. of which one is blank (35,4 × 26,3 cm)
283/Partidöx/til/Zampa=Musiicken/Er No 28 af Wetterannen/B. 283/[...]/No. 28./Dands
Unsigned and undated [c.1830-1832]
[DKKk; MA ms 2982 (KTB 283 (2))
This score is a Danish copy that most was probably was made from a French score brought to Copenhagen from Paris by Bournonville during the early months of 1830.

Répétiteur's copy. Ms. Copy. Brown ink. 1 vol. 8 pp. (32,5 × 23,3 cm)
Repetiteur-Parti / Til / Zampa eller Marmor=/Bruden – /No. 40. [erased]/202/[...]/ Repetiteur Parti/til/ Zampa eller Marmorbruden/No. 10 Finale af 2.den Akt
Unsigned and undated [1832]
[DKKk; MA ms 3060 (KTA 287 (1))
Apart from the incorporated *Pas de deux* this répétiteur's copy contains the complete music for the finale in Act II (score no. 10) of Hérold's opera. The exact place where Bournonville's *Pas de deux* was performed in this opera is indicated by a note (written with brown ink on p. 2) reading: 'Indlagt Dands'.

Répétiteur's copy. Ms. Copy. Brown ink. 1 vol. 6 pp. of which one is blank (32,9 × 23 cm)
287/Repetiteur Parti/til/Zampa/Pas de deux. –/[...]Repetiteur Parti/til/Zampa eller Marmorbruden

Unsigned and undated [1832]
[DKKk; MA ms 3061 (KTA 287 (2))
This répétiteur's copy contains Bournonville's autographed notes
(written with brown ink) which indicate the exact tempi and the
musical phrasing of his *Pas de deux* in Hérold's *Zampa, ou La Fiancée
de Marbre*.

No separate set of parts for Bournonville's 'Pas de deux af Zampa'
has yet been traced.

25.4.1832
Faust.
This three-act romantic ballet on J. W. v. Goethe's *Faust* (set
to a score composed and arranged by Ph. L. Keck) was created as a homage to the great German writer, who had
passed away in Weimar only a month before on 22.3.1832.
Keck incorporated several musical excerpts borrowed from
the works of French, German, and Italian composers. According to Bournonville's memoirs *My Theatre Life* (p. 69)
they included music by J. Schneitzhoeffer, L. Carlini, F. Sor,
G. Spontini, C. M. v. Weber, and G. Rossini, of which four
borrowings are identified as follows:

(1) Act II (score nos. 14, 15, 20, and 21): In these numbers Keck
employed four large excerpts borrowed from F. Sor's and J. Schneitzhoeffer's score to Albert's (François Decombe) three-act fairy-ballet
Cendrillon (premièred at the Paris Opéra on 3.3.1823). According to
the orchestral score and the répétiteur's copy for this ballet (now in
FPo, call no. A 469 [II], and Mat. 19 [63 (3)]) the four excerpts were
all taken from Act II of *Cendrillon*, where they mainly accompanied
dances performed in scenes 5–7 of that act.
(2) Act III (score no. 29): Keck here inserted music borrowed from
F. Hérold's new score to J. Aumer's restaging at the Paris Opéra on
17.11.1828 of J. Dauberval's two-act pantomimic ballet from 1789 *La
Fille mal gardée*. According to the Paris orchestral score and the répétiteur's copy for this production (now in FPo, call nos. A 491 (Acte I),
pp. 245–296, and Mat. 19 [284 (38), pp. 57–67]) Hérold's music originally accompanied a dance in Act I, entitled 'Pas des moissonneurs',
performed by the entire corps de ballet.
(3) Act III (score no. 30): In this number Keck incorporated music
borrowed from the so-called *Pas de soldats* in Act III of G. Rossini's
four-act opera *Guillaume Tell* (premièred at the Paris Opéra on 3.8.
1829).
(4) Act III (the *Finale*): Keck here employed themes borrowed from
C. M. v. Weber's 1826 overture for *Oberon*.

At its 1832 première *Faust* contained (according to the
poster and Bournonville's pencilled autographed notes in
the 1832 répétiteur's copy) one dance divertissement in Act
II, entitled *Pas de deux*. It was performed by P. Funck and S.
C. Møller as score no. '15'. This dance seems later also to
have been given as a separate divertissement in Copenhagen
on 15.10.1839, performed by F. Hoppe and C. Fjeldsted.
   On 17.10.1842 *Faust* was (according to the poster) performed with yet another so-called *New Pas de deux (Ny Pas de
deux)* in Act II. It was choreographed by the French dancer,
F. Lefèbvre, who danced it together with A. Nielsen. According to a pencilled note in the 1832 répétiteur's copy for *Faust*
(p. 13, reading: 'Indlagt No. 15. B.') this dance seems to
have been incorporated immediately after Bournonville's
original *Pas de deux* in the same act, or it may perhaps have
replaced it. Moreover, the 1842 poster identifies for the first
time the two other divertissements in this ballet, which this
year were as follows:

(1) A *Pas de trois*, performed by F. Hoppe, P. Fredstrup, and P. Funck.
(2) A *Mazurka*, danced by Hoppe and P. Funck.

Two years later (on 30.4.1844) the ballet was, according to
the poster and pencilled notes in the orchestral scores and
the parts for *Faust*, performed with two more incorporated
divertissements as follows:

(1) A *Pas de deux* in Act II, set to music by A. Mussi and choreographed by F. Hoppe, who performed it together with C. Fjeldsted.
(2) A Spanish character dance in Act III, entitled *'La Gitana'*, set to
music by E. Helsted with choreography by Hoppe, who performed it
together with C. Fjeldsted between score nos. 30 and 31.

Finally, according to notes written in a separate set of parts
for J. F. Fröhlich's *Pas de deux* (score no. 5) in Bournonville's
pantomimic prologue *The Fatherland's Muses* (*see* 20.3.1840)
this dance (originally performed by F. Hoppe as *Zephyr* and
A. Nielsen as *Aglaë*) was also incorporated as a divertissement in Bournonville's *Faust* some time during the 1840s.
   In Sweden, *Faust* was mounted by Bournonville in a heavily
abridged one-act version at Stockholm's Royal Theatre
(Operahuset) on 9.6.1847. In Copenhagen, the complete
ballet was restaged on 8.12.1849 in a new and slightly extended version. According to Bournonville's pencilled notes
in the orchestral score (p. 161), and other notes in the 1836
répétiteur's copy for *La Sylphide* and in the 1849 répétiteur's
copy for *Faust*, the 1849 staging of this ballet included three
new dances in Act II. They seem to have replaced the earlier
incorporated dances in that act and were as follows:

(1) A *Pas de deux* inserted as score no. '19'. This dance was originally
performed in J. L. Heiberg's three-act play *Princess Isabella, or Three
Nights at the Court* (*see* 29.10.1829) and is set to music by F.-M-A.
Venua. In *Faust* it was performed by W. Funck and J. Price, and replaced the original score no. 19. It seems later also to have been
mounted as a separate divertissement in Copenhagen on 27.12.
1850, 24.4.1851, and 1.9.1857 (at the Court Theatre), and in Norway
(at Christiania's Theatre, Oslo) on 29.6.1852.
(2) A so-called 'Indlagt Contradands C dur' inserted as score no.
'20'. This dance was originally part of Keck's score for Bournonville's
one-act ballet *Victor's Wedding, or The Ancestral House* (*see* 23. 4.1831)
in which it was performed as score no. '6' and notated in E flat major.
(3) A so-called 'Pas de deux D dur (Sylphiden)' inserted between
score nos. 21 and 22. This dance (which is set to music by J. Mayseder) was originally part of Act II (score no. 1 A) in Bournonville's
two-act romantic ballet *The Isle of Phantasy* (*see* 28.10.1838). On 27.9.
1842 it was also incorporated in H. S. v. Løvenskjold's score for
Bournonville's two-act romantic ballet *La Sylphide* (*see* 28.11.1836).
In that ballet it replaced Løvenskjold's original 1836 *Pas de deux* in
Act II (score no. 3) and was danced by Bournonville (as *James*) and A.
Nielsen (as *The Sylph*).

At Bournonville's last restaging of *Faust* in Copenhagen on
25.9.1855, the ballet was (according to a letter written to J. L.
Heiberg on 14.5.1854) mounted in a thoroughly revised version. Acts I and II were now drastically reduced, while the
whole of Act III was completely omitted. This version is described in Bournonville's diary as: 'Reducert de to förste
Akter (1. Akt 20 min., 2. Akt 45 min.)'.
   Furthermore, a third, projected restaging of *Faust* in Copenhagen was (according to Bournonville's diary) prepared
on 6.11.1859, but never carried out.
   Finally, the music for the two opening dances in Act III of

Faust (score nos. 28 and 29) was interpolated in Bournonville's last restaging in Copenhagen of his Danish version of J. Aumer's three-act pantomimic ballet *La Somnambule, ou l'Arrivée d'un nouveau seigneur* on 2.10.1868. In that ballet it replaced the original two opening numbers of Act III. Bournonville's 1868 restaging of *La Somnambule, ou l'Arrivée d'un nouveau seigneur* therefore represents the last time that dances from *Faust* were performed at Copenhagen's Royal Theatre.

The original 1832 version of *Faust* received 43 performances in Copenhagen, the last of which was given on 10.3. 1848. According to the rehearsal book of H. C. J. Fredstrup the ballet was given 35 rehearsals between 8.2. and 25.4. 1832.

Autograph sources:

Manuscript scenario. Ms. Autograph. Black ink. 1 vol. 16 pp. (24,4 × 21 cm)
Faust/romantisk Ballet i 3 Acter./af Auguste Bournonville./1831 -
Signed and dated: '1831'
[DKKk; NKS 3285 4° 2 F

Production note. Ms. Autograph. Black ink. 1 p. (21 × 17 cm)
Faust
Unsigned and undated [1832]
[DKKkt; F.M. (Ballet, læg F)

Musical sources:

Orchestral score. Ms. Autograph (by Ph. L. Keck) and copy. Black and brown ink. 3 vol. Act I 124 pp., Act II 272 pp., Act III 198 pp. (26,8 × 37,5 cm with minor variants)
1.ste Akt/Partituret/til/Balletten Faust/298 [erased] 289/[...]/ 2den Akt/[...]/3die Akt
Unsigned and undated [1832]
[DKKk; C II, 115 (KTB 289)
This score is Keck's autograph except for Act II (score no. 20, pp. 109–126) and Act III (score nos. 29 and 30, pp. 1–90) which are written by an unknown copyist. The score was used for all productions of *Faust* between 1832 and 1855.

Répétiteur's copy (incomplete). Ms. Autographs (by Ph. L. Keck and Bournonville). Black and brown ink. Act I 26 pp., Act II 34 pp., Act III 40 pp. (32,4 × 24,8 cm)
Repetitörparti for To Violiner/til Balletten Faust/No. 1/[...]/2den Akt/[...]/3die Akt
Unsigned and undated [1832]
[DKKk; MA ms 2644 (1–3) (KTB 289)
This répétiteur's copy is Keck's autograph except for Act II (parts of score no. 18, no. 19, and parts of score no. 20) which are Bournonville's autograph, and Act III (score nos. 29 and 30) which are written by an unknown copyist. The volume also contains Keck's autographed notes (written with brown ink) which describe the dramatic action in Act I (score nos. 1–10) and Bournonville's pencilled autographed notes indicating the mime of Act I (score no. 11) and Act III (score no. 29).

Part. Ms. Copy. 29 vol.
3 vl I, 3 vl II, 2 vla, 3 vlc e cb, fl 1/2, ob 1/2, cl 1/2, fag 1/2, cor 1/2, clno 1/2, trb 1/2/3, timp, gr cassa e piatti, tri.
Unsigned and undated [1832]
[DKKk; KTB 289
These parts were used for all productions of *Faust* in Copenhagen between 1832 and 1855.

Other sources:

Drawing by E. Lehmann. Pencil (14,5 × 12,1 cm)
Faust
Unsigned and undated [c.1832–1839]
[DKKt; Lehmann tegninger
According to K. Neiiendam this drawing shows the final scene of Act I in which *Mephistopheles* (A. Stramboe) reveals a vision of the sleeping *Margaretha* (A. Krætzmer or L. Grahn) to *Faust* (Bournonville).

Printed sources:

Printed scenario. 1 vol. 16 pp. (18,7 × 11,1 cm)
Faust./Original romantisk Ballet/i tre Akter/af August Bournonville.
Kjøbenhavn, Bianco Luno & Schneider, 1832.
[DKKk; 17, – 172 8°

5.6.1832
The rôle of *Adolphe* in *Adolphe et Clara, ou les deux Prisonniers (Adolph og Clara eller De to Arrestanter)*.
For this restaging of N. Dalayrac's one-act *comédie en prose* (premièred in Paris at the Opéra-Comique on 10.2.1799, and first performed in Copenhagen on 17.12.1801), Bournonville performed the rôle of Adolphe, a part which his father had played before him on two occasions (8.2. and 20.2.1812). The 1832 staging of this comedy (which was given only once) represents the second and last time that Bournonville performed a singing rôle at Copenhagen's Royal Theatre. Being gifted with a fine (baritone) voice, he had since his childhood appeared in several singing rôles of the Royal Theatre's repertory. The first of these took place in F. L. A. Kunzen's three-act sing-spiel *Rustic Love (Kjærlighed paa Landet)* on 1.3.1817.

Many years later he again performed as a 'singer' in his own one-act ballet-vaudeville *Bellman* (*see* 3.6.1844) in which he performed a song by the great Swedish poet, C. M. Bellman, to his own musical accompaniment on the lute as part of the second and last restaging of this work at Stockholm 's Royal Theatre (Operahuset) on 21.4.1858.

It is not clear from the rehearsal book of H. C. J. Fredstrup exactly how many rehearsals of the rôle of Adolphe in *Adolphe et Clara, ou Les deux Prisonniers* were held by Bournonville in 1832.

Musical sources:

Printed orchestral score. 1 vol. 120 pp. (29,8 × 24, 3 cm)
ADOLPHE/ET/CLARA/OU/LES DEUX PRISONNIERS,
Paris, Huguet, pl. no. 9 [c. 1799]
[DKKk; U 6 (mu 6401.0438)
This printed orchestral score contains J. Baggesen's 1801 Danish translation (written with black ink) of B. J. Marsollier's original French text.

Parts. Ms. Copy. 25 + 2 vol.
4 vlI, 2 vl II, 2 vla, 4 vlc e cb, fl picc, fl 1/2, ob 1/2, cl 1/2, fag 1/2, cor 1/2, timp. 2 vocal parts (*Clara* and *Adolphe*).
Unsigned and undated [1801]
[DKKk; KTA 129

20.7.1832
Cort Adeler in Venice (Cort Adeler i Venedig). **Projected ballet.**
This projected three-act heroic ballet, based on the life and the achievements of the fifteenth-century Norwegian born sea hero, Cort Adeler, was (according to the earliest manu-

script scenario for it) originally dedicated the great Danish sculptor, B. Thorvaldsen. Although Bournonville resumed work on this project during Denmark's war with Germany in 1848, the ballet was not carried out until some 40 years later, when *Cort Adeler in Venice* was premièred at Copenhagen's Royal Theatre on 14.1.1870. It was then set to a new, original score by P. Heise and dedicated to the Danish admiral, E. Suenson.

Autograph sources:

Manuscript scenario. Ms. Autograph. Black ink. 24 pp. (27 × 22 cm)
Cort Adeler/Original heroisk Ballet i 3 [changed to '4'] Acter/af/ Auguste Bournonville/Du Danskes Vej til Roes og Magt/ Sortladne Hav!/Ewald./1832
Signed and dated: 'Frederiksdahl den 20 Julii 1832.' also including a dedication to B. Thorvaldsen dated: 'Kjöbenhavn d: 20 Julii 1832'.
[DKKk; NKS 3285 4° 2 A–E

29.10.1832
Pas de cinq (uncredited) performed by Bournonville, A. Krætzmer, C. A. Bauer, M. Werning, and S. C. Møller in *The Raven (Ravnen eller Broderprøven).*

In his handwritten list of his works, written c.1851 (*see* Additional Sources) this (uncredited) dance is named by Bournonville as 'Ditto [i.e. Pas de Cinq] af Ravnen'. It was an integral part of I. P. E. Hartmann's three-act opera since its première and was performed as the middle section of the chorus in the Act II finale, entitled 'Under Sang og glade Dandse for Kong Millo og hans Brud'. Nearly all of Hartmann's music for this dance was reused many years later by H. S. Paulli in his music for Act I (score no. 3) of Bournonville's three-act ballet *Zulma, or The Crystal Palace* (*see* 14.4. 1852). Moreover, parts of the same music were incorporated by V. C. Holm as the third number in his music arrangement for Bournonville's ballet divertissement *The Mandarin's Daughters* (*see* 23.4.1873).

The *Pas de cinq* was performed 6 times in *The Raven*, the last time on 6.12.1833. It is not clear from the rehearsal book of H. C. J. Fredstrup exactly how many rehearsals were held of this dance in 1832.

Musical sources:

Orchestral score. Ms. Autograph (by I. P. E. Hartmann). Brown and black ink. 1 vol. 132 pp. (26,7 × 38 cm)
Ravnen,/2.den Act/Partitur/I: P: E: Hartmann
Signed and undated [1832]
[DKKk; I. P. E. Hartmanns Samling.
This autographed score was originally Hartmann's private property. The music for the *Pas de cinq* in Act II is written as a separate section inserted at the end of this score (pp. 113–132). It is entitled 'Dands til Finalet af 2.den Act i 'Ravnen' (vide Partiturets Ark 59)'. This circumstance clearly indicates that Hartmann's *Pas de cinq* was written and incorporated in his opera at a rather late stage in the compositional process. The tempo of the dance is indicated by Hartmann with the metronome marking of a dotted crochet equal to '96'.

Orchestral score. Ms. Copy. Black and brown ink. 1 vol. 238 pp. (27,2 × 37,8 cm with minor variants)
Ravnen./Partitur./2.den Akt.
Unsigned and undated [1832]
[DKKk; C II, 114 (KTA 292)
This manuscript orchestral score was used for all performances of *The Raven* in Copenhagen between 1832 and 1833.

No répétiteur's copy for the *Pas de cinq* in *The Raven* has been traced so far.

Parts. Ms. Copy. 32 vol.
3 vl I, 3 vl II, 2 vla, 3 vlc e cb, fl 1/2, ob 1/2, cl 1/2, cor bassetto, fag 1/2, cor 1/2/3/4, tr 1/2, trb 1/2/3, timp, gr cassa e piatti, tri.
Unsigned and undated [1832]
[DKKk; KTA 292
These parts were used for all performances of *The Raven* in Copenhagen between 1832 and 1833.

16.12.1832
Le Cor, Ballade and *Le Retour de Pierre, Romance* sung by Bournonville.

According to the poster for this day, Bournonville performed a ballade and a romance named *Le Cor* and *Le Retour de Pierre*, composed by A. M. Panseron and C.-H. Plantade respectively. The ballade was sung to the accompaniment of a French horn, played by F. C. Drewes. Bournonville's performance of these songs was given at Copenhagen's Royal Theatre as part of a special charity performance for the actor, T. Overskou.

20.12.1832
Pas de deux (uncredited) performed by Bournonville and A. Krætzmer in P. Larcher's *Le Carnaval de Venise, ou Constance à l'Epreuve (Carnavalet i Venedig eller Kjærlighed paa Prøve).*

In his handwritten lists of his works written c.1851 (*see* Additional Sources) Bournonville named this dance 'Pas de deux Carnavalet'. It was danced by himself (in the rôle as Don Carlos) and Krætzmer (in the part of Countess Vittoria). The *Pas de deux* was originally part of L. Milon's two-act pantomimic ballet with the same title (premièred at the Paris Opéra on 22.2.1816 to a score by L.-L. Persuis and R. Kreutzer). According to the orchestral score and the répétiteur's copy for this ballet (now in FPo, call nos. A 444 [II], pp. 121–158, and Mat. 19 [57 (40), pp. 110–111, 130–133, 135–141) it was performed in Act II by the dancers, Albert (François Decombe) and E. Bigottini. It was set to the popular tune in 6/8 time, entitled 'Carneval de Venise', which in its turn is a Neapolitan folk tune named 'La Ricciolella'. It had become widely known through N. Paganini's virtuosic variations of it for solo violin.

The fact that Bournonville lists this *Pas de deux* among his own compositions seems to indicate that it was performed with completely different choreography from that in P. Larcher's original Copenhagen production of *Le Carnaval de Venise* (premièred on 22.12.1823). Bournonville's choreography, however, was most probably very close to that he had seen performed in Milon's ballet in Paris during the late 1820s or early 1830 (*Le Carnaval de Venise* was given for the last time at the Paris Opéra on 1.8.1838). This theory is confirmed by the fact that neither Bournonville nor Larcher was ever credited on the posters for the choreography of this dance.

Many years later Bournonville reused the main musical motif of this *Pas de deux* for a dance named *Polichinel* and performed in Act II of his last ballet on an Italian theme, the two-act ballet-vaudeville *Pontemolle (An Artists' Party in Rome)* (*see* 11.4.1866).

Finally, in 1871 he employed yet another musical excerpt

from Milon's ballet, namely the dance entitled 'La folie'. Most of the music for this dance was this year incorporated by V. C. Holm in his score for the so-called 'En Quadrille af holbergske Figurer' in Bournonville's one-act ballet-vaudeville *The King's Corps of Volunteers on Amager (Livjægerne paa Amager)*, premièred on 19.2.1871.

It is not clear from the rehearsal book of H. C. J. Fredstrup exactly how many rehearsals of the *Pas de deux* in *Le Carnaval de Venise* were held in 1832.

Musical sources:

Orchestral score. Ms. Copy with a partially printed title page. Black ink. 2 vol. Act I 418 pp., Act II 192 pp. (28,9 × 22,5 cm, and a sheet inserted in Act II between p. '302v' and '303r' measuring 27 × 36,5 cm)
Partitur/Le Carnaval de Wenisse [*sic*]/1.ste Akt/[...]/Le Carnaval de Venise/pour Mr Larcher/[...]/De la Composition de M.r Millon/[...]/2.den Akt
Unsigned and dated (on the title-page): '22 Decbr 1823'
[DKKk; C I, 303 (KTB 1009, originally KTB 195)
According to the printed title-page this orchestral score is a French copy made by the music copyist and librarian at the Paris Opéra, F.-C. Lefèbvre. It was brought to Copenhagen by P. Larcher in 1823. According to Bournonville's pencilled autographed note (reading: 'Pas de deux') the *Pas de deux* in Act II was performed as no. 17 (pp. '222r.' to '241r.').

Répétiteur's copy. Ms. Copy (by P. Grønfeldt). Black ink. 1 vol. 52 pp of which two are blank (32,7 × 33,4 cm)
Grønfeldt/Le Carnaval de Wenise/par/Monsieur Larcher./Violino 1.mo/Repetiteur Partie/1823
Signed and dated (on the front cover): 'Grønfeldt/1823'
[DKKk; MA ms 3019 (KTB 1009, originally KTB 195)
According to Bournonville's pencilled autographed notes (reading: 'Pas de deux' and 'Fin') the music for the Act II *Pas de deux* is included on pp. 34–39. His other autographed notes and his choreographic numbers ('1–16') for the so-called 'En Quadrille af holbergske Figurer' in *The King's Corps of Volunteers on Amager* (score no. 15) are written with brown ink on pp. 20–23. They clearly refer to his separate 1871 choreographic description of this dance (*see* 19.2.1871).

Parts. Ms. Copy. 33 vol.
4 vl I, 3 vl II, 2 vla, 4 vlc e cb, fl picc 1/2, fl 1/2, ob 1/2, cl 1/2, fag 1/2, cor princ, cor 1/2, tr 1/2, timp, gr cassa, piatti, tri, arpa.
Unsigned and undated [1823]
[DKKk; KTB 1009 (originally KTB 195)

1833

29.1.1833
The Veteran or The Hospitable House
(Veteranen eller Det gjæstfrie Tag).

According to the poster the score for this one-act idyllic ballet is credited exclusively to L. Zinck and seems (according to the orchestral score) in the main to have been composed by him. However, a pencilled autographed note by Bournonville on p. 16 of the répétiteur's copy (score no. 16) reads 'Overgang til God save the queen'. This seems to indicate that this British national anthem was also included in the ballet, although the actual music for it is not found in the score, nor in the répétiteur's copy or the parts.

Moreover, the ballet's *Pas de deux* (score no. 28) had originally been performed by Bournonville and A. Kraetzmer in Act II of F. Hérold's three-act comic opera *Zampa ou La Fiancée de Marbre* (*see* 30.1.1832).

Later this dance was also given in Copenhagen as a separate divertissement by F. Hoppe and L. Grahn (on 27.4.1836), and by Hoppe and A. Nielsen (on 8.11.1839 and 3.5.1841). Furthermore, according to the posters and Bournonville's pencilled autographed notes in the part for the first violin yet another *Pas de deux* was incorporated in this ballet on 29.9.1837 (between score nos. 27 and 28). It proves to be identical with the so-called 'Pas de deux oriental' (originally performed by Bournonville and A. Kraetzmer in P. Funck's *A Divertissement in Oriental Style* on 26.9.1829), and was performed three times by P. C. Johansson and C. Fjeldsted, the last time on 9.10.1837.

The Veteran or The Hospitable House received a total of 21 performances, the last of which was given on 9.10.1837. According to the rehearsal book of H. C. J. Fredstrup, 49 rehearsals were held of this ballet between 3.10.1832 and 29.1.1833.

Autograph sources:

Production note. Ms. Autograph. Brown ink. 2 pp. (21,4 × 13 cm)
Besætning til Balletten/Det gjæstfrie Tag – Original Ballet i 1 Act.
Unsigned and dated: 'd. 1.steNovbr. 1832.'
[SSm; Daniel Fryklunds samling no. 113 A

Production note. Ms. Autograph. Brown ink. 1 p. (34 × 21,2 cm)
Sainville Oberst/Hr Fredstrup
Unsigned and undated [1833]
[DKKkt; F.M. (Brevregistrant, Bournonville)

Musical sources:

Orchestral score. Ms. Autograph (by L. Zinck) and copy (only the ouverture). 1 vol. 426 pp. (27,2 × 37,1 cm)
283/L. Zinck/Veteranen./Ballet i een Akt./Partitur.
Unsigned and undated [1833]
[DKKk; C II, 125 b (KTB 283)
Pencilled notes written by an unknown hand on p. '168r' ('Indlagt Nummer/Pas de deux') indicates the exact place where Bournonville's so-called 'Pas de deux oriental' was incorporated in thia ballet in 1837.

Repetiteur's copy. Ms. Copy. Black ink. 1 vol. 120 pp. of which two are blank (31,8 × 24,7 cm)
B 283/(Bournonville – Zinck)/Veteranen, eller det/gjæstfrie Tag./Ballet./25/1833/Jan.
Unsigned and dated: '1833/Jan.'
[DKKk; MA ms 2981 (KTB 283 (1))
This répétiteur's copy contains Bournonville's pencilled autographed notes which describe the dramatic action and the mime in score nos. 5, 6, 11, 17, and 18.

Parts. Ms. Copy. 30 vol.
2 vl I, 3 vl II, 2 vla, 3 vlc e cb, fl 1/2, ob 1/2, cl 1/2, fag 1/2, cor 1/2/3/4, tr 1/2, trb 1/2/3, timp, gr cassa e piatti, tri.
Unsigned and undated [1833]
[DKKk; KTB 283
The part for the first violin (no. 1) contains Bournonville's pencilled autographed notes (on p. 76) reading 'Indlagt Nummer/Orientale Pas de deux'. They clearly indicate the exact place where his so-called 'Pas de deux oriental' was incorporated in this ballet in 1837.

The orchestral score for the incorporated 'Pas de deux af Zampa' is now preserved in DKKk (call no. MA ms 2982 (KTB 283 (2)).

The orchestral score, the répétiteur's copy, and the parts for the later incorporated 'Pas de deux oriental' are now preserved in DKKk (call nos. MA ms 2602 (KTB 218), MA ms 2948, and KTB 218).

Printed sources:

Printed scenario. 1 vol. 14 pp. (17,6 × 10,7 cm)
Veteranen/eller/det gjæstfrie Tag./Original pantomimisk Ballet i een Act,/af/August Bournonville./Musikken componeret af L. Zinck.
Kjøbenhavn, Bianco Luno & Schneider, 1833.
[DKKk, 17, – 172 8°

27.4.1833
Romeo and Giulietta (Romeo og Giulietta).
The 1833 restaging of V. Galeotti's and C. Schall's five-act ballet (first performed at Copenhagen's Royal Theatre on 2.4.1811) represents the first and only time Bournonville mounted a work by this choreographer and predecessor of his. His contribution to the ballet was described on the poster as 'paa ny samlet og fremsat af Hr. Dandsedirecteur A. Bournonville'. However, it seems to have been mounted with only minor (if any) changes from Galeotti's original version. Bournonville would certainly have known this work closely from his childhood, and he may also have also have counted on advice received from his father, who had created the rôle of Romeo at the ballet's 1811 première.

The restaging of *Romeo and Giulietta* reached only 5 performances, the last of which was given on 28.9.1833. According to the rehearsal book of H. C. J. Fredstrup 25 rehearsals were held of this ballet between 25.2. and 27.4.1833.

Autograph sources:

Production note. Ms. Autograph (partially in another's hand). Black ink and pencil. 1 p. (34,8 × 20,7 cm)
1812. d: 23.e Maii/Capulet......Hr: Fredstrup
Unsigned and undated [1833]
[SSm; Daniel Fryklunds samling no. 343A

Musical sources:

Orchestral score. Ms. Autograph (by C. Schall). Black and brown ink. 1 vol. 268 pp. (22,7 × 31 cm and 30,9 × 25,7 cm)
171/Romeo
Unsigned and dated (on p. '130v'): 'D. 15 Martz [1811]'
(DKKk; C II, 121 (KTB 171)
A pencilled note on p. '91r' indicates the duration of Act II as 25 minutes.

Prompt's copy. Ms. Copy (by P. Grønfeldt). Brown ink. 1 vol. 122 pp. of which three are blank (23,5 × 29,4 cm)
Balletten/Romeo og Juliette/Hr Galleotti Musikken af Concert Mæster/Schall 1811/Souffleur Partie/Grønfeldt
Signed and dated: '1811'
[DKKk; C II, 121 (KTB 171)
This prompt's copy contains the music for the vocal parts in Galeotti's ballet (Act II, score nos. 1, 5, and 6), Act IV (score nos. 18 and 21), and Act V (score no. 22).

Répétiteur's copy. Ms. Copy. Brown ink. 1 vol. 80 pp. (29,1 × 20 cm)
B 171/Balletten/Romeo og Giulietta/Violino 1.mo/Rept.r Partie
Unsigned and undated [1811]
[DKKk; MA ms 2934 (KTB 171)

This répétiteur's copy contains Bournonville pencilled autographed notes which describe the choreography of the waltz in Act II (score no. 2), and the mime of the finale in Act IV (score no. 21).
Other pencilled notes written in French by an unknown hand (perhaps Bournonville's father?) indicate the casting of the four dances in Act IV. These dances consisted of four numbers as follows:
(1) A 'Gavotta' (score no. 16, originally danced by C. Dahlén).
(2) A 'Pas de deux' (score no. 17, originally performed by C. Dahlén and A. M. Schall).
(3) A so-called 'Danse/Corps de Ballet/Pas de deux/pas de troix/Corps de ballet' (score no. 18).
(4) A 'Pas de deux' (score no. 19, originally danced by C. Dahlén and A. M. Schall).

Parts Ms. Copy. 29 + 9 vol.
2 vl I, 3 vl II, 2 vla, 4 vlc e cb, fl picc, fl 1/2, ob 1/2, cl 1/2, fag, cor 1/2, tr 1/2, trb, timp, gr cassa, cassa, piatti, tri. On stage: fl, ob 1/2, cl 1/2, fag, cor 1/2, trb.
Unsigned and undated [1811]
[DKKk; KTB 171

Printed sources:

Printed scenario. 1 vol. 23 pp. (15,7 × 10 cm)
Romeo og Giulietta./Tragisk Ballet/i/fem Acter/af/Vincenzo Galeotti,/med Chorsange/af/N. T. Bruun./Sat i Musik/af/Hr. Concertmester Schall,/Ridder af Dannebrog.
Kiøbenhavn, N. Christensen, 1811.
[DKKk; UÆ8-A1319 S-1977
This original scenario to *Romeo and Giulietta* was originally part of Bournonville's private collection of printed ballet scenarios, and served most probably for his 1833 restaging of Galeotti's ballet.

Printed scenario. 1 vol. 16 pp. (19 × 10,5 cm)
Romeo og Giulietta./Tragisk Ballet/i/fem Acter/af/Vincenzo Galeotti;/paa ny samlet og fremsat/af/A. Bournonville./Musiken/af/Hr. Professor og Musik=Directeur/Schall,/Ridder af Dannebrogen./Texten til Sangene af N. T. Bruun.
Kjøbenhavn, Irgens Enke, 1833.
[DKKk; 17, – 182 8°
The description of the action in this scenario is completely identical with that in Galeotti's original 1811 scenario (*see* the previous entry).

1834

29.1.1834
Dances in The Guerilla Band (Guerillabanden).
For the Copenhagen première of I. F. Bredal's three-act opera (with text by T. Overskou) Bournonville choreographed two Spanish dances as follows:

(1) a *Seguidilla* performed in Act II (score no. 6).
(2) a *Manchegas* (a variant of a *Seguidilla* deriving from the La Manche region of New Castile) performed in Act III (score no. 12).

Both dances were performed as the middle section of a chorus and appear to have been arranged from popular Spanish folk tunes. They were performed by a group of six dancers dressed as Spanish peasants (in the *Seguidilla*) and gipsies (in the *Manchegas*). According to the poster this troupe consisted of three men and three women (Bournonville, P. Larcher, F. Hoppe, A. Krætzmer, M. Werning, and S. C. Møller).

The Guerrilla Band was performed 9 times, the last time on 9.11.1836. It is not clear from the rehearsal book of H. C. J. Fredstrup exactly how many rehearsals were held of the dances in Bredal's opera in 1834.

Musical sources:

Orchestral score. Ms. Autograph (by L. Bredal) and copy. Brown ink. 1 vol. 390 pp. of which five are blank (27 × 38 cm with minor variants) Guerillabanden/Partitur/2.den og 3.die Akt
Unsigned and dated (p. 210): 'd: 4.de Decbr: [1833]', (p. 327): 'd. 23.de Decbr: [1833]' (p. 389): 'd. 8.de Januar/1834'
[DKKk; C II, 106 (KTA 305)
The music for the so-called 'Sequidillas' (pp. 45-48) and 'Maquegas' (pp. 309–312) are written in a copyist's hand on (unpaginated) pages that were inserted in Bredal's autographed score. This seems to indicate that the music for these dances was borrowed from popular Spanish folk tunes and incorporated (perhaps at Bournonville's wish?) in Bredal's opera at a rather late stage in the compositional process. A pencilled note (on p. 29) indicates the exact tempo of the *Seguidilla* with the metronome marking of a crochet being equivalent to '104'.

Répétiteur's copy. Ms. Copy. Black ink. 1 vol. 26 pp. of which one is blank (32,7 × 24,4 cm)
A. 305/Guerillabanden./215/1834./[…]/Repetiteur=Partie/til/ Guerillabanden.
Unsigned and dated: '1834.'
[DKKk; MA ms 3068 (KTA 305)

Parts. Ms. Copy. 34 vol.
3 vlI, 3 vl II, 2 vla, 3 vlc e cb, fl picc, fl 1/2, ob 1/2, cl 1/2, fag 1/2, cor 1/2, tr 1/2/3, trb, timp, gr cassa, cassa, piatti, tri, tamb, gong, arpa.
Unsigned and undated [1834]
[DKKk; KTA 305

9.3.1834

Dances performed at a soirée given by the Royal Family (The Amalienborg Palace).
A note in the diary of King Christian VIII on this day reads 'Soiré hos Christian Frederik og Caroline Amalie. Bournonvilles Elever dandsede og saas med Fornöielse'. It clearly indicates that Bournonville had arranged a divertissement for his dance students which was performed at the *soirée* given the same evening by Crown Prince Frederik Carl Christian (later King Frederik VII) and Queen Caroline Amalie. It is not possible to identify the dances any further.

23.9.1834

A New Pas de deux composed by Mr. Dance Director Bournonville (En ny Pas de deux, componeret af Hr. Dandsedirecteur Bournonville) performed by F. Hoppe and L. Grahn as an incorporated divertissement in Act I of *La Muette de Portici (Den Stumme i Portici)*.
In Bournonville's handwritten lists of his works, written c.1851 (*see* Additional Sources) this dance is named 'Pas de deux af den Stumme'. In the same source it is listed in the category of dances partially based on the works of other choreographers. The *Pas de deux* was mounted for the début of two of Bournonville's most talented pupils, F. Hoppe and L. Grahn. According to notes found in the printed orchestral score (now in DKKkt, call no. KTA 273) it was inserted between the *Guarache* and the *Bolero* in Act I (score no. 3).

The dance seems to be a choreographically slightly revised version of the earlier (uncredited) *Pas de deux*, originally danced by Bournonville and A. Krætzmer to the same music by M. E. Caraffa as an incorporated divertissement in N. Isouard's three-act comic opera *Jeannot et Colin* (*see* 1.9. 1829). This theory is supported by a letter from Bournon-

ville to his father (written in Paris on 9.12.1829) in which the *Pas de deux* in *Jeannot et Colin* is described as a dance based on an earlier *Pas de deux*, originally performed by the French dancer, Albert (François Decombe), as an incorporated divertissement in the Paris Opéra première on 29.2.1828 of D.-F.-E. Auber's five-act opera *La Muette de Portici*. Moreover, according to another letter from Bournonville to his father (dated 12.8.1828), he had attended a performance of this dance performed at the Paris Opéra during the 1828 season.

Furthermore, Bournonville had himself performed Albert's *Pas de deux* at the Paris Opéra on at least two occasions (6.12. and 7.12.1829) together with the French ballerina, F. A. Duport, after returning to the French capital from his guest performances at Copenhagen's Royal Theatre in the autumn of 1829. It therefore seems most likely that he would already have decided in 1828 to make use of Albert's original *Pas de deux* for his own début in Copenhagen on 1.9.1829.

Finally, during a visit to Paris in the summer of 1834 (on which he was accompanied by his then sixteen-year-old pupil, L. Grahn) Bournonville appeared for the last time at the Paris Opéra in Albert's *Pas de deux* from *La Muette de Portici* on 2.7.1834. He may on that occasion have decided also to use this dance for the later débuts of his two own pupils, Grahn and Hoppe, who made their first appearances at Copenhagen's Royal Theatre the same year.

In Copenhagen the 1834 *Pas de deux* was also given in Auber's opera by Bournonville and Grahn on 3.10.1835, and mounted as a separate divertissement on four later occasions and with the following casts:

(1) on 23.9.1835 at the Royal Theatre (performed by Hoppe and Grahn as an *entr'acte* divertissement between Act II and III of Théaulon de Lambert's and A. Signol's three-act play *Jean*).
(2) on 2.5.1849 at the Court Theatre (danced by S. Lund and S. Price).
(3) on 20.5.1849 at the Casino Theatre (with S. Lund and S. Price).
(4) on 4.12.1872 at the Royal Theatre (performed by D. Krum and A. Scholl).

In Sweden an (uncredited) *Pas de deux from La Muette (Pas de deux utur Den Stumma)* was performed by Bournonville and C. Fjeldsted at Göteborg's Stora Theater (Segerlindska Theatern) on 8.7.1839. It is almost certainly identical with this dance. In Norway the *Pas de deux* was mounted twice at Christiania's Theatre (Oslo) on 29.7.1840 (with Bournonville and C. Fjeldsted), and on 2.7.1847 (with W. Funck and C. Fjeldsted), the last time with the choreography explicitly credited (on the poster) to the French dancer, Albert (François Decombe). During the 1843 summer tour to Hamburg the *Pas de deux* was performed by Bournonville and P. Funck at Hamburg's Stadttheater on 20.7.1843. It was then given as an incorporated divertissement in Auber's two-act opera-ballet *Die Liebende Bayadère oder Der Gott und die Bayadere (Le Dieu et La Bayadère, ou La Courtisane amoureuse)*. On 16.6.1847 the dance was given by Bournonville and his Swedish pupil, M. C. Norberg, at Stockholm's Royal Theatre (Operahuset). That year it was presented on the poster with Bournonville credited for the choreography. The *Pas de deux* was mounted for the last time in Norway (at Christiania's Theatre) with S.

Lund and S. Price on 15.6.1852, this time again with the cho-reography credited exclusively to Bournonville.

For Bournonville's last restaging of Auber's opera in Co-penhagen on 2.9.1873, his 1834 *Pas de deux* was replaced with a new *Pas de deux*, danced by D. Krum and M. Westberg and set to a new score by V. C. Holm. The two male solo varia-tions in this new version were later revised by the French bal-let-master, G. Garey, for the début of H. Beck on 28.11.1879. Moreover, Auber's opera was mounted in Copenhagen with Bournonville's general mise-en-scène in four different pro-ductions on 22.10.1847, 13.10.1850, 12.2.1862 (a staging originally planned by Bournonville, but carried out by L. Gade), and 2.9.1873.

The original 1834 *Pas de deux* was mounted for the last time by Bournonville at Copenhagen's Royal Theatre on 4.12.1872 and was given for the last time there on 18.12. 1872. It is not clear from the rehearsal book of H. C. J. Fred-strup exactly how many rehearsals of *A New Pas de deux* in *La Muette de Portici* were held in 1834.

Musical sources:

The orchestral score, the répétiteur's copy, and the set of parts em-ployed for Bournonville's 1834 *Pas de deux* in Act I of *La Muette de Portici* are now in DKKk (call nos. MA ms 2603 (KTB 209), MA ms 2700, and KTB 209).

30.9.1834

Nina, ou La Folle par amour (Nina, eller Den Vanvittige af Kjærlighed).

The Copenhagen première of L-L. Persuis' and L. Milon's two-act pantomimic ballet *Nina, ou La Folle par amour* (first performed at the Paris Opéra on 23.11.1813) was mounted with Bounonville and the actress, J. L. Heiberg, playing the leading rôles of *Germeuil* and *Nina*. During his Parisian so-journ 1826-1829 Bournonville came to know this ballet closely, and on 5.4.1826 he even made his first début per-formance at the Paris Opéra in this work, when he danced the *Pas de trois* of Act I together with the French ballerinas, E. Lacroix and Julia [de Varennes]. Moreover, in the late 1820s Bournonville wrote a projected casting of Milon's ballet with Danish dancers (*see* 18.4.1829). This clearly indicates that he was planning a Copenhagen production of this ballet well before he was actually appointed director of the Royal Dan-ish Ballet in 1830. For the same purpose, he personally cop-ied the French répétiteur's copy in which he inserted numer-ous notes that describe Milon's mime and the dramatic ac-tion in fine detail. Apart from the opening scene in Act I, the dance divertissements in the same act, and the finale of Act II, this répétiteur's copy contains all of Persuis' music and represents one of the most important sources for the study of the mimic and dramatic contents in Milon's original ver-sion of this ballet. Furthermore, Bournonville's manuscript reveals his great talent at this early stage of his career for giving apt descriptions in written form of even highly com-plex scenes of pantomime.

While he seems to have kept very close to Milon's original mime and dramatic action, he clearly changed the ballet's introduction and most of its dances in the first act, which were set to new music that appears to have been purchased by Bournonville in Paris during late 1829 or early 1830. In Copenhagen this music was interpolated in Persuis' score with the help of J. F. Fröhlich, who also seems to have con-tributed with a few numbers of his own composition. Finally, Fröhlich reorchestrated Persuis' original score in several places.

The new music added by Bournonville in Act I is identified as follows:

(1) Score no. 1 (the *Introduction*): Bournonville here employed mu-sic borrowed from F. Hérold's score to J. Aumer's two-act panto-mimic ballet *Astolphe et Joconde, ou Les coureurs d'aventures* (premièred at the Paris Opéra on 29.1.1827). According to the French orchestral score for this work (now in FPo, call no. A 483 [I], pp. 3–26) it origi-nally served as the overture for Aumer's ballet.

(2) Score no. 6 (a *March*): The music for this dance was borrowed from F. Sor's score to Albert's (François Decombe) three-act fairy-ballet *Cendrillon* (premièred at the Paris Opéra on 3.3.1824). Accord-ing to the répétiteur's copy for this work (now in FPo, call no. Mat. 19. [63 (3), p. 54) the march was originally part of the opening scene of Act II.

(3) A *Pas de deux* in F major: According to pencilled notes in the orchestral score this dance was performed by F. Hoppe and L. Grahn as an incorporated divertissement between score no. 9 A (the *Minuet*) and 9 B (the *Pas de trois*). In Bournonville's handwrit-ten list of his work, written c.1851 (*see* Additional Sources) the same dance is named 'Pas de deux Grahns Debut'. It was set to a score that seems to have been composed by J. Schneitzhoeffer in the year of 1830. This theory is supported by notes written (with brown ink) in the separate orchestral score for this dance reading: 'Mr. Perrot Mlle Taglioni'. They clearly indicate that Bournonville's *Pas de deux* was originally part of the Paris Opéra repertory, where it was per-formed by the dancers, J. Perrot and M. Taglioni.

Moreover, other pencilled notes found in the French répétiteur's copy for L.-S. Le Brun's one-act opera from 1816 *Le Rossignol* (now in FPo, call no. Mat. 19 [244 (93) p. 75) seem to provide more informa-tion about this dance, although no actual music for it is included in this volume. They read: 'Pas de Deux en fa/de m° Perrot et Mlle Taglioni/par m° Schneizhöfer'. These notes seem to indicate that Bournonville's *Pas de deux* (which is also in F major) would have been the same as the *Pas de deux* arranged by A. Vestris and first danced by Perrot and Taglioni on 16.7.1830 for the début of the former at the Paris Opéra. Perrot was a fellow-student and close friend of Bour-nonville during his years of study with Vestris in Paris. It would, there-fore, only be natural if Bournonville had chosen this dance, in which his friend and colleague had made his Paris début, for the débuts of his own two pupils in Denmark. However, because no orchestral score or répétiteur's copy for Perrot's and Taglioni's *Pas de deux* in *Le Rossignol* has yet been traced, the theory of its being identical with Bournonville's F major *Pas de deux* in *Nina, ou La Folle par amour* must remain a hypothesis.

The same seems to the true with regard to the music for the Coda movement in Bournonville's F major *Pas de deux*. According to notes written on p. 31 in the Copenhagen score (reading: 'La Belle, Op-era/Paul/Pas de deux') the music for this section was originally part of yet another French *Pas de deux* which seems to have been choreo-graphed by P. Gardel and was performed by the French dancer, A. Paul, in M. E. Caraffa's three-act fairy-opera *La Belle au bois dormant* (premièred at the Paris Opéra on 2.3.1825). However, the music for this Coda is no longer preserved, neither in the orchestral score nor in the répétiteur's copy for this opera (now in FPo, call nos. A 478 [I–V] and Mat. 19 [51 (111)).

(4) Score no. 9 B (a *Pas de trois*): The music for this dance is identical with that used earlier by Ph. L. Keck in his score for Bournonville's one-act ballet *Victor's Wedding* (*see* 23.4.1831). In that ballet, however, it was listed as score no. 5 and performed as a *Pas de quatre*.

(5) Score no. 9 C (a *Pas de deux* danced by Bournonville as *Germeuil*, and J. L. Heiberg(?) as *Nina*): The music for this dance is borrowed from H. Berton's one-act opera *L'Oriflamme* (premièred at the Paris

Opéra on 1.2.1814). According to the French répétiteur's copy for this work (now in FPo, call no. Mat. 19 [190 (32), pp. 47–59) it was originally choreographed by A. Vestris. Moreover, other notes in the French orchestral score for Milon's *Nina, ou La Folle par amour* (now in FPo, call no. A 435 [I], p. 221) indicate that Berton's *Pas de deux* from *L'Oriflamme* was also performed regularly in Milon's ballet in Paris since 22.7.1813.

(6) Score no. 10 (an unnamed *Dance* for the corps de ballet): The music for this dance (for which no full orchestral score has yet been traced) is most probably composed by J. F. Fröhlich.

(7) Score no. 11 (a *Quadrille*): In the Copenhagen score for *Nina, ou La Folle par amour* the music for this dance is J. F. Fröhlich's autograph. It was most probably written by him especially for this ballet in 1834.

In the second act Fröhlich inserted (according to the orchestral score) some new music for two mime scenes (score nos. 20 and 23), both of which were most probably of his own composition. Moreover, the music for the finale in Persuis' original score (no. 30) was drastically shortened by Fröhlich by omitting four larger sections playing for a total of 479 bars.

According to the rehearsal book of H. C. J. Fredstrup a so-called 'Pas de deux for Jfr. Verning [*sic*] og Hr Hoppe i Nina' was rehearsed on 12.10.1834 in preparation for a performance of the complete ballet on 13.10.1834. This seems to indicate that M. Werning (the elder) had taken over or at least alternated with L. Grahn in the female part of this dance in this early period of the ballet's Danish performances. During the following years this *Pas de deux* was also mounted as a separate divertissement with different casts as follows:

(1) on 12.9.1836 and 21.2.1837 in Copenhagen (performed by F. Hoppe and A. Nielsen).
(2) on 12.7.1839 at Göteborg's Stora Theater, Segerlindska Theatern (performed by Hoppe and C. Fjeldsted).
(3) on 10.10.1847 in Copenhagen (performed by P. C. Johansson and C. Fjeldsted).

Furthermore, most of the music for this dance was many years later reused by Bournonville for two other (uncredited) *Pas de deux*, which he choreographed for the débuts of his pupils, D. Krum (on 12.10.1866), and L. Cetti (on 7.10.1869). The score for the first of these dances was arranged by H. S. Paulli, while the second was done by V. C. Holm.

Nina, ou La Folle par amour was restaged for the last time in Copenhagen by Bournonville on 17.3.1849. For that production the F major *Pas de deux* in Act I and the complete music of score no. 10 appear to have been omitted since these numbers are no longer included in the Copenhagen orchestral score.

The original 1834 version received 18 performances, the last of which was given on 23.10.1837. According to the rehearsal book of H. C. J. Fredstrup, 25 rehearsals were held of *Nina, ou La Folle par amour* between 30.8. and 30.9.1834.

Autograph sources:

Production note. Ms. Autograph. Brown ink. 3 pp. (21,4 × 17,1 cm with minor variants)
Nina eller den Vanvittige/af Kjærlighed/Pantomimisk Ballet i 2 Acter af Milon. Musikken/arrangeret af Persuis, indrettet for den danske Skueplads af/A Bournonville./Personer.

Unsigned and undated [1834]
[SSm; Daniel Fryklunds samling no. 138

Production note. Ms. Autograph. Black ink. 2 pp. (33,4 × 20,9 cm)
Nina eller den Vanvittige af Kjærlighed/Pantomimisk Ballet i 2 Acter af Milon indrettet for/den danske Skueplads af A Bournonville -/Personer.
Unsigned and undated [1834]
[SSm; Daniel Fryklunds samling no. 138

Production note. Ms. Autograph. Black ink. 1 p. (33,3 × 21,6 cm)
Requisiter til Balletten Nina. -
Unsigned and undated [1834?]
[DKKkt; F.M. (Ballet)

Musical sources:

Répétiteur's copy (incomplete). Ms. Copy (made by Bournonville). Black ink. 14 pp. (26 × 34 cm)
1 Acte, 2.me Scène. -
Unsigned and undated [c. late 1820s or early 1830]
[DKKk; MA ms 2640 (KTB 284)
This répétiteur's copy was most probably copied by Bournonville in Paris in the late 1820s. This theory is supported by the French watermark ('D & C Blauw') contained in the répétiteur's copy. It is filled with his autographed annotations describing in fine detail the mime and the dramatic action throughout the ballet.

Répétiteur's copy (*Pas de deux* in Act I, score no. 9 C). Ms Copy. Black ink. 4 pp. (37,7 × 27 cm)
Repetiteur/Violino 1.mo/Andante
Unsigned and undated [between 1813 and 1834]
[DKKk; MA ms 2766 (KTB 284)
This répétiteur's copy contains the music for H. Berton's *Pas de deux* from his one-act opera *L'Oriflamme* (premièred at the Paris Opéra on 1.2.1814). On 30.9.1834 it was incorporated as score no. 9 C in Act I of Bournonville's Copenhagen version of L. Milon's *Nina, ou La Folle par amour*. The manuscript itself, however, seems to date from the period between the 1814 Paris première of Berton's opera and Bournonville's 1834 Copenhagen staging of Milon's ballet.

Orchestral score. Ms. Copy and autograph insertions (by J. F. Fröhlich). Brown ink. 1 vol. 316 pp. of which three are blank (26,5 × 35 cm with several inserts in various sizes)
Partituuren/Til Baletten Nina/1834/Persuis/1849/284
Unsigned and dated: '1834' and '1849"
[DKKk; C I, 303 (KTB 284)
This score was used for all performances of *Nina, ou La Folle par amour* in Copenhagen between 1834 and 1851. It is mainly a French manuscript copy that most probably was brought to Copenhagen by Bournonville in the 1829 or early 1830. The volume contains five autographed sections by J. F. Fröhlich (Act I, score nos. 6, 11, and Act II, score nos. 18, 20, 23, and 30) plus a large insertion with the music for the *Pas de deux* in Act I (score no. 9 C). The latter is entitled '59/No. 9 C/Bournonville/No 5./B.te Petit/Pas de Deux/de l'Oriflâme/donné au jeune bournonville par son ami Baptiste petit'. This insertion (which contains the French watermark 'Andrieu') was clearly a personal gift to Bournonville from his French teacher, B. Petit, who originally performed the *Pas de deux* in H. Berton's opera *L'Oriflamme* at its Paris Opéra première on 1.2.1814, and also gave private lessons to Bournonville before his exam in Paris in 1826.

Orchestral score. Ms. Copy. Brown ink. 1 vol. 54 pp. (30,6 × 23 cm and 26 × 34 cm)
Partidöx/til Ninna [*sic*]/B. 221/M.r Perrot MlleTaglioni/No. 9 A bis/Til Nina/Danses af Hoppe og Grand/Pas de Deux/[...]La Belle, Opera/Paul./Pas de Deux.
Unsigned and undated [c.1832–1834]
[DKKk; MA ms 2949 (KTB 221)
This orchestral score contains the music for the incorporated *Pas de*

deux in Act I (performed by F. Hoppe and L. Grahn between score nos. 9 A and 9 B). It consists of two separate scores, of which the Coda in the second score was used as the finale to the first score. Both scores contain several autographed notes by Bournonville (written with brown ink) which indicate his wishes for the exact tempi and musical phrasing. The scores were most probably purchased by Bournonville in Paris in the early 1830s (most likely during his sojourn there in 1834). This theory is supported by the French watermark (showing a standing lion holding a sword with, underneath, the year '1832') which is contained in the first score.

No répétiteur's copy dating from the 1832 Copenhagen production of *Nina, ou La Folle par amour* has yet been traced.

Parts. Ms. Copy. 33 vol.
3 vl I, 3 vl II, 2 vla, 3 vlc e cb, fl picc, fl 1/2, ob 1/2, cor ingl, cl 1/2, fag 1/2, cor 1/2/3/4, tr 1/2, trb 1/2/3, timp, gr cassa e piatti, tri.
Unsigned and undated [1834]
[DKKk; KTB 284

Other sources:

Drawing by E. Lehmann. Pencil (16,7 × 14,3 cm)
Nina.
Unsigned and dated: 'Nobr. 18..'
[DKKt; Lehmann tegninger
According to K. Neiiendam this drawing dates from the period between November 1834 and November 1836 and shows a scene from Act II in *Nina, ou La Folle par amour* in which *Germeuil* (Bournonville) reappears to the astonished *Nina* (J. L. Heiberg) and her nurse *Elyse* (S. A. Schouw) after his failed attempt of suicide.

Printed sources:

Printed scenario. 1 vol. 14 pp. (19,7 × 12,3 cm)
Nina,/eller/Den Vanvittige af Kjærlighed./Pantomimisk Ballet i to Acter/af/Milon./Musiken arrangeret af Persuis./Indrettet for den danske Skueplads/af/A. Bournonville.
Kiöbenhavn, Thieles Bogtrykkeri, 1834.
[DKKk; 17, – 186 8°

28.10.1834
Pas de deux performed by Bournonville and L. Grahn as an incorporated divertissement in *Le Pré aux clercs* (*Klerkevænget*).

Besides arranging and staging the dances for the masked ball in Act II of F. Hérold's three-act comic opera (in which this incorporated *Pas de deux* was performed) Bournonville was was also responsible for the general mise-en-scène of this work. This is clear from his handwritten list of his works, written c.1872 (*see* Additional Sources), in which he clearly listed the 1834 Danish première of *Le Pré aux Clercs* (first performed at l'Opéra Comique in Paris on 15.12.1832) among his own mises-en-scène (*Arrangements*). According to pencilled notes in the printed orchestral score and the printed piano vocal score for Hérold's opera (now in DKKk, call nos. U 6 and KTA 311) the *Pas de deux* was incorporated immediately after the women's chorus in Act II (score no. 8), entitled «Non, non messieurs votre science ne peut tenter notre désir». Other notes written in the manuscript orchestral score and in the parts for this *Pas de deux* indicate that the music for it is by J. Mayseder. Moreover, according to a note found in the orchestral score, the *Pas de deux* was originally performed by M. Taglioni and J. Perrot at the Paris Opéra. Between 1830 and 1833 they appeared together in at least three different *Pas de deux* as follows:

(1) on 16.7.1830 (in L. S. Le Brun's one-act opera *Le Rossignol*).
(2) on 14.3.1831 (in Ch.-L. Didelot's two-act anacreontic ballet *Flore et Zéphire*)
(3) on 4.12.1833 (in F. Taglioni's three-act fairy-ballet *La Révolte au sérail*)

Since the first two of these dances had already been incorporated by Bournonville in the Copenhagen repertory (*see* 30.9.1834 and 29.10.1829 respectively) the score for his 1834 *Pas de deux* in *Le Pré aux clercs* may derive from *La Révolte au sérail*. If this theory is correct it could have been purchased by him during his sojourn in Paris in the summer of 1834. However, no traces of Mayseder's music for Taglioni's and Perrot's *Pas de deux* have yet been found among the musical sources for *La Révolte au sérail* (now in FPo, call nos. A 507 [I–VI], and Mat. 19 [310 (1–49)). This seems to indicate that the 1834 Copenhagen score may represent the only surviving musical source for Taglioni's and Perrot's *Pas de deux* that has yet come to light.

Meanwhile, according to a printed orchestral score which contains an almost identical version of the music for the *Pas de deux* in *Le Pré aux clercs*, Mayseder's score for this dance was musically based on his much earlier concert-piece for solo violin and orchestra op. 36, entitled *Rondo (Nr. 2)*. This work had already been published in Vienna in 1820–21 by S. A. Steiner & Co., pl. no. 3008 (a copy is now in AWn).

Bournonville's *Pas de deux* in *Le Pré aux clercs* was also mounted by him as a separate divertissement in Copenhagen on 19.2.1835, and restaged there for the last time on 30.10.1840 (then danced by himself and C. Fjeldsted). It was given only 8 times in Hérold's opera by Bournonville and Grahn, the last time on 17.12.1836.

Many years after the *Pas de deux* had gone out of the Copenhagen repertory Bournonville reused Mayseder's music for a completely new *Pas de trois*, which he choreographed for E. Hansen, S. Price, and A. Scholl (*see* 31.10.1870). The score for this dance was rearranged by V. C. Holm, who slightly changed Mayseder's original introduction and reinstated a solo variation that had been omitted earlier and was now performed immediately before the Coda.

Finally, on 30.10.1857 Bournonville included Hérold's *Le Pré aux clercs* in a list of projected opera restagings that he was planning for the 1857–58 and 1858–59 seasons. This project, however, was never carried out.

It is not clear from the rehearsal book of H. C. J. Fredstrup exactly how many rehearsals of Bournonville's *Pas de deux* in *Le Pré aux clercs* were held in 1834.

Musical sources:

Orchestral score. Ms. Copy with autographed insertions (by V. C. Holm). Black ink. 1 vol. 44 pp. of which one is blank (29,1 × 21,7 cm with several variants)
Partidöx/Brugt i Klerkevænget/270/[...]/Introduction/Pas des Deux (M.lle Taglioni.) musique de maiseder./[...]/Brugt i Klerke–vænget
Unsigned and undated [early 1830s and 1870]
[DKKk; C I, 38 g (mu 7402.1981) (KTB 311 a, but originally KTB 270)
This orchestral score is clearly a French copy and was most probably purchased by Bournonville in Paris during the early 1830s. This theory is supported by the French watermark ('J Bouchet') contained in the score. Moreover, notes written with brown ink on p. 3 ('M.lle Taglioni.') and p. 21 ('Variation de M.r Perrot.') clearly indi-

cate that the *Pas de deux* was originally performed in Paris by M. Taglioni and J. Perrot. Furthermore, the score includes Bournonville's pencilled autographed choreographic numbers ('1–2' and '1–14') which seem to refer to a separate (not yet traced) notation he may have made of it. Finally, on pp. 1–2 a music insertion by V. C. Holm is included. It was added in connection with Bournonville's much later reuse of Mayseder's score for a *Pas de trois* that he choreographed for E. Hansen, S. Price, and A. Scholl, and which was premièred on 31.10.1870.

No répétiteur's copy dating from the 1834 Copenhagen première of the *Pas de deux* in *Le Pré aux clercs* has been traced.

Parts. Ms. Copy. 33 vol.
3 vl I, 3 vl II, 2 vla, 3 vlc e cb, fl picc, fl 1/2, ob 1/2, cl 1/2, fag 1/2, cor 1/2/3/4, tr 1/2, trb 1/2/3, timp, gr cassa, piatti, tri.
Unsigned and undated [1834 and 1870]
[DKKk; KTA 311 a
This set of parts dates from the 1834 première of Bournonville's *Pas de deux* in Act II of Hérold's comic opera *Le Pré aux clercs*. It includes several later music insertions made by V. C. Holm. They were added to the parts in 1870 when Mayseder's music was reused by Bournonville for the *Pas de trois* in his so-called *Dance Divertissement (Divertissement af Dands)* which was premièred on 31.10.1870. Holm's insertions clearly indicate that it was the 1834 set of parts that was reused for Bournonville's *Pas de trois* in 1870.

18.11.1834
Pas de deux composed by Mr. Ballet Master Bournonville (componeret af Hr. Balletmester Bournonville) performed by F. Hoppe and L. Grahn.
This dance is probably identical with either Bournonville's *Pas de deux* in *La Muette de Portici* (*see* 23.9.1834), or his *Pas de deux* in *Le Pré aux clercs* (*see* 28.10.1834). It is not possible to identify the dance any further.

1835

19.2.1835
A Pas de deux composed by Bournonville for the singspiel Le Pré aux clercs (En Pas de deux componeret af Hr. Dandse Direkteur Bournonville til Syngestykket: Klerkevænget) performed by Bournonville and C. Fjeldsted.
This *Pas de deux* (set to music by J. Mayseder) was originally performed by Bournonville and L. Grahn as an incorporated divertissement in Act II of F. Hérold's three-act comic opera *Le Pré aux clercs* (*see* 28.10.1834). The 1835 performances represent the first time it was given as separate divertissement in Copenhagen. It was danced four times by Bournonville and Fjeldsted this year (the last time on 11.5.1835).

It is not clear from the rehearsal book of H. C. J. Fredstrup exactly how many rehearsals of this dance were held in 1835.

6.3.1835
The Tyroleans (Tyrolerne).
This one-act idyllic ballet was (according to Bournonville's memoirs *My Theatre Life*, p. 75) freely based on the third Ode of Anacreon, and set to a score composed and arranged by J. F. Fröhlich. In order to add a distinctive local colour he included three excerpts from operas by G. Rossini identified as follows:

(1) Score no. 5 (a *Pas de deux* performed by a Tyrolean couple): For

this dance Fröhlich employed the complete music for the Act I *Pas de six* in *Guillaume Tell* (premièred at the Paris Opéra on 3.8.1829) except for the 6 bars of introduction and the last 35 bars before the Coda movement. Moreover, Rossini's music was (according to the orchestral score) partly reorchestrated by Fröhlich.
(2) Score no. 9 (the so-called 'quarrel scene'): This music is partially borrowed from Rossini's finale in Act I (score no. 11) of his two-act opera *Le Comte Ory* (premièred at the Paris Opéra on 20.8.1828) in which it was sung by Le Comte («Venez amis, retirons nous»).
(3) Score no. 12 (the *Finale*): For the finale Fröhlich employed the concluding *Allegro vivace* section of the overture of *Guillaume Tell* except for its first 14 bars. In *The Tyroleans* it served as an accompaniment for a *Pas de deux* 'in Tyrolean style' performed by Bournonville (as *Fritz*) and L. Grahn (as *Hannchen*).

According to a note in Bournonville's travel-diary on 23.4.1836 (reading 'Dands med Mlle Wagon, indstuderet Pas de deux af Tyrolerne i paakommende Tilfælde') he also seems to have planned a performance at Berlin's Hofoper of the first *Pas de deux* (score no. 5) in *The Tyroleans* during his brief sojourn in that city in the spring of 1836. This project, however, was never carried out.

The Tyroleans was premièred at Stockholm's Royal Theatre (Operahuset) three years later on 8.6.1839, with the new title *The Tyroleans, or: The Mischievous Boy (Tyrolerne, eller: Den Skälmaktige Gossen)*. According to the Swedish orchestral score, this production included a new finale set to music by a not yet identified composer and was followed by a second, additional finale performed after the actual ballet. The latter is almost certainly identical with the so-called *Styrian Dance (Steirisk Dands)*, originally danced at Copenhagen's Royal Theatre as an incorporated divertissement in D.-F.-E. Auber's three-act comic opera *Le Domino noir* (*see* 29.1.1839).

On 21.10.1839 *The Tyroleans* was restaged in Copenhagen with a partially new cast, and a fortnight later it was (according to the poster of 2.11.1839) given with the *Styrian National Dance (den steiriske Nationalandands)* (*see* 29.1.1839). It was incorporated that year as a new finale, thereby replacing the ballet's original 1835 finale to music from Rossini's *Guillaume Tell*.

On 7.2. and 17.2.1842 *The Tyroleans* was performed (according to the posters) with a *Gallopade*, which proves to have been borrowed from Bournonville's two-act romantic ballet *The Isle of Phantasy* (*see* 28.10.1838) and interpolated as a new, extra finale. It is, however, unclear whether this *Gallopade* (which was performed by F. Hoppe and C. Fjeldsted) was that set to music by I. P. E. Hartmann (Act I, score no. 3) or that to music by E. Helsted (Act II, score 7).

The Tyroleans was mounted for the last time in Copenhagen by Bournonville on 8.2.1844, but in a new version that differed from his earlier productions in having two new incorporated dances as follows:

(1) A *New Scenic Pas de deux (Ny scenisk Pas de deux)*, choreographed by F. Lefèbvre and performed by himself and A. Nielsen, thereby replacing Bournonville's original *Pas de deux* (score no. 5).
(2) A *New Hamburg-Scottish, Character Dance (Ny Hamborger=Skotsk, Characteerdands)*, choreographed by Bournonville to new music by H. C. Lumbye and performed by himself and C. Fjeldsted as a new finale to the ballet.

Lumbye's *New Hamburg-Scottish* was later also performed by Bournonville and Fjeldsted as a separate (uncredited) divertissement on 18.12.1844, but with the new title *Hamburg*

Dance (*Hamborger=Dands*). On 24.1.1847 it was restaged with yet another title, *The Vierländers, Hamburg Dance (Vierländerne, Hamborger=Dands)*, with Bournonville credited for the first time on the poster for the choreography.

This dance was also mounted for Bournonville's Swedish pupil, J. G. Gillberg, at Stockholm's Royal Theatre (Operahuset) on 28.5.1847, with the title *Vierländerne, (Hamburger-Dans)*. In Norway it was danced the same year by W. Funck and C. Fjeldsted at Christiania's Theatre (Oslo) on 25.6. 1847 with the title *The Vierländers, Scenic Character Dance (Vierlænderne, scenisk Charakteerdands)*.

Moreover, Fröhlich's score for the *Polonaise* (score no. 10) later became one of his most popular concert pieces, being played numerous times at public concerts in Copenhagen's Tivoli Gardens from the mid-1840s.

Finally, parts of the music for score no. 3 (*Allegretto*, 2/4 time in A major) were many years later reused by H. S. Paulli in his score for Bournonville's Tyrolean divertissement, entitled *The Prophecies of Love, Tyrolean Scene and Dance (Kjærligheds Spaadomme, Tyroler Scene og Dands)* and first performed by the three cousins, J. Price, A. Price, and S. Price, at the Court Theatre on 4.6.1851.

The Tyroleans reached a total of 42 performances in Copenhagen, the last of which was given on 5.3.1844. According to the rehearsal book of H. C. J. Fredstrup 25 rehearsals were held of it between 8.12.1834 and 6.3.1835. Pencilled notes in many of the parts indicate that the entire ballet played for about 1 hour and 5 minutes.

Musical sources:

Orchestral score. Ms. Autograph (by J. F. Fröhlich) and copy. Brown and black ink. 1 vol. 238 pp. (27,4 × 37,5 cm)
Partitur/Til Balletten/Tÿrolerne/Frøhlich/204
Signed and dated (on p. 12): 'JFFrøhlich/Februar 1835.'
[DKKk; C II, 107 (KTB 204)
This orchestral score is Fröhlich's autograph except for nos. 5 and 12 which are written by a copyist. A pencilled note on p. 71 (reading 'Nyt nr:') indicates the exact place where F. Lefèbvre's *New Scenic Pas de deux* was incorporated on 8.2.1844, thereby replacing Bournonville's original *Pas de deux* (score no. 5).

Orchestral score. Ms. Copy. Brown ink. 16 pp. (27 × 38,1 cm)
Pas d'Ensemble./Partitur til Balletten Tÿrolerne/Bournonville.
Unsigned and undated [c.1835]
[DKKk; MA ms 2760 (KTB 204)
This orchestral score contains the music for the *Pas d'ensemble* in *The Tyroleans* (score no. 3, performed by *Hannchen* and the Tyrolean girls). According to Bournonville's autographed notes (written with brown ink on p. 1) it seems to have been his private copy and was probably used for private balls given during the years after the 1835 première of *The Tyroleans*. Thus, no records in the annals of Copenhagen's Royal Theatre indicate that this dance was ever performed there as a separate divertissement.

Répétiteur's copy (fragment). Ms. Copy. Black ink. 6 pp. of which one is blank (32,7 × 24,8 cm)
No. 5. Pas de deux af Wilhelm Tell
Unsigned and undated [1835]
[DKKk; MA ms 2694 (KTB 204)
This fragment of the répétiteur's copy for the *Pas de deux* in *The Tyroleans* (score no. 5 set to music from Rossini's *Guillaume Tell*) represents the only part of the original 1835 répétiteur's copy for *The Tyroleans* that has been traced so far.

Parts. Ms. Copy. 30 vol.
3 vl I, 3 vl II, 2 vla, 3 vlc e cb, fl picc, fl 1/2, ob 1/2, cl 1/2, fag 1/2, cor 1/2/3/4, clno 1/2, trb 1/2/3, timp.
Unsigned and undated [1835]
[DKKk; KTB 204

Parts (*Polonaise*). Ms. Copy. 25 vol.
vl I (conductor's part), 2 vl I, 2 vl II, vla, 2 vlc e cb, fl picc, ob 1/2, cl 1/2, fag 1/2, cor 1/2, tr 1/2, Atrb, Ttrb, Btrb, timp, gr cassa, tri.
Unsigned and undated [c.1840s]
[DKKk; Tivolis musikarkiv no. 949 (mu 9405.1400)
These parts contains the complete music for the *Polonaise* in *The Tyroleans* (score no. 10). It most probably dates from when the dance was played at concerts in The Tivoli Gardens in the 1840s.

Printed sources:

Printed scenario. 1 vol. 15 pp. (17,8 × 10,5 cm)
Tyrolerne./Original idyllisk Ballet i een Act/af/A. Bournonville./ Musiken componeret og arrangeret af Herr Syngemester/Frøhlich. Kjøbenhavn, J. H. Schubothe, 1835.
[DKKk; 17, – 172 8°

17.5.1835
Pas de deux (uncredited) performed by Bournonville and L. Grahn in *Hermann von Unna*.

In Bournonville's handwritten lists of his works, written c.1851 (*see* Additional Sources) this (uncredited) dance is named 'Pas de deux i Hermann v: Unna' and indicated by him as as dance partly based on another choreographer's work. The *Pas de deux* was originally part of G. Spontini's opera *La Vestale* (premièred at the Paris Opéra on 16.12.1807) in which it was performed with choreography by P. Gardel in the final divertissement in Act I, scene 5 (score no. 6). According to several notes in Spontini's autographed score and the opera's original répétiteur's copy (now in FPo, call no. Rés. A 412a, and Mat. 19 [278 (334), pp. 43–51, and 70) the dance was originally named 'Serieux [Pas de] 2/Distributions des Prix' and was first performed by two French dancers, named Beaulieu and Mme Clotilde. Later it also became known in Paris as 'Prix de la Danse' and because of its extremely high technical demands it was used as the touchstone for all aspirant dancers. Bournonville appeared in it at the Paris Opéra five times, together with the French ballerina, L. Noblet, between 1.9.1826 and 25.7.1828.

The rather peculiar nickname of this *Pas de deux* seems to refer to the scene in *La Vestale* in which it was performed. Here a series of six dances were performed after the chorus, entitled «La paix est en ce jour le prix de vos conquêtes». These six dances were named as follows:

(1) 'Guerrère'.
(2) 'sérieux'.
(2) 'tambour'.
(4) 'Lyre'.
(5) 'Distribution des Prix' [i.e. the so-called 'Pas de la Vestale'/ 'Prix de la Danse'].
(6) 'Allegro moderato'.

The name given to the *Pas de deux* (no. 5) thus clearly seems to refer to the text of the hymn to peace that preceded it and is chanted by the people.

A copy of Spontini's orchestral score for this dance was most probably purchased by Bournonville in Paris during the summer of 1834 and brought to Denmark by him the same year. In Copenhagen it was mounted as part of a series of début performances for his pupil, the sixteen-year-old L. Grahn. She performed it together with Bournonville as an incorporated divertissement in A. F. Skjöldebrand's five-act drama *Hermann von Unna* to music by G. J. Vogler (premièred at Copenhagen's Royal Theatre on 30.1.1800). According to a pencilled note on p. '24v' in Vogler's orchestral score for *Hermann von Unna* reading: 'Nÿ Pas' (now in DKKk, call no. C I, 340), the *Pas de deux* was incorporated in Act I (score no. 3) and seems to have replaced V. Galeotti's original so-called 'Ballet' in that place.

The *Pas de deux* received 3 performances by Bournonville and Grahn in *Hermann von Unna*, the last time on 12.9.1835. According to other notes found in the complete set of parts for this dance (reading: '(Erik og Abel)') the *Pas de deux* also seems to have been performed twice as an *entr'acte* divertissement in A. Oehlenschläger's five-act tragedy *Erik and Abel (Erik og Abel)* on 10.9. and 22.9.1835. However, the posters for these performances give no specific information about any dances being incorporated in this work.

After 1835 the *Pas de deux* seems to have survived only at the Copenhagen ballet school, where it was regularly rehearsed and became known as 'Pas de la Vestale'. Finally, at the beginning of this century it was incorporated as an integral part of the repertory of *The Bournonville School*, compiled by Hans Beck between 1902 and 1910. It was here performed as an 'extra' after Saturday's Class.

It is not clear from the rehearsal book of H. C. J. Fredstrup exactly how many rehearsals of the *Pas de deux* in *Hermann von Unna* were held in 1835.

Musical sources:

Orchestral score. Ms. Copy. Black ink. 1 vol. 40. pp. (28,6×21,6 cm)
B 225/Partitur til/Partidöx Hermand/v: unna/225/[...]/Pas de deux de la Vestale/[...]/Spontini
Unsigned and undated [c.1834]
[DKKk; C I, 330 (KTB 225)
This orchestral score is a French copy from the office of the librarian and copyist at the Paris Opéra, F.-C. Lefèbvre. It includes a partially printed title page.

No répétiteur's copy dating from the 1835 Copenhagen staging of the *Pas de deux* in *Hermann von Unna* has yet been traced.

Parts. Ms. Copy. 24 vol.
3 vl I, 3 vl II, 2 vla, 3 vlc e cb, fl 1/2, ob 1/2, cl 1/2, fag 1/2, cor 1/2, clno 1/2, timp.
Unsigned and undated [1835]
[DKKk; KTB 225

5.6.1835
Pas de deux (uncredited) performed by Bournonville and L. Grahn.
This (uncredited) dance is perhaps identical with the *Pas de deux* first performed by Bournonville and Grahn in Act II of F. Hérold's three-act comic opera *Le Pré aux clercs* on 28.10.1834, and later danced as a separate divertissement by Bournonville and C. Fjeldsted on 19.2.1835. It is not possible to identify the dance any further.

9.6.1835
Yelva, ou L'Orpheline Russe (Yelva).
This vaudeville in two parts by E. Scribe, Th. F. V. de Villeneuve, and Desvergers (pen-name for Armand Chapeau) was premièred at the Théâtre de Madame in Paris on 18.3.1828 and may possibly have been seen by Bournonville during his Parisian sojourn in the late 1820s. In Copenhagen he created and mounted the vaudeville's many pantomime scenes, performed by the main character, the mute girl *Yelva* (performed by the actress F. N. Larcher). The music for these scenes was arranged and composed by P. D. Muth-Rasmussen. They consisted of ten numbers which accompanied both the mimic monologues of the protagonist, and her mimic dialogues with the other characters.

Moreover, according to Bournonville's autographed notes written (with brown ink) in the orchestral score he clearly seems to have revised T. Overskou's Danish tranlation as recited by the other characters immediately before and after each mime scene of *Yelva*.

Yelva, ou L'Orpheline Russe reached a total of 27 performances at Copenhagen's Royal Theatre, the last of which was given on 2.4.1842. It is not clear from the rehearsal book of H. C. J. Fredstrup exactly how many rehearsals of the mime scenes in this vaudeville were held in 1835.

Musical sources:

Orchestral score. Ms. Autograph (Muth-Rasmussen). Brown and black ink. 1 vol. 96 pp. of which two are blank (27 × 37,9 cm with minor variants)
Yelva./[...]/Yelva./Drama med Musik i to Acter./(Musiken arrangeret og componeret af Muth Rasmussen)./(Opført første Gang paa Det kongelige Theater d. 9 Juni 1835.)
Unsigned and dated: 'd. 9 Juni 1835.'
[DKKk; C II, 118 (KTA 327)
This orchestral score contains Bournonville's autographed notes (written with brown ink) and his other pencilled notes indicating the action before and after each pantomime scene.

No répétiteur's copy dating from the 1835 staging of *Yelva* has been traced.

Parts. Ms. Copy. 28 vol.
2 vl I, 2 vl II, vla, 2 vlc e cb, fl 1/2, ob 1/2, cl 1/2 fag 1/2 cor 1/2/3/4, tr 1/2, cnt a chiavi 1/2, trb 1/2/3, timp, arpa.
Unsigned and undated [1835]
[DKKk; KTA 327

3.9.1835
In Memory of Schall, Prologue (Schalls Minde, Forspil) (uncredited).
In his handwritten lists of his works, written c.1851 (*see* Additional Sources) Bournonville listed this (uncredited) work among his mises-en-scène (*Scene Arrangements*). It was staged to mark the anniversary of the death of the Danish composer, C. Schall, who had played a prolific rôle in the history of Danish ballet by composing nearly all the scores for V. Galeotti's ballets between 1780 and 1816. The text of the prologue (which was written by A. Oehlenschläger) was accompanied by a series of eight excerpts with highlights from the ballet scores of Schall. According to the poster this series concluded with the overture for Schall's and Galeotti's 1801 three-act pantomimic tragedy from 1801, *Lagertha*. Accord-

ing to an undated manuscript scenario for the prologue (written by an unknown hand and preserved among Bournonville's working papers) the programme and the eight excerpts were as follows:

(1) A chorus with new text by Oehlenschläger sung to the music of the chorus in the first scene of Act V in Schall's and Galeotti's five-act tragic ballet from 2.4.1811 *Romeo and Giulietta (Romeo og Giulietta)*.
(2) A prologue recited by an actor playing the rôle of the monk *Lorenzo* in *Romeo and Giulietta*.
(3) A scene from Schall's and Galeotti's four-act tragic ballet from 13.2.1808 *Bluebeard (Rolf Blaaskjæg)*.
(4) A monologue recited by the monk *Lorenzo*.
(5) A scene from Schall's and Galeotti's two-act comic ballet from 23.9.1802 *The Mountaineers, or The Children and the Mirror (Bjergboerne, eller Børnene og Speilet)*.
(6) A second monologue recited by the monk *Lorenzo*.
(7) A scene of Schall's and Galeotti's four-act comic ballet from 29.4.1788 *The Idol in Ceylon (Afguden paa Ceylon)*.
(8) A third monologue recited by the monk *Lorenzo*.
(9) The sailors' chorus «Fra Chinas Kyst» from Schall's and P. A. Heiberg's two-act singspiel from 2.3.1792 *The China travellers (Chinafarerne)*.
(10) A fourth monologue recited by the monk *Lorenzo*.
(11) A march and dance music from Schall's and Galeotti's three-act pantomimic tragedy from 30.1.1801 *Lagertha*, followed by a dance and two choruses («Saalænge Regnar» and «Saa glade vi drage det lÿnende Sværd») from the same ballet.
(12) A fifth monologue recited by the monk *Lorenzo*.
(13) A duet, with a new text by Oehlenschläger, sung to the melody of the duet «Fra Herrens Straalehiem» in Schall's and Galeotti's tragic ballet *Romeo and Giulietta*.
(14) A chorus, with new text by Oehlenschläger, sung to the music of the finale in Act V of Schall's and Galeotti's tragic ballet *Romeo and Giulietta*.

In Memory of Schall was performed only once. It is not clear from the rehearsal book of H. C. J. Fredstrup exactly how many rehearsals were held of the prologue in 1835.

No separate musical sources have yet been traced for this work. This seems to indicate that no separate orchestral score was actually prepared for it, and that it was performed using the older musical material for Schall's ballets.

Printed sources:

Printed libretto. 6.pp.
Schalls Minde
Published in *Søndagsblad* (Første Aargang, nr. 36, 6.9.1835, pp. 561–566)
DKKk; 57, – 11, 4°

Other sources:

Manuscript libretto. Ms. Copy (by an unknown hand). Black ink. 14 pp. (22,6 × 17,4 cm with minor variants)
Schalls Minde/Et Forspil.
Unsigned and undated [1835]
[DKKk; NKS 3285 4°, kapsel 9, læg 2

23.9.1835

Pas de deux composed by Mr. Ballet Master Bournonville (componeret af Hr. Balletmester Bournonville) performed by F. Hoppe and L. Grahn as an *entr'acte* divertissement between Acts II and III of Théaulon de Lambert's and A. Signol's three-act play *Jean.*

According to the rehearsal-book of F. Hoppe this dance is identical with the *Pas de deux* first performed by Hoppe and Grahn as an incorporated divertissement in Act I of *La Muette de Portici (see 23.9.1834)*. On 21.2. and 21.9.1837 it was also performed as a separate divertissement, by Bournonville and C. Fjeldsted. It is not clear from the rehearsal book of H. C. J. Fredstrup exactly how many rehearsals of this dance were held in 1835.

3.10.1835

Pas de deux in La Muette de Portici (Den Stumme i Portici) performed by Bournonville and L. Grahn.

On this day the poster for D.-F.-E. Auber's five-act opera read for the first time:

'Dandsen componeret af Hr. Dandsedirecteur Bournonville og Hr. Solodandser Funck'.

This clearly indicates that Bournonville's Act I *Pas de deux* (*see* 23.9.1834) was also included in this performance of the opera, and in which it was given for the first time with himself partnering L. Grahn. It is not clear from the rehearsal book of H. C. J. Fredstrup exactly how many rehearsals of the *Pas de deux* were held in 1835.

28.10.1835

Waldemar.

This four-act romantic ballet represents Bournonville's first work on a Danish national historical theme. According to his own account in his memoirs *My Theatre Life* (p. 76), it was drawn from inspirations received from his reading of:

'[L.] Holberg's *History of Denmark*, outlines from the *Knytlinga Saga*, tones from [B. S.] Ingemann's writings, and colours (I make bold to say) from my own imagination'.

Drawing from similar inspirations found in C. Schall's much earlier scores for V. Galeotti's many ballets on Nordic history and medieval legends, J. F. Fröhlich interpolated several Danish songs and medieval tunes in his score for this ballet in order to add a specific national colour and period style to the dramatic action. His musical borrowings are identified as follows:

(1) Act I (score nos. 3 and 12) and Act IV, the finale (score no. 32): In these numbers Fröhlich employed P. E. Rasmussen's 1811 melody to Lavrids Kock's song from 1683, named «Danmark deiligst Vang og Vænge». This song was published in 1812 and in 1814 with the title *Visen om Tyre Danebod* as part of W. H. F. Abrahamson's, R. Nyerup's, and K. L. Rahbek's anthology *Udvalgte Danske Viser fra Middelalderen* (vol. 2, pp. 3–7, and vol. 5, p. LXXIV, no. 56) and was re-versified a few years later by N. F. S. Grundtvig in 1816. In *Waldemar* it was employed either in its complete form or in excerpts. By both framing and uniting the ballet's action musically as well as dramaturgically with this song tune it became a kind of main leitmotif of the national unity so much sought for in the action of Acts I–III and achieved in Act IV.
(2) Act I (score no. 1): In this number Fröhlich employed another medival Danish song, entitled «Den Konning lader en Havfrue gribe». Moreover, for the so-called *Pas de danse* in the same act (score no. 5) he interpolated a tune from yet another Danish medieval song, named «Agnete hun stander paa Høieloft Broe». Both of these songs were published by Nyerup and Rahbek in 1814 (vol. 5, p. XXXVIII no. 69, and p. XXXIV no. 50A). The melody of the latter had been used three years earlier by Fröhlich in his musical arrange-

ment of the score for W. Holst's one-act dramatic idyll *The Feast of May (Maigildet)* from 13.4.1832.

(3) Act II (score no. 20): In this number Fröhlich illustrated musically Bournonville's use of a motif from the Danish medieval ballad *Rolf's Drapa* by incorporating J. E. Hartmann's melody for the song, named «Rolf Skattekonge fejg og ræd». It was originally part of Hartmann's score for B. C. Boye's three-act heroic play *Gorm the old (Gorm den gamle)*, premièred at Copenhagen's Royal Theatre on 31.1.1785. In *Waldemar* it was played on the harp by the character Agnar.

On 28.6.1838 *Waldemar* was mounted as part of a special gala performance for the heir to the Russian throne (later the Czar Alexander II). For this occasion Bournonville wrote a new, revised scenario of the ballet in French.

The ballet was restaged in five thoroughly revised versions on 19.10.1853, 19.12.1857, 21.11.1866, 4.6.1872, and 1.6.1877. Of these the 1872 production included a new recited prologue, named *Dawn (Dæmring)* and set to text by C. Andersen and music by E. Hartmann. Moreover, on 29.5.1867 *Waldemar* was performed for the 99th time as part of a gala performance celebrating the silver wedding of Denmark's King Christian IX and Queen Louise. For this occasion Bournonville again wrote a new and thoroughly revised scenario in French, entitled 'Analyse du Ballet', which included a new explanatory foreword named 'Augment historique'.

Furthermore, the *Pas de deux* from Act II (first danced by Bournonville as *Waldemar* and L. Grahn as *Astrid*) was also mounted as a separate divertissement at the following five theatres:

(1) at Stockholm's Royal Theatre (Operahuset) on 14.6.1839 (performed by Bournonville and C. Fjeldsted).
(2) at Göteborg's Stora Theater (Segerlinska Theatern) on 18.7.1839 (performed by the same dancers).
(3) at Christiania's Theatre (Oslo) on 3.8.1840 (with the same dancers).
(4) at Naples' Teatro San Carlo on 26.6.1841 (performed by Bournonville and L. Taglioni).
(5) at Milan's Teatro alla Scala on 29.8.1841 (performed by Bournonville and G. King).

For two gala performances of *Waldemar* in Copenhagen on 27.6. and 28.6.1838 two (uncredited) dances were (according to the posters) incorporated in Act I and II as follows:

(1) A *Pas de deux* in Act I (performed by P. Larcher and C. Fjeldsted).
(2) A *Pas de trois* in Act II (danced by P. C. Johansson, C. Fjeldsted and A. Nielsen).

According to pencilled notes found in the parts for the former (now in DKKk, call no. KTB 1052) it is identical with the (uncredited) *Pas de deux*, set to music by F.-M.-A. Venua and first performed by Bournonville and A. Krætzmer as a divertissement in J. L. Heiberg's three-act play *Princess Isabella, or Three Nights at the Court* (*see* 29.10.1829).

Finally, according to notes written in the separate musical sources for the *Grand solo variation* of *Astrid* in Act I, score no. 10 (now in DKKk, call nos. MA ms 2718–2720, and KTB 1052 (2)), this solo seems at a later stage to have been been completely omitted from Act I and instead interpolated (in a new musical arrangement by E. Helsted) in the Act II *Pas de deux*. This change, which is also indicated by a pencilled note in Fröhlich's autographed orchestral score for Act II (p. 227, reading: 'her springes tilbage til Pag. 87'), happened most

probably in connection with Bournonville's first revised restaging of *Waldemar* on 19.10.1853.

The original 1835 version of *Waldemar* received 55 performances (the last given on 31.3.1848), and the ballet reached a total of 150 performances during Bournonville's lifetime, the last of which was given on 27.11.1879. According to the rehearsal book of H. C. J. Fredstrup 52 rehearsals were held of it between 24.8.1834 and 28.10.1835.

Autograph sources:

Manuscript scenario (incomplete). Ms. Autograph. Brown ink. 1 vol. 8 pp. (21,3 × 17,4 cm)
Waldemar/1.ste Act./[...]/2.den Act.
Unsigned and undated [1833?]
[DKKt; Brevregistrant: Bournonville

Manuscript scenario. Ms. Autograph. Brown ink. 1 vol. 41 pp. (25,2 × 19,5 cm)
Valdemar/Original romantisk Ballet,/i 4 Acter,/af:/Auguste Bournonville./1833.
Signed and dated: 'Kjøbenhavn d. 2.den Junii, 1833'
[Stockholm, Nordiska Museets Arkiv, Brev- och manuskriptsamling (Inv. nr. 40.090)

Manuscript scenario Ms. Autograph. Brown ink. 1 vol. 10 pp. (21 × 17,3 cm)
Valdemar/Originalt historisk Mimodrama med Dands/af/A Bournonville – 1833 -
Signed and dated: '1833 – '
[DKKk; NKS 3285 4° 3 V-Z

Production note. Ms. Autograph. Brown ink. 4 pp. (35 × 21,5 cm)
Waldemar./1.ste Act./Dandsenummer. [*sic*]
Unsigned and undated [1835?]
[SSm; Daniel Fryklunds samling no. 113

Production note (concerning the costumes of the leading characters). Ms. Autograph. Brown ink. 4 pp. (35 × 21,5 cm)
Svend Eriksön (Hr Pætges) [...]
Unsigned and undated [1835?]
[SSm; Daniel Fryklunds samling no. 113

Production note. Ms. Autograph. Brown ink. 4 pp. (35 × 21,5 cm)
Personerne/i/Balletten Waldemar.
Unsigned and undated [1835?]
[SSm; Daniel Fryklunds samling no. 113

Production note. Ms. Autograph. Brown ink. 1 p. (35 × 21,5 cm)
Decorationerne/til/Balletten Waldemar.
Unsigned and undated [1835?]
[SSm; Daniel Fryklunds samling no. 113

Production note. Ms. Autograph. Brown ink. 2 pp. (35 × 21,5 cm)
Regie af Waldemar. 1.ste Act.
Unsigned and undated [1835?]
[SSm; Daniel Fryklunds samling no. 113

Musical sources:

Orchestral score. Ms. Autograph (by J. F. Fröhlich) and copy. Brown ink. 3 vol. Act I 148 pp., Act II 122 pp., Acts III–IV 148 pp. of which one is blank (23,2 × 33,1 cm with minor variants)
Balletten Waldemar
Signed and dated (on p. 16). 'd. 11.te October 1835/JFFröhlich'
[DKKk; C II, 107 (1909–10. Nr. 369) (KTB 297)
This orchestral score was (according to the date when it was transferred from DKKkt to DKKk) used for all performances of *Waldemar* in Copenhagen between 1835 and c.1907. It contains several con-

ductor's notes which refer to Bournonville's five later revisions of the ballet. Moreover, a great number of pencilled metronome markings are inserted throughout the score.

Répétiteur's copy. Ms. Copy. Brown and black ink. 1 vol. 92 pp. (31,7 × 24, 6 cm)
B. 297/Waldemar./Ballet./244a/d: 28 Oct 1835./[…]/Valdemar/den/Første/Ballet i 4 Acter/af/Aug: Bournonville/Musikken af F: Fröhlich
Unsigned and dated (on p. '89r.'): 'd: 7.de October/1835.'
[DKKk; MA ms 2993 (KTB 297 (1))
This répétiteur's copy was used for all performances of *Waldemar* between 1835 and 1853. It contains Bournonville's pencilled autographed notes which describe the dramatic action, the mime, and the choreography in Act I (score nos. 3, 4, named 'Danse rustique', 5, entitled 'Pas de Danse', 6, and 12), Act II (score nos. 16, i. e. the dance of the Ladies-in-Waiting, 19, 20, and 21, the finale), Act III (score nos. 22–26), and Act IV (score nos. 27, 29, 32, the finale). Moreover, his pencilled autographed numbers ('1–14, 1–4, 1–8, and 1–6') are inserted in the music for the Act II *Pas de deux* (score no. 18). They seem to refer to his separate (not yet traced) choreographic notation of this dance. Furthermore, Bournonville's autographed pencilled notes on the title page, and his other notes (written with brown ink on pp. '7r' and '12r') indicate the later musical changes in score nos. 5, 6, 10, 17, 24, and the omission of score nos. 7–10 made for the revised restaging of *Waldemar* on 19.10.1853. Finally, his autographed pencilled note, written at the end of Act III, seems to indicate that the third act played originally for 20 minutes.

Parts. Ms. Copy. 36 vol.
4 vl I, 4 vl II, 2 vla, 2 vlc, 2 cb, fl picc e fl I, fl II, ob 1/2, cl 1/2, fag 1/2, cor 1/2/3/4, clno 1/2, trb 1/2/3, timp, gr cassa, piatti, tri, arpa.
Unsigned and undated [1835]
[DKKk; KTB 297
These parts were used for all performances of *Waldemar* during Bournonville's lifetime.

Piano score. Ms. Autograph (by J. F. Fröhlich). Brown ink. 1 vol. 40 pp. of which one is blank (26 × 37,2 cm)
F Frøhlich:/Claveerudtog af 'Waldemar'/(Manuscript af Componisten)/H. Rung.
Unsigned and undated [1830s or 40s]
[DKKk; H. & Fr. Rung's Musik-Arkiv. No. 1939a
This piano score contains excerpts from Acts I–IV and was probably arranged by Fröhlich for a projected printed edition which, however, was never carried out. Instead another selection of his music from this ballet was published by C. C. Lose & Olsen in Copenhagen with the title *Ouverture et morceaux choisis de Waldemar* (now in DKKk, call no. D 6, 1912–13.235).

Orchestral score. Ms. Autograph (by J. F. Fröhlich). Brown ink. 1 vol. 8 pp. of which one is blank (26,6 × 36,6 cm)
Triumph – Marsch
Signed (on p. 1): 'Fröhlich', undated [c.1830s or 40s]
[DKKk; C II, 5 (J. F. Fröhlichs samling, kapsel 'Diverse')
This orchestral score contains the music of the triumphal march (*Allegro* in 2/4 time) from Act IV, score no. 32 (the *Finale*) of *Waldemar*. It was most probably made for concert purposes.

Parts. Ms. Copy. 25 vol.
vl I (conductor's part), 2 vl princ, 3 vl I, 4 vl II, 2 vla, 2 vlc, 2 vlc e cb, fl picc, fl, ob, cl 1/2, fag 1/2, cor 1/2.
Unsigned and undated [c.1840s and later]
[DKKk; Tivolis musikarkiv no. 946 (mu 9405.1400)
This set of parts contains two excerpts from Act I of *Waldemar* (score nos. 9 and 10 in the 1835 version). They seem to date from when a selection of Fröhlich's score was first played in The Tivoli Gardens in the mid-1840s. The conductor's part is dated with a pencilled note (reading: 'Anton Bloch/Tivoli Sommer 1892/Dirigent: Georg Lumbye'). This clearly indicates that the excerpts were still part of the

Tivoli concert repertory in the 1892 season. It also reflects the continuous popularity of Fröhlich's music with the audience throughout the last century. Other similar musical excerpts of *Waldemar* were played at three concerts given at the Casino Theatre on 23.4.1847 (entitled *Divertissement af Balletten Waldemar*), on 14.5.1847 (named *Scene og Ballet af Balletten Waldemar*), and on 22.3.1848 (the *Marsch af Balletten Waldemar*).

Parts (the *Shield Dance*). Ms. Copy. 25 vol.
vl I (conductor's part), 2 vl I, 2 vl II, vla, 2 vlc e cb, fl picc, fl, ob 1/2, cl 1/2, fag 1/2, cor 1/2, tr 1/2, Atrb, Ttrb, Btrb, gr cassa, cassa.
Unsigned and undated [c.1840s]
[DKKk; Tivolis musikarkiv no. 944 (mu 9405.1400)
This set of parts contains the music for the so-called *Shield Dance (Vaabendands)* in Act II of *Waldemar* (score no. 20 in the 1835 version). It probably dates from when this dance was first played at a public concert in The Tivoli Gardens in the mid-1840s. Pencilled notes written in the parts indicate the duration of this music as 3 minutes.

Other sources:

Décor for Act II. Pencil, Indian ink, and water colours (32,2 × 49,1 cm)
[Untitled]
Signed and dated: 'Troels Lund inv et fec/1835'
[Academy of the Fine Arts (Copenhagen); Arkitekturtegninger no. A 8696
The extraordinary quality and high degree of completion in this drawing was most probably caused by the fact that it served as Lund's work of admission in 1835 as member of the Danish Academy of the Fine Arts. His 1835 décor for Act II was used until Bournonville's third, revised staging of *Waldemar* on 21.11.1866. That year C. F. Christensen painted a completely new set for this act.

Printed sources:

Printed scenario. 1 vol. 15 pp. (21,8 × 13,3 cm)
Waldemar./Original romantisk Ballet i fire Acter/af/A. Bournonville./Musikken af F. Frölich [*sic*].
Kjøbenhavn, J. H. Schubothe, 1835.
[DKKk; 17, – 172 8°

1836

3.3.1836

Pas de deux composed by Mr. Ballet Master Bournonville (componeret af Hr. Balletmester Bournonville) performed by F. Hoppe and L. Grahn.

This dance is most probably identical with Bournonville's *Pas de deux* performed earlier by Hoppe and Grahn as an *entr'acte* divertissement in the play *Jean* (see 23.9.1835) and, in its turn, is perhaps identical with the *Pas de deux* in *La Muette de Portici* (see 23.9.1834). Another possible identification of this dance is Bournonville's *Pas de deux* in *Nina, ou La Folle par amour* also performed by Hoppe and Grahn (see 30.9.1834). It is not possible to identify the dance any further.

27.4.1836

A Pas de deux, from the ballet 'The Veteran', composed by Mr. Ballet Master Bournonville (En Pas de deux, af Balletten 'Veteranen', componeret af Hr. Balletmester Bournonville) performed by F. Hoppe and L. Grahn.

According to the repertory book of F. Hoppe this dance is

identical with the final *Pas de deux* in Bournonville's one-act idyllic ballet *The Veteran or The Hospitable House* (*see* 29.1. 1833). It represents the first time this dance was given as a separate divertissement. However, the *Pas de deux* (which had been performed in *The Veteran* since its 1833 première) was originally danced by Bournonville and A. Krætzmer as an incorporated divertissement in Act II of F. Hérold's three-act comic opera *Zampa ou La Fiancée de Marbre* (see 30.1. 1832).

According to the repertory book of F. Hoppe it was performed three times by him and Grahn in 1836, the last two times with a slightly different title (*see* 17.9.1836). It is not clear from the rehearsal book of H. C. J. Fredstrup exactly how many rehearsals were held of this dance in 1836.

12.9.1836

Pas de deux composed by Mr. Ballet Master Bournonville (componeret af Hr. Balletmester Bournonville) **performed by F. Hoppe and L. Grahn.**
According to the repertory book of F. Hoppe, this dance is identical with Bournonville's earlier *Pas de deux* in Act I of his Copenhagen version of L. Milon's two-act pantomimic ballet *Nina, ou La Folle par amour* (*see* 30.9.1834). It was performed only once in 1836. It is not clear from the rehearsal book of H. C. J. Fredstrup exactly how many rehearsals of it were held in 1836.

17.9.1836

A Pas de deux composed by Mr. Ballet Master Bournonville (componeret af Hr. Balletmester Bournonville) **performed by F. Hoppe and L. Grahn.**
According to the repertory book of F. Hoppe, this dance is identical with Bournonville's *Pas de deux* originally performed by himself and A. Krætzmer in F. Hérold's three-act comic opera *Zampa ou La Fiancée de Marbre (Zampa eller Marmorbruden)* on 30.1.1832. The dance was given twice by Hoppe and Grahn with this title, the last time on 3.10.1836. They danced it both times as an *entr'acte* divertissement between Acts II and III of Théaulon de Lambert's and A. Signol's three-act play *Jean*. It is not clear from the rehearsal book of H. C. J. Fredstrup exactly how many rehearsals were held of this dance in 1836.

22.9.1836

A Pas de trois, composed by Mr. Ballet Master Bournonville (En Pas de trois, componeret af Hr. Balletmester Bournonville) **performed by P. C. Johansson, L. Grahn, and C. Fjeldsted.**
In Bournonville's handwritten lists of his works, written c.1851 (*see* Additional Sources) this dance is named 'Pas de trois Johansson'. It was mounted especially for the Copenhagen début of his Swedish pupil, P. C. Johansson, and seems to have been based on an earlier work. Thus, the most probable identification of the dance seems to be the *Pas de trois* from the ballet *Soldier and Peasant* (*see* 13.10.1829), which was mounted only fourteen months later by Johansson in Stockholm on 22.1.1838 with the new title *The Homecoming (Hemkomsten)*. On that occasion Bournonville had donated the original French score for the *Pas de trois* as a personal gift to Johansson, with an autographed dedication. Knowing that this dance represented Bournonville's own choreographic

début in Copenhagen, it therefore seems reasonable to assume that he would also have donated the same dance to his Swedish pupil after his début in Copenhagen.

The *Pas de trois* received three performances in Copenhagen by Johansson, Grahn, and Fjeldsted, the last of which was given on 30.9.1836. It is not possible to identify the dance any further.

17.10.1836

Pas de trois, composed by Mr. Ballet Master Bournonville (componeret af Hr. Balletmester Bournonville) **performed by Bournonville, L. Grahn, and C. Fjeldsted.**
This dance is most probably identical with Bournonville's so-called 'Pas de trois Johansson' (*see* 22.9.1836) which was performed three times during the previous month by P. C. Johansson, Grahn and Fjeldsted. It was danced twice by Bournonville, Grahn, and Fjeldsted in 1836, the last time on 22.10.1836. It is not possible to identify the dance any further.

28.11.1836

La Sylphide (Sylphiden).
In his score for this two-act romantic ballet (based on F. Taglioni's and J. Schneitzhoeffer's similar work from 1832 of that name), H. S. v. Løvenskjold incorporated several Scottish folk tunes and dances in order to add a distinctive local colour to the ballet's exotic setting. Thus, in the overture he incorporated a theme of the well-known Scottish song «Auld Lang Syne», while in Act I (score no. 5) he employed a typical *Eccosaise* tune. Moreover, in the following number of the same act (the *Reel*) Løvenskjold seems to improvise freely on motifs of several authentic Scottish *Strathspey* reels, for instance, 'Miss Wedderburn's Reel', and 'Miss Hope's Strathspey' to name only two (both published by M. Keith in *The Complete Repository of Original Scots Slow Strathspeys & Dances*, Glasgow, 1799–1817).

Bournonville, for his part, clearly based his choreography of the Act I *Reel* on an authentic Scottish solo dance, named 'Gille Gàisgeach'. This popular dance was frequently balleticised during the period of the early Romantic ballet and was generally known under the title 'The Highland Laddie'.

La Sylphide was restaged 5 times in Copenhagen during Bournonville's lifetime, by himself or by L. Gade, as follows:

(1) on 22.9.1849 (Bournonville's first, thoroughly revised version mounted for the début of J. Price in the rôle of *The Sylph*).
(2) on 25.11.1856 (a restaging mounted especially for the début of H. Scharff as *James*).
(3) on 4.2.1865 (Bournonville's second, thoroughly revised version, mounted by L. Gade for the début of C. Healey as *The Sylph*).
(4) on 26.4.1867 (Bournonville's third, slightly revised version mounted mainly by L. Gade for the début of M. Price as *The Sylph*).
(5) on 6.9.1871 (Bournonville's last and seemingly unchanged restaging, mounted for the début of M. Westberg in the title rôle).

Moreover, an abridged divertissement version, entitled *Scene from the Ballet La Sylphide (Scen utur Balletten Sylphiden/ Scène de la Sylphide)* was mounted by Bournonville at Stockholm's Royal Theatre (Operahuset) on 14.6.1839 with F. Hoppe playing the rôle of *James*, and A. Nielsen that of *The Sylph*. This version was also performed with a slightly different title at Göteborg's Stora Theater (Segerlindska Theatern) on

15.7.1839. Finally, on 31.7.1840 the ballet was given at Christiania's Theatre (Oslo) in yet another abridged divertissement version in three parts that was arranged by Bournonville and included a cast consisting of *The Sylph* (C. Fjeldsted), *James* (Bournonville), *Madge* (the Danish actor, N. P. Nielsen), and a corps de ballet of sylphs.

The 1840 Norwegian version also included a new incorporated *Pas de deux* for *James* and *The Sylph* which replaced Løvenskjold's original *Pas de deux* (score no. 3) from Act II. This is clear from pencilled notes found in the 1840 répétiteur's copy and in a set of parts for this new dance reading: 'No. 3b 2.d Afd/Sylphiden/Timpani' (now in DKKk, call nos. KTB 1028, and KTB 1052). According to the same sources the new *Pas de deux* is musically identical with the much earlier (uncredited) *Pas de deux*, set to music by F.-M.-A. Venua and originally incorporated by Bournonville in J. L. Heiberg's three-act play *Princess Isabella, or Three Nights at the Court* at Copenhagen's Royal Theatre on 29.10.1829.

In Denmark Løvenskjold's music for the original 1836 *Pas de deux* in Act II (score no. 3) of *La Sylphide* was omitted from the ballet at about the end of the 1837–38 season. This omission resulted from some consistent criticism concerning the fact that the two protagonists (*James* and *The Sylph*) performed with close physical contact in this dance. This physical contact between the ballet's two main characters appeared from a dramaturgical point of view rather unlogical to most of the viewers, including the celebrated actress, J. L. Heiberg. Acknowledging criticism from her and others, Bournonville consequently seems to have replaced Løvenskjold's original *Pas de deux* on 27.9.1842 with yet another (uncredited) dance, entitled *Pas de deux (à la Taglioni)* and set to music by J. Mayseder. This dance, in its turn, was borrowed from Act II of his two-act romantic ballet *The Isle of Phantasy* (*see* 28.10.1838). According to the orchestral score and répétiteur's copy for that ballet (now in DKKk, call nos. C II, 105, and MA ms 2645) the dance is there entitled 'Pas de trois' in spite of being clearly performed as a *Pas de deux* by L. Grahn (as *Phantasiens Dronning*) and P. Larcher (playing *Faunus*).

Mayseder's music for this *Pas de deux* was, according to a printed piano score published in Vienna in 1823 by Artaria & Co (now in AWn, pl. no. 2742), identical with his much earlier concert-piece for violin and piano, entitled *Divertimento nr. 1* (op. 35). It seems to have been purchased by Bournonville in Paris or in Berlin some time during the mid-1830s. This theory is supported by the fact that neither the orchestral score nor the two répétiteur's copies for F. Taglioni's and J. Schneitzhoeffer's original Paris version of *La Sylphide* (now in FPo, call nos. A 501 [I–III], and Mat. 19 [302 (25–26)) contains any traces of Mayseder's *Pas de trois* ever being part of this ballet during its Paris Opéra performances. Consequently, Mayseder's music would have been incorporated in Taglioni's ballet at a later stage, and if so most likely in connection with its staging at Berlin's Hofoper on 25.5.1832.

This assumption is supported by yet another, similar copy of Mayseder's original *Pas de trois*, which was inserted in Act II of Taglioni's *La Sylphide* when it was mounted by the French ballet-master and choreographer, A. Titus, at the Alexandra Theatre in St Petersburg on 28.5.1835. Titus had directed the ballet at Berlin's Hofoper when *Die Sylphide* was mounted there in 1832. Subsequently, he may have brought Mayseder's score for this dance with him to St Petersburg where, according to the Russian orchestral score and répétiteur's copy for *La Sylphide* (now in RF-SPtob, call nos. I 4 Sch 360 (4455), and pe Sylph (1722)), it clearly became part of his 1835 Russian production of Taglioni's ballet.

Another, similar musical source which supports this theory dates from about the same period and consists of a complete set of parts for Mayseder's *Pas de deux* (now in SSkma, call no. KT Dansmusik 43). The label on the box containing this Swedish material reads: 'Pas de deux/La Sylphide/af Maÿseder'. In Sweden, Taglioni's ballet was not given in full until 21.8.1843 (M. Taglioni and P. C. Johansson had appeared in scenes and excerpts of the ballet 4 times in Stockholm, the first time on 24.9.1841). However, Mayseder's *Pas de deux* had already been mounted there by Bournonville as a separate divertissement at Stockholm's Royal Theatre (Operahuset) on 5.6.1839. It was then performed by his pupil, P. C. Johansson, and A. Nielsen with the title *Pas de deux (by Taglioni) (Pas de deux (Af Taglioni))*. When Mayseder's music was incorporated in Act II of Bournonville's *La Sylphide* in Copenhagen on 27.9.1842 it, too, was named *Pas de deux (à la Taglioni)*, and was then danced by Bournonville (as *James*) and A. Nielsen (as *The Sylph*). They performed it 11 times within this ballet, the last time on 20.12.1843.

The same year Bournonville also mounted a separate divertissement in Copenhagen on 28.10.1843, entitled *Pas de deux from the ballet 'La Sylphide' (Pas de deux af Balletten 'Sylphiden')* and performed by F. Hoppe and A. Nielsen. It is unclear whether this dance was set to J. Mayseder's music, or whether it was identical with Løvenskjold's original *Pas de deux* from Act II (score no. 3) of the 1836 version of *La Sylphide*.

Finally, according to Bournonville's pencilled autographed notes in the 1838 répétiteur's copy for Mayseder's *Pas de deux* in *The Isle of Phantasy* and other notes found in the orchestral score and the 1849 répétiteur's copy for *Faust* (now in DKKk, call nos. MA ms 2645, C II, 115, and KTB 289 respectively), Mayseder's music also served for the *Pas de deux* which on 8.12.1849 was interpolated by Bournonville in Act II of his three-act romantic ballet *Faust*.

On 15.6.1857 Bournonville suggested a staging of his complete version of *La Sylphide* to the theatre management of Stockholm's Royal Theatre. This project, which he had originally planned for the spring of 1858, was partially carried out on 12.6.1860 when a new divertissement version of three large excerpts (apparently arranged by Bournonville and entitled *Scene, Solo and Pas de deux, in two sections, from the ballet 'La Sylphide' (Scène, Solo och Pas de deux I två afdelningar, ur Balletten 'Sylphiden')*) were staged at Stockholm's Mindre Theatern with F. Hoppe (as *James*) and J. Price (as *The Sylph*). It was given only twice at Mindre Theatern, the last time on 14.6.1860.

However, only two years later the whole ballet was premièred at Stockholm's Royal Theatre (Operahuset) on 1.4.1862, in a slightly abridged version arranged by Bournonville and mounted for the Swedish ballerina, A. Arrhenius. This production was restaged at the same theatre on 17.9. 1862, with a new, additional *Pas de deux* incorporated by Bournonville in Act I for his English pupils, the sisters A. and C. Healey, and set to music by H. C. Lumbye. That dance proves to be identical with his so-called *Polketta, Pas de deux* (*see* 31.10.1858).

During the year that followed the 1836 Copenhagen première of *La Sylphide* Bournonville also choreographed and published a series of ballroom dances, entitled *Les Sylphides. Contredanses nouvelles*. They were set to a selection of tunes from Løvenskjold's score (*see* 31.10.1837).

The original 1836 version of *La Sylphide* received 55 performances (the last given on 12.1.1849) and the ballet as such reached a total of 80 performances during Bournonville's lifetime, the last of which was given on 12.9.1871. According to the rehearsal book of H. C. J. Fredstrup 49 rehearsals were held of *La Sylphide* between 16.9. and 28.11.1836.

Autograph sources:

Production note. Ms. Autograph. Brown ink. 3 pp. (21,1 × 17,3 cm)
Foreløbigt – Udkast/til/Costumet i Balletten Sÿlphiden.
Signed and undated [1836]
[DKKt; Brevregistrant: Bournonville

Musical sources:

Orchestral score (incomplete). Ms. Autograph (by H. S. v. Løvenskjold) and copy (by V. C. Holm and others). Brown and black ink. 2 vol. Act I 200 pp., Act II 170 pp. + 5 detached pp. (27 × 37 cm with minor variants)
275./Sylphiden./1. Akt/[...]/'Sÿlphiden'/Ballet i to Acter/ved/Auguste Bournonville/sat i Musik/af/H: S: Løvenskiold/[...]/275./Sylphiden./2 Akt/[...]/Anden Act/af/Balletten 'Sylphiden'/af/HSLøvenskiold
Signed and undated [1836]
[DKKk; CII, 117 d (KTB 275)
This autographed orchestral score was used for all performances of *La Sylphide* in Copenhagen during Bournonville's lifetime. It contains several later insertions many of which are written by V. C. Holm (most likely for the 1865 restaging?).

Orchestral score (fragments). Ms. Autograph (by H. S. v. Løvenskjold). Brown and black ink. 24 pp. (27 × 37 cm)
[page] 10/marcato assai
Unsigned and undated [1836]
[DKKk; MA ms 2762 (1) (KTB 275)
These 24 pages contain the music for those sections of the overture for *La Sylphide* (pp. '10–33') which were omitted from Løvenskjold's score at a later restaging of *La Sylphide* (perhaps that of H. Beck on 2.9.1903). The fragments were found among the anonymous musical manuscripts at DKKkt in 1989 and were transferred to DKKk at a later stage.

Orchestral score (fragments). Ms. Autograph (by H. S. v. Løvenskjold). Brown and black ink. 42 pp. (27 × 37 cm)
B 1/Allegro non tanto e grazioso.
Unsigned and undated [1836]
[DKKk; MA ms 2762 (2) (KTB 275)
These 42 pages contain six sections from Løvenskjold's autographed score for *La Sylphide*, Act I (score no. 1, pp. '7–12, 39–44', no. 5, pp. '141–156') and Act II (score no. 5, pp. '96, 100–103, 106–109' + four unpaginated pages). They seem to have been omitted from the ballet at a later restaging (perhaps that of H. Beck on 2.9. 1903). The fragments were found among the anonymous musical manuscripts at DKKkt in 1989 and were transferred to DKKk at a later stage.

Orchestral score (fragments). Ms. Autograph (by E. Helsted). Brown ink. 4 pp. (27 × 37 cm)
No. 1./Anden Act./[...]/No. 2.
Unsigned and undated [1836?]
[DKKk; MA ms 2711 (1–2) (KTB 275)
These pages contain two sections of the music from Act II (score nos. 1 and 2) of *La Sylphide*. They are E. Helsted's autographs and seem to represent those reorchestrations of the music for the brass and wind instruments, which Løvenskjold (according to a letter now in DKKk) had asked I. P. E. Hartmann to revise on 26.11.1836. Hartmann seemingly passed this request on to Helsted, who probably drafted his proposed changes some time around the 1836 première of *La Sylphide*.

Répétiteur's copy. Ms. Copy. Brown ink. 1 vol. 154 pp. (31,2 × 24,2 cm)
Ripiteur Partie/til/Balletten Sÿlphiden/af/Bournonville sat i Musik af Herm: Lövenskjold
Unsigned and undated [1836]
[DKKk; MA ms 2970a (KTB 275)
This répétiteur's copy contains Bournonville's numerous pencilled autographed notes describing the dramatic action, the mime, and the choreography throughout the ballet. The inclusion of the names of several of the dancers who took part in the first performance of the ballet indicate that his notes can confidently be dated to 1836 with the exception of a few later choreographic notations (written on pp.' 63r–65v'), which were clearly written for the 1849 restaging since they include the name of the dancer 'Sophie' [Price]. She appeared for the first time in this ballet in 1849.

Répétiteur's copy (fragments). Ms. Copy. Brown ink. 12 pp. (31,2 × 24,5 with minor variants)
Alla Polacca/[...]/No. 4./[...]/No. 5.
Unsigned and undated [1836]
[DKKk; MA ms 2710 (KTB 275)
These fragments were originally part of the 1836 répétiteur's copy for *La Sylphide*. They contain Løvenskjold's music for Act II, score no. 3 (the *Pas de deux*, incomplete), no. 4 (*All.° agitato*), and parts of no. 5 (the *Andante*, incomplete) and were originally inserted between what is now pp. '49v' and '50r' in the original répétiteur's copy. The pages were most probably taken out of this volume in connection with Bournonville's and L. Gade's revised restaging of *La Sylphide* on 4.2.1865. They include Bournonville's pencilled autographed choreographic notes (all of which would almost certainly date from the 1836 première) and some other notes (written with brown ink on p. 12) which read: 'her indlægges/af den nÿe Penelope/Pas: 28.' These notes indicate the exact place where excerpts from Løvenskjold's score to Bournonville's two-act ballet *The New Penelope, or The Spring Festival in Athens* (*see* 26.1.1847) were incorporated in *La Sylphide* on 22.9.1849.

Parts. Ms. Copy. 38 vol.
5 vl I, 4 vl II, 2 vla, 3 vlc, 2 cb, fl 1/2, ob 1/2, cl 1/2, fag 1/2, cor 1/2/3/4, tr 1/2, trb 1/2/3, tuba, timp, gr cassa e piatti, tri, arpa.
Unsigned and undated [1836]
[DKKk; KTB 275
These parts were used for all performances of *La Sylphide* in Copenhagen during Bournonville's lifetime.

Printed sources:

Printed scenario. 1 vol. 30. pp (20 × 12,7 cm)
LA/SYLPHIDE.,/Ballet en deux Actes,/par M. Taglioni,/Musique de M. Schneitzhoeffer;/Représenté pour la première fois, a Paris,/sur le Théâtre de l'Académie Royal de Musique,/le 12 Mars 1832./Deuxième Édition.
Paris, J.-N. Barba, 1832.
[DKKk; UA Småtryk, kapsel 176 M-Z (1911-12.0208)
This copy of the second edition of the original French scenario for F. Taglioni's *La Sylphide* was (according to his 1834 travel-diary) pur-

chased by Bournonville in Paris on 4.8.1834. It clearly served as the basis for his own later arrangement of this ballet in Copenhagen.

Printed scenario. 1 vol. 16 pp. (21 × 13,4 cm)
Sylphiden,/romantisk Ballet i to Acter./Componeret/af/August Bournonville./Musikken af Hermann Løvenskjold.
Kjøbenhavn, Thieles Bogtrykkeri, 1836.
[DKKk; 17, – 173 8° (expl. 1)
This printed scenario contains Bournonville foreword (*Forerindring*) dated 'Kjøbenhavn, d. 1ste Novbr. 1836'

Printed scenario. 1 vol. 15 pp. (21 × 13,1 cm)
Sylphiden,/romantisk Ballet i to Acter./Componeret/af/August Bournonville./Musikken af Hermann Løvenskjold.
Kjøbenhavn, J. H. Schubothes Boghandel, Trykt i det Nissenske Bogtrykkeri, 1836.
[DKKk; 17, – 173 8° (expl. 2)
This printed scenario is a generic programme without specification of the casting, but is otherwise identical with the previous scenario.

1837

21.2.1837
Pas de deux composed by Mr. Ballet Master Bournonville (componeret af Hr. Balletmester Bournonville) performed by F. Hoppe and A. Nielsen.
According to the repertory book of F. Hoppe this dance is identical with Bournonville's *Pas de deux* in *Nina, ou La Folle par amour* (*see* 30.9.1834). The *Pas de deux* was (according to the rehearsal book of H. C. J. Fredstrup) rehearsed by Bournonville for Hoppe and Nielsen on 18.2.1837 and performed by them as an *entr'acte* divertissement between Act II and III of the play *Jean*.

24.2.1837
Don Quixote at Camacho's Wedding (Don Quixote ved Camachos Bryllup).
This three-act ballet is Bournonville's free version of L. J. Milon's and F.-C. Lefèbvre's much earlier two-act *ballet-pantomime-folie*, entitled *Les Noces de Gamache* (premièred in Paris at Théâtre de la République et des Arts on 18.1.1801). Bournonville had seen that ballet performed on several occasions during his first visit to the French capital in 1820. The 1837 Copenhagen production was set to a completely new score, composed and arranged by L. Zinck. He included numerous musical excerpts and borrowings from works by other composers and which are identified as follows:

(1) Act I (score no. 2): In this number Zinck inserted a solo for L. Grahn (who played *Quiteria*). It was set to music borrowed from F. Sor's and Albert's (François Decombe) three-act fairy-ballet *Cendrillon* (premièred at the Paris Opéra on 3.3.1823). According to the original orchestral score and répétiteur's copy for this ballet (now in FPo, call nos. A 469 [I], pp. 161–169, and Mat. 19 [63 (3), pp. 14–16)) the solo was originally part of a large divertissement performed in Act I of Sor's and Albert's ballet.
(2) Act I (score no. 4): Zinck here incorporated the complete *Boléro* from D.-F.-E. Auber's five-act opera *La Muette de Portici* (premièred at the Paris Opéra on 29.2.1828). According to Bournonville's pencilled autographed notes in the orchestral score it was given in *Don Quixote at Camacho's Wedding* in a musically abridged version as a *Pas de deux* by P. Larcher (who played Pedrillo) and C. Fjeldsted (as Aldonza).

(3) Act II (score no. 9): According to the orchestral score (which here is a manuscript copy) Zinck clearly employed music by another (not yet identified) composer for this number.
(4) Act II (score no. 10): For this scene Zinck interpolated a large excerpt borrowed from the cavatina of *Figaro* in Act I (scene 2) of G. Rossini's two-act opera *Il Barbiere di Sevilla* (premièred at Rome's Teatro Argentina on 20.2.1816).
(5) Act II (score no. 12): Zinck here employed a large excerpt borrowed from the overture of G. Rossini's two-act opera *La Gazza Ladra* (premièred at Milan's Teatro alla Scala on 31.5.1817).
(6) Act III (score no. 13): In this scene Zinck clearly seems (according to the orchestral score which here is a manuscript copy) to have employed music borrowed from a work by another (not yet identified) composer.
(7) Act III (score no. 14): For this number Zinck employed excerpts borrowed from the overture of G. Rossini's two-act opera *Le Comte Ory* (premièred at the Paris Opéra on 20.8.1828).
(8) Act III (score no. 15): According to the orchestral score (which here is a manuscript copy) Zinck incorporated excerpts borrowed from two earlier French ballets in this number. Of these the second excerpt proves to have been borrowed from F. Hérold's score to J. Aumer's three-act pantomimic ballet *Astolphe et Joconde ou Le coureurs d'aventures* (premièred at the Paris Opéra on 29.1.1827). According to Hérold's full orchestral score and the original répétiteur's copy for this ballet (now in FPo, call nos. A 483 [I–II], and Mat. 19 [281 (27)) this music originally served for a *Pas de six* divertissement. Hérold's orchestral score for this dance was most probably purchased by Bournonville in Paris in the late 1820s or early 30s and brought by him to Copenhagen.
(9) Act III (score no. 16): According to the orchestral score for this number (which is a manuscript copy) Zinck here clearly employed music borrowed from the work of another (not yet identified) composer. It consists of two movements, entitled 'Marcia' and a 'Ciaccona', and accompanied a mime scene described as 'Börnecomedie'.
(10) Act III (score no. 17): For this number Zinck incorporated an excerpt in 2/4 time, entitled «Célébrons tour à tour le vin et la folie» which originally was part of the chorus, named «Buvons, buvons, buvons, buvons soudain!» in Act II (score no. 18) of G. Rossini's two-act opera *Le Comte d'Ory* (premièred at the Paris Opéra on 20.8.1828). Many years later the same excerpts were incorporated by H. S. Paulli in Act I (score no. 1) and Act III (score no. 19) of his music for Bournonville's three-act ballet *The Kermesse in Brüges, or The Three Gifts* (*see* 4.4.1851).
(11) Act III (score nos. 18 and 19): According to the orchestral score (which here is a manuscript copy) Zinck clearly must have incorporated music borrowed from works by other (not yet identified) composers.

Moreover, the *Pas de deux* in Act I, score no. 5 (danced by Bournonville as *Basilio*, and L. Grahn as *Quiteria*) is in the orchestral score for *Don Quixote at Camacho's Wedding*, entitled 'Pas de Trois, dansé dans Cendrillon. Musique: Mozart, arrangée par Schneitzhoeffe [*sic*]'. According to Bournonville's pencilled autographed notes in the same score (p. 3) this dance was at a later stage renamed by him to: 'Begyndelsen af Fandango i C Mol som Introduction: -/Pas de deux. Bournonville og Jf. Grahn'. The score for this dance, which also contains Bournonville's own signature (written with black ink), was most likely purchased by him in Paris during the late 1820s or early 30s and brought to Copenhagen at about the same time. It seems to have been revised by Zinck in Copenhagen in 1837 into the Act I *Pas de deux*, that also includes a new *Fandango* introduction of 28 bars in C minor (presumably composed by Zinck). Furthermore, J. Schneitzhoeffer's original score for this dance employs two excerpts borrowed from Act II of W. A. Mozart's four-act singspiel from 1786 *Die Hochzeit des Figaro*, namely the arias «Non più andrai» and «Voi, che sapete» (sung by *Figaro* and *Cherubini* respectively).

Bournonville's *Pas de deux* in Act I of *Don Quixote at Camacho's Wedding* is most probably also identical with the later (uncredited) *Pas de deux* performed in Copenhagen by himself and Grahn as an incorporated divertissement in N. Isouard's three-act lyrical fairy-play *Cendrillon* on 17.12.1837. This theory is based on the fact that the music for the *Pas de deux* in *Don Quixote at Camacho's Wedding* was borrowed from Albert's ballet *Cendrillon*. It therefore would have been natural for Bournonville to incorporate exactly this dance in a work like that of Isouard's *Cendrillon* which is based on the very same plot.

Ten years after the Copenhagen première of *Don Quixote at Camacho's Wedding* the score for the Act I *Pas de deux* was reused for the last time by Bournonville, as an incorporated divertissement in his ballet *The White Rose, or The Summer in Bretagne* (*see* 20.9.1847) in which it was performed in a new, slightly different musical arrangement by H. S. Paulli.

Finally, the *Ciacconne* in Act III (score no. 16) of *Don Quixote at Camacho's Wedding* was eleven years later also incorporated by E. Helsted as no. 6 of his score for Bournonville's one-act ballet *Old Memories, or A Magic Lantern* (*see* 18.12. 1848).

According to Bournonville's pencilled autographed notes in the répétiteur's copy (p. 213) the complete ballet lasted 90 minutes (Act I: 35 minutes, Act II: 15 minutes, Act III: 40 minutes). Other notes found in the parts (reading '2T. 1q') indicate that the total performance played for 2 hours and 15 minutes.

Don Quixote at Camacho's Wedding was only given twice, the last time on 25.2.1837. According to the rehearsal book of H. C. J. Fredstrup 41 rehearsals were held of it between 19.12. 1836 and 24.2.1837.

Autograph sources:

Production note. Ms. Autograph. Brown ink. 4 pp. (34,8 × 21,2 cm)
Udkast til Costumet/i/Balletten D. Quixote ved Gamachos Brÿllup./(Tiden er omtrent den samme hvori Figaro spilles.)
Signed and dated: 'Kbhvn d 30 Decbr 1836.'
[DKKt; Brevregistrant: Bournonville

Production note. Ms. Autograph. Brown ink. 3 pp. (34,8 × 21,2 cm)
Personerne/i/Don Quixote ved Gamachos Brÿllup./original pantomimisk Ballet i 3 Acter/af/August Bournonville.
Unsigned and undated [c.1836–1837]
[DKKt; Brevregistrant: Bournonville

Musical sources:

Orchestral score (*Pas de deux*). Ms. Copy. 1 vol. 26 pp. (29, × 21,8 cm with minor variants)
Bournonville/Pas de Trois, dansé dans Cendrillon. Musique: Mozart, arrangée par Schneitzoeffe[r] [*sic*]
Unsigned and undated [c.1823–1837]
[DKKk; H. & Fr. Rungs Musik-Arkiv, no. 611 (1954–55.661)
This score is clearly a French copy and was most probably purchased by Bournonville in Paris in the 1820s or 30s and brought by him to Copenhagen at about the same time. This theory is supported by the French titles and watermark (showing a bunch of grapes) that are contained in this score.

Orchestral score. Ms. Autograph (by L. Zinck) and copy. Black and brown ink. 2 vol. Act I 268 pp. of which one page is blank, Acts II–III pp. 394 of which six pp. are blank (27,5 × 38 with minor variants)
202/L. Zinck/Don Quixote./Ballet i 3 Acter./Partitur til 1.ste Act,/
[…]/202/L. Zinck/DonQuixote/2
Unsigned and dated (on the title-page) '1837'
[DKKk; C II, 125 (KTB 202)
An autographed page by H. S. Paulli is inserted in Zinck's score between pp. 155 and 156. It contains what appears to be Paulli's first draft for his new introduction to the music of the Act I *Pas de deux* in *Don Quixote at Camacho's Wedding* which some ten years later was incorporated in his score for Bournonville's one-act ballet *The White Rose, or The Summer in Bretagne* (*see* 20.9.1847).

Répétiteur's copy. Ms. Copy. 1 vol. 214 pp. (32,2 × 24,8 cm)
B. 202/Don Quixote/303/Febr 1837./[…]/Repetiteur Partie/til/Don Quixote/Ballet i 3 Acter.
Unsigned and dated: 'Febr. 1837.'
[DKKk; MA ms 2941 (KTB 202)
This répétiteur's copy contains Bournonville's pencilled autographed notes describing the mime and the dramatic action of Act I (score nos. 1–3, 6–8), Act II (score nos. 9–12), and Act III, (score nos. 13–14, 17–18). Moreover, his sporadic autographed choreographic notes are found in Act I (score no. 5, the *Pas de deux*) and Act III (score no. 14, the *Danse rustique*), while other notes (written with black ink by an unknown hand) describes the dramatic action in Act III (score no. 17).

Parts. Ms Copy. 34 vol.
3 vl I, 3 vl II, 2 vla, 3 vlc e cb, fl 1/2, ob 1/2, cor ingl, cl 1/2, fag 1/2, cor 1/2/3/4, tr 1/2, trb 1/2/3, timp, gr cassa, piatti, tri, arpa.
Unsigned and undated [1837]
[DKKk; KTB 202

Printed sources:

Princed scenario. 1 vol. 23 pp. (19,5 × 12,5 cm)
Don Quixote/ved Camachos Bryllup/Original Pantomimisk Ballet i tre Acter/af/August Bournonville./Musikken arrangeret og componeret af Hr. Syngemester/L. Zinck.
Kjöbenhavn, Schubothes Boghandel, trykt hos P. N. Jørgensen, 1837.
[DKKk; 17, – 173 8°

3.10.1837

Pas de deux composed by Mr. Ballet Master Bournonville (componeret af Hr. Balletmester Bournonville) performed by Bournonville and C. Fjeldsted.

This dance is probably identical with the earlier *Pas de deux* performed as an *entr'acte* divertissement in the play *Jean* (*see* 23.9.1835) and, in its turn, is perhaps identical with Bournonville's *Pas de deux* in *La Muette de Portici* (*see* 23.9.1834), or his *Pas de deux* in *Nina, ou La Folle par amour* (*see* 30.9.1834). It is not possible to identify the dance any further.

10.10.1837

Pas de deux composed by Mr. Ballet Master Bournonville (componeret af Hr. Balletmester Bournonville) performed by P. C. Johansson and C. Fjeldsted.

According to the rehearsal book of H. C. J. Fredstrup this dance is identical with Bournonville's *Pas de deux* in *Nina, ou La Folle par amour* (*see* 30.9.1834). It had been performed earlier in that ballet during the same season by Johansson and Fjeldsted on 20.9.1837. The *Pas de deux* seems to have been performed only twice in 1837 by these dancers (the last time on 20.11.1837).

12.10.1837

Pas de deux composed by Mr. Ballet Master Bournonville (componeret af Hr. Balletmester Bournonville) **performed by himself and C. Fjeldsted.**

According to the rehearsal book of H. C. J. Fredstrup this dance is identical with Bournonville's *Pas de deux* in F. Hérold's three-act comic opera *Le Pré aux clercs* (*see* 28.10.1834). It seems to have been given only once in 1837.

28.10.1837

Pas de trois in *Le Postillon de Lonjumeau (Postillonen i Lonjumeau)* **performed by Bournonville, L. Grahn, and C. Fjeldsted.**

In Bournonville's handwritten lists of his works, written c.1851 (*see* Additional Sources), this dance is named 'Pas de trois af Postillonen'. Moreover, according to pencilled notes in the printed orchestral score for A. Adam's three-act comic opera (now in DKKk, call no. U 6, p. '47') it was performed as an incorporated divertissement in the opera's opening chorus of Act I, entitled «Le joli mariage» (score no. 1).

The music for the *Pas de trois* was (according to a note in the manuscript orchestral score for it) originally part of M. E. Caraffa's score to J. Coralli's three-act pantomimic ballet *L'Orgie* (premièred at the Paris Opéra on 18.7.1831). Bournonville had most probably seen this ballet in Paris during his sojourn there in the early 1830s, and may at that time have purchased the copy of Caraffa's orchestral score for the *Pas de trois* in Act II (score no. 12) of *L'Orgie*, which he later clearly brought to Copenhagen. According to Caraffa's orchestral score and the original répétiteur's copy for *L'Orgie* (now in FPo, call nos. A 499 [III], pp. 131–251, and Mat. 19 [297 (21)]) the *Pas de trois* was originally choreographed by J. Perrot, who performed it together with the French ballerinas, P. Montessu, and P. Leroux. Moreover, pencilled autographed notes by Perrot(?) in the same répétiteur's copy indicate the choreography of Montessu's solo variation in the original Paris version of this dance.

Bournonville's 1837 *Pas de trois* in *Le Postillon de Lonjumeau* is most probably also identical with the *Pas de trois* that was performed later the same year as a separate divertissement at Copenhagen's Royal Theatre on 3.11.1837. The same seems to be the case with the even later (uncredited) *Pas de trois* performed at the same theatre by F. Hoppe, C. Fjeldsted, and A. Nielsen on 18.5.1840.

The *Pas de trois* was also mounted twice outside Denmark by Bournonville on 10.7.1839 (at Göteborg's Stora Theater, Segerlindska Theatern), and on 11.6.1852 (at Christiania's Theatre, Oslo). Moreover, in Stockholm Caraffa's music was reused by Bournonville's pupil, S. Lund, in 1858 for his new arrangement of this dance in Sweden. It was then performed at Stockholm's Royal Theatre (Operahuset) on 7.2.1858 as an incorporated divertissement between score nos. 8 and 9 of Bournonville's one-act version of P. Gardel's three-act pantomimic ballet *Paul et Virginie*. The dance was restaged for the last time as a separate divertissement in Copenhagen by Bournonville on 28.1.1861, then performed by F. Hoppe, J. Price, and S. Price.

Finally, on 30.10.1857 Adam's opera was included by Bournonville in a list of projected opera restagings that he was

planning that day for the 1857–58 and 1858–59 seasons. This project, however, was not carried out before 25.9.1873, when *Le Postillon de Lonjumeau* was mounted for the first and only time with Bournonville's own, complete mise-en-scène, but that year without any incorporated dance divertissements.

Caraffa's *Pas de trois* was only performed twice in Copenhagen within Adam's opera, the last time on 30.10.1837. It is not clear from the rehearsal book of H. C. J. Fredstrup exactly how many rehearsals were held of this dance in 1837.

Musical sources:

Orchestral score. Ms. Copy. Black ink. 1 vol. 36 pp. of which one is blank (31 × 22,5 cm)
Pas de troix/Brugt i/Postillionnen [*sic*]/Partitur/29/[…]/l'orgie acte 2.e No 12/Pas de troix
Unsigned and undated [c.1832-1837]
[DKKk; MA ms 2658 (KTB 212)]
This score is clearly a French copy and was most probably purchased by Bournonville in Paris in the early 1830s (perhaps during his Parisian sojourn in the summer of 1834) and brought to Copenhagen by him at about the same time. This theory is supported by the French watermark (showing a standing lion holding a sword and, underneath, the year '1832') contained in this score.

No répétiteur's copy for the *Pas de trois* in *Le Postillon du Lonjumeau* has yet been traced.

Parts. Ms. Copy. 30 vol.
3 vl I, 3 vl II, 2 vla, 3 vlc e cb, fl picc, fl 1/2, ob 1/2, cl 1/2, fag 1/2, cor 1/2/3/4, clno 1/2, trb 1/2/3, arpa.
Unsigned and undated [1837]
[DKKk; KTB 212]
In the part for the tenor trombone a pencilled note reads 'som Pas de deux i Søvngængersken'. This seems to indicate that Bournonville's *Pas de trois* in *Le Postillon du Lonjumeau* was also performed in a revised version and incorporated at a later stage in his version of J. Aumer's three-act ballet *La Somnambule, ou l'Arrivée d'un nouveau seigneur* (*see* 21.9.1829). In that ballet it probably replaced Bournonville's original *Pas de deux* divertissement in Act I (score no. 7 B). However, it is not possible to establish exactly when this change might have happened.

31.10.1837

Les Sylphides. Contredanses nouvelles (Sylphiderne. Nye Françaiser).

This printed work contains a series of five *Contredanses* that are described to be performed by a 'Quadrille de huit paires. Deux paires dans chaque ligne'. The five dances included are entitled:

No. 1. Les fiançailles (Trolovelsen)
No. 2. L'Effy (Effy)
No. 3. La Sylphide (Sylphiden)
No. 4. L'Écharpe (Skjærfet)
No. 5. Le Délire (Forvildelsen)

According to the printed piano score containing the music for these dances it was based 'Sur les motif de la composition de Mr: H. de Løvenskiold' (i.e. *La Sylphide, see* 28.11.1837). It was published by C. C. Lose & Olsen in Copenhagen on 31.10.1837, while the printed choreographic description was printed separately by 'Bianco Luno & Schneiders Officin' at about the same time. The dances appear to have been created with the direct purpose of being taught at private lessons of ballroom dances taught by Bournonville the same year. Moreover, *Les Sylphides* seem to have been performed by members of the Royal Danish Ballet at a masked ball given after the 50th performance of Bournonville's *La Sylphide* on 6.1.1846.

Autograph sources:

Printed choreographic note in Danish and French. 1 vol. 3 pp. (23,1 × 18,8 cm)
Sylphiderne./Nye Françaiser/componerede af/August Bournonville/Les Sylphides./ Contredanses nouvelles/composées par/Auguste Bournonville.
Printed by 'Bianco Luno & Schneiders Officin'; undated [c.1837]
[Private collection (Copenhagen)

Musical sources:

Printed piano score, 1 vol. 5 pp. (24,6 × 32,2 cm)
Les Sylphides/Contredanses françaises pour le Pianoforte/Sur des motifs de la composition de Mr: H. de Løvenskjold/Arrangées et accompagnées de figures nouvelles/par/Aug: Bournonville
Printed by 'C. C. Lose & Olsen'; undated [Published according to *Adresseavisen*, no. 256 on 31.10.1837]
[DKKk; D 24 (mu 7305.0890)

3.11.1837
Pas de trois, composed by Mr. Ballet Master Bournonville (componeret af Hr. Balletmester Bournonville) **performed by Bournonville, L. Grahn, and C. Fjeldsted.**
This dance is probably identical with the *Pas de trois* originally performed by the same three dancers as an incorporated divertissement in A. Adam's three-act comic opera *Le Postillon du Lonjumeau* (*see* 28.10.1837). It is not possible to identify the dance any further.

7.11.1837
Pas de deux (uncredited) **performed by Bournonville and L. Grahn.**
This (uncredited) dance is most probably identical with the *Pas de deux* originally performed by Bournonville and A. Krætzmer in J. L. Heiberg's three-act play *Princess Isabella, or Three Nights at the Court* (*see* 29.10.1829). This assumption is based on the the fact that (according to the rehearsal book of H. C. J. Fredstrup) the 'Pas de deux af Prindsesse Isabella' was rehearsed four times under Bournonville's personal direction between 24.10. and 2.11.1837. It is not possible to identify the dance any further.

17.12.1837
Pas de deux (uncredited) **performed by Bournonville and L. Grahn as an incorporated divertissement in N. Isouard's three-act fairy-play** *Cendrillon (Cendrillon eller Den lille grønne Sko).*
This (uncredited) dance is perhaps identical with the *Pas de deux* first performed by the same dancers in Act I, score no. 5 of Bournonville's three-act pantomimic ballet *Don Quixote at Camacho's Wedding* (*see* 24.2.1837). This theory is based on the fact that according to the orchestral score for this ballet the music of the *Pas de deux* in Act I was borrowed from F. Sor's score to Albert's (François Decombe) three-act fairy-ballet *Cendrillon* (premièred at the Paris Opéra on 3.3.1823).

It therefore would have been natural also to incorporate it in a work like that of Isouard's three-act fairy-opera with the same story.

According to the printed orchestral score for Isouard's opera (p. 267) and the original Danish répétiteur's copy for it (now in DKKk, call nos. U 6, and MA ms 3033 (KTA 166 (1)) the *Pas de deux* was performed as an incorporated divertissement in Act III, scene 10 (score no. 16). It was given only once in Copenhagen within this opera. It is not possible to identify the dance any further.

When Isouard's *Cendrillon* was restaged in Copenhagen on 19.9.1856, Bournonville also choreographed and mounted its complete dances which (according to the printed orchestral score for it) were performed during the so-called 'Choeur du sommeil de Cendrillon' in Act II («ô doux sommeil sur l'innocence daigne répendre tes pavots», score no. 7), and in scene 10 of Act III (score no. 16). Moreover, on 30.10.1857 he included *Cendrillon* in a list of projected opera restagings which he was planning on that day for the 1857–58 and 1858–59 seasons. This project, however, was never carried out, and Isouard's opera was given for the last time in Copenhagen on 25.2.1857.

1838

6.1.1838
Pas de deux (uncredited) **performed by Bournonville and L. Grahn.**
This dance is probably identical with the *Pas de deux* originally performed by Bournonville and A. Krætzmer in J. L. Heiberg's three-act play *Princess Isabella, or Three Nights at the Court* (*see* 29.10.1829). Thus, according to the rehearsal book of H. C. J. Fredstrup that *Pas de deux* was rehearsed by Bournonville and Grahn on this day. It is not possible to identify the dance any further.

22.1.1838
The Homecoming (Hemkomsten) **(Stockholm's Royal Theatre, Operahuset).**
This production represents the first and only staging outside Denmark of Bournonville's pantomimic idyll *Soldier and Peasant* (*see* 13.10.1829). It was mounted by his Swedish pupil, P. C. Johansson, who, apart for a minor cut in score no. 5 (which in the répétiteur's copy is named by Bournonville 'Recit de Victor') mounted the ballet without any significant changes from the Copenhagen version. *Hemkomsten* received 22 performances in Stockholm, the last of which was given on 9.9.1849.

Musical sources:

Répétiteur's copy. Ms. Copy. Brown ink. 1 vol. 23 pp. (32,1 × 25 cm)
Soldat og Bonde./pantomimisk Idÿl af August Bournonville./[...]/Repetiteur Parti/til/Soldat og Bonde
Unsigned and dated (by Bournonville on p. 23): 'Copenhague ce 24 September 1837.'
[SSkma; KT Pantomime-Balletter H 2
This répétiteur's copy was clearly made in Copenhagen in the autumn of 1837. It contains Bournonville's autographed notes (written with brown ink) which describe the dramatic action, the mime, and

the choreography throughout the ballet. Moreover, on p. 1 Bournonville inserted a drawing of the ballet's décor, and on p. 23 he wrote a personal dedication to Johansson reading: 'Auguste Bournonville/A son honnorable Ami & élève P. C. Johansson'.

Orchestral score. Ms. Copy. Brown ink. 1 vol. 176 pp. (score nos. 1–6, and no. 9 measuring 27,5 × 37,8 cm with minor variants, no. 7 measuring 29,5 × 23 cm with minor variants; no. 8 measuring 35 × 26,8 cm with minor variants)
Hemkomsten/Pantomime Ballette/i 1 Akt/[…]/Partituret/til/Soldat og Bonde/Pantomimisk Idyl
Unsigned and undated [1838]
[SSkma; KT Pantomime-Balletter H 2
The music for the *Pas de trois* (score no. 7, p. 63) is entitled: 'Polacca a Rondo/Paul et Virginie/par Mr Caraffa' and also includes Bournonville's autographed dedication (written with brown ink) reading: 'Partition donnée au jeune artiste Johannsson/par son maitre & sincère ami/Auguste Bournonville'. It was clearly purchased by Bournonville in Paris in the late 1820s and brought by him to Denmark in 1829, where it was used by Keck for his musical arrangement of *Soldier and Peasant* at its 1829 Copenhagen première. In 1838 the score seems to have been donated by Bournonville as a personal gift to P. C. Johansson, who that year mounted the ballet at Stockholm's Royal Theatre (Operahuset). Likewise, the music for score no. 8 (p. 133ff) is also a French copy made by F.-C. Lefèbvre in Paris in the 1820s. It too was most probably brought to Denmark by Bournonville in 1829. Its title reads: 'Le devin de Village/All° brillante', which provides the definitive proof that this music was borrowed from F.-C. Lefèbvre's much earlier score for the third, revised staging at the Paris Opéra on 2.5.1779 of J.-J. Rousseau's intermedium *Le Devin de village* (originally performed at Fontainebleau on 18.10.1752).

Parts. Ms. Copy. 31 vol.
3 vl I, 3 vl II, 2 vla, 3 vlc e cb, fl 1/2, ob 1/2, cl 1/2, fag 1/2, cor 1/2/3/4, tr, cnt, trb 1/2/3, timp, gr cassa, tri.
Unsigned and undated [1838]
[SSkma; KT Pantomime-Balletter H 2

Printed sources:

Printed scenario. 1 vol. 7 pp. (20,6 × 12,8 cm)
HEMKOMSTEN,/PANTOMIMISK IDYLL;/af/Aug. Bournonville./Kongl. Dansk Balletmästare./Uppsatt för Kongl. Theatern i Stockholm,/i Jan. 1838,/af/P. C. Johansson.
Stockholm, Nordströmska Boktryckeriet, 1838.
[SSk; Sv. Saml. Vitt. Sv. Dram. Pantom. (Br.)

29.1.1838
Hertha's Offering (Herthas Offer).
This one-act divertissement was created for a Royal red-letter day and is (according to its printed scenario and the poster) given the subtitle *Flower Piece (Blomsterstykke)*. It was set to a score composed and arranged by J. F. Fröhlich. However, according to the orchestral score he seems to have written only two of the ballet's seven numbers, while most of the remaining music appears to be based on borrowed excerpts from works in the then current ballet repertory of the Paris Opéra and Copenhagen's Royal Theatre. Thus, the third scene (showing the awakening of *Hertha*, who symbolises Denmark, and her union with *The Spring* represented by the mythological figure of *Zephyr*) is set to music borrowed from Act III of G. Meyerbeer's five-act opera *Robert le Diable* (premièred at the Paris Opéra on 21.11.1831). It there served as an accompaniment for the three solo variations danced by the abbess *Hélène* during the so-called 'Ballet of the Nuns' (a part created for and first danced by M. Taglioni). Moreover, the first *Pas de deux* in *Hertha's Offering* (score

no. 4, originally performed by Bournonville as *The Spring*, and L. Grahn as *Hertha*) is set to music borrowed from Ph. L. Keck's earlier score to Bournonville's one-act ballet *Victor's Wedding, or The Ancestral House* (*see* 23.4.1831). Furthermore, the second and final *Pas de deux* in *Hertha's Offering* (score no. 5, originally performed by P. Larcher as Ægir's son and C. Fjeldsted as Ægir's daughter) was, according to a separate set of parts for this dance, also given twice as a separate divertissement on 15.11.1838 and 28.2.1840 (both times performed by F. Hoppe and C. Fjeldsted).

In Norway an abridged divertissement version of selected excerpts from *Hertha's Offering*, was mounted by Bournonville at Christiania's Theatre (Oslo) on 5.8.1840 with the title *'The Spring and Hertha'* ('Vaaren og Hertha').

Hertha's Offering reached a total of 19 performances in Copenhagen, the last of which was given on 21.11.1839. According to the rehearsal book of H. C. J. Fredstrup 13 rehearsals were held of this work between 22.1. and 29.1.1838.

Musical sources:

Orchestral score. Ms. Autograph (by J. F. Fröhlich) and copy. Brown ink. 1 vol. 114 pp. (27,5 × 38 cm with minor variants)
Partituur/til/277/Herthas Offer/1838/[…]/Herthas Offer,/Blomsterstykke af Bournonville/[…]/Partitur.
Unsigned and dated (in the front cover): '1838'
[DKKk; C II, 107 (KTB 1005, originally KTB 277)
According to a pencilled note on p. 100 (reading 'Indlagt Nummer') the second *Pas de deux* in *Hertha's Offering* (originally danced by P. Larcher and C. Fjeldsted) was actually performed as an incorporated section in score no. 5. The separate orchestral score for this dance has not yet been traced, but a separate set of parts for it, entitled 'Pas de deux til Herthas Offer' is now in DKKk (call no. KTB 219).

Répétiteur's copy. Ms. Copy. Black ink. 1 vol. 28 pp. (32,5 × 25 cm)
Herthas Offer./204/1838./[…]/Repetiteur Partie/til/Herthas Offer/Blomsterstykke af Bournonville
Signed (on p. 27) 'Lz' and dated (on the front cover): '1838'
[DKKk; MA ms 3018 (KTB 1005, originally KTB 277)
This répétiteur's copy contains Bournonville's pencilled autographed notes which describe the pantomime in score nos. 3 and 6 (the so-called 'Offrande'), and his sporadic choreographic notes for score no. 4 (the first *Pas de deux*) and no. 5 (the second *Pas de deux*).

Parts. Ms. Copy. 33 vol.
3 vl I, 3 vl II, 2 vla, 3 vlc e cb, fl picc, fl 1/2, ob 1/2, cl 1/2, fag 1/2, cor 1/2/3/4, tr 1/2, trb 1/2/3, timp, gr cassa, tri, arpa.
[DKKk; KTB 1005 (originally KTB 277)

Parts (*Pas de deux*, score no. 5). Ms. Copy. 29 vol.
3 vl I, 3 vl II, 2 vla, 3 vlc e cb, fl 1/2, ob 1/2, cl 1/2, fag 1/2, cor 1/2/3/4, cln 1/2, trb 1/2/3, timp.
Unsigned and undated [c.1838]
[DKKk; KTB 219
These parts were also used when the second *Pas de deux* in *Hertha's Offering* was given as a separate divertissement in Copenhagen by F. Hoppe and C. Fjeldsted on 15.11.1838 and 28.2.1840. A pencilled note in the part for the first clarinet (reading 'Pas de Skidt') seems to indicate a rather limited success for this dance.

Printed sources:

Printed scenario. 1 vol. 4 pp. of which one is blank (19,5 × 12 cm)
Herthas Offer,/Blomsterstykke/af/August Bournonville./Fremstilt for første Gang/i Anledning af /Hans Majestæts Kongens høie Fødselsdag,/den 29. Januar 1838.
Kjøbenhavn, Bianco Luno, 1838.
[DKKk; 17, – 173 8°

Printed scenario. 1 vol. 4 pp. of which one is blank (25,1 × 16,9 cm)
L'Offrande d'Hertha./Divertissement allégorique/par/AUGUSTE
BOURNONVILLE/Premier Danseur et Directeur des Ballets de S.
M. le Roi de Danemark.
Copenhague, Imprimerie de Thiele, 1838.
[SSm; Daniel Fryklunds samling nr. 200

13.2.1838
Fiorella.
According to his handwritten list of his mises-en-scène for
operas written c.1851 (*see* Additional Sources) Bournonville
was clearly responsible for mounting the Copenhagen
première of D.-F.-E. Auber's and E. Scribe's three-act comic
opera (premièred in Paris at l'Opéra Comique on 28.11.
1826). The production also included his choreography for
the dances performed by a corps de ballet during the opening chorus in Act I (score no. 1) and at the feast later in the
same act (score no. 4, *Allegretto*, F major, 2/4 time). Moreover, it was in *Fiorella* that L. Grahn for the first time performed her own version of F. Elssler's famous *La Cachucha*
(originally premièred at the Paris Opéra on 1.6.1836 as an
incorporated divertissement in J. Coralli's and C. Gide's
three-act pantomimic ballet *Le Diable boîteux*).
    Fiorella was given only 5 times in Copenhagen, the last time
on 16.3.1838. It is not clear from the rehearsal book of H. C.
J. Fredstrup exactly how many rehearsals were held of this
opera and its dances in 1838.

Musical sources:

Printed orchestral score. 1 vol. 389 pp. (35,5 × 26,5 cm)
FIORELLA/Opéra Comique en trois Actes/Paroles de Monsieur
Scribe,/Musique de /D. F. E. AUBER
Paris, Schlesinger, pl. no. 1998 [1826]
[DKKk; U6 (KTA 342)

Répétiteur's copy (incomplete). Ms. Copy. 6 pp. (33,4 × 25,2 cm)
Repetiteur Partie/til/Fiorella
Unsigned and undated [1838]
[DKKk; MA ms 2780 (KTA 342)
This (incomplete) répétiteur's copy contains the music for the open-
ing chorus in Act I (score no. 4) and parts of the later dance music
in the same number.

Parts. Ms. Copy. 28 vol.
3 vl I, 3 vl II, 2 vla, 3 vlc e cb, fl 1/2, ob 1/2, cl 1/2, fag 1/2, cor 1/2,
tr 1/2, trb, rimp, gr cassa, tri, arpa. 52 vocal parts.
[DKKk; KTA 342

13.3.1838
St. Olave, The Battle at Stiklestad (Olaf den Hellige, Slaget ved Stiklestad).
According to his handwritten list of his mises-en-scène for
operas and plays written c.1851 (*see* Additional Sources)
Bournonville's created the mise-en-scene to I. P. E. Hart-
mann's music for the opening scene in Act V (score no. 4) of
A. Oehlenschläger's five-act tragedy, depicting the battle at
Stiklestad. Hartmann's score was later also incorporated as a
musical *entr'acte* in Oehlenschläger's five-act play *Earl Hakon
(Hakon Jarl)* when it was restaged at Copenhagen's Royal
Theatre on 1.5.1857.
    Moreover, as a result of the great success of Hartmann's
music Bournonville decided to reuse it many years later as

an accompaniment for the battle scenes in Act IV (score no.
33) of his Nordic mythological ballet in four acts *The Valkyrie*
(*see* 13.9.1861). In that ballet it accompanied the end of
scene 2 and the whole of scenes 3–5 which depicted the *Battle at Braavalla Heath*. Thus, apart from a minor omission of 9
bars (meas. 126–134) Hartmann's score was incorporated in
full in *The Valkyrie*, without any significant musical changes.
St Olave and Hartmann's music for *The Battle at Stiklestad*
therefore represent the first in a long series of works for
which Bournonville collaborated with this composer.
    Oehlenschläger's tragedy was given 10 performances with
Bournonville's mise-en-scène, the last of which took place on
1.2.1838. It is not clear from the rehearsal book of H. C. J.
Fredstrup exactly how many rehearsals were held of this
work in 1838. Thus, at least 13 rehearsals were held of the
ballet scenes alone.

Autograph sources:

Manuscript mise-en-scène. Ms. Autograph. Brown ink. 1 vol. 8 pp.
(20,4 × 17,3 cm)
Slaget ved Stiklestad./Componeret til Oelenschlägers [*sic*] Trage-
die/Olaf den Hellige/af/August Bournonville./[...]/Musikken
componeret af Hr Secretair Hartmann.
Unsigned and dated: 'Opfört for förste Gang: Tirsdagen d 13 Marts
1838. – '
[DKKk; NKS 3285 4° 3 R-U

Musical sources:

Musical sketch (fragment). Ms. Autograph. Black ink. 2 pp. (31,5 ×
25 cm)
[Without title]
Unsigned and undated [c.1838]
[DKKk; MA ms 693 (mu 8811.0984)
This fragment for two violins contains Hartmann's early drafts for
the final 38 bars of his music for *The Battle at Stiklestad.*

Orchestral score. Ms. Autograph. Brown ink. 1 vol. 52 pp. (27,2 × 38
cm)
J. P. E. HARTMANN/OLAF DEN HELLIGE/PART./[...]/365/Olaf
den Hellige/Partitur.
Signed and dated (on 52): 'J:P:EHartmann Op: 23-/April 1838.'
[DKKk; C II, 114 (KTA 365)
The music for *The Battle at Stiklestad* is included on pp. 21–56. An
autographed note by Hartmann indicates a later omission of meas.
157–168, which most probably was done when this music was incorporated in Act IV, score no. 33 of Bournonville's *The Valkyrie.*

Répétiteur's copy. Ms. Copy. Brown ink. 1 vol. (32,6 × 25,2 cm)
Slaget ved Stiklestad./212/1838./[...]/Repetiteur Parti til Slaget
ved Stiklestad
Unsigned and dated (on the front cover): '1838.'
[DKKk; MA ms 3081 (KTA 365)
This répétiteur's copy contains Bournonville's pencilled autographed notes from 1838 describing (in general terms) the mime
and choreography for *The Battle at Stiklestad*. His other autographed
notes (written with brown ink) describe the complete mime and
choreography as revised in 1861 for the end of scene 2 and the whole
of scenes 3–5 in Act IV (score no. 33) of *The Valkyrie.*

Parts. Ms. Copy. 34 vol.
3 vl I, 3 vl II, 2 vla, 3 vlc e cb, fl 1/2, ob 1/2, cl 1/2, fag 1/2, cor 1/2/
3/4, tr 1/2/3, cnt a chiavi, trb 1/2/3, timp, gr cassa, tri, arpa. 16
vocal parts.
Unsigned and undated [1838]
[DKKk; KTA 365

1.6.1838

Russian National Dance (Russisk Nationaldands) **composed by Bournonville and performed by himself and R. Lund.**

According to the poster this dance was performed to a Russian song known in Denmark as 'Kalimuska (Skjønne Minka)'. It had become widely known after C. M. v. Weber employed it in Berlin in 1815 for his nine variations for solo piano, entitled *Schöne Minka, Air russe*. In Copenhagen it was arranged and orchestrated by I. P. E. Hartmann, who also added a *Mazurka* of his own composition as a coda. Bournonville's dance was later also incorporated with a new musical introduction in Act I (score no. 8) of Bournonville's two-act romantic ballet *The Isle of Phantasy, or 'From the Shore of China'* at its première on 28.10.1838. The *Russian National Dance* is probably also identical with the so-called '*Mazurka*', *Russian National Dance*, that was performed as a separate divertissement by Bournonville and C. Fjeldsted at Christiania's Theatre (Oslo) on 31.7.1840.

It is not clear from the rehearsal book of H. C. J. Fredstrup exactly how many rehearsals were held of this dance in 1838.

Musical sources:

Orchestral score. Ms. Autograph (by I. P. E. Hartmann). Brown ink. 16 pp. (37,5 × 26,7 cm with minor variants)
Russisk.
Unsigned and undated [c.1838]
[DKKk; MA ms 2631 (1)]

No répétiteur's copy for the 1838 première of this dance has yet been traced.

Parts (incomplete). Ms. Copy. 6 vol.
vl I, vla, Atrb, Ttrb, Btrb, tri.
Unsigned and undated [c.1838]
[DKKk; MA ms 2631 (2–7)]
This (incomplete) set of parts includes Bournonville's autographed signature and title 'Pas-Russe' (written with brown ink). It dates almost certainly from the première of this dance as a separate divertissement on 1.6.1838.

27.6.1838

Pas de deux **(uncredited) performed by P. Larcher and L. Grahn as an incorporated divertissement in Act I of** *Waldemar* **(see 28.10.1835).**

This (uncredited) dance is (except for the introduction) musically completely identical with the similarly uncredited *Pas de deux* to music by F.-M.-A. Venua that was first incorporated by Bournonville in J. L. Heiberg's three-act play *Princess Isabella, or Three Nights at the Court* on 29.10.1829. This is clear from a pencilled note (reading 'til Waldemar') inserted in the part for the first violin to Venua's *Pas de deux*. Other notes found in the part for the second oboe to the same dance (reading 'No. 3/herefter No. 4') seem to indicate that the *Pas de deux* was inserted between score nos. 3 and 4 in Act I of *Waldemar*. According to the poster the *Pas de deux* was also performed at the Royal gala performance of *Waldemar* on the following day.

It is not clear from the rehearsal book of H. C. J. Fredstrup exactly how many rehearsals were held of this dance in 1838.

Musical sources:

No separate orchestral score and répétiteur's copy dating from the incorporation of Venua's *Pas de deux* in *Waldemar* have been traced. This seems to indicate that the dance was performed in this ballet in 1838 with the original orchestral score for *Princess Isabella, or Three Nights at the Court* (now in DKKk, call no. CII, 125 (KTA 276)).

Parts (incomplete). Ms. Copy. 27 vol.
3 vl I, 3 vl II, 2 vla, 3 vlc e cb, fl 1/2, ob II, cl 1/2, fag 1/2, cor 1/2, clno 1/2, Ttrb, Btrb, timp, gr cassa, tri.
Unsigned and undated [c.1838]
[DKKk; KTB 1052 (1) (originally without number)]
This set of parts contains the same music as for F.-M.-A.Venua's *Pas de deux* in *Princess Isabella, or Three Nights at the Court*. However, it must date from the later incorporation of this dance in Act I of *Waldemar* (1838) since a pencilled note in the part for the first violin reads: 'til Waldemar'. The same set of parts was also used for Bournonville's later, abridged version in three parts of his two-act romantic ballet *La Sylphide*, which was mounted at Christiania's Theatre (Oslo) on 31.7.1840. This is clear from pencilled notes found in the part for the kettledrums (reading: 'Sylphiden/2d Afd.').

27.6.1838

Pas de trois **(uncredited) performed by P. C. Johansson, C. Fjeldsted and A. Nielsen as an incorporated divertissement in Act II of** *Waldemar.*

This dance is most probably identical with the *Pas de trois* in *Le Postillon du Lonjumeau* first performed by Bournonville, L. Grahn, and C. Fjeldsted on 28.10.1837. According to the poster the *Pas de trois* was also performed at the Royal gala performance of *Waldemar* on the following day. It is not possible to identify the dance any further.

28.6.1838

Waldemar.

Bournonville's four-act romantic ballet *Waldemar* (*see* 28.10.1835) was on this day restaged as part of a Royal gala performance given in honour of a visit of the heir to the Russian throne, later the Czar Alexander II. For this occasion a new, abridged scenario (written in French) was published which included several historical notes. Moreover, according to the poster, the ballet was enriched with two new dances (a *Pas de deux* and a *Pas de trois* in Act I and II respectively), both of which had been incorporated in *Waldemar* for the first time on 27.6.1838.

Printed sources:

Printed scenario. 1 vol. 16 pp. (24 × 16,6 cm)
Waldemar./Ballet-pantomime en 4 Actes/par Auguste Bournonville/[...]/Musique de Fr. Fröhlich/[...]/Remis sur la scène à l'occasion de l'arrivée de/S. A. Impériale le Grand-Duc Césaréwitch de Russie,/le 28 Juin 1838.
Copenhague, Thiele, 1838.
[DKKk; 17, – 172 8°]

5.7.1838

A Pas de deux, composed by Mr. Ballet Master Bournonville (En Pas de deux, componeret af Hr. Balletmester Bournonville) **performed by P. C. Johansson and C. Fjeldsted.**

This dance is probably identical with Bournonville's incorporated *Pas de deux* in Act I of D.-F.-E. Auber's five-act opera *La Muette de Portici* (*see* 23.9.1834). It is not possible to identify the dance any further.

3.9.1838

A Pas de deux, composed by Mr. Ballet Master Bournonville
(En Pas de deux, componeret af Hr. Balletmester Bournonville)
performed by P. C. Johansson and C. Fjeldsted.

This dance is probably identical with Bournonville's *Pas de deux* in D.-F.-E. Auber's five-act opera *La Muette de Portici* (*see* 23.9.1834), which (according to the rehearsal book of H. C. J. Fredstrup) was rehearsed with Johansson and Fjeldsted on the same day.

28.10.1838

The Isle of Phantasy, or 'From the Shore of China' (Phantasiens Øe eller 'Fra Chinas Kyst').

This two-act romantic ballet with a final tableau was created for a Royal red-letter day and set to a score composed and arranged by seven different composers. The music for the first act (overture and score nos. 1–12) was mainly composed and arranged by I. P. E. Hartmann and E. Helsted. They included several musical excerpts borrowed from the works of nine different composers identified as follows:

(1) Score no. 3: In this number Hartmann employed an excerpt borrowed from J. A. P. Schultz's one-act singspiel from 1790 *The Harvest Festival (Høstgildet)* in which it originally served as an accompaniment for a *Sailor's Dance* ('Matrosdands').
(2) Score no. 4: At the end of this scene Hartmann incorporated a *March* (66 meas.) set to music by E. Dupuy and first published in 1818 in the Danish music anthology, named *Nye Apollo* (IV Aargang, I bind, p. 1). In *The Isle of Phantasy* the first half of Dupuy's *March* is played by an orchestra seated on the stage. Moreover, Hartmann's *Gallopade* which follows Dupuy's *March* was six years later reused by H. S. Paulli, who incorporated it in his overture for Bournonville's one-act ballet-vaudeville *Bellman or the Polish Dance at Grönalund* (*see* 3.6.1844).
(3) Score no. 5: According to notes inserted in the répétiteur's copy, Hartmann incorporated two themes in this number which were borrowed from two (not yet identified) works by N. Dalayrac and C. Schall.
(4) Score no. 7: According to the orchestral score the music for this number is partially E. Helsted's autograph. It includes excerpts borrowed from the *entr'acte* music between Act I and II of D.-F.-E. Auber's three-act fairy-opera *Le Cheval de bronze* (premièred in Paris at l'Opéra Comique on 23.3.1835, and first performed in Copenhagen on 29.1.1836 with the title *Prindsen af China*).
(5) Score no. 8 (the *Russian Dance*): The music for this dance is identical with Hartmann's earlier score for Bournonville's *Russian National Dance (Russisk Nationaldands)* first performed as a separate divertissement on 1.6.1838. It included the Russian song, entitled 'Kalimuska (Skjønne Minka)' and a *Mazurka* of Hartmann's own composition.
(6) Score no. 9 (the *Chinese Dance*): According to the orchestral score this number is E. Helsted's autograph throughout. He incorporated excerpts borrowed from the overture and the Act I finale of Auber's 1835 fairy-opera *Le Cheval de bronze*.
(7) Score no. 10 (the *English Sailor's Dance*): For this dance Hartmann employed two excerpts borrowed from T. Moore's *Irish Melodies* (1807–1834), entitled «The last rose of summer» (also known as 'The Groves of Blarney') and «We may roam thro' this world» (also known as 'Garryowen'). They are followed by a *Hornpipe*, presumably of Hartmann's own composition. Nearly all of Hartmann's arrangement for the *English Sailor's Dance* was many years later incorporated in Bournonville's divertissement, named 'The Sailor's Return', *Scene and English Character Dance ('Matrosens Hjemkomst', Scene og engelsk Characteerdands)*, first performed by E. Stramboe and A. Price at Christiania's Theatre (Oslo) on 9.6.1852.
(8) Score no. 11: This number includes D. L. Rogert's (?) and J. Ewald's Danish national hymn «Kong Christian stod ved højen Mast»

from 1779. It had already been incorporated by F. Kuhlau in his score for J. L. Heiberg's five-act national fairy-play *The Elves' Hill (Elverhøi)* on 6.11.1828.
(9) Score no. 12 (the *Finale*): For this number Hartmann borrowed a theme from the sailors' chorus «Fra Chinas Kyst til Østersøens Grændser» in Act I, scene 6 of C. Schall's score to P. A. Heiberg's two-act singspiel *The China Travellers (Chinafarerne)*, premièred at Copenhagen's Royal Theatre on 2.3.1792.

Act II (score nos. 1–11) was (according to the orchestral score) composed and/or arranged by six composers as follows:

(1) Score no. 1 A (*Pas de deux*): The music for this dance, which in the orchestral score is entitled *Pas de trois*, is by J. Mayseder. According to a printed piano score from 1823 (now in AWn, Artaria & Co., pl. no. 2742) it is musically based on his concert-piece for violin and piano opus 35, entitled *Divertimento nr. 1*. In *The Isle of Phantasy* Mayseder's score accompanied a *Pas de deux* danced by L. Grahn (as *Phantasiens Dronning*) and P. Larcher (as *Faunus*). On 27.9.1842 the same dance was incorporated in Act II of Bournonville's 1836 Copenhagen version of F. Taglioni's two-act ballet *La Sylphide*, in which it was performed by Bournonville and A. Nielsen with the new title *Pas de deux (à la Taglioni)*. Moreover, on 8.12.1849 the *Pas de deux* was interpolated as score no. '19' in Act II of Bournonville's three-act romantic ballet *Faust*. Finally, Mayseder's *Pas de deux* also seems to have been mounted as a separate divertissement in Denmark and abroad on at least eight occasions (*see* 5.6.1839, 4.10.1839, 6.7.1840, 10.8.1840, 7.1.1841, 6.11.1845, 9.11.1850, and 9.6.1852).
(2) Score no. 1 B: Composed by H. S. Paulli.
(3) Score nos. 2–4: Composed by I. F. Bredal.
(4) Score no. 5 (the *Valse bachique*): Composed by H. S. v. Løvenskjold.
(5) Score no. 6: Composed by L. Zinck.
(6) Score no. 7 (the *Pas de deux* and *Gallopade*): Composed by E. Helsted. In the opening *Andantino* movement of this *Pas de deux* Helsted employed the melody of the serenade, entitled «Skjøn Jomfru luk dit Vindue op». It was originally sung by the character *Valentin* in Act II of C. E. F. Weyse's two-act singspiel *The Sleeping-Draught (Sovedrikken)*, premièred at Copenhagen's Royal Theatre on 21.4.1809.
(7) Score no. 8: Composed by E. Helsted.
(8) Score no. 9: Composed by I. F. Bredal.
(9) Score nos. 10 and 11 (the *Final Tableau*): Composed by H. S. Paulli. In his music for no. 10 Paulli employed themes from the same serenade in C. E. F. Weyse's singspiel *The Sleeping-Draught*, which E. Helsted had used before him in his arrangement of the music for the *Pas de deux* in Act II (score no. 7). Moreover, Paulli also employed J. A. P. Schultz's melody for the song, named «Nys fyldte skjøn Sired det attende Aar» which originally was part of Schultz's and Th. Thaarup's one-act singspiel *The Harvest Festival (Høstgildet)*, premièred on 16.9.1790. Finally, in the concluding tableau after score no. 11 Paulli employed a melody by E. Dupuy, that originally had served for a song named «Manden med Glas i Haand, stolt af sin høie Aand» and was first performed in N. F. Bruun's Danish translation of A. Duval's three-act comedy *La Jeunesse d'Henry V (Henrik den femtes Ungdom)* at Copenhagen's Royal Theatre on 6.12.1808. In *The Isle of Phantasy* this tune served (according to Bournonville's printed libretto) as an allusion to the song's third verse which reads: «Skjøndt du, o stolte Hav, var mangen Sømands Grav, elsker han dig». It was reused by A. F. Lincke in the exact same way in Act II, scene 8 (score no. 19) of his music for Bournonville's two-act ballet-vaudeville *Far from Denmark, or: A Costume Ball on Board* (*see* 20.4.1860).

During the summer and autumn of 1839 Bournonville mounted 9 different dance divertissements of selected excerpts from *The Isle of Phantasy*. They were premièred as follows:

(1) on 2.6.1839 (at Copenhagen's Royal Theatre).

(2) on 14.6.1839 (at Stockholm's Royal Theatre, Operahuset).
(3) on 5.7. and 10.7.1839 (at Göteborg's Stora Theater, Segerlindska Theatern).
(4) on 3.9.1839, 17.9.1839, and 10.11.1839 (at Copenhagen's Royal Theatre).
(5) on 31.7 1843 and 2.7.1846 (at Hamburg's Stadttheater).

Moreover, according to a separate set of parts for Helsted's *Gallopade* in Act II, score no. 7 (now in DKKk, call no. MA ms 2757 (1–20)) this dance seems to have been incorporated as a new finale (score no. 12) to Bournonville's one-act idyllic ballet *The Tyroleans* (*see* 7.2.1842). Furthermore, Helsted's *Pas de deux* in Act II (score no. 7) was restaged twice at Stockholm's Royal Theatre (Operahuset) on 2.6.1839 (as a separate divertissement) and on 29.1.1861 (as an incorporated divertissement in S. Lund's staging of V. Galeotti's one-act ballet from 1786 *The Whims of Cupid (Amor's skämt)*. Finally, on 19.1.1860 a freely arranged one-act version of Bournonville's *The Isle of Phantasy* was choreographed by S. Lund and premièred at Stockholm's Royal Theatre (Operahuset) with the title *At the Shore of China (Vid Chinas Kust)*. It was set to a new score composed and arranged by the Swedish composer C. R. af Uhr.

According to notes in several of the parts (reading '2T 1q') the original 1838 Copenhagen version of *The Isle of Phantasy* played for 2 hours and 15 minutes. The ballet received only 9 performances in Copenhagen, the last of which was given on 23.4.1839. According to the rehearsal book of H. C. J. Fredstrup 38 rehearsals were held of it between 19.9. and 28.10.1838.

Autograph sources:

Production note. Ms. Autograph. Brown ink. 2 pp. (34,3 × 20,6 cm)
Personale i Balletten/<u>Phantasiens Øe eller Fra Chinas Kÿst.</u>
Signed and dated: 'Kbhvn d. 20 Sept: 1838.'
[SSm; Daniel Fryklunds samling no. 115

Musical sources:

Orchestral score. Ms. Autograph (by I. P. E. Hartmann, E. Helsted, H. S. Paulli, I. F. Bredal, H. S. v. Løvenskjold, and L. Zinck) and copy. Brown and black ink. 2 vol. Act I 239 pp. of which four are blank, Act II 242 pp. of which two are blank (27,5 × 38 cm with minor variants)
PHANTASIENS ØE/PARTITUR/1/[...]/2
Signed and dated (Act I, p. 239): 'IPE Ha[rtmann]', (Act II, p. 230) '20.e October/1838./HSP.', (Act II, p. 242) '24 Oct/38/HSP'
[DKKk; C II, 105 (KTB 206)
The orchestral score for Mayseder's incorporated *Pas de deux* in Act II (score no. 1 A) was most probably purchased by Bournonville in Berlin during his a sojourn there in the early 1830s. This theory is supported by the clearly non-French watermarks (reading: 'ZOO-NEN/J HONIG/HONIG/J H & Z') contained in the score for this dance.

Répétiteur's copy (incomplete). Ms. Copy and autographs (by I. F. Bredal and H. S. Paulli). Brown and black ink. 1 vol. 124 pp. (32,6 × 24,8 cm)
B 206/Phantasiens Øe/Ballet./(De Danske i China.)/32 Orchst 1 bd Partitur 1 Dirigentst./[...]/Repetiteur Parti/til/Balletten/Phantasiens Ö.
Unsigned and dated (on p. 1): 'Den 28 October 1838'
[DKKk; MA ms 2945 (KTB 206)
This (incomplete) répétiteur's copy contains autographs by Bredal (Act II, score no. 2–4) and Paulli (Act II, score nos. 10–11). Several sections of the music in Act I, score nos. 2 and 7 are missing. The

same is true for the music of the *English Sailor's Dance* in Act I (score no. 10), which in 1852 was incorporated in the répétiteur's copy for Bournonville's divertissement *'The Sailor's Return', Scene and English Character Dance* (*see* 9.6.1852). Similarly, the music for Mayseder's *Pas de deux* in Act I (score no. 1 A) was taken out of the 1838 répétiteur's copy at a later stage, most probably in connection with its incorporation in Act II of Bournonville's two-act ballet *La Sylphide* (*see* 27.9.1842) and/or in *Faust* (*see* 8.12.1849). The répétiteur's copy for *The Isle of Phantasy* contains Bournonville's pencilled autographed notes describing (in rather general terms) the mime and the dramatic action of Act I (score nos. 1, 5, and 6), and Act II (score no. 10).

Parts. Ms. Copy. 35 + 23 vol.
4 vl I, 3 vl II, 2 vla, 3 vlc e cb, fl picc, fl 1/2, ob 1/2, cl 1/2, fag 1/2, cor 1/2/3/4, clno 1/2, cnt a chiavi, trb 1/2/3, timp, gr cassa, tri, arpa. On stage: 3 vl I, 3 vl II, vla, fl 1/2/3, cl 1/2/3, fag 1/2/3, cor 1/2/3, clno, trb, tri, glock.
Unsigned and undated [1838-1839]
[DKKk; KTB 206
This set of parts is a combination of parts dating from the 1838 première of *The Isle of Phantasy* mixed with a later set of parts prepared for an abridged divertissement version of this ballet, named *The Danes in China (De Danske i China)* and premièred on 17.9.1839.

Répétiteur's copy (*Pas de deux*, Act II, score no. 1 A, fragment). Ms. Copy. Black ink. 10. pp. (31,4 × 24,3 cm)
No. 1. A. 2den Akt
Unsigned and undated [c.1838]
[DKKk; MA ms 2645 (KTB 206)
This fragment was originally part of the 1838 répétiteur's copy for *The Isle of Phantasy* in which it was played as the opening number in Act II (*Pas de deux*, score no. 1 A). It seems to have been taken out of that volume in connection with its later incorporations in Bournonville's two ballets *La Sylphide* (*see* 27.9.1842) and *Faust* (*see* 8.12.1849). This is clear from pencilled notes (on p. 1) reading 'Pas de deux/af Balletten Faust'. The fragment also contains Bournonville's pencilled autographed notes indicating (through his use of the initials of the dancers L. 'G'[rahn] and P. 'L'[archer]) which sections of the dance were performed by whom when it was first performed in *The Isle of Phantasy*. A later répétiteur's copy with the same music, dating from the 1840s or 50s, entitled 'Pas de deux af Ball. Sÿlphiden.', is now in DKKk (call no. MA ms 2645 a).

Parts (*Pas de deux*, Act II, score no. 1 A) Ms. Copy. 33 vol.
vl princ, 2 vl I, 3 vl II, 2 vla, 2 vlc e cb, fl picc, fl 1/2, ob 1/2, cl 1/2, fag 1/2, cor 1/2/3/4, tr 1/2, cnt 1/2, trb 1/2/3, timp, gr cassa, piatti e tri.
Unsigned and undated [c.1838]
[DKKk; KTB 1024 (originally KTB 240)
This set of parts is bound together with the parts for H. C. Lumbye's *New Hamburg=Scottish* (first performed as a new, incorporated finale in *The Tyroleans* on 8.2.1844). The parts that contain Mayseder's music were originally part of the original set of parts for *The Isle of Phantasy* (now in DKKk, call no. KTB 206), which seems to have been transformed into a separate set of parts at a later stage. This probably happened when Mayseder's *Pas de deux* was performed as an incorporated divertissement in Act II of Bournonville's ballet *La Sylphide* on 27.9.1842 with the title *Pas de deux (à la Taglioni)*.

Parts (*Gallopade*, Act II score no. 7). Ms. Copy. 20 vol.
2 vl I, 2 vl II, vla, cb, fl picc, fl 1/2, ob 1/2, cl 1/2, fag 1/2, cor 1/2, clno 1/2, timp.
Unsigned and undated [late 1830s or early 40s]
[DKKk; MA ms 2757 (1-20)
This (incomplete) set of parts contains the music for E. Helsted's *Gallopade* in *The Isle of Phantasy* (Act II, score no. 7). It was most probably used for a later, separate performance of this dance in the late 1830s or early 40s (perhaps that on 7.2.1842 when the *Gallopade* was given as a new incorporated finale in Bournonville's ballet *The Tyroleans*).

Printed sources:

Printed scenario. 1 vol. 15 pp. (21 × 12,5 cm)
Phantasiens Øe,/eller:/'Fra Chinas Kyst',/original romantisk Ballet i 2 Acter og et Slutnings=/Tableau,/af August Bournonville./ Musiken til første Act af Hr Secretair Hartmann, til anden/Act af forskjellige Componister./Decorationerne udførte af Dhrr. Wallich og T. Lund.
Kjøbenhavn, Thieles Bogtrykkerie, 1838.
[DKKk; 17, – 173 8°

15.11.1838
A Pas de deux, composed by Mr. Ballet Master Bournonville
(En Pas de deux, componeret af Hr. Balletmester Bournonville)
performed by F. Hoppe and C. Fjeldsted.

This dance is almost certainly identical with the second *Pas de deux* (score no. 5) of Bournonville's divertissement *Hertha's Offering* (*see* 29.1.1838), since that dance was rehearsed (according to the rehearsal book of H. C. J. Fredstrup) for Hoppe and Fjeldsted on this day.

29.11.1838
El Jaleo di Xeres, Spanish Dance (spansk Dands) (uncredited)
performed by L. Grahn.

This (uncredited) Spanish solo dance was also performed by P. Fredstrup on 1.6.1839, and by C. Fjeldsted on 18.3.1848 (then entitled *'El Jaleo de Xerxes'*) and was restaged for the last time in Copenhagen with P. Fredstrup on 26.2.1856. On 12.6.1839 Bournonville mounted a choreographically revised version for a man and a woman. It was set to new music and was first performed at Stockholm's Royal Theatre (Operahuset) as a separate divertissement by F. Hoppe and C. Fjeldsted. This version was later also performed by the same two dancers at Göteborg's Stora Theater (Segerlindska Theatern) on 8.7.1839, and on 24.11.1839 it was given by them for the first time at Copenhagen's Royal Theatre as an incorporated divertissement in D.-F.-E. Auber's five-act opera *La Muette de Portici*.

In a letter to the Copenhagen theatre management, dated 27.9.1839 (now in DKKt), Bournonville noted of Grahn's original version of this dance:

'Dandsen har jeg studeret i sin oprindelige Form, Musikken har jeg ved Auber's Godhed forskaffet mig i Paris ifior og ved min Hjemkomst gjemte jeg den for at dandse den med Jfr. Grahn, der nægtede at udføre den med mig og erholdt Bifald for sin Beslutning'.

The orginal French version of *El Jaleo de Xeres* to Auber's music was premièred at the Paris Opéra as an incorporated divertissement for two women in *La Muette de Portici*. Bournonville had attended a performance of this version at the Opéra on 20.7.1838 and noted about it in his diary on the same day:

'Jaleo de Jeres [*sic*], spansk Nationaldands af begge Noblet [i. e. L. and F. Noblet, the latter later known under her married name as M.me Alexis Dupont]. Livlig men fræk, Opkog af Cachucha men langtfra det mimiske Udtryk som F. Elssler'.

Grahn's *El Jaleo di Xeres* was performed 8 times by her in Copenhagen, the last time on 23.2.1839. It is not clear from the rehearsal book of H. C. J. Fredstrup exactly how many rehearsals were held of this dance in 1838.

Musical sources:

No orchestral score dating from the 1838 Copenhagen première of Grahn's *El Jaleo di Xeres* has yet been traced.

Répétiteur's copy. Ms. Copy. Brown ink. 1 p. (34,5 × 24 cm)
Allegretto <u>udfört af Jfr Grahn</u>/Violino 1-mo Repetiteur/El Jaleo de Xeres
Unsigned and undated [c.1838]
[DKKk; C II, 105, Efterslæt 4 (1)]

Parts. Ms. Copy. 14 vol.
vl I, vl II, vla, vlc e cb, fl, cl, ob, fag, cor 1/2, tr 1/2, Btrb, timp.
Unsigned and undated [c.1838]
[DKKk; C II, 105, Efterslæt 4 (1)]

17.12.1838
A Pas de deux, composed by Mr. Ballet Master Bournonville
(En Pas de deux, componeret af Hr. Balletmester Bournonville)
performed by F. Hoppe and A. Nielsen.

This dance is most probably identical with the second *Pas de deux* (score no. 5) in Bournonville's divertissement *Hertha's Offering* (*see* 29.1.1838), which had been performed by Hoppe and C. Fjeldsted a month earlier on 15.11.1838. It is not possible to identify the dance any further.

1839

29.1.1839
Le Domino noir (Eventyret paa Maskeraden eller Den sorte Domino).

For the 1839 Copenhagen première of D.-F.-E. Auber's three-act comic opera an (uncredited) so-called *Styrian Dance (Steirisk Dands)* was performed by F. Hoppe and C. Fjeldsted as the centrepiece of a dance divertissement that depicted a masked ball at the court of the Queen of Spain. According to pencilled notes in the printed orchestral score for *Le Domino noir* (now in DKKk, call no. U 6, p. 119) this divertissement was performed as an *entr'acte* between Acts I and II.

The *Styrian Dance* was framed by two other, similarly uncredited dances namely a *Pas de deux* (performed by Bournonville and L. Grahn), and a *Boléro* (danced by P. Larcher and A. Nielsen). Moreover, a *Contredanse* to music by H. S. Paulli was performed by the corps de ballet at the very beginning of this divertissement.

According to autographed notes by Bournonville and other notes in a copyist's hand in the orchestral score for the *Pas de deux* (*see* Musical sources) the music for this dance seems to have been borrowed from A. Adam's and A. Guerra's two-act ballet *Les Mohicans* (premièred at the Paris Opéra on 5.7.1837). This theory is supported by notes found in Adam's orchestral score and the répétiteur's copy for this ballet (now in FPo, call nos. A 517 [II], p. 62, and Matériel, shelve 30, pp. 71–72). They indicate that a similar *Pas de quatre* (entitled '2.de Pas à donner/le Pas de Quatre/de Mr Guerra à donner ici') was performed in the second act of *Les Mohicans*. The music for this dance, however, is no longer preserved in the Paris Opéra scores, which seems to indicate the Copenhagen score as the only complete musical source that has yet come to light.

At the restaging in Copenhagen of *Le Domino noir* on 18.2. 1847 this *Pas de deux* was again included, but was then performed by Bournonville and his Swedish pupil, M. C. Norberg. In the two following restagings of the opera on 6.12. 1850 and 12.5.1859 (after 1859 performed with the new title *Den sorte Domino*) no dance divertissements were included at all.

In his handwritten list of his works, written c.1851 (*see* Additional Sources), Bournonville clearly included *Den sorte Domino* under the year of [18]38. Apart from his mis-recollection of the exact year for its Copenhagen première this fact indicates that he was responsible at least for staging the *Pas de deux* and the *Styrian Dance*, while the *Boléro* that year seems to have been choreographed by P. Larcher. This theory is supported by a review of *Le Domino noir* in the Copenhagen paper *Mellemacten* on 9.11.1846. That year the general mise-en-scène of this work is clearly credited to P. Funck, while the *Boléro* is explicitly listed as a dance choreographed by P. Larcher.

The Styrian National Dance (Den Steijermarkska National-dansen) was also performed by F. Hoppe and C. Fjeldsted as a new, incorporated finale to Bournonville's one-act idyllic ballet *The Tyroleans* when this work was given its Swedish première at Stockholm's Royal Theatre (Operahuset) on 8.6.1839. The same dance was later that summer also performed as a separate (uncredited) divertissement at Göteborg's Stora Theater (Segerlindska Theatern) on 5.7. and 18.7.1839. In Norway it was given as a separate (uncredited) divertissement by Bournonville and C. Fjeldsted at Christiania's Theatre (Oslo) on 29.7.1840, then entitled *Den Steierske Nationaldans*.

In Copenhagen *Den Steiriske Nationaldans* was incorporated as a new (uncredited) finale to Bournonville's one-act idyllic ballet *The Tyroleans* (*see* 6.3.1835) at the second performance (on 2.11.1839) of its restaging on 21.10.1839. Moreover, from 1.10.1843 it was mounted at the Royal Theatre as a separate (uncredited) divertissement and reached a total of 42 performances there (with different casts), the last of which took place on 20.3.1865.

On 2.5.1847 another (uncredited) dance for two women, entitled '*The Styrians, National Pas de deux*' ('*Steiermarkeren, Pas de deux National*') was danced by the cousins Juliette and Amalia Price at the Casino Theatre. According to Bournonville's autographed notes written in the parts for this dance it clearly seems to have been arranged and mounted by him and employed (according to the musical sources) the exact same music as that for the 1839 *Styrian Dance* in Act I of Auber's *Le Domino noir*.

On 27.6. and 8.8.1847 W. Funck and C. Fjeldsted performed yet another *Styrian Peasant Dance (Steyersk Bonde-dands)* at Christiania's Theatre (Oslo), the choreography of which is explicitly credited on the poster to 'Balletmester [Jules] Perrot'. That dance, however, was most probably the same as Bournonville's 1839 *Styrian Dance* in Auber's *Le Domino noir*. Consequently, Bournonville's version of this dance may have been based on an earlier dance originally choreographed by Perrot, and which he may have seen and learned during a visit to Paris in the late 1830s (*Le Domino noir* was premièred in Paris at Théatre de l'Opéra-Comique on 2.12.1837).

On 2.7.1852 '*The Styrian National Dance*' ('*Steyrisk National-dands*') was mounted for the third time in Christiania. It was this year performed by E. Stramboe and A. Price, with Bournonville's name explicitly listed on the poster as the choreographer. The '*Styrian Dance*' ('*Steirisk Dands*') was performed for the last time at Christiania's Theatre, by H. Scharff and S. Price on 11.6. and 21.6.1865, but then as a separate (uncredited) divertissement.

On 15.10.1857 a *Styrian Dance (Steirisk Dands)* was mounted as a separate (uncredited) divertissement at the Court Theatre and performed there three times by F. Hoppe and C. Fjeldsted (the last time on 13.11.1857). It, too, is most likely identical with Bournonville's 1839 version of the dance of that name. Moreover, on 30.10.1857 Bournonville included Auber's complete opera in a list of projected opera stagings that he was planning for the 1857–58 and 1858–59 seasons. It was carried out by him in parts on 12.5.1859 when he gave personal stage-instructions to his daughter, the alto C. Bournonville, who that year made her début at Copenhagen's Royal Theatre in the rôle of *Angela*.

During 1839 Bournonville's *Pas de deux* and *Styrian Dance* were performed 14 and 15 times respectively in Auber's opera, while the operas as such reached a total of 85 performances during Bournonville's lifetime (the last given on 30.1. 1872). It is not clear from the rehearsal book of H. C. J. Fredstrup exactly how many rehearsals were held of the opera and its dances in 1839.

Autograph sources:

Production note. Ms. Autograph. Black ink, 2 pp. (19 × 16,8 cm)
For de tre Herrer: Nehm, Bentzen og Ring,/udbedes et forandret Costume i <u>Den sorte Domino</u> […]
Signed and dated: 'Khvn d. 9 Sept: 1846'
[DKKt; Brevregistrant: Bournonville
This note contains Bournonville's indications about new male costumes for a later restaging of *Le Domino noir* on 12.9.1846.

Musical sources:

Orchestral score (*Contredanse*). Ms Autograph (by H. S. Paulli). Black and brown ink. 1 vol. 28 pp. of which one is blank (27,2 × 38 cm)
215/Partitur/til/Contradansen/til/Den Sorte Domino/[…]/No. 1/Contradands.
Signed and dated (on p. 26): 'HSP/J. [18]39'
[DKKk; C II, 119 (KTB 215)

Répétiteur's copy (*Contredanse*, fragment). Ms. Copy. Black ink. 4 pp. (33,4 × 25,5 cm)
[Without title]
Unsigned and undated [1839]
[DKKk; MA ms 2620 (KTB 215)
This fragment of the original répétiteur's copy for Paulli's *Contredanse* in Auber's *Le Domino noir* contains the music of the final 74 bars.

Parts (*Contredanse*). Ms. Copy. 31 vol.
3 vl I, 3 vl II, 2 vla, 3 vlc e cb, fl 1/2, ob 1/2, cl 1/2, fag 1/2, cor 1/2/ 3/4, clno 1/2, trb 1/2/3, timp, piatti, tri.
Unsigned and undated [1839]
[DKKk; KTB 215

Orchestral score (*Pas de deux*). Ms. Copy. Brown ink. 1 vol. 32 pp. (27,2 × 38 cm)

Pas de deux <u>Domino noir.</u>/Pas de Quatre [changed to:] Deux/debuts <u>de Mr.</u> Guerra
Unsigned and undated [c.1837–1839]
[DKKk; MA ms 2605 (KTB 227)
This orchestral score is clearly a French copy that most probably was purchased by Bournonville in Paris in the late 1830s. As a result of its transformation from a *Pas de quatre* to a *Pas de deux* it contains a musical insertion (on p. 18) which replaces parts of Adam's original music.

No répétiteur's copy for Bournonville's *Pas de deux* in *Le Domino noir* has yet been traced.

Parts (*Pas de deux*). Ms Copy. 3 vol.
3 vl I, 3 vl II, 2 vla, 3 vlc e cb, fl 1/2, ob 1/2, cl 1/2, fag 1/2, cor 1/2/3/4, clno 1/2, trb 1/2/3, timp, gr cassa e piatti, tri.
Unsigned and undated [1839]
[DKKk; KTB 227

No orchestral score and répétiteur's copy dating from the 1839 première of Bournonville's *Styrian Dance* in *Le Domino noir* have yet been traced.

Parts (*Styrian Dance*, incomplete). Ms. Copy. 20 vol.
2 vl I, 3 vl II, 2 vla, 3 vlc e cb, fl 1/2, cl 1/2, fag 1/2, cor 1/2, tr 1/2.
Unsigned and undated [c.1839]
[DKKk; KTB 213
This (incomplete) set of parts is entitled *Pas Styrien*. Pencilled notes in the part for the first violin (reading: 'Pas Styrien/til Den sorte Domino') clearly indicate that the parts must date from the 1839 Copenhagen première of the *Styrian Dance* in Auber's opera.

No musical sources dating from the 1839 première of P. Larcher's *Boléro* in *Le Domino noir* have yet been traced. However, a later set of parts for this dance (dating from c.1847) is now in DKKk (call no. MA ms 2702 (1-8)).

12.3.1839
Pas de deux composed by Mr. Ballet Master Bournonville (componeret af Hr. Balletmester Bournonville) **performed by himself and C. Fjeldsted.**
This *Pas de deux* is perhaps identical with Bournonville's earlier *Pas de deux* in *Nina, ou La Folle par amour* (see 30.9.1834). It is not possible to identify the dance any further.

17.4.1839
Aladdin, or The Magic Lantern (Aladdin eller Den forunderlige Lampe).
According to his handwritten lists of his works written c.1851 (see Additional Sources) Bournonville created both the mise-en-scène and the choreography for the Copenhagen première of A. Oehlenschläger's dramatic five-act fairy-play (first published in 1837). It was set to music arranged and composed by the concert-master, P. F. Funck, and by N. W. Gade, both of whom closely followed Bournonville's indications. Their individual contributions were as follows:

(1) Act III (score no. 1): For this number Funck incorporated excerpts of the dance music from Act IV (score nos. 3 and 4) of F. Kuhlau's score to Oehlenschläger's short-lived three-act play *The Trine-Brother of Damascus (Trillingbrødrene fra Damask)*, premièred at Copenhagen's Royal Theatre on 1.9.1830.
(2) Act III (score nos. 2, 9, 10, and 12): In these numbers Funck included a chorus (sung by the spirits of the Lamp) and three dances which (according to Bournonville's pencilled autographed notes in the répétiteur's copy) were all performed by the corps de ballet and set to music by yet another (not yet identified) composer.
(3) Act III (score no 8 A): This number (a *Pas de quatre* performed by

Bournonville, F. Hoppe, C. Fjeldsted, and A. Nielsen) was composed by N. W. Gade and represents the first time Bournonville worked with this composer. Similarly, all of the play's melodramas were written Gade after Bournonville's indications.

According to a letter to the theatre management of Copenhagen's Royal Theatre (now in The State Archive, call no. Det kgl. Teaters Arkiv, Gruppe E, pakke 288) Bournonville asked on 6.5.1839 for permission to 'arrangere Dandsen i 3.die Act uden Pas de quatre'. This was granted and the Act III *Pas de quatre* was replaced on eight occasions (between 13.5.1839 and 25.11.1842) with Bournonville's so-called 'Pas de deux oriental', originally performed by himself and A. Krætzmer on 26.9.1829 as an incorporated divertissement in P. Funck's *A Divertissement in Oriental Style.*

In Oehlenschläger's *Aladdin, or The Magic Lantern* this dance was (according to the repertory book of F. Hoppe) performed 7 times by Hoppe and A. Nielsen (between 13.5. 1839 and 26.11.1841), and once by Hoppe and C. Fjeldsted in the play's 23rd and last performance on 25.11.1842. It is not clear from the rehearsal book of H. C. J. Fredstrup exactly how many rehearsals were held of this play and its dances in 1839.

Musical sources:

Orchestral score. Ms. Autograph (by N. W. Gade). Black and brown ink. 1 vol. 24 pp. (27,1 × 37,8 cm)
N. W. Gade/Aladdin/Supplement Nr 1./[...]/Aladdin 1ste Act.
Unsigned and dated (on p. 1): '11/<u>3. 1839.</u>'
[DKKk; N. W. Gades Samling. Supplement no. 1 (1929-30.14)
This orchestral score contains Gade's music for the melodramas in Act I, II, III, and V of Oehlenschläger's *Aladdin, or The Magic Lantern.*

Répétiteur's copy. Ms. Copy and autograph (by N. W. Gade). Black and brown ink. 1 vol. 44 pp. (33,2 × 25,7 cm with minor variants)
A. 353/Aladdin/Bournonville/46/1839./[...]/Bournonville,/Repetiteur Parti/til/Aladdin
Unsigned and dated (on the front cover): '1839.'
[DKKk; MA ms 3077 (KTA 353)
Apart from the opening *Adagio sostenuto* in the Act III *Pas de quatre* (which proves to be identical with Kuhlau's 'Harmoniemusik' in Oehlenschläger's play from 1830 *The Trine-Brother of Damascus*, score no. 4) the music for the *Pas de quatre* is Gade's autograph throughout. The volume also contains Bournonville's pencilled autographed choreographic notes which indicate the casting of each section in the *Pas de quatre* (score no. 8 A) and describe the steps in the succeeding dance for the corps de ballet (score no. 9).

Parts. Ms. Copy. 33 vol.
3 vl I, 3 vl II, 2 vla, 4 vlc e cb, fl 1/2, ob 1/2, cl 1/2, fag 1/2, cor 1/2/3/4, tr 1/2, trb 1/2/3, timp, gr cassa, tri, arpa. 43 vocal parts.
Unsigned and undated [1839]
DKKk; KTA 353

Printed sources:

Printed libretto. 1 vol. 381 pp. (15,5 × 11 cm)
Aladdin./Dramatisk Eventyr/af/Oehlenschläger.
Kiøbenhavn, J. D. Qvist, 1837.
[DKKk; 55, – 250 8°
The scene in Act III in which Bournonville's dances were interpolated was described by Oehlenschläger (pp. 184-185) as follows:
'Aladdin Pallads. Den store Sal. Aladdin og hans Brud. Soliman, Zulima, Vesiren, Morgiane og Flere sidde til Taffels. [...] Aladdin giver et Vink. Strax aabnes en Dør hvorigennem kommer en Skare Alfer. Nogle kortkjortlede til Dands, andre med Fløiter og Strængeleeg. I det de Dandsende begynde, synge de Andre'.

2.6.1839

Scene, Pas de deux, and Galop (from the ballet The Isle of Phantasy) (Scene, Pas de deux & Galop (utur Balletten: l'Isle des Fantasies [sic])) performed by F. Hoppe and C. Fjeldsted (Stockholm's Royal Theatre, Operahuset).

This work is an abridged divertissement version of selected excerpts in Act II (score no. 7) of *The Isle of Phantasy* (*see* 28.10.1838). It was arranged especially by Bournonville for the 1839 Swedish summer tour and was given twice in Stockholm (the last time on 5.6.1839). Later the same year Bournonville mounted a slightly abridged version of the same dances which was first performed by Hoppe and Fjeldsted at Copenhagen's Royal Theatre on 10.11.1839.

Musical sources:

Orchestral score. Ms. Copy. Brown ink. 1 vol. 56 pp. (32,5 × 24,8 cm)
No. 3 i Amors skämt/Pas de deux/af/Phantasiens Ø/Partitur.
Unsigned and undated [1839/1861?]
[SSkma; KT Dansmusik 97
This orchestral score is a Danish copy made in Copenhagen and most likely brought to Stockholm by Bournonville in 1839. The *Pas de deux* from Act II (score no. 7) of *The Isle of Phantasy* was mounted at Stockholm's Royal Theatre (Operahuset) on two occasions, first as part of a dance divertissement on 2.6.1839, and secondly as an incorporated divertissement in S. Lund's one-act ballet *The Whims of Cupid (Amors Skämt)*, premièred on 29.1.1861. This orchestral score, which seems to have served for both of these stagings, differs slightly from E. Helsted's original 1838 Copenhagen version by some minor musical cuts and omissions.

Répétiteur's copy. Ms. Copy. Brown ink. 1 vol. 6 pp. (34 × 25,8 cm)
Pas de deux/af/Phantasiens Ø/Repetiteur = Partie
Unsigned and undated [1839?]
[SSkma; KT Dansmusik 97
This répétiteur's copy is clearly a Danish copy made in Copenhagen and most likely brought to Stockholm by Bournonville in 1839.

Parts. Ms. Copy. 27 vol.
2 vl I, 2 vl II, vla, 4 vlc e cb, fl picc, fl 1/2, ob 1/2, cl 1/2, fag 1/2, cor 1/2/3/, tr, trb 1/2/3, timp, gr. cassa, tri, arpa.
Unsigned and undated [1839?]
[SSkma; KT Dansmusik 97

2.6.1839

Pas de trois, from Le Postillon du Lonjumeau (Pas de trois, utur Postiljonen i Lonjumeau) (uncredited) performed by F. Hoppe, C. Fjeldsted, and A. Nielsen (Stockholm's Royal Theatre, Operahuset).

This (uncredited) dance is almost certainly identical with Bournonville's so-called 'Pas de trois af Postillonen', that had originally been incorporated in A. Adam's three-act comic opera *Le Postillon de Lonjumeau* at Copenhagen's Royal Theatre on 28.10.1837 (then performed by himself, L. Grahn, and C. Fjeldsted). The dance was given only once at Stockholm's Royal Theatre, performed as an incorporated number in A. Selinder's divertissement, named *A Masquerade Divertissement of Dance (Ett Maskarad-Divertissement af Dans)*. It is not possible to identify the dance any further.

5.6.1839

Pas de deux (by Taglioni) (Pas de deux (Af Taglioni)) performed by P. C. Johansson and A. Nielsen (Stockholm's Royal Theatre, Operahuset).

According to the set of parts in SSkma, this dance was per-

formed to music by J. Mayseder which is identical with that employed for the *Pas de deux* in Act II (score no. 1 A) of Bournonville's two-act romantic ballet *The Isle of Phantasy* (*see* 28.10.1838). The 1839 Stockholm performance of this dance was mounted especially by Bournonville for his Swedish pupil, P. C. Johansson. He danced it together with A. Nielsen as an incorporated number in A. Selinder's *A Masquerade Divertissement of Dance (Ett Maskarad-Divertissement af Dans)*, but later it was also given as an *entr'acte* divertissement in Dinaux's (pen-name for J. F. Beudin and P. P. Goubaux) and G. Legouvé's five-act drama *Louise de Lignerolles*, on 12.6.1839.

During the 1839 summer tour to Sweden the *Pas de deux (by Taglioni)* was also performed three times by Johansson and Nielsen at Göteborg's Stora Theater (Segerlindska Theatern) between 5.7. and 18.7.1839. According to the Danish posters and some pencilled notes found in the Copenhagen set of parts for this dance (which is entitled 'Pas de deux (à la Taglioni)') it also seems to have been mounted as a separate divertissement in Copenhagen and abroad on seven later occasions, and each time with a slightly different title as follows:

(1) *A Pas de deux arranged after Taglioni (En Pas de deux arrangeret efter Taglioni)* mounted by Bournonville for G. Brodersen and A. Nielsen, at Copenhagen's Royal Theatre on 4.10.1839.
(2) *Pas de deux (after Taglioni) (Pas de deux (efter Taglioni))* (uncredited) performed at Copenhagen's Royal Theatre by F. Hoppe and A. Nielsen on 6.7.1840.
(3) *Pas de deux, after Taglioni (Pas de deux, efter Taglioni)* (uncredited) performed in Norway at Christiania's Theatre (Oslo) by Bournonville and C. Fjeldsted on 10.8.1840.
(4) *Pas de deux, à la Taglioni* (uncredited) performed by F. Hoppe and A. Nielsen at Copenhagen's Royal Theatre on 7.1.1841.
(5) *Pas de deux (à la Taglioni)* performed by G. Brodersen and A. Nielsen at Copenhagen's Royal Theatre on 6.11.1845 and described on the poster as a work 'arranged' (*arrangeret*) by Bournonville.
(6) *Pas de deux à la Taglioni* performed by F. Hoppe and J. Price at Copenhagen's Royal Theatre on 9.11.1850 and on 13.3.1851, with Bournonville explicitly credited (according to the poster of the last date) for the choreography.
(7) *'Pas de deux' (à la Taglioni)* performed by S. Lund and J. Price on 9.6.1852 at Christiania's Theatre (Oslo) with the choreography explicitly credited on the poster to Bournonville.

Moreover, on 27.9.1842 the *Pas de deux* was incorporated as score no. '3' in Act II of Bournonville's ballet *La Sylphide*. According to the poster for this performance it was that year entitled *Pas de deux (à la Taglioni)* and given 11 performances by Bournonville (as *James*) and A. Nielsen (as *The Sylph*), the last of which took place on 20.12.1843.

Furthermore, for Bournonville's first, thoroughly revised restaging of *La Sylphide* on 22.9.1849 he reinstated a shortened version of Mayseder's *Pas de deux* in Act II. This version was mixed with other musical excerpts borrowed from Act I of H. S. Løvenskjold's score to Bournonville's two-act ballet *The New Penelope, or The Spring Festival in Athens* (*see* 26.1.1847). The new 1849 version of Mayseder's *Pas de deux* was revised for a third and last time by Bournonville when he made his final restaging of *La Sylphide* in Copenhagen on 4.2.1865.

Finally, the *Pas de deux (à la Taglioni)* was (according to the poster) also incorporated on 12.10.1842 as a divertissement in Act I of Rossini's four-act opera *Guillaume Tell* and was performed there by Bournonville and A. Nielsen.

Musical sources:

No orchestral score and répétiteur's copy for this dance have yet been traced in Stockholm. This seems to indicate that the *Pas de deux* was rehearsed and performed in Stockholm with the Copenhagen orchestral score and répétiteur's copy (now in DKKk, call nos. C II, 105, and MA ms 2645 respectively) while a new set of parts for the dance was clearly made in Stockholm for this performance (*see below*).

Parts. Ms. Copy. 32 vol.
vl princ, 3 vl I, 3 vl II, 2 vla, 3 vlc e cb, fl picc, fl 1/2, ob 1/2, cl 1/2, fag 1/2, cor 1/2/3/4, tr 1/2, trb 1/2/3, timp.
Unsigned and undated [c.1839]
[SSkma; KT Dansmusik 43
The label on the box containing this set of parts reads 'Pas de deux/ La Sylphide/af/ Maÿseder' (*see also* 28.11.1836).

8.6.1839
The Tyroleans, or: The Mischievous Boy (Tyrolerne, eller: Den Skälmaktige Gossen) **(Stockholm's Royal Theatre, Operahuset).**
This performance represents Bournonville's first and only staging outside Denmark of his one-act idyllic ballet *The Tyroleans* (*see* 6.3.1835). According to the orchestral score it differed from the Copenhagen version by the omission of the *Waltz* (score no. 12 in the 1835 version). Moreover, the Stockholm version included a new finale (set to music by a not yet identified composer) which seems to have replaced Bournonville's original 1835 *Finale* (employing music from G. Rossini's overture for his four-act opera *Guillaume Tell*). *The Tyroleans, or: The Mischievous Boy* was performed only three times in Stockholm, the last time on 12.6.1839.

Autograph sources:

Production note. Ms. Autograph. Brown ink. 1 p. (25 × 21 cm)
<u>Hermann</u> Forpagter <u>Hr Wennbom</u>/Spids Hat, [...]
Unsigned and undated [1839]
[SSkma; Lo III: 21,1

Musical sources:

Orchestral score. Ms. Copy. Black ink. 1 vol. 353 pp. (30,9 × 24,5 cm)
Tyrolerne/Pantomime Ballet i 1 Act/Musiken/af/Fröhlich/Partitur.
Unsigned and undated [1839]
[SSkma; KT Pantomime-Balletter T 1

No répétiteur's copy dating from the 1839 Stockholm production of *The Tyroleans* has yet been traced.

Parts. Ms. Copy. 27 vol.
2 vl I, 2 vl II, 2 vla, 2 vlc e cb, fl 1/2, ob 1/2, cl 1/2, fag 1/2, cor 1/2/3/4, tr, trb 1/2/3, timp, gr cassa, tri.
Unsigned and undated [1839]
[SSkma; KT Pantomime-Balletter T 1

Printed sources:

Printed scenario. 1 vol. 8 pp. (20,3 × 14,4 cm)
TYROLARNE,/PANTOMIM-BALLETT I EN AKT;/Uppsatt på Kongl. Theatern i Stockholm/i Juni månad 1839/af/A. BOURNON-VILLE/[...]/Musiken komponerd och arrangerad/af/Konsertmästarn FRÖHLICH.

Stockholm, Nordströmska Boktryckeriet, 1839.
[SSk; Sv. Saml. Vitt. Sv. Dram. Pantom. (Br.)

8.6.1839
The Styrian National Dance (Den Steijermarkska Nationaldansen) **(uncredited) performed by F. Hoppe and C. Fjeldsted (Stockholm's Royal Theatre, Operahuset).**
This (uncredited) dance is almost certainly identical with the *Styrian Dance* first performed in D.-F.-E. Auber's three-act comic opera *Le Domino noir* (*see* 29.1.1839). This theory is confirmed by the existence of a set of parts in SSkma, entitled 'Pas Styrien', containing music completely identical with that employed for Bournonville's *Styrian Dance* in the 1839 Copenhagen première of Auber's opera.
   In Stockholm this dance was performed as a second, additional finale to Bournonville's one-act idyllic ballet *The Tyroleans, or: The Mischievous Boy*. Later the same year it was given twice as a separate divertissement at Göteborg's Stora Theater (Segerlindska Theatern) on 5.7. and 18.7.1839.

Musical sources:

No orchestral score and répétiteur's copy for *The Styrian National Dance* have been traced in Stockholm. This seems to indicate that it was rehearsed and performed in Stockholm with the original (not yet traced) Copenhagen score and répétiteur's copy for it, while a new set of parts was clearly made in Stockholm in 1839 for this performance (*see* the following entry).

Parts. Ms. Copy. 20 vol.
2 vl I, 2 vl II, vla, 2 vlc e cb, fl 1/2, ob 1/2, cl 1/2, fag 1/2, cor 1/2/3/4, trb.
Unsigned and undated [c.1839]
[SSkma; KT Dansmusik 29

12.6.1839
El Jaleo de Xeres (Spanish National Dance) (Spansk Nationaldans) **(uncredited) performed by F. Hoppe and C. Fjeldsted (Stockholm's Royal Theatre, Operahuset).**
This (uncredited) Spanish dance is almost certainly identical with Bournonville's earlier revised version for a couple, of L. Grahn's Spanish solo dance, entitled *El Jaleo di Xeres, Spanish Dance (spansk Dands)* (*see* 29.11.1838). It was set to music by D.-F.-E. Auber and was performed only once during the 1839 summer tour to Stockholm. Later the same year it was mounted at Copenhagen's Royal Theatre with Hoppe and Fjeldsted on 24.11.1839 as an incorporated divertissement in Act I of Auber's five-act opera *La Muette de Portici*.

Musical sources:

Orchestral score. Ms. Copy. Black ink. 1 vol. 15 pp. (25,3 × 20,3 cm with minor variants)
No. 30./Pas de deux/il Jaleo/de Xeres/Partitur
Unsigned and undated [c.1839]
[SSkma; KT Dansmusik 30

No répétiteur's copy and parts for this dance have yet been traced in Stockholm. This seems to indicate that it was rehearsed and performed with the original (not yet traced) Copenhagen material for it. The only musical sources that are still preserved in Copenhagen for this dance all date from its incorporation in Bournonville's two-act idyllic ballet *The Toreador* on 27.11.1840 (now in DKKk, call nos. C II, 114 k, and MA ms 2665).

13.6.1839

Grand Pas de deux composed by Mr. Ballet Master Bournonville (Stor Pas de deux, Componerad af Hr Ballettmästaren Bournonville) **performed by himself and A. Nielsen as an incorporated divertissement in Act II of** *Robert le Diable (Robert af Normandie)* **(Stockholm's Royal Theatre, Operahuset).**

This *Grand Pas de deux* is perhaps identical with Bournonville's *New Pas de deux* performed two years later on 5.12.1841 at Copenhagen's Royal Theatre by himself and C. Fjeldsted as an incorporated divertissement in Act II of G. Meyerbeer's five-act opera *Robert le Diable (Robert af Normandiet)*. This theory is supported by the existence of an orchestral score and set of parts in Stockholm (now in SSkma, call no. KT Dansmusik 85) which contain the music for that dance and was used (according to its title) for a later restaging of it in Stockholm (mounted by Bournonville's pupil, S. Lund, on 13.11.1856).

The 1839 *Grand Pas de deux* was given only once during Bournonville's 1839 summer tour to Stockholm. It is not possible to identify the dance any further.

14.6.1839

Scene from the Ballet La Sylphide (Scen utur Balletten Sylphiden/ Scène de La Sylphide) **(uncredited) performed by F. Hoppe and A. Nielsen (Stockholm's Royal Theatre, Operahuset).**

This (uncredited) work is an abridged divertissement version of Bournonville's two-act ballet *La Sylphide* (*see* 28.11. 1836). According to the set of parts in SSkma it included the *Pas de deux* to music by J. Mayseder, which was originally performed in Act II (score no. 1 A) of Bournonville's two-act romantic ballet *The Isle of Phantasy* (*see* 28.10.1838).

The casting of the divertissement consisted only of the ballet's two protagonists, *James* (Hoppe) and *The Sylph* (Nielsen) and was arranged especially for the Swedish début of these two pupils of Bournonville's. They performed it twice in Stockholm, the last time on 19.6.1839. Later during the same summer Hoppe and Nielsen also performed the divertissement with a slightly different title at Göteborg's Stora Theater (Segerlindska Theatern) on 15.7.1839.

Musical sources:

No orchestral score for the 1839 Stockholm divertissement version of Bournonville's *La Sylphide* has yet been traced.

Répétiteur's copy/Conductor's part. Ms. Copy. 1 vol. 48 pp. of which four are blank (31,9 × 24,4 cm)
Divertissement/N. 1/Balletten 'Sÿlphiden', af Lövenskjold/Repetiteur-Partie./[...]/Divertissement/af Bal:/Sÿlphiden/af/Baron H. von Lövenskiold/Repetiteur Partie.
Unsigned and undated [c.1839]
[DKKk; MA ms 3023 (KTB 1028 (1)) (mu 8608.2273)
This répétiteur's copy also seems to have served as a conductor's part. This is clear from the numerous performance notes and the extensive indications concerning the instrumentation that are contained in this volume. The répétiteur's copy is clearly written by the same copyist who wrote the original répétiteur's copy for the complete Copenhagen version of *La Sylphide*. This proves that the volume was prepared in Copenhagen some time during the late 1830s. The exact place where Mayseder's *Pas de deux* was performed is indicated with a note on p. 29, while the music for this dance is included in a separate répétiteur's copy (*see* the following entry). The present volume, which also includes an owner's signature (reading: 'Aug.

Gjørling'), was for many years preserved in the music archive of Copenhagen's Royal Theatre, but was transferred to DKKk in July 1986.

Répétiteur's copy (*Pas de deux*). Ms. Copy. Black ink. 16 pp. (32,4 × 23,2 cm)
Pas de deux./La Sylphide/Musique de Meiseder [*sic*]./[...]/Repetitör = parti.
Unsigned and undated [c.1839]
[SSkma; KT Dansmusik 43
This répétiteur's copy is the oldest of two répétiteur's copies that are preserved in SSkma and contain Mayseder's music originally employed for the Act II *Pas de deux* in Bournonville's two-act romantic ballet *The Isle of Phantasy*. The volume contains several pencilled notes (written by an unknown hand) that mention the names of the dancers [Conrad Theodor] 'Dahlgren' and 'Theodore' [Ignaz Marckhl]. This seems to indicate that these dancers performed (or at least rehearsed) the male part of this dance in Stockholm some time during the 1840s and/or 50s.

Répétiteur's copy (*Pas de deux*). Ms. Copy. Brown ink. 8 pp. (34,8 × 25,9 cm)
Pas de deux. La Sylphide.
Unsigned and undated [after 1839]
[SSkma; KT Dansmusik 43
This répétiteur's copy contains some minor musical changes from the previous répétiteur's copy and seems to date from a later restaging of Mayseder's *Pas de deux* in Stockholm during the 1840s and/or 50s.

Parts (incomplete). Ms. Copy. 12 vol.
fl II, ob II, cl II, fag II, cor I, tr 1/2, Atrb, Btrb, timp, gr cassa, tri.
Unsigned and undated [c.1839]
[DKKk; KTB 1028 (1) (originally without number)

Parts (*Pas de deux*). Ms. Copy. 30 vol.
vl princ, 3 vl I, 3 vl II, 2 vla, 3 vlc e cb, fl picc, fl 1/2, ob 1/2, cl 1/2, fag 1/2, cor 1/2/3/4, tr, trb 1/2/3, timp.
Unsigned and undated [c.1839]
[SSkma; KT Dansmusik 43

14.6.1839

Grand Pas de deux from the ballet Waldemar (Stor Pas de deux utur Balletten Waldemar/Grand Pas de deux du Ballet de Waldemar) **(uncredited) performed by Bournonville and C. Fjeldsted (Stockholm's Royal Theatre, Operahuset).**

This (uncredited) dance is identical with the *Pas de deux* in Act II of Bournonville's four-act romantic ballet *Waldemar* (*see* 28.10.1835). The Stockholm performance represents the first time it was ever performed outside Denmark. It was given only once in Sweden.

Musical sources:

No orchestral score and répétiteur's copy for this dance are preserved in Stockholm. This seems to indicate that the *Pas de deux* was rehearsed and performed with the 1835 Copenhagen score and répétiteur's copy, which most probably were brought to Stockholm by Bournonville in 1839.

Parts (incomplete). Ms. Copy. 11 vol.
vl I, vl II, vla, cb, cor I, Atrb, Ttrb, gr cassa, tri, arpa.
Unsigned and undated [c.1839]
[DKKk; KTB 1052
This (incomplete) set of parts for what is named 'Pas de deux de Waldemar' seems (according to its French title) to date from the first time this dance was performed outside Denmark. The parts were probably also used on the four later occasions when the Act II *Pas de deux* from *Waldemar* was mounted by Bournonville abroad (*see* 18.7.1839, 3.8.1848, 12.6.1841, and 29.8.1841).

14.6.1839

Edmond in A. Selinder's production of J. Aumer's *La Somnambule, ou l'Arrivée d'un nouveau seigneur (Sömngångersken i Provence)* performed by Bournonville (Stockholm's Royal Theatre, Operahuset).

During the 1839 summer tour to Stockholm Bournonville twice played the rôle of *Edmond* in A. Selinder's production of J. Aumer's ballet (14.6. and 19.6.1839). He knew the rôle by heart from his own, earlier staging of this ballet at Copenhagen's Royal Theatre on 21.9.1829.

In Stockholm, where Aumer's ballet had been premièred on 1.12.1835, Bournonville's two 1839 performances of the rôle of *Edmond* also represent the last times that this ballet was ever given in Sweden.

Musical sources:

The orchestral score and the set of parts for A. Selinder's Stockholm 1835 production of J. Aumer's *La Somnambule, ou l'Arrivée d'un nouveau seigneur (Sömngångersken i Provence)* are now in SSkma (call no. KT Pantomime Balletter S 7). No répétiteur's copy for it has yet been traced in SSkma.

14.6.1839

The English Sailor, (Scene and Hornpipe) (Den Engelska Matrosen, (Scen och Hornpipe)/Le Matelot Anglais (Scène & Hornpipe)) (uncredited) performed by Bournonville (Stockholm's Royal Theatre, Operahuset).

This (uncredited) dance is a revised divertissement version of the *English Sailor's Dance* from Act I (score no. 10) of Bournonville's two-act romantic ballet *The Isle of Phantasy* (*see* 28.10.1838), which seems to have been arranged especially for the 1839 Stockholm tour. Moreover, on the poster Bournonville is explicitly credited for having pieced together the music for it. According to the Swedish set of parts for this solo dance his arrangement consisted of two excerpts from T. Moore's *Irish Melodies* (1807–1834), entitled «The last rose of summer» (also known as 'The Groves of Blarney'), and «We may roam thro' this world» (also known as 'Garry-owen'). They were followed by a *Hornpipe* (presumably composed by I. P. E. Hartmann).

The divertissement was performed twice in Stockholm during the 1839 summer tour (the last time on 19.6.1839). Later the same summer it was also mounted and performed by Bournonville at Göteborg's Stora Theater (Segerlindska Theatern) on 10.7.1839, and in the following year he also danced it at Christiania's Theatre (Oslo) on 14.8.1840.

Musical sources:

No orchestral score and répétiteur's copy for this dance have yet been traced in Stockholm. This seems to indicate that the divertissement was rehearsed and performed with the original 1838 Copenhagen musical material for *The Isle of Phantasy* (now in DKKk, call nos. C II, 105, and MA ms 3016 (KTB 337 (1)).

Parts. Ms. Copy. 27 vol.
3 vl I, 3 vl II, 2 vla, 3 vlc e cb, fl picc, fl 1/2, ob 1/2, cl 1/2, fag 1/2, cor 1/2, tr, trb 1/2/3, timp, gr cassa, tri.
Unsigned and undated [c.1839]
[SSkma; KT Dansmusik 62
This set of parts, which at a later stage was drastically changed by means of musical insertions, omissions etc., was originally named

'Matrosdans'. It contains the exact same music as that for the *English Sailor's Dance* in Act I (score no. 10) of Bournonville's two-act romantic ballet *The Isle of Phantasy*. According to a note written in the part for the first violin the same music was many years later also used as an incorporated divertissement in H. Berens' score for F. Hedberg's Swedish version of Mélesville's, A. De Comberousse's and B. Antier-Chevrillon's four-act play *Le Capitaine de vaisseau, ou le Salamandre (Fregattkaptenen eller 'Salamandern')*, premièred at Stockholm's Royal Theatre on 23.4.1863. In that play it was performed as score no. '3'.

19.6.1839

Pas de deux by Ballet Master Bournonville (Pas de deux, af Balletmästaren Bournonville) performed by F. Hoppe and C. Fjeldsted (Stockholm's Royal Theatre, Operahuset).

This dance is most probably identical with the (uncredited) *Pas de deux* performed by F. Hoppe and A. Nielsen at Copenhagen's Royal Theatre on 17.12.1838. That dance, in turn, is perhaps identical with the second *Pas de deux* (score no. 5) in his divertissement *Hertha's Offering* (*see* 29.1.1838), which had also been performed by Hoppe and Fjeldsted. The *Pas de deux* was given once during the 1839 summer tour to Stockholm. It is not possible to identify the dance any further.

5.7.1839

Scene, Pas de deux and Gallopade from the ballet 'The Isle of Phantasy' (Scene, Pas de deux och Gallopade utur Balletten 'Phantasiens Ö') performed by F. Hoppe and C. Fjeldsted (Göteborg's Stora Theater, Segerlindska Theatern).

This divertissement consists of excerpts from Act II (score no. 7) of Bournonville's two-act romantic ballet *The Isle of Phantasy* (*see* 28.10.1838). It was performed only once in Göteborg.

5.7.1839

Pas de deux (by Taglioni) (Pas de deux (af Taglioni)) performed by P. C. Johansson and A. Nielsen (Göteborg's Stora Theater, Segerlindska Theatern).

This dance is almost certainly identical with the *Pas de deux (by Taglioni) (Pas de deux (Af Taglioni))* to music by J. Mayseder, which was performed by the same two dancers exactly one month earlier at Stockholm's Royal Theatre (Operahuset) on 5.6.1839. That dance, in turn, was originally part of Bournonville's two-act romantic ballet *The Isle of Phantasy* (*see* 28.10.1838). The *Pas de deux* is most probably also identical with the later so-called *Pas de deux (after Taglioni) (Pas de deux (efter Taglioni))*, mounted with F. Hoppe and A. Nielsen at Copenhagen's Royal Theatre on 6.7.1840, and the even later (uncredited) *Pas de deux, à la Taglioni*, performed by the same dancers on 7.1.1841. The *Pas de deux* received three performances at Göteborg's Stora Theater, the last of which was given on 18.7.1839. It is not possible to identify the dance any further.

5.7.1839

The Styrian National Dance (Den Steyermarska Nationaldansen) (uncredited) performed by F. Hoppe and C. Fjeldsted (Göteborg's Stora Theater, Segerlindska Theatern).

This (uncredited) dance is most probably identical with the earlier dance of that name, performed by Hoppe and Fjeldsted at Stockholm's Royal Theatre (Operahuset) on 8.6.

1839. That dance, in turn, is almost certainly the same as Bournonville's *Styrian Dance*, originally incorporated in D.-F.-E. Auber's three-act comic opera *Le Domino noir* at Copenhagen's Royal Theatre on 29.1.1839. *The Styrian National Dance* was performed twice at Göteborg's Stora Theater, the last time on 18.7.1839. It is not possible to identify the dance any further.

8.7.1839

Pas de deux from La Muette de Portici (Pas de deux ur Den Stumma) (uncredited) performed by Bournonville and C. Fjeldsted (Göteborg's Stora Theater, Segerlindska Theatern).

This (uncredited) dance is almost certainly identical with *A New Pas de deux composed by Mr. Bournonville*, first performed by F. Hoppe and L. Grahn at Copenhagen's Royal Theatre on 23.9.1834 as an incorporated divertissement in Act I of Auber's five-act opera *La Muette de Portici*. The *Pas de deux* was given once at Göteborg's Stora Theater. It is not possible to identify the dance any further.

8.7.1839

El Jaleo de Xeres (Spanish National Dance) (El Jaleo de Xeras (Spansk Nationaldans)) (uncredited) performed by F. Hoppe and C. Fjeldsted (Göteborg's Stora Theater, Segerlindska Theatern).

This (uncredited) dance is almost certainly identical with the dance of the same name performed by Hoppe and Fjeldsted at Stockholm's Royal Theatre (Operahuset) on 12.6.1839, and, in turn, is a revised version by Bournonville of L. Grahn's Spanish solo dance, entitled *El Jaleo di Xeres, Spanish Dance* (see 29.11.1838). It was performed once at Göteborg's Stora Theater. It is not possible to identify the dance any further.

10.7.1839

Scene and Pas de quatre from the Ballet La Somnambule (Scene och Pas de quatre utur Balletten Sömngångerskan (uncredited) performed by Bournonville (as *Edmond*), P. C. Johansson (as *Lucas*), C. Fjeldsted (as *Thérèse*), and A. Nielsen (as *Gertrude*) (Göteborg's Stora Theater, Segerlindska Theatern).

This (uncredited) divertissement is based on excerpts from Act I of Bournonville's 1829 Copenhagen version of J. Aumer's three-act pantomimic ballet *La Somnambule, ou l'Arrivée d'un nouveau seigneur* (see 21.9.1829). The divertissement, which represents the first time Bournonville mounted excerpts of this ballet outside Denmark, was performed twice in Göteborg, the last time on 15.7.1839.

10.7.1839

Pas de trois from Le Postillon de Lonjumeau (Pas de trois utur Postillonen i Lonjumeau) (uncredited) performed by F. Hoppe, C. Fjeldsted, and A. Nielsen (Göteborg's Stora Theater, Segerlindska Theatern).

This (uncredited) dance is almost certainly identical with the *Pas de trois* first incorporated by Bournonville for himself, L. Grahn, and C. Fjeldsted, in A. Adam's three-act comic opera *Le Postillon de Lonjumeau* at Copenhagen's Royal Theatre on 28.10.1837. The *Pas de trois* was given once at Göteborg's Stora Theater. It is not possible to identify the dance any further.

10.7.1839

The English Sailor, Scene and Hornpipe (Den Engelska Matrosen, Scene och Hornpipe (uncredited) performed by Bournonville (Göteborg's Stora Theater, Segerlindska Theatern).

This (uncredited) dance is almost certainly identical with the solo dance of that name, mounted and performed by Bournonville the month before at Stockholm's Royal Theatre (Operahuset) on 14.6.1839 and, in turn, is the same as the *English Sailor's Dance* in Act I (score no. 10) of his two-act romantic ballet *The Isle of Phantasy* (see 28.10.1838). The dance was performed twice at Göteborg's Stora Theater, the last time on 18.7.1839.

12.7.1839

Pas de deux from the ballet Nina (Pas de deux utur Balletten Nina) (uncredited) performed by F. Hoppe and C. Fjeldsted (Göteborg's Stora Theater, Segerlindska Theatern).

This (uncredited) dance is almost certainly identical with the *Pas de deux*, first incorporated in Act I (between score nos. 9 A and 9 B) of Bournonville's Copenhagen version of L. Milon's two-act pantomimic ballet *Nina, ou La Folle par amour* (see 30.9.1834). The *Pas de deux* was performed once at Göteborg's Stora Theater.

15.7.1839

Scene and Solo from the Ballet La Sylphide (Scene och Solo utur Balletten Sylphiden) (uncredited) performed by F. Hoppe (as *James*) and A. Nielsen (as *The Sylph*) (Göteborg's Stora Theater, Segerlindska Theatern).

This (uncredited) divertissement consists of excerpts from Bournonville's two-act ballet *La Sylphide* (see 28.11.1836) and is almost certainly identical with the similar divertissement performed (with a slightly different title) by Hoppe and Nielsen at Stockholm's Royal Theatre (Operahuset) on 14.6.1839. The divertissement was given only once at Göteborg's Stora Theater. It is not possible to establish the exact contents of dances in this divertissement any further.

18.7.1839

Grand Pas de deux from the Ballet Waldemar (Stor Pas de deux utur Balletten Waldemar) (uncredited) performed by Bournonville and C. Fjeldsted (Göteborg's Stora Theater, Segerlindska Theatern).

This (uncredited) dance is identical with the *Pas de deux* from Act II of Bournonville's four-act romantic ballet *Waldemar* (see 28.10.1835). It was given only once at Göteborg's Stora Theater.

Musical sources:

The set of parts entitled 'Pas de deux de Waldemar' (see 14.6.1839, now in DKKk, call no. KTB 1052) was most probably also used for this performance.

18.7.1839
Finale (uncredited) performed by Bournonville, F. Hoppe, P. C. Johansson, C. Fjeldsted, and A. Nielsen (Göteborg's Stora Theater, Segerlindska Theatern).

This (uncredited) dance was the last in a series of six guest performances at Göteborg's Stora Theater during the summer of 1839. It seems to be an arrangement of selected excerpts from earlier works by Bournonville. It is not possible to identify the exact contents of dances any further.

3.9.1839
Divertissement from 'The Isle of Phantasy' (Divertissement af 'Phantasiens Øe').

The cast and the exact contents of dances in this divertissement cannot be established from the annals of Copenhagen's Royal Theatre. However, according to the poster the divertissement included 'among other dances' a *Bacchantic Waltz (Bachantisk Vals)*, performed by E. Stramboe and A. Nielsen, and a *Pas de deux* and *Gallopade* performed by F. Hoppe and C. Fjeldsted, both of which were originally part of Act II (score nos. 5 and 7) in Bournonville's two-act romantic ballet *The Isle of Phantasy* (see 28.10.1838).

The divertissement was given once. It is not clear from the rehearsal book of H. C. J. Fredstrup exactly how many rehearsals were held of it in 1839.

17.9.1839
The Danes in China (De Danske i China).

This divertissement is based on seven excerpts from Act I (score nos. 5–11) in Bournonville's two-act romantic ballet *The Isle of Phantasy* (see 28.10.1838). The divertissement was also mounted at Hamburg's Stadttheater on 31.7.1843 and performed there five times (the last time on 7.8.1843). In Copenhagen *The Danes in China* was restaged by Bournonville three more times on 28.1.1842, 27.2.1843, and 26.2. 1865, each time with different contents of dances.

The 1839 version was given 7 performances, the last of which took place on 6.3.1841. It is not clear from the rehearsal book of H. C. J. Fredstrup exactly how many rehearsals were held of it in 1839.

Musical sources:

The orchestral score, the répétiteur's copy, and the set of parts employed for this divertissement version of excerpts from Act I of *The Isle of Phantasy* are now in DKKk (call nos. C II, 119, MA ms 2945, and KTB 206).

4.10.1839
A Pas de deux arranged after Taglioni (En Pas de deux arrangeret efter Taglioni) performed by G. Brodersen and A. Nielsen.

This dance is almost certainly identical with the *Pas de deux (by Taglioni)* to music by J. Mayseder, which was staged by Bournonville as a separate divertissement for P. C. Johansson and A. Nielsen at Stockholm's Royal Theatre (Operahuset) on 5.6.1839. That dance, in turn, was originally performed by L. Grahn and P. Larcher in Act II (score no. 1 A) of Bournonville's two-act romantic ballet *The Isle of Phantasy* (see 28.10.1838). The *Pas de deux* was performed twice by

Brodersen and Nielsen in 1839, the last time on 9.10.1839. It is not possible to identify the dance any further.

15.10.1839
Pas de deux composed by Mr. Ballet Master Bournonville (componeret af Hr. Balletmester Bournonville) performed by F. Hoppe and C. Fjeldsted.

This dance is almost certainly identical with the *Pas de deux* from Act II (score no. 15) of Bournonville's three-act romantic ballet *Faust* (see 25.4.1832). This is clear from the rehearsal book of H. C. J. Fredstrup, according to which that dance was rehearsed with Hoppe and Fjeldsted under Bournonville's direction on 14.10. and 15.10.1839. The *Pas de deux* was given twice in 1839, the last time on 17.10.1839. It is not possible to identify the dance any further.

21.10.1839
The Tyroleans (Tyrolerne).

This performance represents Bournonville's first restaging in Copenhagen of his one-act idyllic ballet *The Tyroleans* (see 6.3.1835). It was this year mounted with a partially new cast, and after 2.11.1839 it was performed with *The Styrian National Dance (den steiriske Nationaldands)* from D.-F.-E. Auber's three-act comic opera *Le Domino noir* (see 29.1.1839) as an incorporated (uncredited) finale. The 1839 version of *The Tyroleans* received 11 performances in Copenhagen, the last of which was given on 17.2.1842.

26.10.1839
Pas de deux composed by Mr. Ballet Master Bournonville (componeret af Hr. Balletmester Bournonville) performed by F. Hoppe and A. Nielsen.

This dance is probably identical with either the *Pas de deux* in *Nina, ou La Folle par amour* (see 30.9.1834), or the *Pas de deux* in *Faust* (see 25.4.1832 and 15.10.1839). According to the posters the dance was given twice during the 1839–40 season, the last time on 5.6.1840. It is not possible to identify the dance any further.

28.10.1839
The Festival in Albano (Festen i Albano).

This, Bournonville's first ballet in the Italian spheres, was created for a Royal red-letter day and set to music composed and arranged by J. F. Fröhlich. He incorporated several Italian and Roman folk tunes and dance rhythms in his score. Moreover, the ballet's choreographic centrepiece (an allegorical *Pas de deux*, score no. 9, performed by Bournonville as *Bacchus*, and A. Nielsen as *Venus*) was composed and arranged by I. P. E. Hartmann. According to a note in the orchestral score, for this dance he employed a theme, borrowed from a (not yet identified) composition of J. W. Kalliwoda. Furthermore, a second note in Hartmann's score for this *Pas de deux* (written on p. 81) seems to indicate that this music may originally have been composed for a projected divertissement in D.-F.-E. Auber's three-act comic opera *Fiorella* (see 13.2.1838), but which was never carried out. Finally, in the ballet's finale (score no. 12) Fröhlich incorporated the melody for a song, entitled «Hr. Oberst, en Skotte maa slaa for sit Land». It was originally part of C. E. F.

Weyse's score for A. Oehlenschläger's four-act singspiel *The Cavern of Ludlam (Ludlams Hule)*, premièred at Copenhagen's Royal Theatre on 30.1.1816.

In a letter to the Swedish count, J. G. Dela Gardie, dated 3.11.1839 (now in Lund's Universitetsbibliotek, sign.: Saml. DLG 382: b) Bournonville gave an interesting assessment of *The Festival in Albano* and the reason for its great success as he saw it:

'J'ai été assez heureuse pour captiver les suffrages de la Cour & du public, et j'ose dire que de tous mes ballets, c'est celui qui m'a donné le plus de Satisfaction [...] l'action n'est que très peu de chose, mais je me suis surtout reposé sur les détails, et je suis parvenu à entretenir les spectateurs pendant une heure; Les voyageurs y ont retrouvé l'image de leur chère Italie, et les sédentaires ont été animés du désir de voyager, j'ai été parfaitement secondé par la peinture et la musique'.

The ballet, which (according to the printed scenario) was inspired by a painting by A. Küchler, was restaged three times by Bournonville in Copenhagen in slightly different versions as follows:

(1) on 8.1.1844 (a staging that included a new sequence of four final *tableaux vivants* depicting some of B. Thorvaldsen's most famous sculptural works).
(2) on 14.1.1858 (this production included a completely new series of incorporated dances).
(3) on 1.1.1869 (this year the ballet was mounted in a thoroughly revised version that included several new or rechoreographed dances and tableaux).

On 2.6. and 9.6.1841 Bournonville's and Hartmann's *Pas de deux* (score no. 9) was replaced by a new (uncredited) *Pas de trois* (danced by P. Taglioni, A. Taglioni, and A. Nielsen). That dance, in turn, was replaced on 22.1.1842 by yet another dance, entitled *New Pas de deux* and choreographed by the French dancer, F. Lefèbvre, who performed it together with C. Fjeldsted. Five years later an uncredited solo dance (entitled *Solo (Incorporated) (Solo (indlagt))* and performed by C. Fjeldsted) was incorporated in *The Festival in Albano* (see 17.5.1847). This dance is almost certainly identical with the later (uncredited) solo dance that (according to the rehearsal book of H. C. J. Fredstrup) was rehearsed for Fjeldsted under Bournonville's personal direction on 4.10.1848 and performed by her as an incorporated divertissement in *The Festival in Albano* on 6.10.1848 with the new title *Pas de solo*.

In Vienna the ballet was mounted by Bournonville in a new, abridged divertissement version at the Kärnthnerthor Theatre on 15.7.1854. This production included two incorporated dances (a *Pas de quatre* and a *Tarantella*) performed to E. Helsted's and H. S. Paulli's music from Act III (score nos. 2 and 3) of Bournonville's three-act ballet *Napoli or The Fisherman and his Bride* (see 29.3.1842). The 1854 Vienna version was given five performances (the last taking place on 8.8.1854). However, on 6.2.1855 a second, slightly different version which included a new incorporated *Pas de deux* by the Italian dancer and choreographer, P. Borri, was mounted without Bournonville's knowledge and performed six times at the Kärnthnerthor Theatre (the last time on 23.3.1855).

In Sweden *The Festival in Albano* was mounted in revised versions at Stockholm's Royal Theatre (Operahuset) on 5.5. 1857, and on 19.2.1862 (Stora Theatern) reaching a total of 22 performances there.

The *Tarantella* in *The Festival in Albano* (originally performed as score no. '10' by the ballet's two protagonists, *Antonio* (F. Hoppe) and *Sylvia* (C. Fjeldsted)) was later also mounted as a separate divertissement at Christiania's Theatre (Oslo) on 10.8.1840 with the title *Tarantella Napolitana*. It was restaged there with W. Funck and C. Fjeldsted on 2.7.1847, but then as an uncredited dance entitled '*La Tarantella neapolitana*'. According to pencilled notes found in a separate set of parts for what is named 'Tarantella Napoletana' (now in DKKk, call no. KTB 1027), Funck and Fjeldsted also performed this dance twice at Flensborg's Theatre and Hamburg's Stadttheater as part of a privately arranged summer tour in Germany (*see* 12.5. and 2.7.1846).

The original 1839 version of *The Festival in Albano* received 29 performances (the last of which took place on 18.11. 1843), and the ballet reached a total of 105 performances during Bournonville's lifetime (the last of which was given on 12.11.1870). According to the rehearsal book of H. C. J. Fredstrup 32 rehearsals were held of *The Festival in Albano* between 13.9. and 28.10.1839.

Autograph sources:

Production note. Ms. Autograph. Black ink. 3 pp. (34,4 × 21 cm)
Festen i Albano./Idyllisk Ballet i en Act af August Bournonville.
Unsigned and undated [1839]
[DKKkt; F.M. (Ballet, læg F)

Musical sources:

Orchestral score. Ms. Autographs (by J. F. Fröhlich and I. P. E. Hartmann). Black and brown ink. 1 vol. 156 pp. of which two are blank (26 × 36,8 cm with minor variants)
282./Festen i Albano./Partitur/[...]/Festen i Albano./idyllisk Ballet i 1 Act af A. Bournonville./Musikken af J. F. Fröhlich
Signed and dated (on p. 118): '21/4 39. I:P:E:Hartmann' and (on p. 156): '11.te Oct. 1839.'
[DKKk; C II, 107 (KTB 282)

Orchestral score (*Pas de deux*, score no. 9). Ms. Copy. Brown ink. 30 pp. (27 × 38 cm)
[Without title]
Unsigned and undated [c.1839]
[DKKk; MA ms 2601 (KTB 282)
This orchestral score for the *Pas de deux* in *The Festival in Albano* (score no. 9) seems to date from a separate performance of it during the late 1830s or early 40s.

Répétiteur's copy. Ms. Copy. Black and brown ink. 1 vol. 76 pp. (32,2 × 25,2 cm)
B. 282/Festen i Albano./(2.den Udgave)/1839./1869./[...]/Festen i Albano./Idyllisk Ballet i 1 Act af,/A: Bournonville/Musikken af J: F: Fröhlich./Repetiteurparti
Unsigned and dated (on the front cover): '1839./1869.'
[DKKk; MA ms 2979 (KTB 282(1))
This répétiteur's copy dates from the 1839 première of *The Festival in Albano*, but was used for all later restagings of this ballet during Bournonville's lifetime. It contains four revised musical insertions (score nos. 8–10 and 11) that were added to the volume at later stages. Of these score no. 11 dates from Bournonville's third and final choreographic revision of the ballet on 1.1.1869, scores nos. 8–10 derive from E. Hansen restaging of it on 1.6.1882.

Moreover, score no. 2 contains Bournonville's autographed notes (written with brown ink) which seem to date from his second re-staging of the ballet on 14.1.1858. They describe (in general terms) the mimic action. Other pencilled choreographic notes (written by an unknown hand and almost certainly dating from 1839) describe the original series of *tableaux vivants* in score no. 12, which showed five of B. Thorvalden's most popular sculptural works. Finally, in score nos. 1–7 and 11–12 Bournonville's autographed choreographic numbers (written with black ink) are inserted. They clearly refer to his similar numbers in the complete notation of the ballet that he wrote in December 1868 in preparation for the 1869 re-staging.

Parts. Ms. Copy. 32 vol.
4 vl I, 3 vl II, 2 vla, 3 vlc e cb, fl picc, fl I e II, ob 1/2, cl 1/2, fag 1/2, cor 1/2, tr 1/2, trb 1/2/3, timp, gr cassa, tamb, tri, glock.
Unsigned and undated [1839]
[DKKk; KTB 282
These parts were used for all performances of *The Festival in Albano* during Bournonville's lifetime.

Other sources:

Sketch by C. F. Christensen for the décor. Pencil and water colours (27,8 × 42 cm)
[Untitled]
Signed (on the reverse with black ink): 'C. F. Christensen', undated [1839]
[DKKt; C. F. Christensens dekorationsudkast

Printed sources:

Printed scenario. 1 vol. 8 pp. (20 × 12,2 cm)
Festen i Albano./Idyllisk Ballet i een Act/af/August Bournonville,/ Musiken af Fr. Frölich. [*sic*]/Opført første Gang i Anledning af/ Hendes Majestæt Dronningens/höie Fødselsdag,/den 28de Octo-ber 1839./[…]/Decorationen er malet af H. Christensen.
Kjøbenhavn, Biano Lunos Bogtrykkeri [1839].
[DKKk; 17, – 173 8°

8.11.1839
Pas de deux composed by Mr. Ballet Master Bournonville (componeret af Hr. Balletmester Bournonville) **performed by F. Hoppe and C. Fjeldsted.**
According to the rehearsal book of H. C. J. Fredstrup, this dance is identical with the *Pas de deux* which Bournonville had incorporated between score nos. 27 and 28 of his one-act idyllic ballet *The Veteran or The Hospitable House* (*see* 29.1.1833) and, in turn, is identical with the even earlier 'Pas de deux oriental' (first performed by Bournonville and A. Kraetzmer as an incorporated divertissement in P. Funck's *A Divertissement in Oriental Style* on 26.9.1829). The 1839 *Pas de deux* was performed once by Hoppe and Fjeldsted during this season.

10.11.1839
Scene, Pas de deux, and Gallopade from the ballet 'The Isle of Phantasy' (Scene, Pas de deux og Galopade af Balletten 'Phantasiens Øe') **performed by F. Hoppe and C. Fjeldsted.**
This divertissement is based on excerpts from Act II (score no. 7) of Bournonville's two-act romantic ballet *The Isle of Phantasy* (*see* 28.10.1838). It was first performed as a separate divertissement by Hoppe and Fjeldsted at Stockholm's Royal Theatre (Operahuset) on 2.6.1839. In Copenhagen it was given 5 times by Hoppe and Fjeldsted, the last time on 17.5.

1841. A second, slightly abridged version of this divertissement was mounted by Bournonville for Hoppe and Fjeldsted on 1.12.1841. That version, which was performed by different casts at Copenhagen's Royal Theatre until 2.1.1866, reached a total of 44 performances.

24.11.1839
El Jaleo de Xerxes [sic] **(uncredited) performed by F. Hoppe and C. Fjeldsted as an incorporated divertissement in Act I of** *La Muette de Portici (Den Stumme i Portici).*
This (uncredited) dance is identical with the earlier *El Jaleo de Xeres (Spanish National Dance) (Spansk Nationaldans)* first performed by Hoppe and Fjeldsted at Stockholm's Royal Theatre (Operahuset) on 12.6.1839 (*see also* 29.11.1838). It was restaged five more times in Copenhagen as follows:

(1) on 10.6.1840 (as an uncredited divertissement, performed by Hoppe and Fjeldsted).
(2) on 12.6.1840 (as an uncredited divertissement, performed by the Spanish dancers, M. Camprubì and D. Serral).
(3) on 17.6.1840 (on this day presented on the poster with the title *New Jaleo de Xeres 'Le Domino noir', Music by Auber (Nye Jaleo de Xeres 'Den sorte Domino', Musik af Auber)* and performed by Camprubì and Serral).
(4) on 10.5.1841 and 17.9.1841 (as an uncredited divertissement, performed by Hoppe and P. Funck).

Moreover, on 27.11.1840 it was renamed *Jaleo de Xeres* and incorporated as a divertissement in Act I (score no. 6) of Bournonville's and E. Helsted's two-act idyllic ballet *The Tore-ador (Toréadoren).* In that ballet it was performed by Bournon-ville (as *Alonzo*) and C. Fjeldsted (as *Maria*). During the following seasons the *Jaleo de Xeres from the ballet The Toreador* was mounted as a separate divertissement on several occasions and with different titles. The first of these took place on 9.1.1842.

It is not clear from the rehearsal book of H. C. J. Fredstrup exactly how many rehearsals were given for the dance in 1839.

Musical sources:

No separate musical material for *El Jaleo de Xerxes* have yet been traced in Copenhagen. However, the complete music for it is in-cluded in the orchestral score, the two répétiteur's copies, and the set of parts for Bournonville's and E. Helsted's *The Toreador* (now in DKKk, call nos. C II, 114 k, MA ms 2665, MA ms 2965, and KTB 1046 (originally KTB 269)).

1840

28.2.1840
Pas de deux **(uncredited) performed by F. Hoppe and C. Fjeldsted.**
According to the rehearsal book of H. C. J. Fredstrup this dance is identical with the *Pas de deux* (score no. 5) from Bournonville's divertissement *Hertha's Offering* (*see* 29.1. 1838), since that dance was rehearsed under Bournonville's personal direction with Hoppe and Fjeldsted on the same day. The *Pas de deux* was given only once this year.

20.3.1840

The Fatherland's Muses (Fædrelandets Muser).

In a letter to the Swedish count, J. G. Dela Gardie, dated 28.5.1840 (now in Lund's Universitetsbibliotek, sign.: Saml. DLG 382: b) Bournonville gave an interesting account about the idea for and the creation of this allegorical one-act pantomimic prologue:

'Je ne sais pas si je Vous ai déjà parlé de mon dernier ballet <u>Les Muses de la patrie</u> (l'Idée d'après l'inscription sur le fronton de Votre belle salle de Spectacle), ce ballet fut donné à l'occasion du Demi-Deuil et de l'arrive au théatre de notre nouveau Roi, il reussit complètement, mais ne peut survivre à la circonstance; cependant j'en ai conservé quelques fragmens, que V. Exc: verra peut-être à Copenhague'.

The inscription on the façade of Stockholm's Royal Theatre, to which Bournonville here refers, reads 'Gustavus III Patriis Musis'. In Bournonville's ballet this inscription clearly served as a similar allusion to Denmark's newly crowned King Christian VIII, who was a great protector of the arts. Consequently, it seems that it was Bournonville's main intention with this work to pay a special tribute to the absolute monarch as protector of the arts on the occasion of his first appearance in the Royal Theatre after his crowning the same year.

The Fatherland's Muses, which in parts also seems to be based on Bournonville's much earlier projected mimic prologue, *The Feast of the Muses* (*see* 1.11.1823), was set to a score composed and arranged by N. W. Gade (the overture and score nos. 1–4 and 7), and J. F. Fröhlich (score nos. 5–6 and 8–9). The ballet's series of eight *tableaux vivants* (score no. 7) illustrated highlights from the Royal Theatre's repertory of operas, plays, and ballets with each tableau being introduced by one of the muses. For these tableaux Gade borrowed music from several works in the current repertory of the Royal Theatre, including F. Kuhlau's music to J. L. Heiberg's five-act play *The Elves' Hill* (*Elverhøi*) premièred at Copenhagen's Royal Theatre on 6.11.1828, and excerpts from J. A. P. Schultz's and Th. Thaarup's one-act singspiel *The Harvest Festival* (*Høstgildet*) premièred on 16.9.1790.

Moreover, in his music for the final tableau (which depicted Denmark's King Waldemar II) Gade incorporated P. E. Rasmussen's melody from 1811 to Lavrids Kock's 1683 song «Danmark deiligst Vang og Vænge» (first published as *Visen om Tyre Danebod* by W. H. F. Abrahamson, R. Nyerup, and K. L. Rahbek in 1812 and 1814 in *Udvalgte Danske Viser fra Middelalderen*, vol. 2, pp. 3–7, and vol. 5, p. LXXIV, no. 56). This song had been used earlier by J. F. Fröhlich in his score for Bournonville's four-act romantic ballet *Waldemar* (*see* 28.10.1835).

Parts of J. F. Fröhlich's music for the divertissement's first *Pas de deux* (score no. 5, performed by F. Hoppe as *Zephyr* and A. Nielsen as *Aglaë*) were later also incorporated by E. Helsted in his score for Bournonville's one-act ballet *Old Memories, or A Magic Lantern* (*see* 18.12.1848) in which they were employed for the finale (score no. 12). Moreover, a later so-called *Dance Divertissement (Divertissement af Dands)* was based on musical excerpts borrowed from *The Fatherland's Muses* and mounted in Copenhagen by Bournonville on 6.10.1840. Furthermore, the ballet's *Pas de deux* (score no. 5) was performed as a separate divertissement in Copen-

hagen by Bournonville and C. Fjeldsted on 3.11.1840. Finally, according to notes found in a separate set of parts for this dance (now in DKKk, call no. KTB 236), Fröhlich's music for the *Pas de deux* seems also to have been performed as an incorporated divertissement in Bournonville's three-act romantic ballet *Faust* (*see* 25.4.1832) at some later (not yet identified) performances during the 1840s.

The Fatherland's Muses received 6 performances in Copenhagen, the last of which was given on 3.6.1840. According to the rehearsal book of H. C. J. Fredstrup 26 rehearsals were held of it between 24.2. and 20.3.1840.

Autograph sources:

Production note. Ms. Autograph. Brown ink. 1 p. (34,5 × 21 cm)
<u>Reqvisiter til Fædrelandets Muser.</u>
Unsigned and undated [1840]
[DKKkt; F.M. (Ballet, læg F)

Musical sources:

Orchestral score. Ms. Autographs (by N. W. Gade and J. F. Fröhlich). Black ink. 1 vol. 180 pp. (27,3 × 38 cm)
Partituret/199/til/Fædrenelandets Muser
Signed and dated (on p. 180): '<u>JFFröhlich</u>/1840.'
[DKKk; C II, 107 (KTB 199)

Répétiteur's copy. Ms. Autograph (by N. W. Gade) and copy. Brown ink. 1 vol. 66 pp. (32,4 × 25 cm)
B. 199/Repetiteur Parti/til/Balletten/Fædrenelandets Muser/ 1840./301/[...]/Musikken af Fröhlich og Gade./1840./Repetitör-partie. til/Fædrenelandets Muser.
Unsigned and dated (on the front cover and on p. 1): '1840.'
[DKKk; MA ms 2939 (KTB 199)
This répétiteur's copy is partially Gade's autograph (score nos. 1–4). It contains Bournonville's pencilled autographed notes, which describe (in general terms) the mime and the choreography in score nos. 1–5, and 8–9. His other autographed notes, written (with brown ink) underneath the music for the *Pas de deux* (score no. 5), describe the new choreography created for A. Nielsen, C. Fjeldsted, and P. Funck in 1848, when parts of Fröhlich's music for this dance were incorporated by E. Helsted in his score for the *Finale* (score no. 12) of Bournonville's one-act ballet *Old Memories, or A Magic Lantern* (*see* 18.12.1848).

Parts. Ms. Copy. 31 vol.
3 vl I, 3 vl II, 2 vla, 3 vlc e cb, fl 1/2, ob 1/2, cl 1/2, fag 1/2, cor 1/2/ 3/4, clno 1/2, trb 1/2/3, timp, gr cassa, tri.
Unsigned and undated [1840]
[DKKk; KTB 1006 (originally KTB 199)

Printed sources:

Printed scenario. 1 vol. 8 pp. (19,7 × 12,2 cm)
Fædrelandets Muser./Pantomimisk Forspil i een Act/af/August Bournonville./Musiken componeret og arrangeret af /DHrr. Fröh-lich og Gade./Decorationerne af DHrr. Wallich og Christensen./ Opført første Gang i Anledning af Deres Majestæters/Kong Chris-tian den Ottendes/og/Dronning Caroline Amalias/Allerhøieste Nærværelse i Skuespilhuset, den 20de Marts 1840.
Kjøbenhavn, Bianco Lunos Bogtrykkeri [1840]
[DKKk; 17, – 173 8°

Printed scenario. 1 vol. 4 pp. (20 × 12,4 cm)
Les Muses de la Patrie./Ballet allégorique en un Acte/par/Auguste Bournonville./Premier Danseur et Maître des Ballet de S. M. le Roi de Danemarck./Musique de M. M. FRÖHLICH et GADE./Repré-senté pour la première fois sur le théâtre Royal de/Copenhague, à

l'occasion de l'arrivée au spectacle de/LL. MM. le roi Christian VIII et la reine/Caroline Amélie/le 20 Mars.
Kopenhague, Bianco Luno, 1840.
[DKKk; 17, – 173 8°

23.4.1840
Mother's Birthday (Moders Födselsdag).
This one-act ballet for children was created for and performed by Bournonville's four daughters, Augusta, Charlotte, Wilhelmine, and Mathilde, and two of his male pupils at the Royal Theatre's ballet school, A. Fredstrup and W. Nehm (who played two angels). It was created as a surprise present to his wife, Helene Bournonville, for her thirty-first birthday on 22.4.1840. The ballet was mounted and performed at Bournonville's private Copenhagen residence in Dronningens Tværgade No. 181. The autographed manuscript scenario gives no indications about the music that accompanied this work.

Autograph sources:

Manuscript scenario. Ms. Autograph. Brown ink. 3 pp. (20,8 × 17,3 cm)
Moders Födselsdag./Ballet i Een Act.
Unsigned and dated: 'Udfört i Dronningens tvergade No. 181. den 23 April/1840.-'
[DKKk; NKS 3285 4° 3 L–P

27.4.1840
Pas de deux (uncredited) performed by F. Hoppe and A. Nielsen.
This (uncredited) dance was performed three times in 1840, the last time on 4.5.1840 (on this day danced by Bournonville and Nielsen). It is not possible to identify the dance any further.

May 1840
A projected series of performances of individual pas and dances at Stockholm's Royal Theatre.
According to a letter from Bournonville to the Swedish count, J. G. Dela Gardie, dated 19.11.1839 (now in Lund's Universitetsbibliotek, sign.: Saml. DLG 382: b) this series of guest performances at Stockholm's Royal Theatre was planned for the month of May 1840. However, the project was never carried out because of some outspoken opposition from the financial director of that theatre, A. Backman, who (according to Bournonville's letter to Dela Gardie) declared rather bluntly about the project:

'Quel besoin avons nous des ballets de Mr. Bournonville'.

Moreover, in a second letter to Dela Gardie (dated 16.2. 1840) Bournonville described in further detail the excerpts of those ballets which he originally intended to mount in Stockholm this year:

'mes projets etaient déjà arretés, je comptais Vous régaler de la Sylphide, des Offrandes d'Hertha, des fêtes d'Albano qui auraient pu être montés à très peu de frais, mais quel que sois le désir que j'aurais de me produire de nouveau sur le théâtre royal de Stockholm, je trouve dans l'opposition de Mr Backmann une raison assez forte pour y renoncer entièrement'.

May 1840
A series of three performances with a (not yet identified) repertory of individual pas and dances (Malmö's Theatre, Sweden).
According to a letter from Bournonville to J. G. Dela Gardie in Stockholm, dated 28.5.1840 (now in Lund's Universitetsbibliotek, sign.: Saml. DLG 382: b) Bournonville gave a series of three guest performances with a (not yet identified) repertory at Malmö's Theatre during the first weeks of May 1840. The dances performed on this tour were most probably the same as those given later the same year during the summer tour to Christiania's Theatre (Oslo) between 29.7. and 12.8.1840.

13.5.1840
A Gallery of ten Danish Kings of the House of Oldenburg, depicted in tableaux vivants, arranged by Mr. Ballet-master Bournonville (Gallerie af 10 danske Konger af den oldenborgske Stamme, fremstillede i levevende Tableauer, arrangerede af Hr. Balletmester Bournonville).
This series of ten *tableaux vivants* was created for a special charity performance given for the actor, A. Stage. They were arranged in six main groups and depicted (in chronological order) ten Danish monarchs from the House of Oldenburg. On the poster these tableaux are described as follows:

1) Christian den Förste, heel Figur;
   Johannes, Christian den Anden
   Frederik den Förste, Christian den Tredie } Brystbilleder
2) Frederik den Anden bygger Frederiksborg;
3) Christian den Fjerde; saaret i Söslaget ved Fehmern;
4) Frederik den Tredie sværger at forsvare sit Folk eller döe i sin Rede;
5) Christian den Femte ved Wismars Beleiring;
6) Frederik den Fjerde skjænker Peter Wessel sit Brystbillede og Navnet Tordenskjold.

In a letter to the Swedish count, J. G. Dela Gardie, dated 28.5.1840 (now in Lund's Universitetsbibliotek, sign.: Saml. DLG 382: b) Bournonville gave a brief, but interesting account of the performance of these tableaux:

'Aussitôt mon retour à Copenhague j'arrangeai pour la recette de Mr Stage (acteur) une gallerie vivante des dix premiers Roi de la race d'Oldenbourg, Christian IV à la bataille de Fehmern, et Frederik IV ennoblissant Tordenskjold obtiennent le plus de succès, du reste tous les rois furent d'une ressemblance parfaite'.

No choreographic or musical sources for this work have yet been traced. The tableaux were performed only once. It is not clear from the rehearsal book of H. C. J. Fredstrup exactly how many rehearsals were held of this work in 1840.

18.5.1840
Pas de trois (uncredited) composed by Bournonville and performed by F. Hoppe, C. Fjeldsted, and A. Nielsen.
This (uncredited) dance is almost certainly identical with the *Pas de trois* first incorporated by Bournonville in A. Adam's three-act comic opera *Le Postillon du Lonjumeau* (see 28.10.1837). This is clear from the rehearsal book of H. C. J. Fredstrup, according to which that dance was rehearsed prior to the second performance of this (uncredited) *Pas de*

trois on 21.5.1840. It is not possible to identify the dance any further.

22.5.1840
Quadrille de fête (Fest Quadrille) for the silver wedding anniversary of Denmark's King Christian VIII and Queen Caroline Amalie (Christiansborg's Palace).

In a letter to the Swedish count, J. G. Dela Gardie, dated 28.5.1840 (now in Lund's Universitetsbibliotek, sign.: Saml. DLG 382: b) Bournonville gave a detailed account about this *Quadrille de fête*, which was choreographed for the silver wedding anniversary of Denmark's royal couple. It reads as follows:

'Les fêtes du marriage d'argent ont été charmantes […] le soir à 8 heures grand Bal-paré au château de Christiansbourg, près de 2000 Personnes étaient invitées, la grande salle des Chevaliers, chef d'oeuvres d'architecture élégante fut inaugurée de la manière la plus pompeuse, plus de mille bougies y répaudaient des flots de lumière, un orchestre de 60 Musiciens exécutait des morceaux charmans, les pièces attenantes des deux côtés donnaient de la place à la foule nombreuse et un second Bal avait lieu dans la grande salle d'appartement avec un orchestre de 50 Musiciens. Le Bal fut ouvert par leurs Majéstés dans une Polonaise oû la Reine honnora de sa main plusieurs gens distingués entre autres [B.] Thorvaldsen, & le vieil architecte du château le conseiller [C. F.] Hansen (85 ans); quand tout le monde etait placé, LL: MM: sur une espèce de trône, nous donnâmes un Quadrille de fête, de ma composition, exécuté par 16 paires, 4 hussards, 4 gardes, 4 régiment de la couronne et 4 gentilhommes de la chambre; parmi les dames plusieurs beautés du premier ordre. Le Quadrille consistait en salut de Menuet, Française, Valse et Final, le tout durait à peu près 20 Minutes, et finissait par des couronnes de Myrthes dont les Dames faisaient hommage au couple royal. […] Tout contribua à rendre cette fête des plus brillante, et plusieurs Etrangers ont avoué qu'on aurait de la peine à trouver un Bal plus magnifique, mieux arrangé et mieux réussi […] Ce bal a fait grand plaisir, on en parle encore & je crois qu'il donnera une bonne portion de bon sang au public'.

The *Quadrille* was performed to music composed by H. C. Lumbye and entitled 'Fest Quadrille', and represents the first time Bournonville collaborated with this composer.

No orchestral score and parts for Lumbye's music have yet been traced. However, a printed piano score of it was published in Copenhagen in 1840 by C. C. Lose and Olsen (a copy is now in DKKk, call no. D 24, × 390204179). According to this edition the *Quadrille de fête* consisted of four dances as follows:

(1) A *Tempo di minuetto* introduction.
(2) A *Française*.
(3) A *Waltz* introduction.
(4) A set of four *Quadrilles* in 3/4 time.

30.5.1840
A projected Intermezzo for *The Healing Spring (Kildereisen)*.

According to a letter to the theatre management of Copenhagen's Royal Theatre, dated 30.5.1840 (now in The State Archive, call no. Det kgl. Teaters Arkiv, Gruppe E, pakke 288) Bournonville was in the spring of 1840 working on a new projected divertissement, which he planned to interpolate as an intermezzo in L. Holberg's three-act comedy from 1750 *The Healing Spring*. In this letter Bournonville reveals a fine instinct for what he thought would work on stage. Moreover, it seems that with this intermezzo he was already conceiving (even if unconsciously) several scenes for his later three-act romantic ballet *Kirsten Piil, or Two Midsummer Festivals* (*see* 26.2.1845):

'La pièce de Kildereisen même du tems de Holberg a dû son succès à l'Intermède, dans lequel était intercallé toutes les folies du jour, et même plusieurs morceaux de ballet. Le tout donnait un tableau sinon digne du théâtre royal, du moins très varié et très vivant; je l'ai vu dans mon enfance, et je me suis beaucoup amusé; mais Vous me permettrez d'observer que le gout a tellement changé, qu'on ne saurait sans danger laisser l'Intermède comme il était; on ne peut réprésenter les folies modernes, et celles du bon vieux temps, ne peuvent être goutées par notre public. On trouvera insipide ce ballet silencieux au milieu d'une pièce enjouée, et l'anachronisme des chants modernes ne sera pas moins senti que l'ennui des melodies du siècle passé; de plus les danses caractéristiques sont usées et demandent à être bien autrement adaptées au sujet; les Pierots et Polichinels qui jadis faisaient les délices, font pitié aujourdhui; par la raison toute simple que les opéras et ballets ont fourni tant de fêtes champêtres, celle de Kildereisen ne peut plus avoir le même attrait et le public sera très étonné de ne pas s'y amuser comme autrefois. – J'en ai déjà fait la remarque il-y-a plusieurs années, aux personnes qui ont desiré remettre cette pièce en scène, il reussirait peut-être à un Bénéficiaire d'éblouir son public par une affiche attrayante, mais la dignité du théâtre, et ma réputation d'Artiste en suffriraient trop. – Ne croyez pourtant pas Mr.: le Chambellan! que je me sois borné à ces réflexions négatives; encouragé par la manière aimable avec laquelle Vous m'avez représenté la chose je me suis mis en devoir de trouver une situation nouvelle et piquante:

Je me suis figuré une pelouse de verdure, près la fontaine de Kirsten Piil au bas de la colline sur laquelle le camp forain est dressé; j'y ai placé des groupes de peuple mangeant sur l'herbe, fumant, dansant folâtrant, enfin un vrai tableau de Teniers. Un carrousel oû de bons bourgeois en perruques courent la bague, des trétaux de Charlatans, des animaux savans, des diseuses de bonne-aventures, des jeux innocenns, des ménétriers, des ivrognes, une voiture surchargée de voyageurs, et à la fin à l'approche de la nuit de la St Jean, un pélérinage à la fontaine; Les veilles femmes et vieillards décréprits jétent leurs hailons, et se transforment en jeunes gens de la ville, qui le verre en mains, au milieu des chants d'allégresse exécutent une bachanale générale. – Le tout assaisonné de couplets, de dialogues, de choeurs et Brouhaha. -

Maintenant daignes Vous figurer la quantité de répétitions qu'un tel spectacle demanderait, les dépenses en decoration et ustensiles, les efforts de verve et de gaité chez les acteurs (pour la plupart improvisans) et après tout, la perte d'un tableau dont j'aurais pu enricher un de mes ballets futurs, et permettez moi d'émettre mon opinion individuelle: Que le resultat ne répondra pas à nos efforts, qu'on ne rira pas, que le souvenir de l'ancien intermède prévaudra, qu'on ne donnera la pièce qu'une seule fois, et que si les Critiques y voient assez clair pour s'appercevoir que le Comique n'est pas tout à fait mon genre, ils prendront à mal les élans de ma gaité forcée, et la méfiance et le découragement qui dans les derniers tems s'est emparé de ma Muse, s'aceroitra par une chute, qui pourrait anéantir l'avenir de les productions chorégraphiques'.

Almost 20 years had to pass before Bournonville's projected intermezzo in Holberg's comedy was carried out in Copenhagen. This happened on 22.5.1859 when his so-called *A new Divertissement as intermezzo in The Healing Spring (Intermedium i Kildereisen)* was premièred at the Royal Theatre.

Autograph sources:

Manuscript synopsis (included in a letter to J. G. Levetzau). Ms. Autograph. Brown ink. 4 pp. (25 × 21,2 cm)
[…] La pièce de Kildereisen même du tems [*sic*] de Holberg a dû son/succès à l'Intermède, dans lequel etait intercallé [*sic*] toutes les folies/du jour, et même plusieurs morceaux de ballet. […]

Signed and dated: 'Auguste Bournonville/Copenhague ce 30 Mai 1840. -'
[Copenhagen, The State Archive (Rigsarkivet); Det kgl. Teaters Arkiv, Gruppe E, pakke 288

1.7.1840
The Seven Sleepers' Day (Syvsoverdag).

According to a letter from J. L. Heiberg to I. P. E. Hartmann written on 13.6.1840 (now in DKKk, call no. NKS 3392 4°) Bournonville was responsible for choreographing and mounting the dances in this romantic three-act comedy. Thus, in his letter Heiberg described Bournonville's involvement in the staging as follows:

'Hermed følger nu N° 10, 11, 12. Hvad <u>Dandsen</u> i N° 10 angaaer, da ønsker jeg, at den maa blive rask, cirklende, hvirvlende, livlig phantastisk, ikke – hvad Balletmester Bournonville synes at have Mod paa – grandiøs, udtrykkende en <u>høitidelig</u> Besværelse. Han vil udentvivl endnu idag henvende sig til Dem, for at gjøre Aftale om Dandsemusiken; jeg maa da bede Dem ei at give efter for hans maaskee min Plan modstridende Fordringer. Tillige anseer jeg det for nødvendigt, at den hele Dands ikke varer længe, omtrent 5 Minuter'.

The dances were performed in Act III, scene 4 (score no. 10) and consisted of an ensemble dance (*Allegro* in 2/4 time, playing for 267 meas.). According to the poster this scene was performed by a corps de ballet of sylphs, elves, nymphs, and gnomes dancing while holding white, green, blue, and red lanterns in their hands. In Heiberg's 1840 libretto the same scene is described as follows:

'(Sylferne komme fra Luften, Alferne fra Skoven, Undinerne fra Søen, Gnomerne fra Jorden. Alle have matlysende Lamper i Haanden: Sylfernes Lamper have et hvidt Skjær, Alfernes et grønt, Undinernes et blaat, Gnomernes et rødt.) […] Dands'.

Bournonville did not include *The Seven Sleepers' Day* in his two handwritten lists of his stagings of operas and plays (written c.1851 and 1871, *see* Additional Sources), nor in the printed list of his works in his memoirs *My Theatre Life* (p. 408).
   The Seven Sleepers' Day was restaged in a thoroughly revised version 27.9.1872. That year the Act III dances were staged by L. Gade in heavily abridged versions, and played for only 74 bars. Of this staging Bournonville noted in his diary:

22.9.1872: 'seet lidt af Prøven paa Syvsoverdagen'
26.9.: 'seet Generalprøven paa <u>Syvsoverdagen</u>'
27.9.: 'I Theatret <u>Syvsoverdag</u> paanÿ indstuderet efter 32 Aars Hvile, blev optaget med samme anerkjendende Kulde som Dengang. Det er et smukt Digt, men intet Theaterstykke. Huset var udsolgt.'

The original 1840 production was given 5 times (the last time on 9.11.1840) and the *Seven Sleepers' Day* reached a total of 22 performances during Bournonville's lifetime, the last of which was given on 21.5.1874. It is not clear from the rehearsal book of H. C. J. Fredstrup exactly how many rehearsals were held of this comedy and its dances in 1840.

Musical sources:

Orchestral score. Ms. Autograph (by I. P. E. Hartmann). Black ink and pencil. 1 vol. 218 pp. of which six are blank (26,8 × 37,6 cm)
Syvsoverdag./B 19/Partitur
Signed and dated (on p. 18): '13/8 72', (p. 217) 'I:P:E Hartmann/op 30./d: 26/6 40.'

[DKKk; C II, 114 (KTA 366)
This autographed orchestral score was used for all performances of *The Seven Sleepers' Day* during Bournonville's lifetime. It contains several later music insertions and pencilled autographed notes by Hartmann, which he made in connection with the later, revised staging of Heiberg's comedy on 27.9.1872. The music for the dances in Act III is included on pp. 163–178.

Orchestral score (*Ouverture*). Ms. Copy. Brown ink. 32 pp. of which one is blank (34,8 × 26,2 cm)
Ouverture til Syvsoverdag.
Signed and dated (by Hartmann with red ink on the cover): 'Første Ouverture/til/Sÿvsoverdag /componeret og instrumenteret paa det Kgl. Theaters Sÿngeskole/Natten 30 Juni – 1 Juli 1840'
[DKKk; I. P. E. Hartmanns samling
This manuscript copy of Hartmann's 1840 ouverture to *The Seven Sleepers' Day* was most probably made for a publishing purpose during the 1850s.

No répétiteur's copy dating from the 1840 première of *The Seven Sleepers' Day* has yet been traced. However, two later répétiteur's copies dating from the 1872 restaging of Heiberg's comedy are now in DKKk (call nos. MA ms 2915 (5–6) (KTA 366 (1–2)).

Parts. Ms. Copy. 34 + 10 vol.
4 vl I, 4 vl II, 2 vla, 4 vlc e cb, fl 1/2, ob 1/2, cl 1/2, fag 1/2, cor 1/2/3/4, tr 1/2, trb 1/2/3, tuba, timp, piatti e tri. On stage: vl I, vl II, vla, vlc e cb, cor 1/2/3/4, tuba, org.
Unsigned and undated [1840]
[DKKk; KTA 366
Another set of parts (49 vol.) which dates from the revised 1872 staging of *The Seven Sleepers' Day* is now in DKKk (call no. KTA 366 a).

6.7.1840
Pas de deux (after Taglioni) (Pas de deux (efter Taglioni)) performed by F. Hoppe and L. Grahn.

This dance is almost certainly identical with *A Pas de deux arranged after Taglioni (En Pas de deux arrangeret efter Taglioni)* which was first performed at Copenhagen's Royal Theatre by G. Brodersen and A. Nielsen on 4.10.1839. That dance, in turn, is probably identical with the *Pas de deux (by Taglioni) (Pas de deux (Af Taglioni))*, originally mounted by Bournonville for P. C. Johansson and A. Nielsen at Stockholm's Royal Theatre (Operahuset) on 5.6.1839. The *Pas de deux* was performed once by Brodersen and Nielsen in 1840.

6.7.1840
El Bolero (arranged for four persons) (El Bolero (arrangeret for 4 Personer)) performed by Bournonville, M. Cambrubì, C. Fjeldsted, and D. Serral.

This Spanish dance was later incorporated in Act II (score no. 11) of Bournonville's two-act idyllic ballet *The Toreador* (*see* 27.11.1840). On 7.6.1865 it was mounted as a separate divertissement with H. Scharff, W. Price, J. Price, and S. Price at Christiania's Theatre (Oslo) and was then performed with the title '*Bolero*' (*spansk Nationaldands*) (*Spanish National Dance*).

29.7.1840
The Styrian National Dance (Den Steierske Nationaldands) (uncredited) performed by Bournonville and C. Fjeldsted (Christiania's Theatre, Oslo).

This (uncredited) dance is almost certainly identical with Bournonville's *Styrian Dance*, first performed at Copenhagen's Royal Theatre as an incorporated divertissement in D.

F. E. Auber's three-act comic opera *Le Domino noir* (*see* 29.1. 1839). It is not possible to identify the dance any further.

31.7.1840

La Sylphide, Romantic Ballet in 3 Parts, arranged by Ballet Master Bournonville (Sylphiden, romantisk Ballet i 3 Afdelinger, arrangeret af Hr. Balletmester Bournonville) (**Christiania's Theatre, Oslo**).

This production is an abridged divertissement version in three parts of Bournonville's two-act ballet *La Sylphide* (*see* 28.11.1836). It was arranged especially for the 1840 summer tour to Norway and included a cast consisting of *The Sylph* (C. Fjeldsted), *James* (Bournonville), *Madge* (played by the Danish actor N. P. Nielsen), and an unnamed corps de ballet of sylphs (seemingly played by a group of actresses from Christiania's Theatre). Moreover, according to the répétiteur's copy the production included most of the music from Act I (score no. 1), and Act II (score nos. 7 and 8) of the original 1836 version. Furthermore, in the second part of this version of *La Sylphide* Bournonville included F.-M.-A. Venua's music for the *Pas de deux* which had originally been performed by himself and A. Krætzmer as an incorporated divertissement in J. L. Heiberg's three-act play *Princess Isabella, or Three Nights at the Court* (*see* 29.10.1829).

The 1840 Norwegian production of *La Sylphide* was given once in Christiania.

Musical sources:

Apart from the incorporated *Pas de deux* to music by F.-M.-A. Venua, no separate orchestral score and set of parts for Bournonville's 1840 Christiania version of *La Sylphide* have yet been traced. This seems to indicate that this version was performed using the 1840 répétiteur's copy (*see below*), which seemingly also served as a conductor's part. This assumption is also supported by the numerous pencilled notes found in it, which indicate the exact instrumentation of the 1840 divertissement version of *La Sylphide*.

Répétiteur's copy/Conductor's part. Ms. Copy. Black ink. 1 vol. 40. pp. (33,5 × 25,7 cm with minor variants)
B 1028/Sylphiden./Ballet/Repititeur Parti/Sylphiden No. 1.
Unsigned and undated [c.1840]
[DKKk; MA ms 3024 (KTB 1028 (2) (originally without number))

Parts (*Pas de deux*). Ms. Copy. 27 vol.
3 vl I, 3 vl II, 2 vla, 3 vlc e cb, fl 1/2, ob II, cl 1/2, fag 1/2, cor 1/2, clno 1/2, Ttrb, Btrb, timp, gr cassa, tri.
Unsigned and undated [c.1838]
[DKKk; KTB 1052 (1) (originally without number)
This set of parts contains the music for F.-M.-A. Venua's *Pas de deux* in J. L. Heiberg's three-act play *Princess Isabella, or Three Nights at the Court* (*see* 29.10.1829). A pencilled note in the part for the first violin reads 'til Waldemar'. This clearly indicates that the parts must date from the incorporation of this dance in Act I of Bournonville's four-act romantic ballet *Waldemar* on 27.6.1838. Moreover, the parts were clearly reused for his revised 1840 Christiania version of *La Sylphide* in three parts since a pencilled note in the part for the kettledrums reads: 'Sylphiden/2d Afd.'.

31.7.1840

'Mazurka', Russian National Dance ('Mazurka', russisk Nationaldands) **performed by Bournonville and C. Fjeldsted (Christiania's Theatre, Oslo).**

This dance is almost certainly identical with the *Russian National Dance (Russisk Nationaldands)*, originally performed by

Bournonville and R. Lund at Copenhagen's Royal Theatre on 1.6.1838, and later incorporated in Act I (score no. 8) of Bournonville's two-act romantic ballet *The Isle of Phantasy* (*see* 28.10.1838).The dance was given once at Christiania's Theatre. However, the final *Mazurka* movement also seems to have been performed by C. Fjeldsted as a solo dance at this theatre (*see* 12.8.1840).

Musical sources:

No separate orchestral score and répétiteur's copy for the 1840 performance of this dance in Christiania have yet been traced. It seems to indicate that it was performed in Norway with the original Copenhagen orchestral score (now in DKKk, call no. MA ms 2631 (1)).

Parts (incomplete). Ms. Copy. 7 vol.
vl I, vl II, vla, vlc e cb, fl, cl, cor I–II.
Unsigned and undated [c.1840]
[DKKk; MA ms 2630 (1–7)
This (incomplete) set of parts is entitled 'Russisk' and seems to date from the 1840 performance of Bournonville's *'Mazurka', Russian National Dance* in Christiania. It excludes the first ten bars of the introduction in Hartmann's original 1838 score for the so-called 'Pas Russe' (now in DKKk, call no. MA ms 2631 (1). The parts also seem to have been used for C. Fjeldsted's later performance at Christiania's Theatre on 12.8.1840 of the (uncredited) solo dance, named *Mazurka*.

3.8.1840

Grand Pas de deux from the ballet Waldemar (Stor 'Pas de deux af Balletten Waldemar') **performed by Bournonville and C. Fjeldsted (Christiania's Theatre, Oslo).**

This dance is identical with the Act II *Pas de deux* from Bournonville's four-act romantic ballet *Waldemar* (*see* 28.10. 1835). It was performed once in Christiania.

Musical sources:

The 1839 set of parts, entitled 'Pas de deux de Waldemar' (now in DKKk, call no. KTB 1052) was most probably also used for this performance.

5.8.1840

'The Spring and Hertha', Divertissement ('Vaaren og Hertha', Divertissement) **performed by Bournonville and C. Fjeldsted (Christiania's Theatre, Oslo).**

This work is in all probability an abridged version of selected scenes and dances from Bournonville's divertissement *Hertha's Offering* (*see* 29.1.1838). It was arranged especially by Bournonville for the 1840 Norwegian summer tour and was given only once in Christiania. No separate musical sources for this divertissement have been traced in Norway. This seems to indicate that it was performed there with the original Copenhagen material for *Hertha's Offering* (now in DKKk, call nos. C II, 107, MA ms 3018, KTB 1005 (originally KTB 277), and KTB 219).

10.8.1840

Pas de deux after Taglioni (Pas de deux efter Taglioni) **performed by Bournonville and C. Fjeldsted (Christiania's Theatre, Oslo).**

This dance is almost certainly identical with the *Pas de deux (after Taglioni) (Pas de deux (efter Taglioni))*, first performed at Copenhagen's Royal Theatre by F. Hoppe and A. Nielsen on

6.7.1840 and, in turn, is probably identical with the even earlier *Pas de deux (by Taglioni) (Pas de deux (Af Taglioni))*, originally danced by P. C. Johansson and A. Nielsen at Stockholm's Royal Theatre (Operahuset) on 5.6.1839. The *Pas de deux* was given once in Christiania. It is not possible to identify the dance any further.

10.8.1840
Tarantella Napolitana, Characterdance from The Festival in Albano (Characteerdands af Festen i Albano) **performed by Bournonville and C. Fjeldsted (Christiania's Theatre, Oslo).**
This dance is identical with the *Tarantella* (score no. 10) from Bournonville's one-act idyllic ballet *The Festival in Albano* (*see* 28.10.1839). It was restaged at the same theatre by W. Funck and C. Fjeldsted on 2.7.1847, as an uncredited dance named '*La Tarantella neapolitana*'. The dance was given once in Norway during the 1840 summer tour.

Musical sources:

No orchestral score and répétiteur's copy dating from the 1840 performance in Christiania of this dance have yet been traced. This seems to indicate that the dance was rehearsed and performed with the Copenhagen material for *The Feast in Albano* (now in DKKk, call nos. C II, 107, and MA ms 2979 (KTB 282)), while a new set of parts was clearly prepared for this tour (*see* the following entry).

Parts. Ms Copy. 22 vol.
2 vl I, 2 vl II, 1 vla, 2 vlc e cb, fl 1/2, ob 1/2, cl 1/2, fag 1/2, cor 1/2, trb 1/2/3, timp, tri.
Unsigned and undated [c.1840]
[DKKk; KTB 282 a
This separate set of parts for the *Tarantella* in *The Feast in Albano* (score no. 10) dates almost certainly from its first performance as a separate divertissement in Christiania. Another set of parts with the music for this (now in DKKk, call no. KTB 1027) was, according to pencilled notes in several of the parts, used for two later privately arranged tours by C. Fjeldsted and W. Funck to Germany (*see* 12.5. 1846) and Norway (*see* 2.7.1847).

12.8.1840
Soldier and Peasant (Soldat og Bonde) **(Christiania's Theatre, Oslo).**
This work is an abridged divertissement version of Bournonville's pantomimic idyll *Soldier and Peasant* (*see* 13.10.1829) that omitted all those dances which were originally performed by the corps de ballet. The new production was arranged especially for the 1840 Norwegian summer tour and included the three leading protagonists, *Victor*, *Lise*, and *Anna*, played by Bournonville, C. Fjeldsted, and the Danish-Norwegian actress, S. Giebelhausen (b. Winsløw) respectively. They were assisted by a group of actors and actresses from Christiania's Theatre who performed the other rôles and/or acted the parts normally performed by the corps de ballet. According to *Norsk Bokfortegnelse* (1814–47, p. 23) a (not yet traced) printed scenario of 'Soldat og Bonde, Pantomimisk Idyl' (4 pp.) was published in Christiania by J. F. Dahl in 1840.

Soldier and Peasant was given only once during the 1840 summer tour to Christiania. No separate musical sources for it have yet been traced in Norway. This seems to indicate that the 1840 version was rehearsed and performed with the

original Copenhagen musical material (now in DKKk, call nos. C II, 115, and KTB 1026 (originally KTB 286)).

12.8.1840
Mazurka **(uncredited) performed by C. Fjeldsted (Christiania's Theatre, Oslo).**
This (uncredited) dance is most probably an adapted solo version of the girl's part in the '*Mazurka*', *Russian National Dance*, performed earlier by Bournonville and C. Fjeldsted at Christiania's Theatre on 31.7.1840 and, in turn, is probably identical with the even earlier *Russian National Dance*, first danced by Bournonville and R. Lund at Copenhagen's Royal Theatre on 1.6.1838 and later incorporated in Act I (score no. 8) of Bournonville's two-act romantic ballet *The Isle of Phantasy* (*see* 28.10.1838).

Fjeldsted's 1840 *Mazurka* was given once in Christiania. It is not possible to identify the dance any further.

14.8.1840
La Somnambule, ou l'Arrivée d'un nouveau seigneur (Søvngængersken) **(Christiania's Theatre, Oslo).**
This performance represents the first of only two complete stagings outside Denmark of Bournonville's 1829 Copenhagen version of J. Aumer's three-act pantomimic ballet (*see* 21.9.1829). According to Bournonville's autographed scenario for it, the dramatic action seems to have kept closely to that of the Danish version. This assumption is supported by the fact that no separate musical sources for the 1840 Christiania staging of *La Somnambule, ou l'Arrivée d'un nouveau seigneur* have yet been traced in Norway. Consequently that ballet was most probably performed with the original musical material for it in Copenhagen (now in DKKk, call nos. C I, 259 f, MA ms 2984, and KTB 287).

The leading rôles of *Edmond* and *Thérèse* were this year played by Bournonville and C. Fjeldsted. They were assisted by a group of actors and actresses from Christiania's Theatre, who performed the other leading mime rôles and/or acted the parts normally performed by the corps de ballet. According to *Norsk Bokfortegnelse* (1814–47, p. 23) the (not yet traced) printed scenario of the Norwegian version of 'Søvngjængersken' (8 pp.) was published in Christiania by J. F. Dahl in 1840.

La Somnambule, ou l'Arrivée d'un nouveau seigneur received one performance in Norway.

Autograph sources:

Manuscript scenario (included in a letter to J. F. Dahl). Ms. Autograph. Brown ink. 6 pp. (31,9 × 23 cm & 26,7 × 22,5 cm)
Søvngængersken/Ballet i 3 Acter af Aumer arrangeret af Hr: Bournonville./Musiken af Herold. ud [erased] opført for första Gang paa Christianias/Theater den 14.de Augusti 1840. -
Unsigned and dated: '14.de Augusti 1840. -'
[DKKk; NKS 2655 4°
This manuscript scenario clearly seems to be Bournonville's final draft for the (not yet traced) printed scenario for 'Søvngjængersken', published by J. F. Dahl in Christiania in 1840.

14.8.1840
'The English Sailor', Scene and Hornpipe ('Den engelske Matros', Scene og Hornpipe) **(uncredited) performed by Bournonville (Christiania's Theatre, Oslo).**
This (uncredited) dance is a divertissement version of the

English Sailor's Dance from Act I (score no. 10) of Bournonville's two-act romantic ballet *The Isle of Phantasy* (*see* 28.10.
1838). It was performed once during the 1840 Norwegian
summer tour.

No orchestral score and répétiteur's copy for this dance
have been traced in Norway. This seems to indicate that it
was rehearsed and performed there with the original 1838
Copenhagen musical material for *The Isle of Phantasy* (now in
DKKk, call nos. C II, 105, and MA ms 3016 (KTB 337 (1)).

6.10.1840
Dance Divertissement (Divertissement af Dands) performed by Bournonville, F. Hoppe, C. Fjeldsted, A. Nielsen, and P. Fredstrup.

According to the rehearsal book of H. C. J. Fredstrup this
divertissement (which was rehearsed between 5.7 and 7.7.
1840) is based on excerpts from Bournonville's one-act pantomimic prologue *The Fatherland's Muses* (*see* 20.3.1840). It is
not possible to identify the exact contents of dances in the
divertissement. The divertissement was given once.

No separate musical sources for this work have yet been
traced. This seems to indicate that it was performed with the
original musical material for *The Fatherland's Muses* (now in
DKKk, call nos. C II, 107, MA ms 2939, and KTB 1006 (originally KTB 199)).

30.10.1840
Pas de deux composed by Mr. Ballet Master Bournonville (componeret af Hr. Balletmester Bournonville) performed by Bournonville and C. Fjeldsted.

According to the rehearsal book of H. C. J. Fredstrup this
dance is almost certainly identical with Bournonville's earlier incorporated *Pas de deux* in F. Hérold's three-act comic
opera *Le Pré aux clercs* (*see* 28.10.1834) since that dance was
rehearsed under his personal direction on 30.10.1840. Another fact that supports this theory is that the *Pas de deux*
from *Le Pré aux clercs* had been performed twice the same
year by Bournonville and Fjeldsted on 30.5. and 10.9.1840. It
is not possible to identify the dance any further.

3.11.1840
Pas de deux composed by Mr. Ballet Master Bournonville (componeret af Hr. Balletmester Bournonville) performed by Bournonville and C. Fjeldsted.

According to the rehearsal book of H. C. J. Fredstrup this
dance (which was rehearsed on 2.11. and 3.11.1840) is identical with the *Pas de deux* (score no. 5) in Bournonville's one-
act pantomimic prologue *The Fatherland's Muses* (*see* 20.3.
1840). Fredstrup describes the dance as 'En grupperet Pas
de deux af Fædrelandets Muser', which seems to indicate
that a small corps de ballet was included forming different
groups around the leading couple.

The *Pas de deux* was given once by Bournonville and Fjeldsted as a separate divertissement.

Musical sources:

No separate orchestral score and répétiteur's copy for this dance has
yet been traced. This seems to indicate that the *Pas de deux* was rehearsed and performed with the original musical material for *The
Fatherland's Muses* (now in DKKk, call nos. C II, 107, and MA ms 2939

(KTB 199)) while a new separate set of parts was clearly prepared for
it (*see below*).

Parts (incomplete). Ms. Copy. 22 vol.
3 vl I, 3 vl II, 2 vla, 3 vlc e cb, fl I, cl 1/2, fag 1/2, cor 1/2, clno 1/2,
timp, tri.
Unsigned and undated [c.1840]
[DKKk; KTB 236
According to notes in several of the parts for this dance (reading:
'Pas de deux/til Faust/af Fædrelandets Muser') it also seems to have
been included in Bournonville's three-act romantic ballet *Faust* (*see*
25.4.1832) at a later (not yet identified) date.

22.11.1840
Pas de deux composed by Mr. Ballet Master Bournonville (componeret af Hr. Balletmester Bournonville) performed by Bournonville and A. Nielsen.

This (unnamed) *Pas de deux* was performed once by Bournonville and Nielsen in 1840. It is not possible to identify the
dance any further.

27.11.1840
The Toreador (Toréadoren).

A fortnight after the première of this two-act idyllic ballet set
in the Spanish spheres, Bournonville gave an interesting assessment of this work in a letter written to the Swedish count,
J. G. Dela Gardie (now in Lund's Universitetsbibliotek, Sweden, call no. Saml. DLG 382: b). In the same letter he also
explained the reason for its extraordinary success as he saw
it:

'Mon nouveau ballet Le Toréador vient d'obtenir un succès d'enthousiasme. La présence des danseurs espagnols m'a donné la
première étincelle de cette idée heureuse – On a trouvé de la gaité
et cette vivacité meridionale que l'on aime tant à voir transplanter
dans le nord; je me serais parfaitement contenté d'un succès comme
celui de la fête d'Albano mais la vogue a de beaucoup surpassé mon
attente, aussi j'ose le dire l'exécution a été parfaite […] Il est singu-
lier de voir l'influence du théâtre sur les esprits: le Toréador a vraiment donné du repos à la controverse politique, les discutions sur les
avantages et défauts des differentes formes de gouvernement ont
céssé un moment pour faire place à des débats beaucoup plus paci-
fiques, et j'ai eu le triomphe de réunir dans les suffrages de mon
ballet les partis les plus opposés, le peuple était d'accord avec le roi,
les aristocrates avec les libéreux, car tout le monde s'est donné le
mot pour s'amuser et m'a applaudi. Ne croyez pourtant pas Votre
Excellence, que cette victoire m'est aveuglé sur mon mérite non!
j'en rends grace à la providence, c'est pour le bien du corps de ballet
entier, la vogue n'est pas toujours l'apanage du mérite, et si j'ai en le
bonheur de réussir célà ne me donne qu'une plus grande respon-
sabilité pour mes prochains ouvrages'.

Moreover, in a letter, written by B. Thorvaldsen, to the Baroness, C. Stampe, at about the same time (now in DKKk, call
no. NKS 3258A 4°, VII, facs. 5, no. 247) this great Danish
sculptor assessed Bournonville's new ballet with the following words:

'i aften gaaer jeg paa Comedien og seer den nÿ Ballet Toréadoren
som er den skjönneste Ballet jeg nogensinde har seet'.

According to an unpublished biographical note, written by
A. F. v. d. Recke on 9.10.1865 (now in DKKk, call no. NKS
3258 A 4°, VII, facs. 9, no. 96), the score for *The Toreador* was
composed and arranged by Recke's father-in-law, H. C. Lumbye, in close collaboration with E. Helsted. Together, these

two composers incorporated several typical traditional Spanish dances like *El Zapatéado* and *El Jaleo de Xeres* in Act I (score nos. 2 and 6 respectively), and *El Boléro* in Act II (score no. 11). However, both the poster and the printed scenario for *The Toreador* give credit exclusively to Helsted. This seems to indicate that it was Helsted who was responsible for the final arrangement and orchestration of this ballet. He incorporated several musical borrowings which are identified as follows:

(1) Act I (score no. 7): Helsted here incorporated several excerpts borrowed from J. Mayseder's *Polonaise nr. 3* for solo violin and strings (opus 12) from 1822. Moreover, in the same number Helsted interpolated N. C. Bochsa's French chansonette, entitled «Je suis la Bayadère dont le gai Tambourin». This tune had been sung at Copenhagen's Royal Theatre by the English soprano, A. Bishop, at four concerts between 15.9. and 6.10.1839 to the accompaniment of Bochsa, and was soon after also published by C. C. Lose & Olsen in Copenhagen (now in DKKk, call no. U 204). Bochsa's song thus clearly seems to have provided Bournonville with the main motif for the grand solo variation, entitled 'Je suis la Bayadère' which he inserted for *Céleste* in Act I of *The Toreador*.
(2) Act II (score no. 12): In this number Helsted (and/or Lumbye?) incorporated J. Strauss the elder's *Jugenfeuer Galop*, opus 90, from 1836. It here served as the ballet's *Finale* and was performed by the entire cast.

Furthermore, the *El Jaleo de Xerxes* in Act I (score no. 6) had earlier been performed at Copenhagen's Royal Theatre by F. Hoppe and C. Fjeldsted as an incorporated divertissement in D.-F.-E Auber's five-act opera *La Muette de Portici* on 24.11. 1839, and was later restaged at the same theatre as separate divertissement on 9.1.1842. Similarly, the *El Bolero* in Act II (score no. 11) was originally premièred at the Royal Theatre as a separate divertissement on 6.7.1840, performed by Bournonville, M. Camprubì, C. Fjeldsted, and D. Serral.

In Italy the *Passo nazionale spagnolo detto EL JALEO DEL TOREADOR* was mounted by Bournonville at Naples' Teatro San Carlo on 26.6.1841 and was performed there by himself and A. Saint-Romain as an incorporated divertissement in G. Briol's two-act comic ballet from 1841, *L'Istituto delle Fanciulle*.

Moreover, on 28.8. and 29.8.1841 the same dance was performed by Bournonville and G. King at Milan's Teatro alla Scala, with the new (uncredited) title *Jaleo de Toreador*, and given as an interpolated divertissement in Act III of P. Hus' restaging of G. Gioja's five-act ballet from 1823, *Il Castello di Kenilworth*.

The complete version of *The Toreador* was staged by Bournonville for the first time outside Denmark at Hamburg's Stadttheater and performed there 6 times between 10.7. and 8.8.1843. This version also included a new, incorporated *Pas de deux* in Act II, danced by the French ballerina, Maria (Jacob) in the rôle of *Céleste* and partnered by a (not yet identified) dancer, named Maximilien.

On 21.6.1845 *The Toreador* was restaged at Copenhagen's Royal Theatre for a special gala performance, given for the visiting King of Prussia, Friedrich William IV. For this occasion Bournonville wrote a new so-called *Analyse du Ballet*, which was published the same day on a specially designed programme-poster.

Two years later the ballet was mounted for a special charity performance at the Court Theatre on 11.3.1847. The same year it was staged by Bournonville at Stockholm's Royal Theatre (Operahuset) and performed there 3 times between 2.6. and 18.6.1847. In Norway an (uncredited) *El Jaleo de Xeres* was performed by W. Funck and C. Fjeldsted on 29.6.1847. It is most likely identical with the similar dance of that name in *The Toreador*. A so-called 'Divertissement from The Toréador' ('Divertissement af Toreadoren') was later also arranged and staged by Bournonville at the same theatre on 11.6.1852.

In Austria the complete ballet was mounted by Bournonville and given nine times at Vienna's Kärnthnerthor Theatre between 15.7.1854 and 18.9.1855 with the first act being performed there separately on one occasion (12.10.1855). In Sweden an (uncredited) *Jaleo de Xeres*, which most probably was arranged and staged by Bournonville, was performed at Stockholm's Royal Theatre (Stora Theatern) on 16.10.1863, while an (uncredited) 'Bolero' (Spanish National Dance) was mounted in Norway by H. Scharff, W. Price, Juliette Price, and S. Price at Christiania's Theatre (Oslo) on 7.6.1865. Both of these dances were most likely arrangements of similar dances in *The Toreador*.

The Toreador was restaged 6 times by Bournonville at Copenhagen's Royal Theatre (see 21.6.1845, 21.10.1850, 21.10. 1866, 6.11.1869, and 28.11.1873), each time with only minor musical and choreographic changes.

The 1840 production received 66 performances (the last given on 4.12.1848), and the ballet reached a total of 137 performances in Copenhagen during Bournonville's lifetime, the last of which was given on 27.3.1876. According to the rehearsal book of H. C. J. Fredstrup 46 rehearsals were held of *The Toreador* between 27.9. and 27.11.1840.

Autograph sources:

Production note. Ms. Autograph. Brown ink. 1 p. (34,5 × 21 cm)
Personerne i Balletten/<u>Toreadoren.</u>
Unsigned and undated [1840]
[DKKkt; F.M. (Ballet)

Musical sources:

Musical draft. Ms. Autograph (by E. Helsted). Brown ink. 4 pp. (32,5 × 23,4 cm)
<u>Torréadoren.</u> [*sic*] <u>Ballet i 2 Acter.</u>/<u>No. 1.</u> <u>Allegretto</u>/[...]/No. 2 <u>Zapatéado.</u>
Unsigned and undated [c.1840]
[DKKk; MA ms 2696 (KTB 269)
This musical draft contains Helsted's early arrangements for the two opening numbers in Act I of *The Toreador*. The titles of each dance are here written (with brown ink) in Bournonville's hand.

Musical draft. Ms. Autograph (by E. Helsted). Brown ink. 2 pp. (34,5 × 24,5 cm)
<u>No. 6.</u>/<u>El Jaleo de Xeres.</u>
Unsigned and undated [c.1840]
[DKKk; MA ms 2665 (KTB 269)
This musical draft contains Helsted's early arrangements for *El Jaleo de Xeres* in Act I of *The Toreador*. The number of the dance is here written (with brown ink) in Bournonville's hand.

Musical draft. Ms. Autograph (by E. Helsted). Brown ink. 2 pp. (34,6 × 24,5 cm)
<u>No. 12.</u>/<u>Finale.</u>
Unsigned and undated [c.1840]
[DKKk; MA ms 2697 (KTB 269)

This musical draft contains Helsted's transcription of J. Strauss the elder's music for *Jugendfeuer Galop* (op. 90), which was incorporated as the *Finale* of Act II in *The Toreador*. The number of this movement ('No. 12.') is here written (with pencil) on the first page by Bournonville. Moreover, his pencilled autographed choreographic notes describe (in general terms) the choreographic evolution of the finale.

Orchestral score. Ms. Autograph (by E. Helsted) and copy. Brown and black ink. 2 vol. Act I 200 pp. of which one is blank, Act II 90 pp. (27,3 × 37 cm with minor variants)
269/Toreadoren/1 Akt/[…]/269/Toreadoren/2 Akt.
Signed and dated (in Act II, p. 88): 'i November 1840./Eduard Helsted.'
[DKKk; C II, 114 k (KTB 269)]
This score was used for all performances of *The Toreador* during Bournonville's lifetime. It also contains several later insertions that were added for the restagings of this ballet at the beginning of the 20th century.

Répétiteur's copy. Ms. Copy and autograph (by H. S. Paulli). Brown and black ink. 1 vol. 102 pp. of which two are blank (30,6 × 24,2 with minor variants)
B. 269/'Toreadoren.'/[…]/Torreadoren [*sic*]./Ball: i 2.de Act/Repiti: Partie
Unsigned and undated [1840]
[DKKk; MA ms 2965a (KTB 269(1))]
This répétiteur's copy contains Bournonville's sporadic autographed notes (written with brown ink) which describe his choreography and the dramatic action in Act I (score nos. 6–7) and Act II (score nos. 9–10). They were most probably written for a later, revised staging of *The Toreador* in the 1850s or 60s. This theory is supported by the fact that most of Bournonville's notes are actually written on pages which are H. S. Paulli's autographs and were inserted in this volume at a later stage (most probably in connection with the restaging of *The Toreador* on 21.10.1866).

Parts. Ms. Copy. 35 vol.
4 vl I, 4 vl II, 2 vla, 4 vlc e cb, fl 1/2, ob 1/2, cl 1/2, fag 1/2, cor 1/2/3/4, tr 1/2, trb 1/2/3, timp, gr cassa, piatti, tri.
Unsigned and undated [1840]
[DKKk; KTB 1046 (originally KTB 269)]

Répétiteur's copy/Conductor's part. Ms. Autograph (by E. Helsted?). Black ink. 4 pp. (33,3 × 25,8 cm)
N [space left open]/Bolero
Unsigned and undated [c.1840s]
[DKKk; MA ms 2675 (KTB 269)]
This répétiteur's copy contains the complete music for the *Boléro* in Act II (score no. 11) of *The Toreador*. It also seems to have served as a conductor's part since it contains several notes which indicate the intrumentation of this dance. The répétiteur's copy was probably used for the later divertissement versions of *The Toreador* that Bournonville mounted on his many tours abroad in the 1840s and 50s.

Other sources:

Drawing by E. Lehmann. Pencil (18,5 × 22,9 cm)
Toreadoren
Signed and dated: 'E. L./1847 -'
[DKKt; Lehmann tegninger
According to K. Neiiendam this drawing shows the scene in Act I (score no. 6) of *The Toreador* in which *Maria* (C. Fjeldsted or P. A. Funck?) and *Alonzo* perform the *El Jaleo de Xeres* while surrounded by *José* (H. C. J. Fredstrup), *Mr. Arthur* (Gott. A. Füssel), *Mr. William* (A. Stramboe), and a group of townspeople.

Painting by E. Lehmann. Oil on canvas (85,5 × 69,5 cm)
[Untitled]
Unsigned and undated [c.1840–1848]
[DKKt; Balletafdelingen (permanent udtilling)

This painting shows A. Nielsen as *Céleste* while performing her solo, named 'Je suis la Bayadère' in Act II (score no. 7) of *The Toreador*. Nielsen performed this rôle for the last time on 4.12.1848, hence the dating of this painting to the 1840s. The painting is curious in that the background depicts a rather strange mixture of Spanish houses set in a Danish landscape with a typical Danish medieval village church in the far distance.

Printed sources:

Printed scenario. 1 vol. 15 pp. (19,3 × 12,8 cm)
TORÉADOREN./Idyllisk Ballet i 2 Acter/af/August Bournonville./Musiken componeret og arrangeret af Edward Helsted./Decorationen af Christensen./Opført for første Gang i November/1840. Kjøbenhavn, Bianco Lunos Bogtrykkeri [1840].
[DKKk, 17, – 173 8°
A second scenario with an identical text was published by Græbes Bogtrykkeri the same year (now in DKKk, call no. 17, – 173 8°).

1841

7.1.1841
Pas de deux, à la Taglioni (uncredited) performed by
F. Hoppe and A. Nielsen.
This (uncredited) dance is most probably identical with the earlier *Pas de deux (after Taglioni)*, performed by Hoppe and Nielsen at Copenhagen's Royal Theatre on 6.7.1840. That dance, in turn, is most likely the same as the even earlier *Pas de deux (by Taglioni)*, set to a score by J. Mayseder and staged as a separate divertissement by Bournonville for his Swedish pupil, P. C. Johansson, and A. Nielsen at Stockholm's Royal Theatre (Operahuset) on 5.6.1839, but originally performed in Act II (score no. 1 A) of his two-act romantic ballet *The Isle of Phantasy* (*see* 28.10.1838). The *Pas de deux, à la Taglioni* was given twice by Hoppe and Nielsen in 1841, the last time on 16.3.1841. It is not possible to identify the dance any further.

19.1.1841
Pas de deux (uncredited) performed by F. Hoppe and
A. Nielsen.
In the rehearsal book of H. C. J. Fredstrup this (uncredited) dance is listed as 'Pas de deux af Det Orientalske Divertissement'. This clearly indicates that it was identical with Bournonville's so-called 'Pas de deux oriental' first performed by himself and A. Krætzmer on 26.9.1829 as an incorporated divertissement in P. Funck's *A Divertissement in Oriental Style*, and later also incorporated by Bournonville in his one-act idyllic ballet *The Veteran or The Hospitable House* (*see* 29.1. 1833). According to the posters the *Pas de deux* was performed only once with this title in 1841. It is not possible to identify the dance any further.

1.2.1841
Pas de deux composed by Mr. Ballet Master Bournonville (componeret af Hr. Balletmester Bournonville) performed by
Bournonville and A. Nielsen.
This dance is beyond doubt an earlier work by Bournonville (perhaps the uncredited *Pas de deux* performed by F. Hoppe and A. Nielsen on 19.1.1841). It is not possible to identify the dance any further.

7.2.1841

Le Dieu et la bayadère, ou La Courtisane amoureuse (Brama og Bayadèren).

According to the poster for the 1841 Copenhagen restaging of D.-F.-E. Auber's two-act opera-ballet (premièred at the Paris Opéra on 13.10.1830 and first performed in Copenhagen on 28.5.1833) the three dance scenes in Act I (score nos. 2 and 5) and Act II (score no. 10) were this year 'arranged' (*arrangeret*) by Bournonville and P. Larcher. However, it is not possible to determine exactly which dances were arranged by whom this year. Meanwhile, according to Bournonville's autographed pencilled choreographic notes in the répétiteur's copy it seems that he was responsible for staging at least the two dance scenes in Act I that are performed by *Zoloé* and the corps de ballet (score nos. 2 and 5).

On 20.7.1843 *Die Liebende Bayadère oder Der Gott und die Bayadere* was mounted at Hamburg's Stadttheater, but then with the dances all credited exclusively to Bournonville. This production also included an incorporated (uncredited) *Pas de deux*, danced by Bournonville and the French ballerina, Maria (Jacob).

During the late 1840s *Le Dieu et la bayadère* was restaged twice by Bournonville at Copenhagen's Royal Theatre on 9.9.1847 and 11.11.1849, each time with the opera's dances credited on the posters to both Bournonville and P. Larcher, despite the fact that that the latter had already died on 15.6.1847.

On 30.10.1857 Bournonville was working on a third projected restaging of the opera, which he carried out on 6.10.1859 when *Le Dieu et la bayadère* was mounted for the first time with his own complete mise-en-scène and choreography. Moreover, for the 1859 production he also gave personal stage instructions to his daughter, the alto Charlotte Bournonville (who played *Ninka*), and the singer A. Zinck (who then made his début in the rôle of *L'inconnu*).

In Sweden a choreographic-mimic adaptation (perhaps arranged by Bournonville?) of two excerpts from the 1859 Copenhagen production of *Le Dieu et La Bayadère* was mounted at Stockholm's Royal Theatre (Mindre Theatern) on 5.6.1860 and performed there twice, the last time on 7.6.1860. Three years later the complete opera was given its Swedish première with Bournonville's mise-en-scène at Stockholm's Royal Theatre (Operahuset) on 14.3.1863.

In Copenhagen *Le Dieu et la bayadère* was restaged for the fourth and last time by Bournonville on 8.10.1871, while Act I was mounted there by him separately on 3.6.1873.

The 1841 production received 18 performances (the last given on 30.5.1847), and between 17.2.1841 and 12.1.1873 Auber's complete opera reached a total of 47 performances. It is not clear from the rehearsal book of H. C. J. Fredstrup exactly how many rehearsals were held of the opera and its dances in 1841.

Musical sources:

Printed score. 2 vol. Act I 439 pp., Act II 240 pp. (32 × 26 cm)
DIE LIEBENDE BAYADERE/oder/Det Gott und die Bayadere/ OPER mit BALLET und PANTOMIME
Mainz und Antwerpen, B. Schott, pl. no. 3410 [February 1831].
[DKKk; U 6 (KTB 301)
This score contains Th. Overskou's Danish translation (written with red ink) and also includes a metronome marking in the dance scene of Act I (score no. 2) that indicates the tempo with a crochet equalling '100'.

Répétiteur's copy. Ms. Copy. Black and brown ink. 1 vol. 20 pp. (32,7 × 24,8 cm)
Repetiteur Parti/A. 301/til/Brama og Bayaderen/61 B./[...]/ Repetiteur Parti/til/Brama og Bayaderen/af/Auber
Unsigned and undated [1833]
[DKKk; MA ms 3063 (KTA 301 (1))
This répétiteur's copy clearly dates from the 1833 Danish première of Auber's opera at Copenhagen's Royal Theatre and contains the music for the three dance scenes in Act I (score nos. 2 and 5), and Act II (score no. 10). Bournonville's sporadic pencilled autographed choreographic notes are found in nos. 2 and 5, while other pencilled notes in score no. 10 (perhaps written by P. Larcher?) indicate the names of the dancers A. Krætzmer and M. Werning, who originally performed the rôles of the two dancing bayadères *Zoloé* and *Fatmé* at the Copenhagen première of Auber's opera.

Parts. Ms. Copy. 37 vol.
4 vl I, 2 vl II, 3 vla, 4 vlc e cb, fl picc, fl 1/2, ob 1/2, cl 1/2, fag 1/2, cor 1/2/3/4, tr 1/2, trb 1/2/3, timp, gr cassa, tri, arpa. On stage: tr 1/ 2. 49 vocal parts.
Unsigned and undated [1833]
[DKKk; KTA 301

2.6.1841

Pas de trois (uncredited) in *The Festival in Albano (Festen i Albano).*

On this day Bournonville's one-act idyllic ballet *The Festival in Albano* (see 28.10.1839) was performed with an incorporated (uncredited) *Pas de trois* choreographed(?) and danced by P. Taglioni, together with his wife, A. Taglioni (b. Galster), and A. Nielsen. It replaced the original *Pas de deux* (score no. 9) and was most probably interpolated in this ballet as a result of Bournonville's absence from Copenhagen during this period because of his enforced six-month exile in 1841. The *Pas de trois* was performed twice in *The Festival in Albano*, the last time on 9.6.1841. No musical sources for this dance have yet been traced. It is not possible to identify the dance any further.

26.6.1841

Nuovo passo a due composto dal signor Bournonville **performed by Bournonville and L. Taglioni as an incorporated divertissement in** *Quadro II* **of S. Taglioni's historical** *ballet d'action* **in eight parts** *Marco Visconti* **(Naples, Teatro San Carlo).**

According to Bournonville's 1841 travel diary this dance is identical with the *Pas de deux* in Act II of his four-act romantic ballet *Waldemar* (see 28.10.1835). It was performed only once at Teatro San Carlo.

Musical sources:

The 1839 set of parts, entitled 'Pas de deux de Waldemar' (now in DKKk, call no. KTB 1052) was most probably also used for this performance.

26.6.1841

Passo nazionale spagnolo detto EL JALEO DEL TOREADOR, composto dal signor Bournonville **performed by Bournonville and A. Saint-Romain as an incorporated divertissement in**

G. Briol's two-act comic ballet *L'Istituto delle Fanciulle* (Naples, Teatro San Carlo).

This dance is identical with Bournonville's *El Jaleo de Xeres* from Act I (score no. 6) of his two-act idyllic ballet *The Toreador* (*see* 27.11.1840). It was given once at Naples' Teatro San Carlo. No separate musical sources for this performance have yet been traced.

28.8.1841

Jaleo del Toreador (uncredited) performed by Bournonville and G. King as an incorporated divertissement in Act III of Gioja's five-act ballet from 1823 *Il Castello di Kenilworth* (Milan, Teatro alla Scala).

This (uncredited) dance is identical with Bournonville's *El Jaleo de Xeres* in Act I (score no. 6) of his two-act idyllic ballet *The Toreador* (*see* 27.11.1840). It was performed twice at Teatro alla Scala, the last time on 29.8.1841. No separate musical sources for this performance have yet been traced.

29.8.1841

Pas de deux serieux (Passo a due serio) (uncredited) performed by Bournonville and G. King as an incorporated divertissement in Act III of P. Hus' restaging of G. Gioja's 1823 ballet *Il Castello di Kenilworth* (Milan, Teatro alla Scala).

According to Bournonville's travel-diary this (uncredited) dance is identical with the *Pas de deux* from Act II of his four-act romantic ballet *Waldemar* (*see* 28.10.1835). It was performed once in Milan.

Musical sources:

The 1839 set of parts, entitled 'Pas de deux de Waldemar' (now in DKKk, call no. KTB 1052) was most probably also used for this performance.

3.9.1841

A Pas de deux, composed by Mr. Ballet Master Bournonville (En Pas de deux, componeret af Hr. Balletmester Bournonville) performed by F. Hoppe and P. Fredstrup.

This dance is beyond doubt a restaging of an earlier work by Bournonville. As a result of Bournonville's enforced six-month exile in 1841 the three rehearsals which were held of this dance (according to the rehearsal book of H. C. J. Fredstrup between 1.9 and 3.9.1841) were directed by either P. Larcher or F. Hoppe. The *Pas de deux* was performed 3 times by Hoppe and Fredstrup in 1841, the last time on 16.12.1841. It is not possible to identify the dance any further.

14.10.1841

New Pas de deux arranged by Mr. Ballet Master Bournonville (Ny Pas de deux arrangeret af Hr. Balletmester Bournonville) performed by Bournonville and C. Fjeldsted.

In his handwritten lists of his works, written c.1851 (*see* Additional Sources) Bournonville named this dance 'Pas de deux de retour'. According to the same source it is clearly indicated by him as a dance based on another choreographer's work. The *Pas de deux*, which was mounted in order to mark Bournonville's homecoming to Denmark after the enforced six-month exile in 1841, is most probably identical with one of those 'two lovely *pas de deux*' that he mentions in a letter to his wife, Helene, written in Paris on 5.5.1841:

'I have already two lovely *pas de deux* and *la Cracovienne* – a famous trifle – which I have decided to be for her [i.e. Caroline Fjeldsted]'.

Moreover, according to his 1841 travel diary Bournonville had two meetings in Paris (on 28.4. and 1.5.1841) with the French choreographer, J. Mazilier. The reason for these encounters may well have been to obtain Mazilier's permission to stage these dances in Copenhagen, in which Bournonville apparently was successful. If this theory is correct, then the 1841 *New Pas de deux* is most likely based on a dance by Mazilier set to music by a (not yet identified) French composer, which Bournonville had seen performed at the Paris Opéra during the spring of 1841. The most likely identification of this dance would, therefore, be a divertissement incorporated in Mazilier's, F. Benoist's and N.-H. Reber's three-act pantomimic ballet *Le Diable amoureux* (first performed at the Paris Opéra on 23.9.1840). In Copenhagen the *New Pas de deux* was performed 3 times by Bournonville and Fjeldsted, the last time on 14.11.1841.

However, a répétiteur's copy, which is H. S. Paulli's autograph and dates from the 1850s (now in DKKk, call no. MA ms 2698), contains an abridged version of the music for this dance. This seems to indicate that the 1841 *New Pas de deux* was either restaged by Bournonville at a later (not yet identified) date during the 1850s, or it may represent Paulli's first draft for the so-called *Festive dance (Festdands)* in Act I (score no. 13) of his and Bournonville's three-act ballet *Zulma, or The Crystal Palace* (*see* 14.4.1852). This theory is supported by the fact that in his music for that ballet Paulli interpolated an excerpt borrowed from the opening *Allegretto* movement in 6/8 time of Bournonville's 1841 *New Pas de deux*.

It is not clear from the rehearsal book of H. C. J. Fredstrup exactly how many rehearsals were held of this dance in 1841.

Musical sources:

Orchestral score. Ms. Copy. Brown ink. 1 vol. 36 pp. (27,2 × 38 cm with minor variants)
229 / Partitturen / til / Pas de döux / Af Hr Borneville [*sic*] / 1841 / [...] / Pas de deux.
Unsigned and dated (on the front cover): '1841'
[DKKk; C II, 127 b (KTB 229)

Répétiteur's copy. Ms. Copy (by H. S. Paulli?). Brown ink. 10 pp. (33,3 × 23,5 cm with minor variants)
Nÿe / Pas de deux / [...] / No. 1. / [...] / 51B. / 1841
Unsigned and dated (on the front cover): '1841'
[DKKk; MA ms 2903 (1) (KTB 229)
This répétiteur's copy (which appears to have been copied by H. S. Paulli) is bound together with the répétiteur's copy for the other 1841 *Pas de deux* that Bournonville incorporated in Act II of G. Meyerbeer's five-act opera *Robert le Diable (Robert af Normandiet)* at Copenhagen's Royal Theatre on 5.12.1841.

Parts. Ms. Copy. 30 vol.
3 vl I, 3 vl II, 2 vla, 3 vlc e cb, fl picc, fl 1/2, ob 1/2, cl 1/2, fag 1/2, cor 1/2, tr 1/2, trb 1/2/3, timp, gr cassa, piatti e tri.
Unsigned and undated [1841]
[DKKk; KTB 229

Répétiteur's copy. Ms. Copy (by H. S. Paulli). Black ink. 4 pp. of which two are blank (34,8 × 25,8 cm)
[Without title]
Unsigned and undated [c.1850s]
[DKKk; MA ms 2698 (KTB 229?)]

26.10.1841

Pas de deux composed by Mr. Ballet Master Bournonville (componeret af Hr. Balletmester Bournonville) **performed by F. Hoppe and C. Fjeldsted.**

This *Pas de deux* is beyond doubt a restaging of an earlier work by Bournonville. It was performed twice by Hoppe and Fjeldsted in 1841, the last time on 16.12.1841. It is not possible to identify the dance any further.

28.11.1841

The Soprano, (Dramatic motif for a new Italian aria) (Sangerinden, (dramatisk Motiv for en ny Italiensk Arie)) **performed by the soprano C. Simonsen, the actor J. F. Kirchheiner, a male chorus and corps de ballet.**

Bournonville created the mise-en-scène for this scenic performance of H. C. Andersen's poem *The Soprano (Sangerinden)*. Moreover, it represents the first time he collaborated with Andersen on the staging of a theatrical work. According to Andersen's autographed libretto for this work, it was created as the framework for an aria from G. Donizetti's three-act tragic opera *Lucia di Lammermoor*, sung on this occasion by C. Simonsen as a separate concert-piece. In 1841 this singer had expressed her wish to Andersen to perform an aria from Donizetti's opera within a kind of scenic presentation. For the same purpose Andersen wrote a dramatic scene that included a plot, which tells of a famous soprano from Naples (named *Maria*), who is held hostage by a group of brigands during a journey to Florence, but regains her freedom by giving them an example of her sublime art of *bel canto*.

The music for Andersen's work was composed and arranged by J. F. Fröhlich and consisted of four numbers as follows:

(1) Score no. 1: A chorus sung by the brigands and the Soprano.
(2) Score no. 2: A chorus sung by the brigands and their Captain.
(3) Score no. 3: An aria sung by the Soprano.
(4) Score no. 4: A finale sung by the entire cast.

In his score Fröhlich employed several excerpts borrowed from works by other composers. They are identified as follows:

(1) In the opening chorus (score no. 1) Fröhlich borrowed excerpts from the chorus, entitled «Hurra Mordjo!» in the Act II finale of F. Kuhlau's three-act singspiel *The Brigands' Castle (Røverborgen)*, first performed at Copenhagen's Royal Theatre on 26.5.1814.
(2) In the second chorus (score no. 2) Fröhlich inserted (according to Andersen's autographed libretto for *The Soprano*) a melody for a song (by a not yet identified composer), entitled «Krokodillen ligger i Sivet».
(3) No separate musical sources for the aria from Donizetti's *Lucia di Lammermoor* (which was said to have been performed as score no. 3 in *The Soprano*) have yet been traced. Thus, according to Andersen's autographed libretto this aria was sung to the text «Per che non ho del vento», a text that, however, is not included in Donizetti's opera.
(4) In score no. 4 Fröhlich incorporated excerpts of the music for

the barcaruola, named «Io son ricco e tu sei bella» and originally sung by *Dulcamara* and *Adina* in Act II of Donizetti's two-act melodrama *L'Elisir d'amore* (premièred at Teatro della Canobbiana in Milan on 12.5.1832).

The Soprano received 5 performances, the last of which took place on 23.3.1842. According to the rehearsal book of H. C. J. Fredstrup only one rehearsal was held of it on 27.11.1841.

Musical sources:

Orchestral score (fragment). Ms. Autograph (by J. F. Fröhlich). Black ink. 4 pp. (27,5 × 38,3 cm with minor variants)
Finale./All.o moderato.
Unsigned and undated [1841]
[DKKk; MA ms 2748 (1) (KTA 512 (1))]
This orchestral score contains the music of the finale (score no. 4) in *The Soprano*, and represents the only autographed musical source that has been traced for this work so far.

Vocal part. Ms. Copy. Black ink. 4 pp. of which one is blank. (25 × 33 cm with minor variants)
Sangerindens Partie til 'Sangerinden'
Unsigned and undated [1841]
[DKKk; MA ms 2748 (2) (KTA 512 (2))]
This vocal part contains the music for score nos. 1 and 4.

Prompt's score. Ms. Copy. Black and brown ink. 1 vol. 12 pp. (24,5 × 32 cm)
512/P. og S.P/446/Sangerinden./Souffleurpartie./[…]/Sangerinden/Dramatisk Scene/af/H. C. Andersen./[…]/Souffleur=Partie
Unsigned and undated [1841]
[DKKk; MA ms 2748 (3) (KTA 512 (3))]
This prompt's score (or 'Souffleur=Partie' in the form of a piano-vocal score) contains the complete music for *The Soprano*. According to the title page it was originally accompanied by vocal parts for the two soloists (the Soprano and the Captain) and seventeen vocal parts for the chorus (the Brigands).

Other sources:

Manuscript libretto. Ms. Autograph (by H. C. Andersen). Brown ink. 5 pp. (20 × 17 cm)
[…]/108./(Afskrift efter en Klade jeg/havde [erased] men her fuldstændigt)/Sangerinden /En dramatisk Scene
Unsigned and undated [after 1841]
[DKKk; Collinske Samling 19, 4° 1. Samlinger af Digte, Hefte 2, no. 108
This autographed libretto was written after the 1841 première of *The Soprano* and was originally part of Andersen's private collection of copies of his poems.

1.12.1841

Pas de deux and Gallopade from the ballet Isle of Phantasy (Pas de deux og Galopade af Balletten 'Phantasiens Øe') **performed by F. Hoppe and C. Fjeldsted.**

This set of dances represents Bournonville's final and definitive version of the divertissement that he had mounted for the first time on 10.11.1839 and, in turn, is based on selected excerpts from Act II (score no. 7) of his two-act romantic ballet *The Isle of Phantasy* (*see* 28.10.1838). The 1841 version of the *Pas de deux and Gallopade* received 44 performances in Copenhagen during Bournonville's lifetime, the last of which was given on 2.1.1866. It is not clear from the rehearsal book of H. C. J. Fredstrup exactly how many rehearsals were held of these dances in 1841.

5.12.1841

New Pas de deux composed by Mr. Ballet Master Bournonville
(Ny Pas de deux componeret af Hr. Balletmester Bournonville)
performed by Bournonville and C. Fjeldsted as an
incorporated divertissement in Act II of *Robert le Diable*
(Robert af Normandiet).

In his handwritten lists of his works, written c.1851 (*see* Additional Sources) Bournonville named this dance 'Pas de deux af Robert'. It is perhaps identical with the so-called *Grand Pas de deux (Stor Pas de deux)* performed two years earlier by Bournonville and A. Nielsen as an incorporated divertissement in Act II of G. Meyerbeer's five-act opera *Robert le Diable* at Stockholm's Royal Theatre (Operahuset) on 13.6.1839. Another possible identification of this dance is one of the two *Pas de deux* mentioned by Bournonville in a letter written to his wife, Helene, in Paris on 5.5.1841:

'I have already two lovely *pas de deux* and *la Cracovienne* – a famous trifle – which I have decided to be for her [i.e. Caroline Fjeldsted]'.

Moreover, according to his 1841 travel diary Bournonville had two meetings in Paris (on 28.4. and 1.5.1841) with the French choreographer, J. Mazilier. The reason for these encounters may well have been to obtain Mazilier's permission to stage these dances in Copenhagen, in which Bournonville apparently was successful. If this theory is correct, then the 1841 *New Pas de deux* is most likely based on a dance by Mazilier set to music by a (not yet identified) French composer, and which Bournonville had seen performed at the Paris Opéra during the spring of 1841. The most likely identification of this dance would, therefore, be a divertissement incorporated in Mazilier's, F. Benoist's and N.-H. Reber's three-act pantomimic ballet *Le Diable amoureux* (first performed at the Paris Opéra on 23.9.1840).

Bournonville's 1841 *New Pas de deux* in *Robert le Diable* is most probably also identical with the later *Pas de deux* 'arranged' (*arrangerad*) by Bournonville and danced by himself and his Swedish pupil, M. C. Norberg, at Stockholm's Royal Theatre (Operahuset) on 28.6.1847, as an incorporated divertissement in Act II of Meyerbeer's *Robert le Diable*.

According to a later set of parts in Sweden, which contains the same music as that for Bournonville's 1841 *New Pas de deux* (now in SSkma, call no. KT Dansmusik 85), this dance was also mounted by Bournonville's pupil, S. Lund, as a separate divertissement at Stockholm's Royal Theatre (Operahuset) on 13.11.1856, but was then presented on the poster as a work 'arranged' (*arrangerad*) by Lund, who performed it together with the Swedish ballerina, J. G. Sundberg.

Bournonville's *New Pas de deux* was (according to a pencilled note in the Danish part for the fourth horn) also mounted in Germany at Hamburg's Stadttheater on 5.7.1843, danced by Bournonville and the French ballerina, Maria (Jacob), as an (uncredited) divertissement in D.-F.-E. Auber's five-act historical opera *Gustave III, ou Le Bal masqué*.

On 29.6.1847 the dance was given for the first time in Norway by W. Funck and C. Fjeldsted at Christiania's Theatre (Oslo) with the title *Grand Pas de deux from 'Robert le Diable'*, *composed by Bournonville (Grand Pas de deux af 'Robert af Normandiet', componeret af Bournonville)*.

In Copenhagen the *Pas de deux from Robert le Diable (Pas de deux af 'Robert af Normandiet')* was given as a separate divertissement for the first time on 26.12.1841, and was restaged there twice on 26.11.1843 and on 29.10.1849 (from 1849 performed by W. Funck and C. Kellermann). It reached a total of 25 performances in Copenhagen, the last of which was given on 19.4.1855.

Finally, during the following years Bournonville worked on five other restagings of Meyerbeer's complete opera as follows:

(1) 18.1.1848 (this performance represents the first restaging in Copenhagen in which the opera's dance scenes and divertissements in Acts II and III were all choreographed by Bournonville).
(2) 23.7.1855 (a restaging at Vienna's Kärnthnerthor Theatre mounted with new choreography in Act III by Bournonville, arranged especially for the début in the Hapsburgian capital of his pupil, J. Price).
(3) 30.10.1857 (a projected restaging in Copenhagen).
(4) 20.12.1862 (a restaging at Stockholm's Royal Theatre, Operahuset).
(5) 19.1.1873 (Bournonville's last restaging of Meyerbeer's opera in Copenhagen, mounted with a completely new mise-en-scène and partially revised choreography).

According to pencilled notes in the printed orchestral score for *Robert le Diable* (now in DKKk, call no. U 6 (KTA 303)) Bournonville's 1841 *New Pas de deux* was performed in Act II of Meyerbeer's opera, where it replaced the original *Pas de cinq* divertissement in that act (score no. 7). It is not clear from the rehearsal book of H. C. J. Fredstrup exactly how many rehearsals were held of this dance in 1841.

Musical sources:

Orchestral score. Ms. Copy. Brown ink. 1 vol. 38 pp. (27,2 × 38 cm) 223/Partitur/Pas de deux/til/Robert af Normandiet,/1841./31 Stemmer/[…]/Andante.
Unsigned and dated (on the front cover): '1841.'
[DKKk; MA ms 2604 (KTB 223)]

Répétiteur's copy. Ms. Copy (by H. S. Paulli?). Brown ink. 14 pp. of which one is blank (33,3 × 23,5 cm with minor variants)
Nye/Pas de deux./til/Robert af Normandiet/No. […] 2./51B./1841
Unsigned and dated (on the front cover): '1841'
[DKKk; MA ms 2903 (2) (KTB 223)]
This répétiteur's copy (which seemingly is copied by H. S. Paulli) is bound together with the répétiteur's copy of the other 1841 *New Pas de deux* that Bournonville mounted as a separate divertissement at Copenhagen's Royal Theatre on 14.10.1841. The volume also contains his autographed choreographic notes (written with brown ink) for the opening *Andante* movement (performed by the woman and the man alternately) as well as his choreography for the male solo variation (*Allegretto*). These notes were probably written for the last restaging of the *Pas de deux* in Copenhagen on 29.10.1849 (that year performed W. Funck and C. Kellermann). This is clear from the terminology and the stenochoreographic signs employed by Bournonville here, which certainly date from around 1848 when he began more systematically to notate his dances. Finally, the music contained on p. 20, including a slightly revised version of the Coda movement, seems to have been copied by Bournonville himself at some later stage.

Parts. Ms. Copy. 31 vol.
3 vl I, 3 vl II, 2 vla, 3 vlc e cb, fl 1/2, ob 1/2, cl 1/2, fag 1/2, cor 1/2/3/4, clno 1/2, trb 1/2/3, timp, gr cassa, piatti e tri.
Unsigned and undated [1841]
[DKKk; KTB 223

1842

9.1.1842

Jaleo from the ballet The Toreador (Jaleo af Balletten Toréadoren) **performed by Bournonville and C. Fjeldsted.**

This dance derives from Act I (score no. 6) of Bournonville's two-act idyllic ballet *The Toreador* (*see* 27.11.1840) and is described in the rehearsal book of H. C. J. Fredstrup as 'Scene og Pas de deux af Balletten Toreadoren'. This fact seems to indicate that it contained a brief mime scene that preceded the actual dance. The *Jaleo* was given once with this title. It is not clear from the rehearsal book of H. C. J. Fredstrup exactly how many rehearsals were held of it in 1841. No separate musical sources for the 1842 divertissement version of this dance have been traced. This indicates that the dance was most probably performed this year with the original musical material for *The Toreador* (now in DKKk, call nos. C II, 114 k, MA ms 2965, and KTB 1046 (originally KTB 269)).

22.1.1842

New Pas de deux (Ny Pas de deux) **in** *The Festival in Albano (Festen i Albano)*, **performed by F. Lefèbvre and C. Fjeldsted.**

On this day Bournonville's one-act idyllic ballet *The Festival in Albano* (*see* 28.10.1839) was performed with a so-called *New Pas de deux (Ny Pas de deux)*, choreographed by the French dancer, F. Lefèbvre, and performed by himself and Fjeldsted in the rôles of two guests at the wedding festival of *Antonio* and *Silvia*. The dance, which replaced Bournonville's original *Pas de deux* (score no. 9), was interpolated in *The Festival in Albano* for Lefèbvre's début performance in Copenhagen and performed twice in this ballet (the last time on 25.1.1842). No separate musical sources for Lefèbvre's *New Pas de deux* have yet been traced. It is not possible to identify the dance any further.

28.1.1842

The Danes in China (De Danske i China).

An earlier divertissement of this name, based on excerpts from Act I (score nos. 5–11) of Bournonville's two-act romantic ballet *The Isle of Phantasy* (*see* 28.10.1838), was premièred in Copenhagen on 17.9.1839. The 1842 version of it differed (according to the poster) by three new dances as follows:

(1) *Chinese* [Dance] *(Chinesisk)* performed by F. Hoppensach.
(2) *A new scenic Pas de deux in Spanish style, named: La Sevilliana. (En ny scenisk Pas de deux i spansk Stiil, kaldet: La Sevilliana)* performed by F. Lefèbvre and C. Fjeldsted.
(3) *The English Sailor (Den Engelske Matros)* performed by Bournonville.

It is unclear whether Bournonville choreographed *La Sevilliana* himself, or whether this dance (which is set to music by a not yet identified composer) was brought to Copenhagen by the French dancer, F. Lefèbvre, who had been engaged in 1842 at Bournonville's request as principal dancer and assistant choreographer of Copenhagen's Royal Theatre, a post he held until April 1847.

The Danes in China was restaged on two later occasions in Copenhagen on 27.2.1843 and 26.2.1865, but each time with different contents of dances. The 1842 version was given 5 times, the last time on 23.2.1842. It is not clear from the rehearsal book of H. C. J. Fredstrup exactly how many rehearsals were held of this divertissement in 1842.

Musical sources:

The orchestral score, the répétiteur's copy, and the set of parts for this divertissement version of excerpts from Act I of *The Isle of Phantasy* are now in DKKk (call nos. C II 119, MA ms 2945, and KTB 206).

No orchestral score and répétiteur's copy for *La Sevilliana* have yet been traced.

Parts (*La Sevilliana*). Ms. Copy. 30 vol.
3 vl I, 2 vl II, 2 vla, 3 vlc e cb, fl 1/2, ob 1/2, cl 1/2, fag 1/2, cor 1/2/3/4, clno 1/2, trb 1/2/3, timp, gr cassa, piatti e tri.
Unsigned and undated [1842]
[DKKk; KTB 210]
The part for the second trombone of *La Sevilliana* contains a pencilled note reading '19½'. It seems to indicate that this Spanish dance was incorporated at a later stage in another ballet as score no. '19½' (perhaps in Bournonville's three-act romantic ballet *Faust* on 17.10.1842).

7.2.1842

Gallopade **performed in** *The Tyroleans (Tyrolerne).*

Bournonville's one-act ballet *The Tyroleans* (*see* 6.3.1835) was (according to the poster) performed on this day with an incorporated *Gallopade*, borrowed from his earlier two-act ballet *The Isle of Phantasy* (*see* 28.10.1838) and given as a new, additional finale to *The Tyroleans*. It is not clear whether this *Gallopade* (which was performed by F. Hoppe and C. Fjeldsted) is identical with that from *The Isle of Phantasy* which is set to music by I. P. E. Hartmann (Act I, score no. 3), or if it is the one with to music by E. Helsted (Act II, score 7). However, the existence of a separate set of parts for Helsted's *Gallopade* (now in DKKk; call no. MA ms 2757 (1–20)) seems to indicate that it was his music which was incorporated on this day as a new finale in *The Tyroleans*. The *Gallopade* was only performed twice in *The Tyroleans*, the last time on 17.2.1842. It is not possible to identify the dance any further.

28.3.1842

Gurre (Evening prospect) (Gurre (Aftenprospect)) **recited by the actor J. C. Hansen accompanied by a chorus of mixed voices.**

This poem by H. C. Andersen (set to music by H. Rung) was mounted with Bournonville's mise-en-scène as part of a charity performance for the actors, C. Faaborg and J. C. Hansen. Bournonville is credited for the mise-en-scène only on the poster for its second performance on 17.4.1842. Twenty-five years later *Gurre* was restaged for the last time by Bournonville on 29.5.1867, as part of a gala performance given in honour of the silver wedding of Denmark's King Christian IX and Queen Louise.

Gurre was received 3 performances, the last of which took place on 29.5.1867. It is not clear from the rehearsal book of H. C. J. Fredstrup exactly how many rehearsals were held of it in 1842.

Musical sources:

Orchestral score. Ms. Autograph (by H. Rung). Brown ink. 1 vol. 24 pp. of which two are blank (29,3 × 34 cm)
H. RUNG/GURRE/PART./[…]/Gurre,/Aftenprospekt af H. C. Andersen./Musiken af H. Rung.
Signed (on the title page): 'H. Rung.', undated [1842]
[DKKk; C II, 157

Piano-vocal score. Ms. Autograph (by H. Rung). Black ink. 4 pp. (24,3 × 32,7 cm)
Gurre/H: Rung./Andante
Signed (on p. 1): 'H: Rung.', undated [c.1842]
[DKKk; C II, 157
This piano-vocal score contains the music for the centrepiece in *Gurre*, namely the romance entitled «Hvor Nilen vander Ægypterens Jord» (originally performed by the actor J. C. Hansen). The score itself most probably dates from a later separate performance of it in Copenhagen.

No parts and vocal parts for *Gurre* dating from the 1842 performances of *Gurre* at the Royal Theatre have yet been traced.

Printed sources:

Printed libretto. 1 vol. 3 pp. (19,8 × 12,2 cm)
Gurre./Aftenlandskab/af/H. C. Andersen./(Musikken componeret af Hr. Syngemester Rung,/Romanzen foredraget af Hr. Hansen den Ældre,/Scenens Arrangement af Hr. Balletmester Bournonville).
Kjøbenhavn, Jens Hostrup Schultz, 1842.
[Private collection (Denmark).
This copy was originally part of Bournonville's private library, and is today owned by his great-great-great-grandson, Mr. Eskil Irminger.

29.3.1842
Napoli or The Fisherman and His Bride
(Napoli eller Fiskeren og hans Brud).
Bournonville's three-act romantic ballet *Napoli or The Fisherman and His Bride* was created from inspirations received during his nine-week sojourn there in the summer of 1841. His first draft for the ballet's scenario was written in Dunkerque on 22.9.1841 on his homebound journey after his six-month enforced exile that year. The score is composed and arranged by four composers, each contributing as follows:

(1) E. Helsted: The *Introduction*, Act I (score nos. 1–4, and no. 7, i.e. the *Finale*), and Act III (score no. 2, i.e. the *Pas de quatre*, later revised into a *Pas de cinq/six*).
(2) H. S. Paulli: Act I (score no. 5, i.e. the *Ballabile*, no. 6, the street singer's mime scene), and Act III (score nos. 1 and 3, i.e. the *Tarantella*).
(3) N. W. Gade: The whole of Act II.
(4) H. C. Lumbye: Act III (score no. 4, i.e. the *Finale Gallop*).

In their respective scores these four composers incorporated several musical borrowings which are identified as follows:

(1) In his music for the *Introduction* to Act I Helsted employed authentic military horn signals used by the British naval army for the evening retreat during the 1803 conquest of the isle of Capri. Moreover, in the scene of Act I (score no. 4) which depicts the calumny of *Peppo* and *Giacomo*, Helsted employed large excerpts from Basilio's aria «La calunnia è un venticello» in Act I (score no. 6) of G. Rossini's two-act comic opera *Il Barbiere di Sevilla* (premièred at Teatro Argentina in Rome on 20.2.1816). Finally, in Act I, score no. 6 (*Moderato*) Helsted employs what clearly appears to be traditional Italian *commedia dell'arte* music to accompany the scene in which the character Carlino and his puppet show enter the stage.

(2) In his music for the *Ballabile* in Act I (score no. 5, the *Allegretto*) Paulli interpolated G. Torrente's Neapolitan arietta to words by the poet Sacco, entitled «Te voglio bene assaje». According to Torrente's autographed manuscript for this song (now in IMc, call no. Noseda) it dates from 1840 and was the most popular song of time in Naples during Bournonville's sojourn in that city. In *Napoli or The Fisherman and His Bride* the tune accompanied the *Pas de deux* section performed by *Gennaro* and *Teresina*, during which they express their mutual love.
(3) In his music for Act II (score no. 6) Gade incorporated Fr. H. Prüme's *Pastorale* op. 1 for solo violin, entitled *La Mélancolie*, except for its second and third variation. This concert piece had been played by Prüme himself at Copenhagen's Royal Theatre on 27.12. 1840, and soon became one of the most popular tunes of the day. Moreover, in score nos. 7 and 8 (*Andante*) Gade incorporated the Sicilian Maria hymn «O sanctissima, o piissima», the first time employed as an accompaniment for the mime scene in which *Gennaro* and *Teresina* overcome the supernatural force of *Golfo* by using their image of Madonna dell'Arco as a protective shield. The hymn, which was published in Germany (Leipzig) by J. G. Herder in the third volume of his music anthology *Adrastea* (1802), became widely known in Denmark in 1841 when it was employed by B. S. Ingemann for his chorale «Dyb af Kjærlighed, Lys og Herlighed, Verdenslivets Forklarer!», written for the marriage of Denmark's crown prince, Carl Frederik Christian (later King Frederik VII) to the German duchess, Caroline Charlotte Marianne. The text for this chorale was first published in Sorø by Peter Magnus' Officin on 27.6.1841, while the melody of *O sanctissima* was published for the first time in Denmark with the original Italian text by A. P. Berggreen in his *Sange til Skolebrug* (Kjøbenhavn, C. A. Reitzel, 1834, no. 11, p. 17).
Furthermore, in Act II of *Napoli or The Fisherman and His Bride* (score no. 3) Gade incorporated G. Torrente's 1840 Neapolitan arietta «Te voglio bene assaje» which Paulli had used before him in the Act I *Ballabile* (score no. 5). The same song tune resurfaces for the third time in the ballet in Paulli's score for the opening section of Act III, and for the fourth and the last time in Lumbye's *Finale Gallop* in the same act (score no. 4) thereby becoming the ballet's main musical leitmotif.
(4) In the opening scene of Act III (score no. 1), Paulli incorporated several excerpts borrowed from a ballade, entitled «Jadis régnait en Normandie». It was originally sung by the character *Raimbaud* and a male chorus of knights in Act I (score no. 1) of Giacomo Meyerbeer's 1831 five-act opera *Robert le Diable*. In Bournonville's ballet these excerpts served to accompany the mime scene in which *Peppo* and *Giacomo* call the attention of the pilgrims at Monte Vergine to the influence of the evil spirits which supposedly caused the cruel fate of *Teresina*.

Helsted's *Pas de quatre* in Act III (which originally was performed by a man and three women) was revised by Bournonville into a *Pas de cinq* on 7.5.1842 (then danced by a man and four women). This version was kept unchanged until 28.1.1844 when the dance was revised a second time into a *Pas de six* (now performed by two men and four women). In a letter from Bournonville to F. Hoppe, dated 29.2.1844 (now in a private collection, Copenhagen) he noted his reasons for making this second revision of the Act III divertissement:

'pas de cinq i Napoli har gaaet deelt som pas de six, for Sig. [S.] Lund og [L.] Gade, da [P.] Funck har erklæret sig ude af Stand, til at gjøre Entrechat à six, om det er Sandhed eller Løgn skal jeg lade være usagt'.

Between 18.5.1844 and 15.9.1866 the divertissement was again performed as a *Pas de cinq*, but after this period it has since been given as a *Pas de six*.

On 27.6.1843 the complete ballet was staged for the first

time outside Denmark at Hamburg's Stadttheater on 27.6. 1843 with the German title *Napoli, oder: Der Fischer und seine Braut*. This production was mounted with new décor by the French scene painter, F. d'Herbès.

On 19.6.1845 the ballet was restaged at Copenhagen's Royal Theatre for a special gala performance given for the visiting King of Prussia, Friedrich William IV. For this occasion Bournonville wrote a new so-called *Analyse du Ballet*, which was published the same day on a specially designed programme-poster.

Six years later the French dancer and choreographer, F. Lefèbvre, mounted a pirated three-act version of *Napoli and The Fisherman and His Bride* at Turin's Teatro Carignano on 30.8.1851. It was entitled *La Grotta Azzurra*, but as it was rather poorly received it went out of the repertory after only a very limited number of performances (the last of which was given on 11.9.1851).

Five years after that the ballet was mounted by Bournonville at Vienna's Kärnthnerthor Theatre on 31.1.1856 with the title *Napoli, oder: Der Fischer und seine Braut*. The Austrian version included two new dances in Act III which replaced Bournonville's original *Pas de cinq* divertissement. They consisted of a *Pas de quatre* (choreographed by L. Gabrielli to music by a not yet identified composer) and a *Pas de deux* (choreographed by L. Vienna and set to music by M. Strebinger). Moreover, the Vienna version included three new solo variations, choreographed by Bournonville and danced by C. Pocchini (as *Teresina*) in Act I and II respectively (all seemingly set to music by Strebinger).

The following year Bournonville proposed a Swedish première of the ballet to the theatre management of Stockholm's Royal Theatre (*see* 15.6.1857). This project was planned to take place in the spring of 1859, but was for unknown reasons never carried out.

Napoli or The Fisherman and His Bride was restaged five more times by Bournonville at Copenhagen's Royal Theatre (*see* 8.1.1860, 23.1.1866, 2.6.1870, 15.3.1873, and 10.9.1875), each time with new casts and in slightly revised versions. Finally, Bournonville also mounted two minor works that have a close relation with this ballet, and were named as follows:

(1) *Masaniello (Neapolitan Tableau) (Masaniello (Neapolitansk Tableau))*, performed as a curtain-raiser for a special charity performance of *Napoli* on 3.6.1842.
(2) *'Italian Genre Picture' Divertissement with Tarantella ('Italiensk Genrebillede' Divertissement med Tarantella)*, premièred at Christiania's Theatre (Oslo) on 2.7.1852.

The original 1842 version of *Napoli or The Fisherman and His Bride* was given 94 times (the last time on 29.5.1855) and the ballet reached a total of 178 performances in Copenhagen during Bournonville's lifetime (the last of which was given on 5.11.1879). According to the rehearsal book of H. C. J. Fredstrup, 56 rehearsals were held of it between 1.12.1841 and 29.3.1842.

Autograph sources:

Manuscript scenario. Ms. Autograph. Brown ink (including a pencilled drawing). 1 vol. 7 pp. (29 × 19,1 cm)
Napoli./eller./Fiskeren og hans Brud./Romantisk Ballet i tre Acter/af/August Bournonville./1841.

Signed and dated: 'skrevet i Dünkirken Onsdagen den 22 Sept: 1841.'
[DKKk; NKS 3285 4° 3 L–P

Manuscript scenario. Ms. Autograph. Brown ink. 3 pp. (22,3 × 17,7 cm)
Napoli/eller/Fiskeren og hans Brud./Romantisk Ballet i 2 Acter af A: Bournonville./[...]/Plan/Første Act./[...]/Anden Act./[...]/Tredie Tableau.
Signed and dated: 'Kjöbenhavn den 30 October 1841.'
[Copenhagen, The State Archive (Rigsarkivet); Det kgl. Teaters Arkiv, Gruppe E, pakke 288

Musical sources:

Musical drafts. Ms. Autograph (by E. Helsted). Black ink. 124 pp. (26,3 × 17,3 cm) 'Napoli.'/Indledning./[...]/No. 1./Tæppet op!/[...]/No. 2. Barcarole./[...]/No. 3.
Signed and dated: (Indledning) 'Januar 1842./Ed. Helsted.', (No. 1) 'September 1841. E. H.', (No. 2) 'September 1841./Ed. H.' October 1841./Ed. Helsted.' [Copied by Helsted in Fredensborg, April 1891]
[DKKk; Collin 120, 2°
These musical drafts are Helsted's own copy of his original drafts for the overture and score nos. 1–3 of Act I in Bournonville's *Napoli or The Fisherman and His Bride*. They were copied in April 1891 as a personal gift to J. Collin and are described by by Helsted in an accompanying letter as follows:
'det er de første Instrumenteringsudkast [...] de første Forsøg paa at iklæde Tonebillederne den karakteristiske Klangdragt hvori de viste sig for mig under Undfangelsen [...] Desværre er det kun Kopier, men egenhændiges og fotografisk nøiagtige Kopier efter Kladderne, hvorefter senere den nu existerende Partitur udfærdigedes'.

Musical draft. Ms. Autograph (by E. Helsted). Black ink and pencil. 4 pp. (33,5 × 26 cm with minor variants)
3.die Act./Napoli/No. 1 Vivace
Unsigned and undated [c.1841-1842]
[DKKk; MA ms 2693
This autographed musical draft for two violins appears to be Helsted's first version of the music of the opening scene in Act III (score no. 1) in Bournonville's *Napoli or The Fisherman and His Bride*.
It contains a note by the composer (on p. 2) reading '(Skuddet falder)'. Helsted's music for this scene, however, was never used in Bournonville's ballet, since the music for the opening scene of Act III was in the end entrusted to H. S. Paulli.

Musical drafts (fragments). Ms. Autographs (by E. Helsted, H. S. Paulli, and N. W. Gade). Brown and black ink. 38 + 2 + 24 + 4 + 4 pp. of which two are blank (34,8 × 24,6 cm with minor variants)
[Act I] Vivace:/[...]/No. 2./[...]/No. 3 Allegretto quasi Allegro./[...]/No. 4. Allegro./[...]/All.° No. 4 [changed to] 5./[...]/No. 5 [changed to] 6/All.°/[...]/fra Helsted/meno mosso/[...]/[Act II] piu lento./[...]/attacca./No. 4/Allegretto/No. 5./Andante./[...]/No. 6./Allegretto./[...]/No. 7./All.° di molto/[...]/No. 8./Presto/[...]/No. 9/Andante/[...]/No. 1. 3.die Akt/No. 4./Finale.
Signed and dated (on p. '28'): 'Fine dell'Atto Seconda / 17 [changed to] 20/1/1842/NWGade' and (on the last page) 'martz 1842'
[Private collection (Copenhagen)
These five autographed musical drafts contain Helsted's and Paulli's music for Act I (score nos. 1–6 and no. 7, fragment), Gade's music for Act II (score no. 3, fragment, and no. 4), Paulli's music for Act III (score no. 1, fragment), and Lumbye's music for the *Finale Gallop* (score no. 4 here copied by Helsted). Moreover, several of the drafts contain music that is found neither in the parts, nor in the full orchestral score for the 1842 version. The drafts also contain Bournonville's autographed pencilled notes describing in fine detail the mime, the dramatic action, and (more generally) the choreography. They were most likely written during the first rehearsals of the ballet held in December 1841 and during the early months of 1842.

Orchestral score. Ms. Autographs (by E. Helsted, H. S. Paulli, N. W. Gade, and H. C. Lumbye). Brown and black ink. 2 vol. Act I 172 pp., Act II–III 244 pp. of which one is blank (26,1 × 36,8 cm)
1.ste Act/[…]/2.den Act./NWGade/[…]/3.die Act.
Signed and dated (Act I, nos. 1, 2, and 3): 'Januar 1842./Eduard Helsted.', (no. 5) 'H. S. Paulli' (no. 6) 'HSPaulli/d: 22 Febr: 1842', (no. 7) 'febr. 1842. Eduard Helsted.', (Act II, no. 9) 'd. 20/2 – 1842.', (Act III, no. 1) 'HSPaulli/Martz 1842.', (no. 2) 'Eduard Helsted/i Martz 1842.', (no. 3) 'HSPaulli/Martz 1842.', (no. 4) 'H. C. Lumbÿe.'
[DKKk; C II, 114 k (KTB 292)]
A later musical insertion in Gade's autographed score for Act II, no. 4 (pp. 45–48, perhaps A. Grandjean's autograph) appears to have been interpolated in this ballet during the late 1890s. This theory is supported by the fact that the insertion is not included in the so-called 'Signalparti' which was made for E. Hansen's restaging of *Napoli or The Fisherman and His Bride* on 29.10.1885 (now in DKKk, call no. MA ms 2989 (KTB 292)).

No répétiteur's copy dating from the 1842 première of *Napoli* has yet been traced. However, a later complete répétiteur's copy (copied by H. S. Paulli) is now in DKKk (call no. C II, 119). It was most probably written in connection with Bournonville's staging of *Napoli, oder: Der Fischer und seine Braut* at Vienna's Kärnthnerthor Theatre (*see* 31.1.1856). It contains his pencilled autographed notes for Act I (score nos. 1–5) describing (in general terms) the mime and the choreography. Moreover, his autographed choreographic numbers (written with brown ink) are included in the same volume underneath the music for Act I and seem to refer to a separate (not yet traced) choreographic notation of this act.

Parts. Ms. Copy. 35 vol.
4 vl I, 4 vl II, 2 vla, 4 vlc e cb, fl 1/2, ob 1/2, cl 1/2, fag 1/2, cor 1/2/3/4, tr 1/2, trb 1/2/3, timp, gr cassa, piatti e tri, arpa.
Unsigned and undated [1842]
[DKKk; KTB 292]
According to several notes and musical insertions added at later stages, this set of parts was used for all performances of *Napoli or The Fisherman and His Bride* in Copenhagen during Bournonville's lifetime and well thereafter (including H. Beck's revised restaging of this ballet in 1907, which was kept in the repertory until 1923).

Other sources:

Sketch by C. F. Christensen for the back curtain in Act II. Pencil and water colours (31,7 × 46 cm)
Napoli/Jan 1842.
Unsigned and dated: 'Jan 1842.'
[DKKt; C. F. Christensens dekorationsudkast
This dated sketch (drawn with pencil and brownish watercolours) clearly represents Christensen's first draft for the back curtain of the blue grotto in Act II of *Napoli or The Fisherman and His Bride*.

Sketch by C. F. Christensen for the décor of Act II. Pencil and water colours (29 × 19 cm)
[Untitled]
Unsigned and undated [c.1842]
[SSm; D. Fryklunds samling no. 289
This sketch shows the décor of the blue grotto in Act II of *Napoli or The Fisherman and His Bride* and dates most probably from the 1842 Copenhagen première of the ballet.

Printed sources:

Printed scenario. 1 vol. 13 pp. (20,9 × 12,1 cm)
Napoli/eller/Fiskeren og hans Brud,/romantisk Ballet i 3 Acter/ August Bournonville./Musiken af Dhrr. Paulli, Ed. Helsted og Gade./Decorationer af Hr. Theatermaler Christensen.
Kjøbenhavn, J. H. Schubothe, Bianco Luno, 1842.
[DKKk; 17, – 173 8°

29.4.1842
The Little Pixie (Den lille Nisse). **Projected ballet.**
This projected ballet in two acts is perhaps identical with the fourth and final work in Bournonville's later series of four projected ballets, named *The Four Seasons, or Cupid's Journey, A Ballet Cycle* (*see* 16.6.1846) and mentioned for the first time in his memoirs *My Theatre Life* (p. 115). However, in spite of the fact that Bournonville's description of this cycle of four ballets is included in his memoirs between the years of 1845 and 1847, he had already mentioned *The Little Pixie* in a letter to the management of Copenhagen's Royal Theatre on 29.4.1842 (now in The State Archive, call no. Det kgl. Teaters Arkiv, Gruppe E, pakke 288). Moreover, this letter is followed by a brief note in a second letter (dated 17.2.1843) in which Bournonville describes his project for *The Little Pixie* in more detail:

'naar Balletten [*The Childhood of Erik Menved*] i løbet af næste Vinter muligen kan have fuldendt sin Løbebane af 25 Forestillinger vil en stor Deel af Costumet og et Par Decorationer tjene mig til min toacts Ballet <u>Den lille Nisse</u> der spiller i Danmark og i Riddertiden'.

Furthermore, the possibility that the plot of *The Little Pixie* is identical with or at least has a close affinity with Bournonville's and A. F. Lincke's much later divertissement, entitled *The Earnest Maiden (Den alvorlige Pige)*, cannot be discarded. Thus, this divertissement (which was premièred at the Court Theatre on 15.10.1856) also includes 'En lille Huusnisse' among its principal characters.

Autograph sources:

Manuscript synopsis (included in a letter to J. Colin). Ms. Autograph. Brown ink. 3 pp. (26,7 × 21,6 cm)
[…]min toacts Ballet <u>Den lille Nisse</u>, der spiller i Danmark og i Riddertiden […]
Signed and dated: 'Kjöbenhavn d: 17 Febr 1843.'
[Copenhagen, The State Archive; Det kgl. Teaters Arkiv, Gruppe E, pakke 288

25.5.1842
Le Nozze di Figaro (the Court Theatre, sung in Italian).
This performance of W. A. Mozart's four-act comic opera from 1786 was given in Italian (by Danish singers) and mounted with Bournonville's mise-en-scène and choreography. It included a *Fandango* (danced by F. Hoppe and P. Funck) and was performed twice at the Court Theatre, the last time on 1.6.1842.

At the restaging at Copenhagen's Royal Theatre of *Die Hochzeit des Figaro (Figaros Bryllup)* on 7.1.1844 (then sung in Danish) Bournonville was again responsible for the staging of the dance scenes, while at the third restaging of this work on 1.5.1849 he supervised the rehearsals of both its dances and the general mise-en-scène. Moreover, on 30.10.1857 Bournonville included *Die Hochzeit des Figaro* in a list of projected opera restagings which he was planning that day for the 1857–58 and 1858–59 seasons. This project was carried out on 21.5.1858 when Mozart's opera was mounted for the first time with Bournonville's own, completely new mise-en-scène. Finally, he restaged *Die Hochzeit des Figaro* on two more occasions, on 7.10.1860 and 30.4.1872 (on the last date with completely new choreography and a partially revised mise-en-scène).

No separate musical sources dating from his 1842 staging at the Court Theatre of *Le Nozze di Figaro* (sung in Italian) have yet been traced. It is not clear from the rehearsal book of H. C. J. Fredstrup exactly how many rehearsals of this opera and its dances were held in 1842.

3.6.1842
Masaniello (Neapolitan Tableau) Overture, Choir of the Fishermen, Barcarola and Duet from 'La Muette de Portici' (Masaniello (Neapolitansk Tableau) Ouverture, Fiskerchor, Barcarola og Duet af 'Den Stumme i Portici').
This tableau was mounted by Bournonville as a curtain-raiser for a charity performance of his three-act romantic ballet *Napoli, or The Fisherman and His Bride* (*see* 29.3.1842), given on this day in order to celebrate his return to Denmark after his enforced six-month exile in 1841. This is clear from his autographed scenario for it (entitled *Improvisatoren paa Molo./Lȳrisk = Genremalerie*) according to which his intention with this tableau was clearly to mark his own homecoming. Moreover, the scenario gives some interesting clues about Bournonville's strong views on the rôle of *Gennaro* in *Napoli* as a nearly autobiographical portrait:

'(Forspil til 2.den Act af den Stumme).
Middagssøvn. Matroser vækker de Sovende og opfordrer Dem til Arbeide. Der hales og læsses. Reisende stige iland. Almue stimler til og nogle Koner omringe en gammel <u>Scrivano</u>, der læser og skriver for Dem.
(Alt under Fisker=Choret)
<u>Rafaello</u> kommer med sin Kone og lille Datter, han er tungsindig og hans Guitar hænger paa hans Skuldre uden at han vil spille paa Den. men han bliver snart muntrere ved at modtage et Brev fra sin Ven <u>Gennaro</u> der nu er riig og förer sit eget Skib. Gennaro har ikke glemt sine fattige Venner og skriver dem til fra det fjerne Norden,, men ak de kunne ikke læse Skrivt. Det er altsaa Skriveren der giver Oplæsning og Brevet hvis Indhold er en Beskrivelse om Indseilingen i Sundet, Ankomsten til Kbhvn og den gode Modtagelse som den neapolitanske Fisker dér har nÿdt. Alle ÿttre deres Glæde over at man i Norden kjender og ÿnder <u>Napoli</u>, og <u>Rafaello</u> maa nu igjen improvisere om <u>Gennaros</u> Kjerlighed og <u>Teresinas</u> forunderlige Frelse fra Havaanden i den blaa Grotte. (<u>Rafaello</u> med Kone og Barn danne den midterste Gruppe). Den talrige Forsamling leirer sig omkring dem og til Guitarens Accorder sÿnger <u>Rafaello</u> en Romance, et melodramatisk recitativ og en <u>Barcarole</u> der istemmes af Choret.
Slutnings Gruppe'.

No separate musical sources containing the excerpts from D.-F.-E. Auber's five-act opera *La Muette de Portici* which accompanied this tableau have yet been traced. It is not clear from the rehearsal book of H. C. J. Fredstrup exactly how many rehearsals were held of this tableau in 1842.

Autograph sources:

Manuscript mise-en-scène. Ms. Autograph. Brown ink. 1 p. (34,8 × 21,6 cm)
<u>Improvisatoren paa Molo./Lȳrisk = Genremaleri/</u>(Forspil til 2.den Act af Den Stumme)
Unsigned and undated [1842]
[DKKk; Den Collinske Manuskriptsamling 95, 4°

10.6.1842
Faust.
On this day Bournonville's three-act romantic ballet *Faust* (*see* 25.4.1832) was restaged with an almost completely new

cast and performed as part of a charity performance given for C. Fjeldsted, who on this occasion played *Margaretha* for the first time. Otherwise, the performance appears to have been mounted with only minor if any changes from Bournonville's original version. It is not clear from the rehearsal book of H. C. J. Fredstrup exactly how many rehearsals were held of this ballet in 1842.

10.6.1842
La Cracovienne, Polish National Dance after Fanny Elssler (Polsk Nationaldans efter Fanny Elssler) **performed by C. Fjeldsted.**
This dance is included in Bournonville's handwritten lists of his works, written c.1851 (*see* Additional Sources) in which it is listed among those dances mounted 'partly from another choreographer's work'. It was originally created for and performed by F. Elssler in Act II of J. Mazilier's three-act pantomimic ballet *La Gipsy* (premièred at the Paris Opéra on 28.1. 1839) and is set to music based on traditional Polish folk tunes, orchestrated by A. Thomas. This is clear from a Polish printed piano score (now in PLKj, call no. Musicalia 1155 III) according to which two excerpts from J. Damse's and K. Kurpinski's score for the ballet, entitled *Wesele w Ojcowie* (premièred at the Narodowy Theatre in Warsaw on 14.3.1823) had provided the main musical motifs for Elssler's *Cracovienne*. The dance is mentioned for the first time by Bournonville in a letter to his wife, Helene, written in Paris on 5.5.1841:

'I have already two lovely *pas de deux* and *la Cracovienne* – a famous trifle – which I have decided to be for her [i.e. Caroline Fjeldsted]'.

Moreover, according to his 1841 travel diary, Bournonville had two meetings in Paris (on 28.4. and 1.5.1841) with J. Mazilier. The reason for these encounters may well have been to obtain Mazilier's permission to mount these dances in Copenhagen, in which Bournonville evidently was successful.
   La Cracovienne was later also performed twice by C. Fjeldsted at Christiania's Theatre (Oslo) on 25.6. and 20.8.1847. On 9.11.1855 it was restaged for S. Price at Copenhagen's Royal Theatre. She also performed it when it was given for the last time in Denmark during Bournonville's lifetime at the Court Theatre on 15.10.1856.
   La Cracovienne reached a total of 33 performances in Copenhagen of which 21 were given by C. Fjeldsted and 12 by S. Price. It is not clear from the rehearsal book of H. C. J. Fredstrup exactly how many rehearsals were held of this dance in 1842.

Musical sources:

Orchestral score. Ms. Copy. Black ink. 1 vol. 46 pp. (30,2 × 23 cm)
Partitur/til/Cracoviennen/la Gibsy [*sic*]/Cracovienne.
Unsigned and undated [c.1841]
[DKKk; MA ms 2664 (KTB 214)
This orchestral score is clearly a French copy since it includes the French embossed stamp 'Dantier Fils'. It was most probably purchased by Bournonville in Paris during one of his two sojourns there in 1841. It contains his autographed pencilled notes which describe the choreography of the entire dance. They were most likely written in Paris shortly after a performance of J. Mazilier's ballet *La Gipsy*, in

which *La Cracovienne* was performed by the French ballerina, Maria (Jacob), who had taken over this part from F. Elssler in 1841.

Répétiteur's copy. Ms. Copy. Brown ink. 1 vol. 8 pp. of which one is black (33,4 × 25,5 cm)
Cracovienne/Repititeurpartie [*sic*]
Unsigned and undated [c.1842]
[DKKk; MA ms 2663 (KTB 214)
This répétiteur's copy is clearly a Danish copy made in Copenhagen and was most likely written immediately before the 1842 première of *La Cracovienne* at the Royal Theatre.

Parts. Ms. Copy. 27 vol.
2 vl I, 2 vl II, vla, 2 vlc e cb, fl 1/2, ob 1/2, cl 1/2, fag 1/2, cor 1/2/ 3/4, clno 1/2, trb 1/2/3, timp, gr cassa, piatti.
Unsigned and undated [1842]
[DKKk; KTB 214

2.8.1842
Pas de trois in *Guillaume Tell (Wilhelm Tell)*.
Projected staging.
According to a letter from Bournonville to the management of Copenhagen's Royal Theatre on 2.8.1842 (now in The State Archive, call no. Det kgl. Teaters Arkiv, Gruppe E, pakke 288) he proposed on this day:

'at jeg for Wilhelm Tell arrangerer Pas de trois'en i tredie Act'.

This project, however, was in the end entrusted to the French dancer, F. Lefèbvre, who was responsible for staging the dances in G. Rossini's four-act opera when it was given its Copenhagen première on 4.9.1842. Lefèbvre's choreography, in turn, was most probably based on the original dances as created by J. Aumer and Albert (François Decombe) for the Paris Opéra première of *Guillaume Tell* on 3.8.1829.

Many years later Bournonville included Rossini's opera in a list of projected opera restagings that he was planning for the 1857–58 and 1858–59 seasons on 30.10.1857. This project was carried out some ten years later, when *Guillaume Tell* was restaged on 23.11.1868 with Bournonville's mise-en-scène and choreography for the first time.

Rossini's opera was mounted two more times in Copenhagen by Bournonville, namely on 16.11.1873 and 21.11.1875 (on the last day with the Act III *Pas de trois* performed in a new, revised version arranged especially for A. Scholl).

8.9.1842
New Pas de deux, composed by Mazilier, music by Fessy (Ny Pas de deux, componeret af Mazilier, Musikken af Fessy), performed by A. Nielsen 'assisted' (*assisteret*) by Bournonville.
This dance by J. Mazilier (to music by A. Fessy) is perhaps identical with one of those two *Pas de deux* Bournonville mentioned in a letter to his wife, Helene, written in Paris on 5.5.1841:

'I have already two lovely *pas de deux* and *la Cracovienne* – a famous trifle – which I have decided to be for her [i.e. Caroline Fjeldsted]'.

If this theory is correct then the dance is most probably a work which Bournonville had seen performed at the Paris Opéra during his sojourn in the French capital in the early spring of 1841.

Another, and perhaps more likely possibility is that the *Pas de deux* was brought to Copenhagen by A. Nielsen in the late spring of 1842. Nielsen had studied with Mazilier in Paris in the early spring of 1842 and made her début at the Paris Opéra in May the same year.

The *Pas de deux* received 4 performances in Copenhagen, the last of which was given on 28.10.1842. No musical sources for a *Pas de deux* to music by A. Fessy have yet been traced in the annals of the music archive of Copenhagen's Royal Theatre. It is not possible to identify the dance any further.

18.9.1842
Undine.
According to his handwritten list of his mises-en-scène for operas, written c.1851 (*see* Additional Sources) Bournonville was responsible for mounting the première of C. Borgaard's five-act melodramatic fairy tale, set to music by A. Adam and I. P. E. Hartmann. The action of this work was based on the same legends and included a cast that was nearly identical with that in Th. Gautier's and J.-H. de Vernoy Saint-Georges' scenario for J. Coralli's and J. Perrot's two-act fantastic ballet *Giselle, ou les Wilis* (premièred at the Paris Opéra on 28.6. 1841). Consequently, *Undine* included five dances as follows:

(1) A *March* in Act II (score no. 6), performed during the chorus named «Hil Dig vor Hersker!».
(2) A *Circle dance* in Act II (score no. 7), performed during the chorus, named «Modtag favre Herskerinde Somrens friske Blomsterpryd!».
(3) A *Solo variation*, borrowed from Act II of Coralli's, Perrot's, and Adam's *Giselle*, performed by A. Nielsen as an interpolated divertissement between Acts III and IV.
(4) An (unnamed) *Dance*, borrowed from Act II of *Giselle* and performed by four undines (P. Funck, P. Fredstrup, N. Borup, and C. Bruun) as an interpolated divertissement between Acts III and IV of *Undine*.
(5) A *Nuptial march (Bryllupsmarsch)* in Act IV (score no. 9), performed during the chorus entitled «Hil dig Undine! Velkommen igjen!».

The interpolated excerpts from A. Adam's *Giselle* represent the first time that parts of this ballet were ever performed in Denmark. Moreover, according to a letter written by A. Nielsen to Bournonville in Paris on 27.7.1842 (now in DKKk, call no. NKS 3258 A 4°, V II, facs. 1, no. 425) the incorporation of these excerpts was the result of an explicit wish on Bournonville's part.

Undine received 9 performances, the last of which was given on 14.4.1844. The interpolated excerpts from *Giselle* were omitted at the sixth and eighth performances (given on 24.10. and 1.12.1843 respectively). According to the rehearsal book of H. C. J. Fredstrup 7 rehearsals of *Undine* and its dances were held between 12.9. and 18.9.1842.

Musical sources:

Orchestral score. Ms. Autograph (by I. P. E. Hartmann). Black and brown ink. 1 vol. 203 pp. of which one is blank (27,2 × 38 cm) [Without title] Introduction/Allegro moderato, grazioso.
Signed and dated (on p. 38): 'IPEHartmann/14/9 – 42.', and (on p. 202) 'I:P:E:Hartmann/Op: 36./d: 6/9 42.'
[DKKk; I. P. E. Hartmanns samling

The exact place where the excerpts from A. Adam's *Giselle* were interpolated is indicated with a pencilled note (on p. 136) reading: 'NB: siehe Einlage'. It was most probably written by the conductor, F. Gläser.

Répétiteur's copy. Ms. Copy. Black ink. 1 vol. 32 pp. of which one is blank (32,3 × 25 cm)
Undine/[...]/Repititeur [*sic*] Partie/til/Undine -
Unsigned and undated [1842]
[DKKk; MA ms 2908 (1) (KTA 378)
This répétiteur's copy contains Bournonville's autographed pencilled notes which describe the choreography for the dance scenes in Act II (score nos. 6–7), and Act IV (score no. 9).

Parts. Ms. Copy. 35 + 8 vol.
3 vl I, 3 vl II, 2 vla, 3 vlc e cb, fl 1/2, ob 1/2, cl 1/2, fag 1/2, cor 1/2/3, tr 1/2, trb 1/2/3, tuba, timp, gr cassa, piatti, tri, arpa, org, kl. On stage: fl 1/2, cl 1/2, fag 1/2, cor 1/2. 48 vocal parts.
Unsinged and undated [1842]
[DKKk; KTA 378

No separate orchestral score and set of parts with the music of the two excerpts from A. Adam's *Giselle* that were interpolated in Borgaard's play have yet been traced.

27.9.1842

Pas de deux (à la Taglioni) (uncredited) performed by Bournonville and A. Nielsen as an incorporated divertissement in Act II of *La Sylphide*.

According to the title of this dance and some pencilled notes in a separate set of parts (now in DKKk, call no. KTB 1024, but originally KTB 240) it is identical with the *Pas de deux* to music by J. Mayseder, that was originally performed in Act II (score no. 1 A) of Bournonville's two-act romantic ballet *The Isle of Phantasy* (*see* 28.10.1838). On 12.10.1842 it was also performed as an incorporated divertissement in Act I of Rossini's four-act opera *Guillaume Tell*, where it was again performed by Bournonville and Nielsen. Moreover, according to the rehearsal book of H. P. J. Fredstrup it was restaged for G. Brodersen and A. Nielsen on 6.11.1845 as a separate divertissement and described on the poster as a work 'arranged' (*arrangeret*) by Bournonville.

The *Pas de deux (à la Taglioni)* was performed 11 times by Bournonville and Nielsen in *La Sylphide*, the last time on 20.12.1843. According to the rehearsal book of H. C. J. Fredstrup 4 rehearsals were held of this dance between 3.9. and 7.9.1842.

17.10.1842

New Pas de deux (Ny Pas de deux) in *Faust*, performed by F. Lefèbvre and A. Nielsen.

According to the poster Bournonville's three-act romantic ballet *Faust* (*see* 25.4.1832) was performed on this day with a so-called *New Pas de deux (Ny Pas de deux)*, choreographed by the French dancer, F. Lefèbvre. Moreover, according to a pencilled note in the 1832 répétiteur's copy for *Faust* (p. 13, reading 'Indlagt No. 15. B.') the dance appears to have been incorporated immediately after Bournonville's original *Pas de deux* in Act II, or perhaps even replaced it. No separate musical sources for Lefèbvre's *New Pas de deux* have yet been traced. It is not possible to identify the dance any further.

1.11.1842

Pas de bouquets (composed by Albert, music by Adam) (componeret af Albert, Musiken af Adam) performed by A. Nielsen (the Court Theatre).

This solo dance was orginally part of the French choreographer, Albert's (François Decombe) three-act pantomimic ballet *La Jolie Fille de Gand* to music by A. Adam (premièred at the Paris Opéra on 22.6.1842). According to Adam's orchestral score and the original répétiteur's copy for this ballet (now in FPo, call nos. A 536 [III], pp. 27–40, and Mat. 19 [339 (23), pp. 9–13) it was originally danced as a *Pas seul* by the French ballerina, Maria (Jacob), in the first tableau of Act III. The music for this solo was most probably brought to Copenhagen by A. Nielsen after her Parisian soujourn in the spring of 1842 during which she most likely had learned it directly from Albert. In Copenhagen it was performed as part of a *New Divertissement (Nyt Divertissement)*, arranged and mounted under the personal supervision of Bournonville and including the première of his own *Polka militaire* (*see* the following entry). Soon after it was transferred to the Royal Theatre, where Nielsen performed it for the first time as a separate divertissement on 10.11.1842.

According to the rehearsal book of H. C. J. Fredstrup Bournonville later also directed a separate rehearsal of *Pas de bouquets* on 6.2.1843, prior to a restaging of it the following day. Moreover, on 25.6.1847 it was mounted for the last time by Bournonville, for his Swedish pupil M. C. Norberg, who danced it at Stockholm's Royal Theatre (Operahuset). Finally, parts of Adam's music for *Pas de bouquets* seem (according to pencilled notes in the parts for this dance) to have been reused by Bournonville for an uncredited Spanish solo dance, entitled *Castilliana* and created for the French ballerina, Maria (Jacob). She performed it for the first time in 1843 as an incorporated divertissement in D.-F.-E. Auber's five-act historical opera *Gustave III, ou Le Bal masqué* at Hamburg's Stadttheater (*see* 5.7.1843).

Pas de bouquets reached a total of 22 performances by Nielsen in Copenhagen, the last of which took place on 12.5. 1848. However, only a few months later C. Fjeldsted appeared in a similar solo dance at the Royal Theatre, entitled *Pas de Diane (af Balletten 'La jolie fille de Gand' af Albert)*, premièred on 22.9.1848. Apart from some minor musical cuts, she employed the exact same music as that which accompanied Nielsen's *Pas de bouquets*.

According to the rehearsal book of H. C. J. Fredstrup, 3 rehearsals were held of this dance under the personal supervision of Bournonville between 30.10. and 31.10.1842.

Musical sources:

No orchestral score dating from the 1842 Copenhagen première of this dance has yet been traced.

Répétiteur's copy. Ms. Copy. Black and brown ink. 8 pp. of which one is blank (27 × 21 cm)
Jolie Fille de Gand/Répétiteur/Pas seul. (maria)
Unsigned and undated [c.1842]
[DKKk; MA ms 2672
According to its title this répétiteur's copy is clearly a French copy that was most probably brought to Copenhagen by A. Nielsen in 1842. It contains the same music as that for the *Pas de bouquets* apart

from the two central movements (*Moderato* in 6/8 time, and *Allegretto* in 3/4 time) which are missing here. Moreover, the title clearly indicates that the music for Nielsen's *Pas de bouquets* was borrowed from A. Adam's score for Albert's three-act pantomimic ballet *La Jolie Fille de Gand*, in which it was originally performed as a *Pas seul* by the French ballerina, Marie (Jacob).

Répétiteur's copy. Ms. Copy. Brown ink. 1 vol. 4 pp. (32,1 × 24,2 cm)
Repetiteur Parti/B. 222/til/Pas de Bouquet
Unsigned and undated [c.1842]
[DKKk; MA ms 2904 (1) (KTB 222 (1))

Parts. Ms. Copy. 30 vol.
3 vl I, 3 vl II, 2 vla, 3 vlc e cb, fl 1/2, ob 1/2, cl 1/2, fag, cor 1/2, clno 1/2, tr 1/2, trb, timp, gr cassa, piatti, tri, arpa.
Unsigned and undated [1842]
[DKKk; KTB 222
A pencilled note in the part for the second horn reads 'Johs. Gentzen, Hamburg d. 5 July 1843'. This clearly indicates that the music for Nielsen's *Pas de bouquets* was reused later for the solo dance, entitled *Castilliana* and performed by the French ballerina, Maria (Jacob), at Hamburg's Stadttheater on 5.7.1843.

1.11.1842
Polka militaire (Polka, (Militairdands)) performed by Bournonville, F. Hoppe, P. Funck, and P. Fredstrup
1.11.1842 (the Court Theatre).

Bournonville's *Polka militaire* was (according to his own account in *My Theatre Life*, p. 417) partially based on a much earlier *Hungarian hussar solo* (choreographed by his father, Antoine Bournonville) in which Bournonville had made his solo début at the Court Theatre as a nine-year-old in the summer of 1814. The 1842 version for two couples was set to a new *Polka* composed by H. C. Lumbye.

As a result of its great success the divertissement was almost immediately transferred to the stage of the Royal Theatre, where it was first performed on 10.11.1842. Later it was performed at Helsingør's Theatre on 16.12.1846 as part of a ballet performance consisting of excerpts from the current ballet repertory of Copenhagen's Royal Theatre.

In Norway it was danced at Christiania's Theatre (Oslo) on 8.8.1847 by W. Funck and C. Fjeldsted in an adapted version for one couple, with the new title '*Military Dance by Bournonville*' ('*Militairdands af Bournonville*'). It was restaged at the same theatre on 9.6.1852 with the original cast for two couples (performed by S. Lund, E. Stramboe, A. Price, and S. Price) and entitled '*Military Polka, Character dance in Hungarian style*' ('*Militair Polka*' *Characteerdands i ungarsk Stiil*'). *Polka militaire* was performed at Christiania's Theatre for the last time by H. Scharff, W. Price, J. Price. and S. Price on 5.6. 1865.

In Sweden the dance was mounted at Stockholm's Royal Theatre (Operahuset) by Bournonville, who that year performed it together with Theodor (stage name for Th. I. Marckhl), M. C. Norberg, and P. A. Watz on 25.6.1847. On 2.6.1848 it was performed once at the Casino Theatre by F. Hoppe, G. Brodersen, J. Rostock, and L. Stramboe. In Stockholm it was restaged for the last time at Mindre Theatern on 12.6.1860, but then in the 1857 Norwegian version for one couple (then performed by F. Hoppe and S. Price) and with the new title *Military Polka (Militär-Polka)*. This version was given twice at Mindre Theatern, the last time on 14.6.1860.

Lumbye's music for *Polka militaire* seems (according to

notes written in the original parts for this dance) also to have been reused by Bournonville in 1843 for a dance entitled *Polka*, mounted at Hamburg's Stadttheater in 1843 for the French ballerina, Maria (Jacob). She performed it as an incorporated divertissement in D.-F.-E. Auber's five-act historical opera *Gustave III, ou Le Bal masqué* (*see* 5.7.1843).

After the 1842 Copenhagen première of *Polka militaire*, the paper *Dagen* (11.11.1842) noted of the dance, which became one of Bournonville most popular divertissements ever:

'Iblandt alle Hr. Bournonvilles artistiske Præstationer ere vistnok hans Characteerdandse de fortrinligste: det Liv, den Sindighed og Gratie, han i dem forener med et elskværdigt Lune og et ægte dramatisk Talent, der gjør, at han aldrig et Øieblik paa Stenen falder ud af den antagne Characteer, give dem Konstværd og langt større Interesse, end nogen anden Dandser vi have seet har været istand til'.

Polka militaire received 105 performances in Copenhagen during Bournonville's lifetime. Moreover, it was the very last dance he saw performed at the Royal Theatre (on 28.11. 1879) only two days before his sudden death on 30.8.1879. According to the rehearsal book of H. C. J. Fredstrup, 3 rehearsals were held of *Polka militaire* between 30.10. and 31.10.1842.

Musical sources:

No autographed orchestral score dating from the 1842 première of *Polka militaire* has yet been traced.

Orchestral score. Ms. copy. Black ink. 1 vol. 12 pp. of which 2 are blank (25,6 × 34,2 cm)
Signed (by the copyist on p. 2): 'H. C. Lumbye.', undated [c.1850s or 60s]
[DKKk; C II, 117 b (KTB 222)
This manuscript copy of Lumbye's score seems to date from a later restaging at Copenhagen' Royal Theatre during the 1850s or 60s.

Répétiteur's copy. Ms. Copy. Brown ink. 1 vol. 2 pp. (32,1 × 24,2 cm)
Polka
Unsigned and undated [c.1842]
[DKKk; MA ms 2904 (1) (KTB 222 (2))

Parts. Ms. Copy. 30 vol.
3 vl I, 3 vl II, 2 vla, 3 vlc e cb, fl 1/2, ob 1/2, cl 1/2, fag, cor 1/2, clno 1/2, tr 1/2, trb, timp, gr cassa, piatti, tri, arpa.
Unsigned and undated [1842]
[DKKk; KTB 222
A pencilled note in the part for the second horn reads 'Johs. Gentzen, Hamburg d. 5 July 1843'. It clearly indicates that Lumbye's music was reused later for the solo dance entitled *Polka*, performed by the French ballerina Maria (Jacob) at Hamburg's Stadttheater on 5.7.1843. Similar notes in the parts for the first horn and the triangle indicate that *Polka militaire* was also performed in Germany (Rendsburg) on 16.6.1846, and in Norway (Bergen) on 26.6.1859. These performances, however, can not be verified any further.

17.12.1842
Pas de deux (uncredited) performed by F. Hoppe and P. Fredstrup.

A note in the repertory book of F. Hoppe (reading: 'Pas de l'Orient') clearly indicates that this (uncredited) *Pas de deux* is identical with Bournonville's so-called 'Pas de deux oriental', first performed by himself and A. Krætzmer on 26.9. 1829 as an incorporated divertissement in P. Funck's *A Diver-*

tissement in Oriental Style. According to the rehearsal book of H. C. J. Fredstrup the dance was rehearsed only once on 17.12.1842 and then under Hoppe's direction.

1843

12.1.1843
The Childhood of Erik Menved (Erik Menveds Barndom).

This four-act romantic ballet (inspired by B. S. Ingemann's 1828 novel of that name) represents the first Bournonville ballet which was performed at its première as a full-length ballet making up the whole evening's programme. Thus, according to an autographed note written by the conductor, F. Gläser, on the poster for its first performance (now in DKKk, Gläser's collection of posters 1842–61, call no. 34 III 4°) the ballet was premièred with L. v. Beethoven's C minor symphony being played as a musical introduction on the same evening.

The score was composed and orchestrated by J. F. Fröhlich, but with the first four numbers of Act I written by the French harpist, N. C. Bochsa. Due to Fröhlich suddenly falling ill, Bochsa (who had given a series of recitals at Copenhagen's Royal Theatre in 1840 together with the soprano, A. Bishop) was commissioned by Bournonville to begin the composition of this ballet during late 1840 and early 1841. This is clear from the orchestral score and a series of letters from Bochsa to Bournonville (now in DKKk, call no. NKS 3258 A 4°, II, 7) according to which Bochsa seems to have completed the music for the whole of Act I. However, having recovered from his illness in early 1842, Fröhlich was still in time to take over the task of completing, rearranging, and orchestrating the entire score. Thus, as a result of assuming sole responsibility for the music at this rather late stage in the creative process, Fröhlich seems to have been forced to incorporate several excerpts of Bochsa's music in the fourth act (score no. 24), although these excerpts were orginally written by Bochsa for Act I (score no. 4).

As in his previous score for Bournonville's national-historical ballet *Waldemar* (*see* 28.10.1835) Fröhlich interpolated several Danish tunes, songs, and medieval ballads in *The Childhood of Erik Menved*. These insertions were made mainly in order to add a historical flavour to the score and to help the audience interpret the ballet's complex dramatic action. These incorporated tunes are identified as follows:

(1) Act I (score no. 7): Fröhlich here employed the romance by H. Rung, entitled «Herr Peder kaster Runer over Spange». It was originally part of H. Hertz's four-act romantic tragedy *The House of Svend Dyring (Svend Durings Huus),* premièred at Copenhagen's Royal Theatre on 5.3.1837.
(2) Act II (score no. 9, *The Proposal Dance (Frierdandsen)*): According to I. Rée's *Musikalsk Anthologie* (1. Aarg., 1856, p. 55) Fröhlich's music for this dance is based on a motif from an old Danish folk tune entitled «Frie vil ærlig, frie vil redelig, frie vil sædelig, frie vil Kongens Bønder Alle». Moreover, both the music and the choreographic motif for *The Proposal Dance* were reused many years later, when it was incorporated in an extended and reorchestrated version (arranged by V. C. Holm) in Act I, scene 3 (score no. 4) of Bournonville's four-act national-historical ballet *Arcona* (*see* 7.5.1875).
(3) Act III (score no. 19): Fröhlich here incorporated the tune of the Danish medieval song «Det var Ridder Hr. Aage, han reed sig under Ø» (published by R. Nyerup, and K. L. Rahbek in 1814 in *Udvalgte Danske Viser fra Middelalderen,* vol. 5, p. XXVI no. 29).
(4) Act III (score no. 21): For this scene Fröhlich interpolated excerpts of the Danish medieval song «Dronning Dagmar ligger i Ribe syg» (also published by Nyerup and Rahbek, vol. 5, p. XXXIX no. 70 A).
(5) Act IV (score nos. 25 and 26): In these two numbers Fröhlich employed the tunes of three Danish medieval songs, entitled «Der gaaer Dands i Borgegaard», «Herr Adelbrand han rider til Lenelilles Gaard», and «Marsk Stig han haver de Døttre to» (all published by Nyerup and Rahbek, vol. 5, p. XLIV no. 95, p. LVIII no. 162 B, and p. XLII no. 79).

Of the many dance divertissements in *The Childhood of Erik Menved* the *Torch Dance (Fakkeldands)* and the *March* in Act II (score nos. 13–14) soon became among the most popular concert pieces of the time, being frequently played at public concerts in the newly opened Tivoli Gardens in Copenhagen. Moreover, parts of Bochsa's music for Act I (score no. 1), and most of Fröhlich's *Finale* for Act III (score no. 23), were rearranged and incorporated with the new title *Torch Dance (Fakkeldands)* in Act II (as score no. '17½') of Bournonville's four-act romantic ballet *Waldemar* when this ballet was restaged in a new, thoroughly revised version on 19.10.1853. After that year this dance became known as 'Riberhus March', and after being reorchestrated for the Tivoli Gardens orchestra by A. F. Lincke on 18.7.1862 it ranked among the most popular concert pieces of the time (Lincke's autographed arrangement of this dance is now in DKKk, call no. C II, 29).

Furthermore, Fröhlich's music for the *Pas de deux* in Act II (score no. 16) of *The Childhood of Erik Menved* was reused by him (except for the two first movements) as accompaniment for a *Pas de trois* in the third tableau of Bournonville's romantic ballet in six tableaux, named *Raphael* (*see* 30.5.1845). Finally, parts of the same music were recycled as an accompaniment for an incorporated solo variation in Act I of Bournonville's 1853 restaging of *Waldemar*.

In a letter written to the theatre management of Copenhagen's Royal Theatre written on 17.2.1843 (now in The State Archive, call no. Det kgl. Teaters Arkiv, Gruppe E, pakke 288) Bournonville gave an interesting assessment of *The Childhood of Erik Menved* and the reason for its strong impact on the audience as he saw it:

'Jeg gaaer først til Arbeidets Natur, der er storartet, altsaa ikke <u>kan</u> nydes saa hÿppigt som det <u>muntre</u>. Jeg troer at Balletten underholder og rører, ja paa sine Steder opvækker Begeistring, men det kan ikke nægtes at den Tendents der gaaer igjennem heele Handlingen, ikke er <u>den</u> der tiltaler Applausen og Journalistikens Formænd. Publicum drives altsaa af egen Lÿst ikke af en larmende udvortes Impuls og vort Publicum maae have Tid at røre og betænke sig'.

Notes in several of the parts (reading '3T 1q') indicate that the ballet played for a total of 3 hours and 15 minutes. *The Childhood of Erik Menved* reached a total of 15 performances, the last of which was given on 15.5.1843. According to the rehearsal book of H. C. J. Fredstrup, 72 rehearsals were held of it between 18.9.1842 and 12.1.1843.

Autograph sources:

Production note. Ms. Autograph. Brown ink. 1 p. (35 × 21 cm)
Balletten Erik Menveds Barndom/[...]/Godtgjörelse for Fodtöi
Signed: 'Auguste Bournonville', undated [1843]
[DKKk; NKS 1576 b fol.

Musical sources:

Répétiteur's copy. Ms. Autograph (by J. F. Fröhlich). Black ink. 1 vol.
88 pp. (25,9 × 37,2 cm)
Charlotte Bournonville/[...]/Første Act./No. 1/All.° modto.
Signed and dated (on p. 36): 'Fredensborg 10/8 42. JFF.', (p. 51)
'quasi Fine/JFFrøhlich', (p. 67) '31/6 42.', and (p. 88) '18/7 42./JF.'
[DKKk; C II, 107 (KTB 207)
While the original 1843 répétiteur's copy from the Royal Theatre's
music archive (originally listed with the call no. KTB 207) has not yet
been traced, this répétiteur's copy was clearly Bournonville's private
copy. According to its dating it represents Fröhlich's earliest known
manuscript for *The Childhood of Erik Menved*. The numbering and the
succession of each section are here completely different from those
in the final orchestral score, reflecting the original progression in
which the music was actually written. The répétiteur's copy was donated to DKKk on 31.3.1910 by Bournonville's daughter, Charlotte
Bournonville. It contains Bournonville's pencilled autographed
notes and his other notes (written with red and brown ink) that describe in fine detail the mime, the dramatic action, and the choreography throughout the ballet.

Orchestral score. Ms. Autograph (by J. F. Fröhlich). Brown and black
ink. 2 vol. Act I–II 198 pp., Act III–IV 154 pp. (27 × 38 cm with minor
variants)
Erik Menveds Barndom/romantisk Ballet i 4 Akter./af/A. Bournonville./Musikken af J. F. Frøhlich./op. 51.
Signed and dated (on p. 16) '8/12 42. JFF.'
[DKKk; C II, 107 (KTB 207)

Piano score. Ms. Autograph (by J. F. Fröhlich). Black ink. 1 vol. 4 pp
(25,9 × 36,1 cm)
J. Fr. Frøhlich:/Erik Menveds Barndom./Marsch af 2' Akt./Klaver./
[...]/Tempo di Marcia.
Unsigned and undated [c.1843]
[DKKk; C II, 107 (1940–41.198)
This autographed piano score contains Fröhlich's complete music
for the *Pas de six* in Act II (score no. 15) and was most likely written
soon after the 1843 première of *The Childhood of Erik Menved*. The
score seems originally to have been in Bournonville's private collection, since it was donated to DKKk on 2.1.1941 by a distant relative of
his, Mrs. Thora Schmidt-Phiseldeck.

Parts. Ms. Copy. 33 vol.
3 vl I, 3 vl II, 2 vla, 3 vlc e cb, fl picc, fl 1/2, ob 1/2, cl 1/2, fag 1/2, cor
1/2/3/4, clno 1/2, trb 1/2/3, timp, gr cassa, piatti e tri, arpa.
Unsigned and undated [1843]
[DKKk; C II, 107 (KTB 207)

Other sources:

Costume drawing by F. Westphal. Pencil (19,5 × 12,9 cm)
[Untitled]
Signed: 'Fritz Westphael', undated [c.1843]
This drawing most probably shows the costume of *Queen Agnes of
Denmark* in *The Childhood of Erik Menved*.

Printed sources:

Printed scenario. 1 vol. 15 pp. (20,2 × 12,7 cm)
Erik Menveds/Barndom,/romantisk Ballet i 4 Acter/af/August
Bournonville./Musikken af Fr. Fröhlich./[...]/Af nye Decorationer
gives fire:/[...]/af Christensen/[...]/af T. Lund./[...]/Costumet
tegnet og anordnet af Westphal.

Kjøbenhavn, J. H. Schubothe, Bianco Luno, 1843.
[DKKk; 17, – 173 8°

27.2.1843
The Danes in China (De Danske i China).
This divertissement was based on selected excerpts from Act
I (score nos. 5–11) of Bournonville's two-act romantic ballet
The Isle of Phantasy (see 28.10.1838). Two earlier divertissements had been mounted with the same title by Bournonville on 17.9.1839 and 28.1.1842, but each time with a different dance content. The 1843 version consisted (according to
the poster) of three dances as follows:

(1) *Russian* [Dance] *(Russisk)* performed by Bournonville and C.
Fjeldsted.
(2) *Chinese* [Dance] *(Chinesisk)* performed by F. Hoppensach.
(3) *The English Sailor (Den Engelske Matros)* performed by Bournonville.

Pencilled notes written in the part for the fourth horn (now
in DKKk, call no. KTB 206) read 'Johs. Gentzen, Hamburg
31/7 1843' and '2/7 1846'. They clearly indicate that the
1843 version of *The Danes in China* was mounted at Hamburg's Stadttheater on at least two occasions.

The 1843 version of *The Danes in China* received 23 performances in Copenhagen, the last of which was given on
28.10.1847. According to the rehearsal book of H. C. J.
Fredstrup, 4 rehearsals were held of it between 23.2. and
25.2.1843.

Musical sources:

The orchestral score, the répétiteur's copy, and the set of parts em-
ployed for this divertissement version of excerpts from Act I of *The
Isle of Phantasy* are now in DKKk (call nos. C II 119, MA ms 2945, and
KTB 206).

9.5.1843
Pas de deux composed by Mr. Ballet Master Bournonville (componeret af Hr. Balletmester Bournonville) performed by Bournonville and C. Fjeldsted.
This dance is perhaps identical with the earlier, so-called *New
Pas de deux* (also named 'Pas de deux de retour') that was
mounted by Bournonville to mark his return to Copenhagen
after his enforced six-month exile in 1841, and first performed by himself and C. Fjeldsted on 14.10.1841. According to the rehearsal book of H. C. J. Fredstrup the *Pas de deux*
was rehearsed twice on 6.5. and 8.5.1843, and is named by
him as 'Pas de deux af Herr Bournonville og Jfr. Fjeldsted'. It
is not possible to identify the dance any further.

27.6.1843
Napoli, oder: Der Fischer und seine Braut (Hamburg's Stadttheater).
This performance represents the first of only two stagings
outside Denmark of Bournonville's three-act romantic ballet
Napoli or The Fisherman and His Bride (see 29.3.1842) during
his own lifetime. In Hamburg the ballet was mounted with
completely new décor by the French scene painter, F.
d'Herbès, and performed with Bournonville and the French
ballerina, Maria (Jacob), in the leading rôles as Gennaro
and Teresina. The ballet was given 5 performances at Ham-

burg's Stadttheater, the last of which took place on 16.7. 1843. No separate musical sources and printed scenario from the 1843 performances of *Napoli* in Hamburg have yet been traced. This seems to indicate that the ballet was performed with only minor if any changes from the original 1842 Copenhagen score.

5.7.1843
Pas de deux (uncredited) performed by Bournonville and Maria (Jacob) as an incorporated divertissement in D.-F.-E. Auber's five-act historical opera *Gustave III, ou Le Bal masqué* (Hamburg's Stadttheater).

According to a pencilled note written in a part for the fourth horn (now in DKKk, call no. KTB 223) this (uncredited) *Pas de deux* is musically completely identical with Bournonville's earlier so-called *New Pas de deux*, first performed at Copenhagen's Royal Theatre by himself and C. Fjeldsted as an incorporated divertissement in Act II of G. Meyerbeer's five-act opera *Robert le Diable* (*see* 5.12.1841). That dance, in turn, is perhaps based on an even earlier work by the French choreographer, J. Mazilier, which Bournonville had most probably had seen performed at the Paris Opéra during the early spring of 1841.

The *Pas de deux* was performed as the centrepiece of a *Divertissement* that contained two other dances, entitled *Castilliana* and *Polka*, both performed by Maria (Jacob). This is clear from notes written in the part for the second horn of what is named *Pas de bouquets* and *Polka militaire* (now in DKKk, call no. KTB 222). In this part, the bugler who played for the 1843 Hamburg performances has inserted his name, the place, and the exact date for the performance of these dances in Hamburg ('Johs. Gentzen, Hamburg d. 5. Jüly 1843'). Moreover, his notes indicate that both the *Castilliana* and the *Polka* performed by Maria in Hamburg on 5.7.1843 were musically identical with the *Pas de bouquets* and the *Polka (Militairdands)*, danced earlier in Copenhagen on 1.11.1842. Furthermore, since the parts for both of these dances were brought to Hamburg by Bournonville in 1843 it also seems likely that the *Pas de bouquets* and *Polka militaire* were rearranged and taught by him to Maria in Hamburg. Consequently, the complete 1843 divertissement in *Gustave III, ou Le Bal masqué* should probably be considered a work arranged and mounted by Bournonville.

The divertissement was performed twice in Hamburg, the last time on 8.7.1843.

10.7.1843
Der Toreador (spanische Stierbekämpfer) und die Tänzerin (Toréadoren) (Hamburg's Stadttheater).

This performance represents Bournonville's first and only staging in Germany of his two-act idyllic ballet *The Toreador* (*see* 27.11.1840). It was performed with himself and the French ballerina, Maria (Jacob), playing the leading rôles of *Alonzo* and *Céleste*. According to the printed German scenario, the ballet included a new, incorporated *Pas de deux* in Act II, performed by Maria (Jacob) and a (not yet identified) dancer named 'Maximilien'. It is most probably identical with the so-called 'Pas de deux af Balletten Toreadoren' that is set to music by a not yet identified composer, and is now in DKKk (call no. MA ms 2902 (9)).

No separate musical sources dating from the 1843 performance of *Der Toreador* in Hamburg have yet been traced. This indicates that the ballet was most likely performed using the original 1840 Copenhagen musical material (now in DKKk, call nos. C II, 114k, MA ms 2965, and KTB 269).

Der Toreador received 5 performances in Hamburg, the last of which took place on 8.8.1843.

Musical sources:

Répétiteur's copy (*Pas de deux* incorporated in Act II?). Ms. Copy. Brown ink. 1 vol. 4 pp. (32,5 × 25,2 cm)
Dands.
Unsigned and undated [c.1843]
[DKKk; MA ms 2902 (9) (KTB 1046, but originally KTB 269a)
On the front cover this répétiteur's copy is named 'Pas de deux af Balletten Toreadoren'. It is most probably identical with the incorporated *Pas de deux* danced by Maria (Jacob) and the dancer 'Maximilien' in Act II of *The Toreador* when this ballet was mouted in Hamburg in 1843. This theory is supported by the fact that the répétiteur's copy is bound together with sixteen other répétiteur's copies that all date from the late 1830s and early 1840s.

No orchestral score and set of parts for this dance have yet been traced.

Printed sources:

Printed scenario. 1 vol. 18 pp. (16,5 × 10,3 cm)
Der Toreador/(spanishe Stierbekämpfer)/und/die Tänzerin./ Idyllisches Ballet in 2 Aufzügen/von/August Bournonville,/[...]/ Die Musik componirt und arrangirt/von/Edward Helsted.
Hamburg, F. H. Nestler und Melle [1843]
[DKKk; 17, – 173 8°

14.7.1843
Divertissement (uncredited).

This (uncredited) *Divertissement* is mentioned for the first time in a letter from Bournonville to the theatre management of Copenhagen's Royal Theatre, dated 14.7.1843 (now in The State Archive, call no. Det kgl. Teaters Arkiv, Gruppe E, pakke 288). It most probably refers to the three dances (entitled *Pas de deux*, *Castilliana*, and *Polka*) that were performed twice by himself and the French ballerina, Maria (Jacob) as an incorporated divertissement in D.-F.-E. Auber's five-act historical opera *Gustave III ou Le Bal masqué* during the 1843 summer tour at Hamburg's Stadttheater (*see* 5.7. 1843). It is not possible to identify the divertissement any further.

20.7.1843
Die Liebende Bayadère oder Der Gott und die Bayadere (Hamburg's Stadttheater).

During Bournonville's 1843 summer tour to Hamburg a performance of D.-F.-E. Auber's two-act opera-ballet (*see* 7.2. 1841) was performed with an (uncredited) *Pas de deux* incorporated in Act II and danced by Bournonville and the French ballerina, Maria (Jacob). While the opera's usual dances were all credited to Bournonville, this *Pas de deux* is identical with the much earlier (uncredited) *Pas de deux*, first performed by Bournonville and A. Krætzmer in Copenhagen as an incorporated divertissement in N. Isouard's three-act comic opera *Jeannot et Colin* (*see* 1.9.1829). This is clear from notes written in several of the parts for this dance (now in DKKk, call no. KTB 209). They clearly indicate that it was performed three times at Hamburg's Stadttheater, on 20.7., 26.7., and 7.8.1843, and later also at Christiania's Theatre (Oslo) on 15.6.1852.

31.7.1843
Therese, die Nachtwandlerin (La Somnambule, ou l'Arrivée d'un nouveau seigneur/Sövngjængersken) (Hamburg's Stadttheater).

This performance represents Bournonville's first and only staging outside Denmark of his Copenhagen version of J. Aumer's three-act pantomimic ballet *La Somnambule, ou l'Arrivée d'un nouveau seigneur* (*see* 21.9.1829). It was the last work that he mounted during the 1843 summer tour to Hamburg's Stadttheater, and received 5 performances there, the last of which was given on 7.8.1843.

According to musician's notes reading: 'Johs. Gentzen, Hamburg 37/7 1843' and '2/7 1846' and written in the part for the fourth horn in Bournonville's divertissement *The Danes in China* (*see* 27.2.1843), it appears that *Therese, die Nachtwandlerin* was given in Hamburg together with Bournonville's 1843 version of this divertissement.

No musical sources and printed scenario dating from the 1843 Hamburg production of *Therese, die Nachtwandlerin* have yet been traced. This seems to indicate that the ballet was performed with only minor if any changes from the 1829 Copenhagen score.

31.7.1843
Divertissement from *The Isle of Phantasy* (Hamburg's Stadttheater).

Pencilled notes written in a part for the fourth horn, reading 'Johs. Gentzen, Hamburg 31/7 1843' (now in DKKk, call no. KTB 206) clearly indicate that this divertissement consisted of dances selected from Bournonville's divertissement *The Danes in China* (*see* 17.9.1839) which, in turn, is based on excerpts from Act I of his two-act romantic ballet *The Isle of Phantasy* (*see* 28.10.1838). Other notes in the same part indicate that a second performance of this divertissement took place in Hamburg three years later on 2.7.1846.

The divertissement was given 5 times during the 1843 summer tour, the last time on 7.8.1843. It is not possible to establish the exact content of the divertissement dances in these performances any further.

11.8.1843
A Ballet Performance (En Ballet=Forestilling) at the theatre in Kiel (Germany).

According to a note in Bournonville's 1843 travel diary he gave a performance on this day at the theatre in Kiel on his way to Copenhagen after the 1843 summer tour to Hamburg. The note reads:

'Forestilling Kl 7 1/2, brilliant Huus og meget Bifald. Jeg dandsede godt'.

The dances performed on this occasion were in all probability some of those given earlier at Hamburg's Stadttheater between 27.6. and 7.8.1843. It is not possible to identify the exact content of dances in this performance any further.

20.9.1843
Moïse (Moses).

According to his handwritten lists of his opera stagings, written c.1851 (*see* Additional Sources), G. Rossini's French version of his four-act opera *Moïse* (first performed at the Paris Opéra on 26.3.1827) was given its Copenhagen première with Bournonville's mise-en-scène on this day. Of the opera's original three dance divertissements in Act III (score no. 11, *Airs nos. 1–3*) only the first (a *Pas de trois* performed by F. Lefèbvre, A. Nielsen, and P. Fredstrup) was included in the Danish production. It was choreographed and mounted by the French dancer, F. Lefèbvre.

Moreover, on 30.10.1857 Bournonville included Rossini's original three-act version of this opera (entitled *Mosè in Egitto*) in a list of projected opera restagings which he was planning on that day for the 1857–58 and 1858–59 seasons. This project, however, was never carried out, and Rossini's opera was given for the last time in Copenhagen on 24.10.1846, reaching a total of 10 performances.

According to the rehearsal book of H. C. J. Fredstrup, 7 rehearsals were held of Rossini's opera and its dance divertissement between 12.9. and 19.9.1843. Of these, 5 were directed by Lefèbvre and 3 by Bournonville.

Autograph sources:

Manuscript mise-en-scène. Ms. Autograph. Brown ink. 2 pp. (35,1 × 21, 5 cm)
Moses. 1.ste Act. 1.ste Scene./[...]/2.den Act./[...]/3.die Act./ [...]/4.de Act.
Unsigned and undated [1843]
[DKKk; NKS 3285 4° 3 L–P

Musical sources:

Printed orchestral score. 2 vol. Act I-II 290 pp. of which ten are manuscript copies, Act III–IV 260 pp. of which one is blank (31,6 × 25 cm)
Moses/Partitur/1.ste og 2.den Act/[...]/3.die og 4.die Act.
[Paris, E. Troupenas, pl. no. 221 [1827]]
[DKKk; U 6 (KTA 384)
This orchestral score (of which the title page is missing) includes ten pp. of manuscript copies containing the music for the overture, which was considerably shortened at the opera's 1843 Copenhagen première.

Répétiteur's copy. Ms. Copy. Brown ink. 12 pp. of which one is blank (33,2 × 25,3 cm)
Moses/[...]/Repetiteur=Parti/til/Sÿngestykket Moses.
Unsigned and undated [1843]
[DKKk; MA ms 2912 (4) (KTA 384)
This répétiteur's copy contains the music for the *Pas de trois* in Act III (score no. 11, *Air* no. 1). It is included on pp. 27–38 in a volume that also contains the répétiteur's copies for five other works, mounted at Copenhagen's Royal Theatre between 1815 and 1873.

Parts. Ms. Copy. 33 vol.
3 vl I, 3 vl II, 2 vla, 3 vlc e cb, fl 1/2, ob 1/2, cl 1/2, fag 1/2, cor 1/2/ 3/4, tr 1/2, trb 1/2/3, tuba, timp, gr cassa, piatti e tri, arpa. 53 vocal parts.
Unsigned and undated [1843]
[DKKk; KTA 384

1.10.1843
Styrian Dance (Steirisk Dands) (uncredited) performed by F. Hoppe and C. Fjeldsted.

This (uncredited) dance is almost certainly identical with

the *Styrian Dance* first performed in Copenhagen by the same dancers as an incorporated divertissement in Act I of D.-F.-E. Auber's three-act comic opera *Le Domino noir* (*see* 29.1.1839), and mounted as a separate divertissement in Norway at Christiania's Theatre (Olso) with Bournonville and C. Fjeldsted (*see* 29.7.1840). After the 1843 performances the dance was restaged 13 times in Copenhagen, with different casts as follows:

(1) on 11.1.1844, 2.5.1846, 7.1.1854, 15.1.1855, 23.1.1856, and 15.10.1857 (all danced by F. Hoppe and P. Fredstrup, on the last day at the Court Theatre).
(2) on 17.1.1851, 3.2.1852, and 23.1.1853 (with F. Hoppe and A. Price).
(3) on 30.1.1862, 1.11.1864, and 20.3.1865 (by H. Scharff and J. Petersen).

During this period it reached a total of 42 performances, the last of which was given on 20.3.1865. In Norway the *'Styrian Dance'* was mounted for the last time at Christiania's Theatre (Oslo) with H. Scharff and S. Price on 11.6.1865. According to the rehearsal book of H. C. J. Fredstrup, only one rehearsal was held of it on 1.10.1843 under the personal direction of F. Hoppe.

Musical sources:

No orchestral score dating from the 1843 restaging of the *Styrian Dance* as a separate divertissement has yet been traced.

Répétiteur's copy. Ms. Copy. Brown ink. 4 pp. (34,6 × 25,5 cm)
10 Stemer/Violino Repititör/til/Pas Stÿrien
Unsigned and undated [c.1843]
[DKKk; MA ms 2701 (KTB 1027, originally KTB 213)
This répétiteur's copy seems (according to the style of the manuscript) to date from the mid-1840s and was most probably written for the first performance of the *Styrian Dance* as a separate divertissement on 1.10.1843.

Parts. Ms. Copy. 9 vol.
vl I, vl II, vla, vlc e cb, fl, cl, fag, cor, tr.
Unsigned and undated [c.1843]
[DKKk; KTB 1027 (originally KTB 213)

11.10.1843
Pas de deux, composed by Mr. Ballet Master Bournonville (Pas de deux, componeret af Hr. Balletmester Bournonville) performed by Bournonville and C. Fjeldsted.
In his handwritten lists of his works, written c.1851 (*see* Additional Sources) Bournonville listed this dance with the title 'Pas de deux. Retour de Fjeldsted'. It was choreographed to mark the return of C. Fjeldsted to Copenhagen's Royal Theatre after her study tour to Paris in the summer of 1843.

According to the orchestral score the music was composed by H. S. Paulli and N. W. Gade(?). Thus, both of the two *Allegretto* movements in this dance (pp. 12–16 and 27–32) appear to be Gade's autograph and are seemingly inserted into Paulli's score. This fact may indicate that Bournonville originally commissioned the score for this dance from Gade, a task which was apparently handed over to Paulli as a result of Gade's imminent departure for Leipzig the same year.

During the following years several excerpts of their music for Bournonville's 1843 *Pas de deux* were reused by Paulli in his musical arrangements for three other Bournonville dances:

(1) *Tableau with Dance (Tableau med Dands)*, premièred on 12.10.1846.
(2) *Flower Dance (Blomsterdands)*, premièred on 20.10.1847.
(3) *Pas des trois cousines*, premièred at the Casino Theatre on 20.5.1848, but later also mounted at the Royal Theatre on 8.9.1849.

The 1843 *Pas de deux* was apparently not very much to Fjeldsted's liking since it was performed only once. According to the rehearsal book of H. C. J. Fredstrup, it received 6 rehearsals between 5.10 and 11.10.1843, and was named by him as 'En nÿe Pas de deux', or 'En nÿe Entrée'.

Musical sources:

Orchestral score. Ms. Autographs (by H. S. Paulli and N. W. Gade?).
Black ink. 1 vol. 42 pp. (34,6 × 29,2 cm)
PAULLI/PAS/DE DEUX/1843/[...]/Pas de deux (du Retour) 1843.
Signed and dated (on p. 11): 'HSPaulli d: 7 Octbr 1843.'
[DKKk; C II, 119 (KTB 211?)
This autographed score contains several pencilled notes indicating the later changes of the music when it was reused by Paulli in his score for Bournonville's *Pas des trois cousines* (*see* 20.5.1848).

No répétiteur's copy and set of parts for the 1843 *Pas de deux* have yet been traced. However, a note reading 'Pas de deux' in the part for the first violin to Bournonville's so-called *Flower Dance* from 20.10.1847 (now in DKKk, call no. KTB 211) seems to indicate that this set of parts actually represents the original parts for Bournonville's 1843 *Pas de deux.*

28.10.1843
Pas de deux from the ballet 'La Sylphide' (Pas de deux af Balletten 'Sylphiden') performed by F. Hoppe and A. Nielsen.
This dance is perhaps identical with H. S. v. Løvenskjold's *Pas de deux* in Act II (score no. 3) of Bournonville's original Copenhagen version of F. Taglioni's two-act pantomimic ballet *La Sylphide* (*see* 28.11.1836). In that ballet it was performed by the two protagonists (*James* and *The Sylph*), rôles which Hoppe and Nielsen had taken over from Bournonville and L. Grahn on 9.9.1840 and 6.9.1839 respectively.

Another possible identification of the dance is the *Pas de deux* (set to music by J. Mayseder) which was incorporated by Bournonville in *La Sylphide* on 27.9.1842 with the title *Pas de deux (à la Taglioni)*. That dance, in turn, is clearly identical with the *Pas de deux* originally performed in Act II (score no. 1 A) of his two-act romantic ballet *The Isle of Phantasy* (*see* 28.10.1838).

The 1843 *Pas de deux from the ballet 'La Sylphide'* was given only once as a separate divertissement by Hoppe and Nielsen. It is not possible to identify the dance any further.

1844

7.1.1844
Die Hochzeit des Figaro (Figaros Bryllup).
In his handwritten chronological list of his opera stagings, written c.1851 (*see* Additional Sources) the 1844 restaging at Copenhagen's Royal Theatre of W. A. Mozart's four-act comic opera from 1786 (sung in Danish) is placed erroneously between Bournonville's stagings of I. P. E. Hartmann's *Undine* (on 18.9.1842), and G. Rossini's *Moïse* on 20.9.1843.

For the 1844 production he was only responsible for mounting the dance scenes in Act III (score nos. 25 and 26).

The *Fandango* (which this year was danced by G. Brodersen and P. Fredstrup) had originally been choreographed by him two years earlier when *Le Nozze di Figaro* was given (in Italian) with his mise-en-scène at the the the Court Theatre (*see* 25.5.1842). However, it was not until his second staging of *Die Hochzeit des Figaro* at the Royal Theatre on 1.5.1849 that Bournonville was officially responsible for directing both the dance scenes and the general mise-en-scène.

Moreover, on 30.10.1857 Bournonville included Mozart's opera in a list of projected opera restagings that he was planning on that day for the 1857–58 and 1858–59 seasons. This project was carried out on 21.5.1858 when *Die Hochzeit des Figaro* was mounted for the first time with his own completely new mise-en-scène. The 1858 version was restaged twice by him with only minor changes on 7.10.1860, and on 30.4. 1872 (on the last date with partially revised choreography).

The 1844 production of *Die Hochzeit des Figaro* received 36 performances, the last of which took place on 15.4.1856. According to the rehearsal book of H. C. J. Fredstrup, 4 rehearsals of the dances in this opera were held between 3.1. and 6.1.1844.

Musical sources:

Orchestral score. Ms. Copy with additions and later changes by various hands. Black ink. 3 vol. Act I 312 pp., Act II 358 pp., Act III-IV 464 pp. (22,5 × 28 cm)
Le Nozze di Figaro/Comedia per Musica/in quattro atti/La Musica del Sigr: Wolf: Amad: Mozart.
Unsigned and undated [c. 1790–1821]
[DKKk; C I, 280 (KTA 215) (mu 7502.0131)
This score contains both the Italian and Danish text and was used for all performances in Copenhagen of *Die Hochzeit des Figaro* during Bournonville's lifetime.

Répétiteur's copy. Ms. Copy. Black ink. 1 vol. 4 pp. (33,3 × 23 cm)
Figaros Giftermaal./Violino 1.mo/Repetiteur Partie/No 15/68./ [...]/Finale/3.die Akt/Figaros Giftermaal/No. 25
Unsigned and undated [1821–1872]
[DKKk; MA ms 3042 (KTA 215)
This répétiteur's copy contains the music for the dance scenes in Act III (score no. 25 including the *Fandango*) and the finale in the same act (score no. 26). It clearly dates from the Copenhagen première of *Die Hochzeit des Figaro* on 9.1.1821. However, according to Bournonville's later pencilled autographed notes it was also used for his 1844 restaging of Mozart's opera as well as for all later restagings of it during his lifetime. Moreover, the volume contains Bournonville's autographed choreographic numbers '1–5' (written with black ink) which most probably were written for his last restaging of this work on 30.4.1872. They seem to refer to his separate choreographic notation of the Act III dances that he wrote on 6.4.1872. Finally, other notes written by Bournonville's father, Antoine Bournonville, indicate the casting of each choreographic section as staged by him at the 1821 Copenhagen première of *Die Hochzeit des Figaro*.

Parts. Ms. Copy. 27 vol.
4 vl I, 4 vl II, 2 vla, 4 vlc e cb, fl 1/2, ob 1/2, cl 1/2, fag 1/2, cor 1/2, tr 1/2, timp. 38 vocal parts. 2 vocal scores.
Unsigned and undated [c.1821]
[DKKk; KTA 215

8.1.1844
The Festival in Albano (Festen i Albano).
Bournonville's one-act idyllic ballet *The Festival in Albano* (*see*

28.10.1839) was restaged on this day with a new finale of *tableaux vivants* (score no. 12) showing four of B. Thorvaldsen's most famous scuptural works and described on the poster as follows:

Ny Række af Thorvaldsenske Billeder:
1. Vulcan. 2. Dandserinden. 3. Den romerske Kriger. 4. Jupiter og Diana.

These tableaux, which represent the only significant change in the 1844 restaging of *The Festival in Albano*, were performed only 3 times (the last time on 4.2.1844) after which the original 1839 series of *tableaux vivants* was reinstated.

According to the rehearsal book of H. C. J. Fredstrup, 24 rehearsals of the 1844 production of *The Festival in Albano* were held by Bournonville between 31.10.1843 and 8.1.1844.

9.1.1844
Serieux solo danced by Miss Fjeldsted, composed for her by Ballet Master Albert in Paris (Serieux solo dandses af Jfr. Fjeldsted, componeret for hende af Balletmester Albert i Paris).
According to a note in the rehearsal book of H. C. J. Fredstrup on this day, both the rehearsals and the actual staging in Copenhagen of this solo dance (by the French choreographer and ballet-master, Albert (François Decombe)) were directed personally by Bournonville. The dance was given only once by Fjeldsted in Copenhagen. No musical sources for it have yet been traced in the annals of Copenhagen's Royal Theatre music archive. It is not possible to identify the dance any further.

8.2.1844
The Tyroleans (Tyrolerne).
This performance represents the last restaging in Copenhagen of Bournonville's one-act idyllic ballet *The Tyroleans* (*see* 6.3.1835). It differed from his original version by having two new incorporated dances:

(1) A *New Scenic Pas de deux (Ny scenisk Pas de deux)* choreographed by the French dancer, F. Lefèbvre, and performed by himself and A. Nielsen.
(2) A *New Hamburg-Scottish, Character Dance (Ny Hamborger=Skotsk), Characteerdands)* choreographed by Bournonville (to music by H. C. Lumbye) and performed by Bournonville and C. Fjeldsted as a new finale (score no. 12).

The *New Hamburg=Scottish* was (according to notes in a part for the first violin) identical with the later (uncredited) *Hamborger=Dands, Pas de deux i Vierländer-Costume*, mounted as a separate divertissement at Copenhagen's Royal Theatre on 18.12. and 20.12.1844 (both times performed by Bournonville and Fjeldsted).

In the rehearsal book of H. C. J. Fredstrup the *New Hamburg=Scottish* is named on 7.2.1844 as 'Hamborger=Dands', while it is listed in the Royal Theatre's *Journal* on 8.2.1844 as 'Tyrolerne (med nye Dandse)'. On 16.12.1846 it was performed by Bournonville and P. Fredstrup at Helsingør's Theatre with the title *The Vierländers, (Hamburger Waltz) (Vierländerne, (Hamborger Vals))*. Moreover, the dance proves to be identical with the later divertissement entitled *The Vierländers (Vierländerne)*, first performed as a separate divertissement at the Royal Theatre by Bournonville and Fjeldsted on 24.1.1847. Finally, it was mounted the same year at Christiania's Theatre (Oslo) by W. Funck and C. Fjeldsted on 25.6.1847, with the (uncredited) title *The Vierländers, Scenic Character Dance (Vierlænderne, scenisk Characteerdands)*.

The 1844 version of *The Tyroleans* was given 5 times, the last time on 5.3.1844. According to the rehearsal book of H. C. J. Fredstrup, 9 rehearsals of this ballet were held by Bournonville between 30.1. and 7.2.1844.

Musical sources:

Répétiteur's copy. Ms. Copy. Black ink. 64 pp. of which two are blank (34,6 × 25,6 cm)
B 204./Tÿrolerne Ballet.
Unsigned and undated [c.1844]
[DKKk; MA ms 2943 (KTB 204)
This répétiteur's copy contains nearly all of the music for *The Tyroleans* except for the *Pas de deux* (score no. 5), the *Polonaise* (score no. 11), and the *Finale* (score no. 12). This seems to indicate that it dates from Bournonville's revised 1844 restaging of this ballet, in which the original 1835 *Pas de deux* was replaced by F. Lefèbvre's *New Scenic Pas de deux* and the original finale (score no. 12) was replaced by Lumbye's *New Hamburg-Scottish, Character Dance*. As a result of the omission of the orginal *Pas de deux* (score no. 5) all successive numbers were changed accordingly throughout the score.

No musical sources for F. Lefèbvre's incorporated *New Scenic Pas de deux* have yet been traced.

No autographed orchestral score and répétiteur's copy for H. C. Lumbye's *New Hamburg-Scottish* which date from its 1844 première in *The Tyroleans* have yet been traced. However, a later orchestral score, entitled 'Vierlaender Dands' is now in NOum (call no. 216 a, Eske 24). It most probably dates from when this dance was mounted with W. Funck and C. Fjeldsted at Christiania's Theatre (Oslo) on 25.6. 1847.

Parts (*New Hamburg=Scottish*). Ms. Copy. 32 vol.
2 vl I, 3 vl II, 2 vla, 2 vlc e cb, fl picc, fl 1/2, ob 1/2, cl 1/2, fag 1/2, cor 1/2/3/4, tr 1/2, cnt 1/2, trb 1/2/3, timp, gr cassa, piatti e tri.
Unsigned and undated [c.1844]
[DKKk; KTB 1024 (originally KTB 240)
This set of parts is bound together with the separate set of parts for J. Mayseder's *Pas de deux* in Act II (score no. 1 A) of Bournonville's two-act ballet *The Isle of Phantasy* (*see* 28.10.1838). A note in the part for the second violin reads 'Hamborgerdands'. Moreover, Lumbye's music for this dance is listed in all of the parts as number '12'. These facts prove beyond doubt that the parts must date from the 1844 performance of the *New Hamburg=Scottish* as a new, incorporated finale in *The Tyroleans*.

18.2.1844
Tableaux vivants. Representés au palais royal d'Amalienborg à l'occasion de la fête de S. A. R. la Princesse Julie de Danemarck **(uncredited).**
This series of eight (uncredited) *tableaux vivants* was choreographed and mounted by Bournonville in his capacity as Court ballet-master. They were performed at the Amalienborg Palace by members of the royal family and the nobility at a party given for Princess Julie of Denmark (later Queen Louise of Denmark). The music that accompanied these tableaux was most probably written (or at least arranged) and conducted by F. Gläser, since a copy of the printed programme for the tableaux is pasted into his private collection of posters of those performances that he conducted between 1842 and 1861 (now in DKKk, call no. 34 III, – 460 4°).

The tableaux (of which two were based on well-known paintings by S. Rosa and F. X. Wintherhalter) were restaged two months later by Bournonville at the Amalienborg Palace on 24.4.1844, then including an added sequence of four new tableaux.

The printed programme for the original series of eight tableaux reads:

1. Le comte d'Oldenbourg et la nymphe des bois, (deux figures).
2. Salvator Rosa peignant la femme du bandit, (cinq figures).
3. La toilette de la mariée, (deux figures).
4. Les bayadères, (cinq figures).
5. Le concert joyeux, (genre flamand, six figures).
6. Tarentelle napolitaine, (quatre figures).
7. La demande en mariage, (genre danois, sept figures).
8. Il Decamerone du Bocace, (d'après *Wintherhalter*).

No musical sources for these tableaux have yet been traced.

Printed sources:

Printed programme. 1 p. (24 × 18,9 cm)
Tableaux vivants./Représentés au palais royal d'Amalienbourg à l'occasion de la fête/de S.A.R. la Princesse Julie de Danemarck, Unsigned and dated: 'le Dimanche 18. fevrier 1844.'
[DKKk; 34 III, – 460 4° (inserted between the Royal Theatre posters for 18.2. and 19.2.1844)

28.2.1844
Les Huguenots (Hugenotterne).
According to his handwritten lists of his stagings of operas, written c.1851 (*see* Additional Sources) Bournonville was responsible for choreographing and mounting the dances in Acts III and V of the 1844 Copenhagen première of G. Meyerbeer's five-act opera *Les Huguenots*. They included a *Gipsy Dance (Danse Bohémienne)* in Act III (score no. 14), a *Nuptial March (Cortège de Noce)* in Act III (score no. 19), and a *Divertissement (Ballet)* in Act V (score no. 23).

Eleven years later he rechoreographed the *Zigeuner-Tanz* in Act III, when *Die Huguenotten* was restaged at Vienna's Kärnthnerthor Theatre on 25.10.1855. Moreover, on 30.10. 1857 Bournonville included *Les Huguenots* in a list of projected opera restagings that he was planning on this day for the 1857–58 and 1858–59 seasons. That project was carried out some 12 years later on 7.4.1869, when the opera was restaged in Copenhagen with Bournonville's complete mise-en-scène and choreography for the first time. However, before that L. Gade had mounted the dances following Bournonville's personal indications when *Les Huguenots* was restaged at the Royal Theatre on 3.10.1867. The 1869 production was restaged for the last time on 22.10.1871, with all the dances rechoreographed by Gade.

The original 1844 production of *Les Huguenots* was given 28 performances, the last of which was given on 9.1.1868 (including a separate performance of Act IV on 20.10.1847). For none of these performances was Bournonville mentioned on the posters. According to the rehearsal book of H. C. J. Fredstrup, 9 rehearsals of the dances in *Les Huguenots* were held between 12.2. and 27.2.1844. Of these 7 were directed by Bournonville, and 2 by Fredstrup.

Musical sources:

Printed orchestral score with several manuscript insertions. 5 vol.

Act I 242 pp. of which two are blank, Act II 168 pp., Act III 246 pp.,
Act IV 160 pp. of which one in blank, Act V 106 pp. (32 × 24,8 cm with
minor variants)
LES HUGUENOTS./OPERA EN 5 ACTES/DE GIACOMO MEYER-
BEER.
[Paris, M. Schlesinger], pl. no. M. S. 2134 [1836]
[DKKk; U6 (KTA 385)

Printed piano vocal score. 2 vol. Act I–II 218 pp. of which three are
blank, Act III–V 261 pp. of which three are blank (32 × 24,8 cm)
Die Hugenotten/(LES HUGUENOTS)
Leipzig, Breitkopf & Härtel, pl. no. 5720 [1836]
[DKKk; U 6 (KTA 385) (1959-60.810)
Pencilled notes in the music for the *Gipsy Dance* (pp. 234–238) seem
to indicate that this dance was drastically shortened at a later re-
staging of *Les Huguenots* (perhaps that on 7.4.1869).

Répétiteur's copy. Ms. Copy. Black ink. 1 vol. 28 pp. (32,3 × 25 cm)
Hügenotterne/[...]/Repetiteur=Partie/til/Huguenotterne.
Unsigned and undated [1844]
[DKKk; MA ms 2908 (2) (KTA 385)
This répétiteur's copy, which is bound together with the répétiteur's
copy for I. P. E. Hartmann's *Undine* (see 18.9.1842), contains Meyerbeer's music for the *Gipsy Dance* in Act III (score no. 14), the *Nuptial
March* in Act III (score no. 19), and the *Divertissement* in Act V (score
no. 23). It also includes Bournonville's pencilled autographed choreographic notes for the *Gipsy Dance* which clearly must date from
the opera's 1844 Copenhagen première. They are inserted next to
his other, later autographed choreographic numbers ('1–14') and
notes (written with black ink), which seem to refer to a (not yet
traced) separate choreographic notation of this dance. These numbers were most probably written for the restaging of Meyerbeer's
opera on either 3.10.1867 (mounted by L. Gade) or on 7.4.1869
(mounted by Bournonville). Finally, Bournonville's autographed
choreographic notes are inserted for the divertissement of Act V
(written with brown ink) and date from the opera's 1844 Copenhagen première.

Parts. Ms. Copy. 45 + 48 vol.
4 vl I, 4 vl II, 2 vla, 4 vlc e cb, fl picc, fl 1/2, ob 1/2, cor ingl, cl 1/2,
cor bassetto, fag 1/2, cor 1/2/3/4, tr 1/2/3/4, trb 1/2/3, tuba,
timp, gr cassa 1/2, piatti 1/2, tri, arpa, org. On stage: 4 vl I, 4 vl II, 2
vla, 4 vlc e cb, fl 1/2, ob 1/2, cl 1/2/3, cor bassetto, fag 1/2/3, cor 1/
2/3/4/5/6, tr 1/2/3/4, cnt 1/2, trb 1/2/3, tuba 1/2, gr cassa 1/2,
piatti 1/2, tri 1/2. 75 vocal parts.
Unsigned and undated [1844]
[DKKk; KTA 385

24.4.1844
Tableaux vivants. Representés au palais royal d'Amalienborg (uncredited).

This series of eleven (uncredited) tableaux was choreographed by Bournonville for a soirée at the Amalienborg
Palace and performed by members of the royal family and
the nobility. The tableaux (of which three were arranged
from well-known paintings by S. Rosa, C. A. Schleisner, and
F. X. Wintherhalter) are in parts identical with those eight
tableaux vivants given only two months earlier at the Amalienborg Palace on 18.2.1844.

The music was most probably written (or at least arranged) and conducted by F. Gläser. This is clear from a copy
of the printed programme for this performance, which is
pasted into Gläser's private collection of posters for those
performances that he conducted between 1842 and 1861
(now in DKKk, call no. 34 III, – 460 4°). It reads as follows:

1. Le comte d'Oldenbourg et la nymphe des bois, (deux figures).
2. Diane et Endymion (trois figures).

3. Salvator Rosa peignant la femme du bandit, (cinq figures).
4. La toilette de la mariée, (deux figures).
5. La damoiselle et le page (deux figures).
6. Les bayadères, (cinq figures).
7. Le concert joyeux, (genre flamand, six figures).
8. Tarentelle napolitaine, (quatre figures).
9. Les joueurs (d'après *Schleisner*).
10. L'Oracle d'amour (deux figures).
11. Il Decamerone du Bocace, (d'après *Wintherhalter*).

No musical sources for these tableaux have yet been traced.

Autograph sources:

Manuscript mise-en-scène. Ms. Autograph. Brown ink. 2 pp. (27,3 ×
22,6 cm)
No. 1. Det oldenburgske Horn. [...]
Unsigned and undated [1844]
[Dkkt; Brevregistrant: Bournonville

Printed sources:

Printed programme. 1 p. (24 × 18,9 cm)
Tableaux vivants./Représentés au palais royal d'Amalienbourg
Unsigned and dated: 'le mercredi 24. Avril 1844.'
[DKKk; 34 III, – 460 4° (inserted between the Royal Theatre posters
for 23.4. and 25.4.1844)

30.4.1844
Faust.

Bournonville's three-act romantic ballet *Faust* (see 25.4.
1832) was on this day performed with two new dances that
were interpolated in Acts II and III as follows:

(1) A *Pas de deux* in Act II. According to pencilled notes in the part for
the first violin this *Pas de deux* was set to music by the Italian composer, A. Mussi, and choreographed by F. Hoppe, who performed it
together with C. Fjeldsted.
(2) A Spanish dance in Act III entitled '*La Gitana*'. This character
dance was set to music by E. Helsted, and choreographed by Hoppe,
who performed it together with C. Fjeldsted as a divertissement between score nos. 30 and 31.

Moreover, Bournonville's own Act II *Pas de deux* was (according to the poster) replaced this year by F. Lefèvre's *Pas de
deux* which had already been performed two years earlier in
Faust (see 17.10.1842).

A. Mussi's music for Hoppe's *Pas de deux* was (according to
Hoppe's 1844 travel diary) brought from Milan to Copenhagen in 1844. It was most probably part of the repertory in
which he had performed (together with L. Grahn) at Milan's
Teatro alla Scala during the winter season of 1843–44. Many
years later Mussi's score was reused by Hoppe, when he
mounted a new (uncredited) *Pas de deux* on 13.11.1868 for
the début of L. Cetti, who danced it (with E. Hansen) under
Bournonville's and Hoppe's personal supervision.

The two interpolated dances in the 1844 restaging of *Faust*
were given twice in this ballet (the last time on 4.5.1844).
However, '*La Gitana*' was later also performed on one occasion as a separate divertissement by Hoppe and Fjeldsted on
6.5.1844, while Hoppe's *Pas de deux* seems (according to the
posters) to have been performed at least one more time in
Faust on 26.9.1845, but then by Hoppe and A. Krætzmer).

According to the rehearsal book of H. C. J. Fredstrup, 5
rehearsals of the two new dances in *Faust* were held between

21.4. and 29.4.1844. Of these, 4 rehearsals were directed by Hoppe and 1 by Bournonville.

Musical sources:

No orchestral and répétiteur's copy for the interpolated *Pas de deux* in *Faust* has yet been traced. However, a later répétiteur's copy containing the complete music for this dance, dating from c.1868, is now in DKKk (call no. KTB 231).

Parts (*Pas de deux*). Ms. Copy. 30 vol.
3 vl I, 3 vl II, 2 vla, 3 vlc e cb, fl picc, fl, ob 1/2, cl 1/2, fag 1/2, cor 1/2, tr 1/2, trb 1/2/3, timp, gr cassa e piatti, tri, arpa.
Unsigned and undated [1844]
[DKKk; KTB 231]
A pencilled note in the part for the first violin (reading: 'af Mussi') clearly indicates that the music for Hoppe's 1844 *Pas de deux* in *Faust* is by the Italian composer, A. Mussi.

Orchestral score ('*La Gitana*'). Ms. Autograph (by E. Helsted). Brown ink. 18 pp. of which one is blank (35,3 × 29,8 cm)
KT (C II, 114 K)/til Faust/B 232
Signed and dated (on p. 17): 'den 27 April/1844/Eduard Helste[d]'
[DKKk; C II, 114 k

No répétiteur's copy for Helsted's and Hoppe's '*La Gitana*' in Act III of *Faust* has yet been traced.

Parts ('*La Gitana*'). Ms. Copy. 29 vol.
3 vl I, 3 vl II, 2 vla, 3 vlc e cb, fl 1/2, ob 1/2, cl 1/2, fag 1/2, cor 1/2, clno 1/2, trb 1/2/3, timp, gr cassa e piatti, tri.
Unsigned and undated [1844]
[DKKk; KTB 232

3.6.1844
Bellman or the Polish Dance at Grönalund
(*Bellman eller Polskdandsen paa Grönalund*).

This one-act ballet-vaudeville was created as a tribute to the great 18th-century Swedish poet-songwriter, C. M. Bellman. According to Bournonville's own account in his memoirs *My Theatre Life* (p. 98), he was inspired by a backcloth transparency painted by the Danish artists, W. Marstrand and J. Sonne, as a décor for a performance given in Copenhagen by the Scandinavian Society in December 1840 to mark the centenary of Bellman's birth.

The music consisted (according to the autographed orchestral score) of an overture and five numbers, composed and arranged by H. S. Paulli (the overture and score nos. 1, 2, and 5) and J. F. Fröhlich (score nos. 3 and 4). They incorporated several musical borrowings, most of which derive from the collection of 82 Bellman songs, named *Fredmans Epistler*, in this way both illustrating and helping the audience interpret the action. These musical borrowings are identified as follows:

(1) In the overture Paulli incorporated I. P. E. Hartmann's *Gallopade* from Act I (score no. 3) of Bournonville's two-act romantic ballet *The Isle of Phantasy* (*see* 28.10.1838).
(2) In score no. 1 Paulli employed an excerpt from Bellman's *Epistler* no. 4 («Hej, musikanter, ge valdthornen väder»). In the same number a later insertion in V. C. Holm's autograph (dating most probably from Bournonville's last restaging of *Bellman* in Copenhagen on 5.2.1869) contains some excerpts from Bellman's *Epistler* no. 58 («Hjertat mig klämmer; Sorgligt jeg stämmer Qvintet på min fiol»).
(3) In score no. 2 Paulli employed three excerpts from Bellman's *Epistler*, namely no. 24 («Kära syster, Mig nu lyster Med dig tala»), no.

82 («Hvila vid denna källa!»), and no. 73 («Fan i fåtöljerna! Stolarna kullra»).
(4) In score no. 3 Fröhlich employed an excerpt from Bellman's *Epistler* no. 67 («Fader Movitz, bror, Spänn igen dina skor»).
(5) In score no. 4 Fröhlich employed two excerpts from Bellman's *Epistler* no. 31 («Se Movitz! Hvi står du och gråter») and no. 13 («Nå, ä nu alla församlade här?»).
(6) In score no. 5 Paulli employed a theme from Bellman's *Epistler* no. 62 («Movitz valdthornet proberar»).

Bellman or the Polish Dance at Grönalund was restaged twice by Bournonville in Copenhagen on 19.12.1849 and 5.2.1869, each time with only minor if any changes. In Sweden the ballet was mounted twice in slightly revised versions at Stockholm's Royal Theatre (Operahuset) on 11.6.1847 and 21.4.1858. Of these the 1858 production represents the last time Bournonville ever performed on stage, playing the title rôle that year.

During his lifetime the ballet received 107 performances in Copenhagen, the last of which was given on 3.11.1876. It is not clear from the rehearsal book of H. C. J. Fredstrup exactly how many rehearsals were held of it in 1844.

Autograph sources:

Production note. Ms. Autograph. Brown ink. 2 pp. (22,3 × 13,4 cm)
Dame = Dragter i Bellman.
Unsigned and undated [1844]
[DKKt; Brevregistrant: Bournonville

Manuscript scenario (included in a letter to J. G. Levetzau?). Ms. Autograph. Brown ink. 3 pp. (27,5 × 22 cm)
[…]/1.ste Scene/[…]/@.den Scene/[…]/3.die Scene/[…]/4.de Scene/[…]/Finale.
Signed and dated: 'Kbhvn d: 31 Mai 1944.'
[Copenhagen, The State Archive (Rigsarkivet); Det kgl. Teaters Arkiv, Gruppe E, pakke 288

Musical sources:

Orchestral score. Ms. Autograph (by H. S. Paulli and J. F. Fröhlich). Brown and black ink. 1 vol. 106 pp. (27 × 37,5 cm with minor variants)
293/293/Bellman/Bellman/(arr af Paulli)/[…]/Ouverture/Moderato.
Signed and dated (p. 106): 'HSPaulli 27/5 44.'
[DKKk; C II, 127 (KTB 293)
This orchestral score contains a later music insertion in V. C. Holm's autograph (pp. 35–38) which most probably dates from Bournonville's last restaging of *Bellman or the Polish Dance at Grönalund* in Copenhagen on 5.2.1869.

No répétiteur's copy for this ballet has yet been traced. However, a later répétiteur's copy copied from the original 1844 Copenhagen répétiteur's copy and dating from 1847 the Stockholm production of this ballet is now in SSkma (call no. KT Pantomime-Balletter B 6).

Parts. Ms. Copy. 35 vol.
3 vl I, 3 vl II, 2 vla, 3 vlc c cb, fl 1/2, ob 1/2, cl 1/2, fag 1/2, cor 1/2/3/4, tr 1/2, cnt 1/2, trb 1/2/3, timp, gr cassa, piatti, tri, arpa.
Unsigned and undated [1844]
[DKKk; KTB 293

Printed sources:

Printed scenario. 1 vol. 4 pp. (21 × 12,8 cm)
Bellman,/eller/Polskdandsen paa Grönalund./Ballet=Vaudeville i een Act/af/A. Bournonville./Musiken tildeels efter Fredmans Epist-

lar/arrangeret af H. Paulli./Opført første Gang til Balletten Walde-
mars Jubelforestilling/den 3.die Juni 1844.
Kjøbenhavn, J. H. Schubothe [1844]
[DKKk; 17, – 173 8°

June–August 1844
The Oresteia, tragic Ballet in 3 parts (unperformed)
(Orestias, Tragisk Ballet i 3 Dele (Uopført.)). **Projected ballet.**
In the first (Danish) edition of Bournonville's memoirs *Mit
Theaterliv* (vol. I, pp. 177–192) a complete libretto for this
projected three-act tragic ballet is included between the
dates of 3.6.1844 and 23.10.1844. According to his 'Anmærk-
ninger' for this work in the same volume, Bournonville had
originally planned to mount this ballet at Copenhagen's
Royal Theatre if its stage were rebuilt and considerably enlarged in depth. This happened some 12 years later, but at
that time Bournonville seems to have decided definitively
not to carry out this rather ambitious project.

The Oresteia was most probably conceived during the summer holiday of 1844, before the end of August, since Bournonville by then had resumed his daily duties at the Royal
Theatre.

Printed sources:

Printed scenario (published in *Mit Theaterliv*, 1848, pp. 177–192). 16
pp. (19 × 11,5 cm)
Orestias./Tragisk Ballet i 3 Dele.
Copenhagen, C. A. Reitzel, 1848.
[DKKk; 42, – 234 8°
In her 1979 English translation of Bournonville's memoirs, *My Theatre Life*, Patricia McAndrew omitted this libretto, but included it later
in her translations of Bournonville's complete scenarios (published
in *Dance Chronicle*, Volume 3 Number 4, pp. 458–469).

12.10.1844
Gioacchino.
For the première of H. P. Holst's four-act drama (to music by
H. Rung) Bournonville was responsible for choreographing
and mounting the finale dance in Act IV (score no. 14). It
consisted of a Neapolitan *Tarantella* and was performed (according to the poster) by Bournonville, E. Stramboe, A. Füssel and G. Brodersen (all dressed as 'four Neapolitan soldiers') together with a corps de ballet. Holst's drama was
restaged 22 years later on 19.3.1866, but then without any
involvement on Bournonville's part in the rehearsals and the
staging of this dance.

Gioacchino received 25 performances, the last of which was
given on 14.4.1866. According to the rehearsal book of H. C.
J. Fredstrup, 6 rehearsals of the finale dance were held by
Bournonville between 7.10. and 11.10.1844.

Musical sources:

Orchestral score. Ms. Autograph (by H. Rung). Black ink. 1 vol. 156
pp. of which one is blank (34,2 × 28,7 cm)
H. Rung/Gioacchino./Partitur./[...]/Gioacchino/romantisk
Drama/Partitur
Signed and dated (p. 156): 'H. Rung/Juli 1844'
[DKKk; C II, 119 k (KTA 388)
The Act IV *Tarantella* is included in this score on pp. 139–156.

No répétiteur's copy dating from the 1844 première of *Gioacchino*
has yet been traced. However, a later copy of it, almost certainly dat-

ing from the 1866 restaging, is now in DKKk (call no. MA ms 2919 (2)
(KTA 388 (2)). According to that copy, the *Tarantella* was at a later
stage performed in a heavily abridged version.

Parts. Ms. Copy. 33 vol.
3 vl I, 3 vl II, 2 vla, 3 vlc e cb, fl 1/2, ob 1/2, cl 1/2, fag 1/2, cor 1/2/
3/4, tr 1/2, trb 1/2/3, timp, guit, arpa, org 1/2. 46 vocal parts.
Unsigned and undated [1844]
[DKKk; KTA 388

23.10.1844
*A Children's Party, New Divertissement (En Børnefest, nyt
Divertissement)* (the Court Theatre).
This divertissement was performed exclusively by children
and consisted of a Christmas evening scene with a group of
orphans being guided to the Christmas tree by the allegorical figures *Flora* and *Zephyr*. It was choreographed and
mounted under the patronage of the Royal Theatre, and
given (according to the poster) as part of a charity performance for an association, named 'den i Aaret 1837 stiftede
Forening til forsømte Børns Frelse'.

The music consisted of an *Introduzione* followed by three
successive dance numbers. It is described on the poster as
'composed and arranged' (*componeret og arrangeret*) by H. S.
Paulli. He incorporated the following musical borrowings in
his score:

(1) In the *Introduzione* Paulli reused a theme from his earlier music to
the introduction for Act II (score no. 1 B) of Bournonville's two-act
romantic ballet *The Isle of Phantasy* (*see* 28.10.1838).
(2) In score nos. 1 and 3 Paulli interpolated excerpts of the music
from the romance «A peine au sortir de l'enfance, quatorze ans au
plus je comptais» in Act I (score no. 2) of E.-H. Méhul's three-act
opera *Joseph et ses frères* (premièred in Paris at l'Opéra Comique on
17.2.1807).

The divertissement was performed by Bournonville's dance
students, headed by his daughter, Augusta (as *Flora*) and S.
Lund (playing *Zephyr*) and accompanied by a groups of six
girls as Flora's suite, and two couples (performing a *Gallopade*). *A Children's Party* was performed only once.

Musical sources:

Musical drafts. Ms. Autograph (by H. S. Paulli). Black ink. 4 pp. (27,6
× 38, 2 cm with minor variants)
Andante sost:/[...]/Romance.
Unsigned and undated [1844]
[DKKk; MA ms 2704 (1–2) (KTB 230)
These untitled drafts contain Paulli's music for score nos. 1 and 2 in
A Children's Party. Moreover, they hold Bournonville's pencilled auto-
graphed choreographic notes describing the chreography per-
formed by *Flora*, *Zephyr* and the suite of six *Nymphs* (score no. 2).

Orchestral score. Ms. Autograph (by H. S. Paulli). Black and brown
ink. 1 vol. 68 pp. of which one is blank (26,7 × 37,7 cm)
H. S. Paulli/En Børnefest/Partitur/230/Børnefest
Signed and dated (p. 67): 'HSPaulli d 18 Octbr 1844.'
[DKKk; C II, 119 (KTB 230)

No répétiteur's copy for *A Children's Party* has yet been traced.

Parts. Ms. Copy. 24 vol.
2 vl I, 2 vl II, vla, 2 vlc e cb, fl 1/2, ob 1/2, cl 1/2, fag 1/2, cor 1/2, clno
1/2, trb, timp, gr cassa, tri, arpa.
Unsigned and undated [1844]
[DKKk; KTB 230

18.12.1844

Hamburg-Dance (Hamborger=Dands) **(uncredited)**
performed by Bournonville and C. Fjeldsted.

According to notes written in a part for the first violin for
this (uncredited) dance, it is identical with the so-called *New
Hamburg-Scottish, Character Dance*, which was originally choreographed by Bournonville and performed by himself and
Fjeldsted as a new, incorporated finale in his one-act idyllic
ballet *The Tyroleans* (*see* 8.2.1844).

On the poster for its second performance on 20.12.1844
the dance is named *Hamborger=Dands, Pas de deux i Vier-
länder=Costume* and is then credited as a work composed
(*componeret*) by Bournonville and set to music by H. C. Lumbye.

The *Hamburg-Dance* was given 7 times as a separate divertissement in Copenhagen, the last time on 2.2.1845.

Musical sources:

While no separate orchestral score and répétiteur's copy from the
1844 performances of this dance have yet been traced, the original
set of parts (dating from when it was first performed in *The Tyroleans*
on 8.2.1844) are now in DKKk (call no. KTB 1024, but originally KTB
240).

22.12.1844

Pas de deux **(uncredited) performed by F. Hoppe and**
C. Fjeldsted.

This (uncredited) *Pas de deux* was mounted as a result of a
last-minute change of this evening's programme. It is most
probably identical with an earlier work by either Bournonville, or F. Lefèbvre, or F. Hoppe (perhaps the *Pas de deux*
choreographed by Hoppe and performed on 30.4.1844 by
himself and Fjeldsted as an incorporated divertissement in
Act II of Bournonville's three-act romantic ballet *Faust*). It is
not possible to identify the dance any further.

1845

8.2.1845

Parisian Polka, Social Dance, (Pariser=Polka, Selskabsdands)
performed by eight couples (the Court Theatre).

This Polka divertissement was created for and performed as
part of the farewell performance the Danish singer-actress,
C. E. Zrza. It is included in Bournonville's handwritten lists
of his works, written c.1851 (*see* Additional Sources) in which
it is listed as 'Zrza's Benefice'. On the poster it is explicitly
presented as a dance 'arranged' (*arrangeret*) by Bournonville
and performed by eight couples of principal dancers from
the Royal Danish Ballet. The music was that of H. C. Lumbye's earlier *Pariser Mode Polka*, played for the first time in
public as part of a concert given in the hall of the Riding
School at Copenhagen's Christiansborg Palace on 16.11.
1844. Bournonville's *Parisian Polka* was performed only
once.

Musical sources:

Orchestral score. Ms. Autograph (by H. C. Lumbye). Brown ink. 1
vol. 4 pp. 27 × 37,4 cm)
Pariser Mode Polka

Signed and dated (p. 1): 'H: C: Lumbÿe/comp: d 12. Novemb: 1844.'
[DKKk; C II, 34 (1931–32.31)

No répétiteur's copy and set of parts dating from the 1845 performance of Bournonville's *Parisian Polka* at the Court Theatre has yet
been traced.

16.2.1845

The Blossom of Happiness (Lykkens Blomst).

According to his handwritten lists of his stagings of operas
and plays, written c.1851 (*see* Additional Sources), Bournonville was responsible for both choreographing and mounting the dances in H. C. Andersen's two-act fairy-tale comedy
(to music by H. Rung). They included a dance in Act II
(score no. 5) performed by a group of elf maidens during
the chorus for female voices, entitled «Hvor Glædens skum-
mende Bølge slaaer». Moreover, brief dance scenes were
performed in the same act as part of the chorus, named
«Stolt Signild lader brygge Viin» (score no. 7) and in the
love scene of the play's two protagonists, *Waldemar* and *Kirsten* (score no. 10).

The Blossom of Happiness was also mounted at the Casino
Theatre on 15.12.1858 and received three performances
there (the last given on 20.12.1858). However, although
Bournonville worked frequently at that theatre during this
period, he does not seem to have been involved in that production of Andersen's comedy.

The Blossom of Happiness received only 6 performances at
Copenhagen's Royal Theatre, the last given on 25.3.1845.
According to the rehearsal book of H. C. J. Fredstrup, 5 rehearsals of its dance scenes were held by Bournonville between 12.2. and 16.2.1845.

Musical sources:

Orchestral score. Ms. Autograph. Black ink. 1 vol. 96 pp. (35,3 × 30
cm with minor variants)
Lykkens Blomst/Partitur./390/[…]/Lÿkkens Blomst/af/H. C. An-
dersen./Musiken af/H. Rung.
Signed and dated (p. 96): 'H. Rung Dec: 1844.'
[DKKk; C II, 119k (KTA 390)

No répétiteur's copy for *The Blossom of Happiness* has yet been traced.

Parts. Ms. Copy. 32 + 22 vol.
3 vl I, 3 vl II, 2 vla, 3 vlc e cb, fl picc, fl 1/2, ob 1/2, cl 1/2, fag 1/2, cor
1/2/3/4, tr 1/2, trb 1/2/3, timp, gong, arpa. On stage: 2 vl I, 2 vl II,
vla, cb, fl 1/2, ob 1/2, cl 1/2, fag 1/2, cor 1/2/3/4, tr 1/2, timp,
gong. 49 vocal parts.
Unsigned and undated [1845]
[DKKk; KTA 390

26.2.1845

Kirsten Piil.

According to a letter from Bournonville to the theatre management of Copenhagen's Royal Theatre, dated 30.5.1840
(now in the The State Archive, call no. Det kgl. Teaters Arkiv,
Gruppe E, pakke 288) Bournonville was in the spring of
1840 working on a projected divertissement intended to be
interpolated as an intermezzo in L. Holberg's three-act comedy from 1750 *The Healing Spring (Kildereisen)*. From the same
letter it is clear that he was then already about to conceive
what became the scenario for the third act of his three-act
romantic ballet *Kirsten Piil*.

'Je me suis figuré une pelouse de verdure, près la fontaine de <u>Kirsten Piil</u> au bas de la colline sur laquelle le camp forain est dressé; j'y ai placé des groupes de peuple mangeant sur l'herbe, fumant, dansant folâtrant, enfin un vrai tableau de <u>Teniers</u>. Un carrousel où de bons bourgeois en perruques courent la bague, des tréteaux de Charlatans, des animaux savans, des diseuses de bonne-aventure, des jeux innocenns, des ménétriers, des ivrognes, une voiture surchargée de voyageurs, et à la fin à l'approche de la nuit de la St Jean, un pélerinage à la fontaine; Les veilles femmes et vieillards décréprits jétent leurs hailons, et se transforment en jeunes gens de la ville, qui le verre en mains, au milieu des chants d'allégresse exécutent une bachanale générale. – Le tout assaisonné de couplets, de dialogues, de choeurs et Brouhaha. -'.

The ballet's score was composed and arranged by E. Helsted. He interpolated several musical borrowings in Acts II and III in order to illustrate and to help the audience interpret the action, which spreads over several centuries. This is particularly true of the scene in Act III (score no. 2) that depicts *Kirsten Piil*'s dream. In this scene the life and the events which unfold during three centuries at the miraculous fountain spring that bears her name are shown in a continuous series of half-mimed, half-danced tableaux. Helsted's musical borrowings for this and the ballet's previous scenes are identified as follows:

(1) Act II (score no. 4): In this number Helsted employed the tune of an old Danish folk song, named «En yndig og frydefuld sommertid», deriving from the region of Neder-Dalby near the towns of Randers and Mariager in Jutland. It was collected and notated by the priest, C. Schütz, in 1843, and was published by A. P. Berggreen in 1860 as part of his musical anthology entitled *Danske Folkesange og Melodier* (Kjøbenhavn, C. A. Reitzel, Anden Udgave, første bind, no. 103, p. 182). The fact that Helsted incorporated this popular love song in Bournonville's ballet indicates, however, that it must have been already well known to the audience in 1845.
(2) Act III (score no. 1): For the opening scene of Act III Helsted employed the melody of a romance, entitled «Jeg gik mig i Lunden». It is borrowed from Act I of F. Kuhlau's score to J. L. Heiberg's five-act play *The Elves' Hill (Elverhøi)*, premièred at Copenhagen's Royal Theatre on 6.11.1828.
(3) Act III (score no. 2, *Kirsten Piil's dream*): For this half-mimed, half-danced scene Helsted employed two more excerpts from Kuhlau's score to *The Elves' Hill*, namely the Act II romance, entitled «Der vanker en Ridder», and the *Minuet* from Act V. Moreover, in the same number he incorporated J. A. P. Schultz's(?) melody to C. Søeborg's then immensely popular parlour song from 1809, entitled «Om hundred Aar er Alting glemt». It is followed by an excerpt borrowed from E. Dupuy's music to N. T. Bruun's song, named «Sankt Hansdag er Glædens og Midsommersfest». After it comes an excerpt from J. A. P. Schultz's song, entitled «Nys fyldte skjøn Sired det attende Aar» (originally written for Th. Thaarup's one-act singspiel *The Harvest Festival (Høstgildet)* from 16.9.1790). Schultz's tune is succeeded by C. E. F. Weyse's melody to C. J. Boye's song, entitled «Der er et Land det Sted er højt mod Norden», but originally written for the five-act tragedy *Svend Grathe* from 10.12.1824. It is followed by a kind of cotilloncoda movement that employs J. Strauss' (the elder) complete *Annen Polka* from 1842 (op. 137).

That the music for the *Pas de deux* in Act II (score no. 8) is written by a copyist (pp. 153–192) seems to indicate that this number was borrowed by Helsted from a work by another (not yet identified) composer.

Finally, excerpts of the music for Helsted's *Waltz* in Act I (score no. 3) were reused many years later by V. C. Holm in his score for scene 6 (score no. 8) of Bournonville's ballet divertissement, *From the Last Century* (*see* 31.10.1875). In that

work it served as an accompaniment for a so-called 'Polskdands', and represents the last time that parts of Helsted's score for *Kirsten Piil* were ever performed at the Royal Theatre.

Kirsten Piil was already revised into two acts at its second performance on 22.3.1846, after which it was given with a new, extended title as *Kirsten Piil or Two Midsummer Festivals (Kirsten Piil eller to Midsommerfeste)*.

Bournonville's pencilled notes in the 1846 répétiteur's copy (p. 16) and other notes found in Helsted's autographed orchestral score indicate several later changes in the succession of the dances in Act I. These changes were most probably made in connection with the ballet's three final performances on 8.10., 11.12., and 28.12.1846.

Kirsten Piil reached a total of 8 performances, the last of which was given on 28.12.1846. According to the rehearsal book of H. C. J. Fredstrup, 53 rehearsals were held of it between 16.11.1844 and 26.2.1845.

Autograph sources:

Production note. Ms. Autograph. Brown and black ink. 3 pp. (22,4 × 13,8 cm; 17,3 × 10,4 cm; 22,1 × 13 cm)
<u>Regie</u>/til/<u>Balletten Kirsten Piil.</u>/-/Decbr. 1844.
Unsigned and dated: 'Decbr. 1844'.
[DKKkt; F.M. (Brevregistrant, Bournonville)

Musical sources:

Musical draft. Ms. Autograph (by E. Helsted). Brown ink. 4 pp. (33,3 × 25,4 cm with minor variants)
i 2.den Act./<u>No. 5</u>. Polonaise/[...]/No. 6 <u>Contradands</u>
Unsigned and undated [c.1845]
[DKKk; MA ms 2708 (KTB 263)
This musical draft contains the music for what at the première became the *Polonaise* in Act II (score no. 6) and the *Contradands* in the same act (score no. 7). It also includes Bournonville's pencilled autographed choreographic notes describing in fine detail the mime and the steps performed in these *pas d'action*.

Orchestral score. Ms. Autograph (by E. Helsted) and copy by an unknown hand. Brown and black ink. 1 vol. 440 pp. of which three are blank (33,2 × 25,6 cm with minor variants)
263/Ed. Helsted,/Kirsten Piil./Ballet.
Signed and dated (on p. 88): '<u>Nytaarsaften 1844. E. H</u>:', (p. 206) '<u>den 22.de Febr 1845. Eduard Helsted.</u>', (p. 439) '<u>Eduard Helsted.</u>'
[DKKk; CII, 114 k (KTB 263)
All those sections which contains musical borrowings in Act III, score no. 2 (pp. 295–356) are here written by a copyist.

Répétiteur's copy. Ms. Copy (with several autographed insertions by E. Helsted). Black ink. 1 vol. 122 pp. of which one is blank (33,7 × 25,8 cm with minor variants)
B. 263/Kirsten Piil/1845/22/[...]/Repit: Partie/til/Balletten/<u>Kirsten Piil</u>.
Unsigned and dated (on the front cover): '1845'
[DKKk; MA ms 2961 (KTB 263)
This répétiteur's copy contains Bournonville's pencilled autographed notes describing both the mime and (in more general terms) the choreography of the Act III finale (score no. 5). His other autographed notes on pp. 52 and 58 (all written with black ink) indicate his later wish to reuse parts of Helsted's music of the *Polska* in Act I (score no. 9) for his so-called *Scandinavian Quadrille (Scandinavisk Quadrille)*, which was part of Bournonville's *'Bouquet Royal', Divertissement*, premièred on 27.1.1870. This is clear from Bournonville's notes in this répétiteur's copy, indicating that the *Polska* from *Kirsten Piil* was to be pieced together with the music for the *Norwegian*

Spring Dance in E. Helsted's score for Bournonville's one-act ballet *Old Memories, or A Magic Lantern (see* 18.12.1848), and concluded with a new 'Galloppe' composed especially by H. C. Lumbye (i.e. the so-called *Bouquet Royal Galop*). Finally, his note on p. 10 indicates Bournonville's later change of the title of Helsted's *Waltz* in Act I (score no. 3) which was renamed 'Polskdands'. This happened when V. C. Holm incorporated this dance in scene 6 (score no. 8) of his score for Bournonville's ballet divertissement *From the Last Century (see* 31.10.1875).

Parts. Ms. Copy. 31 + 9 vol.
3 vl I, 3 vl II, 2 vla, 3 vlc e cb, fl 1/2, ob 1/2, cl 1/2, fag 1/2, cor 1/2/3/4, tr 1/2, trb 1/2/3 timp, gr cassa, tri. On stage: cor 1/2, tr 1/2, cnt 1/2, cnt a chiavi 1/2, trb.
Unsigned and undated [1845]
[DKKk; KTB 263

Répétiteur's copy. Ms Autograph (by E. Helsted). Black ink. 1 vol. 74 pp. of which two are blank (26,5 × 37 cm)
Eduard Helsted/Kirsten Piil/Romantisk Ballet i 3 Akter/af/August Bournonville./[...]/Balletten Kirsten Piil
Signed and dated (p. 72): 'Eduard Helsted. Juli 1846.'
[DKKk; C II, 114 k
This répétiteur's copy was Bournonville's private property and was (according to Helsted dating of it) written the same year the ballet went out of repertory. The volume was for many years in the possession of the Bournonville family, but on 31.3.1910 it was donated to DKKk by his daughter, Charlotte Bournonville. It contains several autographed pencilled notes by Bournonville which describe the dramatic action, the mime, and (more sporadically) the choreography. They were most probably written in connection with the revised 1846 restaging of the ballet.

Printed sources:

Printed scenario. 1 vol. 12 pp. (19,8 × 12,7 cm)
Kirsten Piil./Romantisk Ballet i tre Acter/af/August Bournonville./ Musiken af Edward Helsted.
Kjøbenhavn, J. H. Schubothe [1845]
[DKKk; 17, – 174 8°

30.5.1845
Raphael (Rafael).
According to Bournonville's own account in his memoirs *My Theatre Life* (p. 114) and his two manuscript scenarios, this ballet in six tableaux was conceived during his first visit to Rome in the summer of 1841 and completed in Florence on 7.8.1841. It reached its final form in Paris on 12.9.1841 on his homeward journey back to Denmark after his enforced six-month exile. However, nearly four years had to pass before it was carried out for the occasion of a planned, but at the last minute postponed visit to Denmark of the King of Prussia, Friedrich William IV.

According to his 1841 travel diary Bournonville originally intended to have the impressive series of six décors created by the Danish painter, C. Hansen. This idea, however, was abandoned at an early stage, and *Raphael* was mounted with scenery painted by three different artists of the Royal Theatre, namely A. Wallich (tableaux 1, 2 and 6), C. F. Christensen (tableau 3), and T. Lund (tableaux 4 and 5). The score was composed by Fr. Fröhlich. He incorporated two musical borrowings in his music for the scene in the fourth tableau that depicts a Roman carnival (score no. 21), namely:

(1) The well-known melody in 6/8 time, entitled 'Carneval de Venise'. Originally a Neapolitan folk tune named 'La Ricciolella', this

melody had become famous through N. Paganini's virtuosic variations of it for solo violin. Bournonville had earlier employed it for the *Pas de deux* that he incorporated on 20.12.1832 in P. Larcher's 1823 Copenhagen version of L. Milon's two-act pantomimic ballet *Le Carnaval de Venise, ou Constance à l'Epreuve*. Many years later he reused it as the main musical motif for a solo dance, named *Polichinel*, which was performed in Act II of his last Italian ballet-vaudeville in two tableaux, entitled *Pontemolle (An Artists' Party in Rome) (see* 11.4. 1866).

(2) For the solo variation danced by the character *Pulcinello* Fröhlich employed the same traditional Italian *commedia dell'arte* music which E. Helsted had used before him in Act I (score no. 6) of Bournonville's three-act romantic ballet *Napoli or The Fisherman and His Bride (see* 29.3.1842). In that ballet it served for the scene depicting the entrance of the character *Carlino* and his puppet show.

Moreover, in his music for the *Pas de trois* in the third tableau of *Raphael* (score no. 13), Fröhlich reused (except for the introduction) his own music for the *Pas de deux* in Act II (score no. 16) of Bournonville's four-act romantic ballet *The Childhood of Erik Menved (see* 12.1.1843).

Furthermore, according to Bournonville's pencilled autographed notes in the 1853 répétiteur's copy for his four-act ballet *Waldemar* (now in DKKk, call no. MA ms 2994 (KTB 292 (2)), the choreography and the music for the opening *Allegretto* variation in Fröhlich's *Pas de trois* in *Raphael* was later reused as an incorporated solo variation in the Act I *Pas de six* of *Waldemar* when that ballet was restaged on 19.10. 1853.

Finally, three excerpts of Fröhlich's music for the first and second tableaux of *Raphael* (score nos. 1, 4, and 5) were many years later interpolated by V. C. Holm in his score for Bournonville's ballet divertissement *From the Last Century (see* 31.10.1875). They thereby represent the last time that parts of Fröhlich's music for *Raphael* were performed at the Royal Theatre.

Both of the two first performances of *Raphael* (30.5 and 31.5.1845) were given as full-length ballets making up the whole evening's programme, together with F. Kuhlau's overture for the 1824 opera *Lulu*, which was played as a curtain-raiser before the actual performance.

Raphael reached a total of 7 performances, the last of which was given on 22.11.1845. According to the rehearsal book of H. C. J. Fredstrup, 65 rehearsals were held of this work between 11.5.1844 and 30.5.1845.

Two years after the ballet's last performance, selected excerpts of Fröhlich's score were still frequently played at public concerts in the then newly opened Casino Theatre. The first of these concerts took place on 2.5.1847 and was entitled *Scene og Ballet af Balletten Raphael*. It reflects the continuing success of Fröhlich's music well after the ballet went out of the repertory.

Autograph sources:

Manuscript scenario. Ms. Autograph. Brown ink. 1 vol. 14 pp. (31,5 × 21,5 cm)
Rafaëllo d'Urbino/Ballet i 6 Tableaux./af/Auguste Bournonville./ Rom og i Florentz/1841.
Signed and dated: 'Planen i Rom den 26 Julii 1841. (Programmet udført i) Florentz den 7.de Augusti/1841. -'
[DKKk; NKS 3285 4° 3 R–U

Manuscript scenario. Ms. Autograph. Brown ink. 1 vol. 15 pp. (27 × 20,4 cm)

Rafaëllo d'Urbino/Ballet = pantomime en six tableaux par Auguste Bournonville.
Signed and dated: 'Paris le 12 Septembre 1841.'
[DKKk; NKS 3285 4° 3 R–U

Production note. Ms. Autograph. Brown ink. 3 pp. (34,9 × 22,1 cm)
Rafaël romantisk Ballet i 6 Tableauer./Personer.
Signed and dated: 'Kbhvn d. 15.de April 1845.'
[DKKkt; F.M. (Ballet)

Musical sources:

Orchestral score. Ms. Autograph (by J. F. Fröhlich). Brown and black ink. 1 vol. 366 pp. of which two are blank (26,5 × 36,6 cm with minor variants)
208/Balletten Rafael/[...]/Raffaello./af A. Bournonville./Musikken af J. F. Fröhlich/op. 52.
Signed and dated (p. 2): '17/5 45.'
[DKKk; C II, 107 (KTB 208)

Répétiteur's copy. Ms. Autograph (by J. F. Fröhlich). Brown and black ink. 1 vol. 88 pp. of which two are blank (26,7 × 37,5 cm)
Rafaello d'Urbino
Signed and dated (p. 54): '15/5 45. JFFröhlich'
[DKKk; CII, 107
This répétiteur's copy was Bournonville's private property and remained in the possession of the Bournonville family until 31.3.1910, when it was donated to DKKk by his daughter, Charlotte Bournonville. It contains his pencilled autographed notes describing (in French) the mime, the dramatic action, and (more sporadically) the choreography throughout the ballet. These notes were most probably written during the first rehearsals of *Raphael* during the early months of 1845. Another pencilled note on p. 39 indicates the duration of the first two tableaux as 32 minutes.

Répétiteur's copy. Ms. Copy. Black ink. 1 vol. 160 pp. (33,3 × 25,7 cm with minor variants)
Rafaello/208/1845./[...]/Rafaello d'Urbino./Repit. Partie
Unsigned and dated (on the front cover): '1845.'
[DKKk; MA ms 2946 (KTB 208)
This répétiteur's copy contains Bournonville's pencilled autographed choreographic numbers in the music of the *Pas de trois* in the third tableau (score no. 13, pp. 79–88). They most probably refer to a separate (not yet identified) notation of this dance, which he perhaps made in 1845 or at a later stage. Other Bournonville notes (written with black ink on pp. 4, 8, 31, and 32) refer to V. C. Holm's interpolation of three large excerpts of Fröhlich's music for the first and second tableaux in his score for Bournonville's much later ballet divertissement, entitled *From the Last Century* (*see* 31.10.1875).

Parts. Ms. Copy. 33 vol.
3 vl I, 3 vl II, 2 vla, 3 vlc e cb, fl 1/2, ob 1/2, cl 1/2, fag 1/2, cor 1/2/3/4, clno 1/2, trb 1/2/3, timp, gr cassa, piatti, tri e glock, arpa.
Unsigned and undated [1845]
[DKKk; KTB 208

Other sources:

Costume drawing by E. Lehmann (?). Pencil and water colours (19,4 × 12,6 cm)
[Untitled]
Unsigned and undated [c.1845]
[DKKkt; Kostumetegninger (Lehmann)
This drawing shows the costume of a warrior wearing an iron helmet and holding a sword. It most probably depicts a soldier of the papal guard in Bournonville's ballet *Raphael*.

Printed sources:

Printed scenario. 1 vol. 15 pp. (19,8 × 12,6 cm)
Rafael./Romantisk Ballet i sex Tableauer/af/August Bournonville./

Musiken af Fr. Fröhlich./Decorationerne af Dhrr. Wallich, Lund og Christensen.
Kjøbenhavn, J. H. Schubothe [1845]
[DKKk; 17, – 174 8°

Printed scenario. 1 vol. 6 pp. (27,2 × 17,2 cm)
RAPHAËL,/BALLET-PANTOMIME EN SIX TABLEAUX/PAR/AUGUSTE BOURNONVILLE
Copenhaque, Imprimerie de Berling frères, 1845.
[DKKk; 17, – 174 4°
This is an abridged French version of the original Danish scenario, which was published for the planned, but postponed visit to Denmark of the King of Prussia, Friedrich William IV.

19.6.1845
Napoli or The Fisherman and His Bride (Napoli/Napoli eller Fiskeren og hans Brud).
For a special gala performance given at Copenhagen's Royal Theatre on this day for the visiting King of Prussia, Friedrich William IV, Bournonville wrote a new French *Analyse du Ballet* for his three-act romantic ballet *Napoli* (*see* 29.3.1842). It was printed on a specially designed poster and reads as follows:

ACTE PREMIER.
La main de *Térésina* est convoitée par les deux notabilites du quai de *Ste. Lucia, l'Aquajolo* et le *Macaronaro*; elle leur préfère le pauvre mais aimable *Gennaro* et les rebutes se reunissent pour accuser de sorcellerie leur fortuné rival. Les amants s'étant promenée en nacelle, sont assaillis par une tempête et *Gennaro* à moitié mort, est jeté sur le rivage. La perte de celle qu'il aime, les malédictions de ces accusateurs le réduisent au peur affreux désespoir. L'Aurore cependant, semble ranimer en lui, un rayon d'ésoérance; il reçort un talisman et part à la recherche de sa bien aimée.

ACTE DEUXIEME.
Les esprits de *la grotte d'azur* ont recueilli parmé [*sic*] eux la jeune napolitaine; elle est changée en nayade, l'oubli du passé regne dans son âme, elle ne peut se rappeler les traits de *Gennaro* qui a bravé touts les périls pour venir jusqu'à elle. Le talisman opère son retour à la vis, et dégage les amants de la puissance de Golfo, qui les laisse portir chargés de grésens.

ACTE TROIZIEME.
Retour à Naples. C'est la fête de la *Madonna dell'Arco* à Montevirgine. Le bonheur et la richesse du couple sauvé, ramme les idées de la sorcellerie; frayeur et confusion. Explication: C'est la foi divine qui a été leur talisman, et la joie la plus vive signale union de Gennaro et Térésina.
                                    FIN.

Printed sources:

Printed scenario published on a poster, 1 p. (27,2 × 19, 2 cm)
Théatre Royal de Copenhaque./[...]/Napoli,/[...] Analyse du Ballet.
Published by 'Imprimerie du Bianco Luno' and dated: 'Jeudi le 19 Juin 1845.'
[DKKk; DA (Småtryk; Personalhistorie, Kpsl. B: Bournonville)

21.6.1845
The Toreador (Le Toréador/Toréadoren).
For the second gala performance given at Copenhagen's Royal Theatre on the occasion of a visit by the King of Prussia, Friedrich William IV, Bournonville wrote a new French *Analyse du Ballet* for *Le Toréador* (*see* 27.11.1840). It was printed on a specially designed poster and reads as follows:

ACTE PREMIER.

Alonzo, vainqueur dans une course de taureaux, célèbre sa victoire dans l'auberge de son futur beau-père. Mlle. *Céleste* allant de Paris à Madrid s'arrête à la dite auberge, raffole des danses espagnoles, et prend une leçon de la jolie *Maria* qui lui enseigne le *Jaléo.* Deux anglais-voyageurs, dejeûnant sur le balcon de l'hôtellerie, sont frappés de la grâce de la belle française, en deviennent amoureux et veulent l'épouser. Ils se prennent de querelle dont *Alonzo* est nommé l'arbitre. Le sort en décidera de celui qui le premier fera sa demande en mariage; mais en voulant désigner la dame de leurs pensées, ils marquent l'air et le pas du *Jaléo*; de là, quiproquo et fureur d'*Alonzo,* qui par ses emportements se fait mettre en prison.

ACTE DEUXIEME.

Les gentlemen font leur cour à Mlle. Céleste; après quelques petites aventures qui font ressortir la différence de leurs caractères respectifs, c'est le jovial William qui obtient sa main à condition que la liberté soit rendue au Toréador. Les boléros ramènent la paix et la gaité interrompues par la méprise du Jaléo.

FIN.

Printed sources:

Printed scenario published on a poster. 1 p. (27,2 × 19, 2 cm)
Théâtre Royal de Copenhaque./[...]/Le Toréador,/[...]/ Analyse du Ballet.
Published by 'Imprimerie du Bianco Luno' and dated: 'Samedi le 21 Juin 1845.'
[DKKk; DA (Småtryk; Personalhistorie, Kpsl. B: Bournonville)

6.11.1845
Pas de deux à la Taglioni arranged by Ballet Master
Bournonville (arrangeret af Hr. Balletmester Bournonville)
performed by G. Brodersen and A. Nielsen.
This dance is almost certainly identical with the *Pas de deux (à la Taglioni),* performed by Bournonville and A. Nielsen as an incorporated divertissement in Act II of *La Sylphide* on 27.9. 1842. That dance, in turn, is identical with the even earlier *Pas de deux,* set to a score by J. Mayseder and first performed in Act II (score no. 1 A) of Bournonville's two-act romantic ballet *The Isle of Phantasy (see* 28.10.1838). The dance is most likely also identical with the so-called *A Pas de deux arranged after Taglioni (En Pas de deux arrangeret efter Taglioni),* performed by Brodersen and Nielsen on 4.10.1839, and the *Pas de deux (by Taglioni) (Pas de deux (Af Taglioni)),* mounted by Bournonville at Stockholm's Royal Theatre (Operahuset) for his Swedish pupil, P. C. Johansson, and A. Nielsen, on 5.6.1839.

The 1845 *Pas de deux à la Taglioni* was given only once. According to the rehearsal book of H. C. J. Fredstrup, only one rehearsal was held of this dance by Bournonville on 5.11. 1845.

26.11.1845
Tableaux vivants. Psyché. **(uncredited) (the Amalienborg Palace).**
For a Royal Court ball, given at the Amalienborg Palace on this day on the occasion of a state visit of the Swedish Crown Prince and Crown Princess, Bournonville mounted two series of (uncredited) *Tableaux vivants,* both of which were set to music composed and arranged by F. Gläser. The first of these series was entitled *Psyché* and consisted of seven tableaux. It clearly seems to have been drawn from inspirations

found in B. Thorvaldsen's cycle of bas-relief on the same theme, and may perhaps also represent Bournonville's first draft for his later one-act allegorical ballet *Psyche (see* 7.5. 1850). In the printed programme the tableaux are described as follows:

1. Enlèvement de Psyché.
2. Approche de l'Amour.
3. Curiosité de Psyché.
4. Colère et fuite de l'Amour.
5. Psyché aux enfers.
6. L'amour ranime son amante évanouie.
7. Psyché reçoit les ailes de l'immortalité.

According to Bournonville's diary, his fourteen-year-old daughter, Augusta Bournonville, appeared in one of the leading parts of the tableaux. This is clear from a note on 9.12.1845 reading:

'Excell. [J. G.] Levetzau sagt mig at Kongen vilde forære Augusta [Bournonville] en Confirmations=Kjole i Anledning af Psyche'.

Moreover, in an earlier note on 1.12.1845 Bournonville described his preparations for these tableaux as follows:

'otte Dage tilbragte med Tilberedelser til en Hoffest'.

Finally, Bournonville also arranged and directed the ballroom dances performed at the Royal Court ball on the same evening.

Musical sources:

No orchestral score and répétiteur's copy have yet been traced for this work.

Parts. Ms. Copy. 9 vol.
vl I, vl II, vla, vlc e cb, fl, ob, cl, fag, cor I–II.
Unsigned and dated: '1845'
[DKKk; MA ms 2754 (1–9)
This set of parts is bound together with the parts for the series of four tableaux, entitled *Les Saisons,* which was performed on the same evening (*see* the following entry). On the front cover of the wrapper the parts are entitled: 'Musik til Tableaux/1845/arrangeret/af/Hr. Hof= Kapelmester Glæser'.

Printed sources:

Printed programme. 1 p. (21,4 × 17,1 cm)
[...]/Musique et Tableaux vivants./[...]/Psyché.
Unsigned and dated: 'Mercredi 26. Novembre 1845.'
[DKKk; 34 III, – 460 4° (inserted between the Royal Theatre posters for 26.11. and 27.11.1845)
This programme is part of F. Gläser's private collection of the posters for those performances which he conducted in Copenhagen between 1842 and 1861.

Other sources:

Painting by E. Lehmann(?). Oil on canvas (16,6 × 13,2 cm)
[Untitled]
Unsigned and undated [c.1845]
[DKKt; Balletafdelingen (permanent udstilling)
In all probability this painting shows Bournonville's fourteen-year-old daughter, Augusta, as *Amor* in her father's series of tableaux, named *Psyché* and created especially for a royal soirée at the Amalienborg Palace. This theory is supported not only by the likeness of Augusta with this painting, but also by the fact that the paint-

ing was originally part of the royal collections of King Christian VIII, whose property stamp is found on the back side of the frame. The painting remained in the royal family's property until it was sold at a public auction, together with other properties of Christian VIII's second wife, Queen Caroline Amalie. In 1930 it was purchased by DKKt at another public auction.

The Danish art historian, C. Christensen, regards the painting (which for many years has been credited as a work by E. Lehmann depicting L. Grahn in the title-rôle of Bournonville's two-act romantic ballet *La Sylphide*) as a portrait showing J. Price in the title-rôle of Bournonville'S 1850 ballet *Psyche*. This identification, however, does not seem possible because of the applied property stamp of King Christian VIII, who had died two years before Price appeared in this rôle. Christensen, moreover, is of the opinion that the painting was made by D. Monies.

Another, even less likely identification has recently been advocated by the Danish theatre historian, E. Aasted Neiiendam, in her biographical study of Grahn, entitled *Sylfide og Heks* (Danmarks Købstadsmuseums Skriftrække, bind IV, 1996, pp. 26–28). Aasted Neiiendam is of the opinion that the painting dates from the years 1830–1831 and shown Grahn as *Amor* in P. Funck's Copenhagen version of Ch.-L. Didelot's and F.-M.-A. Venua's two-act anacreontic ballet *Flore et Zéphire* (a ballet that was originally created at the Paris Opéra on 12.12.1815 and was first performed in Copenhagen on 4.11.1820 with a partially new score arrange by L. Zinck).

26.11.1845
Tableaux vivants. Les Saisons (uncredited)
(the Amalienborg Palace).

This series of four (uncredited) *tableaux vivants* (subtitled *Les Saisons*) was created and mounted by Bournonville for a Royal Court ball at the Amalienborg Palace, given for the visiting Crown Prince and Crown Princess of Sweden. The series (set to music composed and arranged by F. Gläser) consisted of four tableaux, described in the printed programme as follows:

L'hiver (sujet danois).
Le Printemps (sujet grec-moderne).
L'été (scène de moisson en Tyrol)
L'automne (scène de vendages aux environs de Naples).

In his music for the tableau representing *Summer,* Gläser employed excerpts from G. Rossini's music for the *Pas de trois* in Act III of his four-act opera *Guillaume Tell.* Moreover, in his score for *Autumn,* Gläser incorporated G. Torrente's Neapolitan arietta «Te voglio bene assaje», which had earlier been extensively used in Bournonville's three-act romantic ballet *Napoli or The Fisherman and His Bride* (*see* 29.3.1842).

In his diary Bournonville noted on 1.12.1845 of the creation of the tableaux:

'otte Dage tilbragte med Tilberedelser til en Hoffest'.

Finally, *Les Saisons* may perhaps represent Bournonville's first draft for his later, projected series of four allegorical ballets, entitled *The Four Seasons, or Cupid's Journey, A Ballet Cycle* (*see* 16.6.1846).

Musical sources:

No orchestral score and répétiteur's copy have yet been traced for this work.

Parts. Ms. Copy. 9 vol.
vl I, vl II, vla, vlc e cb, fl, ob cl, fag, cor I–II.

Unsigned and dated: '1845'
[DKKk; MA ms 2754 (1–9)]
This set of parts is bound together with the parts for the series of seven tableaux, entitled *Psyché*, that was performed on the same evening (*see* the preceding entry). On the front cover of the wrapper the parts are entitled 'Musik til Tableaux/1845/arrangeret/af/Hr. Hof= Kapelmester Glæser' with the title of each tableau listed in German as follows: 'Der Winter', 'Frühling', 'Der Somer', and 'Der Herbst:'.

Printed sources:

Printed programme. 1 p. (21,4 × 17,1 cm)
[…]/Musique et Tableaux vivants./[…]/Les Saisons.
Unsigned and dated: 'Mercredi 26. Novembre 1845.'
[DKKk; 3III, – 460 4° (inserted between the Royal Theatre posters for 26.11. and 27.11.1845)
This programme is part of F. Gläser's private collection of the posters for those performances which he conducted in Copenhagen between 1842 and 1861.

1846

6.1.1846
A Masked Ball given on the occasion of the 50th
performance of *La Sylphide (Sylphiden)* on 21.12.1845.

According to the satirical Copenhagen paper *Corsaren* (9.1. 1846) Bournonville arranged and choreographed the dances given at this masked ball while dressed in an admiral's uniform like that of Napoleon Bonaparte I. Among the dances performed were his earlier series of five *Contredanses*, entitled *Les Sylphides. Contredanses nouvelles (Sylphiderne. Nye Françaiser)* (*see* 31.10.1837). The music for this set of dances was based 'Sur les motif de la composition de Mr: H. de Løvenskiold' (i.e. *La Sylphide, see* 28.11.1836) and had been published in a piano score by C. C. Lose & Olsen on 31.10. 1837. A bilingual choreographic description of the same dances (in Danish and French) was printed separately by Bianco Luno & Schneiders Officin in Copenhagen at about the same time. According to Bournonville's diary the dances were rehearsed and performed by his dance students at the Royal Theatre's ballet school. Thus, on 31.12.1845 he noted:

'ingen Dandskeskole. Jeg arbeidede selv med alle de unge Mennesker'.

This is followed by a second note on 6.1.1846 reading:

'Indtil d. 6.te Januar ingen Dandser=Virksomhed […] Sylphidens Jubelfest'.

Autograph sources:

Production note. Ms. Autograph (partially in another hand). Black ink. 4 pp. (34 × 21,3 and 21,7 × 14,6 cm)
Regnskab for Udgivterne/ved/Festen d: 6 Januari 1846
Signed and dated: 'Hoftheatret d. 10 Januari 1846.'
[SSm; Daniel Fryklunds samling no. 105–106

10.2.1846
In Memory of Wexschall, Prologue (with Tableau)
(Wexschalls Minde, Prolog (med Tableau)) (uncredited).

For a charity performance given for the widow of the ballet répétiteur and concert-master at Copenhagen's Royal Theatre, F. T. Wexschall, Bournonville created this tableau, which was preceded by an (uncredited) prologue also written by him, and recited by the actor. In his diary Bournonville mentioned only two stage rehearsals of the tableau held on 5.2. and 10.2.1846. No autographed and/or musical sources for this work have yet been traced, but the prologue is included in the first volume of Bournonville's memoirs *Mit Theaterliv* (Kjøbenhavn, C. A. Reitzel, 1848, pp. 252–254). Moreover, in an autographed biographical note on Wexschall (now in DKKk, call no. NKS 3285, 4°, kapsel 6) he described how this charity performance and prologue came about:

'Jeg var til Alters i Slotskirken med min Familie og ligesom vi skulde op til Herrens Bord, mødte jeg blandt Nadvergæsterne den bedrøvede Enke! der gjennemfoer mig ligesom en Lysstraale og – Hvad ville de strenge Christne sige til den Slags Andagt! – midt under den hellige Handling modnedes en Plan til hendes og de Faderløses Bedste! – inden jeg var ude af Kirken havde jeg arrangeret en Forestilling paa Hoftheatret til Fordeel for dem. Det var <u>Glucks Orpheus</u> oversat efter det Franske af mig selv, og en Prolog, <u>Wexschalls Minde</u>, som findes blandt mine lyriske Forsøg. Foretagenet iværksattes strax og lykkedes fuldkomment. Desværre nød Enken og de to Børn kun er kort Tid godt af Indtægten'.

In Memory of Wexschall was given only once.

10.2.1846
Act II of Gluck's opera 'Orphée et Euridice'
(2den Act af Glucks Opera Orpheus. (Underverdenen. Elysium.))
(the Court Theatre).

According to his handwritten list of his opera stagings, written c.1851 (*see* Additional Sources), Bournonville was clearly responsible for both the mise-en-scène and the choreography of the dances when Act II of C. W. v. Gluck's 1774 Paris version of his three-act heroic drama *Orphée et Euridice* was performed seperately (in Danish) as part of the charity performance for the widow of F. T. Wexschall (*see* the previous entry). In his diary he listed five rehearsals of this work held between 28.1. and 5.2.1846. They are followed by a note on the opening night reading as follows:

'Ingen Dandseskole formedelst Wexschalls Forestilling. Om Aftenen til Forestillingen paa Hoftheatret'

Furthermore, according to a later (undated) Danish manuscript libretto for *Orpheus* (copied by the alto, J. A. Zinck, some time between 1846 and 1871?) Bournonville also translated the complete French text of Acts II and III into Danish in 1846. This translation was reused many years later by *Musikforeningen* when selected excerpts from *Orphée et Euridice* were performed at the Casino Theatre (Mindre Sal) in four concerts on 25.5.1859, 26.1.1860, 8.11.1870, and 31.1. 1871.

Musical sources:

Printed orchestral score. 1 vol. 222 pp. of which three are blank (29,2 × 24,2 cm)
ORPHÉE/ET/EURIDICE,/TRAGÉDIE/Opera en trois Actes./ MISE EN MUSIQUE/Par/GLUCK.
Paris, Magasin de Musique [1774]
[DKKk; U 6 (KTA 655, 1944–45.367, mu 6403.2535)
Bournonville's pencilled autographed notes in this French printed orchestral score (on pp. 50, 73, 87, 97, 107, and 111) clearly indicate

that it was used for the 1846 performance at the Court Theatre of Act II in Gluck's drama. Moreover, Bournonville's translation of the French text in Act II is here written (with brown ink) by a copyist. Furthermore, according to an owner's stamp on the title page ('Musikforeningen') this score also seems to have served for the two later concerts of selected excerpts from Act II of *Orphée et Euridice* given at the Casino Theatre on 8.11.1870, and 31.1.1871. The same appears to have been true for the concerts of excerpts from Act III of Gluck's drama that were given at the same theatre on 26.1.1860.

Répétiteur's copy. Ms. Copy. Black ink. 1 vol. 24 pp. of which two are blank (33,7 × 25,5 cm with minor variants)
Orpheus./210/1846./[…]/Acte 2.e/Scène 1.r
Unsigned and dated (on the front cover): '1846.'
[DKKk; MA ms 3091 (KTA 655)
This répétiteur's copy contains the complete music for Act II of *Orphée et Euridice*. Bournonville's Danish translation of the drama's French text is here written into the music (with brown ink) by himself and a copyist. Moreover, Bournonville's pencilled autographed choreographic notes in the same volume describe (in more general terms) the dances and the pantomime performed in Act II by the soloists and the corps de ballet alternately.

Parts. Ms. Copy. 20 vol.
3 vl I, 2 vl II, vla, 2 vlc e cb, fl 1/2, ob 1/2, cl 1/2, fag 1/2, cor 1/2, tr, arpa. 22 vocal parts.
Unsigned and undated [1846]
[DKKk; KTA 655
This set of parts contains only the music for the excerpts from Act II of *Orphée et Euridice* that were performed at the Court Theatre in 1846.

Printed sources:

Printed libretto. 4 pp. (20,2 × 12,7 cm)
Orpheus/Opera i 3 Acter af Gluck.
Kjøbenhavn, Bianco Lunos Bogtrykkeri, s. a. [1846]
[DKKk; NKS 3285 4° 8 (læg 'Trykte Digte')

Other sources:

Manuscript libretto. Ms. Copy (by Josephine Amalie Zinck?). Brown ink and pencil. 1 vol. 29 pp. (21 × 17,2 cm)
Orpheus/Opera i 4 Akter af Gluck/Oversættelsen til 2.de og 3.de Akt, som den her er afskrevet,/ er udført af Hr Hof=Balletmester Bournonville og er benyttet tidligere saavel paa Det kgl. Theater, som i Musikforeningens Concerter. Den findes i Theatrets Musik-Archiv./A. Zinck.
Signed and undated [Written most probably between 1846 and 1871(?)]
[SSm; Daniel Fryklunds samling no. 231

18.2.1846
A Procession, entitled 'Cortège de Quintin Durwards', and three Quadrilles named 'Mauresques', 'Polkeurs', and 'Rococo',
choreographed for a Royal masked ball at Bernstorff's palace (Amalienborg).

According to the memoirs of the major general, F. G. von Müller (published by E. Bodenhoff in 1913, Copenhagen, Gyldendal), the dances created for this royal masked ball were all choreographed and rehearsed by Bournonville. In the same source (pp. 234–235) the rehearsals and the performance of the four dances are described by von Müller as follows:

[17.2.1846:] 'Kl. 12 til 3 Generalprøve her i Palaiset paa Quadrillerne og Processionen, som skal udføres her imorgen. *Bournonville* dirigerede som sædvanlig meget godt, men fik ligeledes efter

Sædvane Bersærkergang af og til. Saaledes da Herskabet havde befalet, at der skulde bringes Chocolade efter at flere Prøver vare afholdte, jog han Lakaierne med de fyldte Bakker ud. Jeg beordrede dem strax ind igjen.

Den 18de Februar. Efter Middag en familie hos Kongen var Ballet her, til hvilket der var indbudt 630 Personer. De costumerede samledes alle i Throngemakket og kjørte derfra ind ad Frederiksgade – de øvrige af Bredgade.

Der gaves »Cortège de Quintin Durward«, en Procession af 21 Personer i historiske Costumer. Deltagerne bestode mest af Diplomatiet. Den bevægede sig igjennem samtlige Gemakker. Derefter gaves tre forskjellige Qvadriller 1) Mauresques af 8 Par, 2) Polkeurs af 14 Par og 3) Rococo af 5 Par.

Alt gik meget godt. For ret at se stode Herrer og Damer paa Stole og Sofaer. Derefter gik Ballet med stor Munterhed til Kl. 4.'.

No musical and choreographic sources for this procession and the following set of three quadrilles have yet been traced.

31.3.1846
Tableaux vivants a. Sacrifice to Hygæa b. The wounded Warrior (a. Offer til Hygæa, b. Den saarede Kriger) (the Court Theatre).

This work represents the first in a series of six performances that were arranged and staged by Bournonville for the charity association 'Hygæa'. The official name of this society (of which Bournonville was a leading board member between 1846 and 1852) was 'Selskabet Hygæa til fri Medicinalhjælp for trængende Syge'. The five other concerts/performances for 'Hygæa' took place on 24.4.1847, 11.3.1848, 21.11.1849 (the Court Theatre), 13.9.1851 (Vesterbroe's Theatre), and 4.5.1852 (the Court Theatre).

Of the two tableaux performed on this day, the second was inspired by the sculptural work by B. Thorvaldsen, named 'The Roman Warrior'. It had been mounted two years earlier by Bournonville as part of the new series of final tableaux (score no. 12) in his one-act idyllic ballet *The Festival in Albano* (*see* 8.1.1844). This indicates that the music employed in 1846 was most probably the same as that used in J. F. Fröhlich's original score for *The Festival in Albano*. Both tableaux were restaged at the Court Theatre on 4.6.1846, with a new title (*2 Tableaux*), as part of a charity performance given for the actress, A. Stage.

No autographed and/or musical sources for these tableaux have yet been traced.

12.5.1846
Tarantella Napoletana (uncredited) performed by W. Funck and C. Fjeldsted (Flensborg's Theater).

This (uncredited) dance is identical with the *Tarantella* (score no. 10) in Bournonville's one-act idyllic ballet *The Festival in Albano* (*see* 28.10.1839 and 10.8.1840). This is clear from a pencilled note (reading: 'Th Paulsen 12/5 46 Flensborg') found the part for the first horn of the 'Tarantella Napoletana' in *The Festival in Albano*.

The dance was performed only once at Flensborg's Theater as part of a privately arranged summer tour to Germany by Funck and Fjeldsted. Later it was also danced by them at Hamburg's Stadttheater on 2.7.1846, and at Christiania's Theatre (Oslo) on 2.7.1847.

Musical sources:

No separate orchestral score dating from the 1846 performance of *Tarantella Napolitana* in Flensborg has yet been traced.

Répétiteur's copy/conductor's part. Ms. Copy. Black ink. 6 pp. (33,4 × 25,7 cm)
Violino 1.mo/Tarantella/Napolitana.
Unsigned and undated [c.1846]
[DKKk; MA ms 2623 (KTB 1027, originally KTB 282)
This part for the first violin clearly seems to have served as a répétiteur's copy and/or conductor's part, and most probably dates from when the *Tarantella* from *The Festival in Albano* was performed for the first time as a separate divertissement in Flensborg on 12.5.1846. The same volume seems to have been used by Funck and Fjeldsted at Hamburg's Stadttheater on 2.7.1846, and at Christiania's Theatre (Oslo) on 2.7.1847.

Parts (incomplete). Ms. Copy. 10 vol.
vl I, vl II, vla, vlc e cb, fl, cl, cor 1/2, gr cassa, tri.
[DKKk; KTB 1027 (originally KTB 282)
This (incomplete) set of parts most probably dates from when the *Tarantella* from *The Festival in Albano* was performed for the first time as a separate divertissement in Flensborg on 12.5.1846. The same parts also seem to have been used by Funck and Fjeldsted at Hamburg's Stadttheater on 2.7.1846, and at Christiania's Theatre (Oslo) on 2.7.1847.

4.6.1846
2 Tableaux, a. Sacrifice to Hygæa, b. The wounded Warrior, arranged by Ballet Master Bournonville (2 Tableaux, a. Offer til Hygæa, b. Den saarede Kriger, arrangerede af Hr. Balletmester Bournonville).

Both of these tableaux are identical with those mounted by Bournonville at the Court Theatre on 31.3.1846 as part of a performance for the charity association 'Hygæa'. They were on this day performed as part of a charity performance given for the actress, A. Stage.

16.6.1846
The Four Seasons, or Cupid's Journey, A Ballet Cycle (De fire Aarstider eller Amors Reise. Ballet -Cyclus.). Projected series of four ballets.

The first time Bournonville ever mentioned this projected series of four allegorical ballets dates from a visit to Paris in 1846. During that sojourn he noted in his diary on 16.6.1846:

'componeret 3 Tableauer af Amors Reise'.

This note is followed by a statement on the following day reading:

'skrevet paa Amors Reise'.

Finally, in a letter to the theatre management of Copenhagen's Royal Theatre (written in Paris on 2.7.1846) Bournonville described in fine detail his ideas for this projected series of four ballets situated in four different nations:

'[...] je me fais un plaisir d'annoncer que j'ai élaboré ici mon idée des quatre Saisons. Le sujet étant très riche, me menait à une grande complication de tableaux, qui aurait fait de mon ballet un ouvrage trop long & difficile à monter sous touts les rapports, en sus le considerant dans son ensemble j'ai trouvé en lui le défaut du Tableau de [D. C.] Blunck (les ages) dont une partie nuit à l'effet de l'autre & produit une Masse informe; je l'ai donc entièrement refait, et chaque saison forme aujourd'hui un ballet indépendant, auquel j'ai pu donner le développement necessaires, et qui sera d'autant plus practicables pour le repertoire comme les comédies actuelles ne secondent pas bien les grands ballets, et mes entr'actes ne seront pas la merci de Gunther (comme touts les ballets sont en un acte). J'ai cherché d'y mettre toute la fraicheur et colorés que le sujet comporte & il y aura de l'emplois pour touts nos artistes à talent'.

Two years later *The Four Seasons* was included in the list of Bournonville's works which he published in the first volume of his memoirs *My Theatre Life* (pp. 217–218). Here they are placed immediately after the ballet *Raphael* (*see* 30.5.1846), as the final work of what he labelled 'my first period of ballet compositions' (i.e. 1829–1848). Moreover, in the same volume Bournonville clearly indicates B. Thorvaldsen's well-known bas-reliefs *The Four Seasons* as his main source of inspiration, and also expresses his reasons for choosing this somewhat traditional allegorical theme:

'Cupid, the roguish god of Love plays such a prominent part in most of Thorvaldsen's creations that it makes him the perfect mystic thread which binds the seasons of the year into a garland of four ballet poems'.

Of the four ballets, only the first two (representing Spring and Summer) were carried out, with the ballets *The New Penelope, or The Spring Festival in Athens* (*see* 26.1.1847), and *The White Rose, or The Summer in Brittany* (*see* 20.9.1847). The remaining two (representing Autumn and Winter) are most probably identical with his later projected ballets, entitled *Annitta of The Vintage in the mountains of Albano* (*see* 22.9. 1848) and *The Little Pixie* (*see* 29.4.1842). Of these the former was many years later transformed into the one-act ballet *The Flower Festival in Genzano* (*see* 19.12.1858).

Autograph sources:

Manuscript synopsis (included in a letter to J. G. Levetzau). Ms. Autograph. Brown ink. 4 pp. (27 × 20.9 cm)
[…] mon idée des quatre Saisons. […]
Signed and dated: 'Paris ce 2 juillet 1846.'
[Copenhagen, The State Archive (Rigsarkivet); Det kgl. Teaters Arkiv, Gruppe E, pakke 288

Printed sources:

Printed synopsis. 2 pp. (pp. 217–218) in *Mit Theaterliv* (Første Deel, Kjøbenhavn, C. A. Reitzel, 1848).
De fire Aarstider/eller/Amors Reise./Ballet-Cyclus (English translation by Patricia McAndrew in *My Theatre Life*, pp. 115–116, Middleton, Connecticut, Wesleyan University Press, 1979).
[DKKk; 42–234 8°

2.7.1846
Tarantella Napoletana (uncredited) performed by W. Funck and C. Fjeldsted (Hamburg's Stadttheater).
This (uncredited) dance is identical with the *Tarantella* (score no. 10) in Bournonville's one-act idyllic ballet *The Festival in Albano* (*see* 28.10.1839 and 10.8.1840). This is clear from a pencilled note (reading: 'Johs. Gentzen Hamburg d. 2.te Julÿ 46') in the part for the second cornet of this dance (now in DKKk, call no. KTB 1027). It was performed once at

Hamburg's Stadttheater as part of a private summer tour to Germany arranged this year by Funck and Fjeldsted.

5.9.1846
Polacca guerriera, Pas de deux performed by Bournonville and A. Nielsen.
This dance (to music by H. C. Lumbye) was intended as a homage to the Polish freedom-fighters, and was also frequently played as a musical divertissement at public concerts in the Tivoli Gardens during the late summer of 1846 and, later, at the Casino Theatre after 25.4.1847. It received 5 performances at the Royal Theatre, the last of which was given on 16.10.1846.

Musical sources:

Orchestral score. Ms. Autograph (by H. C. Lumbye). Brown ink. 1 vol. 18 pp. of which one is blank (27 × 37,8 cm with minor variants)
H. C. LUMBYE/POLACCA GUERRIERA/PART./[…]/Polacca Guerriera
Signed and dated: 'par H: C: Lumbÿe/d: 30. August 1846'
[DKKk; C II, 34 (1929–30.853)

No répétiteur's copy dating from the 1846 première of *Polacca guerriera* at Copenhagen's Royal Theatre has yet been traced.

Parts. Ms. Copy. 26 vol.
2 vl I, 2 vl II, vla, 2 vlc e cb, fl 1/2, ob 1/2, cl 1/2, fag 1/2, cor 1/2, tr 1/2, cnt 1/2, trb, tuba, timp, gr cassa, piatti e tri.
Unsigned and undated [1846]
[DKKk; KTB 257

Répétiteur's copy/Conductor's part. Ms. Copy. 1 vol. 4 pp. (33,1 × 23,5 cm)
Polacca Guerriere/af/H: C: Lumbÿe/Violino Repetiteur
Unsigned and undated [c. September 1846]
[DKKk; Tivolis musikarkiv no. 1118 (mu 9405.1400)
This répétiteur's copy was originally part of the musical material for Lumbye's *Polacca guerriera* that was preserved in the music archive of the Tivoli Gardens, but was transferred to DKKk in 1994. It dates from when Lumbye's music was first played as a concert piece in the Tivoli Gardens in the late summer of 1846. The fact that the volume is explicitly entitled as a répétiteur's copy indicates that it was most probably copied from the original (not yet traced) 1846 répétiteur's copy for this dance.

Parts. Ms. Copy. 23 vol.
2 vl I, 2 vl II, vla, 3 vlc e cb, fl picc, fl, ob 1/2, cl 1/2, fag 1/2, cor 1/2, tr 1/2, Btrb, tuba, timp e gr cassa.
Unsigned and dated (in the part for tromba 1.mo): 'den 28/9 46:'
[DKKk; Tivolis musikarkiv no. 1118 (mu 9405.1400)
This set of parts was used when Lumbye's *Polacca guerriera* was played as a concert piece in a new and slightly revised orchestration at the Tivoli Gardens during the late summer of 1846.

10.9.1846
The Elves' Hill (Elverhøi).
According to the rehearsal book of H. C. J. Fredstrup, Bournonville had on this day taken over the responsability of rehearsing and mounting P. Funck's dances in Acts III, IV and V of J. L. Heiberg's and F. Kuhlau's five-act national fairy-play (originally premièred on 6.11.1828). These dances were restaged for a second and last time by Bournonville on 5.11.1848. The 1846 restaging of *The Elves' Hill* was given 6 times between 10.9.1846 and 1.4.1848.

Musical sources:

Orchestral score. Ms. Copy with later manuscript insertions. Brown ink. 1 vol. 248 pp. of which one is blank (27,1 × 37,5 cm)
KUHLAU/ELVERHØJ
Unsigned and dated (on p. 247): 'oct. 1828.'
This orchestral score was used for all performances of *The Elves' Hill* during Bournonville's lifetime.

No répétiteur's copy dating from the 1846 restaging of *The Elves' Hill* has yet been traced.

Parts. Ms. Copy. 34 + 12 vol.
4 vl I, 4 vl II, 2 vla, 2 vlc, 2 cb, fl picc, fl, ob 1/2, cl 1/2, fag 1/2, cor 1/2/3/4, tr 1/2, trb 1/2, timp, gr cassa, piatti, tri. On stage: fl 1/2, ob 1/2, cl 1/2, fag 1/2, cor 1/2, trb 1/2. 65 vocal parts.
Unsigned and undated [1828]
[DKKk; KTA 261
This set of parts was used for all performances of *The Elves' Hill* during Bournonville's lifetime.

18.9.1846
Czaar und Zimmermann (Czaren og Tømmermanden).
According to his handwritten lists of his opera staging, written c.1851 (*see* Additional Sources), Bournonville was clearly responsible for choreographing and staging the dances in the 1846 Copenhagen première of G. A. Lortzing's three-act comic opera (first performed at Städtliches Theater in Leipzig on 22.12.1837). These dances included:

(1) An (unnamed) *Dance*, performed in Act II (score no. 11) during the so-called 'Brautlied', sung by *Maria* and a chorus («Lieblich rötchen sich die Wangen»).
(2) A *Clog Dance* (or 'Tanz mit Holzschuhen') in the finale of Act III (score no. 16), performed by the corps de ballet.

On 30.10.1857 Bournonville included *Czaar und Zimmermann* in a list of projected opera restagings that he was planning on that day for the 1857–58 and 1858–59 seasons. This project was carried out on 7.1.1858, when Lortzing's singspiel was mounted with Bournonville's new and complete mise-en-scène for the first time.
   The 1846 production of *Czaar und Zimmermann* received 17 performances, the last of which was given on 11.5.1849. According to the rehearsal book of H. C. J. Fredstrup, 7 rehearsals of the dances were held by Bournonville between 12.9. and 18.9.1846.

Autograph sources:

Production note. Ms. Autograph. Black ink. 1 p. (15,6 × 22,1 cm)
Classification af Feux/for/Coryphæer [*sic*] i Dandsen/ i/Czar og Tömmermand
Signed and dated: 'Kbhvn d. 22 sept: 1846.'
[Copenhagen, The State Archive (Rigsarkivet); Det kgl. Teaters Arkiv, Gruppe E, pakke 288

Musical sources:

Orchestral score. Ms. Copy. Black ink. 2 vol. Act I 338 pp., Act II–III 400 pp. of which two are blank (26,2 × 33 cm)
Caar [changed to Czar] und Zimmermann/1. Act/Lortzing/[...]/ Caar/und/Zimmermann./Komische Oper in 3 Acten./Music/von/ A. Lortzing.
Unsigned and undated [c.1846]
[DKKk; C I, 274 (KTA 403)
This orchestral score is a German copy that includes A. Vibe's Danish

translation inserted (with brown ink) next to the original text. The music for the two dance scenes in Acts II and III is included in the second volume on pp. 93–104 and 334–357 respectively. The score was used for all performances of *Czaar and Zimmernann* in Copenhagen between 1846 and 1864.

No répétiteur's copy dating from the 1846 première at Copenhagen's Royal Theatre of *Czaar und Zimmernann* has yet been traced. However, a later répétiteur's copy dating from its restaging on 7.1. 1858 is now in DKKk (call no. MA ms 2910 (3) (KTA 403)).

Parts. Ms. Copy. 34 + 8 vol.
4 vl I, 3 vl II, 2 vla, 4 vlc e cb, fl picc, fl 1/2, ob 1/2, cl 1/2, fag 1/2, cor 1/2/3/4, tr 1/2, trb 1/2/3, timp, gr cassa, piatti e tri. On stage: conductor's part, fl, cl, fag 1/2, cor 1/2, glock. 50 vocal parts.
Unsigned and undated [1846]
[DKKk; KTA 403

12.10.1846
Tableau with Dance (Tableau med Dands) performed by A. Nielsen, P. Funck, P. Fredstrup, and a corps de ballet.
In his handwritten lists of his works, written c.1851 (*see* Additional Sources), Bournonville named this tableau 'Kongens Hjemkomst'. It was mounted to celebrate King Christian VIII's return to Copenhagen from a visit to the Duchy of Schleswig Holstein, where the absolute monarch (according to *Berlingske Tidende*) had opposed the growing separatist movement in that region 'with the force of law and state'. According to an article in the Copenhagen paper *Fædrelandet* (7.10.1846) Bournonville's tableau aroused considerable polemics, even before its actual performance. The growing liberal opposition viewed this special performance given in the King's honour as a too evident sign of appreciation by the entire political establishment of the absolute monarch's strong support for Danish nationalism in the border districts. The polemics centred particularly on Bournonville's glorification of the absolute monarch as the only symbol of national identity. *Berlingske Tidende* (13.10.1846) reacted towards this liberal opposition by describing Bournonville's tableau and its accompanying dance (a *Pas de trois* set to music by H. S. Paulli and performed by A. Nielsen, P. Funck, and P. Fredstrup) as follows:

'Forestillingen selv blev indledet ved et af Balletmester Bournonville i denne Anledning særdeles smukt componeret Dands med et Tableau forestillende Kunst, Videnskab, Agerdyrkning, Søfart og det hele Folk, beskyttet af en Throne, hvor Retfærd sidder med Troen og Styrken ved sin Side. Dannebroge svæver i Skyerne, velsignet af Fredens Engle'.

Only the poster for the second and last performance of the tableau (23.10.1846) gives explicit credit to Paulli for the music. The first two movements of his score (the *Adagio* and the *Allegretto*) were actually borrowed from his and N. W. Gade's(?) earlier music for Bournonville's so-called 'Pas de deux. Retour de Fjeldsted' (*see* 11.10.1843), while the remaining music appears to have been composed and arranged especially for this occasion. It includes H. E. Kröyer's melody from c.1820 to A. Oehlenschläger's Danish national hymn «Det er et yndigt Land». The same melody also accompanied a new song, entitled «Kong Christian drager hjem igjen til Axelstad», written especially for this occasion by J. L. Heiberg (now in DKKk, call no. 34 III, 460 4°, poster no. 37).

It was sung by the entire audience at the moment when the monarch entered the theatre, immediately before Bournonville's tableau.

According to the rehearsal book of H. C. J. Fredstrup, 5 rehearsals of the tableau (here listed as 'En nye Dands med Tableaux') were held by Bournonville between 9.9. and 12.9 1846.

Autograph sources:

Production note. Ms. Autograph. Ink. 2 pp. (format unknown)
Tableau./[...]/Costumer ved Slutningstableauet/d. 12.te October 1846./Sujettet.
Signed and dated: 'Kbhvn d. 10 October 1846.'
[USNYp; Dance Collection (microfilm), call nos. *ZBD-71, and (S) *MGZMD 30 (photostat copy)

Musical sources:

Orchestral score (incomplete). Ms. Autograph (by H. S. Paulli). Brown ink. 1 vol. 18 pp. of which three are blank (27,5 × 37,6 cm)
211/Partituur/til/Blomsterdandsen/[...]/Tableaux
Unsigned and undated [1846]
[DKKk; C II, 119 (KTB 211)
According to the title on the front cover of this (incomplete) orchestral score it was also used for Bournonville's later so-called *Flower Dance (Blomsterdands)*. That dance was premièred on 20.10.1847 and performed by the exact same cast that performed his *Pas de trois* in the 1846 *Tableau with Dance*.

No répétiteur's copy for *Tableau with Dance* has been traced.

Parts. Ms. Copy. 30 vol.
3 vl I, 3 vl II, 2 vla, 3 vlc e cb, fl 1/2, ob 1/2, cl 1/2, fag 1/2, cor 1/2, tr 1/2, cnt, trb 1/2/3, timp, gr cassa, piatti e tri.
Unsigned and undated [1846]
[DKKk; KTB 211
Notes written in several of these parts list three different titles of this work ('Tableauerne', 'Pas de trois', and 'Blomsterdandsen'). They clearly indicate that the parts may also have been used for Bournonville's *Flower Dance (Blomsterdands)* (*see* 20.10.1847) and *Pas des trois cousines* (*see* 8.9.1849). Other notes indicate the duration of the music as 12 minutes.

16.12.1846

A Ballet Performance (Helsingør's Theatre).

According to an autographed note, entitled 'Regie til Forestillingen i Helsingør/Onsdagen den 16.de December 1846.', Bournonville was clearly responsible for the mise-en-scène of this performance, which consisted of six individual dances and *pas* from the current ballet repertory of Copenhagen's Royal Theatre. In two advertisements in *Helsingørs Avis* (1846, nos. 186 and 192, pp. [3] and [2], 3. and 14. December) these dances are described as follows:

(1) A *Pas de deux*, choreographed by Bournonville and performed by himself and A. Nielsen.
(2) An (uncredited) *Pas de deux*, danced by F. Hoppe and P. Funck.
(3) Bournonville's (uncredited) *The Vierländers, (Hamburger Waltz) (Vierländerne, (Hamborger-Vals))* (*see* 8.2.1844), performed by himself and P. Fredstrup.
(4) A solo dance entitled *Maritana, (Spanish Gipsy Dance), composed for this occasion by Bournonville ((Spansk Zigeuner-Dands), componeret i denne Anledning af Bournonville)*, performed by A. Nielsen to music by H. C. Lumbye. The score for this solo dance was most probably reused for the *Bolero* movement in Lumbye's and Bournonville's later divertissement named *Maritana (Divertissement in the form of a carnival scene)*, premièred at the Court Theatre on 15.4.1847.

(5) Bournonville's *Polka, (Military Dance) (Militairdands)* (*see* 1.11. 1842), performed by himself, F. Hoppe, P. Funck, and P. Fredstrup.

The performance was given only once. No separate music and printed sources for it have yet been traced.

Autograph sources:

Production note. Ms. Autograph. Black ink. 1 p. (16,8 × 13,3 cm)
Regie til Forestillingen i Helsingør/Onsdagen den 16.de December 1846.
Signed and dated: 'Kbhvn d. 11 Decbr. 1846.
[DKKt; Brevregistrant (Bournonville)

1847

24.1.1847

The Vierländers, Hamburg Dance
(Vierländerne, Hamborger=Dands) performed by
Bournonville and C. Fjeldsted.

According to pencilled notes in the part for the first violin of what is entitled 'Vierländerne Hamborger Dands' (now in DKKk, call no. KTB 1024, but originally KTB 240?) this dance is identical with H. C. Lumbye's so-called *New Hamburg-Scottish*, That dance, in turn, was originally choreographed by Bournonville and danced by himself and C. Fjeldsted as a new, incorporated finale to his one-act idyllic ballet *The Tyroleans* on 8.2.1844. Later the same year it was also performed as a separate divertissement on 18.12.1844. At the 1847 restaging, the title seems to have been different, while Bournonville's original choreography and H. C. Lumbye's music appear to have remained unchanged. Only the poster for its second performance on 13.2.1847 gives explicit credit to Lumbye for the music.

The Vierländers was performed 6 times as a separate divertissement in 1847 (the last time on 5.4.1847). According to the rehearsal book of H. C. J. Fredstrup, 2 rehearsals were held of it by Bournonville on 22.1. and 23.1.1847. It was then listed by Fredstrup as 'Hamborger-Dands'.

Musical sources:

No orchestral score dating from the 1847 Copenhagen performances of *The Vierländers* has yet been traced. However, a later orchestral score, entitled 'Vierlaender Dands' is now in NOum (call no. 216 a, Eske 24). It most probably dates from when this dance was performed by W. Funck and C. Fjeldsted at Christiania's Theatre (Oslo) on 25.7.1847.

Répétiteur's copy. Ms. Copy. Black ink. 4 pp. (34,5 × 225,9 cm)
21 Stem[m]er/Violino Répititör./til/Hamborger=Dans.
Unsigned and undated [c.1847]
[DKKk; MA ms 2626 (KTB 1027, originally KTB 240?)
This répétiteur's copy and the accompanying set of parts (*see* the following entry) were most probably also used for the performance of this dance at Christiania's Theatre (Oslo) on 25.7.1847.

Parts. Ms. Copy. 19 vol.
vl I, vl II e vla, vlc e cb, fl picc, fl, ob 1/2, cl 1/2, fag 1/2, tr 1/2, cnt 1/2, Btrb, timp, gr cassa, tri.
Unsigned and undated [c.1847]
[DKKk; KTB 1027 (originally KTB 240?)

26.1.1847

The New Penelope, or The Spring Festival in Athens
(Den nye Penelope eller Foraarsfesten i Athenen).

This ballet was originally conceived as the first work in Bournonville's projected series of four allegorical ballets, entitled
The Four Seasons, or Cupid's Journey (see 16.6.1846), in which it
represented the season of Spring. According to the autographed orchestral score it was composed by H. S. v. Løvenskjold (Act I, score nos. 1–4, and Act II, score nos. 1–10, 12)
and E. Helsted (Act II, score no. 11, the so-called *Boys' Dance
(Drengedands)*). The *Pas de deux* in the second act, score no. 8
(performed by F. Hoppe and P. Funck) was later the same
year also mounted as a separate divertissement with Hoppe
and Funck on 27.5.1847.

Moreover, the music for the *Allegro vivo e grazioso* movement in the so-called 'Pas af Grækere og Grækerinder' or
'Beltedands' (Act II, score no. 9, performed by three men
and four women) was at a later stage incorporated in the Act
II divertissement (score no. 3) of Bournonville's two-act romantic ballet *La Sylphide (see* 28.11.1836). In that ballet it was
performed by a group of sylphs alternating with *The Sylph.*
The interpolation of Løvenskjold's 1847 music into his own
score for *La Sylphide* most probably happened in connection
with Bournonville's first, revised restaging of this ballet on
22.9.1849.

Finally, the complete music for Løvenskjold's 'Pas af Grækere og Grækerinder' or 'Beltedands' also seems to have been
reused by Bournonville for his later divertissement, entitled
The Flower Maids of Florence (De florentinske Blomsterpiger), created for the three Price cousins, Juliette, Sophie, and Amalia, at the Casino Theatre (*see* 8.6.1850).

The New Penelope, or The Spring Festival in Athens reached a
total of 14 performances, the last of which was given on
10.10.1847. According to the rehearsal book of H. C. J. Fredstrup, 37 rehearsals were held of it between 19.10.1846 and
26.1.1847.

Autograph sources:

Production note. Ms. Autograph. Brown ink. 2 pp. (33,4 × 20,6 cm)
Personer i den nÿe [...] Ballet./Nygræske = Costumer.
Unsigned and undated [c.1846–1847]
[DKKkt; F.M. (Ballet)

Musical sources:

Musical draft (fragment). Ms Autograph (by H. S. v. Løvenskjold).
Brown ink. 6 pp. of which one is blank (33,4 × 26 cm)
[Without title]
Signed and dated (p. 5): 'Fine d'il [changed by Bournonville to:] del
Ballo. -/HSLövenskjold, d: 25.de Novbr: 1846.'
[DKKk; MA ms 2712 (KTA 205)
This musical draft contains Løvenskjold's music for the so-called
Vaabendands (incomplete), the *Marche funèbre*, the *Tableau*, and the
Finaledands in Act II (score no. 12). Moreover, Bournonville's auto-
graphed choreographic notes (written with brown ink and pencil) in
this manuscript describe the dances and the pantomime of the
finale. They were most probably written during late November and/
or early December 1846.

Orchestral score. Ms. Autographs (by H. S. v. Løvenskjold and E.
Helsted). Black and brown ink. 1 vol. 312 pp. (36 × 30 cm including
many inserts in various sizes)
Partituret/til/205/Balletten/Den ny Penelope/[...]/Den nÿ Pene-

lope,/eller:/Foraarsfesten i Athenen,/idÿllisk Ballet/i/to Acter/
af/A: Bournonville;/Musiken/componeret af/HS Lövenskjold./
Partitur.
Signed and dated (p. 108): 'Ende paa förste/Act./d: 4.de December
1846.', (p. 212) 'Endt d: 1.ste Januar 1847.', (p. 312) 'Kjöbenhavn –
/Den 17.de Januar/1847./HSLövenskjold'
[DKKk; C II, 117 d (KTB 205)
Apart from the music for the so-called *Boys' dance (Drengedands)* in
Act II (score no. 11, pp. 251–268) which is Helsted's autograph, this
orchestral score is written exclusively by Løvenskjold. It includes several pencilled notes and a musical transition of four bars (pasted in
on p. 205) which refer to the later interpolation of parts of the music
of no. 11 in Act II of *La Sylphide (see* 22.9.1849). Moreover, an unsigned autographed score by Helsted with some not yet identified
music (36 measures in 3/4 time) is inserted after p. 312.

Répétiteur's copy. Ms. Copy and autographs (by H. S. v. Løvenskjold
and E. Helsted). Black ink. 1 vol. 92 pp. of which one is blank (35,3
× 25,1 cm with minor variants)
B. 205/Repetiteur Parti til Balletten/Den nÿe Penelope/Indstu-
deert/d 9 Decbr 1846/opført d [space left open] Januar 1847./27/
[...]/idÿllisk Ballet/i 2 Acter/af/August Bournonville./Musiken af
Hermann v: Løvenskjold./1846.
Unsigned and dated: ' d. 9 Decbr 1846/[...]/Januar 1847'/[...]/
1846
[DKKk; MA ms 2944 (KTB 205)
This répétiteur's copy contains a musical insertion in Løvenskjold's
autograph (5 bars pasted in on p. 60). Together with pencilled notes
on the same page, it clearly refers to the later interpolation of parts
of Løvenskjold's music for Act II (score no. 9) into Act II of *La Sylphide (see* 22.9.1849). Another insertion in Helsted's autograph (containing an *Allegro* transition of 15 bars in 6/8 time) is inserted in this
volume after p. 92. The répétiteur's copy contains Bournonville's
pencilled autographed notes that describe the mime and the dramatic action in Act I (score nos. 1–3). They were most probably written during late November and/or early December 1846.

Parts. Ms. Copy. 34 vol.
3 vl I, 3 vl II, 2 vla, 3 vlc e cb, fl picc, fl 1/2, ob 1/2, cl 1/2, fag 1/2, cor
1/2/3/4, clno 1/2, trb 1/2/3, timp, gr cassa, tamb rul, piatti e tri,
arpa.
Unsigned and undated [1847]
[DKKk; KTB 205

Printed sources:

Printed scenario. 1 vol. 4 pp. (19,2 × 12,3 cm)
Den nye Penelope/eller/Foraarsfesten i Athenen./Ballet i 2 Akter
af A. Bournonville./Musiken af H. v. Løvenskjold./Decorationerne
af Dhrr. Lund og Christensen.
Kjøbenhavn, Græbes Bogtrykkeri [1847]
[DKKk; 17, – 174 8°

23.2.1847

Pas de deux (uncredited) performed by Bournonville and
M. C. Norberg.

This (uncredited) dance is described in the rehearsal book
of H. C. J. Fredstrup as 'Pas de deux for Jfr. Norberg', and is
most probably identical with Bournonville's *Pas de deux* from
D.-F.-E. Auber's three-act comic opera *Le Domino noir (see*
29.1.1839). That dance had been performed by Bournonville and his Swedish pupil. M. C. Norberg, only a week earlier in D.-F.-E. Auber's opera on 18.2.1847. Norberg had arrived in Copenhagen during the early spring of 1847 to take
lessons with Bournonville. She performed this (uncredited)
Pas de deux with him for the third and last time on 18.4.1847.
It is not possible to identify the dance any further.

14.3.1847

Pas de deux arranged by Ballet Master Bournonville (arrangeret af Balletmester Bournonville) **performed by W. Funck and M. C. Norberg.**

This dance is explicitly described on the poster as a work 'arranged' *(arrangeret)* by Bournonville, and is listed in the rehearsal book of H. C. J. Fredstrup as 'Pas de deux af Hr. Funck og Jfr. Norberg'. It is probably based on an earlier work of Bournonville, which he may have revised in 1847 for his Swedish pupil, M. C. Norberg. The dance was given twice by Funck and Norberg, the last time on 18.4.1847. It is not possible to identify the dance any further.

20.3.1847

Das Diamantkreuz (Diamantkorset).

According to this handwritten list of his opera stagings, written c.1851 (*see* Additional Sources), Bournonville was responsible for choreographing and mounting the dances in this, the world première of S. Saloman's and T. Overskou's three-act Danish singspiel. They included:

(1) A *Processional March* in Act I (scene 4, score no. 3).
(2) An (unnamed) *Dance* in Act II (scene 5, score nos. 9 a–c), performed by the corps de ballet during the so-called 'Chor der Dienerschaft' («Laut Ordre sing wir gern bereit Euch»).
(3) A *Pas de six* in Act II (score no. 9 c), performed by three couples.
(4) An (unnamed) *Dance* in Act II (score no. 9 e), performed by the corps de ballet during chorus, entitled «tra la la la la, O pfui! schäm dich doch».

According to an undated répétiteur's copy and set of parts, entitled 'Pas de quatre af Diamantkorset' (now in DKKk, call nos. MA ms 2622, and KTB 1027), the Act II *Pas de six* seems also to have been performed as a separate divertissement at a later stage during the late 1840s, but with new, revised choreography in the form of a *Pas de quatre*. It is not possible to identify the exact date and location for this performance.

Das Diamantkreuz received 5 performances at Copenhagen's Royal Theatre, the last of which was given on 23.4. 1847. According to the rehearsal book of H. C. J. Fredstrup, 11 rehearsals of the dances in this singspiel were held by Bournonville between 30.1. and 19.3.1847.

Autograph sources:

Production note. Ms. Autograph. Brown ink. 1 p. (24,6 × 19,7 cm)
Dandsen til Diamantkorset./Feu – classification
Signed and dated: 'Kbhvn d. 24 Martz 1847.'
[DKKkt; F.M. (Ballet)

Musical sources:

Orchestral score. Ms. Autograph? (by S. Saloman?). Brown ink. 3 vol. Act I 253 pp., Act II 173 pp., Act III 179 pp. of which one is blank (35,8 × 30 cm with minor variants)
S. Saloman/Diamant=/Korset/Act I./[...]/Act II./[...]/Act III.
Unsigned and undated [c.1847]
[DKKk; C II, 119 p (KTA 394)
In this orchestral score the Act II divertissement is named 'Pas de quatre'. This clearly indicates that Saloman originally intended this dance to be performed by only four persons. However, in the printed piano-vocal score (published in 1850 by Schuberth in Leipzig, pl. no. 1279, now in DKKk, call no. D 6) the same dance is entitled 'Pas de six'. The music for this divertissement is included in the second volume of Saloman's orchestral score (pp. 73a–110a) and contains sev-

eral metronome markings indicating the exact tempo of each section of the dance.

Répétiteur's copy. Ms. Copy. Brown ink. 20 pp. (33,5 × 24,5 cm with variants)
Repetiteur=Parti/til/'Diamantkorset'/2.den act
Unsigned and undated [1847]
[DKKk; MA ms 3084 (KTA 394(1))
This répétiteur's copy contains Bournonville's pencilled autographed choreographic notes for most of the *Pas de six* in Act II. According to these notes the three men performing the *Pas de six* were W. Funck, G. Brodersen, and S. Lund. The notes were most probably written during the early months of 1847.

Parts. Ms. Copy. 34 + 12 vol.
3 vl I, 3 vl II, 2 vla, 3 vlc e cb, fl picc, fl 1/2, ob 1/2, cl 1/2, fag 1/2, cor 1/2/3/4, tr 1/2, trb 1/2/3, tuba, timp, gr cassa, piatti, tri, arpa. On stage: cl 1/2, fag 1/2, cor 1/2/3/4, tr, gr cassa, piatti, tri. 53 vocal parts.
Unsigned and undated [1847]
[DKKk; KTA 394

15.4.1847

Maritana, Divertissement in the form of a Carnival scene (Divertissement i Form af en Carnevals=Scene) **(the Court Theatre).**

This divertissement was created for a charity performance given for an association named 'Den qvindelige Pleieforening'. Its plot seems to be based on A. D'Ennery's (pen name for E. Philippe) and P. Dumanoir's five-act drama *Don César de Bazan* (premièred in Paris at Théâtre de Porte de Saint-Martin on 30.7.1844) in which a similar carnival scene is included. This drama had been performed at Copenhagen's Royal Theatre on 1.5.1846 (with incorporated dances by P. Larcher set to music by H. Rung) and was restaged with Bournonville's choreographic assistance only a year after the première of his own *Maritana* divertissement (*see* 30.11. 1848).

Maritana was performed by 14 soloists of the Royal Danish Ballet (seven men and six women) headed by a leading couple (Bournonville and A. Nielsen, the latter playing *Maritana*). It was restaged and performed once at the Court Theatre on 24.4.1847, but then as part of a performance for the charity association named 'Hygæa', of which Bournonville was a leading board member. The divertissement was given for the first and only time at the the Royal Theatre on 9.5.1847.

The score was composed by H. C. Lumbye and consisted of three numbers:

(1) A *Bolero* (performed by Bournonville and A. Nielsen). This dance is most probably based on Bournonville's and Lumbye's earlier solo dance named *Maritana, (Spanish Gipsy Dance) (Spansk Zigeuner-Dands)*, premièred by A. Nielsen at Helsingør's Theatre on 16.12.1846.
(2) A *Jaleo* (performed by the group of fourteen soloists).
(3) A *Gallop* (performed by the entire cast). This dance was set to Lumbye's 'Champagner Galopp', originally composed in 1845 and first played in public at a concert in the Tivoli Gardens on 22.8.1845.

Moreover, *Maritana* began with a Lumbye waltz, entitled 'Ballet Carnevals-Scene'. This is clear from the original set of parts which is bound together with the parts for his so-called 'Ballet Carnevals-Scene'. This waltz, in turn, proves to be an arrangement of selected excerpts of yet another waltz by

Lumbye that had been published in 1845 as part of his set of three dances, named *Les Souvenirs de Paris* (now in DKKk, call no. D 24, mu 9405.1400). It was played for the first time in public at a concert in the Tivoli Gardens on 21.5.1845. The selected excerpts from this waltz were clearly played as part of the first performance of *Maritana*, since many of the original parts include a note (written with black ink) reading: 'attacca Maritana'.

Musical sources:

Orchestral score. Ms. Autograph (by H. C. Lumbye). Brown ink. 14 pp. of which one is blank (24,3 × 34,2 cm)
Maritana
Signed and dated (p. 1): 'par H: C: Lumbÿe/comp: d: 13 December/ 1846'
[DKKk; MA ms 2728]
This autographed orchestral score contains only the music for the *Bolero* and the *Jaleo* in *Maritana*. Lumbye's original autographed orchestral scores for the waltz, entitled 'Ballet Carnevals-Scene' (i.e. *Les Souvenirs de Paris*) and his 'Champagner Galopp' have not yet been traced.

No répétiteur's copy for *Maritana* has yet been traced.

Parts (incomplete). Ms. Copy. 20 vol.
2 vl I, vl II, fl picc, ob, cl 1/2, fag, cor 1/2, tr 1/2, cnt 1/2, Btrb, tuba, timp, gr cassa, cassa, xyl.
Unsigned and undated [1847]
[DKKk; C II, 105, Efterslæt 3
This set of parts contains a waltz, named 'Ballet Carnevals-Scene' which is followed by the complete music for *Maritana*. The parts for the 'Champagner Galopp' seem to represent the earliest manuscript copies of this work that have been traced so far. Another complete set of parts for *Maritana* dating from the 1940s is now in the music archive of the Tivoli Gardens (call no. 1663).

19.4.1847
Uthal.

E.-H. Méhul's one-act operetta (premièred at l'Opéra Comique in Paris on 17.5.1806) was given its Copenhagen première on 7.7.1846, at a time when Bournonville was away on a trip to Paris. However, at its restaging on 19.4.1847, he was responsible for the mise–en–scène, although his name is not mentioned on the posters, nor in H. C. J. Fredstrup's rehearsal book. Thus, in his handwritten lists of his stagings of operas, written c.1851 (*see* Additional Sources), Méhul's operetta is clearly included under the year of 1847. This seems to indicate that Bournonville's involvement in the 1847 restaging of *Uthal* was a somewhat unofficial engagement that most probably had resulted from the wish of the music conductor, F. Gläser, who may have asked Bournonville personally for his assistance. The 1847 restaging of *Uthal* received 6 performances, the last of which took place on 11.5.1848.

Musical sources:

Orchestral score. Ms. Copy. Black and brown ink. 1 vol. 262 pp. (27,5 × 38 cm)
Uthal. [*sic*]/af/Mehul./Partitur/[…]/Uthal/Opera en un Acte/ Imité d'Ossian/Paroles de Mr. St. Victor/Musique de Mehul.
Unsigned and undated [c.1846]
[DKKk; C I, 278 (KTA 399)
This orchestral score contains C. Borgaard's Danish translation of J. de Saint-Victor's original French text.

No répétiteur's copy for *Uthal* has yet been traced.

Parts (incomplete). Ms. Copy. 25 + 8 vol.
4 vla I, 3 vla II, 3 vlc e cb, fl 1/2, ob 1/2, cl 1/2, fag 1/2, cor 1/2/3/ 4, timp, gong, arpa. On stage: fl 1/2, cl 1/2, fag 1/2, cor 1/2. 27 vocal parts.
Unsigned and undated [1846]
[DKKk; KTA 399

2.5.1847
'The Styrians, National Pas de deux' ('Steiermarkeren, Pas de deux National') (uncredited) performed by Juliette and Amalia Price (the Casino Theatre).

According to Bournonville's autographed notes, written with brown ink in several of the parts for this (uncredited) dance, he personally arranged and staged this dance for his two pupils, the Price cousins Juliette and Amalia.

In the spring and the autumn of 1847 he began (according to his diary) to give private dance lessons to the talented children of the Price dynasty of dancers. As the first result of these lessons he seemingly arranged his earlier *Styrian Dance* (originally performed at Copenhagen's Royal Theatre in D.-F.-E. Auber's three-act comic opera *Le Domino noir* on 29.1. 1839) into this new version for two women, but still set to the same music as that of his 1839 *Styrian Dance*. 'The Styrians, National Pas de deux', therefore, represents the first in the long series of works that he created for the Price children during the late 1840s and early 50s. It was given only once at the Casino Theatre.

Musical sources:

No orchestral score for the 1847 version of this dance has yet been traced.

Répétiteur's copy. Ms. Copy. Black ink. 2 pp. (33,2 × 27 cm)
Repetiteur Stemme/til/Pas Stÿrien.
Unsigned and undated [c.1847]
[DKKk; C II, 105, Efterslæt 5

Parts. Ms. Copy. 15 vol.
2 vl I, 2 vl II, 2 vlc e cb, fl picc, fl, cl 1/2, fag 1/2, cor 1/2, clno 1–2.
[DKKk; C II, 105, Efterslæt 5
This set of parts almost certainly dates from the performance by J. and A. Price of 'Steyermarkeren, Pas de deux National' at the Casino Theatre on 2.5.1847. This theory is confirmed by Bournonville's autographed notes written with brown ink in several of the parts, which clearly indicate that he personally arranged and mounted this dance. The set of parts (which originally was part of the music archive of the Price family) was purchased by DKKk in 1902 from the actor, Carl Price, who was a relative of Juliette Price and may have received it from her previously.

9.5.1847
Maritana, Divertissement in the form of a Carnival scene (Divertissement i Form af en Carnevals=Scene).

This performance represents the first and only time Bournonville's divertissement *Maritana* (*see* 15.4.1847) was performed at the Royal Theatre. According to the rehearsal book of H. C. J. Fredstrup, only one rehearsal was held of it on 8.5.1847. No musical sources for *Maritana* have been traced in the original handwritten catalogues of the Royal Theatre's music archive. It seems to indicate that the divertissement was performed using the original musical material from its Casino Theatre première (now in DKKk, call nos. MA ms 2728, and C II, 105, Efterslæt 3).

11.5.1847
Pas de deux and Polka from the ballet 'Le Diable à quatre' by Mazilier (Pas de deux og Polka af Balletten 'le diable à quatre' af Mazilier) **performed by Bournonville and C. Fjeldsted (the Court Theatre).**

This set of two dances was (according to the orchestral score for it) originally part of the French choreographer, J. Mazilier's two-act ballet-pantomime *Le Diable à quatre* (premièred at the Paris Opéra on 11.8.1845), set to music by A. Adam. The 1847 Copenhagen première took place as part of a special charity performance given for C. Fjeldsted.

According to the rehearsal book of H. C. J. Fredstrup, Bournonville directed all rehearsals of these dances during the following season prior to their restaging on 2.9.1847. This seems to indicate that it may have been he who learned these dances from Mazilier in Paris (perhaps during his sojourn there in the early spring of 1847). According to Adam's original orchestral score and the French répétiteur's copy (both now in FPo, call nos. A 547 [III], pp. 15–64, and Mat. 19 [351 (44), pp. 126–170), Mazilier's dances were originally performed in Act II of *Le Diable à quatre* by the dancers, C. Grisi and L. Petipa.

In Copenhagen the dances were again performed 26 times, the last time on 9.2.1861 (since 21.5.1847 by W. Funck and C. Fjeldsted). Moreover, on 6.6.1851 they were performed as part of a special charity performance at the Court Theatre. Furthermore, on 27.11.1848 H. C. J. Fredstrup renamed the dances as *Pas des Jardiniers* in his rehearsal book when they were rehearsed by Bournonville prior to a restaging on 29.11.1848.

In Norway they were performed 3 times by Funck and Fjeldsted at Christiania's Theatre (Oslo) between 25.6 and 15.8.1847. Finally, the *Pas de deux and Polka from the ballet 'Le Diable à quatre'* are almost certainly also identical with the later *Pas de deux and Polka composed by A. Bournonville (Pas de deux och Polka componerad af A. Bournonville)* which he mounted for the Swedish dancers, C. Th. Dahlgren and J. G. Gillberg, at Stockholm's Royal Theatre (Operahuset) on 4.5. 1848.

Musical sources:

Orchestral score. Ms. Copy. Brown ink. 50 pp. 35,5 × 27 cm with minor variants)
Le Diable à quatre/Pas de Deux 2.e Acte./suivi d'un Polka.
Unsigned and undated [c.1847]
[DKKk; MA ms 2611 (KTB 241)
This orchestral score is clearly a French copy and was most likely purchased by Bournonville in Paris during the early spring of 1847.

Répétiteur's copy. Ms. Copy. Black ink 12 pp. of which three are blank (32,5 × 24 cm with minor variants)
Pas de Deux/Repetiteur
Unsigned and undated [c.1847]
[DKKk; MA ms 2666 (KTB 241)
This répétiteur's copy was most probably made in Paris and brought to Copenhagen by Bournonville in the early spring of 1847.

Parts (incomplete). Ms. Copy. 28 vol.
2 vl I, 2 vl II, vla, 2 vlc e cb, fl 1/2, ob 1/2, cl 1/2, fag 1/2, cor 1/2/3/4, clno 1/2, cnt 1–2, trb 1/2/3, tuba, timp, gr cassa e tri.

Unsigned and undated [c.1847]
[DKKk; KTB 241

Parts (incomplete). Ms. Copy. 1 vol.
vl II.
Unsigned and undated [c.1847]
[DKKk; MA ms 2612 (KTB 241)

Parts (incomplete). Ms Copy. 1 vol.
vlc e cb.
Unsigned and undated [c.1847]
[DKKk; MA ms 2737 (KTB 241)

17.5.1847
Solo (Incoporated) (Solo: (indlagt)) **(uncredited) performed by C. Fjeldsted in** *The Festival in Albano (Festen i Albano).*

This (uncredited) dance is almost certainly identical with the so-called *Pas de solo, after Carlotta Grisi (Pas de solo, efter Carlotta Grisi)* which Fjeldsted had learned in Paris in the winter of 1846–47 during her studies with the French choreographer, J. Mazilier. She performed it twice in Copenhagen as a separate divertissement on 24.4.1847 and 8.1.1848.

Moreover, Grisi's solo was (according to notes in the Copenhagen's répétiteur's copy for it) originally part of Mazilier's and A. Adam's two-act ballet-pantomime *Le Diable à quatre* (premièred at the Paris Opéra on 11.8.1845). According to Adam's original orchestral score (now in FPo, call nos. A 547 [I], pp. 155–172 and 187–215) Mazilier's solo was created for and performed by C. Grisi in Act I of *Le Diable à quatre*. According to the same source Grisi's Paris Opéra version included a final *Allegro con moto* movement, which (according to a pencilled note in the Copenhagen répétiteur's copy on p. 30, reading: 'hertil'), was omitted in Fjeldsted's Copenhagen version of it.

During the 1846–47 Copenhagen season, the solo was performed 3 times as an incorporated divertissement in Bournonville's one-act idyllic ballet *The Festival in Albano* (see 28.10.1839), the last time on 25.5.1847.

Furthermore, according to the Copenhagen posters another (uncredited) dance, named *Solo (danced by Carlotta Grisi in the ballet Le Diable à quatre) (dandset af Carlotta Grisi i Balletten Le Diable à quatre)* was performed 6 times by Fjeldsted as a separate divertissement between 7.5.1847 and 9.4.1853. It is most probably identical with her incorporated 1847 solo in *The Festival in Albano*.

Finally, Fjeldsted's solo in this ballet is most likely the same as the later so-called 'Solo til Jf. Fjeldsted', which Bournonville (according to his diary) rehearsed with her on 4.10. 1848 prior to a restaging of it in *The Festival in Albano* on 6.10.1848.

Musical sources:

Orchestral score. Ms. Copy. Black ink. 1 vol. 48 pp. (35,2 × 26,8 cm)
Adolphe Adam:/Giselle ou les Willis [erased]/Pas Seul de Carlotta/ [KTB 235] C I, 203/[…]/Diable a quatre/ADAM/B. 235/C I, 203/ Pas Seul de Carlotta (acte 1) (adam).
Unsigned and undated [c.1847]
[DKKk; C I, 203 (KTB 235)
This orchestral score is clearly a French copy that was most probably purchased by either Fjeldsted or Bournonville in Paris during the early spring of 1847 and brought to Copenhagen by one of them the same year.

Répétiteur's copy. Ms. Black ink. 14 pp. (32,2 × 24,3 cm)
<u>Caroline</u> [Fjeldsted]/<u>Pas Seul</u>, de Carlotta Grisi/dansé au ballet le diable a quatre.
Unsigned and undated [c.1847]
[DKKk; MA ms 2904 (4) (KTB 235)
This répétiteur's copy is bound together with the répétiteur's copy for five other dances dating from the 1840s and 50s. It is included on pp. 21–34.

Parts (incomplete). Ms. Copy. 32 vol.
2 vl I, 2 vl II, 2 vla, 4 vlc e cb, fl 1/2, ob 1/2, cl 1/2, fag 1/2, cor 1/2/3/4, tr 1/2, cnt, trb 1/2/3, oph, timp, gr cassa, tri.
Unsigned and undated [c.1847]
[DKKk; KTB 235
These parts are written and bound together with the set of parts for the Bohemian solo dance, named *La Redowa* and choreographed by Albert (François Decombe). It was first performed in Copenhagen by C. Fjeldsted on 2.7.1847.

Parts (incomplete). Ms. Copy. 1 vol.
vl I.
Unsigned and undated [c.1847]
[DKKk; MA ms 2714 (KTB 235)

26.5.1847

Pas de deux à la Taglioni arranged by Mr. Ballet Master Bournonville (arrangerad af Herr Balletmästaren Bournonville) **performed by Bournonville and M. C. Norberg (Stockholm's Royal Theatre, Operahuset).**

This *Pas de deux* was given as an incorporated divertissement in Act II of Fr. v. Flotow's three-act opera *Alessandro Stradella*. It is almost certainly identical with the *Pas de deux à la Taglioni*, danced by G. Brodersen and A. Nielsen at Copenhagen's Royal Theatre on 6.11.1845. That dance, in turn, is most likely identical with the even earlier *Pas de deux* set to music by J. Mayseder and originally performed in Act II (score no. 1 A) of Bournonville's two-act romantic ballet *The Isle of Phantasy* (see 28.10.1838).

On 26.5.1847 Bournonville noted of the dance in his diary:

'I Stradellas anden Act dandset pas de deux à la Taglioni til [M. C.] Norbergs Debüt, den gik fortreffeligt, Modtagelse, Applaus og Fremkaldelse'.

It was given two more times at Stockholm's Royal Theatre on 28.5. and 25.6.1847, on the last day as a separate divertissement, with the dancer, Theodore (stage name for Th. I. Marckhl) performing Bournonville's part.

A complete set of parts for Mayseder's *Pas de deux*, which most probably dates from 1839, is now in SSkma (call no. KT Dansmusik 43).

Pas de deux à la Taglioni received 6 performances in Stockholm, the last of which was given on 31.10.1847. It is not possible to identify the dance any further.

27.5.1847

Pas de deux from 'The New Penelope '(Pas de deux af 'Den nye Penelope') **performed by F. Hoppe and P. Funck.**

This dance is identical with the *Pas de deux*, originally performed by Hoppe and Funck in Act II (score no. 8) of Bournonville's two-act allegorical ballet *The New Penelope, or The Spring Festival in Athens* (see 26.1.1847). The dance was performed only once as a separate divertissement in 1847. No

separate musical sources for it have yet been traced. This seems to indicate that it was performed using the original musical material for *The New Penelope, or The Spring Festival in Athens* (now in DKKk, call nos. C II, 117 d, MA ms 2944, and KTB 205).

28.5.1847

The Vierländers, (Hamburger Dance) composed by Mr. Ballet Master Bournonville (Vierländerne, (Hamburger-Dans), componerad af Herr Ballettmästaren Bournonville) **performed by Bournonville and J. G. Gillberg (Stockholm's Royal Theatre, Operahuset).**

This dance is (according to a set of parts for it in SSkma) identical with the *New Hamburg-Scottish*, set to music by H. C. Lumbye and first performed by Bournonville and Fjeldsted in Copenhagen on 8.2.1844 as a new, incorporated finale in his one-act idyllic ballet *The Tyroleans* (see 6.3.1835). Moreover, the dance is the same as the divertissement, named *The Vierländers, Hamburg Dance (Vierländerne, Hamborger=Dands)*, first performed as a separate divertissement by Bournonville and Fjeldsted at Copenhagen's Royal Theatre on 24.1.1847.

The dance was performed once during Bournonville's 1847 summer tour to Stockholm, but remained in the repertory there until the 1884–85 season, thereby reaching a total of 9 performances in the Swedish capital. The last of these took place on 24.1.1885.

In his 1847 diary Bournonville noted about the dance:

24.5.1847: 'Mlle [J. G.] Gillberg lært Hamborgerdandsen'
28.5.: 'Vierländerne […] gik udmærket og blev særdeles applauderet med Fremkaldelse'.

Musical sources:

No orchestral score and répétiteur's copy dating from the 1847 Stockholm performance of this dance has yet been traced in SSkma. This seems to indicate that *The Vierländers* was rehearsed and conducted with the original Copenhagen musical sources, while a new set of parts clearly was made in Stockholm this year (see the following entry).

Parts. Ms. Copy. 33 vol.
3 vl I, 3 vl II, 2 vla, 4 vlc e cb, fl picc, fl I, ob 1/2, cl 1/2, fag 1/2, cor 1/2/3/4, tr 1/2, cnt 1/2, trb 1/2/3, gr cassa, tri.
Unsigned and undated [c.1847]
[SSkma; KT Dansmusik 64
Lumbye's music was in all probability brought to Stockholm by Bournonville in 1847 and copied there. According to a note written by the copyist, A. F. Schwartz, on the box containing this set of parts ('Begagnas i Turken i Italien'), it also seems to have been used as an incorporated divertissement in G. Rossini's two-act comic opera *Il Turco in Italia (Turken i Italien)*. That opera had been given its Stockholm première on 21.4.1824 and was kept in the repertory there until 19.12.1849.

2.6.1847

The Toreador (Toréadoren) **(Stockholm's Royal Theatre, Operahuset).**

This performance represents Bournonville's first and only staging in Sweden of his two-act idyllic ballet *The Toreador* (see 27.11.1840). It was mounted with himself and the Swedish ballerina, C. D. Friebel, playing the leading rôles as *Alonzo* and *Maria*, and with his Swedish pupil, M. C. Norberg, appearing as *Céleste*. Moreover, for this production Bournonville wrote a new, abridged scenario in Swedish which was published on the poster and reads as follows:

'FÖRSTA AKTEN:

Alonzo som segrade uti en tjurfäktning, firart denna seger vid ett värdshus, som tillhör hans blifvande Svärfar. En Fransysk Danseuse, M.lle *Celeste*, som är stadd på en resa från Paris till Madrid, stadnar framför detta värdshus, blir fortjust i de Nationaldansar landtfolket uför, och ber *Marie, Alonzos* fästmö, att ge henne undervisning deruti. Denna lär henne att dansa den Spanska Nationaldansen: 'il Jaleo'. – Två resande Engelsman, som frukostera paa värdshusets balcon, bli betagna uti den sköna Fransyskans behag, forälska sig uti henne och besluta att fria till henne. De råka i strid med hvarandra harom och taga *Alonzo* til skiljedomare emellan sig. – Han föreslår att de skola draga lott om, hvilken som först skall framställa sitt frieri, men för att uttrycka hvem det är som utgör föremålet för deras låga, härma de resande stegen i 'Jaleo', hvarigenom ett missförstand uppkommer. *Alonzo*, som tror att de mena hans fästmö, blir uesinnig, och förgår sig så, att han bli satt i fängelse.

ANDRA AKTEN:

De resande Engelsmannen betyga sin ömhet för *Celeste*. – Efter några små äfventyr, hvarigennom olikheten i begges lynnen röja sig, lyckas det för den mera gladlynte *William* att erhalla den skönas hand, emot vilkor, at Toreadorn åter blir försatt i frihet. Landtfolket firar med sina Boleros denna hädelse, och den glädje, som afbrutits genom *Alonzos* misstag, återställes. – (Slut.)'.

In his diary he noted about the rehearsals and the Swedish première:

25.5.1847: 'Indstuderet de første Scener af Toreadoren, prøvet med Orchester, og arrangeret Decorationerne'
26.5.: 'Prøve paa Toreadoren'
27.5.: 'Prøve fra 9 til 1 paa Toréadoren. – Arrangeret Costumer med Lieut: [U. E.] Mannerhjerta […] Prøve fra 6 til 7'
29.5.: 'Prøvet Toreadoren i Matsalen en time og derpaa fra 11 til 2 paa Theatret. Det er gaaet meget godt og den største Deel lært […] prøvet med Rollerne fra 6–8'
31.5.: 'Paa Theatret Kl 8, prøvet Solonumrene til Kl 10, derpaa indstuderet Finalen og sluttet Balletten'
1.6.: 'Prøve paa Toreadoren fra 9 til 11½ […] Prøvet fra 4 til 6 fuldstændigt paa Toreadoren'
2.6.: 'prøvet Toreadoren udmærket godt Kl 10 til 11½ […] Dandset Toreadoren med overordentligt Held fra alle Sider. Applausen betydelig, men ikke som jeg havde ventet den. Det hele vil gaae og forstaaes endnu bedre næste Gang'.

No musical sources are preserved for this ballet in SSkma and A. F. Schwartz does not even include it in his handwritten catalogue of the music archive of Stockholm's Royal Theatre. These facts seem to indicate that *The Toreador* was performed using the musical material from its 1840 Copenhagen première. If this theory is correct then the ballet must (also according to the Copenhagen set of parts) have been performed with only minor if any musical changes from the original version.

The Toreador received 3 performances in Stockholm, the last of which was given on 18.6.1847.

Printed sources:

Printed scenario. 1 vol. 12 pp. (16,6 × 10 cm)
TORÉADOREN,/IDYLLISK BALLETT I TVÅ AKTER./AF/AUGUST BOURNONVILLE./MUSIKEN KOMPONERAD OCH ARRANGERAD AF/EDWARD HELSTED.
Stockholm, L. J. Hjerta, 1847
[DKKk; 17, – 173 8°

9.6.1847
Faust, Romantic Pantomimic Ballet revised into one act
(Romantisk Pantomime-Ballett, sammandragen i 1 Akt)
(Stockholm's Royal Theatre, Operahuset).

This abridged one-act version represents Bournonville's first and only staging outside Denmark of his three-act romantic ballet *Faust* (*see* 25.4.1832). It was performed with A. Füssel, Bournonville, and M. C. Norberg in the three leading rôles as *Faust, Mephistopheles*, and *Magaretha* respectively. For the production Bournonville wrote a new, abridged scenario in Swedish which was published on the poster and reads:

'*Faust*, fördjupad i sina forskningar, kallar Andeverlden till hjelp. De goda Andar uppenbara sig nu för hon om och *Hoppet* erbjuder honom en ring såsom talisman. Med stolthet försmår den lärde mannen denna gåfva och fordrar en genast lyckobringande vishet. *Mephistopheles* lofvar honom denna och förer honom från hans lärda grubbel ut i verlden til ära och rikedom.
Näre invid det *Faust* tillhöriga Slott är en bondby, hvarest Enken *Johanna* bor tillika med sina tvenne barn, *Valentin* och *Margaretha*. Här firas Enkan *Johannas* födelsedag af hennes vänner, med glada dansar; hvarvid äfven den hvita rosen, såsom priset för oskuld och dygd, tillerkännes *Margaretha*. Denna landtliga glädje blifver snart förstörd genom *Mephistopheles. Faust* tillvinner sig *Margarethas* kärlek och förer henne till förderfvets brant; men hon är nu kommen i besittning af *Hoppets* ring och frälsas af sin goda genius, under det *Faust*, åtföljd af *Mephistopheles*, ilar sin undergång till mötes'.

In his diary Bournonville noted about the rehearsals and the Swedish première:

31.5.1847: '1½ Times Indstudering med Mlle [P. A.] Watz paa Faust'
3.6.: 'Kl 9 paa Faust til Kl 11' […] arrangeret Decorationerne til Faust'
4.6.: 'Waltz til Faust […] Kl 5½ Prøve paa Faust paa Theatret, Finalen og Scener til Kl 7'
5.6.: 'Kl 9 Walsen til Faust. Kl 10 til 12 de vigtigste Situationer for corps de ballet. Kl 12–1 Rollerne'
7.6.: 'Prøve fra 10 til 12 paa Faust færdig'
8.6.: 'Faust med Orchester Kl 11'
9.6.: 'Prøve paa Faust Kl 11 gik meget godt […] spillet Mephistofeles i Faust. […] Kl 10 begyndte Balletten og gik udmærket godt fra alle sider – meget Bifald'.

No musical sources are preserved for this ballet in Stockholm, and A. F. Schwartz does not even include it in his handwritten catalogue of the music archive of Stockholm's Royal Theatre. These facts seem to indicate that the Swedish version was performed using the musical material from the 1832 Copenhagen version, most probably brought to Stockholm by Bournonville in 1847. This theory is confirmed by several pencilled notes (in Swedish) written into the Copenhagen score. They read (in Act I, p. 76) 'hoppas till No. 12', and (in Act II, pp. 11 and 90–91) 'utan repris/utan Repris/mitt repris', thereby clearly indicating the omissions and the musical changes that seem to have been made by Bournonville for the 1847 Swedish production.

The only musical source in Stockholm which holds any relation to *Faust* is a set of parts entitled 'Dansmusik ur Faust' (now in SSkma, call no. KT Dansmusik 61). It contains the music for F.-M.-A. Venua's *Pas de deux*, that was originally performed in Copenhagen by Bournonville and A. Krætzmer in J. L. Heiberg's three-act play *Princess Isabella, or Three Nights at the Court* (*see* 29.10.1829) and later was also incorporated in

Bournonville's first restaging in Denmark of *Faust* (*see* 8.12. 1849). However, no full orchestral score for this dance is preserved in SSkma. Moreover, the label on the box containing the parts for this dance reads: 'Pas de deux, arr: par Bournonville/per [*sic*] Faust'. It is, therefore, unclear whether this *Pas de deux* was performed as part of Bournonville's 1847 Stockholm production of *Faust* or whether it was mounted later on as a separate divertissement in Stockholm.

Bournonville's one-act version of *Faust* was given 3 times in Stockholm, the last time on 13.6.1847.

Musical sources:

Répétiteur's copy (*Pas de deux*). Ms. Copy. Black ink. 1 vol. 5 pp. (34 × 25,7 cm)
No. 61./Pas de deux/af/Faust./Repetiteur = Parti./Cath: No. 61.
Unsigned and undated [1847?]
[SSkma: KT Dansmusik 61
This répétiteur's copy was clearly made in Copenhagen and was perhaps brought to Stockholm by Bournonville in 1847.

Répétiteur's copy (*Pas de deux*) Ms. Copy. Black ink. 1 vol. 7 pp. (32,2 × 23,5 cm)
Repetitör/Repetitör/Pas de deux
Unsigned and undated [1847? or later]
[SSkma: KT Dansmusik 61
According to its title this répétiteur's copy was clearly made in Stockholm. It omits the introduction, and most probably dates from a later period than the previous répétiteur's copy of the same dance.

Parts (*Pas de deux*). Ms. Copy. 30 vol.
3 vl I, 3 vl Il, 2 vla, 3 vlc e cb, fl 1/2, ob 1/2, cl 1/2, fag 1/2, cor 1/2, tr, trb 1/2/3, timp, gr cassa.
Unsigned and undated [1847?]
[SSkma: KT Dansmusik 61

11.6.1847
Bellman, or the Polish Dance at Grönalund (Bellman, eller Polskan på Grönalund) (Stockholm's Royal Theatre, Operahuset).
This production represents the first of two stagings in Sweden of Bournonville's one-act ballet-vaudeville *Bellman or the Polish Dance at Grönalund* (*see* 3.6.1844). It was mounted with himself and the Swedish ballerina, J. G. Gillberg, playing the leading rôles as *Bellman* and *Ulla Wiinblad*. The complete text of the original 1844 Copenhagen scenario was printed in a Swedish translation on the poster and without any changes. In his diary Bournonville noted about the rehearsals and the Swedish première:

3.6.1847: 'Begÿndt Indstuderingen af Bellmann Kl 8 med Børnene [...] Kl 11 derpaa igjen Bellmann til Kl 12 1/2, arrangeret Decorationer'
4.6.: 'Prøve med Børnene til Bellmann'
6.6.: 'Prøve paa Bellmann, Polskdands og Pantomimer'
7.6.: 'Prøve paa Bellmann fra 4 til 6'
8.6.: 'Prøve paa Bellmann Kl 9 1/2 [...] Prøver paa Grupperne til Bellmann, arrangeret Requisiter'
10.6.: 'Prøve paa Bellmann Kl 9 1/2 – 11 – til 1.'
11.6.: 'holdt Prøve paa Bellmann [...] Bellmann der gjorde complet furore. Alt gik fortreffeligt Huset var fuldt og Tilfredsstillelsen almindelig'.

The production was performed 6 times in Stockholm, the last time on 25.6.1847.

Musical sources:

Orchestral score. Ms. Copy. Black ink. 1 vol. 227 pp. (32,6 × 23,5 cm)
Balletten/Bellman./Partitur.
Unsigned and undated [1847]
[SSkma; KT Pantomime-Balletter B 6
This orchestral score was also used for Bournonville's second staging of this ballet in Stockholm on 21.4.1858. It indicates a number of minor musical cuts and also includes some revised sections, which were most probably made for the second Swedish production on 21.4.1858. This is particularly true for the music in score no. 1, in which excerpts of V. C. Holm's music (score no. 3) from Bournonville's Spanish divertissement *La Ventana* (*see* 6.10.1856) were incorporated.

Répétiteur's copy. Ms. Copy. Black ink. 1 vol. 44 pp. (33,1 × 25,5 cm)
Bellmann/eller/Polskdandsen paa Grönalund/Repetiteurparti
Unsigned and undated [1847]
[SSkma; KT Pantomime-Balletter B 6
This répétiteur's copy contains Bournonville's autographed choreographic notes describing the mime and the dramatic action of the entire ballet. Moreover his autographed choreographic numbers ('1–6' and '1–13') are inserted in the *Allegretto* movement before the *Menuet* and the *Polsk Dands* in score no. 5. They seem to refer to a (not yet identified) separate choreographic notation of this movement.

Parts. Ms. Copy. 34 vol.
3 vl I, 3 vl II, 2 vla, 4 vlc e cb, fl 1/2, ob 1/2, cl 1/2, fag 1/2, cor 1/2/ 3/4, tr 1/2, trb 1/2/3, timp, gr cassa, piatti, tri, arpa.
Unsigned and undated [1847]
[SSkma; KT Pantomime-Balletter B 6

16.6.1847
Pas de deux from La Muette de Portici, composed by Mr. Ballet Master Bournonville (Pas de deux af Den Stumma från Portici, componerad af Herr Ballettmästaren Bournonville) performed by Bournonville and M. C. Norberg (Stockholm's Royal Theatre, Operahuset).
This dance is identical with the so-called *A New Pas de deux composed by Mr. Dance Director Bournonville (En ny Pas de deux, componeret af Hr. Dandsedirecteur Bournonville)*, which was set to music by M. E. Caraffa and first performed by F. Hoppe and L. Grahn at Copenhagen's Royal Theatre as an incorporated divertissement in Act I of D.-F.-E. Auber's five-act opera *La Muette de Portici* (*see* 23.9.1834). It was performed twice in Stockholm, the last time on 21.6.1847.

No musical sources for this dance have yet been traced in SSkma. Moreover, A. F. Schwartz does not even include it in his handwritten catalogue of the music archive of Stockholm's Royal Theatre. These facts seem to indicate that the *Pas de deux* was mounted and performed in Stockholm using the original Copenhagen musical material (now in DKKk, call nos. MA ms 2603, MA ms 2700, and KTB 209).

25.6.1847
Pas de bouquets from the ballet: 'La Jolie Fille de Gand' (ur Balletten 'La jolie fille de Gand') (uncredited) performed by M. C. Norberg and a female corps de ballet (Stockholm's Royal Theatre, Operahuset).
This (uncredited) solo dance had been mounted earlier by Bournonville for A. Nielsen at Copenhagen's Royal Theatre on 1.11.1842. It is based on a *Pas seul* in A. Adam's and Albert's (François Decombe) three-act pantomimic ballet *La*

Jolie Fille de Gand (premièred at the Paris Opéra on 22.6. 1842). However, the 1847 Stockholm version seems to have been slightly different from Bournonville's earlier Copenhagen production by its inclusion of a small female corps de ballet. *Pas de bouquets* was given 7 times by Norberg in Stockholm, the last time on 1.4.1848. Moreover, between 16.2. and 1.3.1885 A. Flammé danced it 6 times together with a corps de ballet of 8 women.

Musical sources:

No orchestral score and répétiteur's copy for *Pas de Bouquets* have yet been traced in SSkma.

Parts (incomplete). Ms. Copy. 25 vol.
2 vl I, 3 vl II, 2 vla, 3 vlc e cb, fl 1/2, ob 1/2, cl 1/2, fag 1-2, cor 1/2/ 3/4, timp, tr, trb, gr cassa.
Unsigned and undated [c.1847]
[SSkma; KT Dansmusik 65

25.6.1847
The English Sailor (Den Engelska Matrosen) **performed by Bournonville and a male corps de ballet (Stockholm's Royal Theatre, Operahuset).**
This dance appears to be Bournonville's free adaptation of his own 1838 male solo variation, named *The English Sailor (Den engelske Matros)*, in Act I (score no. 10) of his two-act romantic ballet *The Isle of Phantasy (see 28.10.1838)*. This theory is based on the fact that the Stockholm version differed (according to the poster) from the Copenhagen version by the inclusion of a small male corps de ballet. Another circumstance that supports this theory is the existence of a complete set of parts in SSkma, entitled 'Matrosdans' which contains the exact same music as that for I. P. E. Hartmann's music in Act I (score no. 10) of *The Isle of Phantasy*. *The English Sailor* was only given once in Stockholm.

Autograph sources:

Choreographic note. Ms. Autograph. Brown ink. 3 pp. (18 × 11,3 cm)
Pas de Matelots:
Unsigned and undated [1847?]
[DKKk; NKS 3285 4 ° 3 R–U
This manuscript includes the names of the dancers (Sigurd) Lund and Theodore (stage name for Theodor Ignaz Marckhl) and was most probably written in connection with Bournonville's revised staging of his *The English Sailor (Den Engelska Matrosen)* in Stockholm on 25.6.1847, since both of these dancers took part in this performance. Another possibility is that the manuscript may refer to S. Lund's much later production at the same theatre on 19.1.1860 of a one-act adaptation of Bournonville's two-act romantic ballet *The Isle of Phantasy*, then given with the title *At the Shore of China (Vid Chinas Kust)*.

Musical sources:

No orchestral score and répétiteur's copy for *The English Sailor* have yet been traced in SSkma.

Parts. Ms. Copy. 26 vol.
3 vl I, 3 vl II, 2 vla, 3 vlc e cb, fl picc, fl 1/2, ob 1/2, cl 1/2, fag 1/2, cor 1/2, tr, timp, gr cassa, piatti.
Unsigned and undated [c.1847]
[SSkma; KT Dansmusik 62

25.6.1847
Polka militaire **performed by Bournonville, Theodore (stage name for Th. I. Marchkl), M. C. Norberg, and P. A. Watz (Stockholm's Royal Theatre, Operahuset).**
This performance represents Bournonville's first staging in Sweden of his *Polka militaire (Polka, (Militairdands))*, originally performed at the Court Theatre in Copenhagen on 1.11.1842. In his diary he noted about its reception on the opening night:

'Almindelig Begeistring'.

The dance was given twice in 1847, the last time on 28.6. 1847. *Polka militaire* was restaged 7 times with different casts in Stockholm between the 1847–48 and 1861–62 seasons, thereby reaching a total of 11 performances in the Swedish capital (the last of which was given on 7.2.1862).

Musical sources:

No orchestral score for Lumbye's *Polka militaire* has yet been traced in SSkma.

Répétiteur's copy. Ms. Copy. Black and brown ink. 4 pp. (33 × 24 cm)
Militair Polka/Repetiteur partie
Unsigned and undated [c.1847]
[SSkma; KT Dansmusik 63

Parts. Ms. Copy. 29 vol.
3 vl I, 3 vl II, 2 vla, 3 vcl e cb, fl picc, fl, ob 1/2, cl 1/2, 1 fag, cnt 1/2, cor 1/2, tr 1/2, Btrb, gr cassa, cassa, timp, tri.
Unsigned and undated [c.1847]
[SSkma; KT Dansmusik 63

25.6.1847
The Vierländers, Scenic Character Dance (Vierlænderne, scenisk Charakteerdands) **(uncredited) performed by W. Funck and C. Fjeldsted (Christiania's Theatre, Oslo).**
According to notes written in a part for the first violin (now in DKKk, call no. KTB 1024, but originally KTB 240) this (uncredited) dance is identical with H. C. Lumbye's score for the so-called *New Hamburg-Scottish*, which was first performed by Bournonville and Fjeldsted as a new, incorporated finale (score no. 12) in his one-act idyllic ballet *The Tyroleans (see 8.2.1844)*. *The Vierländers* was given twice by Funck and Fjeldsted in Christiania, the last time on 20.8. 1847.

Musical sources:

Orchestral score. Ms. Copy. Black ink. 1 vol. 26 pp. (24,9 × 34,5 cm)
Vierlaender Dands.
Unsigned and undated [c.1847]
[NOum; Ms. 216, Eske 24 a.
This orchestral score dates almost certainly from when *The Vierländers* was performed for the first and only time at Christiania's Theatre (Oslo) by Funck and Fjeldsted on 25.7.1847. It also represents the only existing full orchestral score for this dance traced so far.

No répétiteur's copy and set of parts dating from the 1847 performance of *The Vierländers* in Norway have yet been traced. However, notes in the Copenhagen set of parts (now in DKKk, call no. KTB 1024, but originally KTB 240)) clearly indicate that it also was used for the 1847 performances in Christiania of this dance.

25.6.1847

*Pas de deux and Polka from the ballet 'Le Diable à quatre',
composed by Mazilier (Pas de deux og Polka af Balletten 'le
diable en [sic] quatre', componeret af Mazilier)* **performed by
W. Funck and C. Fjeldsted (Christiania's Theatre, Oslo).**

This set of dances is identical with the dances of that name
mounted and performed in Copenhagen by Bournonville
and Fjeldsted on 11.5.1847. They were given 3 times in Norway by Funck and Fjeldsted, the last time on 15.8.1847. No
musical sources dating from the 1847 performances in Norway have yet been traced. This seems to indicate that the
Copenhagen musical material was also employed in Norway
this year (now in DKKk, call nos. MA ms 2611, MA ms 2666,
and KTB 241).

25.6.1847

La Cracovienne, Polish National Dance (polsk Nationaldands)
**(uncredited) performed by C. Fjeldsted (Christiania's
Theatre, Oslo).**

This performance represents the first time Bournonville's
Copenhagen version of F. Elssler's solo dance *La Cracovienne*
(*see* 10.6.1842) was ever performed in Norway. It was given
twice in Christiania by Fjeldsted, the last time on 20.8.1847.
No musical sources dating from its performances in Norway
have yet been traced. This seems to indicate that it was rehearsed and performed using the original Copenhagen musical material (now in DKKk, call nos. MA ms 2663, MA ms
2664, and KTB 214).

27.6.1847

*Styrian Peasant Dance by Ballet-master Perrot (Steyersk
Bondedands af Balletmester Perrot)* **performed by W. Funck
and C. Fjeldsted at Christiania's Theatre (Oslo).**

The choreography of this dance is explicitly credited on the
poster to the French dancer and choreographer, J. Perrot.
However, it is in all probability identical with Bournonville's
Styrian Dance, first performed as an incorporated divertissement in D.-F.-E. Auber's three-act comic opera *Le Domino noir*
(*see* 29.1.1839). This theory is supported by the fact that the
1847 *Styrian Peasant Dance* was performed to the exact same
music as that of Bournonville's *Styrian Dance* in Copenhagen.
Consequently, Bournonville's Danish version of this dance
may have been based on choreography by Perrot, which he
had probably seen and learned during a sojourn in Paris in
the late 1830s (*Le Domino noir* was premièred at l'Opéra
Comique in Paris on 2.12.1837). The *Styrian Peasant Dance*
was given 3 times at Christiania's Theatre, the last time on
8.8.1847.

Musical sources:

Orchestral score. Ms. Copy. Black ink. 1 vol. 19 pp. (24,4 × 34 cm)
No. 5/Pas Styrien
Unsigned and undated [c.1847]
[NOum; Ms. 216, Eske 24 a.
This reduced orchestral score almost certainly dates from when the
so-called *Styrian Peasant Dance* was performed for the first time at
Christiania's Theatre (Oslo) by Funck and Fjeldsted on 27.6.1847.

No répétiteur's copy dating from the 1847 performances of the *Styrian Peasant Dance* in Norway has yet been traced.

Parts. Ms. Copy. 9 vol.
vl I, vl II, vla, vlc e cb, fl, cl, fag, cor, tr.
Unsigned and undated [c.1847]
[DKKk; KTB 1027
According to the reduced orchestration in the orchestral score for
the 1847 Norwegian version of the *Styrian Dance* these parts clearly
must date from when the so-called *Styrian Peasant Dance* was performed at Christiania's Theatre (Oslo) by Funck and Fjeldsted on
27.6.1847.

28.6.1847

*Pas de deux, arranged by Mr. Ballet Master Bournonville
(arrangered af Herr Ballettmästaren Bournonville)* **performed
by Bournonville and M. C. Norberg as an incorporated
divertissement in Act II of *Robert le Diable (Robert af
Normandie)* (Stockholm's Royal Theatre, Operahuset).**

This dance is most probably identical with the earlier so-
called *New Pas de deux*, choreographed by Bournonville and
performed by himself and C. Fjeldsted at Copenhagen's
Royal Theatre on 5.12.1841 as a incorporated divertissement
in Act II of G. Meyerbeer's five-act opera *Robert le Diable (Robert af Normandiet)*. The dance is perhaps also identical with
the even earlier *Grand Pas de deux (Stor Pas de deux)* 'composed' (*componerad*) by Bournonville and performed by himself and A. Nielsen at Stockholm's Royal Theatre (Operahuset) on 13.6.1839 as an incorporated divertissement in
Act II of *Robert le Diable*.

No musical sources have yet been traced in SSkma which
can be linked directly to Bournonville's 1847 performances
of this dance in Stockholm. The only sources there thus date
from when his pupil, S. Lund, restaged this *Pas de deux* some
9 years later 13.11.1856. For that production a new set of
parts was made (now in SSkma, call no. KT Dansmusik 85).
This seems to indicate that Bournonville rehearsed and performed this dance in Stockholm in 1847 using the original
Copenhagen musical material for it (now in DKKk, call nos.
MA ms 2903 (2), MA ms 2604, and KTB 223).

The dance was given only once in Stockholm in 1847.

29.6.1847

*Grand Pas de deux from 'Robert le Diable', composed by
Bournonville ('af 'Robert af Normandiet', componeret af
Bournonville)* **performed by W. Funck and C. Fjeldsted
(Christiania's Theatre, Oslo).**

This dance is identical with the *Pas de deux* performed by
Bournonville and M. C. Norberg at Stockholm's Royal Thea-
tre on the previous day. The *Pas de deux* was given twice by
Funck and Fjeldsted in Christiania, the last time on 20.8.
1847. No musical sources from its 1847 performances in
Norway have yet been traced.

29.6.1847

El Jaleo de Xeres **(uncredited) performed by W. Funck and
C. Fjeldsted (Christiania's Theatre, Oslo).**

This (uncredited) dance is most probably identical with *El
Jaleo de Xeres* from Act I (score no. 6) of Bournonville's two-
act idyllic ballet *The Toreador* (*see* 27.11.1840). It was performed only once in Norway by Funck and Fjeldsted. No
musical sources for this dance which date from its 1847 performance in Christiania have yet been traced, and apart
from a printed piano score (published by C. C. Lose & Olsen
in 1843, pl. no. 2009, now in DKKk, call no. D 6) no other

separate musical material for it has been found in Copenhagen.

2.7.1847

Pas de deux from La Muette de Portici, composed by Albert (Pas de deux af den Stumme i Portici, componeret af Albert) **performed by W. Funck and C. Fjeldsted (Christiania's Theatre, Oslo).**

This dance is almost certainly identical with the so-called *A New Pas de deux composed by Mr. Dance Director Bournonville*, that was set to music by M. E. Caraffa and incorporated by Bournonville in Act I of D.-F.-E. Auber's five-act opera *La Muette de Portici* in Copenhagen on 23.9.1834. This is clear from the Norwegian orchestral score for it, which includes the exact same music as that for Bournonville's Danish 1834 *Pas de deux* in *La Muette de Portici*. Moreover, the fact that the Norwegian poster gives explicit credit to Albert (François Decombe) indicates that Bournonville's 1834 *Pas de deux*, too, was most probably based on a dance by this great French dancer. The *Pas de deux from La Muette de Portici* was given only once in Norway by Funck and Fjeldsted.

Musical sources:

Orchestral score. Ms. Copy. Black ink. 1 vol. 40 pp. (24,2 × 33,6 cm)
N I
Unsigned and undated [c.1847]
[NOum; Ms. 216, Eske 24 b.

No separate répétiteur's copy and parts dating from the 1847 performance of this dance in Christiania have yet been traced. This seems to indicate that the *Pas de deux* was rehearsed and performed in Norway with the original Copenhagen musical material for Bournonville's 1834 *Pas de deux* in *La Muette de Portici* (now in DKKk, call nos. MA ms 2700, and KTB 209).

2.7.1847

'La Tarantella neapolitana' (uncredited) **performed by W. Funck and C. Fjeldsted (Christiania's Theatre, Oslo).**

This (uncredited) dance is almost certainly a free arrangement of Bournonville's *Tarantella* in his one-act idyllic ballet *The Festival in Albano* (*see* 28.10.1839 and 10.8.1840). This theory is supported by the existence of a répétiteur's copy/conductor's part and a separate set of parts for that dance, which clearly were written for tour purposes and had earlier been used for a performance of it in Flensborg (*see* 12.5.1846). This musical material (now in DKKk, call no. MA ms 2623, and KTB 1027, originally KTB 282) was most probably also employed by Funck and Fjeldsted for their 1847 performance of *'La Tarantella neapolitana'* in Norway. Bournonville did not take any part in the arrangement of the repertory given by these dancers during the 1847 Norwegian summer tour. *'La Tarantella neapolitana'* was performed only once in Christiania in 1847.

8.8.1847

'Military Dance by Bournonville' ('Militairdands af Bournonville') **performed by W. Funck and C. Fjeldsted (Christiania's Theatre, Oslo).**

This dance seems (according to the musical sources for it in Norway) to be an adapted version for one couple of Bournonville's earlier *Polka militaire (Polka, (Militairdands))*, originally performed by two couples at Copenhagen's Court Theatre (*see* 1.11.1842). *'Military Dance by Bournonville'* was given twice by Funck and Fjeldsted in Christiania, the last time on 15.8.1847.

Musical sources:

Orchestral score. Ms. Copy. Black ink. 1 vol. 11 pp. (24,8 × 33,8 cm)
Militaïr Polka
Unsigned and undated [c.1847? or later]
[NOum; Ms. 216, Eske 24 a.
This orchestral score appears to date from the first 1847 performance of Bournonville's *Polka militaire* in Norway. However, other possible datings of it could be the two later restagings of this dance at Christiania's Theatre on 9.6.1852 and/or 5.6.1865. Whatever the case might be, this score represents the earliest known copy of Lumbye's full orchestral score for *Polka militaire* that has been traced so far.

Répétiteur's copy. Ms. Copy. Black ink. 2 pp. (34,6 × 26 cm)
23 Stemmer./Militair Polka/af Lumbÿe/Violino Repittitör [*sic*]
Unsigned and undated [c.1847]
[DKKk; MA ms 2628 (KTB 1027, originally KTB 222)
This répétiteur's copy seems (according to the style of the manuscript) to date from the first performance in Norway of Bournonville's *Polka militaire.*

Parts (incomplete). Ms. Copy. 23 vol.
2 vl I, 2 vl II, vla, 2 vlc e cb, fl picc, fl, ob 1/2, cl 1/2, fag II, cor, clno, cnt 1/2, Btrb, timp, gr cassa e piatti, tamb rul, tri.
Unsigned and undated [c.1847 and later]
[DKKk; KTB 1027 (originally KTB 222)
According to a pencilled note in the part for the second bassoon (reading 'O. Swendsen Christiania') and the works with which this set of (incomplete) parts is bound, it must certainly date from the first performance in Norway of Bournonville's *Polka militaire.* The same parts were most probably also used for the two later restagings of this dance in Christiania on 9.6.1852 and 5.6.1865.

9.9.1847

Le Dieu et la bayadère, ou La Courtisane amoureuse (Brama og Bayadèren).

For the 1847 Copenhagen restaging of D.-F.-E.Auber's two-act opera-ballet (*see* 7.2.1841) Bournonville seems to have been responsible for creating and mounting at least parts of the choreography and the mise-en-scène. This is clear from notes in his diary reading as follows:

29.6.1847: 'Opskrivning paa Brama og Bayadèren'
8.9.: 'Prøve paa Brama Kl. 5'.

Moreover, according to the rehearsal book of H. C. J. Fredstrup, he directed 3 rehearsals of the dances in Auber's opera between 30.8. and 8.9.1847. Furthermore, Bournonville's extensive autographed choreographic notes in the 1847 répétiteur's copy for Auber's opera clearly indicate that he would have supervised its last stage rehearsal this year.

Finally, according to the same répétiteur's copy and Bournonville's autographed notes on its title page, this volume was especially prepared for his personal use in 1847. On the poster, however, the opera's dances are still credited to both P. Larcher and Bournonville, despite the former having died three months earlier on 15.6.1847.

The 1847 restaging of *Le Dieu et la bayadère* was given 5 performances, the last of which took place on 6.12.1848.

Musical sources:

The printed orchestral score and the set of parts for *Le Dieu et la bayadère* are now in DKKk (call nos. U 6 and KTA 301).

Répétiteur's copy. Ms. Copy (by E. Helsted). Brown ink. 1 vol. 62 pp. of which 4 are blank (32,8 × 25,2 cm)
A. 301/Brama og Bayaderen/61A/[...]/Brama og Bayaderen/Ballet=Partie/1847.
Unsigned and dated (on p. 1): '1847.'
[DKKk; MA ms 3064 (KTA 301 (2))]
According to the title page of this répétiteur's copy (which is Helsted's autograph throughout) it was clearly prepared as Bournonville's personal copy in 1847. It contains his autographed choreographic notes (written with brown ink) which describe the dances in Act I (score nos. 2 and 5) and Act II (score no. 10) and were written (according to his diary) on 29.6.1847. His other autographed choreographic numbers for Act I (score nos. 2–6) and Act II (score no. 10) seem to refer to the separate and only partially traced choreographic description that he wrote connection with his last complete staging in Copenhagen of Auber's opera (*see* 8.10.1871).

20.9.1847
The White Rose, or The Summer in Bretagne (Den hvide Rose eller Sommeren i Bretagne).
This one-act ballet represents the second work in Bournonville's projected series of four allegorical ballets, entitled *The Four Seasons, or Cupid's Journey* (*see* 16.6.1846). It symbolised the season of Summer. The plot was based on the popular medieval tradition in Bretagne every year to choose a Rose-bride, who was allowed to ransom her fiancé from military service. This theme had been used several times in balletic contexts during the 18th and early 19th centuries, for instance, by J.-G. Noverre in his *La Rosière de Salency* (1775) and in M. Gardel's ballet *La Rosière* (1783). Moreover, the same year Bournonville's ballet was premièred the Italian choreographer, G. Casati, had chosen this theme for a ballet, entitled *La Rosiera* (premièred in London, 22.7.1847). It was followed a few years later by the French choreographer, A. Saint-Léon's ballet of the same name (first performed at Lisbon's San Carlo on 13.10.1854).

In his ballet Bournonville focused on the central theme of the choice of the annual Rose-bride by inserting a large dance contest as the choreographic centrepiece. It was performed in the form of a *Pas de quatre* (score no. 13) danced by four women who aspire to the prize of 'The White Rose'.

According to the autographed orchestral score the ballet was divided into 15 numbers, composed and arranged by H. S. Paulli (nos. 1–14) and E. Helsted (the *Finale*, score no. 15). They incorporated several musical borrowings, which are identified as follows:

(1) In score no. 7 Paulli freely employed the same music in 6/8 time by E. L. Müller (originally part of M. Gardel's *La Rosière* at the Paris Opéra on 29.7.1783) which he also incorporated in his later score for the male *brisé* variation in the Act I *Pas d'Ecole* of Bournonville's two-act ballet-vaudeville *The Conservatoire, or A Proposal of Marriage through the Newspaper* (*see* 6.5.1849).
(2) In score no. 7 (the *Pas de deux*) Paulli reused much of the same music by J. Schneitzhoeffer and W. A. Mozart which L. Zinck had employed before him in Act I (score no. 5) of Bournonville's three-act pantomimic ballet *Don Quixote at Camacho's Wedding* (*see* 24.2.1837). In *The White Rose* this music accompanied a *Pas de deux*, performed by F. Hoppe (as *Antoine*) and C. Fjeldsted (as *Alix*). Moreover, in the mimic sections of Hoppe's and Fjeldsted's *Pas de deux* Paulli incorporated a French military song-march by an anonymous com-

poser. It had become widely known in Denmark as 'Pyrenæer=Marschen' after having been published in 1839 by A. P. Berggreen and with a Danish translation by P. A. Heiberg («Hvi sove Frankrigs Helte hen?» in *Sange til Skolebrug*, 4. hefte, no. 43). The original French text for this march was first published in Paris as part of the 1795 edition of *Calendrier republican*, while the march itself seems to have originated in the French army during the 1794 combat with Spain in the Pyrenees. Finally, this tune resurfaces two more times in *The White Rose* (score nos. 14 and 15) thereby becoming the ballet's leading musical motif.
(3) In score no. 12 Paulli interpolated C.-J. Rouget d'Isle's *Chant de guerre pour l'armée du Rhin* from 1792, also known as *La Marseillaise*. It resurfaces one more time in Helsted's *Finale* (score no. 15), but then in the minor key.
(4) In score no. 15 (the *Finale*) Helsted interpolated a march which Bournonville named 'Vaudeville March' in his musical instructions to this composer. This seems to indicates that this march was borrowed from a (not yet identified) French vaudeville.

Moreover, Paulli's music for the so-called 'Danse des battoirs' (score no. 4) was later reused in his score for Bournonville's three-act romantic ballet *The Kermesse in Brügge, or The Three Gifts* (*see* 4.4.1851), in which it was incorporated in a slightly extended version as a clog dance in Act I (score no. 3). Similarly, Paulli's music for the four solo variations in the so-called 'Pas des quatre rosières' (score no. 13) was interpolated in Act II (score no. 12) of *The Kermesse in Brüges, or The Three Gifts*, in which it accompanied a *Pas de quatre* performed at Mme van Everdingen's.

In his diary Bournonville noted about the creation and the 1847 première of *The White Rose or The Summer in Bretagne*:

30.8.1847: 'arbeidet med [H. S.] Paulli fra 5–7'
3.9.: 'Samling med Kmd. Larcher om min nÿe Ballet. – hjemme og componeret hele Aftnen'
4.9.: 'Composition'
5.9.: 'Begyndt Indstuderingen af Den hvide Rose og arbeidet fra 8 1/2 til 1 1/2, meget færdigt'
6.9.: 'Prøve fra 9 1/2 til 1 paa den hvide Rose [...] Kl 4 – Sammenkomst med Theatermaler og Maskinmester'
7.9.: 'Componeret fra 6 til 8 1/2 [...] Prøve fra 10 til 1 1/2'
8.9.: 'Prøve til 1 1/2'
9.9.: 'Prøve til 1 1/2 [...] componeret til 11 1/2'
10.9.: 'Prøve til Kl 1, indstuderet en stor Pas de quatre'
11.9.: 'Prøve til Kl 1 1/2'
13.9.: 'stor og vigtig Indstudering [...] atter Prøve Kl 5 med de fire Damer'
14.9.: 'Hele dagen Prøver'
15.9.: 'Prøver den hele Dag, – förste Aftenprøve paa 'Den hvide Rose''
16.9.: 'Dagen beskjæftiget med [...] Prøver'
17.9.: 'fuldstændig Prøve paa Theatret'
18.9.: 'som Igaar'
19.9: 'Generalprøve paa 'Den hvide Rose''
20.9.: 'Festforestilling i Anledning af Kongens Fødselsdag [...] min nÿe Ballet 'Den hvide Rose' der gik i alle Maader udmærket godt. – H. P. Holst var hjemme hos mig og opmuntrede mig efter dette Arbeide (som ikke en Sjæl udenfor Balletten har sagt mig et Ord for.)'.

Of the second and third performances he noted:

21.9.1847: 'Balletten om Aftnen kold og modvillig Optagelse'
26.9.: 'Balletten Den hvide Rose om Aftnen med Livlighed og Bifald'.

The ballet received 7 performances, the last of which was given on 16.1.1848.

Autograph sources:

Manuscript libretto. Ms. Autograph. Black ink. 1 vol. 7 pp. (22,4 × 17,5 cm)
Den hvide Rose eller Sommerglæderne./Ballet i En Akt af A Bournonville Musiken comp: og arrang: af Paulli
Unsigned and dated: 'Kbhvn d. 10.de Januar 1847.'
[DKKk; NKS 3285 4° 2 G–K]

Musical sources:

Musical draft. Ms. Copy (by Bournonville?). Brown ink. 4 pp. 23 × 30,3 cm)
[Untitled]/allegretto/[...]/Andante/[...]/allegretto/[..]/coda
Unsigned and undated [c.1847]
[DKKk; MA ms 2667]
This musical draft (perhaps written by Bournonville himself?) contains parts of M. E. Caraffa's music for the *Pas de quatre* (score no. 2) in Bournonville's allegorical divertissement *Acclaim to the Graces* (*see* 1.9.1829). Moreover, Bournonville's pencilled autographed notes (on p. 1) indicate the exact structure of Helsted's music for the *Finale* (score no. 15) in *The White Rose, or The Summer in Bretagne*. Finally it also includes a music theme used several times in this ballet. Together these facts seem to indicate that Bournonville originally intended to include Caraffa's music in *The White Rose*, but at a later stage abandoned this idea. Another indication which supports this theory is the existence of an (untitled) autographed score by E. Helsted, containing his complete orchestration of the exact same music (*see* the following entry).

Musical draft. Ms. Autograph (by E. Helsted). Brown ink. 4 pp. (25,5 × 29,8 cm with minor variants)
[Untitled]/[...]/Allegro/[...]/Andante/[...]/Allegretto/[...]/Coda
Unsigned and undated [c.1847]
[DKKk; MA ms 2715]
This orchestral score contains the same music as that contained in the previous musical draft. It seems to represent Helsted's first complete version for the *Finale* in *The White Rose*.

Orchestral score. Ms. Autograph (by H. S. Paulli). Brown ink. 1 vol. 230 pp. of which three are blank (26 × 37,3 cm)
278/Partituret/Paulli/til/Balletten/den hvide Rose
Unsigned and undated [1847]
[DKKk; C II, 119 (KTB 278)]
A pencilled note on p. 175 (reading 'hertil/see den nÿe Partitur. Pag: 195') refers to the later interpolation of parts of Paulli's music for score no. 13 in Act II of Bournonville's 1858 Stockholm version of *The Kermesse in Brüges, or The Three Gifts* (*see* 30.12.1858).

Répétiteur's copy. Ms. Autograph (by H. S. Paulli and E. Helsted). Brown and black ink. 1 vol. 84 pp. (32,8 × 24,4 cm)
B. 278/Den hvide Rose./Bournonville – Paulli/1847./35
Unsigned and dated (of the front cover): '1847.'
[DKKk; MA ms 2972 (KTB 278)]
This répétiteur's copy contains Bournonville's pencilled autographed notes, describing in fine detail the mime, the dramatic action, and the choreography throughout the ballet.

Parts. Ms. Copy. 30 vol.
3 vl I, 3 vl II, 2 vla, 3 vlc e cb, fl 1/2, ob 1/2, cl 1/2, fag 1/2, cor 1/2, tr 1/2, trb 1/2/3, tuba, timp, gr cassa, tri.
Unsigned and undated [1847]
[DKKk; KTB 278]

Printed sources:

Printed scenario. 1 vol. 4 pp. (19,9 × 17,1 cm)
Den hvide Rose/eller/Sommeren i Bretagne./Ballet i een Akt/af/A. Bournonville./Musikken componeret og arrangeret af H. Paulli.
Kjøbenhavn, J. H. Schubothe/Bianco Luno, 1847.
[DKKk; 17, – 174 8°]

13.10.1847
I Capuleti ed i Montecchi (Familierne Montecchi og Capulet).
Although Bournonville's name is not included on the poster for this 1847 Copenhagen restaging of V. Bellini's and N. Vaccai's melodrama in four parts (premièred in Bologna on 27.10.1832, and first performed in Copenhagen on 3.4. 1846) he seems to have been responsible at least for staging the dance scene in the opening chorus of Act II (score no. 6), entitled «Lieta notte» («Fryd og Jubel nu os tilsmile»). It was this year performed by a corps de ballet headed by two couples (danced by G. Brodersen, W. Funck, J. Rostock, and L. Stramboe). This theory is based on notes in Bournonville's diary reading as follows:

13.10.1847: 'Prøve paa Montecchi'
17.10.: 'Inspection ved Forestillingen af Montecchi'.

The dance scene in Act II seems originally to have been choreographed and mounted by P. Larcher, when *I Capuleti ed i Montecchi* was given its Copenhagen 1846 première.

Moreover, although Bournonville never included this work in any of his handwritten lists of his opera stagings (*see* Additional Sources), nor in the printed list of his works in his memoirs, *My Theatre Life* (pp. 409–410), clear historical evidence indicates that he worked on three other restagings in Copenhagen of *I Capuleti ed i Montecchi*:

(1) on 23.3.1849: The first production for which Bournonville is explicitly credited on the poster for the choreography of the dances in the first act.
(2) on 30.10.1857: On this day Bournonville included Bellini's and Vaccai's melodrama in a list of projected operas restagings which he was planning for the 1857–58 and 1858–59 seasons.
(3) on 8.2.1860: A production mounted with Bournonville's completely new mise-en-scène and choreography.

The 1847 restaging was given twice (the last time on 17.10. 1847), and *I Capuleti ed i Montecchi* reached a total of 13 performances during Bournonville's lifetime, the last of which was given on 30.4.1860 (Vaccai's fourth act had originally been premièred separately in Copenhagen on 24.1.1841 with the title *Giulietta e Romeo* and was played as such 10 times until 20.10.1847).

Musical sources:

Orchestral score. Ms. Copy. Black, brown, and red ink. 5 vol. Act I 318 pp. of which two are blank, Act II 160 pp. of which two are blank, Act III 176 pp. of which one is blank, Act IV 74 pp. (22,8 × 31,3 cm with minor variants)
Familierne/Montechi og Capuletti/I Act./[...]/II Act./[...]/III Act./[...]/4.de Act af Vaccai/Partitur
Unsigned and undated [c. early 1840s–1846]
[DKKk; C I, 213 (KTA 395)]
Apart from the score for Act IV (which is a Danish copy) this orchestral score is an Italian manuscript copy that includes N. C. L. Abrahams' Danish translation inserted (with brown ink) next to the original Italian text. Bellini's music for the dance scene in the opening chorus of Act II (score no. 6) is included in the second vol. on pp. 1–32.

Répétiteur's copy, Ms. Copy. Brown ink. 1 vol. 8 pp. (33,8 × 25,5 cm)
Repetiteur=Partie/til/Romeo og Giulietta/Opera af Bellini/1.ste Act Tacet/[...]/Anden Act/No. 6 Chor og Dands
Unsigned and undated [1846]
[DKKk; MA ms 2914 (2) (KTA 395 (1))]

According to the other works bound together with this répétiteur's copy (pp. 19–26) it clearly must date from the first complete production of Bellini's and Vaccai's melodrama in Copenhagen on 3.4.1846. It contains Bournonville's autographed choreographic notes (written with brown ink) which most probably were made from his later restaging of *I Capuleti ed i Montecchi* on 23.3.1849.

Parts. Ms. Copy. 36 + 1 vol.
4 vl I, 3 vl II, 2 vla, 4 vlc e cb, fl 1/2, ob 1/2, cl 1/2, fag 1/2, cor 1/2/3/4, tr 1/2, trb 1/2/3, timp, gr cassa, piatti, tri, arpa 1/2. On stage: tr. 88 vocal parts.
Unsigned and undated [c.1846]
[DKKk; KTA 395
This set of part dates from the first complete performance in Copenhagen of Bellini's and Vaccai's melodrama on 3.4.1846 and was used for all later restagings of this work until 1860.

20.10.1847

Flower Dance (Blomsterdands) performed by A. Nielsen, P. Fredstrup, and J. Rostock.

This dance for three women was choreographed for a special charity performance given for the German singer, W. Schrøder-Devrient, who in the autumn of 1847 had given a series of guest performances at Copenhagen's Royal Theatre. Bournonville had long been an ardent admirer of her vocal art and wanted to contribute to her charity performance with this new dance.

According to the rehearsal book of H. C. J. Fredstrup, only one rehearsal was held of it on 19.19.1847. This seems to indicate that the dance was a somewhat hastily arranged work, probably representing a choreographic and musical adaptation of excerpts of his and H. S. Paulli's earlier divertissement, named *Tableau with Dance* (*see* 12.10.1846). In that work a similar dance for three women (performed by A. Nielsen, P. Fredstrup and P. Funck) was included. It therefore seems likely that Rostock took over the part of P. Funck in this new version. This theory is furthermore supported by the fact that Paulli's original orchestral score for *Tableau with Dance* also includes the title 'Partituur til Blomsterdandsen'. The musical sources for that work are now in DKKk (call nos. C II, 119, and KTB 211).

The *Flower Dance* received 6 performances, the last of which was given on 13.4.1848.

22.10.1847

La Muette de Portici (Den Stumme i Portici).

This performance represents Bournonville's first complete staging of both the dances and the mime in D.-F.- E. Auber's five-act opera (*see* 23.9.1834). For the production the dancer, C. Fjeldsted, had taken over the mimic rôle of *Fenella*, which at the 1830 Copenhagen première of *La Muette de Portici* had been performed by the actress, J. L. Heiberg. In his diary Bournonville noted about the production:

1.10.1847: 'indstuderet den Stumme til [C.] Fjeldsted'
4.10.: 'Prøve paa den Stumme'
6.10.: 'Prøve og Dands (Den Stumme)'
11.10.: 'Prøve paa Tarentellen i den Stumme'
12.10.: 'Prøve paa den Stumme'
14.10.: 'Prøve paa den Stumme med [R. C.] Faaborg'
15.10., 16.10., and 18.10.: 'Prøve paa den Stumme'
19.10.: 'Mangfoldige Prøver'
20.10.: 'Prøve med Fjeldsted'

21.10.: 'Kl 10 Prøve paa Den Stumme indtil Kl. 1½ '
22.10.: 'dandset i Den Stumme, min Dands gik ret godt. Operaen gjorde megen Lykke'.

During the following years Bournonville worked on, or was otherwise involved in, 6 different restagings of Auber's opera as follows:

(1) on 13.10.1850: A restaging at Copenhagen's Royal Theatre with L. Stramboe playing *Fenella* for the first time in Bournonville's instruction.
(2) on 30.10.1857: A projected restaging in Copenhagen.
(3) on 18.1.1862: The first staging in which Bournonville was responsible for the opera's complete mise-en-scène, mounted at Stockholm's Royal Theatre, Operahuset.
(4) on 12.2.1862: A restaging in Copenhagen with the opera's dances partially rechoreographed and rehearsed by Bournonville in September 1861, while the actual staging was carried out by L. Gade.
(5) on 2.10.1865: A restaging in Copenhagen for which Bournonville gave personal mime-instructions to the dancer, J. Petersen, who played *Fenella* for the first time.
(6) on 2.9.1873: Bournonville's last staging of the complete opera in Copenhagen, then performed with a new, incorporated *Pas de deux* in Act I (to music by V. C. Holm), and with a completely revised mise-en-scène except for that of Act IV (which remained unchanged from the 1865 staging).

The 1847 production of *La Muette de Portici* was given 10 performances, the last on 28.12.1848.

Musical sources:

Printed orchestral score with manuscript insertions. 2 vol. Act I–II 384 pp. of which four are blank, Act III–V 353 pp. of which three are blank (31,7 × 25,3 with several variants)
LA MUETTE DE PORTICI/Opéra en 5 actes
Paris, E. Troupenas, pl. no. 240 [1828]
[DKKkt, KTA 273
This printed orchestral score contains several later manuscript insertions. It was used for all performances of Auber's opera in Copenhagen from its première there on 22.5.1830 and throughout Bournonville's lifetime. A note written with red crayon on p. 126 in the first volume (reading: 'Indlagt Dandse Nummer') clearly indicates the exact place in Act I where M. E. Caraffa's *Pas de deux* was incorporated on 23.9.1834. Another note written on the reverse of the front cover in the same volume (reading 'Dansen 316 bruges i Den Stumme') refers to the much later incorporation of V. C. Holm's new *Pas de deux* in the exact same place of the opera (*see* 2.9.1873).

Répétiteur's copy. Ms. Copy (by E. Helsted). Black ink. 1 vol. 72 pp. of which two are blank (32,7 × 24,3 cm)
A. 273/4/Den Stumme i Porticie [*sic*]/60A/[...]/Den Stumme./Ballet=Partie./1847.
Unsigned and dated (on the title page): '1847.'
[DKKk; MA ms 3056 (KTA 273 (2))
This répétiteur's copy (which is Helsted's autograph throughout) was, according to the title page, prepared in 1847 as Bournonville's personal copy. Moreover, it contains his autographed choreographic numbers for the *Guarache* in Act I, score no. 4 ('1–15', written with brown ink), and the *Tarantella* in Act III, score no. 11 ('1–18', written with black ink). They seem to refer to his separate (not yet traced) choreographic notations of these dances, which he most probably wrote in connection with his last restaging of Auber's opera in Copenhagen on 2.9.1873. Furthermore, a later insertion (on pp. 69–72) contains the music for the *Marche* performed during the Act IV chorus, entitled «Honneur – honneur et gloire» (score no. 16). It was most probably added to this volume in connection with the 1873 restaging. Finally, the volume also includes M. E. Caraffa's music for the *Pas de deux* (pp. 4-11) which Bournonville incorporated in Act I of this opera on 23.9.1834.

Parts. Ms. Copy. 38 + 8 vol.
4 vl I, 4 vl II, 2 vla, 4 vlc e cb, fl picc, fl 1/2, ob 1/2, cl 1/2, fag 1/2, cor 1/2/3/4, tr 1/2, trb 1/2/3, tuba, timp, gr cassa, piatti, tri, gong. On stage: fl, cl 1/2, fag 1/2, cor 1/2, gr cassa. 71 vocal parts.
Unsigned and undated [1830]
[DKKk; KTA 273
This set of parts dates from the Copenhagen première of *La Muette de Portici* on 22.5.1830 and was used for all later restagings of it at the Royal Theatre during Bournonville's lifetime.

The orchestral score and the set of parts to M. E. Caraffa's music for the incorporated *Pas de deux* in Act I of *La Muette de Portici* (*see* 23.9. 1834) are now in DKKk (call nos. MA ms 2603, and KTB 209), while the original répétiteur's copy for it is preserved there with the call no. MA ms 2700 (KTB 209).

7.12.1847

Le Maçon (Muurmesteren).
Although Bournonville's name is not included on the poster for the 1847 Copenhagen restaging of D.-F.-E. Auber's three-act comic opera (premièred at l'Opéra Comique in Paris on 3.5.1825, and first performed in Copenhagen on 1.9.1827) he clearly seems to have been responsible for mounting at least parts of this production. This is clear from notes in his diary reading:

2.12. and 3.12.1847: 'Prøve paa Muurmesteren'
7.12.: 'Prøve paa nogle Dandse til Muurmesteren […] Inspiceret ved Forestillingen af Muurmesteren'.

Moreover, in the printed survey of his works in his memoirs *My Theatre Life* (pp. 409–410) Auber's opera is also included. According to a later répétiteur's copy, dating from L. Gade's restaging of *Le Maçon* on 23.4.1880 (now in DKKk, call no. MA ms 2612 (KTA 247)), the opera included a dance scene that was performed during the opening chorus of Act II (score no. 5), entitled «Un instant mes soeurs oublions nos peines». Auber's opera was restaged for a second and last time by Bournonville on 5.12.1868, but that year with his own, partially revised mise-en-scène and choreography.

The 1847 production received 21 performances, the last of which was given on 28.9.1858.

Musical sources:

Printed orchestral score. 1 vol. 326 pp. of which two are blank (32,6 × 25 cm)
Muurmesteren./Partitur/[…]/LE MAÇON/Opéra Comique en trois Actes
Paris, I. Pleyel & Fils, pl. no. 1724 [1825]
[DKKk; U 6 (KTA 247)
The music for the dance scene in Act II (score no. 5) is included on pp. 163–172. A pencilled metronome marking (p. 163) indicates the exact tempo of this dance with a crochet equivalent to '80'.

No répétiteur's copy dating from the 1847 restaging of *Le Maçon* has yet been traced.

Parts. Ms. Copy. 30 vol.
5 vl I, 4 vl II, 2 vla, 4 vlc e cb, fl 1/2, ob 1/2, cl 1/2, fag 1/2, cor 1/2, tr 1/2, timp, gr cassa, piatti, arpa. 55 vocal parts.
Unsigned and undated [1827]
[DKKk; KTA 247
This set of parts was used for all performances of Auber's opera in Copenhagen from its 1827 Danish première (with the dances then probably choreographed by P. Larcher) and throughout Bournonville's lifetime.

1848

6.1.1848

Little Kirsten (Liden Kirsten).
For the 1846 world première of I. P. E. Hartmann's one-act singspiel (with text by H. C. Andersen) the dances were all choreographed by P. Larcher. However, as a result of Larcher's sudden death in 1847, Bournonville appears to have taken over the responsibility for mounting these dances when *Little Kirsten* was restaged in 1848. This theory is supported by notes in his diary that read as follows:

28.12.1847: 'Prøve paa Liden Kirsten'
6.1.1848: 'Prøve paa Liden Kirsten […] hørt Liden Kirsten med sand Fornøielse'.

According to Hartmann's autographed orchestral score, *Little Kirsten* was at its première divided into 11 numbers and included the following 6 dances:

(1) A *Peasant Dance (Bondedands)* in score no. 2, performed by the corps de ballet.
(2) An (unnamed) *Dance scene* in score no. 6, performed during the chorus entitled «Natten lang, Dands og Sang til Musik og Bægerklang».
(3–5) Three dances in score no. 9, consisting of a *Processional March (Optog)*, a *Torch Dance (Fakkeldands)*, and a *Minuet (Menuet)*, performed by the corps de ballet during the chorus «Hil være vor Indgang i Riddersal». Most of Hartmann's music for the *Processional March* was many years later incorporated by himself in his score for Act II (score no. 14) of Bournonville's four-act national historical ballet *Arcona* (*see* 7.5.1875).
(6) A *Circle Dance (Kredsdands)*, performed by the entire cast during the final movement of score no. 12 (*Tempo di Menuetto*).

On 30.10.1857 Bournonville included *Little Kirsten* in a list of projected opera restagings which he planned on that day for the 1857–58 and 1858–59 seasons. That project was carried out on 29.10.1858, when Hartmann's singspiel was restaged in a new, revised two-act version, which was listed as an opera and mounted with Bournonville's own complete mise-en-scène and choreography. *Little Kirsten* was staged by him for the third and last time on 24.4.1869, but then apparently with minor choreographic changes.

The 1848 restaging received 6 performances, the last of which was given on 15.2.1850.

Musical sources:

Orchestral score. Ms. Autograph (by I. P. E. Hartmann) and copy. 1 vol. Black, brown, and red ink. 218 pp. of which three are blank (33,2 × 25,3 cm)
[Untitled]/Indledning
Signed and dated (p. 21): 'I:P:E:Hartmann/28 Decbr 1846.', (p. 46) '25/4 45.', (p. 218) 'I:P:E:Hartmann/d: 10 Novbr: 1845/Op: 44.'
[DKKk; C II, 7 c (I. P. E. Hartmanns samling) (KTA 396)
This orchestral score contains Hartmann's music for score nos. 7–12 (since 29.10.1858 = Act II). It also includes several later insertions and Hartmann's autographed notes (written with red ink) indicating his changes in the music of score no. 7 (made for the 1848 restaging), and his alterations in 1858 for the final two-act revised version of *Little Kirsten*. Hartmann's earliest autographed orchestral score containing the music of score nos. 1–6 (in 1858 = Act I) is now in the (not yet accessible) archive of the Copenhagen music publisher, W. Hansen, while a later two-volume manuscript copy of his

complete score (most probably dating from the restaging of *Little Kirsten* on 14.5.1895) is now in DKKk (call no. CII, 113 (KTA 396)).

Répétiteur's copy. Ms. Copy. Black ink. 1 vol. 34 pp. (33,1 × 25,5 cm)
Liden Kirsten./71B/[…]/Repetiteur=Partie/til/Liden Kirsten
Unsigned and undated [1846]
[DKKk; MA ms 3085 (KTA 396 (1))
This répétiteur's copy contains the complete music for the dances in score nos. 2, 6, 9, and 12. Moreover, it includes Bournonville's pencilled autographed notes and his other choreographic notes (written with brown ink) which describe, in fine detail, the dances performed in score no. 9. They were most probably written for his restaging of *Little Kirsten* on 29.10.1858. Finally, his autographed choreographic numbers and other notes are written (with black ink) in the music for score nos. 2 ('1–5') and 9 ('1–11'). They seem to refer to a later (not yet traced) notation of these dances, which he most probably wrote in connection with his third and last restaging of *Little Kirsten* on 24.4.1869.

Parts. Ms. Copy. 38 vol.
5 vl I, 5 vl II, 3 vla, 6 vlc e cb, fl picc, fl 1/2, ob 1/2, cl 1/2, fag 1/2, cor 1/2/3, tr 1/2, trb 1/2/3, timp, arpa. 31 vocal parts.
Unsigned and undated [1846]
[DKKk; KTA 396
This set of parts was used for all performances in Copenhagen of *Little Kirsten* since its 1846 première there and throughout Bournonville's lifetime.

18.1.1848
Robert le Diable (Robert af Normandiet).
This restaging of G. Meyerbeer's five-act opera represents the first time it was mounted with Bournonville solely responsible for the staging of the dance scenes and divertissements in Acts II and III. They included four numbers as follows:

(1) A *Choeur dansé* (score no. 7) in Act II.
(2) An incorporated *Pas de deux* in Act II which replaced F. Taglioni's and Meyerbeer's original *Pas de cinq* divertissement in that act (*see* 5.12.1841).
(3) The so-called 'Ballet of the Nuns' in Act III (score no. 16).
(4) A *Choeur dansé* in the Finale of Act III.

The choreography of the 'Ballet of the Nuns' (originally mounted in Copenhagen by P. Larcher on 28.10.1833) was, according to Bournonville's autographed pencilled notes in the répétiteur's copy, revised by him especially for this production. This is clear from his note (on p. 5) reading 'dansée par L: F. James -'. This proves beyond doubt that his 1848 production was based on F. Taglioni's original Paris Opéra version that Bournonville had seen performed by the French ballerina, L. Fitzjames (who played the *Abbess Hélène*), during his visits to the French capital in 1841 and 1847. In his diary Bournonville noted about the 1848 Copenhagen production:

30.12.1847, 4.1., 5.1., and 6.1.1848: 'Prøve paa Robert'
7.1.: 'Prøve paa Robert fra 10 til 2 1/2'
17.1.: 'Prøve med Øvelse paa Robert'
18.1.: 'Dands i Robert. Operaen gik særdeles godt. […] Min Pas de deux gjorde complet furore'.

The 1848 restaging of *Robert le Diable* received 13 performances, the last of which was given on 29.9.1864 (Act III was performed separately once on 12.1.1849).

Musical sources:

Printed orchestral score. 5 vol. Act I 220 pp. of which two are blank, Act II 152 pp. of which one is blank, Act III 238 pp. of which two are blank, 170 pp. of which two are blank, Act V 109 pp. of which one is blank (32 × 25 cm with minor variants)
ROBERT LE DIABLE/Opéra en 5 Actes
Paris, M. Schlesinger, pl. no. 1155 [1831]
[DKKk; U 6 (KTA 303)
This printed orchestral score was used for all performances of *Robert le Diable* in Copenhagen from its 1833 première there and throughout Bournonville's lifetime. It includes several conductor's notes and metronome markings (written with black ink) indicating the exact tempi of the three solo variations performed by the *Abbess Hélène* in the Act III divertissement (score no. 16), and the tempo of the final *Choeur dansé* in the same act.

Répétiteur's copy. Ms. Copy. Brown ink. 1 vol. 24 pp. (32,5 × 25,5 cm with minor variants)
Repetiteur Partie af/Robert af Normandiet/1848–/51A/A303/Repetiteur Parti/til/Robert fra Normandiet/af Meyerbeer/[…]/2.den Akt/[…]/3.die Akt
Unsigned and dated (on the front cover): '1848. -'
[DKKk; MA ms 3065 (KTA 303 (1))
According to the style and the paper of the volume this répétiteur's copy clearly dates from the 1833 Copenhagen première of *Robert le Diable*, but was according to the pencilled date on the front cover reused by Bournonville for his 1848 restaging of Meyerbeer's opera. It includes the complete music for the Act II *Choeur dansé* (score no. 7), the divertissement, and the *Choeur dansé* in Act III (score no. 16). Moreover, Bournonville's choreographic notes (written with brown ink) are included for the Act II *Choeur dansé*, while his pencilled notes describe the choreography in the Act III divertissement. Together, these notes were most probably written in connection with the 1848 restaging, while his other pencilled autographed choreographic numbers for the Act III divertissement ('1–16', and '1–9') seem to refer to a later (not yet identified) separate choreographic notation of this ballet (perhaps written for Bournonville's later staging of this divertissement at Vienna's Kärnthnerthor Theatre on 23.7.1855).

Parts. Ms. Copy. 41 + 13 vol.
4 vl I, 4 vl II, 2 vla, 4 vlc e cb, fl picc, fl 1/2, ob 1/2, cor ingl, cl 1/2, fag 1/2, cor 1/2/3/4, tr 1/2/3/4, trb 1/2/3, tuba, timp, gr cassa, piatti, tri e gong, arpa. On stage: conductor's part, stage manager's part, fl, ob, cor 1/2/3, trb 1/2/3, gr cassa, piatti, tri e gong. 82 vocal parts.
Unsigned and undated [1833]
[DKKk; KTA 303
This set of parts was used for all performances in Copenhagen of *Robert le Diable* since its 1833 première there and throughout Bournonville's lifetime.

12.2.1848
The teaching of the rôle of *Teresina* in *Napoli or The Fisherman and His Bride (Napoli eller Fiskeren og hans Brud)* to the Swedish ballerina, J. G. Gillberg (the Court Theatre).
Towards the end of Bournonville's 18-year contract with Copenhagen's Royal Theatre in 1848 he approached the theatre management of Stockholm's Royal Theatre in order to explore the possibilities for a future engagement there. As part of this plan he taught the rôle of *Teresina* in his three-act romantic ballet *Napoli or The Fisherman and His Bride* (*see* 29.3. 1842) to the Swedish ballerina, J. G. Gillberg. Gillberg had come to Copenhagen to take private dance lessons with Bournonville during the winter and early spring of 1848. The fact that Bournonville decided to teach her the part of

Teresina also indicates that he was planning to mount this ballet as the first work in Stockholm should his project for an engagement there have been carried out.

According to a much later letter (written to the Royal Theatre in Stockholm on 15.6.1857, now in SSdt) Bournonville made a second attempt to persuade the theatre management there to mount this ballet, but again with a negative result.

In his diary he noted about the teaching of the rôle of *Teresina* to Gillberg, which he completed during only 5 rehearsals:

25.1.1848: 'begyndt at lære [J. G.] Gillberg, – Teresina'
2.2.: 'Lection [...] for Gillberg'
8.2.: 'Paa Hoftheatret Kl 8 1/2 indstuderet paa Napoli'
11.2.: 'Indstudering til Gillberg'
12.2.: 'Lection, Gillberg fuldendt Indstuderingen af Theresina [*sic*]'.

Napoli or The Fisherman and His Bride was never mounted in Stockholm during Bournonville's lifetime.

21.2.1848
A Quadrille (En Quadrille).
In the winter of 1847–48 Bournonville gave a series of private dance lessons which were concluded with a presentation by his pupils. It took place at the residence of the minister, Professor H. N. Clausen, in Nørregade 243, and a *Quadrille* (choreographed especially for this occasion) was performed. In his diary Bournonville noted about the dance:

9.2.1848: 'Information hos [H. N.] Claussens, tilbragt en behagelig Aften componeret det meste af en Quadrille'
18.2.: 'Information for Chr. Bruuns: Quadrillen færdig, behagelig Aften'
21.2.: 'Lection den sidste hos Claussens. Helene og Augusta vare med. Jeg havde componeret en Quadrille. Vi tilbragte en ȳndig Aften'.

No autographed and/or musical sources for the *Quadrille* have yet been found. It is not possible to identify the dance any further.

7.3.1848
Tarentella for A Students' Carnival (Tarentella til Studenternes Karneval) (the Casino Theatre, mindre sal).
For this masked ball in 'romersk Stiil' (arranged by the students' association at Copenhagen's University, named *Studenterforeningen*), Bournonville choreographed a *Tarentella* that is described in his diary as follows:

5.3. and 6.3.1848: 'Dandset med Studenterne fra 1–3'
7.3.: 'Prøve i Casino med Studenterne [...] Studenternes Carneval i Casinos lille Sal og øvrige Locale. Det hele var paa Romersk, med Promenade i Corsoen (Bazaren), Confetti Optog til Palazzo Casino. Modtagelse hos Prindsen af Casino. Confetti. Væddeløb. Moccoli. – Dands af Masker. Sang. Scener. politiske Taler. Gemȳtlig Spøg, morsomme Charakterer. Hoffets Orchester, min Tarentella gjorde stormende Lȳkke og dandsedes to Gange'.

No autographed and/or musical sources for the *Tarentella* have yet been found. It is not possible to identify the dance any further.

10.3.1848
Soldier and Peasant (Soldat og Bonde).
This performance represents Bournonville's first restaging in Copenhagen of his one-act pantomimic idyll *Soldier and Peasant* (*see* 13.10.1829). It was this year performed with himself and C. Fjeldsted in the leading rôles as *Victor* and *Lise*, but seems otherwise to have been given with only minor if any changes from the original 1829 version. The staging, which was the first in a series of farewell performances mounted for Bournonville's retirement as a dancer at the end of the 1847–48 season, is described in his diary as follows:

21.2., 23.2., and 25.2.1848: 'Prøve paa Soldat og Bonde'
6.3.: 'Prøve fra 10 til 1 paa Soldat og Bonde'
9.3.: 'Prøve paa Soldat og Bonde'
10.3.: 'Dandset min første Afskedsforestilling – Soldat og Bonde og Faust der begge gik udmærket godt og optoges med særdeles Bifald'.

11.3.1848
The Mulatto (Mulatten).
According to his diary Bournonville directed two stage rehearsals (on 9.3. and 10.3.1848) in preparation for this, the last restaging during his lifetime of H. C. Andersen's five-act romantic drama (premièred on 3.2.1840). It was performed to a score by J. F. Fröhlich that included a *Contredands* in Act IV.

The Mulatto is not mentioned in Bournonville's handwritten lists of his stagings of operas and plays (*see* Additional Sources), nor in the printed list of his works in his memoirs *My Theatre Life* (p. 408). This seems to indicate that the choreography of the Act IV *Contredands* (originally mounted by P. Larcher?) was restaged this year with only minor if any changes.

Bournonville did not attend the first performance because of his other commitments at a charity concert given at the Court Theatre on the same evening. The 1848 restaging of *The Mulatto* was given only once.

Musical sources:

Orchestral score. Ms. Autograph (by J. F. Fröhlich). Black ink. 1 vol. 8 pp. of which one is blank (27,1 × 37,4 cm)
J. F. FRÖHLICH/CONTREDANS/TIL MULATTEN/PART./[...]/ Contredands til Mulatten af JFFröhlich.
Signed (on p. 1) 'JFFröhlich' and dated (on p. 7): 'Sept. 1839.'
[DKKk; C II, 5 (J. F. Fröhlichs samling) (KTB 254)

Orchestral score. Ms. Copy. Brown ink. 1 vol. 20 pp. of which one is blank (32 × 27,9 cm)
Mulatten/254/[...]/Contredands til 'Mulatten' af Fröhlich
Unsigned and undated [c.1848]
[DKKk; C II, 107 (KTB 254)
This manuscript copy is musically completely identical with Fröhlich's original autographed score for *The Mulatto* and seems (according to the style of the manuscript) to have been made for the 1848 restaging.

Répétiteur's copy. Ms. Copy. Black ink. 1 vol. 4 pp. (32,5 × 25,2 cm)
Repetiteur Partie/til Mulatten./Contredands
Unsigned and undated [1840]
[DKKk; MA ms 2902 (13) (KTB 254)
According to the other works with which this répétiteur's copy is bound (pp. 63–66) it clearly must date from the 1840 première of *The Mulatto*.

Parts. Ms. Copy. 26 vol.
2 vl I, 2 vl II, vla, 2 vlc e cb, fl 1/2, ob 1/2, cl 1/2, fag 1/2, cor 1/2/
3, tr 1/2, trb 1/2/3, timp, gr cassa, tri.
Unsigned and undated [1840]
[DKKk; KTB 254

11.3.1848
The organisation of a concert for the charity health organisation 'Hygæa' (the Court Theatre).

In his diary Bournonville noted about his organisation of this concert given for the charity health association 'Hygæa' (of which he was a leading board member between 1846 to 1852):

10.2.1848: 'Visit hos [H. W.] Ernst og hört nogle fortreffelige Quartetter'
26.2.: 'begyndt at movere mig om Hygæas Concert'
27.2.: 'Skrevet til [J. G.] Levetzau om Hygæa'
1.3.: 'Möde i Hygæa'
2.3.: 'Forberedelser til Hygæas forestaaende Concert'
4.3.: 'Hygæas Forberedelser'
8.3. and 9.3.: 'Forebereldelser til Hygæa'
11.3.: 'Hele dagen beskjæftiget med Hygæas Concert [...] om Aftnen Concert paa Hoftheatret par Ernst [...] Alt gik godt og Huset var fuldt'.

The concert consisted mainly of pieces composed and played by the Moravian-born violinist, H. W. Ernst.

23.3.1848
Federigo.

In his handwritten list of his mises-en-scène of operas and dramas, written c.1851 (*see* Additional Sources), Bournonville listed the 1848 première of H. Rung's and H. Hertz's three-act singspiel erroneously under the year of 1849. It included no dances, which indicates that Bournonville here worked exclusively on the mise-en-scène. In his diary he noted of his involvement:

5.3.1848: 'Syngeskole paa Federigo'
14.3.: 'Arrangement paa Federigo'
16.3.: 'Prøve paa Federigo'
18.3.: 'marqueret Prøve paa Federigo'
20.3. and 21.3.: 'Prøve paa Federigo'
22.3.: 'Lÿs=Prøve paa Federigo'
23.3.: 'Federigo første Forestilling, gik i det Hele meget godt, men ifølge Omstændighederne tomt Huus'.

Of two later performances the same year he stated:

5.11.1848: 'Prøve (meget kjedelig) paa Federigo'
10.11.: 'overværet Federigo en meget kjedsommelig og tÿndt besøgt Forestilling'.

Federigo received only 4 performances, the last of which was given on 18.11.1848.

Musical sources:

Orchestral score. Ms. Autograph (by H. Rung). Black and red ink. 3 vol. Act I 216 pp. of which one is blank, Act II 214 pp., Act III 158 pp. (34 × 29 cm)
Federigo./Förste Act./I./[...]/Federigo/Syngestykke/i/tre Acter/af/Henrik Hertz/componeret/af/H: Rung/[...]/Anden Act./[...]/Tredie Act.
Signed and dated (vol. 3, p. 158): 'H. Rung September 1847.
[DKKk; C II, 119k (KTA 400)

No répétiteur's copy for *Federigo* has yet been traced.

Parts. Ms. Copy. 34 vol.
3 vl I, 3 vl II, 2 vla, 3 vlc e cb, fl picc, fl 1/2, ob 1/2, cl 1/2, fag 1/2, cor 1/2/3/4, tr 1/2, trb 1/2/3, timp, gong, glock, guit, arpa. 54 vocal parts.
Unsigned and undated [1848]
[DKKk; KTA 400

26.3.1848
The Lucky Wheel or The Last Number-Lottery Office (Lykkens Hjul eller Den sidste Tallotteri=Collecteur).

For the première of H. P. Holst's five-act romantic comedy Bournonville choreographed a series of dances, which were set to music by H. Rung and H. C. Lumbye, although the former is given credit on the poster for having 'composed and arranged' (*comp. og arrangeret*) the music for this work. This included several musical borrowings from popular Spanish dance tunes and French vaudeville tunes. Moreover, in Act I (score no. 8) Rung incorporated the *Minuet (Menuet)* from Act V of F. Kuhlau's and J. L. Heiberg's five-act national fairy-play *The Elves' Hill* (premièred at Copenhagen's Royal Theatre on 6.11.1828). Lumbye's contribution with a (not yet identified) *Polka* was inserted at the beginning of Act III.

In his diary Bournonville noted about the rehearsals and the poor reception of Holst's comedy:

6.1.1848: 'Arbeidet med [H.] Rung paa [H. P.] Holsts Stÿkke'
9.1.: 'Holst besøgt mig to Gange, arbeidet med Rung paa en Polka'
14.1.: 'Besøg af Holst, Ærinde til [H. C.] Lumbÿe'
15.1.: 'smuk Polka af Lumbÿe'
18.2.: 'Componeret til Holsts Stÿkke [...] Indstudering af den nÿ Dands'
19.2.: 'Repetition paa den nÿe Dands'
23.3.: 'Prøve kl. 10 og Kl. 11 paa Holsts Stÿkke. Det gaaer ikke meget godt'
24.3. and 25.3.: 'Prøve paa Lykkens Hjul'
26.3.: 'Ned paa Theatret hvor Alt var udsolgt, men hvor desværre tonen ikke var for Stÿkket. – Det gik ellers meget godt [...] i i det Hele blev det godt spillet, men Bifaldet ledsagedes altid med Hyssen og det der nærmede sig mod Slutningen til en Kamp, som jeg ikke bivaanede'.

The Lucky Wheel or The Last Number-Lottery Office received only one performance.

Musical sources:

Orchestral score. Ms. Autograph (by H. Rung). Black, brown, and red ink. 1 vol. 122 pp. (26,8 × 37,5 cm with minor variants)
Lykkens Hjul./[...]/Lykkens Hjul/eller/Den sidste Tallotterie=Collecteur/af/H: P: Holst./Musiken componeret og arrangeret/af/H. Rung.
Signed and dated (p. 122): 'H: Rung/Januar 1848.'
[DKKk; C II, 119k (KTA 409)
A pencilled note on p. 81 (reading 'begynder med Musik af Lumbÿe') indicates the exact place where Lumbÿe's *Polka* was performed. The music for this dance, however, is not included in the orchestral score, nor in the répétiteur's copy, nor in the parts.

Répétiteur's copy. Ms. Copy. Brown ink. 4 pp. of which one is blank (33,6 × 24,7 cm)
Repetiteur=Partie/til/3.die Act af Lykkens Hjul
Unsigned and undated [1848]
[DKKk; MA ms 2774 (KTA 409)
This répétiteur's copy contains only the music for Act III, score no. 15.

Parts. Ms. Copy. 32 + 1 vol.
3 vl I, 3 vl II, 2 vla, 3 vlc e cb, fl 1/2, ob 1/2, cl 1/2, fag 1/2, cor 1/2/ 3/4, tr 1/2, trb 1/2/3, timp, gr cassa e piatti, guit, arpa. On stage: cor. 54 vocal parts.
Unsigned and undated [1848]
[DKKk; KTA 409

3.4.1848

Il Dissoluto Punito, ossia il Don Giovanni (Don Juan).
In his diary Bournonville noted on this day about his involvement in the 1848 restaging of W. A. Mozart's two-act opera from 1787 (first performed in Copenhagen on 5.5.1807):

'Prøve paa Dandsen til Don Juan'.

The fact that Bournonville did not include Mozart's opera in any of his handwritten lists of his opera stagings (*see* Additional Sources), but mentions it in the much later printed survey of his works in his memoirs *My Theatre Life* (pp. 409– 410), seems to indicate that the *Minuet (Menuetto)* in the Act I finale (scene 20) was mounted in 1848 without any changes from the previous staging of the opera on 23.2.1845 (that year most probably with choreography by P. Larcher).

Five years later Bournonville also directed a stage rehearsal of the *Minuet* on 5.2.1853 prior to a restaging of Mozart's opera on the following day. Moreover, on 30.10.1857 he included *Don Juan* in a list of projected opera restagings which he was planning on that day for the 1857–58 season. This project was carried out on 14.3.1858 when the opera was mounted for the first time with Bournonville's own, original mise-en-scène. *Don Juan* was restaged for a second and last time by Bournonville on 27.1.1870.

The 1848 production of *Don Juan* received 25 performances, the last of which was given on 5.5.1857.

Musical sources:

No orchestral score and répétiteur's copy dating from the 1848 Copenhagen restaging of *Don Juan* have yet been traced.

Parts. Ms. Copy. 31 + 30 vol.
5 vl I, 4 vl II, 2 vla, 5 vlc e cb, fl 1/2, ob 1/2, cl 1/2, fag 1/2, cor 1/2, tr, trb 1/2/3, timp. On stage: 5 vl I, 2 vl II, 2 vla, vlc, 4 cb, 2 ob I, 2 ob II, cl 1/2, fag 1/2, 2 cor I, 2 cor II, trb 1/2/3, 1 unspecified part. 135 (partially printed) vocal parts.
Unsigned and undated [c.1807 and later]
[DKKk; KTA 155
This set of parts dates from the Copenhagen première of *Don Juan* on 5.5.1807, but was later supplied with new (partially printed) parts. It was used for all performances of Mozart's opera in Copenhagen during Bournonville's lifetime.

8.4.1848

Pas de trois (uncredited) performed by S. Lund, P. Fredstrup, and J. Rostock.
This (uncredited) dance is most probably identical with the *Pas de trois* in Act I (score no. 5) of Bournonville's 1829 Copenhagen version of J. Aumer's and F. Hérold's three-act pantomimic ballet *La Somnambule, ou l'Arrivée d'un nouveau seigneur* (*see* 21.9.1829). This theory is supported by the fact that this dance had been performed within *La Somnambule* by the same three dancers only four months earlier on 3.12.1847. Moreover, according to the rehearsal book of H.

C. J. Fredstrup, a separate rehearsal of the 'Pas de trois af Søvngjængersken' was held on 8.4.1848.

Bournonville attended the performance about which he noted in his diary:

'Paa Theatret, hvor jeg gav Pas de trois. [S.] Lund, P. Fredstrup og [J.] Rostock'.

The *Pas de trois* (which was performed a second time by the same dancers on 14.4.1848) is probably also identical with the later (uncredited) *Pas de trois* given during the following seasons on 9.2.1851, 14.12.1852, and 23.1.1853. It is not possible to identify the dance any further.

4.5.1848

Pas de deux and Polka composed by A. Bournonville (Pas de deux och Polka componerad af A. Bournonville) performed by C. Th. Dahlgren and J. G. Gillberg (Stockholm's Royal Theatre, Operahuset).
This set of dances was arranged especially for the début of Bournonville's Swedish pupil, J. G. Gillberg, and performed shortly before her appointment as *première danseuse* of Stockholm's Royal Theatre on 1.7.1848. In his diary Bournonville noted about the dances:

1.3.1848: 'Regleret en Pas for [J. G.] Gillberg'
30.3. and 13.4.: 'Lection til Gillberg'
14.4.: 'Sidste Lection til Gillberg der medbringer to smukke Pas til Stockholm'.

The dances were most probably a slightly revised version of the so-called *Pas de deux and Polka from the ballet Le Diable à quatre*, which were first performed at Copenhagen's Royal Theatre by Bournonville and C. Fjeldsted on 11.5.1847. This theory is supported by an orchestral score and complete set of parts in SSkma, entitled 'Pas de deux suivi d'un Polka' (call no. KT Dansmusik 73). They contain the exact same music as that for the *Pas de deux and Polka from the ballet Le Diable à quatre* in Copenhagen (now in DKKk, call nos. MA ms 2611, MA ms 2666, MA ms 2612, MA ms 2737, and KTB 241). It is not possible to identify these dance any further.

20.5.1848

Pas des trois cousines performed by J. Price, S. Price, and A. Price (the Casino Theatre).
In his dairy Bournonville noted about the creation of this dance, which represents the first in a long series of works that he choreographed for the three Price cousins, Juliette, Sophie, and Amalia, in the 1840s, 50s, and 60s:

16.3.1848: 'Lection til Pricerne, begyndt en Pas de trois'
17.3.: 'Lection til Pricerne'
18.3.: 'Lection til Pricerne. Pas de trois færdig'.

Bournonville did not attend any of their three performances of this dance at the Casino Theatre in the 1848 spring season.

The 1848 posters gives no information about the music composer. However, according to the original set of parts, the music was originally arranged by H. S. Paulli, and consisted of five excerpts (an *Allegro con brio* in 4/4 time, an *Adagio* in 3/4 time, an *Allegretto* in 2/4 time, an *Allegretto* in 2/4 time, and the *Coda*). They were all borrowed from Paulli's and N. W. Gade's (?) earlier score for Bournonville's so-called 'Pas de deux. Retour de Fjeldsted' (*see* 11.10.1843). Moreover, in his score for *Pas des trois cousines* Paulli incorporated two excerpts (*Allegretto* in 2/4, and an *Adagio* transition in 3/4, inserted immediately before the Coda) which were borrowed from his two earlier scores to Bournonville's *Tableau with Dance* (*see* 12.10.1846) and *Flower Dance* (*see* 20.10. 1847).

Pas des trois cousines was restaged at the Casino Theatre on 15.5.1849. About that performance (which represents the first production Bournonville actually saw performed on stage) he noted in his diary:

'Pigebørnene dandsede smukt'.

The poster for the 1849 performance reads: 'NB. Hovedpartiet udføres af Jfr. Juliette Price'. This seems to indicate that this production was a choreographically slightly revised version. Moreover, the 1849 posters gave explicit credit to Paulli for having 'arranged' (*arrangeret*) the music.

As a result of its great success with the audience the dance was soon after also mounted at the Royal Theatre on 8.9. 1849, and on 21.11.1849 it seems to have been performed at the Court Theatre. Furthermore, *Pas des trois cousines* was performed 4 times in Norway at Christiania's Theatre (Oslo) between 7.6. and 12.7.1852 with the Christiania posters then crediting Paulli for having actually composed the music.

In Copenhagen the dance was restaged four more times by Bournonville at the Royal Theatre on the following dates:

(1) on 8.1.1854 (performed by J. Price, S. Price, and J. Rostock, the last being regularly replaced by P. Fredstrup after 2.10.1855).
(2) on 18.10.1867 (then danced by B. Schnell, E. Poulsen, and A. Scholl. For this staging Bournonville made a notation of the complete dance).
(3) on 21.5.1873 (with M. Westberg, A. Scholl, and C. Schousgaard. This year Bournonville re-notated parts of the choreography).
(4) on 24.1.1874 (performed by the same cast as on 21.5.1873).

Pas des trois cousines received 39 performances at the Royal Theatre during Bournonville's lifetime, the last of which was given on 27.2.1874. Because of the many different casts during this period the dance was often listed on the posters simply as *Pas de trois*.

Musical sources:

No orchestral score and répétiteur's copy dating from the 1848 première of *Pas des trois cousines* have yet been traced. However, a later orchestral score, which most probably dates from a restaging of this dance at Copenhagen's Royal Theatre during the 1880s, is now in DKKk (call no. C II, 119 (KTB 318).

Parts (incomplete). Ms. Copy. 22 vol.
2 vl I, vl I, vlc e cb, fl picc, ob 1/2, cl 1/2, fag 1/2, cor 1/2, tr 1/2, cnt, Atrb, Ttrb, Btrb, timp, gr cassa e piatti, tri.
Unsigned and undated [c.1848]
[DKKk; C II, 105 Efterslæt 5
This (incomplete) set of parts represents the earliest known musical source for Bournonville's *Pas des trois cousines* traced so far. It was originally part of the music archive of the Price family and was purchased by DKKk in 1902 from the actor, Carl Price. According to a pencilled note on the part for the first violin, it consisted originally of 25 parts.

Other sources:

Drawing by E. Lehmann. Pencil and water colours (with sight 32,9 × 28,3 cm)
Sophia/Juliette/Amalia
Signed and dated: 'Eduard Lehmann/1848'
[DKKt; Lehmann tegninger
According to Lehmann's pencilled autographed dating of this drawing it clearly shows the original costumes of the *Pas des trois cousines* as worn at its 1848 Casino Theatre première. The drawing was later the same year published as a lithograph, entitled 'Pas des trois cousines', with several copies being sold with applied watercolours.

2.6.1848
Military Polka (Militair-Polka) performed by F. Hoppe, G. Brodersen, J. Rostock, and L. Stramboe (the Casino Theatre).
This dance is identical with Bournonville's *Polka militaire* (*see* 1.11.1842). It represents the first and only time it was performed at the Casino Theatre and was given as part of a special charity performance for the singer, C. E. Simonsen.

22.9.1848
Annitta, or The Vintage in the mountains of Albano (Annitta eller Viinhösten i Albanerbjergene). Projected ballet.
The earliest written source for this projected two-act ballet dates from 22.9.1848, when Bournonville noted in his diary:

'Skrevet en nÿ Ballet (No. 3 periode) Annitta i to Acter'.

This note clearly indicates that the ballet was intended as the third work in his 1846 projected cycle of four allegorical ballets, named *The Four Seasons, or Cupid's Journey* (*see* 16.6. 1846).

Moreover, the 1848 scenario for *Annitta, or The Vintage in the mountains of Albano* seems later to have served him as the basis for most of the dramatic action in the first section of the one-act ballet *The Flower Festival in Genzano* (*see* 19.12. 1858).

Autograph sources:

Manuscript scenario. Ms. Autograph. Brown ink. 10 pp. (20,7 × 17,2 cm)
Annitta./eller/Viinhösten i Albanerbjergene./Ballet i to Akter./af/ August Bournonville./1848.
Signed and dated: 'Fredensborg d. 22 Sept. 1848.'
[DKKk; NKS 3285 4° 2 A–E

4.10.1848
'Solo for Miss Fjeldsted' ('Solo til Jf. Fjeldsted').
On this day Bournonville noted in his diary:

'Prøve paa Hoftheatret (Solo til Jf. [C.] Fjeldsted)'.

This solo dance is most probably identical with the *Pas de solo* performed only two days later by C. Fjeldsted as an incorporated divertissement in Bournonville's one-act idyllic ballet *The Festival in Albano* (*see* 28.10.1839). It was given 4 times within this ballet between 6.10. and 16.11.1848. The dance is most probably also identical with the earlier *Solo (Incorporated)*, first performed by Fjeldsted in *The Festival in Albano* on 17.5.1847. That dance, in turn, is perhaps identical with the even earlier solo dance, named *Pas de solo, after Carlotta*

Grisi and first performed by Fjeldsted as a separate divertissement in Copenhagen on 24.4.1847. It is not possible to identify the dance any further.

7.10.1848
Les Mousquetaires de la Reine (Dronningens Livgarde).

In spite of the fact that the poster for the 1848 Copenhagen première of J.-F. Halévy's three-act comic opera (premièred at l'Opéra Comique in Paris on 3.2.1846) reads: 'Dandsen componeret af Herr Solodandser Hoppe', Bournonville's handwritten mise-en-scène for it is inserted in a volume which originally served him as a notebook for his opera mises-en-scène and is dated (on the front cover) with his inscription: 'fra Sept. 1848'. Moreover, Halévy's opera is included in both of his handwritten lists of his opera stagings in which it is listed under the year of 1848 (*see* Additional Sources). These facts prove that although the dance scene in the finale of Act II (score no. 10), which depicts a *bal masqué*, was officially choreographed by F. Hoppe, the opera's general mise-en-scène was beyond doubt created and mounted by Bournonville.

According to the rehearsal book of H. C. J. Fredstrup, 5 rehearsals were held of *Les Mousquetaires de la Reine* between 3.10 and 6.10.1848, two of which were supervised by Hoppe, and three by Bournonville.

In his diary he noted about the performance:

3.10.1848: 'Prøve paa det kgl. Theater Dronningens Livgarde'
4.10.: 'stor Prøve paa Dronningens Livgarde til Kl. 2'
6.10.: 'Prøve paa Dronningens Livgarde – sidste Prøve'
7.10.: 'Overværet Den første Forestilling af Dronningens Livgarde der blev optaget med Bifald'.

Moreover, on 30.10.1857 Bournonville included *Les Mousquetaires de la Reine* in a list of projected opera restagings which he wrote that day for the 1857–58 and 1858–59 seasons. This project, however, was never carried out and *Les Mousquetaires de la Reine* received a total of 5 performances in Copenhagen, the last of which was given on 23.11.1848.

Autograph sources:

Manuscript mise-en-scène. Ms. Autograph. Brown ink. 1 vol. 8 pp. (16,6 × 11 cm)
Dronningens Livgarde./(Les mousquetaires de la Reine) Musik af Halévy./Decorationer./[…]/Maskin – Requisiter/[…]/Chor = Fordeling./[…]/Dands./[…]/Hovedpersoner./[…]/Scene = Følge.
Unsigned and undated [1848]
[DKKk; NKS 747 8° Vol. 6
This mise-en-scène is included (on pp. 1–8) in Bournonville's 1849 diary (*see* Additional Sources). It served him originally as a notebook for his mises-en-scène for operas and is dated with his autographed inscription (written on the front cover): 'fra Sept. 1848'.

Musical sources:

Printed orchestral score with manuscript insertions. 3 vol. Act I 172 pp. of which two are blank, Act II 166 pp., Act III 100 pp. (31,3 × 25 cm)
LES/MOUSQUETAIRES/DE LA/REINE/Opéra Comique en 3 actes
Paris, Brandus et C.ie, pl. no. 4519 [1846]
[DKKk; U 6 (KTA 402)

No répétiteur's copy for *Les Mousquetaires de la Reine* has yet been traced.

Parts. Ms. Copy. 33 + 7 vol.
3 vl I, 3 vl II, 2 vla, 3 vlc e cb, fl 1/2, ob 1/2, cl 1/2, fag 1/2, cor 1/2/3/4, tr 1/2, trb 1/2/3, timp, gr cassa, piatti, tri, arpa. On stage: fl, cl, fag, cor 1/2, tr, gr cassa. 59 vocal parts.
Unsigned and undated [1848]
[DKKk; KTA 402

20.10.1848
Norma.

In his diary Bournonville noted about his involvement in the 1848 Copenhagen restaging of V. Bellini's two-act lyrical tragedy (premièred in Milan at Teatro all Scala on 26.12. 1831 and first performed in Copenhagen on 20.3.1840):

19.10.1848: 'Prøve paa Norma, Mlle [V. L. T.] Bergnehr meget god.'
20.10.: 'i Theatret hvor jeg overværede Norma. – Stor Bravour for Mlle Bergnehr'.

Bournonville had earlier used words like 'Prøve' (rehearsal) and 'overværede' (attended) about his involvement in the staging of J.-F. Halévy's comic opera *Les Mousquetaires de la Reine* (*see* 7.10.1848), a work for which he created the actual mise-en-scène. These facts indicate that he most likely was also responsible for at least parts of the mise-en-scène for *Norma* in 1848, although he never included this work in his handwritten or printed lists of his works.

However, on 30.10.1857 he mentioned Bellini's lyrical tragedy in a list of projected opera restagings which he wrote on this day for the 1857–58 and 1858–59 seasons. This project was carried out on 5.2.1858, when *Norma* was mounted under his official supervision for the first time. It was restaged on by him two later occasions on 17.4.1860 and 25.9.1865.

The 1848 restaging received 31 performances, the last the last of which was given on 22.9.1856.

Musical sources:

Orchestral score (incomplete). Ms. Copy. Black ink. 1 vol. 276 pp. of which three are blank (24,9 × 31,3 cm)
344./Norma./Partitur/3.die og 4.die Akt/[…]/Norma/Atto secondo & III
Unsigned and undated [c.1840]
[DKKkt; KTA 344
This (incomplete) orchestral score contains the text in both German and Danish and was used for all performances of *Norma* in Copenhagen from its première there in 1840 and throughout Bournonville's lifetime. After the 1845–46 season it was given in three acts, and from the 1865–66 season in four acts, hence the rather confusing titles added to this volume.

No répétiteur's copy for *Norma* has yet been traced.

Parts. Ms. Copy. 35 + 10 vol.
4 vl I, 4 vl II, 2 vla, 4 vlc e cb, fl 1/2, ob 1/2, cl 1/2, fag 1/2, cor 1/2/3/4, tr 1/2, Atrb, Ttrb, Btrb, timp, gr cassa, gong, arpa. On stage: fl picc, cl 1/2, fag 1/2, cor, tr 1/2, trb, gr cassa. 62 vocal parts.
Unsigned and undated [1840]
[DKKk; KTA 344
This set of parts was used for all performances in Copenhagen of *Norma* since its première there in 1840 and throughout Bournonville's lifetime.

5.11.1848
The Elves' Hill (Elverhøi).
According to the rehearsal book of H. C. J. Fredstrup, Bour-

nonville personally directed the rehearsal on 4.11.1848 of P. Funck's dances in F. Kuhlau's and J. L. Heiberg's five-act national fairy-play from 1828 *The Elves' Hill* (*see* 10.9.1846) prior to its restaging on this day. *The Elves' Hill* received 90 performances after the 1848 restaging and during Bournonville's lifetime, the last of which took place on 22.4.1872.

6.11.1848
St. Olave's Day (Sanct Olafs Dag). **Projected drama.**
In his diary Bournonville noted about his involvement in this projected four-act drama by M. W. Brun (pen-name for B. W. Michael) with music by H. Rung:

6.11.1848: 'componeret med [H.] Rung paa Sct: Olafs Dag'.

The drama was for unknown reasons never carried out, although a prompt's book and a set of vocal parts were prepared for it.

Musical sources:

Prompt's book. Ms. Copy. Brown ink. 1 vol. 26 pp. (26,2 × 37,6 cm)
439/439/Sanct Olafs Dag./Souffleurparti./H. Rung
Unsigned and undated [1848]
[DKKk; KTA 439

Vocal parts. Ms. Copy. 8 vol.
Ragnhild, Thora, 6 Tenor I, 6 Tenor II, 6 Basso I, 6 Basso II.
Unsigned and undated [1848]
[DKKk; KTA 439

30.11.1848
Don César de Bazan (Don Cæsar de Bazan).
According to his diary Bournonville directed a rehearsal on 28.11.1848 of the two incorporated dances in A. D'Ennery's (pen-name for E. Philippe) and P. Dumanoir's five-act drama *Don César de Bazan* (first performed in Paris at the Théâtre de Porte de Saint-Martin on 30.7.1844). They were originally choreographed by P. Larcher when *Don César de Bazan* was given its Copenhagen première on 1.5.1846, and were set to music composed and arranged by H. Rung. They consisted of a *Fandango* (performed in Act II, score no. 2), and an unnamed *Spanish Dance* (in Act III, score no. 3), the former being described in the score as an original composition by Rung. As a result of Larcher's sudden death in 1847, Bournonville seems to have taken over the responsibility for mounting these dances in the 1848 restaging of *Don César de Bazan*. It received only 3 performances, the last of which was given on 26.2.1849.

Musical sources:

Orchestral score. Ms. Autograph (by H. Rung). Black ink. 1 vol. 24 pp. of which one is blank (26,6 × 35,4 cm)
467/H. Rung./Don Cæsa de Basa [*sic*]/No. 467./[...]/Don Cesar de Bazan.
Signed (on p. 9): 'H Rung', undated [1848]
[DKKk; C II, 119 k

Répétiteur's copy. Ms. Copy. Brown ink. 1 vol. 6 pp. of which one is blank (33,2 × 24,6 cm)
Repetiteur=Partie/til/Don César de Bazan
Unsigned and undated [1848]
[DKKk; MA ms 2914 (4) (KTA 467)
This répétiteur's copy contains the music for the two incorporated

dances in *Don César de Bazan* and is included on pp. 37–42 in a volume that also contains the répétiteur's copies for four other works mounted at Copenhagen's Royal Theatre during the 1845–46 season.

Parts. Ms. Copy. 21 vol.
2 vl I, 2 vl II, vla, 2 vlc e cb, fl 1/2, ob 1/2, cl 1/2, fag 1/2, cor 1/2, tr 1/2, trb, timp.
Unsigned and undated [1846]
[DKKk; KTA 467

8.12.1848
Die Feuerprobe (Ildprøven).
According to Bournnonville's diary he personally directed the two final stage rehearsals of H. S. v. Løvenskjold's one-act comic operetta, noting about it:

21.11.1848: 'Prøve paa 'Ildprøven' af [H. S. v.] Løvenskiold'
6.12.: 'Prøve paa Byens Theater paa Ildprøven'
8.12.: 'Overværet Ildprøven 1.ste Forestilling'.

In spite of the fact that he never included this work in his handwritten list of his opera stagings, written c.1851 (*see* Additional Sources), nor in the published list of his works in his memoirs *My Theatre Life*, Bournonville thus seems to have been responsible for at least parts of its mise-en-scène. *Die Feuerprobe* received only 6 performances, the last of which was given on 22.2.1849.

Musical sources:

Orchestral score. Ms. Autograph. Black and brown ink. 1 vol. 248 pp. of which two are blank (33,2 × 25,5 cm with several variants)
Ildprøven. -/[...]/Ildprøven,/comisk Operette i een Act/efter Kotzebu[e],/bearbeidet for den danske Scene/af/W: Holst,/Musikken componeret/af/H: S: Løvenskjold./Partitur.
Signed and dated (on p. 248): 'Kbhvn: d: 24.de April 18[48]/H S Lövenskjold'
[DKKk; C II, 117 d (KTA 398)

No répétiteur's copy for *Die Feuerprobe* has yet been traced.

Parts. Ms. Copy. 34 vol.
3 vl I, 3 vl II, 2 vla, 3 vlc e cb, fl picc, fl 1/2, ob 1/2, cl 1/2, fag 1/2, cor 1/2/3/4, tr 1/2, trb 1/2/3, timp, gr cassa e piatti, tri. On stage: cor 1/2. 49 vocal parts.
Unsigned and undated [1848]
[DKKk; KTA 398

18.12.1848
The Childbed Room (Barselstuen).
For this restaging of L. Holberg's five-act comedy from 1749 Bournonville gave personal stage instructions to the actress, J. Fredstrup, who this year played the rôle of *Ane Kandestøbers* for the first time. Of the rehearsals and the performance, which was mounted as part of a gala performance celebrating the centenary of the opening of the first Royal Theatre building at the King's New Square, he noted in his diary:

15.12.1848: 'Instrueret J. Fredstrup som Ane Kandestøber'
18.12.: 'Mandagen d. 18.de Decbr. Comediehusets 100.de Aars =Fest. [...] Besørget Programmer til Kongehuset og andre Honnoratiores. Overværet Fest-forestillingen der begÿndte med et Forspil af [H. C.] Andersen Kunstens Dannevirke, oprigtigt sagt et temmelig mat Product og mere passende til en Benefice for Saarede og Faldnes Efterlatte, end til et Theater=Jubilæum. Derpaa gik 'Barsel-

stuen' som skuespillerne selv paastod ikke paa en Maade der var Høitideligheden værdig'.

Fredstrup played the rôle of *Ane Kandestøber* twice, the last time on 20.12.1848.

18.12.1848
Old Memories, or A Magic Lantern (Gamle Minder eller En Laterna magica).

This one-act ballet was created for a gala performance celebrating the centenary of the opening of the first Royal Theatre building at the King's New Square. Bournonville had originally intended to mount a performance consisting of a series of dioramas like those he had seen at the Parisian theatres during his many visits to the French capital in the 1840s. This plan, however, was abandoned at an early stage in favour of a more traditional series of *tableaux vivants* mingled with several dance scenes.

The dramatic action centred on an invented character, *Philemon*, who is presented with a magic lantern on his one-hundredth birthday. As an ardent theatre-lover, he now relives the many performances he attended at the theatre during his long life.

The score was composed and arranged by E. Helsted. It consists in the main of light arrangements of musical borrowings in order to help the audience interpret the dramatic action and follow the many references to the highlights of the repertory at Copenhagen's Royal Theatre's over a century. These musical borrowings are identified as follows:

(1) In score no. 1 Helsted incorporated J. A. P. Schultz's(?) melody to C. Søeborg's song from 1809, named «Om hundred Aar er Alting glemt», which he had employed three years earlier in his score for Bournonville's three-act romantic ballet *Kirsten Piil* (*see* 26.2.1845).
(2) In score no. 2 Helsted interpolated the *Musset* and the *Second Air de ballet* from Act IV (scene 2) of C. W. v. Gluck's five-act tragedy *Armide* (premièred at the Paris Opéra on 23.9.1777). The exact same music was used many years later by V. C. Holm in his score for scene 5 (score no. 5) of Bournonville's ballet divertissement *From the Last Century* (*see* 31.10.1875).
(3) In score no. 3 Helsted incorporated the *Marsch* from Act I of G. J. Vogler's score for A. F. Skjöldebrand's five-act drama *Hermann von Unna* (premièred at Copenhagen's Royal Theatre on 30.1.1800).
(4) In score no. 4 Helsted employed two excerpts from C. Schall's score to V. Galeotti's three-act pantomimic tragedy *Lagertha* from 30.1.1801, namely the so-called 'Chor en Marsch' in Act I, entitled «Velkommen hid!», and the bridal dance or 'Dands af Regnar og Thora' (*Larghetto Molto Amoroso*) from the same act. The music for the latter served in Helsted's score as accompaniment for an allegorical *Pas de trois*, performed by the three Graces.
(5) In score no. 6 Helsted interpolated the same *Ciaconne* which L. Zinck had earlier employed in Act III (score no. 16) of his score for Bournonville's three-act pantomimic ballet *Don Quixote at Camacho's Wedding* (*see* 24.2.1837). According to Bournonville's printed scenario for *Old Memories, or A Magic Lantern*, this dance was originally part of a (not yet identified) ballet from 1760 by J.-G. Noverre and is described as 'Chaconne fra 1760. Motivet efter Noverre'. It was performed by 'et arcadisk Hyrdepar i Rococo Stiil'.
(6) In score no. 7 Helsted employed two excerpts from J. E. Hartmann's three-act heroic singspiel from 1778 *The Death of Balder (Balder's Død)*, namely *Balder's* aria in Act I (score no. 3) «Taare sig hvorfor du rinder?», and the terzetto «Buldrende brøle Nastronds Flammer» sung by three Valkyries in Act III (score no. 14).
(7) In score no. 8 Helsted interpolated a slightly revised version of the *Norwegian Spring Dance* in J. Lolle's score to V. Galeotti's one-act ballet *The Whims of Cupid and the Ballet-master* from 31.10.1786. To this

dance he added a new introduction and a Coda (presumably of his own composition). According to the set of parts for Galeotti's ballet (now in DKKk, call no. KTB 226), Helsted's new 1848 version of this dance was also interpolated in *The Whims of Cupid and the Ballet-master* when it was restaged by L. Gade on 15.2.1863. There it replaced Lolle's original 1786 version of the same dance.
(8) In score no. 9 Helsted employed an *Allegro* borrowed from Act I of Schall's and Galeotti's *Lagertha*. It is followed by an excerpt from the opening scene of Act I (*Allegro Furioso con Sordine*) in Schall's and Galeotti's four-act tragic ballet *Bluebeard (Rolf Blaaskiæg)*, premièred on 13.12.1808, and concludes with a melody by E. Dupuy that originally served as an accompaniment for a song entitled «Manden med Glas i Haand, stolt af sin høie Aand». It was written for N. F. Bruun's Danish translation of A. Duval's three-act comedy *La Jeunesse d'Henry IV*, premièred at Copenhagen's Royal Theatre on 6.12.1808.

Dupuy's melody had also been interpolated by H. S. Paulli in his music for the final tableau of Act II (score no. 11) in Bournonville's two-act romantic ballet *The Isle of Phantasy*, there serving as an allusion to the song's third verse reading: «Skjøndt du, o stolte Hav, var mangen Sømands Grav, elsker han dig».
(9) In score no. 10 Helsted inserted a *Hornpipe* by Schall, which (according to the printed scenario for *Old Memories, or A Magic Lantern*) was originally performed by Bournonville's father, Antoine Bournonville, in 1798 as an incorporated divertissement in the Act III finale of J. E. Hartmann's three-act singspiel from 1780 *The Fishermen (Fiskerne)*. No musical sources for this *Hornpipe* have yet been traced in the annals of the Royal Theatre's music archive.
(10) In score no. 11 Helsted employed (according to Bournonville's printed scenario) a theme borrowed from a (not yet identified) song in A. Oehlenschläger's five-act tragedy from 1808 *Hakon Jarl*. Moreover, in the same number Helsted incorporated the melody for the song «Fra Orient til Occident basunes höit min Roes» in Act I (score no. 4) of C. E. F. Weyse's two-act singspiel from 1808 *The Sleeping-Draught (Sovedrikken)*.
(11) In score no. 12 (the Finale) Helsted reused parts of J. F. Fröhlich's earlier music for the *Pas de deux* (score no. 5) in Bournonville's pantomimic prologue *The Fatherland's Muses* (*see* 20.3.1840). Finally, in the same number Helsted incorporated Weyse's melody for the song «Der vanker en Konstner ved Tiberens Bred» in Th. Overskou's one-act vaudeville from 1832 *Artists' Life (Kunstnerliv)*.

In his diary Bournonville noted about the creation and the première of *Old Memories, or A Magic Lantern*:

9.11.1848: 'Møde hos [J. G.] Levetzau angaaende Secularfesten [...] Udarbeidet Planen til et Odéon Ballet=Forestilling'
13.11.: 'skrevet et nÿt Program til Secularfesten for det andet som jeg har casseret. Det hedder nu: Gamle Minder eller En Laterna-magica, og vil nok lÿkkes mig [...] fuldendte mit Program'
14.11.: 'talt med Chefen der var tilfreds med mit Arbeide [...] arbeidet med [E.] Helsted'
19.11.: 'modtaget Musik af Helsted'
21.11. and 23.11.: 'arbeidet med Helsted'
26.11.: 'begÿndt med Axel Fredstrup paa Secular=Festens Ballet 'Gamle Minder''
29.11.: 'skrevet og componeret [...] componeret Resten af Aftnen'
30.11.: 'Første Prøve paa 'Gamle Minder' en scène færdig der faldt godt ud. Besøgt [...] Theatermalerne [...] componeret'
1.12.: 'Prøve paa 'Gamle Minder' [...] Møde [...] med Theatermalerne'
2.12.: 'skrevet Lister om Costümet'
3.12.: 'Indstuderet en nÿ Pas til [S.] Lund og Jf. [J.] Rostock [i.e. 'Roccoco Pas de deux' (*Ciacconne*), score no. 6] [...] Componeret hele Eftermiddagen [...] Maskinprøve paa Theatret'
4.12.: 'Prøve paa 'Gamle Minder''
5.12.: 'skrevet og componeret' [...] Prøve paa 'Gamle Minder' [...] componeret'
7.12.: 'componeret og skrevet [...] Prøve paa 'Gamle Minder' componeret den engelske for [F.] Hoppe'
8.12.: 'componeret [...] Prøve paa 'Gamle Minder' Finalen [...] Talt med Theatermalerne [...] Været hos Helsted'

9.12.: 'Prøve og fuldendt Indstuderingen af 'Gamle Minder' Udfald-et var gunstigt'

10.12.: 'Skrevet mit Program den hele Formiddag. Besøgt H. P. Holst, besørget Skriftet til Bogtrykkeren'

11.12.: 'Prøve paa hele Balletten 'Gamle Minder'. [J.] Collin med Damer overværede den og vare særdeles tilfredse [...] Maskinprøve efter Skuespillet. Alt gik smukt og godt'

12.3.: 'Besørget Nødvendigheder til min Ballet'

13.12.: 'Prøve paa Det kgl. Theater paa Gamle Minder. Arrangement der gjorde megen Lÿkke'

14.12.: 'Prøve paa Hoftheatret. Besørget endeel Balletten vedkom-mende paa Theatret om Aftenen'

15.12.: 'Prøve paa Det kgl. Theater. Det Hele gik godt, paa nogle Ubehageligheder nær med [A.] Fredstrup og Jf. [A.] Nielsen (som jeg skal have i Erindring)'

16.12.: 'Prøve paa 'Gamle Minder''

17.12.: 'Generalprøve paa 'Gamle Minder' der gik meget godt og sÿnes at love os en Succès'

18.12.: 'Mandagen d. 18.de Decbr. Comediehusets 100.de Aars= Fest. [...] endelig Kl 9 1/2 Balletten 'Gamle Minder', der gjorde særdeles megen Lÿkke og udførtes fra alle sider meget tilfredsstil-lende. Jeg takkede Gud for mit Held og alle de Medvirkende for deres ufortrødne Iver'.

The *Norwegian Spring Dance (Norsk Springedands)* in *Old Memo-ries, or A Magic Lantern* (score no. 8) was later also mounted as a separate divertissement, with slightly different titles, at four following theatres in Denmark and abroad:

(1) at Copenhagen's Court Theatre on 21.11.1849.
(2) at Copenhagen's Royal Theatre on 12.3.1850.
(3) at Christiania's Theatre (Oslo) on 22.6.1852 and on 7.6.1865.
(4) at Stockholm's Mindre Theatern on 8.6.1860.

Moreover, the music (and probably also the choreography) of this dance was incorporated on 27.1.1870 in H. C. Lum-bye's score for Bournonville's so-called *Scandinavian Quad-rille*, which originally was part of a larger divertissement, named *'Bouquet Royal'*.

Old Memories, or A Magic Lantern reached a total of 20 per-formances, the last of which was given on 20.11.1849.

Autograph sources:

Manuscript scenario. Ms. Autograph. Black ink. 4 pp. (23,2 × 17,8 cm)
Gamle Minder eller En Lanterna = magica./Ballet = Forestilling i Anledning af Det Kgl Theaters Secularfest, d. 18. Decbr 1848./com-poneret af A Bournonville.
Unsigned and dated: 'd. 14 November 1848.' [Written according to the diary on 13.11. and 14.11.1848]
[DKKk; NKS 3285 4° 2 G–K

Musical sources:

Orchestral score. Ms. Autograph (by E. Helsted). Black ink. 1 vol. 128 pp of which four are blank (34 × 28,5 cm)
291/Partituur/til/Gamle Minder/[...]/Balletten/'Gamle Minder' af A: Bournonville.
Signed and dated (on p. 125): '12/12 48 Eduard Helsted.'
[DKKk; C II, 114 k (KTA 291)

Répétiteur's copy. Ms. Autograph (by E. Helsted). Brown ink. 1 vol. 34 pp. of which one is blank (33,5 × 25 cm)
B. 291/Gamle Minder./Bournonville/E. Helsted/36/d. 18. de Dec 1848. 100 Aar=Fest.
Signed and dated (on p. 33): 'Decbr 1848./Eduard Helsted.'
[DKKk; MA ms 2988 (KTB 291)
This répétiteur's copy contains Bournonville's autographed notes

(written with brown ink) which describe, in fine detail, the dramatic action, the mime, and the choreography of score nos. 1–5. His other autographed notes on p. 18 (written with black ink) refer to the later incorporation of the *Norwegian Spring Dance* in H. C. Lumbye's score for Bournonville's *Scandinavian Quadrille* (*see* 27.1.1870).

Parts. Ms. Copy. 32 vol.
3 vl I, 3 vl II, 2 vla, 3 vlc e cb, fl 1/2, ob 1/2, cl 1/2, fag 1/2, cor 1/2/ 3/4, tr 1/2, tr b 1/2/3, timp, gr cassa, tri, arpa.
Unsigned and undated [1848]
[DKKk; KTB 291

Printed sources:

Printed scenario. 1 vol. 8 pp. (20 × 12,1 cm)
Gamle Minder/eller/En Laterna magica,/Ballet i 1 Act/af/August Bournonville./Musiken arrangeret af Edw. Helsted.
Kjøbenhavn, Bianco Luno, 1848.
[DKKk; 17, 174 8°

1849

4.1.1849
Pas de trois **(uncredited) performed by R. C. A. Andersen, S. Price, and J. Rostock (the Casino Theatre).**

This (uncredited) dance was choreographed for a public *Bal en masque* at the Casino Theatre. The music was most probably composed by H. C. Lumbye, who also conducted the Casino orchestra at this ball, during which (according to an advertisement in *Berlingske Tidende*) several 'character dances' (*Characteerdandse*) were performed. Among these were Lumbye's so-called *Casino-Ball-Masque-Ecossaise*, which was written especially for this occasion. In his diary Bour-nonville noted about the dance:

20.12.1848: 'Prøve paa en Pas de trois for [R. C. A.] Andersen, [J.] Rostock og S. Price'
21.12.: 'Prøve for A. Andersen'
3.1.1849: 'componeret en Pas de deux [*sic*]'
4.1.: 'Indstuderet Pas de deux [*sic*] til Andersen, S: Price og Rostock'

Bournonville did not attend the ball.

On 13.1.1849 he noted in his diary: 'Prøve med Price og Andersen'. This rehearsal seems to refer to a later rehearsal of the *Pas de trois* prior to a repeat of the masked ball at the Casino Theatre on 30.1.1849.

No musical sources for this dance have yet been traced. It is not possible to identify the dance any further.

10.1.1849
La Figlia del Regimento (Regimentets Datter) **(the Court Theatre).**

The 1849 Copenhagen restaging (in Italian) of G. Doni-zetti's two-act comic opera (premièred at l'Opéra Comique in Paris on 11.2.1840, and first given in Denmark on 6.10. 1840) is not included in any of Bournonville's handwritten lists of his stagings of operas (*see* Additional Sources), nor in the printed survey of his works in his memoirs *My Theatre Life* (pp. 407–410). However, notes in his diary give clear evi-dence about the mise-en-scène and personal stage instruc-tions he provided this year to the singer, E. Dahl, who played Maria in the 1849 production of Donizetti's opera:

29.12.1848: 'Instruction hos [E.] Dahls'
30.12.: 'Instruction Dahl'
2.1.1849: 'Instruction hos Dahl'
3.1.: 'Instruction hos M.me Dahl'
9.1.1849: 'Prøve med Italienerne paa Regimentets Datter'
10.1.: 'Overværede Forestillingen af La Figlia del Regimento [*sic*] paa Hoftheatret. M.me Dahl's Debüt. Hun sang og spillede smukt, men Stemmen er ikke betÿdelig og Publicum tog hende koldt imod, jeg har Grund til at formode Cabaler fra Italienernes Side'.

About the same performance the Copenhagen paper *Fædre-landet* stated on 11.1.1849:

'Instruktionen i 2. Akt var daarligere end paa Det kongelige Theater og det er vistnok meget sagt'.

Berlingske Tidende noted on the same day:

'Uagtet denne Fremstilling unægtelig vidnede om dramatisk Talent og en ypperlig Methode, fandt vi dog Md. Dahl saa lidt disponeret, mulig tillige Følgen af en naturlig Ængstelighed, at vi udsætter Bedømmelsen af hendes Præstation til en følgende Forestilling'.

La Fille du régiment was also included by Bournonville in a list of projected opera stagings which he wrote on 30.10.1857 while planning the 1857–58 and 1858–59 seasons. This project was carried out two years later on 20.10.1859, when Donizetti's opera was mounted at the Royal Theatre (then sung in Danish) with Bournonville's completely new mise-en-scène. Moreover, about his later supposed involvement in a restaging of this opera on 18.5.1870 he noted in his diary on 1.9.1870: 'Skrevet en Artikel til Dagbladet'. It is followed by a note on the following day reading: 'Dagbladet imødegaaer min Artikel om Regimentets Datter'.

Finally, *La Fille du régiment* was mounted for the last time under Bournonville's general direction in Copenhagen on 4.2.1876.

The 1849 production of *La Figlia del Regimento* at the Court Theatre was given 3 performances, the last of which took place on 14.1.1849. No musical sources dating from this staging have yet been traced.

29.1.1849

The Wedding at Lake Como (Brylluppet ved Como=Søen).

According to his handwritten list of his opera stagings, written c.1851 (*see* Additional Sources), Bournonville was responsible for both the mise-en-scène and the choreography at the 1849 world première of F. Gläser's three-act opera with a libretto by H. C. Andersen, based on A. Manzoni's novel from 1825–26 *Gli Promessi Sposi*. The opera included a mime scene (played by the character Griso appearing as an *Improvisatore*), and a *Saltarello* (danced by the characters *Lucia* and *Renzo*). Both of these numbers were performed during the opening chorus of Act III (score no. 13), entitled «Bravo, bravo godt improviseret, stolte Vers har han leveret!». This scene is described by Gläser in his autographed orchestral score as follows:

'(Lucia og Renzo ere midt i en Saltatrello, Moder Agnese slaaer paa Tamburinen. Tonio stötter sig med Albuen paa Gervasius Skulder og seer paa Dandsen.) (Medens Dandsen agerer Griso Improvisatore.)'.

In his diary Bournonville noted about the rehearsals and the opera's reception:

19.12.1848: 'Sÿngeskole paa [F.] Gläsers Opera Brÿlluppet ved Como-Söen. Musiken forekom mig smuk, livlig og af Virkning for Scenen'
28.12.: 'Claveerprøve paa Glaesers Opera'
6.1.1849: 'Syngeskole paa Gläsers Opera'
20.1.: 'marqueret Prøve paa Gläser's Opera'
21.1.: 'Arrangeret til Gläser's Opera'
22.1., 23.1., and 24.1.: 'Prøve paa Gläsers Opera'
25.1.: 'Reqvisit=Aftale med [C.] Thorup'
26.1.: 'Prøve paa Bryluppet ved Comosøen'
28.1.: 'Prøve paa Como = Söen'
29.1.: 'Første Forestilling af Bryluppet [*sic*] ved Como = Söen. Opera af [H. C.] Andersen og Gläser der gik fortrinligt og gjorde megen LŸkke'.

Moreover, on 30.10.1857 Bournonville included Gläser's opera in his list of projected opera restagings which he was planning on that day for the 1857–58 and 1858–59 seasons. This project, however, was never carried out, and *The Wedding at Lake Como* was given for the last time on 12.3.1852, reaching a total of 12 performances.

Autograph sources:

Manuscript mise-en-scène. Ms. Autograph. Brown ink. 1 vol. 7 pp. (16,6 × 11 cm)
Brÿluppet [*sic*] ved Como = Söen./H. C. Andersen. Musik af Gläser. (Januar 1849)/Decorationer./[...]/ Maskin-Requisiter./[...]/Hovedpartier./[...]/ Chorfordeling. /[...]/Scene = Følge:
Unsigned and dated: '(Januar 1849)'
[DKKk; NKS 747 8° Vol. 6
This manuscript mise-en-scène is included in Bournonville's diary for 1849 that originally served as a notebook for his opera mises-en-scène and is dated (on the front cover) by his autographed inscription 'fra Sept. 1848'.

Musical sources:

Piano vocal score. Ms. Autograph (by F. Gläser). Black ink. 1 vol. 340 pp. (25,5 × 32 cm with minor variants)
Brylluppet ved/Comersøen/Opera med Recitativer/[...]/Brylluppet ved Comer Söen/Opera i 3 Acter/1.ste Act/Ouverture/af/Fr. Glæser
Signed (on p. 1) 'Fr. Glæser', dated (on p. 340): 'Von 14ten Sept. [1848] des Abends/10 Uhr den Entwurf/des 3.tes Ackts beendiegt/vom 15 Sept: bis 29.ten September/gar nicht der weiteren Instrumentierung gearbeitet.'
[DKKk; Dan Fogs Musiksamlinger, Samling nr. 29, Pakke nr. 10

Orchestral score. Ms. Autograph (by F. Gläser). Black ink. 4 vol. Act I a 222 pp., Act I b 284 pp. of which one is blank, Act II 326 pp. of which one is blank, Act III 324 pp. of which one is blank. (25,8 × 32,2 cm with minor variants)
Brylluppet/ved/Como=söen./Act I./F. Glæser./A./[...]/Act I./B:/ [...]/Act II./[...]/Act III.
Signed and dated (in vol. 1, p. 72): 'Den 4.ten September/1848', (in vol. 4, p. 315) 'Den 15.te November 1848/Kl. 3 endt'
[DKKk; C II, 110 (KTA 447)

Répétiteur's copy. Ms. Copy. Black ink. 1 vol. 6 pp. of which one is blank (32,6 × 24,4 cm)
Brÿluppet ved Comosöen/[...]/205/Bournonville/Brylluppet/ved Como=söen. -/Repititions=Stemme/til Dandsen i 3.die Akt./(angaaende: Luzia og Renzo.)
Unsigned and undated [1849]
[DKKk; MA ms 2909 (1) (KTA 447)

This répétiteur's copy is bound together with the répétiteur's copy for H. Rung's music to M. V. Brun's five-act drama *Gustav III (Gustav den Tredie)* (*see* 4.2.1849).

Parts (incomplete). Ms. Copy. 46 + 2 vol.
3 vl I (in 6 vol.). 3 vl II, (in 6 vol.), 2 vla (in 4 vol.), 3 vlc e cb (in 6 vol.), fl picc, fl 1/2, ob 1/2, cl 1/2, fag 1/2, cor 1/2/3/4, tr 1/2, trb 1/2/3, timp, gr cassa, gr cassa e piatti, piatti, tri, arpa. On stage: conductor's part, cor. 64 vocal parts.
Unsigned and undated [1849]
[DKKk; KTA 447

Parts (incomplete). Ms. Copy. 2 vol.
cnt 1/2
Unsigned and undated [1849]
[DKKk; C II, 110 (KTA 447)

4.2.1849
Gustav III (Gustav den Tredie).
In his diary Bournonville noted about the dances choreographed and mounted for the première of M. V. Brun's (pen-name for B. W. Michael) five-act drama. It was set to music composed and arranged by H. Rung. He interpolated several songs by the great 18th-century Swedish poet-songwriter, C. M. Bellman, into his score as follows:

(1) In Act I Rung employed Bellman's song entitled 'Till konnung Gustaf III' («Så lyser din krona, nu kung Gustaf, dubblet dyr»).
(2) In Act III Rung employed six different tunes from Bellman's collection of 82 songs, entitled *Fredmans Epistler.* They are:
　　(a) epistel no. 4 «Hej, musikanter, ge valdhornen vädern» (interpolated in score no. 4).
　　(b) epistel no. 9 «Käraste bröder, systrar och vänner» (interpolated in score no. 5 as accompaniment for a *Minuet (Menuet)* for eight couples).
　　(c) epistel no. 64 («Fäll dina ögon och skäms nu, din tossa» (interpolated in score no. 6).
　　(d) epistel no. 70 «Movitz, vik mössan högt öfver öra» (interpolated in score no. 7).
　　(e) epistel no. 82 «Hvila vid denna källa!» (interpolated in score no. 8).
　　(f) epistel no. 29 «Movitz tag dina pinnar!» (interpolated in score no. 9).
(3) In Act V (score no. '10½') Rung inserted a dance divertissement consisting of four dances, namely a *Polka,* a *Chinese Dance (Chinesisk Dands),* a *Hungarian Dance (Ungarsk Dands),* and a *Minuet (Menuetto).* They all seem to have been set to music borrowed from another (not yet identified) composer. After these dances follows G. J. Vogler's music for the so-called 'Danse à la Ronde mit 4 Characteren' in his score to A. F. Skjöldebrand's five-act drama *Hermann von Unna* (premièred at Copenhagen's Royal Theatre on 30.1.1800).

Only the poster for the drama's second performance on 5.2.1849 gives explicit credit to Rung for having 'arranged' (*arrangeret*) the music.

　In Bournonville's handwritten lists of his stagings of operas and dramas, written c.1851 (*see* Additional Sources), *Gustav III* is listed in the category of 'Arrangements'. This fact seems to indicate that, apart from choreographing the dances in Acts III and V, Bournonville was also responsible for creating at least parts of the drama's mise-en-scène.

　In his diary he noted about the performance:

2.1.1849: 'Forsamling paa Gustav den Tredie'
29.1.: 'Indstuderet Dandsen til Gustav d. III'
30.1.: 'Prøve paa Dandsen til Gustav d. III'
1.2., 2.2., and 3.2.: 'Prøve paa Gustav III'
4.2.: 'Opførelse af Gustav III, temmelig kjedelig og kold Forestilling'.

Gustav III reached a total of 5 performances, the last of which was given on 19.2.1849.

Musical sources:

Orchestral score. Ms. Autograph (by H. Rung) and copy. Black and brown ink. 1 vol. 46 pp. of which one is blank (27,1 × 37,8 cm with minor variants)
436/Gustav den 3.die/Partitur./436/[...]/Gustav den III/Drama/Musiken/arrangeret og componeret/af/H. Rung.
Signed and dated (p. 44): 'H. Rung/Jan. 1849'
DKKk; C II, 119 k (KTA 436)
Three of the dances in Act V (pp. 41–43) are musical insertions written by another hand than Rung's. Since the musical indications for these dances are all given in German, it seems that they were copied from works by either German or Austrian composers.

Répétiteur's copy. Ms. Copy. Black ink. 1 vol. 10 pp. of which one is blank (32,6 × 24,4 cm)
[...]/Gustav den 3.dje./205/Bournonville/Repetiteur=Partie/til/Gustav den 3.die
Unsigned and undated [1849]
[DKKk; MA ms 2909 (2) (KTA 436)
This répétiteur's copy is bound together with the répétiteur's copy for F. Gläser's three-act opera *The Wedding at Lake Como* (*see* 29.1.1849). It contains the complete music for the dances in Act III (score no. 5) and in Act V (score no. 10 1/2). Moreover, Bournonville's autographed choreographic notes (written with brown ink) describe (in general terms) the choreography of the dances in both of these acts.

Parts. Ms. Copy. 22 + 11 vol.
2 vl I, 2 vl II, vla, 2 vlc e cb, fl 1/2, ob 1/2, cl 1/2, fag 1/2, cor 1/2, tr 1/2, trb, timp, arpa. On stage: vl I, vl II, vla, vlc e cb, fl 1/2, ob, cl 1/2, fag 1/2. 42 vocal parts.
Unsigned and undated [1849]
[DKKk; KTA 436

17.3.1849
Nina, ou La Folle par amour (Nina, eller Den Vanvittige af Kjærlighed).
This performance represents Bournonville's second and last staging of his Copehagen version of L. J. Milon's two-act pantomimic ballet (*see* 30.9.1834). L. Stramboe and G. Brodersen then played the leading rôles of *Nina* and *Germeuil* for the first time.

　According to the orchestral score (now in DKKk, call no. C I, 303) the main differences between the 1834 version and the 1849 restaging seem to have consisted in a cancellation of the Act I *Pas de deux* in F major (originally performed between score nos. 9 A and 9 B), and the omittance of the entire music for score no. 10 in the same act. This theory is supported by the fact that neither of these numbers is preserved in the orchestral score.

　Moreover, Bournonville clearly rechoreographed parts of the dances. This is clear from his diary in which he noted about the rehearsals and the first and fifth performances:

13.1.1849: 'begÿndt Indstuderingen af Nina'
14.1.: 'Indstuderet med L. Stramboe'
15.1.: 'Lille Prøve paa Nina'
16.1., 17.1., 18.1., 25.1., 31.1., 2.2., 6.2., 7.2., and 8.2.: 'Prøve paa Nina'
9.2.: 'Prøve paa Nina – Pantomimen færdig'
10.2.: 'indstuderet en Pas de trois'
12.2., 13.2., and 14.2.: 'componeret [...] Prøve paa Nina'
15.2.: 'componeret [...] Det sidste Dandse-Stykke færdigt til Nina'

16.2.: 'Prøve paa Nina'
18.2.: 'arrangeret Costumet til Nina'
19.2.: 'Prøve paa Dandsene til Nina'
20.2.: 'lille Prøve paa Nina'
23.2.: 'Indstuderingen fuldendt paa Balletten Nina'
27.2.: 'stor Prøve paa Nina, [J.]Collin og hans Damer tilstede. L. Stramboe ganske fortrinlig'
1.3.: 'lille Prøve med Jfr. [P. A.] Funck'
2.3.: 'stor Prøve paa Nina'
10.3.: 'Prøve […] paa Pas de trois de Nina for Jfr. [C.] Fjeldsted'
12.3.: 'Prøve paa Dandsene til Nina'
14.3.: 'Prøve paa Nina'
15.3.: 'Fortrinlig generalprøve paa Nina'
17.3.: 'Første Forestilling af den nȳ indstuderede Nina. Balletten gik fortrinligt. Laura Stramboe udførte Hovedrollen med Sandhed og Følelse, og blev meget applauderet, der var almindelig Tilfredshed og Huset var stærkt besat'
30.9.: 'Laura var mange Steder god men trænger til Politur'.

The 1849 production of *Nina, ou La Folle par amour* received 9 performances, the last of which was given on 16.9.1851.

20.3.1849
Echo of Sunday, Dance from Amager (Søndags=Echo. Amagerdands) **performed by Julius Price, Th. Price, W. Price, and C. Price (the Court Theatre).**

This divertissement was created especially for four of Bournonville's youngest pupils from the Price dynasty of dancers. According to its poster the music was 'arranged' (*arrangeret*) by H. S. Paulli. He used a popular 18th-century dance tune from the island of Amager, which J. F. Fröhlich had employed before him in his score for the overture and the finale in J. L. Heiberg's one-act vaudeville *A Sunday on Amager*, premièred at Copenhagen's Royal Theatre on 5.3.1848 (now in DKKk, call no. C II, 114 d (KTA 404)). This tune was orginally published by N. Schiörring in his so-called *Blandinger for Sang og Claveer. No. 2* from 1787 (Kiøbenhavn, Steins Skrifter, p. 8). It is there named *Amager=Dands*. Moreover, the same dance tune was many years later reused by V. C. Holm in his music for Bournonville's one-act ballet-vaudeville *The King's Corps of Volunteers on Amager* (*see* 19.2.1871). There it served as accompaniment for a dance (score no. 11) entitled *Tøndebaands-Dands*.

Finally, in his 1849 musical arrangement for Bournonville's *Echo of Sunday*, Paulli also employed two other minor excerpts borrowed from Fröhlich's score to Heiberg's vaudeville *A Sunday on Amager*, namely parts of the music for score no. '5 a', and a section of the *Allegro molto vivace* movement in score no. '9'.

In his diary Bournonville noted about the creation and the première of *Echo on Sunday*:

8.1.1849: 'Begyndt en Amagerdands for Prices Drenge'
9.1.: 'Amagerdands'
15.3.: 'Prøve paa Hoftheatret'
18.3.: 'Lille Prøve paa Amgerdandsen'
20.3.: 'Aften paa Hoftheatret. – Amagerdandsen ved Navn 'Söndags= Echo' gjorde furore og blev godt udfört af de smaaa Drenge Price'.

Echo of Sunday was given only once at the Court Theatre. However, on 23.3.1849 it was mounted at the Casino Theatre where it reached a total of 36 performances, the last of which was given on 21.4.1851.

Musical sources:

Musical draft. Ms. Autograph (by H. S. Paulli). Black ink. 4 pp. (33,6 × 24,6 cm)
[Untitled]
Unsigned and undated [1849]
[DKKk; MA ms 2618

No orchestral score for *Echo of Sunday* has yet been traced.

Répétiteur's copy. Ms Copy. Black ink. 4 pp. of which one is blank (34,5 × 24 cm with minor variants)
Repetiteur Parti/til/Söndags Echo.
Unsigned and undated [1849]
[DKKk; MA ms 2660

Parts. Ms. Copy. 25 vol.
2 vl I, 2 vl II, vla, 3 vlc e cb, fl picc, fl, ob 1/2, cl 1/2, fag 1/2, cor 1/2, cnt, tr 1/2, Btrb, timp, gr cassa e piatti, tri.
Unsigned and undated [1849]
[DKKk; MA ms 2661 (1-25)
Many of these parts hold Bournonville's autographed note 'Söndags Echo.' (written with brown ink), Moreover, his other autographed note on the part for the first oboe reads: 'Tilhører A: Price'.

23.3.1849
I Capuleti ed i Montecchi (Familierne Montecchi og Capulet).
For this 1849 Copenhagen restaging of V. Bellini's and N. Vaccai's melodrama in four parts (*see* 13.10.1847) Bournonville was for the first time explicitly credited on the poster for the choreography of the dance in Act II (score no. 6), performed by a corps de ballet and two couples during the opening chorus entitled «Lieta notte» («Fryd og Jubel nu os tilsmile»). For the same occasion he appears to have made a complete notation of its choreography in the opera's original répétiteur's copy (now in DKKk, call no. MA ms 2914 (2) (KTA 395 (1)). In his diary he noted about the restaging and its two first performances:

7.3. and 8.3.1849: 'Prøve paa Montecchi'
9.3.: 'Prøve paa Dandsen til Montecchi og General-prøve paa samme Opera'
10.3.: 'Operaen gaaer ikke!'
21.3.: 'Aftenprøve paa Montechi'
22.3.: 'Prøve paa Dandsen til Montechi'
23.3.: 'Overværet Operaen Montechi der gik meget godt. Jf [C.] Lehmann er en talentfuld Pige'.
29.3.: 'seet endeel af Romeo der gik særdeles godt og Jf Lehmann gjorde fortjent Lȳkke'.

The 1849 production of *I Capuleti ed i Montecchi* received 3 performances, the last of which was given on 16.4.1849.

23.3.1849
Echo of Sunday, Dance from Amager (Søndags=Echo. Amagerdands) **performed by Julius Price, Th. Price, W. Price, and C. Price (the Casino Theatre).**

This dance is identical with the divertissement of the same name, premièred at the Court Theatre on 20.3.1849. In his diary Bournonville noted about the only performance he attended of the dance on 15.5.1849:

'Benefice Forestilling i Casino for Rosa Price […] børnene dandsede smukt, der var fuldt Huus'.

Echo on Sunday was performed 36 times at the Casino Theatre, the last time on 21.4.1851. The musical sources employed there were most likely the same as those used for the Court Theatre performance (now in DKKk, call nos. MA ms 2660, and MA ms 2661 (1–25)).

1.5.1849

Die Hochzeit des Figaro (Figaros Bryllyp).

This restaging represents the first time W. A. Mozart's four-act comic opera (*see* 25.5.1842 and 7.1.1844) was mounted by Bournonville after his official appointment as *scene-instructeur* at Copenhagen's Royal Theatre. In his diary he noted about the performance:

27.4.1849: 'lille [...] Prøve paa B[yens]. T[heater]. paa Figaro 2 Akten'
28.4., 29.4., and 30.4.: 'Prøve paa Figaro'
1.5.: 'Overværet Figaro der fra nogle sider gik ȳderst maadeligt'.

The 1849 staging received 25 performances, the last of which was given on 15.4.1856.

2.5.1849

Pas de deux from 'La Muette de Portici' (Pas de deux af 'Den Stumme i Portici') (uncredited) performed by S. Lund and S. Price (the Court Theatre).

This (uncredited) dance is, according to Bournonville's diary, identical with the so-called *A New Pas de deux composed by Mr. Dance Director Bournonville*, first performed on 23.9.1834 by F. Hoppe and L. Grahn as an incorporated divertissement in Act I of D.-F.-E. Auber's five-act opera *La Muette de Portici*. It was mounted this year as part of a charity performance, arranged by the violoncellist in the Royal Theatre orchestra, P. F. Rauch, in order to raise funds for the widows of Danish soldiers who had fallen in the battle at Eckernförde. In his diary Bournonville noted about the performance:

'Prøve paa [P. F.] Rauchs patriotiske Aftenunderholdning [...] Aftenunderhold. paa Hoftheatret. – Sophie Price dandsede Pas de deux af Stumme med Sig. Lund'.

6.5.1849

The Conservatoire, or A Proposal of Marriage through the Newspaper (Conservatoriet, eller Et Avisfrieri).

This two-act ballet-vaudeville, in which Bournonville reflects on his memories from his years of study in Paris, was conceived during the late summer of 1848 and found its final form in the early spring of 1849. It was created for the début of one of his best pupils, Juliette Price, who performed the rôle of the ballerina *Eliza*, and represents the first in a long series of ballets created for this dancer.

The score, which is divided into twelve numbers, was composed and arranged by H. S. Paulli. He incorporated several musical borowings, which are identified as follows:

(1) In the introduction and score no. 1 of Act I Paulli interpolated his own (slightly abridged) orchestral version of C. M. v. Weber's piece for piano *Aufforderung zum Tanze, Rondo brillant*, op. 65 (first published in Berlin in 1821). This popular piano piece (in France known as *Invitation à la valse*) had already been incorporated by the French choreographer, J. Mazilier, as a ballet divertissement (orchestrated by H. Berlioz) in Weber's three-act romantic opera *Le Freyschutz*, when it was given its French première at the Paris Opéra on

7.6.1841. Bournonville had attended several rehearsals of Mazilier's divertissement during his sojourn in Paris in the spring of 1841. He may, therefore, then have conceived his plan of using an orchestral version of Weber's music for a later ballet of his own invention.

(2) In score no. 3 (*Pas d'Ecole*) Paulli interpolated two borrowed excerpts, the first of which (*Allegretto* in 3/4 time, performed by a corps de ballet of children) is based on the main theme of the Act I finale (score no. 4) in H. Berton's three-act opera *Aline, Reine de Golconde* (premièred at the Paris Opéra on 2.9.1803). In that opera it was originally sung by a chorus with the text «Honneur honneur aux français». The same theme was later also used by J. Mayseder in his concert-piece for solo violin from 1812, entitled *Variationen in A-Dur* (op. 3). Moreover, in 1821 it was employed by Archduke J. J. R. Rudolph in his so-called *Ländler mit variazione* and which was originally part of his orchestral suite, named *Serenata en Si bemolle*.

The second borrowed excerpt in Paulli's *Pas d'Ecole* (an *Allegretto* in 6/8 time, performed as a *brisé* variation by the character *Alexis* alternating with the corps de ballet) is according to a source, entitled 'Receuils de Ballets' (now in FPo, call no. Receuil XII, no. 24), identical with the so-called 'Air de danse' which was interpolated by E. L. Müller on 5.4.1788 in his own earlier score for M. Gardel's two-act ballet *La Rosière* (premièred at the Paris Opéra on 29.7.1783). The exact same music was also incorporated by L. J. M. Deland in his two-act pantomimic ballet *The Peasant Wedding or The Corsairs (Bondbröl-loppet eller Corsarerne)*, when it was premièred at Stockholm's Royal Theatre on 22.5.1813. Deland, who was a pupil of Gardel (aîné), may thus have brought Müller's music to Stockholm during the early 19th century. According to the original set of parts for Deland's ballet (now in SSkma, call no. KT Pantomime Balletter C 3) Müller's 'Air de danse' was performed in Act I (score no. 4) in which it accompanied a *Pas de deux*, danced by C. J. Ambrosiani and J. G. Védel-Sainte-Claire. In Copenhagen Paulli, too, had used parts of Müller's music when he arranged the score for Bournonville's one-act allegorical ballet *The White Rose, or The Summer in Bretagne (see* 20.9.1847).

(3) In score no. 4 (a *Pas de trois* performed by the characters *Alexis, Victorine*, and *Eliza*) Paulli employed nearly all of J. P. Rode's *Septième Concerto pour le violin, oeuvre 9*, from 1800 (first published by M. Trentsensky & Vieweg in Vienna, pl. no. A. O W. 2840, c. mid-1830s). This concerto had become widely popular in Denmark in 1814 when F. Kuhlau wrote a *Rondo* for piano based on the main theme of Rode's finale (first published by C. C. Lose in Copenhagen as part of his music anthology, entitled *Nye Apollo*, 1. Aarg., I, pp. 1–5). However, Rode's music was used for the first time in a balletic context by J. Schneitzhoeffer. Thus, in 1826 he had incorporated it in his score for Act I of J. B. Blache's four-act ballet *Mars et Vénus ou Les Filets de Vulcain* (premièred at the Paris Opéra on 29.5.1826). According to the original répétiteur's copy for this ballet (now in FPo, call no. Mat. 19 [151 (1), pp. 129–141) it there accompanied a *Pas de trois* in the ballet's third scene, performed by the French dancers, A. Paul (playing *Zéphyre*), P. Montessu (*Flore*) and L. Noblet (*Venus*). Bournonville had seen this dance on several occasions at the Paris Opéra during his sojourn there in the late 1820s. Consequently, the possibility that he may have reused the orignal choreography of Blache's 1826 *Pas de trois* as model for his own *Pas de trois* in Act I of *The Conservatoire, or A Proposal of Marriage through the Newspaper* cannot be discounted.

(4) In Act II, score no. 10 Paulli incorporated his free arrangement and orchestration of nearly all of F. Chopin's *Grande valse brillante*, op. 18 (first published in Leipzig in 1834). To this popular waltz he added a new Coda movement (presumably of his own composition). It is followed by excerpts from G. Paisiello's duet «Nel cor più non mi sento», that was originally part of Act II (scene 1) in his 1789 opera *L'Amor contrastato* (also known as *La Molinara*). This tune, in turn, is based on a Neapolitan folk song, entitled *Felicella*, and had become widely popular after L. v. Beethoven employed it for his six variations for piano (WoO 70, first published in Vienna in 1796).

Next follows a series of brief repeats of Chopin's waltz and Paisiello's duet and the scene concludes with an excerpt, entitled *Rondo*, borrowed from Fr. H. Prüme's *Concertino* for solo violin and orchestra. Bournonville would probably have known this popular rondo from when Prüme had played it himself in Copenhagen at two concerts, given at the Royal Theatre on 27.12.1840 and the Court Theatre on 12.4.1845. In *The Conservatoire, or A Proposal of Marriage through the Newspaper* this rondo accompanied the *Pas de trois*, danced by *Elisa* and *Victorine* joined by *Fanny*.

(5) In the *Finale* (score no. 12) Paulli incorporated H. C. Lumbye's *Telegraph Galop*, which was first published in Copenhagen by C. C. Lose & Olsen in September 1844, a copy of which is now in DKKk (call no. D 24). This galop is mingled with an excerpt borrowed from the finale movement of a so-called *La véritable Polka Parisienne*, to music by an anonymous composer. The polka, too, had been published in Copenhagen in 1844 by Lose & Olsen (now in DKKk, call no. U 30). Finally, Paulli's *Finale* includes a brief excerpt of F. Elssler's Spanish solo dance *La Cachucha*, first performed at the Paris Opéra on 1.6.1836.

An abridged divertissement version of this ballet (entitled *'Scene and Pas de trois from The Conservatoire'*) was mounted by Bournonville at Christiania's Theatre (Oslo) on 22.6.1852, while the whole ballet was staged at Stockholm's Royal Theatre (Operahuset) on 26.5.1857, in a slightly revised version that omitted the Act I *Pas de trois* (score no. 4).

In Copenhagen the complete ballet was restaged three more times by Bournonville, on 15.9.1865, 28.9.1870, and 4.12.1874, each time with only minor choreographic and musical changes.

In his diary he noted about the ballet's creation and its 1849 première:

19.9.1848: 'begÿndte paa en nÿ Ballet. 'Ungdoms=Luner''
20.9.: 'Jeg fuldendte min Ballet, der forekom mig vellÿkket […] Jeg følte mig usigelig lÿkkelig […] Kunsten skjænkende mig et nÿ Produkt — det bedste Haab for Fremtiden og Tillid til Gud. – Jeg nød Sjælefrÿd og Fred'
21.9.: 'skrevet'
8.10.: 'skrevet, arbeidet med [H. S.] Paulli til Kl 11'
11.10.: 'Arbeidet med Paulli'
30.10.: 'begyndt at componere paa min nÿe Ballet […] hjem hvor jeg componerede lidt paa den første Scene'
2.11.: 'Første Prøve paa min nÿ Ballet 'Ungdoms=Luner'
3.11.: 'Prøve paa Balletten'
4.11.: 'componeret […] Prøve paa Balletten'
6.11.: 'Prøve paa den nÿe Ballet'
8.11.: 'Prøve paa […] min nÿ Ballet […] Möde med [G. F.] Lassen og Malerne'
13.11.: 'Prøve paa den nÿ Ballet'
15.11.: 'componeret paa min nÿe Ballet […] componeret'
16.11.: 'Prøve paa min nÿ Ballet'
18.11.: 'Prøvet paa den nÿe Ballet'
21.11.: 'arbeidet med Paulli'
24.11.: 'skrevet til [P.] Taglioni i Berlin'
25.11.: 'Brev reenskrevet til Paul Taglioni'
26.11.: 'componeret paa den nÿe Ballet'
27.11.: 'Prøve paa den nÿ Ballet'
29.11.: 'Prøve paa Conservatoriet; sluttet 1.ste Act'
22.12.: 'Prøve igjen paa 'Ungdoms Luner' som jeg formodentlig omdöber til 'En Udflugt fra Conservatoriet''
3.1.1849: 'arbeidet med Paulli'
7.1.: 'componeret'
18.2.: 'Musik med Paulli'
13.3.: 'Begÿndt at lære Juliette [Price] sin Debut-Rolle i den nÿe Ballet'
16.3.: 'Prøve med Juliette'
21.3.: 'Prøve paa den nÿ Ballet'
24.3.: 'Prøve og Memorering af den nÿ Ballet'
26.3. and 29.3.: 'Prøve paa den nye Ballet'
30.3.: 'Prøve paa det nÿe. Fuldendt en Række Scener i 2.den Act'
3.4. and 6.4.: 'componeret'
7.4.: 'Prøve paa min nÿ Ballet'

8.4.: 'i Frue Kirke, god christelig Prædiken, Bøn for det betrængte Fædreland…Alle Mænd maatte græde bitterligt, men ikke uden Haab om Frelse, ikke uden Tanke om Gjengjeldelse'
9.4.: 'Lection til Pricerne, indstuderet en scène for at forslaae Sorgen'
11.4.: 'Prøve paa 'Conservatoriet''
14.4.: 'Prøve paa `Conservatoriet´ […] arbeidet med Paulli paa den sidste Scene af Balletten'
17.4.: 'componeret paa den sidste Scene'
18.4.: 'Componeret […] Prøve paa Finalen til den nÿ Ballet'
19.4.: 'Op Kl 6, componeret Slutningen af min Ballet […] Prøve paa 'Conservatoriet' Balletten færdig indstuderet'
20.4..: 'Dandse=Prøve paa 'Conservatoriet' Juliette var fortreffelig'
21.4.: 'Prøve paa Conservatoriet'
24.4.: 'skrevet mit Program'
25.4.: 'begyndt at reenskrive Programmet'
26.4.: 'meget betÿdelig Prøve paa Hoftheatret fuldstændig. [J. G.] Levetzau var tilstede, [C. N.] Rosenkilde, Helene [Bournonville], Eva [Suell] og nogle Børn. Det gik ÿpperligt. Balletten behagede og Juliette dandsede nÿdelgt'
27.4.: 'fuldendt mit Program'
1.5.: 'Prøve paa Balletten'
3.5.: 'fuldstændig Prøve paa Byens Theater. Balletten gik særdeles godt og lovede at gjøre Lÿkke'
5.5.: 'Generalprøve. Juliette præsterede udmærket – med 2.den Acts Udførelse var jeg mindre tilfreds'
6.5.: 'holdt en lille Prøve paa de svage Steder. […] Første Forestilling af Balletten Conservatoriet og Juliettes Debüt. Alt gik fortreffeligt og vandt stormende Bifald. Jeg tror at Det kan regnes som en complet Succes'.

The 1849 production of *The Conservatoire, or A Proposal of Marriage through the Newspaper* received 59 performances (the last given on 16.9.1858) and the ballet reached a total of 93 performances during Bournonville's lifetime, the last of which was given on 24.3.1879.

Autograph sources:

Manuscript scenario. Ms. Autograph. Brown ink. 1 vol. 11 pp. (20,7 × 17,4 cm)
Ungdoms= Luner eller Et Lÿst = Partie./Vaudeville = Ballet i en Akt/ af/Auguste Bournonville./1848.
Signed and dated: 'Fredensborg d. 20 Sept. 1848.'
[DKKk; NKS 3285 4° 3 R–U

Production note. Ms. Autograph (partially by another hand). Black ink. 2 pp. (33,5 × 20,5 cm).
Person = Liste/til/Balletten Conservatoriet eller En Avisfrieri.
Unsigned and undated [1849]
[DKKkt; F.M. (Ballet)

Musical sources:

Musical draft (fragment). Ms. Autopgraph (by H. S. Paulli). Brown ink. 4 pp. (35 × 25,5 cm)
[Untitled]
Unsigned and undated [c.1849]
[DKKk; C II, 10 (H. S. Paullis Efterladte mss. II)
This musical draft contains a fragment of Paulli's first draft for the music in Act II (score no. 10). A pencilled note on p. 4 (reading 'Prume') clearly indicates where Paulli incorporated Fr. H. Prüme's *Rondo* from his *Concertino* for solo violin and orchestra.

Orchestral score. Ms. Autograph (by H. S. Paulli). Brown ink. 1 vol. 236 pp. of which one is blank (25,8 × 36,8 cm with minor variants)
264./Conservatoriet./Partitur
Signed and dated (on p. 236): 'HSPaulli/29 April 1849.'
[DKKk; MA ms 1550 (KTB 264)

Répétiteur's copy. Ms. Autograph (by H. S. Paulli). Ink. 1 vol. 91 pp. (format unknown)
[Untitled]/Allegro vivace No. 1
Unsigned and undated [1849]
[USNYp; Dance Collection (microfilm), call no. *ZBD-74
This répétiteur's copy for *The Conservatoire* was originally part of the Royal Theatre's music archive (call no. KTB 264), but disappeared from there in the early 1950s. It contains several autographed notes by Bournonville, which describe (in general terms) the mime and the choreography throughout the ballet. Moreover, his many other autographed choreographic numbers in this volume seem to refer to the later complete notation of his revised 1865 version of *The Conservatoire* (according to his diary written between 19.6 and 19.7.1865, and certainly prior to its first performance on 15.9.1865).

Parts. Ms. Copy. 37 vol.
4 vl I, 4 vl II, 2 vla, 4 vlc e cb, fl 1/2, ob 1/2, cl 1/2, fag 1/2, cor 1/2/3/4, tr 1/2, cnt, trb 1/2/3, timp, gr cassa, piatti, tri, arpa.
Unsigned and undated [1849]
[DKKk; KTB 264

Other sources:

Drawing by E. Lehmann. Pencil and water colours (17,4 × 12,8 cm)
Conservatoriet
Signed and dated: 'E. L./[18]49.'
[DKKt; Lehmann tegninger
This drawing shows the scene in Act II, scene 3 (score no. 9) of *The Conservatoire* where *Dufour* (F. Hoppensach) declares his love for the disguised *Eliza* (J. Price).

Drawing by E. Lehmann. Pencil and water colours (18 × 13 cm)
[Untitled]
Unsigned and undated [c.1849]
[DKKt; Lehmann tegninger
This drawing is a replica of the previous drawing showing the scene in Act II, scene 3 (score no. 9) of *The Conservatoire* in which *Dufour* (F. Hoppensach) declares his love for the disguised *Eliza* (J. Price).

Drawing by E. Lehmann. Pencil and water colours (23 × 16,9 cm)
(Af Bournonvilles Ballet 'Conservatoriet' -)
Signed and dated: 'E. L./1849'
[DKKk; Ms. phot 125 fol (Helene Bournonvilles stambog, photographic reproduction)
This drawing (the original of which is now in a private collection) shows the same scene from Act II of *The Conservatoire* which is also depicted on the two previous Lehmann drawings. It was made as a personal gift to Bournonville's wife, Helene Bournonville, and pasted into her album on p. 17.

Printed sources:

Printed scenario. 1 vol. 12 pp.
Conservatoriet/eller/Et Avisfrieri./Vaudeville=Ballet i to Akter/af/August Bournonville./Musiken arrangeret og componeret af H. Paulli.
Kjøbenhavn, J. H. Schubothe/Bianco Luno, 1849.
[DKKk; 17, – 174 8°

15.5.1849
Pas des trois cousines **performed by J. Price, S. Price, and A. Price (the Casino Theatre).**
This performance represents Bournonville's second and last staging at the Casino Theatre of his *Pas des trois cousines* (see 20.5.1848). In his diary he noted about it on the opening night:

'Pigebørnene dandsede smukt'.

It was mounted with only two rehearsals, held on 12.5. and 14.5.1849. The posters this year read: 'NB. Hovedpartiet udføres af Jfr. Juliette Price'. This seems to indicate that the dance was mounted in a choreographically slightly revised version which reflected the rapid technical progress of this, one of Bournonville's favourite pupils. Moreover, the 1849 posters give for the first time explicit credit to H. S. Paulli for having 'arranged' (*arrangeret*) the music. The original 1848 musical sources (now in DKKk, call no. C II, 105, Efterslæt 5) seem also to have served for this production.

15.5.1849
Tyrolean Polka composed by Mr. Bournonville (Tyroler=Polka componeret af Hr. Bournonville) **performed by E. Stramboe and A. Price (the Casino Theatre).**
This dance was choreographed for a special charity performance given for the dancer, Rosa Price (mother of Juliette and Sophie Price) and was performed by two of his pupils, E. Stramboe, and the eighteen-year-old Amalia Price. In his diary he noted about the dance, which was performed only once:

12.5.1849: 'Prøve paa Dandsene til Casino'
14.5.: 'Prøve i Casino'
15.5.: 'Benefice- Forestilling i Casino for Rosa Price […] der var fuldt Huus'.

No musical sources for this dance have yet been traced.

20.5.1849
Pas de deux from La Muette de Portici (Pas de deux af den Stumme i Portici) **(uncredited) performed by S. Lund and S. Price (the Casino Theatre).**
This (uncredited) dance is certainly identical with the so-called *A New Pas de deux composed by Mr. Dance Director Bournonville*, first performed by F. Hoppe and L. Grahn on 23.9.1834 as an incorporated divertissement in Act I of D.-F.-E. Auber's five-act opera *La Muette de Portici*. No separate musical sources dating from its 1849 performance at the Casino Theatre have yet been traced. This seems to indicate that the *Pas de deux* (which was given only once at the Casino Theatre) was performed there using the Royal Theatre's musical material (now in DKKk, call nos. MA ms 2603, MA ms 2700, KTB 209).

20.5.1849
'Holmen's Old Guard', Dance for Sailor's children ('Holmens faste Stok', Dands for Matrosbørn) **(the Casino Theatre).**
This dance was choreographed especially for a charity performance given for the actor, A. Price. It was performed by four of the children in the Price dynasty of dancers, Julius, Theodor, Waldemar, and Carl, all of whom were among Bournonville's pupils and later became some of the leading dancers and/or actors at the Royal Theatre.
According to Bournonville's memoirs *My Theatre Life* (p. 173) the performance of this dance concluded with an apotheosis showing a series of Danish naval heroes. The music was based on J. O. E. Horneman's tune to A. F. v. d. Recke's patriotic song, *Sang til Flaaden*, the first line of which reads «Holmens fast Stok, lysteligt hinanden praier, de har

sikkert nok lugtet Tydskens Rævestreger». It was first published in Copenhagen by J. D. Qvist in 1848 (a copy of which is now in DKKk, call no. D 204).

In his diary Bournonville noted about the creation and the first performance of the dance:

16.5.1849: 'nỹ Idée til en Børneballet Holmens faste Stok'
17.5.: 'Componeret Matrosdandsen'
18.5.: 'Indstuderet Matrosdandsen med Børnene fra 9 til 1.'
19.5.: 'Prøve Kl 10 og Kl 1 paa Matrosdandsen'
20.5.: 'Prøve i Casino Kl 11 meget heldig [...] Benefice Forestilling i Casino med min nỹe Dands 'Holmens faste Stok' der gjorde stormende Furore'.

'Holmen's Old Guard', which was given once at the Casino Theatre, was also mounted at the Royal Theatre on 9.6. 1849, and at the fair in the Rosenborg Gardens on 16.8.1849. No separate musical sources dating from its Casino Theatre première have yet been traced.

9.6.1849
Holmen's Old Guard, Divertissement (Holmens faste Stok, Divertissement).

This dance divertissement (originally choreographed for a charity performance at the Casino Theatre on 20.5.1849) was mounted at the Royal Theatre as part of yet another charity performance, this time for the actor H. P. Knudsen. It was performed by four of the children in the Price dynasty of dancers (Julius, Theodor, Waldemar, and Carl Price) who were here joined by students (male and female) from the Royal Danish Ballet School. Thus, the poster describes this new casting as follows:

'The Price children and the students of the Royal dancing school. The leadings parts are performed by Julius Price, [Harald] Scharf[f], Bianca Bills and Gjødesen'.

In his diary Bournonville noted about the rehearsals and the reception of the dance:

8.6.1849: 'Prøve paa Det kgl. Theater for [H.] P Knudsens Benefice'
9.6.: 'Prøve paa Holmens faste Stok [...] Knudsens Forestilling, brilliant Huus. Dandsen gjorde furore'.

The dance was performed 8 times at the Royal Theatre, the last time on 2.11.1850. No separate musical sources dating from its performance at the Royal Theatre have yet been traced.

14.6.1849
Deux mots, ou Une nuit dans la forêt (To Ord eller Natten i Skoven).

For the 1849 restaging of N. Dalayrac's one-act comic opera (premièred in Paris at l'Opéra Comique on 9.6.1806, and first performed in Copenhagen on 19.12.1818) Bournonville gave personal stage instructions to the dancer, L. Stramboe, who this year played the rôle of Rose for the first time. Gifted with an extraordinarily mimic talent, Stramboe made her début as actress within this work, which was mounted as part of a special charity performance for the actor, J. R. Waltz. In his diary Bournonville noted about the performance:

12.6.1849: 'Prøve paa To Ord (Laura Stramboe)'
14.6: 'Prøve paa To Ord [...] [J. R.] Waltz's Sommerforestilling [...] Laura Stramboe meget god i De to Ord'.

The 1849 production of *Deux mots, ou Une nuit dans la forêt* was given only once.

Musical sources:

No orchestral score and répétiteur's copy dating from the 1849 performance of *Deux Mots, ou Une nuit dans la forêt* at Copenhagen's Royal Theatre have yet been traced.

Parts. Ms. Copy. 22 vol.
3 vl I, 3 vl II, 2 vla, 4 vlc e cb, fl 1/2, cl 1/2, fag 1/2, cor 1/2, timp, arpa. 3 vocal parts.
Unsigned and undated [c.1818]
[DKKk; KTA 192
This set of parts dates from the 1818 Copenhagen première of Dalayrac's singspiel and was most probably also used for the 1849 restaging.

16.8.–18.8.1849
The fair in the Rosenborg Gardens on behalf of distressed Jutlanders (Markedet i Rosenborg Have til Fordel for de betrængte Jyder) including a Divertissement of three dances.

The divertissement which Bournonville choreographed for this fair (given on behalf of the distressed Jutlanders, who had been overrun by the German army in the summer of 1849) consisted of three dances:

(1) A so-called *Rosenborg Quadrille*.
(2) A *Hussar Dance*.
(3) A *Reel*.

They were all performed by Bournonville's students at the the Royal Theatre's ballet school, joined by his private pupils among the children of the Price dynasty of dancers. According to the printed programme the music for the three dances consisted of the following works:

(1) H. C. Lumbye's *Rosenborg Quadrille*, composed especially for this occasion.
(2) Lumbye's polka, entitled *Hilsen til Jylland* and composed especially for this fair.
(3) J. O. E. Hornemann's melody to A. F. v. d. Recke's song from 1848, entitled *Sang til Flaaden* (see 20.5.1849).

The *Rosenborg Quadrille* was only given on the first day of the fair (16.8.) and the *Reel* only on its last day (18.8.). The *Hussar Dance* was later the same year mounted as a separate divertissement at the Court Theatre on 21.11.1849, but then with the new title 'Greetings to Jutland' ('Hilsen til Jylland').

For the same fair Bournonville also mounted three allegorical tableaux, which were performed on a stage erected in front of the Herkules Pavilion. They are described in the printed programme (*Markedstidende*) as follows:

'1ste Gruppe: Holger Danske beskyttende en kronet Qvinde' (1st Tableau: Holger Danske protecting a crowned Woman).
'2.den Gruppe: Danneqvinderne løskjøbe Svend Tveskjæg af Fangenskab' (2nd Tableau: The Good women and true ransom Svend Tveskjæg from imprisonment).
'3die Gruppe: Danmark velsigner sine Børn' (3rd Tableau: Denmark blesses her natives).

The tableaux were given only on the two last days of the fair (17.8. and 18.8.1849).

On 21.8.1849 Bournonville noted about his participation in the organisation of the fair:

'Alle disse Dage stærkt beskjæftiget med Markedet i Rosenborg Hauge, hvorved jeg havde Arrangementet af Musiken, Dandsen, Tableauerne, Emblemerne, Mindetavlerne og Blomster-Udsalget, samt en stor Deel af Beværtningen. Søndag d. 12., Mand. d. 13, Tirsd d. 14 og Onsd. d. 15. Forberedelser i Haugen. [...] Rustninger [...], opstillede Krigs-Embl:er, [...] Søe-Emblemet. – [...] Agerdyrknings-Embl:, Styrmand Hansen oprejste en mast ved en høi Estrade og Orchestret fra Ridehuset stilledes under Træerne paa Træsplænen. [C. F.] Christensen besørgede alle Boutiquer og [M. H.] Bing det hele Vareforraad. Helene var meget behjælpelig med Damesagerne, over 80 af Kbhvns vakkreste Damer solgte i Boutiquen [...] og en Deel unge Piger hvoriblandt Augusta [Bournonville] i Blomsterboutiquen. – Veiret var fortreffeligt. Torsdagen havde vi 23,000 Mennesker, Fredagen over 30,000, og om Löverdagen med lidt ustadigt Veir henved 17,000. – Indtægten fra Billetter oversteg 20,000 Rbdl. og Vahrene gik brilliant af og betaltes meget høit. – Folk vare ÿpperligt stemte og Alle takkede mig for min Deel i Arrangementet. Nogle Invalider holdt Vagt ved Trophæerne og høstede rige Gaver, alle Saarede havde fri Adgang. Auctionen gav Anledning til mange humoristiske Træk. Tombolaen og Festbordet gjorde Furore. – Skiveskydningen og den lille Lirekasse indbragte mange Penge. – De gymnastiske Lege og Dandsene bleve stærkt applauderede, Tableauerne ligesaa. Sangforeningerne gjorde en ÿpperlig Virkning. Kongen kom om Fredag formiddag. – Indtægten af det Hele overstiger 50,000 Rbdl!'

Musical sources:

No autographed orchestral scores, répétiteur's copies, and parts for Lumbye's *Rosenborg Quadrille* and *Hilsen til Jylland* have yet been traced. However, a printed piano score of the latter now exists in DKKk (call no. D 24, x39020425x). Moreover, a full manuscript copy score and set of parts containing the full orchestral version of Lumbye's polka *Hilsen til Jylland* are included among the musical material for Bournonville's later *Pas seul*, entitled '*Echo from Denmark*' and premièred at Stockholm's Royal Theatre (Operahuset) on 26.9.1849 (now in SSkma, call no. KT Dansmusik 78).

Other sources:

Miniature book with 8 drawings by E. Lehmann. Pencil and watercolours (5 × 4 cm)
Tegne-Bog/for/Dukker.
Unsigned and undated [c.1849]
[DKKk; Private collection (Copenhagen)
This book contains 8 drawings that capture different scenes from the 1849 fair in the Rosenborg Gardens.

Printed sources:

Printed programmes. 3 vol. 12 pp. (25,7 × 17 cm)
Markeds-Tidende./No. 1./[...]/No. 2/[...]/No. 3/[...]/1849
Copenhagen, Redigeret og forlagt af Eduard Meyer, Trykt hos J. G. Salomon, 16.8.–18.8.1849.
[DKKk; 37, – 429 4°

8.9.1849
Pas des trois composed by Mr. Ballet-master Bournonville (comp. af Hr. Balletmester Bournonville) performed by Juliette Price, S. Price, and A. Price.
This performance marks the first time that Bournonville's *Pas des trois cousines* (*see* 20.5.1848) was performed at Copenhagen's Royal Theatre. In his diary he noted about it on the opening night:

'Pas des trois cousines gik udmærket godt'.

The 1849 staging received 20 performances with the original cast at the Royal Theatre, the last of which was given on 31.5.1853.

Musical sources:

No orchestral score and répétiteur's copy dating from the 1849 staging of *Pas des trois cousines* at the Royal Theatre have yet been traced. However, a later manuscript copy of the orchestral score and a complete set of parts (both probably dating from a restaging of this dance at the Royal Theatre in the 1880s) are now in DKKk (call nos. C II, 119, and KTB 318)

Parts. Ms. Copy. 30 vol.
3 vl I, 3 vl II, 2 vla, 3 vlc e cb, fl 1/2, ob 1/2, cl 1/2, fag 1/2, cor 1/2, tr 1/2, cnt, trb 1/2/3, timp, gr cassa, piatti e tri.
Unsigned and undated [1846]
[DKKk; KTB 211
Notes written in several of these parts give three different titles for this work ('Tableauerne', 'Pas de trois', and 'Blomsterdandsen'). They seem to indicate that these parts were used for at least two other earlier Bournonville's dances, namely the *Tableau with Dance* (*see* 12.10.1846) and the *Flower Dance (Blomsterdands)* (*see* 20.10.1847). Other notes indicate the duration of the music as 12 minutes.

10.9.1849
The decoration of the barracks for a welcome-feast given for the returning soldiers of the artillery (the Barracks of the Artillery in Copenhagen).
In his diary Bournonville noted about his involvement in the organisation of this public feast, given for the returning soldiers from Denmark's war with Germany:

'Jeg passede min Lection, men var fra Kl 6 af beskjæftiget med Festen til Artilleriets Modtagelse. Vi holdt den i Artilleri=Casernens Ridehuus. Jeg havde besørget den hele Decoration i forening med Malermester Bruun. – Damerne stod os bi med Opdækning til 600 Mand. – Borde og Bænke stod som til et Bryllup. Kl 8 kom Batterierne [T.] Jessen og Schultz med General [F. C. A.] v: Bauditz og hele Officeercorpset – Alt gik fortreffeligt. Taler og Sange. – Munterhed og Hjertelighed. Stort Publicum og den herligste Stemning. Festen var forbi Kl 11'.

Two months earlier, when the news of Denmark's victory over the German army in the Battle of Fredericia had reached him, he noted in his diary on 7.7.1849:

'Mageløs Glæde ved Underretningen om et afgjørende Slag under Fredericia, de danske have vunden en fuldstændig Seir over Insnigenterne. 1800 fanger, Alt Beleiringsskytset, endeel Fæltskyts. Beleiringen hævet, Fjenden forfulgt. – Gud jeg takker Dig! Du vil ikke Danmarks Undergang! – Sommerens Varme indfandt sig just Idag. – Hæderens Sol lÿser atter over vore Vaaben. Gud beskÿt mit elskede Fædreland! Jeg var den hele Dag i en høi og religiøs Stemning og hele Hovedstaden deelte denne Stemning. En Masse Mennesker paa Langelinie for at see Fangeskibene ankomme – De ventedes først til Natten'.

16.9.1849
The decoration of a tent erected in the courtyard of the Garnison's Hospital for a feast for the wounded soldiers (the Garnison's Hospital, Copenhagen).
In his diary Bournonville noted about his involvement in the organisation of this public feast, given for the wounded soldiers in Denmark's war with Germany:

11.7.1849: 'Jeg besøgte Garnisons-Hospitalet med Jordbær til de inat ankomne Saarede. – jeg havde megen glæde af dem, – en Tambour og en Jæger gav deres Portioner til andre, det rørte mig særdeles'

12.9.: 'Besøgt Garnisonshospitalet hvor der forberedes et lille Gilde'

15.9.: 'Jeg var ude paa Garnisonshospitalet og hjalp til med Arrangementet'

16.9.: 'Hele Dagen beskjæftiget med en Fest for Garnisonshospitalets saarede. – Jeg hjalp med at reise og decorere et stort Telt midt i Gaarden, stort til 200 Peroner. Commandanten og flere Generaler vare tilstede. Jeg udbragte en Skaal for de Saarede […] Det Hele gik smukt og vandt almindelig Anerkjendelse'.

20.9.1849
Hagbarth and Signe (Hagbarth og Signe).

The 1849 restaging of A. Oehlenschläger's five-act tragedy is not included in any of of Bournonville's handwritten lists of his stagings of operas and plays (*see* Additional Sources) nor in the printed survey of his works in his memoirs *My Theatre Life*. However, according to the rehearsal book of H. C. J. Fredstrup, Bournonville clearly directed two rehearsals of its dances (on 11.9. and 19.9.1849) in preparation for this restaging. These dances (which are set to music by a not yet identified composer) were originally choreographed by his father, Antoine Bournonville, when *Hagbarth and Signe* was given its première at Copenhagen's Royal Theatre on 19.1.1816. They included:

(1) A *March* in Act I.
(2) A *Dands* in Act III followed by an (unnamed) *Dance*, performed during a chorus in that same act.
(4) A *Funeral March* (*Sørge musik*) in Act V.

The 1849 restaging of *Hagbarth and Signe* received 20 performances, the last of which was given on 13.9.1862.

Musical sources:

No orchestral score and répétiteur's copy for *Hagbarth and Signe* have yet been traced.

Parts. Ms. copy. 32 vol.
3 vl I, 3 vl II, 2 vla, 4 vlc e cb, fl 1/2, ob 1/2, cl 1/2, fag 1/2, cor 1/2, tr 1/2, Atrb, Ttrb, Btrb, timp, gr cassa, tamb e cnt a chiavi, piatti, tri. Unsigned and undated (c.1816)
[DKKk; C II, 105
This sets of parts is included in a collection of 32 vols. containing the music which was incorporated in plays given at Copenhagen's Royal Theatre during the late 18th and early 19th century. It is entitled 'Musik til Skuespil (Chor, Romancer, Marscher)' and contains music for 41 plays.

21.9.1849
Pas de deux (uncredited) performed by W. Funck and P. Funck.

This (uncredited) dance is perhaps identical to the *Pas de deux* choreographed by W. Funck to music by the Italian composer, A. Curmi, for which the orchestral score and set of parts are now in DKKk (call nos. C I, 231, and KTB 233). Another possible identification of this dance is the so-called *Pas de deux arranged by Ballet Master Bournonville*, mounted only two years earlier for Bournonville's Swedish pupil, M. C. Norberg, and performed by her and Funck at Copenhagen's Royal Theatre on 14.3.1847. The *Pas de deux* was given only once during the 1849–50 season. It is not possible to identify the dance any further.

22.9.1849
La Sylphide (Sylphiden).

This performance represents the first, revised restaging in Copenhagen of Bournonville's and H. S. v. Løvenskjold's Danish version of F. Taglioni's two-act romantic ballet *La Sylphide* (*see* 28.11.1836). It was mounted especially for Juliette Price, who played the title rôle for the first time, partnered by F. Hoppe as *James*. According to Bournonville's pencilled autographed choreographic notes in the original 1836 répétiteur's copy (now in DKKk, call no. MA ms 2970a) and other notes (written with brown ink) in a separate fragment of the same répétiteur's copy (also in DKKk, call no. MA ms 2710, p. 12), the main difference between the original 1836 version and this restaging seems to relate to the divertissement in Act II (score no. 3), where a musical excerpt (*Allegro vivo e grazioso*), which was borrowed from Act II, score no. 9 of Løvenskjold's earlier score for Bournonville's two-act allegorical ballet *The New Penelope, or The Spring Festival in Athens* (*see* 26.1.1847) was incorporated and performed by the corps de ballet of sylphs alternating with *The Sylph*.

Moreover, parts of the choreography in Act II were notated by Bournonville in the original 1836 répétiteur's copy this year. This is clear from his pencilled notes which include the name of the dancer, S. Price. She appeared in *La Sylphide* for the first time in 1849 in a minor soloist part as one of the leading sylphs of the corps de ballet.

In his diary Bournonville noted about the staging and Juliette Price's début in the title rôle:

23.8.1849: 'Prøve paa Sylphiden med [F.] Hoppe og Juliette [Price]'
29.8., 31.8., and 3.9.: 'Prøve paa Sylphiden'
4.9.: 'Examen for Directionen af Juliette Price der udmærkede sig særdeles og udførte Sylphidens Rolle til stor Tilfredshed'
7.9.: 'Prøve paa Sylphiden'
20.9.: 'Prøve paa Sylphiden der gaaer fortreffeligt med Juliette'
21.9.: 'Generalprøve paa Sylphiden. Stor Satisfaction'
22.9.: 'Om Aftenen Sÿlphiden, der gik for aldeles fuldt Huus. Juliette vakte en stor Sensation og fortjente det Bifald hun erholdt. – Det var en deilig Aften for mig'.

The 1849 production of *La Sylphide* received 7 performances, the last of which was given on 19.12.1853. The musical material employed this year was the same as that used since the 1836 première (now in DKKk, call nos. C II, 117 d, MA ms 2970a, MA ms 2710, MA ms 2762 (1–2), and KTB 275).

26.9.1849
'Echo de Dannemark', Pas Seul, arranged by Aug. Bournonville (Pas Solo, arrangerad af Aug. Bournonville) performed by M. C. Norberg (Stockholm's Royal Theatre, Operahuset).

This dance was created especially for the Stockholm début of Bournonville's Swedish pupil, M. C. Norberg, who had come to Copenhagen in order to study with him during the months of July, August, and September 1849. The music for it was arranged by H. C. Lumbye, who incorporated his own earlier polka *Greeting to Jutland (Hilsen til Jylland)*, which was originally composed for the fair in the Rosenborg Gardens the same year (*see* 16.8–18.8.1849). There it had served as an accompaniment for a so-called *Hussar Dance*. In his score for 'Echo from Denmark' Lumbye mingled this polka with an orchestral version (probably also arranged by him) of J. O E. Horneman's 1848 melody to P. Faber's Danish patriotic song, named *The Valiant Soldier (Den tappre Landsoldat)*. This immensely popular song was first published in Copenhagen in April 1848 and was later reused by Bournonville in two other works, entitled *The Irresistibles* (*see* 3.2.1850), and *The Valiant Soldier, a suite of five tableaux in memory of Faber* (*see* 9.3. 1878).

In his diary he noted about his 1849 creation of Norberg's dance, which he never saw performed on stage:

5.9.1849: 'begyndt at indstudere en Characteerdands til [M. C.] Norberg'
13.9.: 'Lection og Prøve. Farvel til Mlle Norberg'
9.9.: 'Skrevet til Directeuren [S. G.] Schyberg i Anledning af Mlle Norberg'.

'Echo de Dannemark' was performed twice in Stockholm, the last time on 8.10.1849.

Musical sources:

Orchestral score. Ms. Copy. Black ink. 1 vol. 12 pp. (24,8 × 32,9 cm with minor variants)
Echo från Danmark
Unsigned and undated [1849]
[SSkma; KT Dansmusik 78
This orchestral score seems to represent the only existing source for the full orchestral version of Lumbye's polka *Hilsen til Jylland* that has been traced so far.

No répétiteur's copy for *'Echo de Dannemark'* has yet been traced.

Parts. Ms. Copy. 32 vol.
3 vl I, 3 vl II, 2 vla, 4 vlc e cb, fl 1/2, ob 1/2, cl 1/2, fag 1/2, cor 1/2/ 3/4, tr 1/2, trb 1/2/3, timp, gr cassa, tri.
Unsigned and undated [1849]
[SSkma; KT Dansmusik 78

11.11.1849

Le Dieu et la bayadère, ou La Courtisane amoureuse (Brama og Bayadèren).
Bournonville had earlier mounted the dances. in D.-F.-E. Auber's two-act opera-ballet together with P. Larcher on two occasions (*see* 7.2.1841, and 28.5.1847). In spite of the fact that the poster for this restaging still gives credit to both Larcher and Bournonville, the choreography was this year most probably mounted in a new, revised version by Bournonville, since Larcher has passed away more than two years earlier on 15.6.1847. The 1849 production received 8 performances, the last of which was given on 5.9.1854.

21.11.1849

Norwegian Spring Dance (Norsk Springedands) performed by E. Stramboe and L. Stramboe (the Court Theatre).
This dance is identical with E. Helsted's new musical arrangement of the *Norwegian Spring Dance* in Bournonville's one-act ballet *Old Memories, or A Magic Lantern* (*see* 18.12. 1848). It was performed on this day as a separate divertissement in a charity performance, organised by Bournonville for the charity health association 'Hygæa', of which he was a leading board member.

Bournonville restaged this dance for the last time at the Court Theatre on 9.6.1853, when it was then performed by Julius Price and A. Price.

The *Norwegian Spring Dance* was also given as a separate di-

vertissement at the Royal Theatre on 12.3.1850 and restaged there three more times on 7.9.1854, 28.11.1866, and 14.3.1867. In Norway it was mounted at Christiania's Theatre (Oslo) on 22.6.1852 with the new title 'Spring Dance (after Norwegian motifs)' ('Springdands' (efter norske Motiver)'), and again on 7.6.1865, but then named 'Norwegian Spring Dance' ('Norsk Springdands'). Finally, on 8.6.1860 it was performed at Stockholm's Mindre Theatern by W. Price and Juliette Price.

Musical sources:

No orchestral score dating from the 1849 performance of the *Norwegian Spring Dance* at the Court Theatre has been traced.

Répétiteur's copy. Ms. Copy. Black ink. 2 pp. (33,1 × 25 cm)
Springdans./Violino Repetitör
Unsigned and undated [c.1849]
[DKKk; MA ms 2625 (KTB 1027)
According to a note written on p. 2, indicating a reduced orchestration of Helsted's *Norwegian Spring Dance*, this répétiteur's copy almost certainly dates from when it was performed for the first time as a separate divertissement at the Court Theatre in 1849. The répétiteur's copy also seems to have served as the conductor's part, since the reduced intrumentation here is indicated in the actual music.

Parts. Ms. Copy. 16 vol.
2 vl I, vl II, vla, 2 vlc e cb, fl 1/2, ob 1/2, cl 1/2, fag 1/2, cor 1/2.
Unsigned and undated [c.1849]
[DKKk; KTB 1027
This set of parts clearly relates to the répétiteur's copy for the same dance (*see* the previous entry) and almost certainly dates from when the *Norwegian Spring Dance* was performed as a separate divertissement at the Court Theatre in 1849.

21.11.1849

Pas de trois (uncredited) performed by Juliette Price, S. Price, and A. Price (the Court Theatre).
This (uncredited) dance is almost certainly identical with Bournonville's *Pas de trois cousines* (*see* 20.5.1848). According to the poster it is listed simply as *Pas de trois*, and was given as part of a special performance, arranged by Bournonville for the charity health association 'Hygæa'. In his diary he noted about the dance as follows:

'Aftenunderholdning i Hygæa med Dands af Pricerne'.

Pas de trois cousines was mounted for the last time at the Court Theatre on 9.6.1853 and was on that day again performed as part of a charity performance (then given for the brothers, James and A. Price). It was that year listed on the poster with its complete and original title and with the music explicitly credited to be 'by' (*af*) H. S. Paulli.

No separate musical sources dating from the 1849 performance of this dance at the Court Theatre have yet been traced. It is not possible to identify the dance any further.

21.11.1849

'Greetings to Jutland', Hussar Dance from the fair in the Rosenborg Gardens ('Hilsen til Jylland', Husardands fra Rosenborg=Marked) (the Court Theatre).
This dance is identical with Bournonville's and H. C. Lumbye's *Hussar Dance*, first performed by Bournonville's dance students at the fair in the Rosenborg Gardens on 16.8.1849. It was mounted at the Court Theatre as part of a charity per-

formance, organised by Bournonville for the charity health association 'Hygæa'. No separate musical sources dating from the 1849 performance of this dance at the Court Theatre have yet been traced.

8.12.1849
Faust.

This performance represents Bournonville's first restaging in Copenhagen of his and Ph. L. Keck's three-act romantic ballet *Faust* (*see* 25.4.1832). It was mounted with what he describes in his diary as 'flere Forandringer'. According to Bournonville's pencilled notes in the ballet's original orchestral score (p. 161) and other notes found in the new 1849 répétiteur's copy for *Faust*, and in the 1836 répétiteur's copy for *La Sylphide*, this version included three new dances that were all incorporated in Act II. They seem to have replaced the earlier incorporated dances in this act and were as follows:

(1) A *Pas de deux* inserted as score no. '19'. This dance is set to music by F.-M.-A. Venua and was originally performed by Bournonville and A. Krætzmer in J. L. Heiberg's three-act play *Princess Isabella, or Three Nights at the Court* (*see* 29.10.1829). In *Faust* it was danced by W. Funck and J. Price and replaced the ballet's original score no. 19.
(2) A so-called 'Indlagt Contradands C dur' incorporated as score 'no. 20'. This dance was originally part of Ph. L. Keck's music for Bournonville's one-act ballet *Victor's Wedding, or The Ancestral House* (*see* 23.4.1831) in which it was performed as score no. '6' and is notated in E flat major.
(3) A so-called 'Pas de deux D dur (Sylphiden)' interpolated between scores nos. 21 and 22. This dance (which is set to music by J. Mayseder) was originally performed in Act II (score no. 1 A) of Bournonville's two-act romantic ballet *The Isle of Phantasy* (*see* 28.10.1838). It had also been incorporated in H. S. v. Løvenskjold's score for Bournonville's two-act romantic ballet *La Sylphide* on 27.9.1842. In that ballet it was performed by Bournonville (as *James*) and A. Nielsen (as *The Sylph*) in Act II and with the new title *Pas de deux (à la Taglioni)*.

In his diary Bournonville noted about the rehearsals and the first performance of his revised 1849 version of *Faust*:

23.10., 29.10., and 1.11.1849: 'Prøve paa Faust'
10.11.: 'lille Prøve paa Faust'
12.11., 13.11., 16.11., 17.11. and 19.11: 'Prøve paa Faust'
22.11.: 'Prøve paa Faust hele 2.den Akt'
26.11., and 6.12.: 'Prøve paa Faust'
7.12.: 'Prøve paa Faust paa Byens Theater, den gik udmærket godt'
8.12.: 'Opførelse af Faust, med nỹ Indstudering. [L.] Gade Mephistopheles. L. Stramboe Gretchen. Jf, [E.] Larcher Moderen. [C. M.] Eydrup Engelen, og flere Forandringer – Den gik i det Hele meget godt, og vandt sit gamle Bifald'.

The 1849 staging of *Faust* received 5 performances, the last of which was given on 6.3.1852.

Musical sources:

The orchestral score and the set of parts for *Faust* are now in DKKk (call nos. C II, 115, and KTB 289).

Répétiteur's copy. Ms. Copy. Brown ink. 1 vol. 158 pp. (31,3 × 24,7 cm)
Balletten/Faust./(Keck)/B.   289/1849/[...]/Repetiteur/Partie./til/Balletten/Faust./Musik: Keck.
Unsigned and dated (on the front cover): '1849'
[DKKk; MA ms 2987 (KTB 289)

This répétiteur's copy contains Bournonville's autographed choreographic numbers ('1–3') in Act II, score no. 13 (written with brown ink), and his other autographed pencilled notes (on pp. 67 and 85) which indicate the exact places where F.-M.- A. Venua's *Pas de deux* and J. Mayseder's so-called 'Indlagt Pas de deux D Dur' were incorporated respectively. Moreover, his pencilled autographed choreographic numbers ('1–14' and '1–20') in Act III, score nos. 28–29 (pp. 117–135) seem to refer to his later (not yet traced) separate choreographic notation of these dances, which he most probably wrote when the music for these numbers was interpolated (in slightly revised versions) in Act III of his Danish version of J. Aumer's three-act pantomimic ballet *La Somnambule, ou l'Arrivée d'un nouveau seigneur* (*see* 2.10.1868). Finally, his pencilled autographed note on p. 67 reads: 'attacca/Sylphiden/v: p. 85'. It refers to the much later incorporation of an excerpt of Keck's music from Act II (score no. 17) in V. C. Holm's score for Bournonville's one-act ballet epilogue *Farewell to the Old Theatre* (*see* 1.6.1874). In that work the *Faust* music was succeeded by another excerpt borrowed from Act II (score nos. 4–5) of Bournonville's two-act romantic ballet *La Sylphide* (*see* 28.11. 1836).

The orchestral score, the two répétiteur's copies, and the set of parts for F.-M.-A. Venua's incorporated *Pas de deux* (performed as score no. '19' in Act II of *Faust*) are now in DKKk (call nos. C II, 125, MA ms 2926, MA ms 2647 (1), and KTB 1052).

The orchestral score, the two répétiteur's copies, and the set of parts for J. Mayseder's incorporated 'Pas de deux i D dur' (performed between score nos. 20 and 21 in Act II of *Faust*) are now in DKKk (call nos. C II, 119, MA ms 2645, MA ms 2647 (2), and KTB 1029).

12.12.1849
The Masquerade (Maskeraden).

The 1849 restaging of L. Holberg's three-act comedy (premièred at Copenhagen's Royal Theatre on 30.12.1748) represents the first time that the intermedium (performed between Acts I and II) was choreographed and mounted by Bournonville. Although his name is not included on the posters for this production he clearly lists it under the year of 1849 in his handwritten list of his staging of operas and plays, written c.1851 (*see* Additional Sources).

The music for the intermedium (in which a masquerade is shown) was rearranged this year by H. S. Paulli, who employed most of the traditional music that had been used for Holberg's comedy since the end of the 18th and the beginning of the 19th century. According to the 1849 répétiteur's copy, Paulli's new arrangement consisted of the six following dances:

(1) No. 1 'Hanedands'. This *Cock's Dance* was composed especially by Paulli for Bournonville's 1849 restaging of the intermedium in L. Holberg's *The Masquerade*. According to a note in the répétiteur's copy for Paulli's and Bournonville's three-act romantic ballet *The Kermesse in Brüges, or The Three Gifts* (*see* 16.4.1854) it seems that Bournonville also intended to include this dance at a later stage in Act I of that ballet when he was working on a projected staging of it at Vienna's Kärnthnerthor Theatre during the 1856–57 season. This project, however, was never carried out.
(2) No. 2 'Engelsk dands'. This dance is included in the oldest still preserved répétiteur's copy for *The Masquerade* in which it is named 'Engl.' It appears to have been performed as an integral part of the intermedium in Holberg's comedy since the late 18th or early 19th century.
(3) No. 3 'Chiaconne'. According to a pencilled note in the oldest still preserved répétiteur's copy for *The Masquerade* this dance was originally named 'Pochinelle' and seems to have been an integral part of the intermedium in Holberg's comedy since the late 18th or early 19th century.

(4) No. 4 'Contradands'. According to a pencilled note in the oldest still preserved répétiteur's copy for *The Masquerade* (reading 'Cont Dands Træns') this dance was set to music by J. P. Thræn, and seems to have been given as an integral part of the intermedium in Holberg's comedy since the late 18th or early 19th century.

(5) No. 5 'Menuetto'. According to pencilled notes in the oldest still preserved répétiteur's copy for *The Masquerade* this dance was originally named 'Menuetto von Tyboe'. This title seems to indicate that it was originally performed in Holberg's five-act comedy *Jacob von Tyboe* (premièred at Copenhagen's Royal Theatre on 8.10. 1749). However, the music clearly seems to have been incorporated in the intermedium of *The Masquerade* since the end of the 18th century. It consists of a minuet ('Menuetto'), an anglais ('Engl.'), and a 'Coda' (the minuet repeated). Many years later the music for this dance was also incorporated in a slightly revised version by V. C. Holm in his score for Bournonville's ballet divertissement *From the Last Century* (*see* 31.10.1875). There it served as an accompaniment for scene 7 (score no. 9), entitled *Holbergiana*, during which a procession is seen marching across the stage while showing some of the leading characters in Holberg's most popular comedies.

(6) No. 6 'Presto'. According to a note in the oldest still preserved répétiteur's copy for *The Masquerade* (reading 'af Galai= Slaverne') the music for this short finale in 2/4 time was borrowed from Act II (score no. 7 b) of L. Zinck's score for E. Cantiran de Boirie's, P. F. A. Carmouche's and A.-A.-V. Poujol's three-act drama *Les Deux Forçats, ou La meunière du Puy-de-Dôme (De to Galejslaver eller Møllen ved St. Aldervon)*. This drama was performed for the first time at Copenhagen's Royal Theatre on 30.9.1825 and contained some incorporated dances by P. Funck. Zinck's music for the dances (now in DKKk, call no. C II, 125) therefore also seems to have been performed in the intermedium in Holberg's *The Masquerade* since the late 1820s or early 1830s.

In his diary Bournonville noted about the staging:

26.9.1849: 'Talt med [J. L.] Heiberg om `Maskeraden´'
30.9.: '[H. S.] Paulli leveret mig Musik til Maskeraden'
1.10.: 'Componeret endeel paa Intermezzet til Maskeraden. Konfererede med Heiberg, der nu synes at min Composition vil tiltrække sig for megen Opmærksomhed. Efter al Sandsynlighed vil det Hele strande.'
11.10.: 'Prøve paa Maskeraden'
13.10.: 'Prøve og Composition paa Maskeraden'
18.10.: 'Prøve paa Hanedandsen til Maskeraden'
6.12.: 'Stor Prøve paa […] Maskeraden'
10.12.: 'Prøve paa Intermediet til Maskeraden paa Byens Theater'
12.12.: 'Prøve paa Byens Theater paa Maskeraden […] Dirigeret Maskeraden, der gik særdeles godt og gjorde megen Lykke'.

The intermedium was mounted for the second and last time by Bournonville on 11.2.1859, but then with the dances performed in a completely new sequence and with partially revised choreography. This new production was restaged 9 years later by Bournonville's pupil, L. Gade (*see* 15.11.1868), but then with a score containing a new prelude by F. Rung. Rung also seems to have reorchestrated the complete music for the intermedium that year.

Bournonville's 1849 production of *The Masquerade* received 22 performances, the last of which was given on 27.2. 1855.

Musical sources:

Répétiteur's copy (incomplete). Ms. Copy. Black and brown ink. 26 pp. (32,6 × 20,8 cm)
157/Dands/til/Maskeraden/Violino 1.mo/Rept.r Partie
Unsigned and undated [late 18th or early 19th century]
[DKKk; MA ms 2957 (KTB 258 (1))]
This (incomplete) volume represents the oldest, still preserved répé-

titeur's copy for the dances in the intermedium of Holberg's *The Masquerade*. It seems to date from a restaging in the late 18th or early 19th century. Thus, according to notes in the set of parts that relate to this répétiteur's copy (reading '1804') it most probably dates from, or at least was used for, the restaging of *The Masquerade* on 4.1.1804. The fact that an excerpt of L. Zinck's music from 1825 to P. Funck's dances in *Les Deux Forçats, ou La meunière du Puy-de-Dôme (De to Galejslaver eller Møllen ved St. Aldervon)* is also included in this répétiteur's copy clearly proves that it was in use at least until the late 1820s and early 30s. Moreover, Bournonville's autographed choreographic notes (written with brown ink in the music for the 'Chiaconne') provide a definitive proof that it also served him for his preparations of the 1849 restaging of Holberg's comedy.

No orchestral score dating from the 1849 restaging of *The Masquerade* has yet been traced. However, a later score arranged by F. Rung containing his re-instrumentation of the complete music for *The Masquerade* is now in DKKk (call no. C II, 119 (KTB 258)). It dates from L. Gade's restaging of the intermedium in *The Masquerade* on 15.11.1868, a production which was closely based on Bournonville's previous, revised staging on 11.2.1859.

Répétiteur's copy. Ms. Autograph (by H. S. Paulli) and copy. Black ink. 12 pp. 34,8 × 25,1 cm with variants)
B 258/Paulli: Maskeraden/(Hanedans)/[…]/Hanedandsen./No. 1 [changed to] 3. Tempo di menuetto.
Unsigned and undated [1849]
[DKKk; MA ms 2958 (KTB 258 (2))]
This répétiteur's copy dates from the 1849 restaging of *The Masquerade* and contains the complete music for the six dances in Bournonville's new arrangement of the intermedium in Holberg's comedy. The music for the *Cock's Dance* is Paulli's autograph, while the remaining music is a copy of sections from the earlier répétiteur's copy for *The Masquerade*. Bournonville's complete autographed choreographic notes (written with brown ink) describes the steps in the *Cock's Dance*. His other autographed notes (written with black ink) indicate (in more general terms) the choreography for his revised staging of this intermedium on 11.2.1859.

Parts. Ms. Copy. 23 vol.
2 vl I, 3 vl II, 2 vla, 3 vlc e cb, fl 1/2, ob 1/2, cl 1/2, fag 1/2, cor 1/2, tr 1/2, timp.
Unsigned and dated (in the part for the double bass): '1804.'
[DKKk; KTB 258 a]
According to the dating of the part for the double bass, this set of parts seems to have been used for all performances in Copenhagen of the intermedium in *The Masquerade* between 4.1.1804 and Bournonville's 1849 restaging of it.

Parts. Ms. Copy. 20 vol.
2 vl I, 2 vl II, vla, 2 vlc e cb, fl 1/2, ob 1/2, cl 1/2, fag 1/2, cor 1/2, tr 1/2, timp. 1 vocal part.
Unsigned and undated [1849]
[DKKk; KTB 258 b]
This set of parts dates from the 1849 restaging of the intermedium Holberg's *The Masquerade* and seems to have been used for all later performances of it during Bournonville's lifetime.

19.12.1849
Bellman or the Polish Dance at Grönalund (Bellman eller Polskdandsen paa Grönalund).
This performance represents Bournonville's first restaging in Copenhagen of his one-act ballet-vaudeville *Bellman or the Polish Dance at Grönalund* (*see* 3.6.1844). It was mounted for a charity performance celebrating the 50th anniversary of the 'cellist, F. C. Funck, as member of the Royal Theatre orchestra. Funck counted many members of his family among the dancers in the Royal Danish Ballet; three of the most promi-

nent were Pouline Funck, Poul Erik Funck, and Wilhelm Erik Funck.

According to the rehearsal book of H. C. J. Fredstrup, the 1849 restaging (which seems to have been mounted with only minor if any changes from the original 1844 version) demanded only 6 rehearsals between 3.12. and 19.12.1849. The production received 63 performances, the last of which was given on 16.3.1865.

The musical material employed this year was the same as that used for the 1844 première (now in DKKk, call nos. C II, 127, and KTB 293).

1850

21.1.1850
A projected performance in memory of Adam Oehlenschläger (Idée for en Mindefest for Adam Oehlenschläger).
When the news of A. Oehlenschläger's death on 21.1.1850 reached Bournonville noted in his diary:

'Efterretning om [A.] Øehlenschlægers Død Igaar Aftes Kl. 11. Jeg anseer det som en stor Begivenhed for Danmark og som et smerteligt Tab for mig der i ham eiede en sand Ven. – Jeg fik en Idée til hans Sørgefest som jeg meddelte [J. L.] Heiberg – men som efter al Sandsynlighed ikke bliver benyttet'.

A later performance in memory of Oehlenschläger took place at Copenhagen's Royal Theatre on 6.2.1850, but was mounted without any involvement on Bournonville's part.

3.2.1850
The Irresistibles (De Uimodstaaelige).
This divertissement was created as a tribute to the soldiers returning from Denmark's war with Germany, 1848–1850. According to Bournonville's memoirs *My Theatre Life* (pp. 174–175), its title was a clear allusion to the name bestowed upon the infantry regiments of Napoleon Bonaparte I *(Les irresistibles)*, and the divertissement itself was intended as 'a host of modern-day *fylgjur* and *valkyries*, who on the stage would recall the memory of […] the return to Copenhagen of the troops from the Fredericia campaign' after the war.

It was set to a score composed by H. C. Lumbye. In the finale he incorporated his own orchestration of J. O E. Horneman's melody for P. Faber's Danish patriotic song, named *The Valiant Soldier (Den tappre Landsoldat)*, first published in April 1848. The tune for this immensely popular song had earlier been incorporated by Lumbye in his score for Bournonville's *Pas seul, 'Echo de Dannemark'* (see 26.9.1849), and was many years later also reused by C. C. Møller for Bournonville's suite of five tableaux, entitled *The Valiant Soldier, a suite of five tableaux in memory of Faber* (see 9.3.1878).

In his diary he noted about the rehearsals and the 1849 première of *The Irresistibles*:

22.11.1849: 'componeret med [H. C.] Lumbye'
26.11.: 'Møde med Lumbye'
27.11.: 'componeret hjemme'
4.12.: 'Jeg arbeidede med Lumbye'
8.12.: 'componeret hjemme paa en ny Dands'
9.12.: 'componeret'
13.12.: 'componeret til Imorgen'

14.12.: 'Prøve paa den nye Militair=Dands 'De Uimodstaaelige''
17.12. and 20.12.: 'Prøve paa 'De Uimodstaaelige''
21.12.: 'Prøve paa Den ny Dands'
22.12.: 'Prøve paa 'De Uimodstaaelige' Dandsen fædig jeg troer den er vellykket'
29.12.: 'Besørget adskilligt til Divertissementet'
7.1.1850: 'Besøgt Maleren [N.] Simonsen der maler paa Slaget ved Fredericia der bliver fortreffeligt'
12.1.: 'Prøve paa 'De Uimodstaaelige'
25.1.: 'Prøve paa De Uimodstaaelige med Reserver'
28.1.: 'Besørget adskilligt til Divertissementet'
30.1.: 'Prøve med Decoration og Musik paa Divertissementet, der gik særdeles godt'
1.2.: 'Generalprøve paa 'De Uimodstaaelige' der gik særdeles godt'
2.2.: 'Prøve paany med Reserver'
3.2.: 'for første Gang mit divertissement De Uimodstaaelige, der blev meget vel modtaget og fik i Særdeleshed til Slutning stor Applaus. Damerne udførte deres Ting særdeles godt og saae nydelige ud. Det lod til at Publicum var vel tilfreds'
5.2.: 'Dirigeret mit Divertissement der gik særdeles godt, men blev meget koldt optaget af Publicum – der var endog Opposition. Jeg har gjort mit Bedste og mit Arbeide er saavel fra min som de dandsendes Side udført med Begeistring. – Vi faae at see, hvad de næste Gange bringe. – Man kan ikke altid have Lykken med sig'
11.2.: 'De Uimodstaaelige gik godt men koldt, dog uden bestemt Opposition'.

The Irresistibles received 8 performances, the last of which was given 19.3.1850. Soon after it last performance it became one of Lumbye's most popular concert-pieces, and was frequently played by him at public concerts in the Tivoli Gardens.

Musical sources:

Orchestral score. Ms. Autograph (by H. C. Lumbye). Brown ink. 1 vol. 40 pp. (26,6 × 37,2 cm with variants)
288/288./Partitur/til/De uimodstaaelige/[…]/Divertissement/af H: C: Lumbye.
Signed (on p. 1): 'H: C: Lumbye.', undated [1850]
[DKKk; C II, 117 (KTB 288)

Répétiteur's copy. Ms. Copy. Black ink. 1 vol. 12 pp. (32,5 × 24,8 cm)
Divertissement/Musiken af Lumbye
Unsigned and undated [1850]
[DKKk; MA ms 2681 (KTB 1051, originally KTB 288)
The fact that the several notes in this répétiteur's copy indicate the instrumentation of Lumbye's music seems to indicate that it also served as a conductor's part.

Parts. Ms. Copy. 28 vol.
2 vl I, 2 vl II, vla, 2 vlc e cb, fl picc, fl, ob 1/2, cl 1/2, fag 1/2, cor 1/2, tr 1/2, cnt, trb 1/2/3, tuba, timp, gr cassa, piatti, tri,
Unsigned and undated [1850]
[DKKk; KTB 1051 (originally KTB 288)

Parts. Ms. Copy. 30 vol.
3 vl I, 2 vl II, vla, 2 vlc, 2 cb, fl picc, fl, ob 1/2, cl 1/2, fag 1/2, cor 1/2, tr, 1/2, cnt, Atrb, Ttrb, Btrb, timp, gr cassa, piatti, tri.
Unsigned and undated [c.1850]
[DKKk; Tivolis musikarkiv no. 1121 (mu 9405.1400)
These parts were used when Lumbye's music was played for the first time in the Tivoli Gardens. Notes written into several of the parts indicate the duration of the music to between 9½ and 10 minutes.

Printed sources:

Printed scenario. 1 vol. 4 pp. (19,5 × 11,8 cm)
De Uimodstaaelige./Divertissement/af/A. Bournonville./Musiken componeret af Lumbye.

Kjøbenhavn, J. H. Schubothe/Bianco Luno, 1850.
[DKKk; 17, – 174 8°

12.3.1850
Norwegian Spring Dance (Norsk Springedands) (uncredited) performed by E. Stramboe and L. Stramboe).

This (uncredited) dance is identical with E. Helsted's new arrangement of the *Norwegian Spring Dance* (score no. 7) in his and Bournonville's one-act ballet *Old Memories, or A Magic Lantern* (*see* 18.12.1848). The 1850 performance represents the first time it was ever performed as a separate divertissement at Copenhagen's Royal Theatre. It received 6 performances there, the last of which was given on 14.3.1867 (from 7.9.1854 performed by E. Stramboe and L. Stillmann, and after 28.11.1866 by W. Price and L. Stillmann).

Musical sources:

No separate orchestral score and set of parts for the *Norwegian Spring Dance* dating from its 1850 staging as a separate divertissement at the Royal Theatre have yet been traced. This indicates that it most probably was performed using the original musical material for *Old Memories, or A Magic Lantern* (now in DKKk, call nos. CII, 114 k, and KTB 291).

Répétiteur's copy. Ms. Copy. Black ink. 1 vol. 2 pp. of which one is blank (32,2 × 24,3 cm)
Tæppet op./Sringdands [*sic*]
Unsigned and undated [1850]
[DKKk; MA ms 2904 (5) (KTB 291)
According to the other works contained in the same volume this répétiteur's copy dates beyond doubt from the first performance of the *Norwegian Spring Dance* as a separate divertissement at Copenhagen's Royal Theatre. The music is included in this volume on pp. 35–36.

15.3.1850
Marshal Stig (Marsk Stig).

For the première of C. Hauch's five-act tragedy Bournonville choreographed a *Minuet (Minuetto)* which was set to music by H. Rung and performed in Act I (score no. 1) during the song, entitled «Det var ved Midnats tide jeg træn i Hallen ind» (sung by solo voices and a chorus). This dance is concluded by a brief instrumental minuet of 16 bars (score no. 1 b). In his diary Bournonville noted about the performance:

28.2.1850: 'Prøve paa en nÿ Dands til Marsk Stig'
5.3., 9.3., and 12.3.: 'Prøve paa […] Marsk Stig'
15.3.: 'Marsk Stig 1.ste Gang'.

The staging is included in Bournonville's handwritten list of his works, written c.1851 (*see* Additional Sources), but is omitted in the printed list of his works published in his memoirs *My Theatre Life* (p. 408).

Marshal Stig received 7 performances the last of which was given on 30.11.1850.

Musical sources:

Orchestral score. Ms. Autograph (by H. Rung). Black ink. 18 pp. of which one is blank (27,3 × 37,2 cm)
452/Marsk Stig./Partitur./452/H. Rung/[…]/1.ste Act./Minuetto. Moderato assai.
Signed and dated (on p. 13): 'H: Rung Jan: 1850.'
[DKKk; C II, 119 k (KTA 452)

Répétiteur's copy. Ms. Copy. Black ink. 4 pp. of which one is blank (33,2 × 24,7 cm)
Repetiteur=Partie/til/'Marsk Stig'/Tragedie af C: Hauch.
Unsigned and undated [1850]
[DKKk; MA ms 2777 (KTA 452)
This répétiteur's copy contains the music for the minuet performed during the song in Act I (score no. 1). Moreover, C. Hauch's complete autographed text to the song's four verses is pasted in on p. 3.

Parts. Ms. Copy. 19 vol.
2 vl I, 2 vl II, vla, 2 vlc e cb, fl 1/2, ob, cl 1/2, fag 1/2, cor 1/2/3/4, timp. 46 vocal parts.
Unsigned and undated [1850]
[DKKk; KTA 452

7.5.1850
Psyche.

This one-act allegorical ballet, in particular its opening scene depicting the dream of *Psyche*, appears to have been based on Bournonville's earlier series of seven *tableaux vivants*, entitled *Psyché* and originally created for a Royal soirée at the Amalienborg Palace (*see* 26.11.1845). However, the main stimulus which led him to the creation of an actual ballet on this theme came (according to his memoirs *My Theatre Life*, p. 189) from his reading of F. Paludan-Müller's mythological epos *Amor og Psyche* (first published in 1833).

The ballet's score (which is divided into 13 separate numbers) was composed and arranged by E. Helsted. He incorporated several musical borrowings, which are identified as follows:

(1) Scene, 4, score no. 6 (a *Pas de sept* danced by *Psyche, Zephyr, Flora, Myris, Leda*, and two nymphs of Flora's suite): In his music for this dance Helsted incorporated an excerpt (*Allegro non troppo* in 4/4 time) borrowed from the chorus «O séduissante ivresse» in Act III (score no. 13) of D.-F.-E. Auber's three-act fairy-opera *Le Cheval de bronze* (premièred in Paris at l'Opéra Comique on 23.3.1835). In the opera is was originally sung to the text «de la délivrance la douce espérance sourit à mon coeur». The same excerpt resurfaces a second time immediately before Helsted's Coda of the *Pas de sept*.
(2) Scene 9, score no. 12: In this scene (showing *Cupid*'s attempts to fetch his beloved *Psyche* from the Underworld) Helsted incorporated six different excerpts from C. W. v. Gluck's three-act tragic opera *Orphée et Euridice* (premièred at the Paris Opéra on 2.8.1774). Bournonville would have known this opera well from his earlier translation and staging of its second act at the Court Theatre on 10.2.1846. The borrowed excerpts were clearly interpolated (most probably at Bournonville's direct request) to help the audience to follow the dramatic action and the mime during in this scene. They consist of the opening *Moderato* and the *Prélude* in Act II scene 1 of Gluck's opera, which are followed by the first part of the chorus «Quel est l'audacieux» in the same act. Next comes a section from the aria of *Orphée*, entitled «Laissez vous toucher par mes pleurs», after which follows an excerpt of the chorus «C'est le séjour affreux», and the scene concludes with a section from the chorus «Par quels puissants accords, dans le séjour des morts».

In his diary Bournonville noted about the creation and the première of the ballet:

28.5.1849: 'Begÿndt en Bearbeidelse af Psyche'
11.11.: 'corrigeret Programmet til min nÿe Ballet Psyche'
13.1.1850: 'componeret med [E.] Helsted'
21.2.: 'skrevet mit Program færdigt til Psyche, Componeret en scène […] o g den første Prøve paa Balletten Psyche. Scenen med Amor i Mørket'
22.2.: 'begÿndt paa Psyche'
4.3., 5.3., 6.3., 8.3., 11.3., 12.3., and 13.3.: 'Prøve paa Psyche'
14.3.: 'Prøve paa Psyche, talt med Theatermaleren'

20.3.: 'Prøve paa Psyche som sædvanligt. Musiceret med Helsted'
22.3.: 'Prøve, Repetition paa Alt i Psyche det gaaer meget godt'
24.3.: 'componerede paa den store Pas de sept til Psyche'
25.3.: 'Indstudering af Pas de sept til Psyche'
26.3.: 'Prøve og Indstudering af Dandsen der blev færdig'
30.3. and 2.4.: 'Prøve paa Psyche'
3.4.: 'lille Prøve med Juliette [Price] paa Psyche'
4.4.: 'Prøve paa næstsidste Scene af Psyche'
5.4., 11.4., 12.4., and 13.4.: 'Prøve paa Psyche'
17.4.: 'Prøve paa Psyche, for Professor [J. L.] Heiberg'
18.4.: 'Prøve med Maskineriet til Psyche, aftalt Costumet med Fru [C. B.] Rÿge'
20.4.: 'Prøve med Maskinen til Psyche [...] besørget adskilligt til Balletten'
22.4.: 'Prøve med Maskinerne'
24.4.: 'Prøve med Maskinen og Requisiter'
25.4.: 'Prøve, indstuderet den sidste Scene af Psyche. – Skrevet mit Program'
26.4.: 'Skrevet Programmet reent'
27.4.: 'besørget adskilligt til Balletten'
29.4.: 'Prøve fra 11 til 1 1/2 paa Psyche'
1.5.: 'Prøve paa Det kgl. Theater. Balletten begÿnder at gaae meget godt'
2.5.: 'Musikprøve paa Balletten'
3.5.: 'første fuldstændige Prøve paa Psyche, gik særdeles godt [...] Jeg prøvede noget Fyrværkeri til Psyche'
4.5.: 'Prøve paa Psyche Kl. 10, det gik særdeles godt'
6.5.: 'Generalprøve paa Psyche, gik overordentlig godt. Resten af dagen beskjæftiget med Balletten'
7.5.: 'Dagen beskjæftiget med Balletten [...] Første forestilling af Balletten Psÿche', der gik udmærket godt og gjorde megen Lÿkke [...] Jeg forærede Helsted et Kruus i Anledning af hans smukke Musik'.

Psyche reached a total of 19 performances, the last of which was given on 4.1.1855.

Autograph sources:

Manuscript scenario. Ms. Autograph. Brown ink. 8 pp. (22,4 × 17,3 cm)
Psÿche/Ballet i en Akt af August Bournonville.
Signed and dated: 'Kbhvn d. 11 Novbr 1849.'
[DKKk; NKS 3285 4° 3 L–P

Manuscript scenario. Ms. Autograph. Brown ink. 8 pp. (20,8 × 13,5 cm)
Psÿche/Ballet i en Akt af August Bournonville/Musiken af Edw: Helsted.
Unsigned and undated [Written according to the diary on either 21.2. or 26.4.1850]
[DKKk; NKS 3285 4° 3 L–P

Production note. Ms. Autograph. Brown ink. 1 p. (22,4 × 17,3 cm)
Decorationer til Balletten/Psyche.
Unsigned and undated [Written according to the diary most probably in March or April 1850]
[DKKk; NKS 3285 4° 3 L–P]

Musical sources:

Orchestral score. Ms. Autograph (by E. Helsted). Black ink. 1 vol. 272 pp. of which three are blank (32 × 25,3 cm with minor variants)
Partituret/203/til/Balletten/Psyche E. Helsted.
Signed and dated (on p. 271): 'April 1850. Eduard Helsted.'
[DKKk; C II, 114 k (KTB 203)

Répétiteur's copy. Ms. Autograph (by E. Helsted). Black ink. 1 vol. 48 pp. (32,6 × 24,4 cm)
B 203/Psÿche./Ballet i 1 Akt./29./1850([...]/Bournonville/E. Helsted

Signed and dated (on p. 48): 'd: 23 April 1850./Eduard Helsted.'
[DKKk; MA ms2942 (KTB 203)
This répétiteur's copy contains Bournonville pencilled autographed notes describing the mime, the dramatic action, and the choreography in score nos. 1–5 and 7–11. His other autographed notes (written with brown ink) indicate in fine detail the choreography for score no. 6 (the *Pas de sept*, performed by *Psyche, Zephyr, Flora, Myris, Leda*, and two nymphs of Flora's suite) and his mime and dramatic action for score nos. 11–13. According to his diary these notes were almost certainly written between 13.1. and 24.3.1850.

Parts. Ms. Copy. 32 vol.
3 vl I, 3 vl II, 2 vla, 3 vlc e cb, fl 1/2, ob 1/2, cl 1/2, fag 1/2, cor 1/2/ 3/4, clno 1/2, trb 1/2/3, timp, gr cassa e piatti, gong, arpa.
Unsigned and undated [1850]
Notes in several of these parts indicate that the complete ballet played for 1 hour and 3 minutes.

Printed sources:

Printed scenario. 1 vol. 11 pp. (20 × 12,7 cm)
Psyche./Ballet i 1 Akt/af/August Bournonville./Musiken componeret og arrangeret af Eduard Helsted./Decorationerne af Dhrr. Christensen og Lund.
Kjøbenhavn, J. H. Schubothe/Bianco Luno, 1850.
[DKKk; 17, – 174 8°

8.6.1850
The Flower Maids of Florence (De florentinske Blomsterpiger), *Pas de trois* performed by Juliette Price, S. Price, and A. Price (the Casino Theatre).

Bournonville's inspiration for this *Pas de trois* was a reminiscence of his own visit to Florence in the summer of 1841. In that town he had personally experienced the local custom of the young girls of the town meeting all foreigners to present them with a bouquet of flowers as a token of welcome and hospitality. Only at his departure would the visitor be able to thank the girls for this charming sign of welcome by offering them payment for their friendly gesture. This popular Florentine custom was also described by the Danish writer, M. A. Goldschmidt, in his weekly magazine *Nord og Syd* (1850, vol. 5, pp. 517–521). His description this year seems to have provided Bournonville with the choreographic motif for this divertissement, which was created for his three favourite pupils among the Price dynasty of dancers.

The *Pas de trois* was later the same year also performed at Copenhagen's Royal Theatre on 6.10.1850, and on 12.7. 1852 it was mounted in Norway at Christiania's Theatre (Oslo). According to the poster for its second performance in Christiania (on 14.7.1852) the music for it was written by 'Baron H. Lövenskjold'.

Løvenskjold's music for *The Flower Maids of Florence* (for which no separate orchestral score has yet been found) is most likely identical with that of his so-called 'Pas af Grækere og Grækerinder' or 'Beltedands' in Act II (score no. 9) of Bournonville's two-act allegorical ballet *The New Penelope, or The Spring Festival in Athens* (see 26.1.1847). This theory is supported by a note, reading 'C. Herr 1.ste Fagotist ved Christiania Theater d. 30.6.1852', written in the part for the first bassoon of what is entitled 'Pas de trois af "Den nye Penelope"' (now in DKKk, call no. KTB 238). It proves beyond doubt that this excerpt from Løvenskjold's ballet was brought to Christiania and played there during the summer of 1852. Moreover, since *The Flower Maids of Florence* was the only dance with music by Løvenskjold that was performed during the 1852 Norwegian summer tour, it clearly indicates that it was his music from Act II (score no. 9) of *The New Penelope, or The Spring Festival in Athens* which was employed by Bournonville when he created *The Flower Maids of Florence* in Copenhagen in the late spring of 1850.

In his diary Bournonville noted about the creation of the dance and its 1850 Copenhagen première:

29.5.1850: 'componeret en Dands til Pricerne'
31.5.: 'Componeret en nÿ Dands De florentinske Blomsterpiger'
3.6.: 'Prøve paa den nÿe Dands'
8.6.: 'Mine florentinske Blomsterpiger gjorde overordentlig Lÿkke'.

The dance was performed twice at the Casino Theatre, the last time on 13.6.1850. No separate musical sources dating from these performances have yet been traced.

6.7.1850
Tableau mounted for the anniversary of the Battle at Fridericia (Fest-Forestilling til Minde om Fredericia-Slaget) **(Vesterbroe's Theatre).**

In his diary Bournonville noted about this tableau, which was created for a special charity performance that marked the anniversary of the Danish army's victory over the German forces in the battle of Fridericia (on 6.7.1849):

28.6.1850: 'Componeret en Gruppe for Directeur [H. W.] Lange til en Invalidforestilling'
3.7.: 'Arrangeret Gruppen med Maler og Maskinmester paa Vesterbroe'
4.7.: 'Garderobevæsen til Tableauet'
5.7.: 'Prøve paa Tableauet Kl 6-8'
6.7.: 'Aarsdagen for Fredericia-Slaget […] Overværet Forestillingen som Lange gav for Invalider og Enker. Mit Tableau gjorde megen Virkning og gik særdeles godt'.

The tableau, which represents the only work Bournonville ever created for Vesterbroe's Theatre, was given only once. No musical sources for it have yet been traced.

30.8.1850–1.9.1850
Four tableaux, entitled 'Peace', 'War', 'Victory', and 'Memory', performed at the Temple of Memory as part of the fair in the Rosenborg Gardens (Fire Tableauer (Freden, Krigen, Seiren og Mindet) fremstillede i Mindets Tempel ved Høstfesten i Rosenborg Have).

The 1850 fair in the Rosenborg Gardens was arranged in order to raise funds for the widows of soldiers who had fallen in Denmark's war with Germany, 1848-1850. According to the printed programme, the three songs which accompanied Bournonville's series of allegorical tableaux were all written by H. P. Holst and set to the following music:

(1) N. W. Gade's 'Vexelsang' («Herlige Tid, da paa Mark og paa Vang») accompanying the first tableau, entitled 'Danmarks Fredstid'. Gade's song was first published for one voice in Chr. Bull's and P. O. Boisen's *100 Melodier til 'Nye og gamle Viser af og for Danske Folk* (Kjøbenhavn, J. D. Qvist, 1852, p. 18).
(2) H. S. von Løvenskjold's 'Krigerisk Marche' accompanying the second tableau, entitled 'Krigstiden'. This march is identical with Løvenskjold's so-called *Seiersmarch til Minde om Salget ved Isted*, first published in a version for piano by C. C. Lose & Delbanco (Kjøbenhavn, 1850).

(3) H. Rung's 'Hymne' («Hærenes Gud, Du som styrked vor Mod») accompanying the third tableau, entitled 'Seiren'. No printed sources for this song have yet been traced.
(4) I. P. E. Hartmann's 'Mindesang om de Faldne' («Slumrer sødt i Slesvigs Jord») accompanying the fourth tableau, entitled 'Mindet'. Hartmann's song was first published in C. G. Bull's and P. O. Boisen's *100 Melodier til 'Nye og gamle Viser af og for Danske Folk* (Kjøbenhavn, J. D. Qvist, 1852, p. 17–18), and his complete choral score was printed for the first time in *Ni Fleerstemminge Mandssange* (Kjøbenhavn, Foreningen 'Fremtiden', 1866).

The tableaux conluded with P. E. Rasmussen's melody from 1811 to L. Kock's song from 1683, named «Danmark deiligst Vang og Vænge» (first published with the title *Visen om Tyre Danebod* by W. H. F. Abrahamson, R. Nyerup, and K. L. Rahbek in 1812 and 1814 in their anthology *Udvalgte Danske Viser fra Middelalderen*, vol. 2, pp. 3–7, and vol. 5, p. LXXIV, no. 56, and later rewritten with new words by N. F. S. Grundtvig in 1816).

In his diary Bournonville noted about his involvement in the organisation of the fair:

1.8.1850: 'besøgte Christianhavns Lazareth […] bivaanede et Møde hos Pastor Bruun'
2.8.: 'Skrevet Ansøgning og gjort Planer til den Valhalla Fest vi have projecteret'
3.8.: 'talt med Theatermaler [C. F.] Christensen, [M. H.] Bing, [E.] Meyer og [N. H. C. V.] Sallÿ'
8.8.: 'Tour til Kbhvn i Anledning af Festen'
9.8.: 'Aftale med [C. F.] Christensen'
12.8: 'Besøg hos Pastor Bruun. Det hele ordnet under Formen af en Høstfest'
14.8.: 'mange Ærinder for Festen og fundet stor Beredvillighed. Møde med Damerne hos Pastor Bruun'
22.8.: 'Besøg angaaende Festen'
23.8.: 'Møde hos Pastor Bruun'
24.8.: 'Prøve paa […] Tableauerne der bleve indstuderede, foranstaltet det fornødne til Costumer og Maskiner'
25.8.: 'Hele Morgenstunden beskjæftiget med Fest hjemme og i Kongens Have'
26.8.: 'Forretninger og Møde'
27.8.: 'Første dag Arbeide i Rosenborg Hauge, ustadigt Veir'
28.8.: 'Arbeide i Haven og Exercerpladsen. Blæst og Regn'
29.8.: 'Strengt Arbeide med Forberedelserne til Festen'
30.8.: 'Høstfesten i Rosenborghave: En Time førend vi aabnede faldt en frÿgtelig Regn men Kl 4 blev det bedre. Vi aabnede, Alt gik godt og vi havde henved 12,000 Mennesker'
31.8.: '2.den Festdag. […] Haven aaben Kl 4. Kongen kom. Veiret ret ønskeligt, over 20,000 Mennesker. Alt gik godt og Pengene rullede'
1.9.: '3.die Festdag, meget godt Veir, henved 30,000 Mennesker, ypperligt Folkeliv, stor Tilfredshed over Alle. Tableauerne gjorde megen Lykke. – Jeg var meget træt og takkede Gud at det Hele var vel forbi'
2.9.: 'Formiddagen i Haven og Bazaren, der stod aaben for nogle Dage, betalt Regninger. Møde hos Pastor Bruun'
3.9.: 'hævet Penge, tilbragt et Par Timer paa Bazaren hvor der var mange Mennesker, betalt Regninger'
4.9.: 'Sidste Dag paa Bazaren, betydelig Indtægt'
5.9.: 'betalt Regninger'
7.9.: 'Møde Kl 6 hos Sallÿ. Efter en varm Discussion afgjort at vor Comité havde Raadighed over Anvendelsen af Udbyttet i det tilsigtede Øiemed'
9.9.: 'Møde hos Sally fra 7 til 10 1/2. Intet afgjort endnu'
12.9.: 'Skrevet en Artikel i Anledning af Ankerne mod [H. P.] Holsts Vers'
21.9.: 'Besøgt Chrhvns og Garnisons Lazareth for at uddele 18 Rbdlr til 9 saarede (6 paa det første 3 paa det andet). Alt fra en Tombola'.

Musical sources:

Piano vocal score. Ms Autograph (by N. W. Gade). Black ink. 1 vol. 4 pp. 34,7 × 29,5 cm with minor variants)
Vexelsang/for/chor og Orchester/af/Niels W. Gade./(texten af H. P. Holst.)/Componeret til Höstfesten (for de i Krigen Faldnes Efterladte)/den 30.de, 31.e & I sept: 50 i Rosenborg Have.
Signed (on the front cover) and dated (on p. 3): '20 August 50.'
[DKKk; N. W. Gades Samling, Supplement No. 34

Full orchestral and vocal score. Ms Autograph (by N. W. Gade). Black ink. 1 vol. 8 pp. of which one is blank (34,7 × 29,5 cm with minor variants)
Vexelsang/Ordene af H. P. Holst, Musiken af NWGade./comp: til Höstfesten d. 30, 31. Aug & 1 Sept. 50.)
Signed (on the front cover) and dated (on p. 7): 'Oct: 50.'
[DKKk; N. W. Gades Samling, Supplement No. 34
According to the dating of this score it was written well after the actual performances of Gade's song at the fair in the Rosenborg Gardens (perhaps for a publishing purpose).

No autographed musical sources for H. S. v. Løvenskjold's 'Krigerisk Marche' and H. Rung's 'Hymne' have yet been traced.

No autographed orchestral and vocal score for I. P. E. Hartmann's 'Mindesang om de Faldne' («Slumrer sødt i Slesvigs Jord») has been traced.

Piano vocal score. Ms. Autograph (by I. P. E. Hartmann). Brown ink. 4 pp. of which two are blank (35 × 23,8 cm with minor variants)
Mindesang/over de Faldne.
Unsigned and undated [c.1850]
[DKKk; I. P. E. Hartmanns samling, Kapsel F–G (læg betegnet: 'Flerstemmige Sange og Chor')

Printed sources:

Printed programme. 1 vol. 34 pp. (10,8 × 18,6 cm)
Album/til Erindring/om Festen i Rosenborg have/[...]/af H. P. Holst./Musiknumerne/af/Gade, Hartmann og Rung./[...]/Samtlige Tableauer ere arrangerede af Festcomiteens Medlem, Balletmester Bournonville.
Kjøbenhavn, Sally B. Salomon, Brünnichs Efterfølger, 1850.
[Private collection (Copenhagen)

27.9.1850
Soldier and Peasant (Soldat og Bonde).
This performance represents Bournonville's second restaging of his pantomimic idyll *Soldier and Peasant* (*see* 13.10.1829) in which W. Funck played the rôle of *Victor* for the first time. In his diary he noted about the staging, that was mounted with only minor if any changes from his previous 1848 staging:

20.9., 21.9., 23.9., and 24.9.1850: 'Prøve paa Soldat og Bonde'
25.9.: 'Prøve Kl 5 paa Soldat og Bonde'
27.9.: 'Soldat og Bonde med [W.] Funck. Man var ret tilfreds. Funck spillede bedre end jeg havde ventet det, men dandsede ugrazieust og haardt'.

The 1850 restaging of *Soldier and Peasant* was given only 3 times, the last of which took place on 28.11.1850.

1.10.1850
La Dame blanche (Den hvide Dame).
According to his handwritten list of his opera stagings, written c.1851 (*see* Additional Sources), the 1850 Copenhagen restaging of F.-A. Boyeldieu's three-act comic opera (premi-

èred at l'Opéra Comique in Paris on 10.12.1825, and first performed in Copenhagen on 30.10.1826) was clearly mounted with Bournonville's choreography. It included four dance scenes as follows:

(1) A *Circle Dance (Runddands)* in Act I (score no. 1), performed by the corps de ballet during the chorus of the mountaineers «Sonnez, sonnez, sonnez cors et musette» («I Skye, skye skal Horn og Pibe lÿde»).
(2) An (unnamed) *Dance* in Act III (score no. 12), performed by the corps de ballet during the chorus of the mountaineers «Vive à jamais notre nouveau Seigneur!» («Modtag med Frÿd vor brave Herremand!»).
(3) An (unnamed) *Dance* in Act III (score no. 12), performed by six women alternating with six couples during the chorus, entitled «Chantez, chantez joyeux ménestrels» («O syng, o syng i Hallen Minstrel»).
(4) An (unnamed) *Dance* in the Act III finale (score no. 14), performed by the corps de ballet alternating with three soloists (*Pas de trois*) during the repeat of the Act I chorus, entitled «Vive à jamais notre nouveau Seigneur!» («Modtag med Frÿd vor brave Herremand!»).

In his diary Bournonville noted about the staging:

24.9.1850: 'Prøve paa 'Den hvide Dame''
25.9.: 'Prøve paa 'Den hvide Dame' færdig'
28.9.: 'Prøve paa Byens Theater 'Den hvide Dame''
1.10.: 'Hørt 1.ste Act af 'Hvide Dame', hvortil jeg havde componeret Dands'.

On 30.10.1857 he included *La Dame blanche* in a list of projected opera restagings which he wrote on that day for the 1857–58 and 1858–59 seasons. This project was carried out on 17.11.1858 when Boyeldieu's opera was mounted at the Royal Theatre under Bournonville's general supervision for the first time. For that occasion he also made a complete notation of the *Circle Dance* in Act I.
Moreover, in Sweden *La Dame blanche (Hvita Frun på Slottet Avenel)* was restaged with a completely new mise-en-scène by Bournonville at Stockholm's Royal Theatre (Stora Theatern) on 11.1.1864. Furthermore, four years later he gave stage instructions to the singer, H. E. Christophersen, prior to a restaging of this opera in Copenhagen on 4.9.1868. Finally, on 11.1.1875 Bournonville mounted *La Dame blanche* for the last time in Copenhagen when it was given its first performance in the new Royal Theatre building.
His 1850 staging received 16 performances, the last of which was given on 31.3.1854.

Musical sources:

Printed orchestral score with manuscript insertions. 2 vol. Act I 278 pp. of which five are blank, Act II–III 346 pp. of which one is blank. (33,2 × 25 cm)
La/DAME BLANCHE/Opéra Comique en trois Actes/[...]/Par/A. Boieldieu
Paris, Janet et Cotelle, pl. no. 2002 [1826]
[DKKk; U 6 (KTA 246)

Répétiteur's copy. Ms. Copy. Brown ink. 1 vol. 18 pp. of which four are blank (32,6 × 23,3 cm)
A. 246/Repiteur [*sic*] Partie til/Den hvide Dame./Hr: Larcher./57./[...]/Repetiteur Partie/til/Den hvide Dame af Boildieu [*sic*].
Unsigned and undated [1826]
[DKKk; MA ms 3047 (KTA 246)

This répétiteur's copy dates from the Copenhagen première of *La Dame blanche* on 30.10.1826 when the dances were all choreographed and mounted by P. Larcher. It was used for all later performances during Bournonville's lifetime and contains his autographed pencilled choreographic notes describing (in general terms) the choreography and the mise-en-scène of the four dance scenes. These notes were almost certainly written for the 1850 production, while his other pencilled autographed choreographic numbers refer to a later separate choreographic description of the dance scene in Act I which he made for the restaging of *La Dame blanche* on 17.11.1858. Moreover, the répétiteur's copy contains several other choreographic notes (written with black ink) which seem to date from H. Beck's much later staging of the same dances when Boyeldieu's opera was mounted for the last time at Copenhagen's Royal Theatre on 14.5.1904.

Parts. Ms. Copy. 32 vol.
4 vl I, 4 vl II, 2 vla, 5 vlc e cb, fl 1/2, ob 1/2, cl 1/2, fag 1/2, cor 1/2, tr 1/2, trb 1/2, timp 1/2, arpa. 10 vocal parts.
Unsigned and undated [1826]
[DKKk; KTA 246
This set of parts dates from the Copenhagen première of *La Dame blanche* on 30.10.1826 and was used for all performances of this opera during Bournonville's lifetime.

6.10.1850

The Flower Maids of Florence (De florentinske Blomsterpiger), Pas de trois performed by Juliette Price, S. Price, and A. Price.

This performance represents the first time *The Flower Maids of Florence* (see 8.6.1850) was performed at Copenhagen's Royal Theatre. Bournonville did not attend the opening night because of a family visit to Jutland. The dance received 12 performances at that theatre, the last of which was given on 26.4.1853.

Musical sources:

No separate orchestral score and répétiteur's copy dating from the first performance of *The Flower Maids of Florence* at Copenhagen's Royal Theatre have yet been traced. This seems to indicate that it was rehearsed and performed there using the original musical material for H. S. v. Løvenskjold's *The New Penelope, or The Spring Festival in Athens* (now in DKKk, call nos. C II, 117 d, and KTB 205).

Conductor's part. Ms. Copy. Black ink. 8 pp. (34,6 × 24,7 cm)
B. 238/Pas de trois of 'Den ny Penelope.'/Dirigent=Stemme
Unsigned and undated [c.1850 or later]
[DKKk; MA ms 2955 (KTB 238)
This conductor's part seems to have served for the performances at Copenhagen's Royal Theatre of *The Flower Maids of Florence*. It was most probably also used for the later performance of this dance at Christiania's Theatre (Oslo) on 12.7.1852.

Parts. Ms. Copy. 26 vol.
3 vl I, 2 vl II, vla, 2 vlc e cb, fl 1/2, ob 1/2, cl 1/2, fag 1/2, cor 1/2, tr 1/2, trb 1/2/3, timp, gr cassa, tri.
Unsigned and undated [c.1850]
[DKKk; KTB 238
A note in the part for the first bassoon reads: 'C. Herr 1.ste Fagottist ved Christiania Theater d. 30/6. 1852'. This clearly indicates that Løvenskjold's music was part of the repertory in the 1852 summer tour to Norway. Moreover, because no performance was given on the date indicated by the note, and since *The Flower Maids of Florence* is the only work to music by Løvenskjold that was performed in Christiania in 1852, this note almost certainly refers to a rehearsal of *The Flower Maids in Florence* on 30.6.1852 prior to its first performance in Christiania on 12.7.1852.

13.10.1850

La Muette de Portici (Den Stumme i Portici).

This performance represents Bournonville's second complete staging of the dances and the mime scenes in D.-F.-E. Auber's five-act opera (see 23.9.1834 and 28.10.1847). It was mounted with L. Stramboe performing the rôle of Fenella for the first time. According to the poster and Bournonville's pencilled autographed notes in the opera's original répétiteur's copy the *Guarache* in Act I (score no. 3) was this year completely omitted, while the *Bolero* in the same act was mounted in a thoroughly revised version that included several musical cuts and (seemingly) new choreography. The poster, however, gives explicit credit to Bournonville only for having 'arranged' (*arrangeret*) the dances. In his diary he noted about the performance:

17.9., 18.9., 21.9., 28.9., and 30.9.1850: 'Prøve paa Den Stumme'
1.10.: 'Prøve paa Den Stumme. Rollen færdig og særdeles tilfredsstillende'
4.10.: 'Arrangement til Den Stumme'
12.10.: 'Prøve pa Den Stumme – Laura Stramboe meget god. -'
13.10.: 'Om Aftenen dirigeret Dandsen i Den Stumme i Portici. – Laura Stramboe udførte Fenellas Parti meget godt. -'.

The production was given 8 times, the last time on 13.9.1852. During this period the opera was (according to the posters) performed once without the *Bolero* (on 18.11.1850), and once without the incorporated Act I *Pas de deux* (on 9.9.1852).

Musical sources:

The orchestral scores and the sets of parts used for this production were the same as those used for the previous stagings on 23.9.1834 and 28.10.1847 (now in DKKkt and DKKk, call nos. KTA 273, MA ms 2603, MA ms 2700, MA ms 3056, and KTB 209).

Répétiteur's copy (incomplete). Ms. Copy. Brown ink. 1 vol. 22 pp. of which one is blank (33 × 23 cm)
A. 273/Den Stumme i Portici./60 C.
Unsigned and undated [1830]
[DKKk; MA ms 3055 (KTB 273 (1))
This (incomplete) répétiteur's copy contains most of the music for the Act I *Guarache* (score no. 3), the entire *Bolero* in the same act, and the *Tarentelle* in Act III (score no. 11). Moreover, Bournonville's pencilled autographed choreographic notes are included throughout the volume and describe (in general terms) the choreography of all the dances, including an indication of the exact place where the incorporated *Pas de deux* in G major (set to music by M. E. Caraffa) was performed (see 23.9.1834). Furthermore, according to the names of the dancers included here, these notes must almost certainly have been written in connection with Bournonville's 1850 restaging of *La Muette de Portici*. However, the fact that the *Guarache* was omitted in this year's production seems to indicate that Bournonville's notes for this dance only represent his first draft for a revised choreography of it. Finally, Bournonville's later and far more detailed choreographic notes (written in the same volume with brown ink) refer almost certainly to the restaging of *La Muette de Portici* on 12.2.1862, which (according to his diary) was planned and notated by Bournonville on 21.9.1861, and carried out from his notes by L. Gade.

21.10.1850

The Toreador (Toréadoren).

This performance represents Bournonville's first restaging in Copenhagen of his two-act idyllic ballet *The Toreador* (see

27.11.1840). It was mounted this year with W. Funck and A. Price playing the leading rôles of *Alonzo* and *Maria* for the first time. Otherwise, the production seems to have been mounted with only minor if any changes from the original 1840 version. In his diary Bournonville noted about the performance:

26. 9. and 27.9.1850: 'Prøve paa Toreadoren'
2.10.: 'Stor Prøve paa Toreadoren'
3.10., 4.10., 14.10., 15.10., 16.10., and 17.10.: 'Prøve paa Toreadoren'
19.10.: 'Prøve paa Toreadoren, der gik godt med sin nÿ Besætning'
21.10: 'Toreadoren første Gang med den nÿ Besætning. Den gik særdeles godt. Edw. Stramboe var et livagtigt Billede af sin salig Fader [i. e. the mime J. A. F. Stramboe]. – Juliette Price dandsede udmærket godt. Balletten gjorde meget Lÿkke'.

The 1850 restaging received 45 performances, the last of which was given on 9.1.1865. The musical material employed this year was the same as that used since the 1840 première of the ballet (now in DKKk, call nos. C II, 114 k, MA ms 2965, and KTB 1046 (originally KTB 269)).

30.10.1850
The House of Svend Dyring (Svend Dyrings Hus).
Although Bournonville does not include H. Hertz's romantic four-act tragedy (set to music by H. Rung) in any of his handwritten lists of his stagings of operas and plays, nor in the printed survey of his works in his memoirs (*My Theatre Life*, p. 408), he clearly created the mise-en-scène and the choreography for this restaging of it. The work included two half-danced, half-mimed scenes, the first of which is performed in Act I, score no. 4 during the romance and chorus, entitled «Herr Peder kasted Runer over Spange» (sung by young maidens). The second scene takes place during the chorus in Act IV, score no. 9 and is (according to pencilled notes in the répétiteur's copy) described as follows:

'Paa forskjellige Steder i Værelset er et Chor af barnegode Engle med Palmeblade i Hænderne grupperet [...] Choret opløser fire Grupper og udtrykker ved pantomimiske Stillinger og Bevægelser sin Medfølelse for de Sovende'.

In his dairy Bournonville noted about the staging:

28.10.1850: 'Prøve paa [...] Svend Dyrings Huus'
29.10.: 'Prøve paa [...] Svend Dyring'
30.10.: 'Prøve paa Svend Dyring [...] Seet Svend Dyrings Huus. Debut af [L. A.] Eckardt, temmelig 0'.

The 1850 production of *The House of Svend Dyring* received 11 performances, the last of which was given on 19.5.1853.

Musical sources:

Orchestral score. Ms. Autograph (by H. Rung). Brown and black ink. 1 vol. 132 pp. (26,6 × 36,6 cm)
363/Svend Dyrings Hus./Partitur
Signed and dated (on p. 132): 'H. Rung 1836'
[DKKk; C II, 119 k (KTA 363)]
This orchestral score dates from the Copenhagen première of *The House of Svend Dyring* on 15.3.1837 and was used for all performances of this work there during Bournonville's lifetime.

Orchestral score. Ms. Autograph (by H. Rung). Brown ink. 1 vol. 138 pp. (25,9 × 36,8 cm)

'Svend Dyrings Hus'/Musik af H. Rung.
Signed (on p. 1): 'H. Rung', dated (p. 138) 'December 1836'
[DKKK; H. & Fr. Rungs Musik-arkiv no. 72 B]
This orchestral score contains the original Danish text and a German translation added to the score (with red ink) by an unknown hand. It was in the property of H. Rung's son, F. Rung, who sold it to DKKk. The score was probably made for publishing purposes abroad.

Orchestral score. Ms Copy. Black ink. 1 vol. 108 pp. of which one is blank (26,4 × 37,4 cm with minor variants)
H. RUNG/Svend/Dyring/Hus/Part.
Unsigned and undated [1830s]
[DKKk; C II, 119 k (1957-58.796)]
This orchestral score was purchased by DKKk from Knud Larsens Musikforlag on 29.11.1957. The volume, which excludes the overture, was probably made for publishing purposes in Denmark.

Répétiteur's copy, Ms. Copy. Black ink. 1 vol. 4 pp. (31,8 × 25 cm)
A. 363/Svend Dyrings Huus/43B/[...]/Repetiteur Partie./til/ Svend Dyrings Huus.
Unsigned and undated [1837]
[DKKk; MA ms 3079 (KTA 363 (1))]
This répétiteur's copy dates from the Copenhagen première of *The House of Svend Dyring* on 15.3.1837 and was used for all performances of it there during Bournonville's lifetime. It includes his pencilled autographed choreographic notes describing (in general terms) the dance and mime performed during the chorus in Act IV (score no. 9).

Parts. Ms. Copy. 68 vol.
3 vl I, 3 vl II, 2 vla, 3 vlc e cb, fl 1/2, ob 1/2, cl 1/2, fag 1/2, cor 1/2/ 3/4, tr 1/2, trb 1/2/3, timp. On stage: conductor's part, 3 vl I, 2 vl II, vla, vlc, 2 vlc e cb, fl 1/2, ob 1/2, cl 1/2/3/4, fag 1/2/3/4, cor 1/2/ 3/4/5/6, tr 1/2, trb 1/2/3, timp, glock, arpa. Extra parts for the overture: vl I, vl II, cb. 40 vocal parts.
Unsigned and undated [1836 and later]
[DKKk; KTA 363]
This set of parts was used for all performances of *The House of Svend Dyring* in Copenhagen between 1837 and 1877.

9.11.1850
Pas de deux à la Taglioni (uncredited) performed by F. Hoppe and J. Price.
This (uncredited) *Pas de deux* was restaged with the same dancers four months later on 13.3.1851, but then with Bournonville's name listed explicitly on the poster as the choreographer. The dance is almost certainly identical with the so-called *Pas de deux (after Taglioni) (Pas de deux (efter Taglioni))*, performed earlier at Copenhagen's Royal Theatre (by F. Hoppe and A. Nielsen) on 6.7.1840, and at Christiania's Theatre (Oslo) by Bournonville and C. Fjeldsted on 10.8.1840. These dances, in turn, are most probably identical with the so-called *A Pas de deux arranged after Taglioni (En Pas de deux arrangeret efter Taglioni)*, which was first been performed as a separate divertissement at Copenhagen's Royal Theatre by G. Brodersen and A. Nielsen on 4.10.1839, but had originally been danced by P. C. Johansson and A. Nielsen at Stockholm's Royal Theatre (Operahuset) on 5.6.1839 with the title *Pas de deux (by Taglioni) (Pas de deux (Af Taglioni))*. According to a Swedish set of parts for it (now in SSkma, call no. KT Dansmusik 43), that dance, in turn, was performed to music by J. Mayseder, and is identical with the score for the *Pas de deux* in Act II (score no. 1A) of Bournonville's two-act romantic ballet *The Isle of Phantasy* (see 28.10. 1838).

The 1850 *Pas de deux à la Taglioni* is most probably also identical with the later *'Pas de deux' (à la Taglioni)* mounted at Christiania's Theatre (Oslo) for S. Lund and J. Price on 9.6. 1852, the choreography of which is explicitly credited on the poster to Bournonville.

It is not possible to identify the dance any further.

27.12.1850

Pas de deux composed by Mr. Court Ballet Master Bournonville (componeret af Hr. Hofballetmester Bournonville) **performed by S. Lund and P. Fredstrup.**

This dance was (according to the rehearsal book of H. C. J. Fredstrup) rehearsed only once on 26.12.1850. It is most probably identical with the *Pas de deux* set to music by F.-M.- A. Venua (*see* 29.10.1829) and incorporated by Bournonville in Act II of his three-act romantic ballet *Faust* on 8.12.1849. The *Pas de deux* is most likely also identical with the later (uncredited) *Pas de deux* performed as a separate divertissement by S. Lund and S. Price at Copenhagen's Royal Theatre on 24.4.1851, and the even later *'Pas de deux' (from the ballet Faust) composed by Mr. Bournonville*, danced by S. Lund and J. Price at Christiania's Theatre (Oslo) on 29.6.1852.

The *Pas de deux* was performed once by Lund and Fredstrup in 1850. It is not possible to identify the dance any further.

1851

2.2.–20.2.1851

The organisation of the banquets and the decoration of the Riding School at Copenhagen's Christiansborg Palace.

This series of thirteen banquets was given in honour of the returning soldiers from Denmark's war with Germany, 1848– 1850. In his diary Bournonville noted about his involvement in the organisation of the festivities and his personal contribution in addressing the troops in five speeches:

26.1.1851: 'tilkaldt en Comité af Kommunalbestyrelsen for Troppernes Modtagelse – to Möder samme Dag'
27.1.: 'Møde og Foranstaltninger'
28.1.: 'Foranstaltninger og Möde. – 2.det Compagnie af Garden kommer tilveis og uformodet'
29.1.: 'Dagen beskjæftiget med Foranstaltninger'
30.1., 31.1., and 1.2.: 'Foranstaltninger til Festen, den største Deel af Dagen i Ridehuset […] Ridehuset færdig om Løverdag-Aften Kl 10'
2.2.: 'Alt i Hovedstaden beredt til Indtoget. – Gaderne smykkede med Fahner, Billeder og Grønt. Flagning, Salut. Musik. Laugs-Procession. Kl. 12 kom Garden 700 Mand til Ridehuset: Kongen, Ministrene, Generalerne og flere Honnoratiores spiste ved Officeerbordet. Jubel. Sang, Musik og Taler – For de Faldne – For vort Fædreland. – Kl 2 var Collationen forbi, Alt blev nu ordnet paanÿ til Imorgen og saaledes gik den første Dag. -'
3.2.: '2.den Indt. […] Fest i Ridehuset. 1.ste lette Bataillon. Oberstl: Walter. – 1000 Mand – Taler: [H. C.] Christensen for Bataillonen. – Jeg for de Faldne. – &c.'
4.2.: '3 Indt. […] Fest i Ridehuset. 2.den lette Bataillon. Oberstl. Hindenburg: Taler [N. P.] Nielsen for Bataillonen [P. F. A.] Hammerich for de Faldne [H. P.] Holst for [F. R. H.] Bülow'
6.2.: '4.de Indt. […] 3.de Liniebat. Major Vett, Majoren talte meget og godt. Jeg var kun lidet tilstede'
7.2.: '5.te Dag. […] fest i Ridehuset 1.ste Jægercorps Oberstl: Wilster. Taler: for Corpset. Pastor Bruun for de Faldne. Jeg for de Saarede &c.'

8.2.: '6.te Dag: […] Fest i Ridehuset som jeg ikke kunde bivaane. 5.te Bataillon Major [F. R. H.] Bülow, der skal have talt meget godt.'
9.2.: '(7.de Dag.) Fest i Ridehuset 10.de lette Bataillon – Oberst [J.] Ræder. Ing. [M. J.] Hammerich for Bataillonen. Jeg for [C. J. de] Meza. [C. C.] Hall for de troe Skovpiper. – [N. F. S.] Grundtvig for de Tappre Fædrelands Forsvarere. – Oberstel 5 gange. – Kbhvns Borgere, Krigsm: Stænderne – (Rigsdagen), Damerne &c.'
10.2.: '8.e Dag. Hjemkomstfest for Husarerne og 6.te Linie-Bataillon. Vi beværtede circa 1700 Mand. Kongen var tilstede. [P.] F [A.] Hammerich for Velkommen. Oberst Torp proponerede flere Skaaler fortrinligt iblandt andre for Damerne med Hensyn til Jenserne.'
11.2.: '9.de Dag. […] Modtagelse for 7.de Linie Bataillon. – Frederikstads Forsvarere. Dette var Een af de smukkeste Fester, megen Begeistring og deilige Taler af [H. P.] Holst, [N. P.] Nielsen, [J. H. V.] Paulli.'
12.2.: '10.de Dag. […] Ikke fungeret ved 8.de Linie Bataillon. Tale af [N. P.] Nielsen og [P. F. A.] Hammerich'
15.2.: '11.te Dag. […] Festmaaltid for 9.de Liniebataillon. Taler af [N. P.] Nielsen, [E.] Schack, Lacour, Capt. M. Möller, det Hele meget livligt og smukt […] (Batteriet Just)'
16.2.: '(12.de Dag.) fest for Marinen. Udmærket Anordning og Stemning. Taler af [P. F. A.] Hammerich, [F. R. H.] Bülow, [S. A.] Bille, [J. P.] Münster og mig – Jeg gjorde megen Lÿkke Kongen var der og rakte mig Haanden: – circa 150 Officerer og 800 Mand Söfolk. Det Hele gjorde et særdeles godt Indtryk'
20.2.: '(13.de og sidste Dag) […] Artilleriets Fest – Kl 12. – Kongen tilstede, han var brillant og talede særdeles godt. – [N. P.] Nielsen, [P. F. A.] Hammerich, [S. A.] Bille, Bülow, [A. F. v. d.] Recke, [H. C.] Christensen, og Flere, den hele Stemning var fortreffelig, der blev drukken megen Champagne. Kl 3 var det Hele forbi og denne Cyclus af Fester sluttet paa det Herligste'
21.2.: 'Nedtagelse i Ridehuset'
22.2.: 'besørget adskilligt fra Ridehuset'.

Autograph sources:

Manuscripts of five speeches. Ms. Autographs. Black and brown ink. 12 pp. of which two are blank (various sizes)
Naar vi med Begeistring hilse den 1.ste lette Bataillon/[…]/I Slaget ved Fridericia straalede mange Navne/[…]/Til Flaget/[…]/Idet jeg i Eet og Alt slutter mig til den nÿsafsungne/Vise/[…]/Skaal for Troskab, Enighed og Nationalaand.
Unsigned and undated [according to Bournonville's diary these five speeches were given on 2.2, 3.2, 7.2., and 16.2.1851 respectively]
[DKKk; NKS 3285 4°, kapsel 9, facs. III (læg 'Taler')]

9.2.1851

Pas de trois (uncredited) performed by W. Funck, P. Fredstrup, and J. Rostock.

This dance is most likely identical with the (uncredited) *Pas de trois* performed earlier by the same three dancers on 8.4. 1848, and in turn is almost certainly identical with the *Pas de trois* in Act I (score no. 5) of Bournonville's Copenhagen version of J. Aumer's three-act pantomimic ballet *La Somnambule, ou l'Arrivée d'un nouveau seigneur* (*see* 21.9.1829). It is not possible to identify the dance any further.

24.2.1851

Léon, ou Le Château de Monténero (Slottet Montenero).

According to his handwritten list of his opera stagings, written c.1851 (*see* Additional Sources), the 1851 Copenhagen restaging of N. Dalayrac's three-act *comédie en prose* (premièred in Paris at l'Opéra Comique on 15.10.1798) was clearly mounted with Bournonville's choreography. It included a Court dance performed by the corps de ballet in the finale of Act I (score no. 8) as part of the chorus, entitled «Jouissons, jouissons de ce jour d'allegresse» («Jubler höit lad vor Fryd reen og festlig frembryde!»). In his diary on 11.2.1851, Bournonville noted about this dance:

'Prøve, nÿ Dands til Montenero'.

Bournonville did not attend the opening night nor any of the following performances of this work. The 1851 restaging of *Léon, ou Le Château de Monténero* received 7 performances, the last of which was given on 20.10.1851.

Musical sources:

Printed orchestral score. 1 vol. 212 pp. of which two are blank (31,4 × 25 cm with minor variants)
LE CHATEAU/DE/MONTÉNÉRO,/COMÉDIE EN TROIS ACTES ET EN PROSE./[...]/Musique de N. DALAYRAC
Paris, Chez l'auteur, rue de la Michodière, pl. no. 11 [1798]
[DKKk; U 6 (KTA 175)
This score was used for all performances of Dalayrac's comedy in Copenhagen between 1813 and 1851. The music for the Court dance in the finale of Act I is included on pp. 91–97.

Répétiteur's copy. Ms. Copy. Black ink. 1 vol. 4 pp. of which one is blank (32 × 21 cm)
Slottet i Montenero/No. 20./Rept.r Partie/225/No. 6/[...]/195.f/ Dandse Partiet/af/Slottet Montenero
Unsigned and undated [1813]
[DKKk; MA ms 3036 (KTA 175)
This répétiteur's copy dates from the Copenhagen première of Dalayrac's comedy on 28.5.1813 and was used for all performances of it during Bournonville's lifetime. It contains his autographed choreographic notes (written with black ink) for the Court dance in Act I, score no. 8, which most probably were written immediately before the first and only rehearsal held of it on 11.2.1851.

Parts. Ms. Copy. 30 vol.
4 vl I, 4 vl II, 2 vla, 4 vlc e cb, fl picc, fl 1/2, ob 1/2, cl 1/2, fag 1/2, cor 1/2/3, tr 1/2, trb, timp. 89 vocal parts.
Unsigned and undated [1813]
[DKKk; KTA 175
This set of parts dates from the 1813 Copenhagen première of Dalayrac's comedy and was used for all performances of it there during Bournonville's lifetime.

13.3.1851
Pas de deux à la Taglioni composed by Mr. Court Ballet Master Bournonville (componeret af Hr. Hofballetmester Bournonville) **performed by F. Hoppe and Juliette Price.**

This dance is identical with the (uncredited) *Pas de deux à la Taglioni* performed earlier in the same season by Hoppe and Price on 9.11.1850. The dance, which this year was explicitly credited on the poster to Bournonville, is probably also identical with the two earlier dances, entitled *Pas de deux (after Taglioni) (Pas de deux (efter Taglioni))*, performed at the Royal Theatre (by F. Hoppe and A. Nielsen) on 6.7.1840, and at Christiania's Theatre, Oslo, (by Bournonville and C. Fjeldsted) on 10.8.1840.

Both of these dances are most probably identical with the *Pas de deux (by Taglioni) (Pas de deux (Af Taglioni))* set to music by J. Mayseder and first performed as a separate divertissement by Bournonville's Swedish pupil, P. C. Johansson, and A. Nielsen at Stockholm's Royal Theatre (Operahuset) on 5.6.1839. That dance was apparently also performed the same year at Copenhagen's Royal Theatre by G. Brodersen

and A. Nielsen on 4.10.1839, with the new title *A Pas de deux arranged after Taglioni (En Pas de deux arrangeret efter Taglioni)*.

The 1851 *Pas de deux à la Taglioni* dance is almost certainly also identical with the later *'Pas de deux' (à la Taglioni)*, performed by S. Lund and Juliette Price at Christiania's Theatre (Oslo) on 9.6.1852.

It is not possible to identify the dance any further.

25.3.1851
The decoration and the illumination of the main hall in the Royal Shooting Gallery for the celebration of the 50th anniversary after the foundation of the King's Corps of Volunteers (Decorationen og Belysningen af Skydebanen ved Festen for Livjægercorpsets Stiftelsesdag 1801) **(the Royal Shooting Gallery at Vesterbro).**

Apart from arranging the decoration and the illumination of the main hall in the palace of the Royal Shooting Gallery at Vesterbrogade in Copenhagen, Bournonville also wrote two songs for this celebration besides giving the main speech. Like his father before him, Bournonville had, since 1848, been a member of the King's Corps of Volunteers. In his diary he noted about his participation in the organisation of the festivities that marked the fiftieth anniversary of the foundation of this military corps of volunteers:

27.2.1851: Møde hos Waagepetersen i Livjæger Festcomiteen'
2.3.: 'Livjægermøde hos Waagepetersen'
6.3.: 'Besøgt Justitsministeren i Anledning af Livjægerfesten'
9.3.: 'Møde hos Waagepetersen'
16.3.: 'Besørget en Mængde for Livjægerfesten'
19.3.: 'Tour til Skydebanen'
21.3.: 'Hele Dagen paa Skydebanen og arrangeret'
22.3: 'hele Dagen paa Skydebanen for at arrangere Festen'
23.3.: 'Formiddagen paa Skydebanen'
24.3.: 'Hele Dagen Forberedelser til Festen. Prøve paa Belysningen om Aftenen. Decorationen tog sig godt ud'
25.3.: 'Livjægercorpsets Stiftelsesdag 1801. Hele Dagen derude. Jeg iklædte mig Uniformen og Kl 4 1/2 begÿndte Selskabet at samles, der foruden ÿngre og ældre Jægere omtrent 230 i Tallet ogsaa bestod af inviterede Honnoratiores. Prinds [Frederik] Ferdinand, Commandanten Hagemann, Oberst Wilster, Amtmd Tetens og fremfor Alle Hs Excellence General Lieutenant [F. C. v.] Holstein med Søn. Krigs og Justisministrene vare inviterede, den første ved sin Adjudant. Kl 5 kom Holstein og Musikcorpset spillede Corpsets ældste Marsch. Kl henved 6 gik man tilbords. Stemningen var helt igjennem fortreffelig, munter og festlig. Jeg havde skrevet 2 Viser og holdt en Tale til Wilster og de ÿngre Jægere, der gjorde overordentlig Lÿkke. Efter at de ældre vare gaaede blev der dandset indtil Kl 12'.

Printed sources:

Printed songtext. 4 pp. (19,9 × 12,7 cm)
VIII./DAMERNES SKAAL./Den 25. Marts 1851./[...] 'Dannebroge, Dannevang/Danneqvinde
Unsigned and undated [c. 25.3.1851]
[DKKk; Danske Afdeling, Småtryk (Personalhistorie: Bournonville)
Bournonville's text was set to the melody of B. S. Ingemann's song, entitled 'Dannevang ved grønne Bred'. That song, in turn, employed the tune of C. E. F. Weyse's canzonetta, named «Vil du være stærk og fri» (originally part of Weyse's and A. Oehlenschläger's four-act opera *The Cavern of Ludlam (Ludlam's Hule)* from 30.1.1816).

4.4.1851
The Kermesse in Brüges, or The Three Gifts (Kermessen i Brügge eller: De tre Gaver).

This three-act romantic ballet 'in Flemish style towards the close of the seventeeth century' is set to music composed and arranged by H. S. Paulli. In his score (which at the 1851 première consisted of 19 numbers) Paulli included several musical borrowings that are identified as follows:

(1) Act I, score no. 1: Paulli here freely interpolated two excerpts in 6/8 time of the chorus, entitled «Buvons, buvons, buvons, buvons soudain!» from Act II (score no. 18) of G. Rossini's two-act opera *Le Comte Ory* (premièred at the Paris Opéra on 20.8.1828). These excerpts are mingled with a section in 2/4 time from the same Rossini chorus (originally sung to the text «Célébrons tour à tour le vin et la folie»). That section had many years earlier also been used by L. Zinck in Act III (score no. 17) of his score for Bournonville's three-act pantomimic ballet *Don Quixote at Camacho's Wedding* (*see* 24.2. 1837).

(2) Act I, score no. 3: In this number Paulli employed his own, earlier music for the so-called 'Danse des battoirs' that was originally part of his score for Bournonville's one-act allegorical ballet *The White Rose, or The Summer in Bretagne* (*see* 20.9.1847). It was interpolated in *The Kermesse in Brüges, or The Three Gifts* in a new, slightly extended version and was performed as a clog dance by the corps de ballet.

(3) Act I, score no. 6: Paulli here interpolated yet another excerpt from Rossini's *Le Comte Ory*, namely the duet entitled «Une dame du haut parage», originally sung by *Isolière* and *Le Comte* in Act I (score no. 8).

(4) Act II, score no. 8: In this scene Paulli incorporated an anonymous dance tune from the 16th century, entitled 'La Romanesca'. It was first published in Copenhagen in 1847 in a version for piano (*Musikalsk Museum*, 2. Aargang, no. 7), but had already become widely popular in Paris after 1835 when F. Sor employed it in an arrangement for violin and guitar. According to a later rearrangement of Sor's work, made by Paulli for violoncello and piano (now in DKKk, call no. C II, 10, H. S. Paulli's Efterladte mss. II, 1958–59.2) the same tune is identified by him as 'La Romanesca, fameux air de danse du seizième siècle'. In yet another manuscript copy by H. Rung, which dates from about the same period (now in DKKk, call no. H. & Fr. Rungs Musik Arkiv no. 1528), the same tune is entitled 'La Romanesca, scene de Bal' and set to a song the first line of which reads «Le Bal commence, venez belles Dames».

In Paulli's score for *The Kermesse in Brüges, or The Three Gifts* 'La Romanesca' accompanies *Eleonora*'s enforced dance performed by her to the accompaniment of *Carelis* on his magical viola da gamba. The same tune resurfaces later on in the same scene, but then as an accompaniment for a dance performed by *Carelis* and *Eleonora* together.

(5) Act II, score no. 11: Here Paulli incorporated an excerpt from the chorus, entitled «Dans ses présents que de magnificence» in Act I (score no. 1) of F. Hérold's three-act comic opera *Zampa ou La Fiancée de Marbre* (premièred at l'Opéra Comique in Paris on 3.5.1831). In *The Kermesse in Brüges, or The Three Gifts* it served as an accompaniment for the mime scene at *Mme van Everdingen*'s during which the richly dressed *Geert* is much courted by everybody because of the secret powers of his magic ring.

(6) Act II, score no. 12 (*Pas de quatre* and *Menuetto*): For these dances Paulli incorporated his own earlier music for the four solo variations in the so-called 'Pas des quatres rosières' (score no. 13) of his and Bournonville's one-act allegorical ballet *The White Rose, or The Summer in Bretagne* (*see* 20.9.1847). In *The Kermesse in Brüges, or The Three Gifts* it accompanied a *Pas de quatre*, danced by two couples as a divertissement at *Mme van Everdingen*'s. Moreover, during the same dance a brief *Menuetto* section was performed by the corps de ballet before the Coda movement.

(7) Act III, score no. 19 (the *Finale*): In the ballet's finale Paulli inserted the same excerpt in 2/4 time from the chorus in Rossini's *Le Comte Ory*, entitled «Célébrons tour à tour le vin et la folie» which he had employed earlier in Act I (score no. 1).

Only three years after the Copenhagen première of *The Kermesse in Brüges, or The Three Gifts* Bournonville was (according

to a note in his diary on 16.4.1854) planning a revised staging of the complete ballet at Vienna's Kärnthnerthor Theatre. Subsequently, he wrote two new versions of its scenario (in French) and also notated the complete choreography and pantomime in a new répétiteur's copy during the period between 25.5. and 15.7.1855 (now in SSkma, call no. KT Pantomime-Balletter K 4). However, the projected Vienna staging was never carried out, and *The Kermesse in Brüges, or The Three Gifts* was mounted only once outside Denmark during Bournonville's lifetime. That production was carried out by his pupil, S. Lund, who presented the ballet at Stockholm's Royal Theatre (Operahuset) on 30.12.1858.

In Copenhagen *The Kermesse in Brüges, or The Three Gifts* was restaged twice by Bournonville on 19.11.1865, and 8.12. 1872, each time in revised versions that included new incorporated dances and musical excerpts borrowed from his and Paulli's three-act Hungarian ballet *In the Carpathians* (*see* 4.3. 1857). The last of these productions had already been projected by Bournonville in 1.8.1870.

In his diary he noted about the creation and 1851 Copenhagen première of *The Kermesse in Brüges, or The Three Gifts*:

11.9.1850: 'skrevet og componeret'
14.9.: 'componeret'
17.9.: 'Skrevet og fuldendt Programmet til en nÿ Ballet: <u>Kermessen i Brügge</u> eller <u>De tre Brødre</u>'
18.9.: 'Besøg af [H. S.] Paulli og [E.] Lehmann'
2.10.: 'første Gang begÿndt Musiken hos Paulli til min nÿe Ballet'
5.11.: 'componeret paa min nÿe Ballet'
6.11. and 7.11.: 'componeret'
11.11.: 'første Prøve paa min nÿ Ballet. Pas de deux færdig'
14.11.: 'Componeret paa min nÿe Ballet'
15.11. and 16.11.: 'componeret'
17.11.: 'Componeret med Paulli'
18.11.: 'Componeret'
19.11.: 'Prøve paa Kermessen i Brügge. (1.ste Akt.)'
20.11., 25.11., and 26.11.: 'Prøve paa Kermessen'
27.11.: 'Prøve paa Kermessen fuldendt Runddandsen'
29.11.: 'Prøve Kl 10 – læst og componeret'
30.11. 'Prøve paa [...] Kermessen'
1.12.: 'skrevet og componeret'
3.12.: 'Prøve paa Kermessen (pas de Quatre)'
4.12.: 'lille Prøve paa Pas de Quatre'
6.12. and 11.12.: 'Prøve paa Kermessen'
15.12.: 'Componeret, skrevet og arrangeret mine Affairer. Besøg hos Paulli og Maleren [N.] Simonsen'
16.12.: 'Prøve paa Kermessen'
17.12.: 'Prøve med Juliette og Hoppe [...] arbeidet med Paulli'
19.12.: 'Prøve paa Kermessen'
20.12.: 'Skrevet – arrangeret, Prøve Kl 10 paa Kermessen [...] Skrevet og componeret'
21.12.: 'Prøve paa første Akt af Kermessen – heelt igjennem'
26.12. and 27.12.: 'componeret'
28.12.: 'Prøve nÿ Scene af Kermessen [...] componeret'
31.12.1850 and 2.1.1851: 'Prøve paa Kermessen'
3.1.: 'componeret og skrevet. Prøve og nÿe Scener af Kermessen'
4.1.: 'Kermessen'
5.1.: 'arbeidet med Paulli'
10.1. and 11.1.: 'componeret'
13.1.: 'Prøve med Hoppe og Juliette'
14.1.: 'Prøve paa Kermessen nÿ Scene'
15.1.: 'arbeidet med Paulli, componeret, skrevet'
16.1.: 'Prøve paa Kermessen'
17.1.: 'Prøve paa Kermessen, nÿe Scener'
18.1.: 'Prøve paa Kermessens to Akter'
21.1.: 'besluttet Prøve paa Kermessen men formedelst Herr [F.] Hoppes Chicane fandt den ikke Sted [...] besøgt Billedgalleriet'

22.1.: 'skrevet endeel, componeret [...] Prøve og indstuderet en nÿ Scene'

23.1.: 'Prøve paa Kermessen i Directeurens Nærværelse – Det gik meget godt'

24.1.: 'skrevet, componeret'

25.1.: 'indstuderet en nÿ Scene'

5.2.: 'Indstuderet en nÿ Scene til Balletten'

6.2.: 'Fuldendt Scenen'

8.2.: 'Prøve paa Kermessen'

18.2.: 'stor Prøve paa Kermessen'

28.2.: 'Møde med Costumiereren til Balletten'

1.3.: 'Prøve paa [...] Kermessen'

2.3.: 'arrangeret Costumer hos Fru [C. B.] Ryge'

4.3.: 'Første Prøve paa Kermessen – Byens Theater'

6.3.: 'Prøve paa 1.ste og 2.den Act af Kermessen'

9.3.: 'Componeret [...] Jeg blev hjemme den hele Aften og compo‐nerede'

10.3.: 'Prøve paa sidste Scene af Kermessen'

12.3., 13.3., 14.3., 15.3., and 19.3.: 'Prøve paa Kermessen'

20.3.: 'Prøve paa alle tre Akter af Kermessen'

22.3.: 'Prøve paa Kermessen paa Byens Theater'

27.3.: 'Prøve paa Byens Theater. Balletten gik fortreffeligt'

28.3.: 'Skrevet mit Program og befordret det til Trÿkken'

29.3.: 'Prøve paa 3.die Akt af Kermessen'

30.3.: 'Arrangeret Garderoben til Balletten'

31.3.: 'Prøve fuldstændigt paa Kermessen'

1.4.: 'Arrangement til min nÿ Ballet'

2.4: 'Prøve paa Decorationer og Requisiter til Kermessen. Om Efter‐middagen fuldstændig Generalprøve i Costume. Det gik særdeles godt og Alt bebudede Lÿkke'

3.4.: 'Forberedelser til Balletten'

4.4.: 'i Theatret hvor jeg gav for første Gang Balletten Kermessen i Brügge eller de tre Gaver, der gik udmærket godt og gjorde en Sen‐sation, der mindede om Napoli. Jeg var glad og taknemlig for dette Held, der er af Vigtighed for Ballettens hele Bestaaen'.

The original 1851 production of *The Kermesse in Brüges, or The Three Gifts* received 28 performances (the last given on 25.3. 1859) and the ballet reached a total of 63 performances dur‐ing Bournonville's lifetime, the last of which was given on 22.10.1879.

Autograph sources:

Production note. Ms. Autograph. Black ink. 4 pp. (26,9 × 21,5 cm)
Herre = Costumet til Balletten Kermessen.
Signed and dated: 'd: 28 Febr. 1851.'
[DKKkt; F.M. (Ballet)

Production note. Ms. Autograph. Pencil. 1 p. (16,9 × 13,6 cm)
Mandag d: 31 Martz/Prøve paa Kermessen. -
Unsigned and undated [Written most probably on 31.3.1851]
[DKKkt; F.M. (Ballet)

Musical sources:

Orchestral (incomplete) score. Ms. Autograph (by H. S. Paulli and V. C. Holm) and copy. Brown and black ink. 1 vol. 376 pp. of which three are blank (27 × 37 cm with many variants)
271./Kermessen i Brügge./Partitur.
Unsigned and undated [1851]
[DKKk; MA ms 1551 (KTB 271)
This (incomplete) autographed orchestral score was used for all performances of *The Kermesse in Brüges, or The Three Gifts* in Copenha‐gen since the 1851 première and well into the next century. It con‐tains numerous conductor's notes and later manuscript insertions which indicate the many musical and choreographic changes made by Bournonville in his 1865 and 1872 restagings, as well as those done by H. Beck for his staging on 7.11.1909 and those of other successors. Pages 25–40 contain Paulli's music for the *Slowanka*. This

was originally part of his score for Bournonville's three-act Hungar‐ian ballet *In the Carpathians* (*see* 4.3.1857) in which it was performed in Act III (score no. 28). This dance (which is signed and dated on p. 40: 'd. 20 Febr: 1857 HSPaulli') was incorporated by Bournonville in Act I of *The Kermesse in Brüges, or The Three Gifts* on 19.11.1865 and was listed there as no. '2[A]'. Similarly, the music on pp. 55–68 was origi‐nally part of the score for Act I of *In the Carpathians* (score nos. 7 and 8), but was, according to the 1865 répétiteur's copy for *The Kermesse in Brüges, or The Three Gifts* (now in DKKk, call no. MA ms 2966), interpolated in the Act I *Pas de deux* of this ballet on 19.11.1865 (that year listed as score no. '2 B'). The many pages that at later stages were taken out of Paulli's autographed score for *The Kermesse in Brüges, or The Three Gifts* (between 1852 and 1909) were discovered in 1989 at DKKkt and were transferred to DKKk at a later stage (*see* the follow‐ing entry).

Orchestral score (fragments). Ms. Autograph (by H. S. Paulli and V. C. Holm). Brown and black ink. 68 pp. of which five are blank (27,4 × 37,5 cm with many variants)
[Untitled]
Signed and dated (on p. '313'): 'd: 18 Marts 1851. HSPaulli'
[DKKk; MA ms 2762 (3) (KTB 271)
These (untitled) fragments all derive from Paulli's autographed or‐chestral score for *The Kermesse in Brüges, or The Three Gifts*. They con‐tain the music for what originally was Act I pp. '27–38, 45–48, 81–82, 103–107', Act II pp. '135–136', and Act III pp. '175–178, 189–204, 235–236, 309–314'.

Page '28' includes a pencilled note reading: 'herfra til I Karpa‐therne Pag 81'. It refers to the incorporation in *The Kermesse in Brüges, or The Three Gifts* on 19.11.1865 of the *Slowanka* from Act III (score no. 28) of Bournonville's and Paulli's three-act Hungarian ballet *In the Carpathians*. Similarly, the music on pp. '81–82' was origi‐nally part of score no. 7 in Act I of Bournonville's and Paulli's ballet *In the Carpathians* (*see* 4.3.1857). According to the 1865 répétiteur's copy for *The Kermesse in Brüges, or The Three Gifts* (now in DKKk, call no. MA ms 2966 (KTB 271)) it was interpolated in the Act I *Pas de deux* (score no. 2) of *The Kermesse in Brüges, or The Three Gifts* on 19.11.1865. There it accompanied a solo variation danced by Juliette Price (who played the rôle of *Eleonora*).

Moreover, a pencilled note on p. '177' reads: 'I Karpatherne Pag 395. No. 29'. This refers to the incorporation in *The Kermesse in Brüges, or The Three Gifts* on 19.11.1865 of Paulli's music for the so-called 'Pas des piqueurs' (or *Vexeldands*) in Act III (score no. 29) of his and Bournonville's ballet *In the Carpathians*. In *The Kermesse in Brüges, or The Three Gifts* this music served as accompaniment for a *Pas de deux* (on the poster entitled *Jægerdands*) that was danced in Act II by F. Hoppe and S. Price and listed as score number '11'. According to Bournonville's notes in the 1865 répétiteur's copy (p. 79) the same dance was still being performed in *The Kermesse in Brüges, or The Three Gifts* on 8.12.1872, but then in a choreographically revised ver‐sion, arranged by him for E. Hansen and M. Westberg and listed (in the répétiteur's copy) as 'no. 11½' or (in the orchestral score) as 'no. 12b'.

Furthermore, the music on pp. '183–194' contains those excerpts which Paulli had borrowed in 1851 from his own earlier score for Bournonville's one-act allegorical ballet *The White Rose, or The Summer in Bretagne*. It had originally been incorporated in Act II where it served as accompaniment for a *Pas de quatre* (score no. 13).

Finally, a page numbered '203' containing parts of the music from Act III (score nos. 12 and 13) is V. C. Holm's autograph. It was most probably inserted in the score of *The Kermesse in Brüges, or The Three Gifts* in connection with Bournonville's second and last restaging of this ballet on 8.12.1872.

Page '313' which contains the final 13 bars of Act III is signed and dated 'Fine/d: 18 Marts 1851. HSPaulli'.

All fragments seem either to have been taken out of or inserted into Paulli's autographed score in connection with Bournonville's two later restagings of *The Kermesse in Brüges, or The Three Gifts* on 19.11.1865, and 8.12.1872. They were discovered at DKKkt in 1989 and were transferred to DKKk at a later stage.

Répétiteur's copy. Ms. Autograph. Brown ink. 1 vol. 132 pp. of which three are blank (32,9 × 24 cm)
B. 271 3/<u>Kermessen</u>/eller/<u>De tre Gaver</u>/<u>3 Akter</u>/1851.
Unsigned and dated (on the front cover): '1851.'
[DKKk; MA ms 2966a (KTB 271 (1))
This répétiteur's copy (of which only the first three movements in Act I were originally given score numbers) contains several pencilled autographed notes by Bournonville. They describe in fine detail the dramatic action, the mime, and the choreography in Act I (score nos. 1–6), Act II (score nos. 7–12 and 17), and Act III (score no. 18 and parts of no. 19). Moreover, his other notes (written with brown ink) describe the mime and the dramatic action in Act II (score nos. 14–16) and in Act III (the first 30 bars in score no. 19). According to his diary most of these notes must have been written between 5.11. 1850 and 9.3.1851.

The volume also contains several other autographed notes indicating Bournonville's later musical and choreographic changes of this ballet. Thus, a pencilled noted on p. 8 reads 'attacca <u>Slowanka</u>'. This indicates the exact place where the *Slowanka* from Act III (score no. 28) of Bournonville's and Paulli's three-act Hungarian ballet *In the Carpathians* (see 4.3.1857) was incorporated in *The Kermesse in Brüges, or The Three Gifts* in 1865. Similarly, a note on p. 11 (written with brown ink) reads: 'NB. Karpatherne/pag. 31/a Dur/og Segue/ Allegro/pag 34./NB'. This refers to Bournonville's revision in 1865 of the *Pas de deux* in Act I (danced by *Carelis* and *Eleonora*) into which large excerpts of Paulli's music from Act I (score nos. 7 and 8) of *In the Carpathians* were incorporated. In the *Pas de deux* of *The Kermesse in Brüges* this incorporated music served as accompaniment for what in today's performances are still the second solo variations of *Eleonora* and *Carelis* respectively and the beginning of their common Coda.

According to the names of the dancers mentioned in Bournonville's notes for these sections, they must clearly have been written in connection with his 1865 restaging of *The Kermesse in Brüges, or The Three Gifts*. They provide clear evidence that the 1851 répétiteur's copy was still in use by Bournonville when he was preparing the 1865 version, and for which a second répétiteur's copy was made (now in DKKk, call no. MA ms 2966).

Finally, the 1851 répétiteur's copy for *The Kermesse in Brüges, or The Three Gifts* contains large amounts of Bournonville's choreographic numbers, (written with black ink) except for Act I, score no. 2 (the *Pas de deux*), and Act II, score no. 12. These choreographic numbers seem to refer to his later (not yet traced) separate notation of the complete ballet, which he most probably made during the early 1870s (perhaps for the last restaging of the ballet on 8.12.1872).

Parts. Ms. Copy. 33 vol.
3 vl I, 3 vl II, 2 vla, 2 vlc, cb, fl 1/2, ob 1/2, cl 1/2, fag 1/2, cor 1/2/ 3/4, tr 1/2, trb 1/2/3, timp, gr cassa, piatti, tri, arpa.
Unsigned and undated [1851]
[DKKk; KTB 271
This set of parts was used for all performances of *The Kermesse in Brüges, or The Three Gifts* during Bournonville's lifetime.

Other sources:

Costume drawing by E. Lehmann. Pencil and water colours (29,8 × 33,6 cm)
NB. Majordomen
Unsigned and undated [c.1851]
[DKKkt; Kostumetegninger (Lehmann)
This drawing shows the costumes worn by a group of commoners and peasants (three men and two women) in *The Kermesse in Brüges, or The Three Gifts* (Act I? and/or Act III?).

Costume drawing by E. Lehmann. Pencil and water colours (29,8 × 34,9 cm)
[Untitled]
Unsigned and undated [c.1851]
[DKKkt; Kostumetegninger (Lehmann)
This drawing shows the costumes worn by a group of commoners and peasants in *The Kermesse in Brüges, or The Three Gifts* (Act I? and/or Act III?) with the *Jester* dancing a solo in their midst.

Costume drawing by E. Lehmann. Pencil and water colours (27,1 × 38,5 cm)
[Untitled]
Signed: 'Maler Lehmann/Kronprinsessegade 37. 3 Sal', undated [c.1851]
[DKKkt; Kostumetegninger (Lehmann)
This drawing shows eight different types of hats used in *The Kermesse in Brüges, or The Three Gifts*.

Printed sources:

Printed scenario. 1 vol. 8 pp. (19,6 × 12,2 cm)
Kermessen i Brügge/eller/De tre Gaver./Romantisk Ballet i tre Acter/af/August Bournonville./Musikken af H. Paulli.
Kjøbenhavn, J. H. Schubothe/Bianco Luno, 1851.
[DKKk; 17, – 174 8°

24.4.1851
Pas de deux (uncredited) performed by S. Lund and S. Price.
This (uncredited) dance is probably identical with the so-called *Pas de deux composed by Mr. Court Ballet Master Bournonville*, danced by Lund and P. Fredstrup on 27.12.1850 and, in turn, is perhaps identical with Bournonville's *Pas de deux* (to music by F.-M.-A. Venua), that was originally performed in J. L. Heiberg's three-act play *Princess Isabella, or Three Nights at the Court* (see 29.10.1829), and also had been incorporated in Bournonville's three-act romantic ballet *Faust* on 8.12.1849. The *Pas de deux* was given 3 times by Lund and S. Price, the last time on 22.1.1852. It is perhaps also identical with the later (uncredited) *Pas de deux* performed by the same two dancers on 3.3.1854. It is not possible to identify the dance any further.

11.5.1851
Preciosa.
For the 1851 Copenhagen restaging of C. M. v. Weber's lyrical drama in four acts Bournonville rechoreographed and mounted the dances which his father, Antoine Bournonville, had created some 30 years before him for the Danish première of *Preciosa* on 29.10.1822. On the poster Bournonville is explicitly credited for having 'composed and arranged' (*componeret og arrangeret*) the dances. According to the répétiteur's copy they included four numbers as follows:

(1) An (unnamed) *Dance* in Act I, score no. 4, performed by the corps de ballet.
(2) An (unnamed) *Dance* in Act III, score no. 10, performed by two quadrilles (eight pairs).
(3) A *Pas de trois* in Act III, score no. 10, performed by three gipsies.
(4) A *Finale* in Act III, score no. 10, performed by the corps de ballet.

According to pencilled notes written by Antoine Bournonville in the original répétiteur's copy for *Preciosa* (now in DKKk, call no. MA ms 2722 (KTA 217 (1)), Bournonville seems to have remained very close to the original casting and general structure of each of the four dances as devised by his father in 1822.

He did not attend the first performance of his 1851 restaging, but noted in his diary about the dances that he created for it:

7.5.1851: 'componeret'
8.5.: 'Prøve paa Preciosa'.

The 1851 production received 4 performances, the last of which was given on 24.5.1851.

Preciosa was also mounted under Bournonville's general supervision at Stockholm's Royal Theatre (Operahuset) on 10.2.1862. The dances in that production (which included several incorporated numbers to music by J. F. Berwald) were all choreographed by Bournonville's pupil, S. Lund, who served as ballet-master of Stockholm's Royal Theatre between 1856 and 1862.

Musical sources:

Orchestral score. Ms Copy. Black ink. 1 vol. 158 pp of which two are blank (23,2 × 32,1 cm)
217./Preciosa./Partitur./[...]/Preciosa./Schauspiel in 4 Acten mit Gesang und Tanz./von Wolf[f]/Ouverture und zur Handlung gehörige Musick/von Carl Maria von Weber.
Unsigned and undated [c.1822]
[DKKk; C I, 342 (KTA 217)
This orchestral score is a manuscript copy made in Germany, with the text given only in German. It was used for all performances of *Preciosa* in Copenhagen since 1822 and throughout Bournonville's lifetime. The music for the dances in Act I and III are included on pp. 71–83 and 109–120 respectively.

Répétiteur's copy. Ms. Copy. Black ink. 1 vol. 6 pp. of which one is blank (31,8 × 25,4 cm)
Preciosa./55A/Bournonville/[...]/Repetiteur Partiet/til/Præciosa [*sic*]
Unsigned and undated [c. mid-1830s –1851]
[DKKk; MA ms 3043 (KTA 217 (2))
This répétiteur's copy seems (according to the style of the manuscript) to date from a later restaging of *Preciosa* in the mid–1830s. It contains Bournonville's autographed choreographic notes (written with brown ink) for three of the drama's four dances. They describe in fine detail the steps and choreographic evolution of each dance, and were (according to his diary) almost certainly written on 7.5.1851.

Parts. Ms. Copy. 33 + 15 pp.
4 vl I, 4 vl II, 2 vla, 4 vlc e cb, fl picc 1/2, fl 1/2, ob 1/2, cl 1/2, fag 1/2, cor 1/2/3/4, tr 1/2, timp, gr cassa, tri. On stage: vl I, vl II, vla, vlc, fl, cl 1/2, fag 1/2, cor 1/2/3/4, gr cassa, tri. 44 vocal parts.
Unsigned and undated [1822]
[DKKk; KTA 217
This set of parts dates from the 1822 Copenhagen première of *Preciosa* and was used for all performances there during Bournonville's lifetime.

4.6.1851

Pas de debut, arranged by Mr. Court Ballet Master Bournonville (arrangeret af Hr. Hofballetmester Bournonville) **performed by Julius Price and A. Price (the Court Theatre).**

This dance was created for a special charity performance given for the dancer, Rosa Price, and marked the début of her son, Julius Price, who was among Bournonville's most talented pupils. The fact that it is explicitly described on the poster as a work 'arranged' (*arrangeret*) by Bournonville seems to indicate that it was based on an earlier work either by him or by one of the Price dynasty of dancers. This theory is confirmed by the fact that no rehearsals of this dance are mentioned in Bournonville's diary.

A possible choreographic source for it could be the (uncredited) *Pas de deux* performed during the same season by

S. Lund and S. Price at Copenhagen's Royal Theatre on 24.4.1851, which, in turn, is most probably identical with the even earlier *Pas de deux* to music by F.-M.-A. Venua (*see* 29.10.1829), which had been incorporated in Bournonville's three-act romantic ballet *Faust* on 8.12.1849.

Pas de debut was performed once at the Court Theatre. It is not possible to identify the dance any further.

4.6.1851

The Prophecies of Love, Tyrolean Scene and Dance (Kjærligheds Spaadomme, Tyroler Scene og Dands) **performed by J. Price, A. Price, and S. Price (the Court Theatre).**

This Tyrolean *Pas de trois* divertissement was created especially for the Price cousins, Juliette, Amalia, and Sophie, and premièred aa part of a private charity performance given for the dancer Rosa Price (mother of Amalia). The music, which in 1851 consisted of 10 sections, was (according to the poster) 'arranged' (*arrangeret*) by H. S. Paulli. He incorporated an excerpt (*Allegretto*, 2/4 time in A major) borrowed from score no. 3 of J. F. Fröhlich music to Bournonville's one-act idyllic ballet *The Tyroleans* (*see* 6.3.1835).

As a result of the divertissement's great success with the audience it was mounted at the Royal Theatre only three months later on 21.9.1851.

In Norway it was performed by the same three dancers at Christiania's Theatre (Oslo) on 7.6.1852, and in Sweden in was given at Stockholm's Royal Theatre (Operahuset) on 10.5.1858, but then danced by Bournonville's Swedish pupils, J. G. Sundberg, A. Arrhenius, and A. Paulsson.

A second, extended version was mounted by Bournonville at Copenhagen's Royal Theatre on 28.2.1869. It included four new music sections which were borrowed (in parts) from Act I, score no. 6 of Paulli's and Bournonville's three-act Hungarian ballet *In the Carpathians* (*see* 4.3.1857). The 1869 version was performed as a *Pas de six* by the three maidens now joined by their three suitors.

In his diary Bournonville noted about his creation and the 1851 première of *The Prophecies of Love*:

21.5.1851: 'componeret paa en nÿ Dands 'Kjærligheds Spaadomme''
23.5..: 'Kl 4 paa Hoftheatret, componeret nÿe Dandse til Pricerne'
26.5: 'Prøve paà de nÿe Dandse. – Prøve om Eftermiddagen'
27.5.: 'Prøve paa de nÿe Dandse'
28.5.: 'fuldendt 'Kjærligheds Spaadomme'
30.5.: 'Prøve paa Dandsene'
31.5. and 2.6.: 'Prøve'
3.6.: 'Prøve paa Theatret i Costume. Det gik fortreffeligt'
4.6.: 'Prøve paa Prices Forestilling med Orchester [...] Prices Forestilling 1.ste Gang Kjærligheds Spaadomme [...] – De gjorde overordentlig Lÿkke og der var aldeles fuldt Huus'.

The Prophecies of Love was given only once at the Court Theatre during the 1851 season, but on 4.9.1857 it was restaged there (that year with P. Fredstrup replacing A. Price) and received two performances, the last of which was given on 11.9.1857.

Musical sources:

No orchestral score and set of parts dating from the first performance of *The Prophecies of Love* at the Casino Theatre have yet been traced. However, a later full orchestral score and set of parts for this divertissement now exist in SSkma (call no. KT Pantomime-Balletter

K 3) and clearly dates from when it was mounted by Bournonville at Stockholm's Royal Theatre (Operahuset) on 10.5.1858.

Répétiteur's copy. Ms. Autograph (by H. S. Paulli). Brown ink. 18 pp. of which one is blank (33,7 × 24,5 cm)
Kjærligheds Spaadomme/Bournonville/Mai 1851.
Unsigned and dated (on p. 1): 'Mai 1851.'
[DKKk; MA ms 2668 (KTB 1003, originally KTB 268)
This répétiteur's copy contains the music for the original 1851 version of *The Prophecies of Love*. It was also used for its later première at the Royal Theatre on 29.1.1851 and for its second and last restaging there in a new and extended version on 28.2.1869. This is clear from Bournonville's autographed notes on pp. 12–13 (written with brown ink) which include the names of the dancers, M. Price, L. Cetti, and B. Schnell, all of whom performed exclusively in the 1869 production.

4.6.1851
Las Hermanas de Sevilla, Spanish Dance (*Spansk Dands*) performed by Juliette Price, A. Price, and S. Price (the Court Theatre).

This Spanish *Pas de trois* divertissement (the title of which means 'The sisters from Seville') was created for the Price cousins, Juliette, Amalia, and Sophie, and first performed by them at a special charity performance, given for the dancer, Rosa Price (mother of Amalia). On the poster it is explicitly described as a work 'arranged' (*arrangeret*) by Bournonville, while no credit is given for the music.

The score was arranged by C. C. Møller from popular Spanish dance tunes. It represents the first in a long series of minor dances and divertissements that this composer arranged for Bournonville.

As a result of its great success the dance was mounted later the same year at the Royal Theatre on 2.11.1851. Moreover, on 26.2.1865 it was incorporated in Bournonville's divertissement *The Danes in China* (see 17.9.1839).

In Norway '*Las Hermanas de Sevilla*' was given twice by the Price cousins at Christiania's Theatre (Oslo) on 6.7. and 14.7.1852, and again by them at Frederikshald's Theatre (Halden) on 25.7. and 27.7.1852. In Sweden a new version of this divertissement seems to have been mounted by Bournonville, a revised *Pas de deux* version for two women, premièred at Stockholm's Royal Theatre (Operahuset) on 8.12. 1862. This (uncredited) dance was entitled *Las Hermanas, Spanish Characterdance (Spansk Characters-Dans)* and performed by Bournonville's two English pupils, the sisters A. and C. Healey.

The original 1851 version was restaged twice with new casts in Copenhagen on 29.11.1867 and 4.12.1872.

In his diary Bournonville noted about the creation and 1851 première of *Las Hermanas de Sevilla*:

12.5.1851: 'componeret til en spansk Dands'
13.5.: 'componeret og indstuderet spansk Dands'
14.5.: 'Dandsen Las Hermanas færdig'
23.5.: 'Prøve Kl 4 paa Hoftheatret'
24.5.: 'Prøve paa de nye Dandse'
26.5.: 'Prøve paa de nye Dandse. – Prøve om Eftermiddagen'
27.5.: 'Prøve paa de nye Dandse'
30.5.: 'Prøve paa Dandsene'
31.5. and 2.6.: 'Prøve'
3.6.: 'Prøve paa Theatret i Costume. Det gik fortreffeligt'
4.6.: 'Prøve paa Prices Forestilling med Orchester […] Prices Forestilling. 1.ste Gang […] Las hermanas de Sevilla. – De gjorde overordentlig Lykke og der var aldeles fuldt Huus'.

The dance was performed once at the Court Theatre.

Musical sources:

Orchestral score. Ms. Autograph (by C. C. Møller). Brown ink. 1 vol. 12 pp. (26,5 × 38 cm with minor variants)
Carl Chr. Møller./Las Hermanas…/K. T. (C II, 118)/239 B. 239 KT (C II Las Hermanas./Pas de tropie [*sic*] espagnol.
Signed and dated (on p. 1): 'arrang: af Carl. Chr. Møller: d. 12 Mai 51.'
[DKKk; C II, 118 (KTB 239)
This dated autographed orchestral score was beyond doubt used after the first performance of *Las Hermanas de Sevilla* at the Casino Theatre in 1851. Later the same year it was incorporated in the music archive of the Royal Theatre and was used for all performances there during Bournonville's lifetime.

No répétiteur's copy dating from the first performance of *Las Hermanas de Sevilla* at the Casino Theatre in 1851 has yet been traced.

Parts (incomplete). Ms. Copy. 5 vol.
2 vl I, 2 vl II, vla.
Unsigned and undated [1851]
[DKKk; C II, 105 Efterslæt 4
This (incomplete) set of parts was originally part of the music archive of the Price family, and was purchased by DKKk in 1902 from the actor, C. Price, who was a relative of Juliette Price and may have received it from her previously.

6.6.1851
Pas de deux and Polka from the ballet: 'Le Diable à quatre' (Pas de deux og Polka af Balletten: 'le diable à quatre') (uncredited) performed by W. Funck and C. Kellermann (the Court Theatre).

This performance represents the first and only time J. Mazilier's dances from his and A. Adam's two-act pantomimic ballet *Le Diable à quatre* (see 11.5.1847) were performed at the Court Theatre. They were mounted by Bournonville this year as part of a farewell performance given for the singer-actress, I. Rantzau, who retired from the stage after her marriage the same year.

30.8.1851
La Grotta Azzurra (Turin's Teatro Carignano).

This three-act fantastic ballet by the French dancer and choreographer, F. Lefèbvre, is a pirated version of Bournonville's three-act romantic ballet *Napoli or The Fisherman and His Bride* (see 29.3.1842). Lefèbvre had been invited to Copenhagen by Bournonville in 1842 as principal dancer and assistant choreographer at the Royal Theatre, and worked there for nearly five years. Because of a later dispute with Bournonville he left Denmark in 1847 and during the following decade he toured Europe as a dancer and guest choreographer.

His pirated version of Bournonville's ballet, which was mounted with new décors by A. Moja, was most poorly received by the Turin critics. Among them the *Gazzetta Piemontese* stated on 6.9.1851:

'Abbiamo anche un ballo fantastico al quale manca la fantasia, ma non mancarono pur troppo i soliti accompagnamenti disarmonici della platea. Generalmente parlando quel muover di braccia senza nessun costrutto, quegli andirivieni senza scopo, quel piramidale giocar di telegrafia pare che oggi non siano più di moda. In questa *Grotta azzurra* vedemmo al solito le ninfe, le najadi, i pescatori, il mare di Napoli e tante altre belle cose che costarono di certo fatiche e denari, e che non riuscirono a disarmare la severità del pubblico'.

La Grotta Azzura received 5 performances in Turin, the last of which was given on 11.9.1851. No musical sources for it have yet been traced.

Printed sources:

Printed scenario. 1 vol. 8 pp. (17 × 10,6 cm)
LA GROTTA AZZURRA/BALLETTO FANTASTICO IN 3 ATTI/
Composto e prodotto dal Coreografo/FR. LEFÉBVRE
Milan, Giovanni Ricordi, pl. no. 21688, 1851.
[USNYpl; Dance Collection, call no. *MGTY-Res. (Toscanini, Walter, Libretto di ballo no. 619)
This printed scenario is included in the 1851 textbook (pp. 45–52) for S. Cammarano's and G. Verdi's opera *Luisa Miller* with which it was premièred at Turin's Teatro Carignano on 30.8.1851.

13.9.1851
The organisation of a concert for the charity health organisation 'Hygæa' (Vesterbro's Theatre).
In his diary Bournonville noted about his involvement in the organisation of this concert, which was arranged for the charity health association 'Hygæa' of which he was a leading board member:

10.9.1851: 'besørget Hygæas Extra-Concert: Tyrolerne Meister & Bauer'
12.9.: 'besørget Concert for Hygæa'
13.9.: 'Tÿroler-Concert paa Vesterbro til fordeel for Hygæa, tÿndt besat, men dog en lille Gave, der ikke er til at forsmaae. Brødrene Meister og Bauer udførte særdeles smukke Ting, saavel Sang, som Phantasie Instrumenter'.

21.9.1851
The Prophecies of Love, Tyrolean Scene and Dance (Kjærligheds Spaadomme, Tyroler=Scene og Dands) **performed by Juliette Price, A. Price, and S. Price.**
This performance represents the first time Bournonville's *Pas de trois* divertissement *The Prophecies of Love* (*see* 4.6.1851) was performed at Copenhagen's Royal Theatre. In his diary he noted about its reception on the opening night:

'Om Aftenen Kjærligheds Spaadomme for første Gang, gik fortreffeligt for et temmelig lunkent Publicum. Jeg ærgrede mig paa de unge Talenters Vegne, der kues under saa ugunstige Forhold'.

The Prophecies of Love received 23 performances at the Royal Theatre, the last of which was given on 11.4.1864 (since 13.4.1858 with P. Fredstrup replacing A. Price).

Musical sources:

No orchestral score dating from the 1851 Royal Theatre première of this divertissement has yet been traced.

The répétiteur's copy employed for the 1851 première of *The Prophecies of Love* at the Royal Theatre is now in DKKk (call no. MA ms 2668 (KTB 1003, originally KTB 268)).

Parts. Ms. Copy. 28 vol.
3 vl I, 3 vl II, 2 vla, 3 vlc e cb, fl 1/2, ob 1/2, cl 1/2, fag 1/2, cor 1/2, tr 1/2, trb 1/2/3, timp, gr cassa e piatti e tri.
Unsigned and undated [1851 and 1869]
[DKKk; KTB 1003 (originally KTB 268)
This set of parts contains the music for the original 1851 version of

The Prophecies of Love as well as that of the four sections which were added for the second, extended staging of this divertissement in 1869. Notes in several of the parts indicate the duration of the dance as between 20 and 21 minutes. They most probably refer to the 1869 version of the divertissement.

18.10.1851
Romeo and Juliet (Romeo og Julie).
The 1851 Copenhagen restaging of W. Shakespeare's five-act tragedy is not included in any of Bournonville's handwritten lists of his stagings of operas and plays (*see* Additional Sources), nor in the printed survey of his works in his memoirs *My Theatre Life* (p. 408). However, according to his diary and the rehearsal book of H. C. J. Fredstrup he clearly attended and supervised the general mise-en-scène and the rehearsals of the dances in Act I (scene 4) between 13.10. and 17.10.1851, while the tragedy itself was rehearsed with the actors by T. Overskou during the same period. The 1851 restaging received 3 performances, the last of which was given on 26.4.1852. No musical sources for the dances in Act I of Shakespeare's tragedy have yet been traced.

2.11.1851
Las Hermanas de Sevilla, Spanish Dance (Spansk Dands) **performed by Juliette Price, A. Price, and S. Price.**
This performance represents the first time Bournonville's *Las Hermanas de Sevilla* (*see* 4.6.1851) was performed at the Royal Theatre. In his diary he noted about its reception on the opening night:

'Dirigeret Las Hermanas, der gik for første Gang paa Byens Theater og gjorde megen Lÿkke'.

Las Hermanas de Sevilla received 36 performances at the Royal Theatre during Bournonville's lifetime, the last of which was given on 18.12.1872. Four of these were given as an incorporated number in Bournonville's divertissement *The Danes in China* (*see* 26.2.1865).

Musical sources:

The orchestral score used for the 1851 première of *Las Hermanas de Sevilla* at the Royal Theatre is now in DKKk (call no. C II, 118 (KTB 239)).

No répétiteur's copy dating from the 1851 Royal Theatre première of *Las Hermanas de Sevilla* has yet been traced.

Parts. Ms. Copy. 24 vol.
2 vl I, 2 vl II, vla, 2 vlc e cb, fl 1/2, ob 1/2, cl 1/2, fag 1/2, cor 1/2, tr 1/2, cnt 1/2, trb, timp, tri.
Unsigned and undated [1851]
[DKKk; KTB 239

1852

3.2.1852
Pas de deux (uncredited) performed by W. Funck and Juliette Price.
This (uncredited) dance is probably identical with the earlier (uncredited) *Pas de deux* performed three years earlier by W. Funck and P. Funck on 21.9.1849 and, in turn, is most

likely an earlier work by either Funck or Bournonville. The *Pas de deux* was given 3 times by Funck and Price in 1852, the last time on 13.5.1852. It is not possible to identify the dance any further.

14.4.1852

Zulma, or The Crystal Palace (Zulma eller: Krystalpaladset).
According to Bournonville's memoirs, *My Theatre Life* (pp. 193–196), this three-act ballet was drawn from inspirations received from reading several descriptions of the Great Exhibition in London in 1851, and in particular from an illustration showing the interior of Sir Joseph Paxton's glass-and-iron crystal palace in Hyde Park with its many artistic and industrial treasures. This building stood for Bournonville as the symbol of the culmination of Great Britain's imperial might and prestige.

The plot centres on a love story of a Scottish baronet (*Sir Edward*) who, while travelling to India, becomes enamoured of a priestess at a local temple (*Zulma*), and is reunited with her in marriage the following year in London, after her visit to the 1851 Great Exhibition in the Crystal Palace. The ballet's comic character rôle, *Tom* (an English sailor and servant of *Sir Edward*), is based on a real-life incident of the time concerning an English sailor, who, after having deserted the British navy, caused a sensation as an entertainer performing disguised as a Chinaman during the time of the great 1851 London exhibition, but whose true identity was only later revealed by the police.

The music was composed and arranged by H. S. Paulli and, in parts, by V. C. Holm. Several musical borrowings were interpolated in their scores, mainly in order to help the audience interpret the ballet's complex dramatic action and exotic settings. These borrowings are identified as follows:

(1) Act I, score no. 3 (the *Sacred Temple Dances*): In this number Paulli interpolated a section of I. P. E. Hartmann's dance music from his three-act opera *The Raven* in which it originally served as accompaniment for a *Pas de cinq* (choreographed by Bournonville) that was performed during the chorus in the Act II finale, entitled «Under Sang og glade Dandse for Kong Millo og hans Brud» (*see* 29.10.1832). This music, together with most of Paulli's other music for score no. 3, was many years later reused by V. C. Holm in his music arrangement of the score for Act I (score no. 3) of Bournonville's Chinese ballet divertissement, entitled *The Mandarin's Daughters* (*see* 23.4.1873).
(2) Act I, score no. 5: In this number Paulli incorporated an English song, entitled 'Heart(s) of Oak' («Come cheer, up my Lad»). It is set to music by W. Boyce and a text by the great English actor, D. Garrick, and was first performed in London by a not yet identified actor, named Mr Champnes. He sang it in a pantomime-play entitled *Harlequin's Invasion, or a Christmas gamble*, premièred at Drury Lane in London on 31.12.1759. A copy of the first print of this song is now in GBLbm (call no. G 307 [74]). In *Zulma, or The Crystal Palace* the tune of Boyce's song served as an allusion to Garrick's final line in the first verse which was sung by a chorus and reads: «Heart of Oak are our Ships, Heart of Oak are our Men, We always are ready, Steady Boys, steady, We'll fight, and we'll conquer again, and again».
(3) Act II, score no. 8: In this number Paulli incorporated the tune of an aria, entitled «Hurrah for bonnets of blue». It was composed G. A. Lee and rearranged by P. Knapton for the great actress-singer, L. Vestris. A printed piano vocal score of Knapton's arrangement was published in London c.1835 by D'Almaine & Co. (now in GBLbm, call no. h 724 r. [1]). In the same number Paulli also interpolated an Irish song, entitled «I give thee all I can no more». It was written and

arranged by T. Moore from a melody by H. R. Bishop, and was published around 1825 in a piano-vocal score by J. Cole (now in GBLbm, call no. H 1653 i [8]). In *Zulma, or The Crystal Palace* this tune served as an allusion to the text of the last line of the first verse reading «My heart and lute are all the store I can bring to thee».
(4) Act II, score no. 13 (the *Festive Dance*): Paulli here employed an excerpt (*Allegretto* in 6/8 time) which he borrowed from the score of the so-called *New Pas de deux arranged by Mr. Ballet Master Bournonville* (*see* 14.10.1841) and, in turn, is most probably based on a French score from the Paris Opera ballet repertory. In *Zulma, or The Crystal Palace* this excerpt is followed by yet another excerpt (*Allegretto* in 2/4 time), this time borrowed from the duet, named «O bords heureux du gange» and sung by the characters *Ninka* and *L'Inconnu* in Act II (score no. 9) of D.-F.-E. Auber's two-act opera-ballet *Le Dieu et la bayadère, ou La Courtisane amoureuse*.
(5) Act II, score no. 14: Paulli here interpolated the tune of a song(?) which (according to Bournonville's printed scenario for *Zulma, or The Crystal Palace*) was entitled 'Erindringer fra Ganges' (*Memories from Ganges*). The same tune, for which the name of the composer has not yet been identified, resurfaces a second time in Act III (score no. 22).
(6) Act II, score no. 16: Paulli here incorporated S. Nelson's melody to T. H. Bayly's song, named «O steer my Bark to Erin's Isle».
(7) Act III, score no. 17: In this number Paulli incorporated T. A. Arne's melody to *Rule Brittania* («When Britain first at Heav'n's command»), originally composed for the masque *Alfred*, and first performed at Cliefden House on 1.8.1740. After Admiral Nelson's victory in the battle of the Nile in 1798 this melody was elevated to the status of a national anthem. In *Zulma, or The Crystal Palace* it is followed by the excerpt «A charm from the skies seems to hallow us there» from H. R. Bishop's melody to J. Howard Payne's song 'Home, Sweet Home' (originally part of Bishop's three-act opera *Clari, or The Maid of Milan*, first performed at Covent Garden in London on 8.5.1823). Later in the same number Paulli also interpolated C. E. Horn's melody from 1825 to R. Herrick's song, named «Cherry Ripe». This song was apparently first performed by the singer-actress, L. Vestris, in the opera *Paul Pry* in 1826. It is followed by the first theme of *Olifur's* aria, entitled «Sois ma Bayadère» from Act I (score no. 3) of D.-F.-E. Auber's opera-ballet *Le Dieu et la bayadère, ou La Courtisane amoureuse*.
(8) Act III, score no. 22: According to Bournonville's printed scenario Paulli here employed for the second and last time the tune of a not yet identified song(?), named 'Erindringer fra Ganges' (*Memories from Ganges*). It is followed by the English national anthem *God Save our Gracious King*, which dates from about 1742 when it first appears in a collection of part songs, entitled 'Harmonia Anglicana'. However, it became widely known only through T. A. Arne's later arrangement of it.
(9) Act III, score no. 23 (the *Finale*): In the *Polka* that precedes the *Galopin=Finale* (in 6/8 time) Paulli incorporated a brief reminiscence of T. A. Arne's melody for *Rule Brittania* which he had employed earlier in Act III (score no. 17).

In his diary Bournonville noted about the creation and the première of the ballet:

16.8.1851: 'Skrevet den største Deel af Dagen paa en nÿ Ballet. Zulma eller Chrÿstalpaladset. De to Akter færdige'
17.8.: 'skrevet [...] Aftale med Theatermaler [C. F.] Christensen'
18.8.: 'skrevet paa min nÿ Ballet'
19.8.: 'skrevet paa Balletten'
20.8.: 'reenskrevet Balletten'
25.8.: 'modtaget mit Program fra [H. P.] Holst med megen Opmuntring'
27.8.: 'Programmet indleveret til [J. L.] Heiberg. Dagen i Forventning'
28.8.: 'Intet Nÿt!'
29.8.: 'Intet Nÿt. – Vi kunne ikke begribe denne Taushed, men vi ville stole paa Forsÿnet'
1.11.: 'arbeidet med [H. S.] Paulli paa min nÿ Ballet'

30.11.: 'componeret lidt'

1.12., 6.12., and 7.12.: 'componeret'

10.12.: 'Aftenen hjemme componeret paa min nÿ Ballet'

11.11.: 'arbeidet med Paulli, componeret […] senere det ikke componerede'

12.12.: 'lært Juliette [Price] en Solo'

13.12.: 'Første Prøve paa Zulma'

15.12.: 'lille Prøve paa Zulma'

16.12. and 17.12.: 'Prøve paa Zulma'

18.12.: 'skrevet og componeret […] skrevet og componeret til Kl 11'

20.12.: 'Prøve paa Zulma, repeteret den store Dands'

21.12.: 'arbeidet med Paulli'

22.12.: 'Prøve paa Zulma, skrevet, componeret'

23.12., 27.12., 29.12., and 30.12.: 'Prøve paa Zulma'

31.12.: 'Prøve paa Zulma. Divertissementet af 2.den Act færdigt'

1.1.1852: 'componeret lidt'

3.1.: 'componeret med Paulli'

4.1.: 'componeret'

5.1. and 6.1.: 'Prøve paa Zulma'

7.1.: 'skrevet og componeret'

8.1.: 'Prøve paa Zulma'

9.1.: 'Prøve paa Zulma – componeret'

12.1. and 13.1.: 'Prøve paa Zulma'

15.1.: 'Prøve paa Zulma: 1.ste Akt færdig'

18.1.-25.1.: 'Indstudering paa Zulma'

26.1. and 28.1.: 'Prøve paa Zulma'

29.1.: 'Prøve'

31.1.: 'Prøve paa Zulma'

1.2.: 'componeret'

2.2.: 'Prøve paa Zulma'

5.2.: 'Prøve'

6.2.: 'componeret og arrangeret til min nÿe Ballet'

8.2.: 'componeret endeel'

9.2.: 'componeret'

10.2.: 'Prøve paa Zulma […] componeret med Paulli'

11.2.: 'Prøve'

12.2.: 'Prøve paa Bÿens Theater Zulma 2.de Akt […] compneret hos Paulli. Skrevet og componeret hjemme'

13.2.: 'skrevet og componeret. – Prøve paa B. Theater paa to Acter af Zulma'

14.2., 16.2., and 18.2.: 'componeret'

19.2.: 'Prøve paa tredie Act af Zulma'

20.2. and 21.2.: 'Prøve paa Zulma'

22.2.: 'Arbeidet med Paulli'

23.2.: 'componeret'

24.2., 25.2., 27.2., 28.2., amd 1.3.: 'Prøve paa Zulma'

8.3 and 9.3.: 'Prøve paa […] Zulma'

10.3.: 'Prøve paa Zulma […] skrevet og componeret'

11.3.: 'Besørget endeel for Balletten. Prøve paa Byens Theater, der gik meget godt componeret hele Aftenen'

12.3.: 'Prøve paa sidste Scene af Zulma'

13.3.: 'Prøve paa Zulma'

14.3.: 'Besørget meget for Balletten'

15.3.: 'Prøve paa […] Zulma'

16.3.: 'Prøve paa hele Zulma'

17.3.: 'Arrangementsprøve paa Zulma'

18.3.: 'Prøve'

19.3.: 'componeret Slutnings Polka'

20.3.: 'Prøve og indstuderet den sidste Finale der faldt meget heldigt ud. – altsaa Krandsen sat paa Arbeidet'

22.3.: 'stor Prøve paa Balletten. – Dronning Marie [Sophie Frederikke] afgaaet ved Døden Igaar Aftes Kl. 10'

24.3.: 'Alle Prøver standsede formedelst Hofsorgen'

31.3.: 'Prøve paa alle 3 Acter af Balletten. 25, 35 og 25 Minuter'

1.4.: 'Costümeprøve og Decorations – D.o.'

2.4.: 'stor Prøve paa Byens Theater'

4.4.: 'besørget adskilligt for Balletten'

5.4.: 'Musikprøve paa Zulma'

6.4.: 'Prøve paa Zulma med Orchester'

7.4.: 'lille Prøve paa Zulma […] componeret videre'

8.4.: 'Indstuderet en scène'

10.4.: 'Kl 5 Generalprøve med Costumer og Decorationer. Den gik meget godt og lover en god Virkning. Jeg venter mig ingen Begeistring, thi vort Publicum er blaseret'

12.4.: 'besørget en Deel for Balletten'

14.4.: 'Første Forestilling af Balletten Zulma eller Krÿstalpaladset – der gik udmærket godt og vandt stort Bifald. Jeg takkede Gud der har belønnet min Skæbne'.

Acording to a later note in Bournonville's diary (on 31.3. 1852) the ballet played for a total of 1 hour and 25 minutes. *Zulma, or The Crystal Palace* received 20 performances, the last of which was given on 9.1.1855.

Autograph sources:

Manuscript scenario. Ms. Autograph. Brown ink. 1 vol. 16 pp. (22,4 × 17,1 cm)

<u>Zulma eller Chrÿstalpaladset.</u>/<u>Ballet i tre Akter</u>/<u>af</u>/<u>August Bournonville</u>/1851.

Signed and dated: 'Kbhvn d. 20.de August 1851.'

[DKKk; NKS 3285 4° 3 V–Z

Musical sources:

Orchestral score. Ms. Autographs (by H. S. Paulli and V. C. Holm) and copy. Brown and black ink. 1 vol. 322 pp. of which three are blank (27,5 × 37,5 cm)

Partituret/til/Zulma eller Chrystalpaladset/Ballet i 3 Akter/af/August Bournonville/Musikken/Componeret og Arrangeret/af/H. S. Paulli/[…]/Krÿstalpalasset [*sic*]

Signed and dated (on p. 322): 'd: 21 Marts 1852./HSPaulli'

[DKKk; C II, 119 (KTB 1048, originally KTB 294)

This orchestral score is Paulli's autograph except for pp. 141–161 (Act I, score no. 13), pp. 231–239 (Act III, score no. 18), pp. 255–279 (Act III, score nos. 20–21), and pp. 287–303 (Act III, score no. 22) which are all written by different copyists and most probably consist of music borrowed from works by other composers. Moreover, pp. 241–252 (Act III, score no. 19), which are V. C. Holm's autograph, clearly indicate that this composer assisted Paulli in preparing the score for this ballet.

Répétiteur's copy. Ms. Copy. Black ink. 1 vol. 74 pp. of which one is blank (34 × 25,5 cm)

B. 294/<u>Chrystalpaladset.</u>/32 A/[…]/Repetiteurparti/til/Zulma eller Krystalpaladset.

Unsigned and undated [1852]

[DKKk; MA ms 2990 (KTB 1048, originally KTB 294)

This répétiteur's copy contains Bournonville's autographed choreographic numbers (written with black ink) in the music for Act I, score no. 3 ('1–5' and '1–13'). They seem to refer to a (not yet traced) separate choreographic description of the *Sacred Temple Dances (Hellige Tempeldandse)* in Act I. His similar numbers in Act II, score no. 7 ('1–10') and no. 9 ('3–9') indicate that Bournonville also made a separate (not yet traced) notation of these two scenes.

Parts. Ms. Copy. 35 vol.

3 vl I, 3 vl II, 2 vla, 3 vlc e cb, fl 1/2, ob 1/2, cl 1/2, fag 1/2, cor 1/2, tr 1/2, cnt 1/2, trb 1/2/3, timp, gr cassa, piatti, tri, gong, glock, arpa.

Unsigned and undated [1852]

[DKKk; KTB 1048 (originally KTB 294)

Piano score (*Finale*, Act III, no 23). Ms. Autograph (by H. S. Paulli). Brown ink. 4 pp. (26,9 × 37,9 cm)

Polka/[…]/Galopin=Finale

Signed (on p. 1): 'H. S. Paulli.', undated [c.1852]

[DKKk; C II, 10 (H. S. Paullis Efterladte mss. II)

This autographed piano score contains Paulli's complete music for the Act III *Finale* (score no. 23). It was most probably written for publishing purposes.

Other sources:

Costume drawing by E. Lehmann. Pencil and water colours (25,5 × 17,4 cm)
No. 1. Sami (Herr Gade.),
Unsigned and undated [c.1852]
[DKKkt; Kostumetegninger (Lehmann)]
This drawing shows the costume of *Sami* in *Zulma, or The Crystal Palace* (performed by L. Gade).

Costume drawing by E. Lehmann. Pencil and water colours (25,5 × 19,8 cm)
No. 2. Bramin.
Unsigned and undated [c.1852]
[DKKkt; Kostumetegninger (Lehmann)]
This drawing shows the costume of the three *Brahmans* who performed the sacred temple dances in Act I (score no. 3) of *Zulma, or The Crystal Palace.*

Costume drawing by E. Lehmann. Pencil and water colours (26 × 13,3 cm)
[Untitled]
Unsigned and undated [c.1852]
[DKKkt; Kostumetegninger (Lehmann)]
This drawing shows an oriental warrior holding a spear and a knife. It most probably refers to a costume from Act I of *Zulma, or The Crystal Palace.*

Printed sources:

Printed scenario. 1 vol. 15 pp. (18,6 × 12,1 cm)
Zulma/eller/Chrystalpaladset./Ballet i tre Akter/af/August Bournonville./Musiken componeret og arrangeret af Paulli./Decorationerne af DHrr. Christensen og Lund.
Kjøbenhavn, J. H. Schubothe/Bianco Luno, 1852.
[DKKk; 17, – 174 8°

4.5.1852
The organisation of a concert for the charity organisation
'Hygæa' (the Court Theatre).
This concert represents the last in a long series of performances arranged by Bournonville for the charity health organisation 'Hygæa', of which he was a leading board member since 1846 (*see* 31.3.1846). In his diary he noted about the concert:

'Skuespillet var forandret og Balletten [Festen i] Albano skulde gaae Iaften saa at Blomsterpigerne [i. e. *The Flower Maids of Florence, see* 8.6.1850] ikke kunde dandse for Hygæa. Vi maatte give Concerten ligefald, den gik godt (...) Publicum var sig som Medlemmer ikke sin Stilling bevidst og det blev afgjort at denne Aftenunderholdning er den Sidste, jeg arrangerer for Selskabet'.

According to his diary Bournonville wrote a letter six months after this concert announcing his decision on 4.11. 1853 to retire as member of the board of directors of 'Hygæa' ('skrevet og afleveret min Udmeldelse af Bestyrelsen for Hygæa til Garbricht'). The reason for this move is not perfectly clear from either from his letters or his diary.

11.5.–9.7.1852
Two series of drama and dance lessons in Christiania (Oslo).
During his 1852 summer tour to Norway Bournonville arranged and gave a series of dance lessons to 80 private dance students. In the same period he also taught drama lessons to a selected group of young aspirant actors of Christiania's

Theatre. These lessons were (according to his diary) concluded with two public presentations on 7.7. (his dance students) and on 9.7.1852 (the drama students). According to Bornonville's memoirs *My Theatre Life* (p. 201) one of the many dances that he taught at these dance lessons was the *Norwegian Spring Dance* from his one-act ballet *Old Memories, or A Magic Lantern* (*see* 18.12.1848). It is described as follows:

'this bagatelle later became the high point of the ballet repertoire in which I presented by pupils in Norway during the summer of 1852. The fact is that I had established a dancing course that gave me particular satisfaction both in financial respects and through the contacts I made with Christiania's most respected families, whose hospitality greatly enhanced my stay'.

Both of the presentations were assessed in his diary as follows:

7.7.1852: 'Kl. 12. stor Præsentation af 80 Elever for deres Forældre [...] det gik fortreffeligt og jeg havde stor Glæde deraf. Jeg takker Gud, der har givet mig Sundhed og Kraft til at udføre dette Arbeide med Held'
9.7.: 'Præsentation af den dramatiske Skoles Elever – saare lidt Talent, Jfr. Sulestad synes at love. Præsentation af Theatrets yngre Personale. Det gik særdeles godt. Jfr. Svendsen fraværende, skulde hun nogensinde blive Kunstnerinde?'.

7.6.1852
'Pas des trois cousines' performed by Juliette Price, A. Price, and S. Price (Christiania's Theatre, Oslo).
This date marks the first and only time Bournonville's *Pas des trois cousines* (*see* 20.5.1848) was performed outside Denmark during his lifetime. In his diary he noted about its reception on the opening night:

'Pricernes Debüt, [...] de bleve modtagne applauderede og fremkaldte, deres Lÿkke var fuldkommen og de dandsede udmærket. Jeg var ligesom Publicum glad og henrykt'.

'Pas des trois cousines' was given 4 times in Christiania, the last time on 12.7.1852.

The Christiania poster gives explicit credit to H. S. Paulli for having 'composed' (*componeret*) the music. No musical sources dating from the 1852 Norwegian performances of this dance have yet been traced. This seems to indicate that it was performed using of the original 1848 Copenhagen musical material (now in DKKk, call no. C II, 105, Efterslæt 5).

7.6.1852
'The Prophecies of Love' Tyrolean Scene and Dance
(*'Kjærligheds Spaadomme' Tyroler-Scene og Dands*) performed by Juliette Price, A. Price, and S. Price (Christiania's Theatre, Oslo).
This performance represents the first and only time Bournonville's *The Prophecies of Love* (*see* 4.6.1851) was mounted outside Denmark. According to a separate autographed sheet of paper, entitled 'Regie' and inserted in Bournonville's diary next to this date, the dance was mounted with the following accessories:

'Kjærligheds Spaadomme: Et Bord... en Stoel'.

In his diary he noted about its reception on the opening night:

'Pricernes Debŭt [...] Kjærligheds Spaadomme, der blev modtagne, applauderede og fremkaldte. Deres Lÿkke var fuldkommen og de Dandsede udmærket. Jeg var ligesom Publicum glad og henrykt'.

'The Prophecies of Love' received 3 performances in Christiania, the last of which was given on 20.6.1852. No musical sources dating from its 1852 Norwegian performances have yet been traced. This seems to indicate that it was performed using the original Copenhagen musical material (now in DKKk, call nos. MA ms 2668, and KTB 1003 (originally KTB 268)).

9.6.1852
'Pas de deux' (à la Taglioni) composed by Mr. Court Ballet Master, Chevalier Bournonville (componeret af Hr. Hofballetmester, Ridder Bournonville) **performed by S. Lund and Juliette Price (Christiania's Theatre, Oslo)**
This dance is identical with the earlier (uncredited) *Pas de deux à la Taglioni*, performed by F. Hoppe and Juliette Price at Copenhagen's Royal Theatre on 9.11.1850 and 13.3.1851 (on the last day of which Bournonville is explicitly credited on the poster as the actual choreographer). The dance is most probably also identical with the even earlier *Pas de deux (after Taglioni) (Pas de deux (efter Taglioni))*, performed at the Royal Theatre by F. Hoppe and A. Nielsen on 6.7.1840, and at Christiania's Theatre (Oslo) by Bournonville and C. Fjeldsted on 10.8.1840.

Both of these dances are almost certainly identical with the *Pas de deux (by Taglioni) (Pas de deux (Af Taglioni))*, originally mounted as a separate divertissement by Bournonville for P. C. Johansson and A. Nielsen at Stockholm's Royal Theatre (Operahuset) on 5.6.1839, and the so-called *A Pas de deux arranged after Taglioni (En Pas de deux arrangeret efter Taglioni)* performed the same year by G. Brodersen and A. Nielsen at Copenhagen's Royal Theatre on 4.10.1839. These dances, in turn, were seemingly restagings of the even earlier *Pas de deux*, set to music by J. Mayseder and first performed in Act II (score no. 1 A) of Bournonville's two-act romantic ballet *The Isle of Phantasy* (*see* 28.10.1838).

The 1852 Norwegian staging of *'Pas de deux' (à la Taglioni)* was performed once.

Musical sources:

No orchestral score and set of parts dating from the 1852 performance in Norway of *'Pas de deux' (à la Taglioni)* have yet been traced. This seems to indicate that the dance was performed using the original Copenhagen orchestral score and set of parts (now in DKKk, call nos. C II, 105, and KTB 1024 (originally KTB 240), and/or KTB 1029 (originally KTB 307)).

Répétiteur's copy. Ms. Copy. Black ink. 6 pp. (34,6 × 25,8 cm)
Pas de deux af Balletten 'Sÿlphiden.'
Unsigned and undated [c.1852]
[DKKk; MA ms 2647 (2)
This répétiteur's copy is included on pp. 4–9 in an (incomplete) volume of four répétiteur's copies for Bournonville dances that seems to have been made especially for the 1852 Norwegian summer tour. According to its title it certainly dates from the period after 27.9.1842, when this dance was incorporated in Act II of Bour-

nonville's two-act romantic ballet *La Sylphide*, in which it was named (according to the poster) 'Pas de deux (à la Taglioni)'.

9.6.1852
'The Sailor's Return', Scene and English Character Dance ('Matrosens Hjemkomst', Scene og engelsk Characteerdands) **performed by E. Stramboe and A. Price (Christiania's Theatre, Oslo).**
This divertissement was choreographed for the 1852 Norwegian summer tour, but was later also mounted by Bournonville in Copenhagen on four occasions as follows:

(1) at the Court Theatre on 11.6.1855 (performed by Julius Price and S. Price).
(2) at the Royal Theatre on 23.9.1855 (performed by E. Stramboe and L. Stillmann).
(3) at the Court Theatre on 7.9.1857 and 20.2.1867 (on the last date performed by W. Price and S. Price).

Moreover. it was performed in the Danish provinces on two occasions as follows:

(1) at Theatret i Randers on 10.6.1853 (performed by F. Hoppe and J. Rostock).
(2) at Theatret i Aarhus on 14.6.1853 (by the same dancers).

The score was almost certainly pieced together by H. S. Paulli in close collaboration with Bournonville, and consists of the following music:

(1) Following the two opening movements (presumably composed by H. S. Paulli) there is the complete music of I. P. E. Hartmann's earlier music arrangement for the *English Sailor's Dance* in Act I (score no. 10) of Bournonville's two-act romantic ballet *The Isle of Phantasy* (*see* 28.10.1838). The music for this dance is in turn based on two excerpts from T. Moore's *Irish Melodies* (1807–1834), entitled «The last rose of summer» (also known as 'The Groves of Blarney') and «We may roam thro' this world» (also known as 'Garryowen'). They are followed by a *Hornpipe*, presumably of Hartmann's composition.
(2) Following the excerpts from *The Isle of Phantasy* there is a dance set to music by H. C. Lumbye, originally named *The Sailor and His Bride (Matrosen og hans Brud)*. It was composed in 1848 for a divertissement choreographed by R. Price and first performed at the Casino Theatre on 3.12.1848 by six children from the Price dynasty of dancers. In Bournonville's *'The Sailor's Return'* this music by Lumbye (for which the original set of parts is now in DKKk, call no. C II, 105, Efterslæt 3) served as the Coda.

According to a separate autographed sheet of paper, entitled 'Regie' and inserted in Bournonville's diary next to the date of 7.6.1852, the divertissement was mounted with the following accessories:

'Matrosen .... En Baad en Busk'.

In his diary he noted about the creation and 1852 Norwegian première:

2.5.1852: 'Kl. 10 Prøve paa en nÿ Dands til mit Reise-Repertoire Matrosens Hjemkomst, der lÿkkedes mig godt.'
6.5.: 'Prøve paa den nÿ Dands'
8.6.: 'Prøve til Imorgen'
9.6.: 'Alt gjorde megen Lÿkke, Fremkaldelse, fuldt Huus'.

'The Sailor's Return' was also mounted in Sweden at Stock-

holm's Royal Theatre (Operahuset) on 27.12.1856, but then in an adapted version that included a small corps de ballet. It was staged by Bournonville's pupil, S. Lund, who served as ballet-master at Stockholm's Royal Theatre between 1856 and 1862. Moreover, the original 1852 version was performed 3 times by W. Price and S. Price at Stockholm's Mindre Theatern between 1.6. and 19.6.1860. Finally, the divertissement was staged for the last time outside Denmark by W. Price and S. Price, who performed it in Norway at Christiania's Theatre (Oslo) on 9.6.1865, but then with the slightly different title *'The Sailor's Return' (Scene with Dance) ('Matrosens Hjemkomst' (Scene med Dands))*. The divertissement received 6 performances at Christiania's Theatre, the last of which was given on 28.6.1865.

Musical sources:

Répétiteur's copy. Ms. Copy. Black and brown ink. 1 vol. 14 pp. of which two are blank (32 × 24,3 cm with minor variants) Repetiteur=Parti/til/Matrosens Hjemkomst/Bournonville. Unsigned and undated [1838 and 1852] [DKKk; MA ms 2904 (3) (KTB 337, in parts originally KTB 206) This répétiteur's copy clearly dates from Bournonville's creation of this divertissement in Copenhagen during the month of May 1852, well before its later première at Christiania's Theatre on 9.6.1852. It consists of an excerpt borrowed from the original répétiteur's copy for Bournonville's two-act romantic ballet *The Isle of Phantasy* (*see* 28.10.1838). The répétiteur's copy also seems to have been used for all later performance of *'The Sailor's Return'* at Copenhagen's Royal Theatre from 29.9.1855 and throughout Bournonville's lifetime. The music is included on pp. 7–20 in a volume that also contains the répétiteur's copies for four other works. It includes Bournonville's sporadic autographed choreographic notes (written with brown ink) which describe (in general terms) the mime and the choreography. According to his inclusion of the names of the dancers E. Stramboe and A. Price, they clearly must have been written in May 1852.

Orchestral score. Ms. Copy. Black ink. 1 vol. 28 pp. (24,8 × 33,3 cm) Matrosens Hjemkomst Unsigned and undated [c.1852] [NOum; Ms. 216, Eske 24 b. This orchestral score omits the first two movements of the divertissement (both of which were presumably composed by H. S. Paulli).

Conductor's part. Ms. Copy. Black ink. 4 pp. 33,7 × 24,6 cm) Matrosens Hjemkomst./Dirigent Stemme/Introduction/Andantino/[…]/All° Unsigned and undated [c.1852] [DKKk; MA ms 2670 (KTB 337) This conductor's part contains the music of the two opening movements in *'The Sailor's Return'*. It most probably served for the 1852 Norwegian première of this divertissement, but also seems to have been used for the later 1855 Copenhagen performances.

Répétiteur's copy. Ms. Copy. Brown ink. 6 pp. (33,7 × 26 cm) Matrosens Hjemkomst./Repetiteur=Parti Unsigned and undated [c.1852] [DKKk; MA ms 2671 (KTB 337) This répétiteur's copy contains the complete music for *'The Sailor's Return'* and seems to have been used for the 1852 Norwegian première of this divertissement. A note on p. 1 (written with brown ink) indicates that the volume was originally accompanied by 26 parts.

No set of parts dating from the 1852 première in Norway of *'The Sailor's Return'* has yet been traced. However, two later sets of parts dating from the 1855 Copenhagen performances of this divertissement are now in DKKk (call nos. KTB 337 a, and KTB 337 b).

9.6.1852
'Military Polka, Character dance in Hungarian style' ('Militair Polka' Characteerdands i ungarsk Stiil') **performed by S. Lund, E. Stramboe, A. Price, and S. Price (Christiania's Theatre, Oslo).**
This dance is identical with Bournonville's *Polka militaire (Polka, (Militairdands))* first performed by himself, F. Hoppe, P. Funck, and P. Fredstrup at the Court Theatre on 1.11. 1842. It was performed twice in Christiania, the last time on 14.7.1852. The musical material employed for the 1852 summer tour to Norway seems to have been the same as that used when this dance was first given at Christiania's Theatre on 8.8.1847. It is now in NOum (call no. Ms. 216, Eske 24 a.) and DKKk (call nos. MA ms 2628, and KTB 1027 (originally KTB 222)).

11.6.1852
'Divertissement from The Toreador' ('Divertissement af Toréadoren') **(Christiania's Theatre, Oslo).**
This divertissement is based on three excerpts from Bournonville's two-act idyllic ballet *The Toreador* (*see* 27.11.1840) and was arranged especially for the 1852 Norwegian summer tour. According to the poster the excerpts were as follows:

(1) *El Jaleo de Xeres* (performed by E. Stramboe, and A. Price).
(2) *Solo* (danced by Juliette Price).
(3) *Bolero à quatre* (performed by S. Lund, E. Stramboe, A. Price, and S. Price).

In his diary Bournonville noted about its reception on the opening night:

'Divertissementet af Toreadoren, – det gjorde stormende Lykke og Juliette dandsede saa deiligt som hun aldrig endnu har dandset'.

The divertissement was given twice in Norway, the last time on 29.6.1852.

No musical sources dating from the 1852 Norwegian performances have yet been traced. This seems to indicate that the divertissement would have been performed using the original 1840 Copenhagen musical material for *The Toreador* (now in DKKk, call nos. C II, 114 k, MA ms 2965, and KTB 1046 (originally KTB 269)).

15.6.1852
'Pas de deux from La Muette de Portici' composed by Mr. Bournonville ('Pas de deux af den Stumme i Portici' componeret af Hr Bournonville) **performed by S. Lund and S. Price (Christiania's Theatre, Oslo).**
This dance is identical with the so-called *A New Pas de deux composed by Mr. Dance Director Bournonville*, that was set to music by M. E. Caraffa and premièred at Copenhagen's Royal Theatre as an incorporated divertissement in Act I of D.-F.-E. Auber's five-act opera *La Muette de Portici* (*see* 23.9.1834). It was given twice in Christiania in 1852, the last time on 2.7. 1852. The *Pas de deux* was most probably performed this year using the same musical material employed for its earlier staging at this theatre on 2.7.1847 (now in NOum, call no. Ms. 216, Eske 24 b, and DKKk, call nos. MA ms 2700, and KTB 209). This is clear from notes in several of the parts for this dance which clearly indicate that it was performed in Christiania on 15.6.1852.

18.6.1852

'Scene and Pas de quatre from La Somnambule' ('Scene og Pas de quatre af Sövngængersken') **performed by E. Stramboe, S. Lund, A. Price, and S. Price (Christiania's Theatre, Oslo).**

This is a divertissement version of selected excerpts from Act I of Bournonville's Danish version of J. Aumer's three-act pantomimic ballet *La Somnambule, ou l'Arrivée d'un nouveau seigneur* (*see* 21.9.1829). It was arranged by Bournonville especially for the 1852 Norwegian summer. According to a separate autographed sheet of paper, entitled '<u>Regie</u>', inserted in Bournonville's diary next to the date of 7.6.1852, the divertissement was mounted with the following accessories:

'<u>Sövngængersken</u> ... <u>Huse</u>'.

The divertissement was given twice in Norway, the last time on 12.7.1852.

Eight years later a similar (uncredited) divertissement, entitled *Scenes and Pas de quatre from the ballet 'La Somnambule'* (*Scèner och Pas de quatre ur Balletten 'Sömngångerskan'*) was mounted at Stockholm's Mindre Theatern and performed there twice by F. Hoppe, W. Price, Juliette Price, and S. Price on 16.6. and 19.6.1860. It was most probably identical with the 1852 Norwegian divertissement.

Musical sources:

Orchestral score. Ms. Copy. Black ink. 1 vol. 27 pp. (24,4 × 33,8 cm)
No. 6./Pas de deux/af Balletten/Sövngjængersken
Unsigned and undated [c.1852]
[NOum; Ms. 216, Eske 24 a.
This orchestral score is entitled 'Pas de deux' and contains the music for the *Pas de deux* originally danced by *Edmond* and *Thérèse* in Act I (score no. 7 B) of Bournonville's Copenhagen version of *La Somnambule, ou l'Arrivée d'un nouveau seigneur* (*see* 21.9.1829). Because it is the only music from this ballet that has been traced so far in Norway, it seems to refer to Bournonville's 1852 Norwegian arrangement of a *Pas de quatre* divertissement from *La Somnambule*.

No répétiteur's copy and set of parts dating from the 1852 Norwegian performances of this dance have yet been traced. This seems to indicate that the divertissement was rehearsed and performed using the original 1829 music material for Bournonville's Copenhagen version of *La Somnambule, ou l'Arrivée d'un nouveau seigneur* (now in DKK, call nos. MA ms 2984, and KTB 287.

22.6.1852

'Scene and Pas de trois from The Conservatoire' ('Scene og Pas de trois af Conservatoriet') **performed by E. Stramboe (as *Ernest*), S. Lund (as *Alexis*), Juliette Price (as *Celestine*), and S. Price (as *Adèle*) (Christiania's Theatre (Oslo))**

This work is a divertissement version of two excerpts from Act I of Bournonville's two-act ballet-vaudeville *The Conservatoire, or a Proposal of Marriage through the Newspaper* (*see* 6.5. 1849). It was arranged especially by him for the 1852 Norwegian summer tour. For the same occasion Bournonville altered (according to the poster) the names of the two leading ballerinas so that *Eliza* and *Victorine* now became named *Celestine* and *Adèle* respectively. In his diary he noted about the opening night:

'Scene og Pas af Conservatoriet [...] der gjorde overordentlig Lykke. Fremkaldelse'.

The divertissement was performed for the second and last time in Christiania on 9.7.1852, but then (according to the poster) without the opening pantomimic '*Scene*'.

No musical sources for the divertissement have yet been traced in Norway. This seems to indicate that it was rehearsed and performed using the original 1849 Copenhagen musical material for *The Conservatoire* (now in DKKk, call nos. MA ms 1550 and KTB 264, and in USNYp (microfilm)).

22.6.1852

'Spring Dance' (after Norwegian motifs) from the ballet 'Old Memories' ('Springdands' (efter norske Motiver) af Balletten 'Gamle Minder') **performed by E. Stramboe and A. Price (Christiania's Theatre, Oslo).**

This performance represents the first time that the *Norwegian Spring Dance* from Bournonville's one-act ballet *Old Memories, or A Magic Lantern* (*see* 18.12.1848 and 21.11.1849) was ever performed in Norway. It was restaged a second and last time at Christiania's Theatre with W. Price and Juliette Price on 7.6.1865 and was then given with the new title '*Norwegian Spring Dance*' ('*Norsk Springdands*'). The dance reached a total of 5 performances in Christiania between 22.6.1852 and 7.6.1865. No musical sources for it have yet been traced in Norway. This seems to indicate that it was rehearsed and performed in 1852 using the original Copenhagen musical material for *Old Memories, or A Magic Lantern* (now in DKKk, call nos. C II, 114 k, MA ms 2904 (5), and KTB 291).

29.6.1852

'Pas de deux' (from the ballet Faust) composed by Mr. Bournonville ('Pas de deux' (af Balletten Faust) componeret af Hr Bournonville) **performed by S. Lund and J. Price (Christiania's Theatre (Oslo)).**

According to an orchestral score for this dance it is musically identical with Bournonville's much earlier *Pas de deux* to music by F.-M.-A. Venua, which on 8.12.1849 had been incorporated in Act II of his three-act romantic ballet *Faust* (*see also* 29.10.1829). The dance was performed twice in Christiania, the last time on 6.7.1852.

Musical sources:

Orchestral score. Ms. Copy. Black ink. 32 pp. (24,4 × 33,9 cm)
No. III/Pas de deux/af Balletten/Faust
Unsigned and undated [c.1852]
[NOum; Ms. 216, Eske 24 b.

Répétiteur's copy. Ms. Copy. Black ink. 4 pp. (34,6 × 25,8 cm)
<u>Pas de deux af Balletten Faust.</u>
Unsigned and undated [c.1852]
[DKKk; MA ms 2647 (1) (KTB 242 (originally KTB 217))
This répétiteur's copy is included on pp. 1–4 in an (incomplete) volume of four répétiteur's copies for Bournonville dances that seems to have been made especially for the 1852 Norwegian summer tour. According to its title it certainly dates from the period after 8.12.1849 when F.-M.-A. Venua's music had been incorporated for the first time in Act II of Bournonville's three-act romantic ballet *Faust*.

No set of parts for this dance has yet been traced in Norway. This indicates that it most probably was performed using the original Copenhagen music material for Venua's *Pas de deux* (now in DKKk, call nos. KTB 1052 (1) and/or MA ms 2763 (4)).

2.7.1852
'Styrian National Dance' composed by Mr. Bournonville
('Steyrisk Nationaldands' componeret af Hr. Bournonville')
performed by E. Stramboe and A. Price (Christiania's
Theater, Oslo).
This dance is identical with the (uncredited) *Styrian Dance*
(Steirisk Dands), originally performed at Copenhagen's Royal
Theatre as an incorporated divertissement in D.-F.-E.
Auber's three-act comic opera *Le Domino noir* (*see* 29.1.1839).
It was given only once in Christiania in 1852. No separate
musical sources dating from its 1852 performance in Norway
have yet been found.

2.7.1852
'Italian Genre Picture' Divertissement with Tarantella ('Italiensk
Genrebillede' Divertissement med Tarantella) **performed by**
S. Lund, E. Stramboe, A. Price, Juliette Price, and F. Price
(Christiania's Theatre (Oslo).
In his diary Bournonville noted about this Italian divertisse-
ment choreographed during the 1852 Norwegian summer
tour:

23.6.1852: 'Prøve paa Det italienske Genrebillede
2.7.: 'Italiensk Genrebillede der gjorde Lўkke'.

According to a separate autographed sheet of paper, entitled
'Regie', inserted in Bournonville's diary next to the date of
7.6.1852, it was mounted with the following accessories:

'Genrebillede – Et Bord, en Bænk, to Stole, Flaske 5 Glas Dug, –
Kurve med Frugt'.

The divertissement was in all probability based on selected
excerpts from Act I and Act III of Bournonville's three-act
romantic ballet *Napoli or The Fisherman and His Bride* (*see* 29.3.
1842). This theory is confirmed by the fact that the poster
for the second performance on 9.7.1852 includes a cast that
includes many similarities with that of *Napoli*:

Donna Giovannina .... Mad. [Flora] Price,
Theresa [and] Marietta, her daughters .... Juliette and
                                                                                 Amalia Price,
Beppo [and] Carlo, their suitors .... [Edvard] Stramboe
                                                                            and [Sigurd] Lund.

The idea of mounting a miniature version of *Napoli* in Norway thus seems to have come to Bournonville during his stay
in Christiania.
    The music was in all probability pieced together and ar-
ranged by H. S. Paulli. This theory is supported by two orchestral scores in NOum (*see* Musical sources) containing
selected excerpts from *Napoli or The Fisher and His Bride*. According to them the divertissement seems to have consisted
of at least two dances from this ballet, namely E. Helsted's
Pas de quatre in Act III (score no. 2) and H. S. Paulli's *Tarantella* in the same act (score no. 3). Of these the former seems
(according to the title of the first Norwegian score) to have
been performed as a *Pas de trois*.
    The divertissement was given only twice in Christiania, the
last time on 9.7.1852. However, it also seems to be identical
with another work by Bournonville, entitled *Italian Genre
Pictures and Tarantella (Italienske Genrebilder och Tarantella)*,

mounted eight years later at Stockholm's Mindre Theatern
on 5.6.1860.

Musical sources:

Orchestral score. Ms. Copy. Black ink. 1 vol. 30 pp. ($25 \times 33{,}8$ cm)
Pas de trois/af Balletten/Napoli
Unsigned and undated [c.1852]
[NOum; Ms. 216, Eske 24 a.
This orchestral score contains E. Helsted's complete music for the
Pas de quatre in Act III (score no. 2) of Bournonville's *Napoli or The
Fisherman and His Bride* (*see* 29.3.1842). According to its title it clearly
seems to have been performed as a *Pas de trois* in Norway.

Orchestral score. Ms. Copy. Black ink. 1 vol. 30 pp. ($25 \times 33{,}8$ cm)
Tarantella/af Balletten/Napoli
Unsigned and undated [c.1852]
[NOum; Ms. 216, Eske 24 a.
This orchestral score contains H. S. Paulli's complete music for the
Tarantella in Act III (score no. 3) of Bournonville's *Napoli or The Fish-
erman and His Bride*. According to the 1852 Norweigan poster it
seems to have been performed by only two couples in Christiania.

No répétiteur's copy and set of parts for *'Italian Genre Picture'* have yet
been traced in Norway. This fact indicates that the divertissement
probably was performed using the original Copenhagen set of parts
for *Napoli or The Fisherman and His Bride* (now in DKKk, call no. KTB
292).

6.7.1852
'Las Hermanas de Sevilla', Spanish Character Dance (spansk
Characteerdands) **performed by Juliette Price, A. Price, and**
S. Price (Christiania's Theatre, Oslo).
This performance represents the first time Bournonville's
Las Hermanas de Sevilla (*see* 4.6.1851) was performed outside
Denmark. In his diary he noted about its reception on the
opening night:

'Hermanas. – Der var meget godt Huus og stor Applaus'.

The dance was given twice in Christiania, the last time on
14.7.1852.

Musical sources:

Orchestral score. Ms. Copy. Black ink. 1 vol. 24 pp. (25×34 cm)
Las Hermanas
Unsigned and undated [c.1852]
[NOum; Ms. 216, Eske 24 a.

No répétiteur's copy and set of parts dating from the 1852 Norwegian performances of *Las Hermanas de Sevilla* have yet been traced.
This indicates that it most probably was rehearsed and performed in
Christiania using the original Copenhagen set of parts for this dance
(now in DKKk, call no. KTB 239).

12.7.1852
'The Flower Maids of Florence' Character dance ('De florentinske
Blomsterpiger' Characteerdands) **performed by Juliette Price,**
S. Price, and A. Price (Christiania's Theatre, Oslo).
This performance represents the first and only time Bournonville's divertissement *The Flower Maids of Florence, Pas de
trois* (*see* 8.6.1850) was staged outside Denmark. According
to a separate autographed sheet of paper, entitled 'Regie',
inserted in Bournonville's diary next to the date of 7.6.1852,
it was mounted with the following accessories:

'Blomsterpigerne: – Blomster'.

On the poster for its second and last performance in Christiania (14.7.1852) the music is explicitly credited as 'composed' (*componeret*) by 'Baron H. Lövenskjold'. Løvenskjold's music for *The Flower Maids of Florence* (for which no separate orchestral score has yet been found) is most likely identical with that of his so-called 'Pas af Grækere og Grækerinder' or 'Beltedands' in Act II (score no. 9) of Bournonville's two-act allegorical ballet *The New Penelope, or The Spring Festival in Athens* (*see* 26.1.1847). This theory is supported by a note reading 'C. Herr 1.ste Fagotist ved Christiania Theater d. 30.6.1852', written in the part for the first bassoon of what is entitled 'Pas de trois af "Den nye Penelope"' (now in DKKk, call no. KTB 238). It proves beyond doubt that this excerpt from Løvenskjold's ballet was brought to Christiania and played there during the summer of 1852. Moreover, since *The Flower Maids of Florence* was the only dance with music by Løvenskjold that was performed during the 1852 Norwegian summer tour, it clearly indicates that it was his music from Act II (score no. 9) of *The New Penelope, or The Spring Festival in Athens* that Bournonville employed when he created *The Flower Maids of Florence* in Copenhagen in the late spring of 1850.

14.7.1852
'Epilogue' ('Epilog') recited by A. Price (Christiania's Theatre, Oslo).

For the final performance at Christiania's Theatre during the 1852 Norwegian summer tour Bournonville wrote an epilogue in ten verses. It was recited by his pupil, the dancer Amalia Price, who soon after her return to Denmark retired from the ballet in order to become an actress. In his diary Bournonville noted about the epilogue and its reception:

8.7.1852: 'skrevet en Epilog for A. Price'
11.7.: 'gjennemgaaet Epilogen med Amalia'
12.7.: 'Prøve paa Epilogen, der gik godt'
14.7.: 'en Epilog forfattet af mig. Overordentlig Bifald og megen Blomsterregn'.

His text reads as follows:

'Naar Vaaren fletter sine friske Krandse
Og gyder Ungdoms Varme i hvert Brÿst,
Da ÿttrer sig med Stÿrke, Livets Lÿst
I Ved [erased] Sangens Jubelchor og muntre Dandse.

Men, naar den gÿldne Sommers milde Bölger
Bedækker gÿngende en frugtbar Jord,
Da trænger vor Taknemlighed til Ord,
Der kunne tolke, hvad vort Hjerte dölger

Saaledes gaaer det os, vi kom med Varme,
Ret som en Trækfuglskare under Skÿ
Vi svang os let, ved Sommerdands i Bÿ
Mens Øiet smilte gjennem Glædestaarer.

Og Man forstod ret vel vor stumme Tale
Som feerne, der flöi i Svaneham,
Vi baded' os i Mindets dÿbe Dam
Og hented' os en Krands fra Norges Dale.

I denne Krands af Roser og Kjærminder
Staaer Eviggrönt, der visner ei saa let,

Thi, Gjæstevenskab er enAdelsret
Blandt Norges ædle Mænde og hulde Qvinder.

Dog overalt, hvor Gjæstfrihed har hjemme,
Man kan ei reise sig saa taus fra Bord
Og selv Terpsichore bör finde Ord,
Hvis hun ei Folkeskikken rent vil glemme.

Velan, vær hilset fra vor Huldgudinde,
Du Norges unge, friske Muselund!
Hvor Videt sprudler dÿbt fra Elvens Bund
Og Lÿset straaler höit fra Fjeldets Tinde.

Vær takket, at Du ikke har forsmaaet,
En Kunst, der levner kun et flÿgtigt Spore:
'I Rÿthmens Kreds, en Billedverden boer'
Det har din Aand opfattet og forstaaet'

Derfor vor Muse vil Dig kjærlig bringe
Den bedste Skat, hun eier i sit Skjöd,
Et muntert Sind og Sundheds Rosenglöd
Og Tankens Flugt paa Melodiens Vinge

Som hendes Börn, vi har i Kunstens Navn
Af Hjertets Inderste vor frembære,
O skjønne Norge! Du velsignet være!
Tak for hver Blomst, vi sænked i din Favn'.

When A. Price's mother, the dancer, R. Price, informed Bournonville about her daughter's decision to retire as a dancer in order to become an actress he noted in his diary on 25. 7.1852:

'Mme Price fortalte mig at Amalia agter at optræde som Skuespillerinde til næste Sæson [...] at hun har dulgt sin forandrede Kunst-Bestemmelse for mig og er simpeltvæk 'gement' [...] det gjør mig ondt at see det ÿndige Kløverblad [the Price cousins Juliette, Sophie and Amalia] splittet [...] dog vil jeg tage mig det let, og fremfor alt ikke blande mig ind i de private Forhold'.

Autograph sources:

Text. Ms. Autograph. 4 pp. (22 × 17,5 cm)
Epilog./Fremsagt ved Afskedsforestillingen paa/Christiania: Theater, den 14.de Julii 1852, af/Jf. Amalia Price.
Signed and dated: 'den 14.de Julii 1852'
[DKKk; NKS 1770, 2° a)

16.7.–22.7.1852
Three performances at Drammen's Theatre (Norway).

According to Bournonville's diary this series of three performances (given on 16.7., 18.7., and 22.7.1852) consisted of a programme with the three following dances:

(1) '*Italian Genre Picture*' (*see* 2.7.1852).
(2) '*Spring Dance*' (after Norwegian motifs) (*see* 22.6.1852).
(3) '*The Flower Maids of Florence*' (*see* 8.6.1850).

The theatre and the rather awkward décor employed for these performances are described by Bournonville in his memoirs *My Theatre Life* (pp. 202–203) as follows:

'The theatre itself was very poorly equipped as far as scenery and properties were concerned. Thus, for our Italian divertissement we had to make do with a birch forest, and when we needed an image of the Madonna, they came up with a picture which had always done service on such occasions. But since it turned out to be nothing less than a protrait of [P. S.] Griffenfeldt [Chancellor of Denmark during the reign of Christian V] I was forced to renounce my idea – from artistic as well as religious and political considerations'.

According to his diary (15.7.1852) the musical accompaniment for the performances consisted of arrangements for two violins played by Bournonville and H. S. Paulli.

25.7.–27.7.1852
Two performances at Frederikshald's Theatre (Halden, Norway).

According to Bournonville's diary these performances consisted of a programme with the following two dances:

(1) *'Spring Dance' (after Norwegian motifs)* (*see* 22.6.1852).
(2) *'Las Hermanas de Sevilla'* (*see* 4.6.1851).

According to the same source (15.7.1852) the musical accompaniment consisted of arrangements for two violins played by Bournonville and H. S. Paulli.

During the 1852 Norwegian summer tour the same programme was repeated twice at Christianssand's Theatre (Kristiansand) on 1.8. and 3.8.1852, three times at Arendal's Theatre on 6.8., 8.8., and 9.8.1852, and once at Laurvigen's Theatre (Larvik) on 12.8.1852.

About the opening night at Frederikshald's Theatre Bournonville noted:

'fuldt Huus og et dannet Publicum. Megen Applaus'.

The stage of the theatre in Christianssand was described by him on 31.7.1852 as: 'lille Theater og usselt Decorations og Lÿsvæsen', while the theatre in Arendal was assessed on 5.8.1852 as: 'det meget lille Theater'.

2.9.1852
An Episode (En Episode).

For C. Juul's five-act drama about the life of the great 18th-century Danish poet, Johannes Ewald, Bournonville created a series of (uncredited) tableaux which are described on the poster as follows:

Poesiens Genius } Drømmebilleder .... Jfr. [C. M.] Eidrup
Fiskere og Fiskermænd }

In Juul's printed textbook (p. 145) the scene in Act V, during which the so-called 'Drømmebilleder' are revealed to the poet Ewald, is described as follows:

'(Bagteppet gaaer op; man seer et Parti af Stranden. Fiskere og Fiskerinder danne en Gruppe efter [D. N.] Chodowiecki's Billede til anden Handling af 'Fiskerne'. Poesiens Genius træder frem foran Gruppen og fremsiger, medens Musiken tier, langsomt den følgende Replik.).

Genien.
Din Prøvetide er endt for dennesinde;
Det Baand, en natlig Alf i Taarer tvandt,
Skal din Begeistrings Vinger meer ei binde.

I Sorgens Dyb dig selv igjen du fandt,
Kjek skal du atter stræbe mod det Høie,
Der, hvor man skuer Lyset klart og grandt.

Og hun, den Blege, med det matte Øie,

Skal Taaren snart ombytte med et Smiil,
Fri for den Qval, som nu vil hende bøie.

Ryst Støvet af din Fod med Lynets Iil!
Fly Mindet om Fornedrelsen og Nøden!
See, hist i Øst alt blinker Danes Piil!

Fremad! din Vei gaaer imod Morgenrøden!
(Bagtæppet falder. Ewald vaagner og reiser sig)'.

In his diary Bournonville noted about the two rehearsals he directed of these tableaux:

28.8.1852: 'Arrangeret Tableau paa Theatret' [...] prøvet Tableau Kl 5"
2.9.: 'Saisonen aabnet med 'En Episode'.

The tableaux were listed on the poster without giving any credit to Bournonville. Moreover, neither in his handwritten lists of his mises-en-scène for operas and plays (*see* Additional Sources), nor in the printed survey of his works in his memoirs *My Theatre Life* are they included.

No musical sources for Juul's drama have yet been traced. *An Episode* received 3 performances, the last of which was given on 10.9.1852.

Autograph sources:

Choreographic note. Ms. Autograph. Brown ink. 1 p. (10,7 × 13,8 cm)
[Five drawings showing a series of tableaux and in which the following dancers/actors are mentioned by their names: [Laura] Juel, [Arnold] Walbom, [Marie] Eydrup, Sigurd [Lund], [Emil] Hansen, [Petrine] Fredstrup, an unidentified name, Lise [an unidentified artist], [Marie] Werning [the younger], [Ferdinand] Hoppensach, Julie[tte Thorberg], a supernumerary ['Statist'], an unidentified name, [Gustav] Adolf [Füssel], and [Georg] Brodersen]
Unsigned and undated [c.1852]
[DKKk; NKS 3285 4° 1 læg b 10

Since the name of the dancer-actress, M. Eydrup, is included as the central figure in one of the five (untitled) drawings, they clearly represent Bournonville's first drafts for the series of tableaux (entitled 'Drømmebilleder') which he created for C. Juul's 1852 drama *An Episode*. This theory is further supported by the circumstance that the other dancers, whose names are included in this manuscript, were all active members of Copenhagen's Royal Ballet in 1852. The drawings have previously been identified by A. Fridericia (in *August Bournonville*, 1979, p. 249) as showing scenes from Act I of Bournonville's two-act ballet-vaudeville *Far from Denmark, or: A Costume Ball on Board* from 20.4.1860. This theory, however, can be discarded since most of the dancers mentioned in this manuscript were either dead or had long since retired from the stage in 1860.

Printed sources:

Printed text-book. 1 vol. 148 pp. (17 × 10,5 cm)
En Episode./Drama i fem Acter/af/Christian Juul.
Copenhagen, C. G. Iversens Forlag, Thieles Bogtrykkeri, 1852
[DKKk; 55, – 145 8°

7.9.1852
Pas de deux composed by Mr. Court Ballet Master Bournonville (componeret af Hr. Hofballetmester Bournonville) **performed by W. Funck and Juliette Price.**

According to notes in the rehearsal book of H. C. J Fredstrup and other notes in Bournonville's diary, this dance seems to be identical with the so-called *A New Pas de deux composed by*

Mr. Dance Director Bournonville, first performed as an incorporated divertissement in Act I of D.-F.-E. Auber's five-act opera *La Muette de Portici* (*see* 23.9.1834). Thus, Bournonville listed two rehearsals of 'Den Stumme' on 6.9. and 7.9.1852 and describes this performance as:

'Pas de deux, Funck og Juliette meget gode'.

It is not possible to identify the dance any further.

11.9.1852
Pas de deux (uncredited) performed by S. Lund and S. Price.
This (uncredited) dance is most probably identical with the earlier (uncredited) *Pas de deux* performed by the same two dancers on 24.4.1851. It is probably also identical with Bournonville's so-called *'Pas de deux' (from the ballet Faust)*, danced by Lund and S. Price at Christiania's Theatre (Oslo) on 29.6.1852. According to his diary Bournonville attended the performance, but did not make any special comments about it. The *Pas de deux* was given twice by Lund and S. Price in 1852, the last time on 12.10.1852. It is not possible to identify the dance any further.

29.11.1852
Pas de deux (uncredited) performed by W. Funck and J. Rostock.
This dance is most probably identical with the (uncredited) *Pas de deux*, performed by W. Funck and Juliette Price on 3.2.1852 and, in turn, is most likely the same as the even earlier (uncredited) *Pas de deux* danced by W. Funck and P. Funck on 21.9.1849. It was given only once by Funck and Rostock in 1852. It is not possible to identify the dance any further.

1.12.1852
Le Petit Chaperon rouge (Den lille Rødhætte).
Although Bournonville does not include this work in any of his handwritten list of his works (*see* Additional Sources), according to his diary he directed a stage rehearsal on 28.11.1852 of the dances in F.-A. Boyeldieu's three-act fairy-opera (premièred at l'Opéra Comique in Paris on 30.6.1818). *Le Petit Chaperon rouge* included two dance scenes as follows:

(1) An (unnamed) *Dance* in Act I (score no. 7), performed by a corps de ballet during the so-called *Rondo* («Depuis longtemps gentille...Dansez jeunes compagnes, la ronde des montagnes») of *Rose* and a chorus of mixed voices.
(2) A series of *Tableaux* and a *March* in Act II (score no. 12), both performed by a corps de ballet during the dream scene and the cavatine «Charmans plaisirs que l'amour vous rassemble» sung by the characters *Roger* and *Rose*.

According to notes written in the répétiteur's copy from the 1819 Copenhagen première of Boyeldieu's opera (now in DKKk, call no. MA ms 3041 (KTA 198 (1)) the tableaux in Act II are described as follows:

'Les nuages qui masquaient la toille [*sic*] du fond se dissipent et laissent voir un palais magnifique. On voit Roger environné de toute sa cour. De [*sic*] groupes de Danseurs ornent le Tableau [...] les Plaisirs forment de grupes [*sic*] et des tableaux gracieux [...] ici le Plaisirs viennent a lui [...] march des Plaisirs e de la cour de Roger'.

Three years later Bournonville directed another series of rehearsals of the same scenes prior to a restaging of *Le Petit Chaperon rouge* on 25.1.1855. Moreover, on 30.10.1857 he included the opera in a list of projected restagings which he was planning on this day for the 1857–58 and 1858–59 seasons. That project was carried out three years later on 20.12.1860 when *Le Petit Chaperon rouge* was mounted with Bournonville's own and complete mise-en-scène for the first time. Boyeldieu's opera was staged for the fourth and last time by Bournonville in Copenhagen on 8.2.1873.

The 1852 restaging received 7 performances, the last of which was given on 16.1.1855.

Musical sources:

Printed orchestral score. 1 vol. 368 pp. of which four are blank (30,8 × 24,1 cm)
PARTITION/Du Petit Chaperon Rouge,/Opéra-Féerie, en trois Actes/[...]/par/ADRIEN BOIELDIEU
Paris, Boieldieu jeune, pl. no. 707 [1818]
[DKKk; U 6 (KTA 198)
This printed orchestral score was used for all performances at Copenhagen's Royal Theatre since its première there on 29.10.1832 and throughout Bournonville's lifetime.

Répétiteur's copy. Ms. Copy. Brown ink. 1 vol. 4 pp. (32,4 × 25 cm)
Repetiteur Parti/til/Syngestykket Rödhætten/af/Boieldieu
Unsigned and undated [c.1839]
[DKKk; MA ms 2902 (17) (KTA 198 (2))
This répétiteur's copy is included on pp. 89–92 in a volume that also contains the répétiteur's copies for 16 other operas and plays. According to these works it clearly dates from the restaging of *Le Petit Chaperon rouge* at Copenhagen's Royal Theatre on 23.9.1839. The same volume was reused for all later performances of Boyeldieu's opera during Bournonville's lifetime. It contains his autographed choreographic numbers '1–3' written with brown ink in the music for the dance scene of Act I (score no. 7). They seem to refer to a later (not yet traced) choreographic notation of this dance, which Bournonville most probably wrote for one of his restagings of this opera in either 1860 or 1873.

Parts. Ms. Copy. 36 vol.
5 vl I, 4 vl II, 2 vla, 5 vlc e cb, fl picc, fl 1/2, ob 1/2, ob e cl, cl 1/2, fag 1/2, fag e cb, cor 1/2/3/4, tr 1/2, gr cassa e piatti e tri, tamb, arpa. 121 vocal parts.
Unsigned and undated [1819]
[DKKk; KTA 198]
This set of part was used for all performances of Boyeldieu's opera in Copenhagen since its première there on 29.10.1819 and throughout Bournonville's lifetime.

14.12.1852
Pas de trois (uncredited) performed by S. Lund, P. Fredstrup, and J. Rostock.
This (uncredited) dance is most likely identical with the earlier (uncredited) *Pas de trois* performed by the same three dancers on 8.4.1848, and in turn is almost certainly identical with Bournonville's *Pas de trois* in Act I (score no. 5) of his Copenhagen version of J. Aumer's three-act pantomimic ballet *La Somnambule, ou l'Arrivée d'un nouveau seigneur* (*see* 21.9.1829). The *Pas de trois* was given only once in 1852. It is not possible to identify the dance any further.

meas.): Here meas. 13–55, 86–89, 92–98, 122–123, 127–131, 139–

1853

23.1.1853
Pas de trois (uncredited) performed by S. Lund, P. Fredstrup, and J. Rostock.

This dance is almost certainly identical with the (uncredited) *Pas de trois*, performed five weeks earlier by the same dancers on 14.12.1852, and in turn is probably identical with Bournonville's *Pas de trois* in Act I (score no. 5) of his Copenhagen version of J. Aumer's three-act pantomimic ballet *La Somnambule, ou l'Arrivée d'un nouveau seigneur* (*see* 21.9.1829). That dance had first been performed as a separate divertissement by Lund, Fredstrup, and Rostock on 8.4.1848. The *Pas de trois* was given only once in 1853. It is not possible to identify the dance any further.

6.2.1853
Il Dissoluto Punito, ossia il Don Giovanni (Don Juan).

According to a note in Bournonville's diary on 5.2.1853 he directed a stage rehearsal of the *Minuet (Menuetto)* in the Act I finale (scene 20) of W. A. Mozart's two-act opera prior to this, his second restaging of *Il Dissoluto Punito, ossia Don Giovanni* (*see* 3.4.1848). The *Minuet* seems to have been mounted this year without any changes from his previous 1848 production, which reached a total of 25 performances, with the last given on 5.5.1857.

12.2.1853
The Nix (Nøkken).

For the première of F. Gläser's one-act opera (to a libretto by H. C. Andersen) Bournonville was responsible for choreographing its two dance scenes in score nos. 1 and 4, and the general mise-en-scène. The dances included a *Peasant Dance (Bondedands)* performed during the opening chorus, entitled «Dandse vakkert» (score no. 1), and a *Waltz* (also entitled *Allemande*) that was danced by a corps de ballet alternating with four leading couples. The *Peasant Dance* is described by Gläser in his autographed score as follows:

'(En aaben Plads udenfor Jöran Arvedsons Gaard [...] <u>Det er Sol=Nedgang. – Jöran Arvedson, Hedda og en Mængde Gjæster, hvoriblandt Peder Laurin ere samlede og midt i Folkelgen: 'Dandse vakkert' der bestaaer i: at Een indenfor Kredsen dandser i en bestemt, særegen Stilling, hvilken de Andre derefter gjentage.)</u>'.

According to the same source the *Waltz* (score no. 4) is performed by the wedding guests who are joined by a group of young girls during the song, entitled «To Roser, to Roser til Kys sig böie». In his diary Bournonville noted about the staging:

27.1.1853: 'Syngeskole paa Nöcken'
28.1.: 'Indstudering paa Dandsen til Nøkken [...] og prøvet en Decoration'
29.1.: 'Prøve med Chor og Quartet paa Dandsen til Nøkken, der gjorde megen Lÿkke'
3.2.: 'Prøve paa Nøkken paa Bÿens Theater'
9.2.: 'Prøve paa Nøkken – M.d [V.] Fo[s]sum malicieusk Upasselighed, smuk Musik, men det Hele lidt kjedeligt'.

Bournonville did not attend the opera's première, but after its second performance on 15.2.1853 he noted in his diary:

'seet og hørt Nøkken. Smuk Musik af Glaeser, – men det Hele for langtrukket, jeg havde componeret Dands dertil'.

The Nix received 7 performances, the last of which was given on 17.3.1853.

Autograph sources:

Production note. Ms. Autograph. Brown ink. 1 p. (18,4 × 20,6 cm)
<u>Dands i Nökken.</u>
Signed and dated: 'd 30 Januar 1853'
[DKKkt; F.M. (Ballet)

Musical sources:

Orchestral score. Ms. Autograph (by F. Gläser). Black ink. 2 vol. Vol. I 248 pp., Vol. II 244 pp. of which one is blank (25,5 × 32,5 cm with minor variants)
<u>Nökken/Partitur/Nro: I./[...]/Nökken. -/Opera i en Akt./Text af Andersen./Musik/af/Franz Glæser./[...]/Nökken./Partitur/Nro: II./[...]/fortsættelse/af Partituret til 'Operaen'/Nökken/segue: No. 6.</u>
Signed (in vol. I, p. 1): 'Franz Glæser.', undated [1853]
[DKKk; C II, 110 (KTA 450)
The music for the two dance scenes in score nos. 1 and 4 is included on pp. 49–81 and 173–194 respectively.

Répétiteur's copy. Ms. Copy (with autographed insertions by F. Gläser on p. 1). Black ink. 1 vol. 14 pp. (32,3 × 25 cm)
<u>Ballet=Repetitions=/Stemme/til: Nökken./206/[...]/Ballett= Repititions=Stemme/til/Operaen: 'Nökken.'</u>
Unsigned and undated [1853]
[DKKk; MA ms 3087 (KTA 450)
This répétiteur's copy contains the dance music in score nos. 1 and 4. Moreover, Bournonville's pencilled autographed choreographic notes and his other notes (written with brown ink) describe (in general terms) the choreography and the casting of each dance scene.

Parts. Ms. Copy. 30 vol.
3 vl I, 3 vl II, 2 vla, 3 vlc e cb, fl I, fl II e picc, ob 1/2, cl 1/2, fag 1/2, cor 1/2/3/4, tr 1/2, trb 1/2/3, timp, arpa. 49 vocal parts.
Unsigned and undated [1853]
[DKKk; KTA 450

4.3.1853
The Wedding Festival in Hardanger (Brudefærden i Hardanger).

This two-act ballet is drawn from inspirations received during Bournonville's 1852 summer tour to Norway as well as from his later reading of Norwegian literature, in particular N. R. Østgaard's book *En Fjeldbygd. Billeder fra Østerdalen* (first published in Christiania, 1852) and the collections of poems by J. S. C. Welhaven (published in Christiania in 1839 and 1845). According to his diary, Bournonville had originally planned to commission the music for this ballet from N. W. Gade, but this project was abandoned at an early stage because of Gade's many other commitments abroad during this period. Instead the score was composed and arranged by H. S. Paulli. He incorporated several Norwegian and Danish folk songs and dances, which are identified as follows:

(1) Act I, score no. 1: In the ballet's opening scene Paulli incorporated the melody of a Norwegian folk song from the region of Smaalenene, entitled «Jeg veet en liten Jente». It was first published in 1842 by L. M. Lindeman in his five-volume collection of Norwegian mountain songs, named *Norske Fjeld=Melodier* (Christiania, P. T. Malling, 2. oplag, vol. II, no. 26). This melody is followed by another

Norwegian song tune, entitled «Aa kjöre Ve aa kjöre Vann» (also published by Lindeman, vol. IV, no. 41).

(2) Act I, score no. 2: In this number Paulli employed the tune of the Norwegian folk song «Je sku au ha Löst t'aa jifte mei san» (published by Lindeman, vol. I, no. 90).

(3) Act I, score no. 6: Paulli here interpolated the tune of the Norwegian folk song, named «Aa Ola, Ola, min ejen Onge, kvi la du meg den Sorg saa tonge?». It was published in Christiania by W. Lindorff as no. 10 in his collection of songs, entitled *50 Norske Nationalsange og Folkemelodier*.

(4) Act I, score no. 11: For this scene Paulli incorporated the tune of the Norwegian folk song, named «Stusle Söndags Kvællen» (published by Lindeman, vol. II, no. 11).

(5) Act II, score no. 12 (the so-called 'Bord Dands'): In his music for this dance Paulli incorporated the tune of the Norwegian folk song, entitled «En liten Gut ifra Tistedalen» (published by Lindeman, vol. I, no. 2).

(6) Act II, score no. 14: In this number Paulli incorporated the melody of a Danish folk song from c.1815, entitled «En deilig ung Ridder i Lunden mon gaae», rewritten with new words by H. Hertz in c.1851. This melody was reused by E. Lembcke in 1859 for his national Danish song «Vort Modersmaal er deiligt». Moreover, Bournonville employed this melody again in 1860 for his so-called *Feast-Quadrille (Fest-Quadrille)*, choreographed for a Royal Golden Anniversary (*see* 10.11.1860).

(7) Act II, score no. 15 (the *Halling*): In his music for this dance Paulli incorporated the melody of an authentic Norwegian *Halling* from the region of Telemarken (published by Lindeman, vol. V, no. 67). The opening section of this dance was in Paulli's arrangement used as the coda. The *Halling* is followed by another Norwegian folk dance, entitled 'Vosserull'. It was first published as no. 10 in H. Kierulf's collection of Norwegian folk dances, named *XXV Udvalgte Norske Folkedandse* (Stockholm, A. Hirsch, pl. no. 1077).

The Wedding Festival in Hardanger was also mounted twice by Bournonville at Stockholm's Royal Theatre (Operahuset) on 22.6.1857 and 1.11.1861. In Copenhagen it was restaged on 25.4.1869 (by L. Gade), and on 7.12.1870 (by Bournonville).

In his diary Bournonville noted about the ballet's creation and its 1853 première:

5.6.1852: 'Aftnen hos Lieut. [J.] Ræders hvor der var charmant Selskab. Sang af Fru Lasson en smuk Dame med en kunstuddannet stemme, men i særdeleshed blev jeg henrevet af to Søstre fra Tromsöe, Fru Kjerulf og hendes Søster Jf. Norbÿ. De sang saa ÿndigt tilsammen og den sidste foredrog en norsk Klagesang saa deiligt at jeg blev inderlig rört. Aftenen var ÿderst behagelig'
30.8.: 'læst i Fjeldbygder'
3.9.: 'læst i Fjeldbygder'
4.9.: 'læst og componeret'
5.9.: 'størstedelen af Dagen læst og skrevet lidt'
6.9.: 'Læst og skrevet hele Eftermiddagen'
8.9.: 'læst og skrevet'
13.9.: 'Ordnet mine Idéer til den nÿ norske Ballet, begÿndt Programmet til Brÿlluppet i Hardanger'
14.9.: 'Skrevet min Ballet færdig'
15.9.: 'reenskrevet min nÿ Ballet, <u>Brudefærden i Hardanger</u>, sendt den til H: P. Holst for at høre hans Mening'
17.9.: 'Besøg hos Holst, skrevet'
21.9.: 'talt med [N. W.] Gade om min nÿ Ballet. Talt med [J. L.] Heiberg. [E.] Lehmann hos os til Aften'
22.9.: 'Besøg hos Gade og paa Malersalen. – Gade kan ikke skrive Musiken formedelst sine Arbeider for Leipzig'
3.10.: 'componeret med [H. S.] Paulli'
10.10.: 'Arbeidet med Paulli'
16.10.: 'Besøg […] paa Malersalen'
24.10.: 'Arbeidet med Paulli og Theatermalerne'
3.11.: 'Arbeidet med Paulli […] componeret paa min nÿe Ballet'

7.11.: 'componeret paa min nÿe Ballet'
9.11.: 'skrevet, componeret'
11.11.: 'besørget adskilligt paa Theatret og hos Paulli'
14.11.: 'arbeidet med Paulli'
16.11.: 'componeret'
24.11.: 'arbeidet med Paulli'
13.12.: 'componeret'
14.12.: 'Første Indstuderingsprøve paa Brudefærden i Hardanger, den første Scene lovede godt. Gud forunde mig Held og Kraft!'
15.12.: 'Prøve paa den nÿ Ballet'
16.12.: 'lille Prøve med Juliette [Price], skrevet og componeret'
18.12.: 'Prøve og Indstudering. Arbeide med Paulli […] skrevet og componeret den hele Aften'
19.12.: 'componeret og arrangeret min nÿ Ballet hele dagen og Aftenen'
20.12.: 'Prøve og Indstudering'
31.12.: 'componeret paa min nÿ Ballet'
5.1.1853: 'componeret'
6.1.: 'Indstudering af Barbeerdandsen der faldt godt ud'
8.1.: 'Prøvet Alt igjennem. [F.] Høedt tilstede'
9.1.: 'arbeidet med Paulli'
21.1.: 'hjemme hele Aftenen og componeret'
22.1.: 'Kl 10 aabnede jeg vort nÿ Locale med en almindelig Lection for Alle. Kl 11 prøvedes der tre Dandse og Kl 11 1/2 samlede jeg hele Personalet, holdt en Tale for dem, aflagde Regnskab for Subscriptionen og begÿndte derpaa i Guds Navn Prøve med Indstudering af en nÿ Dands til Brudefærden i Hardanger […] Etatsraad Heiberg kom Kl 1 1/2 og Cultusminister [C. F.] Simony Kl 2 for a tage Localet i Øiesyn som vi have benævnet <u>Conservatoriet</u>''
24.1.: 'Prøve paa den nÿ Ballet, stor Indstudering, (Vrøvl med nogle Figurantinder om Konepartierne.) […] arbeidet med Lehman: Costumer'
25.1.: 'Prøve og Indstudering, flere Dandse og Scener indstuderede […] componeret den hele Aften'
26.1.: 'Indstudering af Hallingdandsen […] arbeidet med Lehmann'
28.1.: 'stor Prøve paa Brudefærden'
30.1.: 'Lehmann hos mig med Costümer'
1.2.: 'Prøve og Indstudering paa den nÿ Ballet'
2.2.: 'stor Prøve paa Brudefærden'
3.2.: 'Costüme-Møde med Garderobe-Forvalteren &c'
4.2.: 'Indstudering'
5.2.: 'Prøve paa […] Brudefærden'
6.2.: 'componeret'
8.2.: 'Prøve – Juliette lært sit Parti'
9.2.: 'Prøve paa Balletten (Juliette)'
10.2.: 'componeret'
11.2.: 'Indstudering af Springdandsen […] Costume-Arrangement'
14.2.: 'Prøve paa Brudefærden'
16.2.: 'Stor Prøve paa Brudefærden, sidste Haand paa Indstuderingen'
19.2.: 'Prøve paa Brudefærden'
21.2.: 'Prøve paa Brudefærden […] skrevet mit Program til Trÿkken'
22.2.: 'Prøve paa Brudefærden, Arrangement paa Byens Theater'
23.2.: 'Prøve paa Brudefærden. Ubehageligheder med Jf [E.] Larcher og [F. J. G.] Berner. Prøven hævet, jeg gik sÿg hjem'
25.2.: 'Prøve paa Bÿens Theater'
28.2.: 'Prøve paa Byens Theater, det gik meget godt'
2.3.: 'Generalprøve paa Brudefærden. Den gik fortræffeligt og gjorde meget Indtryk'
4.3.: 'Første Forestilling af min Ballet 'Brudefærden i Hardanger'. Den gik fortreffeligt og gjorde overordentlig Lÿkke. Alle Roller bleve udførte med Talent og Præcision. – Jeg takkede Gud'
6.3.: 'Brev til Helene. Balletten gik udmærket godt og for fuldt Huus, men for et ulideligt dvask Publicum'.

The original 1853 version was given 80 times (the last time on 6.3.1867) and the ballet reached a total of 95 performances during Bournonville's lifetime, the last of which took place on 31.5.1872.

Autograph sources:

Manuscript scenario. Ms. Autograph. Black ink. 1 vol. 12 pp. (20,2 × 16,3 cm)
Brudefærden i Hardanger/Ballet i to Akter./af/August Bournonville./1852.
Signed and dated: 'Kbhvn d. 14.de September 1852.'
[DKKk; NKS 3285 4° 2 A–E

Production note. Ms. Autograph. Brown and black ink. 3 pp. (32,8 × 20,7 cm)
Personerne i Balletten/Brudefærden i Hardanger.
Unsigned and dated: 'Kjøbenhavn den 30.de Januar 1853.'
[DKKkt; F.M. (Ballet)

Musical sources:

Musical draft(?). Ms. Autograph (by H. S. Paulli). Brown and black ink. 2 pp. (33,4 × 25 cm)
Norske Viser.
Unsigned and undated [c.1852–1853]
[DKKk; C II, 10 (H. S. Paullis Efterladte mss. II)
This manuscript contains the tunes of twelve (untitled) Norwegian songs, of which four were later incorporated in Paulli's music for *The Wedding Festival in Hardanger* (Act I, score nos. 1 and 6, and Act II, score no. 11). This seems to indicate that this manuscript represents Paulli's compilation of those Norwegian folk tunes and songs which he originally planned to make use of in his score for this ballet.

Orchestral score. Ms. Autograph (by H. S. Paulli). Brown and black ink. 1 vol. 186 pp. (26 × 37 cm with minor variants)
266./Brudefærden/i Hardanger./Partitur
Signed and dated (on p. 186): 'HSPaulli d: 14 Februar 1853.'
[DKKk, C II, 119 (KTB 266)

Répétiteur's copy. Ms. Autograph (by H. S. Paulli). Brown and black ink. 1 vol. 76 pp. of which two are blank (33,2 × 24,3 cm with minor variants)
Brudefærden/i/Hardanger./Ballet i to Akter/af/August Bournonville./1853.
Unsigned and dated (on the title page): '1853.'
[DKKk; MA ms 2963 (KTB 266)
This répétiteur's copy contains Bournonville's autographed choreographic notes (written with brown ink). Apart from the *Halling* dance in Act II (score no. 15) they include detailed descriptions of the choreography, the mime, and the dramatic action throughout the ballet.

Parts. Ms. Copy. 33 vol.
4 vl I, 3 vl II, 2 vla, 4 vlc e cb, fl 1/2, ob 1/2, cl 1/2, fag 1/2, cor 1/2, tr 1/2, trb 1/2/3, timp, gr cassa, piatti, tri, arpa.
Unsigned and undated [1853]
[DKKk; KTB 266

Piano score (excerpts). Ms. Autograph (by H. S. Paulli). Black ink. 4 pp. (27 × 38 cm)
[Untitled]
Signed (on p. 1): 'H. S. Paulli.', undated [c.1853]
[DKKk; C II, 10 (H. S. Paullis Efterladte mss. II)
This (untitled) autographed piano score contains nine excerpts of Paulli's music for *The Wedding Festival in Hardanger* and was most probably made for publishing purposes.

Other sources:

Lithograph with applied water colours after a drawing of E. Lehmann (23,7 × 18,5 cm)
Det Kongl. Theater./Brudefærden
Signed (in print): 'E. Lehmann del/J. W. Tegner & [J. A.] Kittendorff's Lith. Inst.', undated [c.1853 or later]

[DKKt; Balletafdelingen (permanent udstilling)
This lithograph shows the opening mime scene in Act I (score no. 1) between the characters *Ragnhild*, *Guri*, and *Halvor*.

Costume drawing by E. Lehmann. Pencil and water colours (25 × 18 cm)
No. 2/[...]/Kirsti
Unsigned and undated [c.1853]
[Private collection (Copenhagen)
This drawing show the second costume worn by *Kirsti* in Act II of *The Wedding Festival in Hardanger* (performed by P. Fredstrup).

Printed sources:

Printed scenario. 1 vol. 15 pp. (19,6 × 12,8 cm)
Brudefærden i Hardanger./Ballet i to Akter/af/August Bournonville./Musiken af H. Paulli./Decorationerne af Christensen og Lund./Costumerne tegnede af E. Lehmann.
Kjøbenhavn, J. H. Schubothe/Bianco Luno, 1853.
[DKKk; 17, – 174 8°
A second, almost identical scenario was published by J. H. Schubothe and Græbes Bogtrykkeri at about the same time as this scenario.

10.3.1853
Dances for an artists' carnival (Dandse ne til Kunsterkarnevallet) (the Casino Theatre).
In his diary Bournonville noted about his involvement in the organisation of this masked ball, arranged by the association of younger artists in Copenhagen named *Den yngre Kunstnerforening*:

15.2. and 21.2.1853: 'Møde i Kunstforeningen'
27.2.: 'Kunstner-Carnevals Møde'
2.3.: 'Møde i den yngre Kunstnerforening for at træffe en Aftale om Carnavalet. – Flouhed og Uvillighed'
5.3.: 'Maskerade=Forberedelser'
6.3.: 'Den største Deel af Dagen beskjæftiget med Kunstnercarnavalet'
7.3.: 'Quadrille=Prøve for 42 Par'
9.3.: 'Quadrille-Prøve'
10.3.: 'Hele Formiddagen beskjæftiget med Carnavalet. Prøve i Casino. Alle tre Pigebørn vare med. Kl 8 kjørte vi derhen [...] Carnavalet var særdeles livligt – circa 2000 Mennesker. Scene paa Theatret (Pulcinella og Arlecchino). Parade af Do Dulcimara... Quadrille med Sang og Polka i tre Quadriller, derpaa blev Dandsen almindelig, der var en Masse ÿndige Damer og Stemningen fortreffelig. En Schnitzelbank blev sungen og en Tombola med sang af [H. P.] Holst'.

According to the poster 12, dances were performed at this ball:

Nr. 1. Vals, Nr. 2. Galop, Nr. 3. Polka & Polka-Mazurka, No. 4. Quadrille, Nr. 5. Vals, Nr. 6. Polka & Polka-Mazurka, Nr. 7. Galop, Nr. 8. Quadrille, Nr. 9. Vals, Nr. 10. Polka & Polka-Mazurka, Nr. 11. Galop, Nr. 12. Vals.

No musical sources for these dances have yet been traced.

14.3.1853
Pas de deux (uncredited) performed by W. Funck and S. Price.
This (uncredited) dance is perhaps identical with one of the two earlier (uncredited) *Pas de deux* performed on 11.9.1852 (by S. Lund and S. Price) and on 29.11.1852 (by W. Funck and J. Rostock). Another possible identification of the dance is the (uncredited) *Pas de deux* performed by S. Lund and S.

Price on 24.4.1851. The *Pas de deux* was given only once in 1853. It is not possible to identify the dance any further.

5.4.1853
A song and a dance written and choreographed for the celebration of the rentrée of the actress, Johanne Louise Heiberg, **performed by the singer J. E. Egense and members of the Royal Danish Ballet in a rehearsal studio of the ballet school in Ny Vestergade (known as 'Conservatoriet').**
In his diary Bournonville noted about this song and dance, which were created on the occasion of the *rentrée* of the celebrated actress, J. L. Heiberg, after her long illness in the winter of 1852–53:

30.3.1853: 'I Theatret. Fru Heibergs første Optrædelse efter hendes Sygdom. Hun blev modtaget med Blomsterregn og hilset med Jubel.'
31.3.: 'Løbet endeel i Anledning af et Balproject til Ære for Fru Heiberg, men strandede paa [N. P.] Nielsen og den Clique, der hører til.'
2.4.: 'componeret en lille Ting til fru Heibergs Modtagelse'
3.4.: 'Prøve paa Damerne af en Modtagelse af Fru Heiberg 12–2. Møde hos Heibergs. Møde bestemt til tirsd. Kl 1'
4.4.: 'besørget Visen i Trykkeriet'
5.4.: 'Modtagelse og Hilsen til Fru Heiberg i Ballet-Conservatoriet Kl 1. Hele Personalet ([F.] Hoppe undtagen) modtog hende med en Sang og en Dands som jeg havde componeret og som gjorde et dybt Indtryk baade paa hende og Manden. Der blev drukket Chokolade og dandset lidt. Det hele var forbi Kl 2 1/2'

Bournonville's song (which was performed by the singer J. E. Egense) was many years later published in Heiberg's memoirs, entitled *Et Liv gjenoplevet i Erindringen*. It there reads:

Velkommen i sin Hal dig byder
Den yngste af de Søstre ni.
Thi Kjærlighed og Poesi,
igjennem Dandsens Tone lyder:
See Vaarens Blomst udfolder sig
Med Sundhedsglød paa dine Kinder!
En Krands af venlige Kjærminder
I Rhytmers Leg vi flette dig.

Blandt Alfers lyse Regioner,
I Laurens By, din Vugge stod,
Og gjerne rører sig din Fod
Alt til de velbekendte Toner.
Musiken Dig paa Armen bar,
Nu kan Du selv en Lyra stemme,
Men dog du aldrig vil forglemme
Den Melodi, du dandset har.

Saa mangt et Billed for vor Øie
Fremtryller du ved Ordets Magt,
Og i dit stumme Spil er lagt
En Toneverden fra det høie;
Men hvor du end os fører hen,
Blandt Nordens Iis, til sydens Dale,
Dit Ord er Sang, din Dands er Tale,
Geniet følger dig som Ven.

En Guddom skærmer dine dage
Paa Kunstens farefulde Vei
Og strøer den med Forglemmigei,
Naar glad og stolt du seer tilbage.
Dog bliv hos os en liden Stund
Og lyt til Alfechorets Stemme;
'At du vor Musa ei vil glemme',
Vi gjerne hører af din Mund.'

This text (the original print of which is now in DKKk, call no. NKS 3285, 4°, 8, læg, 'Trykte Digte') was set to H. Rung's melody for a song that Heiberg had performed 5 years earlier when performing the rôle of *Maritana* in A. D'Ennery's and P. Dumanoir's five-act drama *Don César de Bazan* (premièred at Copenhagen's Royal Theatre on 30.11.1848).

Moreover, according to Heiberg's memoirs, the music for the dance also choreographed by Bournonville for this occasion was that of a solo variation in C. Schall's and V. Galeotti's two-act comic ballet *The Mountaineers, or The Children and the Mirror (Biergbeboerne eller Börnene og Speilet)* from 23.9.1802. In that ballet Heiberg had made her début as a dancer at the tender age of eleven when she performed a solo on 23.1.1824 created especially for her.

The répétiteur's copy and the set of parts for Schall's and Galeotti's ballet *The Mountaineers, or The Children and the Mirror* are now in DKKk (call no. KTB 1015, but originally KTB 165).

14.5.–1.7.1853
Thirty-three private drama lessons **for the students of the Norwegian Drama School.**
In his diary Bournonville noted about the series of private drama lessons which he taught to the students of the Norwegian Drama School in Christiania (Oslo) during the summer of 1853:

14.5.1853: 'modtaget Elver'
17.5.: 'ventet Elever'
18.5.: 'tegnet elever'
20.5.–30.6.: [Thirty-three] 'Lectioner' [given mainly between 'Kl. 5–7 1/2']
1.7.: 'præsenteret Elverne af den norske dramatiske Skole [...] pakket, takket Gud for en lykkelig Reise og Ophold endskjøndt Fortjensten har været forholdsmæssig ringe, i det Hele en Netto-Beholdning af 150 rb! men jeg er dog fornøiet'.

The lessons took place in a rented apartment in Nedre Slotsgade no. 1.

On 15.6.1853 Bournonville also inserted an advertisement in the Christiania papers announcing his intention to give a 'Valse-Kursus for Herrer' which was planned to last for three weeks. This course, however, was cancelled because, as Bournonville puts it in his diary on the same day: 'Intet Herrecursus formedelst total Mangel paa Tegning'.

9.6.1853
Norwegian Spring Dance (Norsk Springdands) **performed by Julius Price and A. Price (the Court Theatre).**
This performance represents the second and last staging at the Court Theatre of Bournonville's *Norwegian Spring Dance* from his one-act ballet *Old Memories, or A Magic Lantern* (see 18.12.1848 and 21.11.1849). It was this year performed as part of a charity performance for the actors Adolph and James Price. Bournonville did not attend the performance because of a trip to Norway during the months of May, June, and July 1853. No separate musical sources dating from the performance at the Court Theatre this year have yet been traced. This seems to indicate that the dance was given using the same musical material as when it was mounted for the first time at the Court Theatre on 21.11.1849 (now in DKKk, call nos. MA ms 2625 and KTB 1027).

10.10.1853

Varsovienne (Varsoviana).

According to a note in his diary on this day (reading: 'Varsoviana vist til hele Personalet') Bournonville directed a rehearsal for all members of Copenhagen's Royal Ballet during which he taught the newest of ballroom dances of the time, the *Varsovienne*. Moreover, according to his previous correspondence with the French choreographer, A. Saint-Léon, Bournonville had received a complete choreographic description of it a few weeks earlier from this French colleague of his. The dance was most probably taught in preparation for a ball given for the members of Copenhagen's Royal Ballet on 8.11.1853. This ball took place in the main ballet rehearsal room in Ny Vestergade (also known as 'Conservatoriet'). No musical sources for the *Varsovienne* have yet been traced.

19.10.1853

Waldemar.

The 1853 Copenhagen restaging of Bournonville's four-act romantic ballet *Waldemar* (*see* 28.10.1835) represents his first, thoroughly revised production of this work. It was this year reduced to three acts and mounted with W. Funck and C. Kellermann in the leading rôles as *Waldemar* and *Astrid*. According to the 1853 répétiteur's copy, the major changes occurred in the ballet's first act, in which score nos. 8–11 were completely omitted.

Moreover, a new *Pas de six* (danced by F. Hoppe, S. Lund, J. Price, P. Fredstrup, J. Rostock, and S. Price) was incorporated in Act I (score no. 5) where it replaced Bournonville's original *Pas de cinq*. The music for this new dance was the same as that of the original *Pas de cinq* except for an additional solo variation (performed by Juliette Price), which was borrowed from J. F. Fröhlich's earlier score to Bournonville's ballet in six tableaux *Raphael* (*see* 30.5.1845). In that ballet it was part of the *Pas de trois* divertissement in the third tableau (score no. 13). Fröhlich's music for this solo was, in turn, originally composed for his and Bournonville's even earlier four-act romantic ballet *The Childhood of Erik Menved* (*see* 12.1.1843), in which it was performed as part of the Act II *Pas de deux* (score no. 16).

Another significant change in Bournonville's 1853 restaging of *Waldemar* regards the *Grand solo variation* performed by *Astrid* in Act I (score no. 10). According to a pencilled note in Act II (p. 227) of Fröhlich's autographed score for *Waldemar* (reading: 'her springes tilbage til Pag 87'), this solo seems to have been omitted from the first act in 1853 and instead interpolated as a solo variation in the Act II *Pas de deux*. This theory is supported by a separate set of parts for this dance, which was reorchestrated by E. Helsted and clearly differs from Fröhlich's original 1835 version of it by having a new intrada of seven bars (presumably composed and added by Helsted).

Finally, according to the 1853 répétiteur's copy for *Waldemar* the original *Torch Dance (Fakkeldands)* in Act II was omitted this year and replaced by another *Torch Dance*. It was based on selected excerpts borowed from Bournonville's three-act ballet *The Childhood of Erik Menved*, namely parts of N. C. Bochsa's music for Act I (score no. 1) and Fröhlich's *Finale* in Act III (score no. 23). This new version of the *Torch Dance* was incorporated in Act II of *Waldemar*, where it was listed as score no. '17½' and was since then known as 'Riberhus March'. However, according to some later notes in the 1853 répétiteur's copy, Fröhlich's original 1835 *Torch Dance* seems to have been reinstated in *Waldemar* at its fourth staging in Copenhagen on 21.11.1866.

In his diary Bournonville noted about the revised 1853 version of *Waldemar*:

5.8.1853: 'Brev fra [J. L.] Heiberg om Saisonens Udsættelse til den 1.ste October'
2.9. and 5.9.: 'Prøve paa Waldemar'
8.9.: 'Prøve paa Waldemar med Choret'
24.9.: 'Costume Prøve paa Waldemar'
25.9.: 'Costume=Møde hos Directionen. Alt afgjort til Fordeel for Balletten der skal gaae den 19.e October'
27.9.: 'Prøve paa Waldemar'
28.9. and 1.10.: 'Prøve paa Theatret paa Waldemar'
3.10.: 'Prøve paa Rollerne til Waldemar'
4.10.: 'Prøve paa Dandsene til Waldemar'
5.10.: 'stor Arrangementsprøve paa Theatret'
7.10.: 'omskrevet Programmet til Waldemar [...] Prøve paa Dandsene'
11.10.: 'Prøve paa Waldemar'
12.10.: 'Stor Prøve paa Waldemar de to Akter som gik særdeles godt, jeg kom temmelig fatigueret hjem'
13.10.: 'Kl 10 paa Theatret i det Haab at kunde holde min Prøve paa Waldemar tredie Akt, men jeg maatte kjøre hjem igjen og overlade den til [L.] Gade og [H. C. J.] Fredstrup'
16.10.: 'Prøve paa Waldemar'
17.10.: 'Generalprøve paa Waldemar. Det gik meget godt'
19.10: 'Foreberedelser til Balletten. Ondt i Foden. Maskinprøve Kl 4½. Balletten gik godt og gjorde overordentlig Lykke; min Fod blev rask af bare Glæde'.

Less than a year after the revised 1853 staging of *Waldemar* Bournonville noted about it in his diary on 21.9.1854:

'Waldemar i Theatret (Nu begynder den at trætte mig)'.

The 1853 production received 19 performances, the last of which was given on 21.5.1855.

Autograph sources:

Production note. Ms. Autograph. Brown ink. 1 p. $(23,9 \times 22,8$ cm)
Drabanter
Unsigned and undated [early 1850s]
[DKKkt; F.M. (Ballet)]

Production note. Ms. Autograph. Black ink. 2 pp. $(36,3 \times 22,8$ cm)
Personliste til Balletten Waldemar.
Unsigned and undated [1853]
[DKKkt; F.M. (Ballet)]

Production note. Ms. Autograph. Black ink. 4 pp. $(32,6 \times 20$ cm)
Bönder
Signed and dated: '24.Sept. 1853'
[DKKkt; F.M. (Ballet)]

Production note. Ms. Autograph. Black ink. 1 p. $(22,2 \times 17,4$ cm)
Drabantdragterne:
Signed and dated: 'd 25 Sept 1853'
[DKKkt; F.M. (Ballet)]

Musical sources:

Fröhlich's autographed orchestral score for *Waldemar* is now in DKKk (call no. C II, 107 (KTB 297)).

Répétiteur's copy. Ms. Copy. Brown and black ink. 1 vol. 166 pp. (32,2 × 23,8 cm with minor variants)
B. 297/1/'Valdemar'/[...]/Waldemar/den Förste/Ballet i 4 Acter / af/August Bournonville/Musikken af F. Fröhlich.
Unsigned and undated [1853]
[DKKk; MA ms 2994 (KTB 297 (2))]
This répétiteur's copy was beyond doubt used for all performances of *Waldemar* given between 1853 and 1877. This is clear from the volume's original division in three acts which dates it beyond any doubt to Bournonville's 1853 three-act version. Later the same volume was revised into four acts in connection with the ballet's third restaging on 21.11.1866. The répétiteur's copy contains Bournonville's autographed choreographic notes (written with brown ink) in the music for the Act I *Pas de six* (score no. 5), while his other autographed notes describe the dramatic action in Act I, (score no. 7). Moreover, his autographed choreographic numbers (written with brown ink) are included throughout the score except for Act III (score nos. 27–32). They most probably refer to his (not yet traced) separate choreographic notation of the entire ballet, which was made (according to his diary) between 27.8. and 27.9.1866. Finally, several pencilled metronome markings are inserted throughout the volume, indicating the exact tempi of most of the dances.

Orchestral score (the Act I *Grand solo variation*). Ms. Autograph (by E. Helsted). Brown ink. 12 pp. (35,1 × 26,3 cm)
Af Balletten 'Waldemar'
Unsigned and undated [1853?]
[DKKk; MA ms 2720 (KTB 1052 (2)]
This autographed orchestral score contains the complete music for the *Grand solo variation* in Act I of *Waldemar* (performed by *Astrid*). It is reorchestrated by E. Helsted and seems to have been incorporated in Act II of the 1853 restaging.

Répétiteur's copy (the Act I *Grand solo variation*). Ms. Copy. Brown ink. 12 pp. of which one is blank (34,4 × 24,5 cm)
Af Balletten Valdemar
Unsigned and undated [1853?]
[DKKk; MA ms 2718 (KTB 1052 (2))]
This répétiteur's copy contains the complete music for the *Grand solo variation* in Act I of *Waldemar* (performed by *Astrid*). It seems to have been incorporated in Act II of the 1853 restaging.

Part for the vlc princ (the Act I *Grand solo variation*). Ms. Autograph (by E. Helsted). Brown ink. 4 pp. of which one is blank (34,6 × 26,7 cm)
Violoncello Solo til Pas de deux af Waldemar.
Unsigned and undated [1853?]
[DKKk; MA ms 2719 (KTB 1052 (2))]
The title of this part proves beyond doubt that Helsted's reorchestration of the *Grand solo variation* from Act I of *Waldemar* was incorporated at a later stage in the Act II *Pas de deux* of the same ballet.

Parts (the Act I *Grand solo variation*, incomplete). Ms. Copy. 11 vol. vl princ, vl I, vl II, vla, vlc e cb, fl, cl 1/2, fag, cor 1/2.
Unsigned and undated [1853?]
[DKKk; KTB 1052 (2)]
This (incomplete) set of parts contains the complete music for the *Grand solo variation* in Act I of *Waldemar* (performed by *Astrid*). It is reorchestrated by E. Helsted and seems to have been incorporated in Act II of the 1853 restaging. In the handwritten catalogue of the music archive at Copenhagen's Royal Theatre the parts were originally entitled 'Indlæg til Waldemar' and listed under the call. no. '218'.

Printed sources:

Printed scenario. 1 vol. 15 pp. (19 × 12 cm)
Valdemar./Romantisk Ballet i 3 Acter/af/August Bournonville./ Musikken af Fr. Fröhlich/[...]/paany indstuderet og sat i Scenen den 19de October 1853.
Kjøbenhavn, J. H. Schubothe and Bianco Luno, 1853.
[DKKk; 17, – 172 8°

20.11.1853
La Fiancée (Bruden).
The 1853 Copenhagen restaging of D.-F.-E. Auber's three-act comic opera (premièred at l'Opéra Comique in Paris on 10.1.1829, and first performed in Copenhagen on 22.4. 1831) was listed erroneously by Bournonville under the year of 1854 in his handwritten survey of his stagings of operas and plays, written c.1872 (*see* Additional Sources). This is clear from his other notes in his diary according to which the 1853 production of *La Fiancée* represents the first time he ever mounted the dances of this work. They included two numbers as follows:

(1) A *Contredanse* (or *Quadrille*) in the opening scene of Act II (score no. 7), danced by four couples during the chorus «Sous ce riant feuillage sous ces ombrages frais un jour de mariage que la danse a d'attraits».
(2) A *Waltz* (or *Tyrolienne*) in the same act, performed by six couples during the chorus «Montagnard ou berger votre sort peut changer».

These dances were restaged by Bournonville for the second time, without any significant changes, on 16.1.1855. Moreover, on 30.10.1857 he included *La Fiancée* in a list of projected opera stagings that he wrote on this day for the 1857–58 and 1858–59 seasons. That project was carried out on 7.10.1858, when Auber's complete opera was mounted under his general supervision for the first time. *La Fiancée* was restaged for the fourth and last time by Bournonville on 28.12.1873, but then with a completely new mise-en-scène and a partially revised choreography.

About the 1853 production he noted in his diary on 16.11. 1853:

'Componeret Dands til Bruden [...] Prøve paa Bruden [...] Prøve paa Theatret (Bruden)'.

Bournonville did not attend the opening night.

The 1853 staging received 6 performances, the last of which was given on 12.12.1853.

Musical sources:

Printed orchestral score with manuscript insertions. 2 vol. Act I 244 pp. of which three are blank, Act II–III 268 pp. of which two are blank (32,9 × 25,9 cm)
LA FIANCÉE/Opéra Comique/en trois actes/[...]/Musique de D. F. E. Auber
Paris, E. Troupenas, pl. no. 309 [1829]
[DKKk; U 6 (KTA 281)]
This printed orchestral score was used for all performances of *La Fiancée* at Copenhagen's Royal Theatre after its première there on 22.4.1831 and throughout Bournonville's lifetime. The music for the two dances in Act II are included on pp. '240–260' and pp. '264–287' respectively.

Répétiteur's copy. Ms. Copy. Brown ink. 1 vol. 8 pp. (32,6 × 23 cm)
A 281./Dandsen i/Bruden./52/[...]/Repetiteur Parti/til/Bruden af Auber
Unsigned and undated [1831]
[DKKk; MA ms 3059 (KTA 281)]
This répétiteur's copy dates from the 1831 Copenhagen première of *La Fiancée* and was used for all later performances of it during Bournonville's lifetime. It contains the music for the *Contredanse* (or *Quadrille*) in Act II (score no. 7), and the *Waltz* (or *Tyrolienne*) performed in the same act. Moreover, Bournonville's autographed choreographic notes (written with brown ink) are included for both of these dances. According to his diary they were most likely written on

16.11.1853. Furthermore, his other autographed choreographic numbers ('1–16' and '1–12', written with brown ink) clearly refer to the much later separate choreographic notation that he made on 13.12.1873 in preparation for his last restaging of Auber's opera on 28.12.1873. According to these notations the *Quadrille* was that year performed by eight couples, and the *Tyrolienne* by six couples who were joined in the end by six other couples of supernumeraries.

Parts. Ms. Copy. 34 vol.
4 vl I, 3 vl II, 2 vla, 4 vlc e cb, fl picc, fl 1/2, ob 1/2, cl 1/2, fag 1/2, cor 1/2/3/4, tr 1/2, trb 1/2/3, timp, gr cassa, tri. 43 vocal parts.
Unsigned and undated [1831]
[DKKk; KTA 281]
This set of parts dates from the 1831 Copenhagen première of *La Fiancée* and was used for all performances of it there throughout Bournonville's lifetime.

1854

8.1.1854
Pas des trois cousines performed by Juliette Price, J. Rostock, and S. Price.
This performance represents Bournonville's second staging at Copenhagen's Royal Theatre of his *Pas des trois cousines* (*see* 20.5.1848), mounted this year with J. Rostock replacing A. Price. In his diary he listed only one rehearsal (on 7.1.1854) and noted about the dance on the opening night:

'Pricerne og Rostock dandsede le pas des trois Cousins, Juliette var fortreffelig'.

Between 2.10.1854 and 24.9.1861 P. Fredstrup alternated with J. Rostock in this dance.

23.1.1854
Pas de trois (uncredited) performed by S. Lund, P. Fredstrup, and J. Rostock.
This (uncredited) dance is most probably identical with the (uncredited) *Pas de trois* performed exactly one year before by the same three dancers on 23.1.1853 and, in turn, is perhaps identical with Bournonville's *Pas de trois* in Act I (score no. 5) of his Danish version of J. Aumer's three-act pantomimic ballet *La Somnambule, ou l'Arrivée d'un nouveau seigneur* (*see* 21.9.1829). The *Pas de trois* was given only once in 1854. It is not possible to identify the dance any further.

28.2.1854
A Procession and two Quadrilles choreographed for the Royal Masked Ball given for Friedrich Wilhelm of Hesse-Cassel (Et Optog, en Mousquetair=Quadrille, og en Polka Quadrille ved Maskeraden for Frederik Wilhelm af Hessen) performed at the Copenhagen residence of the Heir presumptive, Prince Frederik Ferdinand.
In his diary Bournonville noted about the dances he choreographed for this royal masked ball:

18.2.1854: 'Möde hos Pr. Frederik [Wilhelm] af Hessen'
20.2.: 'Møde hos Pr. Ferdinand'
21.2.: 'Conference [...] hos Pr. Ferdinand'
22.2.: 'om Aftenen Quadrille prøve hos Prinds Ferdinand'
23.2.: 'Quadrilleprøve hos Prinds Frederik [Wilhelm af Hessen]'
25.2.: 'Prøve fra 2–4 hos Prinds Frederik [Wilhelm af Hessen] [...]

og Prøve hos Prinds Ferdinand 8 til 10 1/2. Begge Quadriller færdige, men meget træt'
27.2.: 'Prøve hos begge Prindserne [...] Prøve hos Arveprindsen, det gik udmærket godt. Brodersen assisterede'
28.2.: 'Forberedelser til Festen [...] Møde hos Arveprindsen, hvor Optoget og Quadriller blev prøvet for Enkedronningen [i.e. Queen Caroline Amalie of Denmark], derpaa stor Maskerade hos Prinds Frederik [Wilhelm af Hessen] hvor Alt gik paa det splendideste til. Kl 9 3/4 begyndte Optoget og der dandsedes En Mousquetaire= Quadrille og en Polka ditto af <u>min</u> Composition med Musik af Lumbÿe. I den første figurerede Prinds Christian af Danmark [i.e. the later King Christian IX] med Gemalinde og Prinds Frederik [Wilhelm af Hessen] med Gemalinde tilligemed 12 andre Herrer og Damer. I den Anden var 16 rigtklædte Par. Dernæst en lille Farce udført af Pr: Ferdinand og Kammerherre G: Sehested, som Dame og Herre. Det Hele gik udmærket og gjorde stor Lÿkke. Ballet fortsatte. Tafflet serveredes Kl. 1 og jeg tog hjem Kl. 1½ '.

The music by H. C. Lumbye employed by Bournonville for his dances at this ball was most probably from older works by this composer.

3.3.1854
Pas de deux (uncredited) performed by S. Lund and S. Price.
This (uncredited) dance is most likely identical with the (uncredited) *Pas de deux* performed by the same dancers on 24.4.1851. That dance, in turn, is probably identical with F.-M.-A. Venua's *Pas de deux*, originally performed in J. L. Heiberg's three-act play *Princess Isabella, or Three Nights at the Court* (*see* 29.10.1829). The *Pas de deux* was given twice by Lund and S. Price, the last time on 11.3.1854. It is not possible to identify the dance any further.

19.3.1854
A new Quadrille choreograped for and performed by Bournonville's private dance students.
During the winter of 1853–54 Bournonville gave a series of private lessons in ballroom dances for three groups of pupils. They took place in the studio of the Royal Danish Ballet Schoolst in Ny Vestergade (also known as 'Conservatoriet') and were concluded by two presentations on 17.3. and 19.3. 1854. In his diary Bournonville noted about the last four lessons and the new *Quadrille* that he choreographed for this occasion:

14.3.1854: 'Lection 5–8 i Conservatoriet for 3 Hold Elever og Indstudering af en nÿ Quadrille'
15.3.: 'Lection 1–3 og 5–7'
17.3.: 'Lection 2–3 og Præsentation af de mindre Hold fra 5–7, særdeles tilfredsstillende'
18.3.: 'Lection og Prøve for <u>mine større Hold</u>'
19.3.: 'præsenteret de større Hold med stort Bifald, Menuet, Quadrille &c.'.

No musical sources for this *Quadrille* have yet been traced.

20.3.1854
A Folk Tale (Et Folkesagn).
According to Bournonville's own account in his memoirs *My Theatre Life* (pp. 205–221), this three-act romantic ballet was drawn from inspirations received from his reading of J. M. Thiele's collection of *Danmarks Folkesagn* (first published in 1818–1823, with a 2nd edition in 2 vols. published by C. A.

Reitzel in 1843). Among this collection of popular Danish tales and legends several situations and characters from the legends, named *Marbierg* (vol. I), *Alterbægeret i Vigersted Kirke* (vol. II), *Troldfolket i Fibjerg Bakke* (vol. I), *Fru Birthe* (vol. I), *Ellepigerne* (vol. II), *Hagbro* (vol. II), *Den gamle Brud* (vol. II), *Bondevette* (vol. II), and *Gillesbierg* (vol. II) can thus be clearly retraced in Bournonville's ballet. Moreover, the tale named *Alterbægere II* (vol. II) seems to have provided him with the main inspiration for the ballet's second act depicting the diabolic underworld of the trolls.

According to the posters the ballet's *Pas de quatre* divertissement in the Act III *Finale* (score no. 20) was originally performed by a man and three women (dressed a gipsies), but was revised into a *Pas de cinq* on 5.10.1858 (then danced by a man and four women).

The ballet's music is composed by N. W. Gade (Act I and III) and I. P. E. Hartmann (Act II). Gade's *Bridal Waltz (Brudevals)* in the Act III *Finale* (score no. 20) soon became one of this composer's most popular tunes. Thus, only three years after the première of *A Folk Tale* this dance tune had become so widely known that it was also incorporated as a wedding song (entitled «Medens vort Hjærte frydefuldt slaar») in J. C. Hostrup's immensely popular one-act vaudeville *A Family Dispute, or The Strange Year (Familietvist eller Det mærkværdige Aar)*, premièred at Copenhagen's Folketheatret on 7.10.1857.

Furthermore, a later score based on Hartmann's and Gade's music was arranged on 26.12.1892 by N. Hansen for a five-act dramatisation of Bournonville's ballet, written by E. Collin, A. Ipsen, and V. Østergaard. It, too, was premièred at Folketheatret, but was soon after also mounted at several other theatres in Copenhagen and the Danish provinces.

Three years after the ballet's Copenhagen première Bournonville proposed a Swedish production of *A Folk Tale* in a letter written to the theatre management of Stockholm's Royal Theatre on 15.6.1857 (now in SSdt). This project was planned to be carried out during the spring of 1859, but did not find approval in Stockholm, and to Bournonville's great disappointment the ballet was never mounted outside Denmark in his lifetime.

In Copenhagen *A Folk Tale* was restaged 4 times under his personal supervision (*see* 20.9.1867, 3.4.1871, 1.6.1874, and 3.11.1877). Each of these productions was mounted in a slightly revised version, with partially rechoreographed dances.

In his diary Bournonville noted about the ballet's creation and the first three performances in 1854:

8.7.1853: 'Tilbragt Dagen med at læse, spadsere, skrive og tænke paa min nÿ Ballet'
9.7. and 10.7.: 'læst og skrevet'
11.7.: 'Læst og skrevet. Kjørt med Omnibus til Jægersborg Allé hvor Prof. H. P. Holst boer, tilbragt en yndig Dag med Spadseren i Charlottenlund og Dyrehaugen, mødt megen Venlighed'
14.7.: 'Skrevet paa en nÿ Ballet Et Folkesagn [...] da jeg kom hjem skrev jeg Balletten færdig'
15.7.: 'Skrevet paa min nÿ Ballet'
16.7.: 'hjem, skrevet. Balletten færdig'
29.7: 'reenskrevet paa Et Folkesagn og Brev til [J. L] Heiberg'
30.7.: 'færdigskrevet Et Folkesagn'
3.8.: 'besøgt [E.] Helsted (der har været temmelig hårdt angrebet af sin Nÿresten)'

23.8.: 'Brev til [...] Heiberg hvilket [...] ikke blev expederet, da jeg fik Brev fra ham selv med Programmet som han bifaldt'
17.9.: 'arbeidet med [N. W.] Gade 1.ste Gang'
20.9.: 'Brev til Heiberg og [J. G.] Levetzau'
29.9.: 'Musik hos [I. P. E.] Hartmann [...] ([E.] Lehmann Tegning)']
30.9.: 'Musik hos Gade'
10.10.: 'Musik hos Hartmann'
20.10.: 'Musik hos Gade'
22.10.: 'talt med Maleren og faaet Musik hos Hartmann'
23.10.: 'Læst, skrevet, componeret'
26.10.: 'første Indstudering paa min nÿ Ballet 'Et Folkesagn'. Det lover godt – Gud give mig Held dertil!'
27.10.: 'skrevet, componeret'
28.10.: 'Prøve og Indstudering, nÿ Scene'
29.10.: 'Musik hos Gade'
1.11.: 'besøgt [...] Hartmann'
2.11.: 'skrevet, componeret [...] skrevet, componeret'
4.11.: 'lille Prøve paa Et Folkesagn'
5.11.: 'Møde med [T.] Lund og [A. P.] Wedden [...] componeret'
6.11.: 'componeret'
8.11.: 'Musik hos Hartmann'
9.11.: 'Musik med Gade, skrevet og componeret'
10.11.: 'fra 10-12 Indstudering'
11.11.: 'Skrevet og componeret [...] Indstudering'
12.11.: 'Indstudering [...] Aftenen hjemme, componeret'
13.11.: 'componeret'
14.11: 'Componeret [...] og Indstudering [...] componeret og læst'
15.11: 'Indstudering [...] Musik hos Hartmann og Gade'
16.11.: 'hjem og componeret en Time'
17.11.: 'Instudering'
18.11.: 'Componeret, besøgt Hartmann, Indstudering fra 10–12 1/2 [...] componeret og skrevet'
19.11.: 'Componeret [...] og Indstudering; talt med Malerne'
20.11.: 'Componeret [...] Prøve paa 1.ste og det Halve af 2.den Akt af den nÿ Ballet. Vrøvl og Gemenhed af [E.] Stramboe'
22.11.: 'Componeret'
23.11.: 'Musik hos Gade' [...] componeret'
24.11.: 'Musik hos Hartmann'
28.11.: 'Musik hos Gade og Hartmann'
30.11.: 'lille Prøve'
1.12.: 'Hjemme den hele Dag [...] Jeg læste og componerede'
2.12.: 'Musik af Gade'
3.12.: 'Musik af Hartmann'
5.12.: 'Musik hos Gade'
6.12.: 'Indstudering paa Et Folkesagn'
7.12.: 'Prøve paa Et Folkesagn'
8.12.: 'lille Prøve paa Et Folkesagn. Musik hos Gade'
9.12.: 'Componeret [...] Indstudering'
10.12.: 'Prøve med Indstudering. Musik hos Gade [...] Brev og Indstilling til Heiberg. Gud give det Held!'
11.12.: 'componeret'
12.12.: 'Componeret [...] arbeidet med Lehmann'
13.12.: 'Indstudering'
14.12.: 'Prøve'
15.12.: 'besørget adskilligt. Musik, Decorationer &c'
16.12.: 'componeret'
17.12.: 'Indstudering paa Et Folkesagn. Musik hos Gade'
20.12. and 21.12.: 'Prøve paa Et Folkesagn'
23.12.: 'stor Prøve paa Balletten for Hartmann og Gade, der vare henrÿkte. Det Hele gik ÿpperligt og lover godt'
24.12.: 'besøgt Gade. Costumer af Lehmann'
26.12.: 'Lehmann hos os, skrevet og componeret'
27.12. and 28.12.: 'Musik hos Gade'
29.12.: 'skrevet og componeret'
30.12.: 'Prøve og Indstudering. Costume-Mõde'
31.12.: 'Prøve. Costumelister'
2.1.1854: 'Cõstûme Møde med Fru [C. B.] Rûge'
3.1.: 'stor Prøve paa 'Et Folkesagn', min Famillie saae derpaa og vare henrykte. Musik hos Gade'

4.12.: 'componeret og læst'

5.12.: 'besøgt Gade'

9.1.: 'ladet Napoli skjøtte sig selv, skrevet og componeret'

10.1.: 'Prøve paa [...] en Solo til M.d [C.] Kellermann [...] componeret'

11.1.: 'componeret'

12.1.: 'Indstuderet Størstedelen af den nÿ Pas de quatre til [F.] Hoppe, Mme Kellermann, [J.] Rostock og S. Price. Samtale med Theatermalerne, ubehagelig Explication med T. Lund, endte godt, men en god Lection om at bevare min Tunge for Fremtiden'

13.1.: 'indstuderet Dandsen færdig'

14.1.: 'Prøve paa Dandsene til 'Et Folkesagn' [...] Musik hos Gade og Hartmann'

16.1.: 'Prøve paa Dandsene. Costume-Møde'

17.1.: 'større Prøve paa Balletten [...] componeret'

18.1.: 'lille Prøve'

19.1.: 'Indstudering'

20.1.: 'Indstudering. Troldgalloppen færdig'

21.1.: 'indstuderet Slutningsfinalen til Balletten og saaledes fuldendt Compositionen af mit nÿ Arbeide, som Gud forunde mig Lÿkke med!'

23.1.: 'Repetition paa Balletten [...] besørget adskilligt Balletten vedkommende'

24.1.: 'stor Prøve i Conservatoriet paa største Deel af Balletten. Componisterne og H. C. Andersen tilligemed H. E. og Mormor vare tilstede; efter Prøven havde vi et lille Reisegilde som jeg bestod med Café og Viin, der blev dandset og var meget gemÿtligt'

25.1.: 'Forberedelse til en Prøve paa Theatret. Kl 11 Arrangement hele 2.den Akt'

26.1.: 'Prøve paa 1.ste og 2.den Akt af Balletten paa Theatret, det gik meget godt og jeg havde megen Glæde af Maskinmester [A. P.] Weddén'

27.1.: 'besørget adskilligt til Balletten'

28.1.: 'arrangeret med Maskinmesteren'

30.1.: 'Prøve paa Theatret 1.ste og 2.den Akt. Jeg besøgte Gade og Hartmann'

31.1.: 'skrevet og arrangeret'

2.2.: 'Prøve paa 3.die Akt'

3.2.: 'Prøve paa Dandsene'

4.2.: 'Prøve paa 3.die Akt Theatret fra 11 til 2'

6.2.: 'besørget endeel til Balletten, reenskrevet mit Program'

8.2.: 'Prøve paa Theatret paa 3.die Akt'

9.2.: 'Prøve paa alle tre Akter paa Theatret, det gik udmærket godt. [F.] Høedt var der og gjorde nogle Bemærkninger som jeg vil tage ad notam [...] skrevet og udført mit Program'

11.2.: 'lille Prøve paa Balletten'

13.2.: 'lille Prøve. Costume=Arrangement'

14.2.: 'Musikprøve paa Balletten, et deiligt Værk af Gade og Hartmann. Høedt trakterede med Champagne i Parkettet'

15.2.: 'Prøve paa Balletten'

16.2.: 'Stor Prøve paa Balletten med Musik og Requisiter, den gik ÿpperligt'

17.2.: 'Arrangement til Balletten [...] lille Decorationsprøve, forandret Høi'

24.2.: 'besørget endeel til Balletten'

27.2.: 'Decorationsprøve paa Balletten til henved Kl 12'

2.3.: 'Prøve paa 'Et Folkesagn' uden Juliette [Price]'

5.3.: 'besørget adskilligt til Prøven imorgen'

6.3.: 'Prøve paa Et Folkesagn Kl 12, baade Juliette og Petrine [Fredstrup] vare i Gadeklæder og ÿderst angrebne, saa det Hele gik temmelig lunkent. Balletten blev atter sat ud i det Ubestemte og mit Humeur var temmelig tungt'

16.3.: 'stor Prøve paa Et Folkesagn'

17.3.: 'Generalprøve med Costume. Det gik fortreffeligt'

19.3.: 'sidste Prøve paa Balletten 12–2'

20.3.: 'Forberedelser til Forestillingen Iaften. Hele familien i Theatret. 'Et Folkesagn' for første Gang, udmærket udført fra alle Sider og optaget med overordentlig Bifald. Jeg takkede Gud for al hans Godhed imod mig. Der samledes hos mig [A.] Drewsen, Helsted, Prices, Høedt, [J. J. G. P.] Jacobson og tilfældigvis Gundersen, og vi jublede sammen indtil Kl 1''

22.3.: 'Balletten for anden Gang stort Bifald'

25.3.: 'Balletten gik for fuldt Huus og i enhver Henseende fortreffeligt men Publicum i den Grad koldt, at man maa forbande den Stund, da man blev Kunstner i Danmark'

Two years after the première *A Folk Tale* was mounted as part of a special gala performance on 24.9.1856, given on the occasion of a state visit to Denmark by the French Prince Napoléon (the nephew of Napoléon Bonaparte I, and later Napoléon III). Bournonville, who had deliberately chosen this ballet as the most suitable work for that occasion, subsequently wrote a new 'Motif' and 'Analyse du Sujet' for it, stating that the trolls were to be regarded as creatures of Lapp(!) origin. This new 'Analyse du Sujet' was printed on the evening's poster and the performance assessed in his diary as follows:

23.9.1856: 'Om Aftenen Bud at Prinds Napoléon kom i Theatret Imorgen og jeg valgte 'Et Folkesagn' som den Ballet, der var den meest passende. Jeg tilbragte Aftenen indtil 11½ med at skrive et fransk Program'

24.9.: 'reenskrevet det franske Program og besørget det til Trÿkken. Stor Prøve paa 'Et Folkesagn' [...] Forestillingen gik udmærket og Juliette har aldrig dandset saa smukt, som denne Aften'.

The 1854 version of *A Folk Tale* received 64 performances, the last of which was given on 2.2.1864.

Autograph sources:

Manuscript scenario. Ms. Autograph. Brown ink. 4 pp. (21,3 × 13,4 cm)
Et Folkesagn./Romantisk [erased] Ballet i 3 Akter af A Bournonville./Udkast.
Unsigned and undated [Written according to the diary between 8.7. and 15.7.1853]
[DKKk; NKS 3285 4° 2 F]

Manuscript scenario. Ms. Autograph. Brown ink. 1 vol. 8 pp. (21,3 × 13,4 cm)
Et Folkesagn./Ballet i 3 Akter af A Bournonville/(Udkast)
Signed and dated: 'Kbhvn d 16.de Julii 1853.'
[DKKk; NKS 3285 4° 2 F]

Manuscript scenario. Ms. Autograph. Brown ink. 1 vol. 15 pp. (21 × 13,5 cm)
Et Folkesagn./Ballet i tre Akter/af/August Bournonville/1853.
Signed and dated: 'Kbhvn d. 16.de Julii 1853.'
[DKKk; NKS 3285 4° 2 F]

Production note. Ms. Autograph. Black ink. 2 pp. (35,2 × 21,9 cm)
Det mandlige Costume til Et Folkesagn/Ballet i tre Akter
Signed and dated: 'den 29.de Decbr 1853'
[DKKkt; F.M. (Ballet)]

Manuscript scenario. Ms. Autograph. Brown ink. 1 vol. 12 pp. (27,1 × 21,1 cm)
'Et Folkesagn'./ Ballet i tre Akter af August Bournonville./Musiken componeret af Gade og Hartmann./Decorationerne af Dhrr. Christensen og Lund. (Costümet tegnet af Edv. Lehmann/(Maskineriet anordnet af Herr Weddén:)/Opfört første Gang den 27.e Februar 1854.
Unsigned and undated [Written according to the diary on 6.2., 9.2., and 24.2.1854]
[DKKk; NKS 3285 4° 2 F]
Bournonville had originally planned the première of *A Folk Tale* to take place on 27.2.1854, hence his date '27. februar 1854' on the title-page of this scenario. As a result of Juliette Price's sudden illness the première was postponed for nearly a month until 20.3.1854.

Musical sources:

Musical draft/Répétiteur's copy. Ms. Autograph (by N. W. Gade). Brown and black ink. 56 pp. of which four are blank (35,5 × 29,5 cm with several variants)
Et Folkesagn./Repetiteurens Parti
Unsigned and undated [Written according to Bournonville's diary between 17.9.1853 and mid-January 1854]
[DKKk; C II, 108 (KTB 274)

This manuscript contains Gade's music for Act I (score nos. 1–3, parts of no. 4, and no. 5), and Act III (score nos. 14–20 except for his *Bridal Waltz*). Although the title indicates that it was written as a répétiteur's copy, the manuscript clearly represents Gade's first compositional drafts for *A Folk Tale*, and was most probably used for the first working sessions between Bournonville and the composer. This theory is supported by the inclusion of Bournonville's pencilled autographed notes indicating his first draft for the choreography of the *Minuet (Menuet)* in Act I (score no. 3).

Moreover, his other autographed notes (written with brown and black ink) describe in fine detail the dramatic action, the mime, and the choreography throughout Act III. Furthermore, Gade's pencilled autographed notes describe (in general terms) the dramatic action throughout his music. Finally, Gade's other (partially smeared) autographed pencilled notes (written on p. 17 after the music for Act I, score no. 5) read: 'Hermed sender jeg Dem Dette – rigtignok for 2 Viol. lidt tarvelige -/Repetiteurpartie. Jeg haaber Det nu er Dem tilpas, hvis ei lad mig da snart vide det./Denne Slutning paa dette Ark maa jeg bede at <u>faae</u>/<u>igjen</u> til at instrumentere efter./Deres hengivne/Niels W. Gade'.

Orchestral score. Ms. Autographs (by N. W. Gade, I. P. E. Hartmann, and V. C. Holm). Brown and black ink. 2 vol. Act I–II 176 pp., Act III 152 pp. of which one is blank (26,8 × 37,5 cm with minor variants)
Et Folkesagn./Ballet af A. Bournonville./Musikken af Hartmann/og/Gade.
Signed and dated (vol. I, p. 82): 'G-A-D-E [music anagram]/21. November 53.', (p. 176) 'I:P:E:Hartmann/d: 9. Februar 1854.', (vol II, p. '327') 'G-A-D-E [music anagram]/Feb: 1854.'
[DKKk; C II, 108 (KTB 274)

The second volume of this orchestral score contains two later music insertions in V. C. Holm's autograph (vol. II, pp. '299–308' and '313–315a'). They replaced at a later stage what in 1854 was Gade's original pp. '123–126' (a solo variation performed by C. Kellermann, and a section danced by two gipsy women). Holm's autographed insertions contain the music for those additional sections which were interpolated in the Act III *Pas de quatre* (score no. 20) when this dance was revised by Bournonville into a *Pas de sept* on 20.9.1867 (then danced by three men and four women). The fact that these two later additions are both written by Holm seems to indicate they were at least orchestrated and perhaps also composed by him. This theory is supported by the fact that in none of the later printed piano scores of *A Folk Tale* (published between Bournonville's 1867 restaging and well into the next century) are these new insertions included. Subsequently, they have never officially been credited as music actually composed by Gade.

Moreover, in a répétiteur's copy for *A Folk Tale* that was written some time in the mid-1850s (*see* 15.6.1857), the new insertions are described by Bournonville (on pp. 77 and 80) through his notes written at a later stage for his musical collaborator of that time and without any explicit mentioning of Gade's name. These notes read: '<u>NB</u> Her ønskes en munter 6/8 i fire Dele (afvexlende <u>Forte</u> og <u>Pi-</u><u>ano</u>) med en rask Slutning. Det Hele i A dur med de efter Componistens Skjön nødvendige Overgange. Derpaa gaaes ind til Tempo di Marcia <u>D Dur</u> (Nr. 18.) pag 79. [...] × NB × Her kommer Tempo primo alla Polacca No. 20 pag. 77, som da gaaer umiddelbar ind til <u>Coda</u>'en der ønskes repeteret som betegnet staaer nemlig efter de förste 16 Takter og da videre indtil Slutningen, der naaes fuldkommen <u>oplöst</u>, hvorimod Overgangen til Walsen maa staae særskildt'.

Répétiteur's Copy (incomplete). Ms. Copy. Brown and black ink. 1 vol. 126 pp. of which two are blank (33,7 × 25 cm with minor variants)

Et Folkesagn./Ballet i 3 Akter/af/August Bournonville/Musiken af Gade & Hartmann./1854.
Unsigned and dated (on p. 1): '1854.'
[DKKk; MA ms 2968 (KTB 274 (1))

This 1854 répétiteur's copy contains Bournonville's autographed pencilled notes, which describe the dramatic action, the mime, and the choreography for Act I, score nos. 1 and 2 (the *Reel*), no. 5 (the *Elf maidens' dance*), no. 9 (*Hilda's dream*), and no. 10. Moreover, his other autographed notes (written with brown ink) describe in fine detail the mime and the choreography for Act I, score no. 2 (the *Peasant Dance*), Act II, score no. 10–12, and Act III, score nos. 14–15. According to his diary they were most probably written between late October 1853 and 21.1.1854. Furthermore, his autographed choreographic numbers ('1–7' and '1–4', written with brown ink) are inserted in the music for the two solo variations of *Hilda* in Act II, score no. 12 (pp. 51–55). They refer to his later separate notation of these dances, written for his third revised staging of *A Folk Tale* on 3.4.1871. Finally, a pencilled note (written by an unknown hand on p. 117) reads: 'spilles for den engelske Dandserinde'. This indicates that the solo variation, which originally was danced by S. Price before the Coda in the Act III *Pas de quatre* (score no. 20), was omitted at a later stage, but was reinstated when Bournonville's English pupil, C. Healey, performed it four times between 26.12.1864 and 2.2.1865.

The 1854 répétiteur's copy was used for all performances of *A Folk Tale* during Bournonville's lifetime. Consequently it also includes several other notes and indications (written by unknown hands) which indicate the many later musical changes made for his four revised stagings of this ballet (*see* 20.9.1867, 3.4.1871, 1.6.1874, and 3.11.1877.

Répétiteur's copy (fragment). Ms. Copy. Black ink. 6 pp. (34,5 × 25,7 cm)
[...] Allegro/No. 13/[...]/V: S: Galop.
Unsigned and undated [1854]
[DKKk; MA ms 2692 (KTB 274)

This fragment contains what originally was pp. '53–58' in the 1854 répétiteur's copy for *A Folk Tale*. It also includes Bournonville's autographed choreographic notes (written with brown ink) which describe the last five bars of *Hilda's* second solo variation in Act II (score no. 12). Moreover, the fragment includes a complete version of Hartmann's music for the so-called *Trolls' Gallop (Trolde Galop)* in the same act (score no. 13). It plays for 202 bars, but seems to have been taken out of the 1854 répétiteur's copy in connection with a later restaging of *A Folk Tale* (most likely that on 20.9.1867). This theory is supported by the fact that the *Trolls' Gallop* which is now included the 1854 répétiteur's copy (pp. 55–62) plays for only 153 bars and contains music that is significantly different from that in this fragment. Another possibility is that the music included in this fragment represents Hartmann's very first version for the Act II finale, which may have been replaced by himself well before the ballet's actual première. This theory is supported by the fact that in the later répétiteur's copy for *A Folk Tale* (made in the late 1850s for Bournonville's projected staging at Stockholm's Royal Theatre, *see* 15.6.1857) Hartmann's shorter version of the Act II *Trolls' Gallop* is included. Whatever the case might be, this fragment represents the only musical source of this hitherto unknown version of Hartmann's *Trolls' Gallop* that has come to light so far.

Parts (incomplete). Ms. Copy. 36 vol.
4 vl 1, 4 vl II, 2 vla, 5 vlc e cb, fl 1/2, ob 1/2, cl 1/2, fag 1/2, cor 1/2/3/4, tr 1/2, trb 1/2/3, timp, gr cassa e piatti, tri, arpa.
Unsigned and undated [1854]
[DKKk; KTB 274

Parts (incomplete). Ms. Copy. 4 vol.
2 vl II, vla, glock
Unsigned and undated [1854]
[DKKk; KTB 1054 (KTB 274)

Piano score. Ms. Autograph (by N. W. Gade). Brown ink. 4 pp. (34,4 × 24,2 cm with minor variants)

Ved Elverhöi./Scherzo [erased]/Allegretto./N. W. Gade
Signed (on p. 1): 'N. W. Gade', undated [c.1854]
[DKKk; N. W. Gades Samling, kapsel C–E
This autographed piano score contains Gade's arrangement of his
music for Act I (score no. 4) in *A Folk Tale* and was most probably
made for publishing purposes.

Piano score. Ms. Autograph (by N. W. Gade). Brown ink. 4 pp. of
which one is blank (34,6 × 25,8 cm)
Elverpigerne./[smeared word]/Allegro con fuoco [changed to:]
non troppo/N. W. Gade.
Signed (on p. 1): 'N. W. Gade', undated [c.1854]
[DKKk; N. W. Gades Samling, kapsel C–E
This autographed piano score contains Gade's arrangement of his
music for Act I (score no. 5) in *A Folk Tale* and was most probably
made for publishing purposes.

Orchestral score. Ms. Copy. Brown ink. 28 pp. (35 × 26,3 cm with
minor variants)
Et Folkesagn./Andantino con moto/[3. Akt. No. 19. Troldenes Af-
rejse]
Unsigned and undated [c.1854–1870s]
[DKKk; N. W. Gades Samling, kapsel C-E
This orchestral score contains a copy of Gade's music for Act III
(score no. 19) in *A Folk Tale* and was most probably made for a concert version of this number played during the 1860s or 70s.

Other sources:

Costume drawing by E. Lehmann. Pencil and water colours (23,5 ×
14 cm)
Et Folkesagn.
Untitled and undated [c.1854]
[SSm; Daniel Fryklunds samling no. 256 (F 1331)
This drawing shows the costumes of *Diderik* and *Viderik* in Act III(?)
of *A Folk Tale* (performed by F. Hoppensach and E. Stramboe respec-
tively).

Drawing by E. Lehmann. Pencil and water colours (format un-
known)
Folkesagnet 2 Act –
Signed and dated: 'Ed. Lehmann/1865.' [c.1854(?) –1865]
[Private collection (Copenhagen)
This drawing depicts the opening scene in Act II of *A Folk Tale* showing the characters *Diderik* (F. Hoppensach), *Hilda* (Juliette or S.
Price, *Muri* (N. Møller or L. Juel), and *Viderik* (E. Stramboe or A.
Fredstrup). According to A. Fridericia (who first published it in
1989) the drawing may date from the period between the ballet's
1854 première and Lehmann's autographed pencilled dating of it
('1865'). It is drawn into an album which dates from 1855 and was
originally owned by the Copenhagen stockbroker, M. R. Henriques
and his wife Thérèse (b. Abrahamsen), who were close friends of the
Bournonvilles. A microfilm of the complete album is now in DKKk
(call no. Ms. micro 2468).

Printed sources:

Printed scenario. 1 vol. 15 pp. (20 × 12,6 cm)
Et Folkesagn./Ballet i 3 Acter/af/August Bournonville./Musiken
componeret af Gade og Hartmann./Decorationerne af Dhrr. Christensen og Lund. Costumet tegnet af Hr. Edw. Lehmann. Maskineriet
anordnet af Hr. Weddén.
Kjøbenhavn, J. H. Schubothe/Bianco Luno, 1854.
[DKKk; 17, – 174 8°

Printed scenario (in French) published on a poster. 1 p. (30 × 24 cm)
Théâtre royal de Copenhague./Representation extraordinaire [...]
/24 Septembre 1856:/UNE LÉGÉNDE DU NORD./[...] MOTIF./
[...]/ANALYSE DU SUJET.
s. l., dated: '24 Septembre 1856:'

[DKKk; Danske Afdeling, Småtryk (Personalhistorie: Bournonville)

16.4.1854
The Kermesse in Brüges, or The Three Gifts (La Kermesse de Brüges ou Les trois dons). Projected staging at Vienna's Kärnthnerthor Theatre.

During a trip to the Austrian capital in the spring of 1854
Bournonville planned a staging at Vienna's Kärnthnerthor
Theatre of his three-act romantic ballet *The Kermesse in
Brüges, or The Three Gifts* (*see* 4.4.1851). It was his clear intention to mount it there during the 1855–56 season. Subsequently, he wrote two new versions (in French) of its scenario, the first of which is dated 16.4.1854, while the second
undated scenario was (according to notes in his diary) almost certainly written on 6.4.1855. Moreover, according to
the diary, Bournonville notated the complete choreography
and mime of this ballet (in French) between 25.5. and 15.7.
1855. These notes were written in a new répétiteur's copy
that dates from about the same period and is now in SSkma
(call no. KT Pantomime-Balletter K 4).

However, the projected Vienna staging of *The Kermesse in
Brüges, or The Three Gifts* was never carried out, and Bournonville's 1855 French notation of it was not used until some
four years later, when the ballet was staged for the first and
only time outside Denmark during his lifetime. That production was mounted by his pupil, S. Lund, and premièred at
Stockholm's Royal Theatre (Operahuset) on 30.12.1858.

In his diary Bournonville noted about his original 1854
plan and preparations for a Vienna production of this ballet:

16.4.1854: 'skrevet og arrangeret'
18.4.: 'reenskrevet det franske Program til Kermessen'
6.4.1855: 'beskjæftiget mig den hele Dag med min Arbeidsplan for
Wien og med Oversættelsen paa Fransk af flere Programmer'
25.5.: 'skrevet Noter til Kermessen'
28.5.: 'noteret i Kermessen'
29.5.: 'skrevet og noteret [...] Noteret i Kermessen'
30.5.-15.7.: 'skrevet og noteret'
14.11.: 'skrevet den hele Formiddag fuldendt Programmet af Kermessen'
16.11.: 'Forgjæves Forsøg paa at faae [J.] Cornet i Tale angaaende
mit Repertoire'
17.11.: 'Besøg hos Herr [J. R.] v. Raymond der lovede at tage sig af
min Sag'
19.11.: 'Directionsbrev fra Cornet med frit Valg imellem tre Programmer, jeg vælger naturligvis Napoli'.

Autograph sources:

Manuscript scenario. Ms. Autograph. Black ink. 6 pp. (21,1 × 13,7
cm)
La Kermesse de Brüges/ou/Les trois dons./Ballet = pantomime en
3 actes par Bournonville.
Signed and dated: 'Vienne ce 16 avril 1854.' [Written according to
the diary on 16.4.–18.4.1854]
[DKKk; NKS 3285 4° 2 G–K

Manuscript scenario. Ms. Autograph. Black ink. 1 vol. 28 pp. (22,1 ×
13,8 cm)
La Kermesse de Brüges/ou/Les trois dons./Ballet en trois actes./
par/Auguste Bournonville./1855.
Unsigned and dated: '1855.' [Written according to the diary almost
certainly on 6.4.1855]
[DKKk; NKS 3285 4° 2 G–K

Musical sources:

Répétiteur's copy. Ms. Copy. Black ink. 1 vol. 96 pp. (26,6 × 37,2 cm)
La Kermesse de Brüges./(Ballet en trois Actes)/(Kermessen)/
(eller)/(De tre gaver)/par/Auguste Bournonville/Musique composée et arrangée par H. Paulli
Unsigned and undated [c.1854–1855]
[SSkma; KT Pantomime-Balletter K 4
This répétiteur's copy dates almost certainly from 1854–1855, when Bournonville was in the midst of preparing a projected staging of *The Kermesse in Brüges, or The Three Gifts* at Vienna's Kärnthnerthor Theatre for the 1856–57 season. His autographed notes included in this volume (all written with brown ink) thus seem to describe the mime and choreography such as he intended it to be performed in Vienna. This theory is supported by a note (in French) on p. 14 reading: 'NB Entre ce pas [i.e. the Act I *Pas de deux* danced by *Carelis* and *Eleonora*] et No. 3 on place une danse comique (La danse du coq) et un galop militaire'. This seems to indicate that Bournonville was planning the inclusion in the first act of his earlier *Cock's Dance (Hanedands)*, originally performed to music by H. S. Paulli in Bournonville's intermedium for J. L. Holberg's three-act comedy *The Masquerade* (*see* 12.12.1849).

Bournonville's notes in this volume seem (according to his diary) in the main to have been written between 25.5 and 15.7.1855. However, the same répétiteur's copy was also used by S. Lund for his later staging of *The Kermesse in Brüges, or The Three Gifts* at Stockholm's Royal Theatre (Operahuset) on 30.12.1858. For this occasion Bournonville appears to have inserted a few other pencilled notes indicating his changes in the choreography of the Act II *Pas de quatre* as well as some other notes regarding a number of minor musical cuts.

29.5.1854

Pas de trois performed by Julius Price, S. Price, and E. Garlieb.

In his handwritten list of his works, written c.1872 (*see* Additional Sources), this dance is listed by Bournonville as 'Pas de trois (Julius Price)'. It was choreographed especially for the débuts of his two pupils, Julius Price, and E. Garlieb. The score was composed and arranged by H. S. Paulli, who incorporated several musical borrowings as follows:

(1) Following the brief introduction of only 14 bars (presumably composed by Paulli) there is the same *Adagio* movement by R. W. v. Gallenberg which Bournonville had also used many years earlier for his *Pas de trois* in Act I (score no. 9) of his Danish two-act version of J. Aumer's one-act ballet *Les Pages du Duc de Vendôme* (*see* 3.9.1830).
(2) Following the *Adagio* there is a large *Allegretto* movement, the three middle-sections of which were borrowed by Paulli from earlier works. The first of these sections (which according to Bournonville's pencilled notes in the répétiteur's copy was a solo variation for E. Garlieb) was originally part of F. Sor's score to Albert's (François Decombe) three-act fairy-ballet *Cendrillon* (premièred at the Paris Opéra on 3.3.1823). In the original French orchestral score and répétiteur's copy for this ballet (now in FPo, call nos. A 469 [II], pp. 325–328, and Mat. 19 [63 (3), pp. 125–126) this music served as accompaniment for a *Pas de deux* danced immediately before the Act II finale by the characters *Le Comte* (Albert) and *Cendrillon* (E. Bigottini). The music for the second and third middle-sections in Paulli's *Allegretto* movement (according to Bournonville's choreographic notes, two solo variations performed by Julius Price and S. Price respectively) had already been used by Bournonville in his much earlier *Pas de cinq* in Act III (score no. 14) of N. Paccini's three-act singspiel *La Gioventù di Enrico V* (*see* 28.10.1831). This *Pas de cinq*, in turn, is musically completely identical with an even earlier *Pas de trois*, set to music by R. W. v. Gallenberg, originally performed at the Paris Opéra as an incorporated divertissement in N. Isouard's and A.-M. Benincori's three-act fairy-opera *Aladin, ou La Lampe merveilleuse* sometime in the 1820s.
(3) In the Coda Paulli incorporated a large excerpt which he borrowed from a much earlier Bournonville *Pas de trois* to music by S. Mercadante. It was originally part of the score for the *Pas de trois* (score no. 7) in Bournonville's one-act ballet *Victor's Wedding, or The Ancestral House* (*see* 23.4.1831). Mercadante's music for this dance, however, derives from an even earlier *Pas de trois*, first performed at Naples' Teatro San Carlo on 4.11.1825 as part of the Franco-Italian choreographer, L. Henry's ballet *L'Arrivo del Gran Signore*.

According to a later manuscript copy of Paulli's orchestral score (now in SSkma, call no. KT Dansmusik 87) Bournonville's 1854 *Pas de trois* was also mounted in Sweden by his pupil, S. Lund. He mounted it in a choreographically slightly revised version at Stockholm's Royal Theatre (Operahuset) on 16.3.1857. This version received 5 performances, the last of which was given on 29.3.1857.

In his diary Bournonville noted about the creation and the Copenhagen première of his 'Pas de trois (Julius Price)':

27.3.1854: 'arbeidet med Paulli'
2.4.: 'skrevet, arrangeret og componeret'
5.4.: 'Indstudering af en nў Pas de trois'
7.4.: 'Prøve paa Pas de trois'
9.5.: 'Prøve paa den nўe Pas de trois'
10.5.: 'Prøve paa den nўe Pas'
13.5.: 'Prøve paa Pas de trois'
16.5.: 'Pas de trois, der gik udmærket'
29.5.: 'Debut af Julius Price og Elisa [*sic*] Garlieb. Han især gjorde megen Lўkke og Pas de trois blev optaget med Bifald'.

The *Pas de trois* received 9 performances in Copenhagen, the last of which was given on 3.4.1856 (with S. Lund replacing Julius Price since 26.2.1856).

Musical sources:

Orchestral score. Ms. Autograph (by H. S. Paulli). Black ink. 1 vol. 24 pp. (26,2 × 37,4 cm)
Partituret./247./til/Pas de trois Debŭt.
Signed and dated (on p. 24): 'HSP–/arr: April 1854'
[DKKk; C II, 119 (KTB 247)

Répétiteur's copy. Ms. Autograph (by H. S. Paulli). Ms. Black ink. 14 pp. (32,1 × 24,5 cm with variants)
Pas de trois/composé pour/Mr. Jules Price, Mlles Garlieb &/Sophie Price/par/Auguste Bournonville/1854
Unsigned and dated (on p. 1): '1854'
[DKKk; MA ms 2638 (KTB 247)
This répétiteur's copy contains Bournonville's autographed choreographic notes (written with brown ink) which describe in fine detail the choreography of the opening *Adagio* movement. Moreover, his pencilled autographed notes indicate the casting of each of the solo variations and also describe (in more general terms) the choreography of the Coda. According to his diary all of these notes were most probably written on 2.4.1854.

Parts. Ms. Copy. 25 vol.
2 vl I, 2 vl II, vla, 2 vlc e cb, fl 1/2, ob 1/2, cl 1/2, fag 1/2, cor 1/2, cnt 1/2, trb 1/2/3, timp, gr cassa, tri.
Unsigned and undated [1854]
[DKKk; KTB 247

5.6.1854

The organisation of the celebrations of the Constitution day at the Royal Hermitage (Grundlovsfesten paa Eremitagen).

This open-air celebration of the fifth anniversary for Denmark's new constitution was accompanied by several songs, anthems and choruses, composed and conducted by H.

Rung, and also included a selection of gallopades and polkas by H. C. Lumbye. In his diary Bournonville noted about his involvement in the organisation of this event:

23.5.1854: 'særdeles godt Møde i Studenterforeningen angaaende Høitideligholdelsen af d. 5.e Juni. Jeg maatte gaae til Theatret, men der blev mig sagt at jeg var valgt til Medlem af en Comité'
26.5.: 'Møde hos Sadelmager Christensen i Anledning af Grundlovsfesten, af 9 Medlemmer undskyldte sig de fem. Det blev besluttet at overrække Kongen en Medaille, præget af [P.] Petersen'
27.5.: 'Aftale med Dhrr Comiterede'
28.5.: 'til Frederiksborg, hvor vi drak Café og jeg traf mine Med-comiterede. Vi blev stedede til Audients hos H. Majestæt [Frederik VII] Kl 16 1/2, og Kongen modtog os med en Anstand, Værdighed og Hjertelighed, der i høi Grad rørte og opbyggede os'
29.5.: 'Foranstaltninger til Grundlovsfesten. – Møde og antaget Program'
30.5.: 'Fest-Anstalter, megen Lunkenhed hos vore Medborgere og Uvillighed hos de Assisterende'
31.5.: 'Fest-Anstalter – Tour til Eremitagen med [N. H. C. V.] Sallÿ og Christensen og Magnus'
1.6.: 'Kjørt omkring og gjort Anstalter med meget Besvær'
2.6.: 'hele Eftermiddagen besørget Anstalter til Festen'
3..6.: 'Kl 3 kjørt ud paa Eremitagen hvor Arbeidet gik rask fra Haanden, hjem og tilsengs Kl 10 1/2'
4.6.: 'Hele Dagen paa Eremitagen. – Arbeidet skrider fremad. – En herlig Søile reises ved Tribunen paa Plænen høieste Punkt og Slottet Decoreres af [E.] Lehmann. [H. V.] Bissen modelerer en collosal Buste af Kongen'
5.6.: 'Prøve paa [H.] Visbys og Rungs Hymne. [...] Kjørt ud Kl 8 1/2. – Søilen og Slottet færdigt Kl 12. Veiret klart og skjønt, men stærk Nordenvind. Kl 4 samledes circa 30.000 Mennesker paa Plænen, der frembød et imponerende Skue, Laugene og Foreningerne droge op med flyvende Faner og Hymnen istemmedes fra Søilen med Borger-væbningens Musik og 100 Mandsstemmer. Christensen (Formanden) udbragte et Leve for Kongen, Spandst [?] var Dirigent. Instructeur [N. P.] Nielsen holdt en begeistret Tale for Danmark, og Provst [P. F. A.] Hammerich for Grundloven. – [C. V.] Rimestad talte for Festen. Der var megen Begeistring men den bedste Tone og gemytligste Stemning. Talerstolen blev lukket Kl 7 1/2. – Dands paa Græsset. Beværtning i Teltene, alt gik med Orden, kun ikke Billetsalget, der var overladt til Dhrr J. A. Hansen og Kunstdreier [H.] Andersen. Festen var fuldkommen lykket og Alle vare glade. – Jeg har havt endeel Besvær, men jeg føler mig belønnet ved det for hele Landet saa lykkelige Udfald. Jeg tog hjem Kl 9 og gik meget træt tilsengs'.

Autograph sources:

Production note. Ms. Autograph. Black ink. 4 pp. 32,2 × 22 cm)
Udkast til Grundlovsfestn 1854.
Signed and dated: 'Kjøbenhavn d. 29.de Mai 1854.'
[DKKk; NKS 3285 4°, kapsel 6 (læg 'Grundlovsfesten 1854')

19.6.1854

Pas de deux (new) by Mr. Ballet Master Bournonville (Pas de deux (ny) af Hr. Balletmester Bournonville) **performed by S. Lund and Juliette Price (the Court Theatre).**
According to the poster for this performance this *Pas de deux* was performed to music 'arranged' (*arrangeret*) by V. C. Holm. This makes this dance into the first of a long series of individual *pas* and minor divertissements that Bournonville created together with this composer. The *Pas de deux* was choreographed for a special charity performance given for Juliette Price. Bournonville did not attend the opening night because of his departure on 17.6.1854 for Vienna, where he was engaged at the Kärnthnerthor Theatre in the 1854–55 season. In his diary he noted about the dance:

11.5.1854: 'begyndt et Arrangement til Juliettes Benefice'
15.5.: 'Arrangeret Musik [...] besørget endeel til Juliettes Aften-underholdning [...] besøgt [N. W.] Gade, [E.] Helsted og [H. C.] Lumby[e]'
16.5.: 'Musik med [V. C.] Holm'
20.5.: Spadseretour til Frederiksberg Allée for at [...] tale med Holm'
22.5.: 'skrevet og componeret'
29.5. 'Indstuderet nye ting til J. P.'
30.5.: 'Prøve. – Indstudering'
31.5.: 'Prøve'
6.6.: 'lille Prøve'
7.6.: 'Prøve. – Juliette fortreffelig'
14.7.: 'Prøve paa Hoftheatret'
16.6.: 'Prøve paa Juliettes Aftenunderholdning'
17.6.: 'Kl 11 Prøve paa Juliettes Aftenunderholdning til Kl 1. Alt gik smukt.

No musical sources for this *Pas de deux* (which was given once at the Court Theatre) have yet been traced.

19.6.1854

Divertissement (The motif from Gardel's Paul et Virginie) (Divertissement (Motivet fra Gardel's Paul og Virginie)).
This abridged one-act version of Bournonville's earlier Copenhagen production of P. Gardel's three-act panto-mimic ballet *Paul et Virginie* (*see* 29.10.1830) was arranged for a special charity performance given for Juliette Price. Its score consisted of excerpts from Acts I and II (score nos. 1, 8, 10–12, and 17–20) of the 1830 version, but this year arranged by H. S. Paulli and presented in a completely new sequence and with new, additional music (presumably composed by Paulli).

The divertissement was so successful with the audience that Bournonville soon after decided to transfer it to the Royal Theatre, where it was premièred on 21.1.1855. Moreover, in Sweden it was mounted by Bournonville's pupil, S. Lund at Stockholm's Royal Theatre (Operahuset) on 7.2. 1858 and was performed there 9 times until 15.4.1859. Lund's staging differed from the Copenhagen version by the inclusion of an (uncredited) *Pas de trois*, performed as an incorporated divertissement between score nos. 8 and 9. Finally, on 16.1.1866 Bournonville planned a restaging of the divertissement in Copenhagen for the début of his pupils, B. Schnell and D. Krum. However, this project (which was planned for the 1866–67 season) was for unknown reasons never carried out.

In his diary he stated about the 1854 creation and rehearsals of the one-act version of *Paul et Virginie*:

11.5.1854: 'begyndt et Arrangement til Juliettes Benefice'
15.5.: 'Arrangeret Musik [...] besørget endeel til Juliettes Aften-underholdning [...] besøgt [N. W.] Gade, [E.] Helsted og [H. C.] Lumby[e]'
18.5.: 'componeret paa Paul & Virginie'
22.5.: 'skrevet og componeret'
24.5.: 'første Prøve paa Divertissementet af Paul & Virginie'
27.5. and 29.5. and 30.5. and 31.5.: 'Prøve'
3.6.: 'Prøve. – Paul og Virginie færdig'
9.6.: 'Prøve for Juliette'
14.6.: 'Prøve paa Hoftheatret'
16.6.: 'Prøve paa Juliettes Aftenunderholdning'
17.6.: 'Kl 11 Prøve paa Juliettes Aftenunderholdning til Kl 1. Alt gik smukt'.

Bournonville did not attend the première because of his departure for Vienna on 17.6.1854 where he was engaged as guest choreographer of the Kärnthnerthor Theatre during the 1854–55 season.

The divertissement was given only once at the Court Theatre.

Musical sources:

Orchestral score. Ms. Autograph (by H. S. Paulli). Black ink. 1 vol. 76 pp. (26 × 37,3 cm).
290/Poul [*sic*] og Virginie.
Signed and dated (on p. 76): 'HSP. d: 8 Juni 1854'
[DKKk; C I, 270 b (KTB 290)]
This orchestral score was used for all performances in Copenhagen of Bournonville's 1854 version of *Paul et Virginie* at the Court Theatre and (later on) at the Royal Theatre.

Répétiteur's copy. Ms. Autograph (by H. S. Paulli). Brown ink. 1 vol. 36 pp. (33,1 × 25,5 cm)
B 170/Paul og Virginie/Divertissement./Bournonville/(arranger-et)/28/1854./Paulli/
(arrang)/[...]/Divertissement/arrangeret af Bournonville/efter/Motiver af Gardels/Paul og Virginie
Unsigned and dated (on the front cover): '1854.'
[DKKk; MA ms 2933 (KTB 170 (2), originally KTB 290)]
This répétiteur's copy contains Bournonville's autographed notes (written with brown ink) which, except for the finale, describe the dramatic action, the mime, and the choreography in fine detail. Moreover, his autographed choreographic numbers ('1–8') are included in music for the divertissement's final *Allegro* movement in 6/8 time (pp. 30–36). They seem to refer to a separate (not yet traced) choreographic description of the divertissement's finale. According to Bournonville's diary all of these notes were most probably written on 18.5 and 22.2.1854. The répétiteur's copy was used for all performances in Copenhagen of the 1854 version of *Paul et Virginie* at the Court Theatre and (later) at the Royal Theatre.

Parts. Ms. Copy. 29 vol.
3 vl I, 3 vl II, 2 vla, 3 vlc e cb, fl picc e II, fl I, ob 1/2, cl 1/2, fag 1/2, cor 1/2, clno 1/2, Atrb, Ttrb, Btrb, timp, gr cassa, tri.
Unsigned and undated [1854]
[DKKk; KTB 290]
This set of parts was used for all performances in Copenhagen of Bournonville's 1854 version of *Paul et Virginie* at the Court Theatre and (later) at the Royal Theatre.

19.6.1854

La Ventana, Spanish Solo (new) (spansk Solo (ny)) **performed by Juliette and S. Price (the Court Theatre).**
This mirror-dance was created as the finale of a special charity performance at the Court Theatre given for Juliette Price. It was performed by her and her sister, Sophie, for the third and last time on the same stage exactly one year later on 19.6.1855. The music consisted of an abridged version of H. C. Lumbye's so-called *Eugenie Walzer (Eugenie vals)*, which had been published in Leipzig by Breitkopf & Härtel during the early spring of 1854 (pl. no. 9002). This waltz was preceded by a brief mime scene, performed to the waltz's introduction and its first section, to which Lumbye added two completely new movements (a *Præludium ad Libitum*, and an *Andantino* in 6/8 time) that seem to have been composed especially for this occasion.

As a result of the divertissement's great success, Bournonville decided later the same year to mount it at the Royal Theatre, where it was premièred on 26.12.1854. Moreover,

on 7.12.1858 it was performed by Bournonville's pupil, B. Bills, and the Irish ballerina, C. Saint Louin, at Stockholm's Mindre Theatern and given there 4 times until 12.12.1858. Furthermore, two years later it was again performed at that theatre, but then by Juliette and S. Price, who danced it twice on 16.6. and 19.6.1860. Finally, in Norway *La Ventana* was performed 3 times by the Price sisters at Christiania's Theatre (Oslo) between 16.6. and 3.7.1865.

In his diary Bournonville noted about the creation and the 1854 Copenhagen première of this divertissement:

11.5.1854: 'begyndt et Arrangement til Juliettes Benefice'
15.5.: 'Arrangeret Musik [...] besørget endeel til Juliettes Aften-underholdning [...] besøgt [N. W.] Gade, [E.] Helsted og [H. C.] Lumby[e]'
22.5.: 'skrevet og componeret'
8.6.: 'indstuderet La Ventana spansk Dands for Juliette Price'
9.6.: 'Prøve for Juliette'
14.6.: 'Prøve paa Hoftheatret. Costume=Tegning af [E.] Lehmann'
16.6.: 'Prøve paa Juliettes Aftenunderholdning'
17.6.: 'Kl 11 Prøve paa Juliettes Aftenunderholdning til Kl 1. Alt gik smukt'.

Bournonville did not attend the opening night because of his departure on 17.6.1854 for Vienna, where he was about to begin a one-year tenure as guest choreographer of the Kärnthnerthor Theatre.

After his return to Copenhagen in 1856 he mounted a revised and extended version of this divertissement at the Royal Theatre. It consisted of two tableaux and included a number of new dances that were set to music composed and arranged by V. C. Holm (*see* 6.10.1856).

Musical sources:

No autographed orchestral score dating from the 1854 première of *La Ventana* at the Court Theatre has yet been traced. However, a later manuscript copy of Lumbye's orchestral score (dating from the revised and extended 1856 version of this divertissement) is now in DKKk (call no. MA ms 1127 (KTB 300)).

Répétiteur's copy/Conductor's part. Ms. Copy. Brown ink. 1 vol. 8 pp. of which one is blank (33,8 × 24,1 cm)
B. 300/'La Venatana.'/1/No. 6 A/[...]/La Ventana/Danse Espagnole/composèe [*sic*] par A: Bournonville./executée par M.lle Juliette Price/le 19 Juin 1854.
Unsigned and dated (on p. 1): 'le 19 Juin 1854.'
[DKKk; MA ms 2997 (KTB 300)]
According to the title page, this répétiteur's copy clearly dates from the 1854 première of *La Ventana* at the Court Theatre. It is bound together with the new additional music, composed and arranged by V. C. Holm for the second, extended 1856 version of this divertissement. The fact that the volume includes several notes about the instrumentation and is not explicitly entitled as a répétiteur's copy seems to indicate that it also served as the conductor's part in 1854.

No set of parts dating from the 1854 première of *La Ventana* at the Court Theatre has yet been traced.

Parts. Ms. Copy. 24 vol.
vl I (conductor's part), 2 vl I, 2 vl II, vla, 2 vlc, 2 cb, fl picc, fl, ob, cl 1/2, fag, cor 1/2, tr 1/2, trb, tuba, tri e tamb, gr cassa e timp e cast.
Unsigned and undated [c.1854]
[DKKk; Tivolis Musikarkiv no. 2030 (mu 9405.1400)]
This set of parts was used when Lumbye's concert version of *Eugenie vals* was played for the first time in the Tivoli Gardens during the summer of 1854. They differ drastically from the later 1856 orches-

tral score for *La Ventana* in that the concert version plays for a total of 285 meas. against the 177 bars in *La Ventana*. Moreover, a brief *Bolero* section of only 10 bars (which is not included in *La Ventana*) is inserted between the opening *Allegro* movement and the actual waltz. According to notes written in several of these parts, the concert version played for 6 minutes.

15.7.1854

Das Fest in Albano (Festen i Albano) (**Vienna's Kärnthnerthor Theatre**).

This performance represents Bournonville's first staging outside Denmark of his one-act idyllic ballet *The Festival in Albano* (*see* 28.10.1839). It was mounted in a heavily abridged divertissement version that included the following three dances:

(1) a *Pas de quatre*. According to the conductor's part in AWn this dance is identical with E. Helsted's *Pas de quatre* from Act III, score no. 2 of Bournonville's three-act romantic ballet *Napoli or The Fisherman and His Bride* (*see* 29.3.1842). In Vienna it was performed by the Italian dancer, F. Croce, and the Austrian ballerinas, K. Lanner, C. Dittrich, and E. Baseg.

(2) a *Pas de deux* performed by P. Borri (in the rôle of *Antonio*) and A. Levasseur (as *Silvia*). This dance is (according to the conductor's part in AWn) the same as Bournonville's and I. P. E. Hartmann's original *Pas de deux* in *The Festival in Albano* (score no. 9).

(3) a *Tarantella*. According to the set of parts in AWn this dance is identical with H. S. Paulli's Act III *Tarantella* (score no. 3) in Bournonville's ballet *Napoli or The Fisherman and His Bride* (*see* 29.3.1842).

This 1854 Vienna version of *Das Fest in Albano* received 5 performances until 8.8.1854.

At its restaging at the Kärnthnerthor Theatre on 6.2.1855 it was given without Bournonville's incorporated *Pas de quatre* and the original *Pas deux*. Instead a new *Pas de deux*, choreographed by P. Borri and performed by himself and A. Levasseur was incorporated (*see* 6.2.1855). This second version of the divertissement was mounted without Bournonville's approval and reached 6 performances (the last given on 23.3.1855) after which the ballet went out of the Vienna repertory.

In his diary Bournonville noted about the original 1854 production of *Das Fest in Albano*:

5.7.1854: 'skrevet og componeret. Prøve i Redouten fra 6 til 8¼ paa de to Pas til Divertissementet'
6.7.: 'componeret. – Prøve fra 6 til 8½. Begge Pas færdige'
7.7.: 'Prøve fra 5 – 6½ paa Tarentellen'
8.7.: 'Prøve i Redouten fra 5 til 7'
10.7.: 'Prøve 6 til 7½'
11.7.: 'Prøve fra 6 til 7½'
12.7.: 'Prøve Redouten fra 12 – 2"
13.7.: 'Fuldstændig Prøve med Orchester Kl 9 til 12 der gik særdeles godt og gjorde et smukt Indtryk. Jeg var
i meget godt Humeur derover'
14.7.: 'Generalprøve Kl 10. – Den gik særdeles godt, paa min gode [P.] Borri nær, der mangler en heel Deel af
hvad der hörer til Rollen og Dandsene'
15.7.: 'Paa Theatret K. 6 og foreberedt Alt til min Forestilling Festen i Albano som Divertissement [...] Tarentellen henrev til Begeistring og efter Divertissementet blev jeg fremkaldt med overordentlig Bifald'.

According to several notes in the Vienna set of parts (reading 'dauert 35 Minuten') the 1854 version of *Das Fest in Albano* lasted 35 minutes.

Musical sources:

No full orchestral score dating from the 1854 Vienna performances of *Das Fest in Albano* has yet been traced.

Conductor's score/Répétiteur's copy. Ms. Copy. Brown ink. 1 vol. 76 pp. (32,8 × 25,2 cm)
1026/Fest in Albano./Direction Stimm./O. A. 1026/Ouverture / [...]/Repetiteurparthie/No. 1
Unsigned and undated [1854]
[AWn; O. A. 1026

Parts. Ms. Copy. 45 vol.
5 vl I, 5 vl II, 3 vla, 2 vlc, 3 cb, fl picc, fl, ob 1/2, cl 1/2, fag 1/2, cor 1/2/3/4, tr 1/2, trb 1-2, trb 3, oph, timp, gr cassa, cassa, tamb, piatti, tri, glock, arpa 1/2.
Unsigned and undated [1854]
[AWn; O. A. 1026 (Orchesterstimmen)
This set of parts includes (as the only musical source in Vienna) the music for the *Tarantella*, which is that from Act III, score no. 3 of Bournonville's ballet *Napoli or The Fisherman and His Bride*. Here it amounts to a total of 497 played bars(!), but was at a later stage shortened by the omission of three repeats of 16, 8, and 8 bars, thereby playing for 465 meas. Moreover, the same set of parts includes H. S. Lumbye's *Finale Gallop* from Act III (score no. 4) of Bournonville's *Napoli or The Fisherman and His Bride*. However, notes in all of the parts clearly indicate that this dance was omitted from the very outset and was never performed in *Das Fest in Albano* in Vienna. The presence of Lumbye's music for this dance therefore seems to indicate that Bournonville had planned its inclusion in *Das Fest in Albano*, but abandoned this idea at an early stage.

15.7.1854

Der Toreador (Toréadoren) (**Vienna's Kärnthnerthor Theatre**).

This performance represents Bournonville's first staging in Austria of his two-act idyllic ballet *The Toreador* (*see* 27.11. 1840). It was mounted with the Italian and French dancers, P. Borri and A. Levasseur, in the leading rôles as *Alonzo* and *Maria*, and the Austrian ballerina, K. Lanner, performing the part of *Céleste*. According to the musical material in AWn the ballet was mounted with some minor changes in Act I (score nos. 2 and 4) and Act II (score nos. 8 and 10).

In his diary Bournonville noted about the production and its reception:

23.6.1854: 'Kl 9 Prøve i den lile Redoutensal, indstuderet den store Solo med Frln. [K.] Lanner og endeel Pantomime med [P.] Borri og Mlle [A.] Levas[s]eur. Det gik udmærket godt og Personalet synes besjelet af den bedste Villie. Kl 1 var jeg færdig med mit Dagsværk'
24.6.: 'Prøve med Corps de Ballet fra Kl. 9 til 11 og med Solodandsen fra 11-1. Det gaaer meget godt. – [...] Prøve med Borri Kl 5.'
26.5.: 'Arbeidet med Decorationsmalerne. Prøve fra 9–1, indstuderet meget [...] Prøve fra 5–7'
27.6.: 'Arrangeret Decorationer paa Theatret Kl. 8. Prøve fra 9–11'
28.6.: 'Skrevet og arrangeret. Prøve fra 12–2 [...] arrangeret'
30.6.: 'Prøve fra 9–11 og 12.2. [Gott. A.] Füssel ankommen og deeltaget i Prøven'
1.7.: 'Prøve paa Theatret 9–11 og i Redouten 12–2. [L.] Frappard lærte sin Rolle'
2.7.: 'Prøve med Begynderinden Passeg [i. e. E. Baseg] fra 8 til 11'
3.7.: 'arbeidet med Mlle Passeg [*sic*] fra 8–9. Prøve 9–11 og fra 12 til 1½'
4.7.: 'Prøve med [F.] Croce og Passeg [*sic*] fra 8 1/2 til 10. Derpaa en Time med det Hele paa Theatret [...] Prøve med Mlle Ditrich [i.e. C. Dietrich] fra 1–2 [...] Prøve med Borri fra 5 1/2 til 7'
5.7.: 'Prøve med Boleroen fra 9 til 11½ [...] skrevet og componeret'

6.7.: 'componeret. Prøve fra 9 til 11½ paa første Akt af Toreadoren'

7.7.: 'skrevet og arrangeret. Prøve fra 9–11½'

8.7.: 'skrevet og componeret. Prøve fra 10–12 paa Theatret, fra 12–1½ i redouten'

10.7.: 'Prøve fra 9–12, fra 12½ – 2'

11.7.: 'Prøve fra 9–11. Arrangements […] Indstuderingen færdig. Champagner drukket'

12.7.: 'Prøve for Orchestret. Musiken gik udmærket godt. [J.] Mayseder spillede selv sin Polonaise og gjorde stor Lykke. Alle vare henrykte over Instrumentationen'

13.7.: 'skrevet og arrangeret, Fuldstændig Prøve med Orchester Kl 9 til 12 der gik særdeles godt og gjorde et smukt Indtryk. Jeg var i meget godt Humeur derover'

14.7.: 'Generalprøve Kl 10. – Den gik særdeles godt, paa min gode Borri nær, der mangler en heel Deel af hvad der hörer til Rollen og Dandsene, Med Guds Hjælp vil det nok gaae godt'

15.7.: 'lille Prøve paa Dandsene Kl 10 […] Toreadoren gik fra Publicums Side fortrinlig. Mlle Lanner var fortreffelig som Celeste. [Gott. A.] Füssel spillede sin Rolle med fuldstændig Virtuositet. Frappart som Sir William var paa mange Steder overdreven, men behagede Publicum overmaade meget. De øvrige Roller og Partier bleve mere eller mindre svagt udførte og uagtet jeg nød al mulig Ære og fremkaldtes, fandt jeg mig kun ufuldkommen tilfredsstillet. Dog takkede jeg Gud for det lykkelige Udfald'.

According to notes in several of the Vienna parts (reading: '1¼ St.') the complete ballet played for a total of 75 minutes. *Der Toreador* reached a total of 9 performances at the Kärnthnerthor Theatre, the last of which was given on 18.9. 1855. Moreover, Act I was given there once as a separate divertissement on 12.10.1855. Finally, according to an (undated) letter written by K. Lanner to Bournonville in Vienna (now in DKKk, call no. NKS 3258 A 4°, VI, facs. 4, no. 149), it appears that *Der Toreador* or an excerpt of it was performed by her in Hamburg later the same year. It has not been possible to verify the exact date and place of this performance.

Musical sources:

No full orchestral score dating from the 1854 Vienna première of *Der Toreador* has yet been traced.

Violin I/Conductor's score/Répétiteur's copy. Ms. Copy. Brown ink. 1 vol. 116 pp. (31,9 × 25,2 cm)
1024/Der Toreador./Violino 1.mo/Directoren/O.A. 1027.
Unsigned and undated [1854]
[AWn; O. A. 1027

Parts. Ms. Copy. 38 vol.
vl princ, 4 vl I, 5 vl II, 3 vla, 2 vlc, 3 cb, fl 1, fl picc e II, ob 1/2, cl 1/2, fag 1/2, cor 1/2/3/4, tr 1/2, trb 1-2, trb 3, timp, gr cassa, cassa, piatti, tri.
Unsigned and undated [1854]
[AWn; O. A. 1027 (Orchesterstimmen)

Other sources:

Costume drawing by G. Franceschini. Lithograph with applied watercolours (22,2 × 14,2 cm)
messiers [*sic*] Croci [i.e. F. Croce, who played the rôle of *Pedro*]
Unsigned and undated [1854]
[AWth; HM 3877a

Costume drawing by G. Franceschini with two figures. Lithograph with applied water colours (22,2 × 14,2 cm)
M. Schellenberger [i.e. V. Schellenberger, who played the rôle of *Ein Gensd'arm=Korporal*]/M. Pitrot [i.e. D. Pitrot, who played the rôle of *José, Gastwirth*]

Unsigned and undated [1854]
[AWth; HM 3878

Costume drawing by G. Franceschini with two figures. Lithograph with applied water colours (22,2 × 14,2 cm)
Mr. Winkler [i.e. J. Winkler, who played the rôle of *Ein Kutscher*]/Mr. Destefano [i.e. G. Distefano, who played the rôle of *Ein Jokay*]
Unsigned and undated [1854]
[AWth; HM 3879

Costume drawing by G. Franceschini with two toreadors. Lithograph with applied water colours (22,2 × 14,2 cm)
16 Figurang [*sic*]
Unsigned and undated [1854]
[AWth; HM 3880

Costume drawing by G. Franceschini with two figures. Lithograph with applied water colours (22,2 × 14,2 cm)
Mad. Finard [performed by E. Baseg]/Mlle Celeste [performed by K. Lanner]
Unsigned and undated [1854]
[AWth; HM 3881

Costume drawing by G. Franceschini. Lithograph with applied water colours (22,2 × 14,2 cm)
Maria/[performed by] Ml. [A.] Levasseur
Unsigned and undated [1854]
[AWth; HM 3882

Printed sources:

Printed scenario. 1 vol. 14 pp. (18,5 × 11,7 cm)
Der Toreador./Idyllisches Ballet in Zwei Akten
Wien, A Pichler's Witwe & Sohn, 1854
[AWn; 802.558 B Th.
[DKKk; 17, – 173 8°

26.12.1854
La Ventana, Spanish Character Dance (La Ventana, spansk Characteerdands) **performed by Juliette and S. Price.**

This performance represents the first time that Bournonville's mirror-dance *La Ventana* (*see* 19.6.1854) was mounted at Copenhagen's Royal Theatre. In his diary he listed only one stage rehearsal of it on 23.12.1854 and noted about its reception on the opening night:

'La Ventana gik for første Gang, yndigt men lunkent fra Publicums Side'.

The 1854 version of *La Ventana* received 9 performances at the Royal Theatre, the last of which was given on 12.5.1855.

Musical sources:

No autographed orchestral score dating from the 1854 première of *La Ventana* at the Royal Theatre has yet been traced. However, a later manuscript copy of Lumbye's full orchestral score, dating from the second and extended 1856 version of it, is now in DKKk (call no. MA ms 1127 (KTB 300)).

The répétiteur's part employed for the 1854 première of *La Ventana* at the Royal Theatre is now in DKKk (call no. MA ms 2997 (KTB 300)).

No separate set of parts dating form the 1854 première of *La Ventana* at the Royal Theatre has yet been traced.

1855

16.1.1855
La Fiancée (Bruden).

This performance represents Bournonville's second staging of the dances in the second act of D.-F.-E. Auber's three-act comic opera (*see* 20.11.1853). They seem to have been mounted this year with only minor if any changes from his previous staging. This theory is supported by the fact that according to the rehearsal book of H. C. J. Fredstrup and notes in Bournonville's diary only three rehearsals were held of this opera on 12.1., 13.1., and 15.1.1855. The 1855 re-staging received 5 performances, the last taking place on 3.3.1855. The musical material employed this year was the same as that used for the previous 1853 production (now in DKKk, call nos. U 6, MA ms 3059, and KTA 281).

21.1.1855
Paul et Virginie, Divertissement (The motif from Gardel) (Paul og Virginie, Divertissement (Motivet efter Gardel)).

This performance represents the first time Bournonville's abridged one-act version of P. Gardel's three-act ballet *Paul et Virginie* (*see* 29.10.1830) was performed at the Royal Theatre. Originally it was created for a special charity performance given for Juliette Price at the Court Theatre on 19.6.1854. For its 1855 restaging Bournonville directed (according to his diary) one rehearsal on 19.1.1855, and noted about the performance on the opening night:

'Jeg maatte først bivaane Forestillingen af Paul og Virginie. Diver-tissement, der gik smukt og gjorde megen Lykke'.

The divertissement was given 12 times at the Royal Theatre, the last time on 17.4.1857. The musical material used for these performances was the same as that used for the Court Theatre première (now in DKKk, call nos. C I, 270 b, MA ms 2933, and KTB 290).

25.1.1855
Le Petit Chaperon rouge (Den lille Rødhætte).

According to the rehearsal book of H. C. J. Fredstrup Bournonville directed two rehearsals (on 23.1. and 24.1.1855) of the dances in Act I (score no. 7) and Act II (score no. 12) of F.-A. Boyeldieu's three-act fairy-opera (*see* 1.12.1852) prior to its restaging this year. The performance, which seems to have been mounted with only minor (if any) changes from the previous staging, represents the second time Bournon-ville was involved in a staging of this opera. It received only 3 performances, the last of which was given on 12.2.1855.

6.2.1855
Das Fest in Albano (Festen i Albano) **(Vienna's Kärnthnerthor Theatre).**

This performance represents the second and last time Bour-nonville's 1854 Vienna version of his one act idyllic ballet *The Festival in Albano* was mounted at the Kärnthnerthor Theatre (*see* 28.10.1839 and 15.7.1854). It was staged during his absence from the Habsburg capital and differed from Bournonville's previous staging by the omittance of his own

incorporated *Pas de quatre* (which is identical with that from Act III, score no. 2, of *Napoli or The Fisherman and His Bride*).

Moreover, a new *Pas de deux* (choreographed by the Italian dancer, P. Borri, and performed by himself and the French ballerina, A. Levasseur) was incorporated and replaced Bournonville's and I. P. E. Hartmann's original *Pas de deux*. According to a note in the part for the harp (reading: 'Rob-ert und Bertram' [*sic*]) the music for Borri's *Pas de deux* was played immediately before the *Tarantella* and was, in parts, borrowed from H. Schmidt's score to P. Taglioni's new ver-sion of F.-M. Hoguet's three-act ballet *Robert und Bertrand* (premièred in Vienna on 8.12.1854). In that ballet it origi-nally served as accompaniment for a 'Gran Ballabile'. To this music Borri added a Coda movement, borrowed from a so-called 'Spanisch' which originally was part of yet another Italian choreographer's work, namely G. Golinelli's new pro-duction of P. Taglioni's two-act comic ballet *Don Quixote* (also premièred at the Kärnthnerthor Theatre on 6.2.1855). A note written in the part for the side drum to Golinelli's pro-duction of Taglioni's ballet (now in AWn, call no. O. A. 1032 Orchesterstimmen) thus indicates that this Spanish dance was originally performed as score no. '20' in *Don Quixote*.

The 1855 Vienna version of *Das Fest in Albano* (which was mounted without Bournonville's approval) received 6 per-formances, the last of which was given on 23.3.1855.

Musical sources:

Parts for the harp (*Pas de deux*). Ms. Copy. 2 vol.
Arpa/Das Fest in Albano.
Unsigned and undated [1854–55]
[AWn; O. A. 1026 (Orchesterstimmen)]
These parts represent the only musical sources for P. Borri's incorpo-rated *Pas de deux* in the 1855 version of *Das Fest in Albano* that have been traced so far in Vienna.

28.3.1855
Abdallah.

This three-act ballet was conceived by Bournonville in 1848, reworked by him in 1853, and reached its final form during the autumn and winter of 1854-55. According to his own ac-count in his memoirs *My Theatre Life* (p. 211) the plot was inspired from a tale in an English collection of Arabian tales (most likely E. W. Lane's *Arabian Anecdotes and Tales*, pub-lished in London, 1845, and part of Bournonville's own li-brary). The music for it was (according to Bournonville's di-ary) already drafted by H. S. Paulli in 1848. With his score for this work Paulli wrote for the first time a full-length ballet without incorporating any musical borrowings. Conse-quently, *Abdallah* should be regarded as his first original work in this sphere.

Abdallah seems to have been created with the explicit in-tention of also mounting it at the Paris Opéra. This is clear from a series of notes in Bournonville's 1855 diary, accord-ing to which he made a copy of the scenario in French, which he mailed to the director of the Paris Opéra, N. Roqueplan, as early as on 9.2.1855. This scenario was thus written while Bournonville was still in the midst of the crea-tive process of the ballet and well before the exact date for its Copenhagen première had been established.

Abdallah was never given in Paris, but on 5.9.1855 it was

mounted by Bournonville in a slightly revised version at Vienna's Kärnthnerthor Theatre with the new title *Die Gazelle von Bassora*. It received 4 performances there, the last of which was given on 12.1.1856. The Vienna version included a new *Solo* (choreographed by Bournonville for *Palmyra* in Act II, score no. 9), and an incorporated *Pas de deux* and a *Solo* in Act III (both inserted after the first 28 bars of score no. 16). The two incorporated dances in Act III were both choreographed by the Italian dancer, P. Borri, and performed by him and his wife, the Italian ballerina, C. Pocchini. The latter also appeared as *Palmyra* in Act II, although from a dramaturgical point of view this reappearance might seem rather unlogical.

In Sweden the *Pas de cinq* from *Abdallah* (Act III, score no. 15) was mounted as a separate divertissement by Bournonville's pupil, S. Lund, at Stockholm's Royal Theatre (Operahuset) on 12.2.1857 and performed there 6 times until the 1857–58 season.

Moreover, several years later Bournonville created a new *Pas de trois* which employed most of Paulli's music for the so-called *Changing Dance (Vexeldands)* in Act I, score no. 2 of *Abdallah* (originally performed by *Irma, Abdallah,* and two unnamed girls). This new *Pas de trois* was choreographed especially for Bournonville's pupils, D. Krum, M. Westberg, and A. Scholl, and premièred by them at Copenhagen's Royal Theatre on 10.10.1872. According to Bournonville's 1872 autographed notation of this dance, the choreography of the Coda was nearly identical with that originally devised for the Coda in his 1854 *Changing Dance* from Act I of *Abdallah*.

Finally, in 1873 V. C. Holm borrowed three excerpts from the harem scene in Act II (score no. 9) of *Abdallah*, which he interpolated in his score for Bournonville's Chinese ballet divertissement *The Mandarin's Daughters* (*see* 23.4.1873). This music (which in *Abdallah* served as accompaniment for the scene in which *Palmyra* and her suite of odalisques are revealed to *Abdallah*) represents the last time that excerpts from Paulli's score were performed during Bournonville's lifetime.

In his diary Bournonville noted about the rather long creative process of *Abdallah* and its 1855 Copenhagen première:

30.8.1848: 'begyndt paa min Ballet Abdalla [*sic*] skrevet'
31.8. and 1.9.: 'skrevet paa min Ballet'
7.9.: 'Brev til [H. S.] Paulli [...] Brev til [J.] Collin'
9.9. and 10.9.: 'skrevet'
11.9.: 'skrevet lidt'
12.9.: 'Paulli ankom Kl 3½'
13.9.: 'arbeidet med Paulli'
12.7.1853: 'Skrevet den hele Formiddag og ordnet efter en nÿ Form min Ballet Abdallah, der sÿntes at være lÿkkes mig godt'
28.7.: 'Skrevet og reenskrevet Abdallah'.
1.9.1854: 'skrevet og speculeret paa min nÿ Ballet'
17.9.: 'Brev til [J. L.] Heiberg'
19.9.: 'Brev fra Heiberg. Ordre til at iværksætte Abdallah, componeret strax, arbeidet med Paulli'.
20.9.: 'Op Kl 6 skrevet og componeret [...] besørget adskilligt den nÿ Ballet angaaende'
22.9.: 'Besøg og Aftale paa Malersalen'
25.9.: 'skrevet og componeret'
28.9.: 'Møde med Theatermalerne og [A.P.] Weddén'
30.9.: 'Musik med Paulli'
9.10.: 'Besøg hos H. P. Holst og Paulli – Musik'

11.10., 12.10., 13.10., and 14.10: 'componeret'
16.10.: 'Lehmann hos os til Aften'
18.10.: 'componeret [...] og den første Indstuderingsprøve paa Abdallah [...] componeret'
19.10.: 'Prøve og 2.den Indstudering af Abdallah. – Veddestriden færdig'
20.10.: 'componeret'
21.10.: 'Prøve og 3.die Indstudering paa Abdallah' [...] skrevet og componeret lidt'
24.10.: 'Prøve paa Abdallah (4.de)'
26.10.: skrevet og componeret'
31.10.: '5.te Indstuderingsprøve paa Abdallah'
2.11.: 'arbeidet med Paulli [...] 6.te Indstudering. – 1.ste Akt færdig' [...] componeret'
4.11.: 'skrevet componeret [...] 7.de Indstudering. 2.den Akt begyndt'
5.11.: 'componeret'
6.11.: '(8.de Indstudering)'
8.11.: 'lille Repetition paa Balletten [...] componeret'
9.11.: 'Musik af Paulli' [...] componeret og skrevet'
10.11: '9.de Indstudering'
11.11.: 'Prøve paa Balletten'
12.11. and 13.11.: 'componeret'
14.11.: 'Musik hos Paulli [...] Napoli gik men jeg blev hjemme og componerede den hele aften'
15.11.: '(10.de Indstudering) M.d [C.] Kellermann [...] componeret og skrevet'
16.11: 'Prøve og 11.te Indstudering' [...] componeret og skrevet'
17.11.: '(12.de Indstudering)'
19.11.: 'componeret og skrevet'
20.11.: 'componeret [...] og Repetitionsprøve paa [...] Abdallah'
21.11.: 'skrevet, componeret'
24.11.: 'Prøve (13.de Instudering) Haremscenen færdig'
25.11.: 'Musik med Paulli'
26.11.: 'skrevet og componeret'
27.11.: 'Repetitionsprøve paa Alt hvad der er færdigt i Balletten [...] componeret Resten af Aftnen'
28.11.: 'Prøve (14.de Indstudering)'
30.11.: 'componeret'
1.12.: '15.de Indstuderingsprøve'
2.12.: '16 Indstudering'
4.12.: 'Skrevet og componeret [...] componeret fra 11 til 12'
5.12.: '17.de Indstuderingsprøve'
6.12.: 'componeret [...] 18.de Indstudering (2.den Akt færdig) [F.] Hoppe høist ubehagelig'
8.12.: 'stor Repetitionsprøve paa de to færdige Akter. Det gik udmærket godt'
21.12.: 'Musik hos Paulli [...] skrevet og componeret'
22.12.: 'skrevet og componeret'
24.12.: 'componeret lidt'
26.12.: 'skrevet og componeret paa Conservatoriet'
27.12.: 'besørget Costumer til Lehmann [...] 19.de Indstuderingsprøve fra 10–1½, skrevet og componeret i Conservatoriet'
28.12.: 'skrevet og componeret [...] og 20.de Indstuderingsprøve (Pas de cinq) meget Besvær med M.d [L.] Stillmann'
29.12.: 'stor Repetitionsprøve paa Abdallah, halvtredie Akt'
30.12.: '21.de Indstuderingsprøve, pas de Cinq færdig'
2.1.1855: 'Prøve paa den nÿ Pas de cinq'
3.1.: 'Arrangeret Costûm med Lehmann'
4.1.: 'arbeidet med Paulli'
5.1.: 'componeret [...] og lille Prøve paa Abdallah'
6.1.: '22.de Indstudering (Vaabendandse)'
8.1.: 'skrevet og componeret [...] lille Prøve paa Abdallah'
10.1.: 'Prøve pa 3.die Akt Repetition'
11.1.: 'Musik hos Paulli [...] talt med Theatermaler [C. F.] Christensen'
12.1.: 'componeret [...] og 23.de Indstudering'
13.1.: '24.de Indstudering Balletten færdig – med Undtagelse af Slutningsdandsen (som jeg først componerer sidst i Februar)'
14.1.: 'skrevet og arrangeret Costûmer'
15.1.: 'talt med Decorationsmalerne'

16.1.: 'Repetitionsprøve paa Abdallah'
17.1.: 'Repetition Abdallah'
18.1.: 'Malersalen. Costümer'
22.1.: 'Arrangementsprøve paa Abdallah'
25.1.: 'Costüme – Möde'
26.1.: 'Malersal. Program begyndt paa Dansk og Fransk'
30.1.: 'Prøve paa 2.den Akt af Abdallah (Theatret)'
31.1.: 'skrevet paa mine Programmer'
1.2.: 'skrevet Program'
2.2.: 'skrevet en stor Deel af Programmet. – Statistprøve og Reqvisit-møde paa Theatret'
3.2.: 'Jeg sad oppe og skrev paa mit franske Program til Kl 12'
4.2.: 'fuldført mit franske Program, bragt det til Copiering til Prof. [N. C. L.] Abrahams'
5.2.: 'skrevet paa mit danske Program'
8.2.: 'besørget mit franske Program'
9.2.: 'Brev til Operadirecteuren Mr <u>Nestor Roqueplan</u> der skal gaae til Paris med det franske Program af Abdallah, besørget ved Kbm [M. C.] Levÿsohn […] Prøve – Theatret paa 2.den Akt af Balletten'
10.2.: 'Brev til Mr Duchesne de Belleroust [?] med Posten for at bede ham interessere sig for min sag for Operadirecteuren'
11.2.: 'Leveret min Pakke med Brev og Program til Levÿsohn der besørger det gjennem Mr Duchesne til Operadirecteuren Nestor Roqueplan'
24.2.: 'Prøve paa Dandsene til Abdallah'
25.2.: 'Besøg paa Malersalen'
5.3.: 'Vrøvl og Ondskab af Hoppe'
6.3. and 7.3.: 'Repetitionsprøve paa Abdallah'
8.3.: 'Besøg paa Malersalen'
9.3.: 'Theaterprøve paa Abdallah'
11.3.: 'Musik hos Paulli, skrevet, componeret'
12.3.: 'componeret Finalen til Abdallah'
13.3.: 'Indstudering til Juliette [Price]'
14.3.: 'Orchesterprøve paa Musiken til Abdallah. 1 og 2.den Akt'
15.3.: '25.de Instuderingsprøve Finalen'
16.3.: 'besørget en heel Deel til min Theaterprøve paa de to første Akter med Orchester. Den gik udmærket godt og slog godt til; prøvet Costümer'
17.3.: 'Prøve paa Abdallah'
19.3.: 'Detailprøve med Juliette'
20.3.: 'Prøve paa Balletten'
21.3.: 'Theaterprøve paa Abdallah med Orchester 3.die Akt. Det gik særdeles godt'
24.3.: 'Fuldstændig Prøve i Directeurens Nærværelse. Den gik særdeles godt og det Hele tager sig ypperligt ud'
25.3.: 'besørget adskilligt til min Ballet'
26.3.: 'Generalprøve med Costumer. Det gik særdeles godt'
27.3.: 'lille Prøve'
28.3.: 'Første Forestilling af 'Abdallah' for meget fuldt Huus og et særdeles livligt Publicum. Balletten gik fortreffeligt og gjorde stor Lÿkke. Den blev udført godt fra alle Sider, men navnlig <u>Juliette Price</u> som Gazellen var udmærket og vil hævde sig i Rÿ i denne Rolle'.

About his later restaging in Copenhagen after the return from Vienna he noted in his diary on 6.9.1856:

'Balletten gik heelt igjennem fortreffeligt (paa to Hoppeske Uheld nær). Vi tilbragte en glad Aften, til Erindring om den Modsætning der var imellem <u>her og Wien</u>!'.

The Copenhagen production of *Abdallah* reached a total of 5 performances in Copenhagen, the last of which was given on 12.3.1858.

Autograph sources:

Manuscript scenario. Ms. Autograph. Brown ink. 1 vol. 12 pp. (20,8 × 17,5 cm)
<u>Abdalla.</u> [*sic*]/Ballet i 2 Acter af A Bournonville./1848.
Signed and dated: 'Fredensborg d. 1.ste Sept. 1848.
[DKKk; NKS 3285 4° 2 A-E

Manuscript scenario. Ms. Autograph. Brown ink. 1 vol. 4 pp. (21,2 × 13,6 cm)
<u>Abdalla.</u> [*sic*]/Eventÿr – Ballet i 3 Akter af A. Bournonville./(<u>Udkast</u>)
Signed and dated: 'Kbhvn d. 12.de Julii 1853'.
[DKKk; NKS 3285 4° 2 A–E]

Manuscript scenario. Ms. Autograph. Brown ink. 1 vol. 10 pp. (21 × 13 cm)
Abdallah./eventÿr – Ballet i tre Akter/af/August Bournonville/·1853.
Signed and dated: 'Kbhvn d. 12.de Julii 1853.'
[DKKk; NKS 3285 4° 2 A-E

Manuscript scenario. Ms. Autograph (partially in another's hand). Black ink. 1 vol. 16 pp. (26,8 × 21,2 cm) Abdallah/ou/La gazelle de Bassora./Ballet en 3 actes composé par/Auguste Bournonville/<u>1855.</u>
Signed and dated: 'Copenhague ce 4 fevrier 1855' [Written according to Bournonville's diary between 26.1. and 4.2.1855]
[DKKkt; F.M. (Ballet)
A photocopy of this scenario is now in DKKk (call no. Ms. Phot. 233, 4°).

Musical sources:

Orchestral score. Ms. Autograph (by H. S. Paulli). Brown ink. 1 vol. 386 pp. (26,3 × 37 cm with minor variants)
273/Abdallah.
Signed and dated (on p. 385): 'HSPaulli/Kjöbenhavn d: 21 Marts 1855.'
[DKKk; C II, 119 (KTB 273)
This autographed orchestral score contains three musical insertions that were all added at later stages. Two of them are Paulli's autograph and one by M. Strebinger. Paulli's insertions clearly date from his rearrangement of the music for the *Changing Dance (Vexeldands)* in Act I (score no. 2) when it was reused by Bournonville for his much later *Pas de trois* (premièred on 10.10.1872). Strebinger's insertion consists (according to notes in the orchestral score and the répétiteur's copy, pp. 187 and 64 respectively) of the new *Solo* in 2/4 time, which Bournonville inserted for *Palmyra* in Act II (score no. 9) when *Abdallah* was mounted in Vienna on 5.9.1855. Other notes written in Paulli's score on pp. 7 and 12 indicate that Strebinger may also have interpolated two (not yet traced) insertions in the overture in connection with the 1855 Vienna première. Moreover, a later insertion (written by a copyist on pp. 111–112) indicates that a new and slightly different ending to Act I was made for the Vienna production. Finally, a conductor's note (written with red crayon on p. 310) indicates the exact place where P. Borri's *Pas de deux* and *Solo* were incorporated in Act III (score no. 16) of the 1855 Vienna production. Other pencilled notes (in German) indicate the duration of each act as: Act I '30 Minuten', Act II '45 M:', and Act III '3 Viertel Stund'. All together these notes indicate beyond any doubt that Paulli's autographed orchestral score was brought to Vienna by Bournonville in 1855 and served there if not for the actual performances of the ballet then at least for his preparation of the Vienna conductor's score for this ballet (now in AWn, call no. O. A. 1034).

Répétiteur's copy. Ms. Autograph (by H. S. Paulli). Brown ink. 1 vol. 142 pp. (33,5 × 25 cm)
B. 273/Abdallah./<u>Ballet i 3 Akter</u>/<u>Bournonville</u>/<u>Paulli</u>/1855
Unsigned and dated (on the front cover): '1855'
[DKKk; MA ms 2967 (KTB 273)
This répétiteur's copy contains Bournonville's autographed notes (written with brown ink). Apart from Act II (score no. 9) and Act III (the *Finale*, score no. 19) they describe the dramatic action, mime, and choreography in fine detail. His other (partially smeared) pencilled autographed notes (written on pp. 68–74) indicate the dramatic action and the mime for Act II, score no 9. All together these notes seem (according to his diary) to have been written between 20.9.1853 and 12.1.1854.

Other later notes in German (written with brown ink) indicate the exact places where Strebinger's new *Solo* for *Palmyra* in Act II (score no. 9), and P. Borri's *Pas de deux* and *Solo* in Act III (score no. 16) were incorporated when *Abdallah* was premièred in Vienna on 5.9.1855. They provide clear evidence that the Copenhagen répétiteur's copy must also have been brought to Vienna by Bournonville in 1855, serving him there for the rehearsals at the Kärnthnerthor Theatre. Moreover, the many other minor musical cuts made in this volume probably relate to Bournonville's slightly revised version of *Abdallah* which he made for its third performance in Vienna on 10.9.1855. Finally, his autographed choreographic numbers and notes (written with brown ink) in the music for the *Changing Dance (Vexeldands)* in Act I (score no. 2, pp. 6–20) clearly refer to similar numbers in his much later choreographic notation of the *Pas de trois* which he created on 10.10.1872 and set to Paulli's music from *Abdallah*.

Parts. Ms. Copy. 34 vol.
3 vl I, 3 vl II, 2 vla, 3 vlc e cb, fl picc e II, fl I, ob 1/2, cl 1/2, fag 1/2, cor 1/2/3/4, tr 1/2, trb 1/2/3, timp, gr cassa, tamb, piatti e tri, gong, arpa.
Unsigned and undated [1855]
[DKKk; KTB 273

Other sources:

Costume drawing by E. Lehmann. Pencil and water colours (24,1 × 10,5 cm)
1.
Unsigned and undated [c.1855]
[DKKkt; Kostumetegninger (Lehmann)
This drawing shows the first costume of sheik *Ismail* in Acts I and II of *Abdallah*.

Costume drawing by E. Lehmann. Pencil and water colours (24,1 × 11,8 cm)
No. 1/Ubestemt
Unsigned and undated [c.1855]
[DKKkt; Kostumetegninger (Lehmann)
This drawing shows the first costume of *Abdallah* in Acts I–II of the ballet of that name.

Costume drawing by E. Lehmann. Pencil and water colours (25 × 12,3 cm)
Abdallah/No. 3/2/1 Paaklædning/samme Underdragt
Unsigned and undated [c.1855]
[DKKkt; Kostumetegninger (Lehmann)
This drawing shows the second costume of *Abdallah* in Acts II and III of the ballet of that name.

Costume drawing by E. Lehmann. Pencil and water colours (24, 4 × 19,3 cm)
Omar/No. 5.
Unsigned and undated [c.1855]
[DKKkt; Kostumetegninger (Lehmann)
This drawing shows the costume of *Omar* in Acts II and III of *Abdallah*.

Costume drawing by E. Lehmann. Pencil and water colours (21,5 × 17,2 cm)
Jf. Rostock/Jf S. Price
Unsigned and undated [c.1855]
[DKKkt; Kostumetegninger (Lehmann)
This drawing shows the costumes of the two friends of *Irma* in Act I of *Abdallah* (performed by J. Rostock and S. Price).

Costume drawing by E. Lehmann. Pencil and water colours (24,1 × 18,5 cm)
Forskjellige Turbaner/No. 8./No. 2.
Unsigned and undated [c.1855]
[DKKkt; Kostumetegninger (Lehmann)

This drawing shows the costumes and the turbans worn by five men of the corps de ballet in Act I (?) of *Abdallah*.

Costume drawing by E. Lehmann. Pencil and water colours (24 × 33,7 cm)
Ismails Sønner/No. 7.
Unsigned and undated [c.1855]
[DKKkt; Kostumetegninger (Lehmann)
This drawing shows the costumes and the armory worn by the sons of *Ismail* in Act III of *Abdallah*.

Costume drawing by E. Lehmann. Pencil and water colours (30,5 × 24,5 cm)
2./3./Irma./4./Abdallah
Unsigned and undated [c.1855]
[SSm; Daniel Fryklunds samling no. 253 (F 1330 a)
This drawing shows the three costumes worn by *Irma* in Acts I–III of *Abdallah*.

Costume drawing by E. Lehmann. Pencil and water colours (20 × 25 cm)
Scheik Ismail/2./Ubestemt/No. 4./Abdallah
Unsigned and dated (on the back side): '1855'
[SSm; Daniel Fryklunds samling no. 254 (F 1330 b)
This drawing shows the costumes worn in Act III of *Abdallah* by sheik *Ismail* and *Abdallah* respectively.

Printed sources:

Printed scenario. 1 vol. 16 pp. (19,9 × 12,6 cm)
Abdallah./Ballet i 3 Acter/af/August Bournonville./Musiken componeret af Paulli./Decorationerne af Dhrr. Christensen og Lund./Costumet tegnet af Edw. Lehmann. Maskineriet anordnet af Hr. Weddén.
Kjøbenhavn, J. H. Schubothe/Bianco Luno, 1855
[DKKk; 17, – 174 8°

2.6.1855
Pas de deux (uncredited) performed by S. Lund and S. Price (the Court Theatre).
This dance was given as part of a charity performance for the 'cellist in the Royal Theatre Orchestra, F. Rauch, and is perhaps identical with the so-called *Pas de deux (new)* by *Mr. Ballet Master Bournonville*, performed at the Court Theatre by S. Lund and Juliette Price on 19.6.1854. Other possible identifications of this dance are:

(1) the (uncredited) *Pas de deux*, danced by Lund and S. Price at the Royal Theatre on 24.4.1851.
(2) the Bournonville *Pas de deux*, performed by Lund and P. Fredstrup at the Royal Theatre on 27.12.1850.
(3) the *Pas de deux* from Act II (score no. 15) of Bournonville's three-act romantic ballet *Faust* (see 25.4.1832), which had been given as a separate divertissement at the Royal Theatre on 15.10.1839.

According to his diary Bournonville attended the performance; but he made no specific comments about this dance. It is not possible to identify the dance any further.

11.6.1855
Pas de deux (uncredited) performed by Julius Price and Juliette Price (the Court Theatre).
This dance was given as part of a special charity performance for the dancer, Amalia Price (sister of Julius Price), and is perhaps identical with the so-called *Pas de debut* arranged by Bournonville for her and her brother four years earlier at the Court Theatre on 4.6.1851. It is not possible to identify the dance any further.

11.6.1855

The Sailor's Return, Divertissement (Matrosens Hjemkomst, Divertissement) **performed by Julius Price and S. Price (the Court Theatre).**

This performance seems to represent the first time Bournonville's divertissement *The Sailor's Return (see* 9.6.1852) was ever mounted in Copenhagen, and was this year given as part of a special charity performance for the dancer, Amalia Price. Bournonville did not attend the performance. *The Sailor's Return* was restaged with the same dancers at the Court Theatre on 18.6.1855 and reached a total of 10 performances there, the last of which was given on 20.2.1867.

Musical sources:

No orchestral score and répétiteur's copy dating from the 1855 performance of *The Sailor's Return* at the Court Theatre have yet been traced. This seems to indicate that the divertissement was performed with partial use of the music material employed for its 1852 première in Norway (now in DKKk, call nos. MA ms 2670 and MA ms 2671).

Parts. Ms. Copy. 21 vol.
2 vl I, 2 vl II, vla, 2 vlc e cb, fl 1/2, ob 1/2, cl 1/2, fag 1/2, cor 1/2, tr 1/2, timp, gr cassa.
Unsigned and undated [c.1855]
[DKKk; KTB 337 a
This (reduced) set of parts for *The Sailor's Return* probably dates from its first performance in Copenhagen at the Court Theatre in 1855.

23.7.1855

Robert le Diable (Robert der Teufel) **(Vienna's Kärnthnerthor Theatre).**

In his diary Bournonville noted about this, his first and only staging outside Denmark of the divertissement in Act III (score no. 16) of G. Meyerbeer's five-act opera *(see also* 5.12. 1841 and 18.1.1848):

2.7.1855: 'Besøg hos Directeuren, hjertelig Modtagelse overalt. Strax afgjort at Juliette [Price] skulde debutere den 12.e Juli som Helene i Robert le Diable'
4.7.: 'Prøve paa Robert [...] Componeret Juliettes Dands'.
19.7.: 'Prøve paa Burgtheatret Kl. 8 Robert som gik fortreffeligt'
20.7.: 'Prøve paa B Theatret Kl. 8. Det gik udmærket'
21.7.: 'Kl. 8–11 Generalprøve paa Robert le diable. Juliette udførte Helenes Parti, det gik udmærket godt og Mange ÿttrede stor Tilfredhed dermed.'
23.7.: 'Robert af Normandiet. Juliettes første Debut. Hun præsterede ganske udmærket, men nød kun en kold Modtagelse. Det kunde ikke andet end nedslaae os Noget, men vi fattede dog snart Mod igjen, da vi fik Vished om at hun ikke havde mishaget, men kun frapperet ved det højst forskjellige i hendes hele Methode fremfor det, som man er vant til at see her. Vi haabe bedre Lÿkke for Fremtiden. Pigebarnet viste ved denne Leilighed en fortreffelig Characteer'.

Juliette Price performed the part of the abbess *Hélène* seven times in Vienna, the last time 9.3.1856. According to his diary, Bournonville later also taught this rôle to the Italian dancer, P. Ricci, on 24.10.1855. She, however, did not perform the part until 29.10.1856, long after Bournonville had left Vienna.

Musical sources:

Orchestral score. Ms. Copy. Black and brown ink. 1 vol. 632 pp. (30,9 × 24,6 with minor variants)
Robert der Teufel/Partitur/3. Akt.

Unsigned and undated [c.1833]
[AWn; O. A. 1314
According to the numerous conductor's notes (written with pencil, and red and black crayon) this score was used for all performances of Meyerbeer's opera at Vienna's Kärnthnerthor Theatre between 31.8.1833 and 25.1.1870. It is made of several manuscript copies originating from different periods and places. This is clear from the fact that several sections are given French titles, while others include German and/or Italian headings. Conductor's notes (written on pp. 200r – 316r) indicate several later omissions and musical cuts in the Act III divertissement. According to these the entire divertissement played as follows:
(1) 'Recit.vo et Evocation', Molto moderato in 4/4 time (69 meas.): In this number meas. 13–25 were omitted.
(2) 'Procession der Nonnen', Andante sostenuto in 3/4 time (54 meas.): No omissions are made in this section.
(3) 'Recitativo' in 4/4 time (25 meas.): No omissions are made in this number.
(4) 'Bacchanale', Allegro con moto in 4/4 time (alla breve, 300 meas.): Here meas. 13–55, 86–89, 92–98, 122–123, 127–131, 139–144, 155–156 were initially omitted, but were (according to conductor's notes reading: 'Gilt') reinstated at a later stage.
(5) Without title, Allegro vivace in 6/8 time (65 meas.): A pencilled metronome marking for this section indicates the tempo with a dotted crochet being equal to '76'. Moreover, a conductor's note indicates that a general pause ('halten/Pause') was added to this movement between meas. 40 and 41.
(6) 'Recitativo', Andante in 4/4 time (53 meas.): No omissions are made in this number.
(7) Without title and indication of tempo, in 4/4 time (alla breve) [i.e. 1st solo variation for *Hélène*] (33 meas.): This movement proceeds into a 'poco meno' section in 4/4 time (16 meas.) and for which a pencilled metronome marking indicates the tempo with a crochet equal to '104'. That movement, in turn, continues into a 'Tempo I°' section in 4/4 time (alla breve, 25 meas.) after which follows a section of 14 meas. in 3/4 time, the first 9 bars of which were cancelled.
(8) 'IIme Air de Ballet', Un peu moins vite, Moderato assai in 3/4 time (113 meas.): No omissions are made in this dance.
(9) 'II [i.e. III] Air Ballet' (54 meas.): No omissions are made in this number except for the very first bar, which at some later stage became shortened to the upbeat only.
(10) 'Tanz mit Chor', Allegro vivace, All.o in 4/4 time (alla breve, 69 meas.): In this number meas. 59–62 were omitted.

Printed piano vocal score. 1 vol. 462 pp. (26,6 × 18,2 cm)
Roberto/Il Diavolo/Opéra en 5 Actes [...] avec Paroles/Italiennes et Allemandes
Paris, Brandus & C.ie, pl. no. B. & C.ie 5284 [c.1846]
[AWn; O. A. 1945

No répétiteur's copy and set of parts dating from the 1855 performances of *Robert der Teufel* in Vienna have yet been traced.

Printed sources:

Printed libretto. 1 vol. 42 pp. (17,1 × 11,4 cm)
Robert der Teufel./Grosse romantische Oper in fünf Akten
Wien, A. Pichler's Witwe & Sohn, 1854.
[AWn; 987.6680 – A M. TB
The décor and the ballet divertissement in Act III, scene 7 is in this libretto described (on pp. 30–31) as follows:
'Verwandlung. Die Bühne zeigt den innern Theil einer in Ruinen zerfallenen Burg mit einem Kirchhofe. Die Gegend ist vom Mond erhellt. Auf einer Statue erblickt man einem grünen Zweig. [...] Tanz [...] Robert will entfliehen, wird aber von phantastischen Gestalten durch Tanz verleitet, den Zweig zu brechen. er widersteht lange, unterliegt aber am Ende, er bricht den Zweig, schwingt ihn durch unterliegt aber am Ende, er bricht den Zweig, schwingt ihn durch die luft, und eilt ab.'

At the restaging on 3.1.1854 in Vienna of *Robert der Teufel* the divertissement in Act III was choreographed and mounted by P. Taglioni, with the abbess *Hélène* then being danced by M. Taglioni (the younger).

27.7.1855
Pas de trois **performed by Julius Price, P. Ricci, and Juliette Price as an incorporated divertissement in Act II of** *Robert und Bertrand* **(Vienna's Kärnthnerthor Theatre).**

This dance represents the Viennese debut of Bournonville's pupil, Julius Price. Because H. Schmidt's orchestral score for P. Taglioni's Vienna production of F.-M. Hoguet's three-act comic ballet *Robert und Bertrand* (premièred on 8.12.1854) is no longer preserved, it is impossible to establish exactly where in the second act of this ballet Bournonville's *Pas de trois* was incorporated.

According to notes in his diary, the same *Pas de trois* was later also performed 14 times in a slightly abridged version at the Kärnthnerthor Theatre. These performances took place between 2.8.1855 and 1.3.1856 and were given as an incorporated divertissement in Act III of P. Borri's staging of J. Mazilier's and Th. Labarre's three-act pantomimic ballet *Carita* (premièred at Vienna's Kärnthnerthor Theatre on 2.8.1855, but originally created for the Paris Opéra on 11.11.1853 with the title *Jovita, ou les Boucaniers*). Notes in the orchestral score for this ballet (now in AWn, call no. O. A. 1033) indicate that Bournonville's *Pas de trois* was incorporated as score no. '28' immediately before the ballet's final 'Grand Ballabile'. Moreover, a conductor's note on p. '98r' in the same score reads: 'Pas/Trois/v. Strebinger'. This gives clear evidence that the music for Bournonville's 1855 *Pas de trois* (for which no musical sources have yet been traced) was composed by M. Strebinger. Finally, the *Pas de trois* was also performed 3 times as part of a so-called *Divertissement dansant* given at the Kärnthnerthor Theatre on 29.9., 9.11., and 18.12.1855.

In his diary Bournonville noted about his creation, the 1854 première, and the later performances in Vienna of this dance:

7.7.1855: 'Hørt lidt af [Guillaume] Tell og set den lille [P.] Ricci som dandsede meget godt til sin Debut'
11.7.: 'skrevet og componeret'
12.7.: 'componeret [...] Lection hos [G.] Carey til Julius [Price] som begyndte en nÿ Pas de trois'
13.7.: 'componeret lidt'
14.7.: 'Prøve for Juliette [Price] og Julius'. Mr. og M.me Bretelle saae dem med stor Fornøielse'
16.7.: 'skrevet og componeret [...] Lection til Julius Kl 1. – componeret'
17.7.: 'componeret [...] Prøve fra Kl 9 til 11. Det gik udmærket godt'
18.7.: 'componeret [...] og Prøve paa Burgtheatret Kl 8 1/2 – 10 fuldendt Pas de trois'
24.7.: 'Prøve paa B. Theatret Kl 8. – Det gik ypperligt'
25.7.: 'Prøve paa Theatret'
26.7.: 'Prøve paa Burgtheatret og i Operaen. Beslutning at Pas de trois skulde dandses Imorgen i Robert og Bertrand'
27.7.: 'lille Prøve med Mlle Ricci [...] Forberedelser til Iaften. Juliette og Julius dandsede den nÿ Pas de trois med meget Bifald og det gik udmærket godt'
31.7.: 'Generalprøve paa [P.] Borris Ballet. (Pas de trois forkortet)'
2.8.: 'Første Forestilling af Carita (Her den franske Jovita[, ou les Boucaniers] af Borri) – meget Applaus. Min pas de trois gik med særdeles Applaus (Juliette tiltaler mere og mere)'
3.8.: 'Balletten gik igjen. Dandsen gik meget godt og med Bifald'
6.8.: 'Carita i Theatret. Pas de trois høstede meget Bifald'

9.8.: 'Balletten Carita, pas de trois meget applauderet'
26.9.: 'Carrita. Juliette dandsede smukt'
9.11.: 'lille Prøve paa Pas de trois til Iaften, med [G.] Hel[l]mesberger i [J.] Mayseders Sted [...] Om Aftenen Divertissement – Juliette dandsede smukt og med meget Bifald'
18.12.: 'Divertissement i Operaen, hvor Juliette og Julius dandsede deres pas de trois med meget Bifald'.

5.9.1855
Die Gazelle von Bassora (Abdallah) **(Vienna's Kärnthnerthor Theatre).**

This production represents Bournonville's first and only staging outside Denmark of his three-act ballet *Abdallah* (*see* 28.3.1855). It differed from the original Copenhagen version by a series of completely new dances which (according to the poster) included:

(1) A new *Solo* to music by M. Strebinger, incorporated by Bournonville for the character *Palmyra* and performed by the Italian ballerina, C. Pocchini, in Act II (score no. 9).
(2) A *Pas de deux* followed by a *Solo* and interpolated in Act III after the first 28 bars of score no. 16.

These dances were both created by the Italian choreographer, P. Borri, who himself performed the *Pas de deux* together with his wife, C. Pocchini (the latter also dancing the *Solo*).

Notes in the Vienna conductor's score for *Abdallah* (reading: 'Pas/Solo/v. Carita./in E') indicate that Borri's two dances in Act III were originally part of his then recent Vienna production of J. Mazilier's and Th. Labarre's three-act pantomimic ballet *Carita* (first performed at the Kärnthnerthor Theatre on 2.8.1855, but originally premièred at the Paris Opéra on 11.11.1853 with the title *Jovita, ou les Boucaniers*). Moreover, according to the orchestral score for *Carita* (now in AWn, call no. O. A. 1033), Borri's two dances were originally performed in that ballet in Acts I and II respectively, with the *Solo* being set to music by M. Strebinger and entitled *Pas de tambourin*.

As a result of the incorporation of these dances in *Die Gazelle von Bassora* Bournonville was forced to omit his own so-called *Pas de caractère* in Act I (score no. 3) when the ballet was given its third performance on 10.9.1855. This is clear from notes in his diary, according to which this change was ordered directly by the threatre director, J. Cornet. His commands also induced Bournonville to accept several other minor cuts made throughout the ballet (in Act I, score nos. 2, 3, and 5, Act II, score nos. 6, 7, 8, 9, 12, and Act III, score nos. 15, 18, and 19). Thus, a note written in the part for the first flute indicates that *Die Gazelle von Bassora* originally played for a total of 2 hours and 15 minutes, while other pencilled notes (written in the part for the first violin) describe the reduced duration of each act as: Act I, 30 minutes; Act II, 35 minutes; and Act III, 45 minutes.

Die Gazelle von Bassora received 5 performances in Vienna, the last of which took place on 12.1.1856.

In his diary Bournonville noted about his preparations for the Vienna production, its rehearsals and 1855 première:

26.1.1855: 'Program begyndt paa Dansk og Fransk'
28.1.: 'skrevet den hele Formiddag'
31.1.: 'skrevet paa mine Programmer'
2.2.: 'skrevet en stor Deel af Programmet'
3.2.: 'Jeg sad oppe og skrev paa mit franske Program til Kl 12'

4.2.: fuldført mit franske Program, bragt det til Copiering til Prof.
[N. C. L.] Abrahams'
6.2. 'Brev til [J.] Cornet'
8.2.: 'besørget mit Franske Program'
28.2.: 'skrevet den hele Formiddag og besøgt Abrahams [...] expederet Programmet af Abdallah til Cornet'
28.7.: 'Prøve i Redout=salen. 1.ste Indstudering til Abdallah'
30.7.: 'Indstudering paa Abdallah'
1.8.: '3.die Indstudering paa Abdallah fra Kl 9–11½'
3.8.: 'Prøve i R. Salen 4.de Indstudering paa Abdallah [...] componeret.'
4.8.: 'componeret [...] Prøve i Redouten 5.te'
6.8.: 'lille Prøve i Redouten [...] arbeidet med Maskinmesteren [G.]
Dreylich og med Capelmester [F. (or L.?)] Ricci'
7.8.: 'Prøve i R. S. indtil 12 [...] componeret, modtaget Musik af
Ricci'
10.8.: 'Prøve paa den store pas de cinq. Vi mister formodentlig Localet formedelst Reparationer'
11.8.: 'Prøve fra 12–1 samt i [G.] Careys Sal 5–6.'
12.8.: 'besørget adskilligt Ballettens Decorationer vedkommende'
13.8.: 'lille Prøve i Salongen paa Theatret – lært endeel af 2.den Akt'
16.8.: 'Prøve i Salonen fra 10–12½'8.8.: 'Prøve indtil Kl 12, en heel
Deel færdig'
17.8.: 'Prøve i Salonen 10–11½'9.8.: 'Prøve i R. S.
18.8.: 'Prøve paa Theatret'
20.8.: 'Prøve paa Theatret. Decorationsmøde. Costumemøde'
21.8.: 'Min 50.de Aars Fødselsdag [...] En god Prøve paa Theatret'
22.8.: 'Prøve paa Theatret, hele 1.ste Akt, gik udmærket. Det var en
fortreffelig Dag for mig!'
23.8.: 'Prøve fra 9 til 1. [C.] Pocchini!! Det gik meget heldigt'
24.8.: 'Prøve paa Abdallah fra 9 til 1½, det gaaer godt fremad [...]
Lille Prøve med [P.] Ricci og]E.] Roll'
25.8.: 'Prøve paa Theatret fra 10–12, det gik brillant' [...] Prøve kl 4
for Carey. [L.] Frappart lærte sin Rolle færdig'
27.8.: 'Paa Theatret fra 8½ til 1, god Prøve og Indstuderingen af
2.den Akt færdig. – Lille Prøve paa 3.die Akt fra 4–6'
28.8.: 'Prøve paa Theatret. (3.die Akt) indtil Kl 12½'
29.8.: 'Prøve fra 10–1½'
30.8.: 'besørget og skrevet til Balletten. Prøve fra 10. til 11½. Indstuderingen færdig'
31.8.: 'Prøve paa alle tre Akter, meget gik godt men der fattes Disci-
plin i Personalet'
1.9.: 'Musikprøve fra 9 indtil 11½. Prøve paa Dandsene. Det gik
særdeles godt, færdig Kl 1½'
2.9.: 'Decorationsprøve paa Theatret'
3.9.: 'Hele dagen beskjæftiget med Balletten. 1.ste Generalprøve,
stor Uorden med Reqvisiter'
4.9.: 'Som igaar, sidste Generalprøve, lidt bedre, (men det gaaer hulter til bulter ved dette Theater)'
5.9.: 'besørget adskilligt til den første Fremstilling af min Ballet, der
skal gaae Iaften. Lille Prøve med Maskiner og Requisiter [...] Balletten gik under Navnet 'Die Gazelle von Bassora' og blev i det Hele
meget godt udført. Juliette [Price] overgik sig selv baade i Kraft og
Sikkerhed. Udstyrelsen var Pragtfuld og Musiken gik ypperligt. Decorationerne vare smukke og intet gik feil i Maskineriet, men Balletten blev optaget med en Kulde, der gav mig den Overbevisning at
mine Kunstbestræbelser her i Wien ere spildte. Applausen er i Italienernes Hænder og Wienerne forlange Overdrivelser, som jeg ikke
kan gaae ind paa. Uagtet alle de Vidnesbyrd om Tilfredshed jeg har
modtaget ved Prøverne kan jeg dog betragte mit Arbeide som faldet
igjennem'
6.9.: 'De fleste Blade behandle Balletten med Strenghed og under
Indflydelse af de Anskuelser der herske hos det større Publicum [...]
Jeg modtog et mærkeligt Brev fra Cornet om forkortelser i Balletten.
2.den Forestilling om Aftnen, den gik ganske fortrinlig. Juliette
udførte sit Parti fortreffelig men Applausen var for Herr [P.] Borri og
Mlle Pocchini i en frygtelig Pas de deux; – dog jeg mærkede allerede
paa mig selv at man kan vænne sig af med den larmende Erkjendelse.
Jeg kom fornøiet hjem'
7.9.: 'Prøve paa væsentlige Forkortninger i Abdallah'
10.9.: 'Balletten gik for 3.die gang og særdeles godt. Juliette dandsede udmærket og nød Anerkjeldelse'.

About the rehearsals prior to the fifth and last performance
of *Die Gazelle von Bassora* in Vienna on 12.1.1856 he noted:

6.1.1856: 'Sceneprøve paa Abdallah'
7.1.: 'Prøve fr a 10–1 paa Abdallah'
8.1.: 'Prøve fra 10–1 1/2 paa Abdallah'
11.1.: 'Paa Theatret fra 9 1/2 til 1 1/2, Generalprøve paa Abdallah'
12.1.: 'lille Prøve paa Abdallah [...] Abdallah gik for godt Huus, ved
Keiserhoffets Nærværelse og med Bifald. Juliette dandsede og spillede sin Rolle fortrinligt og hele Balletten gik med Liv. Jeg var meget
glad og takkede Gud i mit Hjerte'.

Autograph sources:

Manuscript scenario. Ms. Copy (perhaps written by N. C. L. Abrahams and including Bournonville's autographed signature and
notes reading: 'Presenté à la Direction Imperiale & Royale du
théâtre de l'Opéra à Vienne'). Brown ink. 1 vol. 14 pp. (25,9 × 18,6
cm)
Abdallah/ou/La gazelle de Bassora,/Ballet en 3 actes composé par/
Auguste Bournonville/1855.
Dated: 'Copenhague ce 28 février 1855.'
[DKKk; NKS 3285 4° 2 A–E

Musical sources:

Conductor's score/Répétiteur's copy. Ms. Copy. Brown ink. 1 vol.
174 pp. (31,7 × 25,2 cm)
1034/Foglietto/Abdallah/[Fogli]etto/O. A. 1034.
Unsigned and undated [1855–56]
[AWn; O. A. 1034

Orchestral score (*Solo* in Act II). Ms. Autograph (by M. Strebinger).
Black ink. 4 pp. (32,9 × 26 cm)
Einlage zum Ballet Abdalla/Agitato
Signed (on p. 1): 'Strebinger', undated [1855]
[DKKk; C II, 119 (KTB 273, *Abdallah*, ad p. 187)
This autographed orchestral score contains M. Strebinger's music
for Bournonville's incorporated *Solo* in Act II (score no. 9) of *Die
Gazelle von Bassora*, performed by the Italian ballerina, C. Pocchini
(as *Palmyra*).

Répétiteur's copy (*Solo* in Act II). Ms. Autograph (by M. Strebinger).
Black ink. 1 p. (32,9 × 25,5 cm)
Agitato assai./foglietto
Signed: 'Strebinger', undated [1855]
[DKKk; MA ms 2749 (1) (KTB 273)
This autographed répétiteur's copy contains M. Strebinger's music
for Bournonville's incorporated *Solo* in Act II (score no. 9) of *Die
Gazelle von Bassora*, performed by the Italian ballerina, C. Pocchini
(as *Palmyra*).

Parts. Ms. Copy. 41 vol.
vl princ, 5 vl I, 5 vl II, 3 vla, 2 vlc, 3 cb, fl 1, fl picc e 2, ob 1/2, cl 1/2,
fag 1/2, cor 1/2/3/4, tr 1/2, trb 1 e 2, trb 3, timp, oph, gr cassa,
tamb, tri, arpa.
Unsigned and undated [1855–56]
[AWn; O. A. 1034 (Orchesterstimmen)
A musician's note written in the part for the first trumpet ('morte e
taci') clearly reflects the ballet's poor success with the Vienna audience.

Other sources:

Sketch by C. Brioschi(?) for the back curtain employed in Act III of
Die Gazelle von Bassora. Pencil and water colours (32,5 × 42,5 cm)
Fas. 2/36/zum Ballet/Zhea [erased]/zu Gazelle v Bassora/462/2.
Unsigned and undated [1855]
[AWth; HOpÜ/5025
This décor was originally made for Act II of P. Taglioni's and C.
Pugni's two-act fantastic ballet *Thea, oder Die belebten Blumen*

(premièred at Vienna's Kärnthnerthor Theatre on 30.10.1853 and given there for the last time on 16.11.1853). It was reused in 1855 for Act III of Bournonville's *Die Gazelle von Bassora*, which (according to the 1855 Vienna libretto) takes place in 'Ein grosser Garten mit Brunnen verziert'.

Printed sources:

Printed scenario. 1 vol. 16 pp. (18 × 11,4 cm)
Die Gazelle von Bassora./Ballet in Drei Akten/von August Bournonville.
Wien, A. Pichler's Witwe & Sohn, 1855.
[AWn; 802.551 B Th., and DKKk; 17, – 174 8°

23.9.1855
The Sailor's Return, Scene and Dance (Matrosens Hjemkomst, Scene og Dands) **performed by E. Stramboe and L Stillmann.**
This performance represents the first time Bournonville's divertissement *The Sailor's Return* (*see* 9.6.1852) was performed at Copenhagen's Royal Theatre. Bournonville did not attend its performance because of his engagement as ballet-master at Vienna's Kärnthnerthor Theatre in the same season. *The Sailor's Return* received 7 performances at the Royal Theatre, the last of which was given on 12.12.1858.

Musical sources:

Conductor's part. Ms. Copy. Black ink. 10 pp. (34,8 × 25,5 cm)
Matrosens Hjemkomst./Matrosens Hjemkomst/Dirigent Stemme
Unsigned and undated [c.1855]
[DKKk; MA ms 3016 (KTB 337 (1))
This conductor's part most probably dates from the first performance of *The Sailor's Return* at the Royal Theatre.

The répétiteur's copy used for the 1855 première of *The Sailor's Return* at the Royal Theatre is now in DKKk (call no. MA ms 2904 (3) (KTB 337), but in parts originally KTB 206)).

Parts. Ms. Copy. 25 vol.
2 vl I, 2 vl II, vla, 2 vlc e cb, fl 1/2, ob 1/2, cl 1/2, fag 1/2, cor 1/2, tr 1/2, trb 1/2/3, timp, gr cassa e piatti, tri.
Unsigned and undated [c.1855]
[DKKk; KTB 337 b
This set of parts represents the only orchestral material for *The Sailor's Return* that has been traced so far. It most probably dates from its first performance at the Royal Theatre.

25.9.1855
Faust.
This performance represents Bournonville's second and last restaging in Copenhagen of his three-act romantic ballet *Faust* (*see* 25.4.1832). According to a letter written in Copenhagen on 14.5.1855 to the director of the Royal Theatre, J. L. Heiberg (now in the State Archive, call no. Det kgl. Teaters Arkiv, Gruppe E, pakke 288), it was this year mounted in a thoroughly revised version in only two acts. Moreover, in a note in his diary on the same day Bournonville indicated the duration of this new version as: 'Reducert de to förste Akter (1. Akt 20 min., 2. Akt 45 min)'. Furthermore, in his letter to Heiberg, Bournonville gave an interesting account of his reasons for mounting this new version:

'Ved Arrangementet af det Repertoire jeg ønsker at efterlade ved min Afreise er jeg kommen til den Erfaring at Balletten Faust, med lidt forandring reduceret til de to første Akter vilde afgive et særdeles brugbart Stykke og vinde forøget Interesse derved, at den bedste Deel blev bibeholdt og ikke vilde spille længere tid end <u>fem</u>

Quarteer. Da saaledes sujettet kom til at sluttes omtrent paa samme Maade som i [J. W. v.] Goethes Mesterværk d. er: Gretchen afslaaer Frelsen ved den Ondes Bistand, hvorved alle Hendes Lidelser i tredie Akt bortfaldt tilligemed Markedet og de Partier der altid have været svage og slet udstyrede, vilde det Hele blive smukt afrundet i Særdeleshed naar det kunde bringes til at gaae foran et muntert Stykke, Vaudeville eller deslige; som sagt 1.ste Akt vare 20 Minutter og 2.den Akt 45 Min. Altsaa med Mellemakten fem Quarteer i det Hele'.

Bournonville did not attend any of the performances of his two-act version of *Faust* because of his engagement in the same season as ballet-master at Vienna's Kärnthnerthor Theatre. However, according to his diary he directed two rehearsals of it on 14.5. and 31.5.1855 before leaving for Vienna on the last date.

The 1855 production of *Faust* received 5 performances, the last of which took place on 17.11.1855.

Musical sources:

Répétiteur's copy. Ms. Copy. Black ink. 1 vol. 86 pp. of which two are blank (33,7 × 26 cm)
Repetiteur/Partie/til/Balletten/Faust/1855.
Unsigned and dated (on the front cover by Bournonville?): '1855.'
[DKKk; MA ms 2642 (KTB 289)
This répétiteur's copy contains the music for Bournonville's abridged two-act version of *Faust* (Act I, score nos. 1–8, and Act II, score nos. 9–21) which he arranged during the spring of 1855.

13.10.1855
Pas de trois **(uncredited) performed by S. Lund, P. Fredstrup, and J. Rostock.**
This dance is most probably identical with the earlier (uncredited) *Pas de trois*, performed by the same three dancers on 23.1.1854 and, in turn, is most likely identical with the even earlier *Pas de trois* in Act I (score no. 5) of Bournonville's Copenhagen version of J. Aumer's three-act pantomimic ballet *La Somnambule, ou l'Arrivée d'un nouveau seigneur* (*see* 21.9.1829). That dance was first given as a separate divertissement by Lund, Fredstrup, and Rostock on 8.4.1848. According to the rehearsal book of H. C. J Fredstrup, all rehearsals of the *Pas de trois* in 1855 were directed by S. Lund. Bournonville did not attend its performance because of his engagement as ballet-master at Vienna's Kärntherthor Theatre in the same season. It is not possible to identify the dance any further.

21.10.1855
La Juive (Die Jüdin) **(Vienna's Kärnthnerthor Theatre).**
The 1855 Vienna restaging of J.-F. Halévy's five-act opera (originally premièred at the Paris Opéra on 23.2.1835) represents the first time Bournonville was ever involved in a staging of this work by choreographing and mounting its dances. These included four numbers as follows:

(1) A *Waltz* in Act I (score no. 6), performed by a corps de ballet of townspeople.
(2) A *Processional March* in the Act I finale (score no. 7), performed during the chorus «Hieher! hieher! hieher! seht nur, seht ganz von fern».
(3) A *Pantomime scene* and a *Ballet divertissement* in Act III (score no. 14).
(4) A *Processional March* in Act V (score no. 21).

Two years later Bournonville included *La Juive* in a list of projected opera restagings, which he wrote in Copenhagen on 30.10.1857 for the 1857–58 and 1858–59 seasons. Moreover, on the same day he appears to have written a new mise-en-scène for Halévy's opera. That project was carried out on 4.1.1869, when *La Juive* was mounted at Copenhagen's Royal Theatre with Bournonville's new and complete mise-en-scène for the first time.

Meanwhile, during his three-year tenure at Stockholm's Royal Theatre between 1861–1864 Bournonville made two other mises-en-scène for this opera on 5.10. and 6.10.1863 in preparation for a projected Swedish première of *La Juive*. That project, however, was never carried out by Bournonville, but both his 1857 and the two 1863 mises-en-scènes seem later to have served as a basis for the first staging of this opera at Stockholm's Royal Theatre (Stora Theatern) on 6.6.1866, mounted by his pupil and personal friend, the Swedish actor and director, L. Josephsson. This theory is supported by the fact that one of Bournonville's 1863 manuscripts for *La Juive* is still preserved among Josephsson's working papers (now in SSk, *see* 5.10.-6.10.1863).

Halévy's opera was restaged for a second and the last time by Bournonville in Copenhagen on 29.10.1870.

In his diary he noted about the choreography he created for the 1855 Vienna production of *Die Jüdin*:

11.10.1855: 'componeret en Dands til Jödinden [...] componerede'
12.10.: 'Prøve paa en nÿ Dands til <u>Jødinden</u> (indstuderet færdig.)'
13.10.: 'lille Prøve paa mine Dandse i [...] <u>Jødinden</u>'
16.10.: 'Prøve paa Jødinden'
17.10.: 'Arrangement=prøve paa Jødinden'
18.10.: 'Prøve paa Jødinden'
19.10.: 'Theaterprøve paa Jødinden'
20.10.: 'Generalprøve paa Jødinden'
21.10.: 'Man gav Jødinden for aldeles fuldt Huus og udstyret med særdeles Pragt. Min Dands gik godt. Jeg saae kun 1.ste Akt'.

The *Waltz* in Act I (score no. 7) was also described in his diary on 27.10.1855 as: 'min lille Dands i Jødinden'.

The 1855 Vienna production of *Die Jüdin* received 11 performances during Bournonville's engagement there, the last of which was given on 30.3.1856.

Autograph sources:

Choreographic note. Ms. Autograph. Blue ink. 3 pp. (22,2 × 13,9 cm)
<u>Choeur et Danse.</u>/Du 1.er Acte de <u>la Juive.</u>/<u>Arrangement de Bournonville.</u>
Unsigned and dated: 'Vienne ce 11 Octobre 1855.'
[DKKk; NKS 3285 4° 2 G–K

Musical sources:

Printed orchestral score. 2 vol. Act I-II 188 pp., Act III–V 346 pp. (33,2 × 25,7 cm)
La Juive/Die Jüdin/[...]/Neue correcte Original-Ausgabe.
Berlin, [M.] Schlesinger, pl. no. S. 1966 [1835?]
[AWn; O. A. 1330

No répétiteur's copy and set of parts dating from the 1855 Vienna restaging of *Die Jüdin* have yet been traced.

Other sources:

Manuscript mise-en-scène. Ms. Autograph (by an unknown hand). Black ink, pencil and red crayon. 1 vol. (33,5 × 20,9 cm)

Oper: Die Jüdin
Unsigned and undated [c.1855]
[AWn; Suppl. mus. 32.666
Because of the inclusion in this volume of the names of those singers who performed the leading rôles in the 1855 Vienna restaging of Halévy's opera, this manuscript must certainly date from (or at least was used for) the 1855 production. The volume also contains several stage diagrams and includes a description of the *Processional March* in the Act I finale which reads:
'<u>Ritornell</u>[e] <u>18 takt</u>[e] <u>All</u>[egr]<u>o C dur C.</u> <u>Zuerst kom</u>[m]<u>t die Chor</u> [...] dan[n] ballet. [...] <u>Dann, wen</u>[n] <u>die Gesang angefanz</u> [*sic*] is[t] <u>Ballet</u> n[e]be hin v[on] <u>R</u>[echt] gr[osse] <u>Marsch</u>'.

Printed sources:

Printed libretto. 1 vol. 36 pp. (17,5 × 11 cm)
Die Jüdin./Grosse Oper in fünf Acten/mit Divertissement.
Wien, A. Pichler's Witwe & Sohn, 1855
[AWn; 987.428 A. M. TB
According to this libretto the *Waltz* in Act I, scene 7 (here named 'Tanz') was actually performed during the end of and repeated after the chorus «Hier ist Wein!! edler Wein». Moreover, the *Processional March* in the Act I finale is in this libretto named 'Marsch und Eingang des Königs'.

25.10.1855

Gipsy Dance (Zigeuner=Tanz) in Act III of *Les Huguenots (Die Hugenotten)* performed by L. Frappart, Julius Price, E. Roll, A. Millerceck, and a corps de ballet (Vienna's Kärnthnerthor Theatre).

Bournonville had earlier choreographed the dances in Act III and Act V of G. Meyerbeer's five-act opera *Les Huguenots* when it was given for the first time in Copenhagen on 28.2.1844. In his diary he noted about the new *Gipsy Dance* that he choreographed for Act III (score no. 16) in the 1855 Vienna restaging of *Die Huguenotten*:

24.9.1855: 'componeret efter Ordre en nÿ Dands til <u>Hugenotterne</u>'
25.9.: 'skrevet og componeret [...] Componeret Dandsen færdig'
26.9.: 'Prøve paa Hugenotterne fra 10–11'
2.10. and 6.10.: 'Prøve paa <u>Hugenotterne</u>'
8.10.: 'Prøve paa Hugenotterne Dandsen færdig og vellÿkket'
9.10.: 'Repetition paa Hugenotterne hvordi Dandsen gik særdeles vel'
13.10.: 'Lille Prøve paa mine Dandse til <u>Hugenotterne</u>'
25.10.: 'prøvet Dandsen til Hugenotterne [...] Dirigeret min Dands der gik smukt og blev optaget med Bifald'.

During Bournonville's engagement in Vienna the *Gipsy Dance* was performed 5 times within Meyerbeer's opera, the last time on 4.3.1856.

At the first performance of the opera after Bournonville had left Vienna (31.3.1856) the dance was still being performed by the same cast, but was then presented on the poster without credit to Bournonville for its choreography.

Musical sources:

No orchestral score, répétiteur's copy, and set of parts dating from the 1855 restaging in Vienna of *Die Hugenotten* have yet been traced.

Prompt's book. Ms. Copy. Brown ink. 1 vol. 180 pp. (24,1 × 31,6 cm)
<u>Hugenotten.</u>/<u>Souffleurpart.</u>/<u>III. Band.</u>/[...]/Dritter Akt
Unsigned and undated [c.1839]
[AWn; O. A. 366
This 'Souffleurpart.' was (according to notes written on the inside front cover) used for all performances of Meyerbeer's opera at Vien-

na's Hofoper between 1839 and 1876. In the volume for Act III the *Zigeuner=Tanz* is described (on p. 34) as follows:
'No. 16 Tanz Tacet / Tanz Zigeuner / La Tarentella / Tanz Musik / Gregorius'.

Other sources:

Manuscript 'Soufflierbuch'. Ms. Copy (by an unknown hand). Black ink. 1 vol. 115 pp. (23,9 × 19 cm)
Die Hugenotten. /oder/ Raoul de [changed to] von Nangis. /oder/ Valentine von St: Bris. /Grosse oper in fünf Aufzügen, /auf dem französischen des Scribe/ bearbeitet.
Unsigned and undated [1848?]
[AWn; Suppl. mus. 32.145
According to its title-page this 'Soufflierbuch' clearly seems to date from the restaging of *Die Hugenotten* at Vienna's Kärnthnerthor Theatre on 12.7.1848 (Meyerbeer's opera was first performed there on 19.12.1839 with the title *Die Welfen und Gibellinen*). Thus, the 1848 production represents the first time that the opera was performed in Vienna with the title *Die Hugenotten*. The décor and the *Zigeuner=Tanz* in Act III (Scene 1) are described on pp. 48 and 54 as follows:
'Die Bühne stillt die pré aux clercs [...] Zigeuner eintriern und führen seinen Tanz aus, in welchen die Studenten [erased], die Soldaten und die jungen Mädchen grif manegen'.

Printed sources:

Printed libretto. 1 vol. 87 pp. (15,5 × 9,4 cm)
Die Hugenotten/Oper in 5 Aufzügen/nacch dem Französischen des Sribes/übersetzt von Castelli.
Berlin, s. l., s. a.
[AWn; 987.452 A. M. TB
For the restaging on 12.7.1848 of Meyerbeer's opera at Vienna's Kärnthnerthor Theatre this German translation by Ignaz Franz Castelli was used. In his libretto the Act III *Zigeuner=Tanz* is listed on p. 43 as 'No. 15'.

9.11.1855

La Cracovienne (uncredited) performed by S. Price.

This performance represents the first and only time Bournonville's 1842 version of F. Elssler's Polish character dance *La Cracovienne* (*see* 10.6.1842) was restaged at Copenhagen's Royal Theatre. It was this year performed for the first time by S. Price, who also danced it when it was given its last performance in Copenhagen during Bournonville's lifetime at the Court Theatre on 15.10.1856. The 1855 restaging was most probably mounted by C. Kellermann, as Bournonville was away from Copenhagen this year because of his one-year tenure at Vienna's Kärnthnerthor Theatre in the 1855–56 season. *La Cracovienne* reached a total of 12 performances by S. Price at the Royal Theatre, the last of which took place on 19.6.1856. The musical material employed this year was most probably the same as that used for the 1842 première (now in DKKk, call nos. MA ms 2664, MA ms 2663, and KTB 214).

29.12.1855

L'Etoile du Nord (Der Nordstern) (Vienna's Kärnthnerthor Theatre).

This performance represents the Vienna première of G. Meyerbeer's three-act comic opera (first performed at l'Opéra Comique in Paris on 16.2.1854). It was mounted with Bournonville's mise-en-scène, including his choreography for the opera's three dance scenes. They were as follows:

(1) According to the printed 1855 Vienna libretto for *Der Nordstern* an (unnamed) dance was performed in Act I (scene 7) by the character *Katharina* (disguised as a 'Marketenderin') and joined by a group of 'Kalmücken und Tartaren'. This dance was an integral part of Meyerbeer's so-called *Scène et ronde bohémienne* (score no. 6).
(2) A *Waltz* at the beginning of Act II (score no. 10), performed by a group of eight women.
(3) A *Marche sacrée* in Act II, scene 16 (score no. 13), performed during the chorus entitled «Dieu protecteur, viens, sois son sauveur!».

According to an (anonymous) 1855 Vienna manuscript mise-en-scène for *Der Nordstern* the casts of dancers employed in this production were as follows:

Act I: '8 Damen zum Ballabile'.
Act II: '12 Damen als Husarren, 12 Damen als Infanteristen, 12 Marketenderinnen'.

In his diary Bournonville noted about his staging and the Vienna première of Meyerbeer's opera:

7.11.1855: 'instrueret Frlns [E.] Hofmann og [B.] Holm i en Fægtescene'
8.11.: 'Claveerprøve med Flns H og H'
9.11.: 'prøvet paa Syngeskolen og talt med [G.] Meyerbeer, der er en meget behagelig Mand'
12.11.: 'Claveerprøve med Hofmann og Holm'
13.11.: 'Claveerprøve Kl 4'
15.11.: 'Visit hos Meyerbeer'
16.11.: 'skrevet og componeret paa Dandsen til Nordstjernen'
17.11.: 'skrevet og componeret'
18.11., 19.11., 20.11., and 21.11.: 'skrevet og arrangeret'
23.11.: 'skrevet, confereret om Scene-Arrangementet i Nordstjernen'
26.11. and 27.11.: 'skrevet og arrangeret'
28.11. 'arrangeret Prøverne til Nordstjernen'
29.11.: 'componeret Dandse til Nordstjernen'
30.11.: 'Skrevet og componeret. Indstudering paa Nordstjernen'
1.12.: 'skrevet og arrangeret. Prøve fra 10–1 i Redoutsalen [...] componerede'
2.12.: 'componerede'
3.12.: 'skrevet og arrangeret. Prøve i Redouten paa Dandsene til Nordstjernen, som jeg gjorde færdige; exercerede med Choristinderne'
4.12.: 'Repetition i Redouten [...] skrevet og componeret'
5.12.: 'skrevet og arrangeret. Prøve i Redouten [...] fra 11-1 for Ballettens og Chorets Damer'
6.12.: '2. Arrangementprøve paa Nordstjernen'
7.12.: 'Prøve Arrangement paa Nordstjernen'
11.12.: 'Arrangementprøve paa Nordstjernen'
12.12.: 'Excerceerprøve fra 9–10. Arrangementprøve'
13.12.: 'Prøve'
14.12. and 15.12.: 'Prøve paa Nordstjernen'
17.12.: 'Prøve fra Kl 9 til 12½ paa Nordstjernen [...] skrevet og componeret'
18.12., 19.12., and 20.12.: 'Prøve paa 'Nordstjernen''
21.12.: 'Skrevet og arrangeret Prøve paa Nordstjernen'
22.12.: 'Prøve paa Nordstjernen'
27.12.: 'Prøve i Costume paa Nordstjernen'
28.12.: 'General=Prøve paa Nordstjernen'
29.12.: 'Arrangementsprøve [...] Første Forestilling hertillands af Meyerbeers Opera 'Der Nordstern' der gik i alle Maader udmærket godt. Mesteren var selv tilstede og blev gjentagne gange fremkaldt. Bifaldet var størst i første Act, men aftog noget i de sidste Acter, flere stærkt beregnede Effekter gjorde ikke den forønskede Virkning. Dog var det Hele en stor Succés og tilløbet ganske overordentligt. Mine Dandse og Evolutioner gik smukt og bleve modtagne med Bifald'
30.12.: '2.den Forestillng af Nordstjernen der gik udmærket med stormende Bifald'.

Der Nordstern received 16 performances during Bournonville's engagement in Vienna, and the opera reached a total of 78 performances in the old Kärnthnerthor Theatre, the last of which was given on 16.11.1867.

Musical sources:

Printed orchestral score containing several manuscript insertions and conductor's notes (written with red and black ink). 3 vol. Act I 366 pp. (including 22 ms. pp. between pp. '134–135'), Act II 250 pp. (including 1 ms. p. pasted on p. '402', 40 ms. pp. between pp. '434–435', 8 ms. pp. between pp. '454–455', 4 ms. pp. between pp. '488–489', and 24 ms. pp. between pp. '560–561'), Act III 166 pp. (including 2 ms. pp. between pp. '624–625', 7 ms. pp. between pp. '638–639', 50 ms. pp. between pp. '688–689', 10 ms. pp. between pp. 696–697", 4 ms. pp. between pp. '716–717', 11 printed pp. containing the 'Arioso/[...]/Einlage in Act III' and inserted between pp. '716–717', 3 ms. pp. between pp. '716–717', 2 ms. pp. between pp. '746–747', and 1 ms. p. between pp. '774–775') (31,8×24,8 cm).
L'ÉTOILE/DU NORD,/Opéra comique en trois actes
Paris, Brandus et C.ie, pl. no. B. et C.ie 9404 (1–19) [1855]
[AWn; O. A. 1300
According to notes (written with black ink) on the title-page of this volume, it is a revised edition prepared especially for the 1855 Vienna première of *L'Etoile du Nord*.

No répétiteur's copy and set of parts dating from the 1855 Vienna première of *Der Nordstern* have yet been traced.

Other sources:

Manuscript mise-en-scène. Ms. Autograph (or copy?) by unknown hand. Black and brown ink. 1 vol. 76 pp. (21,3 × 17,9 cm)
Der Nordstern,/Oper 3 A v Meyerbeer/10899
Unsigned and undated [1855–1856?]
[AWn; 987.071 C M. TB
A copy of the complete 1854 printed libretto for the Stuttgart version of *Der Nordstern* (published by M. Schlesinger in Berlin) is pasted into this (anonymous) manuscript mise-en-scène. Moreover, the manuscript parts of this volume contain several stage diagrams and pencilled notes which describe the movements on stage throughout the opera. Furthermore, according to a note written (with brown ink) on the title-page of the inserted Stuttgart libretto (reading: 'Nur zur Aufführung auf dem K. K. Hofoperntheater zum Kärnther Thore in Wien bestimmt') this mise-en-scène clearly dates from the 1855 Vienna première of Meyerbeer's opera. Consequently, it represents the most extensive written source that has been traced so far for Bournonville's 1855 Vienna production of *Der Nordstern*.

Manuscript mise-en-scène. Ms. Autograph (or copy?) by an unknown hand. Brown ink. 1 vol. 76 pp. (24,1 × 18,8 cm)
Der/Nordstern/10981
Unsigned and undated [1855–1856?]
[AWn; 987.072 C M. TB
A copy of the complete 1856 printed Vienna libretto for *Der Nordstern* (published by A. Pichler's Witwe & Sohn) is pasted into this (anonymous) manuscript mise-en-scène. Moreover, the manuscript parts of this volume contain several stage diagrams and notes (written with blue and red crayon) which describe the movements on stage throughout the opera. They clearly indicate that this volume reflects the 1855 Vienna staging of Meyerbeer's opera.

Costume drawing by G. Franceschini. Pencil and water colours (19,9 × 12,5 cm)
Catharine/I Costume
Unsigned and undated [1855]
[AWth; HM 3941 [1855]
This drawing shows the costume of *Katharina* in disguise as a 'Marketenderin' in Act I (score no. 6) during the so-called *Scène et ronde bohémienne* (performed by 'Frln. [M.] Wildauer').

Costume drawing by G. Franceschini. Pencil and water colours (19,8 × 12,5 cm)
Untitled
Unsigned and undated [1855]
[AWth; HM 3946
This drawing shows the costume of a 'Marketenderin' in Act I (score no. 6) during the so-called *Scène et ronde bohémienne* (performed by 'Frl. [B.] Holm').

Costume drawing by G. Franceschini. Pencil and water colours (19,8 × 12,5 cm)
Frl. Hofman
Unsigned and undated.
[AWth; HM 3947 [1855]
This drawing shows the costume of a 'Marketenderin' in Act I (score no. 6) during the so-called *Scène et ronde bohémienne* (performed by E. Hofmann).

Costume drawing by G. Franceschini. Pencil and water colours (19,7 × 12,5 cm)
8 Herrn Ballet/I Ackt [*sic*]
Unsigned and undated.
[AWth; HM 3957 [1855]
This drawing shows the costume of a Russian nobleman. It most probably relates to the costumes worn by the corps de ballet in Act I (score no. 6) during the so-called *Scène et Ronde Bohémienne*.

Costume drawing by G. Franceschini. Pencil and water colours (19 × 12,5 cm)
8 Ballet Damen
Unsigned and undated.
[AWth; HM 3956 [1855]
This drawing shows the costume of a 'Cossack'. It most probably relates to the costumes worn by the eight women, who performed the *Waltz (en travestie)* in Act II (score no. 10).

Costume drawing by G. Franceschini. Pencil and water colours (19 × 12,5 cm)
Ballet
Unsigned and undated.
[AWth; HM 3958 [1855]
This drawing shows the costume of a military person and relates most probably to the costumes worn by the corps de ballet during the *Marche sacrée* in Act II (score no. 13)

Printed sources:

Printed libretto. 1 vol. 78 pp. (17,2 × 11 cm)
Der Nordstern./Oper in drei Akten/[...]/Für das k. k. Hoftheater nächst dem Kärnthnerthore.
Wien, A Pichler's Witwe & Sohn, 1856.
[AWn; 987.768 A M. TB
This volume includes several manuscript notes written by an unknown hand (with pencil and black ink) and indicating the movements on stage throughout the opera.

1856

21.1.1856
***Pas de trois* (uncredited) performed by S. Lund,
P. Fredstrup, and J. Rostock.**

This (uncredited) dance is most probably the same as the similarly uncredited *Pas de trois*, performed by the same dancers on 13.10.1855 and, in turn, is probably identical with Bournonville's *Pas de trois* in Act I (score no. 5) of his Copenhagen version of J. Aumer's three-act pantomimic ballet *La Somnambule, ou l'Arrivée d'un nouveau seigneur (see*

21.9.1829). That dance had been given for the first time as a separate divertissement by Lund, Fredstrup, and Rostock on 8.4.1848. According to the rehearsal book of H. C. J Fredstrup, only two rehearsals were held of this dance on 15.1. and 19.1.1856, both of which were directed by S. Lund. Bournonville did not attend the performance because of his engagement in Vienna this season. It is not possible to identify the dance any further.

31.1.1856
Napoli, oder: Der Fischer und seine Braut (Napoli eller Fiskeren og hans Brud) (Vienna's Kärnthnerthor Theatre).
Bournonville's 1856 Vienna staging of his three-act romantic ballet *Napoli or The Fisherman and His Bride (see* 29.3.1842) represents the second and last time this ballet was mounted outside Denmark during his lifetime. According to a note in his diary on 7.12.1855 and the poster for the Vienna première, it included two new solo variations, entitled *Solo* and *La canzonetta,* incorporated in the Act I *Ballabile* (score no. 5). They were both performed by the Italian ballerina, C. Pocchini (who played *Teresina*). The music for these variations is today preserved only in the Vienna conductor's score for *Napoli, oder: Der Fisher und seine Braut.* It is inserted there on pp. 43–46 immediately before the Coda of the Act I *Ballabile.* Both of these dances were in all probability composed by the Austrian composer, M. Strebinger, and consist of the following music:

(1) 'Var. 1.mo' in 6/8 time, D major (27 meas.).
(2) 'Var. 2.do' in 3/8 time, A major (66 meas.).

Moreover, according to the Vienna posters, Act II included a new, incorporated solo variation (*Moderato assai* in 2/4 time, 41 meas.), which was entitled *La najade* and danced by Pocchini. It, too, seems to have been composed by Strebinger, although it is not possible to establish the exact place in the second act where this dance was performed.

Finally, two completely new divertissements were incorporated in Act III, where they replaced E. Helsted's original 1842 *Pas de quatre* (score no. 2). They consisted of:

(1) A *Pas de quatre,* choreographed by the Italian dancer, L. Gabrielli, and performed by him and three women (P. Ricci, E. Roll, and C. Dietrich). According to the part for the ophicleide in *Napoli, oder: Der Fisher und seine Braut* this dance consisted of eight movements as follows:
(a) 'Scherzoso e vivo' in 6/8 time, E flat major (29 meas.)
(b) 'Adagio' in 12/8 time, C major (21 meas.)
(c) '1.ster Variat:' (time signature, key, and number of bars unknown)
(d) 'Var: 2.do Allegretto' in 2/4 time, F major (44 meas.)
(e) '3tes Variation' (time signature, key, and number of bars unknown)
(f) 'Var: 4.to' in 3/4 time, B flat major (58 meas.)
(g) 'Coda' in 2/4 time, G major (52 meas.) followed by a section in 6/8 time, E flat major (26 meas.)
(h) 'Galop' in 2/4 time, C major (111 meas.)
(2) A *Pas de deux,* choreographed by the Italian dancer, L. Vienna, and performed by him and C. Pocchini. In the part for the first violin for *Napoli, oder: Der Fisher und seine Braut* the complete music for this *Pas de deux* is included. Apart from the introduction it is nearly identical with that in H. S. Paulli's score from three years later for Bournonville's *Pas de deux* (score no. 12) in his one-act ballet *The Flower Festival in Genzano* (premièred at Copenhagen's Royal Theatre

on 19.12.1858). This indicates that the music for Bournonville's 1858 *Flower Festival Pas de deux,* which hitherto has been regarded as a work composed exclusively by Paulli, already existed and was performed during Bournonville's sojourn in Vienna 1855–56. A pencilled note in the part for the first violin (reading 'v[on]: Strebinger') provides the name of its composer, M. Strebinger, who clearly must have written this dance in Vienna during late 1855 or early 1856. However, the definitive proof that Strebinger is the true composer of this music comes from the existence of his autographed score for those parts of the music which were played by an accompanying brass ensemble seated on the stage (the so-called 'Banda'). This score, together with another manuscript copy of Strebinger's full orchestral score, is now in DKKk (*see* Musical sources). They provide clear evidence that Paulli should today only be credited with having arranged and/or reorchestrated Strebinger's music when it was incorporated (most likely at Bournonville's wish) in his 1858 score for *The Flower Festival in Genzano.*

In his diary Bournonville noted about his preparations for the 1856 Vienna production of *Napoli, oder: Der Fisher und seine Braut* and its première there:

6.4.1855: 'beskjæftiget mig den hele Dag med min Arbeidsplan for Wien og med Oversættelsen paa Fransk af flere Programmer'
12.4.: 'oversat min Ballet Napoli paa Fransk'
22.5.: 'skrevet fransk Program til Napoli'
16.11.: 'Forgjæves Forsøg paa at faae [J.] Cornet i Tale angaaende mit Repertoire'
17.11.: 'Besøg hos Herr [J. R.] v. Raymond der lovede at tage sig af min Sag, arrangeret Musik'
18.11.: 'Musikmøde med]M.] Strebinger'
19.11.: 'Directionsbrev fra Cornet med frit Valg imellem tre Programmer, jeg vælger naturligvis Napoli'
21.11.: 'brev fra Rgd. Raymond om Napolis Antagelse [...] 1.ste Prøve for [C.] Pocchini'
22.11.: 'tilbragt den største Deel af Dagen med at skrive Regien til Napoli'
23.11.: 'skrevet [...] 2.den Prøve for Pocchini'
26.11.: 'Prøve for Mlle Pocchini'
29.11.: 'arbeidet med Strebinger'
30.11.: 'Prøve for Mlle Pocchini'
4.12.: 'componeret'
5.12.: 'Prøve i Redouten fra 10–11 for [J.] Beau'
6.12.: 'Besøg hos Strebinger [...] Indstudering til Beau hele Golfos Rolle'
7.12.: 'componeret 2 Variationer til Mlle Pocchini'
14.12.: '(indstuderet Napoli)'
15.12: 'Indstudering paa Napoli'
19.12.: 'Repetition af Napoli, der gik meget godt'
20.12.: 'Prøve paa Dandse til Napoli'
22.12.: 'Prøve paa [...] Napoli'
31.12.: 'besørget adskilligt Napoli angaaende'
2.1.1856: 'Decorationsmøde [...] arrangeret mine Balletlister, skrevet til Cornet angaaende Theatermaleren'
3.1.: 'Decorationsmøde Kl 9, afgivet Lister til Reqvisitøren og Maskinmesteren'
4.1.: 'Maskinprøve og Localebelysning for Napoli'
9.1.: 'læst, skrevet og arrangeret hele Eftermiddagen paa Napoli'
10.1.: 'Paa Theatret fra 9 til 1½ paa Napoli (1.ste Indstudering)'
11.1.: 'Rollevrøvl med [L.] Frappard [*sic*]'
12.1.: 'Costumemøde med [G.] Franceschini'
13.1.: 'skrevet og arrangeret til Napoli'
14.1.: 'Prøve paa Napoli fra 10 til 1½ – Frappard [*sic*] betydelig uforskammet'
15.1.: 'Prøve paa Napoli fra 10 til 12½'
16.1.: 'Napoli med Mlle Pocchini og Julius [Price] der lærer Beppos Partie. Prøve igjen fra 5–7 hvor jeg fik færdig den største deel af 3.die Akt.'
17.1.: 'Prøve paa Theatret fra 10–1 (Finalen af 3.die Akt og det meste af 2.den)'

18.1.: 'Prøve fra 10–12 i Redoutsalen og derpaa i Foyen [*sic*] for Mlle Pocchini. Jeg var meget vel fornøiet og haaber godt af Udførelsen'
19.1.: 'Besøg paa Maskinværkstedet. Prøve fra 10–12 i Redoutsalen'
20.1.: 'Jeg tilbragte den største Deel af dagen med at omarbeide det tydske Program til Napoli'
21.1.: 'Prøve fra 10 til 1 paa Napoli, der avrunder stærkt'
22.1.: 'Prøve fra 10–1 paa Napoli'
23.1.: 'Prøve paa Napoli [...] Aftenprøve paa Napoli (Tarentellen). Indstuderingen færdig'
24.1.: 'Prøve med Corps de Ballet paa Napoli, skrevet Lister og Regier den hele Dag'
25.1.: 'besøgt Malersalen hvor det gik godt med mine Decorationer. Prøve paa alle Dandsene til Napoli og Scene=Arrangement'
26.1.: 'Prøve fra 9 til 1½, alle tre Akter med Repetiteur (Nogle slemme Fyre blandt det mandlige Balletpersonale)'
28.1.: 'Dagen tilbragt med møjsommelige Prøver paa Napoli, ond Villie hos Cornet og blandt flere af Personalet'
29.1.: 'Første Generalprøve – ret godt men i mange Henseender ufuldstændig'
30.1.: 'Stor Generalprøve'
31.1.: 'Styrket ved en inderlig Bøn til Gud begyndte jeg mit Dagværk. Jeg forberedte Alt til den første Forestilling af Napoli [...] Alt gik efter Ønske. Balletten blev godt udført. Mlle Pocchini og Vienna gjorde stor Bravour i Hovedpartierne og Julius var ypperlig som Beppo. Balletten gjorde overordentlig Lykke og jeg blev fremkaldt efter 2.den og 3.die Akt. Stor Glæde.'
1.2.: 'tilbragt dagen i Glæde over det lykkelige Udfald af Balletten, der er velomtalt i Bladene'
2.2.: 'Napoli for fuldt Huus og stort Bifald med Fremkaldelse (Jeg blev i Coulissen)'
5.2.: 'en smuk Anmeldelse om Balletten i Wiener Theater Zeitung'
9.2.: 'Balletten gik for tredie gang med godt Huus og stormende Bifald. Vi vare alle meget glade'.

Napoli received 3 performances in Vienna, the last of which was given on 9.2.1856.

Autograph sources:

Manuscript scenario. Ms. Autograph. Brown and blue ink. 1 vol. 27 pp. (21,8 × 14 cm)
Napoli ou La Fiancée du pêcheur [*sic*]/Ballet en trois actes/par Auguste Bournonville./Musique de Gade, Helsted & Paulli.
Signed and dated: 'Ce 23 Mai 1855.' [Written according to Bournonville's diary on 22.5. and 23.5.1855]
[DKKk; NKS 3285 4° 3 L–P

Production note. Ms. Autograph. Blue ink. 3 pp. (27,8 × 22,3 cm)
Napoli ou La fiancée du pêcheur/[...]/<u>Décors.</u>
Signed and dated: 'Vienne ce 23 Novbr 1855.' [Written according to Bournonville's diary on 22.11. and 23.11.1855]
[DKKk; NKS 3285 4° 3 L–P

Production note. Ms. Autograph. Blue ink. 4 pp. (27,8 × 22,3 cm)
Napoli ou La fiancée du pêcheur/[...]/Personnages.
Signed and dated: 'Vienne ce 23 Novbr 1855.' [Written according to Bournonville's diary on 22.11. and 23.11.1855]
[DKKk; NKS 3285 4° 3 L–P

Production note. Ms. Autograph. Blue ink. 4 pp. (27,8 × 22,3 cm)
Napoli ou La fiancée du pêcheur/[...]/Costumes.
Unsigned and undated [Written according to Bournonville's diary on 22.11.1855]
[DKKk; NKS 3285 4° 3 L–P

Musical sources:

Répétiteur's copy. Ms. Copy (by H. S. Paulli). Black and brown ink. 1 vol. 68 pp. (26,4 × 37 cm)
Napoli/romantisk Ballet i 3 Acter/af/A. Bournonville/Musiken af/Paulli, Helsted og Gade.

Unsigned and undated [c.1854–1855]
[DKKk; C II, 119
This répétiteur's copy was most likely made as a private copy for Bournonville's stagings abroad of *Napoli and The Fisherman and His Bride*. This theory is supported by the fact that it remained in the property of the Bournonville family long after his death, and was donated to DKKk by his daughter, Charlotte Bournonville, on 31.3. 1910. The volume includes Bournonville's autographed pencilled notes which describe his changes in both the mime and the choreography when he mounted this ballet in Vienna. Thus, as a result of his incorporation of two new solo variations for *Teresina* (C. Pocchini) in the Act I *Ballabile* (score no. 5) that divertissement was completely rechoreographed, as can clearly be seen from Bournonville's choreographic notes for it. Moreover, his other pencilled notes indicate the many minor cuts and musical changes which he made in both Act II and Act III for the Vienna production. Finally, his autographed choreographic numbers (written with brown ink) are inserted throughout Act I. They seem to refer to a later (not yet traced) choreographic notation that he made of this act.

Conductor's score/Répétiteur's copy. Ms. Copy. Brown ink. 1 vol. 170 pp. (32,3 × 25,2 cm)
1036/Napoli/Foglietto/O. A. 1036.
Unsigned and undated [1855–1856]
[AWn; O. A. 1036
In Act III of this conductor's score a note immediately after score no. 2 reads 'Pas'. It is inserted in the place where E. Helsted's original *Pas de quatre* used to be performed. A similar note is also found in most of the instrumental parts together with other notes reading: 'Pas de deux', 'Pas de quattre/Pas 2', 'Pas de 4', or 'Pas 4'. Together they indicate the exact place where L. Gabrielli's *Pas de quatre* and L. Vienna's *Pas de deux* were incorporated when *Napoli, oder: Der Fischer und seine Braut* was premièred in Vienna.

Because the succeeding *Tarentella* is listed in the conductor's score and the Vienna set of parts as the ballet's final number ('No. 3'), it seems that Bournonville had from the very outset planned to omit Helsted's *Pas de quatre* divertissement. This dance was, in fact, already known in Vienna since it had been incorporated in Bournonville's *Das Fest in Albano* on 15.7.1854. Consequently, he seems to have decided early on to incorporate L. Gabrielli's and L. Vienna's new dances before his own *Tarentella*, while he completely omitted H. C. Lumbye's *Finale Gallop*.

Parts. Ms. Copy. 36 vol.
vl princ, 4 vl I, 3 vl II, 2 vla, 2 vlc, 2 cb, fl picc, fl 1, ob 1/2, cl 1/2, fag 1/2, cor 1/2/3/4, tr 1/2, trb 1 e 2, trb 3, timp, oph, gr cassa, tri, tamb, arpa.
Unsigned and undated [1855–1856]
[AWn; O. A. 1036 (Orchesterstimmen)

Parts (Act II, *La najade*, incomplete). Ms. Copy. 9 vol.
2 vl I, 2 vl II, 2 vlc e cb, arpa 1/2.
Unsigned and undated [1855–1856]
[DKKk; KTB 292 a
According to notes in the parts for the first violins reading: 'Einlage Balett/Napoli/Zweiter Akt/[...]/La Najade' this (incomplete) set of parts contains the music for Bournonville's incorporated solo variation in Act II for C. Pocchini (who played *Teresina*). The parts were most probably brought to Copenhagen by Bournonville in 1856 and have ever since been part of the Royal Theatre's music archive, although this music (which almost certainly is composed by M. Strebinger) was never played in the Copenhagen perfomances of *Napoli or The Fisherman and His Bride*. The two parts for the harp also contain the complete music played by this instrument in both Acts I and II.

Orchestral score for a brass ensemble (the so-called 'Banda') seated on stage (Act III, *Pas de deux*). Ms. Autograph (by M. Strebinger). Brown and black ink. 1 vol. 14 pp. (33 × 25,6 cm)
<u>Ballo – Napoli. Pas de deux.</u> <u>Strebinger</u> /[...]/<u>Banda.</u>/[...]/<u>Herrn v. Bournonville.</u> – Propriété de M.lle Price –
Signed '<u>Strebinger</u>', undated [1855–1856]

[DKKk; C II, 105, Efterslæt 3 (M. Strebinger, Ballo Napoli) [1]
This autographed score by M. Strebinger seems (according to its title-page) to have been purchased by Bournonville in Vienna. Moreover, according to his autographed note ('Propriété de M.lle Price') it was later donated to Juliette Price. She performed the *Flower Festival Pas de deux* together with H. Scharff at its Copenhagen première on 19.12.1858, for which nearly all of Strebinger's music was employed. In 1902 the score was bought by DKKk from the actor, Carl Price, who was a relative of Juliette Price and may have received it from her previously.

Musical insertion in the part for the first violin (Act III, *Pas de deux*). Ms. Copy. Brown ink with numerous pencilled notes. 1 vol. 12 pp. of which four are blank (33,4 × 25,7 cm)
v: Strebinger/Violino 1.mo/(1./Pas de deux/Allegretto/[...]/ And.te/[...]/Allegretto/[...]/Var: 1.mo/ Mod.to/[...]/Var: 2.do/ Brillante assai/[...]/Coda/[...]/Banda/All.o/[...]
Unsigned and undated [1855–1856]
[AWn; O. A. 1036 (Orchesterstimmen, 'Violino primo, no. 1, 3.ter Act')
This musical insertion is found in the part for the first violin, no. 1 (pp. 13–23). It contains the complete music for L. Vienna's and M. Strebinger's incorporated *Pas de deux* in Act III of *Napoli, oder: Der Fisher und seine Braut*. It was danced by Vienna (as *Gennaro*) and C. Pocchini (as *Teresina*). The *Pas de deux* is inserted between the incorporated *Pas de Quatre* (choreographed by L. Gabrielli) and the *Tarantella* (score no. 3). Numerous pencilled notes indicate the original orchestration of Strebinger's score, while other notes give information about the musical phrasing and tempi. They clearly testify to the fact that Strebinger's music was actually played as part of the Vienna performances of Bournonville's *Napoli, oder: Der Fisher und seine Braut*.

Orchestral score (Act III, *Pas de deux*). Ms. Copy. Black ink. 1 vol. 54 pp. (32,7 × 25,7 cm)
Propriété de M.lle Juliette Price./von Strebinger/Pas de Deux./Jfr Prices Eiendom
Unsigned and undated [c.1855–1856]
[DKKk; C II, 105, Efterslæt 3 (M. Strebinger, Ballo Napoli) [2]
This score is musically completely identical with the part for the first violin to Strebinger's *Pas de deux* in Act III of Bournonville's 1856 Vienna version of *Napoli, oder: Der Fisher und seine Braut*. According to Bournonville's autographed notes on the title-page ('Propriété de M.lle Price'/'Jfr Prices Eiendom') it was most probably purchased by him in Vienna and later on donated to Juliette Price, who was the first to perform the *Flower Festival Pas de deux* in Copenhagen in 1858. The score must almost certainly have been copied in Vienna, at Bournonville's direct request (perhaps by the Italian 'Capelmester Ricci' from whom he regularly received music copies during his sojourn in Vienna 1855–56). This theory is confirmed by the fact that the title of each movement and the names of the instruments are all given in Italian.

Moreover, the score clearly refers to Strebinger's autographed score for the accompanying brass ensemble seated on stage (*see* previous entry) with a note on p. 25 reading: 'Con Banda Tutta'. Furthermore, the score also holds a number of minor rhythmical differences from Paulli's later 1858 rearrangement of it for the *Flower Festival Pas de deux*. It is also orchestrated differently in that it includes an ophicleide, which does not appear at all in Paulli's 1858 orchestration.

The score was bought by DKKk in 1902 from the actor, Carl Price, who was a relative of Juliette Price and may have received it from her previously.

Other sources:

Costume drawing by G. Franceschini. Pencil and water colours (21,1 × 13,8 cm)
[Untitled]
Signed 'Franceschini'; undated [1855–1856]
[AWth; HM 3966

This drawing shows a white festive dress with attached yellow ribbons and was probably worn by *Teresina* (?) in Act III. It is peculiar that the girl is here wearing white gloves(!).

Costume drawing by G. Franceschini. Pencil and water colours (20,8 × 13,4 cm)
[Untitled]
Unsigned and undated [1855–1856]
[AWth; HM 3983
This drawing shows a Neapolitan sailor (Act I?).

Costume drawing by G. Franceschini. Pencil and water colours (20,4 × 13,5 cm)
[Untitled]
Unsigned and undated [1855–1856]
[AWth; HM 3984
This drawing shows a Neapolitan police officer (Act I?).

Costume drawing by G. Franceschini. Pencil and water colours (20,3 × 13,4 cm)
[Untitled]
Unsigned and undated [1855–1856]
[AWth; HM 3985
This drawing shows a Neapolitan girl in festive dress adorned with red ribbons (Act III?)

Printed sources:

Printed scenario. 1 vol. 12 pp. (17,2 × 11 cm)
Napoli,/oder:/Der Fischer und seine Braut./Ballet in drei Akten/ von August Bournonville/Musik von verschiedenen Meistern. Wien, A Pichler's Witwe & Sohn, 1856.
[AWn; 802.562 B Th.

26.2.1856

***Pas de trois* composed by Mr. Court Ballet Master Bournonville (*componeret af Hr Hofballetmester Bournonville*) performed by S. Lund, S. Price, and E. Garlieb.**
This dance is most probably identical with Bournonville's earlier so-called 'Pas de trois (Julius Price)', which he created for the Copenhagen début of his pupils, Julius Price and E. Garlieb, and was premièred by them and S. Price on 29.5.1854. Julius Price had followed Bournonville to Vienna in 1855 and remained there for the rest of his professional life. Subsequently his part in the 1854 *Pas de trois* seems to have been taken over by Lund in this 1856 restaging. This theory is supported by the fact that Bournonville's 1854 *Pas de trois* was also mounted by Lund in a slightly revised version at Stockholm's Royal Theatre on 16.3.1857. That staging was entitled *New Pas de trois, (Debut.) arranged by Ballet-master Sigurd Lund (En af Herr Balletmästaren Sigurd Lund arrangerad ny Pas de Trois, (Debut.))* and performed by Lund, M. W. H. Wiegand, and A. Paulsson. It is not possible to identify the dance any further.

8.3.1856

***Pas de deux* performed by Julius Price and Juliette Price as an incorporated divertissement in Act II of P. Taglioni's *Robert und Bertrand* (Vienna's Kärnthnerthor Theatre).**
According to four entries in Bournonville's diary (on 17.10., 24.10., 18.11., and 29.11.1855) the music for this *Pas de trois* was written by M. Strebinger, premièred as an incorporated divertissement in P. Taglioni's and H. Schmidt's new Vienna version of M. Hoguet's three-act comic ballet *Robert und Bertrand* (first performed at Vienna's Kärnthnerthor Theatre on 8.12.1854). Since Schmidt's 1854 score for *Robert und Ber-*

trand is no longer preserved (only a later score dating from its 1873 Vienna restaging exists now in AWn, call no. O. A. 1361) it is not possible to determine the exact place in Act II of *Robert und Bertrand* where Bournonville's new *Pas de deux* was incorporated. In his diary he noted about its creation and première:

1.10.1855: 'Besøg hos [M.] Strebinger om nÿ Musik'
7.10.: 'til Strebinger om en nÿ pas de deux'
12.10.: 'besøgt Strebinger og besørget adskilligt'
13.10.: 'modtaget nogen Musik af Strebinger, componeret lidt paa en pas de deux'
14.10.: 'componeret'
15.10.: 'begyndt Indstuderingen af en Pas de Deux'
16.10.: 'Indstudering med Pricerne […] componeret'
17.10.: 'Besøgt <u>Strebinger</u> angaaende Musiken til Pas de deux'
18.10.: 'skrevet og componeret […] Musikmøde med Strebinger (Coda'en omgjort.)'
19.10.: 'modtaget Musik af Strebinger (Coda) studeret lidt derpaa'
20.10.: 'Indstudering til Julius [Price] Pas de deux færdig. Besøg hos Strebinger'
10.11.: 'Prøve til Pricerne (Pas de deux)'
5.12. and 6.12.: 'Lection til Pricerne med Repetiteur'
16.1.1856: 'Prøve paa Pas de deux til Julius og Juliette [Price]'
7.2.: 'Lection til Pricerne og Prøve paa deres pas de deux'
8.2.: 'Lection og Prøve til Pricerne'
12.2.: 'Prøve paa pas de deux paa Theatret'
13.2.: 'betalt Strebinger'
7.3.: 'Pludseligt Forlangende af den nÿ Pas de deux (Juliette meget ilde tilmode)'
8.3.: 'besørget endeel med Hensyn til den ovennævnte pas de deux. Prøve med Orchester paa denne […] Om Aftenen <u>Robert og Bertrand</u> Ballet hvori Juliette og Julius dandsede min nÿ Pas de deux med særdeles Bifald og de vare selv meget tilfredse derover'.

The dance, which represents the last work Bournonville mounted in Vienna, was given only once.

Musical sources:

Orchestral score. Ms. Autograph (by M. Strebinger). 1 vol. Brown ink. 33 pp. + 1 p. including a so-called 'Einlage' and inserted between pp. 24 and 25 (33 × 25,9 cm)
Propriété de/<u>M.lle Juliette Price</u>/Pas de Deux./Math: Strebinger
Signed: 'Math: Strebinger'; undated [October 1855]
[DKKk; C II, 105, Efterslæt 3 (M. Strebinger, Pas de deux) [3]
According to notes in Bournonville's diary this score was written betweeen 1.10. and 20.10.1855 and was clearly purchased by him in Vienna the same year. Moreover, his autographed note on the title-page (reading: 'Propriété de M.lle <u>Juliette Price</u>') indicates that it was donated later to Juliette Price, who originally had performed it together with Julius Price in Vienna on 8.3.1856. In 1902 the score was bought by DKKk from the actor, Carl Price, who was a relative of Juliette Price and may have received it from her previously.

Répétiteur's copy. Ms. Copy. Brown ink. 1 vol. 10 pp. (33,7 × 25,7 cm)
Propriété de/M.lle Juliette Price./Pas de Deux:/Strebinger
Unsigned and undated [October 1855]
[DKKk; C II, 105, Efterslæt 3 (M. Strebinger, Pas de deux) [4]
According to notes in Bournonville's diary this répétiteur's copy was written betweeen 1.10. and 20.10.1855 and was clearly purchased by him in Vienna the same year. Moreover, according to his autographed note on the title-page (reading: 'Propriété de M.lle <u>Juliette Price</u>.') it was later donated to Juliette Price, who had originally performed it together with Julius Price in Vienna on 8.3.1856. The volume also contains Bournonville's autographed pencilled choreographic numbers, which seem to refer to a separate (not yet traced) notation of the *Pas de deux* that he may have written (according to his diary) in Vienna on 13.10. and 14.10.1855. In 1902 the score was bought by DKKk from the actor, Carl Price, who was a relative of Juliette Price and may have received it from her previously.

No set of parts for Bournonville 1856 Vienna *Pas de deux* has yet been traced.

14.3.1856
Pas de deux (uncredited) performed by W. Funck and B. Bills.
This (uncredited) dance was mounted for the Copenhagen début of B. Bills and is perhaps identical with an earlier (uncredited) *Pas de deux*, first danced by W. Funck and P. Funck on 21.9.1849. This theory is supported by the fact that the (anonymous) orchestral score for Funck's 1849 *Pas de deux* (now in Copenhagen's Royal Library, call no. C I, 231) also includes the names of [W.] 'Funck' and [B.] 'Bills' on its title-page. Another possibile identification of this dance is the even earlier *Pas de deux*, arranged by Bournonville in 1847 and first performed by Funck and Bournonville's Swedish pupil, M. C. Norberg (*see* 14.3.1847).

According to the rehearsal book of H. C. J. Fredstrup only two rehearsals were held of this dance on 11.3. and 13.3. 1856, both of which were directed by Funck. Bournonville did not attend the performance because of his engagement at Vienna's Kärnthnerthor Theatre in the same season. It is not possible to identify the dance any further.

19.9.1856
Cendrillon (Cendrillon eller Den lille grønne Sko).
Many years before this Copenhagen restaging of N. Isouard's three-act fairy play (originally premièred in Paris at L'Opéra Comique on 22.2.1810, and first performed in Copenhagen on 29.10.1812) Bournonville had danced an (uncredited) *Pas de deux* together with L. Grahn as an incorporated divertissement in Act III (*see* 17.12.1837). The poster for the 1856 restaging gives no specific information about the choreography except from stating: 'med tilhørende Dands'. It consisted of a *Danse* performed by a group of children in the first scene of Act II (score no. 7) during the so-called 'Choeur du sommeil de Cendrillon' («ô doux sommeil sur l'innocence daigne répendre tes pavots»). This dance is also described in Isouard's printed orchestral score (p. 117) as follows:

'La scène se passe dans le palais du Prince. Le théâtre représente un salon magnifiquement décoré pour une fête; à droite du théâtre est élevé un trône, sur les dégrés duquel on aperçoit Cendrillon, avec une parure très-élégante: elle dort profondémt [*sic*], et se trouve absolument dans la même position où elle s'est endormie auprès du feu à la fin du premier acte, en face du trône on aperçoit un grouppe [*sic*] d'hommes et de femmes vétus en blanc, tenant des lyres à la main et représentant des génies. De jeunes enfants également vetus en blanc ont des guirlandes de fleurs à la main'.

Moreover, according to the same source a so-called *Danse générale* and a *Pas de deux* were performed by 'un groupe de danseurs' in Act III, scene 10 (score no. 16).

In his diary Bournonville noted about the performance:

29.8.1856: 'Prøve og Indstudering af Dandsen til Cendrillon'
1.9.: 'Prøve […] Cendrillon'
11.9.: 'Theaterprøve paa Cendrillon'
19.9.: 'bivaanet de første halvanden Akt af Cendrillon'.

The 1856 restaging of *Cendrillon* received 11 performances, the last of which was given on 25.2.1857.

Musical sources:

Printed orchestral score. 1 vol. 292 pp. of which one is blank (31,4 × 24,7 cm)
Cendrillon./Partitur.
s. l., s. a., pl. no. 91 [c.1810]
[DKKk; U 6 (KTA 166)]
This French orchestral score was used for all performances of Isouard's *Cendrillon* in Copenhagen since its 1812 première there until its last performance on 25.2.1857. According to conductor's notes (on pp. 118–123) and the music contained in the two 1856 répétiteur's copies for *Cendrillon* (*see* the following entries) the dance scene in Act II (score no. 7) was mounted by Bournonville in 1856 in a heavily abridged version that omitted 77 bars. The music for the *Danse générale* and *Pas de deux* in Act III (score no. 16) is in this score included on pp. 261–277.

Répétiteur's copy (Act II). Ms. Copy (made by Bournonville). Brown ink. 1 p. (32,9 × 25,5 cm)
Chor og Dands/Andantino con moto.
Unsigned and undated [1856]
[DKKk; MA ms 2749 (2) (KTA 166 (4))]
This répétiteur's copy is written in Bournonville's hand and contains his abridged 1856 version of the music for the dance scene in Act II (score no. 7) of Isouard's *Cendrillon*. It also includes his pencilled autographed choreographic notes which describe the actual steps as performed by a group of children while holding flower garlands in their hands.

Répétiteur's copy. Ms. Copy. Black ink. 1 vol. 6 pp. (33,5 × 25,3 cm)
Repetiteur=Parti til Cendrillon
Unsigned and undated [1856]
[DKKk; MA ms 2915 (8) (KTA 166 (5))]
This répétiteur's copy contains Bournonville's abridged 1856 version of the dance scene in Act II (score no. 7) and Isouard's complete music for the two dances in Act III (score no. 16).

Parts. Ms. Copy. 40 vol.
4 vl I, 4 vl II, 2 vla, 4 vlc e cb, fl picc 1/2, fl 1/2, ob 1/2, 2 cl I, 2 cl II, 2 fag I, 2 fag II, 3 cor I, 3 cor II e cor princ, 2 tr I, 2 tr II, timp, arpa. 68 vocal parts.
Unsigned and undated [1812]
[DKKk; KTA 166
This set of parts dates from the 1812 Copenhagen première of *Cendrillon* and was used for all performances of it there until 25.2.1857.

6.10.1856
La Ventana, Ballet Divertissement (Balletdivertissement).
This work represents Bournonville's second and revised version of his earlier mirror-dance divertissement, entitled *La Ventana, Spanish Character Dance* (*see* 19.6.1854). It was this year extended to two tableaux, of which the second included three new dances as follows:

(1) A *Solo* for *The Señor*, performed by F. Hoppe to music by V. C. Holm.
(2) A *Pas de trois*, danced by W. Funck, C. Kellermann, and P. Fredstrup to music by V. C. Holm.
(3) A Spanish dance, named *La Seguedilla (after Taglioni) (efter Taglioni)* and performed by three men and three women. This dance is a free arrangement of a divertissement named *La Seguidilla* that was originally choreographed by P. Taglioni (to music perhaps written by M. Strebinger?) and was seen by Bournonville on two occasions at Vienna's Kärnthnerthor Theatre, when it was danced there by M. Taglioni (the younger) and C. Müller on 30.10. and 24.11.1855.

The new 1856 version of *La Ventana* was later also mounted at the the Court Theatre on 21.9.1857.

Holm's music for the *Pas de trois* was incorporated by Bournonville in his ballet-vaudeville *Bellman or the Polish Dance at Grönalund* (*see* 3.6.1844) when this work was restaged for the second and last time at Stockholm's Royal Theatre (Operahuset) on 21.4.1858. It was that year performed by three women (A. Arrhenius, J. Hjorth, and A. Paulsson) who appeared in it dressed as the three Graces(!). Two months later the complete 1856 version of *La Ventana* was mounted by Bournonville at Stockholm's Royal Theatre (*see* 15.6.1858), but then with the Swedish subtitle, *Fönstret*. For this performance the music was for the first time credited on the poster as 'partially composed and arranged' (*delvis komponerad och arrangerad*) by Lumbye and Holm. Moreover, the Swedish staging differed from the Copenhagen version by having the *Pas de trois* performed by the same three women who also danced it when it was incorporated in *Bellman or the Polish Dance at Grönalund* on 21.4.1858, replacing the original cast of this dance for a man and two women.

Furthermore, on 1.6.1860 a *Seguidille (Spanish Dance) (Spansk Dans)* was performed by F. Hoppe, W. Price, Juliette Price, and S. Price at Stockholm's Mindre Theatern. It was described on the poster as a dance 'composed by Bournonville' and was in all probability an free adaptation for two couples of his *Seguedilla* in *La Ventana*. This version was performed 4 times at Mindre Theatern (the last time on 17.6.1860). On 3.10.1862 yet another (uncredited) *Seguidilla* was mounted at Stockholm's Royal Theatre (Operahuset) and was performed by Bournonville's pupils, S. Lund and J. G. Sundberg, together with a small corps de ballet. It, too, is almost certainly identical with his 1856 *La Seguedilla (after Taglioni)* in *La Ventana* and was performed 4 times by them in Stockholm (the last time on 10.11.1862). Finally, on 18.6. 1865 a third arrangement of this dance, performed by four persons and entitled '*La Seguedille*' *(Spanish National Dance)*, was mounted as a separate divertissement at Christiania's Theatre (Oslo).

In Copenhagen a so-called *Seguedilla* was incorporated as a divertissement in Bournonville's two-act idyllic ballet *The Toreador* when it was restaged at the Royal Theatre on 21.10. 1866. It was almost certainly identical with that in *La Ventana*.

The complete 1856 version of *La Ventana* was restaged twice in Copenhagen on 5.12.1868 and 4.3.1871. Of these the 1868 production was mounted with partially revised choreography, arranged especially for B. Schnell who this year played the rôle of *The Señorita* for the first time. On 20.12. 1874 Bournonville mounted the *Pas de trois* and *Seguedilla (after Taglioni)* as two separate divertissements. They represent the last time that he worked on this divertissement.

In his diary he noted about his preparations, the creation, and the 1856 Copenhagen première of the new, extended version of *La Ventana*:

30.10.1855: '*Kjøbt mig en Billet* for at see [P.] Taglionis første Forestilling […] Jeg saa den første Forestilling af [P. & M.] Taglionis og med stor Fornøielse. Den oprindelig franske Ballet <u>Die verwandelten Weiber</u> (Le Diable à quatre) er af ham arrangeret med megen Smag, navnlig den choreographiske Deel. Flere Dandse passe ikke i Sujettet, men de ere nødvendige ved det herværende Publicums Fordringer […] Glands punktet var en indlagt spansk Dands <u>Segui-</u>

dilla. Det var en ÿpperlig Composition fuld af romantisk Liv og slaaende Virkning. Jeg havde Leilighed at takke de vakkre Kunstnere og gik hjem, meget tilfreds med min Aften'

24.11.: 'i Operaen, hvor jeg fra Orchestret saae Die verwandelten Weiber, stort Bifald for Seguidilla'en, der er et udmærket Nummer, men fra Marie Taglionis Side dandses med frygtelig Overdrivelse, men det er desværre derfor at Publicum sværmer. – Ak! Den Kunst her øves og ÿndes er ikke min Kunst'

6.8.1856: 'Brev til [G.] Carey'

10.8.: 'Brev fra Carey […] skrevet til [M.] Strebinger'

11.8.: 'Brev til Careÿ i Wien'

3.9.: 'skrevet til Carey og sendt ham 20 fl. C.M. recommanderet'

4.9.: 'Musiceret med [V. C.] Holm'

6.9.: 'Musiceret med Holm (nÿ pas de trois)'

7.9.: 'Eftermiddagen hjemme og componeret paa pas de trois'

8.9.: 'skrevet og componeret […] Indstudering af en nÿ Pas de trois for Mme [C.] Kellermann, [W.] Funck og Jf. [J.] Rostock […] skrevet og componeret'

10.9.: 'Brev fra Carey med Seguidillen i Claverudtog'

13.9.: 'Prøve paa La Ventana'

16.9.: 'Prøve og Indstudering […] La Ventana […] Eftermiddag Indstudering paa La Seguidilla'

17.9.: 'componeret'

18.9.: 'musiceret med Holm […] Indstudering paa La Seguidilla (færdig). Prøve indtil Kl 2'

19.9.: 'Prøve paa La Ventana […] skrevet og arrangeret til Divertissementet'

20.9.: 'arrangeret for Musik og Costûmer'

22.9.: 'Prøve paa Divertissementet'

27.9.: 'Prøve paa La Ventana'

29.9. and 30.9.: 'skrevet og componeret'

3.10.: 'Musikprøve paa La Ventana – Dandseprøve […] paa Conservatoriets Locale'

4.10.: 'skrevet og arrangeret. Generalprøve paa La Ventana der lover godt'

6.10.: 'Første Forestilling af det nÿe Divertissement La Ventana som gjorde megen Lÿkke og hvori Juliette [Price] udmærkede sig særdeles. M.me Kellermann var ÿderst ubehagelig men jeg holdt mig godt og det forstÿrrede ingenlunde min Glæde. Jeg takkede Gud og gik tilsengs'.

The complete 1856 version of *La Ventana* reached a total of 110 performances during Bournonville's lifetime, the last of which was given on 16.5.1879.

Autograph sources:

Choreographic note. Ms. Autograph. Ink. 3 pp. (format unknown)
La Seguedilla. (d'après Taglioni.)/[…]/Entrée scenique/[…]/ Boléro./[…]/Jaleo/[…]/Coda.
Unsigned and undated [c.1855–1856]
[USNYp; Dance Collection, call nos. *ZBD-71 (microfilm), and (S)*MGZMD 30 (photostat copy)
This choreographic note (which is written exclusively in French) was most probably made in Vienna and soon after Bournonville had attended a performance of P. Taglioni's *La Seguidilla* at the Kärnthnerthor Theatre on 30.10.1855.

Musical sources:

Printed piano score. 1 vol. 7 pp. (30,2 × 24,2 cm)
La Seguidilla./[…]/in dem Ballet: Die Weiberkur/getanzt von/ Fräulein Marie Taglioni/für Clavier arrangirt/von/Louis Engel./ […]/OP. 25.
Vienna, C. A. Spina, pl. no. 9656 [c.1853–1854]
[AWn; M. S. 43770
It was probably from a copy of this printed piano score (including L. Engel's arrangement of the music for P. Taglioni's *La Seguidilla*) that V. C. Holm made his later arrangement for Bournonville's *La Seguedilla (after Taglioni)* in *La Ventana*. This theory is supported by notes

in Bournonville's diary which clearly indicate that he received a piano score of this dance from G. Carey in Vienna on 10.9.1856.

Musical drafts. Ms. Autograph (by V. C. Holm). Black ink. 8 pp. (34,5 × 25,5 cm)
La Ventana/Moderato
Unsigned and undated [1856]
[DKKk; MA ms 2713 (KTB 300)
These musical drafts contain V. C. Holm's first arrangement of the music for *La Seguedilla* in *La Ventana*. They also include Bournonville's autographed choreographic numbers (written with brown ink) for what is named 'La Seguidilla' ('1–6'), 'Moderato' ('1–4'), 'Bolero' ('1–6'), and 'Tempo primo' ('1–2'). These numbers most probably refer to Bournonville's earlier, separate choreographic notaton of this dance, entitled 'La Seguedilla. (d'après Taglioni)'.

Répétiteur's copy. Ms. Copy and autograph (by V. C. Holm). Brown and black ink. 1 vol. 28 pp. of which one is blank (33,8 × 24,1 cm with variants)
B. 300/'La Ventana.'/1/No. 6 A/[…]/La Ventana/Danse Espagnole/composèe [*sic*] par A: Bournonville./executée par M.lle Juliette Price/le 19 Juin 1854.
Unsigned and dated (on p. 1): 'le 19 Juin 1854.' [1854 and 1856]
[DKKk; MA ms 2997 (KTB 300)
The first eight pp. of this répétiteur's copy date from the première at the Court Theatre on 19.6.1854 of Bournonville's and Lumbye's mirror-dance, *La Ventana*. The remaining pages (pp. 9–28) contain the new music, composed and arranged by V. C. Holm for Bournonville's second, extended 1856 version of this divertissement. His pencilled autographed notes are included on pp. 9–11 and describe in fine detail the choreography of the *Señor*'s solo. They were most probably written during September 1856. Moreover, in the music for the *Pas de trois* Bournonville inserted a long series of choreographic numbers (written with black). They seem to refer to similar numbers in a (not yet traced) choreographic notation of this dance which Bournonville may have written for a later restaging (perhaps that mounted on 20.12.1874?).

Orchestral score. Ms. Copy and autogaph (by V. C. Holm). Black and brown ink. 1 vol. 116 pp. of which one is blank (24,6 × 34 cm)
300/La Ventana/Partitur/[…]/La Ventana./MUSIK: H. C. LUMBYE
Signed and dated (on p. 40): 'WCHolm/Den 23 September 1856', (p. 80) 'WCHolm d: 20.e September 1856', (p. 115) 'W C Holm den 29 September 1856'
[DKKk; MA ms 1127 (KTB 300) (mu 8903.1098)
This orchestral score was used for all performances of *La Ventana* in Copenhagen during Bournonville's lifetime (including those with selected excerpts given separately). Pages 1–30 (which include Lumbye's music) are written by a copyist, while pp. 31–116 are V. C. Holm's autograph.

Parts (incomplete). Ms. Copy. 29 + 3 vol.
3 vl I, 3 vl II, vla, vlc, cb, fl 1/2, ob 1/2, cl 1/2, fag 1/2, cor 1/2, tr 1/ 2, trb 1/2/3, timp, gr cassa, tamb, piatti e tri, arpa. On stage: fl 1/2, guit.
Unsigned and undated [1856]
[DKKk; KTB 300
This and the following set of parts were used for all performances of *La Ventana* in Copenhagen during Bournonville's lifetime.

Parts (incomplete). Ms. Copy. 6 vol.
2 vla, 2 vlc e cb, fl, cl II.
Unsigned and undated [1856]
[DKKk; KTB 1055 (originally KTB 300)

Other sources:

Drawing by E. Lehmann. Pencil (16,5 × 11,1 cm)
1856/'La Ventana'

Unsigned and dated: '1856'
[DKKt; Lehmann tegninger]
This drawing shows a situation from the mirror dance in the 1856 version of *La Ventana* (performed by Juliette and S. Price).

Drawing by E. Lehmann. Pencil and water colours (18,2 × 13,1 cm)
'la Ventana'
Signed and dated: 'E. L./1870'
[DKKk; Ms. phot 125 fol of Helene Bournonville's 'Stambog' (photographic reproduction in black and white)]
This drawing (the original of which is now in a private collection) shows the same scene from the mirror-dance in *La Ventana* depicted in the previous Lehmann drawing. It was apparently made as a more refined and hand-coloured replica in 1870 and was donated the same year to Bournonville's wife, Helene, who pasted it into her album on p. 44.

15.10.1856
Pas de deux (uncredited) performed by S. Lund and S. Price (the Court Theatre).

This (uncredited) dance was given as part of a charity performance for the Price dynasty of dancers. It is probably identical with the earlier (uncredited) *Pas de deux*, performed at the Court Theatre by the same dancers on 2.6.1855 which, in turn, is probably identical with Bournonville's even earlier *Pas de deux (new)* first by Lund and Juliette Price at the Court Theatre on 19.6.1854.

Another possible identification of this dance is the (uncredited) *Pas de deux*, performed by Lund and S. Price on 24.4.1851 and, in turn, is perhaps identical with either the (uncredited) *Pas de deux* danced by Lund and P. Fredstrup on 27.12.1850, or Bournonville's *Pas de deux* from his three-act romantic ballet *Faust* (first performed as a separate divertissement on 15.10.1839)

Bournonville attended the performance about which he noted in his diary:

'i en foregaaende pas de deux havde [Juliette Price] udfoldet Alt hvad Gratie og Elegance kan udtænke'.

It is not possible to identify the dance any further.

15.10.1856
La Cracovienne (uncredited) performed by S. Price (the Court Theatre).

This performance, which represents the first and only time that Bournonville's version of F. Elssler's *La Cracovienne* (*see* 10.6.1842) was given at the Court Theatre, was mounted as part of a special charity performance given for the Price dynasty of dancers. According to his diary Bournonville attended the performance; but he made no specific remarks about the *Cracovienne*, which he saw performed for the last time on this occasion. The musical material used at the Court Theatre was most probably the same as that used since the 1842 Royal Theatre première of this dance (now in DKKk, call nos. MA ms 2664, MA ms 2663, and KTB 214).

15.10.1856
The Earnest Maiden, A Pastoral Picture in form of a Ballet (Den alvorlige Pige, Landligt Billede i Balletform) (the Court Theatre).

This divertissement was created especially for a charity per-

formance given for the Price dynasty of dancers. It was drawn from inspirations received from Bournonville's reading of C. Winther's 1828 collection of eleven poems, entitled *Træsnit* (first published in Copenhagen, by C. A. Reitzel, 1828). Of these Winther's final poem, named *Erik og Ellen* seems to have provided the most significant elements for the divertissement's plot.

The Earnest Maiden represents the first time that Bournonville collaborated with the composer, A. F. Lincke, who during the following years wrote and/or arranged the scores for several other minor divertissements and dances by Bournonville. Apart from incorporating some motifs in his overture, borrowed from H. E. Kröyer's melody from 1820 to A. Oehlenschläger Danish national hymn «Der er et yndigt Land» (1819), Lincke's score for this divertissement seems to be completely his own.

Since it was highly successful with the audience Bournonville decided soon after also to mount the divertissement at the Royal Theatre, where it was premièred only a month later on 23.11.1856. In his memoirs *My Theatre Life* (p. 177) he characterised it as follows:

'This little idyll, or more properly speaking, this woodcut after Chr. Winther's model, had a great deal of bravura when it was first performed at the small Court Theatre, but completely lost its effect when it appeared on the larger stage'.

Moreover, in a letter to the editor of the Copenhagen paper *Dagbladet*, dated 21.11.1856 (now in DKKk, call no. NBD III, 212), he described it as:

'Handlingen foregaaer i Sjælland for mange Aar siden. Det Hele maa betragtes som et landligt Billede, fornemlig paavirket af Chr. Winthers Træsnit'.

In his diary he noted about its creation and the première:

29.9.1856: 'bestilt Musik hos [A. F.] Lincke'
30..9.: 'skrevet en lille Ballet til Prices Aftenunderholdning kaldet 'Den alvorlige Pige'
1.10.: 'reenskrevet Programmet til 'den alvorlige Pige', musiceret med Lincke [...] drukket Café hos [F.] Høedt, der morede sig over min lille Ballet'
2.10. and 3.10.: 'componeret'
4.10.: 'musiceret med Lincke'
7.10.: 'componeret paa den lille Ballet til Prices. Prøve derpaa Kl 4, musiceret med Lincke'
8.10.: 'Prøve og Indstudering paa Den alvorlige Pige' [...] Musik med Lincke'
9.10.: 'skrevet og componeret [...] Prøve paa [...] Den alvorlige Pige Kl 1–3 paa Hoftheatret [...] (musiceret to Gange med Lincke)'
10.10.: 'skrevet og arrangeret [...] Prøve paa Hoftheatret – Indstudering [...] hjemme skrevet og componeret'
11.10.: 'Prøve Kl 9 1/2 paa Hoftheatret. Indstuderingen færdig'
12.10.: 'besørget Revisiter til 'Den alvorlige Pige''
13.10.: 'Prøve paa Hoftheatret 'Den alvorlige Pige'
14.10.: 'Prøve paa [...] Den alvorlige Pige i Costume'
15.10.: 'Generalprøve paa Forestillingen til Iaften [...] Prices forestilling paa Hoftheatret [...] 'Den alvorlige Pige' Juliette [...] var som den klodsede Bondepige ganske fortreffelig og gjorde stormende Lykke. Jeg har grund til at formode at mit Arbeide gjorde Sensation uagtet flere Steder ikke bleve saaledes givne som jeg havde ventet det – Nok der var stor Velsignelse ved denne Aften, thi Huset var udsolgt'.

The Earnest Maiden received 3 performances at the Court Theatre, the last of which was given on 4.9.1857.

Musical sources:

Orchestral score. Ms. Autograph (by A. F. Lincke). Brown ink. 1 vol. 110 pp. (24,9 × 33,3 cm)
265/265/Lincke:/Den alvorlige/pige/[…]/'Den alvorlige Pige'/Ballet/af/A. Bournonville/Musikken af A. F. lincke.
Signed (on the title-page): 'A. F. Lincke', undated [1856]
[DKKk; C II, 117 b (KTB 265)
This orchestral score was most likely used for all performances of *The Earnest Maiden* at both the Court Theatre and the Royal Theatre.

Répétiteur's copy. Ms. Copy. Brown ink. 1 vol. 36 pp. (33,1 × 25,4 cm)
B. 265/Den alvorlige Pige./33/1856./[…]/Repetiteur Partie/til/Den alvorlige Pige.
Unsigned and dated (on the front cover): '1856.'
[DKKk; MA ms 2962 (KTB 265)
This répétiteur'c copy was most likely used for all performances of *The Earnest Maiden* at both the Court Theatre and the Royal Theatre.

Parts. Ms. Copy. 28 vol.
3 vl I, 3 vl II, 2 vla, 3 vlc e cb, fl 1/2, ob 1/2, cl 1/2, fag 1/2, cor 1/2, tr 1/2, trb 1/2/3, timp, gr cassa.
Unsigned and undated [1856]
[DKKk; KTB 265]
This set of parts was most likely used for all performances of *The Earnest Maiden* at both the Court Theatre and the Royal Theatre.

13.11.1856

A Pas de deux arranged by Mr. Ballet Master Sigurd Lund (En af Herr Balletmästaren Sigurd Lund arrangerad Pas de deux) performed by S. Lund and J. G. Sundberg (Stockholm's Royal Theatre, Operahuset).

According to the Swedish musical sources for this dance (now in SSkma) it is identical with the much earlier *New Pas de deux*, originally mounted by Bournonville in Copenhagen as an incorporated divertissement in Act II of G. Meyerbeer's five-act opera *Robert le Diable* (*see* 5.12.1841). The 1856 Swedish staging of it represents the first time S. Lund ever mounted a work at Stockholm's Royal Theatre after his appointment as ballet-master there on 1.11.1856.

According to A. F. Schwartz's handwritten catalogue of the music archive of Stockholm's Royal Theatre, the musical material for Lund's staging is entitled 'Pas de deux (af Robert af Normandie)' with the label on the box containing the orchestral parts reading: 'Pas de deux arr: af Balletm: Lund'. This clearly indicates that Lund must have revised Bournonville's choreography in 1856. Moreover, according to the musical sources in Stockholm, he clearly made some minor cuts in the Coda movement, which in Sweden played for 95 bars against the original 135 bars in the 1841 Copenhagen version.

Lund's *Pas de deux* received a total of 10 performances in Stockholm during the 1856–57 and 1857–58 seasons.

Musical sources:

Orchestral score. Ms. Copy. Black ink. 1 vol. 66 pp. (33,4 × 25,5 cm)
Pas de deux.
Unsigned and undated [c.1856]
[SSkma; KT Dansmusik 85

Répétiteur's copy. Ms. Copy. Black ink. 1 vol. 8 pp. (34 × 25,8 cm)

Pas de deux/af/Robert af Normandiet/Repetiteur = Parti
Unsigned and undated [c.1856]
[SSkma; KT Dansmusik 85
This répétiteur's copy was clearly made in Copenhagen and seems to have been brought to Stockholm by S. Lund in 1856.

Parts. Ms. Copy. 33 vol.
3 vl I, 3 vl II, 2 vla, 4 vlc e cb, fl picc, fl, ob 1/2, cl 1/2, fag 1/2, cor 1/2/3/4, tr 1/2, trb 1/2/3, timp, gr cassa, piatti, tri.
Unsigned and undated [c.1856]
[SSkma; KT Dansmusik 85

23.11.1856

The Earnest Maiden, Ballet Divertissement (Den alvorlige Pige, Balletdivertissement).

This performance represents the first time Boiurnonville's and A. F. Lincke's divertissement *The Earnest Maiden* (*see* 15.10.1856) was mounted at the Royal Theatre. In his diary Bournonville noted about the staging on 20.10.1856:

'Den alvorlige Pige antagen til Opførelse'.

It is followed by a series of other notes indicating six rehearsals of it held between 29.10. and 20.11 1856, and a description of its first performance reading as follows:

'mit Divertissement 'Den alvorlige Pige' for første Gang. – Det gjorde temmelig Lykke men fandt dog ikke den fornøden stemning'.

When the ballet was given its fifth performance on 28.2.1857 Bournonville stated:

'Bivaanet Den alvorlige Pige, der mere og mere vinde Publicums Bifald'.

The Earnest Maiden received a total of 7 performances at the Royal Theatre, the last of which was given on 14.9.1857. The musical material used for the Royal Theatre performances were most likely the same as those employed for performances at the Court Theatre earlier the same year (now in DKKk, call nos. C II, 117 b, MA ms 2962, and KTB 265).

Autograph sources:

Manuscript scenario. Ms. Autograph (included in a letter to C. S. A. Bille). Brown ink. 2 pp. (21,2 × 13,3 cm)
[…] Den alvorlige Pige/Ballet-Divertissement af A. Bournonville/Musiken componeret af Lincke/Personerne/[…]/Handlingen […]
Signed and dated: 'd. 21.e Novbr 1856.'
[DKKk; NBD III, 212, 21.11.1856

25.11.1856

La Sylphide (Sylphiden).

This performance represents Bournonville's second staging in Copenhagen of his Danish version of F. Taglioni's two-act romantic ballet *La Sylphide* (*see* 28.11.1836 and 22.9.1849). It was mounted for the début of his pupil, H. Scharff, as *James*, and seems (according to his diary) to have been staged with only minor if any changes from the previous 1849 production. In his diary Bournonville noted about the performance:

23.8.1856: 'Kl 5 indstuderet James' Parti til [H.] Scharff'

25.8.: 'Indstudering til Scharff'
26.8.: 'Indstudering paa Sylphiden'
12.9.: 'Prøve paa Sylphiden, corps de ballet'
16.9.: 'Prøve og Indstudering <u>Sylphiden</u>'
29.9.: 'Repetition med Scharff <u>Kl 5</u>'
9.10.: 'Kl 10. Prøve paa Sylphiden'
22.10.: 'Costumemøde til Sylphiden'
27.10.: 'Prøve paa Sylphiden (Juliette [Price] fortreffelig)'
28.10., 29.10., and 31.10.: 'Prøve paa Sylphiden'
7.11.: 'Prøve paa Sylphiden. Juliette dansed saaledes som jeg endnu aldrig før har seet hende'
10.11.: 'Prøve paa Sylphiden'
11.11.: 'Prøve paa Sylphiden. Juliette lidt upasselig'
21.11.: 'Prøve paa Sylphiden'
24.11.: 'Prøve paa Theatret paa Sylphiden'
25.11.: 'I Theatret Sylphiden for første Gang efter flere Aars Hvile. Den gik ÿpperligt og behagede overordentlig. Juliette var i sandhed mesterlig og <u>Scharff</u> udførte James' Rolle med Ild og Ungdomsfriskhed. M.d [L.] Stillmann var nydelig som Effÿ. Det var en meget tilfredsstillende Aften'.

The 1856 restaging received 8 performances, the last of which was given on 15.11.1859. The musical material employed this year was the same as that used for the previous 1849 production (now in DKKk, call nos. C II, 117 d, MA ms 2970a, MA ms 2710, MA ms 2762 (1–2), and KTB 275).

27.12.1856
The Sailor's Return, Dance Divertissement arranged by Mr. Ballet Master Sigurd Lund (Sjömannens hemkomst, Divertissement af Dans arrangeradt af Herr Ballettmästaren Sigurd Lund) performed by S. Lund, J. G. Sundberg, and a Corps de Ballet (Stockholm's Royal Theatre, Operahuset).

This divertissement is a choreographically free adaptation of Bournonville's 'The Sailor's Return', Scene and English Character Dance (see 9.6.1852). It was mounted by his pupil, S. Lund, who served as ballet-master at Stockholm's Royal Theatre from 1856 to 1862. According to the poster Lund's version seems to have differed from Bournonville's version by the inclusion of a small corps de ballet, while the music is completely identical with that of the original 1852 score. The Stockholm version received 4 performances, the last of which was given on 4.1.1857.

Musical sources:

Orchestral score. Ms. Copy. Brown ink. 1 vol. 56 pp. + cover (33,3 × 24 cm)
Matrosens Hjemkomst/86
Unsigned and undated [1856]
[SSkma; KT Dansmusik 86
Although the title on the cover of this orchestral score is written in Danish, the music itself is clearly a Swedish copy made in Stockholm.

Répétiteur's copy. Ms. Copy. 8 pp. (34 × 25,6 cm)
Vl.o repetiteurstemmen./Matrosens Hemkomst/<u>Violino 1.mo</u>
Unsigned and undated [1856]
[SSkma; KT Dansmusik 86

Parts. Ms. Copy. 19 + 8 vol.
2 vl I, 2 vl II, vla, 2 vlc e cb, fl 1/2, ob 1/2, cl 1/2, fag 1/2, cor 1/2, tr, timp. 8 extra parts.
Unsigned and undated [1856]
[SSkma; KT Dansmusik 86

1857

1.2.1857
The King on Fuurland (Kongen paa Fuurland).

The première of C. Brosbøll's two-act play (to music by H. Rung) is not included in Bournonville's handwritten list of his stagings of operas and plays, written c.1872 (see Additional Sources), nor in the printed survey of his works in his memoirs *My Theatre Life* (p. 408). However, in his diary he clearly noted about the dance, which he choreographed for this play:

11.1.1857: 'componeret og skrevet'
12.1.: 'Indstudering og Prøve [...] Kongen paa Fuurland (som jeg gjorde færdig)'
21.1.: 'Prøve paa Theatret – Kongen paa Fuurland'
1.2.: 'min Familie med i Theatret. Man gav for første Gang <u>Kongen paa Fuurland</u> af Brosböl, der var Dands i af min Composition'

This dance consisted of a *Minuet* (also named 'Dands') performed in the fourth scene of Act I (score no. 2) during the chorus, entitled «Fru Ingeborg hun var saa deilig og skjøn!». According to a note in Rung's autographed score (p. 14) the tune of this chorus was based on a (not yet identified) Danish folksong. The *King on Fuurland* received 4 performances, the last of which was given on 12.2.1857.

Musical sources:

Orchestral score. Ms. Autograph (by H. Rung). Black ink. 1 vol. 44 pp. (33,1 × 25 cm)
468/Partituret/til/Kongen paa Fuurland/Musikken af H: Rung./468./[...]/<u>Kongen paa Fuurland.</u>/Musiken/af/H: Rung
Signed and dated (on p. 44): <u>H. Rung Novb: 1856</u>'
[DKKk; C II, 119 k (KTA 468)
The music for the *Minuet* of Act I (score no. 2) is included in this score on pp. 14–23.

Répétiteur's copy. Ms. Copy. Brown ink. 1 vol. 4 pp. of which one is blank (33,3 × 24,5 cm)
Kongen paa Fuurland./207/1857./[...]/Repetiteurparti/til/Kongen paa Fuurland/Musikken af H: Rung.
Unsigned and dated (on the front cover): '1857.'
[DKKk; MA ms 3088 (KTB 468)
This répétiteur's copy contains the music for the *Minuet* in Act I (score no. 2). Moreover, Bournonville's autographed choreographic numbers '1–4' (written with black ink) are included in the music for this dance. They seem to refer to his separate (not yet traced) choreographic notation of it, which (according to his diary) most probably was made on 11.1.1857.

Parts. Ms. Copy. 21 + 2 vol.
2 vl I, 2 vl II, vla, 2 vlc e cb, fl 1/2, ob 1/2, cl 1/2, fag 1/2, cor 1/2, tr 1/2, trb, timp. On stage: cor 1/2. 45 vocal parts.
Unsigned and undated [1857]
[DKKk; KTA 468

12.2.1857
Pas de cinq from the ballet 'Abdallah' arranged by Mr. Ballet Master Sigurd Lund (En af Herr Ballettmästaren S. Lund arrangerad Pas de cinq ur balletten 'Abdallah') performed by S. Lund, Théodore [i.e. Th. I. Marckhl], A. Arrhenius, C. G. Edberg, and M. W. H. Wiegand (Stockholm's Royal Theatre, Operahuset).

This dance is identical with the *Pas de cinq* in Act III (score no. 15) of Bournonville's three-act ballet *Abdallah* (*see* 28.3. 1855). It was mounted in Stockholm by S. Lund, who (according to the poster) seems to have revised Bournonville's choreography. Lund had himself performed in this dance at the 1855 Copenhagen première in *Abdallah*. The *Pas de cinq* reached a total of 6 performances in Stockholm (3 during the 1856–57 season and 3 in the 1857–58 season), the last of which was given on 25.9.1857.

Musical sources:

Orchestral score. Ms. Copy. Brown ink. 1 vol. 52 pp. (33,6 × 25,5 cm) <u>Pas de cinq af Ball. Abdallah.</u>
Unsigned and undated [c.1857]
[SSkma; KT Dansmusik 84

No répétiteur's copy dating from the 1857 Stockholm performances of Bournonville's *Pas de cinq* from *Abdallah* has yet been traced.

Parts. Ms. Copy. 34 vol.
3 vl I, 3 vl II, 2 vla, 4 vlc e cb, fl 1/2, ob 1/2, cl 1/2, fag 1/2, cor 1/2/ 3/4, tr 1/2/3/4, trb 1/2/3/4, timp, arpa.
Unsigned and undated [c.1857]
[SSkma; KT Dansmusik 84

16.2.1857
A *Quadrille Noble* (*Ridder Quadrille*) and a *Tarantella* choreographed for a masked ball at the Copenhagen home of Baron J. F. von Zytphen in Store Kongensgade no. 52.
In his diary Bournonville noted about these dances, which were choreographed for a privately arranged costume ball:

3.2.1857: 'Aftenen hjemme, componeret en Tarentella Quadrille til en Maskerade hos [J.F. von] Zeüphens [*sic*]'
4.2.: 'Indstudering hos Baronesse [C.] Stampe af den nÿ Quadrille, der faldt meget godt ud'
7.2.: 'Lection 5–7 – Quadrille hos Baronesse Stampe'
8.2.: 'conciperet en Ridder=Quadrille […] Indstuderet min Ridder-quadrille'
10.2.: 'Ridderquadrille fra 3 til 4 1/2 – Hidsighed fra min Side (over en uartig Scavenius) jeg fortrød det og ønskede det usagt hvad jeg udtalte. Jeg haaber at gjøre det godt igjen'
11.2.: 'Om Aftenen Quadrilleprøve hos Baronesse Stampe. Tarentellen gik udmærket godt'
12.2.: 'Ridderquadrille Kl 3'
14.2.: 'Quadrilleprøve paa Landgrevens Palais […] Generalprøve paa Tarentellen hos Baronesse Stampe i Costüme'
15.2.: 'skrevet og arrangeret, Lection i Tarentelle til Chr Stampe og Cont.ssa Rewentlov'
16.2.: 'Prøve paa Ridderquadrillen i Landgrevens Palais […] klædte mig paa til den store Maskeradefest hos <u>Baron Zütphen Adler</u> og Baronesse. Det var i høi Grad smagfuldt og magnifikt, den livligste Tone herskede og flere muntre og gratieuse Optog forskjønnede det Hele; min Ridderquadrille gik smukt og Tarentellen gjorde complet Furore. Jeg gik hjem Kl 1 1/2 men Ballet har varet til Kl 5'.

On 23.2.1857 the *Quadrille* and the *Tarentella* were performed for a second time at a ball given at the Copenhagen residence of the Landgrave and sometime Governor of Copenhagen, Wilhelm of Hesse-Cassel, and his wife, the Danish Princess Louise Charlotte. It was described by Bournonville in his diary as follows:

21.2.1857: 'Quadrilleprøve hos Landgrevens'
23.2.: 'fra Prøven gik jeg hen og repeterede Quadrillen for Prindsen af Danmark [i. e. the later King Chrstian IX] […] Stort Bal hos

Landgrevens, hvor jeg var inviteret, der var yderst magnifikt. Dronningen Caroline Amalia var tilstede og Quadrillerne gjorde megen Lÿkke, navnlig Tarentellaen, der blev dandset to Gange. Jeg kom hjem Kl 2'.

No choreographic and musical sources for these dances have yet been traced.

4.3.1857
In the Carpathians (*I Karpatherne*).
According to Bournonville's diary the creation of this three-act Hungarian ballet took exactly one year. Thus, he had already begun working on it during his sojourn in Vienna 1855– 56, and its scenario was completed soon after his return to Copenhagen in the early summer of 1856. Among his main sources of inspiration for this work was J. G. Elsner's two-volume description of the history of Hungary and its popular and national customs (published in Leipzig in 1840).

According to the orchestral score, the music was for the main part composed and arranged by H. S. Paulli, and includes four Hungarian National dances in Act III, three of which (score nos. 27, 29, and 30) were orchestrated by V. C. Holm. Notes in Bournonville's diary seem to indicate that he may have received the music for these national dances from the Austrian composer, M. Strebinger, who perhaps is the true composer behind all of the four Hungarian dances in this ballet. They are as follows:

(1) A so-called 'Kör' or *Czardas* in Act III (score no. 27), performed by two leading couples and a corps de ballet.
(2) A *Slowanka* in Act III (score no. 28), performed by five couples.
(3) A so-called 'Pas des piqueurs' (or *Vexeldands*) in Act III (score no. 29), performed as a *Pas de deux* by F. Hoppe and Juliette Price accompanied by a group of four men (*Les piqueurs*).
(4) A *Frisckha* in Act III (score no. 30), performed by the entire cast.

Moreover, in Act III, score no. 24 Paulli incorporated (according to his notes in the orchestral score) an authentic Austrian *Ländler*.

In the Carpathians reached a total of 15 performances, the last of which was given on 1.3.1859. However, shortly after the ballet had gone out of repertory Bournonville mounted an abridged divertissement version of the first act, named *The Pitman's Dream (Bjergmandens Drøm)* and premièred on 6.11.1859.

The *Slowanka* from Act III (score no. 28) was many years later incorporated in Act I (listed as score no. '2[A]') of Bournonville's and Paulli's three-act romantic ballet *The Kermesse in Brüges, or The Three Gifts* when that ballet was restaged in a new, revised version on 19.11.1865. The same thing happened with the music of the so-called 'Pas des piqueurs' from Act III (score no. 29), which in 1865 was interpolated in Act II of the *The Kermesse in Brüges, or The Three Gifts* and performed there as score no. '11'. It was still being performed in this ballet, its second and last restaging by Bournonville on 8.12.1872, but was that year renumbered in the répétiteur's copy as no. '11½' and in the orchestral score as no. '12 b'.

Furthermore, parts of Paulli's music for Act I (score no. 6) were in 1869 reused in Bournonville's second, extended version of his and Paulli's divertissement *The Prophecies of Love* (*see* 28.2.1869).

Finally, five excerpts from Act I (score no. 6) and nearly all of the music for the *Frischka* in Act III (score no. 30) were incorporated by V. C. Holm in his 1870 arrangement of the music for Bournonville's so-called *Dance Divertissement* (*see* 31.10.1870). For that divertissement the borrowed excerpts were pieced together in a completely new sequence by Holm and performed as a *Czardas* by the corps de ballet.

In his diary Bournonville noted about the creation of *In the Carpathians* during his sojourn in Vienna, his later rehearsals of it in Copenhagen, and its 1857 première:

4.3.1856: 'Dandseøvelse med [E.] Reyssinger [*sic*] i Ungarske [...] Dandse'
5.3.: '2. Dandseøvelse med Reissinger'
6.3.: '3. Dandse Øvelse'
10.3.: 'Dandseøvelse og begge Dandsene Kör og Alliance lærte'
4.6.: 'Udkastet Plan for min Virksom (eventualiteter) i næste Saison'
7.6.: 'Besørget Affairer hos Im. Rhé [*sic*] angaaende Musik'
9.6.: 'Jeg hentede Bøger paa Classens Bibliothek'
11.6.: 'læst om Ungarn'
12.6.: 'læst i Elsners Ungarn'
22.6.: 'expederet [...] Repertoire til Secretair [H. C.] Christensen. Brev fra Maleren [I.] Stephanini i Mailand med Skizzer'
12.7.: 'Brev fra [...] Stephanini'
24.7.:'skrevet og componeret'
29.7.: 'skrevet en Akt af min nÿ Ballet'
30.7.: 'Den største Deel af Dagen beskjæftiget med min nÿ Ballet'
31.7.: 'Fuldendt min Ballet i tre Akter som jeg kaldte I Karpatherne'
1.8.: 'Hele Dagen tilbragt med at reenskrive mit Program færdigt'
2.8.: 'Brev til Secrt Christensen og afsendt Programmet til [N. V.] Dorph'
6.8.: 'Brev [...] fra Dorph og Christensen'
10.8.: 'skrevet til [M.] Strebinger'
19.8.: 'Brev til Prof. Dorph angaaende Repetiteurerne da [H. S.] Paulli er bleven sÿg'
25.8.: 'Møde om Decorationerne til min nÿ Ballet'
4.9.: 'besøgt Paulli, der nu er meget bedre'
8.9.: 'Besøg hos Prof. Dorph om Costumer'
21.9.:'skrevet og componeret'
23.9. and 25.9.: 'musiceret med Paulli'
26.9.: 'skrevet og componeret'
29.9.: 'skrevet og componeret [...] musiceret med Paulli'
30.9.: 'skrevet og componeret'
6.10.: 'Musik fra Strebinger [...] Pakke og Brev, Strebinger'
7.10.: 'musiceret med Paulli'
8.10.: 'Musik med Paulli'
14.10.: 'musiceret med Paulli'
17.10.: 'hævet mit Musik=Udlæg paa Theatercompoiret, köbt 50 fl til Strebinger [...] Musik med Paulli'
20.10.: 'skrevet Brev til [G.] Carey (med Penge til Strebinger recommanderet)'
21.10.: 'musiceret med Paulli'
26.10.: 'skrevet Person- og Reqvisitlister til den nÿ Ballet'
27.10.: 'componeret og skrevet'
28.10.: 'musiceret hos Paulli'
29.10.: 'componeret'
31.10.: 'skrevet og componeret [...] Møde i Garderoben og paa Malersalen'
1.11.: 'componeret'
3.11.: 'skrevet og componeret'
5.11.: 'componeret'
6.11. 'skrevet og componeret. Første Indstudering af min nÿ Ballet, I Karpatherne'
12.11.: 'Prøve og Indstudering paa den nÿ Ballet'
13.11.: 'skrevet og componeret. – Indstudering'
14.11. and 15.11.: 'skrevet og arrangeret. Indstudering'
16.11.: 'musiceret med Paulli, aftalt Costüme med [E.] Lehmann. Besøgt [J. F.] Fröhlich i Eftermiddagen, skrevet og componeret'
17.11.: 'Møde hos Lehmann'

18.11.: 'componeret Prøve og Indstudering fra 10–12½. Musikmøde hos Paulli'
19.11.: 'componeret'
20.11.: 'componeret'
22.11.: 'Indstudering fra 10–12'
23.11. and 24.11.: 'componeret'
26.11.: 'skrevet og componeret. Indstudering'
27.11.: 'Indstudering paa den nÿ Ballet'
28.11.: 'componeret. Prøve paa Balletten 1.ste og et Stykke af 2.den Akt [...] skrevet, componeret. – Indstudering'
29.11.: 'Prøve fra 10–1½'
1.12.: 'Indstudering og Prøve fra 10½ til 1'
2.12.: 'høfligt Svar paa en uhøflig Skrivelse fra Theatermaler [C. F.] Christensen [...] Indstudering, Costumemøde [...] componeret'
3.12.: 'skrevet og componeret. Indstudering (1.ste Scene af 2.den Akt) [...] Costüme=Møde'
4.12.: 'skrevet til H[. C.] Christensen [...] Prøve paa den nÿ Ballet [...] componeret'
5.12.: 'componeret'
6.12.: 'Prøve og Indstudering'
7.12.: 'skrevet og componeret'
8.12.: 'skrevet og componeret. Prøve og Indstudering 2.den Akt færdig'
9.12.: 'componeret og speculeret'
10.12.: 'Prøve paa [...] 2.den Akt af Karpatherne. – Efter megen eftertanke endelig lykkes det mig at omarbeide den 3.die Akt, der ikke tilfredstillede mig. – Nu vil det Hele faae et bedre Sving'
11.12: 'reenskrevet [...] fuldendt Reenskrivningen af 3.die Akt'
18.12.: 'skrevet og componeret'
19.12.: 'componeret'
20.12.: 'Prøve paa den nÿ Ballet'
3.1.1857: 'musiceret med Paulli [...] Besøg paa Malersalen'
5.1.: 'lang Tour udaf Porten til Capelmusicus [V. C.] Holm, der skal hjelpe ved Instrumentationen til Balletten [...] lille Prøve paa den nÿ Ballet'
6.1.: 'stor Prøve paa den nÿ Ballet'
8.1.: 'Musik med Paulli [...] Prøve paa den nÿ Ballet [...] componeret'
9.1.: 'skrevet og componeret'
10.1.: 'Indstudering paa den nÿ Ballet [...] Lehmann hos os til Aften'
11.1.: 'componeret og skrevet [...] Costume Møde'
12.1.: 'Indstudering og Prøve, I Karpatherne'
13.1.: 'componeret'
14.1.: 'skrevet og componeret. Prøve og Indstudering fra 11–12'
15.1.: 'Prøve og Indstudering paa den nÿ Ballet [...] componeret'
16.1.: 'skrevet og componeret. Prøve og Indstudering'
17.1.: 'stor Prøve paa den nÿ Ballet (Repetition)'
18.1.: 'Udarbeidet en Reqvisitliste med [A.] Fredstrup'
19.1.: 'skrevet og componeret. – Indstudering. [...] paa Malersalen [...] componeret den hele Aften'
20.1.: 'musiceret med Paulli [...] Indstudering [...] componeret'
21.1.: 'Møde hos Lehmann [...] Indstudering til [F.] Hoppe'
22.1.: 'Musik hos Paulli [...] Costüme-Møde paa Theatret [...] skrevet og componeret'
23.1.: 'besøgt Lehmann. Prøve paa den nÿ Ballet'
24.1.: 'Indstudering. Handlingen færdig'
25.1.: 'skrevet og componeret'
26.1.: 'Prøve paa 3.die Akt af Balletten'
28.1.: 'Prøve Kl 10 1/2, sidste Indstudering paa I Karpatherne: Finalen færdig'
30.1.: 'Prøve paa den nÿ Ballet 11–1'
31.1. and 2.2.: 'Prøve paa den nÿ Ballet'
3.2.: 'stor Prøve paa min Ballet for Directeurerne og H. C. Andersen. Den gik ganske udmærket og jeg havde megen Glæde deraf'
4.2.: 'Møde om Reqvisiterne paa Theatret'
5.2.: 'Scene=Arrangement paa I Karpatherne'
10.2.: 'Arrangementsprøve paa Theatret 3.die Akt'
11.2.: 'skrevet Personlister til Bladene m.m. Besøg paa Malersalen'
18.2.: 'Arrangementsprøve fra 6–9'
19.2.: 'Prøve for at besætte Pladsen for Mme [N.] Møller, der nu møder med sin tredie store Upasselighed'

20.2.: 'skrevet hele Formid. paa mit Balletprogram'
21.2.: 'Prøve for at remplacere Mme Møller'
22.2.: 'Maskinprøve paa min nÿ Ballet […] Eftermiddagen tilbragt med at reenskrive mit Program, besørget adskilligt i Theatret'
23.1.: 'Prøve paa 1.ste Akt af Balletten med Maskiner, det gik særdeles godt'
24.2.: 'Prøve først paa Consv: og derpaa paa Theatret'
25.2.: 'Prøve paa Balletten fra 11 til henved 3. Alt gaaer godt'
26.2.: 'Musikprøve paa 1.ste og 2.den Akt'
27.2.: 'Fuldstændig Prøve paa 1.ste og 2.den Akt af Balletten' […] besørget adskilligt til Balletten. Decorationsprøve efter Theatret'
28.2.: 'Prøve paa 3.die Akt af Balletten, der gik udmærket godt'
2.3.: 'Generalprøve i Costüme paa Balletten I Karpatherne. Den gik udmærket godt og lovede at give en god første Forestilling. [F.] Høedt viste sig som en sand Ven for mig'
3.3.: 'sÿslet med Balletten'
4.3.: 'Uddeelt Programmer, prøvet Maskiner til Ballettens første Forestilling Iaften […] I Karpatherne gik for første Gang og opnaaede heelt igjennem en overordentlig Succès, som jeg efter Indtrykket at bedømme venter skal blive af Varighed. Alle udførte deres Partier fortreffeligt, men hvad jeg aldrig vil glemme er Juliette [Price], der i fire Dage har skjult en Halsbetændelse for mig og nu overvandt sin Upasselighed i den Grad, at hun dandsede og spillede med høi Grad af Udmærkelse. Høedt [H.P.] Holst Lehmann [E.] Helsted og [M.] Henriques med Kone drak The med os og deelte vor Glæde'

Autograph sources:

Manuscript scenario. Ms. Autograph. Brown ink. 1 vol. 34 pp. (21,3 × 13,4 cm)
I Karpatherne./Ballet./[…]Ballet i tre Akter/af August Bournonville/1856.
Signed and dated: 'Fredensborg d. 31.de Juli 1856'
[DKKk; NKS 3285 4° 2 G–K]

Manuscript scenario. Ms. Autograph. Brown ink. 1 vol. 24 pp. (22,8 × 18,1 cm)
I Karpatherne./Ballet i tre Akter/af./August Bournonville./1856.
Signed and dated: 'Fredensborg d. 31 Juli 1856'
[DKKk; NKS 3285 4° 2 G–K]

Manuscript scenario (Act III). Ms. Autograph. Brown ink. 1 vol. 12 pp. (21,2 × 13,4 cm)
Tredie Akt./af./Balletten 'I Karpatherne'/2.den forandrede Udgave.
Signed and dated: 'd. 11.de Decbr 1856.'
[DKKk; NKS 3285 4° 2 G–K]

Production note. Ms. Autograph. Brown ink. 4 pp. (21 × 13,3 cm)
I Karpatherne/Ballet i tre Akter af Bournonville./Musiken af Paulli./Personerne:/[…]/Handlingen
Signed and undated [1857]
[DKKk; Troensegaards Autografsamling II]

Production note. Ms. Autograph. Black ink. 7 pp. (36,4 × 23,1 cm)
I Karpatherne. Ballet i 3 Akter./Requisiter./1.ste Akt.
Unsigned and undated [1857]
[DKKkt; F.M. (Ballet, læg I–J)]

Musical sources:

Orchestral score (incomplete). Ms. Autograph (by H. S. Paulli and V. C. Holm). Brown and black ink. 2 vol. Act I–II 188 pp., Act III 206 pp. of which two are blank (26,5 × 37 cm with several variants)
I Karpatherne./Atto 1.mo & 2do/276/Paulli/[…]/I Karpatherne./276/Atto 3.tio
Signed and dated (on p. 10): 'd: 21 Febr. 1857 HSPaulli', (p. 164) 'd. 18 Febr: 1857. HSPaulli'
[DKKk; C II, 119 (KTB 276)]

The two missing pages in this score (originally paginated '81–82') are now preserved in DKKk (call no. MA ms 2762 (3)). Moreover, the pages which originally were paginated '83–98' are now inserted as pp. '55–68' of Paulli's autographed score for Bournonville's three-act romantic ballet *The Kermesse in Brüges, or The Three Gifts* (now in DKKk, call no. MA ms 1551). They contain what originally was the music for Act I (score nos. 7 and 8) of *In the Carpathians*, but were interpolated by Bournonville in the Act I *Pas de deux* of *The Kermesse in Brüges, or The Three Gifts* on 19.11.1865 and were listed there as score no. '2 B'. Similarly, the music for the *Slowanka* in Act III, score no. 28 of *In the Carpathians* (originally paginated '379–394') is now preserved in the orchestral score for Act I of *The Kermesse in Brüges, or The Three Gifts* (pp. '25–40'). It, too, was incorporated in this ballet on 19.11.1865 and performed there as score no. '2 [A]'. Finally, the music of the so-called 'Pas des piqueurs' (or *Vexeldands*) in Act III, score no. 29 (originally paginated '395–412') is now preserved as a separate manuscript (see the following entry), but had been interpolated in *The Kermesse in Brüges, or The Three Gifts* on 19.11.1865 and performed there score no. '11' in Act II.

Orchestral score (fragment). Ms. Autograph (by V. C. Holm) and copy. Black ink. 18 pp. (26,2 × 35,5 cm with variants)
No. 29 [changed to:] 12b/Allegretto.
Unsigned and undated [1857]
[DKKk; MA ms 2762 (5) (KTB 271)]
This fragment of the orchestral score for *In the Carpathians* was discovered at DKKkt in 1989 among those separate orchestral score fragments which had been either incorporated or taken out of Paulli's autographed score for *The Kermesse in Brüges, or The Three Gifts*. It was originally paginated '395–412' and contains the music for the so-called 'Pas de piqueurs' (or *Vexeldands*) in Act III, score no. 29 of *In the Carpathians*. According to the 1865 répétiteur's copy for *The Kermesse in Brüges, or The Three Gifts* (now in DKKk, call no. MA ms 2966), it was interpolated on 19.11.1865 in Act II of *The Kermesse in Brüges, or The Three Gifts*, where it was listed as score no. '11' and danced (according to the poster) by F. Hoppe and S. Price as a *Pas de deux* (also named 'Jægerdands'). Moreover, at Bournonville's second restaging of *The Kermesse in Brüges, or The Three Gifts* on 8.12.1872 the same music served for a new *Pas de deux* (performed by E. Hansen and M. Westberg). It, too, was performed in the second act, but was this year listed in the répétiteur's copy as 'no. 11 1/2' and in the orchestral score as 'no. 12 b'. This is clear from Bournonville's autographed note on p. 79 in the 1865 répétiteur's copy for *The Kermesse in Brüges, or The Three Gifts* reading: 'Kermessen i Brügge Pas de deux (Herr E Hansen og Frk Westberg.)'). Finally, in H. Beck's much later restaging of *The Kermesse in Brüges, or The Three Gifts* on 7.11.1909 the 1872 *Pas de deux* was replaced by yet another Bournonville *Pas de deux*, this time dating from 2.9.1873 and set to a score by V. C. Holm. That dance was originally choreographed for D. Krum and M. Westberg, and had first been performed by them together with a small female corps de ballet as an incorporated divertissement in Act I of D.-F.-E Auber's five-act opera *La Muette de Portici*.

Répétiteur's copy. Ms. Autograph (by H. S. Paulli) and copy. Black and brown ink. 1 vol. 160 pp. of which two are blank (33,1 × 25 with minor variants)
B. 276/I Karpatherne./31A/Bournonville/1857./Paulli
Unsigned and dated (on the front cover): '1857.'
[DKKk; MA ms 2971 (KTB 276)]
This répétiteur's copy contains Bournonville's autographed notes (written with brown ink) which describe the dramatic action, the mime, and parts of the choreography for Act I (score nos. 1–4 and 6–10), Act II (score nos. 11–13 and 15), and Act III (score nos. 16–23 and 26). Moreover, his autographed choreographic numbers are included in Act I (score nos. 5–8), Act II (score nos. 11–15), and Act III (score nos. 28–29). Most of the numbers in Act I seem to refer to some later (not yet traced) separate choreographic notation which he probably made in 1859 for the divertissement, entitled *The Pitman's Dream* (see 6.11.1859). Similarly, the numbers in the music for the *Slowanka* and the so-called 'Pas des piqueurs' (or *Vexeldands*)

in Act III (score nos. 28–29) may also refer to some later (not yet traced) separate choreographic notations, that perhaps were written when these dances were incorporated in *The Kermesse in Brüges, or The Three Gifts* on 19.11.1865.

This répétiteur's copy also contains music which in several cases is not included in the orchestral score, which bears witness to the fact that it was written well before Paulli's full orchestral score was completed.

Parts. Ms. Copy. 33 vol.
3 vl I, 3 vl II, 2 vla, 3 vlc e cb, fl picc e II, fl I, ob 1/2, cl 1/2, fag 1/2, cor 1/2/3/4, tr 1/2, trb 1/2/3, timp, gr cassa, piatti, tri, arpa.
Unsigned and undated [1857]
[DKKk; KTB 276

Other sources:

Costume drawing by E. Lehmann. Pencil and water colours (15 × 24 cm)
No. 3/I Karpatherne
Unsigned and undated [c.1857]
[SSm; Daniel Fryklunds samling no. 267 (F 1327)
This drawing most probably shows the costume of *Gregor* in Act I of *In the Carpathians* (performed by H. Scharff).

Costume drawing by E. Lehmann. Pencil and water colours (24,2 × 15 cm)
No. 1.
Unsigned and undated [c.1857]
[DKKkt; Kostumetegninger (Lehmann)
This drawing most probably shows the costume of the miners in Act I of *In the Carpathians* (performed by the corps de ballet).

Costume drawing by E. Lehmann. Pencil and water colours (24,2 × 15 cm)
No. 12.
Unsigned and undated [c.1857]
[DKKkt; Kostumetegninger (Lehmann)
This drawing most probably shows the costume of the miners in Act I of *In the Carpathians* (performed by the corps de ballet).

Costume drawing by E. Lehmann. Pencil and water colours (24,1 × 15 cm)
No. 6.
Unsigned and undated [c.1857]
[DKKkt; Kostumetegninger (Lehmann)
This drawing most probably shows the costumes of the *Elf-maidens* in the divertissement, entitled *'The Dream'* in Act I of *In the Carpathians* (performed by a groups of twelve children).

Costume drawing by E. Lehmann. Pencil and water colours (24,1 × 15,1 cm)
No. 9.
Unsigned and undated [c.1857]
[DKKkt; Kostumetegninger (Lehmann)
This drawing shows the costume of *Count Bathyani* in Act III of *In the Carpathians* (performed by Gott. A. Füssel).

Costume drawing by E. Lehmann. Pencil and water colours (24,3 × 15,1 cm)
No. 10.
Unsigned and undated [c.1857]
[DKKkt; Kostumetegninger (Lehmann)
This drawing most probably shows the costume of *Matthias* in Act III of *In the Carpathians* (performed by G. Ad. Füssel).

Costume drawing by E. Lehmann. Pencil and water colours (23,9 × 15 cm)
No. 11.
Unsigned and undated [c.1857]

[DKKkt; Kostumetegninger (Lehmann)
This drawing most probably shows the costume of the hussar *Farkas* in Act III of *In the Carpathians* (performed by L. Gade).

Printed sources:

I Karpatherne./Ballet i 3 Akter/af/August Bournonville./Musiken componeret af H. Paulli./Decorationerne af Hr. Christensen. Maskineriet af Hr. Wedén./Costumerne tegnede af Hr. Lehmann. Kjøbenhavn, J. H. Schubothe/Bianco Luno/F. S. Muhle, 1857. [DKKk; 17, – 175 8°

16.3.1857

New Pas de trois, (Debut.) arranged by Ballet-master Sigurd Lund (En af Herr Balletmästaren Sigurd Lund arrangerad ny Pas de Trois, (Debut.)) **performed by S. Lund, M. W. H. Wiegand, and A. Paulsson (Stockholm's Royal Theatre, Operahuset).**

This dance is musically completely identical with Bournonville's so-called 'Pas de trois (Julius Price)', premièred three years earlier (to a score composed and arranged by H.S. Paulli) at Copenhagen's Royal Theatre on 29.5.1854. A copy of Paulli's score for Bournonville's *Pas de trois* thus seems to have been brought to Stockholm in 1856 by S. Lund, who mounted the dance there for the début of the Swedish dancer, A. Paulsson, seemingly (according to the poster) with Lund's slightly revised choreography. The *New Pas de trois, (Debut.)* received 5 performances in Stockholm, the last of which was given on 29.3.1857.

Musical sources:

Orchestral score. Ms. Copy. Black ink. 1 vol. 47 pp. (33,4 × 25 cm)
No. 87./Pas de trois debüt/Partitur
Usigned and undated [c.1856–1857]
[SSkma; KT Dansmusik 87
This score is a Danish copy made in Copenhagen and was most probably brought to Stockholm by S. Lund in the late months of 1856.

No répétiteur's copy dating from the 1857 Stockholm performances of this dance has yet been traced.

Parts. Ms. Copy. 29 vol.
3 vl I, 3 vl II, 2 vla, 3 vcl e cb, fl picc, fl, ob 1/2, cl 1/2, fag 1/2, cor 1/2, cnt 1/2, trb 1/2/3, timp, gr cassa, tri.
Unsigned and undated [1857]
[SSkma; KT Dansmusik 87

5.5.1857

The Festival in Albano (Festen i Albano) **(Stockholm's Royal Theatre, Operahuset).**

In his diary Bournonville noted about this, his first staging in Sweden of his one-act idyllic ballet *The Festival in Albano* (*see* 28.10.1839):

11.4.1857: 'besat Partierne i Festen i Albano'
13.4.: 'noteret Albano'
14.4.: 'Indstudering paa Festen i Albano fra 10 til 1 3/4, ringe Kræfter men god villie'
15.4.: 'Prøve fra Kl 9 1/2 til 2. Arbeidet gaaer godt fra Haanden'
16.4.: 'Prøve fra 9 til 2'
17.4.: 'Prøve fra 10 til Kl. 1'
18.4.: 'Prøve fra 9 til 1. Decorationsmøde i Anledning af Balletterne (Decorationsmaler [E.] Roberg)'
19.4.: 'skrevet og noteret'
20.4.: skrevet og componeret. Prøve fra 10 – 1 og fra 4 – 5"

21.4.: Prøve fra 10–1 […] Costume=Møde for festen i Albano'
22.4.: Skrevet og arrangeret. Prøve fra 10 til 1" […] (Indstuderingen af Festen i Albano færdig)'
23.4.: 'Prøve paa Dandsene til Albano […] Requisitmøde Kl. 5'
24.4.: 'Prøve paa Theatret fra 9–11½ derpaa i Matsalen paa Albano'
25.4.: '9-10 Prøve paa Albano'
27.4.: 'Prøve paa Albano paa Theatret'
30.4.: 'Orchesterprøve paa Festen i Albano Kl 10 og Kl 12 Arrangementsprøve paa samme Ballet'
1.5.: 'modereret Alt til Prøven paa Albano der fandt Sted Kl 10 fuldstændig og gik udmærket godt'
2.5.: 'Paa Theatret Kl 11 og afprøvet Costumet til Festen i Albano. General Prøve Kl 1 gik aldeles udmærket'
5.5.: 'leveret Programmer til Balletten […] første Forestilling af Balletten Festen i Albano der gik fortreffeligt og gjorde overordentlig Lykke. Jeg blev stormende fremkaldt og vi havde Aarsag til at glæde os over en complet Succès'.

The main difference between the Stockholm production and the original Copenhagen version seems (according to the Swedish musical material) to have been the *Pas de deux* (score no. 9), which this year was rechoreographed by Bournonville for his Swedish pupil, J. Hjorth. It was now transformed into an allegorical *Pas de trois*, danced by three pilgrims representing the *Flower* (*Blomma*), the *Fruit* (*Frukt*), and the *Grape* (*Drufva*). This new dance was performed by Hjorth, A. Arrhenius, and the Austrian born dancer, Théodore (stage name for Th. I. Marckhl). Moreover, the ballet's final series of four *tableaux vivants* (score no. 12), which depicts the sculptural works of B. Thorvaldsen, was this year replaced by yet another allegorical dance, namely a *Pas de deux* performed by *Amor* and *Psyche*. As a result of these and several other minor choreographic changes, many musical cuts were made in score nos. 7 (the *Pas de six*), 9, and 12.

The Festival in Albano was restaged a second time in Stockholm by Bournonville's pupil, S. Lund, on 19.2.1862 and reached a total of 22 performances in the Swedish capital, the last of which was given on 19.2.1862.

Musical sources:

Orchestral score. Ms. Copy. Black ink. 1 vol. 288 pp. of which one is blank (35 × 26 cm)
Festen i Albano/Pantomime-Ballett i 1 Akt/af/Bournonville,/Musiken/af/Fr. Fröhlich./Första gången uppförd å Kongl. Theatern d. 5 Maj 1857.
Unsigned and dated (on the title page): '5 Maj 1857'
[SSkma; KT Pantomime-Balletter F 10

Répétiteur's copy. Ms. Copy. Black ink. 1 vol. 76 pp. (33,6 × 25,2 cm)
Festen i Albano/Idyllisk Ballet i 1 Act/af/A Bournonville/Musikken af J F Fröhlich/Repetiteurparti
Unsigned and undated [1857]
[SSkma; KT Pantomime-Balletter F 10
This répétiteur's copy contains Bournonville's autographed notes (written with brown ink) which describe in fine detail nearly all of the mime and the choreography as devised for the 1857 Stockholm production. According to his diary these notes were all written on 13.4.1857.

Parts. Ms. Copy. 34 vol.
3 vl I, 3 vl II, 2 vla, 4 vlc e cb, fl 1/2, ob 1/2, cl 1/2, fag 1/2, cor 1/2/3/4, tr 1/2, trb 1/2/3, timp, gr cassa, piatti, tri, glock.
Unsigned and undated [1857]
[SSkma; KT Pantomime-Balletter F 10

Other sources:

Sketch by E. Roberg for the back curtain. Pencil and water colour (38,5 × 62,5 cm)
Fond till Balletten Festen i Albano – […]/gifven i Kongl. Theatern d 5 Maj 1857.
Unsigned and dated: 'd 5 Maj 1857.'
[SSdt; 2515/1939?

Printed sources:

Printed scenario. 1 vol. 7 pp. (18,3 × 11,1 cm)
FESTEN I ALBANO./BALLETT I EN AKT/AF/August Bournonville./Musiken af Fr. Fröhlich./Dekorationen af E. Roberg. Stockholm, Hörbergska Boktryckeriet, 1857.
[DKKk; 17, – 173 8°

26.5.1857
The Conservatoire, or A Proposal of Marriage through the Newspaper (Conservatoriet, eller Ett Frieri i Tidningarne) (Stockholm's Royal Theatre, Operahuset).
In his diary Bournonville noted about this, the first and only complete staging outside Denmark of his two-act ballet-vaudeville *The Conservatoire* (*see* 6.5.1849) during his lifetime:

23.4.1857: 'begyndt paa Conservatoriet'
24.4.: 'Prøve paa Theatret fra 9–11 1/2 derpaa i Matsalen paa […] Conservatoriet'
25.4.: 'Conservatoriet 10–1'
28.4.: 'Prøve paa Conservatoriet'
29.4.: 'Indstudering Conservatoriet 10–1'
4.5.: 'Prøve paa Conservatoriet og Skole til Dandsene'
6.5. and 7.5.: 'Prøve og Indstudering paa Conservatoriet'
8.5.: 'Lection til den lille Pige. Skole. Prøve paa Conservatoriet'
9.5.: 'Indstudering paa Conservatoriet'
11.5.: 'Prøve paa Conservatoriet. <u>Indstuderingen færdig</u>'
12.5.: 'Decorationsmøde Kl 11'
14.5.: 'Prøve paa Conservatoriet paa Theatret. Decorationsmøde'
16.5.: 'Prøve paa Conservatoriet'
18.4.: 'Prøve paa Theatret paa Conservatoriet'
19.4: 'arrangeret for Costume og Requisiter. Musikprøve paa Conservatoriet'
22.4.: 'fuldstændig Prøve paa Conservatoriet'
23.4.: 'besørget Garderobevæsen'
24.5.: 'Generalprøve i Costume paa Conservatoriet ikke fuldkommen tilfredsstillende, altsaa Forestillingen opsat til paa Tirsdag'
25.5.: 'Prøve paa Conservatoriet (fint gjemmengaaet)'
26.5.: 'Paa Theatret hvor jeg holdt en fuldstændig Prøve paa Conservatoriet […] første Forestilling af Balletten Conservatoriet (fuldt Huus), der gik udmærket godt fra alle Sider og gjorde overordentlig Lykke, Fremkaldelse m. m.'.

The Stockholm production differed from the original 1849 Copenhagen version by a series of musical cuts in the *Pas d'Ecole* of Act I (score no. 3) as well as some other minor omissions in Act II (score nos. 7, 8, 9, and the *Finale*). Moreover, the complete music for the Act I *Pas de trois* (score no. 4, performed by *Alexis*, *Victorine*, and *Eliza*) seems, according to the Swedish répétiteur's copy, to have been completely omitted in the Stockholm production. Finally, according to the poster, the action of the ballet is said to take place in and outside Paris in the year 1835.

The Conservatoire received 9 performances in Stockholm, the last of which was given on 22.10.1857.

Musical sources:

Orchestral score. Ms. Copy. Black ink. 1 vol. 367 pp. (Act I pp. 1–152, Act II pp. 153-367) (35,2 × 26,2 cm)
Conservatoriet/eller/et Frieri i Tidningarne/Vaudeville – Ballet/i 2 Akter,/af/A. Bournonville./Musiken dels componerad, dels arrangerad/af/H. Paulli./Första gången uppförd å Kongl. Theatern d. 26 Maj 1857.
Unsigned and dated (on the title page): '26. Maj 1857'
[SSkma; KT Pantomime-Balletter C 3

Répétiteur's copy. Ms. Copy. Black ink. 1 vol. 84 pp. (33,1 × 25,5 cm)
Balletten/Conservatoriet,/af./Balletmester A Bournonville.
Unsigned and undated [1857]
[SSkma; KT Pantomime-Balletter C 3
This répétiteur's copy contains Bournonville's autographed notes (written with brown ink) which describe the mime and the dramatic action throughout the ballet. Moreover, his choreographic notes are included in Act II for the *Can Can* (score no. 7, danced by the students and the *grisettes*), the *Polka* (score no. 8, performed by *Victorine* and *Dufour*), the *Pas de trois* (score no. 9, danced by *Victorine, Eliza,* and *Fanny*), and the *Finale* (score no. 12, performed by the entire cast). These notes were most probably written before the first rehearsal of the ballet was held on 23.4.1857. As a result of the omission of what in the original Copenhagen version was Act I, score no. 4 (the *Pas de trois*), all the following score numbers in Act I were changed accordingly.

Parts. Ms. Copy. 32 vol.
3 vl I, 3 vl II, 2 vla, 4 vlc e cb, fl 1/2, ob 1/2, cl 1/2, fag 1/2, cor 1/2, tr 1/2, cnt, trb 1/2/3, timp, gr cassa, piatti, tri.
Unsigned and undated [1857]
[SSkma; KT Pantomime-Balletter C 3

Other sources:

Sketch by E. Roberg for the back curtain in Act II. Pencil and water colour (25,3 × 61 cm)
[...]/Till Balletten Conservatoir/Gifven å Kongl. Theatern i Maj 1857.
Unsigned and dated: 'Maj 1857.'
[SSdt; 790/1967

Printed sources:

Printed scenario. 1 vol. 12 pp. (17,5 × 10,9 cm)
CONSERVATORIET/ELLER/ETT FRIERI I TIDNINGARNE./VAUDEVILLE-BALLET I TVÅ AKTER/AF/August Bournonville./Musiken dels komponerad dels arrangerad af H. Paulli.
Stockholm, Hörbergska Boktryckeriet, 1857.
[DKKk; 17, – 174 8°

15.6.1857
La Sylphide (Sylphiden). Projected staging at Stockholm's Royal Theatre.
According to a letter to the theatre management of Stockholm's Royal Theatre, dated 15.6.1857 (now in SSdt, call no. KTA, E 2A, Indkomne breve) Bournonville suggested on this day a Stockholm première of his and H. S. v. Løvenskjold's Copenhagen version of F. Taglioni's two-act romantic ballet *La Sylphide* (*see* 28.11.1836). It was planned to be carried out two years later during the spring of 1858. The project was carried out in part three years later on 12.6.1860, when a divertissement version of three excerpts (most probably arranged by Bournonville and named *Scene, Solo and Pas de deux, in two sections, from the ballet 'La Sylphide'*) was mounted at Stockholm's Mindre Theatern with F. Hoppe as *James*, and Juliette Price as *The Sylph*. Moreover, two years after that, the complete ballet was premièred at Stockholm's Royal Theatre (Operahuset) on 1.4.1862 and given there 12 times during Bournonville's engagement as artistic director. This slightly abridged version was mounted especially for the Swedish ballerina, A. Arrhenius, and was restaged by Bournonville on 17.9.1862, but then with a new, incorporated *Pas de deux* in Act I (set to music by H. C. Lumbye and performed by his two English pupils, A. and C. Healey).

15.6.1857
Napoli or The Fisherman and His Bride (Napoli eller Fiskeren og hans Brud). Projected staging at Stockholm's Royal Theatre.
According to a letter to the theatre management of Stockholm's Royal Theatre, dated 15.6.1857 (now in SSdt, call no. KTA, E 2A, Indkomne breve) Bournonville suggested on this day a Stockholm première of his three-act romantic ballet *Napoli or The Fisherman and His Bride* (*see* 29.3.1842). It was planned to be carried out during the spring of 1859. Although Bournonville had already taught the rôle of *Teresina* to the Swedish ballerina, J. G. Gillberg, some 9 years earlier, (*see* 12.2.1848) this projected staging was never carried out.

15.6.1857
A Folk Tale (Et Folkesagn). Projected staging at Stockholm's Royal Theatre.
According to a letter to the theatre management of Stockholm's Royal Theatre, dated 15.6.1857 (now in SSdt, call no. KTA, E 2A, Indkomne breve) Bournonville suggested on this day a Stockholm première of his three-act romantic ballet *A Folk Tale* (*see* 20.3.1854). It was planned to be carried out during the spring of 1859 as the last in a series of nine projected premières and/or restagings of his works in the Swedish capital. For the same project Bournonville seems to have ordered a new répétiteur's copy to be made, in which he inserted an almost complete notation of the ballet's dramatic action, mime, and choreography. However, the projected Swedish staging of *A Folk Tale* was never carried out, and *A Folk Tale* has to this day not been performed in Stockholm.

Musical sources:

Répétiteur's copy. Ms. Copy. Brown ink. 84 pp. of which one is blank (27,2 × 37,7 cm with minor variants)
Et Folkesagn/Ballet i 3 Acter/August Bournonville./Musiken af/N. W. Gade & I. P. E. Hartmann
Unsigned and undated [c.1854–1857]
[DKKk; C II, 108
This répétiteur's copy contains the complete music of the 1854 version of *A Folk Tale*. It was originally in Bournonville's private property, but was donated to DKKk on 31.3.1910 by his daughter, Charlotte Bournonville. It seems to have been made for a later projected staging of this ballet abroad (most likely that for Stockholm's Royal Theatre planned on 15.6.1857). This theory is supported by Bournonville's many autographed notes in this volume which describe (in French) the ballet's action, mime, and choreography of Acts I–II and most of Act III. His other autographed notes (written on pp. 77–80) indicate that the répétiteur's copy was also used for his later preparation of a revised staging of *A Folk Tale* in Copenhagen on 20.9.1867. In that production the original Act III *Pas de quatre* was transformed into a *Pas de sept* by the insertion of two new music sections, both of which appear (according to the orchestral score for *A Folk Tale*, now in DKKk, call no. C II, 108) to be orchestrated and perhaps also composed by V. C. Holm.

22.6.1857

The Wedding Festival in Hardanger (Brudefärden i Hardanger) **(Stockholm's Royal Theatre, Operahuset).**

This performance represents the first of two stagings in Sweden of Bournonville's and H. S. Pauli's two-act ballet *The Wedding Festival in Hardanger* (*see* 4.3.1853), both of which were mounted personally by Bournonville. The 1857 production differed from the original Copenhagen version mainly by three major musical cuts in Act II, score no. 14 (scene 4), no. 15 (the *Halling Dance*), and no. 16 (the *Spring Dance*). Moreover, several indications about the exact musical tempi in the Stockholm orchestral score and répétiteur's copy are significantly different from those given in Paulli's 1853 autographed orchestral score.

In his diary Bournonville noted about the rehearsals and Stockholm première:

7.5.1857: 'Begyndt paa Brudefærden i Hardanger'
13.5.: 'Indstudering paa Brudefærden (godt Haab om Udførelsen)'
15.5.: 'Prøve og Indstudering Brudefærden i Hardanger'
16.5.: 'Prøve paa [...] Brudefærden'
27.5.: 'Costumemøde paa Brudefærden i Hardanger'
29..5.: 'arrangeret til Brudefærden [...] Kl 11 Indstudering paa Brudefærden'
30.5.: 'Indstudering paa Brudefærden'
2.6.: 'Prøve paa [...] Brudefærden'
3.6. and 4.6.: 'Indstudering paa Brudefærden'
5.6.: 'Theaterprøve paa Brudefærden 1.ste Akt, som gaaer meget godt'
6.6.: 'Theaterprøve paa Brudefærden, godt mimeret'
8.6.: 'Prøve i Foyer og paa Theatret paa Brudefærden. <u>Indstuderingen færdig</u>'
9.6.: 'Prøve paa Brudefærden'
10.6.: 'Besørget Costume og requisiter til Brudefærden'
12.6.: 'Marqueret Musikprøve. Prøve fra 10–12 paa Brudefærden'
13.6.: 'Prøve paa Brudefærden'
15.6.: 'Prøve paa Brudefærden [...] Musikprøve paa Brudefærden'
16.6.: 'besørget adskilligt i Garderoben, skrevet og noteret'
17.6.: 'Theaterprøve paa Brudefærden Kl. 1. Hjem Kl 3'
18.6.: 'Prøve paa Brudefærden 1.ste Akt.'
19.6.: 'Prøve paa forskjellige Costumer'
20.6.: 'Generalprøve i Costume paa Brudefærden i Hardanger der gik meget godt og gjorde overordentlig Lÿkke'
22.6.: 'I Theatret stor Festforestilling til Ære for Prinds [Frederik] Oscar og Gemalinde [Princess Sophie of Nassau] [...] min Ballet Brudefærden, der gik fortrinligt og vandt saa stort Bifald, som Aftenens Høitidelighed vilde tillade det. Jeg modtog mange Complimenter'
25.6: 'Brudefærden i Theatret, gik meget godt og med Bifald uden synlig Enthousiasme'.

The Wedding Festival in Hardanger was restaged for the second and last time in Stockholm on 1.11.1861 and reached a total of 10 performances in the Swedish capital, the last of which was given on 7.11.1861.

Musical sources:

Orchestral score. Ms. Copy. Black ink. 1 vol. 232 pp. (Act I pp. 1–184, Act II pp. 185-232) (34,6 × 26 cm)
Brudefärden/i/Hardanger./Pantomime-Ballett/i 2 Acter,/af/A. Bournonville./Musiken dels componerad dels arrangerad/af/H. Paulli.
Unsigned and undated [1857]
[SSkma; KT Pantomime-Balletter B 5

Répétiteur's copy. Ms. Copy. Black ink. 1 vol. 86 pp. (33 × 25,5 cm)

Brudefærden/i/Hardanger/Ballet i 2.de Akter,/af,/August Bournonville.
Unsigned and undated [1857]
[SSkma; KT Pantomime-Balletter B 5
This répétiteur's copy contains Bournonville's autographed notes (written with brown ink) which describe the complete mime and choreography, except for that of the so-called 'Danse du barbier' in Act II (score no. 13). Moreover, the volume contains several other pencilled notes which most probably were written by S. Lund in preparation for the ballet's second staging in Stockholm on 1.11.1861.

Parts. Ms. Copy. 31 vol.
3 vl I, 3 vl II, 2 vla, 4 vlc e cb, fl 1/2, ob 1/2, cl 1/2, fag 1/2, cor 1/2, tr, trb 1/2/3, timp, gr cassa, piatti, tri, arpa.
Unsigned and undated [1857]
[SSkma; KT Pantomime-Balletter B 5

Other sources:

Manuscript scenario. Ms. Copy (by an unknown hand). Brown ink. 1 vol. 11 pp. (33,1 × 20,3 cm)
Brudfärden i Hardanger
Unsigned and undated [1857]
[SSdt; KTA, Lit. B No. 72 a

Sketch by E. Roberg for the back curtain in Act II. Pencil and water colours (39 × 61,8 cm)
[...]/Till Balletten en Brudfärd på Hardanger fjorden/gifven å Kongl. Theatern i Juni 1857.
Unsigned and dated: 'i Juni 1857.'
[SSdt; 789/1967

Printed sources:

Printed scenario. 1 vol. 11 pp. (17,6 × 11,2 cm)
BRUDFÄRDEN I HARDANGER./BALLETT I TVÅ AKTER/AF/ August Bournonville./Musiken af H. Paulli.
Stockholm, Hörbergska Boktryckeriet, 1857.
[DKKk; 17, – 174 8°

22.6.1857

A Circle Dance (En Runddands) **arranged for** *A Cup of Welcome (Ett Hemkomstöl)* **(Stockholm's Royal Theatre, Operahuset).**

This circle dance was arranged by Bournonville for J. Jolin's two-act play *A Cup of Welcome*, created for the occasion of the nuptials of the Swedish Crown Prince, Oscar Fredrik of East Götland (later King Oscar II), and Princess Sophie of Nassau (later Queen Sophie of Sweden and Norway). According to the poster it was set to music arranged and composed by J. Foroni. In his diary Bournonville noted about the dance:

8.6.1857: 'arrangeret en Runddands for [J.] Jolins Leilighedsstykke'
22.6.: 'Man gav et Leilighedsstykke af Jolin Hemkomstøllet'.

A Cup of Welcome received 3 performances, the last given on 30.6.1857. No musical sources have yet been traced for this work in SSkma.

23.6.1857

Thirty-six drama lessons and a performance presentation **of Bournonville's Swedish drama students (Stockholm's Royal Theatre).**

According to his diary Bournonville gave 36 drama lessons (between 29.4. and 22.6.1857) to a selected group of aspirant actors at Stockholm's Royal Theatre. These lessons were an official part of his engagement at Stockholm's Royal Theatre during the spring and summer of 1857. In his diary he noted on 23.6.1857 about the result of his efforts:

'jeg præsenterede de dramatiske Elever for Directionen og et Udvalg af Kunstnere og Theatervenner. De gjorde deres Ting særdeles vel og [G. O. Hyltén-] Cavallius takkede mig i en Tale. Jeg har saaledes fuldendt mit Hverv for Iaar og Alt er lÿkkes over Forventning'.

26.6.1857
Epilogue (Epilog) **(Stockholm's Royal Theatre, Operahuset).**
This epilogue by J. Jolin ended with an allegorical tableau by Bournonville, set to music by A. Randel. According to Jolin's autographed synopsis it depicted the allegorical figure *Svea* sheltering Muses and Graces, and the Four Estates of the Swedish Realm, and was mounted on the occasion of the nuptials of the Swedish Crown Prince Frederik Oscar of East Götland and Princess Sophie of Nassau. The epilogue was played by Bournonville's drama students at Stockholm's Royal Theatre headed by the Swedish actor, E. M. Swartz, and the tableau was performed by the dance students of the Royal Swedish Ballet. In Jolin's synopsis the tableau was originally drafted as follows:

'(Melodramens musik slutar i några triumferande toner, Konstens Genius döljis af ett molen, som sänker sig ned mellan honom och den [words illegible]. Ridån faller)'.

This text was later on changed by an unknown hand to:

'(Melodramens musik slutar i några triumferande toner, Konstens Genius återgår till sitt altare blandt skyarna. Dessa dela sig och öfverst på molnbådden synes Svea, omgifven af allegoriska figurer, föreställande dom fyra Rikständer. Nedanför ser man Apollo och Sånggudinnorna grupperade)'.

Finally, a third and definitive version was written over the revised text and reads as follows:

'(Melodramens musik slutar i några triumferande toner, Konstens Genius återgår till sitt altare blandt skyarna. Dessa dela sig och öfverst på molnbådden synes Svea, omgifven af allegoriska figurer, föreställande Kriget, Akerbruket, Vetenskapen, Handel och Sjöfart, alle utsträckande sin Krans åt Sångudinnorna, grupperade kring Apollo och Minerva/(Ridån faller!!!!)'.

In his diary Bournonville noted about the performance:

20.5.1857: 'Composition til en Epilog'
28.5.: 'Gruppering til Epilogen'
29.5.: 'Prøve paa Epilogen, som jeg sætter i scene til stor Tilfredsstillelse for Vedkommende'
25.6.: 'Prøve paa Epilogen'
26.6.: 'Prøve paa Epilogen [...] Stor Upvisning af Theatrets Localer og Magaziner, samt Elevforestilling for Rigets Stænder der in corpore vare inviterede til Forestillingen med deres Damer. Man gav [...] Epilogen, hvortil jeg havde componeret en lille Børnedands og et Tableau forestillende Svea der beskytter Kunsten og videnskaben, der gjorde stormende Lÿkke og fremkaldte Folkesangen, der blev af afsjungen med stor Høitidelighed'.

Musical sources:

Orchestral score. Ms. Autograph. Brown ink. 1 vol. 35 pp (23 × 37,5 cm)

Epilog af Jolin./Musik af A. Randel.
Signed and undated [1857]
[SSkma; KT Epiloger 7

No répétiteur's copy for this work has yet been traced in SSkma.

Parts. Ms. Copy. 39 vol.
3 vl I, 3 vl II, 2 vla, 4 vlc e cb, fl 1/2, ob 1/2, cl 1/2, fag 1/2, cor 1/2/3/4, tr 1/2, trb 1/2/3, timp, gr cassa, tri. On stage: cl 1/2, fag 1/2, cor 1/2, arpa.
Signed and undated [1857]
[SSkma; KT Epiloger 7

Other sources:

Manuscript synopsis. Ms. Autograph (by J. Jolin) and copy. Black and blue ink with numerous pencilled notes. 1 vol. 17 pp. (33,5 × 20,8 cm)
Epilog.
Unsigned and undated [1857]
[SSdt; KTA Lit. E No. 87

1.9.1857
Pas de deux composed by Mr. Court Ballet Master Bournonville (componeret af Hr. Hofballetmester Bournonville) **performed by F. Hoppe and Juliette Price (the Court Theatre).**
According to the repertory book of F. Hoppe this dance is identical with a *Pas de deux* from Bournonville's three-act romantic ballet *Faust* (*see* 25.4.1832). It is most likely the same as that to music by F.-M.-A. Venua which had been incorporated in *Faust* on 8.12.1849, but dates back to J. L. Heiberg's three-act play *Princess Isabella, or Three Nights at the Court* (*see* 29.10.1829). In his diary Bournonville mentions three rehearsals of this dance on 28.8., 29.8., and 31.8.1857, but makes no specific comments about its performance on this day. The *Pas de deux* was mounted at the Court Theatre this year as the result of a temporary closing of the Royal Theatre at the King's New Square, which was rebuilt during the autumn of 1857. The 1857 Court Theatre season began on 1.9.1857 and ended on 22.11.1857, followed by the reopening of the newly rebuilt Royal Theatre on 5.12.1857. The *Pas de deux* was given twice by Hoppe and J. Price at the Court Theatre, the last time on 25.9.1857. It is not possible to identify the dance any further.

6.9.1857
La Ventana, Ballet Divertissement (Balletdivertissement) **(the Court Theatre).**
This performance represents the first time Bournonville's second and final version of *La Ventana* (*see* 6.10.1856) was performed at the Court Theatre. It was mounted there because of the temporary closure and rebuilding of the Royal Theatre at the King's New Square, which made the Court Theatre the only stage available during the autumn of 1857. In his diary he noted about its second and last performance at the Court Theatre on 21.9.1857:

'I Theatret for meget daarligt Huus [...] *La Ventana* som gjorde overordentlig Lÿkke'.

7.9.1857
'The Sailor's Return', Scene and English Character Dance ('Matrosens Hjemkomst', Scene og engelsk Characteerdands)

performed by E. Stramboe and L. Stillmann (the Court Theatre).

This performance represents the second staging in Copenhagen of Bournonville's divertissement *The Sailor's Return* (*see* 9.6.1852). It was mounted at the Court Theatre because of the temporary closure and rebuilding of the Royal Theatre at the King's New Square, which made the Court Theatre the only stage available during the autumn of 1857. In his diary Bournonville listed only two rehearsals of the dance on 4.9. and 5.9.1857. The divertissement was given 22 times at the Court Theatre during the 1857-58 season, the last time on 19.11.1857. The musical material employed this year was most probably the same as that used for the first performance of this divertissement at the Royal Theatre (now in DKKk, call nos. MA ms 3016, MA ms 2904, and KTB 337 b).

29.9.1857

La Somnambule, ou l'Arrivée d'un nouveau seigneur (Sövngjængersken) (the Court Theatre).

This production represents Bournonville's first restaging in Copenhagen of his Danish version of J. Aumer's three-act pantomimic ballet *La Somnambule, ou l'Arrivée d'un nouveau seigneur* (*see* 21.9.1829) and the first time it was ever performed at the Court Theatre. It received 8 performances there (the last given on 13.11.1857) and seems to have been mounted with only minor if any changes from the original 1829 production. Thus, in his diary Bournonville noted about the performance:

10.9, 11.9., and 12.9.1857: 'Prøve paa Søvngængersken'
19.9.: 'lille Prøve paa Søvngængersken'
21.9., 23.9, and 25.9.,: 'Prøve paa Søvngængersken'
26.9.: 'Theaterprøve paa Søvngængersken'
28.9.: 'Generalprøve paa Søvngængersken. Juliette |Price] sÿg!!! Eftermiddagsprøve for at remplacere hende med Jf.]B.] Bills.'
29.9.: 'Dandseprøve paa Søvngængersken […] der i det Hele gik meget godt. [H.] Scharff havde mange gode Ting. M.e [L.] Stillmann var meget interessant og [F.] Hoppe dandsede fortræffeligt. Lille Bills var Nul'.

The musical material employed this year was the same as that used since the 1829 première (now in DKKk, call nos. C I, 259 f (+ b), MA ms 2984, and KTB 287).

5.10.1857

Adriana. **Projected ballet in two acts.**

This projected ballet, which takes place in sixteenth-century Venice, represents the last collaboration ever between Bournonville and N. W. Gade. In his diary Bournonville described their work of the project, which for unknown reasons remained unfinished:

23.7. and 27.7.1857: 'Læst og speculeret paa mine nÿe Balletter'
28.7.: 'læst, skrevet'
30.9. and 1.10.: 'componeret'
2.10.: 'skrevet, componeret'
3.10.: 'skrevet og componeret'
4.10.: 'Resten af Dagen conciperet hele min nÿ Ballet, Adriana, der lover at blive god'
5.10.: 'Resten af Dagen, vexelviis spadseret og reenskrevet Balletten'
6.10.: 'Besøg hos [F.] Høedt, der har læst Balletten […] Løbet endeel for at faae fat paa Directeur [H. C.] Christensen, leveret ham Programmet'

8.10.: 'Conference med Directeuren angaaende min nÿ Ballet, ditto med [N. W.] Gade om Musiken'
9.10.: 'leveret Theatermaler [C. F.] Christensen Program til Balletten'
27.10.: 'Conference med Directeuren'
31.10.: 'Conference med Christensen'
1.11.: 'Besøg hos […] Prof. Gade'
22.11.: 'Aftalt Arbeidstimer med N. W. Gade i Anledning af vor nÿ Ballet'
25.11.: 'Hos Prof. Gade Kl 9 og begyndt paa Adriana'
7.12.: 'Musik og Cafe hos Gade'
8.12.: 'Musik hos Gade'
2.1.1858: 'musiceret med Gade'
9.1.: 'besøgt N. Gade'
16.3.: 'Besørget endeel Ærinder […] N. V. Gade som jeg traf Aftale med'
24.8.: 'Brev til […] N. Gade'.

Although *Adriana* was never carried out, a number of dramatic situations and scenic elements clearly resurface in Bournonville's much later three-act ballet, entitled *Cort Adeler in Venice* (*see* 14.1.1870).

Autograph sources:

Manuscript scenario. Ms. Autograph. Brown ink. 1 vol. 19 pp. (22,5 × 18 cm)
Adriana./Ballet i to Akter/af/August Bournonville./1857.
Signed and dated: 'Kjøbenhavn den 5.te October 1857.'
[DKKk; NKS 3285 4° 2 A–E

Musical instruction. Ms. Autograph (in parts also by N. W. Gade). Brown and black ink. 10 pp. (17,8 × 11,3 cm with minor variants)
Adriana/1.ste Act. 1.ste Scene/[…]/No. 2./[…]/No. 3/[…]/No. 4./[…]/No. 5./[…]/No. 6. /[…]/[Scene 8:] Bølgende 4/4/[…]/ Grand Pas/[…]/9.de Scene
Signed and dated (on p. 6) 'd. 30.e Novbr 1857.' and (on p. 8) 'd. 7.e Decbr. 1857.'
[DKKk; N. W. Gade's samling, Kpsl. A–B
This manuscript contains Bournonville's indications and personal wishes for the musical lay-out of Act I in *Adriana*.

Musical sources:

Musical draft. Ms. Autograph (by N. W. Gade). Brown ink. 6 pp. (27 × 37,4 cm with minor variants)
Adriana. 1ste Akt./No. 1/[…]/No. 2/[…]/No. 3/[…]/N4./[…]/ N 5.
Unsigned and undated [1857–1858]
[DKKk; N. W. Gade's samling, Kpsl. A–B
This piano score manuscript contains Gade's first drafts for the music in Act I, score nos. 1–5 of *Adriana*. It also includes his autographed notes which describe the ballet's dramatic action and mime. According to Bournonville's diary the drafts were most probably written between late November 1857 and 16.3.1858.

Other sources:

Manuscript scenario. Ms. Copy (by an unknown hand). Black ink. 1 vol. 30 pp. (22,3 × 17,6 cm)
Adriana./Ballet i to Akter/af/August Bournonville./1857.
Unsigned and dated: 'Kjöbenhavn 5.te October 1857.'
[DKKk; N. W. Gade's samling, Kpsl. A–B

15.10.1857

Styrian Dance (Steirisk Dands) **(uncredited) performed by F. Hoppe and C. Kellermann (the Court Theatre).**

This (uncredited) dance is almost certainly identical with

Bournonville's *Styrian Dance*, first performed in Act I of D.-F.-E. Auber's three-act comic opera *Le Domino noir* (*see* 29.1. 1839). The 1857 restaging represents the first time it was mounted at the Court Theatre. It received 3 performances there by Hoppe and Kellermann, the last of which took place on 13.11.1857. Bournonville did not attend any of these performances.

Musical sources:

Répétiteur's copy. Ms. Copy. Black ink. 4 pp. (34,8 × 26 cm)
Violino 1.mo/til/Pas Styrien
Unsigned and undated [c.1857]
[DKKk; MA ms 2703 (KTB 213)
According to the style of the handwriting in this répétiteur's copy it clearly seems to date from the late 1850s and was most probably used for the 1857 performances at the Court Theatre of Bournonville's *Styrian Dance.*

18.10.1857
Pas de deux (uncredited) performed by W. Funck and S. Price (the Court Theatre).

According to the rehearsal book of H. C. J. Fredstrup this (uncredited) dance was rehearsed under Bournonville's personal direction on 14.10. and 17.10.1857. It is probably identical with the (uncredited) *Pas de deux* performed six years earlier by S. Lund and S. Price at the Court Theatre on 24.4.1851. It is not possible to identify the dance any further.

30.10.1857
Plan for an opera repertory for the 1857–58 and 1858–59 seasons.

According to his diary and two autographed manuscripts, entitled 'Opera Repertoire' and 'Operaens Besætning/Indstudering og Opförelse.' (now in The State Archive, call no. Det kgl. Teaters Arkiv, Gruppe E, pakke 288), Bournonville made an extensive list on this day, including the titles of 82 operas, operettas, and singspiels which he intended to mount and/or restage at Copenhagen's Royal Theatre during the 1857–58 and 1858–59 seasons. The plan was written as a result of a meeting he had on 27.10.1857 with the theatre management at which he was offered the sole responsibility for the mises-en-scène of all operas and plays at Copenhagen's Royal Theatre. After some initial hesitation he accepted this offer on 9.11.1857, but initially only for a period of four months.

The repertory list is interesting in that it reflects Bournonville's great familiarity with and personal preferences among the opera repertory of his time. Thus, out of 82 works, 39 were French, 17 German, 16 Italian, and 9 Danish. Moreover, 11 works in this list had never before been performed at the Royal Theatre. Among these were G. Rossini's *Otello,* C. M. v. Weber's *Oberon, or The Elf King's Oath,* G. Meyerbeer's *Le Prophète,* and G. Verdi's *Ernani* and *Il Trovatore.* The 82 works are grouped according to the nationality of their respective composers and include the following works:

Danish composers (Danske Componister):

Lulu.
The projected restaging of F. Kuhlau's three-act romantic opera from 1824 (which Bournonville proposed again on 20.1.1858) was never carried out, and the opera has not been performed at Copenhagen's Royal Theatre since 8.1.1838 to this day.

The Brigands' Castle (Røverborgen).
The projected 1857 restaging of F. Kuhlau's three-act singspiel from 1814 was carried out three years later on 7.3.1860, when *The Brigands' Castle* was mounted for the first and only time with Bournonville's mise-en-scène.

Faruk.
The projected restaging of C. E. F. Weyse's three-act singspiel from 1812 was never carried out by Bournonville, and since 8.4 1834 to this day *Faruk* has not been performed at Copenhagen's Royal Theatre.

The Feast at Kenilworth (Festen paa Kenilworth).
The projected restaging of C. E. F. Weyse's three-act singspiel from 1836 was never carried out by Bournonville. and *The Feast at Kenilworth* has not been performed at Copenhagen's Royal Theatre since 24.9.1836 to this day.

The Sleeping-Draught (Sovedrikken).
The projected restaging of C. E. F. Weyse's two-act singspiel from 1809 (which in 1858 was divided into three acts, and in 1866 into four acts) was carried out by Bournonville on 15.1.1858, when *The Sleeping-Draught* was mounted under his personal direction for the first time. It was restaged for a second and last time by Bournonville on 5.3.1874, but then with his own, completely new mise-en-scène.

Youth and Folly, or Trick upon Trick (Ungdom og Galskab eller List over List).
The projected restaging of E. Dupuy's two-act singspiel from 1806 was carried out by Bournonville on 20.3.1869, when *Youth and Folly* was mounted for the first and only time with his mise-en-scène.

Mariotta.
The projected restaging of N. W. Gade's three-act opera from 1850 was never carried out by Bournonville, and *Mariotta* has not been performed at Copenhagen's Royal Theatre since 13.1.1851 to this day.

Little Kirsten (Liden Kirsten).
I. P. E. Hartmann's one-act singspiel from 1846 had been restaged on 6.1.1848 with the dances rehearsed and staged by Bournonville. The projected 1857 restaging was carried out on 29.10.1858, when *Little Kirsten* was mounted in an enlarged two-act version with Bournonville's own complete mise-en-scène and choreography for the first time.

The Wedding at Lake Como (Brylluppet ved Como=Søen).
Bournonville had earlier created the mise-en-scène for F. Gläser's three-act opera when it was given its world première on 29.1.1849. The projected 1857 restaging was never carried out, and the opera has not been performed at Copenhagen's Royal Theatre since 12.3. 1852 to this day.

German Composers (Tydske Componister):

Die Zauberflöte (Tryllefløiten).
The projected 1857 restaging of W. A. Mozart's two-act opera from 1791 was carried out by Bournonville on 27.1.1869 when it was mounted for the first and only time with his complete mise-en-scène.

Il Dissoluto Punito, ossia il Don Giovanni (Don Juan).
The projected 1857 restaging of W. A. Mozart's two-act opera from 1787 (*see also* 3.4.1848) was carried out by Bournonville during the following year on 14.3.1858 when he gave personal stage instructions to the singers and created for the first time a completely new mise-en-scène for the entire opera.

Die Hochzeit des Figaro (Figaros Bryllup).
Bournonville had earlier been involved in the restagings of W. A. Mozart's four-act comic opera from 1786 on three occasions, namely at the Court Theatre on 25.5.1842 (sung in Italian), and at the Royal Theatre on 7.1.1844 and 1.5.1849 (both given in Danish). The projected 1857 restaging was carried out with Bournonville's new, original mise-en-scène and personal stage instructions to the singers on 21.5.1858.

La Clemenza di Tito (Titus).
The projected 1857 restaging of W. A. Mozart's two-act opera from 1791 was carried out by Bournonville on 8.9.1860, when it was mounted with his mise-en-scène for the first and only time.

Die Entführung aus dem Serail (Bortførelsen af Seraillet).
The projected 1857 restaging of W. A. Mozart's three-act comic opera from 1782 was carried out by Bournonville on 21.5.1859, when *Die Entführung aus dem Serail* was mounted with his mise-en-scène for the first and only time.

Der Doktor und Apotheker (Apothekeren og Doktoren).
The projected 1857 restaging of C. D. v. Dittersdorf's two-act comic opera from 1786 was never carried out by Bournonville. It was mounted for the last time in Copenhagen on 13.1.1865, at a time when Bournonville was not under contract with the Royal Theatre.

L'Amore Artigiano/Die Liebe unter den Handwerksleuten (De forliebte Haandværksfolk).
The projected 1857 restaging of F. L. Gassmann's three-act singspiel from 1767 was never carried out by Bournonville. It was, however, restaged for the last time at Copenhagen's Royal Theatre on 14.1.1877, but then at a time when Bournonville (according to his contract) was no longer obliged to direct the stagings of operas and plays.

Der Freischütz (Jægerbruden).
The projected 1857 restaging of C. M. v. Weber's three-act romantic opera from 1821 was partially carried out by Bournonville on 27.3.1858 when he gave personal stage instructions to the singer, J. A. Steenberg, who played *Max* in its restaging that year on 4.5.1858. Not until 21.2.1869 was *Der Freischütz* actually mounted under Bournonville's general direction and with his complete mise-en-scène.

Oberon, or The Elf King's Oath.
The projected 1857 restaging of C. M. v Weber's three-act romantic fairy-play from 1826 was never carried out by Bournonville, although he resumed working on it on two later occasions (*see* 6.10.1859 and 8.6.1871). In Stockholm, however, he succeeded in mounting *Oberon* on 21.5.1858 when it was given its Swedish première at Stockholm's Royal Theatre (Operahuset).

Abu Hassan.
The projected 1857 restaging of C. M. v. Weber's one-act singspiel from 1811 was never carried out by Bournonville, and *Abu Hassan* has not been performed at Copenhagen's Royal Theatre since 23.3.1824 to this day.

Fidelio, oder Die ehelich Liebe (Fidelio).
The projected 1857 restaging of L. v. Beethoven's three-act singspiel from 1805 (after 1814 reduced to two acts) was carried out by Bournonville on 18.12.1858, when it was mounted with his mise-en-scène for the first time. It was restaged by him for a second and last time on 17.12.1870.

Hans Heiling.
The projected 1857 restaging of H. Marschner's three-act romantic opera from 1833 was carried out by Bournonville on 20.2.1858, when *Hans Heiling* was mounted for the first time with his mise-en-scène. The opera was restaged by him for the second and last time on 4.11.1868.

Der Templer und Die Jüdin (Tempelherren og Jødinden).
The projected 1857 restaging of H. Marschner's three-act opera from 1829 was carried out by Bournonville on 16.4.1871, when *Der Templer und Die Jüdin* was mounted for the first and only time with his dances and mise-en-scène.

Martha oder Der Markt zu Richmond (Martha eller Markedet i Richmond).
The projected 1857 restaging of F. v. Flotow's four-act romantic comic opera from 1847 (which was reproposed by Bournonville on 20.1.1858) was carried out by him three years later on 15.5.1860, when *Martha* was restaged with his mise-en-scène in Copenhagen for the first and only time.

Alessandro Stradella (Stradella).
Bournonville would certainly have known F. v. Flotow's three-act opera from 1844 from his summer tour in 1847 to Stockholm, where he danced the so-called *Pas de deux à la Taglioni* together with his Swedish pupil, M. C. Norberg as an incorporated divertissement in this opera's second act at Stockholm's Royal Theatre (Operahuset) on 26.5.1847. The projected 1857 Copenhagen première of this opera (sung in Danish) was never carried out by Bournonville, and *Alessandro Stradella* has to this day not been performed at Copenhagen's Royal Theatre. However, on 7.6.1858 the opera was given its Copenhagen première by a visiting German opera company, who performed it four times in the Danish capital (sung in German). The first three performances took place at Vesterbroes Theater, while the last was given at the Alhambra Theatre on 13.6.1858. Bournonville could not have attended any of these performances because of his summer tour to Stockholm during the period between 1.4. and 21.6.1858.

Czaar und Zimmermann (Czaren og Tømmermanden).
Bournonville had earlier choreographed the dances in G. Lortzing's three-act comic opera from 1837 when it was given its Copenhagen première on 18.9.1846. His 1857 projected restaging of it was carried out on 7.1.1858, when *Czaar und Zimmermann* was mounted with his complete mise-en-scène for the first and only time.

Des Adlers Horst (Ørnens Rede).
The projected 1857 restaging of F. Gläser's three-act comic opera from 1832 was never carried out by Bournonville, and the opera has not been performed at Copenhagen's Royal Theatre since 5.1.1844 to this day.

French Composers (Franske Componister):

Joseph (Joseph og hans Brødre i Ægypten).
The projected 1857 restaging of E.-H. Méhul's three-act opera from 1807 was carried out by Bournonville on 13.10.1858, when *Joseph* was mounted with his mise-en-scène for the first time. After having attended a performance of it on 5.1.1857 Bournonville noted about this opera in his diary: 'hørt Joseph og hans Brødre med Steenberg, der har en smuk stemme – hvilken guddommelig Musik!'. This very positive experience clearly seems to represent the main reason why he decided to include this work among his projected opera restagings for the 1857–58 and 1858–59 seasons. *Joseph* was mounted by Bournonville for the last time at Stockholm's Royal Theatre (Operahuset) on 19.1.1864.

Héléna.
The projected 1857 restaging of E.-H. Méhul's three-act opera from 1803 was never carried out by Bournonville and the work has not been performed at Copenhagen's Royal Theatre since 21.5.1819 to this day.

Le Trésor supposé, ou Le Danger d'écouter aux portes (Skatten eller Staa ikke paa Lur).
The projected 1857 restaging of E.-H. Méhul's extraordinary successful one-act *comédie en prose* from 1802 was never carried out by Bournonville. However, it was mounted by Th. Overskou(?) on 17.3.

1858 at a time when Bournonville was otherwise occupied preparing a summer tour to Stockholm. *Le Trésor supposé, ou Le Danger d'écouter aux portes* remained in the Copenhagen repertory until 5.12.1888 and reached a total of 160 performances.

Les Deux Journées, ou Le Porteur d'eau (De to Dage eller Flygtningene).
The fact that both of the two works by L. Cherubini in Bournonville's list were premièred in Paris seems to have induced him to list them here as works by a French composer. His projected 1857 restaging of Cherubini's three-act opera from 1800 was carried out some three years later when *Les Deux Journées* was mounted for the first and only time with his mise-en-scène in Denmark (*see* 30.10.1860). Moreover, on 19.11.1863 he proposed a restaging of this opera at Stockholm's Royal Theatre. That project, however, was never carried out during his tenure at that theatre.

Lodoiska.
The projected 1857 restaging of L. Cherubini's three-act heroic comedy from 1791 was never carried out by Bournonville, and from 27.3.1838 to this day *Lodoiska* has not been performed at Copenhagen's Royal Theatre.

Léon, ou Le Château de Monténero (Slottet Montenero).
Bournonville had earlier choreographed a dance in Act I of N. Dalayrac's three-act singspiel from 1798 when it was restaged at Copenhagen's Royal Theatre on 24.2.1851. His projected 1857 restaging of this work was never carried out and *Léon, ou Le Château de Montenero* has not been performed at Copenhagen's Royal Theatre since 20.10.1851 to this day.

L'Opéra-comique (Operetten).
The projected 1857 restaging of D. Della Maria's one-act comic opera from 1798 was never carried out by Bournonville and *L'Opera-comique* has not been performed at Copenhagen's Royal Theatre since 15.11.1849 to this day.

Une Heure de mariage (En Times Ægteskab).
The projected 1857 restaging of N. Dalayrac's one-act opera from 1804 was never carried out by Bournonville, and *Une Heure de mariage* has not been performed at Copenhagen's Royal Theatre since 13.2.1834 to this day.

L'Intrigue aux fenêtres (Kærlighedsintriguen i Vinduerne).
This projected restaging of N. Isouard's one-act opera from 1805 was never carried out by Bournonville, and *L'Intrigue aux fenêtres* has not been performed at Copenhagen's Royal Theatre since 11.12.1823 to this day.

Jeannot et Colin (Jeannot og Colin eller Fosterbrødrene).
For his Copenhagen début Bournonville performed a *Pas de deux* together with A. Krætzmer on 1.9.1829 as an incorporated divertissement in N. Isouard's three-act comic opera from 1814. This projected 1857 restaging of *Jeannot et Colin* was never carried out, and Isouard's opera has not been performed at Copenhagen's Royal Theatre since 23.5.1834 to this day.

Joconde, ou Les Coureurs d'aventures (Joconde eller Frierne paa Eventyr).
The projected 1857 restaging of N. Isouard's three-act comic opera from 1814 was never carried out by Bournonville, and *Joconde, ou Les Coureurs d'aventures* has not been performed at Copenhagen's Royal Theatre since 18.4.1850 to this day.

Cendrillon (Cendrillon eller Den lille grønne Sko).
On 17.12.1837 Bournonville performed a *Pas de deux* together with L. Grahn as an incorporated divertissement in N. Isouard's three-act lyrical fairy-play from 1810. Later he also directed a restaging of *Cendrillon* which was performed on 19.9.1856. His projected 1857 restaging of this work was never carried out, and *Cendrillon* has not been performed at Copenhagen's Royal Theatre since 25.2.1857 to this day.

Le Colporteur, ou L'Enfant du Bucheron (Skovhuggerens Sön).
The projected 1857 restaging of G. Onslow's three-act comic opera from 1827 was never carried out by Bournonville and *Le Colporteur, ou L'Enfant du Bucheron* has not been performed at Copenhagen's Royal Theatre since 13.12.1828 to this day.

L'Alcade de la Véga (Alcalden af Vega).
Bournonville's projected 1857 Danish première of G. Onslow's one-act lyrical drama from 1824 was never carried out, and *L'Alcade de la Véga* has not been performed at Copenhagen's Royal Theatre to this day.

Le Nouveau Seigneur de village (Den nye Jordegodseier).
The projected 1857 Copenhagen restaging of F.-A. Boyeldieu's one-act comic opera from 1813 was never carried out by Bournonville, although he proposed a staging of it again on 20.1.1858. However, a production of it was carried out in Copenhagen by I. F. Bredal on 6.11.1861 at a time when Bournonville was under contract with Stockholm's Royal Theatre. Moreover, *Le Nouveau Seigneur de village* was mounted with Bournonville's mise-en-scène at Stockholm's Royal Theatre (Operahuset) on 13.12.1861.

Jean de Paris (Johan fra Paris).
The projected 1857 restaging of F.-A. Boyeldieu's two-act comic opera from 1812 was not carried out by Bournonville until 12 years later on 17.12.1869, when *Jean de Paris* was mounted in Copenhagen with his mise-en-scène for the first and only time.

Les Voitures versées/Le Séducteur en voyage, ou Les Voitures versées (De væltede Vogne).
The projected 1857 restaging of the 1820 version of F.-A. Boyeldieu's two-act comic opera from 1808 was never carried out by Bournonville, and *Le Séducteur en voyage* has not been performed at Copenhagen's Royal Theatre since 7.4.1829 to this day.

Ma Tante Aurore ou Le Roman impromtu/Ma Tante Aurore (Tante Aurora).
The projected 1857 restaging of F.-A. Boyeldieu's three-act comic opera from 1803 (later reduced to two acts) was never carried out by Bournonville, and *Ma Tante Aurore* has not been performed at Copenhagen's Royal Theatre since 26.11.1821 to this day.

Le Calife de Bagdad (Califen af Bagdad).
The projected 1857 restaging of F.-A. Boyeldieu's one-act opera from 1800 was never carried out by Bournonville, but was mounted under his general supervision at Stochkolm's Royal Theatre (Operahuset) on 20.2.1862.

Le Petit Chaperon rouge (Den lille Rødhætte).
Bournonville had earlier directed the rehearsals of the dances in F.-A. Boyeldieu's three-act fairy-opera from 1818, when it was restaged in Copenhagen on 1.12.1852 and 25.1.1855. His projected 1857 restaging of this work was carried out three years later on 20.12.1860, when *Le Petit Chaperon rouge* was mounted with his own, complete mise-en-scène for the first time. It was restaged for the last time by him on 8.2.1873.

La Dame blanche (Den Hvide Dame).
Bournonville had earlier choreographed the dances in F.-A. Boyeldieu's three-act comic opera from 1825 when it was restaged in Copenhagen on 1.10.1850. His projected 1857 restaging was carried out on 17.11.1858, when *La Dame blanche* was mounted under his general direction for the first time.

La Muette de Portici (Den Stumme i Portici).
Bournonville had mounted the dances and the mime scenes in D.-F.-E. Auber's five-act opera from 1828 on three earlier occasions in Copenhagen (*see* 23.9.1834, 22.10.1847, and 13.10.1850). His projected 1857 restaging was not carried out before on 2.10.1865, when he gave personal mime instructions to the dancer, J. Petersen, who that year played *Fenella* for the first time. Moreover, on 2.9.1873

Bournonville restaged *La Muette de Portici* for the last time in Copenhagen. It was that year performed with a new incorporated *Pas de deux* in Act I (to music by V. C. Holm) and with a completely new mise-en-scène (except for that of Act IV, which remained unchanged from the previous 1865 staging). Finally, in Sweden *La Muette de Portici* was mounted with Bournonville's mise-en-scène at Stockholm's Royal Theatre (Operahuset) on 18.1.1862.

Fra-Diavolo, ou l'Hôtellerie de Terracine (Fra Diavolo eller Værtshuset i Terracina).
The projected 1857 restaging of D.-F.-E. Auber's three-act comic opera from 1830 was carried out by Bournonville on 20.12.1857, when *Fra-Diavolo, ou l'Hôtellerie de Terracine* was mounted for the first and only time with his mise-en-scène and choreography.

La Fiancée (Bruden).
Bournonville had choreographed and mounted the dances in Act II of D.-F.-E. Auber's three-act comic opera from 1829 on two earlier occasions in Copenhagen (*see* 20.11.1853 and 16.1.1855). His projected 1857 restaging was carried out on 7.10.1858, when *La Fiancée* was mounted under his general direction for the first time. The opera was restaged for the second and last time by him on 28.12.1873, but then with a completely new mise-en-scène and partially revised choreography.

Le Concert à la cour, ou La Débutante (Hof-Concerten eller Debutaninden).
The projected 1857 restaging of D.-F.-E. Auber's one-act comic opera from 1824 was never carried out by Bournonville, and *Le Concert à la cour, ou La Débutante* has not been performed at Copenhagen's Royal Theatre since 28.10.1839 to this day.

Lestocq (Lestocq eller Stats=Intrigen).
The projected 1857 restaging of D.-F.-E. Auber's four-act opera from 1834 was never carried out by Bournonville, and *Lestocq* has not been performed at Copenhagen's Royal Theatre since 12.10.1840 to this day.

Le Dieu et la bayadère, ou La Courtisane amoureuse (Brama og Bayadèren).
Bournonville had choreographed the dances in D.-F.-E. Auber's two-act opera-ballet from 1830 on three earlier occasions in Copenhagen (*see* 7.2.1841, 9.9.1847, and 11.11.1849). His projected 1857 restaging was carried out on 6.10.1859, when *Le Dieu et la bayadère* was mounted with his own, complete mise-en-scène and choreography for the first time. The opera was staged 4 more times by Bournonville on 6.10.1859, 14.3.1863 (in Stockholm), 8.10.1871, and 3.6.1873 (only the first act).

Le Cheval de bronze (Prindsen af China).
The projected 1857 restaging of D.-F.-E. Auber's three-act fairy-opera from 1835 was not carried out by Bournonville until almost 14 years later, when *Le Cheval de bronze* was mounted on 22.1.1871 with the title *Broncehesten* and with his own mise-en-scène and choreography for the first time.

Le Domino noir (Eventyret paa Maskeraden eller Den sorte Domino).
For the 1839 Copenhagen première of D.-F.-E. Auber's three-act comic opera (*see* 29.1.1839) Bournonville had choreographed and/or staged some of the dances in Act I. At the restaging of this production on 6.12.1850 (in which Bournonville was not personally involved) none of his 1839 dances was included any more. The same was true of the restaging of *Le Domino noir* on 12.5.1859. That year Bournonville carried out, in parts, this projected 1857 restaging of Auber's opera by giving personal stage instructions to his daughter, the alto Charlotte Bournonville, who made her début at Copenhagen's Royal Theatre this year in the rôle of *Angela*.

La Clochette ou Le Diable Page (Alfen som Page).
F. Hérold's three-act fairy-play from 1817 was given for the first time in Copenhagen on 29.10.1825 with an incorporated divertissement, choreographed by P. Funck, entitled *Pas de clochette*. The music for

this dance (now in DKKk, call no. KTB 228) was later reused by F. Hoppe for a *Pas de deux* choreographed by himself and performed together with C. Fjeldsted as a separate divertissement on 22.10. 1841. Bournonville's 1857 projected restaging of *La Clochette ou Le Diable Page* was never carried out and this work has not been performed at Copenhagen's Royal Theatre since 10.11.1826 to this day.

Le Pré aux clercs (Klerkevænget).
For the 1834 Copenhagen première of F. Herold's three-act comic opera from 1832 Bournonville mounted a *Pas de deux* (to music by J. Mayseder) which was performed as an incorporated divertissement by himself and L. Grahn (*see* 28.10.1834). His projected 1857 restaging of *Le Pré aux clercs* was never carried out and this opera has not been performed at Copenhagen's Royal Theatre since 17.12.1 836 to this day.

Les Mousquetaires de la Reine (Dronningens Livgarde).
Bournonville had earlier directed the staging of J.-F. Halévy's three-act comic opera from 1846, when it was given its Copenhagen première on 7.10.1848. His projected 1857 restaging of it was never carried out, and *Les Mousquetaires de la Reine* has not been performed at Copenhagen's Royal Theatre since 23.11.1848 to this day.

Le Postillon du Lonjumeau (Postillonen i Lonjumeau).
For the 1837 Copenhagen première of A. Adam's three-act comic opera from 1836 Bournonville had mounted a *Pas de trois* to music by M. E. Caraffa. It was performed by himself, L. Grahn, and C. Fjeldsted as an incorporated divertissement in Act I (*see* 28.10.1837). His projected 1857 restaging of *Le Postillon du Lonjumeau* was not carried until some 16 years later, when it was mounted on 25.9.1873 with Bournonville's complete mise-en-scène for the first and only time.

La Juive (Jødinden).
Bournonville had two years earlier choreographed and mounted a dance in Act I of J.-F. Halévy's five-act opera from 1835, when it was restaged at Vienna's Kärnthnerthor Theatre on 21.10.1855. The projected 1857 Copenhagen restaging was not carried out by him until 12 years later on 4.1.1869, when *La Juive* was mounted at Copenhagen's Royal Theatre with his complete mise-en-scène for the first and only time. However, an undated autographed manuscript mise-en-scène (written in Danish) seems to have been written by Bournonville in connection with the 1857 projected restaging, and was probably only reused by him for his later projected Swedish première of *La Juive* (*see* 5.10. and 6.10.1863). The same manuscript also seems to have served as a basis for the première of Halévy's opera at Stockholm's Royal Theatre (Stora Theatern) on 6.6.1866, which was mounted by Bournonville's personal friend and pupil, the Swedish actor and director L. Josephsson.

Robert le Diable (Robert af Normandiet).
Bournonville had been involved in five earlier restagings in Copenhagen of G. Meyerbeer's five-act opera from 1831 (*see* 13.6.1839, 5.12.1841, 18.1.1847, 18.1.1848, and 23.7.1855). His projected 1857 restaging was first carried out in Sweden at Stockholm's Royal Theatre (Operahuset) on 20.12.1862. Not until 11 years later did he actually succeed in mounting this opera in Copenhagen, where it was restaged on 19.1.1873 with Bournonville's completely new mise-en-scène and partially revised choreography.

Les Huguenots (Hugenotterne).
Bournonville had choreographed and mounted the dances in G. Meyerbeer's five-act opera from 1836 in connection with two earlier stagings in Copenhagen (*see* 28.2.1844 and 21.10.1855). His projected 1857 restaging was not carried out until almost 12 years later, when *Les Huguenots* was mounted on 7.4.1869 with his own, complete mise-en-scène for the first time. Moreover, on 22.10.1871 he staged this opera for the last time in Copenhagen, but then with the dances rechoreographed by his pupil, L. Gade.

Le Prophète (Profeten).
Bournonville's projected 1857 Copenhagen première of G. Meyerbeer's five-act opera from 1849 was never carried out, although he resumed working on it on 10.3.1858. However, his ideas for a staging of this opera were partially carried out at Stockholm's Royal Theatre (Operahuset) where *Le Prophète* was restaged under his general direction and choreographic supervision on 18.4.1863. Meyerbeer's opera has to this day never been performed at Copenhagen's Royal Theatre.

Guillaume Tell (Wilhelm Tell).
The fact that G. Rossini's four-act opera from 1829 was premièred at the Paris Opéra seems to have induced Bournonville to list it here as a French work. On 2.8.1842 he had asked (in a letter to the management of Copenhagen's Royal Theatre) to be commissioned to choreograph and stage the *Pas de trois* in Act III of Rossini's opera, prior to its Danish première on 4.9.1842. This task, however, was entrusted the French dancer, F. Lefèbvre. Bournonville's projected 1857 restaging of *Guillaume Tell* was not carried out until 11 years later, when the opera was mounted on 23.11.1868 with his own, complete mise-en-scène for the first time. *Guillaume Tell* was restaged two more times by Bournonville on 16.11.1873 and 21.11.1875 (in 1875 with a new, revised version of the Act III *Pas de trois*, arranged especially for his pupil, A. Scholl).

The Bohemian Girl (Zigeunerinden).
Although M. W. Balfe was Irish, his three-act opera from 1843 was for unknown reasons listed by Bournonville among the works of French composers. His projected 1857 Danish première of it was never carried out and *The Bohemian Girl* has not been performed at Copenhagen's Royal Theatre to this day

Die Lustigen Weiber von Windsor (De lystige Koner i Windsor).
Although O. Nicolai's three-act fantastic comic opera from 1849 was premièred in Berlin (in German) Bournonville listed it here among the works of French composers. During a summer tour to Stockholm in 1857 he had attended a Swedish performance of Nicolai's opera and noted about it in his diary on 18.5.1857: 'De muntre Fruer i Windsor Opera af Nicolai, smuk Musik blev i det Heele god udført og gjorde Lykke'. This positive experience may have led to his projected 1857 Copenhagen première of it, which, however, was not carried out until almost a decade later, when *Die Lustigen Weiber von Windsor* was given its first Danish performance on 14.9.1867. That staging also included a divertissement in Act III with choreography by Bournonville.

Italian composers (Italienske Componister):

Almaviva o sia l'inutile precauzione/Il Barbiere di Siviglia (Barberen i Sevilla).
The projected 1857 restaging of G. Rossini's two-act comic opera from 1816 was carried out on 23.1.1858. For this performance Bournonville directed the opera's final stage rehearsal on 22.1.1858.

La Donna del Lago (Pigen ved Söen).
The projected 1857 restaging of G. Rossini's two-act melodrama from 1819 was never carried out by Bournonville, and *La Donna del Lago* has not been performed at Copenhagen's Royal Theatre to this day.

Otello ossia Il Moro di Venezia (Othello).
G. Rossini's three-act tragic drama from 1816 had been performed four times in Copenhagen (in Italian) by foreign opera companies at Vesterbroes Nye Theater between 27.8.1834 and 14.7.1840. Bournonville's projected 1857 Danish restaging of it was never carried out and *Otello ossia Il Moro di Venezia* has not been performed at Copenhagen's Royal Theatre to this day.

Mosè in Egitto (Moses).
Bournonville had on 20.9.1843 been responsible for the mise-en-scène of G. Rossini's French version in four acts (entitled *Moïse*) of this three-act opera seria from 1818. This projected 1857 staging of the Italian version was never carried out by him, and *Mosè in Egitto* has not been performed at Copenhagen's Royal Theatre to this day.

I Puritani di Scozia/I Puritani ed i Cavalieri (Puritanerne).
The projected 1857 restaging of V. Bellini's 1835 melodrama in three parts was never carried out by Bournonville in Copenhagen, and *I Puritani ed i Cavalieri* has not been performed at Copenhagen's Royal Theatre since 13.1.1842 to this day. However, in Sweden it was mounted once under Bournonville's general supervision at Stockholm's Royal Theatre (Stora Theatern) on 18.9.1863.

Norma.
Bournonville had earlier participated in the Copenhagen restaging on 20.10.1848 of V. Bellini's two-act lyrical tragedy from 1831. His projected 1857 staging of it was carried out on 5.2.1858, when *Norma* was officially mounted under his general supervision for the first time. It was restaged two more times by him in Copenhagen (*see* 17.4.1860, and 25.9.1865).

I Capuleti ed i Montecchi (Familierne Montecchi og Capulet).
Bournonville had choreographed and staged the dance scene in Act II (score no. 6) of V. Bellini's and N. Vaccai's 1832 melodrama in four parts on two earlier occasions (*see* 13.10.1847 and 23.3.1849). His projected 1857 restaging of it was not carried out until some three years later, when *I Capuleti ed i Montecchi* was mounted by him for the last time on 8.2.1860, but that year with a completely new mise-en-scène and choreography.

La Sonnambula (Søvngængersken).
V. Bellini's two-act melodrama from 1831 was performed three times in Copenhagen (in Italian) by foreign opera companies at Vesterbroes Nye Theater between 22.7. and 25.8.1840. Bournonville's projected 1857 Danish première of it was not carried out by himself, but was mounted at Copenhagen's Royal Theatre on 2.11.1864, when he was not under contract with this theatre.

Lucia di Lammermoor (Lucia af Lammermoor).
The projected 1857 première at Copenhagen's Royal Theatre of G. Donizetti's three-act tragic drama from 1835 was carried out by Bournonville on 8.12.1857, when *Lucia di Lammermoor* was mounted for the first and only time with his mise-en-scène and choreography.

La Fille du régiment (Regimentets Datter).
Bournonville had already participated in a staging of G. Donizetti's two-act comic opera from 1840, when it was mounted (in Italian) by a foreign opera company at the the Court Theatre on 10.1.1849. His projected 1857 Danish restaging of it (which he reproposed on 20.1.1858) was carried out two years later, when *La Fille du régiment* was mounted on 20.10.1859 (sung in Danish) with his complete mise-en-scène for the first time. The opera was restaged for a third and last time in Copenhagen under his general direction on 4.2.1876.

L'Elisire d'Amore (Elskovsdrikken).
Bournonville's projected 1857 restaging of G. Donizetti's two-act comic opera from 1832 was carried out on 28.11.1859, when *L'Elisire d'Amore* was mounted under his personal direction for the first time. The opera was restaged for the second and last time by him in Copenhagen on 22.11.1872.

Lucrezia Borgia.
G. Donizetti's 1833 melodrama in two acts and a prologue was performed for the first time in Denmark (in Italian) by a foreign opera company at the Court Theatre on 11.2.1842 and was kept continuously in the repertory there until the 1853–54 season, reaching more than 60 performances. Bournonville's projected 1857 première of it at Copenhagen's Royal Theatre (which he reproposed on 20.1.1858) was carried out on 15.4.1859, when *Lucrezia Borgia* was mounted

(sung in Danish) with his mise-en-scène for the first time. This production was rehearsed again by Bournonville on 6.10.1859, and restaged for the last time under his personal direction in Copenhagen on 21.9.1860.

Linda di Chamounix (Linda af Chamounÿ).
G. Donizetti's three-act opera from 1842 was first performed in Denmark (in Italian) by a foreign opera company at the Court Theatre on 12.1.1845, and was kept continuously in the repertory there until 26.2.1854, reaching a total of 41 performances. Bournonville's projected 1857 première at Copenhagen's Royal Theatre was never carried out, and *Linda di Chamounix* has not been performed at that theatre to this day.

Anna Bolena.
G. Donizetti's two-act lyrical tragedy from 1830 was first performed in Denmark (in Italian) by a foreign opera company at the Court Theatre on 14.2.1844, and was kept in the repertory there until 29.3.1844 reaching a total of 8 complete performances. Bournonville's projected 1857 première of it at Copenhagen's Royal Theatre was never carried out, and *Anna Bolena* has not been performed at this theatre to this day.

Ernani (Hernani).
Verdi's four-act lyrical drama from 1844 was first performed in Denmark (in Italian) by a foreign opera company at the Court Theatre on 1.3.1846, and was kept continuously in the repertory there until 12.3.1854, reaching a total of 59 complete performances. Bournonville's projected 1857 première at Copenhagen's Royal Theatre was never carried out and *Ernani* has not been performed at that theatre to this day. However, *Ernani* was restaged 6 years later with a completely new mise-en-scène by Bournonville at Stockholm's Royal Theatre (Stora Theatern) on 28.10.1863. Moreover, 10 years after Bournonville's 1857 projected Copenhagen staging of *Ernani* it was mounted in that town by a foreign opera company at the Casino Theatre (then sung in Italian) and received 6 performances there between 1.5. and 28.5.1867.

Il Trovatore (Troubadouren).
Bournonville's 1857 projected Copenhagen première of G. Verdi's four-act lyrical drama from 1853 was carried out by him eight years later on 10.9.1865, when *Il Trovatore* (sung in Danish) was mounted with his mise-en-scène for the first time. This production also included a new ballet divertissement in Act III, set to music arranged and composed by A. F. Schwartz and H. C. Lumbye, replacing Verdi's original ballet in that act, written for the French 1857 Paris Opéra version of this opera. However, three years before the 1865 Copenhagen première of *Il Trovatore* Bournonville had been involved in a Swedish restaging of this opera at Stockholm's Royal Theatre (Operahuset) where he personally directed its four final stage rehearsals prior to a performance on 20.11.1862.

30.10.1857
La Juive (Jødinden). Projected Danish staging.
During his engagement at Vienna's Kärnthnerthor Theatre Bournonville had choreographed the dances in J.-F. Halévy's five-act opera, when it was restaged there on 21.10.1855. His projected 1857 Copenhagen restaging of it was not carried out until 4.1.1869, when *La Juive* was mounted for the first with Bournonville's mise-en-scène and choreography at the Royal Theatre. However, Bournonville's earliest (undated) manuscript mise-en-scène for this work (written in Danish) clearly seems to have been made immediately after he wrote his repertory plan of operas and singspiels on 30.10.1857. Moreover, this manuscript appears to have been reused by him six years later when he was preparing yet another mise-en-scène for *La Juive*, but this time at Stockholm's Royal

Theatre (*see* 5.10. and 6.10.1863). The projected Swedish production, however, was never carried out by him, but both his 1857 and 1863 mises-en-scène for this opera seem to have served as a basis for the later Swedish première of *La Juive*, mounted at Stockholm's Royal Theatre (Stora Theatern) on 6.6.1866 under the direction of Bournonville's pupil and personal friend, the Swedish director L. Josephsson.

Autograph sources:

Manuscript mise-en-scène. Ms. Autograph. Brown ink. 3 pp. (22,6 × 18 cm)
Jødinden (1.ste Akt)/[...]/2.den Akt
Unsigned and undated [c. 30.10.1857]
[SSm; Daniel Fryklunds samling no. 130
This manuscript mise-en-scène is inserted in Bournonville's later 1863 manuscript mise-en-scène (written in Swedish) which he clearly made in Stockholm on 6.10.1863.

8.12.1857
Lucia di Lammermoor (Lucia af Lammermoor).
The Copenhagen première of G. Donizetti's three-act tragic drama (first performed at Naples' Teatro San Carlo on 26.9.1835) was originally projected by Bournonville on 30.10.1857 and represents the first and only time it was mounted with his mise-en-scène and choreography. It included two dance scenes as follows:

(1) A *Procession* and an (unnamed) *Dance* in 4/4 time, performed in the Act II finale (score no. 7) by a corps de ballet of six men and twelve women during the chorus and cavatina of *Arturo*, named «Per te d'immenso giubilo».
(2) An (unnamed) *Dance* in 2/4 time, performed in Act III (score no. 9) by the corps de ballet(?) during the chorus, entitled «D'immenso giubilo s'innalzi un grido».

Moreover, between 1.11. and 10.11.1858 Bournonville directed four other rehearsals of Donizetti's drama prior to a performance of it on 11.11.1858. They represent the last time he ever worked on *Lucia di Lammermoor* in Denmark. Finally, five years later the opera was mounted under his personal supervision and with a completely new mise-en-scène at Stockholm's Royal Theatre (Operahuset) on 30.9.1862. In his diary he noted about the 1857 Copenhagen première:

11.11.1857: 'Skrevet og læst Bogen til Lucia [...] skrevet og arrangeret'
12.11.: 'Forvenetet Instruction til [J. A.] Steenberg men han var sÿg og kunde ikke prøve [...] Costumemøde med Lehmann'
14. 11: 'skrevet og besørget Opera=Forretninger [...] Instruction til Steenberg'
17.11.: 'Instruction Steenberg'
18.11.: 'Skrevet og arrangeret Costüme=Møde hos [J. A.] Pätges [...] Instruction 7–8'
19.11.: 'Instruction Steenberg'
20.11.: 'Instruction forfeilet da [J. C.] Hansen var upasselig'
21.11.: 'skrevet og arrangeret. Indstuderet Dands til Lucia'
22.11. and 25.11.: 'Instruction 7–9'
27.11.: 'Prøve paa Lucia paa Conservatoriet fra 6 til 8½'
28.11.: 'Indstuderingen af Vanvids-Scenen med M.d. [V. L. T.] Fossum til 2½'
30.11.: 'Lille Prøve paa Opera=Dands. Stor Quartett-Prøve paa Lucia. Den gik udmærket'
2.12.: 'Theaterprøve paa Det kgl. Theater Kl 11, hele Lucia. Den gik særdeles veel'

3.12.: 'Aftenprøve paa Theatret paa Lucia, der gik meget smukt, forbi Kl 9½.'
5.12.: 'Theaterprøve fra 12 til 2¼ paa Lucia. Den gik udmærket godt'
7.12.: 'Generalprøve paa Lucia Kl 12. [...] fra 9½ til henved 11
prøvet Decorationerne til Lucia'
8.12.: 'Kl 6 i Theatret for at besørge Alt. Lucia af Lammermoor, gik
særdeles godt og med et Bifald – der var eenstemmigt, skjønt ikke
varmt. M.e Fossum vare fortræffelig. Steenberg meget brav og lov-
ende for Fremtiden'.

Lucia di Lammermoor received 22 performances at the Royal
Theatre, the last of which was given on 30.11.1866.

Autograph sources:

Manuscript mise-en-scène. Ms. Autograph. Brown ink. 15 pp. (10,8 ×
16,9 cm)
<u>Lucia di Lammermoor</u>
Unsigned and undated [Written according to the diary most probably on 11.11.1857]
[DKKk; NKS 3285 4° 3 L–P]
The 15 pages containing Bournonville's mise-en-scène for *Lucia di
Lammermoor* were originally part of a notebook, entitled: '<u>Fire Opera
Scene</u>/<u>Instructioner.</u>/1857.', but were taken out of this volume by
him at a later stage, when it was transformed into his diary and given
the new title: '<u>Journal.</u>/<u>d. 24.de October 1861.</u> til/d. <u>1.te Novbr</u>/
1862.' (now in DKKk, call no. NKS 747 8°, 4, vol. 23).

Choreographic note. Ms. Autograph. Brown and black ink. 2 pp.
(18,2 × 11,3 cm)
<u>2' Akt 4.de Scene</u> Ritournelle
Unsigned and undated [Written according to the diary most probably between 11.11. and 21.11.1857]
[SSm; Daniel Fryklunds samling no. 134]
This manuscript describes the *Procession* performed by six 'officiers',
fourteen couples of 'Riddere og Damer', six couples of 'Skotske
Bønder, and six 'Karle med Fahner' during the Act II finale (score
no. 7). It also includes the names of the characters *Henry, Arthur,* and
Norman. Moreover, Bournonville's choreographic notes for the (unnamed) *Dance* performed in the same scene by 'les trois bonniers'
and 'les jeunes filles' are included. According to these notes it was
performed by a corps de ballet of six men and twelve women. Finally,
Bournonville's autographed choreographic numbers ('1–6', '1–3'
and 'C1–6') are inserted in this manuscript for the Act II finale. They
refer to similar numbers written into the music for this finale (on pp.
1–3) in the 1857 répétiteur's copy for *Lucia di Lammermoor* (now in
DKKk, call no. MA ms 2910 (1) (KTB 466 (1)).

Musical sources:

Orchestral score. Ms. Copy. Brown and black ink. 3 vol. Act I 232 pp.
of which one is blank, Act II 278 pp. of which four are blank, Act III
280 pp. of which two are blank (26 × 33 cm with minor variants)
<u>Lucie af Lammermoor</u>/<u>Partitur.</u>/1.ste Akt./[...]/Lucia von Lam-
mermoor/Oper in 3 Acten/nach dem Italienischen des Salvatore
Cammerano./Musik von Donizetti./Für das königliche Hoftheater
zu <u>Koppenhagen</u> [*sic*]/durch die Theater=Agentur/des <u>P. Gläser</u> in
Wien./[...]/2.den Akt./[...]/3.die Akt.
Unsigned and undated [c.1857]
[DKKk; C I, 236 n (KTA 466)
Donizetti's music for the dance scenes in Acts II and III is included
in the second and third volume of this score (on pp. 151–171 and 73–
93 respectively).

Répétiteur's copy. Ms. Copy. Brown ink. 1 vol. 4 pp. of which one is
blank (33,6 × 25,5 cm)
<u>Dandse</u>/<u>til</u>/<u>Lucia.</u>/[...]/81./<u>1858.</u>./Bournonville./[...]/Repeti-
teurparti 2.den Akt. til Lucia
Unsigned and dated (on the front cover): '<u>1858.</u>.'
[DKKk; MA ms 2910 (1) (KTA 466 (1))

This répétiteur's copy contains the music for the (unnamed) *Dance*,
performed in the Act II finale (score no. 7) during the chorus and
the cavatina of *Arturo*, entitled «Per te d'immenso giubilo». The
voume also includes Bournonville's autographed choreographic
numbers for this dance ('1–3' and '1–6', written with brown ink).
They seem to refer to his separate (not yet traced) choreographic
notation of it, which (according to his diary) he wrote during early
November 1857. The music is included on pp. 1–4 in a volume that
also contains the répétiteur's copies for three other operas and singspiels, mounted at Copenhagen's Royal Theatre between December
1857 and March 1858.

Répétiteur's copy. Ms. Copy. Black ink. 1 vol. 4 pp. of which one is
blank (33 × 25,3 cm)
<u>Lucia af Lammermoor.</u>/[...]/Repetiteurpartie/til/Dands i 3.die
Act af Lucia di Lammermoor.
Unsigned and undated [c.1857]
[DKKk; MA ms 2912 (6) (KTA 466 (2))
This répétiteur's copy contains the music for the (unnamed) *Dance,*
performed in Act III (score no. 9) during the chorus «D'immenso
giubilo s'innalzi un grido». The music is included on pp. 66–69 in a
volume that also contains the répétiteur's copies for five other operas and plays, mounted at Copenhagen's Royal Theatre between
1815 and 1871.

Parts. Ms. Copy. 35 vol.
4 vl I, 3 vl II, 2 vla, 4 vlc e cb, fl picc, fl 1/2, ob 1/2, cl 1/2, fag 1/2, cor
1/2/3/4, tr 1/2, trb 1/2/3, timp, gr cassa, piatti e tri, arpa. 57 vocal
parts.
Unsigned and undated [1857]
[DKKk; KTA 466

19.12.1857
Waldemar.

This performance represents Bournonville's second staging
of his revised three-act version of *Waldemar* (*see* 28.10.1835
and 19.10.1853). The divertissement in Act I (score no. 5)
was this year explicitly listed on the poster as *Pas de six* and
performed by A. Fredstrup, H. Scharff, P. Fredstrup, L. Stillmann, E. Garlieb, and B. Bills. This seems to be the only significant change from the previous 1853 production. In his
diary Bournonville noted about the production:

8.12., 9.12. 11.12., 12.12., and 14.12.1857: 'Prøve paa Waldemar'
15.12.: 'Prøve paa Waldemar fra 10–12½'
16.12.: 'stor Arrangementsprøve paa Waldemar'
17.12.: 'Prøve paa Waldemar (i Conservatoriet)'
18.12.: 'Prøve fuldstændig paa Waldemar'
19.12.: 'Stort arbeide med at remplacere S. Price der atter var upasselig!! [...] 1.ste Forestillingen af Gjentagelsen af Balletten Waldemar der gik udmærket godt og blev særdeles paaskjønnet'
22.12: ' I Theatret Waldemar der fra Ensemblets Side gik udmærket
godt. Dandsen derimod svagt. – [H.] Scharff var doven og ligegyl-
dig'.

The 1857 production received 5 performances (the last of
which was given on 7.2.1858) and the ballet was rehearsed
and performed using the same musical material employed
for the 1853 staging (now in DKKk, call nos. C II, 107, MA ms
2994, and KTB 297).

20.12.1857
*Fra-Diavolo, ou l'Hôtellerie de Terracine (Fra Diavolo eller
Værtshuset i Terracina).*
The 1857 Copenhagen restaging of D.-F.-E. Auber's three-act
comic opera (premièred at l'Opéra Comique in Paris on

28.1.1830) was projected by Bournonville on 30.11.1857. It represents the first and only time this opera was mounted in Copenhagen with his mise-en-scène and choreography, and includes an (unnamed) *Dance* in Act III (score no. 13) performed by a group of eight persons during the chorus, entitled «C'est grande fête». Moreover, on 1.5.1862 Bournonville wrote a new mise-en-scène for Auber's opera in preparation for a projected restaging of it at Stockholm's Royal Theatre during the late spring of 1862. This project, however, was never carried out. In his diary he noted about the 1857 Copenhagen staging:

17.12.1857: 'indstuderet Dands til Fra Diavolo'
19.12.: 'Prøve paa Fra Diavolo, hvor jeg arrangerede en Deel af 3.die Act.'
20.12.: 'Fra Diavolo med nyt Arrangement i 3.die Akt'.

The 1857 production of *Fra-Diavolo* reached a total of 24 performances during Bournonville's lifetime, the last of which was given on 2.4.1870.

Autograph sources:

Choreographic notes. Ms. Autographs. Brown ink. 2 sheets (17,8 × 11,4 cm)
Diavolo/18 Takter/Entrée/[...]/Prière.
Unsigned and undated [c. December 1857]
[SSm; Daniel Fryklunds samling no. 140 f
In these manuscripts Bournonville describes in fine detail the (unnamed) *Dance* in Act III (score no. 3) of *Fra Diavolo*, performed by eight persons during the chorus, entitled «C'est grande fête», and the dance performed in the same scene during the chorus «O sainte Vierge».

Musical sources:

Printed orchestral score. 2 vol. Act I 220 pp. of which two are blank, Act II–III 222 pp. of which one is blank (31,6 × 25,2 cm)
Fra Diavolo/OU/l'Hotellerie de Terracine/[...]/musique de D. F. E. Auber
Paris, E. Troupenas, pl. no. 334 [1830]
[DKKk; U 6 (KTA 282)
This orchestral score was used for all performances in Copenhagen of *Fra-Diavolo* during Bournonville's lifetime. A metronome marking (written with brown ink on p. '345') indicates the tempo of the (unnamed) *Dance* in Act III with a crochet equivalent to '120'.

Répétiteur's copy. Ms. Copy. Brown ink. 1 vol. 10 pp. of which one is blank (33,6 × 25,5 cm)
Dandse/til/Fra   Diavolo./[...]/81./1858../Bournonville./[...]/Dands/til/Fra Diavolo/Repetiteur=Parti.
Unsigned and dated (on the front cover): '1858..'
[DKKk; MA ms 2910 (2) (KTA 282)
This répétiteur's copy contains the music for the (unnamed) *Dance*, performed in Act III (score no. 13) during the chorus, entitled «C'est grande fête». It also includes Bournonville's pencilled autographed choreographic numbers ('1–2') which refer to similar numbers contained in the separate choreographic note which he most probably wrote in the month of December 1857. The music for the Act III dance is included on pp. 5–14 in a volume that also contains the répétiteur's copies for three other operas and singspiels mounted at Copenhagen's Royal Theatre between December 1857 and March 1858.

Parts. Ms. Copy. 46 + 11 vol.
4 vl I, 4 vl II, 2 vla, 4 vlc e cb, fl picc e II, fl I, 2 ob I, ob II, cl 1/2, 2 fag I, fag II, 2 cor I, 2 cor II, cor III, cor IV, 2 tr I, tr II, 2 Atrb, 2 Ttrb, Btrb, timp 1/2, 2 gr cassa, tamb, 2 piatti, tri. On stage: 2 cor I, cor II, clno II, clno II, 2 Atrb, 2 Ttrb, Btrb. 52 vocal parts.

Unsigned and undated [c.1830]
[DKKk; KTA 282
This set of parts was used for all performances of *Fra-Diavolo* in Copenhagen from its première there on 19.5.1831 and throughout Bournonville's lifetime.

Other sources:

Manuscript mise-en-scène. Ms. Autograph (by T. Overskou?). Brown ink. 1 vol. 15 pp. (26 × 21 cm)
Nöiagtig Opgivelse/af/Scenens Arrangement/i Sÿngespillet: Fra Diavolo./med de for Stÿkkets Opförelse paa den danske Skueplads nödvendige Forandringer.
Unsigned and undated [c.1831–1857?]
[SSm; Daniel Fryklunds samling no. 356 a
This manuscript mise-en-scène appears to have been in Bournonville's possession and probably served him as a basis for his 1857 staging of Act III of *Fra-Diavolo*.

1858

7.1.1858
Czaar und Zimmermann (Czaren og Tømmermanden).
The 1858 Copenhagen restaging of G. A. Lortzing's three-act comic opera was originally projected by Bournonville on 30.10.1857 and represents the only time this work was mounted with his complete mise-en-scène (*see also* 18.9. 1846). The (unnamed) *Dance*, performed during the so-called 'Brautlied' in Act II (score no. 11), and the *Clog Dance* (or 'Tanz mit Holzschuhen') in the Act III finale (score no. 16) seem both to have been mounted this year with only minor if any changes from Bournonville's previous 1846 staging. In his diary he noted about the production:

23.11.1857: 'Prøve paa Dandsen til Czar og Tømmermand'
25.11.: 'Arrangementsprøve fra 10–12 [...] Instruction 7–9'
27.11.: 'Prøve Kl. 11 paa Dandsen til Czar og Tømmermand'
30.11.: 'Lille Prøve paa Opera Dands'
3.12.: 'Prøve paa [...] Czaren'
4.12.: 'Instruction paa Czar og Tømmermand'
21.12.: 'Quartettprøve paa Czar og Tømmermand'
23.12.: 'Prøve paa Dandsen til [...] Czar og Tømmermand'
29.12.: 'Theaterprøve paa Czar og Tømmermand'
2.1.1858: 'Theaterprøve med Quartett paa Czar og Tømmermand'
4.1.: 'Theaterprøve paa Czar og Tømmermand'
5.1.: 'noteret Scene Arrangementet for Czar og Tømmermand'
6.1.: 'Generalprøve paa Czar og Tømmermand'
7.1.: '1.ste Forestilling af Czar og Tømmermand (nyt indstuderet). Meget gik godt, men Md. [A. K.] Rosenkildes pludselige Hæshed forstemte en heel deel. Publicum var ubeskrivelig lunkent. Dandsen og [J. C.] Hansens Arie gjorde Lÿkke'.

The 1858 production of *Czaar und Zimmermann* received 12 performances, the last of which was given on 21.3.1864.

Autograph sources:

Manuscript mise-en-scène. Ms. Autograph. Brown ink. 16 pp. (10,8 × 16,9 cm)
Czar og Tømmermand.
Unsigned and undated [Written according to the diary on 5.1.1858]
[DKKk; NKS 3285 4° 3 L–P
The 16 pages containing Bournonville's mise-en-scène for *Czaar und Zimmermann* were originally part of his notebook, entitled: 'Fire Opera Scene/Instructioner./1857.'. They were detached by him at a

later stage from this volume when it was transformed into his diary and given the new title: 'Journal./d. 24.de October 1861. til/d. 1.te Novbr/1862.' (now in DKKk, call no. NKS 747 8°, 4, vol. 23).

Musical sources:

The orchestral score and the parts for *Czar und Zimmermann* are now in DKKk (call nos. C I, 274, and KTA 403).

Répétiteur's copy. Ms. Copy. Black ink. 1 vol. 10 pp. of which one is blank (33,7 × 25,8 cm)
Dandse/til:/[...]/Czar og Tömmermand./[...]/81./1858../Bournonville./[...]/Dands/af/ Czar og Tömmermand./Repetiteur=Parti./[...]/Brude=Vise
Unsigned and dated (on the front cover): '1858.'
[DKKk; MA ms 2910 (3) (KTA 403)]
This répétiteur's copy contains the music for the (unnamed) *Dance*, performed during the so-called 'Brautlied' («Lieblich röthen sich die Wangen») in Act II (score no. 11), and the music for the *Clog Dance* (or 'Tanz mit Holzschuhen') in the Act III finale (score no. 16). It is included on pp. 15–24 in a volume that also contains the répétiteur's copies for three other operas and singspiels mounted at Copenhagen's Royal Theatre between December 1857 and March 1858.

11.1.1858
Le Tonnelier (Bødkeren). Projected restaging(?).
In his diary Bournonville noted on this day about what seems to be a projected staging of N.-M. Audinot's one-act comic opera from 1761 (set to music by various composers):

'Skrevet og arrangeret, – Arrangement paa Bødkeren'.

This indicates that a restaging of *Le Tonnelier* (which had performed for the first time in Copenhagen on 27.10.1780) was planned for the early spring of 1858. This project, however, was never carried out, and *Le Tonnelier* has not been performed at Copenhagen's Royal Theatre since 28.4.1845 to this day. No indications have been found in the Copenhagen musical sources for *Le Tonnelier* (now in DKKk, call nos. C I, 279 m, KTA 95, and U 6 (KTA 501, mu 6609.0236)) which bear witness to Bournonville ever having worked on this material. Another possibility is that Bournonville may have been referring in this note to a (not yet traced) mise-en-scène written for the first performance of Audinot's opera at Copenhagen's Folketheatret, where it was staged on 7.3. 1858 with a new, revised version of H. Gram's original Danish translation from 1780.

14.1.1858
The Festival in Albano (Festen i Albano).
This performance represents Bournonville second restaging in Copenhagen of *The Festival in Albano* (*see* 28.10.1839). It was performed with H. Scharff and S. Price playing the leading rôles of *Antonio* and *Silvia*. According to the poster the four dances in this production were as follows:

(1) a *Pas de six.*
(2) a *Pas de trois* (this dance is musically completely identical with the ballet's original *Pas de deux*, score nos. 8–9).
(3) a *Tarantella.*
(4) a *Solo* performed by P. Fredstrup.

In his diary Bournonville noted about the performance:

14.11.1857: 'Prøve paa Festen i Albano'
16.11. and 17.11.: 'Prøve paa Albano'
19.11.: 'Prøve paa Pas de trois til Albano'
21.11.: 'prøve Dandsene til Albano'
22.11.: 'Prøve paa Festen i Albano'
3.12.: 'Prøve paa Albano'
5.1. and 6.1.1858: 'Prøve paa Festen i Albano'
10.1.: 'talt med Theatermaler [C. F.] Christensen'
12.1.: 'Prøve paa Theatret paa Festen i Albano. Etatsraad [C.] Hauch var tilstede. [E.] Stramboe negligerede og fortjente ved sin Adfærd en Mulkt'
13.3.: 'Decorationsmøde'
14.1.: 'Festen i Albano der gik smukt, men manglede noget Liv. [H.] Scharff dandsede for [F.] Hoppe'.

The 1858 staging received 14 performances, the last of which was given on 15.3.1864.

The music material employed this year was the same as that used for the original 1839 version (now in DKKk, call nos. C II, 107, MA ms 2979, and KTB 282).

15.1.1858
The Sleeping-Draught (Sovedrikken).
The 1858 restaging of C. E. F. Weyse's three-act singspiel (premièred at Copenhagen's Royal Theatre 21.4.1809) was originally projected by Bournonville on 30.10.1857. According to his diary it represents the first time this work was mounted under his personal direction. However, it is not included in his handwritten list of his stagings of operas and plays, written c.1872 (*see* Additional Sources), nor in the printed survey of his works in his memoirs *My Theatre Life* (p. 408). *The Sleeping-Draught* was restaged for the second and last time by Bournonville on 5.3.1874, but this with his own and completely new mise-en-scène. In his diary he noted about the 1858 production:

14.1.1858: 'Theaterprøve paa Sovedrikken'
15.1.: 'I Theatret Sovedrikken ([P. L. N.] Schramm) der gik udmærket godt for godt Huus og gjorde megen Lykke'.

The 1858 staging received 6 performances, the last of which was given on 27.12.1866.

Musical sources:

Orchestral score. Ms. Copy. Brown and black ink. 2 vol. Act I 380 pp. of which one is blank, Act II 256 pp. of which one is blank (21,4 × 29,2 cm)
Sove – Drikken/af Weyse./1.ste Akt./1.ste og 2.den Akt/[...]/Sovedrikken/Syngestykke i 2 Acter/sat i Musik/af/Weise/[...]/Sovedrikken/Anden Act./No. 162./3.die og 4.die Akt
Unsigned and undated [c.1809]
[DKKk; C II, 123 (KTA 150)]
This orchestral score is a copy of Weyse's autographed score (now in DKKk, call no. C. E. F. Weyses Samling, Box A 5.2017). It dates from the 1809 première and was used for all later performances of *The Sleeping-Draught* during Bournonville's lifetime (divided into three acts in 1858, and into four acts after 1866).

No répétiteur's copy for *The Sleeping-Draught* has yet been traced.

Parts. Ms. Copy. 28 vol.
4 vl I, 4 vl II, 2 vla, 2 vlc, 2 cb, fl 1/2, ob 1/2, cl, cor basseto 1–2, fag 1/2, cor 1/2, tr 1/2, timp, arpa. 34 vocal parts.
Unsigned and undated [1809]
[DKKk; KTA 150]

This set of parts dates from the 1809 Copenhagen première of Weyse's singspiel and was used for all performances of *The Sleeping-Draught* during Bournonville's lifetime.

20.1.1858
Plan for a repertory of operas in the months of March, April, and May 1859 (Plan til Operaens Virksomhed i Martz, April og Mai 1859).

According to his diary Bournonville wrote on this day a detailed plan (copies of which are now in the State Archive, call no. Det kgl. Teaters Arkiv, Gruppe E, pakke 288, and in SSm, call no. Daniel Fryklunds samling no. 102) in which he included the repertory of operas that he intended to mount during the months of March, April, and May 1859. It contains the following seven works:

March 1859:

Ludovic.
The projected 1859 restaging of F. Hérold's two-act comic opera from 1833 (completed by J.-F. Halévy) was carried out by Bournonville on 20.3.1859, when *Ludovic* was mounted in Copenhagen with his mise-en-scène for the first and only time.

Lucrezia Borgia.
The projected 1859 restaging of G. Donizetti's 1833 melodrama in two acts and a prologue had been planned by Bournonville since 30.10.1857 and was carried out by him on 15.4.1859.

La Fille du régiment (Regimentets Datter).
The projected 1859 restaging of G. Donizetti's two-act comic opera from 1840 had been planned by Bournonville since 30.10.1857 and was carried out by him on 20.10.1859.

Le Nouveau Seigneur de village (Den nÿ Jordegodseier).
The projected 1859 restaging of F.-A. Boyeldieu's one-act comic opera had been planned by Bournonville since 30.10.1857 and was carried out in Copenhagen by I. F. Bredal on 6.11.1861, and later in Sweden by Bournonville at Stockholm's Royal Theatre (Operahuset) on 13.12.1861.

April 1859:

Le Domino noir (Eventyret paa Maskeraden eller Den sorte Domino (Den sorte Domino)).
The projected 1859 restaging of D.-F.-E. Auber's three-act comic opera from 1837 had been planned by Bournonville since 30.10. 1857 and was carried out by him in parts on 12.5.1859.

Lulu.
The projected 1859 restaging of F. Kuhlau's three-act romantic opera from 1824 had been planned by Bournonville since 30.10.1857, but was never carried out by him.

Martha oder Der Markt zu Richmond (Martha eller Markedet i Richmond)
The projected 1859 restaging of F. v. Flotow's four-act romantic comic opera from 1847 had been planned by Bournonville since 30.10.1857 and was carried out by him on 15.5.1860.

May 1859:

Projected performances of all the above-mentioned works.

23.1.1858
Almaviva o sia l'inutile precauzione/Il Barbiere di Siviglia (Barberen i Sevilla).
The 1858 Copenhagen restaging of G. Rossini's two-act

comic opera (premièred in Rome at Teatro Argentina on 20.2.1816, and first performed in Denmark on 14.9.1822) was originally projected by Bournonville on 30.10.1857. However, it is not included in his handwritten list of his stagings of operas and plays, written c.1872 (*see* Additional Sources), nor in the printed survey of his works in his memoirs *My Theatre Life* (p. 408). The 1858 production represents the first and only time he directed a final stage rehearsal of this work. In his diary he noted about the performance:

22.1.1858: 'skrevet og arrangeret Prøve paa Barberen'
23.1.: 'I Theatret <u>Barberen i Sevilla</u> der gik udmærket smukt'.

The 1858 restaging was given only once, and the opera was not restaged in Copenhagen until 18.11.1861, when Bournonville was under contract with Stockholm's Royal Theatre.

Musical sources:

No orchestral score and répétiteur's copy for *Almaviva/Il Barbiere di Siviglia* dating from the 1858 performance have yet been traced.

Parts. Ms. Copy. 32 vol.
4 vl I, 4 vl II, 2 vla, 4 vlc e cb, fl picc, fl 1/2, ob 1/2, cl 1/2, fag 1/2, cor 1/2, tr 1/2, timp, gr cassa, piatti e tri, guit, arpa. 45 vocal parts.
Unsigned and undated [1822]
[DKKk; KTA 216
This set of parts dates from the 1822 Copenhagen première of Rossini's opera and was used for all performances of it there during Bournonville's lifetime.

5.2.1858
Norma.
The 1858 Copenhagen restaging of V. Bellini's two-act lyrical tragedy (*see* 20.10.1848) was originally projected by Bournonville on 30.10.1857. However, it is not included in his handwritten list of his stagings of operas and plays, written c.1872 (*see* Additional Sources), nor in the official list of his works published in his memoirs *My Theatre Life* (p. 408). About the staging, which represents Bournonville's second production of this work in Copenhagen, he noted in his diary:

4.2.1858: 'Theaterprøve paa Norma',
5.2.: 'Norma der gik fortræffeligt – Decorationsprøve'.

The 1858 production, which clearly seems to have been mounted with only minor if any changes from the previous 1848 staging, received only 2 performances, the last of which was given on 2.3.1858. The musical material employed this year was the same as that used in 1848 (now in DKKkt and DKKk with the call no. KTA 344).

7.2.1858
Paul et Virginie, Dance Divertissement after Gardel and A. Bournonville, mounted by Ballet-master S. Lund (Paul och Virginie, Divertissement af Dans, efter Gardel och A. Bournonville, uppsatt af Hr Balletmästaren S. Lund) (Stockholm's Royal Theatre, Operahuset).
The first five rehearsals of the 1858 Swedish production of Bournonville's abridged divertissement version of his Copenhagen version of P. Gardel's three-act pantomimic ballet *Paul et Virginie* (*see* 19.6.1854) were directed by himself

as an official part of his engagement at Stockholm's Royal Theatre in the spring and summer of 1857. The ballet's final rehearsals and its actual staging, however, were carried out by his pupil, S. Lund, who served as ballet-master in Stockholm between 1856 and 1862. The Swedish production differed from the 1854 Copenhagen version by a number of minor musical cuts in score nos. 1, 5, and 8. Moreover, it included an (uncredited) *Pas de trois*, which was incorporated between score nos. 8 and 9 and is named 'Pas de trois arr. af Lund' by A. F. Schwartz in his handwritten catalogue of the music archive at Stockholm's Royal Theatre (now in SSkma). Furthermore, an autographed note by S. Lund (written in the part for the harp in this dance) reads: 'begagnas i Balletten Paul & Virginie nya som No. 8½'. This bears clear witness to this dance actually being performed as an integral part of Lund's 1858 Stockholm staging of *Paul et Virginie*.

The music for Lund's *Pas de trois* proves to be identical with that by M. E. Caraffa which was originally used by Bournonville in Copenhagen for his so-called 'Pas de trois af Postillonen' and performed as an incorporated divertissement in A. Adam's three-act comic opera *Le Postillon de Lonjumeau* (*see* 28.10.1837).

Finally, another (uncredited) *Pas de trois* (danced by Théodore [stage name for Th. I. Marchkl], M. C. Törner, and J. G. Sundberg) was staged during the following year by S. Lund at Stockholm's Royal Theatre (Operahuset) on 28.9.1859. It was restaged by him as an incorporated divertissement in G. Rossini's four-act opera *Guillaume Tell* on 28.9.1859 and was kept in the Stockholm repertory until 22.6.1861, receiving a total of 8 performances there. That *Pas de trois*, too, is most probably identical with the *Pas de trois* performed by the same three dancers in Lund's 1858 Stockholm staging of Bournonville's divertissement version of *Paul et Viriginie*.

Paul et Virginie received 9 performances in Stockholm, the last of which was given on 15.4.1859.

In his diary Bournonville described his involvement in this production as follows:

17.6.1857: 'Indstudering paa Paul og Virgine for Mlle [J.] Hjorth og [M. W. H.] Wigandt'
18.6.: 'Prøve paa Paul og Virginie'
19.6.: 'Indstudering Paul og Virginie'
23.6.: 'noterede paa Paul og Virginie'
25.6.: 'sidste Indstudering paa Paul og Virginie'.

Musical sources:

Orchestral score. Ms. Copy. Black ink. 1 vol. 144 pp. (35 × 26,3 cm)
Paul och Virginie/Divertissement/af/A. Bournonville
Unsigned and undated [c.1857–1858]
[SSkma; Pantomime-Balletter P 4

Répétiteur's copy. Ms. Copy. Black ink. 1 vol. 48 pp. (33,1 × 25,4 cm)
Divertissement,/arrangeret af Bournonville/efter/Motiver af Gardels [changed to:] Gardel./Paul og Virginie
Unsigned and undated [c.1857–1858]
[SSkma; Pantomime-Balletter P 4
This répétiteur's copy contains Bournonville's autographed notes (written with brown and black ink) that describe the mime in score nos. 1, 2, 4, and 6, and the choreography for score no. 7. Moreover, his autographed choreographic numbers ('1–16') are inserted in

the music for score no. 8 and seem to refer to his (not yet traced) choreographic notation of this movement.

Parts. Ms. Copy. 30 vol.
3 vl I, 3 vl II, 2 vla, 4 vlc e cb, fl 1/2, ob 1/2, cl 1/2, fag 1/2, cor 1/2, tr, trb 1/2/3, timp, gr cassa, tri, arpa.
Unsigned and undated [c.1857–1858]
[SSkma; Pantomime-Balletter P 4

Harp's part (*Pas de trois*). Ms. Copy. 1 vol. 7 pp. (32 × 23,3 cm)
Paul Virginie/Pas de trois/Harpa/[…]/begagnas i Balletten Paul & Virginie nya som No. 8 1/2/[…]/Pas de trois/Harpa
Unsigned and undated [1858?]
[SSkma; KT Pantomime-Balletter P 1

Parts (*Pas de trois*). Ms. Copy. 34 vol.
3 vl I, 3 vl II, 2 vla, 4 vlc e cb, fl 1/2, ob 1/2, cl 1/2, fag 1/2, cor 1/2/3/4, tr 1/2/3/4, trb 1/2/3/4, timp, arpa.
Unsigned and undated [1858?]
[SSkma; KT Dansmusik 83

10.2.1858
William Shakespeare. Epilogue and Apotheosis (Efterspil: Oberon og Titannia […] Apotheose: Britannia bekrandser Shakspeare [sic], der staaer omringet af sine Digterværker.').
For the 1858 restaging of C. J. Boye's four-act romantic play from 1826 (set to music by F. Kuhlau) Bournonville created both the general mise-en-scène and the choreography. It included five dances, mime scenes, and tableaux as follows:

(1) A *Circle Dance (Ringdands)* in the opening scene of Act I, score no. 1, performed by a group of elves during the chorus «Frem til Ringdands Alfer! Frem!».
(2) A *Pantomime scene* in Act I, score no. 3, performed by *Oberon*, *Titania*, and the dancing elfs during the chorus of the singing elves, entitled «Holloh! Holloh! Holloh!».
(2) An (unnamed) *Dance* in Act IV, score no. 6, performed during the chorus «I Ring, i Ring saa lystig og let vi snoe os omkring!» by the same group of elves as those in the previous two numbers.
(3) A mimic *Epiloque (Efterspil)* in Act IV (score no. 8), performed by *Oberon* and *Titania* during the final chorus of the elves, entitled «Til Flugt, afsted!».
(4) A final *Apotheosis (Apotheose)*, described on the poster as 'Britannia bekrandser Shakspeare [sic], der staaer omringet af sine Digterværker', performed to two musical excerpts of Kuhlau's pantomime music from Act IV, (score no. 7) of Boye's *William Shakespeare*.

The staging is not included in Bournonville's handwritten list of his stagings of operas and plays, written c.1872 (*see* Additional Sources), nor in the printed survey of his works in his memoirs *My Theatre Life* (p. 408).

In his diary he noted about the performance:

5.1.1858: 'gjennemlæst William Shakespeare'
8.1.: 'arrangeret til William Shakespeare'
12.1.: 'skrevet og componeret […] componeret Grupper til William Shakespeare. Decorationsmøde'
18.1.: 'Indstudering paa Alfedandsen til William Shakespeare'
20.1.: 'Indstudering paa William Shakespeare'
21.1.: 'fuldendt Indstuderingen af William Shakespeare'
23.1., 27.1. and 28.1.: 'Prøve paa William Shakespeare'
30.1. and 1.2.: 'Theaterprøve paa William Shakespeare'
2.2.: 'Theaterprøve paa W. Sh. uden Dands'
5.2.: 'Prøve paa Shakespeare-Grupper […] Decorationsprøve'
6.2.: 'Prøve i Conservatoriet paa Grupperne til W. Shakespeare'
7.2.: 'Gruppe-Prøve paa Det kongelige Theater'
8.2.: 'Theaterprøve paa <u>Shakespeare</u>'
9.2.: 'skrevet og arrangeret. Theaterprøve med <u>Belysning</u> paa <u>Wil-</u>

liam Shakespeare. Costumet blev prøvet men Belysningen var til Fortvivlelse slet […] Paa Theatret, hvor jeg føiede Anstalter til en bedre Belysning'

10.2.: 'Belysnings- og Grupperingsprøve til iaften […] William Shakespeare (1.ste Gang) udsolgt Huus og rundeligt Bifald. – Alfe-dandsen og Grupperingen gik fortræffeligt'.

The 1858 staging of *William Shakespeare* received 16 perform-ances, the last of which was given on 16.9.1859.

Autograph sources:

Manuscript mise-en-scène. Ms. Autograph. Brown ink. 4 pp. (22,6 × 17,9 cm)
<u>William Shakespeare.</u>/<u>4.de Act. 5.te Scene.</u>
Signed and dated: 'Kbhvn d 12 Januar 1858.'
[DKKk; NKS 3285 4° 3 V-Z

Manuscript mise-en-scène. Ms. Autograph. Brown ink. 2 pp. (21,1 × 13,5 cm)
<u>Shakespeares – Apotheose.</u>/Slutnings – Chor i Skuespillet/(William Shakespeare)
Signed and dated: 'd 2.d[en] Febr 1858.'
[DKKk; NKS 3285 4° 3 V–Z

Production note. Ms. Autograph. Brown ink. 2 pp. (21,1 × 13,5 cm)
<u>Personerne</u>/i/Macbeth – Synet./<u>Personerne</u>/i/<u>Shakespeares Apo-theose</u>
Signed and dated: 'd 2.d[en] Febr 1858.'
[DKKk; NKS 3285 4° 3 V–Z

Production note. Ms. Autograph. Brown ink. 1 p. (20,3 × 13,9 cm)
<u>Shakespeares = Apotheose.</u>/<u>Opstilling</u>
Unsigned and undated [January-February 1858]
[DKKk; NKS 3285 4° 3 V–Z

Production note. Ms. Autograph. Brown ink. 1 p. (21,7 × 13,9 cm)
<u>Shakespeares – Sӱn.</u>/(Allegorisk Tableau)
Unsigned and undated [January–February 1858]
[DKKk; NKS 3285 4° 3 V–Z

Musical sources:

Orchestral score. Ms. Copy. Brown ink. 1 vol. 262 pp. of which two are blank (26,8 × 37 cm)
Partituret/til/William Shakpear [*sic*]/af/Kammer Musikus Kuhlau
Unsigned and undated [1826]
[DKKk; C II, 115 (KTA 260)]
This score dates from the Copenhagen première of *William Shake-speare* on 28.3.1826 and was used for all performances of it in Copen-hagen during Bournonville's lifetime. Pages 222–238 contain Bour-nonville's pencilled autographed notes which seem to describe the action of the final *Apotheosis* and was performed to two musical ex-cerpts from Act IV (score no. 7) of Boye's play. Metronome markings (written with black ink on pp. 89 and 199) indicate the tempo of the two dances, performed by the elves in Act I and III respectively, with dotted crotchets being equivalent to '84'.

Répétiteur's copy. Ms. Copy. Black ink. 1 vol. 58 pp. of which two are blank (33,7 × 25,5 cm)
A. 260/William Shakspeare/45 A/[…]/Repititeur=Parti/til/Wil-liam Shakespeare/af/Kuhlau./1.ste Akt/1.ste Scene
Unsigned and undated [1858]
[DKKk; MA ms 3049 (KTA 260 (2))]
This répétiteur's copy contains the music in Act I (score nos. 1 and 3), Act III (score no. 5), and Act IV (score nos. 6–8). Bournonville's autographed choreographic numbers ('1–10', '1–11', '1–5', and '1–9', all written with brown ink) are inserted in the music for Act I. They almost certainly refer to his separate (not yet traced) choreo-

graphic notation of the *Circle Dance*, performed by the elves in this act, which he wrote (according to his diary) on 12.1.1858.

Parts. Ms. Copy. 32 + 21 + 8 vol.
4 vl I, 4 vl II, 2 vla, 4 vlc e cb, fl 1/2, ob 1/2, cl 1/2, fag 1/2, cor 1/2/3/4, tr 1/2, trb, timp, gr cassa, piatti e tri. On stage (Act III): vl I, vl II, vla, vlc e cb, fl 1/2, ob 1/2, 2 cl I, 2 cl II, 2 fag I, 2 fag II, cor 1/2/3/4, gr cassa e piatti. On stage (Act IV): fl, ob, cl 1/2, fag 1/2, cor 1/2. 43 vocal parts.
Unsigned and undated [1826]
[DKKk; KTA 260]
This set of parts dates from the 1826 première of *William Shakespeare* and was used for all performances of it in Copenhagen during Bournonville's lifetime.

20.2.1858
Hans Heiling.
The 1858 Copenhagen restaging of H. Marschner's three-act romantic opera (premièred at Berlin's Hofoper on 24.5.1833, and first performed in Copenhagen on 13.5.1836) was originally projected by Bournonville on 30.10.1857. It repre-sents the first time this opera was mounted with his mise-en-scène in Copenhagen. During his later engagement as man-aging director of Stockholm's Royal Theatre Bournonville also became involved in the planning of the Swedish premi-ère of *Hans Heiling*, which he projected on 16.10.1862. That première, however, was not carried out by him, since Mar-schner's opera was mounted in Stockholm on 11.10.1865, nearly a year after Bournonville had left the Swedish capital. *Hans Heiling* was restaged for the last time by Bournonville in Copenhagen on 4.11.1868, but that year with a seemingly slightly revised mise-en-scène. In his diary he noted about the 1858 production:

29.1.1858: 'Hele Formiddagen paa Syngeskolen til <u>Hans Heiling</u>. Kl 5 Scene=Instruction paa samme Opera'
1.2.: 'Directionsmøde om Hans Heilings Sceneri'
2.2.: 'componeret'
3.2.: 'skrevet og arrangeret […] Instruction paa Hans Heiling'
8.2.: 'Instruction paa Hans Heiling 5-7-'
10.2.: 'bivaanet Quartetprøve paa Hans Heiling'
12.2.: 'Instruction paa Hans Heiling'
13.2.: 'skrevet, stort Arrangement paa Hans Heiling'
15.2.: '1.ste Theaterprøve paa Hans Heiling'
16.2.: 'Theaterprøve paa <u>Hans Heiling</u>'
18.2.: 'Theaterprøve paa Hans Heiling fra 10–1 1/2'
19.2.: 'Generalprøve paa Hans Heiling, det Hele gik meget godt'
20.2.: 'i Theatret <u>Hans Heiling</u> 1.ste Gang, gik udmærket godt og med Bifald, fuldt Huus'.

The 1858 restaging of *Hans Heiling* received 24 perform-ances, the last of which was given on 13.1.1868.

Autograph sources:

Manuscript mise-en-scène. Ms. Autograph. Brown ink. 1 vol. 7 pp. (21,2 × 13,6 cm)
<u>Scene = Arrangement</u>/til/Operaen <u>Hans Heiling.</u>
Unsigned and undated [Written according to Bournonville's diary on 13.2.1858]
[SSm; Daniel Fryklunds samling no. 126

Manuscript mise-en-scène. Ms. Autograph. Brown ink. 16 pp. (10,8 × 16,9 cm)
<u>Hans Heiling.</u>

Unsigned and undated [Written according to Bournonville's diary most probably on 13.2.1858]
[DKKk; NKS 3285 4° 3 L–P]
The 16 pages containing Bournonville's mise-en-scène for *Hans Heiling* were originally part of his notebook, entitled: '<u>Fire Opera Scene/Instructioner./1857.</u>' They were detached from this volume at a later stage, when it was transformed into Bournonville's diary and given the new title: '<u>Journal./d. 24.de October 1861.</u> til/d. <u>1.te Novbr/</u>1862.' (now in DKKk; NKS 747 8°, 4, vol. 23).

Musical sources:

Orchestral score. Ms. Copy. Black ink. 2 vol. Act I 378 pp. of which two are blank, Act II–III 344 pp. of which two are blank (24 × 33,5 cm with minor variants)
<u>Hans Heiling</u>/<u>Partitur.</u>/1.ste Akt/[…]/Hans Heiling/romantische Oper in 3 Acten/nebst einen Vorspiel/von Edouard Devrient/Music/von/<u>Heinrich Marschner</u>/<u>nach Kopenhagen.</u>/[…]/2. den Act./[…]/3.ter Act.
Unsigned and undated [c.1836]
[DKKk; C I, 275 (KTA 320)
This orchestral score is a German copy dating from the 1836 Copenhagen première of *Hans Heiling*. It was used for all performances during Bournonville's lifetime.

No répétiteur's copy for *Hans Heiling* has yet been traced.

Parts. Ms. Copy. 37 + 9 vol.
4 vl I, 4 vl II, 2 vla, 4 vlc e cb, fl 1/2, ob 1/2, cl 1/2, fag 1/2, cor 1/2/3/4, tr princ, tr 1/2, 2 trb I, 2 trb II, 2 trb III, timp, org. On stage: fl, cl 1/2, fag 1/2, cor 1/2/3/4. 59 vocal parts.
unsigned and undated [1836]
[DKKk; KTA 320]
This set of parts dates from the 1836 Copenhagen première of *Hans Heiling* and was used for all performances of it there during Bournonville's lifetime.

10.3.1858
Le Prophète (Profeten). Projected Danish staging.
On 30.10.1857 Bournonville considered a Danish staging of G. Meyerbeer's five-act opera (premièred at the Paris Opéra on 16.4.1849) for the first time, when he included it in a list of projected opera stagings planned for the 1857–58 and 1858–59 seasons. This project was never carried out at Copenhagen's Royal Theatre, but was partially realised by him at Stockholm's Royal Theatre (Operahuset), where he supervised if not actually directed the restaging of *Le Prophète* on 17.4.1863. In his diary he noted about the 1858 projected Copenhagen première of *Le Prophète*:

10.3.1858: 'besørget text og Musik til Profeten'
25.3.: 'Modtaget igaar Partituret til <u>Profeten</u>. Sendt det idag til [F.] <u>Gläser</u> […] skrevet paa Decorationslisterne til Profeten'
26.3.: 'skrevet og fuldendt Decorationslister, talt med Theatermaler [C. F.] Christensen'.

14.3.1858
Il Dissoluto Punito, ossia il Don Giovanni (Don Juan).
The 1858 Copenhagen restaging of W. A. Mozart's two-act opera (*see* 3.4.1848) was originally projected by Bournonville on 30.10.1857. It represents the first time this opera was mounted with his complete mise-en-scène and personal stage instructions. In his diary he noted about the performance:

1.3.1858: 'Opera-Instruction i Conservatoriet paa Don Juan'
2.3.: 'Scene-Instruction paa D. Juan'

4.3.: 'Sceneprøve paa D. Juan'
8.3.: 'Forfeiltet Generalprøve paa Don Juan formedelst [P. L. N.] Schramms Upasselighed'
13.3.: 'Theaterprøve paa Don Juan'
14.3.: 'I Theatret <u>Don Juan</u>, der gik udmærket godt og for aldeles udsolgt Huus'.

The opera's dances in Act I clearly seem to have been mounted without any changes from the previous 1848 staging. The 1858 production of *Don Juan* received 40 performances, the last of which was given on 2.6.1869.

Musical sources:

No orchestral score dating from the 1858 restaging of *Don Juan* has yet been traced.

Répétiteur'c copy. Ms. Copy. Black ink. 1 vol. 8 pp. of which three are blank (33,7 × 25,6 cm)
<u>Dandse</u>/til:/[…]/<u>Don Juan</u>/81./<u>1858.</u>/Bournonville./[…]/Dands/til/<u>Don Juan.</u>/Repetiteur=Parti
Unsigned and dated (on the front cover): '<u>1858.</u>.'
[DKKk; MA ms 2910 (4) (KTA 155 (1))]
This répétiteur's copy contains the complete dance music in the Act I finale (scene 20) of *Don Juan*. The music is included on pp. 25–32 in a volume that also contains the répétiteur's copies for three other operas and singspiels, mounted at Copenhagen's Royal Theatre between December 1857 and January 1858.

The set of parts used for the 1858 restaging of *Don Juan* is now in DKKk (call no. KTA 155).

21.4.1858
Bellman or the Polish Dance at Grönalund (Bellman, eller Polskan på Grönalund) (Stockholm's Royal Theatre, Operahuset).
This performance represents the second and last staging in Stockholm of Bournonville's one-act ballet-vaudeville *Bellman or the Polish Dance at Grönalund* (*see* 28.2.1844 and 11.6.1847). It differed from his previous Swedish production by a completely new décor (painted by E. Roberg) and a slightly revised scenario (the latter being published on the programme-poster).

Moreover, according to the Swedish musical material for this work, the 1858 production was radically different in that Bournonville this year made several musical cuts in score nos. 1, 3, and 5. Furthermore, in score no. 2 he incorporated V. C. Holm's complete music for the *Pas de trois* in his Spanish ballet divertissement, entitled *La Ventana* (*see* 6.10.1856), while the whole of score no. 4 was completely omitted. According to the poster the incorporated music from *La Ventana* was performed by the Swedish ballerinas, A. Arrhenius, J. Hjorth, and A. Paulsson, who appeared as the three Graces in this dance.

Finally, the 1858 staging is interesting in that Bournonville this year played the title rôle himself, in spite of the fact that nearly a decade had passed since his official retirement from the stage in 1848. The Stockholm performances, therefore, represent the very last time he ever performed on stage, and during which he even accompanied himself on the lute when playing one of the tunes from C. M. Bellman's popular songs (cf. J. Svanberg, *Kungl. Teatrarne under ett halft sekel 1860–1910*, Stockholm, 1917, vol. I, pp. 55).

In his diary Bournonville noted about the 1858 Stockholm production:

17.3.1858: 'øvet og gjennemgaaet Bellman'
20.3.: 'Prøve for mig selv paa Bellman'
10.4.: 'Prøve paa Bellman med fru [J. G.] Sundberg'
11.4.: 'Regi- og Costüme=Møde. Item [*sic*] for Decorationerne med [E.] Roberg'
12.4.: 'Prøve paa Bellman, først med Børnene Kl. 9, derpaa med [A.] Elmlund (Molberg), derpaa med Fru Sundberg, [F.] Bechman (Movits) og Krögaren ([[G.] Sandström), forbi Kl. 1.'
13.4.: 'Prøve paa Bellman Kl. 10–1.'
14.4.: 'skrevet, besørget Beskeed med Dilligencekudsken [...] Prøve paa Bellman Kl. 11–2 [...] Besørget adskilligt med Repertoiret. Bellman er bestemt til at gaa næste Onsdag'
15.4.: 'Prøve paa Bellman Kl. 10'
16.4.: 'Prøve paa Bellman Kl. 10. Indstuderingen færdig.'
17.4.: 'Prøve paa Bellman fra 10 til henved 3. Jeg var meget træt'
18.4.: 'Besørget Costume-væsenet'
19.4.: 'Prøve paa Bellmann fra 11–1 [...] og paa Theatret med Orchester Kl. 1'
20.4.: 'Generalprøve i Costume paa Bellmann der gik udmærket godt.'
21.4.: 'Bellman, pragtfuldt Huus, glimrende Modtagelse, fuldstændig Succes og jublende Fremkaldelser. Alt gik godt og jeg takkede Gud af mit ganske Hjerte'.

The 1858 Stockholm production of *Bellman* received 5 performances, the last of which was given on 2.5.1858. The musical material employed this year was mainly the same as that used for the 1847 Stockholm première of this work (now in SSkma, call no. KT Pantomime-Balletter B 6).

Autograph sources:

Advertissement for the press. Ms. Autograph. Blue ink. 2 pp. (26,9 × 21,5 cm)
Unsigned and undated [14.4.1858?]
[SSdt; KTA, E2A Ink. breve 1857/58, 14.4.1858]
This seemingly unpublished manuscript is dated '14/4 [18]58.' by an unknown hand and reads as follows:
'Balletten Bellman eller Polskan på Grönalund, der er et Glandspunkt i det kgl danske Theaters mimiske Repertoire, skylder sin Oprindelse, ikke alene til de scandinaviske Sympathier, men til det Venskabsforhold der bestod imellem den uforlignelige Lyriker, og Componistens forlængst afdøde Fader – den i sin Tid saa feirede Premier-Danseur Antoine Bournonville, der selv ofte havde den Lykke af være Gjenstanden for Bellmans Improvisationer ved de Kunstnergilder, der udmærkede hiin muntre Periode. Maaden hvorpaa Bellmans Individualitet er opfattet af Bournonville vidner om en nedarvet Begeistring og Kjærlighed – Den Portrætlighed, hvormed han selv gjengiver Digteren, der fra Ironiens Standpunkt beetragter og idealiserer sine comiske Typer, gjør denne Ballet til et selvstændigt Hele, der, mærkelig nok – er den eneste vellykkede Reproduktion af det Liv, der rører sig i Fredmans Epistler, thi ligesaa umuligt det er, at oversætte i et fremmed Sprog disse lyriske Mesterstykker, ligesaa svært ja formasteligt er det, at ville sammenbinde dem med en Handling og en Dialog, der er ligesaa langt fra Tidens Aand og Duft, som fra Skjaldens Tone og Lune. I Balletten derimod fremtræder Alt i Form af Illustration: Melodien følger de plastiske Figurer. Enhver Bellmans=Dyrker kan selv lægge Ordene til medens det hele Skuespil bæres frem paa Phantasiens Vinger.
    Allerede ifjor imødesaae Publicum med Længsel en Gjentagelse af den Kunstaabenbaring der i Aaret 1847 havde sat hele Stockholm i Bevægelse og [erased] frembragt taareblandet Glæde med Stolthed over at see den svenske Anacreon saaledes paaskjønnet i Naboriget – men Ulla's eneste berettigede Fremstillerinde – vor talentfulde og gratieuse Johanne Sundberg laae farlig syg og man frygtede for at see hende tabt for Scenen, dog denne Vaar seer hende opblomstre

paanÿ og Bournonville vil feire hendes Gjenoptrædelse ved selv at fremstille Bellmans Rolle maaske paa det eneste sted hvor han [erased] og den kgl Theater Direction har grebet denne Leilighed for at bÿde Publicum en sand national Kunstnÿdelse, ved foreløbig at engagere Herr Bournonville for fem Gjæsteforestillinger der tilligemed Arrangementet af flere nÿe Balletter skulle betegne hans Virksomhed for denne Saison.

———

Efter Forlydende vil den 1.ste Forestilling af Bellmann samt Fru Sundbergs Rentrée finde Sted Onsdagen den 21.e April'.

Other sources:

Sketch by E. Roberg for the back curtain. Pencil (23,5 × 27,7 cm)
Till Bellman på Grönalund gifven på kongl./Theater.. d. 22 April 1858.
Unsigned and dated: 'd. 22 April 1858.'
[SSdt; 406/1929

4.5.1858
Der Freischütz (Jægerbruden).
For the 1858 Copenhagen restaging of C. M. v. Weber's three-act romantic opera (first projected on 30.10.1857) Bournonville gave (according to a note in his diary on 27.3. 1858) personal stage instructions to the singer, J. A. Steenberg, who this year played *Max* for the first time. The 1858 production is not included in Bournonville's handwritten list of his stagings of operas and plays, written c.1872 (*see* Additional Sources), nor in the printed survey of his works in his memoirs *My Theatre Life* (p. 408). Bournonville did not attend the first performance because of his engagement at Stockholm's Royal Theatre during the spring and summer of 1858. The 1858 production received 29 performances, the last of which was given on 29.9.1862. However, 11 years later he mounted *Der Freischütz* for the second and last time in Copenhagen, but then with his own complete mise-en-scène (*see* 21.2.1869).

Musical sources:

Orchestral score. Ms. Copy. Black and brown ink. 3 vol. Act I 194 pp., Act II 194 pp. of which one is blank, Act III 164 pp. of which two are blank (23,2 × 32 cm with minor variants)
213./Jægerbruden./Partitur./1.ste Akt./[...]/Der Freÿschütz/romantische Oper in 3 Aufzügen./Dichtung Gedicht [erased] von F: Kind./in Music gesetzt [erased]/von [erased]/Music von Carl Maria von Weber./Atto. I.mo/[...]/Atto II.do/[...]/Atto III.
Unsigned and dated (by Weber's autographed note on p. 1): 'für das königl. Theater/zu Koppenhagen. [*sic*]/Carl Maria von Weber / 1821.'
[DKKk; C I, 342 (KTA 213)
This orchestral score is a German manuscript copy that contains both the original German text and A. Oehlenschläger's Danish translation. It was used for all performances of *Der Freischütz* in Copenhagen during Bournonville's lifetime.

No répétiteur's copy for *Der Freischütz* has yet been traced.

Parts. Ms. Copy. 34 + 7 vol.
4 vl I, 4 vl II, 2 vla, 2 vlc, 2 cb, fl picc 1/2, fl 1/2, ob 1/2, cl 1/2, fag 1/2, cor 1/2/3/4, clno 1/2, trb 1/2/3, timp. On stage: vl I, vl II, vlc, cl, cor 1/2, clno. 70 vocal parts.
Unsigned and undated [1822]
[DKKk; KTA 213]
This set of parts dates from the Copenhagen première of *Der Freischütz* on 26.4.1822 and was used for all performances of it there during Bournonville's lifetime.

10.5.1858
The Prophecies of Love, Tyrolean Scene and Dance (*Kärleks Spådomar, Scen och Tyrolienne*) performed by J. G. Sundberg, A. Arrhenius, and A. Paulsson (Stockholm's Royal Theatre, Operahuset).

This Swedish staging represents the second and last time Bournonville's divertissement *The Prophecies of Love* (*see* 4.6. 1851) was mounted outside Denmark. According to the musical sources for it (now in SSkma) it differed from the Copenhagen version by two cuts (of 6 and 74 measures each) in the movements entitled *Allegro non troppo* (in 4/4 time) and *Allegretto* (in 3/4 time). In his diary Bournonville noted about the performance:

11.4.1858: 'Regi- og Costüme=Møde. Item [*sic*] for Decorationerne med [E.] Roberg'
24.4.: 'Skrevet og arrangeret Indstuderingen paa [...] Kjærligheds Spaadomme'
26.4.: 'Prøve og Indstudering paa [...] Kjærligheds Spaadomme'
27.4.: 'Prøve og Indstudering paa [...] Kjærligheds Spaadomme, som jeg gjorde færdig'
29.4., 30.4., and 6.5.: 'Prøve paa [...] Kjærligheds Spaadomme'
7.5.: 'Orchesterprøve paa 'Kjærligheds Spaadomme' Kl 7"
8.5.: 'Generalprøve paa Kjærligheds Spaadomme'
10.5.: 'Første Forestilling af Kjærligheds Spaadomme der gik særdeles godt men blev temmelig koldt modtaget'.

The divertissement received 5 performances in Stockholm, the last of which was given on 10.9.1858.

Musical sources:

Orchestral score. Ms. Copy. 1 vol. 57 pp. (33,3 × 25,4 cm)
Musiken af Paulli/Kjærligheds Spaadomme (Ballet)
Unsigned and undated [1858]
[SSkma; KT Pantomime-Balletter K 3

No répétiteur's copy dating from the 1858 Stockholm production of this work has yet been traced.

Parts. Ms. Copy. 23 vol.
2 vl I, 2 vl II, 2 vla, 3 vlc e cb, fl 1/2, ob 1/2, cl 1/2, fag 1/2, cor 1/2, tr, trb, timp, gr cassa.
Unsigned and undated [1858]
[SSkma; KT Pantomime-Balletter K 3

21.5.1858
Die Hochzeit des Figaro (*Figaros Bryllup*).

The 1858 Copenhagen restaging of W. A. Mozart's four-act comic opera (*see also* 25.5.1842 and 7.1.1844) was originally projected by Bournonville on 30.10.1857. It represents the first time *Die Hochzeit des Figaro* was mounted with his own, complete mise-en-scène. Moreover, for this production he gave personal stage instructions to the singer, J. H. Wiehe, who made his début this year in the rôle of *Figaro*. Bournonville did not attend the first performance because of his engagement in Stockholm during the spring and summer of 1858. In his diary he noted about the rehearsals:

10.1.1858: 'hørt Lieut. J. [H.] Wiehe hos [E.] Helsted; særdeles smuk Basstemme'
17.1.: 'bivaanet Syngeprøve (J. Wiehe) hos Helsted'
18.1.: 'Lection til J: Wiehe'
3.2.: 'Instruction til J. Wiehe'
9.3.: 'Instruction til J. Wiehe paa Figaro'
27.3.: 'Kl 5. stort Scene-Arrangement paa Figaros Bryllup'

29.3.: 'Scene Arrangement paa Figaro'.

When Bournonville restaged this production on 9.3.1859 he noted in his diary:

5.3.1859: 'Kl 11 Theaterprøve paa Figaros Bryllup'
7.3.: 'Prøve Kl 10 1/2 paa Dandsen til Figaro'
8.3.: 'Generalprøve paa Figaro'
9.3.: 'I Theatret Figaros Bryllup. M.e [V. L. T.] Fossum fortrinlig; Johan [H.] Wiehe meget heldig'.

The 1858 production of *Die Hochzeit des Figaro* received 8 performances, the last of which was given on 26.3.1859. The musical material employed this year was the same as that used for the previous 1844 staging of Mozart's opera (now in DKKk, call nos. C I, 280, MA ms 3042, and KTB 215).

21.5.1858
Oberon, or The Elf King's Oath (*Oberon*) (Stockholm's Royal Theatre, Operahuset).

The 1858 Swedish première of C. M. v. Weber's three-act romantic fairy-play (first performed in London at Covent Garden on 12.4.1826) also represents the first and only time this work was mounted with Bournonville's mise-en-scène and choreography (*see also* his three projected Copenhagen restagings, dated 30.10.1857, 6.10.1859 and 8.6.1871). The Swedish production included two dance scenes, performed by a corps de ballet in the Act II *Finale* (score no. 15) during the so-called 'Choeur et Ballet' of Act III (score no. 21). Moreover, the production was performed with his daughter, the alto Charlotte Bournonville, who this year played *Fatima* for the first time. The performance is not included in Bournonville's handwritten list of his stagings of operas and plays, written c.1872 (*see* Additional Sources), nor in the printed survey of his works in his memoirs *My Theatre Life* (p. 408). In his diary he noted about the production:

21.4.1858: 'Jeg skrev en deel Scene-Arrangement til Oberon'
23.4.: 'skrevet Scene=Arrangements. Møde paa Oberon. Chorprøve paa den Samme'
25.4.: 'Regimøde paa Oberon'
28.4.: 'Skrevet og componeret. Indstudering paa Oberon Kl 9½ til 12'
29.4.: 'skrevet og componeret. Indstudering paa Oberon'
30.4.: 'Indstudering paa Oberon'
3.5.: 'skrevet og arrangeret. Prøve og Indstudering paa Oberon fra 9½ til 1½'
4.5.: 'Arrangements prøve paa Oberon'
7.5.: 'Stor Arrangementsprøve paa Oberon'
10.5.: 'Prøve paa Oberon'
11.5.: 'Aftenprøve paa Oberon, meget Besvær'
12.5.: 'Prøve paa Oberon 2.den og 3.die Akt 10–1'
13.5.: 'Kl 6 Prøve paa Oberon dog uden Balletten. Charlotte [Bournonville] sang og spillede særdeles godt'
14.5.: 'Theaterprøve paa Oberon Kl 10–1'
16.5.: 'Charlotte havde Halspine og jeg maatte melde at hun ikke kunde prøve iaften eller synge imorgen, hvilket voldte stor Ubehagelighed. Stakkels Pige! Det kalder man at være ret uheldig!'
17.5.: 'Charlotte meget bedre [...] Da vi kom hjem var det værre med Charlottes Hals og vi gik meget bedrøvede tilsengs'
18.5.: 'musiceret og passet Charlotte, der har det meget bedre og haaber at kunne synge paa fredag'
20.5.: 'Generalprøve i Costume paa Oberon. Charlotte var endnu ikke ganske vel, spillede og sang kun med halv Stemme og uden Costüme'
21.5.: 'Kl 6 gik jeg paa Theatret, hvor man gav Oberon for første

Gang. Den gik i det Hele udmærket godt paa Strandberg nær, – og blev heelt igjennem applauderet. Charlotte holdt sig tappert, uagtet sin Indisposition, som Gud være lovet ikke var til at bemærke. Hun sang yndigt og høstede meget Bifald, hendes Spil i det franske Sprog vidnede om et virkeligt Talent og hun gjorde det behageligste Indtryk. Mine Dandse gik godt og behagede. Vi takkede Gud for dette heldige Udfald'.

The 1858 production received 33 performances in Stockholm, the last of which was given on 28.9.1862.

Musical sources:

Orchestral score. Ms. Copy. Black ink with several pencilled manuscript insertions. 3 vol. Act I 206 pp., Act II 196 pp., Act III 180 pp. (23,4 × 31,3 cm)
Kongl. Theatern/Oberon/Romantische Oper in dreÿ Acten./Nach dem Englischen des J[ames] Planché/von/Theodor Hell./Musik von Carl Maria von Weber./Tilhörer kongl: Theatern
Unsigned and undated [c.1858]
[SSkma; KT Operor O 11

Répétiteur's copy. Ms. Copy. Brown ink. 1 vol. 54 pp. (32,6 × 24,5 cm)
A. 267/OBERON./1858/-/63A/Repetiteur./[…]/Oberon./Romantisk Oper i 3.ne Akter./Musiken/af/C. M. v: Weber./Dansar och Grupperingar af A Bournonville/Repetiteur.
Unsigned and dated (on the front cover): '1858/–'
[DKKk; MA ms 3054 (KTA 267 (2))
This répétiteur's copy was clearly made in Stockholm in 1858, but was at a later stage brought to Copenhagen (probably by Bournonville himself) where it became part of the Royal Theatre's music archive. It contains Bournonville's autographed choreographic numbers ('1–17') in the music for the Act II *Finale* (score no. 15). They most probably refer to a (not yet traced) separate choreographic description of this scene. The volume also includes his autographed choreographic notes for the so-called 'Choeur et Ballet' in Act III (score no. 21). According to his diary these were most probably written during late April and early May 1858. The répétiteur's copy also seems to have served for Bournonville's two later projected restagings of *Oberon* in Copenhagen (*see* 6.10.1859 and 8.6.1871).

Parts. Ms. Copy. 36 + 12 vol.
3 vl I, 3 vl II, 2 vla, 4 vlc e cb, fl 1/2, ob 1/2, cl 1/2, fag 1/2, cor 1/2/3/4, tr 1/2/3/4, trb 1/2/3, timp, gr cassa, cassa, piatti, tri. On stage: fl 1/2, ob 1/2, cl 1/2, fag, vl, Bcl, gr cassa, piatti, arpa.
Unsigned and undated [c.1858]
[SSkma; KT Operor O 11

Other sources:

Manuscript mise-en-scène. Ms. Copy. Black ink. 1 vol. 26 pp. (35 × 22,3 cm)
Oberon./Sceneri i utdrag ur franska/mise-en-scène.
Unsigned and undated [1858?]
[SSdt; KTA, Lit. O No. 43

15.6.1858
La Ventana (The Window) (La Ventana, (Fönstret.)), Ballet-Divertissement in 2 Tableaux (i 2 Tablåer) (Stockholm's Royal Theatre, Operahuset).
This performance represents the first and only time Bournonville's second and extended version of his Spanish ballet divertissement, entitled *La Ventana* (*see* 6.10.1856) was mounted outside Denmark during his lifetime. It was staged especially for his two pupils, M. C. Törner and S. Lund, who performed the leading rôles of *The Señorita* and *The Señor*. The Swedish production differed from the Danish version

mainly by having the *Pas de trois* danced by three women (A. Arrhenius, M. W. H. Wiegand, and A. Paulsson) instead of the original cast of a man and two women. In his diary Bournonville noted about the production:

11.4.1858: 'Regi- og Costüme=Møde. Item for Decorationerne med [E.] Roberg'
12.4.: 'eftermiddagsprøve paa La Ventana for Fru [M. C.] Törner'
13.4. and 14.4.: 'Prøve paa La Ventana'
16.4. and 19.4.: 'Eftermiddagsprøve med Fru Törner'
24.4.: 'skrevet og arrangeret Indstuderinger paa La Ventana […] om Eftermiddagen Prøve med Fru Törner og S. Lund'
26.4.: 'skrevet og arrangeret. Prøve og Indstudering paa La Ventana'
27.4: 'skrevet og componeret. Prøve og Indstudering, først paa La Ventana'
29.4.: 'Skrevet og componeret […] Prøve paa La Ventana'
30.4.: 'Prøve paa La Ventana'
1.5.: 'skrevet og arrangeret. Indstudering Kl 10 paa Pas de trois til La Ventana, hvorved jeg fuldendte dette Divertissement'
11.5, 26.5. and 28.5.: 'Prøve paa La Ventana'
29.5.: 'Theaterprøve med Orchester paa La Ventana'
10.6.: 'prøvet La Ventana'
11.6.: 'Generalprøve paa La Ventana'
14.6.: 'Generalprøve paa La Ventana meget godt'
15.6.: 'Första Gang La Ventana og Fru Törners Gjenoptrædelse paa Scenen. Stort Bifald og Fremkaldelse for Fru Törner. Det Hele gik meget godt'.

La Ventana reached a total of 19 performances in Stockholm during Bournonville's lifetime, the last of which was given on 12.9.1861.

Musical sources:

Orchestral score. Ms. Copy. Black ink. 1 vol. 162 pp. (34,1 × 25,9 cm)
1.ste Afdeling./La Ventana./Ballet/componeret af/A Bournonville./Musikken af Lumbye & Holm.
Unsigned and undated [1858]
[SSkma; KT Pantomime-Balletter V 2

No répétiteur's copy dating from the 1858 Stockholm performance of *La Ventana* has yet been traced.

Parts. Ms. Copy. 29 + 3 vol.
2 vl I, 2 vl II, 2 vla, 4 vlc e cb, fl 1/2, ob 1/2, cl 1/2, fag 1/2, cor 1/2, tr, trb 1/2/3, timp, gr cassa, piatti, tri, arpa. On stage: fl 1/2, guit.
Unsigned and undated [1858]
[SSkma; KT Pantomime-Balletter V 2

7.10.1858
La Fiancée (Bruden).
The 1858 Copenhagen restaging of D.-F.-A. Auber's three-act comic opera (*see* 20.11.1853) was projected by Bournonville on 30.10.1857 and represents the first time this work was mounted under his general supervision. According to his diary it seems to have been mounted without any major changes from the previous 1853 and 1855 productions. Bournonville noted about the performance:

30.9.1858: 'Prøve paa Bruden'
1.10.: 'lille Prøve paa Bruden'
3.10.: 'Textprøve paa Bruden'
4.10. and 6.10.: 'Prøve paa Bruden'
7.10.: 'Bruden i Theatret'.

The 1858 production of *La Fiancée* was given only once. The musical material employed this year was the same as that used for the previous 1855 production (now in DKKk, call nos. U 6, MA ms 3059, and KTA 281).

13.10.1858
Joseph (Joseph og hans Brødre i Ægypten).

The 1858 Copenhagen restaging of E.-H. Méhul's three-act opera was originally projected on 30.10.1857 and represents the first time this work was mounted with Bournonville's own mise-en-scène and choreography. However, prior to a performance of *Joseph* in Copenhagen on 20.1.1848 Bournonville had decided to omit the dance in Act III which is performed by a group of young girls during the chorus, entitled «Aux accens de notre harmonie unissez vous fils d'Israël». It was originally choreographed by his father, Antoine Bournonville, for the Copenhagen première of *Joseph* on 10.10.1816. Bournonville's decision to omit this dance was caused by the serious health conditions of Denmark's King Christian VIII, which resulted in the monarch's death on the following day (21.1.1848). Under these serious circumstances Bournonville regarded it as too tasteless for the Act III dance to be performed in that evening's performance. Consequently he ordered its omission and noted about this decision in his diary:

'Der skal spilles til Iaften. – Joseph og hans Brödre men jeg fik dem til at slette Dandsen ud – da det under nærværende Omstændigheder forekom mig forargeligt'.

In the printed orchestral score for Méhul's *Joseph* (p. '140') the scene in Act III during which this dance is performed is described as follows:

'Le théâtre représente le palais de Joseph. Une longue table tient un des côtés du théâtre, mais sans gêner l'avant-scène. Jacob et tous ses enfans sont autour de cette table, couchés à la manière antique. Au côté opposé sont des musiciens jouant des divers instrumens connus dans ce tems-là. Sur l'avant-scène sont des esclaves de toutes couleurs, occupés à remplir de grands vases d'or, &c.'

Joseph was mounted for a second and last time by Bournonville at Stockholm's Royal Theatre (Stora Theatern) on 19.1.1864.

In his diary he noted about the 1858 Copenhagen production:

2.10.1858: 'Eftermiddag Costume-Møde med [J. A.] Pätges paa Joseph'
7.10.: 'Costume Møde paa Joseph'
8.10: 'Scene og Arrangement=prøve paa Joseph'
9.10.: 'Theaterprøve paa Joseph'
12.10.: 'Theaterprøve paa Joseph [...] Costumemøde i Theatret'
13.10.: 'Costumeprøve paa Joseph [...] 1.ste forestilling af Gjentagelsen af Joseph. Jf. [J. A.] Lund debuterede som Benjamin (deilig Stemme). Operaen gik smukt og Scene-Arrangementet tog sig godt ud'.

About a later performance of *Joseph* in Copenhagen on 5.1.1860 he stated on 23.12.1859:

'arrangeret et nyt Costume for Joseph'.

That performance represents the last time Bournonville ever worked on Méhul's opera in Denmark.

The 1858 production received 11 performances, the last of which was given on 1.5.1860.

Musical sources:

Printed orchestral score. 1 vol. 196 pp. of which one is blank (30,9 × 24 cm)
Joseph./[...]/181/[...]/JOSEPH/Opéra en trois Actes/[...]/MUSIQUE DE/MÉHUL
Paris, Magasin de Musique [1807]
[DKKk; U 6 (KTA 181)
This French printed orchestral score was used for all performances of Méhul's opera in Copenhagen since its première there on 10.10.1816 and throughout Bournonville's lifetime.

No répétiteur's copy for *Joseph* has yet been traced.

Parts. Ms. Copy. 39 vol.
5 vl I, 5 vl II, 2 vla, 6 vlc e cb, fl picc 1/2, fl 1/2, ob 1/2, cl 1/2, fag 1/2, cor 1/2/3/4, tr 1/2/3/4, trb, timp, arpa. 73 vocal parts.
Unsigned and undated [1816]
[DKKk; KTA 181
This set of parts dates from the 1816 Copenhagen première of *Joseph* and was used for all performances given during Bournonville's lifetime.

29.10.1858
Little Kirsten (Liden Kirsten).

The 1858 Copenhagen restaging of I. P. E. Hartmann's one-act singspiel (performed this year in a revised two-act version and named as an opera) was originally projected by Bournonville on 30.10.1857. It represents the first time *Little Kirsten* was mounted with his own, complete mise-en-scène. Moreover, the 1858 production included his partially revised choreography including a completely new *Processional March* in Act II, score no. 9 (the so-called *Optog*) which this year was named *Mummespil*. In his diary Bournonville noted about the staging:

20.10.1858: 'Indstudering [...] paa Liden Kirsten'
21.10.: 'Prøve paa Liden Kirsten færdig med Dandsen dertil'
22.10.: 'Prøve paa Liden Kirsten. Costumeprøve til Samme'
23.10.: 'Prøve paa [...] Liden Kirsten'
24.10.: 'componeret Costume-Optog til Liden Kirsten. Costume-Møde 9–11'
25.10.: 'Prøve fra 11–2 paa Liden Kirsten 1.e Theaterprøve'
27.10.: 'Theaterprøve paa Liden Kirsten'
28.10.: 'Generalprøve paa Liden Kirsten'
29.10.: 'I Theatret Liden Kirsten der gik udmærket smukt; men for halvt Huus!!'.

The 1858 production of *Little Kirsten* received 17 performances, the last of which was given on 13.5.1864.

The music material employed this year was the same as that used for Bournonville's previous staging on 6.1.1848 (now in DKKk, call nos. C II, 7 c (Hartmanns samling), MA ms 3085, and KTB 396).

Autograph sources:

Production note. Ms. Autograph. Black ink. 3 pp. (22,9 × 18,1 cm)
Liden Kirsten./(Characteerdragter for Chorets Damer)
Signed and dated: 'd. 24' October 1858.
[DKKkt; F.M. (Opera)

Production note. Ms. Autograph. Black ink. 3 pp. (22,9 × 18,1 cm)
Liden Kirsten./Characteerdragter til Chorets Herrer.

Signed and dated: 'd. 24.e October 1858'
[DKKkt; F.M. (Opera)

Production note. Ms. Autograph. Brown ink. 1 p. (36 × 11,6 cm)
Optog.
Unsigned and undated [c. October 1858]
[DKKkt; F.M. (Opera)

Production note. Ms. Autograph (partially in another's hand).
Brown ink. 2 pp. (20,8 × 13,5 cm)
Dands i Liden Kirsten
Unsigned and undated [c. October 1858]
[DKKkt; F.M. (Opera)

29.10.1858

***The Girls from Xeres, Spanish National Dance arranged by
Mr. Ballet Master S. Lund (Flickorna från Xeres, spansk
Nationaldans; arrangeradt af Herr Ballettmästaren Sigurd
Lund)* performed by J. G. Sundberg, A. Arrhenius, and
A. Paulsson (Stockholm's Royal Theatre, Operahuset).**

This Spanish dance is perhaps identical with a (not yet identified) dance by Bournonville. Thus, according to a note in
A. F. Schwartz's handwritten catalogue of the music archive
of Stockholm's Royal Theatre (now in SSkma, call no. KT
Dansmusik 96), the musical material for it consisted originally of an orchestral score and 23 parts, of which only the
orchestral score is preserved in SSkt (Vinstocken). Moreover, according to Schwartz's musical incipit for this dance,
it is identical with the music that Bournonville had received
from Schwartz (according to a note in his diary) during the
late summer of 1865, and reused for his divertissement in
Act III of G. Verdi's four-act lyrical drama *Il Trovatore*, when
that work was given its Copenhagen première on 10.9.1865
(*see also* 20.11.1862). *The Girls from Xeres* received 7 performances in Stockholm, the last of which was given on 30.12.
1859. It is not possible to identify the dance any further.

Musical sources:

Orchestral score. Ms. Copy. Black ink. 1 vol. 20 pp. (30,6 × 24,5 cm)
Flickorna från Xeres/Spansk-Nationaldans.
Unsigned and undated [c.1858]
[SSkt (Vinstocken), but formerly SSkma with the call no. KT Dansmusik 96.
This orchestral score clearly dates from the 1858 Stockholm première of S. Lund's *The Girls from Xeres*, but was later incorporated among
the dances that he created for the Stockholm première of G. Verdi's
four-act lyrical drama *Il Trovatore* on 31.5.1860 (*see* 20.11.1862). The
score is today preserved as an insertion in the Stockholm orchestral
score for Verdi's *Il Trovatore (Trubaduren)*. No separate répétiteur's
copy and set of parts for *The Girls of Xeres* have yet been trace in
Stockholm.

31.10.1858

***Polketta, Pas de deux* (uncredited) performed by A. and
C. Healey (the Casino Theatre).**

This (uncredited) dance is set to music by H. C. Lumbye and
is described on the poster as a work 'composed' (*componeret*)
for the Healey sisters, but with no mention of Bournonville's
name. According to his memoirs *My Theatre Life* (p. 178),
Bournonville regarded it as the best in the long series of individual *pas* and smaller divertissements that he choreographed for these two English pupils of his. Before their
Copenhagen début at the Casino Theatre in 1858 they had

(according to Bournonville's diary) taken 42 private dance
lessons with him between 27.8.–30.10.1858, each of which
lasted approximately two hours.

Polketta represents the Bournonville divertissement that,
with regard to its number of performances, became the most
widely performed dance during his lifetime, reaching a total
of well over 150 performances. Moreover, it was included in
all of the privately arranged tours of the Healey sisters in the
Danish provinces and abroad, being performed in five countries and eleven cities as follows:

(1) in Denmark, at Odense Theater between 4.4. and18.4.1859, at
the theatres of Aarhus, Aalborg, and Randers during the months of
November–December 1859, and at Copenhagen's Folketheatret between 13.2. and 17.2.1861.
(2) in Norway, at Christiania's Lille Theater (Oslo), and at Det
Norske Teater in Bergen during April-May 1859 and in the summer
of 1861.
(3) in Sweden, at Stockholm's Royal Theatre, Operahuset, between
23.4.1860 and 17.9.1862, on the last date performed as an incorporated divertissement in Act I of Bournonville's two-act romantic ballet *La Sylphide*.
(4) in England, at London's King's Theatre, Royal Italian Opera,
Covent Garden, and Theatre Royal Haymarket during the 1860s and
early 1870s.
(5) in Scotland, at Glasgow's Theatre Royal during the 1860s and
early 1870s.
(6) in Ireland, at Dublin's Theatre Royal during the 1860s and early
1870s.

In Copenhagen the *Polketta* was danced by the Healey sisters
for the last time in the Tivoli Gardens (Theatret) as part of a
series of ten guest performances there between 13.7. and
18.8.1870.

In his diary Bournonville noted about his first encounter
with the Healeys, and his creation and the 1858 première of
Polketta:

24.8.1858: 'Eftermiddag, talt med Miss's [*sic*] Healey paa Vesterbro
angaaende Lectioner'
25.8.: 'Lection til Miss Healley [*sic*], der synes at have gode Anlæg'
22.9.: 'Lection til Healley's [*sic*]'
26.9.: 'Lection Kl 8–9½ til M Healey'
24.9.: 'skrevet til Casinodirectionen'
28.9.: 'Erik Boehg [i.e. Bøgh] bragte mig Svar paa mit Brev at Miss'
Healey vare engagerede i Casino fra 1.ste Novbr til 1.ste April for 150
r. om Maaneden'
29.9.: 'Aftenen paa Tivoli med Edmond [Bournonville]'
1.10.: 'Brev til Just. [H. C.] Christensen i Anledning af anonym Ind-
sigelse imod Lectionerne'
11.10.: 'Musik med [H. C.] Lumby[e] for Søstrene Healey der ere
engagerede til Casino'
12.10.: 'Lection, arrangeret en Pas de deux for Mis' [*sic*] Healey'
13.10.: 'Lection, sluttet pas de deux [...] arbeidet med Lumbÿ'
16.10.: 'Lection og Indstudering til Søstrene Healey'
18.10.: 'Lection til Søstrene Healey indtil Kl 3½'
19.10.: 'Prøve med Healey'
20.10.: 'afleveret Healey'ernes Contract i Casino'
26.10.: 'Lection og Prøve med Healey'erne'
29.10.: 'Prøve med Healey'erne i Casino'
31.10.: 'Casino, Debut for Søstrene Healey i en ny pas de deux af mig,
Polketta, der gjorde stormende Lÿkke'.

Musical sources:

Orchestral score. Ms. Autograph (by H. C. Lumbye). Brown ink. 1
vol. 20 pp. of which one is blank (29,7 × 35 cm with minor variants)

'Polketta' Pas de deux, (for M.lles Christine og Agnes Healey)/(af Hoff Balletmester Ridder Bournonville)
Signed and dated (on p. 1): 'par H: [C: Lumbÿe]/(d: 16. October [1858])'
[DKKk; C II, 34 (mu 6510.2570) [6410.3004]
This autographed orchestral score was part of the music archive of Denmark's Broadcasting (Danmarks Radio) until it was donated to DKKk on 30.10.1964.

Orchestral score. Ms. Copy. Brown ink. 14 pp. (25,5 × 34,2 cm)
Polketta.
Signed and dated (by the copyist on p. 1): 'H: C: Lumbÿe/October 1858.'
[DKKk; MA ms 2723
This manuscript copy of Lumbye's orchestral score of *Polketta* appears to have been made by C. F. Bomholt in 1858, since his owner's signature is written on p. 1.

Orchestral score (the *Polka Mazurka*). Ms. Copy. Brown ink. 6 pp. of which one is blank (29,7 × 35 cm with variants)
Polka Mazurka (af Balletten Polketta.)
Signed and dated (by the copyist on p. 1): 'H: C: Lumbye/October 1858.'
[DKKk; MA ms 2727
This orchestral score contains only the music of the final *Polka Mazurka* and coda movement of *Polketta*. It was probably a copy made in October 1858 for use at public concerts in the Casino Theatre.

No répétiteur's copy and set of parts dating from the 1858 Casino Theatre première of *Polketta* have yet been been traced. However, a later set of parts dating from the 1860 Stockholm performances of this dance is now in SSkma (call no. KT Dansmusik 101).

Parts. Mc. Copy. 31 vol.
5 vl I, 4 vl II, 3 vla, 5 vlc e cb, fl 1/2, ob, cl 1/2, fag, cor 1/2, tr 1/2, trb, tuba, gr cassa, piatti e tri.
Unsigned and undated [c.1860s]
[DKKk; Mf. A. nr. 73
This set of parts seems to date from the 1860s and was (according to several pencilled notes in it) used for public concerts given at the Casino Theatre and abroad (in Hamburg on 23.10.1865 and 11.3. 1867, in Berlin on 7.11.1865, in Breslau in 1866, in Dresden on 12.3. 1866, and in Paris on 12.5.1867). A pencilled note (written in the part for the first trumpet) indicates that the music played for a total of 7 minutes.

17.11.1858
La Dame blanche (Den Hvide Dame).
The 1858 Copenhagen restaging of F.-A. Boyeldieu's three-act comic opera (*see* 1.10.1850) was projected by Bournonville on 30.10.1857. It was mounted for a special charity performance given for the singer-actor, L. F. Sahlertz, and represents the first time *La Dame blanche* was staged under Bournonville's general supervision. According to his separate choreographic notation of the *Circle Dance* in Act I, score no. 1 (performed by a corps de ballet during the chorus of the mountaineers, entitled «Sonnez, sonnez, sonnez cors et musette») it seems that Bournonville had revised this dance for this particular occasion. In his diary he noted about the performance:

12.11.1858: 'Dandseprøve paa 'Den hvide Dame' og Sceneprøve paa Samme'
13.11. and 16.11.: 'Theaterprøve paa Den hvide Dame'
17.11.: 'I Theatret 'Den hvide Dame' til Extra Indtægt for Sahlertz, der blev modtaget med stor Acclamation'.

The 1858 restaging received 25 performances, the last of which was given on 13.12.1867.

The musical material employed this year was the same as that used for the previous 1850 staging (now in DKKk, call nos. U 6, MA ms 3047, and KTA 246).

Autograph sources:

Choreographic note. Ms. Autograph. Brown ink. 2 pp. (22,3 × 18,2 cm)
La dame Blanche/(Ballets du 1.ier acte)
Unsigned and undated [Written almost certainly before the first rehearsal on the dances on 12.11.1858]
[DKKk; NKS 3285 4° 2 A–E
The choreographic numbers contained in this manuscript ('1–11' and '1–5') refer to similar pencilled numbers written in the original répétiteur's copy for *La Dame blanche* (now in DKKk, call no. MA ms 3047 (KTA 246)).

17.11.1858
Pas de deux gracieux (uncredited) performed by A. and C. Healey (the Casino Theatre).
This (uncredited) dance is presented on the poster as a work 'arranged' (*arrangeret*) for the Healey sisters, but with no mention of Bournonville's name. The music is credited as having been arranged by 'Hr. [C. J.] Malmqvist'.

The *Pas de deux gracieux* is almost certainly identical with the (uncredited) *Pas de deux*, given twice by the Healeys at Copenhagen's Folketheatret (*see* 18.2. and 22.2.1861), and the similarly uncredited *Pas de deux gracieux*, performed 8 times in the Tivoli Gardens (Theatret) between 5.8. and 13.8.1870. It was probably also included in their many tours abroad to Norway (April–May 1859 and the summer of 1861), Germany, England, Scotland, and Ireland (during the 1860s and early 1870s). Moreover, on 17.5.1860 they performed a similar (uncredited) dance at Stockholm's Royal Theatre (Operahuset), named *Grand Pas de gracieux, (förut dansad af systrarne Elssler)*. Its title seems to indicate that it is identical with the 1858 *Pas de deux gracieux*. If this theory is correct then this dance is most likely a freely adapted version of the so-called *Pas de châle* in which the sisters, F. and T. Elssler, performed for the last time at the Paris Opéra on 30.1. 1840. That dance also represents the last work which the Elssler sisters performed together.

In his diary Bournonville noted about his involvement in arranging the 1858 *Pas de deux gracieux* for his English pupils:

13.11.1858: 'Prøve med M.lles Healey'
15.11.: 'Prøve i Casino'
16.11.: 'Prøve med Orchestret i Casino paa en Pas de deux gracieux'
17.11.: 'Jeg bivaanede Healey'ernes Dands i Casino, en nÿ pas de deux gracieux arrangeret af mig'.

The dance received 13 performances at the Casino Theatre, the last of which was given on 9.2.1859. No musical sources for the *Pas de deux gracieux* have yet been traced.

21.11.1858
The Fisher Girls, Hornpipe and Reel (Fiskerpigerne, Hornpipe og Reel) (uncredited) performed by A. and C. Healey (the Casino Theatre).
This (uncredited) divertissement is set to music by H. C. Lumbye and described on the poster as a work 'composed' (*componeret*) for the Healey sisters, but with no mention of Bournonville's name. In his score Lumbye incorporated the

English national anthem *God Save our Gracious King*, which dates from about 1742 when it first appeared in a collection of part songs entitled 'Harmonia Anglicana'. It became widely known, however, only through T. A. Arne's later arrangement of it.

Moreover, the poster for *The Fisher Girls* includes a brief scenario that reads:

'(Paa den engelske Kyst vente to Søstre paa en bortreist Sømand, der er forlovet med den ældste. De øine Skibet, hvorpaa han er ombord, og tilvifte ham Velkommen, medens den engelske Nationalsang toner fra Orlogsmanden.)'.

In his diary Bournonville noted about his creation and the 1858 Copenhagen première of this divertissement:

3.11.1858: 'Eftermiddag arbeidet med [H. C.] Lumbÿ[e]'
6.11.: 'Møde hjemme med Lumbÿ'
8.11.: 'componeret en ny Dands til de engelske Elever. Musik af Lumbÿ'
9.11. and 10.11.: 'Lection og Indstudering paa 'Fiskerpigerne''
13.11.: 'Prøve med M.lles Healey'
15.11.: 'Prøve i Casino'
19.11.: 'Lection og Prøve med Healey's'
20.11.: 'Prøve i Casino paa'Fiskerpigerne''
21.11.: 'Fiskerpigerne, der gjorde overordentlig Lÿkke'.

The divertissement reached a total of 13 performances at the Casino Theatre, the last of which was given on 7.3.1859.

The Fisher Girls was most probably also included by the Healeys in their many privately arranged tours to Norway (April–May 1859, and the summer of 1861), Germany, England, Scotland, and Ireland (during the 1860s and early 1870s).

Musical sources:

Orchestral score. Ms. Autograph (by H. C. Lumbye). Black and brown ink. 1 vol. 18 pp. (29,4 × 34,5 cm with minor variants)
H. C. Lumbye:/Fiskerpigerne./[…]/Fiskerpigerne,
Signed and dated (on p. 1): 'Musikken af H: C: Lumbÿe/d: 13 November 1858.'
[DKKk; C II, 34 (1930–31.57)
This autographed orchestral score was purchased by DKKk from Lumbye's grandson, the journalist T. Lumbye, on 3.7.1930.

Orchestral score. Ms. Copy. Brown ink. 1 vol. 28 pp. (34,7 × 26,1 cm with minor variants)
Lumbye, H. C./Fiskerpigerne./Partitur/[…]/Fiskerpigerne/Pas de deux/H. C. Lumbye.
Unsigned and undated [c.1860s]
[DKKk; C II, 34 (mu 6510.2568)
This orchestral score seems to date from the 1860s and was most probably made for use at public concerts in the Tivoli Gardens. It was donated to DKKk by the music archive of Denmark's Broadcasting (Danmarks Radio) on 30.10.1964, but was previously part of the music archive of the Tivoli Gardens.

No répétiteur's copy for *The Fisher Girls* has yet been traced.

Parts. Ms. Copy. 26 vol.
3 vl I, 2 vl II, 2 vla, 2 vlc e cb, fl 1/2, ob 1/2, cl 1/2, fag 1/2, cor 1/2, tr 1/2, trb 1/2, tuba, gr cassa, piatti e tri.
Unsigned and dated (in the part for the first trumpet): 'Frederiksberg/d: 17. April 1859'
[DKKk; Mf. A nr. 55
This set of parts clearly dates from 1859 and was used for public concerts in Copenhagen (most likely at the Albambra Theatre on

Frederiksberg) and abroad. This theory is supported by the dating of the part for the first trumpet and several other pencilled notes indicating that the parts also served for concerts in Germany (Stettin and Hamburg). They represent the oldest orchestral material for *The Fisher Girls* that has been traced so far. Pencilled notes in several of the parts indicate that the music played for a total of between 6½ and 7 minutes. The parts were originally the property of H. C. Lumbye'e son, Carl Lumbye, who sold them to DKKk. Another, much later set of parts for this dance (dating from the 1940s) exists in the music archive of the Tivoli Gardens (call no. 1077).

1.12.1858
El Capricio, Jaleo (uncredited) performed by A. and C. Healey (the Casino Theatre).

This (uncredited) Spanish dance duet is to music by H. C. Lumbye and was premièred as an incorporated divertissement in E. Bøgh's one-act vaudeville *The Caprice (Capricen)*, which was performed on this day as part of a special charity performance given for the actor, C. H. Hagen. On the poster the dance is described as a work 'composed' (*componeret*) for the Healey sisters, but with no mention of Bournonville's name.

On 12.12.1858 it was given separately from the vaudeville by A. Healey as a solo divertissement. Moreover, *El Capricio* was performed by the Healey sisters at Stockholm's Royal Theatre (Operahuset) on 30.4.1860, but this time with Bournonville explicitly credited on the poster for having 'arranged' (*arrangerad*) the dance.

El Capricio was most probably also included in the many other privately arranged tours by the Healeys to Norway (April–May 1859 and the summer of 1861), Germany, England, Scotland, and Ireland (during the 1860s and early 1870s).

In his diary Bournonville noted about its creation and 1858 Copenhagen première:

12.11.1858: 'Musik med [H. C.] Lumbÿ[e]'
18.11.: 'Indstuderinger af en spansk Dands til Healey's'
19.11.: 'Lection og Prøve med Healey's'
23.11.: 'Prøve paa den spanske Dands med Healey'
29.11.: 'Prøve i Casino paa den nÿ Vaudeville med min spanske Dands'
30.11.: 'Generalprøve i Casino'
1.12.: 'Om Aftenen Beneficeforestilling i Casino for [C. H.] Hagen […] Capricen, hvori min nÿ spanske Dands, stort Bifald, udsolgt Huus'
12.12.: 'bivaanet Casino hvor Agnes Healey dandsede allene 'El Capriccio'.

El Capricio reached a total of 13 performances at the Casino Theatre, the last of which was given on 21.2.1859.

Musical sources:

Orchestral score. Ms. Autograph (by H. C. Lumbye). Black ink. 1 vol. 12 pp. of which two are blank (25,7 × 34,5 cm)
H. C. Lumbye:/El Capricho/[Jaleo af 'Capricen' af Erik Bøgh]/ […]/367/El Capriccio Jaleo.
Signed and dated (on p. 1): 'par H: C: Lumbÿe/d: 19.de November 1858.'
[DKKk; C II, 34 (1944–45.65 a)
This autographed orchestral score was part of the music archive of the Tivoli Gardens before it was transferred to DKKk in 1944. According to Lumbye's autographed dating, it most probably also served for the première of this dance at the Casino Theatre.

No répétiteur's and set of parts for *El Capricio* have yet been traced.

7.12.1858

La Ventana (The Window) (fönstret.) Ballet-Divertissement
**performed by B. Bills and C. Saint Louin (Stockholm's
Mindre Theatern).**

This performance represents the first staging in Sweden of
Bournonville's original Spanish mirror-dance, entitled *La
Ventana* (*see* 19.6.1854 and 6.10.1856). It was given as part of
a series of 17 guest performances by Bournonville's Danish
pupil, B. Bills, and the Irish ballerina, C. Saint Louin, from
Dublin's Theatre Royal. On the poster the leading rôle of
The Señorita (danced by Bills) was then named 'Rosina, en
ung Spanjorska'. Moreover, the poster contains an interesting scenario (in Swedish) that was possibly written by Bournonville himself. It represents the only detailed description
of this work that has yet come to light from during his lifetime. This scenario reads:

'Innehållet af La Ventana:
Scenen är uti en ung Spanjorskas boudoir.
Spanjorskan kommer hem til sig efter en promenad; hon återkallar
i sitt minne att hon blifvit förföljd af en herre på gatan. Efter några
koketta ställningar ser hon med harm att alla hennes rörelser här-
mas i spegeln. Full af blygsel öfver sitt kokketeri drager hon hastigt
förhänget för sin sjelfsvåldiga spegelbild. Sedan hon verkställt detta
höres plösligt från gatan en serenad, deruti hennes älskare genom
flöjtens ljufva toner förklarer henne sin glödande kärlek. Derefter
öfvergår musiken til hennes favorit-melodi, den spanska nationaldansen; hänförd af tonernas förtrollande välde börjar hon en lång-
sam och stilla dans, hvilken småningom upplifvas af den spanska
dansmusiken. Kämpande mot sin glödande kärlek, vinner denna lik-
väl seger, och under inflytelsen af sin passion, kastar hon åt sin
tilbedjare ner rosetten, som hon bär vid sitt bröst'.

La Ventana received 4 performances at Stockholm's Mindre
Theatern, the last of which was given on 12.12.1858. No musical sources that date from these performances have yet
been traced in Sweden.

18.12.1858

Fidelio, oder Die ehelich Liebe (Fidelio).

The 1858 Copenhagen restaging of L. v. Beethoven's two-act
singspiel (premièred in Vienna at Theater auf der Wieden
on 20.11.1805, and first performed in Copenhagen on 17.9.
1829) was originally projected by Bournonville on 30.10.
1857. It represents his first staging of *Fidelio*, for which he
also gave personal stage instructions to the singer, J. A.
Steenberg, who played *Florestan* for the first time this year.
Fidelio was restaged for the second and last time by Bournonville in Copenhagen on 17.12.1870.

In his diary he noted about the 1858 production (which
was mounted with new costumes drawn by E. Lehmann):

7.9.1858: 'Møde med T. Lund om Decorationerne til Fidelio'
8.9.: 'Decorations-prøve paa Fidelio, Eftermiddag skrevet Scene-
følgen i Fidelio'
11.9.: 'Opæsning paa Fidelio – meget slet'
22.11.: 'Quartettprøve paa Fidelio'
27.11.: 'Instruction til [J. A.] Steenberg'
29.11. and 30.11.: 'Instruction paa Fidelio'
2.12.: 'Prøve paa Fidelio'
3.12.: 'Prøve paa Fidelio. 1.ste Theaterprøve gÿseligt Vrøvl med M.d
[V. L. T.] Fossum'
7.12.: 'Prøve pa Fidelio'
8.12.: 'Prøve paa […] en Akt af Fidelio'
11.12.: 'Theaterprøve paa Fidelio'

13.12.: 'Prøve paa Fidelio'
15.12.: 'Generalprøve paa Fidelio'
16.12.: 'Ingen Fidelio iaften formedelst [C. L. L.] Ferslews Sygdom'
18.12.: 'Første Forestilling af Fidelio nÿ indstuderet, det gik udmærket godt. M.me Fossum havde ypperlige Momenter. Godt Huus
og eenstemmigt Bifald'.

The 1858 restaging of *Fidelio* received 7 performances, the
last of which was given on 7.12.1860.

Musical sources:

No orchestral score and répétiteur's copy dating from the 1858
Copenhagen restaging of *Fidelio* have yet been traced.

Parts. Ms. Copy. 38 + 1 vol.
5 vl I, 5 vl II, 3 vla, 3 vlc, 3 cb, fl picc, fl 1/2, ob 1/2, cl 1/2, fag 1/2/
3, cor 1/2/3/4, tr 1/2, trb 1/2, timp. On stage: tr. 57 vocal parts.
Unsigned and undated [1829]
[DKKk; KTA 231
This set of parts dates from the 1826 Copenhagen première of *Fidelio*
and was used for all performances of it there during Bournonville's
lifetime.

19.12.1858

The Flower Festival in Genzano (Blomsterfesten i Genzano).

Most of the dramatic action in this one-act ballet appears to
have been based on Bournonville's much earlier scenario
for the projected allegorical ballet, entitled *Annitta, or The
Vintage in the Mountains of Albano* (*see* 22.9.1848). That work,
in turn, was originally planned as the third in a series of four
projected allegorical ballets, named *The Four Seasons, or Cupid's Journey* (*see* 16.6.1846). To his 1848 scenario Bournonville added new elements, borrowed from the third chapter
of H. C. Andersen's 1835 novel *The Improvisatore (Improvisatoren)* in which a detailed description of the annual flower
festival in Genzano is included. Andersen's description was
combined with additional narrative material borrowed from
A. Dumas' *Impressions du Voyage* (1834).

The Flower Festival in Genzano was set to music composed
and arranged by E. Helsted (the introduction and score nos.
1–10) and H. S. Paulli (score nos. 11–13 and the *Saltarello*).
In his music for the *Pas de deux* (score no. 12, danced by H.
Scharff as *Paolo*, and J. Price as *Rosa*, and a group of six girls)
Paulli employed nearly all of M. Strebinger's earlier music
for a *Pas de deux* by the Italian dancer and choreographer, L.
Vienna. It was originally performed as an incorporated divertissement in Act III of Bournonville's Vienna production
of his three-act romantic ballet *Napoli, oder: Der Fischer und
seine Braut* (*see* 31.1.1856).

In Sweden an (uncredited) *Grand pas de deux from the ballet
The Flower Festival (Stor Pas de deux, ur Balletten 'Blomsterfesten')*
was performed twice by Bournonville's English pupils, A.
and C. Healey, at Stockholm's Royal Theatre (Operahuset)
on 26.4. and 13.5.1860. This dance, which seems to be a revised version for two women of the *Pas de deux* in *The Flower
Festival in Genzano*, was most likely arranged by Bournonville.
Moreover, the *Pas de deux and Balabile from the ballet The Flower
Festival in Genzano* were given the same year at Stockholm's
Mindre Theatern on 1.6. and 3.6.1860 in yet another adaptation for two couples, also probably arranged by Bournonville
and performed by F. Hoppe, W. Price, Juliette Price, and S.
Price. Furthermore, in Norway the same dances were per-

formed twice by H. Scharff, W. Price, Juliette Price, and S. Price at Christiania's Theatre (Oslo) on 9.6. and 28.6.1865, but then with the title *'Pas de deux'* and *'Ballabile'* *(from the ballet The Flower Festival)*.

The 1860 Swedish adaptation of the (uncredited) so-called *Grand pas de deux* for two women was also mounted some 10 years later in Copenhagen by the Healey sisters, who danced it 16 times in the Tivoli Gardens (Theatret) between 28.6. and 4.8.1870. The same dance was restaged at that theatre by the French ballerinas, F. and L. Carey, who performed it 19 times between 14.5.1871 and 30.8.1872.

Finally, the complete version of *The Flower Festival in Genzano* was restaged by Bournonville in Copenhagen in a choreographically slightly revised version on 11.9.1872, while the ballet's so-called *Section II ('2. Afd.')* was mounted by him there as a separate divertissement on 1.1.1875.

On 31.3.1877 he also made a notation of the ballet's complete mime and most of its choreography prior to his last restaging of it in Copenhagen on 1.5.1877.

In his diary he noted about the creation and the 1858 première of this ballet:

23.7. and 27.7.1857: 'Læst og speculeret paa mine nÿe Balletter'
28.7.: 'læst, skrevet'
31.8.1858: 'Reenskrevet et Program til en lille nÿ Ballet, Blomsterfesten i Genzano'
6.9.: 'begyndt den nÿ Ballet 1.ste Deel med Helsted'
7.9.: 'Møde [...] med H[. S.] Paulli, der gav mig Saltarellen af den nÿ Ballet'
14.9.: 'arbeidet med Paulli og senere paa Eftermiddagen med [E.] Helsted'
16.9.: 'arbeidet med Paulli'
25.9.: 'Eftermiddag arbeidet med Helsted – endelig!'
27.9.: 'Op Kl 6, componeret paa min nÿ Ballet' [...] componeret den Hele Eftermiddag'
28.9.: '1.ste Indstuderingsprøve paa 'Blomsterfesten i Genzano' [...] componeret'
29.9.: '2.den Indst:prøve paa 'Genzano' [...] Eftermiddagen skrevet og componeret'
30.9.: 'skrevet og componeret, arbeidet med Helsted'
1.10.: 'componeret'
2.10.: '3.die Indstudering paa Blomsterfesten [...] arbeidet med Helsted'
3.10.: 'Møde med [E.] Lehmann'
4.10.: 'skrevet og componeret'
6.10.: 'en Times Indstudering paa Blomsterfesten'
8.10.: 'besøgt [...] Helsted [...] arbeidet med Helsted'
9.10.: '5.te Indst: paa Blomsterfesten'
10.11.: 'Skrevet og componeret den hele Formiddag'
11.10.: 'Skrevet Regien til min nÿ Ballet'
12.10.: 'Prøve Kl 10. 6.te Indst. paa Blomsterfesten'
13.10.: 'Prøve 7.de Indstudering Blomsterfesten'
14.10.: '8.de Indst. paa Blomsterfesten'
15.10.: 'componeret paa Saltarello'en'
16.10.: 'lille Prøve paa Saltarello'en [...] componerede lidt'
18.10.: 'skrevet, arrangeret, componeret [...] Prøve 9.e Indstudering [...] Eftermiddagen hjemme og componeret indtil Kl 9'
19.10.: '10.de Indstudering'
20.10.: 'componeret [...] 11.e Indstudering paa den nÿ Ballet [...] Decorations=Möde med Troels Lund paa den nÿ Ballet'
24.10.: 'Arbeidet med Helsted. – Frokost der'
25.10.: 'skrevet og componeret'
26.10.: '12 Indstudering paa Blomsterfesten'
28.10.: 'skrevet og componeret'
29.10.: 'Modtaget den sidste Scene af Helsted'
30.10. and 31.10.: 'skrevet og componeret'

1.11.: 'skrevet og arrangeret, indleveret Regien til den nÿ Ballet. Prøve [...] fuldendt pas de deux til Balletten'
2.11.: 'Prøve paa Blomsterfesten'
3.11.: '14.de Indstudering paa Blomsterfesten'
4.11.: 'Prøve paa Blomsterfesten 15.de Indstudering'
6.11.: '16.de Indstudering paa Blomsterfesten'
8.11.: '17.de og sidste Indstudering paa Blomsterfesten'
9.11.: 'Prøve paa Pas de deux til Blomsterfesten'
10.11.: 'Costumemøde pa Blomsterfesten'
11.11.: 'Prøve paa hele Blomsterfesten, der varer 53 Minutter'
12.11.: 'lille Prøve paa Blomsterfesten'
17.11.: 'Prøve paa Blomsterfesten for Directeurerne'
24.11. and 27.11.: 'Prøve paa Blomstefesten'
9.12.: 'passet Prøver paa <u>Blomsterfesten</u>'
10.12.: 'Arrangement prøve paa Blomsterfesten'
11.12.: 'lille Prøve paa Blomsterfesten'
12.12.: 'Musikprøve Kl 12 paa Blomsterfesten. Reenskrevet Programmet til Balletten'
13.12.: 'Prøve paa [...] 1.ste Deel af Blomsterfesten [...] fuldført Programmet og bragt det til Bogtrykkeren'
14.12.: '1.ste fuldstændige Prøve paa Blomsterfesten, der gik udmærket'
15.12.: 'Correctur paa Balletprogrammet [...] Aftenprøve paa Blomsterfesten'
17.12.: 'Generalprøve paa Blomsterfesten der gik udmærket godt'
18.12.: 'Costumeprøve og Reqvisitprøve paa Balletten'
19.12.: 'Afsendt Programmer [...] 1.ste Forestilling af <u>Blomsterfesten i Genzano</u>, for fuldt Huus og et særdeles livligt Publicum. Balletten gik udmærket godt og Juliette [Price] vandt Publicum. Det var en stor Succès, med stormende Bifald. Jeg havde atter Aarsag at takke Gud for al hans Miskundhed imod os'.

About the ballet's second performance on 23.12.1858 he stated:

22.12.1858: '<u>Blomsterfesten</u> 2.den Gang uden Abonnement 2/3 Huus og glimrende Succès. Da jeg kom hjem, fik jeg Brev med Tilsigelse at møde til Audients hos H. M. Kongen [i.e. Christian IX], Imorgen Kl 9'
23.12.: 'til Audients for H. M. Kongen, der i de naadigste Udtryk bevidnede mig sin Tilfredshed med Forestillingen iaftes'.

The 1858 version of *The Flower Festival in Genzano* received 34 performances (with the last given on 16.5.1865) and the complete ballet reached a total of 50 performances during Bournonville's lifetime, the last of which was given on 18.5.1877.

Autograph sources:

Manuscript scenario. Ms. Autograph. Black ink. 1 vol. 10 pp. (22,8 × 16,9 cm)
<u>Blomsterfesten i Genzano./Ballet i een</u> akt/af/August Bournonville/1858.
Signed and dated: '<u>Kbhvn</u> d 31.e August 1858.'
[DKKk; NKS 3285 4° 2 A-E

Choreographic note. Ms. Autograph. Black ink. 2 pp. (21,4 × 13,7 cm)
<u>Saltarello. Blomsterfesten.</u>
Unsigned and undated [Written according to the diary on 15.10. and 16.10.1858]
[Private collection (Copenhagen)
This manuscript contains Bournonville's complete choreography for the final *Saltarello* as danced in 1858 by C. Kellermann (*Gelsomina*), A. Fredstrup (*Pasquale*), F. Hoppe, N. P. Stendrup (*Matteo*), W. Funck, R. C. A. Andersen (*Christoffano*), L. Stillmann (*Giacinta*), S. Price (*Lila*), E. Stramboe (*Giacomo*), P. Fredstrup (*Violetta*), H. Scharff (*Paolo*), Juliette Price (*Rosa*), G. Brodersen, and E. Garlieb

(*Fiorabella*). The dance is divided into 19 sections, each of which is given a choreographic number ('1–19') that most likely refers to a similar number inserted by Bournonville in the (not yet traced) original 1858 répétiteur's copy for *The Flower Festival in Genzano*.

Production note. Ms. Autograph. Black ink. 2 pp. (22,9 × 18 cm)
Blomster-Requisiter til Balletten/<u>Blomsterfesten i Genzano</u>.
Unsigned and undated [Written according to the diary between 11.10. and 1.11.1858]
[Private collection (Copenhagen)
This note clearly dates from the 1858 première since the names of the dancers, C. Kellermann, Juliette Price, and P. Fredstrup, are mentioned in it.

Production note. Ms. Autograph. Black ink. 1 p. (22,9 × 18 cm)
<u>Requisiter til Balletten</u>/<u>Blomsterfesten i Genzano</u>.
Unsigned and undated [Written according to the diary between 11.10. and 1.11.1858]
[Private collection (Copenhagen)
This note clearly dates from the 1858 première because the names of the dancers, L. Stillmann, E. Stramboe, H. Scharff, G. A. Füssel, and F. Hoppensach, are mentioned in it.

Production note. Ms. Autograph. Black ink. 2 pp. (20,9 × 13,4 cm)
<u>Blomsterfesten.</u>/<u>11.te   Scene</u>/[...]/<u>Optog.</u>/[...]/<u>Allegro.</u>/[...]/
<u>Pas de six.</u>
Unsigned and undated [1858?]
[Private collection (Copenhagen)

Musical sources:

Orchestral score. Ms. Autograph (by E. Helsted and H. S. Paulli). Black and brown ink. 1 vol. 234 pp. of which two are blank (25,2 × 33,5 cm)
267/Blomsterfesten i Genzano./Partitur
Signed and dated (on p. 127): 'December 1858/Eduard Helsted.', (p. 233) 'Nov: 1858 HSPaulli'
[DKKk; C II, 114 k (KTB 267)

The original 1858 répétiteur's copy for *The Flower Festival in Genzano* has not yet been traced, but a photostat copy is now in a private collection (Copenhagen).

Part for the first violin/Répétiteur's copy. Ms. Copy. Black ink. 1 vol. 62 pp. (33,2 × 25,1 cm)
267/<u>Repetiteur</u>/Blomsterfesten/i/<u>Genzano</u>./Violino 1. No. 1./
[...]/<u>Violino 1.</u>/Blomsterfesten i Genzano.
Unsigned and undated [1858]
[DKKk; MA ms 2964 (KTB 267)
This part for the first violin also seems to have served as a répétiteur's copy at a later stage.

Parts (incomplete). Ms. Copy. 15 vol.
3 vl I, vl II, vla, 2 vlc e cb, fl, cl1/2, tr 1/2, trb, timp, gr cassa.
Unsigned and undated [1858]
[DKKk; KTB 267
This (incomplete) set of parts is the only one that dates from the 1858 première of *The Flower festival in Genzano* traced so far.

Piano score. Ms. Copy. Brown ink. 12 pp. (35,5 × 26,2 cm)
Pas de deux/af/'Blomsterfesten i Genzano'/af/Paulli
Unsigned and undated [c. late 1850s or early 60s]
[DKKk; C II, 119
This piano score contains the complete music of Paulli's 1858 version of the *Pas de deux* in *The Flower Festival in Genzano* (score no. 12). It was most probably prepared for publishing purposes.

Printed sources:

Printed scenario. 1 vol. 11 pp. (19,8 × 12.6 cm)

Blomsterfesten i Genzano./Ballet i een Akt/af/August Bournonville./Musiken af DHrr. Ed. Helsted og H. Paulli./Decorationerne af DHrr. Christensen og Lund.
Kjøbenhavn, J. H. Schubothe/Bianco Luno/F. S. Muhle, 1858.
[DKKk; 17, – 175 8°

30.12.1858

The Kermesse in Brüges, or The Three Gifts (Kermessen i Brügge eller De tre gåfvorna) (**Stockholm's Royal Theatre, Operahuset**).

The 1858 Stockholm première of Bournonville's three-act Flemish ballet *The Kermesse in Brüges, or The Three Gifts* (*see* 4.4.1851) represents the only time this work was staged outside Denmark during his lifetime. While the first 19 rehearsals were directed personally by Bournonville as part of his engagement at Stockholm's Royal Theatre during the summer of 1858, the final rehearsals and the actual staging were carried out by his pupil, S. Lund, who served as ballet-master in Stockholm between 1856 and 1862. Lund mounted the ballet mainly from Bournonville's autographed choreographic notes, written three years earlier in a new répétiteur's copy. These notes (which according to his diary were made between 25.5. and 15.7.1855) were revised by Bournonville during his sojourn in Stockholm between 1.4. and 21.6.1858. Moreover, Lund would have known this ballet by heart, having performed in it himself at its 1851 Copenhagen première.

According to the Swedish musical sources (now in SSkma) the ballet was mounted with only few changes from the original 1851 Copenhagen version. They consisted of ten minor musical cuts and/or omissions of repeats in Act I (score no. 2), Act II (score nos. 7, 13, 14), and Act III (score no. 18).

In his diary Bournonville noted about the Swedish production:

20.3.1858: 'Prøve for mig selv paa [...] Kermessen'
30.3.: 'Prøve paa <u>Kermessen i Brügge</u>'
5.5.: 'skrevet og arrangeret [...] Om Eftermiddagen begÿndt paa Kermessen'
6.5. and 8.5.: 'Indstudering og Prøve paa [...] Kermessen'
9.5.: 'skrevet'
10.5.: 'Indstudering paa Kermessen. Eftermiddagsprøve'
11.5.: 'Indstudering paa Kermessen'
12.5.: 'skrevet'
14.5.: 'skrevet og componeret. Prøve Kl 9 indstuderet en pas de deux til Kermessen'
15.5.: 'arrangeret, Indstudering og Prøve fra 9–12'
17.5.: 'skrevet og arrangeret. Prøve og Indstudering paa Kermessen'
18.5.: 'skrevet og componeret. Indstudering og Prøve fra 10–2'
19.5.: 'skrevet og arrangeret. Indstudering og Prøve paa Kermessen [...] skrevet, arrangeret'
20.5.: 'skrevet og arrangeret'
21.5.: 'skrevet [...] Prøve og Indstudering paa Kermessen [...] Arrangeret mine Personlister'
22.5.: 'skrevet og arrangeret. Stor Arrangementsprøve paa Kermessen 1.ste og 2.den Akt. Aftale med [G. O. Hyltén-] Cavallius, at denne Ballets Opførelse skulde gjemmes til Høsten'
24.5. and 25.5.: 'skrevet og arrangeret'
27.5.: 'Theaterprøve paa Kermessen'
31.5.: 'Indstudering paa Kermessen i Brügge'
1.6.: 'Indstudering paa Kermessen'
2.6.: 'skrevet, Indstudering og Prøve paa Kermessen'
3.6.: 'skrevet'
4.6.: 'skrevet [...] Prøve paa Kermessen. Indstuderingen aldeles færdig'

7.6: 'Prøve paa Kermessen'
16.6: 'skrevet og arrangeret sidste Prøve paa Kermessen'
24.9. and 3.10.: 'Skrevet til […] [S.] Lund'
2.1.1859: 'Brev til Sigurd Lund'
8.1.: 'Brev fra Sigurd Lund med behagelig Efterretning om Kermessens lykkelige Opførelse i Stockholm d. 30.e December'.

The Kermesse in Brüges, or The Three Gifts received only 2 performances in Stockholm, the last of which was given on 3.1. 1859.

Autograph(?) sources:

14 costume drawings (containing Bournonville's autographed notes and seemingly copied by him from E. Lehmann's originals drawings from 1851?). Pencil and water colour (29,5 × 19 cm with minor variants).
[1.] Fru [J. G.] Sundberg/Johanne [erased]/(Jf. [L.] Stramboe [erased]/Marchen./(Jf. A Price) [DTM 653/63
[2.] D:lle [A.] Paulsson/Marchen [erased]/(Jf. A Price)/Johanne./ (Jf [L.] Stramboe) [DTM 655/63
[3.] Grevinnan (M.de [N.] Møller) [DTM 654/63
[4.] Eleonora (Jf Juliette Price.)/Fru [M. C.] Törner [DTM 656/63
[5.] Cavaleer, modificeres [DTM 649/63
[6.] Mirewelt/Herr [Gott. A.] Füssel. [DTM 650/63
[7.] Fem Borgerkoner /(Jf [P.] Fredstrup)/modif. [DTM 651/63
[8.] D:lle Hallberg./Trutje/(Jfr. [J.] Fredstrup.)/modif. [DTM 652 /63
[9.] Geert 1.sta Costymen [DTM 644/63
[10.] 2.dra Costymen [DTM 643/63
[11.] Adrian/[G.] Brodersen [DTM 645/63
[12.] Geert [erased]/Adrian ([G.] Brodersen) [DTM 648/63
[13.] Carel/(Herr [F.] Hoppe.) [DTM 646/63
[14.] Van der Steen/([L.] Gade) [DTM 647/63
Unsigned and undated [1858 and/or 1859?]
[SSdt; 643–656/63
This set of 14 costume drawings appears to have been prepared especially for the 1858 Swedish première at Stockholm's Royal Theatre of *The Kermesse in Brüges, or The Three Gifts*. The fact that Bournonville inserted the names of several Danish dancers who later played the leading rôles of this ballet in Copenhagen indicates that the drawings were also used for a later restaging in Copenhagen (most probably on 25.3.1859, when the ballet was mounted with a partially new cast). Another, similar drawing that clearly belongs to this series and shows the costume worn by *Geert* in Act II (*see* the following entry) includes a pencilled note (written by an unknown hand) which reads: 'Tegning af A. Bournonville'. This indicates that it may have been Bournonville who personally prepared this set of 15 costume drawings, which to a large extent seem to have been based on (or perhaps even copied directly from) E. Lehmann's original (not yet traced) drawings of the costumes for the 1851 Copenhagen première of *The Kermesse in Brüges, or The Three Gifts*.

Costume drawing by Bournonville? (seemingly copied by him after an original drawing by E. Lehmann and containing his extensive autographed notes which indicate his wishes for changes and additions). Pencil and water colour (29,6 × 19 cm).
Geert/i 'Kermessen i Brügge'./(Trøien af en lysere Farve)/[…]/ Tegning af A. Bournonville.
[Unsigned and undated [1858 and/or 1859?]
[SSm; Daniel Fryklunds samling no. 271 a
Bournonville's autographed notes on this drawing (written with brown and black ink) read as follows: ' Vide guule Benklæder nedenfor Knæet;/' blaae Strømper./' carmosinrøde Sløifer./' sort Trøie med carmosin Besætning./———/Omklædning./Tre Sløifer med Sölv paa hver Buxe./——/Lÿseblaae Vams, med guule Ærmer med sort Velvet og Sölv-Besætning./——/Bred Hat – mørkebrun med Sölvkant og Smaafjer over Skyggen (blaae) [erased] (røde)./ Sløifer til Skoene: (Barbouille farver)'.

Musical sources:

Orchestral score. Ms. Copy. Black ink. 2 vol. Act I 207 pp., Act II–III 373 pp. (34,8 × 25,9 cm with minor variants)
Kermessen./Partitur./1.Ak…n./[…]/2:3. Ak…n.
Signed and dated (on p. 373): 'Copierat af [C. F. A.] Holmström i Junii 1858'
[SSkma; KT Pantomime-Balletter K 4

Répétiteur's copy. Ms. Copy. Black ink. 1 vol. 96 pp. (26,6 × 37,2 cm)
La Kermesse de Brüges./(Ballet en trois Actes)/(Kermessen)/ (eller)/(De tre gaver)/par/Auguste Bournonville/Musique composée et arrangée par H. Paulli
Unsigned and undated [c.1854–1855]
[SSkma; KT Pantomime-Balletter K 4
This répétiteur's copy dates almost certainly from 1854–55, when Bournonville was working on a projected staging of *The Kermesse in Brüges, or The Three Gifts* at Vienna's Kärnthnerthor Theatre for the 1856–57 season. This is clear from his autographed notes included in this volume (all written with brown ink), which describe the ballet's complete mime and choreography such as he planned it to be performed in Vienna. According to his diary these notes were written between 25.5 and 15.7.1855. The projected Vienna staging was never carried out. Consequently this répétiteur's copy and Bournonville's autographed notes in it came into use only when S. Lund mounted the ballet at Stockholm's Royal Theatre on 30.12.1858. For that production Bournonville added a number of pencilled notes which indicate his changes in the choreography for the Act II *Pas de quatre*, performed by the Swedish ballerinas, A. Arrhenius, M. W. H. Wiegand, J. Hjort, and H. E. C. Ek. His other pencilled notes indicate the ten minor musical cuts or omissions of repeats which he also made for the 1858 Stockholm production.

Parts. Ms. Copy. 30 vol.
2 vl I, 2 vl II, 3 vla, 3 vlc e cb, fl 1/2, ob 1/2, cl 1/2, fag 1/2, cor 1/2/ 3/4, tr, trb 1/2/3, timp, gr cassa, piatti e tri, arpa.
Unsigned and undated [1858]
[SSkma; KT Pantomime-Balletter K 4

Other sources:

Manuscript scenario. Ms. Copy. Brown ink. 1 vol. 14 pp. (21,8 × 17,1 cm)
Kermessen i Brügge/eller/De tre gåfvarna./Romantisk Ballet i 3 Akter/af August Bournonville./Musiken af H. Paulli
Unsigned and undated [1858]
[SSdt; KTA, Lit K No. 47

Production note. Ms. Copy. Brown ink. 43 pp. (33,6 × 21 cm)
Kostumlista till 'Kermessen i Brügge.'
Unsigned and undated [1858]
[SSdt; KTA, F3CD, Nr. 313 Kermessen i Brügge

Costume drawing. Ms. Autograph (by an unknown hand). Brown ink. 1 p. (18,5 × 20,8 cm)
[Untitled]
Unsigned and undated [1858]
[SSdt; KTA, F3CD, Nr. 313 Kermessen i Brügge
This drawing shows the costume of a nobleman in *The Kermesse in Brüges, or The Three Gifts*.

Production note. Ms. Autograph (by P. Allennbom?). Brown ink. 1 p. (33,2 × 21,2 cm)
Chor lista till Balletten: 'Kermessen i Brügge'/den 21 November 1858.
Signed and dated: 'Stockholm d. 21 Novemb: 1858./P Allennbom.' [?]
[SSdt; KTA, F3CD, Nr. 313 Kermessen i Brügge

Production note. Ms. Autograph (by S. Lund, partially in another's hand). Brown ink. 1p. (18,5 × 20,8 cm)

Personal af Machineriet Till Kermessen i Brugge/1.ste & 2. Akt
Signed and undated [1858]
[SSdt; KTA, F3CD, Nr. 313 Kermessen i Brügge

Production note. Ms. Autograph (by S. Lund). Brown ink. 3 pp. (33,6 × 21 cm)
Personalet/i/Kermessen i Brügge.
Signed and undated [1858]
[SSdt; KTA, F3CD, Nr. 313 Kermessen i Brügge

Printed sources:

Printed scenario. 1 vol. 12 pp. (17,1 × 10,2 cm)
Kermessen i Brügge/ELLER/DE TRE GÅFVORNA./ROMANTISK BALLETT I TRE AKTER/AF/AUGUST BOURNONVILLE./Musiken af Paulli.
Stockholm, Hörbergska Boktryckeriet, 1858.
[DKKk; 17, 174 8°

1859

21.1.1859
Galop militaire (uncredited) performed by A. and C. Healey (the Casino Theatre).

This (uncredited) dance is described on the poster as a work 'composed' (*componeret*) for the Healey sisters, but with no mention of Bournonville's name. It was most likely also included in their many privately arranged tours to Norway (in April–May 1859 and the summer of 1861), Germany, England, Scotland, and Ireland (during the 1860s and early 1870s). In his diary Bournonville noted about the creation and the première of this dance:

7.1.1859: 'Lection og componeret en Gallope [*sic*] militaire for Søstrene Healey'
8.1.: 'Prøve paa Galoppen'
13.1.: 'Dandseprøve for Healey's'
19.1.: 'Orchesterprøve paa Galop militaire'
21.1.: 'i Casino min nỹ Galop militaire for meget daarligt Huus og smukt Bifald'.

Galop militaire reached a total of 9 performances at the Casino Theatre, the last of which was given on 4.3.1859.

Musical sources:

Orchestral score. Ms. Autograph (by H. C. Lumbye). Black ink. 1 vol. 12 pp. (25,7 × 34,3 cm)
H. C. Lumbye:/Militair Galop./(Pas de deux)/[...]/369./Pas de deux/Militair Galop.
Signed and dated (on p. 1): 'par H: C: Lumbye/d: 15. Januar 1859.', (p. 12) 'Fine Kl 2½ Onsdag Morgen d: 19.de/Januar 1859.'
[DKKk; C II, 34 (1944–45.65 a)
This autographed orchestral score was part of the music archive of the Tivoli Gardens before it was transferred to DKKk in 1944. According to Lumbye's autographed dating, it most probably also served for the première of this dance at the Casino Theatre.

No répétiteur's copy and set of parts dating from the 1859 première of Lumbye's *Galop militaire* have yet been traced.

Orchestral score. Ms. Copy. Brown ink. 18 pp. of which one is blank (25,9 × 34,3 cm)
Pas de Deux/Militair Galop.
Signed and dated (by the copyist on p. 1): 'H: C: Lumbÿe./1859.'
[DKKk; MA ms 2724

This orchestral score was originally the property of the musician, C. Jensen, and was probably made for public concerts in Denmark and abroad in the 1860s.

Orchestral score. Ms. Copy. Brown ink. 17 pp. (29,3 × 35,3 cm)
Pas de Deux/Militair Galop
Signed and dated (by the copyist on p. 1): 'H: C: Lumbÿe 1859'
[Music archive of Denmark's Broadcasting (Danmarks Radio, Nodearkivet), Islands Brygge 81, DK-2300 Copenhagen S.
This orchestral score seems to date from 1859 and was most probably made for public concerts in Denmark and abroad in the 1860s. A photocopy of it is now in DKKk (call no. MA ms 2831 (mu 9310. 2961)).

10.2.1859
2 Tableaux entitled 'The Storming at Vestervold' ('Stormen paa Vestervold') and 'The Blessing of Peace' ('Fredens Velsignelse'), staged on the occasion of the bicentenary of the Storming of Copenhagen (Borgerfesten ved To=Hundrede=Aars Jubilæet for Stormen paa Kjøbenhavn) (the Casino Theatre, Lille Sal).

These tableaux were created for the celebration of the bicentenary of the storming of Copenhagen by the occupying forces of Sweden between 10.2. and 11.2.1659. This assault was heroically repelled by the population of Copenhagen. In his diary Bournonville noted about the tableaux, which were mounted with costumes and décor by E. Lehmann:

27.1.1859: 'Comité for Festen d. 10.de Februar (200 Aar siden Stormen paa Kjøbenhavn)'
29.1.: 'Udkast til en Decoration ved Festen. – Comité=Möde fra 6–8 1/2'
30.1.: 'brev til [...] Agent Clausen, musiceret og componeret'
31.1.: 'Conference med Clausen og [E.] Lehmann. Brev til Comitéen'
1.2.: 'Comité=Möde'
2.2.: 'Aftenen hjemme, componeret (besørget en heel Deel til Festen.)'
3.2.: 'confereret med Lehmann [...] besørget adskilligt til Festen [...] Comitémøde'
4.2.: 'talt med Lehmann [...] Om Eftermiddagen læst (Kjøbenhavns Beleiring 1659)'
5.2.: 'Comité for Festen'
6.2.: 'Costumemöde til Festen, besørget endeel'
7.2.: 'i Casino, arrangeret adskilligt der'
8.2.: 'Prøve paa [...] de to Tableauer. Decorationsprøve i Casino'
9.2.: 'Den øvrige Deel af Dagen beskjæftiget med Festen [...] Belysningsprøve i Casino'
10.2.: 'Allene beskjæftiget med Festen til iaften [...] Borgerfesten i Casino, der aabnedes Kl 8. 530 Herrer spiste ved Bordene og ligesaa mange Damer prudede Balconen og Amphitheater. Pr. [Frederik] Ferdinand repræsenterede Kongens Person, Overpræsidenten som Formand, Rector magnificus. (Lüttichau og [J. G.] Forchhammer) udbragte Skaalerne for Kongen og Kongehuset, Brix for Danmark, [P. F. A.] Hammerich for Norden, [J. N.] Madvig for Nationens Udvikling, Broberg for Armee og Marine, [C. H.] Schepellern for Kbhvns Borgere, cand Hansen Studenternes Tak og endelig C Ploug ganske udmærket for Damerne. Kl. 10½ var Bordet forbi. Herrene hentede Deres damer og Konversationen varede i Pergolaen og den lille Sal indtil Kl. henved 12. – Da fremstod W. [C.] Holst som Prologus for et Tableau af mig, der forestillede Stormen paa Vestervold, udført af 46 Mandfolk og 3 Damer. Det gjorde overordentlig Lỹkke. ½ Time efter viste jeg det andet Tableau: Fredens Velsignelse der ogsaa fik meget Bifald.'
11.2.1859: 'leverede et Referat til Berlingske'.

No musical sources for these two tableaux (which were give only once) have yet been traced.

11.2.1859
The Masquerade (Maskaraden).

The 1859 restaging of L. Holberg's three-act comedy (*see* 12.12.1849) represents the second and last time when its intermedium (performed between Acts I and II) was mounted by Bournonville. According to his autographed notes in the 1849 répétiteur's copy (written with black ink) it was mounted this year in a choreographically completely new version and with the six (renamed) dances performed in a new sequence as follows:

(1) 'Contra-ça-ira!' (in 1849 entitled 'Contradands' and listed as score no. 4).
(2) 'Grand Menuet de la cour!' (in 1849 entitled 'Menuetto' and listed as score no. 5).
(3) 'Hanedandsen' (in 1849 listed as score no. 1).
(4) 'Den skotske Sextour' (in 1849 entitled 'Engelsk dands' and listed as score no. 2).
(5) 'Pas de trois gracieux' (in 1849 entitled 'Chiaconne' and listed as score no. 3).
(6) 'Kehraus!' (in 1849 entited 'Presto' and listed as score no. 6).

The 1859 version of the intermedium was restaged by L. Gade on 15.11.1868 with only minor if any choreographic changes, but was then performed to a score which included a new, additional prelude composed by Fr. Rung, who on this occasion also seems to have reorchestrated the music for the entire intermedium.

In his diary Bournonville noted about the 1859 production:

18.1. and 24.1.1859: 'Prøve paa Maskeraden'
4.2.: 'Prøve og Theaterprøve paa Maskeraden'
8.2: 'Prøve paa Maskeraden'
11.2.: 'Gratis-Forestilling i Det kongelige Theater Maskeraden [...] samme gode Stemning som igaar'.

The production received 14 performances, the last of which was given on 30.4.1864.

The musical material employed in 1859 was mainly the same as that used for the previous 1849 staging (now in DKKk, call nos. MA ms 2958, and KTB 258 b).

Musical sources:

Parts (incomplete). Ms. Copy. 3 vol.
vl I, vl II, cb.
Unsigned and undated [1859?]
[DKKk; KTB 258 b
According to pencilled notes in these (extra) parts, they seem to have been made in connection with the revised 1859 restaging of Bournonville's intermedium in Holberg's *The Masquerade*.

1.3.1859
Tarantella=Napolitana (uncredited) performed by A. and C. Healey (the Casino Theatre).

This (uncredited) dance was set to a new score by H. C. Lumbye and premièred as part of a performance, entitled *Tableau with Song and Dance (Tableau med Sang og Dands)*. It began with a duet by the Italian composer, V. Gabussi, named *I Pescatori* (sung by the actors H. Albrecht and T. Rasmussen), after which followed Bournonville's dance. It is presented on the poster as a work 'composed' (*componeret*) for the Healey sisters, but with no mention of Bournonville's name. The

first performance was given as part of a special charity performance for the actor, T. Rasmussen and his wife.

The *Tarantella=Napolitana* is almost certainly also identical with the later (uncredited) '*La Tarantella*' which was performed twice by the Healey sisters at Stockholm's Royal Theatre (Operahuset) on 17.5. and 18.5.1860. It was most probably also included in their many other, privately arranged tours to Norway (in April–May 1859 and the summer of 1861), Germany, England, Scotland, and Ireland (during the 1860s and early 1870s).

In his diary Bournonville noted about the creation of the dance:

22.1.1859: 'besøgt [...] [H. C.] Lumbÿ[e] om en [...] Tarantella'
7.2: 'componeret en nÿ Tarantella og indstuderet den'
22.2.: 'Dandseprøve paa Tarentellen i Casino'
23.2.: '(intet Engagement for Søstrene Healey!)'
28.2.: '<u>Kl 4</u> Prøve i Casino'
1.3.: 'Prøve paa Tarentellen i Casino'.

Tarantella=Napolitana reached a total of 6 performances at the Casino Theatre, the last of which was given on 20.3.1859. Bournonville did not attend any of these performances, and it appears that he never saw it performed on stage before an audience.

Autograph sources:

Choreographic note. Ms. Autograph. Ink. 1 p. (format unknown)
<u>Tarentella.</u>
Unsigned and undated [1859?]
[USNYp; Dance Collection (microfilm)]
This (undated) choreographic note includes the name of the English dancer 'Christine' [Healey]. It most probably refers to the *Tarantella=Napolitana* performed by her and her sister, Agnes Healey, at the Casino Theatre on 1.3.1859. This theory is supported by the fact that during C. Healey's later engagement at Copenhagen's Royal Theatre in the 1864–65 season she never appeared in the *Tarantella* of Act III (score no. 3) in Bournonville's three-act romantic ballet *Napoli or The Fisherman and His Bride*, nor did she dance in the Act III *Tarentella* of D.-F.-E. Auber's five-act opera *La Muette de Portici*. Consequently, the only possible identification of this choreographic note seems to be Bournonville's 1859 *Tarantella=Napolitana* at The Caino Theatre. However, because Bournonville here explicitly mentions a 'garçon' as partner of 'Christine' [Healey] the note can only be identified as his 1859 *Tarantella=Napolitana* if A. Healey had performed her part *en travestie*. No indications proving that this was the case have yet been found.

Bournonville's choreography in this note holds a certain similarity with his choreography for the opening section of the *Tarantella* in Act III of *Napoli or The Fisherman and His Bride* as danced by *Teresina* and *Gennaro* in today's performances of this ballet.

Musical sources:

Orchestral score (incomplete). Ms. Autograph (by H. C. Lumbye). Black ink. 1 vol. (25,5 × 34,4 cm)
H. C. <u>Lumbye:</u>/Tarantel/[...]/Tarantel
Signed and dated (on p. 1): 'par H: C: Lumbÿe/comp. 20. Februar 1859.'
[DKKk; C II, 34 (1930–31.82)]
This (incomplete) autographed orchestral score lacks the final 77 measures. It was purchased by DKKk on 3.7.1930 from Lumbye's grandson, the journalist T. Lumbye.

No répétiteur's copy and set of parts for *Tarantella=Napolitana* have yet been traced. The only complete musical source for this work is thus a printed piano score, first published by C. Plenge in Copenhagen in October 1859 as part of a series of Lumbye dances, entitled *H. C. Lumbyes Dandse for Pianoforte* (now in DKKk, call no. D 24).

20.3.1859
Ludovic.

The 1859 Copenhagen restaging of F. Hérold's two-act comic opera (completed by J.-F. Halévy and first performed at l'Opéra Comique in Paris on 16.5.1833) was originally projected by Bournonville on 30.10.1857 and reproposed by him on 20.1.1858. It is not included in his handwritten list of his stagings of operas and plays, written c.1872 (*see* Additional Sources), nor in the printed survey of his works in his memoirs *My Theatre Life* (p. 409). About the staging, which represents the first and only time this opera was mounted with Bournonville's mise-en-scène, he noted in his diary:

22.2.1859: 'Læseprøve paa Ludovic'
23.2.: 'skrevet Scene=Arrangement til Ludovic'
24.2.: 'Decorationprøve paa Ludovic'
1.3.: 'Arrangementprøve paa Ludovic'
3.3.: 'Prøve paa Ludovic'
11.3.: 'Ludovic prøvet ved Höedt'
16.3.: 'bivaanet Generalprøven paa Ludovic'.

Bournonville was not present on the opening night, but attended the opera's second performance on 24.3.1859 about which he noted in the diary:

'I Theatret, seet og hørt Ludovic (uinteressant.)'.

The 1859 production received 4 performances, the last of which was given on 5.4.1859.

Musical sources:

Printed orchestral score. 1 vol. 316 pp. of which two are blank (34,5 × 26 cm)
Ludovic./Partitur/[…]/LUDOVIC/Opéra Comique/EN 2 ACTES /[…]/Musique de/F. HÉROLD ET F. HALÉVY
Paris, M. Schlesinger, pl. no. M. S. 1426 [1833]
[DKKk; U 6 (KTA 307)
This French orchestral score contains Th. Overskou's Danish translation (written with red ink) and was used for all performances of *Ludovic* in Copenhagen since its première there on 24.5.1834 and throughout Bournonville's lifetime.

No répétiteur's copy for *Ludovic* has yet been traced

Parts. Ms. Copy. 32 vol.
4 vl I, 3 vl II, 2 vla, 4 vlc e cb, fl 1/2, ob 1/2, cl 1/2, fag 1/2, cor 1/2/ 3/4, tr 1/2, trb 1/2/3, timp, gong. 48 vocal parts.
Unsigned and undated [1834]
[DKKk; KTA 307
This set of parts dates from the 1834 Copenhagen première of *Ludovic* and was used for all performances of it there during Bournonville's lifetime.

31.3.1859
Polonaise (uncredited) performed by A. and C. Healey (the Casino Theatre).

This (uncredited) dance was the last that Bournonville choreographed for the Healey sisters during their 1859 engagement at the Casino Theatre. On the poster it is described as a work 'composed' (*componeret*) for the Healeys, but without any mention of Bournonville's name. It was mounted as part of a special charity performance for the actor, A. Smidth, and was performed only once at the Casino Theatre.

The dance is almost certainly identical with the later (uncredited) *'Pas de Polonaise'*, performed by the Healey sisters at Stockholm's Royal Theatre (Operahuset) on 18.5.1860. The following year it was again performed by them in Copenhagen, but then at Folketheatret (on 24.2., 25.2., and 26.2.1861), with the (uncredited) title *La Polonaise*. The dance was most probably also included in the many later, privately arranged tours of the Healeys to Norway (April–May 1859 and the summer of 1861), Germany, England, Scotland, and Ireland (during the 1860s and early 1870s).

In his diary Bournonville noted about his 1859 *Polonaise* and its Copenhagen première:

22.1.1859: 'besøgt […] [H. C.] Lumbÿ[e] om en Polonaise'
3.3.: 'Aftenen hjemme, componeret og skrevet'
4.3.: 'Lection og Begÿndelse paa Lumbyes Polonaise'
5.3.: 'skrevet og componeret'
7.3.: 'Lection og Indstudering med Healey's […] skrevet og componeret'
8.3.: 'Lection og fuldendt Polonaisen for Healey's'
26.3.: 'besørget adskilligt for Søstrene Healeÿ'
29.3.: 'Prøve i Casino'
30.3.: 'Prøve paa Polonaisen i Casino'
31.3.: 'Smiths Benefice i Casino. Søstrene Healey dandsede for sidste Gang En Polonaise af min Composition og vandt meget Bifald'.

Musical sources:

Orchestral score. Ms. Autograph (by H. C. Lumbye). Black ink. 1 vol. 10 pp. (25,5 × 34 cm)
H. C. Lumbye:/La Polonaise/[…]/372/La Polonaise
Signed and dated (on p. 1): 'par H: C: Lumbÿe/comp: d. 2.den Martz/1859.'
[DKKk; C II, 34 (1944–45.65a)
This autographed orchestral score was part of the music archive of the Tivoli Gardens before it was transferred to DKKk in 1944.

No original répétiteur's copy and set of parts for Lumbye's 1859 *Polonaise* have yet been traced. However, a much later set of parts (arranged, signed and dated: 'Marts 1944 [B.] Bjerregaard-Jensen') is now in the music archive of the Tivoli Gardens (call no. 1070).

1.4.1859
The Treasure of Claus Rigmand (Claus Rigmands Skat).

The 1859 première of J. M. Thiele's five-act play was set to music by N. W. Gade and mounted with Bournonville's mise-en-scène and choreography. However, this work is not included in Bournonville's handwritten list of his stagings of operas and plays, written c.1872 (*see* Additional Sources), nor in the printed survey of his works in his memoirs *My Theatre Life* (p. 408). His dances for it included:

(1) A *Procession* in Act V, performed during the chorus entitled «Thi bære vi Dig Mai i bÿ!».
(2) A *Minuet* in the same act, performed by a corps de ballet during the so-called 'Maisang' («Her kommer vi Karle og Piger smaa») sung by a chorus.

These dances represent the last time Bournonville ever choreographed to Gade's music. In his diary he noted about the staging and its first two performances:

17.3.1859: 'Læst Claus Rigmands Skat af [J. M.] Thiele'
29.3.: 'Arrangement paa Claus Rigmands Skat'
31.3.: 'Generalprøve paa Claus Rigmands Skat'
1.4.: 'Første Forestilling af Thieles Genrestÿkke Claus Rigmands Skat. Det er ingen Comedie altsaa lidt kjedeligt, gjorde maadelig Lÿkke'
6.4.: 'Claus Rigmand […] gik udmærket godt'.

The Treasure of Claus Rigmand reached a total of 7 performances, the last of which was given on 25.4.1859.

Musical sources:

Orchestral score, Ms. Autograph (by N. W. Gade). Black ink. 1 vol. 18 pp. of which two are blank (25,1 × 33,8 cm)
471/Klaus Rigmands Skat./Partitur./471./[…]/'Klaus Rigmands Skat'/Skuespil i fem Acter./Partitur.
Signed and dated (on p. 16) 'G-A-D-E [musical anagram]/18. Martz/1859.'
[DKKk; C II, 108 (KTA 471)

Répétiteur's copy. Ms. Copy. Black ink. 1 vol. 4 pp. of which one is blank (34,1 × 25,2 cm)
2a. Klaus Rigmands Skat A 471/[…]/Repetiteurstemme/til/Klaus Rigmands Skat
Unsigned and undated [1859]
[DKKk; MA ms 2911 (3) (KTA 471)
This répétiteur's copy contains Gade's music for the *Minuet* in Act V, performed by a corps de ballet during the so-called 'Maisang med Dands' («Her kommer vi Karle og Piger smaa»). It also includes Bournonville's autographed choreographic numbers ('1–7', written with black ink) that seem to refer to his (not yet traced) separate notation of this dance, and which he most probably wrote during March 1859. The music is included on pp. 31–34 in a volume that also contains the répétiteur's copies for three other operas, mounted at Copenhagen's Royal Theatre between 1860 and 1863.

Parts. Ms. Copy. 20 vol.
2 vl I, 2 vl II, vla, 2 vlc e cb, fl 1/2, ob 1/2, cl 1/2, fag 1/2, cor 1/2, tr 1/2, cnt. 44 vocal parts.
Unsigned and undated [1859]
[DKKk; KTA 471

15.4.1859
Lucrezia Borgia.
G. Donizetti's melodrama in two acts and a prologue (premièred at Milan's Teatro alla Scala on 26.12.1833) was performed for the first time in Copenhagen by a foreign opera company at the Court Theatre on 11.2.1842 (then sung in Italian), and reached a total of more than 60 performances there until the 1853–54 season. The 1859 Danish staging at the Royal Theatre had been projected by Bournonville on 30.10.1857 and was reproposed by him on 20.1.1858. It represents the first and only time this work was mounted at Copenhagen's Royal Theatre. The production, which is not included in Bournonville's handwritten list of his stagings of operas and plays, written c.1872 (*see* Additional Sources), is, however, mentioned in the printed survey of his works in his memoirs *My Theatre Life* (p. 409). In his diary he noted about his mise-en-scène and the première of Donizetti's melodrama:

28.1.1859: 'skrevet paa Scene=Arrangementet til Lucretia [*sic*] Borgia'
31.3.: 'Claveerprøve paa Lucretia'
1.4.: 'Arrangementprøve paa Lucretia'

4.4.: 'skrevet, Arrangementprøve paa Lucretia Borgia 5–8'
5.4.: 'skrevet og arrangeret. Kl 10. Prøve paa Lucretia, der gik ind formedelst Sygdom'
7.4.: '1.ste Theaterprøve paa Lucretia'
12.4.: 'Theaterprøve paa Lucretia Borgia (gik mindre godt.)'
14.4.: 'Generalprøve paa Lucretia Borgia, ret godt. M.me [V. L. T.] Fossum ÿderst ubehagelig […] Efter Theatret Prøve paa Belysningen til Lucretia færdig Kl 12'
15.4.: 'Arrangement paa Lucrezia, der gik om Aftenen, særdeles godt og med udeelt Bifald'.

The 1859 production was rehearsed again by Bournonville on 6.10.1859 and restaged by him for the last time on 21.9. 1860, in this way reaching a total of 8 performances (the last of which was given on 3.11.1866).

Autograph sources:

Manuscript mise-en-scène. Ms. Autograph. Brown ink and pencil. 6 pp. (22,8 × 18 cm)
Scene = Arrangement til Operaen/Lucrezia Borgia
Unsigned and undated [Written according to the diary on 28.1. 1859]
[SSm; Daniel Fryklunds samling no. 135

Musical sources:

Orchestral score. Ms. Copy. Brown and black ink. 4 vol. Act I 224 pp. of which two are blank, Act II 287 pp. of which two are blank, Act III 274 pp. of which one is blank, 'Anhang' (Act I, score nos. 1 and 4, Act II, Finale, Act III, score nos. 6, 8, and 9) 60 pp. of which one is blank (24,2 × 31,5 cm with several variants)
Lucrezia Borgia./Partitur./1.ste Act./[…]/Lucrezia Borgia./Oper in 3 Acten,/v Donizetti./Förste Akt./[…]/2.den Act./[…]/3.die Act./[…]/469/Anhang/til/Lucrezia Borgia./No. 469.
Unsigned and undated [c.1859]
[DKKK; C I, 236 n (KTA 469)
This manuscript orchestral score is a German (or Austrian?) copy that dates from the première of *Lucrezia Borgia* at Copenhagen's Royal Theatre on 15.4.1859. In contains several musical insertions and conductor's notes, most of which are written by the conductor, F. Gläser.

No répétiteur's copy for *Lucrezia Borgia* has yet been traced.

Parts. Ms. Copy. 35 vol.
4 vl I, 3 vl II, 2 vla, 4 vlc e cb, fl 1/2, ob 1/2, cl 1/2, fag 1/2, cor 1/2/ 3/4, tr 1/2, trb 1/2/3, timp, gr cassa, piatti, tri, arpa. 60 vocal parts.
Unsigned and undated [1859]
[DKKk; KTA 469

13.5.1859
The Mountain Hut, or Twenty Years (Fjeldstuen eller Tyve Aar).
This pantomimic ballet is divided into three tableaux consisting of seven, four, and fourteen music numbers respectively. It represents the second and last ballet Bournonville choreographed in the Norwegian spheres and was mainly drawn from inspirations received from his reading of the Norwegian writer B. Björnson's *Norske Bondefortællinger* (1856), in particular the novel *Synnöve Solbakken* (first published in Christiania, i.e. Oslo, in 1857).

The music was composed by two of the youngest Danish composers of the time, A. Winding (a student of N. W. Gade), and E. Hartmann (son of I. P. E. Hartmann). Winding wrote the complete music of the first tableau, and Hartmann most of the score for the second and third tableaux.

Moreover, Hartmann's father, I. P. E. Hartmann, clearly seems (according to the autographed score and E. Hartmann's musical drafts for this ballet) to have orchestrated at least 5 of the 14 numbers in the ballet's third tableau (score nos. 7–11). Of these, score no. 9 even appears to have been actually composed by I. P. E. Hartmann.

Furthermore, Winding clearly also wrote sections of the music for the third tableau. This is clear from the earliest autographed orchestral score for *The Mountain Hut, or Twenty Years*, according to which his contributions to the third tableau are the so-called *Danse sauvage* (performed by *Asta* in scene 8, score no. 12) and nearly all of the music for score no. 13 (scene 9). The main musical motif for the *Danse sauvage* had earlier been employed by Winding in his music for the *Reel* in the ballet's first tableau (scene 7, score no. 8). This motif, in turn, appears to be based on a refrain (named «Huldre Kvæe») in the Norwegian folk-song, entitled 'Huldre aa en Elland' (first published by L. M. Lindeman in his *Ældre og nyere Norske Fjeldmelodier*, Andet Hefte, no. 71, Christiania, 1853).

Finally, according to several pencilled autographed notes by N. W. Gade (inserted in Winding's earliest autographed score for the ballet's first tableau), Gade also contributed to this ballet by making numerous corrections and additions to Winding's orchestration. These changes were all followed in the final manuscript copy of the ballet's full orchestral score, which was used at its 1859 première.

The Mountain Hut, or Twenty Years was restaged twice by Bournonville in Copenhagen on 9.10.1865 (that year reduced to only two acts) and on 27.3.1877. Each of these productions was mounted in a thoroughly revised version.

In his diary Bournonville noted about the ballet's creation and 1859 première:

8.1.1858: 'læst i Synnøve Solbakken, hvori der er ypperlige Characteer=Skildringer'
22.12.: 'arrangeret endeel til en nÿ Ballet. Musiken skal skrives af Emil Hartmann og A Winning [i.e. Winding]'
23.12.: 'Eftermiddag skrevet paa en nÿ Ballet'
24.12.: 'Op Kl 7½, skrevet [...] skrevet 1.ste Akt færdig' [...] Jeg skrev lidt paa min nÿ Ballet'
26.12.: 'skrevet paa min nÿ Ballet [...] fuldendt Programmet til Fjeldstuen eller Tyve Aar, læst det for Famillien'
27.12.: 'skrevet og arrangeret'
28.12.: 'reenskrevet Programmet til min nÿ Ballet'
29.12.: 'Op Kl 7½, skrevet Programmet færdigt [...] arbeidet 1.ste Gang med Emil Hartmann, afgivet mit Program til Copien'
11.1.1859: 'læst Fjeldstuen for nogle af Rollerne'
12.1.: 'arbeidet med E Hartmann, componeret'
14.1.: 'arbeidet med gl [I. P. E.] Hartmann og modtaget god Musik af Winding'
16.1.: 'arbeidet med E Hartmann og besøgt Theatermaler [C. F.] Christensen' [...] skrevet og componeret'
21.1.: 'arbeidet med Winning [*sic*]'
25.1.: 'arbeidet med Winding, componeret paa min nÿ Ballet, i mit Værelse paa Theatret'
26.1.: '1.ste indstudering paa Fjeldstuen'
28.1.: 'arbeidet med Winning [...] componeret paa Fjeldstuen'
29.1.: '2.den Indstudering paa Fjeldstuen'
31.1.: 'componeret'
1.2.: '3.die Indstudering paa Fjeldstuen'
2.2.: 'arbeidet med E Hartmann. Aftenen hjemme componeret'
3.2: '4.de Indstudering paa Fjeldstuen'
4.2.: 'arbeidet med Winding'
5.2.: '5.te Indstudering paa Fjeldstuen'

8.2.: 'Prøve paa Fjeldsten'
14.2.: 'hjemme den hele Dag, læste og componerede'
15.2.: '6.te Indstudering paa Fjeldstuen'
16.2.: 'Prøve paa det færdige i Fjeldstuen i Nærværelse af de to unge Componister'
17.2.: 'Skrevet i mit Kammer paa Theatret og componeret to Dandse til min nÿ Ballet'
18.2.: 'Arbeidet med E Hartmann'
192.: '7.de Indstudering paa Fjeldstuen (Menuet og Reel)'
21.2.: 'Prøve Repetition paa Fjeldstuen [...] skrevet og componeret'
22.2.: 'arbeidet med Vinding [...] Aftenen hjemme, skrevet og componeret'
23.2.: '8.de Indstudering paa Fjeldstuen (Vuggesangen.)'
27.2.: 'Composition'
2.3.: '9.de Indstudering paa Fjeldstuen'
3.3.: 'componeret og skrevet'
4.3.: '10.de Indstudering paa Fjeldstuen'
5.3.: 'arbeidet med Emil Hartmann'
7.3.: 'Repetition paa Fjeldstuen [...] skrevet og componeret'
9.3.: 'Prøve paa 1.ste Act af Fjeldstuen 11.e Indstudering'
10.3.: 'Prøve paa 2.det Tableau af Fjeldstuen, skrevet og arrangeret. Besøg hos unge Hartmann'
11.3.: 'arrangeret Decorations=Regien for [...] Fjeldstuen, confereret med Theatermaler Christensen'
13.3.: 'componeret lidt'
15.3.: 'Prøve paa Fjeldstuen'
21.3. and 22.3.: 'arbeidet med Hartmann'
25.3.: 'arbeidet med Winding'
27.3.: 'Om Eftermiddagen skrevet og componeret'
28.3. and 29.3.: 'Indstudering paa Fjeldstuen'
30.3.: 'Repetition paa Fjeldstuen'
6.4.: 'arbeidet med Winding [...] Prøve-Repetition paa Fjeldstuen'
8.4.: 'Indstudering til M.e [L.] Stillmann'
11.4.: 'Kl 6 Prøve og Indstudering pa Fjeldstuen'
13.4.: 'Aftenen hjemme, skrevet og componeret'
14.4.: 'skrevet og arrangeret [...] Kl 6 Indstudering paa Fjeldstuen'
15.4.: 'Op Kl 6, skrevet og arrangeret [...] Indstudering paa Fjeldstuen (Repetition)'
20.4.: 'arrangeret og componeret [...] Prøve paa Fjeldstuen. – Eftermiddagen hjemme skrevet og componeret'
21.4.: 'skrevet og arrangeret [...] besøgt [J. F.] Fröhlich!!!'
22.4.: 'skrevet og arrangeret'
23.4.: 'Prøve paa Fjeldstuen'
24.5. and 25.5.: 'skrevet og arrangeret'
26.4.: 'indstuderet den sidste Scene af Fjeldstuen'
27.4.: 'sidste Indstudering af Fjeldstuen, som det sÿnes vellÿkket'
28.4.: 'lille Prøve med [W. E.] Funck'
29.4.: 'skrevet og arrangeret [...] lille Prøve'
3.5.: 'skrevet og arrangeret. 1.ste Arrangementprøve paa Fjeldstuen fra 10–2 1/2'
4.5.: 'Jeg prøvede [...] om Eftermiddagen for Funcks Skyld'
5.5.: 'skrevet og arrangeret. Prøve paa Theatret fra 10-12 paa 1.ste og 3.die Act af Balletten, afgivet Programmet til Trykken'
6.5.: 'skrevet og arrangeret. Theaterprøve Kl 10, og lille Prøve paa Rollerne Kl 11–12'
7.5.: 'Prøve paaa hele Balletten Kl 10 oppe i Salen for Directionen, H. C. Andersen og [F.] Høedt. Det gik meget smukt. Correcturprøve paa endeel af Musiken [...] Eftermiddagen hjemme og i nedtrykt Humeur, besørgeet adskilligt paa Theatret'
9.5.: 'skrevet og arrangeret [...] Prøve paa 1.te og 2.den Akt af Balletten med Orchester (adskillige Gjenvordigheder med Musiken)'
10.5.: 'lille Prøve Kl 11. Theaterprøve paa 2.den og 3.die Akt. Det gik bedre idag'
11.5.: 'Om Eftermiddagen Kl 7 Generalprøve paa Fjeldstuen der ligeledes gik udmærket godt'
12.5.: 'Theaterprøve paa Fjeldstuen'
13.5.: 'I Theatret [...] den første Forestilling af min nÿ Ballet Fjeldstuen eller Tÿve Aar, der gik udmærket godt og med et storartet Bifald. Alle gratulerede os og vi havde atter Aarsag at takke Gud for al hans Naade og Miskundhed'
14.5.: 'Bladene omtalte Balletten paa den meest glimrende Maade'

15.5.: 'Festforestilling i Anledning af den ægÿptiske Prindses Mehemed Ali Pascha's Nærværelse [...] <u>Fjeldstuen</u> der gjorde overordentlig Lÿkke ligesom første Gang'
16.5.: '3.die Forestilling af Balletten, der gik udmærket godt og
gjorde stor Lÿkke'.

The 1859 version of *The Mountain Hut, or Twenty Years* received 14 performances (the last given on 29.12.1860), and
the ballet as such reached a total of 28 performances during
Bournonville's lifetime, the last of which took place on 13.5.
1878.

Autograph sources:

Manuscript scenario. Ms. Autograph. Brown ink. 1 vol. 32 pp. (22,1
× 18 cm)
<u>Fjeldstuen</u>/<u>Ballet af Bournonville.</u>/[...]/Fjeldstuen eller Tÿve Aar/
Pantomimisk Ballet i 3 Tabelauer/<u>af</u>/August Bournonville/Musi-
ken af E Hartmann og A Winding/<u>1858.</u>
Signed and dated: 'Fredensborg den 26.e Decbr 1858.' [Written according to the diary on 23.12., 24.12., and 26.12.1858]
[DKKk; NKS 3285 4° 2 F

Production note. Ms. Autograph. Brown ink. 1 p. (20,8 × 16,6 cm)
<u>Fjeldstuen eller Tÿve Aar.</u>
Unsigned and undated [1859]
[DKKkt; F.M. (Ballet, læg F)

Musical sources:

Musical draft. Ms. Autograph (by E. Hartmann). Brown ink. 4 pp.
(34,8 × 29,7 cm)
No. 4. (3die 4de og 5te Scene)
Signed (on p. 1): 'Emil Hartmann', undated [c. January–February
1859]
[DKKk; MA ms 2721 (1) (KTB 281)
This autographed manuscript for two violins contains E. Hartmann's
first draft for what became the music for the second tableau, score
no. 4 (i.e. scenes 3 and 4) in the 1859 première of *The Mountain Hut,
or Twenty Years*. It also includes Hartmann's autographed notes (written with brown ink) which describe (in more general terms) the
dramatic action.

Musical draft. Ms. Autograph (by E. Hartmann). Brown ink. 2 pp.
(34,9 × 29,6 cm)
(Fortsættelse af No. 4 i 2den Act)/<u>2 Act. 5te Scene</u>.
Unsigned and undated [c. January–February 1859]
[DKKk; MA ms 2721 (2) (KTB 281)
This autographed manuscript for two violins contains E. Hartmann's
first draft for what at the 1859 première of *The Mountain Hut, or
Twenty Years* became the music for the end of score no. 4 in the second tableau (i.e. scene 5). The manuscript also includes Bournonville's autographed notes (written with brown ink) which describe in
fine detail the mime performed during this scene.

Musical draft. Ms. Autograph (by E. Hartmann). Brown ink. 4 pp.
(29,7 × 35 cm)
4de Scene
Unsigned and undated [c. January–February 1859]
[DKKk; MA ms 2721 (3) (KTB 281)
This autographed manuscript for two violins contains E. Hartmann's
first draft for what became the music for the third tableau, score no.
4 (i.e. scene 4) at the 1859 première of *The Mountain Hut, or Twenty
Years*. The manuscript also includes Bournonville's autographed
notes (written with brown ink) which describe in fine detail the
mime and the dramatic action during this scene.

Musical draft. Ms. Autograph (by E. Hartmann). Brown ink. 8 pp. of
which one is blank (29,7 × 35 cm with variants)

3die Act No. 5
Unsigned and undated [c. January–February 1859]
[DKKk; MA ms 2721 (4) (KTB 281)
This autographed manuscript for two violins contains E. Hartmann's
first draft for what became the music for the third tableau, score no.
5 (i.e. scene 5 and the beginning of scene 6) in *The Mountain Hut, or
Twenty Years* at its 1859 première. It also includes Hartmann's autographed notes (written with brown ink) which describe in fine detail
the mime and the dramatic action performed during these scenes.

Musical draft. Ms. Autograph (by E. Hartmann). Brown ink. 4 pp. of
which one is blank (29,7 × 35 cm)
Anden Act. No 11 (Duet imellem Ingrid og Erik.)/[...]/No. 12
(Menuet)/[...]/No. 13
[DKKk; MA ms 2721 (5) (KTB 281)
This autographed manuscript for two violins contains E. Hartmann's
first draft for what became the music in the third tableau, score nos.
6–7, and the beginning of no. 8 (i.e. scene 6 and the beginning of
scene 7) of *The Mountain Hut, or Twenty Years* at its 1859 première.
The manuscript also includes Bournonville's and Hartmann's autographed notes (written with brown ink) which describe in fine detail
the mime and the dramatic action performed during these scenes.

Musical draft. Ms. Autograph (by I. P. E. Hartmann). Brown ink. 4
pp. (35,2 × 29,8 cm)
Allegro non troppo. – 8.de Scene
Unsigned and undated [c. January–February 1859]
[DKKk; MA ms 2721 (6) (KTB 281)
This manuscript for two violins seems to represent the first draft for
what became the music for the third tableau, score no. 9 (i.e. scene
8) in the 1859 première of *The Mountain Hut, or Twenty Years*. The fact
that the music is here written by E. Hartmann's father, I. P. E.
Hartmann, seems to indicate that he was the actual composer of it.

Orchestral score (*First tableau*). Ms. Autograph (by A. Winding and
N. W. Gade). 1 vol. Black ink and pencil. 166 pp. of which one is
blank (28,5 × 34,2 cm)
15/Fjeldstuen 1ste Akt./af/Aug. Winding.
Signed (on the front cover): 'Aug. Winding', dated (on p. 165) 'd.
22de April 18[59]'
[DKKk; C II, 15 (1943–44.592)
Winding's autographed orchestral score contains numerous pencilled corrections and additions, written by another hand throughout
the volume. According to an autographed pencilled note on p. 1
(reading 'Blyantrettelser el. Tilføjelser af N. W. Gade') they were
made by Winding's music teacher, N. W. Gade. These corrections
and additions were all inserted in the later manuscript copy of Winding's score, and from which the ballet was actually performed. Winding's autographed score was originally part of the music library of
the Danish Music Academy (Det kgl. Danske Musikkonservatorium),
but was dontated to DKKk on 15.3.1944. According to a pencilled
note on p. 165 the first tableau played for a total of 37 minutes.

Orchestral score (*Second and third tableau*). Ms. Autograph (by E.
Hartmann, I. P. E Hartmann, and A. Winding). Black and brown ink.
1 vol. 226 pp. of which one is blank (29,7 × 35 cm with minor variants)
[Untitled]
Signed (on p. 1): 'Emil Hartmann.', (p. 206) 'August Winding/April
1859. –'
[DKKk; Emil Hartmanns Samling No. 15 (1929–30.998)
This autographed orchestral score contains the complete music for
the second and third tableaux of *The Mountain Hut, or Twenty Years*.
The music for the second tableau (score nos. 1–5 (pp. 1–80)), and
that for the third tableau, (score nos. 1–6, the end of score no. 13,
and score no. 14 (pp. 81–144 and 210–226)) are E. Hartmann's autographs. Moreover, the pages containing the music for score nos. 7–
11 (pp. 145–198) in the third tableau is here written in I. P. E.
Hartmann's hand, while that for score no. 12 (pp. 199–206) is signed
and dated by A. Winding. The score was originally E. Hartmann's
property, but was donated to DKKk by his heirs on 13.11.1929.

Orchestral score. Ms. Copy. Black ink. 2 vol. 1st tableau 202 pp. of which two are blank, 2nd and 3rd tableau 200 pp. (28,7 × 34,2 cm with several variants)
281/Fjeldstuen./I./[...]/Fjeldstuen/Ballet i 3 Tableauer af Bournonville/med Musik/af/August Winding og Emil Hartmann./1.ste Tableau./Mai 1859./[...]/Fjeldstuen./2.den Act/Musiken af/Emil Hartmann
Unsigned and dated (vol I, p. 1): 'Mai 1859.'
[DKKk; C II, 122 m (KTB 281)
In the second volume of this manuscript orchestral score numerous musical cuts occur. They were most probably made in connection with Bournonville's later revised stagings of *The Mountain Hut, or Twenty Years* on 9.10.1865 and 27.3.1877. This theory is supported by the fact that the pages, which in 1859 were paginated '37–42', '47–50', '71–74', '87–104', '111–114', '145–148', and '149–176', were later either completely omitted, or transferred to other places in this score, or were replaced with new, heavily revised insertions. It is not possible from this score to establish exactly which changes were made for each of Bournonville's two restagings of this ballet.

Répétiteur's copy. Ms. Copy. Black ink. 1 vol. 130 pp. (33,6 × 25,3 cm with minor variants)
2/B. 281/Fjeldstuen./Ballet i 3 Tableauer/1859./[...]/Fjeldstuen eller tyve Aar./Ballet i 3 Tableauer/af/August Bournonville./Musiken af Aug. Vinding og Emil Hartmann./1859.
Unsigned and dated (on the front cover and p. 1): '1859.'
[DKKk; MA ms 2977 (KTB 281 (1))
This répétiteur's contains several autographed notes by Bournonville (written with brown ink). They describe in fine detail the dramatic action and the mime in the first tableau, scenes 1–4 and 7 (i.e. score nos. 1, 2, 5, and parts of no. 12), the second tableau, scenes 3–4 (i.e. parts of score no. 4), and the whole of score no. 4), and the third tableau, scenes 6–8 (i.e. score nos. 7–12). Moreover, his many autographed choreographic numbers in this volume (written with black ink) refer to his later separate notations of the complete ballet, written (according to his diary) in connection with the 1865 and 1877 restagings. Finally, his autographed note on p. 85 (reading: 'NB Changement og lille Mellemscene') clearly indicates that this répétiteur's copy also served in his preparations for the last restaging of this ballet, for which a second, heavily revised répétiteur's copy was made (*see* 27.3.1877).

Parts. Ms. Copy. 35 + 3 vol.
4 vl I, 3 vl II, 2 vla, 3 vlc e cb, fl 1/2, ob 1/2, cl 1/2, fag 1/2, cor 1/2/3/4, tr 1/2/3, trb 1/2/3, tuba, timp, gr cassa, piatti, tri. On stage: tr, Tcor, bells.
Unsigend and undated [1859]
[DKKk; KTB 281
This set of parts was used for all performances of *The Mountain Hut, or Twenty Years* in Copenahgen (including the two revised restagings in 1865 and 1877).

Other sources:

Two sketches by C. F. Christensen for the décor of the second tableau. Pencil (20,3 × 14,8 cm)
Fjeldstuen/[...]/Klippe Partie til Fjeldstuen
Unsigned and undated [1859]
[DKKt; C. F. Christensens dekorationsudkast
These sketches of two set pieces in *The Mountain Hut, or Twenty Years* are drawn on each side of the paper and show a Norwegian mountain hut and part of a mountain.

Costume drawing by E. Lehmann. Pencil and water colours (20 × 15,9 cm)
Jon Grimstad/Hr. Füssel jun.
Unsigned and undated [c.1859]
[DKKt; Kostumetegninger (Lehmann)
This drawing shows the costume worn by *Jon Grimstad* in the first tableau of *The Mountain Hut, or Twenty Years* (performed by G. Ad. Füssel).

Costume drawing by E. Lehmann. Pencil and water colours (17 × 20 cm)
(Hr Hoppensach)/1 Act./Balletten Fjældstuen.
Unsigned and undated [c.1859]
[SSm; Daniel Fryklunds samling no. 258 (F 1323 b)
This drawing shows the costume worn by *Guldbrand Skaffer* in the first tableau of *The Mountain Hut, or Twenty Years* (performed by F. Hoppensach).

Costume drawing by E. Lehmann. Pencil and water colours (19,9 × 16,5 cm)
Sigrid
Unsigned and undated [c.1859]
[DKKkt; Kostumetegninger (Lehmann)
This drawing shows the costume worn by *Sigrid* in the first tableau(?) of *The Mountain Hut, or Twenty Years* (performed by N. Møller).

Costume drawing by E. Lehmann. Pencil and water colours (16,5 × 20 cm)
Svend (1 Acte)/(Hr Gade/Balletten Fjældstuen.
Unsigned and undated [c.1859]
[SSm; Daniel Fryklunds samling no. 257 (F 1323 c)
This drawing shows the costume worn by *Svend* in the first tableau of *The Mountain Hut, or Twenty Years* (performed by L. Gade).

Costume drawing by E. Lehmann. Pencil and water colours (20 × 16 cm)
Christoffer (Hr. Füssel)
Unsigned and undated [c.1859]
[DKKkt; Kostumetegninger (Lehmann)
This drawing shows the costume worn by *Christoffer* in the first tableau of *The Mountain Hut, or Twenty Years* (performed by Gott. A. Füssel).

Costume drawing by E. Lehmann. Pencil and water colours (19,9 × 16,1 cm)
Svend (2 Acte) Gade
Unsigned and undated [c.1859]
[DKKkt; Kostumetegninger (Lehmann)
This drawing shows the costume worn by *Svend* in the second and third tableaux of *The Mountain Hut, or Twenty Years* (performed by L. Gade).

Costume drawing by E. Lehmann. Pencil and water colours (16,5 × 20 cm)
Asta/Balletten: Fjældstuen.
Unsigned and undated [c.1859]
[SSm; Daniel Fryklunds samling no. 259 (F 1323 a)
This drawing shows the costume worn by *Asta* in the second and third tableaux of *The Mountain Hut, or Twenty Years* (performed by L. Stillmann).

Costume drawing by E. Lehmann. Pencil and water colours (20,3 × 15,9 cm)
Guldbr – 2 Act/Hoppensach
Unsigned and undated [c.1859]
[DKKkt; Kostumetegninger (Lehmann)
This drawing shows the costume worn *Guldbrand Skaffer* in the second and third tableaux of *The Mountain Hut, or Twenty Years* (performed by F. Hoppensach).

Printed sources:

Printed scenario. 1 vol. 23 pp. (19,4 × 12,4 cm)
Fjeldstuen eller Tyve Aar./Pantomimisk Ballet i 3 Tableauer/af/August Bournonville./Musiken af August Vinding og Emil Hartmann.
Kjøbenhavn, J. H. Schubothe/Biano Luno/F. S. Muhle, 1859
[DKKk; 17, – 175 8°

12.5.1859

Le Domino noir (Den sorte Domino).

The 1859 Copenhagen restaging of D.-F.-E. Auber's three-act comic opera (*see also* 29.1.1839) was originally projected by Bournonville on 30.10.1857 and reproposed by him on 20.1. 1858. Only parts were mounted by him, since this year he only gave personal stage instructions to his daughter, the alto Charlotte Bournonville, who made her début performance at Copenhagen's Royal Theatre in the rôle of *Angèle*.

The restaging is not mentioned in Bournonville's hand-written list of his stagings of operas and plays, written c.1872 (*see* Additional Sources), but is included in the printed list of his works in his memoirs *My Theatre Life* (p. 410). In his diary he noted about the 1859 production and the début of his daughter:

13.2.1859: 'Brev til Justitsraad [H. C.] Christensen i Anledning af Charlottes Ønske at søge
Engagement ved den danske Scene. Svar foreløbigt'
18.2.: 'virket endeel for Charlotte og faaet Sagen ret godt igang [...] Brev fra Charlotte. Svar tilbage med gode Forhaabninger'
20.2.: 'Breve til Justitsraad Christensen i Anledning af Charlotte'
21.2.: 'Conference med Christensen'
23.2.: 'Brev fra [...] Charlotte'
7.3.: 'Læst med Charlotte'
24.3.: 'Charlotte 1.ste Claveerprøve paa 'Den sorte Domino''
26.3.: '(Charlotte 3.e Claveerprøve)'
19.4.: 'Charlotte havde været paa to meget heldige Prøver'
24.4.: 'Charlotte Prøve paa Den sorte Domino'
1.5.: 'Charlottes første fuldstændige Prøve var gaaet udmærket godt'
4.5.: 'Charlotte forkjölet og ude af stand til at holde Generalprøve eller til at debutere imorgen'
11.5.: 'overværet Generalprøve paa Den sorte Domino der gik udmærket godt og hvori Charlotte sang og spillede fortrinligt'
12.5.: 'Dagen hengik med Forberedelser til Charlottes Debüt. Den sorte Domino, gik fortrinligt og Charlotte præsterede berömmeligt baade som Sangerinde og Skuespillerinde. Hun nød ogsaa velfortjent Bifald – men jeg maatte med stor Bitterhed erfare at Stemningen i Publicum ikke var til hendes Gunst, hun maatte kæmpe sig frem og lidt mindre Dygtighed og Talent hos hende, saa havde man gjort hende Fortræd! Jeg følte med Smerte at det er <u>mine</u> gamle Forfølgere som ad denne Vei ville mig tillivs. Imidlertid gik Alt godt og jeg havde Aarsag at takke Gud, der efter sin uransagelige Viisdom styrer vor Skjæbne [erased:] tilmaaler mig Denne ydre Verdens Gaver med knap Haand. Charlotte var ved godt Mod og [F.] <u>Høedt</u>, der har viist sig som en sand Ven baade i Raad og Daad, tilbragte Aftenen med os'.

C. Bournonville played *Angèle* 7 times in *Le Domino noir*, the last time on 29.3.1860.

Musical sources:

Printed orchestral score. 1 vol. 356 pp. of which three are blank (30,5 × 24,7 cm)
298./Den sorte Domino./Partitur/[...]/LE DOMINO NOIR/ OPÉRA COMIQUE EN TROIS ACTES/[...]/Musique de/D. F. E. Auber
Paris, E. Troupenas, pl. no. T. 544 [1837]
[DKKk; U 6 (KTA 298)
This French printed orchestral score was used for all performances of *Le Domino noir* in Copenhagen during Bournonville's lifetime. It contains T. Overskou's Danish translation (written with red ink) next to the original French text. A note written with red crayon on p. '173' reads: 'Transponeres in G for fr. Bornonville [*sic*]'. It indicates a transposition from A flat major to G major (made for Charlotte

Bournonville in 1859) of the so-called *Ronde Aragonaise* («La belle Inès fait florès»), sung by *Angèle* in Act II, score no. 8.

No répétiteur'c copy for *Le Domino noir* has yet been traced.

Parts. Ms. Copy. 35 + 14 vol.
4 vl I, 4 vl II, 2 vla, 4 vlc e cb, fl 1/2, ob 1/2, cl 1/2, fag 1/2, cor 1/2/ 3/4, tr 1/2, trb 1/2/3, timp, gr cassa, piatti e tri, org. On stage: vl I, vl II, vla, vlc e cb, fl picc, ob 1/2, cl 1/2, fag 1/2, cor 1/2, glock. 58 vocal parts.
Unsigned and undated [1839]
[DKKk; KTA 298
This set of parts dates from the 1839 Copenhagen première of *Le Domino Noir* and was used for all performances of it there during Bournonville's lifetime.

21.5.1859

Die Entführung aus dem Serail (Bortførelsen af Seraillet).

The 1859 restaging of W. A. Mozart's three-act comic opera (premièred at Vienna's Burgtheater on 16.7.1782, and first performed at Copenhagen's Royal Theatre on 1.4.1813) was originally projected by Bournonville on 30.10.1857. It represents the first and only time this opera was mounted with his mise-en-scène. The restaging is not included in Bournonville's handwritten list of his stagings of operas and plays, written c.1872 (*see* Additional Sources), but is mentioned in the printed survey of his works in his memoirs *My Theatre Life* (p. 410). For this production Bournonville also contributed with personal stage instructions given to the singer, A. G. L. Zinck, who this year made his début in the rôle of *Belmonte*.

In his diary Bournonville noted about the performance:

10.3.1859: 'skrevet og arrangeret'
11.3.: 'Arrangeret Decorations-Regien for Seraillet'
6.5.: 'hørt lidt af Bortførelsen af Seraillet'
15.5.: 'skrevet og arrangeret, bivaanet en Textprøve paa <u>Seraillet</u>'
16.5.: 'Prøve paa [...] Seraillet'
17.5.: 'Instruction til Sangeren [A. G. L.] Zinck'
18.5.: 'Theaterprøve paa Seraillet'
19.5.: 'Prøve paa [...] Seraillet'
21.5.: '1.ste Forestilling af den ny Indstudering af Bortførelsen fra Seraillet. Zinck jr. Debut – meget heldig'.

The 1859 production of *Die Entführung aus dem Serail* received 5 performances, the last of which was given on 1.12. 1859.

Autograph sources:

Production note. Ms. Autograph. Black ink. 3 pp. (22,4 × 17,5 cm)
<u>Decorationer til Bortførelsen af Seraillet.</u>
Signed and dated: 'Kbhvn d. 10.de Martz 1859.'
[SSm; Daniel Fryklunds samling no. 118

Musical sources:

No orchestral score and répétiteur's copy dating from the 1859 restaging of *Die Entführung aus dem Serail* have yet been traced.

Parts. Ms. Copy. 32 vol.
4 vl I, 4 vl II, 2 vla, 4 vlc e cb, fl picc, fl 1/2, ob 1/2, cl 1/2, cor bassetto 1/2, fag 1/2, cor 1/2, tr 1/2, timp, gr cassa, piatti e tri. 70 vocal parts.
Unsigned and undated [1813]
[DKKk; KTA 171
This set of parts dates from the 1813 Copenhagen première of *Die Entführung aus dem Serail* and was used for all performances of it there during Bournonville's lifetime.

22.5.1859

A new Divertissement (after Holberg's indications) as an intermezzo in The Healing Spring (Intermedium, Et nyt Divertissement (efter Holbergs Opgave) i Kildereisen).

The 1859 Copenhagen restaging of L. Holberg's two-act comedy from 1750 *The Healing Spring* represents the first and only time this work was mounted with Bournonville's complete mise-en-scène. It also included a new intermezzo, performed between Acts II and III to a new score by I. P. E Hartmann and with text (in the choruses) by H. C. Andersen.

Nearly twenty years earlier Bournonville had worked for the first time on a projected staging of this intermezzo (*see* 30.5.1840). His 1859 version of it is not included in his handwritten list of his stagings of operas and plays, written c.1872 (*see* Additional Sources), nor in the printed survey of his works in his memoirs *My Theatre Life* (p. 408). It consisted of the following five numbers:

(1) An Introduction and a song, entitled «Alverdens Skaber mild og blid» (*Indledning og Sang af Bønder, som gaar Sommer i Bÿ*), sung by a chorus of peasants as a celebration and inauguration of the summer season. The melody employed for H. C. Andersen's new text to this song was originally from an old Danish folk tune.
(2) A song for the spring (*Wexelsang ved Kilden*), sung by the chorus to the text «Sanct Hans du bringer os Sommertid». The motifs of this song were composed by the cantor at Copenhagen's Ganisons Kirke, A. W. Hartmann, who was a relative of I. P. E. Hartmann.
(3) A *Reel*, performed by the corps de ballet.
(4) A *Processional March (Optog)*, performed by the entire cast.
(5) A finale song («Nu er her i Skoven en Stilhed og Fred») and a *Dance (Slutnings-Sang og Dands)*, performed by the entire cast.

In his diary Bournonville noted about the performance:

8.11.1858: 'Komponeret et nyt Intermedium til Kildereisen, meddelt det til [F.] Høedt'
9.11.: 'Møde med [H. C.] Andersen og [I. P. E.] Hartmann'
22.11.:' Arbeidet med Hartmann til Kildereisen'
2.12.: 'arbeidet med Hartmann'
30.12.: '1.ste Indstudering paa Dandsene til Kildereisen'
1.1.1859: 'componeret paa Kildereisen'
3.1.: 'Prøve paa Kildereisen'
13.1.: 'Indstudering til Kildereisen'
15.1.: 'Prøve paa Kildereisen'
17.1.: 'Prøve paa Kildereisen'
25.1.: 'Prøve paa Kildereisen ([L.] Gade)'
14.5.: 'Prøve paa Kildereisens Divertissement'
17.5.: 'Theaterprøve paa Kildereisen'
18.5.: 'lille Prøve paa Kildereisen'
19.5.: 'Prøve paa Kildereisen'
21.5.: 'Generalprøve paa Kildereisen'
22.5.: 'I Theatret gaves Kildereisens Optagelse for 1.ste Gang med mit nÿ Divertissement, der gjorde megen Lÿkke'.

The 1859 restaging of *The Healing Spring* received 5 performances, the last of which was given on 4.10.1859.

Autograph sources:

Production note. Ms. Autograph. Black ink. 2 pp. (26,8 × 21,1 cm)
Kildereisen (Mellemact)/1.ste deel/Farten til Skoven (fra D. S. til K S:)/Theatrets Disposition:
Unsigned and undated [1858–1859]
[DKKk; NKS 3285 4° 2 G–K

Musical sources:

Orchestral score. Ms. Autograph (by I. P. E. Hartmann). Brown ink. 1 vol. 90 pp. of which two are blank (25 × 34,3 cm with minor variants)
470/Kildereisen/Partitur/470./[...]/Kildereisen./Partitur./hertil/32 Orchesterstemmer/44 Chorstemmer
Signed and dated (on p. 88): 'I:P:E:Hartmann/19/4 58.'
[DKKk; C II, 114 (KTA 470)

The répétiteur's copy dating from the 1859 restaging of *The Healing Spring* has not yet been traced. However, a later répétiteur's copy, which includes the complete music of the intermezzo and dates from H. Beck's restaging of it on 2.9.1894, is now DKKk (call no. MA ms 3089 (KTA 470 (2)).

Parts. Ms. Copy. 29 + 32 vol.
3 vl I, 3 vl II, 3 vla, vlc, 4 cb, fl 1/2, ob 1/2, cl 1/2, fag 1/2, cor 1/2/3, tr 1/2, timp, gr cassa. The intermedium: 3 vl I, 3 vl II, 2 vla, 2 vlc, 2 cb, fl 1/2, ob 1/2, cl 1/2, fag 1/2, cor 1/2/3/4, tr 1/2, trb 1/2/3, timp, gr cassa, tri. 41 vocal parts.
Unsigned and undated [1859]
[DKKk; KTA 470

25.5.1859

Scenes from 'Orphée et Euridice' for Alto, Chorus and Orchestra (Scener af 'Orpheus og Eurydice' for Alt solo, Chor og Orchester) **performed by J. A. Lund with the chorus and orchestra of** *Musikforeningen* **conducted by N. W. Gade (the Casino Theatre, Mindre Sal).**

For this concert with excerpts from Act II of C. W. v. Gluck's three-act heroic drama Bournonville's 1846 Danish translation of the opera's French text was employed (*see* 10.2.1846). Although he was a member of *Musikforeningen* and frequently attended its concerts, Bournonville was (according to his diary) not present on this evening.

Musical sources:

Orchestral score. Ms. Copy (by N. W. Gade) and copy. Brown ink. 1 vol. 72 pp. (34 × 25,7 cm)
Gluck/Orpheus og Eurydice/2.den Akt/Part. og Clav. Udtog/[...]/Orpheus og Eyrydice./2.den Akt.
Signed and dated (on p. 72): 'G-A-D-E [musical anagram]/1858.'
[DKKk; C I, 245 (Musikforeningens Archiv, no. 153 b) (1944–45. 367)
This manuscript orchestral score was copied by N. W. Gade and contains several of his musical changes and additions to Gluck's score. Bournonville's Danish translation from 1846 is here inserted next to an Italian version of the opera's text.

Parts. Ms. Copy. 37 vol.
8 vl I, 5 vl II, 4 vla, 3 vlc, 3 cb, fl 1/2, ob 1/2, cl 1/2, fag 1/2, cor 1/2, trb e tuba 1/2/3, arpa. 137 vocal parts.
Unsigned and undated [1859]
[DKKk; Mf. 153 b

Printed sources:

Printed programme. 1 vol. 8 pp. of which one is blank (20,6 × 13,3 cm)
MUSIKFORENINGENS/CONCERT/Onsdagen den 25. Mai 1859./[...]/2. Gluck, W. C.: Scener af «Orpheus og Eurydice» for Alt solo, Chor og Orchester (comp. 1762).
[Copenhagen], Bianco Luno/F. S. Muhle [1859]
[DKKk; Musikforeningens Arkiv, kapsel 68 (1858–59)
Bournonville's Danish translation of the French text for Gluck's *Orphée et Euridice* (for which he is not credited in this programme) is included on pp. 3–5.

6.10.1859

Lucrezia Borgia.

On this day Bournonville noted in his diary:

'Bivaanet Claveerprøven paa <u>Lucrezia</u> [Borgia] med lidt Instruction'.

G. Donizetti's two-act melodrama had been mounted 6 months earlier by Bournonville (*see* 15.4.1859).

In spite of his rehearsal of it on this day it was not performed at all during the 1859–60 season. Consequently it does not seem to have been aimed at any specific performance or imminent restaging of *Lucrezia Borgia*.

6.10.1859

Le Dieu et la bayadère, ou La Courtisane amoureuse (Brama og Bayadèren).

The 1859 Copenhagen restaging of D.-F.-E. Auber's opera-ballet (*see* 7.2.1841, 9.9.1847, and 11.11.1849) was originally projected by Bournonville on 30.11.1857. It represents the first time *Le Dieu et la bayadère* was mounted with his complete mise-en-scène and was (according to notes in the répétiteur's copy and in Bournonville's diary) mounted with slightly revised choreography, arranged especially for Juliette Price. Moreover, for the 1859 production Bournonville gave personal stage instructions to his daughter, the alto Charlotte Bournonville (playing *Ninka*), and the singer, A. G. L. Zinck, who made his début this year in the rôle of *L'inconnu*. Furthermore, the two dancing bayadères, *Zoloé* and *Fatmé*, were this year performed by Juliette Price and P. Fredstrup respectively.

In his diary Bournonville noted about the performance:

23.8.1859: 'Studeret Dandsen til Brama og Bayaderen'
24.8.: 'Decorationsmøde paa Brama. Eftm. componeret'
25.8.: 'Costumemøde paa Brama'
26.8.: 'Indstudering paa Brama og Decorationsmøde'
27.8.: 'Prøve paa Brama [...] eftm. skrevet og componeret'
28.8.: 'skrevet og arrangeret'
29.8.: 'Indstuderet Pas de deux til Brama og Bayaderen'
30.8.: 'Eftermiddagsprøve for [A. G. L.] Zinck og Juliette [Price] '
5.9.: 'Prøve paa Brama 5 – 6½'
7.9.: 'Eftermiddagsprøve med Zinck og Charlotte [Bournonville]'
8.9.: 'Quartettsprøve paa Brama'
9.9. and 10.9.: 'Prøve paa Brama'
12.9.: 'Arrangement og Theater-Prøve paa Brama og Bayaderen'
13.9.: 'Prøve paa Brama og Bayaderen'
14.9.: 'Aftenprøve paa Brama og Bayaderen [...] Prøven gik udmærket godt'
16.9.: 'Prøve paa Brama. Generalprøve paa ditto. Zinck indisponeret. Alt gik iøvrigt meget godt.'
17.9.: 'Charlotte forkjølet og Sygemelding for Brama'
23.9.: 'Charlotte fuldkommen rask'
1.10.: 'Eftermiddag prøvet Costume med Charlotte'
4.10.: 'Prøve paa [...] Brama'
5.10.: 'Generalprøve paa Brama, med Haab om Forestilling imorgen'
6.10.: 'I Theatret Brama og Bayaderen for udsolgt Huus. Juliette war fortræffelig. Charlotte havde udmærket Succès, men var ikke saa sikker som sædvanlig. Zinck was ilde disponeret og [P. L. N.] Schramms fyldest gjorde slet ikke som Olifur. Operaen gjorde megen Lykke'.

The 1859 production of *Le Dieu et la bayadère* received 8 performances, the last of which was given on 22.2.1865.

The musical material employed this year was the same as

that used for the previous staging on 9.9.1847 (now in DKKk, call nos. U 6, MA ms 3064, and KTA 301).

6.10.1859

Oberon, or The Elf King's Oath (Oberon). **Projected Danish restaging.**

The projected 1859 restaging of C. M. v. Weber's 1826 three-act romantic fairy-play (premièred in London at Covent Garden on 12.4.1826, and first performed at Copenhagen's Royal Theatre on 31.1.1831) was originally planned by Bournonville on 30.10.1857. For almost a month after 6.10.1859 he worked on a new mise-en-scène for it. This project, however, was for unknown reasons never carried out, although he resumed working on it some 12 years later (*see* 8.6.1871).

In his diary he noted about the projected 1859 staging:

6.10.1859: 'Skrevet Scenearrangement til <u>Oberon</u>'
7.10.: 'Skrevet og fuldendt Decorationslister paa <u>Oberon</u>'
17.10. and 19.10: 'skrevet lister til Oberon'
21.10.: 'skrevet til Oberon'
29.10.: 'Audients hos Chefen [F. F. v. Tillisch] angaaende Oberon'
31.10. and 1.11.: 'Decorations Møde paa Oberon'
3.11.: '(Conference med Chefen)'.

Autograph sources:

Manuscript mise-en-scène. Ms. Autograph. Brown ink. 4 pp. (22,7 × 17,8 cm)
<u>Oberon</u>./Trÿlle = Opera i 3 Akter (7 Tableauer) af C. M Weber./ <u>Indhold</u>:
Unsigned and undated [Written according to Bournonville's diary on 6.10.1859]
[SSm; Daniel Fryklunds samling no. 139 e

Production note. Ms. Autograph. Brown ink. 3 pp. (35,8 × 22,4 cm)
<u>Oberon</u> (Damer.)/Trÿlle = Opera i 3 Acter (7 Tableauer) af C. M. v. Weber./Decorationer/<u>Forslag</u>:
Signed and dated: 'Kbhvn d. 19.e October 1859.'
[SSm; Daniel Fryklunds samling no. 139 c

Production note. Ms. Autograph. Brown ink. 3 pp. (35,8 × 22,4 cm)
<u>3 Acter</u>/<u>7 Tableauer.</u>/Decorationer til Oberon/Trÿlle = Opera efter [C. M.] Wieland, af C. M: v: Weber:
Signed and dated: '<u>d. 19.e Octbr</u>/1859.'
[SSm; Daniel Fryklunds samling no. 139 d

Production note. Ms. Autograph. Brown ink. 4 pp. (35,8 × 22,4 cm)
<u>Costumet til Oberon</u> (Herrer.)/<u>Trÿlle = Opera af C M v. Weber:</u>
Signed and dated: 'Kbhvn d. [space left empty by Bournonville] October 1859.'
[SSm; Daniel Fryklunds samling no. 139 a

Production note. Ms. Autograph. Brown ink. 1 p. (35,8 × 22,4 cm)
<u>Costumer til Oberon</u> (Damer.)/Trÿlle = Opera af C. M v. Weber.
Signed and dated: 'Kbhvn d. [space left empty by Bournonville] October 1859.'
[SSm; Daniel Fryklunds samling no. 139 b

20.10.1859

La Fille du régiment (Regimentets Datter).

The 1859 Copenhagen restaging of G. Donizetti's two-act comic opera (premièred in Paris at l'Opéra Comique on 11.2.1840, and first performed in Danish at Copenhagen's Royal Theatre on 6.10.1840) was originally projected by Bournonville on 30.10.1857 and reproposed by him on 20.1.1858 (*see also* 10.1.1849). It represents the first time *La Fille du régiment* was mounted with his complete mise-en-scène at Copenhagen's Royal Theatre. The restaging is not included in Bournonville's handwritten list of his stagings of operas and plays, written c.1872 (*see* Additional Sources), nor in the printed survey of his works in his memoirs *My Theatre Life* (p. 408). In his diary he noted about the staging:

14.10.1859: 'Skrevet Scene-Arrangementet til Regimentets Datter'
15.10.: 'Arrangementsprøve paa Regimentets datter'
16.10: 'Theaterprøve paa Regimentets Datter'
18.10.: Theaterprøve paa Regimentets Datter, der skulde gaae til Festforestilling imorgen, men ved Kgl. Befaling blev ombyttet med Bagtalelsens Skole'
20.10.: 'Regimentets Datter, der gik udmærket og for fuldt Huus'.

The 1859 production of *La Fille du régiment* received 17 performances, the last of which was given on 16.9.1866.

Autograph sources:

Manuscript mise-en-scène. Ms. Autograph. Brown ink. 1 vol. 7 pp. (21,9 × 13,8 cm)
Regimentets Datter./Scene Arrangement.
Signed and dated: 'd. 14.e October 1859.'
[SSm; Daniel Fryklunds samling no. 144

Musical sources:

Printed orchestral score. 1 vol. 342 pp. of which two are blank (32,5 × 25 cm)
LA/Fille du Régiment/Opera Comique en 2 actes,/[...]/Musique de/G. DONIZETTI
Paris, Schonenberger, pl. no. S. 653 [1840]
[DKKkt; KTA 300
This French orchestral score includes T. Overskou's Danish translation (written with black ink) next to the original French text. It served for all performances of Donizetti's opera in Copenhagen after its première there on 6.10.1841 and throughout Bournonville's lifetime.

No répétiteur's copy for *La Fille du régiment* has yet been traced.

Parts. Ms. Copy. 36 + 6 vol.
4 vl I, 4 vl II, 2 vla, 4 vlc e cb, fl 1/2, ob 1/2, cl princ, cl 1/2, fag 1/2, cor 1/2/3/4, tr 1/2, trb 1/2/3, timp, gr cassa, piatti, tri. On stage: vl I, vla, vlc e cb, cnt 1/2, gr cassa. 13 vocal parts.
Unsigned and undated [1840]
[DKKk; KTA 300
This set of parts dates from the 1840 Copenhagen première of *La Fille du régiment* and was used for all performances of it there during Bournonville's lifetime.

6.11.1859
Faust. Projected restaging.
On this day and during the following two weeks Bournonville worked on a revised staging of his three-act romantic ballet *Faust* (*see* 25.4.1832), which he intended to mount during the 1859–60 season. This is clear from his diary in which he noted about the project:

6.11.1859: 'Brev til Chefen [F. F. v. Tillisch] om [...] Faust'
7.11.: 'Arbeidet paa en Forandring af min gamle Ballet Faust og til den ende læst meget i Göthes [*sic*] Mesterværk'
8.11.: 'Jeg skrev og beskjæftigede mig meget med [J. W. v.] Goethes Faust med Hensyn til en nÿ tredie Akt til min Ballet'
11.11.: 'fuldendt Programmet til 3die Akt af Balletten Faust'
12.11.: ' Skrevet paa Faust'
16.11.: 'arbeidet paa Faust med [H. S.] Paulli'

22.11.: 'arbeidet med Paulli'.

The projected restaging of *Faust* was for unknown reasons never carried out, although a completely new répétiteur's copy for this revised version was made.

Autograph sources:

Manuscript scenario/Production note. Ms. Autograph. Brown ink. 1 vol. 8 pp. (20,7 × 17,3 cm)
<u>Faust</u>/Romantisk Ballet i tre Akter af A Bournonville/[...]/<u>Forandringer.</u>/til/Anden – Udgaven af Balletten <u>Faust</u>. (vide Rep. Partiet.)
Signed and dated: 'Kjøbenhavn d. 12.de November 1859.'
[DKKk; NKS 3285 4° 2 F

Production note. Ms. Autograph. Brown ink. 1 p. (34,2 × 12,4 cm)
<u>Personnages.</u>
Unsigned and undated [1859]
[DKKk; NKS 3285 4° 2 F

Mimic-choreographic note (incomplete). Ms. Autograph. Brown ink. 1 p. (21,2 × 14,3 cm)
<u>Faust</u>./<u>Scène 1.</u> [incomplete]
Unsigned and undated [1859?]
[DKKk; Utilg. 828 (Harald Landers Arkiv, Kapsel 182)
This (incomplete) manuscript for *Faust* was later reused as wrapping for Bournonville's separate notations of his four-act nordic mythological ballet *The Valkyrie* (*see* 13.9.1861). This seems to indicate that the manuscript dates from the projected 1859 restaging of *Faust*.

Musical sources:

Répétiteur's copy (incomplete). Ms. Copy. Black ink. 48 + 16 pp. of which one is blank (34,5 × 25,7 cm)
Repetiteur = Partie/til/'Faust'
Unsigned and undated [c.1859]
[DKKk; MA ms 2643 (1–2) (KTB 289)
This répétiteur's copy includes the music for Act I, score nos. 1–12, Act II, score nos. 13–15 (incomplete), and Act III, score nos. 22 (incomplete), 23, and 24. Because no signs are left indicating that it was ever used for rehearsals, it was most probably from Bournonville's 1859 projected restaging of *Faust*.

24.11.1859
The Wedding of the Dryad, Mythological Poem for Solo voices, Chorus and Orchestra (Dryadens Bryllup, mythologisk Digt for Solostemmer, Chor og Orchester) conducted by N. W. Gade (the Casino Theatre, Mindre Sal).
In his diary Bournonville noted this day about his involvement in the first complete performance of I. P. E. Hartmann's and F. Paludan-Müller's mythological poem:

'Prøve i Casino for Dryadens Bryllup af Hartmann'.

This seems to indicate that Bournonville took part in the stage arrangement of this quasi-scenic concert-performance.
Hartmann's music had earlier been performed by *Musikforeningen* in the minor auditorium of the Casino Theatre on 22.2.1859, but then in a reduced version that omitted the introduction.

Musical sources:

Orchestral score. Ms. Autograph (by I. P. E. Hartmann). Brown ink. 1 vol. 204 pp. (33,5 × 29 cm with minor variants)
J. P. E. Hartmann,/Dryadens Bryllup./op. 60./Partitur,/[...]/Drÿadens Brÿllup/Digt af Fr: Paludan = Müller/componeret for Solostemmer, Chor/og Orchester/af/I:P:E: Hartmann.

Signed and dated (on p. 204): 'I:P:E: Hartmann/3 Decbr. 1858.'
[DKKk; I. P. E. Hartmanns samling

Parts. Ms. Copy. 52 + 112 vol.
7 vl I, 6 vl II, 4 vla, 6 vlc e cb, fl picc, fl 1/2, ob 1/2, cl 1/2, fag 1/2, cor
1/2, tr 1/2, trb 1/2/3, tuba, timp, gr cassa, piatti e tri, arpa, 8 piano
scores. 112 vocal parts.
Unsigned and undated [c.1859 and later]
[DKKk; Mf. 654
This set of parts seems to have been used for all performances of *The
Wedding of the Dryad* given by *Musikforeningen* in Copenhagen between 1859 and the beginning of this century (1913).

6.11.1859
*The Pitman's Dream, Hungarian Ballet Divertissement in 1 Act
(Excerpt from the Ballet In the Carpathians) (Bjergmandens
Drøm, Ungarsk Balletdivertissement i 1 Act (Uddrag af Balletten
I Karpatherne).*

This work is an abridged divertissement version of Act I,
scene 4 (score nos. 5–9) of Bournonville's and H. S. Paulli's
three-act Hungarian ballet *In the Carpathians* (*see* 4.3.1857),
and was performed by six couples. In his diary Bournonville
noted about its rehearsals and the première:

11.10.1859: 'Prøve paa Karpatherne forkortet'
12.10.: 'Prøve paa Karpatherne'
26.10.: 'Prøve paa Bjergmandens Drøm, Forkortelse af I Karpatherne'
30.10.: '(afleveret Costumelisterne til [J. A.] Pätges)'
1.11.: 'Prøve paa Bjergmandens Drøm'
2.11.: 'skrevet og arrangeret, besørget adskilligt, Prøve paa Bjergmandens Drøm paa Theatret'
5.11.: 'Prøve paa […] Bjergmandens Drøm'
6.11.: 'Kl 12 Lille Maskinprøve paa Bjergmandens Drøm […] Bjergmandens Drøm (Uddrag af Karpatherne) gik […] for halvt Huus og
et temmelig lunkent Publicum'.

The Pitman's Dream received 6 performances, the last of
which was given on 30.1.1860.

The musical material employed this year was the same as
that used for *In the Carpathians* (now in DKKk, call nos. C II,
119, MA ms 2971, and KTB 276).

Autograph sources:

Production note. Ms. Autograph. Brown ink. 1 p. (36,2 × 22,7 cm)
Bjergmandens Dröm./Ballet = Divertissement i En Akt (Uddrag af
Balletten/'I Karpatherne') af Herr Hofballetmester Bournonville.
Musiken/af Herr Koncertmester Paulli./Personerne.
Unsigned and undated [Written according to the diary most prob-
ably between 30.10. and 2.11.1859]
[DKKkt; F.M. (Ballet, læg I–J)

Production note. Ms. Autograph (partially in another's hand).
Brown ink. 1 p. (36,2 × 22,7 cm)
Bjergmandens Dröm/Ballet i 1 Akt (uddraget af Balletten I Karpa-
therne.)
Unsigned and undated [Written according to the diary most prob-
ably between 30.10. and 2.11.1859]
[DKKkt; F.M. (Ballet, læg I–J)

Production note. Ms. Autograph. Black ink. 1 p. (18,3 × 22,9 cm)
Classification af Skopenge/til/Balletdivertissementet Bjergmand-
ens Dröm:
Unsigned and undated [Written according to the diary most prob-
ably between 30.10. and 2.11.1859]
[DKKk; Musikafdelingen (Box, Bournonville manuskripter)

28.11.1859
L'Elisire d'Amore (Elskovsdrikken).

The 1859 Copenhagen restaging of G. Donizetti's two-act
comic opera (premièred in Milan at Teatro della Canobbiana on 12.5.1832, and first performed at Copenhagen's
Royal Theatre on 16.6.1856) was originally projected by
Bournonville on 30.10.1857. It represents the first time this
opera was mounted under his general direction. However,
the staging seems to have been mounted with only minor if
any changes from the original 1856 Copenhagen production. Donizetti's opera is not included in Bournonville's
handwritten list of his stagings of operas and plays, written
c.1872 (*see* Additional Sources), nor in the printed survey of
his works in his memoirs *My Theatre Life* (p. 409). It was restaged for the second and last time by Bournonville on
22.11.1872.

In his diary he noted about the 1859 production:

24.11.1859: 'Prøve paa […] Elskovsdrikken fra 11–1½'
27.11.: 'Theaterprøve paa Elskovsdrikken'
28.11.: 'Eftermiddagsprøve 5 – 7, Elskovsdrikken for maadeligt
Huus, men levende og fortjent Bifald'.

The staging received 22 performances, the last of which took
place on 5.2.1867.

Musical sources:

Orchestral score. Ms. Copy. Black and red ink. 4 vol. Act I 300 + 300
pp., Act II 322 + 155 pp. of which seven are blank + 8 pp. (23,2 × 32
cm with minor variants)
Elskovsdrikken./Partitur./Första Akt/I./[…]/L'Elisir d'Amore/
Musica/Del Sig:r Maestro Donizetti/Atto Primo/Proprietà di Giovanni Ricordi a Milano/[…]/Första Akt./II./[…]/Anden Akt/III.
/[…]/Anden Akt/IV.
Unsigned and undated [c.1856]
[DKKk; C I, 236 n (KTA 464)
This Italian manuscript orchestral score dates from the 1856 premi-
ère at Copenhagen's Royal Theatre of *L'Elisire d'Amore*. It contains T.
Overskou's Danish translation (written with brown ink) next to the
original Italian text. The score, which also includes an incorporated
aria for *Adina* in Act III (score no. 20) entitled «Bliv Du! Nei, jeg tör
ei klage», was used for all performances of Donizetti's opera at the
Royal Theatre during Bournonville's lifetime.

No répétiteur's copy for *L'Elisire d'Amore* has yet been traced.

Parts. Ms. Copy. 33 + 2 vol.
4 vl I, 4 vl II, 2 vla, 4 vlc e cb, fl picc e II, fl I, ob 1/2, cl 1/2, fag 1/2,
cor 1/2, tr 1/2, trb 1/2/3, timp, gr cassa, piatti e tri. arpa. On stage:
cnt 1/2. 41 vocal parts.
Unsigned and undated [1856]
[DKKk; KTA 464
This set of parts dates from the 1856 Copenhagen première of *L'Elisire d'Amore* and was used for all performances of it at the Royal Theatre during Bournonville's lifetime.

1860

2.1.1860
Cyprianus.

The first performance of I. Nielsen's one-act play (with songs
set to music by H. Rung) was mounted in part by Bournonville, who gave personal stage instructions to his daughter,

the alto Charlotte Bournonville, who played the rôle of *Else*. The play contained an (unnamed) *Dance* in the Finale (score no. 13), performed by the entire cast during the chorus «Det gaaer lÿstigt til og i Dands som Leg saa fro». Nielsen's play is not included in Bournonville's handwritten list of his stagings of operas and plays, written c.1872 (*see* Additional Sources), nor in the printed survey of his works in his memoirs *My Theatre Life* (p. 408). In his diary Bournonville noted about the staging:

23.11.1859: 'Charlotte [Bournonville] Oplæsning paa Cyprianus'
20.12.: 'besøgt [H.] Rung'
22.12.: 'overværet Prøve paa Cyprianus, hvori Charlotte har en Rolle'
23.12.: 'bivaanet en Deel af Prøven paa Cyprianus'
24.12.: 'Prøve paa Cyprianus for Charlotte'
27.12.: 'Theaterprøve paa Cyprianus Kl 10'
29.12.: 'overværet en Prøve paa Cyprianus'
31.12.: 'overværet Generalprøven paa Cyprianus'
1.1.1860: 'I Theatret og prøvede Dragt med Charlotte'
2.1.: 'I Theatret, første Forestilling af Cyprianus. Charlotte spillede og sang meget smukt, men da hele Stÿkket fattes Pointer faldt der ingen Applaus og det Hele gik temmelig lunkent af'.

Cyprianus received 8 performances, the last of which was given on 14.2.1860.

Musical sources:

Orchestral score. Ms. Autograph (by H. Rung). Brown ink. 1 vol. 80 pp. of which one is blank (34,3 × 29,2 cm)
474 / H. Rung / <u>Cyprianus.</u> / <u>Partitur</u> / No. 474 / […] / <u>Cyprianus.</u>/ <u>Sangspil i 1 Akt.</u>
Signed and dated (on p. 79): 'H. Rung. Aug: 1859.'
[DKKk; C II, 119 k (KTA 474)

No répétiteur's copy for *Cyprianus* has yet been traced.

Parts. Ms. Copy. 25 vol.
vl princ, 3 vl I, 3 vl II, 2 vla, 3 vlc e cb, fl 1/2, ob 1/2, cl 1/2, fag 1/2, cor 1/2, tr 1/2, timp. 32 vocal parts.
Unsigned and undated [1860]
[DKKk; KTA 474

8.1.1860
Napoli or The Fisherman and His Bride (Napoli eller Fiskeren og hans Brud).
This performance represents the first time Bournonville's three-act romantic ballet *Napoli or The Fisherman and His Bride* (*see* 29.3.1842) was restaged in Copenhagen with a completely new cast. The leading rôles of *Teresina* and *Gennaro* were this year performed by Juliette Price and H. Scharff for the first time. Moreover, the production represents the first time this ballet was performed after the 1857 restoration of the stage area in Copenhagen's old Royal Theatre building.

In his diary Bournonville noted about the production, which otherwise seems to have been mounted with only minor if any changes from the original 1842 version:

12.11.1859: 'Skrevet og arrangeret'
19.11.: '1.ste Prøve paa Napoli (nÿ Indstudering) […] Eftermiddagsprøve paa <u>Napoli</u>'
21.11.: 'Prøve paa Napoli. Costume=Møde paa D.o
22.11.: 'Møde paa Malersalen […] arbeidet med [H. S.] Paulli'

23.11.: 'Prøve paa Napoli fra 10–12 […] Decorationsskue paa Napoli'
24.11.: 'Prøve paa Napoli fra 10–11'
25.11.: 'Prøve paa Napoli 11–1½. Decorationsskue, Eftermiddagsprøve paa Napoli'
26.11.: 'Prøve paa Napoli'
28.11.: 'Prøve paa Napoli fra 10½ til 1. – Eftermiddagsprøve 5–7'
29.11.: 'Prøve paa Napoli fra 11–1½'
30.11.: 'Prøve paa Napoli'
1.12.: 'Rolleprøve paa Napoli'
3.12.: 'Sceneprøve paa Napoli'
6.12. and 7.12.: 'Prøve paa Napoli'
8.12.: 'Prøve paa de sidste Akter af Napoli, udmærket godt'
9.12.: 'Decorationsprøve paa Napoli'
10.12.: 'Arrangementprøve paa Napoli 1.ste Akr 10–12'
13.12.: 'Arrangementprøve paa Napoli Kl 10–12'
14.12.: 'Prøve paa Dandsene til Napoli'
15.12.: 'Theaterprøve paa 2.den Akt af Napoli'
17.12.: 'Jeg passede min Prøve paa Napoli, der gik udmærket'
19.12.: 'Prøve paa alle tre Acter af Napoli'
20.12.: 'Juliette meldt sÿg for det første!!! ingen Napoli'
2.1.1860: 'Lection til Juliette [Price] og [H.] Scharff – Sceneprøve paa Napoli'
3.1.: 'Theaterprøve med Orchester paa Napoli'
4.1.: 'Sceneprøve paa Napoli'
6.1.: 'Generalprøve paa <u>Napoli</u>, der gik udmærket'
8.1.: '<u>Napoli</u> for fuldt Huus. Balletten gik i det Hele udmærket godt og høstede stor Bifald'.

The 1860 production received 29 performances, the last of which took place on 6.11.1865.

The musical material employed this year was the same as that used since the 1842 première of this ballet (now in DKKk, call nos. C II, 114 k, and KTB 292).

Autograph sources:

Production note. Ms. Autograph. Black ink. 2 pp. (36,5 × 22,9 cm)
<u>Personalet i Napoli</u>/ (Novbr 1859.) nÿt indstuderet.
Signed and dated: 'Kbhvn d. 12 Novbr 1859.'
[DKKkt; F.M. (Ballet)

Production note. Ms. Autograph. Black ink. 1 p. (18,3 × 22,9 cm)
[…]/<u>Ballabile af Napoli.</u>/[…]/Giovannina — [H.] Hammer [erased] [N.] Borup/[…]/ <u>Pas de cinq:</u>/[…]/<u>Najader:</u>/[…]/ <u>Neapolitanerinder:</u>/[…]/<u>Neapolitanere:</u>/[…]/<u>Tarentella.</u>
Unsigned and undated [Written most probably during the late 1859 or early January 1860?]
[DKKk; Musikafdelingen (Box, Bournonville manuskripter)
According to the names of the two dancers (Hammer and Borup) in this note, it was most probably written for the 1860 restaging.

10.1.1860
Dance of the Witches in Macbeth (Hexenes Dands i Macbeth) (uncredited).
The 1860 Copenhagen restaging of W. Shakespeare's five-act tragedy with music by C. E. F. Weyse represents the last time this work was mounted at Copenhagen's Royal Theatre during Bournonville's lifetime. Moreover, it represents the first time it was staged with Bournonville's choreographic arrangement of the figurative dance, performed by the three witches in Act IV (score no. 6). This dance was originally choreographed by his father, Antoine Bournonville, for the Copenhagen première of *Macbeth* on 15.11.1817. According to the 1860 poster it was performed by Bournonville's daughter, C. Bournonville, the singer-actresses, J. A. Lund,

and A. Holm, all of whom appeared for the first time in this work.

The staging is listed on the poster with no mention of Bournonville's name. Furthermore, it is not included in his handwritten list of his stagings of operas and plays, written c.1872 (see Additional notes) nor in the printed survey of his works in his memoirs *My Theatre Life* (p. 408).

In his diary he noted about the performance:

21.12.1859: 'arrangeret Hexenes Dands i Macbeth'
22.12.: 'Prøve paa [...] Hexenes Dands'
10.1.1860: 'I Theatret Macbeth med Fru [J. L.] Heiberg som Ladÿ – Flere Scener med stort Mesterskab. Det Hele noget manieret og [N. P.] Nielsen selv var tung. Der var aldeles udsolgt'.

The 1860 production of *Macbeth* received 4 performances, the last of which was given on 11.2.1860.

Musical sources:

Orchestral score. Ms. Copy and autograph (by F. Rung). Brown and black ink. 1 vol. 214 pp. of which six are blank (24,2 × 34 cm with minor variants)
C. E. F. <u>Weyse</u>/<u>Macbeth</u>./Partitur/201/Macbeth./Partitur/[...]/ Macbeth/Sörgespil/<u>5 Acter. -</u>/<u>Partitur</u> -/[...]/Macbeth/comp. af. C E F Weyse
Unsigned and undated [1817]
[DKKk; C II, 123 (KTA 201)
This orchestral score dates from the 1817 Copenhagen première of *Macbeth* and was used for all performances of it there during Bournonville's lifetime. It includes five musical insertions by F. Rung (on pp. 67–68, 97–104, 141–148, 157–160, and 165–166) and also contains his autographed signature on p. 102 (reading: 'Fr. Rung, Januar 1894.'). Rung's additions to Weyse's score were made for a much later restaging of Shakespeare's tragedy, premièred on 21.1.1894. Weyse's original music for the dance of the three witches in Act IV is included on pp. 156, 161–164, and 167.

No répétiteur's copy for *Macbeth* has yet been traced.

Parts. Ms. Copy. 26 + 16 vol.
3 vl I, 3 vl II, 2 vla, 4 vlc e cb, fl 1/2, ob 1/2, cl 1/2, fag 1/2, cor 1/2, tr 1/2, trb, timp. On stage: fl 1/2, ob 1/2, cl 1/2, cor 1/2, tr 1/2, trb 1/2/3, tuba, gr cassa, piatti e tri. 3 vocal parts.
Unsigned and undated [1817]
[DKKk; KTA 201]
This set of parts dates from the 1817 Copenhagen première of *Macbeth* and was used for all performances of it there during Bournonville's lifetime.

16.1.1860

Le Quadrille des Lanciers: La Dorset, La Victoria, Les Moulinets, Les Visites, Les Lanciers.

For a series of private lessons in social dance given during the winter of 1859–60 (mainly on Wednesday evenings) Bournonville notated and taught his own, seemingly slightly revised version of one of the most popular ballroom dances of the time, *Le Quadrille des Lanciers*. It was performed by his pupils at his Copenhagen residence in Nørregade no. 33 as a conclusion to his private dance lessons taught this season.

In his diary he noted about the dance:

5.11.1859: 'Studeret Quadrille des Lanciers'
2.1.1860: 'aftalt nÿe Lectioner hos [...] Prof. [M.] Sommer'
6.1.: '1.ste Lection paa Lanciers-Quadriller hos Prof. Sommer.'
7.1.: '2.den Lection i Lanciers-Quadrillen færdig indstuderet'
9.1.: 'sidste Lection i Lanciers-Quadrillen hos Enkefru Bruuns'
12.1.: 'Lanciers indstuderet herhjemme for Børnene og flere unge Mennesker'
15.1.: 'Jeg var inviteret i Aftenselskab hos Enkefru Gether hvor mine Lanciers vare samlede og hvor der var meget hÿggeligt'
16.1.: 'Lanciers Quadrille hjemme'.

No musical sources for Bournonville's 1860 version of *Le Quadrille des Lanciers* have yet been traced. However, he most likely employed the music composed and arranged by J. Mikel (pseudonym for Joseph Meykiechel?) in about 1857, entitled *3.me Quadrille des Lanciers. Hommage à Madame La Marquise Aguado*. This arrangement was first published as the third in a series of five sets of quadrilles, named *Les Lanciers*, the choreography of which was arranged by the French dancing teacher at the court of Napoleon III, H. Laborde. Laborde, in turn, based his choreography on a much earlier *Les Lanciers Quadrilles*, first published by J. Hart in London in 1819. The theory that Mikel's and Laborde's *3.me Quadrille des Lanciers* from c.1857 was the immediate source for Bournonville's 1860 Copenhagen version of *Le Quadrille des Lanciers* is supported by the fact that except from some minor differences in the fifth and last quadrille (entitled 'Les Lanciers'/'The Lancers') Bournonville's choreographic description of this set of five dances is practically identical with Laborde's description in Mikel's printed piano score (published by M. Ménestrel in Paris, c.1857, pl. no. H. 2421, now in FPc, call no. K 17030). Furthermore, Mikel's music was published in Copenhagen by W. Hansen in the same year that Bournonville taught these quadrilles, and was advertised on 28.1.1860 in *Dansk Boghandlertidende* (6. Aarg., 1859–60, p. 134) as follows:

'Paa mit Forlag er udkommet Quadrille des Lanciers af Mikel, arr. f. pfte, som den bruges her ad d'Hrr. Dandsere ved det kongl. Theater'.

Finally, W. Hansen's 1860 piano score (a copy of which is now in DKKk, call no. U 24) also includes Mikel's original dedication to 'Madame La Marquise Aguado'. This clearly indicates that Hansen's score was based on Laborde's quadrilles (the heading of which also reads: 'Les Cours Laborde').

Another possible musical source for Bournonville's *Le Quadrille des Lanciers* could be the so-called *Les Lanciers à Copenhague, ny Quadrille*, published for piano by J. O. E. Horneman and J. E. Erslev in Copenhagen in 1859–60, during the very same period in which Bournonville notated these dances. Thus, the music for Horneman's and Erslev's edition (for which the composer's name has not yet been identified) must certainly have been used in Copenhagen during the winter of 1859–60. It is included in the musical anthology, entitled *Musikalsk Museum* (14. Aarg., hefte 9, pp. 52-54), a copy of which is now in DKKk (call no. D 2).

A third possibility for a musical source to Bournonville's quadrilles is the so-called *Quadrille des Lanciers*, composed by N. Behrendt and published (according to an advertisement in *Dansk Boghandlertidende*, 6. Aarg., 1859–60, p. 167) by Sally B. Salomon in March 1860 as a supplement to V. Pio's weekly magazine *For Alle* (2. Aargang Nr. 11). A piano score of this version is now in DKKk (call no. D 2, x827-0160).

Bournonville's 1860 choreographic notation of *Le Quadrille des Lanciers* seems to represent one of the earliest, if not the very first written description made in Denmark of this social dance. *Le Quadrille des Lanciers* is still among the most popular ballroom dances in Denmark.

Autograph sources:

Choreographic note. Ms. Autograph. Brown ink. 3 pp. (20,8 × 17,2 cm)
Le Quadrille des Lanciers./Explication des figures/[…]/No. 1 La Dorset./[…]/No. 2 La Victoria/[…]/No. 3 Les Moulinets/[…]/No. 4. Les Visites./[…]/No. 5. Les Lanciers.
Unsigned and undated [Written according to the diary between 5.11.1859 and 16.1.1860]
[DKKk; NKS 3285 4° 1 læg B 9

19.1.1860
At the Shore of China (Vid Chinas Kust) (Stockholm's Royal Theatre, Operahuset).
This one-act ballet is exclusively credited to S. Lund on the poster. However, according to the musical sources for it (now in SSkma) it was a free arrangement of selected excerpts from Act I (score nos. 5–11) of Bournonville's two-act romantic ballet, entitled *The Isle of Phantasy, or 'From the Shore of China'* (*see* 28.10.1838). On the Stockholm poster this music is described as being 'arranged' (*arrangerad*) by the Swedish composer, C. R. af Uhr. *Vid Chinas Kust* received 4 performances in Stockholm, the last of which was given on 2.2. 1860.

Musical sources:

Orchestral score. Ms. Autograph. Black ink. 1 vol. 123 pp. (32,3 × 23,6 cm with minor variants)
Vid Kinas kust,/Ballett/i/En Akt/af/Sigurd Lund./Musiken arrangerad af C, R, af, Uhr/Partitur.
Unsigned and dated (on p. 123): 'December 1859'
[SSkma; Pantomim-Balletter V 3

No répétiteur's copy for *At the Shore of China* has yet been traced.

Parts. Ms. Copy. 28 vol.
2 vl I, 2 vl II, 2 vla, 2 vlc e cb, fl 1/2, ob 1/2, cl 1/2, fag 1/2, cor 1/2/3/4, tr, trb 1/2/3, timp, gr cassa, piatti, tri.
Unsigned and undated [1860]
[SSkma; Pantomim-Balletter V 3

24.1.1860
Il Matrimonio Segreto (Det hemmelige Ægteskab).
The 1860 Copenhagen restaging of D. Cimarosa's two-act comic opera (premièred at Vienna's Burgtheater on 7.2. 1792, and first performed at Copenhagen's Royal Theatre on 26.9.1797) represents the first time this work was mounted under Bournonville's general supervision. Fourteen years later it was restaged by him for the second and last time on 3.2.1874, and was then mounted with a completely new mise-en-scène. In his diary he noted about the 1860 production:

4.1.1860: 'Quartettprøve paa 'Det hemmelige Ægteskab' […] Arrangementprøve paa 'Det hemmelige Ægteskab' 7 – 9"
10.1.: 'Arrangement paa Det hemmelige Ægteskab – 12 – 2½'
11.1., 12.1., and 14.1.: 'Theaterprøve paa 'Det hemmelige Ægteskab''
15.1.: 'Theaterprøve paa 'Det hemmelige Ægteskab' der lover at blive jævnt kjedeligt'
23.1.: 'Generalprøve paa 'Det hemmelige Ægteskab''

24.1.: 'I Theatret 'Det hemmelige Ægteskab' der gik særdeles godt med meget Bifald men for maadeligt Huus. [P. L. N.] Schramm fortræffelig'.

Bournonville's 1860 production was given twice, the last time on 15.1.1860.

Musical sources:

Orchestral score. Ms. Copy. Black ink. 4 vol. Act I 316 + 370 pp. of which two are blank, Act II 448 + 320 pp. of which two are blank (22,3 × 31 cm)
Det hemmelige Ægteskab./1.ste Akt: A: 1./Partitur./[…]/IL MATRIMONIO SEGRETO./Drama giocoso/per musica/in due Atti./La musica è del Sig.r Domenico Cimarosa./ATTO I.mo./[…]/1.ste Akt: B./[…]/2.den Akt. A:/[…]/2.den Akt: B:
Unsigned and undated [c. 1797]
[DKKk; C I, 231 (KTA 116)
This orchestral score is an Italian copy that dates from the 1797 Copenhagen première of *Il Matrimonio Segreto*. It contains F. G. Sporon's and T. Overskou's Danish translations (written with black ink and pencil) dating from 1797 and 1854 respectively.

No répétiteur's copy for *Il Matrimonio Segreto* has been traced.

Parts. Ms. Copy. 27 vol.
4 vl I, 4 vl II, 2 vla, 4 vlc, fl 1/2, ob 1/2, cl 1/2, fag 1/2, cor 1/2, tr 1/2, timp. 11 vocal parts.
Unsigned and undated [1797]
[DKKk; KTA 116
This set of parts dates from the 1797 Copenhagen première of *Il Matrimonio Segreto* and was used for all performances of it there throughout Bournonville's lifetime.

26.1.1860
Orphée at the tomb of Euridice, Scene for Alto, Chorus and Orchestra (Orpheus ved Eurydices Grav, Scene for Alt solo, Chor og Orchester) performed by J. A. Lund and the chorus and orchestra of *Musikforeningen* conducted by N. W. Gade (the Casino Theatre, Mindre Sal).
For this concert of excerpts from Act III of C. W. v. Gluck's three-act heroic drama Bournonville's 1846 Danish translation of its original French text was employed (*see* 10.2.1846). Although he was a member of *Musikforeningen* and frequently attended its concerts, Bournonville was (according to his diary) not present on this evening.

Musical sources:

The orchestral score employed for the concert was most probably the same as that used for the much earlier performance of excerpts from *Orphée et Euridice* at the Court Theatre (see 10.2.1846). That score is now in DKKk (call no. U 6 (1944–45.367, mu 6403.2535)).

No separate set of parts dating from the 1860 performance of excerpts from Act III of *Orphée et Euridice* has yet been traced.

Printed sources:

Printed programme. 1 vol. 8 pp. of which one is blank (20,2 × 13 cm)
MUSIKFORENINGENS/3.die/ABONNEMENTS – CONCERT/Torsdagen den 26.de Januar 1860./[…]/2. Gluck, W. C.: Orpheus ved Eurydices Grav, Scene for Alt solo, Chor og Orchester.
[Copenhagen], Bianco Luno/F. S. Muhle [1860]
[DKKk; Musikforeningens Arkiv, kapsel 69 (1859-60)
Bournonville's (uncredited) 1846 Danish translation of the French text for the excerpts from Act III of Gluck's *Orphée et Euridice* is included in this printed programme on pp. 2–3.

8.2.1860

I Capuleti ed i Montecchi (Familierne Montecchi og Capulet).
The 1860 Copenhagen restaging of V. Bellini's and N. Vaccai's melodrama in four parts (*see* 13.10.1847) represents Bournonville's third and last restaging of this work. It was mounted with a completely new mise-en-scène and choreography. Thus, the dance scene in Act II, score no. 6 (originally performed by a corps de ballet headed by two couples of soloists) seems this year to have been performed by a completely new cast. This theory is supported by the fact that the 1860 poster no longer included the original casting of two couples of soloists.

In his diary Bournonville noted about the performance:

28.1.1860: 'skrevet, Quartettsprøve paa Montecchi'
29.1.: 'studeret paa Montecchi'
30.1.: 'besørget min Arrangementsprøve'
31.1.: 'skrevet og arrangeret, Prøve og Indstudering af en ny Dands til Montecchi [...] Eftermiddag Arrangement af Operaens 4.de Akt'
1.2.: 'Theaterprøve paa Montecchi'
3.2.: 'Sceneprøve paa [...] Montecchi foranlediget ved Jf. Hammers Upasselighed'
6.2.: '2.den og sidste Theaterprøve paa Romeo'
8.2.: 'I Theatret Montecchi og Capuletti, Jf. [J. A.] Lund Romeo og Mme [J. E.] Liebe Giulietta, det gik vidunder let og navnlig Jf. Lund vandt stort Bifald'.

About a later performance during the same season (in which the singer, C. Lehmann, played the rôle of *Romeo* for the first time) he noted:

11.4.1860: 'Theaterprøve paa Montecchi, Jf [C.] Lehmann'
12.4.: 'I Theatret Montecchi og Capuletti med Jf Lehmann som Romeo. – Hendes Fædrene og underschwenglische [*sic*] Manerer gjorde et skadeligt Indtryk, og hendes Sang skjøndt meget virtuos, var i det Hele manieret. Dog gav hun den fjerde Akt udmærket. – fuldt Huus og Bifald'.

The 1860 restaging of *I Capuleti ed i Montecchi* received 6 performances, the last of which was given on 30.4.1860.

While the orchestral score and the set of parts this year were the same as those used for the previous 1847 and 1849 productions (now in DKKk, call nos. C I, 213, and KTA 395) a completely new répétiteur's copy was made for this staging.

Autograph sources:

Manuscript mise-en-scène. Ms. Autograph. Brown ink and pencil. 2 pp. (22,4 × 17,9 cm)
Montecchi og Capuletti/tragisk Opera i 4 Akter
Unsigned and undated [Written according to the diary between 28.1. and 31.1.1860]
[SSm; Daniel Fryklunds samling no. 136

Musical sources:

Répétiteur's copy. Ms. Copy. Black ink. 1 vol. 8 pp. of which one is blank (34 × 25,6 cm)
3. Montechi [*sic*] og Capuletti/A 395/[...]/Repetiteurstemme/til/ Montechi og Capuletti/2.den Act.
Unsigned and undated [1860]
[DKKk; MA ms 2911 (4) (KTA 395 (2))
This répétiteur's copy contains the complete music for the (un-named) *Dance* performed in *I Capuleti ed i Montecchi* during the opening chorus of Act II (score no. 6), entitled «Lieta notte» («Fryd og Jubel nu os tilsmile»). Moreover, it includes Bournonville's auto-

graphed choreographic numbers ('1–14', written with black ink), which seem to refer to his separate (not yet traced) notation of this dance that he made (according to his diary) between 28.1. and 30.1 1860. The music for this dance is included on pp. 35–42 in a volume that also contains the répétiteur's copies for three other operas and plays, mounted at Copenhagen's Royal Theatre between 1859 and 1863.

7.3.1860

The Brigand's Castle (Røverborgen).
The 1860 Copenhagen restaging of F. Kuhlau's three-act singspiel (premièred in Copenhagen on 26.5.1814) was originally projected by Bournonville on 30.10.1857. It represents the first and only time this work was mounted with his mise-en-scène. The staging is not included in his handwritten list of his stagings of operas and plays written c.1872 (*see* Additional Sources), nor in the printed survey of his works in his memoirs *My Theatre Life* (p. 409). In his diary he noted about the production:

21.2.1860: 'Costumeprøve paa Røverborgen'
23.2.: 'Arrangementsprøve paa Røverborgen 12–2'
28.2.: 'Text og Arrangementsprøve paa Røverborgen'
1.3.: 'partiel Theaterprøve paa Røverborgen'
3.3.: 'Theaterprøve paa Røverborgen'
6.3.: 'Textprøve Kl 10, Generalprøve paa Røverborgen'
7.3.: 'Røverborgen gik for fuldt Huus meget godt. Charlotte [Bournonville] udførte Birgittes Rolle med stort Talent, men vor Fornøielse blev noget forstyrret ved en lille privat Cabale'.

About some later rehearsals held prior to a performance on 18.11.1860 he stated:

9.4.1860: 'lille Prøve paa Røverborgen'
13.11.: 'Prøve paa Røverborgen'
14.11.: 'Sceneprøve paa Røverborgen'
15.11.: 'Røverborgen med M.d B. Hansen som Birgitte'
18.11.: 'I Theatret Røverborgen for halvt Huus'.

The 1860 production of *The Brigand's Castle* received 3 performances, the last of which was given on 10.12.1860.

Music sources:

Orchestral score. Ms. Copy. Black ink. 2 vol. Act I 288 pp. of which one is blank, Act II–III 222 pp. of which one is blank (24,5 × 33,8 cm)
177/Røverborgen/Første Act./Partitur/[...]/Röverborgen/Syngespil i 3 Akter/af/A. Ølenschlæger. [*sic*]/sat i Musik/af/Kuhlau/ [...]/Anden og Tredie Act/Partitur.
Unsigned and undated [1814]
[DKKk; C II, 115 (KTA 177)
This orchestral score dates from the 1814 Copenhagen première of *The Brigand's Castle* and was used for all performances of it there during Bournonville's lifetime. An autographed note by H. S. Paulli (written with black ink on p. 2) reads: 'NB. Metronom-Angivelsen, tilføiet af Concertmester Bredahl,/er, navnlig for alle hurtige Tempi, for langsom./HS Paulli.'.

No répétiteur's copy for *The Brigand's Castle* has yet been traced.

Parts. Ms. Copy. 31 vol.
4 vl I, 4 vl II, 2 vla, 5 vlc e cb, fl 1/2, ob 1/2, cl 1/2, fag 1/2, cor princ, cor 1/2, tr princ, tr 1/2, timp, gr cassa e piatti e tri. 68 vocal parts.
Unsigned and undated [1814]
[DKKk; KTA 177
This set of parts dates from the 1814 Copenhagen première of *The Brigand's Castle* and was used for all performances of it there during Bournonville's lifetime.

14.3.1860

A performance **given by A. and C. Healey
(the Court Theatre).**

In his diary Bournonville listed 52 private dance lessons for his English pupils, the sisters A. and C. Healey, taught between 12.1. and 10.4.1860. They were given in preparation for a privately arranged tour to Sweden, where the Healeys performed a series of Bournonville dances at Stockholm's Royal Theatre between 23.4. and 18.5.1860. During this period of study the Healeys appeared at the Court Theatre on this day, where they took part in a special charity performance about which Bournonville noted in his diary:

3.12.1859: 'Brev til Svar paa Hartkopffs Propositioner til Healey's'
10.12.: 'Besøg af Herr Hartkopff i Anledning af et fordeelagtigt Engagement for Healey's. Jeg skrev umiddelbar til de Damer, der ere i Aalborg'
4.1.1860: 'Velkommen til Søstrene Healeÿ, der igaar kom hjem fra en meget behagelig og indbringende Reise i Jylland'
10.1.: 'indfundet mig i Apollo-salen for at give Lection til Søstrene Healeÿ, men de kom for silde'
11.1.: 'Møde hos Chefen [F. F. v. Tillisch] der meddelte mig Tilladelse til Healeyerne at öve sig paa Theatret'
13.2.: 'Telegraf fra Hartkopff om Healeys'
18.2.: 'Brev og Penge fra Hartkopff'
24.2.: 'Lection-Prøve Healeys
13.3.; 'Prøve paa Hoftheatret for Søstrene Healey'
15.3.: 'Lection til Healey's, der igaar Aftes havde gjort overordentlig Lÿkke paa Hoftheatret'.

It has not been possible yet to identify the titles of the dance(s) performed by the Healeys on this evening.

17.4.1860

Norma.

The 1860 restaging of V. Bellini's two-act lyrical tragedy (*see* 20.10.1848) represents the third time Bournonville mounted this work in Copenhagen. It seems to have been staged with only minor if any changes from his previous staging on 5.2.1858. About the production, which is not included in Bournonville's handwritten list of his stagings of operas and plays, written c.1872 (*see* Additional Sources), nor in the printed survey of his works in his memoirs *My Theatre Life* (p. 408), he noted in his diary:

16.4.1860: 'Theaterprøve paa Norma'
17.4.: 'I Theatret for udsolgt Huus. Norma med Jf [c.] Lehmann: Hovedrollen meget ypperligt i Sangen, men Spillet i det Hele svagt. – Udsolgt Huus og stor Applaus'.

The 1860 production received 3 performances the last of which was given on 27.4.1860.

The musical material employed this year was the same as that used for the 1848 staging (now in DKKkt and DKKk with the call no. KTA 344).

20.4.1860

Far from Denmark: or A Costume Ball on Board (Fjernt fra Danmark eller: et Costumebal ombord).

This two-act ballet-vaudeville is set to a score, composed and arranged by J. Glæser, H. C. Lumbye (Act II, score no. 17), and A. F. Lincke (Act II, score no. 8–9, and 18–19). However, according to the autographed orchestral score the orches-

tration of Glæser's music was carried out by four other composers as follows:

(1) V. C. Holm (Act I, the Introduction, score nos. 1–6, and parts of Act II, score no. 16).
(2) C. C. Møller (Act II, the Introduction and score nos. 6–7, 10–12, and 14).
(3) L. W. T. Carlsen (Act II, score nos. 13 and parts of no. 16).
(4) H. S. Paulli (Act II, score no. 15).

The score includes several musical borrowings, which are identified as follows:

(1) Act I, score no. 3 (scenes 6 and 7): In these numbers Glæser incorporated R. Bay's melody for H. P. Holst's poem, entitled 'Syd og Nord' («Du er rig, du er deilig, o Syd»). It was first published in Holst's *Ude og Hjemme Reise=Erindringer* (Kjøbenhavn, C. A. Reitzel, 1843) in which it is entitled *Meta. Syracusa* («Her ved Bredden af Anapos Strøm»). According to Bournonville's printed scenario for *Far from Denmark*, Bay's tune served as an allusion to the third verse in Holst's poem reading: «Over Havet, hvis blaanende Speil».
(2) Act I, score no. 6 (scene 9): Glæser here incorporated a slightly abridged version of L. M. Gottschalk's piano piece (opus 5), entitled *Le Bananier, chanson nègre (The Banana Tree)*. It was composed c.1845–46 and was published in Paris in about 1850.
(3) Act II, score no. 11 (scene 3): For this number Glæser incorporated B. Parera's melody for V. López y Planes' Argentine National Anthem from 1813, entitled «Oid mortales! el grido sagrado, Libertad!».
(4) Act II, score no. 19 (scene 8): For this scene Lincke incorporated a popular Danish broadside ballad from 1854 (with text by J. Helms), named 'En svensk konstabel fra Sverrig' («Nu vil jeg indvie jer i»). It is followed by a tune by E. Dupuy, originally written for a song in N. F. Bruun's Danish translation of A. Duval's three-act comedy *La Jeunesse d'Henry V (Henrik den femtes Ungdom)*. In that comedy it was entitled «Manden med Glas i Haand, stolt af sin høie Aand» and was first performed at Copenhagen's Royal Theatre on 6.12.1808. According to Bournonville's printed scenario for *Far from Denmark*, Dupuy's tune served as an allusion to the song's third verse, which reads: «Skjøndt du, o stolte Hav, var mangen Sømands Grav, elsker han dig». Dupuy's melody (which is also included in V. C. Holm's overture for *Far from Denmark: or A Costume Ball on Board*) had many years earlier been used by H. S. Paulli in a very similar way as an accompaniment for the concluding tableau in Act II (score no. 11) of Bournonville's two-act romantic ballet *The Isle of Phantasy* (*see* 28.10.1838).

After Dupuy's song Lincke incorporated yet another piece by this composer, namely an *English Dance (Lang=Engelsk)*. According to the first printed piano score for *Far from Denmark: or A Costume Ball on Board* (now in DKKk, call no. D 6) this music, too, was borrowed from a much earlier (not yet identified) work by Dupuy.

Next follows R. Bay's melody from c.1823 for B. S. Ingemann's poem 'Til Dannebroge' («Vift stolt paa Codans Bølge»). It was first published in his collection of poems, entitled *Julegaven* (1816). However, Bay's melody for this poem seems to be based on a much earlier German song. This is clear from F. L. Schubert's *Concordia, Anthologie classischer Volkslieder* (Leipzig, M. Schäfer, 1863, Erster Band, p. 174). In here the same melody is described as 'Volkslied' and is said to have been used in 1813 for a hymn, entitled *Allen Helden*, dedicated to 'die Gefallenen den 18. Juni und 18. October 1813'.

In his diary Bournonville noted about the long and rather troublesome creation of *Far from Denmark: or A Costume Ball on Board* and its well-received première:

13.12.1859: 'Besøg hos Anton Melbÿ i Anledning af en Tegning til et nÿt Ballet-Divertissement'
20.12.: 'besøgt […] Capt. [H.] Rothe og Melbÿ'
21.12.: 'Modtaget en Tegning af Melbÿ'

23.12.: 'skrevet og componeret'

27.12.: 'Breve til […] Capt. Møller'

5.1.1860: 'hjem og componeret paa en nÿ Ballet […] reenskrevet 1.ste Akt'

6.1.: 'componeret paa min nÿ Ballet'

7.1.: 'reenskrevet paa min nÿ Ballet […] fuldført Reenskrivningen af min nÿ Ballet – 'Langt fra Danmark eller Et Costumebal ombord''

15.1.: 'Talt med den unge [J.] Glaëser [*sic*] om Musikcompositionen til min nÿ Ballet'

16.1.: 'Arbeidet første Gang med Glaëser jr der skal componere Musik til min nÿ Ballet'

24.1.: 'første Møde med Glaëser jun'

28.1.: 'fortsat mit Skrivt om Balletten'

31.1.: 'J Glaëser'

3.2.: 'Musik med J Glaëser'

5.2.: 'arbeidet med J Glaëser. Besøg hos Capt Rothe i Anledning af Balletten'

9.2.: 'skrevet og arrangeret, arbeidet med J Glaëser'

13.2. and 15.2.: 'arbeidet med J Glaëser'

17.2.: 'skrevet til [J. O. E.] Hornemann […] besøg hos [E.] Lehmann […] arbeidet med J Glaëser'

20.2.: 'componeret lidt paa min nÿ Ballet'

22.2.: 'skrevet og componeret'

23.2.: 'componeret'

24.2.: 'skrevet og componeret'

25.2.: 'skrevet og arbeidet med J Glaëser […] min første Indstudering af den nÿ Ballet 'Fjernt fra Danmark', Prøve fra 11–2"

26.2.: 'componeret'

27.2.: 'skrevet og componeret. 2.den Indst: paa den nÿ Ballet fra 11–1 1/2

28.2.: 'skrevet og componeret, Repetition fra 10–11 […] Hele Aftenen componeret'

29.2.: '3.die Indst: paa den nÿ Ballet […] arbeidet med Lehmann'

1.3.: 'hjemme og componeret'

2.3.: 'Repetiton Kl 10 paa den nÿ Ballet og 4.de Indstudering (Negerdandsen.)'

3.3.: 'Fra 10–11 5.e Indstudering og 1.ste Akt færdig'

6.3.: 'Aftenprøve paa 1.ste Akt af min nÿ Ballet'

8.3.: 'skrevet og arrangeret. 6.te Indstudering Eskimo-Dandsen […] componeret den hele Aften'

9.3.: 'skrevet og componeret. Lille Prøve paa den nÿ Ballet […] Efterm arbeidet med Glaëser'

10.3.: 'skrevet og componeret. Repetition paa Fjernt fra Danmark […] componeret den hele Efterm:'

11.3.: 'componeret'

12.3.: 'skrevet og componeret. 7.de Indst (Styrmandsdandsen) […] Efterm. arbeidet med Lehmann og Glaëser'

13.3.: 'Prøve Kl 10–12, 8.de Indstudering Chineserdandsen […] Eftermiddagen componeret'

14.3.: 'skrevet og arrangeret, 9.de Indst. (Quadrillen og Bayadèredandsen)'

16.3.: 'skrevet og arrangeret. Repetition paa 'Fjernt fra Danmark' […] Afleveret Costume=Regiet. Efterm. skrevet og componeret'

17.3.: 'skrevet og arrangeret. Repetition paa den nÿ Ballet. Den større Prøve forhindret ved Skuespilforandring'

18.3.: 'arrangeret og componeret'

20.3.: '1.ste Theaterprøve, Arrangement og 11.te Indstudering paa Fjernt fra Danmark, det gik meget godt og varede fra 10–1 […] Om Aftenen Costumemøde paa Theatret […] besøgt Glaëser og arbeidet lidt med ham'

21.3.: 'Prøve paa Fjernt fra Danmark og Præsentation for Chefen [F. F. v. Tillisch], der var særdeles tilfreds […] Aftenen hjemme og componeret'

22.3.: 'skrevet og componeret. Ingen Prøve men Lection og conference med Glaëser (lidet glædelig, da han aldeles er standset med Arbeidet og maa tvinges til at tage Hjælp)'

23.3.: 'Theaterprøve fra 10–12'

24.3.: 'Kl 11 den 12.e Indstudering `Fandangoen´, Conference med Chefen og afgjort at der skulde requireres Assistance ved Instrumenteringen […] Eftermiddag talt med [L. W. T.] Carlsen, [C. C.]

Møller og [A. F.] Lincke der lovede mig den fornødne Bistand, desværre [H. S.] Paulli kan ikke hjælpe os formedelst en daarlig Haand. – Jeg skrev til Glaëser og traf alle fornødne Anstalter til Ballettens musikalske Fuldendelse'

25.3.: 'skrevet og componeret, besørget endeel og ærgret mig over Glaëser, der skulker fra Alting'

26.3.: 'componeret, 13.de Indst. Juliette [Price] og [H.] Scharff 'Fandango' (de assisterende med)'

27.3.: 'componeret […] 14.e Indst Fandangoen og tilhørende Jaleo […] Brev fra J Glaëser med Rendez-vous. Aftale med ham og reen Besked at han ikke har skrevet en eneste Takt Partitur, men nu vil overlade Instrumentationen til Andre!! – Strax hen til [E.] Helsted'

28.3.: 'skrevet, besørget adskilligt for mine Partitur skrivere! Theaterprøve paa 1.ste Akt af Fjernt fra Danmark. Bryderier med Helsted […] Besøg hos Lincke, der gav mig Udkastet til Finalen, [N. W.] Gade, der fortalte mig hvorlunde det forholdt sig med Glaësers Kundskaber!'

29.3.: 'skrevet og arrangeret, beørget adskilligt i Anledning af Balletten. Repetition paa Dandsene'

30.3.: 'componeret. 15.de Indstudering – Finalen. […] talt med mine Instrumentister, der arbeide rask – Intet endnu fra Glaëser, [H. C.] Lumbÿ[e] componerer Krigerdandsen – arbeidet med Lincke'

31.3.: 'componeret og skrevet Noter. Prøve Kl 11 paa den nÿ Ballet og 16.de Indstudering, Vildmandsdandsen […] besøgt Instrumentisterne […] Besøg hos Lumbÿ, derfra meget træt hjem'

1.4.: 'componeret. Besøg hos Holm og Lincke […] Om Eftermiddagen skrevet og arrangeret'

2.4.: 'skrevet og arrangeret. Møde med Lincke […] Prøve og 17.de Indstudering […] Besøg hos Prof [F.] Glaëser'

3.4.: 'skrevet og arrangeret, Arrangementprøve paa Ballettens 2.den Akt […] Om Eftermiddagen Kl 5½–7 Prøve med 16 Mand fra Holmen, der skal udføre Matroser i Balletten, de vare ganske fortræffelige og det morede mig særdeles'

4.4.: 'skrevet og arrangeret […] Prøve og 18. sidste Indstudering paa 'Fjernt fra Danmark' Eftermiddagsprøve paa hele 2.den Akt, der gik meget tilfredstillende (6–8)'

6.4.: 'skrevet mit Program til Trykken'

7.4.: 'skrevet og arrangeret […] Prøve paa Dandsene til den nÿ Ballet […] besørget adskilligt ved min Ballet, – fuldendt Programmet som [F.] Høedt besørger til Trykken. – Langt Besøg hos ham'

8.4.: 'Jeg besørgede endnu adskilligt og overbeviste mig om at hele 2.den Akt af Balletten nu var instrumenteret […] Brev til [F. F. v.] Tillisch i Anledning af Musiken til Fjernt fra Danmark'

10.4.: 'Theaterprøve Kl 10 paa 'Fjernt fra Danmark' 1.ste Akt […] Brev fra [J.] Glaëser – Svar'

11.4.: 'Prøve paa Dandsene og med Holst Kl 11'

12.4.: 'Theaterprøve paa Ballettens begge Akter – som gik meget godt'

14.4.: 'besørget adskilligt med Hensÿn til Programmet. – Musikcorrecturprøve paa Balletten. Heldigt Udfald af Instrumentationen'

15.4.: 'Fuldstændig Prøve paa Balletten Kl 12–2, – den gik udmærket godt'

16.4.: 'fuldstændig Prøve paa 1.ste Akt af Balletten […] Efter Theatret Decorationsprøve, hvor [C. F.] Christensen i høieste Grad har udmærket sig. – færdig Kl 1½'

17.4.: 'Theaterprøve paa 2.den Akt, uden Orchester. – Sendt Programmer'

18.4.: 'Lille Prøve paa Costumer og Forvandlinger […] Generalprøve Kl 7 paa Fjernt fra Danmark. Den gik udmærket godt og gjorde god Virkning'

19.4.: 'Brev og Program til Admiral [S. A.] Bille. Besørget adskilligt paa Theatret […] Svar fra Admiral Bille og et smukt Vers fra [H. C.] Andersen'

20.4.: 'Musikprøve Kl 10 […] Første Forestilling af min Ballet 'Fjernt fra Danmark' der gik udmærket godt og gjorde stormende Lÿkke. Ethvert Point blev grebet med Begeistring og det Hele gjorde et fortræffeligt Indtryk – Billetterne vare revne bort og Kongen overværede Forestillingen. – [F.] Høedt, Consul Unnas og Capt Rohtes [*sic*] var hos os til Aften og Glæde herskede i min Famillie der Alle, paa Helene nær havde været i Theatret. – Jeg takkede Gud af mit inderste Hjerte'

27.4.: 'Møde paa Theatercomptoiret [J.] Glaëser modtaget sig Honnorar'.

Apart from some later minor cuts in the Act II *Fandango*, and partially new casts (on 7.3.1872, 20.9.1876, and 5.3.1878), the ballet was (according to Bournonville's diaries and the posters) performed without any significant changes throughout Bournonville's lifetime. During that period it reached a total of 130 performances, the last of which was given on 30.5.1879.

Autograph sources:

Production note. Ms. Autograph (partially in another's hand, perhaps by H. Rothe?). Brown and black ink. 7 pp. (20,2 × 13,4 & 22,1 × 13,8 cm)
Spørgsmaal med Hensyn til/Forholdene ombord i en Orlogsmand / i de tropiske Farvande/[...]/Svar!
Unsigned and undated [Written probably in December 1859]
[DKKk; NKS 3285 4° 2 F

Manuscript scenario (incomplete). Ms. Autograph. Brown ink. 8 pp. (21, 5 × 13,7 cm)
Et Costumebal Ombord./Ballet i to Tableauer.
Unsigned and undated [Written probably between 5.1 and 7.1. 1860]
[DKKk; NKS 3285 4° 2 F

Manuscript scenario. Ms. Autograph. Brown ink. 1 vol. 14 pp. (21,4 × 13,7 cm)
Langt [changed by an unknown hand to: Fjernt] fra Danmark./ eller/Et Costumebal ombord./Ballet i to Akter/af/August Bournonville/1860.
Signed and dated: 'd. 6 Januar 1860.' [Written according to the diary on 6.1. and 7.1.1860]
[DKKk; NKS 3285 4° 2 F

Musical instructions. Ms. Autograph. Black ink. 3 pp. (21,4 × 13,4 cm)
2.den Akt 6.te Scene./[...]/7.e Scene./[...]/8.de Scene (forandret Program)
Unsigned and undated [Written probably in late March, 1860]
[DKKk; NKS 3285 4° 2 F

Production note. Ms. Autograph. Black ink. 2 pp. (20,7 × 17cm)
Fjernt fra Danmark./eller,/Et Costûmebal ombord./Vaudeville = Ballet i Akter af A Bournonville./(Musiken tildeels componeret [erased] af Herr Joseph Gläser)/Decorationerne af Dherr Lund og Christensen./Costûmerne tegnede af Herr E Lehmann.l/Personerne.
Unsigned and undated [Written probably in late March 1860]
[DKKk; NKS 3285 4° 2 F

Production note. Ms. Autograph. Black ink. 4 pp. (20,8 × 17,1 cm)
Personale i 1.ste Act/[...]/Personale i 2.den Act:/[...]/Dandse i 2.den Akt.
Unsigned and undated [written probably in February–March 1860]
[DKKk; NKS 3285 4° 2 F

Production note. Ms. Autograph. Brown ink. 4 pp. (21,4 × 13,4 cm)
Personale i 2.den Akt/af/Et Costumebal ombord/[...]/Dandsenes Fölge./[...]/1.e Akt./Negerdands.
Unsigned and undated [written probably in February–March 1860]
[DKKk; NKS 3285 4° 2 F

Production note. Ms. Autograph. Black ink. 2 pp. (21,6 × 13,5 cm)
Assistenternes Partie/i/Balletten Fjernt fra Danmark.
Unsigned and undated [written probably in February–March 1860]
[DKKk; NKS 3285 4° 2 F

Mimic-choreographic note. Ms. Autograph. Brown ink. 4 pp. (20,9 × 16,9 cm)
Fjernt fra Danmark/1.ste Akt. 1.ste Scene. No. 1./[...]/2.den scène No. 2./[...]/4.de Scene./[...]/No. 3. 6.te Scene.
Unsigned and undated [written probably in February–March 1860]
[DKKk; NKS 3285 4° 2 F

Choreographic note. Ms. Autograph. Black ink. 1 p. (20,9 × 16,9 cm)
1. [choreographic diagram] a. Polonaise en – avant/b & c tour de main.
Unsigned and undated [written probably in February–March 1860]
[DKKk; NKS 3285 4° 2 F

Choreographic note. Ms. Autograph. Black ink. 2 pp. (20,9 × 11,5 cm)
Esquimaux:
Unsigned and undated [written probably in February–March 1860]
[DKKk; NKS 3285 4° 2 F

Choreographic note. Ms. Autograph. Black ink. 2 pp. (20,3 × 13,4 cm)
Pas Chinois/[F.] Hoppe o [A.] Fredstrup & [E.] Stramboe x. [L.] Stillmann & Petrine [Fredstrup] ·.
Unsigned and undated [written probably in February–March 1860]
[DKKk; NKS 3285 4° 2 F

Choreographic note. Ms. Autograph. Black ink. 1 p. (20,6 × 16,9 cm)
Danse des Bayadères.
Unsigned and undated [written probably in February–March 1860]
[DKKk; NKS 3285 4° 2 F

Choreographic note. Ms. Autograph. Brown ink. 5 pp. (21,6 × 13,6 cm)
Jaleo/[...]/Juliette [Price] seule/[...]/[F.] Hoppe [W.]Funck [E.] Stramboe:/[...]/[H.] Scharff entre en scène/[...]/Jaleo suite./ [...]/Coda./[...]/Fandango (1.ière Partie)/[...]/Ensemble des Dames & Cavaliers:/[...]/Fin du Fandango.
Unsigned and undated [written probably in February–March, 1860]
[DKKk; NKS 3285 4° 2 F

Choreographic note [i.e. 'Fandango (1.ière Partie)'?]. Ms. Autograph. Brown ink. 1 p. (12,6 × 10,4 cm)
1. Cp. br. [stenochoreographic sign] cp. br. [stenochoreographic sign]. Bis en remontant
Unsigned and undated [written probably in February–March 1860]
[DKKk; NKS 3285 4° 2 F

Choreographic note. Ms. Autograph. Brown ink. 1 p. (20,5 × 16,8 cm)
Danse (guèrrière des Indiens.)
Unsigned and undated [written probably in February–March 1860]
[DKKk; NKS 3285 4° 2 F

Choreographic note. Ms. Autograph. Brown ink. 2 pp. (20,5 × 19,4 cm)
La Chansonnière. (Les lanternes sont allumées.)/[...]/Anglaise./ [...]/Coda.
Unsigned and undated [written probably in February–March 1860]
[DKKk; NKS 3285 4° 2 F

Choreographic note. Ms. Autograph. Brown ink. 1 vol. 30 pp. (20,2 × 13,5 cm)
Fjernt fra Danmark./eller,/Et Costumebal ombord./Notes choré-graphiques.
Unsigned and undated [written probably in February–March 1860]
[DKKk; NKS 3285 4° 2 F

Mimic note. Ms. Autograph. Ink. 2 pp. (format unknown)
Wilhelms Rolle i Fjernt fra Danmark/1.ste Akt 1.ste Scene/No. 1/ [...]/No. 2/[...]/7.de Scene/[...]/8.de Scene/[...]/No. 5

Unsigned and undated [written probably in February–March 1860] [USNYp; Dance Collection, call nos. *ZBD-71 (microfilm), and (S)*MGZMD 30 (photostat copy)

Production note. Ms. Autograph. Black ink. 2 pp. (21,4 × 13,7 cm)
Dame – Costumer til Balletten/'Fjernt fra Danmark'
Unsigned and undated [written probably in February–March 1860]
[DKKk; NKS 3285 4° 2 F

Production note. Ms. Autograph. Black ink. 4 pp. (21,4 × 13,7 cm)
Costumer til Balletten/Fjernt fra Danmark.
Unsigned and undated [written probably in February–March 1860]
(DKKk; NKS 3285 4° 2 F

Manuscript scenario. Ms. Copy (with Bournonville's autographed corrections). 1 vol. 24 pp. (22,2 × 17,6 cm)
Fjernt fra Danmark/eller et Costumebal ombord./Ballet i to Acter/af/August Bournonville./1860.
Unsigned and dated: '1860.'
[DKKk; NKS 3285 4° 2 F

Musical sources:

Orchestral score. Ms. Autographs (by V. C. Holm, C. C. Møller, A. F. Lincke, L. W. T. Carlsen, H. S. Paulli, and H. C. Lumbye). Brown and black ink. 1 vol. 366 pp. of which one is blank (29,7 × 34,7 cm with several variants)
Fjernt fra Danmark/eller/Et Costumebal ombord,/Vaudeville Ballet/i/2 Acter/af/A Bournonville/Musiken tildeels af Hr. Glæser jun:
Signed and dated (on p. 170): 'A. F. Lincke', (p. 268) 'HSPaulli 1860.', (p. 307) 'af H: C: Lumbÿe', (p. 366) 'A. F. Lincke/A. F. L. (: 8/4 [18]60:)'
[DKKk; C II, 110 (KTB 285) (mu 7911.1161)

Répétiteur's copy. Ms. Copy. Brown ink. 1 vol. 108 pp. of which one is blank (32,9 × 24,7 cm)
3/B. 285/'Fjernt fra Danmark.'/[…]/Repetiteurstemme/til/Fjernt fra Danmark
Unsigned and undated [1860]
[DKKk; MA ms 2983 (KTB 285) (mu 8608.2279)
This répétiteur's copy contains Bournonville's autographed notes (written with brown ink) describing in fine detail the dramatic action, the mime, and the choreography of Act I and Act II (the Introduction, score nos. 7–10, and parts of no. 16). Moreover, apart from Act II, score nos. 16–19 his autographed choreographic numbers (written with black ink) are inserted throughout the volume. They refer to his eleven separate choreographic descriptions of this ballet, which (according to his diary) were written during the months of February and March 1860.

Parts (incomplete). Ms. Copy. 35 + 12 vol.
3 vl I, 4 vl II, 2 vla, 2 vlc, 2 cb, fl 1/23, ob 1/2, cl 1/2, fag 1/2, cor 1/2/3/4, tr 1/2, trb 1/2/3, timp, gr cassa, piatti, tri, arpa. On stage: fl, cl 1/2, fag, cor 1/2, trb, tuba, 4 inserts.
Unsigned and undated [1860]
[DKKk; KTB 285

Part. Ms. Copy. 1 vol.
On stage: trb.
Unsigned and undated [1860]
[DKKk; KTB 1057 (originally KTB 285)

Other sources:

Costume drawing by E. Lehmann. Pencil and water colours (23,2 × 12,3 cm)
Fernandes (Hr Füssel sen.) 1 D/No. 1
Unsigned and undated [c.1860]
[DKKkt; Kostumetegninger (Lehmann)

This drawing shows the first costume of *Fernandez* in Act I of *Far from Denmark* (performed by Gott. A. Füssel)

Costume drawing by E. Lehmann. Pencil and water colours (23,8 × 13 cm)
Jason (Hr. Fredstrup)/No. 5.
Unsigned and undated [c.1860]
[DKKkt; Kostumetegninger (Lehmann)
This drawing shows the costume of *Jason* in Act I of *Far from Denmark* (performed by A. Fredstrup).

Costume drawing by E. Lehmann. Pencil and water colours (23,8 × 13,2 cm)
No. 5./Medea (Jfr Borup)
Unsigned and undated [c.1860]
[DKKkt; Kostumetegninger (Lehmann)
This drawing shows the costume of *Medea* in Act I of *Far from Denmark* (performed by N. Borup).

Costume drawing by E. Lehmann. Pencil and water colours (13 × 24 cm)
Rosita (Jfr J. Price) 1 Dr./Fjærnt fra Danmark
Unsigned and undated [c.18 60]
[SSm; Daniel Fryklunds samling no. 260 (F 1325 e)
This drawing shows the first costume worn by *Rosita* in Act I of *Far from Denmark* (performed by Juliette Price).

Costume drawing by E. Lehmann. Pencil and water colours (13 × 24 cm)
N° 2./2 Dragt/Juliette Price i/'Fjærnt fra Danmark'
Unsigned and undated [c.1860]
[SSm; Daniel Fryklunds samling no. 261 (F 1325 f)
This drawing shows the second costume worn by *Rosita* in Act I (scenes 8 and 9) and Act II of *Far from Denmark* (performed by Juliette Price).

Costume drawing by E. Lehmann. Pencil and water colours (23,7 × 12,4 cm)
1 Dragt/No. 2
Unsigned and undated [c.1860]
[DKKkt; Kostumetegninger (Lehmann)
This drawing shows the second costume worn by *Fernandez* in Act I (scenes 8 and 9) and Act II of *Far from Denmark* (performed by Gott. A. Füssel).

Costume drawing by E. Lehmann. Pencil and water colours (13 × 24 cm)
Ole (Hr Gade)./Fjærnt fra Danmark
Unsigned and undated [c.1860]
[SSm; Daniel Fryklunds samling no. 262 (F 1325 d)
This drawing shows the costume of *Ole the Bargeman* in *Far from Denmark* (performed by L. Gade).

Costume drawing by E. Lehmann. Pencil and water colours (23,7 × 13,2 cm)
No. 12./Jungmænd (Damer)
Unsigned and undated [c.1860]
[DKKkt; Kostumetegninger (Lehmann)
This drawing shows the costumes of the ordinary seamen in Act II of *Far from Denmark* (performed by the women of the corps de ballet *en travestie*).

Costume drawing by E. Lehmann. Pencil and water colours (23,7 × 13,2 cm)
No. 13./Skibsdrenge (Elever)
Unsigned and undated [c.1860]
[DKKkt; Kostumetegninger (Lehmann)
This drawing shows the costume of the ship's boys in Act II of *Far from Denmark* (performed by the apprentices of the ballet school).

Costume drawing by E. Lehmann. Pencil and water colours (23,8 × 13,1 cm)
No. 7./2 Dragt
Unsigned and undated [c.1860]
[DKKkt; Kostumetegninger (Lehmann)
This drawing shows the costume of *The Chief Boatswain* disguised as *Neptune* in Act II (scene 3) of *Far from Denmark* (performed by G. Ad. Füssel).

Costume drawing by E. Lehmann. Pencil and water colours (13 × 24 cm)
N° 14./De fire Vinde
Unsigned and undated [c.1860]
[SSm; Daniel Fryklunds samling no. 263 (F 132 c)
This drawing shows the costume of the four seamen disguised as the *Four Winds* in the procession with *Neptune* in Act II (scene 3) of *Far from Denmark*.

Costume drawing by E. Lehmann. Pencil and water colours (23,3 × 13,2 cm)
Najader – No. 7.
Unsigned and undated [c.1860]
[DKKkt; Kostumetegninger (Lehmann)
This drawing shows the costumes of the corps de ballet of naiads who accompanied *Neptune* in Act II of *Far from Denmark*.

Costume drawing by E. Lehmann. Pencil and water colours (13 × 24 cm)
Eskimodandsen i 'Fjernt fra Danmark'/Tegn af Edv. Lehmann.
Unsigned and undated [c.1860]
[SSm; Daniel Fryklunds samling no. 263 [a] (F 1325 a)
This drawing shows the costume of the women in the *Eskimo Dance* in Act II (scene four) of *Far from Denmark* (performed by J. Tardini).

Costume drawing by E. Lehmann. Pencil and water colours (13 × 24 cm)
Eskimodandsen i 'Fjernt fra Danmark'/Tegn af Edv. Lehmann.
Unsigned and undated [c.1860]
[SSm; Daniel Fryklunds samling no. 263 [b] (F 1325 b)
This drawing shows the costume of the man in the *Eskimo Dance* in Act II (scene 4) of *Far from Denmark* (performed by F. Gold).

Costume drawing by E. Lehmann. Pencil and water colours (23,3 × 13,1 cm)
Bayadere/No. 4.
Unsigned and undated [c.1860]
[DKKkt; Kostumetegninger (Lehmann)
This drawing shows the costume of the corps de ballet of bayadères in Act II (scene four) of *Far from Denmark*.

Costume drawing by E. Lehmann. Pencil and water colours (23,9 × 16,3 cm)
Indianerinde
Unsigned and undated [c.1860]
[DKKkt; Kostumetegninger (Lehmann)
This drawing shows the costume of the Indian women performing the *Indian War Dance* in Act II (scene seven) of *Far from Denmark*.

Printed sources:

Printed scenario. 1 vol. 15 pp. (20 × 12,7 cm)
Fjernt fra Danmark,/eller:/Et Costumebal ombord./Vaudeville=Ballet i to Akter/af/August Bournonville./Musiken tildeels af Hr. Glæser jun. Decorationerne af/DHrr. Lund og Christensen. Costumerne tegnede/af Hr. Edw. Lehmann.
Kjøbenhavn, J. H. Schubothe/Bianco Luno/F. S. Muhle, 1860.
[DKKk; 17, – 175 8°

23.4.1860
Polketta, arranged by A. Bournonville (arrangerad af A. Bournonville) **performed by A. and C. Healey (Stockholm's Royal Theatre, Operahuset).**
This dance is identical with the (uncredited) *Polketta, Pas de deux*, first performed by the Healey sisters at Copenhagen's Casino Theatre on 31.10.1858. It was performed by them 10 times in Stockholm, the last time at Stora Theatern on 6.1.1864.

Musical sources:

No orchestral score and répétiteur's copy for Bournonville's and H. C. Lumbye's *Polketta* have yet been traced in Stockholm.

Parts. Ms. Copy. 26 vol.
3 vl I, 3 vl II, 2 vla, 3 vcl e cb, fl picc, fl, ob 1/2, cl 1/2, fag 1/2, cor 1/2, tr 1/2, trb, gr cassa, cassa.
Unsigned and undated [c.1860]
[SSkma; KT Dansmusik 101

23.4.1860
Scene and Pas de trois from The Return (Scen och Pas de trois från Hemkomsten) **(Stockholm's Royal Theatre, Davidsons Paviljong).**
This divertissement was arranged and mounted by Bournonville's pupil, S. Lund. It is based on excerpts from his pantomimic idyll *Soldier and Peasant* (*see* 13.10.1829), which had been mounted for the first time in Stockholm (Operahuset) by Bournonville's Swedish pupil, P. C. Johansson, with the title *Hemkomsten* (*see* 22.1.1838). Lund's 1860 divertissement version was performed only once at Davidsons Paviljong. The musical material employed this year was most probably the same as that used for *Hemkomsten* in 1838 (now in SSkma, call no. KT Pantomime-Balletter H 2).

26.4.1860
Grand Pas de deux from the ballet 'The Flower Festival' (Stor pas de deux, ur Balletten 'Blomsterfesten') **(uncredited) performed by A. and C. Healey (Stockholm's Royal Theatre, Operahuset).**
This (uncredited) dance is most likely an adapted version for two women (perhaps arranged by Bournonville himself?) of the *Pas de deux* (score no. 12) danced by the characters *Rosa* and *Paolo* in Bournonville's one-act ballet *The Flower Festival in Genzano* (*see* 19.12.1858). It was given twice in Stockholm by the Healey sisters, the first time as an *entr'acte* divertissement in J. F. A. Bayard's and J. de Wailly's three-act comedy *Le Mari à la campagne (Den gifta Mannen i staden och på landet)*, and the second time as an incorporated divertissement between Acts I and II of C. M. v. Weber's three-act romantic opera *Der Freischütz (Friskytten)* on 13.5.1860.

Musical sources:

Orchestral score. Ms. Copy. 1 vol. 128 pp. (34,3 × 25,8 cm)
Blomsterfesten/i/Genzano/Partitur
Unsigned and undated [c.1860?–1887]
[SSkma; KT Pantomime-Balletter B 8

Répétiteur's copy. Ms. copy. 12 pp. (35 × 26 cm with minor variants)
Repetitörstämma/till/'Blomsterfesten'/af A. Bournonville./2.ra Afdelingen.

Unsigned and dated (on the title-page): '[18]88./ d. 28/1, 4/2, 24/ 2, 18/4.'
[SSkma; KT Pantomime-Balletter B 8

This répétiteur's copy seems to date from (or at least was used for) the much later Stockholm staging of *Section II of 'The Flower Festival in Genzano' (Andra Afdelingen af 'Blomsterfesten i Genzano')*, mounted on 25.3.1887 by Bournonville's pupil, E. Hansen. This theory is supported by the four datings (written by an unknown hand) on the title-page.

Parts. Ms. Copy. 35 vol.
3 vl I, 3 vl II, 2 vla, 4 vlc e cb, fl 1/2, cl 1/2, ob 1/2, fag 1/2, cor 1/2/ 3/4, tr 1/2, trb 1/2/3, timp, gr cassa, piatti, tamb, tri, arpa.
Unsigned and undated [1860?–1887]
[SSkma; KT Pantomime-Balletter B 8

30.4.1860
'El Capricio', arranged by A. Bournonville (arrangerad af A. Bournonville) **performed by A. and C. Healey (Stockholm's Royal Theatre, Operahuset).**
This dance is identical with the (uncredited) *El Capricio, Jaleo*, first performed by A. and C. Healey to a score by H. C. Lumbye at Copenhagen's Casino Theatre on 1.12.1858. It was given twice by them in Stockholm in 1860. No musical sources for this dance have yet been traced in Sweden.

15.5.1860
Martha oder Der Markt zu Richmond (Martha eller Markedet i Richmond).
The 1860 restaging of F. v. Flotow's four-act romantic comic opera (premièred at Vienna's Kärnthnerthor Theatre on 25.11.1847, and first performed at Copenhagen's Royal Theatre on 23.12.1852) was originally projected by Bournonville on 30.10.1857 and reproposed by him on 20.1.1858. It represents the first and only time this work was mounted under his direction in Copenhagen. The restaging is not included in Bournonville's handwritten list of his stagings of operas and plays, written c.1872 (*see* Additional Sources), nor in the printed survey of his works in his memoirs *My Theatre Life* (p. 409).

In his diary he noted about the performance:

23.4.1860: 'Arrangement paa Martha'
24.4.: 'Kostumemøde paa Martha'
25.4.: 'Quartett og Arrangementprøve paa Martha'
27.4.: 'Seneprøve paa Martha'
28.4.: 'Theaterprøve paa Martha med Orchester'.

Bournonville did not attend the opening night because of a trip to Germany and France between 29.4.1860 and 31.5. 1860. Later on the same year he directed a stage rehearsal of *Martha* on 15.10.1860 in preparation for a performance on 16.10.1860 which he attended, but made no specific comments about.

The 1860 restaging received 4 performances, the last of which was given on 16.10.1860.

Musical sources:

Printed orchestral score with several manuscript insertions. 3 vol. Act I 298 pp., Act II–III 122 pp., Act IV 128 pp. (32,8 × 25,2 cm)
Als Manuscript/Martha/oder/Der Markt zu Richmond/Opera in vier Abtheilungen
s. l. s. a. [c.1847]
[DKKkt; KTA 451

This specially printed orchestral score dates from the 1847 Copenhagen première of *Martha*, and was used for all performances of it there during Bournonville's lifetime.

No répétiteur's copy for *Martha* has yet been traced.

Parts. Ms. Copy. 35 + 2 vol.
4 vl I, 3 vl II, 2 vla, 2 vlc, 2 cb, fl 1/2, ob 1/2, cl 1/2, fag 1/2, cor 1/ 2/3/4, tr 1/2, trb 1/2/3, timp, gr cassa, piatti, tri, arpa. On stage: cassa, glock.
Unsigned and undated [1847]
[DKKk; KTA 451

This set of parts dates from the 1847 Copenhagen première of *Martha*, and was used for all performances of it there during Bournonville's lifetime.

17.5.1860
Grand pas de gracieux, (previously danced by the Elssler sisters) (förut dansad af systrarne Elssler) **(uncredited) performed by A. and C. Healey (Stockholm's Royal Theatre, Operahuset).**
This (uncredited) dance is most probably identical with the earlier, similarly uncredited *Pas de deux gracieux*, which was originally arranged by Bournonville for the Healey sisters and first performed by them in Copenhagen at the Casino Theatre on 17.11.1858. The dance was given only once in Stockholm and was performed as an *entr'acte* divertissement between Act I and II of C. M. v. Weber's three-act romantic opera *Der Freischütz (Friskytten)*. No musical sources for this dance have yet been traced in Stockholm.

17.5.1860
'La Tarantella' **(uncredited) performed by A. and C. Healey (Stockholm's Royal Theatre, Operahuset).**
This dance is almost certainly identical with Bournonville's and H. C. Lumbye's earlier *Tarantella=Napolitana*, premièred by the Healey sisters at Copenhagen's Casino Theatre on 1.3.1859. *'La Tarantella'* was performed twice by them in Stockholm, the last time on 18.5.1860. No musical sources for this dance have yet been traced in Sweden.

18.5.1860
'Pas de Polonaise' **(uncredited) performed by A. and C. Healey (Stockholm's Royal Theatre, Operahuset).**
This dance is almost certainly identical with the (uncredited) *Polonaise*, choreographed by Bournonville to a score by H. C. Lumbye and first performed by the Healey sisters at Copenhagen's Casino Theatre on 31.3.1859. *'Pas de Polonaise'* was performed only once in Stockholm where it was given as an *entr'acte* divertissement between Acts II and III in J. F. A. Bayard's and J. de Wailly's three-act comedy *Le Mari à la campagne (Den gifta Mannen i staden och på landet)*. No musical sources for this dance have yet been traced in Sweden.

1.6.1860
Pas de deux and Balabile from the ballet The Flower Festival in Genzano (Pas de deux et Balabile ur Balletten Blomsterfesten i Genzano) **performed by F. Hoppe, W. Price, Juliette Price, and S. Price (Stockholm's Mindre Theatern).**
Both of these dances are adaptations (perhaps arranged by Bournonville himself?) of excerpts from his one-act ballet *The Flower Festival in Genzano* (*see* 19.12.1858). They were especially arranged this year for a summer tour to Stockholm

of four of the most outstanding dancers of the Royal Danish Ballet. The dances were given twice in Stockholm, the last time on 3.6.1860. Bournonville did not attend any of the eleven performances given during the 1860 Stockholm summer tour of these four leading Danish dancers.

Musical sources:

Printed piano score. 1 vol. 3 pp. (34,9 × 26,7 cm)
Scene ur Balletten Blomsterfesten,/[...]/dansade af/Juliette och Sophie Price.
Stockholm, Abr. Lundquist, pl. no. 465 [c.1860]
DKKk; D 6 (mu 7912.2926)
This Swedish piano score represents the only known music source that dates from the 1860 Stockholm version of Bournonville's *Pas de deux et Ballabile from the ballet The Flower Festival in Genzano*. It contains the same music as that of the introduction, the girl's second solo variation, and the coda in H. S. Paulli's 1858 score for the *Pas de deux* (score no. 12) in *The Flower Festival in Genzano*.

1.6.1860

The Sailor's Return (Matrosens Hjemkomst) **performed by W. Price and S. Price (Stockholm's Mindre Theatern).**

This dance is identical with Bournonville's 1852 divertissement *'The Sailor's Return', Scene and English Character Dance ('Matrosens Hjemkomst' Scene og engelsk Characteerdands)*, first performed at Christiania's Theatre (Oslo) on 9.6.1852. In Sweden the divertissement had been staged on one earlier occasion at Stockholm's Royal Theatre (Operahuset) on 27.12.1856, but in a freely adapted version, arranged by Bournonville's pupil, S. Lund. Bournonville's original 1852 version of it was given 3 times at Stockholm's Mindre Theatern, the last time on 19.6.1860.

Musical sources:

Printed piano score. 1 vol. 2 pp. (34,9 × 26,7 cm)
Engelsk Matrosdands,/[...]/dansade af/Juliette och Sophie Price.
Stockholm, Abr. Lundquist, pl. no. 465 [c.1860]
DKKk; D 6 (mu 7912.2926)
This Swedish piano score represents the only known musical source for the 1860 Stockholm version of Bournonville's *The Sailor's Return*. It contains only the music by I. P. E. Hartmann for the *Hornpipe* in this divertissement.

1.6.1860

Seguidille, Spanish Dance (Spansk Dans) **performed by F. Hoppe, W. Price, Juliette Price, and S. Price (Stockholm's Mindre Theatern).**

This dance is most probably a free adaptation (perhaps arranged by Bournonville himself?) of *La Seguedilla (after Taglioni)* in the second and final version of his Spanish Ballet divertissement *La Ventana* (see 6.10.1856). It was performed 4 times in Stockholm, the last time on 17.6.1860.

Musical sources:

Printed piano score. 1 vol. 3 pp. (34,9 × 26,7 cm)
[...]/Seguidille, (Spansk dans)/dansade af/Juliette och Sophie Price.
Stockholm, Abr. Lundquist, pl. no. 465 [c.1860]
DKKk; D 6 (mu 7912.2926)
This Swedish piano score represents the only known musical source for the 1860 Stockholm version of Bournonville's *La Seguedilla (after Taglioni)*. It contains an abridged version of V. C. Holm's original 1856 musical arrangement of this dance.

5.6.1860

Scene and Pas de deux from the opera Le Dieu et la bayadère (Scène och Pas de deux ur Operan Brama och Bayadéren) **performed by W. Price, Juliette Price, and S. Price (Stockholm's Mindre Theatern).**

According to the musical sources for this work it was a choreographic-mimic adaptation of selected excerpts from Act II (score no. 10) of Bournonville's 1859 Copenhagen mise-en-scène for D.-F.-E. Auber's two-act opera-ballet (see 6.10.1859, and also 7.2.1841). Thus, on the poster it is explicitly presented as a work 'composed' (*komponerad*) by Bournonville. The excerpts appear to have been especially arranged and choreographed in Copenhagen for the 1860 privately arranged summer tour to Stockholm of four of Bournonville's leading dancers. It differed from his previous 1859 Copenhagen mise-en-scène for *Le Dieu et la bayadère* by having a new, brief intrada (*Allegretto*) of four bars. Moreover, a male dancer (W. Price) now performed in mime the rôle of the opera's leading character, the Indian prince *L'inconnu*. He was accompanied by two dancing bayadères *Zoloé* (Juliette Price) and *Fatmé* (S. Price).

The divertissement was given twice at Stockholm's Mindre Theatern, the last time on 7.6.1860.

Musical sources:

No orchestral score and répétiteur's copy for this divertissement have yet been traced.

Parts. Ms. Copy. 11 vol.
vl I, vl II, vla, vlc e cb, cor III, cor IV, Atrb, Ttrb, Btrb, gr cassa e piatti, tri.
Unsigned and undated [c.1860]
[DKKk; MA ms 2763 (1) (KTA 301)
This (incomplete) set of parts contains the dance music from Act II (score no. 10) of *Le Dieu et la bayadère*. It most probably dates from the 1860 Stockholm summer tour. This theory is supported by the fact that it contains a new intrada (*Allegretto*) which was never included in the Copenhagen performances of Auber's opera-ballet. Moreover, no other separate musical sources for this divertissement have been traced in the Stockholm music archives.

5.6.1860

Italian Genre Pictures and Tarantella (Italienska Genrebilder och Tarantella) **performed by F. Hoppe, W. Price, Juliette Price, S. Price, and F(?). Price (Stockholm's Mindre Theatern).**

This work is almost certainly identical with Bournonville's earlier *'Italian Genre Picture' Divertissement with Tarantella ('Italiensk Genrebillede' Divertissement med Tarantella)*, first performed by S. Lund, E. Stramboe, A. Price, Juliette Price, and F. Price at Christiania's Theatre (Oslo) on 2.7.1852. It was given three times at Stockholm's Mindre Theatern, the last time on 7.6.1860. No musical sources for this work have yet been traced in Stockholm.

8.6.1860

Norwegian Spring Dance (Norsk Spring-Dans) **performed by W. Price and Juliette Price (Stockholm's Mindre Theatern).**

This dance is identical with the *Norwegian Spring Dance* in Bournonville's one-act ballet *Old Memories, or A Magic Lantern* (see 18.12.1848). It was given only once at Stockholm's

Mindre Theatern. No musical sources dating from its 1860 Stockholm performance have yet been traced.

12.6.1860
Scene, Solo and Pas de deux, in two sections, from the ballet 'La Sylphide' (Scène, Solo och Pas de deux I twå afdelningar, ur Balleten 'Sylphiden') **performed by F. Hoppe and Juliette Price (Stockholm's Mindre Theatern).**

This divertissement consisted of three excerpts from Bournonville's two-act romantic ballet *La Sylphide* (*see* 28.11.1836). They seem to have been arranged especially for the 1860 summer tour to Stockholm, perhaps by Bournonville himself. Since no musical sources for this version have yet been traced it is not possible to establish the exact contents of dances in this divertissement. It was given twice at Stockholm's Mindre Theatern, the last time on 14.6.1860.

12.6.1860
Military Polka (Militär-Polka) **performed by F. Hoppe and S. Price (Stockholm's Mindre Theatern).**

This dance is identical with the 1847 Norwegian version for one couple of Bournonville's *Polka militaire (Polka, (Militairdands))*, originally choreographed for two couples (*see* 8.8.1847 and 1.11.1842). It was performed twice at Stockholm's Mindre Theatern, the last time on 14.6.1860. No musical sources dating from the 1860 Stockholm performances of this dance have yet been traced.

16.6.1860
Scenes and Pas de quatre from the ballet 'La Somnambule' (Scèner och Pas de quatre ur Balletten 'Sömngångerskan') **(uncredited) performed by F. Hoppe, W. Price, Juliette Price, and S. Price (Stockholm's Mindre Theatern).**

This (uncredited) divertissement is almost certainly identical with Bournonville's divertissement, entitled *'Scene and Pas de quatre from La Somnambule' ('Scene og Pas de quatre af Söunngængersken')* first performed at Christiania's Theatre (Oslo) by E. Stramboe, S. Lund, A. Price, and S. Price on 18.6.1852. That work was, in turn, based on excerpts from Act I of Bournonville's 1829 Copenhagen staging of J. Aumer's three-act pantomimic ballet *La Somnambule, ou l'Arrivée d'un nouveau seigneur* (*see* 21.9.1829). The 1860 excerpts were performed twice at Stockholm's Mindre Theatern, the last time on 19.6.1860. No musical sources for this divertissement version have been traced in Stockholm.

16.6.1860
La Ventana, (Mirror Dance) (Spegeldans) **performed by Juliette Price (Stockholm's Mindre Theatern).**

This performance represents the second and last time Bournonville's 1854 mirror-dance *La Ventana* was mounted at Stockholm's Mindre Theatern (*see* 19.6.1854 and 7.12.1858). In spite of the fact that the poster lists only the name of Juliette Price, she was undoubtedly accompanied by her sister, S. Price, appearing in the rôle as her mirror image. *La Ventana* was given twice at Stockholm's Mindre Theatern, the last time on 19.6.1860. No separate musical sources dating from the 1860 Stockholm performances of this dance have yet been traced in Sweden.

8.9.1860
La Clemenza di Tito (Titus).

The 1860 Copenhagen restaging of W. A. Mozart's two-act lyrical drama (premièred at Prague's Nationaltheater on 6.9.1791, and first performed in Copenhagen on 29.1.1823) was originally projected by Bournonville on 30.10.1857. It represents the first and only time this work was mounted with his mise-en-scène. The production is not included in Bournonville's handwritten list of his stagings of operas and plays, written c.1872 (*see* Additional Sources), nor in the printed survey of his works in his memoirs *My Theatre Life* (p. 410). In his diary he noted about the performance:

25.8.1860: 'Skrevet Scene=Arrangementet til Titus'
29.8.: 'Prøve paa Titus og Arrangement om Eftermiddagen'
31.8.: 'Theaterprøve paa Titus 5–8'
6.9.: 'Theaterprøve paa Titus Kl 11'
7.9.: 'Generalprøve paa Titus'
8.9.: 'I Theatret 1.ste Forestilling af Operaen Titus, meget godt. <u>Frk.</u> [J. A.] <u>Lund</u> sang udmærket smukt'
10.9.: 'I Theatret <u>Titus</u> for daarligt Huus'.

The 1860 production of *La Clemenza di Tito* received 5 performances, the last of which was given on 17.1.1861.

Autograph sources:

Manuscript mise-en-scène. Ms. Autograph. Brown ink. 4 pp. (22,5 × 18 cm)
<u>Titus.</u> (Scene = Arrangement)
Signed and dated: 'Kbhvn d. 25.de August 1860.'
[SSm; Daniel Fryklunds samling no. 149

Production note. Ms. Autograph. Brown ink and pencil. 1 p. (22,5 × 18 cm)
<u>Decorationer til Titus.</u>
Unsigned and undated [Written according to the diary probably in August–September 1860]
[SSm; Daniel Fryklunds samling no. 149

Musical sources:

Printed orchestral score with several later manuscript insertions. 1 vol. 348 pp. of which four are blank (34,8 × 25,7 cm with variants)
LA/Clemenza di Tito/Dramma in due Atti/[...]/Titus/Oper in Zwey Akten/[...]/von/W. A. Mozart
Leipzig, Breitkopf & Härtel, pl. no. 620 [1809]
[DKKkt; KTA 218
This German printed orchestral score was used for all performances of *La Clemenza di Tito* at Copenhagen's Royal Theatre from its première there in 1823 until its last performance on 17.1.1861.

No répétiteur's copy for *Titus* has yet been traced.

Parts. Ms. Copy. 28 vol.
4 vl I, 4 vl II, 2 vla, 4 vlc e cb, fl 1/2, ob 1/2, cl 1/2, cor bassetto, fag 1/2, cor 1/2, tr 1/2, timp. 42 vocal parts.
Unsigned and undated [1823]
[DKKk; KTA 218
This set of parts dates from the 1823 Copenhagen première of *La Clemenza di Tito* and was used for all performances of it there during Bournonville's lifetime

16.9.1860
Saltarello **in** *The Heart on Trial (Hjærtet paa Prøve)* **(uncredited).**

For the première of T. Overskou's' one-act singspiel, set to music by N. Behrendt, Bournonville choreographed and mounted a *Saltarello*. It was performed by his daughter, the alto Charlotte Bournonville (playing the rôle of *Giudetta*), and the singer, P. Schramm (playing *Benetto*), during the duet, entitled «Ak jeg at bede er saa frie» (score no. 8). *The Heart on Trial* is not included in Bournonville's handwritten list of his stagings of operas and plays, written c.1872 (*see* Additional Sources), nor in the printed survey of his works in his memoirs *My Theatre Life* (p. 408), nor is his name mentioned on the posters for this work. In his diary he noted about the *Saltarello* and its first performance:

1.9.1860: 'Indstudering paa en Saltarello til Hjertet paa Prøve for [P. L. N] Schram[m] og Charlotte [Bournonville]'
7.9.: 'Saltarello med Schram og Charlotte'
9.9.: 'Overværet 1.ste Theaterprøve paa 'Hjertet paa Prøve'
11.9.: 'overværet Hjertet paa Prøve – gaaer endnu svagt'
12.9.: 'Theaterprøve paa Hjertet paa Prøve'
15.9.: 'Generalprøve paa Hjertet paa Prøve. Charlotte meget tilfredsstillende'
16.9.: 'I Theatret 1.ste Forestilling af Hjertet paa Prøve der gik smukt og vandt meget Bifald. Charlotte udførte sin Rolle og sit Partie udmærket og gjorde megen Lykke'.

Berlingske Tidende reported about the *Saltarello* on 17.9.1860:

'...navnlig gjorde Hr. Schrams of Frøken Bournonvilles charakteristiske Dands megen Lykke; man modtog ved at see den et uvilkaarligt Indtryk af, at tvende Figurer fra de [Wilhelm] Marstrandske Genremalerier pludselig vare traadte ud af Rammen og havde faaet Liv og Bevægelse...'.

The Heart on Trial received 6 performances, the last of which was given on 5.12.1860.

Musical sources:

Orchestral score. Ms. Autograph. Black ink. 1 vol. 226 pp. of which two are blank (24,8 × 34,1 cm)
Hjertet paa Prøve./Syngespil i 1 Akt./af Nic. Berendt. -/476./[...]/ Hjertet paa Prøve./Syngespil i 1 Act./af./Th: Overskou./Professor. /Musiken./componeret af:/Nicolai Berendt.
Unsigned and undated [1860]
[DKKk; C II, 105 k (KTA 476)
The music for the *Saltarello* (score no. 8) is included in this score on pp. '169–188'. The scene in which the dance is performed is here described as follows:
'[Benetto] griber en Mandolin og spiller og dandser./ [...]/[Giudetta] griber en/Tamburin/[...]/[Benetto] synker om paa Stolen/ [...]/Benetto har drukket af Flasken, medens Guidetta dandser, henrykt over hendes bevægelser/farer han op, og begynder at svinge sig med endnu større Heftighed./[...]/Paa den sidste Accord, kaster Guidetta sig udmattet paa en Stol.'.

No répétiteur's copy for *The Heart on Trial* has yet been traced.

Parts. Ms. Copy. 33 vol.
3 vl I, 3 vl II, 2 vla, 3 vlc e cb, fl picc, fl 1/2, ob 1/2, cl 1/2, fag 1/2, cor 1/2/3/4, tr 1/2, trb 1/2/3, tuba, timp, gr cassa, tri. 10 vocal parts.
Unsigned and undated [1860]
[DKKk; KTA 476
Another, similar set of parts for Overskou's and Behrendt's singspiel (26 vol.) is now in DKKk with the same call no. (KTA 476). It seems to have been made for touring purposes.

21.9.1860
Lucrezia Borgia.
This performance represents the last time G. Donizetti's two-act melodrama (*see* 15.4.1859 and 6.10.1859) was mounted under Bournonville's personal direction. It was this year performed without any significant any changes from his previous 1859 mise-en-scène. This is clear from his diary in which he noted about the performance:

18.9.1860: 'Theaterprøve paa Lucrezia Borgia'
20.9.: 'Generalprøve paa Lucrezia'
21.9.: 'I Theatret Lucrezia Borgia'.

The 1860 production of *Lucrezia Borgia* received 3 performances, the last of which was given on 5.11.1866.

The musical material employed this year was the same as that used for the 1859 production (now in DKKk, call nos. C I, 236 n, and KTA 469).

5.10.1860
Terpsichore. **Projected Divertissement.**
This projected allegorical divertissement was conceived by Bournonville during a journey between his country residence in Fredensborg and Copenhagen. In his diary he noted about it:

5.10.1860: 'Op Kl 6, pakket og lavet mit til Reisen. Farvel og afsted Kl 9 med Dilligencen, ganske allene i Vognen componerede jeg et Ballet Divertissement – Terpsichore. – Ankomst Kl 2. – Alt vel, – stærkt Regnveir, skrevet mit Program'.

The project was for unknown reasons never carried out. However, its subject seems to have formed the basis for Bournonville's *A Ballet Divertissement (Ett Ballet=Divertissement)*, premièred three years later at Stockholm's Royal Theatre on 12.9.1863. That work, which was created for the inauguration of Stockholm's Dramatiska Theatern, was (according to Bournonville's diary) given the subtitle 'Terpsichore hos Thalia'. Moreover, according to his 1863 autographed manuscript mise-en-scène for this divertissement (now in DKKk, call no. NKS 3285 4° 5 læg 21) it holds many similarities with his 1860 scenario for *Terpsichore*.

Autograph sources:

Manuscript scenario. Ms. Autograph. Brown ink. 4 pp. (22,5 × 18 cm)
Terpsichore./Ballet = Divertissement/af/August Bournonville.
Unsigned and undated [written according to the diary on 5.10. 1860]
[DKKk; NKS 3285 4° 3 R–U

7.10.1860
Die Hochzeit des Figaro (Figaros Bryllup).
The 1860 Copenhagen restaging of W. A. Mozart's four-act comic opera represents Bournonville's second, complete staging of this work at Copenhagen's Royal Theatre. It was mounted without any significant changes from his previous mise-en-scène (*see* 21.5.1858). This is clear from his diary in which he noted about the production:

6.10.1860: 'Theaterprøve paa Figaros Bryllup'
7.10.: 'Figaros Bryllup gik meget smukt'.

The 1860 production of *Die Hochzeit des Figaro* received 36 performances, the last of which was given on 23.12.1869.

The musical material employed this year was the same as that used for the previous 1844 and 1858 stagings (now in DKKk, call nos. C I, 280 MA ms 3042, and KTB 215).

24.10.1860
Pas de trois (uncredited) arranged for F. Hoppe, Juliette Price, and S. Price.

This (uncredited) dance is most probably a revised version of Bournonville's *Pas de trois* (score no. 5) in his Copenhagen version of J. Aumer's three-act pantomimic ballet *La Somnambule, ou l'Arrivée d'un nouveau seigneur* (see 21.9.1829), given only a week later on 3.11.1860. Another possible identification of this dance is the (uncredited) *Pas de trois* that was performed some three months later as a separate divertissement by Hoppe, Juliette Price, and S. Price on 28.1. 1861, which in turn is identical with Bournonville's and M. E. Caraffa's 1837 *Pas de trois* incorporated in A. Adam's three-act comic opera *Le Postillon du Lonjumeau* (see 28.10.1837). In his diary Bournonville noted about the dance:

24.10.1860: 'regleret en pas de trois for [F.] Hoppe, J. og S. Price (Vrøvl med Sophie!) – Eftermiddagsprøve – Søvngængersken færdig indstuderet'
29.10.: 'Prøve fra 10–11 pas de trois'.

It is not possible to identify the dance any further.

26.10.1860
The Elves (Alferne).

For the 1860 Copenhagen restaging of J. L. Heiberg's one-act fairy-play to music by L. Zinck (premièred on 29.1.1835) Bournonville directed the stage rehearsals and also mounted its dances (originally choreographed by P. Funck). These included two numbers as follows:

(1) An (unnamed) *Dance scene* in 3/8 time, performed by a group of children during the opening chorus, entitled «See, o see, hvor smukt Dandsen gaaer! hvor de muntre Börn sig svinge!» (score no. 1).
(2) A *Divertissement (Ballet)* in 4/4 and 6/8 time, performed by a group of elves (score no. 4).

Both of these dances seem to have been mounted this year with only minor if any changes from P. Funck's original versions. The 1860 production of *The Elves* is not included in Bournonville's handwritten list of his stagings of operas and plays, written c.1872 (see Additional Sources), nor in the printed survey of his works in his memoirs *My Theatre Life* (p. 408). Moreover, for a later restaging of *The Elves* on 30.11. 1870 Bournonville seems, according to his pencilled notes in the 1870 répétiteur's copy for Heiberg's play (now in DKKk, call no. MA ms 3070 (KTA 313 (1)) to have made a separate (not yet traced) choreographic notation of at least the first of the two dances in this work. They were that year mounted by L. Gade.

In his diary he noted about the 1860 production:

19.10.1860: 'Prøve paa Alferne'
26.10.: 'I Theatret Alferne'.

The 1860 staging of *The Elves* received 25 performances, the last of which was given on 26.2.1866.

Musical sources:

Orchestral score. Ms. Autograph (by L. Zinck). Brown, black, and red ink. 1 vol. 118 pp. of which three are blank (27 × 38 cm with several variants)
Alferne. -/Partitur.
Unsigned and undated [1835]
[DKKk; C II, 125 (KTA 313)]
This autographed orchestral score was used for all performances of *The Elves* during Bournonville's lifetime. The music for the two dance scenes are included on pp. 34–43 and 69–79 respectively. Metronome markings indicate the tempo of each dance with a quaver being equal to '160' (in score no. 1), and a crochet equal to '116' (in score no. 4).

Conductor's part. Ms. Copy. Black ink. 1 vol. 46 pp. of which two are blank (25,4 × 34,3 cm with several variants)
313/313/Alferne/Musiken paa Theatret/Dirigentpartie/[…]/Alferne. -/Musikken paa Theatret./Dirigent = Partie.
Unsigned and undated [c.1835–1912]
[DKKk; C II, 125 (KTA 313)]
This conductor's part contains the music in *The Elves* which was played by an orchestra seated on the stage. It also includes several later insertions added for the restagings of Heiberg's play on 18.4. 1886 and 22.11.1912.

No répétiteur's copy dating from the 1860 restaging of *The Elves* has yet been traced.

Parts. Ms. Copy. 31 + 16 vol.
3 vl I, 3 vl II, 2 vla, 3 vlc e cb, fl picc, fl 1/2, ob 1/2, cl 1/2, fag 1/2, cor 1/2, tr 1/2, trb 1/2/3, timp, gr cassa, piatti e tri, arpa. On stage: vl I, vl II, vla, vlc e cb, fl 1/2, ob 1/2, cl 1/2, fag 1/2, cor 1/2, trb, gr cassa e piatti e tri. 38 vocal parts.
Unsigned and undated [1835]
[DKKk; KTA 313]
This set of parts dates from the 1835 Copenhagen première of *The Elves* and was used for all performances of it there during Bournonville's lifetime.

28.10.1860
Pas de deux composed by Mr. Court Ballet Master Bournonville (componeret af Hr. Hofballetmester Bournonville) performed by F. Hoppe and A. Healey.

According to a note on this day in the rehearsal book of A. Fredstrup this *Pas de deux* is identical with Bournonville's *Pas de deux* from Act I (score no. 7 B) of his Copenhagen version of J. Aumer's three-act pantomimic ballet *La Somnambule, ou l'Arrivée d'un nouveau seigneur* (see 21.9.1829). It was arranged as a separate divertissement this year for the début at Copenhagen's Royal Theatre of Bournonville's English pupil, A. Healey, who performed it three times with F. Hoppe (the last time on 12.11.1860). In his diary Bournonville noted about the dance:

18.10.1860: 'Ordres de débuts for Agnes Healey'
19.10.: 'Prøve paa […]Pas de deux […] Eftermiddagsprøve for Miss Healey'
20.10.: 'Prøve for Agnes Healeÿ'
23.10.: 'Prøve for pas de deux […] Eftermiddagsprøve for Miss Healey'
24.10.: 'Theaterprøve paa Pas de deux'
25.10.: 'Prøve med A Healey'
27.10.: 'Prøve for Agnes Healey'
28.10.: 'I Theatret […] første Debut af Agnes Healey i pas de deux med Hoppe. Det gik udmærket godt og hun blev modtaget med særdeles Bifald'

2.11.: 'Pas de deux Agnes Healey dandsede charmant og vandt meget Bifald'
12.11.: 'pas de deux, Agnes Healey der gjorde megen Lўkke'.

No separate musical sources for this dance have yet been traced. This seems to indicate that the *Pas de deux* was rehearsed and performed using the original 1829 musical material for *La Somnambule, ou l'Arrivée d'un nouveau seigneur* (now in DKKk, call nos. C I, 259 f, MA ms 2984, and KTB 287).

30.10.1860
Les Deux Journées, ou Le Porteur d'eau (De to Dage eller Flygtningene).
The 1860 Copenhagen restaging of L. Cherubini's three-act opera (premièred in Paris at Théâtre de la rue Faydeau on 16.1.1800, and first performed in Copenhagen on 14.4. 1803) was originally projected by Bournonville on 30.10. 1857. It represents the first and only time this opera was mounted with his mise-en-scène in Denmark. The production is not included in Bournonville's handwritten list of his stagings of operas and plays, written c.1872 (*see* Additional Sources), nor in the printed suvey of his works in his memoirs *My Theatre Life* (p. 409).

On 19.11.1863 Bournonville also proposed a restaging of this opera at Stockholm's Royal Theatre. That project, however, was never carried out by him.

The same was the case with his later proposal on 1.8.1870 for a Copenhagen restaging of *Les Deux Journées, ou Le Porteur d'Eau*. It was carried out on 20.5.1871, but not by Bournonville, since that year he considered Cherubini's opera as what he called 'en svag Forestilling'.

In his diary he noted about the 1860 Copenhagen restaging:

17.10.1860: 'Instruction paa De to Dage'
23.10.: 'Arrangement og Textprøve paa De to Dage'
26.10.: 'Arrangement= og Theaterprøve paa De to Dage'
27.10.: 'Theaterprøve paa De to Dage'
29.10.: 'Prøve [...] fra 11–1½ De to Dage'
30.10.: 'Første forestilling af Reprisen af De to Dage. Det gik meget godt'.

The 1860 production received 8 performances, the last of which was given on 15.2.1862.

Musical sources:

Printed orchestral score. 1 vol. 310 pp. of which one is blank (32,8 × 25 cm)
Les/DEUX JOURNÉES/OPERA EN TROIS ACTES/[...]/MIS EN MUSIQUE/Par le C.en Chérubini
Paris, frères Gaveaux [1800]
[DKKk; U 6 (KTA 136) (mu 6405.1330)
This printed orchestral score was used for all performances of *Les Deux Journées* in Copenhagen during Bournonville's lifetime. It contains N. T. Bruun's Danish translation, written (with brown ink) next to the opera's original French text.

No répétiteur's copy for *Les Deux Journées* has yet been traced.

Parts. Ms. Copy. 30 + 1 vol.

5 vl I, 4 vl II, 2 vla, 4 vlc e cb, fl 1/2, ob 1/2, cl 1/2, fag 1/2, cor 1/2/ 3, tr 1/2, Btrb, timp. On stage: cassa. 68 vocal parts.
Unsigned and undated [1803]
[DKKk; KTA 136]
This set of parts dates from the 1803 Copenhagen première of *Les Deux Journées* and was used for all performances of it there during Bournonville's lifetime.

3.11.1860
La Somnambule, ou l'Arrivée d'un nouveau seigneur (Sövngjængersken).
This performance represents Bournonville's second complete restaging in Copenhagen of his Danish version of J. Aumer's three-act pantomimic ballet (*see* 21.9.1829). It was mounted especially for the début of his English pupil, A. Healey, who played *Thérèse* this year for the first time. Otherwise the ballet seems to have been mounted with only minor if any changes from the original 1829 version. In his diary Bournonville noted about the staging and A. Healey's début:

18.10.1860: 'Ordre de débuts for Agnes Healey'
22.10.: 'Prøve paa Søvngængersken'
24.10.: 'Eftermiddagsprøve – Søvngængersken færdig indstuderet'
29.10.: 'Prøve fra 10–11 pas de trois [...] 1½–2½ pas de quatre [...] fra 5–7½ Prøve paa Søvngængersken'
30.10.: 'Prøve paa Søvngængersken'
1.11.: 'Generalprøve paa Søvngængersken. Agnes Healey udmærket god'
3.11.: 'I Theatret Søvngængersken Agnes Healey var fortræffelig som Therese og høstede glimrende Bifald'.

The 1860 staging received 9 performances, the last of which was given on 2.12.1864.

No separate musiccal sources dating from the 1860 performances of this ballet have yet been traced. This seems to indicate that it was mounted this year using the original 1829 musical material (now in DKKk, call nos. C I, 259 f, MA ms 2984, and KTB 287).

10.11.1860
Feast-Quadrille in honour of Landgrave Wilhelm of Hesse-Cassel's and Princess of Denmark, Countess Charlotte's Golden Anniversary (Fest-Quadrille i Anledning af [...] Landgreve Wilhelm af Hessens og [...] Landgrevinde Charlotte, født Prindsesse til Danmarks høie Guldbryllup) **performed at the Copenhagen residence of the Heir presumptive, Prince Frederik Ferdinand).**
This series of dances and tableaux was choreographed by Bournonville for the Royal Golden Anniversary of the Landgrave (and sometime Governor of Copenhagen) Wilhelm of Hesse-Cassel, and the Danish princess, Louise Charlotte. It consisted of a series of separate sections, each of which was centred on the allegorical figure of *Cupid*, played by the seven-year-old Danish Princess Thyra. Most of Bournonville's dances for this *Feast-Quadrille* were arranged either from his own ballets or from his current stagings of operas. They included the following four dance numbers:

(1) The *Minuet* from Act I (score no. 9 A) of Bournonville's Copenhagen version of L. Milon's two-act pantomimic ballet *Nina, ou la Folle par amour (Nina, eller Den Vanvittige af Kjærlighed)*, premièred on 30.9.1834.

(2) The *Bridal Waltz* from Bournonville's three-act romantic ballet *A Folk Tale* (*see* 20.3.1854).
(3) The *Dance of the bridal maids* from D.-F.-E. Auber's three-act comic opera *La Fiancée* (*see* 20.11.1853).
(4) A *March* and a *Dance*, performed to the chorus «Rataplan rataplan rataplan» from the Act I finale of G. Donizetti's two-act comic opera *La Fille du régiment* (*see* 20.10.1859).

In the printed programme the complete series of dances and tableaux is described as follows:

(1) '1. Dands af otte Brudepiger (Mel.: af La fiancée.)'.
(2) 'Amor aabenbares imellem dem. (Mel.: Hjertet veed af ingen Fare.)'. The tune employed for this tableau has not yet been identified.
(3) '2. Alferne bringe et Portrait der bekranses med Roser. (Mel.: Og hun var saa ung og saa yndig saae hun ud)'. The tune employed for this tableau is that of a Danish folk song daring from c.1815, named «En deilig ung Ridder i Lunden mon gaae» (rewritten with new words by H. Hertz c.1851). It had been earlier used by H. S. Paulli in his music for Act II (score no. 14) of Bournonville's two-act Norwegian ballet *The Wedding Festival in Hardanger* (*see* 4.3.1853).
(4) '3. Et Corps af smaa Trommeslagere marschere op. De dandse med Alferne. (Mel.: Rataplan af Regimentets Datter)'.
(5) '4. Otte Officerer med deres Damer træde frem og bringe deres Hyldning. (Revue-Marsch fra Frederik den Sjettes Tid.)'. The march accompanying this number is most probably identical with P. D. Muth-Rasmussen's so-called *Revuemarsch for Kongens Regiment* from 1836 (first published in Copenhagen by C. C. Lose).
(6) 'Menuet (af Balletten Nina.)'.
(7) '5. De gamle Faner bæres ind og hilses med Begeistring. (Mel.: Til Jyllands Kyst.)'. The tune employed for this number was originally part of the aria «God Nat, Cabaler!» sung by the character *Johan* in Act I (score no. 5) of E. Dupuy's two-act singspiel *Youth and Folly* (*Ungdom og Galskab*), premièred at Copenhagen's Royal Theatre on 19.5.1806.
(8) '6. Amor med fakkel, fulgt af Brudepigerne, der bringe Guldbryllupskrandse, træder ind for det høie Par. Slutningsdands. (Brudedands af Et Folkesagn.)'.

In his diary Bournonville noted about the rehearsals and the performance of the divertissement:

28.10.1860: '(componeret en Guldbryllups-Quadrille)'
1.11.: 'Besørget Musik til Guldbryllupsquadrillen'
2.10.: 'begyndt paa Guldbryllupsquadrillen med Börnene)'
3.10.: 'Prøve paa Guldbryllupsquadrillen (Børnene)'
4.11.: '1.ste Indstudering hos Arveprindsen [Frederik Ferdinand]'
5.11.: 'Lection til den lille Prindsesse Dagmar. – Eftermiddagsprøve hos Arveprindsen'
6.11.: '3.die Indstudering hos Prinds [Frederik] Ferdinand (færdig)'
7.11.: 'besørget adskilligt til Festen for Landgreven [...] Aftenprøve hos Arveprindsen, Quadrillen færdig, gik allerede smukt'
8.11.: 'Prøve hos Arveprindsen'
9.11.: 'Generalprøve hos Arveprindsen. Det gik fortræffeligt og gjorde stor Effect'
10.11.: 'Landgreve Wilhelms og Prindsesse Charlottes Guldbryllupsfest. [...] besørget flere Ting til Festen. [...] Kl 8 1/2 kjørte jeg til Festen hos Arveprindsen. Det var i høieste Grad fyrsteligt. Kongen [i.e. Frederik VII], Enkedronningen [i.e. Caroline Amalie] og det hele Kongehuus vare nærværende. Kl 10 aabnedes Salsdørene og Guldbryllupsparret hilsedes med en Sang af H. P. Holst, foredraget af [J. C.] Hansen, [J. A.] Steenberg, [P. L. N.] Schramm og [C. L. L.] Ferslew. Derpaa gik min Quadrille, der gjorde et begeistret og dybt Indtryk – Den naadigste Tak og hjerteligste Paaskjønnelse mødte mig overalt og Dandsen maatte gjentages. Jeg overværede den glimrende Fest indtil Kl 2 og kom meget tilfreds hjem'.

No separate musical sources for Bournonville's 1860 *Feast-Quadrille* have yet been traced.

Autograph sources:

Choreographic note. Ms. Autograph. Black ink. 2 pp. (22,4 × 14,1 cm)
Quadrille (Rataplan)/[...]/Menuet.
Unsigned and undated [Written according to the diary on 28.10.1860]
[DKKk; NKS 3285 4° 3 V–Z

Printed sources:

Printed programme. 1 vol. 6 pp. (22,7 × 14 cm)
FEST-QUADRILLE/i Anledning af/[...] Wilhelm af Hessens/og/[...]/Landgrevinde Charlotte,/[...]/GULDBRYLLUP/[...]/Componeret af Hofballetmester Bournonville.
Berlingske Bogtrykkeri ved N. H. Stenderup, dated: 'den 10. November 1860.'
[DKKk; NKS 3285 4° 2 F

20.12.1860
Le Petit Chaperon rouge (Den lille Rødhætte).
The 1860 Copenhagen restaging of F.-A. Boyeldieu's three-act fairy opera (*see* 1.12.1852) was originally projected by Bournonville on 30.10.1857. It represents the first time this work was mounted in Copenhagen with his complete mise-en-scène and choreography (*see also* 25.1.1855). According to Bournonville's autographed choreographic numbers (written in the original répétiteur's copy for Boyeldieu's opera, now in DKKk, call no. MA ms 2902 (17)) he seems this year to have revised the (unnamed) *Dance* in Act I (score no. 7) and at the same time to have made a (not yet traced) choreographic notation of it. In his diary he noted about the performance:

15.11.1860: 'Indstudering paa Dands til Rødhætten'
20.11.: 'Indstudering paa Den lille Rødhætte'
21.11.: 'Indstudering færdig til Rødhætten'
24.11.: 'Prøve paa [...] Dandsen til Rødhætten'
30.11.: 'Oplæsning paa Den lille Rødhætte'
1.12.: 'lille Prøve paa Dandsen til Rødhætten'
3.12.: 'Lille Prøve paa Rødhætten'
8.12.: 'Instructionsprøve paa Den lille Rødhætte'
10.12.: 'Instruction og Arrangementsprøve paa Rødhætten'
11.12.: 'Eftermiddags=Instr. 6–8 paa Rødhætten'
12.12.: 'Theaterprøve pa Rødhætten'
15.12.: '1.ste fuldstændige Prøve paa Rødhætten'
17.12.: 'fuldstændig Theaterprøve paa Rødhætten'
19.12.: 'Generalprøve paa Rødhætten, der gik udmærket [...] Jeg prøvede Charlottes [i.e. C. Bournonville] Costume'
20.12.: 'I Theatret Rødhætten 1.ste Gang med den nÿ Besætning. Charlotte var heelt igjennem fortræffelig, sang og spillede som en sand Kunstnerinde, men blev af Publicum behandlet med usædvanlig Lunkenhed, det kan ikke nægtes at der er en Cabale tilstede der skjult venter paa en Applaus for at yttre Mishag – det var derfor vore Venner taug. – Charlotte tog Sagen meget smukt og er en herlig Pige'.

The 1860 production received 4 performances, the last of which was given on 7.1.1861.

The musical material employed this year was the same as that used for the previous 1852 staging (now in DKKk, call nos. U 6, MA ms 2902 (17), and KTA 198).

1861

26.1.1861
The Cavern of Ludlam (Ludlams Hule).
The 1861 Copenhagen restaging of C. E. F. Weyse's and A. Oehlenschläger's three-act singspiel from 1816 represents the first and only time this work was mounted with Bournon-ville's mise-en-scène. It is not included in his list of his stagings of operas and plays, written c.1872 (*see* Additional Sources), nor in the printed survey of his works in his memoirs *My Theatre Life* (p. 410). In his diary he noted about the performance:

26.12.1860: 'Læst og studeret Ludlams Hule!'
28.12.: 'Decorationsmøde paa <u>Ludlams Hule</u>'
13.1.1861: 'ordnet Scene=Arrangement til Ludlams Hule'
14.1. and 18.1.: 'Prøve paa Ludlams Hule <u>to Akter</u>'
18.1.: '2 Akters Prøve paa Ludlams Hule'
19.1.: 'Theater=arrangementprøve paa Ludlams <u>kjedelige</u> Hule – 3.e og 4.e Akt'
20.1.: 'Costumemøde paa <u>Ludlams Hule</u>. Seneprøve paa ditto'
21.1.: 'Prøve paa Ludlams Hule til Kl 2¹/₂.
23.1.: 'Theaterprøve paa Ludlams Hule'
25.1.: 'Generalprøve paa Ludlams Hule'
26.1.: 'I Theatret <u>Ludlams Hule</u> gik i det Hele meget smukt, godt Huus men temmelig kjedeligt'.

The 1861 staging of *The Cavern of Ludlam* received 5 performances, the last of which was given on 18.3.1861.

Musical sources:

Orchestral score. Ms. Copy. Black ink. 2 vol. Act I 298 pp. of which four are blank, Act II–IV 326 pp. of which one is blank (23,5 × 34,5 cm)
<u>Ludlams</u>/<u>Hule. I.</u>/[…]/Ludlams Hule/Syngespil/af/Adam Øhlen-schläger/sat i Musik/af Weÿse/[…]/<u>Ludlams</u>/<u>Hule. II.</u>
Unsigned and undated [1816]
[DKKk; C II, 123 (KTA 202)
This orchestral score dates from the Copenhagen première of Weyse's singspiel on 30.1.1816 and was used for all performances of it there during Bournonville's lifetime.

No répétiteur's copy for *The Cavern of Ludlam* has yet been traced.

Parts. Ms. Copy. 33 + 9 vol.
4 vl I, 4 vl II, 2 vla, 5 vlc e cb, fl picc, fl 1/2, ob 1/2, cl 1/2, fag 1/2, cor 1/2, tr 1/2, trb, timp, gr cassa, piatti e tri, arpa. On stage: ob 1/2, cl 1/2, fag 1/2, cor 1/2, trb. 57 vocal parts.
Unsigned and undated [1816]
[DKKk; KTA 202
This set of parts dates from the 1816 Copenhagen première of Weyse's singspiel and was used for all performances of it there during Bournonville's lifetime.

28.1.1861
Pas de trois (uncredited) performed by F. Hoppe, Juliette Price, and S. Price.
According to two entries in Bournonville's diary this (un-credited) dance is identical with Bournonville's and M. E. Caraffa's much earlier incorporated *Pas de trois* in A. Adam's three-act comic opera *Le Postillon du Lonjumeau* (*see* 28.10.1837). His notes read as follows:

26.1.1861: 'Prøve paa pas de trois'
28.1.: 'Pas de trois (af Postillonen)'.

Moreover, in the rehearsal book of A. Fredstrup three other rehearsals of this dance are listed on the dates 5.1., 23.1., and 25.1.1861.

The *Pas de trois* received 2 performances during the 1860–61 season, the last of which was given on 11.5.1861.

29.1.1861
Pas de deux from The Isle of Phantasy incorporated in S. Lund's The Whims of Cupid (Amor's skämt) (Stockholm's Royal Theatre, Operahuset).
For S. Lund's freely adapted Stockholm staging of V. Gale-otti's 1786 ballet *The Whims of Cupid and the Maître de Ballet (Amor og Balletmesterens Luner)* the *Pas de deux* (to music by E. Helsted) from Act II, score no. 7 of Bournonville's two-act romantic ballet *The Isle of Phantasy* (*see* 28.10.1838) was incorporated as score no. '3'. According to the Swedish musical material for this dance (now in SSkma) it differed from the original 1838 Copenhagen version by two larger musical cuts each totalling 43 and 30 measures. Moreover, according to the poster Bournonville's *Pas de deux* was this year entitled *Pas de deux Français* and performed by S. Lund and J. G. Sundberg. The *Pas de deux* received 10 performances in Stockholm, the last of which was given on 1.12.1861.

Musical sources:

Orchestral score (the *Pas de deux*). Ms. Copy. Brown ink. 1 vol. 56 pp. (32,5 × 24,8 cm)
No. 3 i Amors skämt/<u>Pas de deux</u>/af/<u>Phantasiens Ø</u>/<u>Partitur.</u>
Unsigned and undated [1839 or 1861]
[SSkma; KT Dansmusik 97
This orchestral score was clearly made in Copenhagen and seems to have been brought to Stockholm by Bournonville perhaps as early as 1839(?).

Répétiteur's copy. Ms. Copy. Brown ink. 1 vol. 29 pp. (33,5 × 25 cm)
Amors Skämt
Unsigned and undated [1861]
[SSkma; KT Pantomime-Balletter A 6
According to a note written in this répétiteur's copy for *Amors skämt* the incorporated 'Pas de deux Phantasiens ö' was performed as score no. '3'. The volume also includes numerous autographed notes by S. Lund which describe the ballet's mimic and dramatic action. From these notes it is clear that *Amors skämt* (which was set to a score composed and arranged by A. F. Schwartz) was a free adapta-tion of V. Galeotti's allegorical ballet *The Whims of Cupid and the Maître de Ballet (Amor og Balletmesterens Luner)*, first performed at Co-penhagen's Royal Theatre on 31.10.1786.

Répétiteur's copy (the *Pas de deux*). Ms. Copy. Brown ink. 1 vol. 6 pp. (34 × 25,8 cm)
<u>Pas de deux</u>/af/<u>Phantasiens Ø</u>/<u>Repetiteur = Partie</u>
Unsigned and undated [1839?]
[SSkma; KT Dansmusik 97
This répétiteur's copy was clearly made in Copenhagen and seems to have been brought to Stockholm by Bournonville perhaps as early as 1839(?).

Parts (the *Pas de deux*). Ms. Copy. 28 vol.
2 vl I, 2 vl II, vla, 4 vlc e cb, fl picc, fl 1/2, ob 1/2, cl 1/2, fag 1/2, cor 1/2/3, tr, trb 1/2/3, timp, gr cassa e tri, arpa.
Unsigned and undated [1839?]
[SSkma; KT Dansmusik 97

13.2.1861
Polketta (uncredited) performed by A. and C. Healey (Folketheatret).

This (uncredited) dance is identical with Bournonville's and H. C. Lumbye's *Polketta, Pas de deux*, first performed by the Healey sisters at Copenhagen's Casino Theatre on 31.10. 1858. It was given 3 times by them at Folketheatret, the last time on 17.2.1861. Bournonville, whose name is not mentioned on any of the posters, did not attend these performances. No separate musical sources dating from the 1861 performances of *Polketta* have yet been traced.

18.2.1861
Pas de deux (uncredited) performed by A. and C. Healey (Folketheatret).

This (uncredited) dance is almost certainly identical with the so-called *Pas de deux gracieux*, first performed by the Healey sisters three years earlier at Copenhagen's Casino Theatre (*see* 17.11.1858). It was given twice by them at Folketheatret, the last time on 22.2.1861. Bournonville, whose name is not mentioned on the posters, did not attend any of these performances. It it not possible to identify the dance any further.

24.2.1861
La Polonaise (uncredited) performed by A. and C. Healey (Folketheatret).

This dance is almost certainly identical with the (uncredited) *Polonaise*, choreographed two years earlier by Bournonville (to a score by H. C. Lumbye) and premièred by the Healey sisters at Copenhagen's Casino Theatre on 31.3. 1859. It was performed 3 times by them at Folketheatret, the last time on 26.2.1861. Bournonville, whose name is not mentioned on the posters, did not attend any of these performances. No separate musical sources dating from the 1861 Copenhagen performances of *La Polonaise* have yet been traced.

28.2.1861
Echo from the Ballroom, Character Dance (Echo fra Balsalen, Characteerdands) (uncredited) performed by A. and C. Healey (Folketheatret).

This (uncredited) divertissement is listed on the poster simply as a work 'performed' (*udført*) by the Healey sisters, with no mention of Bournonville's name. The score is explicitly credited as being 'composed' (*componeret*) by H. C. Lumbye. It consists of seven movements as follows:

(1) 'Hurtig Vals' (71 meas.).
(2) 'Lento' (7 meas.).
(3) 'Langsom Vals' (76 meas.).
(4) 'Hurtig Vals' (24 meas.).
(5) 'Hopsa' (70 meas.).
(6) 'Lento' (9 meas.).
(7) 'Galop' (146 meas.).

Of these the music for the final 'Galop' was first published in 1869 by C. F. E. Horneman and H. C. Lumbye in a version for piano as part of their musical anthology, entitled *Musikalske Nyheder* (9. Aarg., No. 3, pp. 14–15, now in DKKk, call no. D 2). In this edition the gallop was named *Velocipedes Galop*. However, it was clearly composed in 1861 for Bournonville's

Echo from the Ballroom. The divertissement received 12 performances by the Healey sisters at Folketheatret, the last of which took place on 21.3.1861.

Echo from the Ballroom, New Pas de deux (Echo från Balsalen, Ny Pas de deux) was also mounted by Bournonville for the same two dancers at Stockholm's Royal Theatre (Operahuset) on 3.10.1862 and was performed there 4 times until 13.11.1862. During the following years the divertissement was most probably also included in their many other privately arranged tours to Norway (in the summer of 1861), Germany, England, Scotland, and Ireland (in the 1860s and early 1870s). *Echo from the Ballroom* was restaged for the last time in Copenhagen in the Tivoli Gardens (Theatret) on 19.8.1870, and was given there by the Healeys 4 times until 23.8.1870.

In his diary Bournonville noted about the creation and 1861 première of this divertissement:

6.2.1861: 'Lection Healeÿ – componeret med [H. C.] Lumbÿ[e]'
7.2.: '(Healeyerne engagerede for nogle Forestillinger paa Folketheatret)'
12.2.: 'Modtaget Musik af Lumbÿ[e] til en nÿ pas for Søstrene Healey; hjemme hele Eftermiddagen, skrevet og componeret den nÿ pas'
13.2.: 'Skole og en lille Indstudering for Healey's'
14.2.: 'Tour ud til Lumbÿe'
16.2.: 'Lection og Prøve til Healey'ernes nÿe Dands'
19.2.: 'besøgt Lumbÿ[e]'
20.2.: 'Prøve med Healey's paa en nÿ pas de deux 'Echo fra Balsalen' Musik af Lumbÿe'
25.2.: 'Ubehageligheder med Healeys!'
28.2.: 'I Folketheatret hvor jeg […] overværede den første Gang af 'Echo fra Balsalen' hvori Søstrene Healey gjorde stormende Lÿkke'.

About the third performance he noted on 3.3.1861:

'I Folketheatret […] Echo fra Balsalen stormende Applaus'.

Lumbye's music was frequently also played at public concerts in the Tivoli Gardens, the first time on 1.6.1861.

Musical sources:

Orchestral score. Ms. Copy. Black ink. 1 vol. 24 pp. ($28,8 \times 33,8$ cm with minor variants)
H. C. LUMBYE/ECHO FRA BALSALEN/PART./[…]/Echo fra Balsalen/Echo zum Ballsaal/402
Signed by the copyist (on p. 1): af H. C. Lumbye', dated (on p. 24): '1861.'
[DKKk; C II, 34 (1941–42.329)
This orchestral score seems to be the oldest, still preserved copy of Lumbye's *Echo from the Ballroom*. It was purchased by DKKk on 8.1. 1942 from the antiquarian and music seller, Einar Møller (Klosterstræde 22, Copenhagen) and seems to have been originally made for touring and/or concert purposes.

Orchestral score. Ms. Copy. Brown ink. 1 vol. 28 pp. ($28,8 \times 33,825,9 \times 34,7$ cm with minor variants)
Lumbye, H. C./Echo fra Ballsalen./Partitur/[…]/Echo fra Ballsalen.
Signed by the copyist (on p. 1): 'af H. C. Lumbye', dated (on p. 24): 'Kopenhagen d. 9.e April 1861./A. Pracht.'
[DKKk; C II, 34 (mu 6410.3004) (6510.2562)
This orchestral score was originally part of the music archive of Denmark's Broadcasting (Danmarks Radio), before it was donated to DKKk on 30.10.1964. It appears to have been originally made for touring and/or concert purposes.

No répétiteur's copy and set of parts dating from the 1861 première of *Echo from the Ballroom* have yet been traced. However, a later set of parts (dating from 1941 and seemingly copied from H. C. Lumbye's not yet traced autographed orchestral score) is now in the music archive of the Tivoli Gardens (call no. 1111).

13.3.1861
Soldier and Peasant (Soldat og Bonde).

This performance represents Bournonville's third and last restaging in Copenhagen of his one-act pantomimic idyll *Soldier and Peasant* (*see* 13.10.1829). It was this year presented on the poster as a 'Divertissement' and was mounted especially for the débuts of his two young pupils, J. Petersen and J. Thorberg, who played the rôles of *Lise* and *Anna* respectively. For the same production Bournonville made numerous notes in the original 1829 répétiteur's copy between 28.2. and 4.3.1861. They describe in fine detail the choreography and the mime of most of the ballet as mounted. According to his diary the choreography seems to have been staged in a slightly revised version in 1861:

28.2.1861: 'componeret [...] Indstudering paa Soldat og Bonde'
1.3.: 'Indstudering paa Soldat og Bonde [...] Eftermiddagsprøve paa Soldat og Bonde'
2.3.: 'skrevet [...] Indstudering paa Soldat og Bonde'
4.3.: 'skrevet og componeret [...] Prøve paa Soldat og Bonde'
5.3.: 'Prøve paa Pantomimen til Soldat og Bonde'
6.3. and 7.3.: 'Prøve paa Soldat og Bonde'
9.3.: 'Theaterprøve paa Soldat og Bonde der gik meget smukt'
11.3.: 'lille Prøve paa Soldat og Bonde'
12.3.: 'Theaterprøve paa Soldat og Bonde'
13.3.: ' I Theatret Soldat og Bonde nÿt Indstuderet med <u>Johanne Petersen</u> og <u>Juliette Thorberg</u> som Debut. Det gik udmærket godt og de høstede meget Bifald'.

The 1861 restaging of *Soldier and Peasant* received 12 performances, the last of which was given on 27.4.1862.

The musical material employed in 1861 was the same as that used since the 1829 première (now in DKKk, call nos. C II, 115, MA ms 3021, and KTB 1026).

23.3.1861
Twenty-one dance lessons for the Prince of Denmark (the Amalienborg Palace).

Between 9.1. and 23.3.1861 Bournonville gave 21 dance lessons to Prince Christian Frederik Wilhelm Carl of Denmark (later King Frederik VIII). The lessons were concluded with a performance at the Amalienborg Palace of the *Minuet* and the *Gavotte* from F. Kuhlau's score to J. L. Heiberg's five-act national fairy-play *The Elves' Hill* (*see* 10.9.1846). Both of these dances were arranged by Bournonville especially for this occasion. In his diary he carefully listed all 21 dance lessons (which took place on Monday and Wednesday afternoons) and also noted about the last five lessons and the concluding performance:

6.3.1861: '16 Lection hos Prindsen [i.e. the later King Frederik VIII], indstuderet en Gavotte'
11.3.: '17.e Lection for Prindsen af Danmark, smukke Fremskridt'
13.3.: '18.de Lection hos Prindsen'
18.3.: '19.de Lection for Prindsen af Danmark'
20.3.: '20.e Lection hos Prindsen'
23.3.: 'Om Aftenen 21.e og sidste Lection hos Prindsen af Danmark. Dronningen [i.e. Queen Louise Wilhelmine Friederike Caroline Auguste Julie], Landgreven [i.e. Landgrave and sometime Governor

of Copenhagen Wilhelm of Hesse-Cassel], Landgrevinden [i.e. the Danish princess, Louise Charlotte], og Prindsesse Auguste af Hessen vare tilstede og der blev udført Menuetten og Gavotten af Elverhøi arrangeret af mig. Jeg har havt den største Glæde af denne Undervisning og jeg skal aldrig glemme de elskværdige Børn, de ophøiede Forældre og den smukke Behandling jeg der har nÿdt som Kunstner og Lærer'.

No separate musical sources employed for this performance of the *Minuet* and the *Gavotte* from *The Elves' Hill* have yet been traced.

27.4.1861
Iphigenia in Aulis (Iphigenia i Aulis).

The 1861 Copenhagen staging represents the first time R. Wagner's 1846 revision of C. W. v. Gluck's three-act opera (premièred at Königlich Sächsisches Hoftheater in Dresden on 24.2.1847) was performed in Denmark, and the first time it was mounted with Bournonville's mise-en-scène and choreography. *Iphigenia in Aulis* was staged a second time by him on 11.1.1870, but then with a number of minor choreographic changes. Thus, the *Dance of the priestesses of Lesbos*, performed in Act II, score no. 17 (during the chorus, entitled «Wir preisen, besingen die Holde/Vi prise vi hædre vor Dronning») was originally performed by six women, but was revised that year into a dance for only four women. Moreover, at the last Copenhagen restaging of Gluck's opera in Bournonville's lifetime (mounted by L. Gade on 18.4. 1874) this dance was revised again for only three women.

Finally, during a sojourn in Stockholm in 1871, Bournonville gave personal stage instructions to the singer, F. Stenhammer, on 30.4.1871. She performed the title-rôle in Gluck's opera 7 times during the same season at Stockholm's Royal Theatre (Stora Theatern).

In his diary Bournonville noted about the 1861 Copenhagen première of *Iphigenia in Aulis*:

27.1.1861: 'Eftermiddagen læst Iphigenia [in Aulis]'
16.3.: 'udarbeidet en Personliste til Iphigenia'
18.3.: 'skrevet Scene=Arrangement til Iphigenia'
20.3.: 'skrevet paa Scene-Udstyret til Iphigenia – arbeidet med [E.] Lehmann'
30.3.: 'Costumemøde paa Iphigenia'
2.4.: 'componeret Dands til Iphigenia'
3.4.: 'overværet Claveerprøve paa Iphigenia'
4.4.: 'Indstudering paa Dandsene til Iphigenia'
5.4.: 'Indstudering paa Dandsene til Iphigenia (færdig)'
6.4.: 'Repetition paa Iphigenia'
8.4.: 'Repetition paa Dandsene til Iphigenia'
9.4.: 'skrevet og arrangeret – Arrangementsprøve paa Iphigenia fra 10½ til 1½ – componeret til Kl 3'
10.4.: 'skrevet og arrangeret [...] indstuderet paanÿ Lesbeindernes Dands til Iphigenia'
11.4.: 'skrevet og arrangeret [...] Stor Arrangementsprøve paa Iphigenia [...] Eftermiddags Instruction paa Iphigenia'
12.4.: 'Dandseprøve paa [...] Iphigenia [...] Eftermiddags-Instruction paa Ihpigenia'
13.4.: 'skrevet, – Arrangement=Repetition paa Iphigenia'
14.4.: 'sidste Arrangementsprøve paa Iphigenia'
15.4.: 'Eftermiddagsprøve paa Iphigenia'
17.4.: 'Quartettprøve paa Iphigenia'
18.4.: 'Theaterprøve med Quartett paa Iphigenia ([P. L. N.] Schramm og [J. A.] Steenberg sÿge)'
20.4.: '1.ste fuldstændige Prøve paa Iphigenia, gik udmærket'
22.4.: '2.den Theaterprøve paa Iphigenia'
23.4.: 'Maskinprøve paa Iphigenia'

24.4.: 'fuldstændig Prøve paa Iphigenia'
25.4.: 'Costumeprøve Kl 11. – Generalprøve i Costume paa Iphigenia'
27.4.: 'Første Forestilling af Iphigenia i Aulis. Den gik meget smukt og for fuldt Huus, dog uden Tilstrømning og med maadeholdent Bifald'.

The 1861 production of *Iphigenia in Aulis* received 15 performances, the last of which was given on 5.4.1866.

Autograph sources:

Production note. Ms. Autograph (partially in another's hand). Black ink. 4 pp. (36,3 × 22,9 cm)
Personale i Operaen Iphigenia./[...]/Bipersonerne i 1.ste Akt./ [...]/2.den Akt./[...]/3.die Akt.
Signed and dated: 'Kjøbenhavn den 16.de Martz 1861.
[Copenhagen, The State Archive (Rigsarkivet); Det kgl. Theaters Arkiv, Gruppe E, pakke 217 (Indk. Breve 1861)

Musical sources:

Orchestral score. Ms. Copy. Black ink. 3 vol. Act I 122 pp. of which one is blank, Act II 120 pp., Act III 106 pp. (26 × 33,3 cm)
Iphigenia i Aulis/Partitur/1.ste Act/478/[...]/2.den Act/[...]/ 3.die Act.
Unsigned and undated [c.1861]
[DKKkt; KTA 478
This orchestral score is a German copy that dates from the 1861 Copenhagen première of *Iphigenia in Aulis* and was used for all performances of it there during Bournonville's lifetime. It contains the opera's German text and A. Hertz's Danish translation of it (written with black ink).

Répétiteur's copy. Ms. Copy. Brown ink. 1 vol. 16 pp. (34,1 × 25,8 cm)
2. Iphigenia [*sic*] i Aulis A 478/[...]/Repetiteurpartie/til/Iphigenia i Aulis
Unsigned and undated [1861]
[DKKk; MA ms 2911 (2) (KTA 478)
This répétiteur's copy contains the music for Act I (score nos. 5, and 7–8), Act II (score nos. 16–17), and the Act III finale. Moreover, it includes Bournonville's autographed choreographic numbers (written with black ink), which (according to his diary) seem to have been written for his second and last restaging of Gluck's opera on 11.1.1870. They clearly refer to a separate (not yet traced) choreographic notation of the dance scenes in Act I (score nos. 5, and 7–8), and Act II (score no. 17). The music is included on pp. 15–30 in a volume that also contains the répétiteur's copies for three other operas and plays, mounted at Copenhagen's Royal Theatre between 1859 and 1863.

Parts. Ms. Copy. 32 + 11 vol.
4 vl I, 4 vl II, 2 vla, 2 vlc e cb, fl 1/2, ob 1/2, cl 1/2, fag 1/2, cor 1/2/ 3/4, tr 1/2, trb 1/2/3, timp. On stage: fl 1/2, ob 1/2, fag 1/2, cor 1/ 2, tr 1/2, gong. 73 vocal parts.
Unsigned and undated [1861]
[DKKk; KTA 478
This set of parts dates from the 1861 Copenhagen première of *Iphigenia in Aulis* and was used for all performances of it there during Bournonville's lifetime.

24.7.1861
Plan for a Repertory at Stockholm's Royal Theatre in September 1861 (Repertoire for Stockholms Theater i September 1861).
According to a note in his diary on this day (reading: 'forfattet et Repertoire for Stockholms Theater i September') Bournonville wrote a (not yet traced) plan of the repertory of operas and plays that he intended to mount in September 1861 as part of his three-year-long engagement as managing director of Stockholm's Royal Theatre. It is not possible to identify the exact contents of works included in this repertory plan.

13.9.1861
The Valkyrie (Valkyrien).
This four-act ballet represents Bournonville's first full-length work within the Nordic mythological sphere. According to his diary it seems to have been created under the influence of his recent reading of R. Wagner's *Oper und Drama* during the summer of 1860 (first published by J. J. Weber in Leipzig in 1852).

However, a note given ten years earlier in the Copenhagen paper *Flyve Posten* (1851, no. 223, September 25) indicates that Bournonville may at that time already have conceived his first ideas for *The Valkyrie* and initially asked N. W. Gade to write the music:

'Ligeledes har Bournonville forberedet Udarbeidelsen af en større Ballet: "Valkyrierne", hvortil N. W. Gade componerer Musiken.'

The Valkyrie was in the end set to a score by I. P. E. Hartmann which consists of 4 acts and is divided into 36 numbers. For parts of scene 2 and the whole of scenes 3–5 in Act IV (score no. 33) Hartmann employed nearly all of his much earlier music for A. Oehlenschläger's five-act tragedy *St. Olave* (*see* 13.3.1838) in which it originally served as the accompaniment for a pantomimic scene depicting *The Battle at Stiklestad*. In *The Valkyrie* this music (to which Hartmann added three transitory bars at the end) accompanied the pantomimic scene depicting *The Battle at Bravalla Heath*. Moreover, for this reuse of Hartmann's music Bournonville made a complete notation of both the choreography and the pantomime in *The Battle at Bravalla Heath*, which he wrote into the 1838 répétiteur's copy for *St. Olave* (now in DKKk, call no. MA ms 3081 (KTA 365)).

The Valkyrie was restaged 3 times by Bournonville in Copenhagen (*see* 1.9.1869, 29.1.1873, and 5.9.1876), each time with only minor if any changes from the original version.

In his diary he noted about the ballet's creation and its 1861 première:

9.6.1860: 'Anlæg til en nỹ Ballet (Valkyrien)'
3.7.: 'Brev til [I. P. E.] Hartmann om Balletten Valkyrien'
5.8.: 'Læst den største Deel af Dagen i R: Wagners Bog Die Oper und das Drama'
8.8.: 'fuldendt Læsningen af Wagners 'Oper und Drama''
9.8.: 'Begyndt Redactionen af min nỹ Ballet 'Valkyrien''
10.8.: 'Skrevet paa min nỹ Ballet'
11.8.: 'som igaar'
12.8.: 'Fuldendt Programmet til Balletten Valkyrien'
13.8.: 'reenskrevet mit Program'
14.8.: 'Fuldendt Reenskrivningen af mit Program og læst det for min Familie'
17.8.: 'besøgt [F.] Paludan-Müllers der vare særdeles tilfreds med min nỹ Ballet'
3.9.: 'Besøgt H. P. Holst. – Om Eftermiddagen læst Tannhäuser af Wagner'
4.9.: 'Brev til Hartmann med Program'
5.9.: 'Första Sammenkomst med Prof. Hartmann i Anledning af Balletten Valkyrien'

7.9.: 'Balletprogram afleveret til Chefen [i.e. F. F. v. Tillisch]'

10.9.: 'Brev fra H. P. Holst om min Ballet'

11.9.: '2.den Sammenkomst med Hartmann, der bragte mig god Musik'

17.9.: 'reenskrevet og Besøg hos [F.] Höedt'

19.9.: 'Decorations og Maskinmøde paa <u>Valkyrien</u> Kl 9'

26.9.: 'talt med Hartmann'

15.10.: 'Leveret mit Program og et Brev <u>Til Kongen</u> [i.e. Frederik VII] i hans Forgemak'

27.10.: 'Musik med Hartmann – Rescript fra Cabinettet at Kongen ikke kunde indlade sig paa at understøtte Balletten Valkyriens Udstyr'

1.12.: 'Musik med Prof. Hartmann'

2.12.: 'skrevet og componeret paa Valkyrien'

4.12.: '<u>Første</u> Indstudering paa Valkyrien fra 11 1½'

5.12.: 'Indstudering 2.den paa Valkyrien […] skrevet og componeret'

9.12.: 'Musik og Composition'

10.12.: 'Prøve Kl 10–12½ 3.die Indst.'

11.12.: '4.de Indstudering paa Valkyrien. Musik med Hartmann'

13.12.: '5.te Indst. [erased] Repetition paa Valkyrien, hjem og componeret'

14.12.: '5.te Indst paa Valkyrien'

16.12.: 'Skrevet og componeret den hele Formiddag'

17.12.: '6.te Indstudering paa Valkyrien'

18.12.: '7.e Indstudering paa Valkyrien […] Jeg gik hjem og componerede'

19.12.: '8. Indstudering paa Valkyrien'

21.12.: '9.e Indstudering fuldendt den 1.ste Akt af Valkyrien'

27.12.: 'Repetition paa Valkyrien'

29.12.: '(Besøg hos Hartmanns)'

30.12.: 'componeret'

31.12.: '<u>10.de Indst</u> paa Valkyrien […] Arbeidet med Hartmann'

1.1.1861: 'Eftermiddag skrev jeg og componerede paa en scène af 2.den Act til Valkyrien'

2.1.: 'skrevet og arrangeret […] 11.e Indstudering paa Valkyrien'

4.1.: 'Repetition paa Valkyrien […] componeret'

5.1.: 'componeret […] 12.e Indstudering paa Valkyrien – 2.den Akt færdig'

7.1.: 'Breve fra Chefen'

8.1.: 'begyndt paa Besvarelser, reduceret Plan til Valkyriens Udstyr […] Repetition paa Balletten'

9.1.: 'arbeidet med Hartmann, skrevet mine Breve til Chefen og Planerne færdige'

10.1.: 'expederet mine Breve til Chefen […] Repetition af 2.den Akt for Hartmann'

11.1.: 'Repetition paa 1.ste Akt af Valkyrien'

12.1.: 'arbeidet med Hartmann'

14.1. and 15.1.: 'componeret'

16.1.: 'Prøve og 13.de Indstudering paa Valkyrien 3.die Akt […] Møde med Hartmann'

17.1.: 'Prøve paa Valkyrien'

19.1.: 'componeret. <u>14.e Indstudering</u> paa <u>Valkyrien</u>'

21.1.: 'Om Eftermiddagen, componeret'

22.1.: '15.e Indstudering paa Valkyrien

24.1.: '16.e Indstudering paa Valkyrien – Decorationsmøde paa Samme'

25.1.: 'Arbeidet med Hartmann […] og componeret'

26.1.: '17.e Indstudering paa Valkyrien'

28.1.: 'Brev til Theatermaler [C. F.] Christensen'

29.1.: 'Repetition paa 2½ Akt af Valkyrien'

31.1.: 'Decorationsmøde'

1.2.: 'componeret, Decorationsmøde, 18.e Indstudering paa Valkyrien […] arbeidet med Hartmann, Eftermiddagen hjemme skrevet, componeret'

2.2.: 'skrevet og arrangeret […] 19.e Indst paa Valkyrien'

4.2.: 'Repetition paa Dandsen til Valkyrien'

8.2.: 'arbeidet med Hartmann. Conference med Chefen – givet min bestemte Erklæring. – Valkyrien udsat til Efteraaret'

12.2.: '19.e Indstudering paa Valkyrien 3.die Akt færdig'

14.2.: 'Repetition paa 3.die Akt af Valkyrien'

15.2.: 'arbeidet med Hartmann'

16.2.: 'Sceneprøve paa Valkyrien'

18.2.: 'Repetition paa 1.ste og 2.den Akt af Valkyrien. Møde hos Hartmann'

19.2.: 'Theaterprøve paa Valkyrien'

20.2.: 'Theaterprøve paa 1.te og 2.den Akt af Valkyrien, der gik særdeles godt'

21.2.: 'lille Prøve paa Dandse'

22.2.: 'lille Prøve paa Valkyrien'

23.2.: 'skrevet og arrangeret […] Prøve med Comparser paa 3.die Akt af Valkyrien, arbeidet med Hartmann'

25.2.: 'Underretning om at jeg har faaet Lehmanns Engagement som Costumetegner sat igjennem'

26.2.: 'Theaterprøve paa 3.die og 2.den Akt af Valkyrien […] Eftermiddag arbeidet med Lehmann; modtaget af ham en smuk Skizze, som jeg betalte med <u>40</u>.d i Betragtning af hans mangfoldige Artigheder imod <u>os</u>'

28.2.: 'componeret […] Prøve paa Valkyrien 1ste Akt'

1.3.: 'arbeidet med Hartmann'

4.3.: 'skrevet og componeret'

9.3.: 'skrevet og componeret, arbeidet med Hartmann, Eftermiddag componeret paa 4.de Akt'

11.3.: '20.de Indstudering paa Valkyrien. – Eftersyn af nordisk Armatur'

12.3.: '21.de Indstudering paa Valkyrien 4.e Akt. – Armatur Gjennemsyn'

14.3.: '22.de Indstudering paa <u>Valkyrien</u>'

16.3.: 'Repetition paa Valkyrien'

17.3.: 'Møde i Theatret i Anledning af Costumet til Valkyrien'

18.3.: 'Costumemøde paa Valkyrien'

20.3.: 'stor Prøve paa Valkyrien for Hartmann og H C Andersen, Costümemøde paa Valkyrien […] arbeidet med Lehmann'

22.3.: 'Modtaget det sidste Numer af Hartmann – componeret'

23.3.: '23.e Indstudering paa Valkyrien (sidste Scene)'

24.3.: 'tilbragt hele Formiddagen med Composition af Einheriadandsen Finale til Valkyrien'

25.3.: '24.e Indstudering paa Valkyrien (Finale)'

26.3.: '25.de Indstudering paa Valkyrien. <u>Compositionen fuldført</u>'

27.3.: 'Repetition paa Valkyrien. Costumemøde paa Valkyrien'

29.3.: 'skrevet endeel med Hensyn til Ballettens Udstÿr'

30.3.: 'skrevet […] Costumemøde paa […] Valkyrien, prøve paa […] Valkyrien'

8.4.: 'Repetition paa […] endeel af Valkyrien'

12.4.: 'skrevet og besørget 'Et forslag for Ballettjenesten til Theaterchefen'

18.4.: 'Endelig Afgjørelse af Valkyrie=Sagen og mit Engagements Forlængelse til 1.ste October i to underlige Skrivelser'

23.4.: 'Repetition paa Valkyrien'

25.4.: 'Besøg hos Hartmann'

1.5.: 'Sidste Costüme Møde med [J. A.] Pätges […] Decorations= Møde paa Theatret'

15.6., 16.6., and 20.6.: 'noteret i Valkyrien'

25.6. and 26.6.: 'noteret paa Valkyrien'

27.6.: 'Noteret i Valkyrien, skrevet en Forerindring til Ballettens Repetiteur=Partie'

28.6.: 'noteret'

1.7.: 'Møde med [C. F.] Christensen og [A. P.] Weddén'

4.7.: and 5.7.: 'skrevet og noteret'

12.7.: 'talt med Theatermaler Christensen'

23.7.: 'skrevet en Fortale til min Ballet'

25.7.: 'Brev fra Pätges'

1.8.: 'Breve til [A.] Fredstrup, Hartmann'

5.8.: 'læste og reenskrev paa Valkyrien'

6.8.: 'Brev fra Hartmann'

7.8.: 'skrevet og fuldendt Programmets Reenskrivning. Brev til Hartmann'

14.8.: 'skrevet og noteret'

20.8.: 'Paa Theatret – prøvet Valkyrien igjennem, den gik udmærket godt'

22.8.: 'Prøve paa Valkyrien [...] Eftermiddags Arrangements prøve fra 6–8¹/₂. Jeg havde megen Fornøielse deraf og Alt slog godt til. – Jeg kom dygtig træt hjem'
23.8.: 'Prøve paa Einheriadandsen'
24.8.: 'Repetition paa 3.die og 4.die Akt'
26.8.: 'Ankomst Kl 11¹/₂, besørget flere Ting til Balletten. Eftermiddagsprøve paa 1.ste og 2.den Akt'
27.8.: 'Arrangement paa Finalen af Valkyrien. Eftermiddagsprøve paa de to første Akter af Musiken – Det er et storartet Kunstværk af Hartmann!'
28.8.: 'Prøve paa Valkyriens Dandse [...] 2.den Musikprøve fortræffelig'
29.8.: 'Theaterprøve med Orchester paa tre Akter. Det gik fortræffeligt'
30.8.: 'Eftermiddagsprøve og sidste Arrangement paa Valkyrien, – dygtig træt tilsengs'
31.8.: 'besørget adskilligt paa Theatret'
4.9.: 'Eftermiddagsprøve paa 1.ste og 4.de Akt med Orchester'
5.9.: 'Costümeprøve'
7.9.: '1.ste Generalprøve paa Valkyrien gik ÿpperligt'
8.9.: 'besørget adskilligt paa Theatret'
9.9.: '2.den Generalprøve paa Valkyrien, gik ÿpperligt'
10.9.: 'arrangeret for Balletten [...] besørget Programmer. Decorationsprøve om Aftenen indtil Kl 1¹/₂'
12.9.: 'Tour til Bakkegaarden for at levere Program til Geheimeraad [C. C.] Hall'
13.9.: 'Forberedelser til Balletten. Billetterne solgte til forhøiet Priis, fuldt Huus naturligviis [...] Mit sidste og som jeg troer det bedste Arbeide, gik for et Publicum, der er mæt af mig, og jeg – det veed Gud – inderlig kjed af Det. – Naar jeg undtager [Gott. A.] Füssels store Scene, der gik i Lÿset, formedelst hans gamle Uheld med Skjægbaandet, blev Balletten i alle sine Details udmærket udført. De store Effectsteder rev Publicum med sig og til Slutning lød et vedvarende Applaus, der skulde betyde en Fremkaldelse, men i det Hele var der Lunkenhed, som bragte mig til at takke Gud, fordi jeg fra nu af er befriet for at componere, og ikke skal beroe af den ulidelige Dvaskhed, der maa dræbe al Lÿst og Kraft. [...] Vi kom hjem til vort Logis Kl 1 og jeg gik tilsengs med den Bøn til Gud at Jeg maa lære at nedstemme mine Fordringer paa Løn for min Skæbne. Jeg kan ikke nægte at det, vort Publicum giver synes mig altfor ringe'.

About the reviews of the ballet and the following four performances he noted:

14.9.1861: 'Megen Ros og Berømmelse for Balletten'
15.9.: '2.den Forestilling af Valkyrien for fuldt Huus og meget livlig Applaus. Alt gik ÿpperligt og Indtrykket var storartet. Glimrende Anmeldelse i Den Berlingske'
16.9.: 'udmærket Artikel i Dagbladet'
18.9.: 'I Theatret Walkyrien [*sic*] for fuldt Huus, gik udmærket og fik særdeles Bifald'
21.9.: 'I Theatret Valkyrien for fuldt Huus men for et ubeskriveligt lunkent Publicum!!! Nei, det er ikke muligt at udholde den fornemme Tilbageholdenhed. – Theatret maa sÿgne hen eller forfalde til Farcer!'
22.9.: 'I Theatret Valkyrien efter allerhøieste Befaling for aldeles fuldt Huus og med Det sædvanlige Bifald!'.

The last performance which Bournonville attended on 8.10.1860 before his departure to Stockholm was assessed as follows:

'I Theatret Valkyrien for udsolgt Huus og et taust Publicum. Jeg sagde Farvel til den danske Skueplads med blandede Følelser'.

The 1861 production of *The Valkyrie* received 39 performances (the last given on 16.10.1865) and the ballet reached a total of 61 performances during Bournonville's lifetime, the last of which was given on 28.1.1879.

Autograph sources:

Musical instructions. Ms. Autograph. Brown and black ink. 16 pp. of which two are blank (21,2 × 13,2 cm)
N° 1. /[...]/2.den Akt. (1.ste Scene)/[...]/Valkyrien 3.die Akt/1.ste Scene./[...]/4.de Akt. 1.ste Scene: –
Unsigned and undated [Written, according to the diary, most likely between 3.7. and 4.9.1860]
[DKKk; NKS 2982, 4°, II

Manuscript mise-en-scène. Ms. Autograph. Brown ink. 4 pp. of which two are blank (28,5 × 22,9 cm)
Momenter af Slaget/paa [changed to:] ved Stiklestad/til/Øehlenschlägers Tragedie Olaf den Hellige/fremstillede og ordnede efter Hartmanns Musik/af/August Bournonville
Unsigned and undated [c. summer 1860]
[DKKk; NKS 2982, 4°, III
This manuscript contains Bournonville's new mise-en-scène for the scene named *The Battle at Stiklestad* that he arranged in 1860 especially for his new ballet *The Valkyrie* (Act IV, scenes 2–5).

Manuscript scenario. Ms. Autograph. Brown ink. 1 vol. 24 pp. of which three are blank (26,8 × 20,9 cm)
Valkÿrien./[...]/Valkyrien/Ballet i fire Akter./af./August Bournonville./1860.
Signed and dated: 'Fredensborg d 12. August 1860.' [Written, according to the diary, between 9.8 and 14.8.1860]
[DKKk; NKS 2982, 4°, I

Manuscript scenario. Ms. Autograph. Brown ink. 1 vol. 22 pp. (22,5 × 18 cm)
Valkÿrien./Ballet i fire Akter./af./August Bournonville./1860.
Signed and dated: 'Fredensborg d 12.de August 1860.' [Written according to the diary between 9.8. and 14.8.1860]
[DKKk; NKS 3285 4° 3 V–Z

Choreographic note. Ms. Autograph. Brown ink. 4 pp. (17,9 × 11,3 cm)
La danse des Valkyries../[...]/Marche. [= Act I, scene 1]
Unsigned and undated [c. December 1860?]
[DKKt; Brevregistrant: Bournonville
This manuscript contains a complete description of the *Dance of the Valkyries* and the 'Valhalla Marsch' in Act I (score nos. 1–2) of *The Valkyrie*. It seems to represent Bournonville's first drafts for these numbers, since it is slightly different from his notes for the same dances written into the répétiteur's copy for *The Valkyrie* (pp. 2–7) during the summer of 1861. The manuscript also includes his autographed choreographic numbers ('1–14') which refer to similar numbers inserted in the répétiteur's copy underneath the music for these dances.

Choreographic note. Ms. Autograph. Brown ink. 2 pp. (21,1 × 13,6 cm)
Valkyrien/1.ste Akt 1.ste Scene (Valkyriernes Dands)/[...]/Valhalla-Marsch.
Unsigned and undated [c. December 1860?]
[DKKk; Utilg. 828 (Harald Landers Arkiv, Kapsel 182)
This manuscript seems to represent Bournonville's second draft for the choreography of the *Dance of the Valkyries* and the 'Valhalla Marsch' in Act I (score nos. 1–2) of *The Valkyrie*. This theory is based on the fact that its contents are slightly different both from the above-mentioned manuscript and from the notes for the same dances which he wrote in the répétiteur's copy for *The Valkryrie* (pp. 2–7) during the summer of 1861. The manuscript also includes Bournonville's autographed choreographic numbers ('1–4') which refer to a series of similar numbers inserted in the répétiteur's copy underneath the music for these dances.

Choreographic and mimic note. Ms. Autograph. Black ink. 2 pp. (17,8 × 13 cm)

1.er Acte – Scene 2:me
Unsigned and undated [c. December 1860]
[DKKk; Utilg. 828 (Harald Landers Arkiv, Kapsel 182)
This manuscript seems to represent Bournonville's first choreographic and mimic draft for the second scene in Act I of *The Valkyrie*, since it differs slightly from his notes for the same scene written into the répétiteur's copy for this ballet (pp. 8–12) during the summer of 1861. The manuscript also includes his autographed choreographic numbers ('1–17') which refer to a similar series of numbers inserted in the répétiteur's copy underneath the music for this scene.

Mimic note. Ms. Autograph. Black ink. 2 pp. (20,5 × 13,4 cm)
[Act I] Scène 3.me/[…]/Scène 4.me
Unsigned and undated [c. December 1860?]
[DKKk; Utilg. 828 (Harald Landers Arkiv, Kapsel 182)
This manuscript seems to represent Bournonville's first draft for the mime of the third and fourth scenes in Act I of *The Valkyrie*, since it is slightly different from his notes for these scenes written into the répétiteur's copy for this ballet (pp. 12–18) during the summer of 1861. The manuscript also includess his two sets of choreographic numbers ('1–17' and '1–15') which refer to similar numbers inserted in the répétiteur's copy underneath the music for these scenes.

Mimic-choreographic note. Ms. Autograph. Brown ink. 2 pp. cut into two pieces (17,9 × 10,3 cm and 17,9 × 10,4 cm).
Scène 5.me/[…]/Allo molto: [= Scene 6]/[…]/poco Andantino.
Unsigned and undated [c. December 1860]
[DKKk; Utilg. 828 (Harald Landers Arkiv, Kapsel 182)
This manuscript seems to represent Bournonville's first draft for the mime and the choreography in the fifth and sixth scenes of Act I in *The Valkyrie*, since it is slightly different from his notes written into the répétiteur's copy for this ballet (pp. 18–28) during the summer of 1861. The manuscript also includes his autographed choreographic numbers ('1–17', '1–19', and '1–4') which refer to similar numbers inserted in the répétiteur's copy underneath the music for these scenes.

Mimic note. Ms. Autograph. Black ink. 1 p. (22,4 × 17,9 cm)
Finale (Poco Andantino) [= Act I, scene 7]
Unsigned and undated [c. December 1860?]
[DKKk; Utilg. 828 (Harald Landers Arkiv, Kapsel 182)
This manuscript describes the mimic action in the first part of the seventh scene in Act I of *The Valkyrie*. It seems to represent Bournonville's first draft since it is slightly different from his notes for this scene that he wrote in the répétiteur's copy for *The Valkyrie* (pp. 28–32) during the summer of 1861. The manuscript also includes his autographed choreographic numbers ('1–19') which refer to similar numbers inserted in the répétiteur's copy underneath the music for this scene.

Choreographic note. Ms. Autograph. Black ink. 1 p. cut into two pieces (17,9 × 12,9 and 17,9 × 12,7 cm)
Apparition des Valkyries./Final. [= Act I, scene 7]
Unsigned and undated [c. December 1860?]
[DKKk; Utilg. 828 (Harald Landers Arkiv, Kapsel 182)
This manuscript describes the choreography for the second part of the seventh scene in Act I of *The Valkyrie*. It seems to represent Bournonville's first draft, since it is slightly different from his notes for the same scene written into the répétiteur's copy for this ballet (pp. 32–36) during the summer of 1861. The manuscript also includes his autographed choreographic numbers ('1–12') which refer to similar numbers inserted in the répétiteur's copy underneath the music for this scene.

Choreographic note. Ms. Autograph. Brown ink, 1 p. (22,4 × 17,9 cm)
Notes chorégraphiques./du ballet/de la Valkyrie./1861.
Unsigned and dated: '1861.'
[DKKk; Utilg. 828 (Harald Landers Arkiv, Kapsel 182)

This manuscript was originally used as a cover for Bournonville's complete collection of sheet manuscripts for *The Valkyrie*.

Mimic note. Ms. Autograph. Black ink. 2 pp. (20,4 × 16,9 cm)
2.me Acte – Scene 1.ière
Unsigned and undated [c. late December 1860 or early January 1861?]
[DKKk; Utilg. 828 (Harald Landers Arkiv, Kapsel 182)
This manuscript describes the mimic action in the first scene of Act II in *The Valkyrie*. It seems to represent Bournonville's first draft for it, since it is slightly different from his notes for the same scene written into the répétiteur's copy for *The Valkyrie* (pp. 38–44) during the summer of 1861. The manuscript also includes his autographed choreographic numbers ('1–25') which refer to similar numbers inserted in the répétiteur's copy underneath the music for this scene.

Mimic-choreographic note. Ms. Autograph. Brown ink. 4 pp. (21,5 × 13,1 cm)
Acte 2.me Scène 2.me/[…]/Scène 3:me
Unsigned and undated [c. late December 1860 or early January 1861?]
[DKKk; Utilg. 828 (Harald Landers Arkiv, Kapsel 182)
This manuscript describes the mimic action and the choreography in the second and third scenes of Act II in *The Valkyrie*. It seems to represent Bournonville's first draft, since it is slightly different from his notes for the same scenes written into the répétiteur's copy for this ballet (pp. 44–53) during the summer of 1861. The manuscript also includes his autographed choreographic numbers ('1–30' and '1–13') which refer to similar numbers inserted in the répétiteur's copy underneath the music for these scenes.

Production note. Ms. Autograph. Brown ink. 3 pp. (28,5 × 22,4 cm)
Bilag A./Motiveret Plan til Udstyrelsen/af/Balletten 'Valkyrien'
Signed and dated: 'Kjøbenhavn den 10.de Januar 1861.' [Written according to the diary on 9.1.1861]
[SSm; Daniel Fryklunds samling no. 104

Mimic-choreographic note. Ms. Autograph. Brown ink. 8 pp. (22,2 × 14,3 cm)
Valkyrien, 3.die Akt./2.den scène./[…]/Pas grece. [*sic*]
Unsigned and undated [c. mid-January to mid-February 1861?]
[DKKk; Utilg. 828 (Harald Landers Arkiv, Kapsel 182)
This manuscript describes the complete mime and the choreography in the first and second scenes of Act III in *The Valkyrie*. It seems to represent Bournonville's first draft, since it is slightly different from his notes for the same scenes written into the répétiteur's copy for *The Valkyrie* (pp. 58–80) during the summer of 1861. The manuscript also includes his six autographed sets of choreographic numbers ('1–10', '1–20', '1–6', '1–15', '1–13, and '1–14') which refer to similar numbers inserted in the répétiteur's copy underneath the music for these scenes.

Mimic-choreographic note. Ms. Autograph. Black ink. 4 pp. (22,2 × 14,2 cm)
Acte 3.me: Scène 3:me [= Act III, scene 3-5]
Unsigned and undated [c. mid-January to mid-February 1861?]
[DKKk; Utilg. 828 (Harald Landers Arkiv, Kapsel 182)
This manuscript describes the mime and the choreography in the third, fourth, and fifth scenes of Act III in *The Valkyrie*. It seems to represent Bournonville's first draft since it is slightly different from his notes for the same scenes written into the répétiteur's copy for *The Valkyrie* (pp. 80–92) during the summer of 1861. The manuscript also includes his autographed choreographic numbers ('1–34') which refer to similar numbers inserted in the répétiteur's copy underneath the music for these scenes.

Mimic-choreographic note. Ms. Autograph. Brown ink. 2 pp. (20,5 × 13,5 cm)
Scène 6.me [= Act III, scene 6 (incomplete)]
Unsigned and undated [c. mid-January to mid-February 1861?]

[DKKk; Utilg. 828 (Harald Landers Arkiv, Kapsel 182)
This manuscript describes the mime and the choreography in the sixth scene of Act III of *The Valkyrie*. It seems to represent Bournonville's first draft, since it is slightly different from his notes for the same scene written into the répétiteur's copy for this ballet (pp. 92–97) during the summer of 1861. The manuscript also includes his autographed choreographic numbers ('1–13' and '1–8') which refer to similar numbers inserted in the répétiteur's copy underneath the music for this scene.

Choreographic note. Ms. Autograph. Black ink. 2 pp. (20,5 × 13,2 cm)
1. La toile levée montre Brune & Svava/a gauche. [= Act IV, scene 1 (incomplete)]
Unsigned and undated [c. March 1861?]
[DKKk; Utilg. 828 (Harald Landers Arkiv, Kapsel 182)
This manuscript describes parts of the mime and the choreography in the first part of scene 1 in Act IV of *The Valkyrie*. It seems to represent Bournonville's first draft, since it is slightly different from his notes for the same scene written into the répétiteur's copy for *The Valkyrie* (pp. 106–109) during the summer of 1861. The manuscript also includes his autographed choreographic numbers ('1–14') which refer to similar numbers inserted in the répétiteur's copy underneath the music for this scene.

Choreographic note. Ms. Autograph. Black ink. 3 pp. (21,7 × 17,9 cm)
Valkyrien/4.de Akt: 1.ste Scene/[…]/2.den scène [incomplete]
Unsigned and undated [c. March 1861?]
[DKKk; Utilg. 828 (Harald Landers Arkiv, Kapsel 182)
This manuscript describes parts of the mime and the choreography in the first and second scenes of Act IV in *The Valkyrie*. It seems to represent Bournonville's first draft, since it is slightly different from his notes for the same scenes written into the répétiteur's copy for *The Valkyrie* (pp. 108–118) during the summer of 1861. The manuscript also includes his two autographed sets of choreographic numbers ('1–8' and '1–7'), the last of which clearly refers to similar numbers inserted in the répétiteur's copy underneath the music for this scene.

Mimic-choreographic note. Ms. Autograph. Black ink. 3 pp. (17,7 × 11,4 cm)
Acte 4.me Scène 6.me/[…]/Scène 7.me [incomplete]
Unsigned and undated [c. March 1861?]
[DKKk; Utilg. 828 (Harald Landers Arkiv, Kapsel 182)
This manuscript describes the mime and the choreography in the sixth and seventh scenes of Act IV. It seems to represent Bournonville's first draft, since it is slightly different from his notes for the same scenes that he wrote into the répétiteur's copy for *The Valkyrie* (pp. 128–133) during the summer of 1861. The manuscript also includes his two sets of autographed choreographic numbers ('1–8' and '1–16') which refer to similar numbers inserted in the répétiteur's copy underneath the music for this scene.

Choreographic note. Ms. Autograph. Brown ink. 6 pp. (21,5 × 13,3 cm)
Einheria=Dands./(Finale til Valkyrien.)
Signed and dated: 'Copenhague ce 24 Mars 1861.'
[DKKk; Utilg. 828 (Harald Landers Arkiv, Kapsel 182)
This manuscript describes the choreography for the finale of the seventh scene of Act IV. It seems to represent Bournonville's first draft since it is slightly different from his notes for the same scene written into the répétiteur's copy for *The Valkyrie* (pp. 133–141) during the summer of 1861. The manuscript also includes his autographed choreographic numbers ('1–28') which refer to similar numbers inserted in the répétiteur's copy underneath the music for this scene.

Production note. Ms. Autograph. Black ink. 3 pp. (34,8 × 21,2 cm)
Nÿe Costümer og nÿ (og tildels restaureret) Armatur/til Balletten Valkÿrien.

Signed and dated: 'Kjøbenhavn d. 30.de Martz 1861.' [Written according to the diary on 29.3. and 30.3.1861]
[SSm; Daniel Fryklunds samling no. 116

Production note. Ms. Autograph. Brown ink. 2 pp. (35,8 × 22,4 cm)
Decorationer til Valkÿrien
Unsigned and undated [Written according to the diary most probably on 30.3.1861]
[DKKk; NKS 3285 4° 3 V–Z

Manuscript scenario. Ms. Autograph. Brown ink. 1 vol. 34 pp. (22,5 × 17,9 cm)
Valkÿrien./Valkÿrien./Ballet i fire Akter/af/August Bournonville./(Musiken af J. P. E. Hartmann sen.)/Decorationerne malede af C. F. Christensen./Costumerne tegnede af Edv. Lehmann./Opfört förste gang i September/1861.
Signed and dated: '1861.' [Written according to the diary between 23.7. and 7.8.1861]
[DKKk; NKS 3285 4° 3 V–Z

Musical sources:

Orchestral score. Ms. Autograph (by I. P. E. Hartmann). Brown ink and pencil. 2 vol. Act I–II 185 pp. of which one is blank, Act III–IV 266 pp. of which four are blank (34 × 29 cm)
Valkyrien/Partitur/1.ste og 2.den Act./Valkÿrien/Ballet/af Aug. Bournonville/Musik af/J:P:E:Hartmann./[…]/Valkÿrien/Partitur/3.die og 4.de Act.
Signed and dated (on p. '445'): 'd: 14 Aug: 1861./J:P:E:Hartmann/Op: 62.'
[DKKk; C II, 114 (KTB 298)
Hartmann's autographed orchestral score was used for all performances of *The Valkyrie* since its 1861 première and throughout Bournonville's lifetime.

Répétiteur's copy. Ms. Copy. Black ink. 1 vol. 2 title pages (pp. i–ii) and 142 pp. of which three are blank (33,6 × 25 cm)
B. 298/5/[…]/Valkyrien./Ballet i 4 Acter/af/August Bournonville/Musiken af Professor J. P. E Hartmann./1861.
Unsigned and dated (on p. 1): '1860/1861'
[DKKk; MA ms 2995 (KTB 298)
This répétiteur's copy contains Bournonville's autographed notes (written with brown ink) which describe the dramatic action, the mime, and the choreography throughout the ballet. The répétiteur's copy itself is dated by Bournonville (on p. 141) with his inscription: 'Chorégraphien sluttet den 24.e Martz 1861./Composition og Indstudering d. 27.e do do.'. Moreover, this volume contains numerous choreographic numbers (written by Bournonville and an unknown hand) which refer to his separate production notes and/or choreographic drafts that he wrote (according to his diary) between mid-January and 24.3.1861. Finally, according to his diary he made most of the notes in this volume during the three weeks between 15.6. and 5.7.1861, well after the complete ballet had been taught and rehearsed. This fact indicates that Bournonville's notes in this répétiteur's copy could be regarded as his final and definitive version of *The Valkyrie*, in this way reflecting what actually took place on stage.

Parts. Ms. Copy. 40 + 4 vol.
5 vl I, 4 vl II, 2 vla, 2 vlc, 2 cb, fl picc, fl 1/2, ob 1/2, cl 1/2, fag 1/2, cor 1/2/3/4, tr 1/2/3, trb 1/2/3, tuba, timp, gr cassa, piatti, tri, arpa. On stage: tr 1/2, gr cassa, piatti e tri.
Unsigned and undated [1861]
[DKKk; KTB 298
This set of parts dates from the 1861 première of *The Valkyrie* and was used for all performances of this ballet during Bournonville's lifetime.

Piano score (fragment). Ms. Copy. Black ink. 6 pp. of which two are blank (34,9 × 25,9 cm)

Indledning til Balletten 'Valkyrien'
Signed by the copyist (on p. 2): 'I. P. E. Hartmann. Op. 62', undated [c. mid-1860s or later]
[DKkk; I. P. E. Hartmanns samling, voksende samling, I, Ms. (1939–40.448)
This piano score for four hands contains the first 52 measures of Hartmann's music for *The Valkyrie*. It was most probably arranged for publishing purposes. The score was donated to DKKk on 15.2. 1940 by the physician and amateur composer, A. Liebmann.

Orchestral score (fragment). Ms. Copy. Black ink. 4 pp. (35,2 × 26 cm)
Scene af Valkyriens 3 <u>Akt.</u>
Unsigned and undated [c. mid-1860s or later]
[DKKk; I. P. E. Hartmanns samling, kapsel V–Ø
This orchestral score contains the first 32 measures of Hartmann's music for Act III, scene 3 (score no. 21) in *The Valkyrie*. It was most probably written for concert purposes.

Orchestral score (excerpt). Ms. Copy. Brown ink. 12 pp. (34,8 × 26,1 cm with minor variants)
Valhalla-Marsch/aus dem Ballet: 'Die Walküre'
Unsigned and undated [c. mid-1860s or later]
[DKKkI. P. E. Hartmanns samling, kapsel V–Ø
This orchestral score contains the complete music of the so-called 'Valhalla March' in Act I, scene 1 (score no. 2) of *The Valkyrie*. According to Hartmann's pencilled autographed title, it was most likely made for publishing purposes in Germany.

Orchestral score (excerpt). Ms. Copy. Brown ink. 48 pp. of which two are blank (34,8 × 26,1 cm with minor variants)
Der nordische Kämpfer Bjørn/von die Griecherinnen zu Verführung/geführt, aus dem Ballet: 'Die Walküre.'
Unsigned and undated [c. mid-1860s or later]
[DKKk; I. P. E. Hartmanns samling, kapsel V–Ø
This orchestral score contains the complete music of Act III, scene 4 (score no. 22) of *The Valkyrie*. According to Hartmann's pencilled autographed title it was most likely made for publishing purposes in Germany.

Other sources:

Manuscript scenario. Ms. Copy. Brown ink. 1 vol. 22 pp. (25,3 × 21,2 cm)
<u>Valkyrien.</u>/<u>Valkyrien</u>/Ballet i fire Akter/af./August Bournonville./<u>1860.</u>
Unsigned and dated: '1860.'
[DKKk; NKS 3285 4° 3 V–Z

Manuscript scenario. Ms. Copy. Brown ink. 1 vol. 61 pp. (22,9 × 18 cm)
Valkyrien./<u>Ballet i fire Akter.</u>/<u>af.</u>/<u>August Bournonville.</u>/<u>1860.</u>
Unsigned and dated: '1860.'
[DKKk; NKS 3285 4° 3 V–Z

Costume drawing by E. Lehmann. Pencil and water colours (16 × 25 cm)
<u>Heimdal</u>/Valkyrien/Hr. Fredstrup.
Unsigned and undated [c.1861]
[SSm; Daniel Fryklunds samling no. 286 (F 1326 c)
This drawing shows the costume of *Heimdal* in Acts I and IV of *The Valkyrie* (performed by A. Fredstrup).

Costume drawing by E. Lehmann. Pencil and water colours (16 × 25 cm)
W. Price./Valkyrien.
Unsigned and undated [c.1861]
[SSm; Daniel Fryklunds samling no. 285 (F. 1326 b)
This drawing shows the costume of *Odin* in Act I, scene 1 (score nos. 1–2) of *The Valkyrie* (performed by W. Price).

Costume drawing by E. Lehmann. Pencil and water colours (16 × 25 cm)
W. Price./Valkyrien.
Unsigned and undated [c.1861]
[SSm; Daniel Fryklunds samling no. 284 (F 1326 a)
This drawing shows the costume of *Brune* (i.e. *Odin* in disguise) in *The Valkyrie* (performed by W. Price).

Costume drawing by E. Lehmann. Pencil and water colours (17 × 24 cm)
Harald Hildetand/Valkyrien./Füssel sen.
Unsigned and undated [c.1861]
[SSm; Daniel Fryklunds samling no. 287 (F 1326 d)
This drawing shows the costumes of *Harald Hildetand* and his grandson *Helge* in Act I of *The Valkyrie* (performed by Gott. A. Füssel and H. Scharff respectively).

Costume drawing by E. Lehmann. Pencil and water colours (16 × 24 cm)
Björn/Valkyrien./Gade.
Unsigned and undated [c.1861]
[SSm; Daniel Fryklunds samling no. 288 (F 1326 e)
This drawing shows the costume of *Bjørn* in *The Valkyrie* (performed by L. Gade).

Costume drawing by E. Lehmann. Pencil and water colours (24,3 × 16 cm)
<u>Kongens Hirdmænd</u>/[…]/Valkyrien.
Unsigned and undated [c.1861]
[DKKkt; Kostumetegninger (Lehmann)
This drawing shows the costume of the Danish royal housecarls in Act I of *The Valkyrie*.

Costume drawing by E. Lehmann. Pencil and water colours (24,6 × 16 cm)
Livvagt 3die Akt Byzantinske Krigere/Valkyrien/[…]/12 milt. Statister.
Unsigned and undated [c.1861]
[DKKkt; Kostumetegninger (Lehmann)
This drawing shows the costume of the Greek warriors in Act III of *The Valkyrie* (performed by twelve surnumeraries).

Costume drawing by E. Lehmann. Pencil and water colours (24,1 × 17,5 cm)
Græsk Høvedmand. /[…]/Valkyrien
Unsigned and undated [c.1861]
[DKKkt; Kostumetegninger (Lehmann)
This drawing shows the costume of *Greek Chieftains* in Act III of *The Valkyrie*.

Costume drawing by E. Lehmann. Pencil and water colours (24,8 × 16,1 cm)
<u>Græsk Dandserinde</u>
Unsigned and undated [c.1861]
[DKKkt; Kostumetegninger (Lehmann)
This drawing shows the costume of the *Greek Women* in Act III of *The Valkyrie*.

Costume drawing by E. Lehmann. Pencil and water colours (24,4 × 16 cm)
Valkyrien./[…]/<u>Einheriar.</u>
Unsigned and undated [c.1861]
[DKKkt; Kostumetegninger (Lehmann)
This drawing shows the costume of the *Einheriar* in the finale of Act IV (score no. 36) of *The Valkyrie* (performed by 24 men).

Drawing of accessories by E. Lehmann. Pencil and water colours (22,3 × 13,9 cm)
Valkyrien./[…]/Bronce Drage
Unsigned and undated [c.1861]

[DKKkt; Kostumetegninger (Lehmann)
This drawing shows a standard with a dragoon painted on it.

Costume drawing by E. Lehmann. Pencil and water colours (22,1 ×
28 cm)
Valkyrien/[...]/Valkyrien
Unsigned and undated [c.1861]
[DKKkt; Kostumetegninger (Lehmann)
This drawing shows two different banners.

Printed sources:

Printed scenario. 1 vol. 23 pp. (20,8 × 13,5 cm)
Valkyrien./Ballet i 4 Akter/af/August Bournonville./Musiken af I.
P. E. Hartmann sen./Decorationerne malede af C. F. Christensen./
Costumerne tegnede af Edw. Lehmann.
Kjøbenhavn, J. H. Schubothe/Bianco Luno/F. S. Muhle, 1861
[DKKk; 17, – 175 8°

31.10.1861
Recommendation notes concerning the projected (re)stagings of
several plays at Stockholm's Royal Theatre.
In his diary Bournonville noted on this day about the recom-
mendation notes he wrote to the mangement of Stockholm's
Royal Theatre:

'Læst flere stykker og afgivet min Mening om dem'.

This note is followed by a more detailed description in his
Swedish *Journal* on the following day reading:

'Läst 'Les chaises à porteurs.' anm: t.- Chefen [i.e. E. F. O. L. von
Stedingk]'.

Apart from his (not yet traced) recommendation note for
the projected Stockholm restaging this year of J. M. Monvel's
two-act comedy *Jerôme le porteur de chaise (Portechaisebäraren)* it
is not possible to identify the titles of the other plays recommended by Bournonville during this early period of his
three-year tenure as managing director of Stockholm's Royal
Theatre.

1.11.1861
The Wedding Festival in Hardanger (Brudfärden i Hardanger)
(Stockholm's Royal Theatre, Operahuset).
This performance represents Bournonville's first staging after his appointment as artistic director of Stockholm's Royal
Theatre and his second and last staging in Sweden of his two-
act Norwegian ballet *The Wedding Festival in Hardanger* (*see*
4.3.1853 and 22.6.1857). In his diary and in his Swedish *Journal* he noted about the performance:

25.10.1861: 'Eftermds Prøve paa Brudefærden i Hardanger'
26.10.: 'Prøvet Rollerne til Brudefærden i Hardanger fra 10–1'
27.10.: 'lille Prøve paa Brudefærden 1–2½'
29.10.: 'Prøve fra 10–1 paa Brudefærden'
39.10.: 'Prøve paa Brudefärden 11–1'
30.10.: 'Prøve paa Brudefærden 10–11'
31.10.: 'Prøve paa Brudefærden'
1.11.: 'Generalprøve paa Brudefærden [...] Brudefærden der gik ret
godt [...] H M Konungen [i.e. King Carl XV] bevistade spektaklen'.

The 1861 production, which seems to have been mounted
with only minor if any changes from the previous Stockholm
staging, was performed twice, the last time on 7.11.1861. It
employed the same musical material as that used for the
1857 Stockholm première of this ballet (now in SSkma, call
no. KT Pantomime-Balletter B 5).

6.11.1861
Flickarnas Ja. **Projected staging at Stockholm's Royal
Theatre.**
A note in Bournonville's diary on this day reads:

'læst en Oversættelse efter det Spanske 'Flickornas Ja' og afgivet min
Erklæring derom'.

This clearly indicates that he wrote a (not yet traced) recommendation note to the theatre management of Stockholm's
Royal Theatre in which he expressed his opinion about a
projected staging of this Spanish play by a not yet identified
writer. *Flickarnas Ja* was never mounted in Stockholm.

6.11.1861
Le Nouveau Seigneur de village (Den nye Jordegodsejer).
The 1861 Copenhagen restaging of F.-A. Boyeldieu's one-act
comic opera (premièred at l'Opéra Comique in Paris on
29.6.1813, and first performed in Copenhagen on 6.2.1819)
was originally projected by Bournonville on 30.10.1857 and
reproposed by him on 20.1.1858. However, as a result of his
three-year tenure with Stockholm's Royal Theatre between
1861 and 1864, it was at Bournonville's personal request carried out by the concert-master of the Royal Theatre orchestra, I. F. Bredal. The 1861 production received 8 performances (the last of which was given on 24.11.1866) after which
it went out of the Copenhagen repertory.

18.11.1861
Les Diamants de la Couronne (Kronjuvelerna) **(Stockholm's
Royal Theatre, Operahuset).**
The 1861 Stockholm restaging of D.-F.-E. Auber's three-act
comic opera (premièred in Paris at l'Opéra Comique on 6.3.
1841, and first performed in Sweden on 17.9.1845) represents the first time this work was ever mounted with Bournonville's mise-en-scène. Seven years later he also mounted
it in Copenhagen, but then with a completely new mise-en-
scène (*see* 10.10.1868). In his diary and in his Swedish *Journal*
Bournonville noted about the 1861 Stockholm production:

23.10.1861: 'Eftermiddags Costumemøde paa Kronjuvelerne. Instruction paa Samme med M.lle [W. C.] Gelhaar og [C. O.] Arnoldson'
24.10.: 'Instruction paa Kronjuvelerne'
25.10.: 'skrevet Scene=Arrangementet til Kronjuvelerne'
26.10.: 'skrevet Scene=Arrangement [...] Instruction paa Kronjuvelerne'
28.10.: 'Efterm: 5–7 paa Kronjuvelerne'
29.10.: '11–1 Arrangement paa Kronjuvelerne'
30.10.: 'Arrangement paa Kronjuvelerne 11–12½'
1.11.: 'Kl 5: Dialogen af Kronjuvelerne [...] Efterm 5–7½ Instruction paa Kronjuvelerne'
2.11.: 'Theaterprøve med Claveer paa 1.ste og 2.den Akt af Kronjuvelerne, gik meget godt'
11.11.: 'Prøve paa Kronjuvelerne ved Piano'
12.11.: 'Dialog prøve paa Kronjuvelerne'
13.11.: 'paa Theatret, hvor jeg prøvede Kronjuvelerne fra 10½ til 2,
men blev blot færdig med 2 Akter [...] Gen. Rep.'
15.11.: 'til Prøven paa Kronjuvelerne'

16.11.: 'Generalprøve paa Kronjuvelerne i Costume, gik meget godt'
18.11.: 'I Theatret 1.ste Gang (paa nÿ indstuderet) Kronjuvelerne, der gik udmærket godt og gjorde megen Lykke'.

The 1861 production received 23 performances during Bournonville's engagment in Stockholm.

Autograph sources:

Manuscript mise-en-scène. Ms. Autograph. Brown ink. 1 vol. 18 pp. (21,4 × 17,5 cm)
Kronjuvelerna./Opéra = comique.
Signed and dated: 'd 25 October 1861.'
[DKKk; NKS 3285 4° 5 læg 1

Manuscript mise-en-scène (incomplete). Ms. Autograph. Brown ink. 1 vol. 7 pp. (21,5 × 17,5 cm)
Kronjuvelerna./Personer./Hufvudpersonernes./Costüm/Decorationer./Attributer./
Répetitioner./Representationer
Unsigned and undated [Written according to the diary on 25.10. and 26.10.1861]
[DKKk; NKS 3285 4° 4 læg 1

Musical sources:

Printed orchestral score with manuscript insertions. 3 vol. Act I 188 pp., Act II 136 pp., Act III 116 pp. of which one is blank (31 × 24 cm)
Les Diamans [*sic*] de la Couronne/Opéra Comique en trois Actes/ [...]/Musique/DE/D. F. E. Auber
Paris, E. Trupenas & C.ie, pl. no. T 1041 [1841]
[SSkma; KT Operetter K 8

No répétiteur's copy for *Les Diamants de la Couronne* has yet been traced in SSkma.

Parts. Ms. Copy. 32 vol.
3 vl I, 3 vl II, 2 vla, 4 vlc e cb, fl 1/2, ob 1/2, cl 1/2, fag 1/2, cor 1/2/ 3/4, tr, trb 1/2/3, timp, gr cassa, piatti, tri.
Unsigned and undated [c.1845–1861]
[SSkma; KT Operetter K 8

23.11.1861
La Ciguë (Giftbägaren) **(Stockholm's Royal Theatre, Operahuset).**
This performance represents the Swedish première of E. Augier's two-act comedy (first performed in Paris at the Second Théâtre Français on 13.5.1844). It was mounted with Bournonville's mise-en-scène and was set to a score of two numbers (*Allegretto*, 26 meas., and *Andante mosso*, 40 meas.) composed and arranged by J. A. Söderman. Söderman's music, which was played by an orchestra seated on the stage ('Bakom Scenen'), was performed in Act I (scene 1) and Act II (scene 10) respectively. Moreover, according to pencilled notes in the parts, the music accompanying the so-called 'Hymn' in Act II (*Andante mosso*) was later reused by Bournonville in his Stockholm staging of W. Shakespeare's five-act play *Richard II* (*see* 8.10.1863).

In his diary and in his Swedish *Journal* he noted about the 1861 Stockholm première of *La Ciguë*:

21.10.1861: 'læst La Ciguë af E Augier'
4.11.: 'Skrevet Scene=Arrangement til Giftbägaren'
15.11.: 'Eftermidagsprøve paa Giftbägaren'
16.11.: 'Prøve paa Giftbägaren fra 10½ til 12½ [...] Sceneri [...] Gen. Rep.'

17.11.: 'Kl. 10. Rep: Giftbägaren. ([C. G.] Sundberg.)'
18.11.: 'Prøve paa Giftbägaren Kl 10½ [...](Gen. Rep.)'
19.11.: 'Paa Theatret, Giftbägaren [...] (Gen. Rep.)'
20.11.: 'Generalprøve i Costume paa Giftbägaren, der gik usikkert og fordrer to Prøver til'
21.11.: 'Prøve paa [...] Giftbägaren [...] (Rollrepetition)'
22.11.: 'Sidste Prøve paa Giftbägaren, der nu gaaer med stor Sikkerhed [...] (Gen. Rep.)'
23.11.: '1.ste Forestilling af Giftbägaren, der gik fortræffeligt'.

Augier's comedy received 10 performances during Bournonville's engagment in Stockholm, the last of which was given on 14.1.1863.

Autograph sources:

Manuscript mise-en-scène. Ms. Autograph. Brown ink. 1 vol. 10 pp. (21,4 × 17,5 cm)
Giftbägaren./Komedi på vers i två Akter./af./Emil Augier.
Signed and dated: 'Stockholm d. 6.e Novbr 1861.' [Written according to the diary on 4.11.1861]
[DKKk; NKS 3285 4° 5 læg 2

Musical sources:

Orchestral score. Ms. Autograph. Black ink. 3 pp. (32,4 × 26,2 cm)
Theatermusik./Giftbägaren/1.ste akt. 1ste Scen./[...]/2.dra Akt 10.de Scen
Unsigned and undated [1861]
[SSkma; KT Tal-Pjeser med Musik G 21

Parts. Ms. Copy. 6 vol.
On stage: fl 1/2, cl 1/2, fag, arpa.
Unsigned and dated: '17.nov.1861'
[SSkma; KT Tal-Pjeser med Musik G 21

2.12.1861
After Fifty Years (Efter femtio år) **(Stockholm's Royal Theatre, Operahuset).**
The 1861 Stockholm restaging of Z. Topelius's five-act play with a prologue and epilogue (first performed in Stockholm at Djurgårds-theatern on 25.5.1851) was mounted with Bournonville's new original mise-en-scène. It included two scenes with music by a not yet identified composer played by an orchestra seated on the stage, entitled *Polonäs*, *Menuett*, and *Hymn*. In his diary and in his Swedish *Journal* Bournonville noted about the performance:

15.10.1861: 'Læst et originalt Stÿkke af [Z.] Topelius För 50.e År'
18.10.: 'På Theatret Klokken 9½. Møde med Regisseur [C. O.] Lindmark, derpaa med Costumier Drake og Herr P. [J.] Deland i Anledning af Efter 50 år'
19.10.: 'prøvet Efter 50 år, som blev udsat formedelst en mangelfuld Rollebesætning'
18.11.: 'Prøve paa [...] Prologen til 50 år, Eftermiddagen skrevet Arrangement'
19.11.: 'Paa Theatret [...] Efter 50 år, som [C. G.] Sundberg besørgede'
26.11.: 'Prøve paa Prologen til 50 år'
28.11.: 'Theaterprøve paa Efter 50 år'
29.11.: 'Efterm: Prøve paa Efter 50 år'
30.11.: 'Aftenprøve i Costume paa Efter 50 år'
2.12.: 'Gen. Prøve med [A.] Randell (der ikke besidder Personalets Tillid) [...] bivaanet den 1.ste Forestilling af 'Efter 50 år' Debut for det gamle Kunstnerpar [P. J. and H. L. C.] Deland. Megen Lykke!!!'.

The 1861 restaging of *After Fifty Years* received 6 performances, the last of which was given on 13.1.1862.

Musical sources:

No orchestral score and répétiteur's copy for *After Fifty Years* have yet been traced in SSkma.

Parts. Ms. Copy. 2 vol.
vl I–II, vla e cb.
Unsigned and undated [c.1861]
[SSkma; KT Tal-Pjeser med Musik E 35

12.12.1861
Cora, ou l'Esclavage (Cora eller Slafveriet). **Projected staging at Stockholm's Royal Theatre (Operahuset).**
In his diary and in his Swedish *Journal* Bournonville noted about his involvement in the projected 1861 restaging of P. J. Barbier's five-act play with songs:

12.12.1861: '(läst Cora.)'
3.4.1862: 'Utlemnadt roler till Cora'
11.4.: 'Collationering på Cora'
3.6.: 'Skrifvit sceneri till Cora'
6.6.: 'Sceneprøve paa Cora […] (Sceneri)'
11.6.: 'Cora (på theatern)'
24.8.: 'Conference med Hofkammerer [D.] Hwasser Cora gifves ick af twå skäl: (Decorationerne fela. Piesen utspelt på södra theatren.)'.

Barbier's play was never staged at Operahuset.

Autograph sources:

Manuscript mise-en-scène. Ms. Autograph. Black ink. 16 pp. (22,2 × 18,2 cm)
Cora
Signed and dated: 'Stockholm d 3.die Junii 1862.'
[DKKk; NKS 3285 4° 5 læg 7

12.12.1861
The Little Treasure (La Joie de la maison/En liten Skatt/Gertrude eller En lille Skat) **(Stockholm's Royal Theatre, Operahuset).**
The 1861 Stockholm restaging of A. Bourgeois' and A. Decourcelle's three-act comedy (premièred in Paris at Théâtre de la Vaudeville on 6.3.1855, and first performed in Stockholm on 10.6.1860 with the title *En liten demon*) was mounted with Bournonville's mise-en-scène. It was this year given in a new Swedish translation by F. N. Berg, who employed F. Thomsen's earlier Danish translation of A. Harris's English version of this comedy (dating from its Danish première at Copenhagen's Royal Theatre on 11.3.1860). In his diary and in his Swedish *Journal* Bournonville noted about the production:

19.11.1861: 'skrevet Scene Arrangement til En liten skatt'
21.11.: 'Prøve paa En lille Skat […] Sceneri til En liten skatt'
22.11.: 'Instruction paa En liten skatt'
25.11.: 'Efterm: Prøve paa En liten skatt […] (Scener)'
30.11.: 'besørgede min Prøve paa En liten skatt […] Gen. Rep.'
2.12.: 'Kl 11. En liten skatt. Rep. Salen'
3.12.: 'Kl 11. En liten skatt'
5.12.: 'Kl 10, En liten skatt.'
6.12.: 'Prøve paa En liten skatt'
9.12.: 'Kl 10. En liten skatt'
10.12: 'Kl½ 5. En liten skatt. (Gen. Rep.)'
11.12.: 'Prøve paa […] En liten skatt'
12.12.: '1.ste Forestilling af En liten skatt (Gertrud) der gjorde megen Lykke'.

The Little Treasure received 5 performances during Bournonville's engagement in Stockholm, the last of which was given on 26.1.1862.

Autograph sources:

Manuscript mise-en-scène. Ms. Autograph. Brown ink. 1 vol. 10 pp. (21,4 × 17,5 cm)
En liten skatt./Komedi i tre Akter./efter engelska originalet: 'The little treasure'/af/A. Harris
Signed and dated: 'Stockholm d. 20 Novbr 1861.' [Written according to the Swedish *Journal* on 19.11.1861]
[DKKk; NKS 3285 4° 5 læg 2

13.12.1861
Le Nouveau Seigneur de village (Den nya Egendomsherrn) **(Stockholm's Royal Theatre, Operahuset).**
The 1861 Swedish restaging of F.-A. Boyeldieu's one-act comic opera (first performed in Stockholm on 20.1.1818, *see also* 30.10.1857 and 6.11.1861) represents the first time it was ever mounted with Bournonville's mise-en-scène. In his diary and in his Swedish *Journal* he noted about the production:

30.11.1861: 'Collationeringer paa Den nya egendomsherrn'
3.12.: 'Kl. 10 Decorations=Möte paa Egendomsherrn'
4.12.: 'Kl 12 skrifvit sceneri till Egendomsherrn'
3.12.: 'Costume möte paa Egendomsherrn […] Kl ½ 12 Dialog och sceneri paa D.o'
7.12.: 'Aftenprøve paa Egendomsherrn […] (vid Fortepiano)'
9.12.: 'Kl. 12 Egendomsherrn'
10.12.: 'Kl ½ 11 Egendomsherrn. Gen. Rep.'
11.12.: 'Kl 1 [F.] Arlberg'
12.12.: 'Prøve paa […] Den nÿa egendomsherrn […] sista Gen. Rep.'
13.12.: 'Den nÿa egendomsherrn der gik særdeles godt. Arlberg høstede meget og fortjent Bifald'.

The production received 4 performances during Bournonville's engagement in Stockholm, the last of which was given on 1.2.1862.

Autograph sources:

Manuscript mise-en-scène. Ms. Autograph. Brown ink. 1 vol. 12 pp. (21,4 × 17,5 cm)
Nya egendomsherrn./Operetta af Boyeldieu. (1 Akt.)
Signed and dated: 'Stockholm d. 3 December 1861.' [Written according to the diary on 4.12.1861]
[DKKk; NKS 3285 4° 5 læg

19.12.1861
Comedy of Errors (Förvexlingarne) **(Stockholm's Royal Theatre, Operahuset).**
In his diary and in his Swedish *Journal* Bournonville noted about his staging of this, the Stockholm première of W. Shakespeare's three-act play from c.1592–93:

9.11.1861: 'Jeg gjennemlæste Shakespeares Forvexlinger''
20.11.: 'Costume Möte till Forvexlingarne'
27.11.: 'skrifvit Sceneri till Förvexlingarna'
1.12: 'Oplæsning paa Forvexlingarna […] Collationering på Förvexlingarna'
7.12.: 'Mllerne [A. H. M.] Sandberg och [G. J. C.] Åberg på Förvexlingarne'
10.12: 'Förvexlingarne. 1.ste och 2dra Akten'
11.12.: 'Förvexlingarne. 1.ste och 2.dra Akten. (Rep. salen)'

12.12.: 'Förvexlingarne. 2.dra och 3.die Akten.'
13.12., 14.12., and 16.12.: 'Förvexlingarne. (Gen. Rep.)'
18.12.: 'Generalprøve i Costüme paa Förvexlingarne (comedy of errors)'
19.12.: 'I Theatret 1.ste Gang Forvexlingarne'.

Bournonville's staging received 8 performances during his engagement in Stockholm, the last of which was given on 8.11.1862.

Autograph sources:

Manuscript mise-en-scène. Ms. Autograph. Brown ink. 1 vol. 12 pp. (21,4 × 17,5 cm)
Förvexlingarne./Lustspel i tre Akter/(Fri bearbetning efter 'Comedy of errors' af Shakespeare.)
Signed and dated: 'Stockholm d. 27 Novbr 1861.'
[DKKk; NKS 3285 4° 5 læg 2
The Swedish 1861 version of W. Shakespeare's play was translated by F. A. Dahlgren from K. E. v. Holtei's earlier German version of it.

1862

18.1.1862
La Muette de Portici (Den Stumma från Portici) (Stockholm's Royal Theatre, Operahuset).

This performance represents the first time D.-F.-E. Auber's five-act opera (*see* 23.9.1834) was mounted with Bournonville's own complete mise-en-scène. In his diary and in his Swedish *Journal* he noted about the staging:

19.12.1861: 'Kl 11. Den stumme (sångrummet)'
26.12.: 'Kl 12. Fru [E.] Hvasser <u>Fenella</u>'
27.12.: 'skrifvit sceneri'
31.12.: 'Sceneri=Prøve paa Den Stumme'
1.1.1862: 'Kl 6: Costume=Möde på <u>Den Stumma</u>'
3.1.: 'Kl 11 sångr: Den Stumma'
4.1.: 'Kl 11 sångr: Den Stumma. Kl 12 Fru Hvasser Fenella'
7.1.: 'Kl 11 sångr: Den Stumma'
9.1.: 'Stor Claverprøve paa Den Stumme'
10.1.: 'Stor Sceneriprøve paa Den Stumme. Skrevet og arrangeret'
11.1.: 'Stor Prøve paa Den Stumme'
13.1. and 14.1.: 'Prøve paa Den Stumme'
16.1.: 'Generalprøve paa den Stumme, der gik meget godt'
17.1.: 'Generalprøve i Costume paa den Stumme. Alt gik godt, med Undtagelse af Fru Hvasser, der negligerede i en scandaløs Grad. – Jeg yttrede mig ikke desangaaende men skal ved Leilighed erindre denne mindre heldige Opførsel'
18.1.: '1.ste forestilling af La reprise de la Muette de Portici. Storartet succès, almindelig Begeistring, fuldt Huus og vedvarende Bifald'.

The 1862 production of *La Muette de Portici* was given 20 times during Bournonville's engagement in Stockholm, the last time on 16.4.1863.

Musical sources:

No orchestral score for *La Muette de Portici* has yet been traced in SSkma.

Répétiteur's copy. Ms. Copy. Black ink. 1 vol. 52 pp. (34 × 24,4 cm)
Den Stumma från Portici/[...]/Balleterna af Th Martin/[...]/Repetiteur.
Unsigned and dated (on the front cover): '1866' [c.1861]
[SSkma; KT Operor S 2
This répétiteur's copy was most probably also used for Bournon-

ville's 1861 Stockholm restaging of *La Muette de Portici*. According to the dating on its front cover it was still in use when Auber's opera was restaged during the 1866–67 season with new dances choreographed by T. Martin. The volume contains pencilled metronome markings indicating the tempo of the Act I *Bolero*, with a crochet being equal to '104' and the *Animato* section equal to '88'.

Parts. Ms. Copy. 35 + 8 vol.
3 vl I, 3 vl II, 3 vla, 5 vlc e c, fl picc, fl 1/2, ob 1/2, cl 1/2, fag 1/2, cor 1/2/3/4, tr, trb 1/2/3, oph, timp, gr cassa, cassa e tri. On stage: fl, cl 1/2, fag 1/2, cor 1/2, org.
Unsigned and undated [1836?]
[SSkma; KT Operor S 2
This set of parts seems to date from the Swedish première of *La Muette de Portici* on 19.3.1836 and was used for all performances of Auber's opera during Bournonville's engagement in Stockholm.

24.1.1862
Torkel Knutson (Stockholm's Royal Theatre, Operahuset).

According to his diary Bournonville began working on the mise-en-scène for B. v. Beskow five-act tragedy with a prologue while he was still in Copenhagen, well before he departed for Stockholm on 14.10.1861. His staging, which represents the première of this work, included several musical insertions composed and arranged by J. A. Söderman (score nos. 1–3, and 5–8), L. Norman (score no. 4), and A. Randel ('Sorgmarsch', and 'Marsch'). According to the orchestral score and notes written into the parts, these composers employed several excerpts borrowed from older works. These excerpts were as follows:

(1) L. v. Beethoven's *Egmont* overture (op. 84) from 1809–10, here employed as the overture for Beskow's tragedy.
(2) G. J. Vogler's so-called 'Karl XII:s marsch vid Narva', here also used as an overture.
(3) The overture from H. Purcell's opera *Dido and Aeneas* from 1689, here used as an *entr'acte* between Acts I and II.
(4) P. D. Muth-Rasmussen's overture from his score to the vaudeville in two parts *Yelva, ou L'Orpheline Russe* (*see* 9.6.1835), used here as an *entr'acte* between Acts II and III.
(5) a Swedish folksong and hymn, entitled «Ur svenska hjärtans djup», employed here as an *entr'acte* between Acts III and IV.

Torkel Knutson was mounted with décor made, for the main part, by the Swedish scene painter, F. Ahlgrensson, who only a few years later came to Copenhagen and created many imporant décors for Bournonville's later ballets.

In his diary and in his Swedish *Journal* Bournonville noted about his staging of *Torkel Knutson* and its first three performances:

7.5.1861: 'læst [...] ([B. v.] Beskow)'
4.6.: 'studeret Beskows Tragedie <u>Torkel Knutzon</u>'
5.6.1861: 'læst Grev [G.] Lagerbjelkes Sceneri til Torkel Knutzon, mesterlig udarbeidet'
16.9: 'arbeidet paa Torkel Knutzon'
17.9.: 'skrevet Arrangement paa T. K.'
18.9.: 'skrevet og arrangeret'
19.9.: 'skrevet og fuldendt Arrangementet af Torkel Knutson'
18.10.: 'Confererede med Chefen [i.e. E. F. O. L. von Stedingk] og derpaa hos Baron Beskow om Torkel Knutson'
26.10. and 28.10.: 'Costumemøde paa <u>Torkel Knutson</u>'
29.10.: 'Costume og Decorationsmøde paa Torkel Knutson'
30.10.: 'Costumemøde og confererede med [C. G.] Dahlqvist'
7.11.: 'Arrangement till <u>Torkel Knutson</u>'
8.11.: 'skrifvit sceneri til <u>Torkel Knutson</u>'

9.11.: 'Uppgjordt Musik=Arrang: til Torkel Knutson'
27.12.: 'skrifvit sceneri'
30.12.: 'Collationering på Torkel Knutson [...] Stor Oplæsning paa Torkel Knutson. Eftermiddagen skrevet Sceneri'
4.1.1862: 'skrifvit sceneri'
7.1.: 'Instruction Torkel Knutson [...] Smaaprøver paa Torkel Knutson'
10.1. and 13.1.: 'Efterm: Instruction paa Torkel Knutson (skrifvit sceneri) [...] Scener ur Torkel Knutson'
14.1.: 'Fullfört sceneriet till Torkel Knutson [...] Efterm: Instruction paa Torkel Knutson [...]Prologen till Torkel Knutson å barn theatern'
15.1.: '1.ste Theaterprøve paa Torkel Knutson [...] (1.ste, 2.dra och 3.die Akten)'
17.1.: 'Prøve paa Torkel Knutson [...] (1.e, 2.a, 3.e och 4.e Akten)'
18.1.: 'Prøve paa Torkel Knutson, der lover godt [...] (Prolog och de fyra Akten)'
20.1.: 'Formiddagen Prøve paa Torkel Knutson [...] (Gen. Rep.)'
21.1.: 'Sceneri til Torkel Knutson [...]Formiddag og Eftermiddag, Prøve paa Torkel Knutson [...] (Gen. Rep.)'
22.1.: 'Prøve paa Torkel Knutson'
23.1.: 'Hele Dagen beskjæftiget med Torkel Knutson. Generalprøve i Costüme, der gik udmærket til stor Fornøielse for Forfatteren Baron Beskow, der takkede mig paa det forbindtligste. Jeg kom høist silde tilsengs'
24.1.: 'Torkel Knutson gik for første Gang og det ved et mærkeligt Træf paa Gustaf den Tredies Fødselsdag. Kong Carl [XV] med Hof var tilstede, og et udvalgt Publicum bivaanede Forestillingen, der gik med udmærket Talent og Held. Alle gjorde deres Bedste og Dahlqvist var virkelig stor i Hovedrollen. Stykket varede 3 1/4 time'
25.1.: 'Besøg af Baron Beskow, der takkede mig for min Virken til hans Stykkes udmærkede Gang' [...] I Theatret 2.den Gang Torkel Knutson med ligemeget Bifald, men middelmaadigt Huus!!'
28.1.: 'I Theatret Torkel Knutson med Forkortninger og fuldt Huus'.

On 24.3.1862 he noted in his diary about a personal gift received on that day from Beskow:

'Stor Overraskelse ved en kostbar Present og Brev fra Baron Beskow i Anledning af hans Torkel Knutson. Det var et deiligt Sölv=Skrivetøi – En Foræring der virkelig gjorde mig skamfuld, – men glad paa samme Tid'.

Torkel Knutson received 13 performances during Bournonville's engagement in Stockholm, the last of which was given on 19.10.1862.

Autograph sources:

Manuscript mise-en-scène. Ms. Autograph. Brown ink. 1 vol. 24 pp. (21,4 × 17,5 cm)
Torkel Knutson/Sorgespel i 5 Akter med Prolog./af./B v: Beskow.
Signed and dated: 'Stockholm d. 14.de Januar 1862.' [Written according to the diary between 8.11.1861 and 14.1.1862]
[DKKk; NKS 3285 4° 5 læg 3

Production note. Ms. Autograph. Brown ink. 1 p. (21,5 × 13,5 cm)
Högtärade Herr Secretair Drake!/Om det vore möjligt att foretage en liten färgförändring i Grefvinnan/Hedvigs husdrägt (och i stället för/den ljusblaa klädning sätta en svart/sidensaat med sammet garnitur/hvortill ljusblaa underärmer och/guld prydelsen.) så gjorde Titulus/oss en verklig tjenst. –/[...]
Signed and dated: '15. Januar 1862.'
[SSkma; Lo III: 21,1

Musical sources:

Orchestral score. Ms. Autographs (by J. A. Söderman, L. Norman, and A. Randel) and copies. 1 vol. 88 pp. (33,4 × 27 cm with minor variants)

Torkel Knutson/Musiken af Norman, Randel och Söderman./Partitur.
Signed and dated (7.de scen No. 4. Hyllnings marsch): 'Stohm 22 Januar 1862/Ludvig Norman'.
[SSkma; KT Tal-Pjeser med Musik T 27

Orchestral score (*Marsch*). Ms. Copy. 1 vol. 12 pp. (33,4 × 25,6 cm)
Torkel Knutson./Andra Akten./Marsch/på/Theatern./Partitur
Unsigned and undated [1862]
[SSkma; KT Tal-Pjeser med Musik T 27

Parts. Ms. Copy. 27 vol. + 14 vol.
2 vl I, 2 vl II, vla, 2 vlc e cb, fl 1/2, ob 1/2, cl 1/2, fag 1/2, cor 1/2/3/4, tr, trb 1/2/3, timp, gr cassa, piatti, tri. On stage: fl 1/2, ob 1/2, cl 1/2, fag 1/2, ob 1/2, tr, trb, gr cassa, piatti.
Unsigned and undated [1862]
[SSkma; KT Tal-Pjeser med Musik T 27

30.1.1862

***Pas de trois* (uncredited) performed by F. Hoppe, J. Price and S. Price.**

This (uncredited) dance is most probably identical with Bournonville's and M. E. Caraffa's much earlier incorporated *Pas de trois* in A. Adam's three-act comic opera *Le Postillon du Lonjumeau* (*see* 28.10.1837). That dance, in turn, had been performed by the same three dancers during the previous Copenhagen season on 28.1.1861. The *Pas de trois* was given only once in 1862. It is not possible to identify the dance any further.

1.2.1862

***La Pluie et le beau temps (Regn och Solsken)* (Stockholm's Royal Theatre, Operahuset).**

In his diary and in his Swedish *Journal* Bournonville noted about his involvement in the Swedish première of L. Gozlan's one-act comedy (first performed in Paris at Théâtre Français on 21.10.1861):

18.12.1861: 'läst Regn och Solsken'
19.1.1862: 'Utdelat rolerna till Regn och solsken'
28.1.: 'Regn och solken (Gen. Rep.) [C. G.] Sundberg'
29.1., 30.1., and 31.1.: 'Regn och solsken (Gen. Rep.)'
1.2.: 'Jeg gik et Øjeblik i Theatret, hvor man gav 1.ste gang Regn og Solsken, der gik meget godt'.

Gozlan's comedy received 7 performances in Stockholm, the last of which was given on 27.3.1862.

10.2.1862

***Die Töchter des Cid (Cids döttrar)*. Projected staging at Stockholm's Royal Theatre.**

On 10.2.1862 Bournonville wrote a recommendation note to the theatre management of Stockholm's Royal Theatre in which he expressed his opinion about the projected Swedish staging of Ph. J. Meyer's four-act drama (premièred in Berlin in 1857). It reads as follows:

'Les filles du Cid:
Pièce remplie d'interêt & de caractères bien dessinés. – avec quelques modifications dans les longueurs du dialogue je crois qu'elle pourra obtenir un véritable succès.
Je proposerais comme superflue la première partie du 1.ier Acte. i.e. La Scène au palais du roi.
La distribution naturelle des rôles se présente à mon esprit de la manière suivante:

Le Cid .... M. [N. W.] Almlöf
Le Roi .... '[C. G.] Sundberg ?
Le prince .... '[A. T.] Schwartz
Ximène .... M.me [Z.] Hedin
Christine ....M.lle [A. H. N.] Sandberg
Maria .... M.me [E.] Hwasser
Ramon .... Hr [A. W. J.] Elmlund
Alvar .... '[[A. F.] Westermarck ?
Sebastian .... '[L.] Josephsson

Les décors & costumes me semblent point présenter de grandes difficultés.
Stockholm ce 10 Fevrier/1862./très humblement/August Bournonville.'

In spite of Bournonville's very positive statements about this play it was not mounted during his engagement at Stockholm's Royal Theatre. Thus *Cids döttrar* was not staged in Stockholm until 2.1.1867, when it was premièred at Stockholm's Royal Theatre (Stora Theatern), receiving only 6 performances that year.

Autograph sources:

Recommendation note. Ms. Autograph. Brown ink. 2 pp. (21,5 × 13,8 cm)
[…]Les filles du Cid […]
Signed and dated: 'Stockholm ce 10 Fevrier/1862.'
[SSdt; KTA, E2A Ink. breve 1861/62, 10.2.1862

10.2.1862
Preciosa (Préciosa) (Stockholm's Royal Theatre, Operahuset).
The 1862 Swedish restaging of C. M. v. Weber's four-act lyrical drama (*see also* 11.5.1851) was mounted under Bournonville's general direction. The dances, however, which this year included six new incorporated numbers in Acts I and III (composed by J. F. Berwald) were all choreographed by his pupil, S. Lund, who served as ballet-master at Stockholm's Royal Theatre between 1856 and 1862. In his diary and in his Swedish *Journal* Bournonville noted about the production:

29.1.1862: 'Efterm. Preciosa […] (M.lle [G. J. C.] Åberg)'
31.1.: 'Eftermiddag Prøve paa Preciosa […] Melodram.'
2.2.: 'M.lle Åberg. Preciosa'
4.2.: 'Preciosa=Instruction […] Preciosa om Eftermiddagen […] Scener'
5.2., 6.2., and 7.2.: 'Prøve paa Preciosa […] Decoration=möte […] Partiel Repetition […] Costym=möte[…] Sceneri […] Dialog]…] (Gen. Rep. vid Piano)'
8.2.: 'Generalprøve paa Preciosa, der gaaer meget godt'
10.2.: 'Generalprøve paa Preciosa […] 1.ste gang Gjenoptagelsen af Preciosa, der gik meget smukt og for fuldt Huus'.

Bournonville's 1862 Stockholm production of *Preciosa* received 6 performances, the last of which was given on 25.3.1862.

Musical sources:

Orchestral score. Ms. Copy. Brown and Black ink. 1 vol. 204 pp. (25,9 × 34 cm)
Preciosa./Schauspiel in IV Acten mit Gesang u [*sic*] Tanz/von/[P. A.] Wolf[f]./Ouverture und zur Handlung gehörige Music/von Carl Maria von Weber.
Unsigned and undated [1824 ?–1862]

[SSkma; KT Operetter P 7
This orchestral score and the other musical material for *Preciosa* in SSkma seem to date from the 1824 Swedish première of Weber's drama and was used for all performances of this work during Bournonville's engagement in Stockholm. The new, incorporated dance music by J. F. Berwald consists of the following six numbers:
(1) Act I, score no. 2½ (*Allegretto* in 2/4 time, 91 meas.).
(2) Act III, score no. 10 (*Marche* in 4/4 time alla breve, 66 meas.).
(3) Act III, score no. 13 (*Allegretto Grazioso* in 2/4 time, 130 meas.).
(4) Act III, score no. 14 (*Allegro moderato* in 3/4 time, 55 meas.).
(5) Act III, score no. 15 (*Allegro moderato* in 3/4 time, 24 meas. This music is an arranged excerpt of meas. 9–32 from Weber's overture to *Preciosa*).
(6) Act III, score no. 16 (*Allegro vivace* in 6/8 time, 85 meas.).

Répétiteur's copy. Ms. Copy. Black ink. 1 vol. 15 pp. (28,4 × 23,3 cm)
N.ro 245/Preciosa/Repetiteur Partie.
Unsigned and undated [1824?–1862]
[SSkma; KT Operetter P 7

Parts. Ms. Copy. 28 vol. + 14 vol.
3 vl I, 3 vl II, 2 vla, 4 vlc e cb, fl picc, fl 1/2, ob 1/2, cl 1/2, cor 1/2/3/4, tr, timp, gr cassa, piatti, tri. On stage: fl 1/2, cl 1/2, fag 1/2, cor 1/2/3/4, tri, gr cassa, tamb, glock.
Unsigned and undated [1824?–1862]
[SSkma; KT Operetter P 7

12.2.1862
La Muette de Portici (Den stumme i Portici).
The 1862 Copenhagen restaging of D.-F.-E. Auber's five-act opera (*see* 22.10.1847) was mounted under the general direction of L. Gade, since Bournonville was not under contract with Copenhagen's Royal Theatre this year. However, Bournonville personally directed 8 rehearsals of the opera before his contract expired on 1.10.1861. Moreover, according to notes in his diary and his autographed choreographic notes written into the opera's original répétiteur's copy (now in DKKk, call no. MA ms 3055 (KTB 273 (1)), he also created a completely new choreography for the Act I *Guarache* (this year mounted in a heavily abridged version) and the Act III *Tarantella*. Finally, the incorporated *Pas de deux* in Act I (to music by M. E. Caraffa) was performed by W. E. Funck and Juliette Price in this staging.

In his diary Bournonville noted about his involvement in the 1862 production, which represents his last professional duty in Copenhagen before his departure on 9.10.1861 for the three-year-long engagement in Stockholm:

3.9.1861: 'Prøve paa Den Stumme i Portici, Fenellas Rolle'
5.9.: 'Prøve med M.e [L.] Stillman'
6.9.: 'Prøve paa Den Stumme'
12.9.: 'Prøve paa […] Pantomimen til Den Stumme i Portici'
16.9.: 'Prøve med M.e Stillman paa 'Den Stumme''
21.9.: 'Noteret og componeret Dandse til Den Stumme'
23.9.: 'Indstudering af Dandse til Den Stumme'
24.9.: 'Prøve paa Den Stumme'
30.9.: 'Lille Prøve paa Dandsen til Den Stumme'

The 1862 production received 42 performances, the last of which was given on 18.5.1865.

The musical material used for this production was the same as that employed for the previous 1834, 1847 and 1850 stagings (now in DKKkt and DKKk with the call nos. KTA 273, MA ms 3055, MA ms 3056, and (for the Act I *Pas de deux*) MA ms 2603, MA ms 2700, KTB 209).

19.2.1862
The Festival in Albano (Festen i Albano) (Stockholm's Royal Theatre, Operahuset)

This performance represents the second and last restaging in Sweden of *The Festival in Albano* (*see* 28.10.1839) during Bournonville's lifetime. It was directed by his pupil, S. Lund, and seems to have been mounted with only minor if any changes from the previous Stockholm production (*see* 5.5. 1857). The ballet was given only once and was performed using the earlier musical material for it (now in SSkma, call no. KT Pantomime-Balletter F 10). Bournonville did not attend the performance.

4.3.1862
A Military Quadrille for the Royal Masked Ball (En Militair Quadrille for Hof=Masqueraden) performed by twenty-four men dressed as musketeers and four boys dressed as drummers and trumpeters (Stockholm's Royal Palace).

In his diary Bournonville noted about this *Quadrille*, choreographed for a royal masked ball:

8.2.1862: 'Møde hos H. M. Kongen [i.e. Carl XV] i Anledning af en Maskerade = Quadrille. Kongen var meget naadig og kaldte mig 'Du'. Det klang underligt for mine Øren!'

13.2.: 'Aftenen hjemme for at componere Militair-Quadriller til Hoffet.'

14.2.: 'arbeidet med [A. J.] Schnötzinger paa Quadriller, beseet Localerne paa Slottet'

15.2.: '1.ste Indstudering af Hofquadrillen, modtaget og behandlet med overordentlig Naade af Kongen og Dronningen [i.e. Queen Louise Wilhelmina Frederika Alexandra Anna]'

18.2.: 'Quadrilleprøve paa Slottet'

19.2.: 'Quadrillen med de fire Drenge'

20.2.: 'Quadrille med Drengene'

21.2.: 'Quadrille paa Slottet'

25.2.: 'Quadrille paa Slottet. Den gaaer nu ubehindret og De Kongelige ere særdeles fornöiede'

1.3.: 'Generalprøve paa Slottet. Quadrillen gaaer ubehindret og gjøre megen Lykke'

4.3.: 'Ballet var i höieste Grad glimrende circa 800 Personer vare inbudne og Maskeraden gik igjennem to Etager, der forenedes ved en indre pragtfuld Trappe. Der blev dandset flere Quadriller. 1° Af Kongen og 24 Herrer. Et slags Polichinel Optog, som jeg ikke fik at see. 2° Et Domino Spil af 12 Par, arrangeret af Lund (temmelig kjedeligt). 3° Militair Quadrille af mig. 12 Par Mousquetairer & med 2 trommeslagere og 2 trompeter af Balletdrenge. Den gik udmærket godt og gjorde megen Lykke. 4° Et andet Polichinel = Optog, der skulde byde paa de fire Aarstider, med Sköitelöber, Blomster, Tarantell og Paraplyer arrangeret af [A.] Selinder, men ikke videre heldigt – 5° En Hyrdequadrille à la Wateau [*sic*] udført af 16 damer og 4 Herrer og tog sig yndigt ud, baade formedelst de smukke Damefigurer og de elegante Phantasidragter. For resten var der Overflod paa rige Costumer og der blev dandset i to sale Spegelsalongen nede hos Dronningen og Palace salen ovenpaa. Quadrillerne 2–3–5 bleve gjentagne, min tre Gange, den Sidste efter Demaskeringen. Sceneringen var i alle Henseender Kongelig, men stod ikke over hvad vi ved lignende Leiligheder have ved Hofferne i Kbhvn. H. M. Kongen havde 4 forskjellige Omklædninger. Jeg kjendte ham først i den Sidste. Turcesisk Dragt udmærket smuk. Jeg selv var klædt i Hægadragt og Domino, men jeg kunde ikke blive ukjendt – mit Navn blev udtalt hvert Øieblik. Jeg traf mange bekjendte Personer: – Iøvrigt var denne Maskerade som de fleste i Norden, med Undtagelse af Kunstnercarnevalerne enoï [*sic*] ved Alt Humor og indtil Demaskeringen temmelig tør og sløv. Soupéen satte lidt mere Liv i det Hele og efter Kl. 12 tog Dandsen sin fulde Ret. Musiken var langtfra fortrinlig, men min Quadrille gik upaa-

klageligt. Jeg forlod Maskeraden Kl. 1 og fortrød ikke at jeg havde været der endskjøndt jeg først havde undskyldt mig, men fik en gjentagen Indbydelse, hvilket kunde gjælde for en naadig Befaling'.

No musical sources for Bournonville's *Military Quadrille*, which clearly seems to have been composed and/or arranged by A. J. Schnötzinger, have yet been traced.

7.3.1862
Mozartiana, Four Apotheotic Tableaux (fyre apotheotiska Tablåer) (Stockholm's Royal Theatre, Operahuset).

In his choreographic note for this series of four tableaux Bournonville stated about the music that accompanied them:

'La musique, qui conviendrait à cette suite de tableaux serait à mon avis un abrégé de l'ouverture de la flûte enchantée (Die Zauberflöte)'.

The tableaux were mounted for the celebration of the centenary of W. A. Mozart's birth and were performed as an epilogue to *Die Hochzeit des Figaro (Figaros Bröllop)*. They are described on the poster as follows:

'Mozart vid sitt Claver, bekransad af sin Sånggudinna och omgifven af Genier, framkallar fantasiens rike:
a) Figaros Bröllopsfest, med alle dess hufvudroller och figurer.
b) Titus förlåtande Sextus och Sarastro förenande Tamino och Pamina.
c) Don Juan bjudande Guvernören till sin aftonmåltid.
d) Religionen lyftande Psychen till de sällas boninger (häntydande på Requiem.). Under Tablåerna udföres ouverturen til »Trollflöjten.»'.

Almost ten years later a similar series of tableaux was mounted by Bournonville with the exact same title as part of a charity performance at Copenhagen's Royal Theatre on 2.6.1871.

In his diary and in his Swedish *Journal* he noted about the 1862 version of *Mozartiana*:

23.1. and 24.1.1862: 'Figaros bröllopp: (sångrummet.) [...] Statist= repetition'

4.3.: 'Om Eftermiddagen stillede jeg Tableauerne til Mozartiana.'

6.3.: 'Figaros bröllop (Gen. rep.) [...] Forberedelser til tableauerne som jeg prøvede Kl 4½ med Belysning og Costumer og som gik aldeles fortræffeligt. Mozartiana gjorde forlods megen Lykke'

7.3.: 'aldeles udsolgt Huus: Figaro, der gik temmelig kjedeligt og Mozartiana, der tog sig fortræffeligt ud og blev meget applauderet dog uden egentlig Enthusiasme'.

No separate musical sources for *Mozartiana* have yet been traced in SSkma.

Autograph sources:

Manuscript mise-en-scène. Ms. Autograph. Ink. 2 pp. (format unknown)

l'Apotheose de Mozart/après la repésentation/du Mariage de Figaro/le 27 Janvier 1862./(Jour anniversaire de la naissance de Mozart)

Signed and dated: 'Stockholm ce 23 Janvier 1862.'

[USNYp; Dance Collection, call nos. *ZBD-71 (microfilm), and (S)*MGZMD 30 (photostat copy)

13.3.1862
At Sunset (I Solnedgången/Naar Solen gaar ned) **(Stockholm's Royal Theatre, Operahuset).**

In his diary and in his Swedish *Journal* Bournonville noted about his staging of this one-act play by the Danish writer, C. Brosbøll (pen-name for C. Etlar):

30.1.1862: 'skrifvit sceneri till I Solnedgången'
1.2.: 'Collationnering på I Solnedgången [...] 'Oplæsning paa 'I Solnedgången' af Carit Etlar'
11.2.: 'I Solnedgången (Barntheatern)'
12.2.: 'Ny Collationnering pa Solnedgången'
20.2.: 'I Solnedgången (1.ste Rep.)'
4.3., 5.3., 7.3., 10.3., and 11.3.: 'I Solnedgången (Gen. Rep.)'
12.3.: 'I Solnedgången (Gen. Rep. i Costym.)'
13.3.: 'I Theatret, to nye Stykker. Begge danske: I Solnedgången og En arfs och kärleksfråga. De gjorde megen Lykke og bleve godt fremstillede. Huset var mærkelig nok kun lidt over halvfuldt! Sørgelige Omstændigheder for den dramatiske Scene'.

At Sunset (which had been given for the first time at Copenhagen's Royal Theatre on 11.10.1859) reached a total of 9 performances in Stockholm, the last of which was given on 9.3.1863.

Autograph sources:

Manuscript mise-en-scène. Ms. Autograph. Brown ink. 1 vol. 5 pp. (21,4 × 17,5 cm)
I Solnedgången./Skådespel i en Akt./af/Carit Etlar (Bråsböll.) [*sic*]/(Fri öfversättning från Danskan.)
Signed and dated: 'Stockholm d: 30 Januar 1862.'
[DKKk; NKS 3285 4° 5 læg 3

13.3.1862
A Benefactor's Testament (En Arfs- och Kärleks-fråga/En Velgjörers Testamente) **(Stockholm's Royal Theatre, Operahuset).**

In his diary and in his Swedish *Journal* Bournonville noted about his staging of this three-act play by the Danish writer, C. Andersen:

23.2.1862: 'Oplæsning paa En Velgjörers Testamente [...] Collationnering på 'Arf och Kärlek'
26.2.: 'Sceneri skrifvit til 'En arfs och kärleks fråga. (En Velgjörers Testamente)'
27.2.: 'Sceneri till Ark och kärlek (skrifvit)'
28.2.: 'Prøve og Scene=arrangement til En arfs of kärleks fråga (En Velgjörers Testamente)'
5.3., 7.3., 8.3., 10.3., 11.3., and 12.3.: 'En arfs och kärleksfråga (Gen. Rep.)'
13.3.: 'I Theatret, to nye Stykker. Begge danske: I Solnedgången og En arfs och kärleksfråga. De gjorde megen Lykke og bleve godt fremstillede. Huset var mærkelig nok kun lidt over halvfuldt! Sørgelige Omstændigheder for den dramatiske Scene'.

The play included five dance numbers set to music by a not yet identified composer and played by an orchestra seated on the stage. According to Bournonville's manuscript mise-en-scène for *A Benefactor's Testament* these numbers seem to have been performed during scenes 6 and 10.

The play (which had been given for the first time at Copenhagen's Royal Theatre on 18.10.1858) reached a total of 13 performances in Stockholm, the last of which was given on 27.5.1862.

Autograph sources:

Manuscript mise-en-scène. Ms. Autograph. Brown ink. 1 vol. 10 pp. (21,4 × 17,5 cm)
En arfs och kärleks fråga./Comedie i 3 Akter. Öfversättning från/det danska Originalet:/('En Velgjörers Testamente.')/(M.lle Andersen.)
Signed and dated: 'Stockholm d 27 Februar 1862.'
[DKKk; NKS 3285 4° 5 læg 3

Musical sources:

No orchestral score and répétiteur's copy for *A Benefactor's Testament* have yet been traced in SSkma.

Parts. Ms. Copy. 6 vol.
On stage: vl I, vl II, vla, vlc, cb, fl.
Unsigned and undated [c.1862]
[SSkma; KT Tal-Pjeser med Musik E 36
This set of parts contains the music for five dance numbers which are named: (no. 1) 'Kadrilj', (no. 2) untitled, (no. 3) 'Polka', (no. 4) 'Vals', (no. 5) 'Vals'.

18.3.1862
The Gipsy (Zigeunaren). **Projected staging at Stockholm's Royal Theatre, Operahuset.**

On this day Bournonville noted in his Swedish *Journal* about a projected staging of this play(?) by a not yet identified author: 'Läst Zigeunaren i en Akt'. The work does not seem to have been mounted in Stockholm.

1.4.1862
La Sylphide (Sylphiden). **(Stockholm's Royal Theatre, Operahuset).**

This performance represents Bournonville's first complete staging in Sweden of his two-act romantic ballet *La Sylphide* (*see* 28.11.1836). According to his foreword in its printed scenario, it was mounted especially for the Swedish ballerina, A. Arrhenius, who had returned to the Swedish capital after a study tour to Paris, and performed the title-rôle for the first time. She was partnered by Bournonville's Danish pupil, S. Lund, who similarly played the rôle of *James* for the first time this year. The Stockholm production, which was premièred as part of a special charity performance given for Bournonville, was (according to his diary) presented in a slightly abridged version. According to the 1862 répétiteur's copy, the changes made this year consisted in the main of two musical cuts in the opening scene of Act I (score no. 1), and a series of minor cuts and musical rearrangements of the Act II divertissement (score nos. 2–5). This version was restaged six months later at the same theatre on 17.9.1862, but then with an incorporated *Pas de deux* in Act I, choreographed by Bournonville and set to music by H. C. Lumbye. It was performed by Bournonville's English pupils, A. and C. Healey.

In his diary and in his Swedish *Journal* he noted about the 1862 production of *La Sylphide* and its reception:

19.12.1861: 'M.lle [A.] Arrhenius & [F. W.] Forsberg (Sylfiden)'
2.1.1862: 'Indstudering for Mlle Arrhenius'
3.1.: 'Arrhenius Sylphiden'
4.1.: ' Eftermiddag Arrhenius Sylphiden'
6.1.: 'Forkortadt Sylphiden'
8.1.: 'Mlle Arrhenius. (Sylphiden.)'

9.1.: 'Sylphiden med Arrhenius'
11.1. and 15.1.: 'eftermiddag Arrhenius paa Sylphiden'
19.1.: 'Skrevet til [...] [J. A.] Pätges angaaende Sylphidevingerne'
20.1.: 'Eftermiddagen paa Sylphiden'
26.1.: 'Noteradt på Sylphiden'
27.1. and 28.1.: 'Indstuderet paa Sylphiden [...] (Barntheatern)'
29.1., 31.1., 1.2., 3.2., 4.2., and 5.2.: 'Prøve paa Sylphiden [...] (Barntheatern)'
10.2.: 'Prøve paa Sylphiden [...] (Barntheatern) [...] flou Underretning fra Pätges'
11.2.: 'Prøve og Indstuderinger paa Sylphiden [...] (Barntheatern) [...] Telegram til Pätges'
12.2.: 'Prøve paa Sylphiden [...] (Barntheatern)'
13.2.: 'Thaterprøve paa Sylphiden [...] Brev til Pätges'
17.2. and 18.2.: 'Prøve paa Sylphiden [...] (Bartnhteatern)'
19.2.: 'Telegram fra Pätges'
22.2.: 'Sylphiden (1.ste akten på theatern).'
24.2.: 'Eftermiddagsprøve paa Scener af Sylphiden'
27.2.: 'Prøve paa Sylphiden [...] å barntheatern'
4.3.: 'Sylphiden: 2.dra Akten med répétiteur'
5.3.: 'skrifvit listarna till Sylphiden'
12.3.: 'Sÿlphiden (M.lle Arrhenius)'
14.3.: 'Arrangement paa [...] 1.ste Akt af Sylphiden'
17.3.: 'Sylphiden 2.dra Akten (Gen.) Repetituers. [...] Musik=Collationnering på Sylphiden'
18.3.: 'Scener ur Sylphiden'
19.3.: 'skrifvit Program till Sylphiden. [...] Sylphiden med repetiteurs'
20.3.: 'Prøve paa Sylphiden [...] (å Barntheatern)'
22.3.: 'Prøve paa hele Sylphiden med Repetiteurs [....] Modtaget Vingeværkerne fra Toldboden De vare fuldkommen tilfredsstillende'
23.3.: 'Jeg skrev til Pätges'
24.3.: 'Lection til Arrhenius og [S.] Lund [...] Besørget adskilligt med Henseende til min Benefice'
25.3.: 'M.lle Arrhenius & [S.] Lund [...] Audientz hos Kongen [i.e. Carl XV] og Enkedronningen [i.e. Queen Joséphine Maximilienne Eugénie Napoléone], for at levere Programmet til min Benefice'
26.3.: 'Prøve paa 1.ste Akt af Sylphiden [...] (med Orchester)'
27.3.: 'Maskinprøve paa Sylphiden, derpaa Generalprøve som gik ret godt'
28.3.: 'Prøve paa Sylphiden [...] Maskiner'
29.3.: 'Maskinprøve paa Sylfiden. Aften=Generalprøve paa Balletten, der gik meget godt'
30.3.: 'Maskineri paa Theatret [...] Sendt Programmer til Allerhøiste og Høie Vedkommende'
31.3.: 'Prøve paa Sylphiden, der gik udmærket godt [...] Maskiner och kostymer'
1.4.: 'Sylfiden for første Gang til min Benefice og for aldeles udsolgt Huus. Balletten gik udmærket godt og vandt meget Bifald. Mlle Arrhenius blev særdeles vel modtaget af Publicum, og efter Forestillingens Slutning fremkaldt tilligemed mig. Jeg tracterede Personalet med Champagne og Punch, og gik hjem med mine kjære med hvem jeg glædede mig af Hjertet og takkede Gud for al hans Naade imod os'
2.4.: 'Der stod en udmærket Artikel om Balletten i Aftonbladet'
3.4.: 'I Theatret [...] Sylfiden desværre kun for temmelig godt Huus! Det er virkelig daarlige Tider, Theatret lever i! Balletten gik i det Hele mindre godt end første Gang'.

La Sylphide received 12 performances in Stockholm during Bournonville's lifetime, the last of which was given on 12.2. 1863.

Musical sources:

Orchestral score. Ms. Copy (with several manuscript insertions in Act II which most probably are written by either H. S. Paulli, or V. C. Holm). Black and brown ink. 2 vol. Act I 222 pp., Act II 137 pp. (27,5 × 37 cm with minor variants)

Sylphiden/af/Lövenskjold.
Unsigned and undated [1862]
[SSkma; KT Pantomime-Balletter S 9

Répétiteur's copy. Ms. Copy. Brown and black ink. 1 vol. 136 pp. of which one is blank (33,6 × 25,3 cm with minor variants)
S 9/Sylfiden:/Ballet./Piano./[...]/Ripiteur [*sic*] Parti./til/Balletten Sÿlphiden/af [*sic*]/Bournonville sat i Musick [*sic*] af Hr. Lövenskjold./1:ste Akt
Unsigned and undated [1862]
[SSkr (Vinstocken), but formerly in SSkma with the call no. KT Pantomime-Balletter S 9
This répétiteur's copy contains several autographed notes by Bournonville (written with brown ink) which describe the mime performed by *Madge* and her suite of eight witches in the opening scene of Act II (score no. 1), and the choreography danced by *The Sylph*, *James* and the corps de ballet of sylphs in the large divertissement of the same act (score nos. 2–5). Musically, the répétiteur's copy is an exact copy of Bournonville's earlier revised 1849 Copenhagen version of this ballet. However, several pencilled notes indicate at least two major musical cuts made personally by Bournonville in the opening scene of Act I (score no. 1). Moreover, a series of other omissions and musical rearrangements of the divertissements in Act II (score nos. 2–5) were beyond doubt also made by Bournonville for this production. This is clear from his autographed pencilled notes on p. 104 (reading: 'vide pag./93/&94/G dur/till slutet af/No. 3 pag 98.' The new musical arrangement of the Act II divertissements was followed closely in the later revision that Bournonville made some three years later, when *La Sylphide* was restaged in Copenhagen under the direction of L. Gade (*see* 4.2.1865).

Parts. Ms. Copy. 33 vol.
3 vl I, 3 vl II, 2 vla, 3 vlc e cb, fl 1/2, ob 1/2, cl 1/2, fag 1/2, cor 1/2/3/4, tr 1/2, cnt, trb 1/2/3, timp, gr cassa, piatti e tri, arpa.
Unsigned and undated [1862]
[SSkma; KT Pantomime-Balletter S 9

Printed sources:

Printed scenario. 1 vol. 7 pp. (18 × 10,6 cm)
SYLFIDEN./BALLETT I TVÅ AKTER./MUSIKEN/AF/H. LÖVENSKJOLD.
Stockholm, E. Westrell, 1862.
[DKKk; 17, – 173 8°
This bilingual scenario (Swedish and French) contains a new foreword by Bournonville, dated 'Stockholm 20 Mars 1862', and a highly abridged description of the ballet's dramatic action.

5.4.1862

The Slanderer (Smädeskrifvaren, eller: Vänner och Ovänner) **(Stockholm's Royal Theatre, Operahuset).**

In his diary and in his Swedish *Journal* Bournonville noted about his rehearsals, the première and the following three performances of J. Jolin's five-act play:

12.1.1862: 'Tilbragt den øvrige Deel af Dagen hos [J.] Jolin, der forelæste for mig Smädeskriveren, et efter min Mening fortjenstfuldt Lystspil. Vi bleve der til Middag og Aften og havde det meget hyggeligt'
8.3.: 'Collationnering på Smädeskrifvaren'
12.3.: 'arbeidet paa forkortninger i Smädeskrifvaren. Decorationsmøde til Samme'
17.3.: 'skrifvit sceneri på Smädeskrifvaren'
20.3.: '1.ste Prøve paa [...] Smädeskrifvaren. 1.ste och 2.dra Akten'
21.3.: 'Skrifvit sceneri till Smädeskrifvaren'
24.3.: 'Smädeskrifvaren. 1.ste, 2.dra & 3.die Akten'
26.3.: 'Smädeskrifvaren. (4.de och 5.te Akten.)'
28.3.: 'Smädeskrifvaren: (1.e 2.a 3.e & 4.de Akten) Rep: salen.'
29.3.: 'Smädeskrifvaren (5.te Akten) (Rep: salen)'

1.4.: 'Costȳm=Möte på Smädeskrifvaren. [...] Smädeskrifvaren (General=Repetition)'
2.4., 3.4., and 4.4.: '<u>Smädeskrifvaren</u> (Gen. Rep.)'
5.4.: 'I Theatret 1.ste Forestilling af <u>Smädeskrifvaren</u> Comedie af Jolin, der gjorde ganske overordentlig Lȳkke og fortjente det baade for Digtningen og den udmærkede Udførelse'
7.4.: 'I Theatret '<u>Smädeskrifvaren</u>' for fuldt Huus og stormende Bifald (svage men forurettede Demonstrationer fra <u>de Truffnes</u> Side. – Alle Bladskrivere rasende imod Stykket, Forfatteren, Theatret og Publicum'
8.4.: 'I Theatret tredie Forestilling af Smädeskrifvaren, fuldt Huus og savidt jeg hørte indtil tredie Akts Slutning ingen Opposition'
10.4.: 'I Theatret Smädeskrifvaren for fuldt Huus. Jeg saae blot 1.ste Akt, og gik tidlig hjem. – Bladene vedblive at rase imod Stykket og Publicum applauderer'.

The play included two dance numbers with music composed and arranged by A. Randel, and two students' songs, entitled «O yngling om du hjerta har» (to a tune by E. G. Geijer) and «Brüder lass uns lustig sein». According to Bournonville's manuscript mise-en-scène, the two dances consisted of a *March (Marsch)* and a *Circle Dance (Ringdans)* both of which were performed in Act I, scene 4, and are described as follows:

'Marsch från fonddøren H. rundt, igenom Ørners rum och tilbaka, fördela i båda rummene [...] Ringdans igenom båda rummena. Grupp på bord och stolar'.

The Slanderer received 15 performances during Bournonville's engagement in Stockholm, the last of which was given on 30.11.1862. According to a series of later notes in Bournonville's diary (on 21.4., 5.5., and 6.5.1862) and three letters written to him by the Danish author, H. P. Holst, on 16.4., 30.4. and 13.9.1862 (now in DKKk, call nos. NKS 3258 A 4°, V, facs. 6, nos. 469–471) the 1862 Stockholm mise-en-scène also seems to have been employed by Holst, when he mounted Jolin's play at Copenhagen's Casino Theatre on 2.12.1862 with the Danish title *Smædeskriveren eller Talentet paa Afvej*. It was given there 9 times, the last time on 9.1.1863.

Autograph sources:

Manuscript mise-en-scène. Ms. Autograph. Brown ink. 1 vol. 13 pp. (21,4 × 17,5 cm)
<u>Smädeskrifvaren.</u>/eller/<u>Vänner och Ovänner.</u>/<u>Komedi i fem Akter.</u>
Unsigned and undated [Written according to the diary on 17.3. and 21.3.1862]
[DKKk; NKS 3285 4° 5 læg 2]

Musical sources:

No orchestral score and répétiteur's copy for *The Slanderer* have yet been traced in SSkma.

Parts. Ms. Copy. 6 vol.
cl 1/2, cor 1/2, Btrb, piano. Vocal parts.
Unsigned and undated [c.1862]
[SSkma; KT Tal-Pjeser med Musik S 45 (vocal parts in kapsel S)]

9.4.1862
Estrella de Soria **(Stockholm's Royal Theatre, Operahuset).**
In his diary and in his Swedish *Journal* Bournonville noted about the staging and the première of F. Berwald's five-act grand romantic opera:

3.11.1861: 'genomläst Libretto'en til <u>Estrella</u>!'
13.11.: '<u>Hemma</u>. Skrifvit Sceneri til <u>Estrella</u>'
21.11.: 'skrifvit sceneri til <u>Estrella</u>'
6.2.: 'Lister till <u>Estrella</u>'
7.2.: 'Costym=möte på <u>Estrella</u>'
14.2.1862: 'Första Sceneprøve ved Claveer paa Estrella Opera af F Berwald'
15.2.: '2.den scèneprøve paa Estrella'
19.2.: 'Prøve i Sångrummet paa Estrella [...] Sceneri [...] 3.die Akten. (Rep: salen.)'
20.2.: 'Indstudering paa Estrella [...] (scener)'
21.2.: 'Eftermiddagsprøve paa Estrella [...] Sceneri 1.ste Akt'
22.2.: 'Eftermiddagsprøve paa Sceneriet til Estrella [...] 2.dra och 3.die Akten [...] <u>sceneri</u>'
25.2.: 'Collationnering paa Musiken til Estrella (meget interessant) [...] Estrella. (vid Piano.)'
27.2.: '<u>Estrella</u> Musik=Collationnering'
1.3.: 'Prøve paa 1.ste Akt af Estrella med Orchester og Alt. Den gik efter Omstændighederne særdeles godt'
3.3.: 'Sång och Musik-repetition på theatern <u>Estrella</u>'
8.3.: 'Prøve paa Estrella – men vi naaede ikke længere end til Halvdelen. Jeg maatte derfor arrangere et nȳt Repertoire for næste Uge'
11.3.: 'Estrella (2.dra Akten) Gen. Rep. [...] Estrella (3.die Akten (Gen Rep.))'
13.3.: 'Generalprøve paa Estrella'
14.3.: 'Arrangement paa sidste Akt af Estrella [...] 1.ste Akten (Rep: salen.) [...] Sceneri till 3.die Akten'
15.3.: 'Generalprøve paa Estrella [...] 2.dra Akten (Rep. salen)'
4.4. and 7.4.: 'Prøve paa Estrella [...] (General=Repetition)'
8.4.: 'Sidste Generalprøve paa Estrella, der gik udmærket godt og i Costume'
9.4.: 'I Theatret 1.ste Forestilling af <u>Estrella de Soria</u> Opera af Berwald, fra Musikens Side et særdeles interessant Værk, men som næppe vil erhverve sig nogen Popularitet, da det lider af <u>Længde</u> og som en Følge deraf, af <u>Kjedelighed</u>. Udførelsen var meget god og Bifaldet eenstemmigt skjønt temmelig sparsomt. Componisten fremkaldtes'.

On 22.4.1862 he noted: 'Forkortninger til Estrella', and about a performance on the following day he stated: 'Estrella for lidt over halvt Huus!!'. The fifth and last performance on 28.4.1862 was assessed by him as follows:

'I Theatret meget daarligt Huus til <u>Estrella</u>, der formodentlig nu bliver henlagt!'.

According to Bournonville's manuscript **mise-en-scène**, the production included a ballet divertissement, named 'Polonaise', performed by a corps de ballet in Act II, scene 9 (score no. 21). The music for this dance was published in Stockholm in 1843 by A. Hirsch in a version for piano score (pl. no. 173, now in SSkma). It was first played at Stora Börssalen in Stockholm on 6.2.1843 as part of the anniversary celebrations of King Carl Johan XIV's 25th year on the throne (Berwald's first autographed orchestral score for this 'Polonäse' is now in SSk, call no. Handskrifter, S. 194).
Estrella de Soria received 5 performances during Bournonville's engagement in Stockholm, the last of which was given on 28.4.1862.

Autograph sources:

Manuscript mise-en-scène. Ms. Autograph. Brown ink and pencil. 1 vol. 14 pp. (21,4 × 17,5 cm)
<u>Estrella de Soria.</u>/Opera i 3 Akter./af/<u>Otto Prechtler.</u> Musiken af <u>Frantz Berwald.</u>

Signed and dated: 'Stockholm d. 21 Novbr 1861.' [Written according to Bournonville's Swedish *Journal* on 13.11. and 21.11.1862]
[DKKk; NKS 3285 4° 5 læg 1

Musical sources:

Orchestral score. Ms. Autograph (by F. Berwald) and copy. 5 vol.
(34,2 × 25 with minor variants)
Estrella de Soria/Grosse romantische Oper mit Tanz in 3 Akten/von
Otto Prechtler/Musik/von/Franz Berwald
Unsigned and undated [1862]
[SSkma; KT Operor E 5

No répétiteur's copy for *Estrella de Soria* has yet been traced in SSkma.

Parts. Ms. Copy. 33 vol. + 21 vol.
3 vl I, 3 vl II, 2 vla, 4 vlc e cb, fl 1/2, ob 1/2, cl 1/2, fag 1/2, cor 1/2/
3/4, tr, trb 1/2/3/4, timp, gr cassa, piatti, arpa. On stage: fl 1/2, ob
1/2, cl 1/2/3, fag 1/2, cor princ, cor 1/2/3/4, tr 1/2, trb 1/2/3/4,
gr cassa e piatti.
Unsigned and undated [1862]
[SSkma; KT Operor E 5

1.5.1862
Fra-Diavolo, ou l'Hôtellerie de Terracine (Fra Diavolo eller Värdshuset i Terracina). Projected restaging at Stockholm's Royal Theatre (Operahuset).
On this day Bournonville noted in his Swedish *Journal* about
a projected Swedish restaging of D.-F.-E. Auber's three-act
comic opera from 1830 (*see also* 20.12.1857):

'skrifvit sceneri till Fra Diavolo'.

About the same project (which he never carried out) he
later wrote:

2.5.1862: 'Kl 1/2 11. Fra Diavolo (sångr.)
4.5.: 'Fra Diavolo. (sångr.) (skall icke gå, förmedelst [F.] Arlbergs
omöjlighet i sångpartiet.)'.

No autographed sources for Bournonville's projected 1862
mise-en-scène of Auber's opera have yet been traced.

9.5.1862
Hamlet, Prince of Denmark (Hamlet, Prins af Danmark) (Stockholm's Royal Theatre, Operahuset).
In his diary and in his Swedish *Journal* Bournonville noted
about his 1862 Swedish restaging of W. Shakespeare's five-act
tragedy from c.1600–01 (first performed in Stockholm on
26.3.1819):

9.4.1862: 'Paa Theatret, hvor jeg idag ingen Prøve havde men arbeidede paa Sceneriet til Hamlet'
10.4.: 'Sceneri till Hamlet'
11.4.: 'Hamlet med [A. F.] Westermarck'
12.4.: 'Beskjæftiget mig meget med Hamlet. [...] Sceneri på Hamlet'
14.4.: 'Prøve paa Hamlet (3 første Akter) med de af mig foreslaaede
Modificationer'
15.4.: 'Hamlet (4.e och 5.te Akten.) [...] Decorationsmöte på Hamlet'
16.4.: 'Generalprøve paa Hamlet [...] (alla fem Akter.)'
22.4.: 'Hamlet. (sceneri)'
29.4. and 30.4.: 'Hamlet. (Gen. Rep:)'
2.5.: 'Hamlet (roler) [*sic*]'
7.5.: 'Hamlet (Gen: Rep:) 1.ste 2.dra 3.die Akten'
8.5.: 'Hamlet. (Gen: Rep.) 4.de och 5.te Akten'
9.5.: 'I Theatret, Hamlet der gik udmærket godt og hvori [A. T.]

Schwartz viste sig som betydelig Skuespiller. Huset var ikke stærkt
besat, men Tilfredsheden almindelig'.

The 1862 production received 7 performances, the last of
which was given on 29.10.1862.

No autographed sources containing Bournonville's
changes for his staging of Shakespeare's *Hamlet, Prince of Denmark* have yet been traced. However, musical material dating
from the two previous Stockholm stagings of Shakespeare's
tragedy (mounted on 26.3.1819 and 7.11.1853) are still preserved in SSkma (call no. KT Tal-Pjeser med Musik H 6). It is,
though, uncertain whether this material (which also includes
some pantomime music composed by E. Dupuy) was reused
by Bournonville's for his 1862 production.

17.5.1862
Hothouse Flowers (Blommor i drifbänk) (Stockholm's Royal Theatre, Operahuset).
In his diary and in his Swedish *Journal* Bournonville noted
about his involvement in the staging and première of F. Hedberg's four-act comedy:

24.4.1862: 'Collationnering på Blommor i Drifbänk'
28.4.: 'Blommor i Drifbänk (sceneri.)'
5.5.: 'Blommor i drifbänk ([C. G.] Sundberg.)'
6.5.: 'Blommor i drifbänk (4.de Akten) Sundberg'
10.5.: 'Blommor i drifbänk. (Gen. Rep.) (Sundberg)'
11.5.: 'Blommor i drifbänk. (3.die & 4.de Akten) Sundberg'
12.5.: 'sceneri=skrifning'
13.5.: 'Sceneri till Blommor i drifbänk'
14.5.: 'overværet Prøven paa Blommor i drifbänk, der styres af Sundberg'
15.5. and 16.5.: 'Blommor i drifbänk. (Gen. Rep.)'
17.5.: 'Blommor i drifbänk. (4.de Akten.) [...] Første Forestilling af
Blommor i drifbänk af Hedberg. Der gjorde Lykke formedelst en
vittig Dialog og morsomme Situationer'
18.5.: 'I Theatret Blommor i drifbänk for daarligt Huus. Sommeren
kalder alle ud i det Grønne'.

The staging included two dance numbers, a so-called
'Marsch', composed by A. Leonhardt, and a 'Galopp' by E.
A. Förster. According to Bournonville's manuscript mise-en-
scène, Leonhardt's 'Marsch' was performed during the
finale of Act I (scene 14) and is described as follows:

'paraden som hörts en stund under förra scenen, men på afstand
kommer nu allt närmare och närmare, och man ser på torget näre
alléen en massa folk inkomma, somliga springande, andra marsche-
rande i takt, och då man just väntar att musiken skall inkomma på
scenen, fallar ridåen hastigt, hvarefter orchestern spelar marschen
till slut'.

It has not been possible to establish exactly where in the
comedy Förster's 'Galopp' was performed.

Hothouse Flowers received 20 performances during Bournonville's engagement in Stockholm, the last of which was
given on 17.6.1863.

According to a later note Bournonville's diary (on 30.7.
1863) and two letters to him from the Danish writer, H. P.
Holst (dated 23.7. and 1.8.1863, now in DKKk, call nos. NKS
3258 A 4°, V, facs. 5, no. 456, and facs. 6, no. 475), Bournonville's 1862 Stockholm mise-en-scène also seems to have
been employed by Holst in Copenhagen. This happened
when Holst mounted Hedberg's comedy in his own transla-

tion at the Casino Theatre on 13.5.1864 with the Danish title *Drivhusplanter*. It was performed there 6 times, the last time on 20.6.1864.

Autograph sources:

Manuscript mise-en-scène. Ms. Autograph (partially in another's hand). Brown ink. 1 vol. 22 pp. (21,5 × 17,5 cm)
<u>Blommor i drifbänk</u>/Lustspel i 4 Akter af <u>Hedberg.</u>/<u>svenskt original.</u>
Unsigned and undated [Written according to Bournonville's Swedish *Journal* most probably on 12.5.1862]
[DKKk; NKS 3285 4° 4 læg 2

Musical sources:

No orchestral score and répétiteur's copy for *Hothouse Flowers* have yet been traced in SSkma.

Parts. Ms. Copy. 14 vol. + 8 vol.
vl I, vl II, vla, 2 vlc e cb, fl, ob 1/2, fag 1/2, tr, trb, gr cassa, piatti. On stage: fl, cl 1/2, cor, cnt, Btuba, gr cassa, piatti.
Unsigned and undated [1862]
[SSkma; KT Tal-Pjeser med Musik B 26

5.6.1862
Faust (Stockholm's Royal Theatre, Operahuset).
The 1862 Stockholm première of the original version of C. Gounod's five-act opera (first performed in Paris at the Théâtre Lyrique on 19.3.1859) was mounted with Bournonville's mise-en-scène. According to his diary and the original music material in Stockholm (now in SSkma and SSkt), Gounod's opera was mounted with some major cuts and changes in Acts III and IV respectively. These cuts (which were made mainly because of the opera's long duration) appear to have included the condemnation scene of *Mephistopheles* in the garden of *Margaretha* (Act III, score no. 7), and the seduction scene between *Faust* and *Margaretha* at the end of the same act (score no .11). These changes were followed by a new sequence of the three main scenes of Act IV (showing *Margaretha's* dwelling – the church – and the street scene).The production also included Bournonville's choreography for the dance scenes in Act I, score no. 9 ('Valse et Chœur', entitled «Ainsi que la brise légère» and performed by three couples), and in Act V, score nos. 28 and 29 (entitled '<u>Chör och Ballet</u>', and 'Dans af Demoner' respectively). *Faust* was mounted for the second and last time by Bournonville at Copenhagen's Royal Theatre on 16.3.1873.

In his diary and in his Swedish *Journal* he noted about the 1862 Stockholm première:

12.3. and 14.3.1862: 'Decorationsmöte på <u>Faust</u> [...] Opera af [C.] Gounod'
14.4.: 'Faust. (sångrummet) [J. A.] Söderman)'
15.4.: 'Faust. (Sångr.)'
16.4.: 'Costumemøde paa Faust'
23.4.: 'Faust (Mephistofeles:)'
24.4.: 'Faust. (sångr.)'
25.4., 28.4., and 1.5.: 'Faust (Mephistofeles.)'
2.5.: 'Componerat Dands till Faust [...] 'Faust (Mephistofeles.)'
3.5.: 'Componeret Dands til Faust [...] <u>Faust</u>. (balletterna.) [...] Faust (sångr.)'
5.5.: 'Componeret og indstuderet Waltsen til Faust [...] <u>Faust</u>. (Balletterna)'
6.5.: '<u>Faust</u> (conference med Machiner och Decors.) [...] D.° (sångr.) [...] Faust ([C. O.] Arnoldsson och [P. A. J.] Willman.)'

7.5.: 'Eftermiddagsarbeide paa Faust'
8.5.: '<u>Faust</u>. (Instruction, Barntheatern.)'
9.5.: '<u>Faust</u>. sångr. D.° skrifvit sceneri [...] <u>Faust</u> (Instr: Barntheatern.)'
10.5.: '<u>M.lle</u> [F.] <u>Andrée</u> (instr: Faust.)'
12.5.: 'sceneri=skrifving [...] <u>Faust</u>. (Instr: Barntheatern.)'
13.5. and 14.5.: 'Faust (Barntheatern.) [...] Eftermiddagsprøve'
15.5.: 'Sceneri=arbete till <u>Faust</u>.'
16.5.: '<u>Faust</u> (Barntheatern.) [...] indstuderet'
19.5.: 'Faust (4.de Akten (Rep. salen)) [...] Sceneri och Ballet till 5 Akten. [...] componeret Dands til Faust'
20.5.: 'Faust (sångr.) [...] D.° Balletten 5.te Akten. [...] indstuderet Dands til Faust's 5.te Akt [...] D° <u>Instruction</u> 5.te Akten'
21.5.: 'Faust (sångr.) [...] D.° Balletten 5.te Akten. [...] indstudering paa Dands til Faust [...] D° Scener i 5.te Akten'
22.5.: '<u>Faust</u>. (Trollscenen i 5.te Akten.) [...] D.° Barntheatern'
23.5.: 'Dandseprøve og Musik=Collationnering paa Faust. [...] Faust. Balletterne å Barntheatern. [...] D.o Scener Barntheatern'
24.5.: 'Faust (Rep: salen) [...] Hela Dagen paa Theatret, beskjæftiget med Decorationerne til Faust [...] Decorations uppsättning'
26.5.: 'Sceneri till Faust (2.e och 4 Akten)'
27.5.: 'Faust. 1.ste, 3.die och ½ 4 Akterne (Piano)'
28.5.: 'Faust (Gen Rep) 1.ste 2.dra 3die Akten'
29.5.: '<u>Faust sceneri till 4.de Akten</u>. (Piano.)'
30.5.: '<u>Faust</u>. 3.die och 4.de Akten (Gen Rep.)
31.5.: 'Orchester=Collationnering. <u>5.te Akten</u>.' [...] <u>Faust</u>. 5.te Akten (Gen Rep) [...] <u>Faust</u>. (Gen: Repetition) <u>1.e 2.dra 3.e Akten</u>'
1.6.: '<u>Faust</u> (Gen. Repetition) 2.dra 3.e 4. [...] Aftenprøve paa Faust der varede fra 6 – ³/₄ 11. Endnu en Time gik vi med Decorationerne og alligevel maa Operaen opsættes!!'
2.6.: 'Faust 5.te Akts sceneri vid piano'
3.6.: 'Generalprøve paa Faust, der gik ret godt'
4.6.: 'Costymprof. [...] General=Repetition i Costym <u>Faust</u> [...] der gik udmærket godt, men de sidste Akter behøve Forkortninger. Jeg kom meget silde hjem og tilsengs Kl 12'
5.6.: 'Kl 6-7 på morgonen skrifvit och moveratt för nödiga förkortningar i Faust. [...] Inspicerat maskinerna [...] Repeteradt förkortningarna [...] Første Forestilling af Faust, der gik udmærket godt og vandt stort Bifald. Jeg gjorde Underværker med Mellemakterne, men Operaen varede dog indtil ³/₄ 11.!'.

Faust received 26 performances in Stockholm during Bournonville's engagement there, the last of which was given on 20.6.1864.

Autograph sources:

Manuscript mise-en-scène (incomplete). Ms. Autograph. Brown ink. 1 vol. 23 pp. (21,5 × 17,5 cm)
<u>Faust.</u>
Unsigned and undated [Written according to the diary on 9.5. and 12.5.1862]
[DKKk; NKS 3285 4° 4 læg 1

Musical sources:

Orchestral printed score with manuscript insertions. 3 vol. Act I–II 183 pp., Act III 108 pp., Act IV-V 236 pp. (26,2 × 17,5 cm)
Faust/Opéra en cinq actes/[...]/Musique de/CH. GOUNOD
Paris, Choudens, Exemplaire N. 53 [1859–1862]
[SSkma; KT Operor F 4

Répétiteur's copy. Ms. Copy. Black ink. 1 vol., 60 pp. of which two are blank (30 × 23,5 cm)
24/<u>Faust</u>/Kongl. teatern/Repetitör./Ballet/[...]/Faust/Oper i 5 Akter/af/Ch: Gounod,/<u>Repetieur</u>
Unsigned and undated [1862]
[SSkt (Vinstocken), but formerly in SSkma with the call no. KT Operor F 4
This répétiteur's copy dates from the 1862 Stockholm première of

Gounod's *Faust*. It contains the complete music for the so-called 'Valse et Chœur' («Ljuftig daft på vestvindens vingar») and the finale in Act II (score no. 9), followed by the complete music in Act V (score no. 29) for the so-called 'Sabat de démons'. The volume also contains Bournonville's autographed notes describing the mime and the choreography performed during these two scenes. Finally, his autographed choreographic numbers are included throughout this volume. They may refer to a (not yet traced) separate notation of the choreography and mise-en-scène that he created for this opera, which (according to his diary) may have been written between 2.5 and 19.5.1862.

Parts. Ms. Copy. 39 + 1 vol.
4 vl I, 4 vl II, 3 vla, 4 vlc e cb, fl picc, fl 1/2, ob 1/2, cl 1/2, fag 1/2, cor 1/2/3/4, tr, trb 1/2/3, timp, gr cassa, cassa, piatti, tri, 2 arpa. On stage: org.
Unsigned and undated [1862]
[SSkma; KT Operor F 4

1.8.1862
Plan for a repertory at Stockholm's Royal Theatre from 28.8. to 15.9.1862.
During a summer holiday at his residence in Fredensborg, Bournonville wrote on this day a plan for the repertory he intended to stage at Stockholm's Royal Theatre during the first three weeks of the 1862–63 season. This plan, which has not yet been traced, is described in his diary as follows:

'udarbeidet Repertoiret for Det kgl svenske Theater indtil den 15 Sept. og sendt det tilligemed Brev til [D.] Hwasser recommenderet'.

It is not possible to identify the exact content of works included in this repertory plan.

29.8.1862
On ne badinez pas avec l'amour (Lek ej med kärleken).
Projected staging at Stockholm's Royal Theatre.
On this day Bournonville wrote a recommendation note to the theatre management of Stockholm's Royal Theatre expressing his opinion about a projected Swedish staging of A. de Musset's three-act comedy (first performed at the Théâtre Français in Paris on 18.11.1861). This note reads as follows:

'Ne badinez pas avec l'amour/par/Alfred de Musset.
On ne peut autrement que déplorer la penurie du repertoire dramatique en pensant que cette pièce forme aujourd'hui une partie des délires du théâtre français!
    J'y trouve une tendance très prononcée à la comedie d'avenir composée de parfums & d'harmonies tourmenties, à l'égal des chants sans mélodies des opéras du célèbre novateur. On y cherche en vain une situation, des caractères un nœud, une solution, enfin ce qui constitue aux yeux d'un public habitué aux oeuvres de [J. B.] Molière, e [P. A. C. de] Beaumarchais ou de [E.] Scribe, une pièce dramatique.
    J'ai peut-être grand tort, mais c'est avec regrets que je me suis apperçu que lorsque les Français du temps moderne soît dans leurs romans, soît dans leurs drames, veulent sortie de la voie des situations scabreuses, pour faire de la morale ou de la réligion, ils tombent dans une affectation mielleuse.
    C'est ça que forme l'essence de la présente comedie, qui en dépit d'un jeu magistral ne pourra jamais produire sur des affects sains, qu'un effet de muse & d'oppiat.
    Je dois en déconseiller la traduction, comme un travail perdu pour le théâtre royal.
    ce 29 Août 1862./très humblement/August Bournonville'.

De Musset's play was not mounted at Stockholm's Royal Theatre during Bournonville's engagement there, and was not given in the Swedish capital until twenty years later, when it was premièred (in a translation by E. Lundquist) at Nya Theatern on 21.10.1882 with the Swedish title *Lek ej med kärleken*.

Later it was also mounted at Stockholm's Royal Theatre (Dramatiska Theatern) on 14.11.1894, but then in a new translation by E. Thyselius. The 1894 production was given 13 times until 1908, when de Musset's play play was restaged for the third and last time in Stockholm in a completely new production at Dramatiska Theatern.

Autograph sources:

Recommendation note. Ms. Autograph. Brown ink. 2 pp. (14,2 × 11,4 cm)
Ne badinez pas avec l'amour/par/Alfred de Musset. [...]
Signed and dated: 'ce 29 Août 1862'
[SSdt; KTA, E2A Ink. breve 1862/63, 29.8.1862

17.9.1862
Pas de deux **performed by A. and C. Healey in Act I of *La Sylphide (Sylphiden)*.(Stockholm's Royal Theatre, Operahuset).**
According to the poster for this Swedish performance of Bournonville's two-act romantic ballet *La Sylphide (see also* 1.4.1862), a *Pas de deux* to music by H. C. Lumbye was incorporated by Bournonville in the first act, where it was performed by his two English pupils, A. and C. Healey. Moreover, a note in his diary on the same day clearly indicates that this dance was identical with his earlier *Polketta, Pas de deux*, originally performed by the Healey sisters at Copenhagen's Casino Theatre on 31.10.1858 and first danced by them in Stockholm on 23.4.1860.

About the performance in *La Sylphide* Bournonville noted in his diary:

26.8.1862: 'Sylphïden (på theatren.)'
10.9.: 'Sylphiden'
12.9.: 'Sylphiden (med repetiteur)'
16.9.: 'Sylphiden (Gen. Rep.) ([A. and C.] Healeys)
17.9.: 'Sylphiden, Huset var fuldt og Healeyerne debuterede med deres polketta, der gjorde overordentlig Lykke og de bleve fremkaldte med stormende Applaus. Balletten gik smukt og jeg var meget glad'.

The *Polketta* was danced 4 times in *La Sylphide*, the last time on 12.2.1863. Later the same year it also seems to have been performed as an incorporated divertissement in C. Gounod's three-act comic opera *Le Médecin malgré lui (Läkaren mot sin Vilja) (see* 14.12.1863).

The musical material employed for the *Polketta* this year was the same as that employed for the 1860 Stockholm première of it (now in SSkma, call no. KT Dansmusik 101).

30.9.1862
Lucia di Lammermoor (Lucie eller Bruden från Lammermoor) **(Stockholm's Royal Theatre, Operahuset).**
Bournonville had earlier mounted G. Donizetti's three-act tragic drama, when it was given its first performance at Copenhagen's Royal Theatre (sung in Danish) on 8.12.1857.
    In his diary and in his Swedish *Journal* he noted about the

1862 Swedish restaging, which was the last production he ever directed of this work:

17.9.1862: 'Costume=Möte på <u>Lucie</u> [...] Kl 11. <u>Lucie</u> (sångr.)'
18.9.: '<u>Lucie</u> [...] Efterm: Instruction <u>Berends</u> [*sic*]'
19.9. and 20.9.: '<u>Lucie</u> (sångr.)'
22.9.: 'skrevet og læst'
23.9.: 'læst, skrevet; Prøve paa Lucie m. m. [...] (sceneri vid Piano)'
26.9.: 'Prøve og Embedsforretninger (Lucie) [...] (Gen Rep)'
27.9. and 29.9.: '<u>Lucie</u> (Gen Rep)'
30.9.: '<u>Lucie</u> gik for fuldt Huus og meget Bifald. [C. B.] <u>Behrens</u> Ashton'.

The 1862 restaging received 5 performances during Bournonville's engagement in Stockholm, the last of which was given on 17.11.1862.

Autograph sources:

Manuscript mise-en-scène. Ms. Autograph. Black ink. 1 vol. 5 pp. (21,5 × 17,5 cm)
<u>Lucia från Lammermoor</u>/<u>Opera i 4 Akter.</u>/af/<u>Donizetti.</u>/(nytt sceneri af 22.de Sept. 1862.)
Signed and dated: 'd 22.e September 1862.'
[DKKk; NKS 3285 4° 4 læg 1

Manuscript mise-en-scène. Ms. Autograph. Brown ink and pencil. 4 pp. (22,9 × 14,3 cm)
<u>Lucie</u> (Opera)/<u>Første Akten</u> (Skog)/[...]/<u>Anden Akten:</u> (Sal.)/[...]/<u>3.die Akten:</u> (Sal)/[...]/<u>Fjerde Akten:</u> (Park med grafvårdar)
Signed and dated: 'd. 22.de Septbr.' [1862]
[SSm; Daniel Fryklunds samling no. 134

Musical sources:

Orchestral score. Ms. Copy. 2 vol. Act I–II: 468 pp., Act II–IV: 278 pp. (35 × 27 cm)
Lucie/1.a och 2.a Act:
Unsigned and undated [c.1840–1862]
[SSkma; KT Operor L 1
This orchestral score dates from the Stockholm première of *Lucia di Lammermoor* on 16.4.1860 and was used for all performances of it there during Bournonville's engagement.

No répétiteur's copy for *Lucia di Lammermoor* has yet been traced in SSkma.

Parts. Ms. Copy. 28 vol.
4 vl I, 4 vl II, 2 vla, 4 vlc e cb, fl picc, fl 1/2, ob 1/2, cl 1/2, fag 1/2, cor 1/2/3/4, tr 1/2, trb, tuba, timp, gr cassa, piatti, tri, arpa.
Unsigned and undated [c.1840–1862]
[SSkma; KT Operor L 1

3.10.1862
La Papillonne (Fjärilsfebern) (Stockholm's Royal Theatre, Operahuset).
The Stockholm première of C. C. Jungberg's Swedish translation of V. Sardou's three-act comedy (first performed at the Théâtre Français in Paris on 11.4.1862) was mounted with Bournonville's mise-en-scène. It was staged as part of an experiment aimed at testing the judgement of Stockholm's critical establishment, and was premièred only two days before the staging of the same work at Stockholm's then privately run Mindre Theatern (5.10.1862). At that theatre it was given in another Swedish translation by L. E. Stjernström and with a completely different cast and mise-en-scène. With this action of surprise Stockholm's Royal Theatre intended (according to Bournonville's memoirs *My Theatre Life*, p. 310) to present Sardou's comedy 'under cover of secrecy and by the the attractive force of intrigue' immediately before it was to be performed 'by our astounded and indignant neighbours'. The result of this experiment is described in the same memoirs as follows:

'The blow was violent and decisive; the public opened its eyes, and this time dared to pass an independent sentence in spite of the desperate efforts of the protecting powers [of the press]. We held the battlefield, and from now on there was no more talk of rivalry [...] Mindre Theatern hoisted all its sails, both classical and romantic, but in vain; it fell further and further behind, and scarcely three months after the aforesaid defeat we learnt this establishment was to be sold or leased'.

In his diary and in his Swedish *Journal* Bournonville noted about the staging and its first two performances at Stockholm's Royal Theatre:

16.9.1862: 'Comité i Theatercancelliet. Chefen [i.e. E. F. O. L. von Stedingk], [D.] Hwasser, Jeg, [F. N.] Berg, [L.] Norman, [J. A.] Söderman og [W.] Kjellberg'
24.9.: 'Hemmelig <u>Collationnering</u> paa La papillonne'
27.9.: 'skrifvit sceneri till Fjärillsfebern'
28.9.: 'Efterm: hemmelig Prøve paa Fjärilsfeberen. [...] (Barntheatren)'
29.9.: 'Decorationsmöte på Fjärilsfebren [...] hemmelig Prøve paa Fjärilsfebren [...] (Barntheatren.)'
30.9.: 'Fjärilsfebren (Barntheatren.)'
1.10.: 'Kl 11. Fjärilsfebren. (Gen. Rep.) [...] Fjärilsfeberen (Gen. Rep.)'
2.10.: '<u>Fjärilsfebren</u> (Gen. Rep.)'
3.10.: 'Fjärilsfebren. (Gen Rep) [...] Første Forestilling af Fjärilsfeberen [...] gjorde overordentlig Lykke. Det var en udmærket Aften'
5.10.: 'Fjärilsfeberen, der gik udmærket'.

Bournonville's staging of *La Papillonne* reached 21 performances during his engagement in Stockholm, the last of which was given on 26.12.1863. The rival production at Mindre Theatern reached only 6 performances during this period.

Autograph sources:

Manuscript mise-en-scène. Ms. Autograph. Brown ink and pencil. 1 vol. 12 pp. (21,5 × 17,5 cm)
<u>Fjärilsfebern.</u>/Comedie i tre Akter/af/Victorien Sardou./uppförd 1.ste Gången d. [space left open] October./<u>1862</u>.
Signed and dated: 'Stockholm d 27.e Septbr 1862.'
[DKKk; NKS 3285 4° 4 læg 2

3.10.1862
Echo from the Ballroom, New Pas de deux (Echo från Balsalen, Ny Pas de deux) (uncredited) performed by A. and C. Healey (Stockholm's Royal Theatre, Operahuset).
This dance is identical with Bournonville's *Echo from The Ballroom, Character Dance*, first performed by the Healey sisters at Copenhagen's Folketheatret on 28.2.1861. In Stockholm it was described on the poster as 'New Pas de deux danced by' (*Ny Pas de deux dansad af*) A. and C. Healey, but with no mention of Bournonville's name. Apart from two minor cuts in the 'Galopp' and the 'Finale' (of 7 and 16 bars each) the dance seems to have been mounted without any differences from the original Copenhagen production. It was given 4 times in Stockholm, the last time on 13.11.1862.

In his Swedish *Journal* Bournonville listed three reheasals and noted about the dance after having attended its first performance:

'Echo fra Balsalen […] Balletten gjorde overordentlig Lÿkke. Det var en udmærket Aften'.

Musical sources:

No orchestral score and répétiteur's copy for *Echo from the Ballroom* have yet been traced in SSkma.

Parts. Ms. Copy. 30 vol.
3 vl I, 3 vl II, 2 vla, 3 vlc e cb, fl picc, fl, ob 1/2, cl 1/2, fag 1/2, cor 1/2, tr 1/2, trb 1/2/3, timp, gr cassa, cassa, tri.
Unsigned and undated [1862]
[SSkma; KT Dansmusik 102

3.10.1862
Seguidilla (uncredited) performed by S. Lund, J. G. Sundberg, and a corps de ballet (Stockholm's Royal Theatre, Operahuset).

This dance is almost certainly identical with the so-called *La Seguedilla (after Taglioni)* in Bournonville's Spanish ballet divertissement *La Ventana*. That divertissement was staged only four years earlier at Stockholm's Royal Theatre on 15.6.1858 and had been kept in the repertory there until 12.9.1861. The (uncredited) 1862 *Seguidilla* received 4 performances in Stockholm, the last of which was given on 10.11.1862.

In his 1862 diary Bournonville mentioned only one rehearsal of it on 2.10.1862 and noted after its first performance:

'Seguidilla […] gjorde overordentlig Lÿkke. Det var en udmærket Aften'.

Musical sources:

No orchestral score and répétiteur's copy for the (uncredited) 1862 *Seguidilla* have yet been traced in SSkma.

Parts. Ms. Copy. 24 vol.
2 vl I, 2 vl II, vla, 2 vlc e cb, fl picc, fl, ob 1/2, cl 1/2, fag 1/2, cor 1/2, tr 1/2, trb 1/2, Btrb, gr cassa, cassa.
Unsigned and undated [1862?]
[SSkma; KT Dansmusik 95
Apart from a slightly different intrada this music is completely identical with that of the so-called *La Seguedilla. (after Taglioni)* in Bournonville's 1856 version of *La Ventana*. It was most likely used for the (uncredited) *Seguidilla* given at Stockholm's Royal Theatre (Operahuset) on 3.10.1862.

20.10.1862
Les Contes de la Reine de Navarre, ou la Revanche de Pavie (En Saga af Drottningen af Navarra) (Stockholm's Royal Theatre, Operahuset).

Bournonville's 1862 Swedish restaging of E. Scribe's and G. Legouvé's five-act comedy (premièred at the Théâtre Français in Paris on 13.10.1850, and first performed in Stockholm on 3.3.1851) was mounted from F. Høedt's 1851 Danish version (entitled *Dronning Marguerites Noveller*) which had been translated into Swedish by F. N. Berg (in 1851) and by I. Högfeldt (in 1853). In his diary and in his Swedish *Journal* Bournonville noted about the performance:

25.8.1862: 'rolerna utdelade till Drottningen af Navarra'
29.8.: 'Læst En Saga…'
10.9.: 'skrifvit sceneri till En Saga af D af N.'
12.9.: 'skrifvit sceneri till En Saga'
15.9.: 'En Saga af Drottn: af Navarra (Sceneri.)'
17.9.: 'En Saga (1.ste Akten).'
18.9.: 'En Saga (1.ste och 2.dra Akten.)'
20.9.: 'En Saga (1.ste 2.dra 3.die Akten.)'
22.9.: 'En Saga (3.die och 4.de Akten)'
23.9.: '3.die 4.de och 5.te Akten En Saga'
24.9.: 'En Saga (1.e 2.dra 3.e Akten) (Gen Rep)'
25.9.: '4.de och 5.te Akten. En Saga'
26.9.: 'En Saga (Gen Rep.)'
30.9.: 'Generalprøve af Drottningen af Novarra […] En Saga inställd (Fru [Z.] Hedin sjuk.)'
10.10. and 18.10.: 'En Saga (Gen Rep)'
20.10.: 'I Theatret En Saga af Drottningen af Novarra, for fuldt Huus. [A. T.] Schwartz og Fru [E.] Hwasser vare ÿpperlige. De større Roller derimod leed af Usikkerhed og Stykket gik i det Hele med mindre Liv end det burde'
23.10.: 'I Theatret En Saga som gik meget bedre end sidst.'
2.11.: 'En Saga for fuldt Huus men temmelig svagt udført. Den er virkelig over Kræfterne (Schwartz og Fru Hwasser fortræffelige)'.

Les Contes de la Reine de Navarre was only given once during Bournonville's engagement in Stockholm.

Autograph sources:

Manuscript mise-en-scène. Ms. Autograph. Brown ink. 1 vol. 18 pp. (21,5 × 17,5 cm)
En Saga/af/Drottningen af Navarra./Comedie i 5 Akter./af/Scribe./genupptagen och uppförd d. [space left open] October/1862.
Signed and dated: 'd 12.de Septbr 1862.' [Written according to the diary on 10.9. and 12.9.1862]
[DKKk; NKS 3285 4° 4 læg 2

4.11.1862
Les Projets de ma Tante (Min tants planer) (Stockholm's Royal Theatre, Operahuset).

In his diary and in his Swedish *Journal* Bournonville noted about his 1862 staging of H. Nicolle's one-act comedy (first performed at the Théâtre Français in Paris on 8.10.1859) which was translated into Swedish by F. Hedberg:

25.10.1862: 'Collationnering. (Min tants planer.)'
30.10. and 31.10.: 'Min tants planer (Gen Rep.)'
1.11.: 'Min tants planer […] Instruction (Frederiksson [i.e. G. Fredriksson]) Barntheatern'
3.11.: 'Min tantes planer. (Gen Rep.)'
4.11.: 'Min tantes planer. (Gen Rep.) […] I Theatret Min tantes planer 1.ste Gang. (Herr Frederikssons Debut) […] Alt for brilliant Huus'.

Nicolle's play was given 8 times during Bournonville's engagement in Stockholm, the last time on 22.1.1863.

7.11.1862
Forward! National divertissement in four tableaux (Framåt! National-Divertissement i 4 tablåer) (Stockholm's Royal Theatre, Operahuset).

This divertissement (with text by J. Jolin and music composed and arranged by L. Norman) was mounted with Bournonville's mise-en-scène and choreography, and with décor painted by F. Ahlgrensson. It was created to celebrate the inauguration of the new railway-line that linked the Swedish capital with the town of Gothenborg. In his diary and in his Swedish *Journal* Bournonville noted about the divertissement and its first three performances:

15.10.1862: 'Op Kl 7. skrevet, Kl 9 hos [J.] Jolin med en nŷ Composition til Jernbanens Aabning d. 3. Novbr […] Möte for Svea och Götha (composition) […] Confererede om Leiligheds-Stykket der vandt meget Bifald'
16.10.: 'Möte med [L.] Normann [*sic*] och [F.] Ahlgrensson'
21.10.: 'Conference om […] Svea och Götha'
22.10.: 'arbeidet med Jolin'
23.10.: 'Costume=möte på (d 7.e Novbr: piès.)'
25.10.: 'Decorations=arrangement (för d. 7.de Novbr.)'
27.10.: 'skrevet og componeret […] Componeret til Leilighedsstykket […] Kl 1/2 12 Grupperingar till d. 7.de Novbr: Kl 5: Ditto till D.°'
28.10.: 'Collationnering på d 7.de Novbr. […] Componeradt Elfdansen: […] Componeret dandse och Grupperinger […] Maskin= möte'
29.10.: 'Costÿm=möte […] Indstudering af dans till d. 7.de Novbr. […] Arrangement på scenen af D.°'
30.10.: '1.ste och 2.dra Tablåerna till d 7.de Novbr […] componeret'
31.10.: 'skrevet og componeret […] Indstudering af 3.die Tablå […] 1.ste och 2.dra Tablå på scenen […] vi benyttede Eftermiddagen til en grundig Prøve og Indstudering af tredie Akt […] 3.die Tablå på scenen'
1.11.: 'Prøve og Indstudering […] Framåt! 1.ste 2.dra 3.die Tablå på scenen […] 4.de Tablå (Barntheatern)'
2.11.: 'Requisit-möte'
3.11.: 'Imorges Kl 8.45 aabnedes Jernbanen fra Stockholm til Götheborg med stor Høitidelighed. Kongen med samt endeel af det diplomatiske Corps og en stor Deputation af Rigets Stænder fulgte med […] 3.die och 4.de Tablåer ur Framåt'
4.11.: 'Elfvor och dvärgar (Barntheatern) […] Framåt. (alla fÿra tablåer.)'
5.11.: 'Musik=Collationnering Framåt […] Dans på Barntheatern D.°'
6.11.: 'paa Theatret, hvor jeg var sysselsat den hele Dag med Framåt […] 4.de Tablaa (vid piano) […] D.° General=repetiton […] Musik= Collationnering […] Framåt. Gen Rep (i Costÿm)'
7.11.: 'Framåt. (partiel Gen Rep:) […] Costumeprøve paa Framåt, der nu gaaer udmærket godt. Alt i Orden til Forestillingen iaften. – Parket, første og anden Etage opfyldtes af Rigsdagsmænd og Honnoratiores. Kongen [i.e. Carl XV] og hele den kongelige Famillie. Folkesangen spillet […] Lumbyes nordiske Fostbrodergallop som Entre'acte. Derpaa Søstrene [A. and C.] Healeys Polketta, der gjorde stormende Lykke og endelig vort nye Arbeide Framåt der paa et Par Maskinforseelser nær, gik udmærket godt, men hvis Momenter ikke bleve grebne af det tilstedeværende Publicum der efter pas de deux'en atter træk sig tilbage i det kolde stive Ceremoniel. Ikke et eneste af de patriotiske Steder blev pointeret af Tilhörerne. Det er en Dvaskhed, der langt overgaaer den, som jeg har liidt saa meget af i Kjøbenhavn!!!'
8.11.: 'Framåt, der gik særdeles godt og uden Anstød'
10.11.: 'Framåt med adskillige Forkortninger'.

Framåt! reached a total of 9 performances, the last of which was given on 23.11.1862.

Autograph sources:

Manuscript mise-en-scène. Ms. Autograph. Brown ink. 2 pp. (36,2 × 22,8 cm)
Götha och [erased] Svea och Götha./Tillfällighetspies i Anledning af Vestbanens öppning/d 3.die Novbr 1862.
Unsigned and undated [Written according to the diary on 15.10. 1862]
[DKKk; NKS 3285 4° 5 læg 25

Musical sources:

Orchestral score. Ms. Autograph. Black ink. 1 vol. 84 pp. (26,9 × 34,3 cm)
Svea och Götha/(Framåt)./Tillfällighets stycke i 4 Tablåer/af/Johan Jolin/Musik/af/L. Norman./Partitur.
Signed: 'L. Norman.', undated [1862]
[SSkma; KT Tal-Pjeser med Musik 40

Répétiteur's copy. Ms. Copy. Black ink. 2 pp. (33,7,24,1 cm)
Framåt/Repetitör/No. 13./Gallopp
Unsigned and undated [1862]
[SSkma; KT Tal-Pjeser med Musik 40
This répétiteur's copy contains the music for the divertissement's *Finale Gallop* (score no. 13) and also includes Bournonville's autographed numbers ('1–6' written with black ink) which seem to refer to a separate (not yet traced) choreographic description of this dance.

Parts. Ms. Copy. 34 vol. + 20 vol.
3 vl I, 3 vl II, 2 vla, 4 vlc e cb, fl 1/2, ob 1/2, cl 1/2, fag 1/2, cor 1/2/ 3/4, tr 1/2/3, trb 1/2/3, timp, gr cassa, piatti, tri. On stage: fl, ob 1/ 2, cl 1/2, fag, cor 1/2/3/4, tr 1/2, trb 1/2/3/4, gr cassa, cassa, arpa, org.
Unsigned and undated [1862]
[SSkma; KT Tal-Pjeser med Musik 40

Printed sources:

Printed libretto. 1 vol. 36 pp. (16,2 × 10,2 cm)
Framåt!/National-Divertissement/I en Akt./af/Johan Jolin./(Planen och den sceniska anordningen af A. Bournonville; musiken af L. Norman.)
Stockholm, J. L. Brudin, 1862.
This libretto contains J. Jolin's autographed dedication to Bournonville reading: 'Til Vännen A. Bournonville./När De – ett snille ifrån topp till tå,/Sjelf ovan vid at följa jordens strät,/På mina tunga tankar, satte wingar;/Hvem undrar, om de sökta fluga då ?/Lik Moses watten der ur klippan tvingar,/Så föddes mit 'Framåt!' på ditt – 'framåt'/J.J.'.
[Private collection (Denmark).

19.11.1862
Der Fechter von Ravenna (Fäktaran från Ravenna)
(Stockholm's Royal Theatre, Operahuset).

F. Halm's (pen-name for Eligius Freiherr v. Münch-Bellinghausen) five-act tragedy had first been performed at Vienna's Hof-Burgtheater on 18.10.1854, and was translated into Swedish by the Danish writer, M. A. Goldschmidt in 1862. In his diary and in his Swedish *Journal* Bournonville noted about his staging and the Stockholm première of this work:

5.9.1862: 'Ingen Collationnering paa Fäktaren i Ravenna formedelst Vrøvl af Fru [F.] Westerda[h]l'
20.9.: 'Collationnering på Fäktaren'
7.10.: 'skrifvit sceneri till Fäktaren'
9.10.: 'Fäktaren (scener på Barntheatern.)'
10.10.: 'skrifvit Régie (Fäktaren) […] Instruction […] till Fäktaren'
13.10.: 'Instruction (Fäktaren Bth.)'
14.10.: 'Eftermiddags-Instruction […] Fäktaren (Barnth.)'
18.10.: 'Eftermiddagsprøve paa Fäktaren […] (1.ste 3.die och 4.de Akten.)'
22.10.: 'Eftermiddags=Instruction paa Fäktaren […] (scener å Barntheatern)'
24.10.: 'Fäktaren. (1.e 3.e 4.e Akten Rep: salen) […] D.° 2.dra och 5. Akten (scenen)'
25.10.: 'Fäktaren Gen Rep (utan comparser.)'
28.10.: 'Fäktaren (Gen Rep)'

13.11.: 'Fäktaren från Ravenna (Rolerna)'
15.11.: 'Fäktaren från Ravenna'
17.11.: 'Fäktaren (Gen Rep.)'
18.11.: 'Eftermiddagsprøve paa Fäktaren i Ravenna […] (Gen Rep i Costym) […] den gik udmærket godt og bidrog meget til at hæve mit gjennem Sygdommen sjunkne Humeur'
19.11.: 'I Theatret første Forestilling af Fäktaren från Ravenna der gik udmærket godt og gjorde megen Lÿkke'.

Der Fechter von Ravenna received 8 performances during Bournonville's engagement in Stockholm, the last of which was given on 7.1.1863.

Autograph sources:

Manuscript mise-en-scène. Ms. Autograph. Brown ink. 1 vol. 11 pp. (21,5 × 17,5 cm)
Fäktaren från Ravenna./af/Halm (Munch – Bellinghausen.)/öfver-sättning från tyskan./uppförd 1.ste Gången på Stockholms kongl Theater/d 19.de Novbr/1862.
Unsigned and undated [Written according to the diary on 7.10.1862]
DKKk; NKS 3285 4° 4 læg 2

Manuscript mise-en-scène. Ms. Autograph. Brown ink. 7 pp. (22,6 × 18,2 cm)
Fäktaran från Ravenna./Sceneri
Unsigned and undated [Written according to the diary on 10.10.1862]
[DKKk; NKS 3285 4° 5 læg 12

20.11.1862
Il Trovatore (Trubaduren) (Stockholm's Royal Theatre, Operahuset).
When Bournonville first saw a performance of G. Verdi's four-act lyrical drama in Stockholm on 24.5.1861 he noted in his diary:

'Troubaduren, en rigtig verdisk Opera godt udført'.

Although he did not include *Il Trovatore* among those works mounted personally by him in Stockholm, he was (according to his Swedish *Journal*) supervising all the song and stage rehearsals of this work held between 11.11. and 18.11.1862.

Moreover, the incorporated ballet divertissement in Act III was this year choreographed by his pupil, S. Lund. Lund's choreography (which was also rehearsed by Bournonville on one later occasion on 29.12.1863) seems to have served Bournonville as a model for his own later divertissement in *Il Trovatore*, which he mounted for the 1865 Copenhagen première of this work (*see* 10.9.1865). This is clear from the dance music incorporated by Bournonville in Verdi's lyrical drama in Copenhagen, which uses most of the exact same music employed by Lund in Stockholm in 1862.

In his diary and in his Swedish *Journal* Bournonville noted about his involvement in the 1862 Stockholm performance of *Il Trovatore*.

11.11.1862: 'Trubaduren (sångr.)'
12.11.: 'Trubaduren (Manricos scener.)'
14.11.: 'Trubaduren (scener på sångr.)'
15.11.: 'Trubaduren (Gen. Rep.)'
18.11.: 'Trubaduren (Gen. Rep.)'
19.11.: 'I Theatret Trubaduren for fuldt Huus [O. F.] Stenhammer (Manrico)'

Il Trovatore received 15 performances during Bournonville's engagement in Sweden, the last of which took place on 25.5.1864.

Musical sources:

Orchestral score. Ms. Copy. Black and brown ink. 2 vol. Act I–II 564 pp. of which five are blank, Act III–IV 444 pp. of which two are blank (31,5 × 25,2 cm)
TRUBADUREN/Partitur/1° – 2°/Der Troubadour./1. Act/von G. Verdi/[…]/3° – 4°
Unsigned and undated [c.1860]
[SSkt (Vinstocken), but formerly in SSkma with the call no. KT Operor T 3
This orchestral score is clearly a copy made in Germany and includes only the Swedish translation by C. W. A. Strandberg of S. Cammarano's original text (written underneath the music with black ink). The score was employed for all performances of *Il Trovatore* in Stockholm throughout Bournonville's lifetime and seems to have been in use there until the 1920s. A pencilled note in the second volume (p. 8, reading: 'Ballett') indicates the exact place in Act III (score no. 9) where A. F. Schwartz's music for S. Lund's incorporated divertissement was played.

Orchestral score (Act III divertissement). Ms. Autograph (by A. F. Schwartz). Black ink. 1 vol. 36 pp. (35,2 × 25,3 cm with minor variants)
Balett Musik/till/Trubaduren/Componerad/af/A: F: Schwartz/Partitur
Signed (on the title page): 'A: F. Schwartz', undated [1860]
This orchestral score contains the complete music for A. F. Schwartz's and S. Lund's incorporated divertissement in Act III of Verdi's *Il Trovatore*, except for that of the so-called 'Spansk-National-dans' (*see* the following entry). According to a pencilled note on p. 10 reading: '(Indlæg Spansk dands)' this section (which was danced by three gipsy women) was incorporated between Schwartz's opening *Allegro* movement in G major and the following *meno* section in C major, the latter leading directly into the divertissement's final *Galopp*. Another pencilled note on p. 25 reads: '(Af Lumbye)'. It indicates the *Galopp* to be a work by H. C. Lumbye.

Orchestral score (Act III divertissement). Ms. Copy. Black ink. 1 vol. 20 pp. (30,6 × 24,5 cm)
Flickorna från Xeres/Spansk-Nationaldans.
Unsigned and undated [c.1858]
[SSkt (Vinstocken), but formerly in SSkma with the call no.KT Dans-musik 96.
This orchestral score clearly dates from the 1858 Stockholm premi-ère of S. Lund's Spanish dance, entitled *The Girls from Xeres (Flickorna från Xeres)*, but was at a later stage incorporated in the divertissement that he created for the Stockholm première of G. Verdi's four-act lyrical drama *Il Trovatore*. The score is today preserved as a musical insertion in the Stockholm orchestral score for Verdi's *Il Trovatore*. Lund's original choreographic arrangement of *Flickorna från Xeres, Spansk Nationaldans* was first performed as a separate divertissement at Stockhom's Royal Theatre (Operahuset) on 29.10.1858, and given there 7 times until 30.12.1859. At the later Stockholm premi-ère of Verdi's *Il Trovatore* on 31.5.1860 it was incorporated in Act III, where (according to the poster) it was performed with the new title *Spanish Dance (Spansk dans)*.

Répétiteur's copy (Act III divertissement). Ms. Copy. Black ink. 1 vol. 12 pp. (31,9 × 25 cm with several variants)
4/Trubaduren/Kongl. Teatern/Repetiteur/[…]/Balletten/till/Trubaduren/Repetiteur
Unsigned and undated [c.1860]
[SSkt (Vinstocken), but formerly SSkma with the call no. KT Dans-musik 96.
The répétiteur's copy contains the complete music for A. F. Schwartz's and S. Lund's so-called 'Spansk-Nationaldans' from

1858. The latter is here inserted after the final 'Gallopp' although it was clearly performed as the middle-section of the whole divertissement. Pencilled notes indicate the names of the dancers who performed each section of the divertissement.

No set of parts for the divertissement in the 1862 Stockholm restaging of Verdi's *Il Trovatore* has yet been traced.

26.11.1862
The King's Goddaughter (Konungens guddotter). **Projected staging at Stockholm's Royal Theatre.**
On 20.11.1862 Bournonville wrote a recommendation note to the theatre management of Stockholm's Royal Theatre in which he expressed his opinion about a projected staging of W. Bohlin's one-act so-called 'genre comedy' (*genreteckning*). This note reads as follows:

'Kungens Guddotter
La donnée de cette petite comédie est assez plaisante, jouée avec esprit & finesse elle pourra fournir une addition agréable à notre menu-repertoire.
   Quelques longueurs de dialogue, quelque expressions un peu trop naïves de 'Blanche' pourrant aisément être modifiées. En général, je crois que la pièce réduite en un acte gagnerait considerablement.
   J'ai l'honneur d'être/avec le plus profond respect/M le Baron [i.e. E. F. O. L. von Stedingk]/Votre dévoué serviteur/Stockholm ce 26 Novbr/1862./Auguste Bournonville'.

In spite of Bournonville's positive assessment of this work it was never mounted during his engagement at Stockholm's Royal Theatre. Bohlin's comedy was not given its Stockholm première until some twenty years later, when it was premièred at Dramatiska Theatern on 18.12.1882 receiving 11 performances there.

Autograph sources:

Recommendation note. Ms. Autograph. Brown ink. 2 pp. (23 × 14,3 cm)
[...] Kungens Guddotter/[...]/cette petite comedie [...]
Signed and dated: 'Stockholm ce 26 Novbr/1862.'
[SSdt; KTA, E2A Ink. breve 1862/63, 26.11.1862

29.11.1862
Les Ganaches. **Projected staging at Stockholm's Royal Theatre.**
In his diary Bournonville noted on this day about V. Sardou's four-act comedy (first performed at the Théâtre Gymnase in Paris on 29.10.1862), which was planned by the theatre management to be staged at Stockholm's Royal Theatre during the 1862–63 season:

'Eftermiddagen hjemme og læst Les Ganaches af [V.] Sardou. I mine Tanker et Makværk og umuligt paa vor Scene'.

As a result of Bournonville's strong opposition to this project it was never mounted in Stockholm.

2.12.1862
The Slanderer (Smædeskriveren eller Talentet paa Afvej) **(the Casino Theatre).**
According to a series of notes in Bournonville's diary and three letters written to him from the Danish writer, H. P.

Holst, on 16.4., 30.4., and 13.9.1862 (now in DKKk, call no. NKS 3258 A 4°, V, facs. 6, nos. 469–471), Bournonville's earlier Stockholm mise-en-scène for J. Jolin's five-act play (*see* 5.4.1862) seems to have been reused by Holst when *The Slanderer* was given its Copenhagen première in his Danish translation. This theory is supported by Bournonville's notes in his Stockholm diary, in which he stated about the Copenhagen staging:

21.4.1862: 'Brev fra [...] H P Holst, om Smädeskrifvaren hvilken Affaire jeg strax klarede med [J.] Jolin og besvarede paa staaende Fod'
5.5.: 'Brev fra Holst om Jolins Manuscript'
6.5.: 'Expederet Manuscriptet til H P Holst med Dam[p]skibet Carl X'.

Moreover, in his letter to Bournonville on 30.4.1862 Holst stated:

'Jeg venter Stykket med Længsel for at kunne tage en Bestemmelse; Mod Conditionerne har jeg Intet at indvende under den Forudsætning, at Stykket er brugeligt for os. Det tvivler jeg ikke om, da Du troer det; men det er dog nødvendigt, at jeg selv faaer Troen i Hænderne. Tjen mig derfor i at paaskynde Afsendelsen, for at vi snart kan komme til et endeligt Resultat. At Du vil sende dit Scenearrangement med er naturligviis en yderst behagelig Tilgift; ligeledes er jeg aldeles enig med Dig om at Stykket ikke bør localiseres for ikke at berøve det det piquante, der kan ligge i dets couleur local'.

Smædeskriveren eller Talentet paa Afvej reached a total of 9 performances at the Casino Theatre, the last of which was given on 9.1.1863.

   No autographed sources by Bournonville relating to the Copenhagen mise-en-scène of Jolin's play have yet been traced. This seems to indicate that it was his own personal copy of the Stockholm's mise-en-scène which was sent to Holst in Copenhagen on 6.5.1862 (now in DKKk, call no. NKS 3285 4° 5 læg 2).

8.12.1862
Las Hermanas, Spanish Charactersdance (Spansk Characters-Dans) **(uncredited) performed by A. and C. Healey (Stockholm's Royal Theatre, Operahuset).**
This (uncredited) dance is almost certainly a revised version, arranged by Bournonville for two women, based on his much earlier *Pas de trois* divertissement, entitled *Las Hermanas de Sevilla, Spanish Dance (Spansk Dands).* That dance, in turn, was originally created for and first performed by the three Price cousins, Juliette, Amalia and Sophie, as part of a special charity performance given at Copenhagen's Court Theatre on 4.6.1851.

   In his 1862 diary and in his Swedish *Journal* Bournonville listed three rehearsals of *Las Hermanas* and noted after the first Stockholm performance:

'Las hermanas, der behagede meget'.

No musical sources for this dance have yet been traced in the music archive of Stockholm's Royal Theatre (now in SSkma). This seems to indicate that the 1851 Copenhagen orchestral score and set of parts for C. C. Møller's *Las Hermanas de Sevilla* (now in DKKk, call nos. C II, 118, and KTB 239) might have been brought to Stockholm either by the Healey sisters, or by Bournonville in the early autumn of 1862. *Las Hermanas* was given twice in Stockholm, the last time on 12.1.1863. It is not possible to identify the dance any further.

20.12.1862
Robert le Diable (Robert af Normandie) (Stockholm's Royal Theatre, Operahuset).

The 1862 Stockholm restaging of G. Meyerbeer's five-act grand opera from 1831 (first performed in Stockholm on 10.5.1839) represents the second time Bournonville mounted this work outside Denmark (*see* 15.12.1841 and 23.7. 1855). While the opera was clearly produced under his general direction, the choreography of the Act III divertissement was explicitly credited on the poster to the French dancer and choreographer, T. Martin – in spite of the fact that (according to his diary) Bournonville directed all rehearsals of 'Balletscenen i 3.de Akten' held between 8.12. and 19.12.1862. About the production he noted in the diary and in his Swedish *Journal* as follows:

12.11.1862: 'Decorationsprof till <u>Robert</u>'
3.12.: 'Scene = Arrangement paa Robert [...] 1.ste och 2.dra Akten'
4.12.: '<u>Robert</u> sceneri (4.de och 5.te Akten.)'
5.12.: 'Eftermiddagsprøve paa Robert med [C. O.] Arnoldsson [...] och [P. A. J.] Willman'
6.12.: 'Robert. (Instruction Barntheatern)'
8.12.: 'Robert. 1.e och 2.dra Akten vid piano [...] D.° Balletscenen i 3.e Akten'
10.12.: '<u>Robert</u> 3.die Akten (vid piano)'
13.12.: 'Robert (4.de och 5.te Akten vid piano)'
16.12.: '<u>Robert</u> 1.ste 2.dra 3.e Akten. (Gen Rep) [...] D.° 4.e 5.e Akten (Gen Rep.) [...] D.° <u>Decorationer</u>'
18.12.: 'Prøve paa Robert [...] Gen Rep'
19.12.: 'Generalprøve paa Robert. [T.] Martins Ballet gjør en charmant Virkning – frappant'
20.12.: 'Robert som blev ÿpperlig udført. Balletten gjorde stormende Lÿkke. Huset var aldeles fuldt'.

The 1862 production of *Robert le Diable* received 15 performances during Bournonville's engagement in Stockholm, the last of which took place on 10.6.1864.

Autograph sources:

Manuscript mise-en-scène (incomplete). Ms. Autograph. Black ink. 1 pp. (17,3 × 11,4 cm)
<u>4.° Akten.</u>
Unsigned and undated [Written most probably in December 1862]
[DKKk; NKS 3285 4° 4 læg 1 ad 24r
This (incomplete) mise-en-scène (written in Swedish) almost certainly dates from Bournonville's 1862 staging of *Robert le Diable* in Stockholm.

Musical sources:

Orchestral printed score with several manuscript insertions. 3 vol.
Act I–II 367 pp., Act III 246 pp., Act IV–V 268 pp. + 16 pp. of 'Supplements' (33,7 × 23,8 cm)
Robert le Diable/Opéra en 5 Actes
Paris, M. Schlesinger, pl. no. 1155 [1831]
[SSkma; KT Operor R 3
This printed orchestral score was used for all performances of *Robert le Diable* in Stockholm since its première there on 10.5.1839 and throughout Bournonville's lifetime.

No répétiteur's copy for *Robert le Diable* has yet been traced in SSkma.

Parts. Ms. Copy. 34 vol + 18 vol.
3 vl I, 3 vl II, 2 vla, 4 vlc e cb, fl picc, fl 1/2, ob 1/2, cl 1/2, fag 1/2, cor 1/2/3/4, tr, trb 1/2/3, oph, timp, gr cassa e piatti, gong, arpa. On stage: fl picc, ob, cl 1/2, fag 1/2, tr princ, tr 1/2/3/4, trb 1/2/3, oph, gr cassa, piatti, tri.
Unsigned and undated [1839–1863]
[SSkma; KT Operor R 3
This set of parts dates from the 1839 Stockholm première of Meyerbeer's opera and was used for all performances of it there throughout Bournonville's lifetime.

1863

12.1.1863
Le Jeu de l'Amour et du hasard (Kärlekens Försyn) (Stockholm's Royal Theatre, Operahuset).

The Stockholm première of P. C. de C. de Marivaux's three-act comedy (first performed by *Les Comediens Italiens ordinaires du Roi* in Paris on 23.1.1730, and freely translated into Swedish by L. Josephsson in 1863) was mounted by Bournonville with a new ending written in collaboration with the Swedish play-writer F. Hedberg. In the diary and in his Swedish *Journal* Bournonville stated about the performance:

26.11.1862: 'Læst Theaterstykker'
19.12.: 'Collationnering paa <u>Kärleken och Slumpen</u>'
23.12.: 'Skrifvit sceneri till <u>Kärleken och Slumpen</u>'
27.12., 29.12., 30.12., and 31.12.: '<u>Kärleken och Slumpen</u> (Instruction Barnth.)'
2.1.1863: '<u>Kärleken och Slumpen</u> (Rep salen.) [...] K & S. (Instr. Barntheatren) [...] Prøve paa Les jeux de l'amour & du hazard'
3.1., 5.1., and 6.1.: '<u>Kärleken och Slumpen</u> (Gen Rep.)'
7.1.: 'Prøve paa Les jeux de l'amour & du hazard der nu har faaet Navnet <u>Kärlekens försÿn</u> og en ny Slutning som jeg har lavet i Forening med [F.] Hedberg'
9.1. and 10.1.: '<u>Kärlekens försÿn.</u> (Gen Rep.)'
12.1.: 'Kärlekens försÿn (Minnesrep. R. S:) [...] for første Gang <u>Kärlekens forsÿn</u> der gik udmærket godt paa Fru [Z.] <u>Hedin</u> nær, der overdrev sin Rolle i en betydelig Grad og forstyrrede den Glæde, jeg havde ventet mig af Stÿkket'.

Le Jeu de l'Amour et du hasard received 14 performances during Bournonville's engagement in Stockholm, the last of which was given on 3.2.1864.

Autograph sources:

Manuscript mise-en-scène. Ms. Autograph. Brown ink and pencil. 7 pp. (22,7 × 18,1 cm)
<u>Kärleken och Slumpen</u>/Comedie i 3 Akter./af/<u>Marivaux.</u>/<u>Sceneri.</u>
Unsigned and dated: '<u>d 23 Decbre</u> 1862.'
[DKKk; NKS 3285 4° 5 læg 16

Manuscript mise-en-scène. Ms. Autograph. Black ink. 1 vol. 9 pp. (21,5 × 17,5 cm)
<u>Kärlekens försÿn.</u>/(Le jeu de l'amour & du hazard [*sic*])/Comedie i tre Akter/af/Marivaux./uppförd <u>d 12.de Januari</u> 1863.
Unsigned and dated: '<u>d 23.de Decbr 1862.</u>'
[DKKk; NKS 3285 4° 4 læg 2

24.1.1863
Day Waxes! (Dagen gryr!) (Stockholm's Royal Theatre, Operahuset).

On 26.11.1862 Bournonville wrote a recommendation note

to the theatre management of Stockholm's Royal Theatre in which he expressed his opinion about a planned staging of F. Hedberg's new five-act historical drama. This note reads as follows:

'Dagen grẙr.

Ce drame, quant au dialogue est ecrit avec un talent incontestable, il-y-a des scènes d'une facture excellente (p: ex: celle du paysan dale-carlien avec le Roi). Le caractère du Roi et celui de Brask me semblent tracés de main de maître et la petite intrigue d'amour tissue dans ce grand évenement politique est touchée très délicatement.

Voilà à mes yeux les vrais mérites de la pièce et qui la rendent superieure au drame de Børjeson 'Solen sjunker' [i.e. *Sunset. The final Days of Gustaf I (Solen sjunker. Gustaf I:s sista dagar)*. Historical play in four acts by J. Börjesson, premièred at Stockholm's Royal Theatre (Mindre Theatern) on 13.3.1856 and performed there 29 times until 11.2.1863].

———

Il ne peut donc nullement être question de rejetter un pareil ouvrage, mais il ne faut pas non plus s'en dissimuler les imperfections. Il est par exemple toujours scabreux de mêler dans les arts – une dose trop forte de politique & de religion.

Sans doute on ne peut faire de l'histoire sans ces deux éléments mais nous arrivons là ou problème si c'est l'histoire qui doit servir au développement des caractères & des situations ou bien vice versa. Ici l'on a peut-être trop compté sur les allusions locales & momentanées. – Si dans l'effervesence des passions de parties l'on réussit à exciter une démonstration par l'effet des phrases fortement accentuées. La pièce aura le mérite d'attirer la foule mais est-ce là une mission digne du théâtre royal? Si au contraire les tirades sentencieuses passent tranquillement – elles risquent de tomber dans le fastidieux et présenter plutôt un compté rendu des debats parlementaires qu'un drame à caractères. – En général, je crois qu'il foudra diminuer autant que possible les éffets d'église, de même que le bal de la cour pourrait comme dans le comédies de Scribe être supposée dans la pièce atténuée.

La romance du [word illegible] semble tout à fait hors-d'oeuvre et la conclusion de la pièce est un peu trop languissante'.

In his diary and in his Swedish *Journal* he noted about the staging of this work, which was mounted in a reduced four-act version with music by J. A. Söderman, A. F. Schwartz and other (not yet identified) composers:

25.11.1862: 'Läst: Dagen grẙr ([F.] Hedberg)'
26.11.: 'Conférence med Hedberg'
20.12.: 'Collationnering. Dagen grẙr'
22.12.: 'Collationnering 4.e & 5' Akten af Dagen gryr, arbeidet med Hedberg'
23.12.: 'Decorationsmøte för Dagen grẙr'
30.12.: 'skrifvit sceneri'
13.1.1863: 'Sceneriprøve paa Dagen grẙr […] (1.e 2.dra & 3.die Akten.)'
15.1.: 'Prøve og Indstudering paa Dagen grẙr […] (4.de Akten. 5.te borttfallen) […] Personallister till Dagen grẙr'
16.1.: 'Eftermiddags Arrangementsprøve paa Dagen grẙr […] (3.die Akts sceneri)'
17.1.: 'Dagen gryr (Gen Rep.)'
19.1.: 'Stor Prøve paa Dagen grẙr […] 4.e 3.e och 1.ste Akterne (Gen Rep:) […] D.° (Instruction.)'
21.1. and 22.1.: 'Dagen grẙr (Gen Rep)'
23.1.: 'Generalprøve paa Dagen grẙr. Alt i Orden'
24.1.: 'Forberedelser til Aftenens første Forestilling. Det var ligesom ifjor paa Gustaf den Tredies Fødselsdag at et nyt national Stykke blev opført og Dagen grẙr gik med overordentligt og fortjent Bifald. [A. T.] Schwartz som Gustaf Wasa [C. G.] Dahlqvist som Biskop Brask og Swensson [i.e. W. C. A. Svenson] som Dalkarlen Peder Ulfson vare

fortræffelige og det Hele gik med Kraft og Ensemble. Jeg var meget glad over denne Succès og gratulerede Hedberg der ogsaa takkede mig for min Medvirkning'.

According to the musical sources in SSkma, Söderman's music was performed in Act I, in which it accompanied the opening chorus, entitled «Heliga Guds moder», sung by the nuns.

Moreover, a *March* (originally composed by A. F. Schwartz for the Stockholm restaging on 12.4.1859 of J. G. Naumann's three-act lyrical drama from 1786 *Gustaf Wasa*) was included in scene 3 of Act III. It had been choreographed by S. Lund in 1859. In *Day Waxes!* this *March* is followed by a series of five fanfares, all of which were composed by Söderman.

Finally, in the opening scene of Act IV two more dance numbers (a *Molto maestoso* and a *Molto moderato*) were included and played by an orchestra seated on the stage. They employed music by a not yet identified composer and are described by Bournonville in his manuscript mise-en-scène as follows:

'Dans i tredie rummet i fonden (sakta musik)/Dansen upphörer./ […]/Konungen […] går atföljd af de andra Par in i Dans=/salongen, hvor dansen börjar ånye/NB Stegena äro gående och långsamma.)/figurerne helt enkla. (Rond och Chaîne.)'.

Day Waxes! received 17 performances during Bournonville's engagement in Stockholm, the last of which was given on 28.8.1863.

Autograph sources:

Recommendation note. Ms. Autograph. Brown ink. 3 pp. (23 × 14,3 cm)
[…]Dagen grẙr […]
Signed and dated: 'Stockholm ce 26 Novbr/1862.'
[SSdt; KTA, E2A Ink. breve 1862/63, 26.11.1862]

Manuscript mise-en-scène. Ms. Autograph. Black ink and pencil (including a pencilled drawing for 'A Midsummernight's Dream' ('En Midsommernatsdrøm'). 19 pp. (22,8 × 18,1 cm)
Dagen grẙr./Sceneri.
Signed and dated: 'Stockholm d 29.de Decbr 1862.' [Written according to Bournonville's Swedish *Journal* on 30.12.1862]
[DKKk; NKS 3285 4° 5 læg 8

Manuscript mise-en-scène. Ms. Autograph. Black ink. 1 vol. 15 pp. (21,5 × 17,5 cm)
Dagen grẙr./Historiskt Skådespel/i fẙra akter/af./Fr. Hedberg:/ uppförd 1.ste Gången d 24.de Januari/1863.
Signed and dated: 'Stockholm d 29 Decbr 1862.' [Written according to Bournonville's Swedish *Journal* on 30.12.1862]
[DKKk; NKS 3285 4° 4 læg 2

Musical sources:

Orchestral score. Ms. Autograph. Black ink and pencil. 1 vol. 7 pp. (33,4 × 23,5 cm)
Dagen gryr!/Fanfarer./Partitur
Unsigned and undated [1863]
[SSkma; KT Tal-pjeser med Musik D 18

No répétiteur's copy for *Day Waxes!* has yet been traced in SSkma.

Parts. Ms. Copy. 17 + 4 vol.
fl 1/2, ob 1/2, cl 1/2, fag 1/2, cor 1/2, tr 1/2/3, trb 1/2/3, timp. On

stage: 'Enkel Quartett' (vl I, vl II, vla, vlc). Vocal parts (Soprano 1/2, Alto 1/2).
Unsigned and undated [1863 and earlier]
[SSkma; KT Tal-pjeser med Musik D 18

16.2.1863
L'Avare (Den Girige) (Stockholm's Royal Theatre, Operahuset).
On 20.11.1862 Bournonville wrote a recommendation note to the theatre management of Stockholm's Royal Theatre in which he expressed his opinion about the then planned re-staging of J. B. Molière's five-act comedy from 1668–69 (first performed in Stockholm on 2.10.1755, and retranslated into Swedish by M. Schück in 1863). His note reads as follows:

'<u>Den Girige</u> af Molière
————

La traduction me parait très convenable, mais succeptible de quelques petites retouches ça & là.

Sans profaner le chef=d'œuvre je crois que les tirades des amoureux pourraient subir quelques raccourcissements. (opérés par Mr [F.] Hedberg.)
La distribution des rôles:
me semble la suivante:

Harpagon .... Mr. [C. G.] Dahlqvist.
Anselme .... '[R. G.] Broman
Elise. Harpagons dotter Mlle .... [A. H. M.] Sandberg
Marianne Anselmes Dotter .... '[A. O.] Ramstén
Cléante (Harpagons son) .... Herr [G.] Fredriksson
Valérie (Anselmes son) .... '[C. G.] Sundberg
Frosine .... Fru [B. C. M.] Bock
Simon (mäklare) .... Herr [L.] Josephs[s]on
Mäster Jacques Kock och Kusk Herr .... [G. V.] Sandstedt
La flèche (betjent hos Cléante) .... '[J.] Jolin
En Poliskommissairie .... '[C.] Lundin
Brindavoine .... '[G.] Nor[r]by
La Merluche .... '[G. R.] Ohlsson
Jungfru Claude (slave person) .... M.lle [Z. A.] Lindqvist

Stockholm ce 20 Novbr 1862./très humblement/August Bournonville'.

In his diary and in his Swedish *Journal* he noted about his staging of the work:

20.11.1862: 'Embedsforretninger, læst og skrevet hjemme'
19.1.1863: '<u>skrifvit sceneri</u>'
25.1.: 'skrifvit sceneri till <u>Den Girige</u>'
30.1.: '<u>skrifvit sceneri</u>'
3.2.: 'Prøve paa <u>Den Girige</u> (Sceneri) […] (Arrangement)'
6.2.: 'Prøve paa Den Girige […] (Gen Rep.) <u>1.ste 2.dra och 3.die Akten</u>'
7.2.: 'Eftermiddagsprøve paa <u>Den Girige</u> […] (Gen. Rep.) 3.die 4.de och 5.te akten'
9.2.: '<u>Den Girige</u> (Instr Barnth.)'
10.2., 11.2., 12.2., and 14.2.: '<u>Den Girige</u> (Gen. Rep.)'
16.2.: '<u>Den Girige</u> (Gen. Rep.) […] I Theatret <u>Den Girige</u> […] Stykket gik i mange Heenseender godt men i andre svarede det hverken til Publikums eller mine Forventninger. Dahlqvist havde ypperlige Momenter. I det Hele maa det ansees for en skole til Opretholdelse af den dramatiske Kunst'.

L'Avare received 3 performances during Bournonville's engagement in Stockholm, the last of which was given on 22.2. 1863.

Autograph sources:

Recommendation note. Ms. Autograph. Brown ink. 2 pp. (23 × 14,3 cm)
[…]<u>Den Girige</u> af Molière […]
Signed and dated: 'Stockholm ce 20 Novbr 1862.'
[SSdt; KTA, E2A Ink. breve 1862/63, 20.11.1862

Manuscript mise-en-scène (incomplete). Ms. Autograph. Black ink. 1 p. (21,5 × 17,5 cm)
<u>Den Girige</u>/<u>Comedie i fem Akter af Molière</u>/<u>Personerne</u>.
Unsigned and undated [Written according to Bournonville's Swedish *Journal* on either 19.1. or 25.1.1863]
[DKKk; NKS 3285 4° 4 læg 2

Manuscript mise-en-scène. Ms. Autograph. Brown ink. 8 pp. (22,8 × 18,3 cm)
<u>Den Girige</u>/<u>Sceneri</u>.
Signed and dated: 'Stockholm d 30. Januar 1863' [Written according to Bournonville's Swedish *Journal* between 25.1. and 30.1 1863]
[DKKk; NKS 3285 4° 5 læg 13

3.3.1863
A Bridal Dance (Brudesang og Dands) projected for a ball at Stockholm's Royal Theatre to celebrate the nuptials of the Danish Princess Alexandra, and the Prince of Wales.
According to entries in Bournonville's diary he planned on this day to choreograph a bridal dance for a ball given by the Danish ambassador to Sweden, Count W. Scheel-Plessen, in the foyer of Stockholm's Royal Theatre (Operahuset) on 10.3.1863. The ball was given to celebrate the nuptials of the Danish Princess Alexandra and the Prince of Wales (later King Edward VII). Bournonville's notes about this projected dance read as follows:

3.3.1863: 'En Idée til Minister Grev [W. Scheel-] Plessens Bal i Anledning af Prindsesse Alexandras Bryllup'
4.3.: 'Løbet den hele Eftermiddag om Iværksættelsen af min Idée, nemlig en Brudesang og Dands – <u>Dansk</u> og <u>Engelsk</u>'
5.3.: 'Min Idée uudførlig'.

The dance (for which no written choreographic sources have yet been traced) was not carried out because, as Bournonville himself put it: 'Min Idée uudførlig'.

9.3.1863
Eine Familie (En Familj). Projected restaging at Stockholm's Royal Theatre.
On this day Bournonville wrote an interesting recommendation note to the theatre management of Stockholm's Royal Theatre, in which he expressed his strong opposition to a projected restaging of C. Birch-Pfeiffer's five-act play with an epilogue (originally premièred at Berlin's Königlichen Theater on 19.11.1846, and first performed in Stockholm on 8.4.1847). This note reads as follows:

'En Famille.
Il est très possible que ce soit une bonne pièce, mais je dois m'avouer incompétent par la raison toute simple qu'ayant vécu pour <u>l'idéal d'une profession d'artiste capable d'ennoblir & non d'avilir l'âme</u>, je ressens la plus grande répugnance devant le portrait d'une courtisanne=actrice ou danseuse.

Les misères de ce monde appartiennent à tous les états, pourquoi donc le théâtre doit-il toujours servir à corroborer un préjugé aussi cruel qu'injuste?

Très humblement/ce <u>9 Mars</u>/<u>1863</u>/August Bournonville'.

In spite of Bournonville's outspoken opposition towards the staging of Birch-Pfeiffer's play it was mounted during his engagement in Stockholm at Dramatiska Theatern on 11.1. 1864, but without any involvement on Bournonville's part.

Autograph sources:

Recommendation note. Ms. Autograph. Black ink. 2 pp. (18,1 × 11 cm)
[…]<u>En Famille.</u> […]
Signed and dated: 'ce <u>9 Mars</u>/<u>1863</u>'
[SSdt; KTA, E2A Ink. breve 1862/63, 9.3.1863

14.3.1863
Le Dieu et la bayadère, ou La Courtisane amoureuse (Brama och Bajaderen) (Stockholm's Royal Theatre, Operahuset).
This performance represents the Stockholm première of D.-F.-E. Auber's two-act opera-ballet (*see also* 7.2.1841). Its first performance was given as part of a special charity performance for Bournonville. In his diary and in his Swedish *Journal* he noted about the staging:

20.10.1862: 'Begyndt Indstudering paa Brama og Bayadèren til Søstrene [A. and C.] Healey'
22.10.: 'Dansen till <u>Brama</u>'
23.10.: 'Indstudering til Healeys […] (Brama.)'
25.10., 28.10., and 29.10.: 'Brama med Healeys'
21.11.: 'Om Eftermiddagen Indstudering paa Brama'
24.11.: 'Paa Theatret, indstuderet Dands til Brama og Bayaderen […] (Barntheatern)'
25.11.: 'Indstuderinger […] <u>Brama</u> (Ballett.)'
26.11.: 'Brama (Healeys)'
27.11.: 'Brama (Ballett.)'
28.11.: 'Lection (Healey.) Brama'
23.12.: 'Decorationsmöte för […] <u>Bayaderen</u>'
1.2.1863: 'skrifvit <u>régie</u> till <u>Brama och Bayaderen</u>'
8.2. and 9.2.: '<u>Brama och Bayadèren</u> (sångr.)'
10.2.: 'Indstudering paa Bayaderen begyndt'
11.2.: 'Prøve paa […] Bayaderen […] (sångr.) […] <u>Brama</u> (Barntheatern) […] <u>Brama</u> (Zoloé Barntheatern)'
13.2.: 'Komponeret og indstuderet den sidste Dands til Bayaderen […] Eftermiddagsprøve paa Bayaderen […] (sangr) […] (Ballet: Barntheatern) […] (Ensemble Barntheatern)'
14.2.: '<u>Brama</u> […] Indstudering med Agnes Healey'
15.2.: 'Brama (sångr)'
16.2.: 'Brama (Barntheatern) […] D.° (sångr)'
17.2.: 'Costym=Möte på Brama[…] Brama (Ballet=repetition)'
18.2.: '<u>Brama</u> (piano Barntheatern.)'
19.2.: '<u>Brama</u> (Instr: Healey.)'
20.2.: 'Stor Claverprøve paa Brama […] (Rep. salen Chör och Sång) […] D.° ([C. O.] Arnoldson och Agnes Healey))'
21.2.: 'Prøver paa Bayaderen […] (Scener och Ballett vid piano)'
23.2.: 'Brama (Ballett, Barntheatern)'
24.2.: 'Eftermiddagsprøve paa Bayaderen […] (scener, Barntheatern)'
26.2.: '<u>Brama</u> […] Prøve med Healeyerne'
2.3.: '<u>Brama</u> (Healey's)'
3.3.: 'Arrangement paa Brama og Bayaderen […] (sceneri vid piano.)'
4.3.: 'Musikprøve paa Brama […] (Musik=Collationnering)'
5.3.: 'besørget Annoncer om min Benefice Forestilling […] Brama (Ballet.) […] D.° (Scener [C. J. J.] Uddman & [A.] Healey.)'
6.3.: 'Første Generalprøve paa Brama og Bayaderen […] (1.ste Akten)'
7.3. and 8.3.: 'Brama (sångr)'
9.3.: '(de fleste Billetter til min Beneficeforestilling udsolgte) […] <u>Brama</u> (Musik=Collationnering) […] D.° (Grupper och Ballett.)'
10.3.: '1.ste Generalprøve paa Brama'
11.3.: 'Generalprøve paa Brama der gik smukt'
12.3.: 'Brama (Ballet) Barnth.'
13.3.: 'Tidlig paa Theatret, prøvet Decorationer, derpaa Generalprøve paa min Benefice'
14.3.: 'spektakel. (Bournonvilles recet.) […] Brama og Bayaderen, der gik udmærket godt uagtet Mlle [F.] Andrée var meget syg. Agnes Healey gjorde Underværker i Zoloés Parti og høstede stormende Bifald. Huset var paa det Nærmeste aldeles fuldt, men Enkedronningens [i.e. Queen Joséphine Maximilienne Eugénie Napoléone] Fødselsdag med tilhørende Sager forhindrede Hoffet fra at bivaane Forestillingen. Publikum var i Begjyndelsen meget lunkent, men varmedes op til Slutning indtil virkelig Begeistring. Jeg blev stærkt fremkaldt og mødte med Agnes Healey ved Haanden'.

Bournonville's 1863 staging of *Brama och Bajaderen* reached a total of 6 performances in Stockholm (the last given on 22.5. 1863) after which it went out of the Swedish repertory.

Autograph sources:

Manuscript mise-en-scène (incomplete). Ms. Autograph. Brown ink. 1 vol. 3 pp. (21,5 × 17,5 cm)
<u>Brama och Bayadèren</u>/Opera i twå [*sic*] <u>Akter</u>/af/<u>Scribe och Auber</u>/uppförd første Gången d 14.de Mars 1863.
Unsigned and undated [Written according to Bournonville's Swedish *Journal* on 1.2.1863]
[DKKk; NKS 3285 4° 4 læg 1

Musical sources:

Orchestral printed score with manuscript insertions. 2 vol. Act I 439 pp., Act II 240 pp. (32 × 25,4 cm).
Die Liebende Bayadere/oder/Der Gott und die Bayadere/Oper mit Ballet und Pantomime/in 2 Aufzügen
Mainz, B. Schott´s Söhnen, pl. no. 3410 [February 1831]
[SSkma; KT Operor B 3
This orchestral score was used for all performances of *Le Dieu et la bayadère* in Stockholm.

No répétiteur's copy for *Le Dieu et la bayadère* has yet been traced in SSkma.

Parts. Ms. Copy. 35 vol.
3 vl I, 3 vl II, 2 vla, 4 vlc e cb, fl picc, fl 1/2, ob 1/2, cl 1/2, fag 1/2, cor 1/2/3/4, tr 1/2, trb 1/2/3/4, timp, gr cassa, tri, arpa.
Unsigned and undated [1863]
[SSkma; KT Operor B 3

26.3.1863
The Mail Robbers (Poströfvarne). Projected staging at Stockholm's Royal Theatre.
On this day Bournonville wrote a recommendation note to the theatre management of Stockholm's Royal Theatre, in which he exressed his opinion about a projected staging of this play by a not yet identified Swedish writer. This note reads as follows:

'Poströfvarne
J'ai trouvé dans cette pièce des étincelles de verve comique et une idée primitive capable de produire une intrigue assez plaisante <u>mais</u> … l'auteur s'est fourvoyé dans des longueurs interminables en s'éloignant sans cesse du bu de l'action – Il-y-a la-dedans des scènes jouables mais la pièce entière me parait impossible – autant pour les spectateurs que pour les acteurs.
    très humblement/ce 26 Mars 1863./August Bournonville'.

No play of this title was ever mounted in Stockholm.

Autograph sources:

Recommendation note. Ms. Autograph. Black ink. 1 p. (21,3 × 13,4 cm)
[…]Poströfvarne […]
Signed and dated: 'ce 26 Mars 1863'
[SSdt; KTA, E2A Ink. breve 1862/63, 26.3.1863

26.3.1863
Rosa and Rosita (Rosa och Rosita/Rosa og Rosita) (Stockholm's Royal Theatre, Operahuset).

In his diary and in his Swedish *Journal* Bournonville noted about his staging of this, the Swedish première of the Danish playwright, C. Andersen's two-act comedy (first performed at Copenhagen's Royal Theatre on 11.2.1862, and in 1863 freely arranged and translated into Swedish by F. Hedberg):

12.9.1862: 'Modtaget Rosa og Rosita Manuskript'
21.10.: 'Collationnering Rosa och Rosita'
4.11. and 5.11.: 'Eftermiddags=Instruction paa Rosa och Rosita'
11.11.: '(Barntheatern) […] Prøve paa Rosa og Rosita, høist ufuldkommen da Fru [H. L. C.] Deland var borte formedelst Mandens [i.e. P. J. Deland] høist betænkelige Tilstand – Han ligger for Døden!'
10.3.1863: 'Collationnering, Rosa och Rosita'
14.3.: 'skrevet og arrangeret'
19.3.: 'Første Repetition paa Rosa och Rosita […] (sceneri og Dialog.)'
21.3.: 'Prøve paa Rosa och Rosita der begynder at gaae meget godt […] (Gen. Rep.) […] Eftermiddags Instruction paa samme Stykke […] (M.lle [G. J. C] Åberg och Herr [V. L.] Hartman.)'
23.3., 24.3., and 25.3.: 'Rosa och Rosita (Gen Rep.)'
26.3.: 'Rosa och Rosita (Gen Rep.) […] I Theatret for første Gang Rosa och Rosita der gik udmærket godt og gjorde megen Lykke […] Huset var kun halvt besat!'.

Rosa and Rosita was given 18 times during Bournonville's engagement in Stockholm, the last time on 16.12.1863.

Autograph sources:

Manuscript mise-en-scène (incomplete). Ms. Autograph. Black ink. 1 p. (21,5 × 17,5 cm)
Rosa och Rosita./Comedie i två Akter af Författaren/til 'En arfs och kärleks fråga./Personarna.
Unsigned and undated [1862–1863]
[DKKk; NKS 3285 4° 4 læg 2

Manuscript mise-en-scène. Ms. Autograph. Brown ink and pencil. 8 pp. (22,2 × 18,1 and 22,8 × 18,5 cm)
Rosa och Rosita/Comedie i två Akter./Ofversättning/Sceneri
Signed and dated: 'Stockholm d. 14 Mars 1863'
[DKKk; NKS 3285 4° 5 læg 23

18.4.1863
Le Prophète (Profeten) (Stockholm's Royal Theatre, Operahuset).

The 1863 Stockholm restaging of G. Meyerbeer's five-act opera (premièred at the Paris Opéra on 16.4.1849, and first performed in the Swedish capital on 8.11.1852, *see also* 10.3. 1858) was carried out under Bournonville's direction and choreographic supervision. It was mounted this year as a result of the temporary engagement of the famous German tenor, J. A. Tichatscheck, who performed the rôle of *Johan von Leyden*. The Act III ballet divertissement *Les Patineurs* was on this occasion choreographed and staged by the Swedish choreographer, A. Selinder.

Bournonville had included *Le Prophète* in a list of projected opera stagings which he had written for Copenhagen's Royal Theatre six years earlier, on 30.10.1857. That project, however, was never carried out by him, and the opera has to this day not been performed in Denmark. Consequently, the 1863 Swedish restaging represents the first and only time he was involved in a staging of Meyerbeer's opera.

In his Swedish *Journal* and his diary he included an interesting description of Tichatscheck's stage appearance and also wrote of his own involvement in the production of *Le Prophète*. They read as follows:

4.4.1863: 'Besøg af [J. A.] Tichatscheck, den berømte Dresdener Tenorist (høit oppe i de 50!)'
7.4.: 'Tichatscheck (Han besidder endnu betydelige Stemmemidler og er fuld af Ild og Kraft)'
9.4.: '1.ste Debut af Tichatscheck […] han har virkelig endnu betydelig Volumen i Stemmen, skjøndt Omfanget er ringere, Matheden er langtfra correct men Foredraget interessant. Der er meget indre Liv hos ham og han henriver i visse Momenter. Dog er hans Spil og hele Holdning hverken godt eller smukt, og der er en vis tydsk Travlhed over ham, der ofte bliver latterlig. Summa Summarum. Det er en rigtig Kunstner med store Egenskaber og store Feil. – Man kan lære Endeel af ham men han bør ikke efterlignes'
10.4.: 'mangfoldige Embedsforetninger i Anledning af ovennævntes Gæsteroller […] Kl 6 Profeten (sång)'
11.4.: 'Kl 11 Profeten (sång)'
12.4.: 'Kl 11 Profeten (scener vid Piano)'
13.4.: 'Kl 1/2 11. Profeten (vid Piano) […] Prøve paa Profeten bestyret af [F.] Arlberg'
15.4.: 'Kl 6 Profeten (Gen. Rep.) […] Aftenprøve paa Profeten'
16.4.: 'Skridtskoballetten (på theatern) […] Profeten (Gen Rep. 5.te Akten)'
17.4.: 'Kl 1/2 11. Profeten (Gen. Rep.)'
18.4.: 'I Theatret Profeten med Tichatscheck i Titelrollen, der var udsolgt Huus og stort Bifald'.

Le Prophète received 5 performances during Bournonville's engagement in Stockholm, the last of which was given on 26.4.1863.

The musical sources for the opera and the Act III divertissement *Les Patineurs* are now in SSkma (call no. KT Operor P).

28.4.1863
Le Gamin de Paris (Pariser-Pojken) (Stockholm's Royal Theatre, Operahuset).

In his diary and in his Swedish *Journal* Bournonville noted about his 1863 Stockholm restaging of J.-F.-A. Bayard's and E. L. Vanderburch's two-act comedy (premièred at the Théâtre Gymnase Dramatique in Paris on 30.1.1836, and first performed in Stockholm on 23.1.1837):

27.3.1863: 'Collationnering på Pariserpöjken'
9.4.: 'skrifvit sceneri till Pariserpöjken'
10.4.: 'Pariserpöjken. (Gen. Rep.) […] Pariser pöjken (Instruction Klefberg.)''
14.4.: 'Eftermiddags=Instruction paa Pariserdrengen […] (Barntheatern.)'
15.4.: 'Pariserpöjken (Gen Rep.)'
18.4.: 'Pariserpöjken (Rep: salen.)'
20.4.: 'Eftermiddags Instruction paa Pariserdrengen […] (Barnth:)'
22.4., 24.4., and 27.4.: 'Pariserpöjken (Gen Rep)'
28.4.: 'Pariserpöjken (med [H. A.] Klefberg meget god i Titelrollen) […] fuldt Huus og storartet Bifald'.

Le Gamin de Paris received 4 performances during Bournonville's engagement in Stockholm, the last of which was given on 13.5.1863.

Autograph sources:

Manuscript mise-en-scène. Ms. Autograph. Brown ink. 4 pp. (22,6 × 18 cm)
Pariserpojken.
Unsigned and undated [Written according to Bournonville's Swedish *Journal* on 9.4.1863]
[DKKk; NKS 3285 4° 5 læg 20]

4.5.1863
Les Dragons de Villars (Villars' Dragoner) (Stockholm's Royal Theatre, Operahuset).
The Swedish première of L. A. Maillart's three-act comic opera (first performed at the Théâtre Lyrique in Paris on 19.9.1856) also represents the first time this work was mounted with Bournonville's mise-en-scène and choreography. It included an (unnamed) *Dance* performed by a group of dragoons and young girls in the Act I finale (score no. 6) during the so-called 'Chanson des soldats' («Pour séduire une fillette, faut-il un air de musette»).

The Stockholm production was restaged by Bournonville with only minor if any changes on 12.2.1864, and Maillart's opera reached a total of 17 performances in the Swedish capital, the last of which was given on 7.3.1866.

On 1.8.1870 Bournonville proposed a Danish première of this work to the theatre management of Copenhagen's Royal Theatre. It was carried out by him the same year with completely new mise-en-scène and choreography (*see* 19.10.1870).

In his diary and in his Swedish *Journal* he noted about the rehearsals and the 1863 Stockholm première of *Les Dragons de Villars*:

26.2.1863: 'Om Eftermiddagen Collationnering paa Villars Dragoner'
27.2.: 'skrivfit sceneri til Villars Dragoner'
12.3.: 'Eftermiddagsprøve paa Villars Dragoner'
13.3.: 'Decorations-prof.'
17.3.: 'Villars Dragoner (sångr)'
19.3.: 'Eftermiddags Instruction paa Villars Dragoner.'
23.3.: 'Villars Dragoner (sångr) [...]Eftermiddags Instruction [...] (på Barntheater)'
28.3. and 31.3.: 'Villars dragoner (Dialog. Rep: salen.)'
10.4.: 'Villars Dragoner'
13.4.: 'Eftermiddagsprøve paa Villars Dragoner [...] (1.ste Akt Barntheatern)'
17.4.: 'Eftermiddagsprøve paa Villars dragoner [...] (2.dra Akten piano Barnth:)'
19.4.: 'Formiddagen paa Prøve [...] Villars Dragoner (1.e & 2.dra Akten vid piano)'
21.4.: 'Eftermiddagsprøve paa Villars dragoner (M.lle [W. C.] Gelhaar ubehagelig) [...] (piano Barntheatern.)'
23.4.: 'Musik=Collationnering på Villars Dragoner'
24.4.: 'Sceneri skrifvit'
25.4.: 'Sceneri till Villars Dragoner [...] Musik=Collationnering på D.°'
26.4.: 'Villars dragoner (sångrepetition Rep salen) [...] Villars dragoner. (Dans å Barntheatern)'
27.4.: 'Eftermiddags Indstudering paa Dandsen til Villars Dragoner [...] (Dans å Barntheatern)'
28.4.: 'Generalprøve paa Villars Dragoner. [...] Sceneri [...] 1.ste och 2.dra Akten af D.° (Gen Rep:)'

29.4.: 'Generalprøve paa Villars dragoner [...] 3.die Akt m m'
30.4.: 'Generalprøve paa Villars dragoner der gik meget godt'
1.5.: 'Villars dragoner (Ballett.) [...] D.° (Gen Rep:)'
2.5.: 'Villars dragoner (sista Gen: Rep:)'
4.5.: 'i Theatret Villars dragoner 1.ste Gang blev modtaget med lunkent Bifald, men gik alligevel udmærket godt, paa M.lle Gelhaars Sang nær der led af stærk Indisposition og gjorde meget Skade paa alle hendes Numere. Hendes Spil derimod lykkedes særdeles vel'.

Autograph sources:

Manuscript mise-en-scène (incomplete). Ms. Autograph. Brown ink. 1 vol. 1 pp. (21,5 × 17,5 cm)
Villars Dragoner/Opera = comique i tre Akter./Musiken af Maillart.
Unsigned and undated [Written according to Bournonville's Swedish *Journal* on either 27.2. or 24.4.1863]
[DKKk; NKS 3285 4° 4 læg 1]

Musical sources:

Orchestral printed score with manuscript insertions. 3 vol. Act I 258 pp., Act II 150 pp., Act III 142 pp. (32,5 × 24,5 cm).
Als manuscript gedruckt / LES / DRAGONS de VILLARS / Opéra comique en 3 Actes/ [...] /Musique de/AIMÉ MAILLART
Paris, G. Brandus, Dufour et C.ie, pl. no. B. et C.ie 9744 (1–16) [1856]
[SSkma; KT Operetter V 19
This orchestral score was used for all performances of *Les Dragons de Villars* during Bournonville's engagement in Stockholm. The music for the (unnamed) *Dance* in the Act I finale is included on pp. '223–258'.

No répétiteur's copy for *Les Dragons de Villars* has yet been traced in SSkma.

Parts. Ms. Copy. 34 vol. + 3 vol.
3 vl I, 3 vl II, 2 vla, 4 vlc e cb, fl picc, fl 1/2, ob 1/2, cl 1/2, fag 1/2, cor 1/2/3/4, tr 1/2, trb 1/2/3, timp, gr cassa, cassa, piatti, tri. On stage: tr 1/2, glock.
Unsigned and undated [1863]
[SSkma; KT Operetter V 19

26.5.1863
Le Télégramme (Telegrammet) (Stockholm's Royal Theatre, Operahuset).
In his diary and in his Swedish *Journal* Bournonville noted about this, the Stockholm première of P. Poirson's one-act comedy (first performed at the Théâtre Vaudeville in Paris on 28.2.1863, and translated into Swedish by F. Hedberg in 1863):

18.5.: 'Eftermiddagsprøve paa Telegrammet [...] (Barntheatern)'
20.5.: 'første Prøve paa Telegrammet'
22.5. and 23.5.: 'Telegrammet. (Gen Rep.)'
26.5.: 'Telegrammet. (Gen Rep.) [...] den 1.ste Forestilling af Telegrammet, som gik meget smukt'.

Le Télégramme received 4 performances during Bournonville's engagement in Stockholm, the last of which was given on 4.6.1863.

Autograph sources:

Manuscript mise-en-scène. Ms. Autograph. Brown ink. 3 pp. (22,9 × 18,1 cm)
Telegrammet/Lustspel i en Akt. af Poirson.
Signed and dated: 'Stockholm d 11.de Mai 1863'
[DKKk; NKS 3285 4° 5 læg 26]

1.6.1863
La Vida es Sueno (Lifvet en Dröm) (Stockholm's Royal Theatre, Operahuset).

P. Calderon de la Barca's five-act dramatic poem from 1635 had been given its Stockholm première in a Swedish translation by F. A. Dahlgren on 15.11.1858. It included several musical insertions among which were three movements (named *Allegro, Menuett,* and *Rondo*) that were borrowed from a (not yet identified) symphony by C. R. af Uhr and used as *entr'acte* music. Moreover, a chorus (entitled «Hell, hell! Hell dig ädle Sigismund!») and some other additional instrumental pieces by anonymous composers were incorporated as accompaniment for the combat scenes, and were played by an orchestra seated on the stage. This music (for which no complete orchestral score has yet been traced) is now preserved in SSkma (call no. KT Tal-pjeser med Musik L 21).

For the 1863 restaging of *La Vida es Sueno* Bournonville wrote a note to the theatre management of Stockholm's Royal Theatre on 12.5.1863, in which he asked for permission to make a series of cuts in those sections of Dahlgren's Swedish translation, which (according to his diary) he regarded as both tasteless and indecent. These cuts concerned the scene at the end of Act V in which the sudden death of the comic character *Clarin* (performed by C. G. Dahlqvist) is shown. It was regarded by Bournonville as without true dramatic motivation, and consequently he intended to omit it. In this, however, he was not successful.

In his diary and in his Swedish *Journal* he noted about the staging:

12.5., 22.5., and·28.5.1863: 'Lifvet en dröm (Gen Rep.)'
29.5.: 'Lifvet en dröm (Gen Rep.) [...] Lang samtale med [C. G.] Dahlqvist om hans Smagløsheder i Lifvet en drøm!'
1.6.: 'I Theatret Lifvet en dröm (der ikke gjorde sÿnderlig Virkning)'.

La Vida es Sueno was given only twice during Bournonville's engagement in Stockholm, the last time on 5.6.1863.

Autograph sources:

Production note (included in a letter to F. A. Dahlgren). Ms. Autograph. Brown ink. 2 pp. (21,2 × 13,4 cm)
[...]Lifvet en dröm./[...]/Jeg udbeder mig derfor Deres Velbaarenheds Consens til at maatte foretage följende Coupure [...]
Signed and dated: 'Stockholm den 12.de Mai 1863.'
[SSk; L. 13:1 a

12.9.1863
A Ballet Divertissement (Ett Ballet=Divertissement) (Stockholm's Royal Theatre, Dramatiska Theatern).

This allegorical divertissement was choreographed for the inauguration of Dramatiska Theatern in Stockholm (identical with the earlier privately run Mindre Theatern). In spite of Bournonville's outspoken protest it had been bought by Stockholm's Royal Theatre on 1.7.1863, and after the 1863–64 season was used as the main stage for plays and minor ballet performances.

The four leading characters in Bournonville's inaugural divertissement for this theatre (representing *Terpsichore* and the three graces) were performed by his English pupils, the sisters A. and C. Healey, and the Swedish ballerinas, A. Forsberg, and A. Paulsson.

The divertissement appears to have been based, at least in part, on Bournonville's earlier projected allegorical ballet, entitled *Terpsichore*, which he drafted (according to his diary) on 5.10.1860. This theory is further supported by the poster for *A Ballet Divertissement*, on which the action is described as follows:

'(Therpsichore, gifvande Thalia en hyllningsgärd, bjuder Gracerna att deruti deltaga och frammanar till samma ändamål bilder ur svenska folklifvet.)'.

The score for this divertissement (for which no musical sources have yet been traced in the music archive of Stockholm's Royal Theatre, now in SSkma) was according to Bournonville's diary most probably composed and/or arranged by the then newly-appointed conductor of the orchestra of Dramatiska Theatern, H. Berens.

In his diary and in his Swedish *Journal* Bournonville stated about the performance:

1.9.1963: 'Faaet Ideen til en Indvielses-Prolog for Dramatiska Theatern der blev modtaget med Glæde, tidlig Middag og derpaa Udfart til Waxholm for at tale med [F.] Hedberg om Prologen, Capelmester [H.] Berens var med mig'
2.9.: 'Componeradt dansar! [...] Inöfvadt dansar (Bth.) [...] Indstudering med [A. and C.] Healeyerne, [A.] Forsberg og [A.] Paulsson'
3.9.: 'Indstudering [...] Dans (Bth.)'
4.9.: 'Indstudering paa min Dandseprolog [...] (Bth.)'
5.9.: 'Indstudering færdig paa mit lille Divertissement Thalias ÿngre Søster [...] (Barnth.)'
8.9.: 'Prøve paa mit nÿ Divertissement [...] Thalias yngre syster'
9.9.: 'Repetition paa mit Divertissement, der nu skal hedde Terpsichore hos Thalia [...] (dr th.)'
10.9.: 'Eftermiddagsprøve paa mit Divertissement [...] Terpsichore (Gen Rep.)'
11.9.: 'Prøve paa mit Divertissement som [...] gik udmærket [...] Terpsichore (Gen Rep) dr th.'
12.9.: 'Første Forestilling paa Dramatiska Theatern (Mindre Theatern) der blev indviet med en Prolog fremsagt af [N. W.] Almlöf, derpaa Gustav den III's Skuespil Siri Brahe [*och Johan Gyllenstjerna*, originally premièred on 8.3.1788] og til Slutning mit Ballet=Divertissement, der gjorde overordentlig Lÿkke og gik meget smukt. Huset var udsolgt. Efter Forestillingen blev der paa H. M. Kongens [i.e. Carl XV] Bekostning drukket et Glas Chamopagne til en lykkelig Indvielse af dette Theaters Virksomhed. – Jeg har aldrig været for denne Affaire, men skal den stedes vil jeg gjøre min Pligt i første Række'.

Bournonville's *A Ballet Divertissement* reached 4 performances, the last of which was given on 28.9.1863.

Autograph sources:

Manuscript mise-en-scène. Ms. Autograph. Brown ink. 6 pp. (22,8 × 18,1 cm)
Motiv till en Prolog/før/Dramatiska theaterns Invigelse/September 1863:
Signed and dated: 'Stockholm d. 1.de Septbr 1863'
[DKKk; NKS 3285 4° 5 læg 21

17.9.1863
Les Faux Bonshommes (Så kallade Hedersmän) (Stockholm's Royal Theatre, Dramatiska Theatern).

When Bournonville saw T. Barrière's and E. Capendu's four-act comedy for the first time at Copenhagen's Royal Theatre on 18.3.1860 he stated about it in his diary:

'Skikkelige Folk Les faux bonshommes (1.ste Gang) Det blev udført med meget Talent og interesserede heelt igjennem. – Lidt Opposition lod sig høre hist og her, men hidrører kun fra urene Kilder'.

In his diary and in his Swedish *Journal* he noted about his own 1863 Stockholm staging of the comedy (originally premièred at the Théâtre Vaudeville in Paris on 11.11.1856):

24.8.1863: 'skrifvit sceneri'
25.8.: '1.ste Prøve paa Hedermän? (skikkelige Folk) [...] (Barntheatern)'
27.8.: 'Eftermiddagsprøve [...] Såkallade Hedersmän (1.ste och 2.a Akten (Bth.))'
28.8.: 'Prøve paa Hedermän [...] (Bth.)'
29.8.: 'Eftermiddagsprøve paa Såkallade Hedersmän [...] (dr: theatern.)' 3' Akten.'
1.9.: 'Prøve paa Hedermän [...] (Bth) 4.e Akten'
3.9.: 'Eftermiddagsprøve [...] Såkallade Hedersmän (dr: theatern)'
5.9.: 'Prøve pa Dr: Theater paa Såkallede Hedersmän. 4.e Akt færdig'
7.9.: 'Såkallade Hedersmän: Gen. Rep: (dr. th.)'
8.9.: 'Costym-möte'
10.9.: 'Prøve paa Såkallade Hedersmän, der nu begynder at gaae udmærket godt'
11.9.: 'Såkallade Hedersmän: Gen. Rep: (dr. th.)'
14.9.: 'Prøve paa Hedersmän [...] (Gen rep)'
16.9.: 'holdt Generalprøve i Costume paa Såkallade Hedersmän, der gik meget godt (paa et Par Usikkerheder nær)'
17.9.: 'Første Forestilling paa Dramatiska theatern af Såkallade Hedersmän for fuldt Huus og med stor Succès – Alt gik udmærket godt'.

Les Faux Bonshommes received 24 performances during Bournonville's engagement in Stockholm, the last of which was given on 2.6.1864.

Autograph sources:

Manuscript mise-en-scène. Ms. Autograph. Black ink. 1 vol. 15 pp. (22,5 × 18,1 cm)
Sceneri/till./Såkallade Hedersmän/Comedie i 4.ra Akter./af/Th. Barrière och Ernest Capendu
Signed and dated: 'Stockholm d. 28.e Augusti 1863.' [According to Bournonville's Swedish *Journal* probably written between 24.8. and 28.8.1863]
[DKKk; NKS 3285 4° 5 læg 4

Production note. Ms. Autograph. Brown ink., 1 p. (18,1 × 11,2 cm)
Costym förslag/till (Vertillac (Herr Josephsson.)/Såkallade Hedersmän.
Signed and dated: 'd 31 Augusti 1863'
[SSk; Ep. J 7:1

Manuscript mise-en-scène (incomplete). Ms. Autograph. Black ink. 1 p. (21,5 × 17,5 cm)
Såkallade Hedersmän./Comedie i 4 Akter af Th Barrière./ (Les faux bons hommes.)/Personerna.
Unsigned and undated [August–September 1863]
[DKKk; NKS 3285 4° 4 læg 2

18.9.1863
I Puritani di Scozia (Puritanerne) (Stockholm's Royal Theatre, Stora Theatern).
The 1863 Swedish restaging of V. Bellini's melodrama in three parts (originally premièred at the Théâtre Italien in Paris on 25.1.1835) represents the first and only time this work was mounted with Bournonville's mise-en-scène (*see also* his projected restaging of it at Copenhagen's Royal Theatre, dated 30.10.1857). It included an (unnamed)

Dance in Act I, scene 2 (score no. 1) performed by a group of Plymouth villagers during the so-called 'Coro di Castellane e Castellani' («A festa! a festa!»). At the Stockholm première of *I Puritani di Scozia* on 7.4.1851 this scene was choreographed and mounted by the then ballet-master, A. Selinder. His choreography seems to have been restaged by Bournonville in 1863 with only minor if any changes, since no notes in his diary indicate that he choreographed this scene anew this year.

In his diary and his Swedish *Journal* Bournonville stated about the production:

19.5.1863: 'Kl. 11 Puritanerna (sångr)'
20.5.: 'Kl 11 Puritanerna (sångr)'
26.5.: 'Læst og skrevet [...] Eftermiddagen Indstudering paa Puritanerne [...] Kl 5 Puritanerna (sceneri)'
27.5.: 'Eftermiddagsprøve paa Puritanerne [...] Kl 5 Puritanerna (Barnth.)'
30.5.: 'Eftermiddagen Instruction paa Puritanerne'
1.6.: 'Eftermiddagsprøve paa Puritanerne [...] (Instruction)'
8.6.: 'Kl 11. Puritanerna (stor sång rep.:)'
28.8.: 'Kl 11 Puritanerna (Rep. salen) [...] Eftermiddagsprøve paa Puritanerne [...] Bth.'
29.8.: 'Kl 1/2 11. Puritanerna (Gen Rep)'
31.8.: 'Prøve paa Puritanerne der er sat tilbage for [F.] Stenhammers Sygdom'
15.8.: 'Prøve paa Puritanerne [...] (Gen. Rep)'
17.8.: 'Generalprøve paa Puritanerne, der gaaer meget smukt (paa Stenhammer nær) [...] Kl. 6. Puritanerna'
18.9.: 'I Theatret Puritanerne for fuldt Huus, gik som ovennævnt'.

I Puritani di Scozia received 3 performances during Bournonville's engagement in Stockholm, the last of which was given on 27.9.1863.

Autograph sources:

Manuscript mise-en-scène. Ms. Autograph. Brown ink. 1 vol. 7 pp. (22,5 × 18,2 cm)
Puritanerna (Sceneri)
Signed and dated: 'Stockholm d. 26 Mai 1863.'
[DKKk; NKS 3285 4° 3 L.–P

Musical sources:

Orchestral score. Ms. Copy. Black ink. 2 vol. Act I 432 pp., Act II–III 304 pp. (30,5 × 37,3 cm with minor variants)
I. Puritani/dell M.o/Bellini./Atto 1.mo
Unsigned and undated [c.1851–1863]
[SSkma; KT Operor P 4
This Italian manuscript orchestral score dates from the 1851 Stockholm première of Bellini's *I Puritani di Scozia* and was used for all performances of it there during Bournonville's lifetime.

Répétiteur's copy. Ms. Copy. Black ink. 5 pp. (33,4 × 24,5 with minor variants)
Repetiteur Partie till Puritaner
Unsigned and undated [c.1851–1863]
[SSkma; KT Operor P 4
This répétiteur's copy contains the complete music (177 meas.) of the chorus, entitled «A festa! A festa!» in Act I, scene 2 (score no. 1) of Bellini's *I Puritani di Scozia*, during which an (unnamed) *Dance* is performed by a group of villagers. The volume itself dates from the 1851 Stockholm première of Bellini's melodrama, but also seems to have been used by Bournonville for his 1863 restaging of this work.

Parts. Ms copy. 33 vol. + 5 vol.
3 vl I, 3 vl II, 2 vla, 4 vlc e cb, fl 1/2, ob 1/2, cl 1/2, fag 1/2, cor 1/2/

3/4, tr, trb 1/2/3, timp, gr cassa, cassa, tri, arpa. On stage: cor 1/2/3, gr cassa, cassa.
Unsigned and undated [c.1851–1863]
[SSkma; KT Operor P 4
This set of parts dates from the 1851 Stockholm première of Bellini's *I Puritani di Scozia* and was used for all performances of it there during Bournonville's lifetime.

26.9.1863

Les Fourberies de Scapin (Scapins Skälmstycken) (Stockholm's Royal Theatre, Dramatiska Theatern).

In his diary and in his Swedish *Journal* Bournonville noted about his mise-en-scène and staging of the Stockholm première of J. B. Molière's three-act comedy from 1671:

19.8.1863: 'skrifvit sceneri'
23.8.: 'fuldendt Sceneriet til Scapins Skälmstykken'
24.8.: 'skrifvit sceneri'
26.8.: 'Collationnering <u>Scapins skälmstycken</u>'
11.9. and 14.9.: 'Eftermiddag=Instruction for K Almlöf paa <u>Scapins Skälmsstycken</u>'
15.9., 17.9., and 18.9.: '<u>Scapin</u> Instruction'
20.9., 22.9., 23.9., and 24.9.: '<u>Scapins skälmsstycken</u> (Gen Rep <u>dr th</u>:)'
25.9.: 'fuldstændig Generalprøve paa <u>Scapin</u> der gaaer udmærket godt'
26.9.: '<u>Scapin</u> (scener) [...] for første Gang <u>Scapins Skälmsstycken</u> som Debut for Knut Almlöf. Det gik udmærket godt og blev stærkt applauderet (fuldt Huus)'.

Molière's comedy received 10 performances during Bournonville's engagement in Stockholm, the last of which was given on 21.2.1864.

Autograph sources:

Manuscript mise-en-scène. Ms. Autograph. Black ink. 7 pp. (22,9 × 18,2 cm with minor variants)
<u>Scapins Skälmsstycken.</u>/Lustspel i tre Akter af Molière.
Signed and dated: 'Stockholm d 23 Augusti 1863'
[DKKk; NKS 3285 4° 5 læg 24

Manuscript mise-en-scène (incomplete). Ms. Autograph. Black ink. 1 p. (21,5 × 17,5 cm)
<u>Scapins skälmstycken</u>/Comedie af Molière. (3 Akter.)/<u>Personerna</u>.
Unsigned and undated [August-September 1863]
[DKKk; NKS 3285 4° 4 læg 2

5.10.–6.10.1863

La Juive (Judinnan). Projected staging at Stockholm's Royal Theatre.

On these days Bournonville noted in the diary and in his Swedish *Journal* about his preparations for a projected Swedish première of J.-F. Halévy's five-act opera from 1835:

'Læst, skrevet [...] Sceneri til Judinnan [...] arrangeret Sceneri'.

In a later recommendation note written to the theatre management of Stockholm's Royal Theatre on 16.10.1863 he explained in further detail his reasons for wanting to stage *La Juive* during November 1863:

'Je suis chargé de la mission délicate de vous annoncer de la part de M.me Michaelli [i.e. L. Michaëli] qu'a date de la fin de Décembre, elle sera obligée de suspendre le cours de ses représentations à cause d'une circonstance fortuite [...] Je proposerais une mise à l'étude

très énergique de La Juive pour qu'elle puisse aller en scène à la mi-novembre et nous fournir une brillante série, jusqu'à la fin de l'année'.

The projected 1863 Stockholm première of *La Juive* (*see also* 21.10.1855 and 30.10.1857) was never carried out by Bournonville. However, his two manuscript mises-en-scène for it (written according to his diary and his Swedish *Journal* on 5.10. and 6.10.1863) seem later to have served as a basis for the first Swedish production of Halévy's opera at Stockholm's Royal Theatre (Stora Theatern) on 5.6.1866. This theory is supported by the fact that the first of Bournonville's two manuscript mises-en-scène (dated 5.10.1863) is now preserved in SSk among the working papers of his pupil, the Swedish actor and director L. Josephsson. Moreover, Josephsson was solely responsible for the 1866 Stockholm première of this opera (*Die Jüdin* had been given for the first time in Sweden at Gothenborg's Nya Theatern on 3.11.1864, but then sung in German and mounted with mise-en-scène by C. Gaudelius).

Josephsson's 1866 Stockholm production reached a total of 22 performances, the last of which was given on 21.10.1869.

Autograph sources:

Production note. Ms. Autograph (partially in another's hand). Brown ink and pencil. 4 pp. (22,3 × 17,8 cm)
Decorations – Forslag/till/Opran Judinnan.
Signed and dated: 'Stockholm d 5.e October 1863.'
[SSk; Ep. J. 7:1

Manuscript mise-en-scène. Ms. Autograph. Brown ink. 1 vol. 13 pp. (22,4 × 18 cm)
<u>Judinnan</u>/Opera i 5 Akter af Halevÿ/<u>Sceneri.</u>
Unsigned and undated [Written according to the diary on 6.10. 1863]
[SSm; Daniel Fryklunds samling no. 130
This autographed manuscript mise-en-scène (written in Swedish) is bound together with Bournonville's earlier (undated) projected Danish mise-en-scène for *La Juive*, which he most probably wrote on 30.10.1857.

Recommendation note. Ms. Autograph. Brown ink. 2 pp. (26,8 × 21,3 cm)
[...] à Monsieur/Mr le Baron E de Stedingk./[...]/Je proposerais une mise à l'étude très énergique de La Juive [...]
Signed and dated: 'Stockholm ce 16 Octobre 1863'
[SSdt; KTA, E2A Ink. breve 1862/63, 16.10.1862
Due to a misreading of the date of this letter it has erroneously been placed among the correspondance of the 1862–63 season and is listed under the date of 16.10.1862.

8.10.1863

Richard II (Konung Richard den Andre) (Stockholm's Royal Theatre, Stora Theatern).

In his diary and in his Swedish *Journal* Bournonville noted about this, the Swedish première of W. Shakespeare's five-act play from c.1595–96:

17.3.1863: 'Collationnering paa Konung Richard II'
18.3., 20.3., and 24.3.: 'skrifvit sceneri till Richard d. 2.dre'
7.9.: 'Prøve paa Sceneriet til Konung Richard den Andren [...] 1' 2. 3.'
9.9.: 'Sceneriprøve paa Richard [...] <u>4.e & 5.e Akten</u>'

16.9.: 'Konung Richard (Recit:)'
19.9.: 'Konung Richard 1.ste 2.a 3.e Akt. (Gen Rep.)'
21.9.: 'Konung Richard 3.de 4.e 5.e Akten Gen Rep.'
22.9.: 'Rolerna ur Konung Richard.'
23.9.: 'Konung Richard Gen Rep. 1.ste 2' 3.e Akten'
25.9.: 'Konung Richard (3.e 4.e 5.te Akten Gen Rep.)'
2.10.: 'Compars=repetition på Konung Richard [...] Konung Richard (Gen Rep.) [...] fra Kl. 9 til 2! Det begynder at gaae udmærket godt'
4.10.: 'Costymprof på Richard [...] Konung Richard (5.te akten)'
5.10.: 'Konung Richard (Gen Rep.)'
7.10.: 'Generalprøve i Costume paa Konung Richard d. 2.dre som lover udmærket godt'
8.10.: 'I Theatret 1.ste Forestilling af Shakespeares' Konung Richard den Andre, der gik udmærket godt og skaffede [E. M.] Swartz en stor Triumph'.

The staging (which was in part arranged by Bournonville's pupil, L. Josephsson) was based on C. A. Hagberg's Swedish translation and included 17 music numbers. These numbers served mainly for *entr'actes* and fanfares, or accompanied the battle scenes in Act III (score no. 5) and the *Funeral March* in Act V (score no. 15). This music, of which eight pieces (score nos. 5–9 and 11–13) were played by an orchestra seated on the stage, was written by various composers, two of which are identified as follows:

Act III, score no. 3: For this number Bournonville employed J. Drinnenberg's *Hommage à Pelissier. Grande Marche Triomphale* (op. 22), first published by J. André in Offenbach s. M. between 1856 and 1858 (pl. no. 7730).
Act V, score nos. 16 and 17: In these numbers Bournonville reused parts of the music from J. A. Söderman's so-called 'Hymn' (*Andante mosso*), which was originally composed for the Stockholm première of E. Augier's two-act comedy *La Ciguë* (*see* 23.11.1861).

Richard II received 3 performances during Bournonville's engagement in Stockholm, the last of which was given on 20.10.1863.

Autograph sources:

Manuscript mise-en-scène. Ms. Autograph. Brown ink and pencil. 16 pp. (22,4 × 18,4 cm)
Konung Richard den Andre./Tragedie i 5 akter./af/Shakespeare/Sceneri.
Signed and dated: 'afslutat den 24 Mars 1863' [Written according to Bournonville's Swedish *Journal* between 18.3. and 24.3.1863]
[DKKk; NKS 3285 4° 5 læg 14
Because of a sudden illness in spring 1863 of the actor, E. M. Swartz (who played *Richard II*), the première of Shakespeare's play was postponed from late spring to the autumn of 1863, hence the early dating of Bournonville's manuscript mise-en-scène for this play.

Manuscript mise-en-scène (incomplete). Ms. Autograph. Black ink. 1 p. (21,5 × 17,5 cm)
Konung Richard den Andre./Historisk Skådespel i fem Akter af Shakespeare./Personerna:
Unsigned and undated [1863]
[DKKk; NKS 3285 4° 4 læg 2

Production note. Ms. Autograph. Brown ink and pencil. 3 pp. (36,4 × 22,4 cm)
Personalen i Konung Richard d. 2.den.
Unsigned and undated [1863]
[DKKk; NKS 3285 4° 5 læg 14

Musical sources:

Conductor's score ('Anförerparti'). Ms. Copy with inserted printed music. 1 vol. 18 pp. (31,8 × 24,1 cm with minor variants)
KONUNG RICHARD/den andre/Anförarparti/Violino 1.mo/No. 1
Unsigned and undated [c.1863]
[SSkma; KT Tal-Pjeser med Musik K 18

No répétiteur's copy for *Richard II* has yet been traced in SSkma.

Parts. Ms. Copy. 23 vol. + 10 vol.
vl I, vl II, vla, 2 vlc e cb, fl 1/2, ob 1/2, cl 1/2, fag 1/2, cor 1/2, tr 1/2, trb 1/2, timp, gr cassa, piatti, tri. On stage: fl 1/2, cl 1/2, fag, tr, cor 1/2, trb, arpa.
Unsigned and undated [c.1863]
[SSkma; KT Tal-Pjeser med Musik K 18
The three numbers which contain music composed by J. A. Söderman (Act V, score nos. 16 and 17) are here entitled:
(1) 'Hymne/Psalmsång utanför'.
(2) 'Richards liktog der stannar i midten af trädgården'.
(3) 'Processionen slutar piesen'.

14.10.1863
Carl XII (Karl den tolfte). Projected staging (Stockholm's Royal Theatre).
According to a letter written by the Swedish author, T. Hagberg, to the theatre management of Stockholm's Royal Theatre on 14.10.1863 (now in SSdt), Bournonville had written a letter to Hagberg in the early autumn of 1863, in which he firmly rejected the author's suggestion for a Stockholm staging of this play. According to the same letter, Bournonville's reason for not recommending a staging of Hagberg's five-act historical play derived from his determined view that it belonged to a genre which he described rather bluntly by his stating:

'tous les genres sont bons hors le genre ennuyeux'.

Hagberg's play, which was eventually published by W. Schultz in Uppsala (1864), was never mounted in Stockholm.

16.10.1863
Le Roman d'Elvire (Drottning Elviras Saga). Projected staging (Stockholm's Royal Theatre).
On this day Bournonville wrote a recommendation note concerning the projected Stockholm staging of A. Thomas's three-act comic opera (originally premèred l'Opéra Comique, Salle Favart, in Paris on 4.2.1860). This note reads:

'Aussitôt nous métterons en scène une autre nouveauté – Le roman d'Elvire [...] avec les ressources eclartantes que nous possedons, car l'ancien repertoire se trouvera completement impossible par l'absence de nos deux Primedonne'.

During an earlier visit to Paris in 1860 Bournonville had attended a performance of *Le Roman d'Elvire* at l'Opéra Comique on 25.5.1860 and made on that day the following comment about it in his diary:

'Le roman d'Elvire, moret mig godt (det Hele meget smukt)'.

The 1863 projected Stockholm première of Thomas's opera was carried out six months later on 26.4.1864, when it was mounted with Bournonville's mise-en-scène.

Autograph sources:

Recommendation note (included in a letter to E. F. O. L. von Stedingk). Ms. Autograph. Brown ink. 2 pp. (26,8 × 21,3 cm)
[…] à Monsieur/Mr le Baron E de Stedingk./Chambellan du Roi./
Chef de la Chapelle & des théâtres Royaux/[…]Aussitôt nous métterons en scène une autre nouveauté – le roman d'Elvire […]
Signed and dated 'Stockholm ce 16 Octobre 1863'
[SSdt; KTA, E2A, Ink. breve 1862/63, 16.10.1862
Due to a misreading of the date of this letter it has erroneously been
placed among the correspondence of the 1862–63 season and is
listed under the date of 16.10.1862.

16.10.1863
Hans Heiling. **Projected staging (Stockholm's Royal Theatre).**
According to a letter from Bournonville to the theatre management of Stockholm's Royal Theatre, he proposed on this
day a Swedish première of H. Marschner's three-act romantic opera from 1833 (*see also* 30.10.1857 and 20.2.1858).
However, the project was for unknown reasons never carried
out during Bournonville's engagement at Stockholm's Royal
Theatre, and *Hans Heiling* was not mounted at that theatre
until 11.10.1865.

Autograph sources:

Recommendation note (included in a letter to E. F. O. L. von Stedingk). Ms. Autograph. Brown ink. 2 pp. (26,8 × 21,3 cm)
[…] à Monsieur/Mr le Baron E de Stedingk./Chambellan du Roi./
Chef de la Chapelle & des théâtres Royaux/[…]Aussitôt nous métterons en scène une autre nouveauté/[…] Hans Heiling avec les
ressources eclartantes que nous possedons […]
Signed and dated 'Stockholm ce 16 Octobre 1863'
[SSdt; KTA, E2A, Ink. breve 1862/63, 16.10.1862
Due to a misreading of the date of this letter it has erroneously been
placed among the correspondence of the 1862–63 season and is
listed under the date of 16.10.1862.

16.10.1863
Jaleo de Xeres, Spanish Dance (Spansk Dans) **(uncredited)**
performed by S. Lund and H. M. Lund (Stockholm's Royal
Theatre, Dramatiska Theatern).
According to several notes in Bournonville's diary and in his
Swedish *Journal* it seems that this (uncredited) Spanish
dance was a work choreographed and mounted by him. If
this theory is correct, then it is probably identical with *El
Jaleo de Xeres*, originally performed in Act I (score no. 6) of
Bournonville's two-act idyllic ballet *The Toréador* (*see* 27.11.
1840).
　　Another fact which points to *El Jaleo de Xeres* from *The Tore-
ador* is the existence of an orchestral score and an (incomplete) set of parts in SSkma, that contain E. Helsted's 1840
musical arrangement of this dance (*see* Musical sources).
Moreover, *The Toreador* had also been mounted by Bournonville at Stockholm's Royal Theatre (Operahuset) on
2.6.1847.
　　On 29.10.1858 yet another similar Spanish National
Dance was performed in Stockholm by three women (J. G.
Sundberg, A. Arrhenius, and A. Paulsson) with the title *The
Girls from Xeres (Flickarna från Xeres)*. It was mounted by Bournonville's pupil, S. Lund, who (according to the poster) was
credited for having 'arranged' (*arrangeradt*) this dance. It,
too, seems to have been based on the choreography of Bour-

nonville's *El Jaleo de Xeres* from *The Toreador*, in spite of being
performed to different music from that in *The Toreador*.
　　With this knowledge it is, therefore, reasonable to assume
that the (uncredited) 1863 *Jaleo de Xeres* was based – at least
in part – on either one or both of these previous dances.
　　In his Swedish *Journal* Bournonville noted on 10.10.1863
about the dance:

'Presentation af två dansar'.

This note is followed by indications of two rehearsals of this
dance on 12.10 and 15.10.1863, and on the opening night
he commented about it in his diary:

'Jaleo de Xeres […] gik meget smukt og for ret godt Huus'.

The 1863 *Jaleo de Xeres* received 3 performances at Dramatiska Theatern, the last of which took place on 27.10.1863.
　　It is not possible to identify the dance any further.

Musical sources:

Orchestral score. Ms. Copy. Black ink. 1 vol. 15 pp. (31 × 24,6 cm)
Pas de deux/Il Jaleo de Xeres
Unsigned and undated [1860s? or earlier]
[SSkma; KT Dansmusik 30

No répétiteur's copy for this dance has yet been traced in SSkma.

Parts. (incomplete). Ms Copy. 1 vol.
vl II.
Unsigned and undated [1860s? or earlier]
[SSkma; KT Dansmusik 30

21.10.1863
Le Train du minuit (Goda exempel). **Projected staging at**
Stockholm's Royal Theatre.
On this day Bournonville wrote a recommendation note to
the theatre management of Stockholm's Royal Theatre
about a projected Stockholm première of H. Meilhac's two-
act comedy (set to music by J.-F. Halévy and originally premièred at the Théâtre Gymnase in Paris on 15.6.1863). This
note reads:

'Goda Exempel (le train de minuit.)
Cette pièce, jouée avec l'entrain voulu, pourir fournir agréable-
ment la moitié d'une soirée de comédie […] je crois que Mr [C. G.]
Sundberg pourra soigner la mise-en-scène de la présente si toutefois
mon trés honoré Chef [i.e. E. F. O. L. von Stedingk] n'en décide
autrement.
très respecteusement/ce 21 Octobre 1863./August Bournonville'.

Meilhac's play was premièred the same year at Dramatiska
Theatern on 30.11.1863, but without any involvement on
Bournonville's part. Thus, in his diary he assessed it on the
opening night simply as a 'smukt lille Lystspil'.

Autograph sources:

Recommendation note. Ms. Autograph. Brown ink. 1 p. (21,2 × 13,4
cm)
[…] Goda Exempel (Le train de minuit) […]
Signed and dated: 'ce 21 Octobre 1863.'
[SSdt; KTA, E2A Ink. breve 1863/64, 21.10.1863
According to an earlier note in his diary ('læst nogle Franske Styk-
ker') Bournonville probably read Meilhac's comedy for the first time
on 26.8.1863.

27.10.1863

Corpus Kirsti (Korp=Kirsti) **(Stockholm's Royal Theatre, Dramatiska Theatern).**

In his diary and in his Swedish *Journal* Bournonville noted about this, the première of F. Hedberg's one-act Swedish fairy play (or *dalaäfventyr*):

31.8.1863: 'læst [F.] Hedbergs ny Vaudeville'
29.9.: 'Collationnering: Korp-Kristi'
12.10.: 'Korp-Kirsti (Barnth)'
14.10.: 'Første Prøve paa Korp-Kirsti [...] (vid piano.)'
15.10.: 'Korp-Kirsti (vid piano.)'
21.10.: 'Prøve paa Korp-Kirsti med Orchester [...] (Chör) [...] Korp-Kirsti (Gen – Rep:)'
22.10.: 'Korp-Kirsti (Gen Rep.)'
23.10. and 24.10.: 'Korp-Kirsti Gen Rep (vid piano)'
26.10.: 'Prøve paa Korp-Kirsti Formiddag og Eftermiddag i Costume. Den lover os megen Fornøielse'
27.10.: 'for første Gang Korp-Kirsti, der gik udmærket godt og gjorde Lykke, dog ikke i den Grad, som jeg havde ventet af en saa god Nationalvaudeville'.

The play included 11 song and dance numbers composed and arranged by H. Berens. In his score Berens incorporated several Norwegian and Swedish folksongs and dance tunes, which he borrowed mainly from two song collections by I. Hallström (entitled *Svenska folkvisor*) and R. Dübeck (entitled *Svenska vallvisor och hornlåtar*), the latter dating from 1846.

    Corpus Kirsti received 15 performances during Bournonville's engagement in Stockholm, the last of which was given on 10.5.1864.

Autograph sources:

Manuscript mise-en-scène. Ms. Autograph. Brown ink and pencil. 1 vol. 9 pp. (22,9 × 18,2 cm)
Korp = Kirsti./Ett daläfventyr i 1 Akt/med sång och dans/af/Fr Hedberg./Sceneri
Signed and dated: 'Stockholm d 27.de Septbre 1863.'
[DKKk; NKS 3285 4° 5 læg 15

Manuscript mise-en-scène (incomplete). Ms. Autograph. Black ink. 1 p. (21,5 × 17,5 cm)
Korp – Kirsti/Vaudeville i en Akt af Fr Hedberg./Personerna
Unsigned and undated [1863]
[DKKk; NKS 3285 4° 4 læg 2

Musical sources:

The musical material for Berens' arrangement for *Corpus Kirsti* (for which no complete orchestral score has yet been traced) is now preserved in SSkma (call no. KT Dramat. teat. kapsel 20 and kapsel K).

28.10.1863

Ernani **(Stockholm's Royal Theatre, Stora Theatern).**
The 1863 Stockholm restaging of G. Verdi's four-act lyrical drama (premièred in Venice at Teatro La Fenice on 9.3. 1844, and first performed in the Swedish capital on 25.5. 1853) represents the first and only time *Ernani* was mounted with Bournonville's mise-en-scène. It also marks the first time he mounted a work by Verdi (*see also* the projected staging of *Ernani* in Copenhagen, dated 30.10.1857).

    In his diary and in his Swedish *Journal* he noted about the performance:

6.10.1863: 'arrangeret sceneri [...] Ernani (sångr)'
8.10. and 13.10.1863: 'Ernani (sångr)'
16.10.: 'skrevet, læst [...] Ernani (sångr)'
17.10.: 'Sceneriprøve paa Ernani'
19.10.: 'Ernani sång och Chör (Rep. Salen) inställt i betraktning af Fru Michaellis [i.e. L. Michaëli] utförande af Donna Anna [in *Il Dissoluto Punito, ossia il Don Giovanni*] istället för Fru [F.] Stenhammar'
20.10.: 'Ernani Sång och Chör (Rep. Salen)'
22.10.: 'Prøve paa Ernani [...] (Gen. Rep.)'
24.10.: 'Ernani (Gen. Rep.)'
27.10.: 'Prøve paa Ernani [...] (Gen. Rep.)'
28.10.: 'I Theatret Ernani for fuldt Huus og med stor Bravour fra Fru Michaelli'.

Ernani received 8 performances during Bournonville's engagement in Stockholm, the last of which took place on 8.4. 1864 (three performances of Acts I and III were also given on 6.5., 8.5., and 18.5.1864).

Autograph sources:

Manuscript mise-en-scène. Ms. Autograph. Black ink. 1 vol. 11 pp. (18 × 11,4 cm)
Ernani./Sceneri.
Unsigned and dated: 'd 16.de October 1863.'
[DKKk; NKS 3285 4° 5 læg 10

Musical sources:

Orchestral score. Ms Copy. 3 vol. Black ink with pencilled annotations. Act I 227 pp., Act II 194 pp, Act III 145 pp. (29,4 × 34,5 cm)
Ernani/Maestro Verdi/Preludio/Atto 1.o/Kungl. Theatern
Unsigned and undated [1853–1863]
[SSkma; KT Operor E 4
This Italian manuscript orchestral score dates from the 1853 Stockholm première of Verdi's *Ernani* and was used for all performances of it there during Bournonville's lifetime.

No répétiteur's copy for *Ernani* has yet been traced in SSkma.

Parts. Ms. Copy. 27 vol. + 19 vol.
3 vl I, 3 vl II, 2 vla, 4 vlc e cb, fl 1–2, ob 1–2, cl 1–2, fag 1–2, cor 1/2/3/4, tr 1–2, trb 1/2/3/4, timp, gr cassa, arpa. On stage: fl 1–2, ob 1–2, cl 1/2/3, fag 1/2, cor princ, cor 1/2/3/4, tr 1/2, trb 1/2/3/4, gr cassa e piatti.
Unsigned and undated [1853–1863]
[SSkma; KT Operor E 4
This set of parts dates from the 1853 Stockholm première of *Ernani* and was used for all performances of it there during Bournonville's lifetime.

9.11.1863

Horace et Lydie, Une ode d'Horace (Horatius och Lydia). **Projected staging at Stockholm's Royal Theatre.**
On this day Bournonville wrote a recommendation note to the theatre management of Stockholm's Royal Theatre, in which he expressed his strong opposition to the projected Swedish staging of F. Ponsard's one-act comedy (originally premièred at the Théâtre Français in Paris on 19.6. 1850). This note reads as follows:

'Horatius och Lydia

Je n'ai pas eu l'avantage de lire l'original français, mais il me sem[b]le appartenir au genre parfumé qui cherche à travestir les chef d'oeuvre plastiques de l'antiquité en héros & heroines de boudoires plus ou moins adaptés aux moeurs du quartier de Breda. – Je ne doute nullement que la comédie versifiée de [F.] Ponsard ne se soutienne pas les beautés du langage mais le traducteur suèdois n'a pas été heureux ni dans le <u>mètre</u> (qui manque absolument la variété de <u>l'anapeste</u>, qui fait le charme de l'alexandrin français) ni dans <u>la rime</u>, qui en plusieurs endroits m'a paru d'une platitude désespérante.

J'avou que je n'ai fait que parcourir le manuscrits, n'ayant pas en la patience de l'aprofondir dans tous ses détails – mais j'ai lieu de croire cette disposition partagée par une grande fraction du public. <u>ce 9 Novbr 1863.</u> très humblement/August Bournonville'.

According to an earlier note in Bournonville's diary ('læst nogle Franske Stykker') he probably read Ponsard's comedy for the first time on 26.8.1863.

Horace et Lydie, Une ode d'Horace was never mounted at Stockholm's Royal Theatre, but received its Stockholm première some 18 years later when it was staged (in a new Swedish translation by H. Molander) at the then privately run Nya Theatern on 17.3.1880, receiving only 4 performances there.

Autograph sources:

Recommendation note. Ms. Autograph. Brown ink. 2 pp. (13,3 × 10,5 cm)
<u>Horatius och Lydia</u>
Signed and dated: 'ce 9 Novbr 1863.'
[SSdt; KTA, E2A Ink. breve 1863/64, 9.11.1863

17.11.1863
La Demoiselle à marier, ou La Première Entrevue (Friaran kommer) (Stockholm's Royal Theatre, Dramatiska Theatern).
According to a recommendation note written to the theatre management of Stockholm's Royal Theatre on 21.10.1863, Bournonville explicitly asked to be solely responsible for the 1863 restaging of E. Scribe's and Mélesville's (pen-name for J. Duveyrier) one-act vaudeville-comedy (originally premièred at the Théâtre de Madame in Paris on 18.1.1826, and first performed in Stockholm on 23.4.1827 with the title *Första mötet*). Moreover, an earlier note in his diary (reading: 'læst nogle Franske Stykker') seems to indicate that Bournonville would have read this work for the first time on 26.8.1863. It had been translated into Swedish in 1863 by K. Almlöf after F. Printzlau's much earlier Danish translation from 1832.

In his diary and in his Swedish *Journal* Bournonville described the staging as follows:

28.10.1863: 'Collationnering af Frierens Besøg'
3.11.: 'Instruction (Friaren kommer)'
4.11.: 'Friaren kommer (sceneri)'
11.11.: '<u>Friaren kommer</u> (Gen. Rep.)'
13.11., 14.11.: '<u>Friaren kommer</u>'
16.11.: '<u>Friaren kommer</u> (Gen. Rep.)'
17.11.: '<u>Friaren kommer</u> (Gen. Rep.) […]Friaren kommer for 1.ste Gang under nærværende Form. Den gik udmærket godt og Fru [H.] Kinmansson høstede meget Bifald'.

The 1863 production of *La Demoiselle à marier* received 16 performances during Bournonville's engagement in Stockholm, the last of which was given on 5.6.1864.

Autograph sources:

Recommendation note. Ms. Autograph. Brown ink. 1 p. (21,2 × 13,4 cm)

[…] Comme je me charge des pièces suivantes […] <u>Friaran</u> […]
Signed and dated: '<u>ce 21 Octobre 1863.</u>'
[SSdt; KTA, E2A Ink. breve 1863/64, 21.10.1863

Manuscript mise-en-scène. Ms. Autograph. Black ink. 1 vol. 7 pp. (22,9 × 18,5 cm)
<u>Friaren kommer</u>/Comedie i 1 Akt af Scribe och Melesville/<u>Sceneri</u>
Signed and dated: 'd 31.de October 1863.'
[DKKk; NKS 3285 4° 5 læg 11

Manuscript mise-en-scène (incomplete). Ms. Autograph. Black ink. 1 p. (21,5 × 17,5 cm)
<u>Friaren kommer</u>/Comedie i 1 Akt af Scribe och Melesville/<u>Personerna.</u>
Unsigned and undated [1863]
[DKKk; NKS 3285 4° 4 læg 2

19.11.1863
Les Deux Journées, ou Le Porteur d'eau (Wattendragaren).
Projected restaging (Stockholm's Royal Theatre).
According to a letter written to the theatre management of Stockholm's Royal Theatre, Bournonville proposed on this day a restaging of L. Cherubini's three-act opera from 1800 (first performed in Stockholm on 2.12.1803; *see also* 30.10.1857 and 30.10.1860). His reasons for wanting it restaged this year read as follows:

'Je prends en même temps la liberté de vous proposer la remise des <u>Deux journées</u> (Vattendragaren) de Cherubini, ouvrage ardemment desiré par tous les amateurs de musique […] avec <u>Joseph</u> <u>Les Dragons de Villars</u> & <u>La muette</u> [de Portici] pourront assez bien remplir la lacune laissié par l'absence des premières cantatrices (Janvier & Fevrier.)
d. 19.e Novbr 1863. très humblement/August Bournonville'.

Les Deux Journées, ou Le Porteur d'eau was not mounted during Bournonville's engagement in Stockholm, but was restaged there during the 1867–68 season, receiving 8 performances (the last of which was given on 14.5.1869).

Autograph sources:

Recommendation note (included in a letter to E. F. O. L. von Stedingk). Ms. Autograph. Brown ink. 2 pp. (21,2 × 13,4 cm)
[…] La remise des Deux Journées (Vattendrageren) […]
Signed and dated: 'd. 19.e Novbr 1863.'
[SSdt; KTA, E2A, Ink. breve 1863/64, 19.11.1863

25.11.1863
The Ticket of Leave Man. **Projected staging at Stockholm's Royal Theatre.**
On this day Bournonville wrote a recommendation note to the theatre management of Stockholm's Royal Theatre in which he expressed his strong opposition to the projected Stockholm première of T. Taylor's four-act drama. It reads as follows:

<u>'The Ticket-of-Leave Man.</u>
Drame en 4 actes par <u>Taylor.</u>
Cette pièce jouée sur un des théâtres secondaires de Londres porte l'empreinte du goût de la classe ouvrière de cette cité immense, mais si elle était jouée a <u>Coventgarden</u> ou <u>Drury=Lane</u> elle fournerait une preuve marquante de la décadence du théâtre anglais. – Comme la scène royale de Stockholm est en chemin de progrès, je dois <u>déconseiller</u> la mise-en-scène du drame surnommé.
très humblement/ce 25 Nbr 1863./August Bournonville'.

Taylor's drama was originally premièred at London's Olympic Theatre on 27.1.1863 where it was an instant hit, and reached a total of 407 performances.

As a result of Bournonville's outspoken opposition to a Swedish staging of this work, it was never mounted at Stockholm's Royal Theatre, nor was it staged at any of the many private theatres in the Swedish capital.

Autograph sources:

Recommendation note. Ms. Autograph. Brown ink. 2 pp. (13,4 × 10,5 cm)
[…]The Ticket-of-Leave Man./Drame en 4 Actes par Taylor. […]
Signed and dated: 'ce 25 Nbr 1863.'
[SSdt; KTA, E2A Ink. breve 1863/64, 25.11.1863

8.12.1863
Le Chef-d'œuvre inconnu (Törne och Lager). Projected staging at Stockholm's Royal Theatre (Dramatiska Theatern).

According to a note in his diary (reading: 'læst nogle Franske Stykker'), Bournonville probably read C. Lafont's one-act drama for the first time on 26.8.1863. The play (which was originally premièred at the Théâtre Français in Paris on 17.6.1837) had earlier been performed in Stockholm at the privately run theatre in Humlegården on 21.7. 1853. In his diary and in his Swedish *Journal* he noted about the projected 1863 Stockholm restaging of this work:

1.12.1863: 'Collationnering Törne och Lager'
8.12.: 'Jeg fuldendte Sceneriet til Törne och Lager'.
9.1.1864: '1.ste Prøve paa Törne och Lager […] (sceneri)'
13.1.: 'Törne och Lager (Gen Rep)'
14.1.: 'Prøve paa Törne och Lager'
23.1.: 'Prøve paa Törne och Lager'.

In spite of the fact that four rehearsals of *Törne och Lager* were clearly held by Bournonville, the staging of it was for unknown reasons never carried out during his engagement at Stockholm's Royal Theatre. It was two years after he left Stockholm that Lafont's drama premièred at Dramatiska Theatern, on 10.1.1866, but then with mise-en-scène by Bournonville's pupil, the Swedish director L. Josephsson.

No autographed sources for Bournonville's projected 1863 mise-en-scène for *Törne och Lager* have yet been traced.

14.12.1863
Le Médecin malgré lui (Läkaren mot sin Vilja) (Stockholm's Royal Theatre, Stora Theatern).

The 1863 Stockholm première of C. Gounod's three-act comic opera (originally premièred at the Théâtre Lyrique in Paris on 15.1.1858) was mounted only partially by Bournonville. This is clear from a letter he wrote to the theatre management of Stockholm's Royal Theatre on 19.11.1863, in which he expressed his reasons from not wanting to be solely responsible for this production:

'Je vien d'assister à la répétition musicale du Médecin malgré lui. Charmé de la composition de Mr [C.] Gounod, j'ai trouvé les caractères de la pièce et principalment celui de Sganarelle ([F.] Arlberg) conçus et esquisser d'une manière si diamétralement opposier au comique du grand [J. B.] Molière que je me suis senti incapable d'en tirer le moindre tel pour l'éxécution dramatique.

Mr Arlberg ayant ses théories que je réspecte, et n'ésperant pour ma part excercer aucune influence sur un talent de sa dimension, je crois dans l'intérêt de la pièce de lui en laisser la direction entière. – Je vous demande donc Mr le Baron [i.e. E. F. O. L. von Stedingk], la permis[s]ion de le charger à son tour, comme régisseur, de la mise-en-scène du dit Opera-comique, dont tout le succès repose sur la conception du rôle principal'.

About the actual staging and the première he noted in his diary and in his Swedish *Journal*:

21.11.1863: 'skrevet paa Theatret'
22.11.: 'Collationnering. Läkaren mot sin villja'
23.11. and 27.11.: 'Läkaren mot sin villja (sångr)'
28.11.: 'Eftermiddagsprøve paa Läkaren mot sin villja […] (Dialog å scenen)'
30.11.: 'Läkaren mot sin villja (vid piano.)'
1.12.: 'Läkaren &c (vid piano)'
2.12.: 'Läkaren mot sin villja (piano.)'
5.12.: 'Läkaren mot sin villja (vid piano)'
8.12.: '1.ste Generalprøve paa Läkaren mot sin villja'
10.12.: 'Läkaren mot sin villja (Gen Rep.)'
11.12: 'Läkaren &c (Gen Rep.)'
12.12.: 'Läkaren mot sin villja. G. R. (i Costÿm)'
14.12.: 'I Theatret første Forstilling af Läkaren mot sin villja opera-comique af [C.] Gounod som gik meget godt, men blev temmelig koldt optaget'.

According to the Swedish musical sources for Gounod's opera the performance included a so-called 'Dans' and a 'Pastoral – Grupp -' in the Act I finale (scene 7), and a 'Dans' in the Act II finale (scene 12).

Moreover, on the back cover of the part for the bass drum to H. C. Lumbye's so-called 'Pas de deux, Polka et Mazurka' (i.e. the *Polketta, Pas de deux*, now in SSkma, call no. KT Dansmusik 101) a musical excerpt of a piece for piano from Gounod's 'Läkaran mot sin Vilja' (G major, 19 meas. in 4/4 time) is included with the title 'Chor/Dansen börjar'. This seems to indicate that Bournonville's *Polketta, Pas de deux* (*see* 31.10.1858) was included at a later stage as an incorporated divertissement in Gounod's opera.

Le Médecin malgré lui received 6 performances during Bournonville's engagement in Stockholm, the last of which was given on 31.1.1864.

Autograph sources:

Recommendation note (included in a letter to E. F. O. L. von Stedingk). Ms. Autograph. Brown ink. 2 pp. (21,2 × 13,4 cm)
[…] la répétition musicale du Médecin malgré lui. […]
Signed and dated: 'd. 19.e Novbr 1863.'
[SSdt; KTA, E2A, Ink. breve 1863/64, 19.11.1863

Manuscript mise-en-scène. Ms. Autograph. Black ink and pencil. 10 pp. (22,8 × 18,1 cm)
Läkaren mot sin villja/Opera=comique i 3 Akter (Musik af Gounod)/Sceneri.
Signed and dated: 'Stockholm den 21.e Novbr 1863.'
[DKKk; NKS 3285 4° 5 læg 18

Musical sources:

No orchestral score for Gounod's *Le Médecin malgré lui* has yet been traced in SSkma.

Piano vocal score.
According to A. F. Schwartz's handwritten catalogue of the music

archive of Stockholm's Royal Theatre (now in SSkma) a piano vocal score existed originally for this work (call no. KT Operetter L 24), but has not yet been traced.

Parts. Ms. Copy. 31 vol.
3 vl I, 3 vl II, 3 vla, 4 vlc e cb, fl picc, fl 1/2, ob 1/2, cl 1/2, fag 1/2, cor 1/2/3/4, tr 1/2, timp, gr cassa, piatti.
Unsigned and undated [c.1863]
[SSkma; KT Operetter L 24

1864

2.1.1864

La Maison sans enfants (Ett Barnlöst Hem) (Stockholm's Royal Theatre, Dramatiska Theatern).

The 1864 Swedish première of P. F. P. Dumanoir's three-act comedy (originally premièred at Théâtre Gymnase in Paris on 26.3.1863) was already planned by Bournonville during the spring of 1863. This is clear from a recommendation note that he wrote to the theatre management of Stockholm's Royal Theatre on 6.5.1863, which read as follows:

'La maison sans enfants
par
Dumanoir
La nouveauté du sujet présente quelques effets hazardés – sans être précisément scabreux. – Les quatre rôles joués a un certain degré de perfection pourront assurer du succès à cette pièce, remplie d'esprit et d'observations psychologiques'.

In his diary and in his Swedish *Journal* he noted about the staging:

6.5.1863: 'Embedsforretninger'
29.11.: Collationnering paa <u>Barnlös</u>'
7.12.: '1.ste Prøve paa <u>Barnlös</u> […] (sceneri)'
11.12. and 14.12.: 'Prøve paa <u>Barnlös</u> […] (Gen Rep.)'
18.12. and 30.12.: '<u>Ett barnlöst Hem</u> (Gen Rep.)'
2.1.1864: '<u>Ett barnlöst hem</u> (Gen Rep) […] i <u>dr. Th:</u> <u>Ett barnlöst hem</u> for første Gang […] gik udmærket godt'.

La Maison sans enfants received 10 performances during Bournonville's engagement in Stockholm, the last of which took place on 6.6.1864.

Autograph sources:

Recommendation note. Ms. Autograph. Brown ink. 1 p. (13,3 × 10,7 cm)
<u>La maison sans enfants.</u>/par/<u>Dumanoir</u>
Signed and dated: 'ce 6 Mai 1863.'
[DKKk; NKS 3285 4° 4, læg 3, pp. 66v – 67r]

Manuscript mise-en-scène. Ms. Autograph. Black ink. 1 vol. 9 pp. (22,5 × 18,1 cm)
<u>Barnlös.</u>/<u>Comedie i tre Akter</u>/<u>af</u>/<u>Dumanoir</u> (Öfversattning)/<u>Sceneri.</u>
Signed and dated: 'Stockholm d. 4.de Decbr 1863.'
[DKKk; NKS 3285 4° 2 A–E]

11.1.1864

La Dame blanche (Hvita Frun på Slottet Avenel) (Stockholm's Royal Theatre, Stora Theatern).

In a letter to the theatre management of Stockholm's Royal Theatre (dated 19.11.1863) Bournonville expressed his intention of mounting F.-A. Boyeldieu's three-act comic opera in Stockholm with the following words:

'Pour ma part je serai charmé de donner tous mes soins à la remise de <u>la Dame blanche</u>, où une retouche scenique pourra contribuer à faire ressortir dignement toutes les beautés de ce Chef d'oeuvre lyrique'.

The restaging, which was the only complete production Bournonville mounted of this opera (*see also* 1.10.1850), is described in his diary and in his Swedish *Journal* as follows:

3.12., 9.12., 11.12., 13.12., and 14.12.1863: '<u>Hvita frun</u> (sångr)'
15.12.: 'Eftermiddagsprøve paa <u>Hvita frun</u> […] (Dialog å barntheatern.)'
17.12.: 'Instructionsprøve paa <u>Hvita frun</u> […] (piano)'
18.12.: '<u>Hvita frun</u> (piano)'
19.12.: 'Indstudering af Balletterne til <u>Den hvide Dame</u>. Eftermiddagsprøve paa samme Opera […] (vid piano)'
21.12.: 'Ballet og Operaprøve paa <u>Hvita frun</u> […] (vid piano)'
22.12.: 'Generalprøve paa <u>Hvita frun</u>'
28.12.: '<u>Hvita frun</u> (Balletterna)'
2.1.1864: 'Generalprøve paa […] tredie Alt af <u>hvita frun</u> med tilhørende Balletter'
7.1.: 'Prøve […] om Aftenen <u>Hvita frun</u> […] (Gen Rep.) '
9.1.: 'Eftermiddagsprøve paa <u>Hvita frun</u> […] (Gen. Rep.)'
11.1.: 'Musikprøve paa <u>Hvita frun</u> […] (2' Akts Finale) […] I Operaen for første Gang efter flere Aars Hvile <u>Hvita frun</u> (ny Indstudering) og gjorde megen Lykke'.

The 1864 staging received 13 performances during Bournonville's engagement in Stockholm, the last of which took place on 1.6.1864.

Moreover, the production was such a success with the audience that it remained continuously in the Stockholm repertory until the 1874–75 season, reaching a total of 58 performances in this decade.

Autograph sources:

Recommendation note (included in a letter to E. F. O. L. von Stedingk). Ms. Autograph. Brown ink. 2 pp. (21,2 × 13,4 cm)
[…] A Monsieur le Baron E de Stedingk […] la remise de <u>la Dame blanche</u> […]
Signed and dated: 'd. 19.e Novbr 1863.'
[SSdt; KTA, E2A, Ink. breve 1863/64, 19.11.1863]

Musical sources:

Printed orchestral score with manuscript insertions. 3 vol. Act I 269 pp., Act II 192 pp., Act III 114 pp. + 'Variante' 1 p. (31,2 × 23,8 cm)
La/DAME BLANCHE/Opéra Comique en trois Actes
Paris, Janet et Cotelle, pl. no. 2002 [1825]
[SSkma; KT Operetter H 7]
This French printed orchestral score was used since the Stockholm première of Boyeldieu's *La Dame blanche* on 31.1.1827 and for all later performances of it there during Bournonville's lifetime.

No répétiteur's copy for *La Dame blanche* has yet been traced in SSkma.

Parts. Ms. Copy. 27 vol.
3 vl I, 3 vl II, 2 vla, 3 vlc e cb, fl 1/2, ob 1/2, cl 1/2, fag 1/2, cor 1/2/3/4, tr, trb, timp, arpa.
Unsigned and undated [c.1827–1864]
[SSkma; KT Operetter H 7]
This set of parts dates from the 1827 Stockholm première of *La Dame blanche* and was used for all performances of it there during Bournonville's lifetime.

18.1.1864

***Daniel Hjort* (Stockholm's Royal Theatre, Stora Theatern).**

In a recommendation note written to the management of Stockholm's Royal Theatre on 21.10.1863 Bournonville expressed his explicit wish to be solely responsible for mounting the Swedish première of J. J. Wecksell's five-act tragedy (written under the pen-name Lagus, and mounted as an anonymous work). In his diary and in his Swedish *Journal* he noted about the actual staging:

18.11.1863: 'Collationnering på Daniel Hjort'
20.11.: 'skrevet paa Sceneri m m.'
23.11: 'Decorationsmöte på Daniel Hjort'
30.12.: 'Første Prøve paa Daniel Hjort [...] (1.e och 2.dra Akten)'
3.1.1864: 'Prøve paa Daniel Hjort'
4.1.: 'Daniel Hjorth (fyra Akter rolerna)'
5.1.: 'Prøve paa Daniel Hjort [...] (4.e & 5.e Akten.)'
7.1.: 'Daniel Hjort (Gen Rep rolerna)'
11.1.: 'Sceneriprøve paa Daniel Hjort'
12.1., 14.1., and 15.1.: 'Daniel Hjort (Gen Rep.)'
16.1.: 'Prøve [...] om Aftenen paa Daniel Hjort i Costym ÷ Fru [E.] Hwasser, modstræbende som forhen'
18.1.: 'Første Forestilling af Sørgespillet Daniel Hjort, der gik udmærket godt og gjorde et Slags Lykke! Fremtiden vil vise'.

No complete orchestral score for *Daniel Hjort* has yet been traced. However, according to several notes in the (incomplete) musical sources for this work, the staging included a dance scene in Act I (scene 11), entitled 'Polonaise', set to music most probably by L. Norman. Moreover, a song in the same act (score no. 5) is entitled 'Soldatvisa' («När jeg var barn») and was performed to music by a not yet identified composer. It is followed by three other songs, the first of which (named 'Suomis sång') is composed by F. Pacius and was employed as a musical *entr'acte* between Acts I and II. In the following acts a song by a not yet unidentified composer (entitled «Nu skördas den gröna sommarskatt i hemmet dal») is performed by a chorus of soldiers. It is followed by yet another song by L. Norman (named «Sanct Göran han var en riddare god»), sung by the character *Oluf* together with a chorus. After this song follows F. Pacius' arrangement from 1860 of a popular French military tune, which in Sweden was known as *Björneborgarnes marsch*. It seems to have been employed as a musical *entr'acte* between Acts III and IV of *Daniel Hjort*. Finally, a 'Chaconne' was performed (most likely in Act V?) by an orchestra seated on the stage.

Of these numbers only a few vocal parts and an orchestral score for the song «När jeg var barn», plus two complete sets of parts for Pacius' *Björneborgarnes marsch* and the 'Chaconne', have been preserved (*see* Musical sources).

Daniel Hjort received 8 performances during Bournonville's engagement in Stockholm, the last of which was given on 14.2.1864.

Autograph sources:

Recommendation note (included in a letter to E. F. O. L. von Stedingk). Ms. Autograph. Brown ink. 1 p. (21,2 × 13,4 cm)
[...] Comme je me charge des pièces suivantes [...] Daniel Hjorth. [...]
Signed and dated: 'ce 21 Octobre 1863.'
[SSdt; KTA, E2A Ink. breve 1863/64, 21.10.1863

Manuscript mise-en-scène. Ms. Autograph. Black ink and pencil. 1 vol. 19 pp. (22,6 × 18 cm)
Daniel Hjort./historiskt Skådespel i fem Akter./Lagus (finskt Original.)/Sceneri.
Signed and dated: ' d. 20 Novbr 1863.'
[DKKk; NKS 3285 4° 5 læg 9

Manuscript mise-en-scène (incomplete). Ms. Autograph. Black ink. 1 p. (21,5 × 17,5 cm)
Daniel Hjorth/Historisk Skådespel i fem Akter af Lagus./Personerna.
Unsigned and undated [c.1863]
[DKKk; NKS 3285 4° 4 læg 2

Musical sources:

Orchestral score ('Soldatvisa', Act I, score no. 5). Ms. Copy. 1 vol. 12 pp. (34,6 × 25,8 cm)
(När jeg var barn)/[...]/No. 5./Soldat visa i [word illegible] Akten.
Unsigned and undated [c.1864]
[SSkma; KT Tal-Pjeser med Musik D 19 (vocal parts in 'kapsel D')

Parts (*Björneborgarnes marsch/Björneborgermarschen*). Ms. Copy. 20 vol.
vl I, vl II, vla, vlc e cb, fl 1/2, ob 1/2, cl 1/2, fag 1/2, cor 1/2, tr 1/2, Btrb, timp, gr cassa, piatti.
Unsigned and undated [c.1864 or earlier]
[SSkma; KT Tal-Pjeser med Musik D 19

Parts ('Chaconne' in Act V?). Ms. Copy. 14 vol.
vl I, vl II, vla, vlc e cb, fl, ob, fag 1/2, cor 1/2, tr 1/2, Btrb, timp.
Unsigned and undated [c.1864 or earlier]
[SSkma; KT Tal-Pjeser med Musik D 19

19.1.1864

***Joseph (Joseph i Egypten)* (Stockholm's Royal Theatre, Stora Theatern).**

The 1864 Stockholm restaging of E.-H. Méhul's three-act opera (*see also* 13.10.1858) represents the last time this work was ever mounted under Bournonville's supervision. Its restaging this year had been proposed by him to the Stockholm theatre management in a recommendation note written on 19.11.1863. In his diary and in the Swedish *Journal* Bournonville noted about the production:

19.11.1863: 'Embedsforretninger'
6.1., 7.1., and 8.1.1864: 'Joseph (sångr:)'
9.1.: 'Joseph mid Chör (Rep. salen)'
10.1.: 'Piano-Repetition paa Joseph'
12.1.: 'Eftermiddagsprøve paa Joseph [...] (vid Piano)'
14.1.: 'Eftermiddag paa Joseph [...] (vid Piano)'
16.1.: 'Prøve paa Joseph [...] (Gen. Rep.)'
18.1.: 'Generalprøve paa Joseph'
19.1.: 'Sceneriprøve paa Joseph [...] I Theatret – Joseph i Egypten, der med Undtagelse af Hovedrollen gik udmærket godt og vederqvægede mig baade musikalsk og [i] dramatisk Henseende [...] Huset var maadeligt besat'.

Joseph received 5 performances during Bournonville's engagement in Stockholm, the last of which was given on 20.3. 1864.

Autograph sources:

Recommendation note (included in a letter to E. F. O. L. von Stedingk). Ms. Autograph. Brown ink. 2 pp. (21,2 × 13,4 cm)
[...]La remise de [...] Joseph [...]
Signed and dated: 'd. 19.e Novbr 1863.'
[SSdt; KTA, E2A, Ink. breve 1863/64, 19.11.1863

Musical sources:

Printed orchestral score with manuscript insertions. 1 vol. 194 pp. (34,4 × 26 cm)
JOSEPH/Opéra en trois Actes
Paris, Magasin de Musique, pl. no. 505 [1807]
[SSkma; KT Operetter I 5
This French printed orchestral score was used since the Stockholm première of Méhul's opera on 15.10.1856 and for all later performances of it there during Bournonville's lifetime.

No répétiteur's copy for *Joseph* has yet been traced in SSkma.

Parts. Ms. Copy. 28 vol. + 5 vol.
3 vl I, 3 vl II, 2 vla, 4 vlc e cb, fl 1/2, ob 1/2, cl 1/2, fag 1/2, cor 1/2, tr, tuba, timp, arpa 1/2/3. On stage: vl, cor 1/2, tr 1/2.
Unsigned and undated [c.1856]
[SSkma; KT Operetter I 5
This set of parts dates from the 1856 Stockholm première of *Joseph* and was used for all later performances of it there during Bournonville's lifetime.

20.1.1864

Souvenir de Taglioni, Pas de deux (uncredited) performed by A. and C. Healey (Stockholm's Royal Theatre, Dramatiska Theatern).

This (uncredited) dance was choreographed and mounted by Bournonville for his two English pupils, A. and C. Healey. Musically it is based on the much earlier *Pas de deux* to music by F.-M.-A. Venua, which Bournonville first incorporated in J. L. Heiberg's three-act play *Princess Isabella, or Three Nights at the Court* at Copenhagen's Royal Theatre on 29.10.1829.

Venua's music (to which Bournonville added a new, brief introduction of 16 bars) is mingled with an excerpt from H. S. Paulli's score for the Act I *Pas d'Ecole* (score no. 3) in Bournonville's two-act ballet-vaudeville *The Conservatoire, or A Proposal of Marriage through the Newspaper* (*see* 6.5.1849). This excerpt is inserted immediately before Venua's *Coda* movement of 29 measures.

Souvenir de Taglioni received 3 performances in Stockholm, the last of which took place on 3.2.1864. Later the same year it was also performed by the Healey sisters at Copenhagen's Royal Theatre on 19.9.1864 and reached a total of 5 performances there.

In his diary and in his Swedish *Journal* Bournonville noted about the 1864 Stockholm première of this dance:

19.1.1864: 'Kl 1/2 11 pas de deux […] Kl 1. […] Prøve med Orchester paa 'Souvenir de Taglioni' pas de deux for Søstrene [A. and C.] Healey'
20.1.: 'Prøve paa […] Souvenir de Taglioni […] i D.T. […] Souvenir de Taglioni, der gik meget smukt'.

Musical sources:

Orchestral score. Ms. Autograph (by H.S. Paulli?) and copy. Brown and black ink, and pencil. 30 pp. (28,2 × 38,4 cm)
Pas de deux./Nr. 107./[…]/Adagio. No. 19 [changed to:] 107/Partitur og Stemmer tilhører Bournonville.
Unsigned and undated [1864]
[SSkma; KT Dansmusik 107
This orchestral score consists of excerpts from two older scores that are pieced together. Of these the first section (the 'Introduction') includes the subtitle 'Pas de deux'. The following movement ('Adagio') and most of the remaining music seems to be written in H. S. Paulli's hand. The score was renamed at a later stage by a pencilled

note (written by an unknown hand) on the front cover which reads: '107 Partitur og Stemmer tilhører Bournonville'.

Répétiteur's copy. Ms. Copy. 1 vol. 11 pp. (33,5 × 24 cm)
Souvenir de Taglioni./Pas de deux/pour/Mlles Agnes & Christine Healey
Unsigned and undated [1864]
[SSkma; KT Dansmusik 107
This répétiteur's copy includes Bournonville's autographed inscription (written with black ink): 'Souvenir de Taglioni./Pas de deux/pour/Mlles Agnes & Christine Healey'. It also contains his autographed notes about the musical phrasing, the dymanics, and the exact tempi of the dance together with some other, more specific choreographic indications describing who performed which sections.

Parts. Ms. Copy. 30 vol.
3 vl I, 3 vl II, 2 vla, 3 vlc e cb, fl 1/2, ob 1/2, cl 1/2, fag 1/2, cor 1/2, tr 1/2, Atrb, Ttrb, Btrb, timp, gr cassa, cassa, tri.
Unsigned and undated [1864]
[SSkma; KT Dansmusik 107

6.2.1864

Un Homme de rien (Richard Sheridan) (Stockholm's Royal Theatre, Dramatiska Theatern).

Although Bournonville did not include A. Langlé's four-act comedy (first performed at the Théâtre Vaudeville in Paris on 25.4.1863) in his list of those plays that he mounted in Stockholm (published in *My Theatre Life*, pp. 313–318), he wrote a recommendation note about it to the theatre management at Stockholm's Royal Theatre on 20.6.1863, expressing his hesitations about the planned staging of *Richard Sheridan*. This note reads as follows:

'Un Homme de rien
(par l'Anglé)
Des situations piquantes, mais trop souvent invraisemblables, des effets de mise-en-scène parfois trop compliqués pour la comédie; un interêt trop envisagé du point de vue des Français, un dialogue calculé sur des talents spéciaux me rendent trés incertain sur la reception, que cette pièce pourait espérer sur la scène de Stockholm et sur la manière, dont elle serait rendue par nos acteurs actuels'.

In the diary and in his Swedish *Journal* he stated about his later involvement in the actual staging of Langlé's comedy:

8.1.1864: 'Collationnering Sheridan (foyéen.)'
22.1.: 'Richard Sheridan (1.ste rep)'
25.1.: 'Richard Sheridan'
26.1.: 'Richard Sheridan (Gen Rep) inställd.
27.1. and 28.1.: 'Sheridan'
30.1.: 'Sheridan (Gen Rep)'
1.2.: 'Kl 10 Sheridan (sceneri) Kl 11. 1.ste och 2' Akten Gen Rep'
3.2.: 'Sheridan (Gen Rep)'
4.2.: 'Sheridan'
5.2.: 'Kl 6 Sheridan (Gen Rep i Costym)'
6.2.: 'Sheridan (Minnesrep:) […] Jeg gik ud på Dramatiska theatern for at see 1.ste Forestilling af Sheridan'.

No musical sources for *Un Homme de rien* have yet been traced in SSkma, in spite of the fact that the Swedish textbook for this work clearly indicates the performance of several fanfares and horn signals.

Un Homme de rien received 17 performances during Bournonville's engagement in Stockholm, the last of which was given on 19.4.1864.

Autograph sources:

Recommendation note. Ms. Autograph. Brown ink. 1 p. (18,4 × 11,1 cm)
Un Homme de rien / (par l'Anglé)
Signed and dated: 'ce 20 Juin 1863.'
[SSm; Daniel Fryklunds samling no. 100

20.2.1864
The Order of the Amaranth (Amarather-Orden) including an
Intermezzo in Act V, entitled *Le Ballet des cinq sens*
(Stockholm's Royal Theatre, Dramatiska Theatern).
On 29.10.1863 Bournonville wrote a recommendation note
to the theatre management of Stockholm's Royal Theatre
about the projected première of O. Wijkander's historical
five-act play. In this note he expressed his favourable opinion about mounting this play and also discussed the possibility of interpolating a ballet divertissement in the form of a
court ball in Act V. It read as follows:

'Amaranther = Orden:
Cette pièce qui se présente sous le titre modeste de 'Charactersteck-
ning' me semble remplir toutes les conditions d'une comédie de
mœurs et d'un tableau historique. Le dialogue est palpitant d'espert
& d'interêt, les situations bien amenées et à quelques scènes d'une
controverse trop abstracte près [?], la marche est rapide et parfaitement adaptée aux jeux de théâtre.
  Avec un public aussi blasé que le nostre il est très difficile de pré-
dire quelle sorte de succès la pièce pourra obtenir et quelles objec-
tions elle aura à subir du côté de la critique. – Une consideration
assez delicate qui à mon avis mériterait d'être mise en regard est: –
Les sentiments de piété envers un personage auguste – exemple de
la plus haute vertu – professant le culte, qui détacha de la Suède, la
fille du grand Gustav Adolphe.
  Sous le point de vue économique & pour obtenir une serie de
représentations fructueuses, je suis d'avis de monter cette pièce
pour le théâtre dramatique.
  L'intermède de l'institution de l'Ordre e l'Amarather (dont l'ori-
gine papale étonnera singulièrement la grands majorité du public)
hors-d'oeuvre qui n'ajoutera rien à l'interêt de la pièce, si ce n'est le
spectacle d'une fête de cour, dont l'Opera fournit à chaque pas le
pareil – pourra s'effectuer avec le même luxe de danses costume &
cortèges – au petit théâtre et n'occasionerait pas la même dépense.
Comme Intendant de la mise-en-scène je dois necéssairement m'op-
poser aux privilèges donnés par l'auteur à l'artiste chargée du rôle
principal -dans l'ouvrage – même du 3.me Acte. Je conviendrai avec
plaisir des dispositions les plus comodes mais comme employé res-
ponsable je ne dois pas avoir les mains liées.
  très respectueusement./29 Octbr 1863./August Bournonville'.

In the printed 1864 textbook of Wijkander's play (pp. 82–
84) a detailed description is included of the opening scene
in Act V, in which Bournonville incorporated his allegorical
Le Ballet des cinq sens. The text for this scene (which was most
probably written by Bournonville himself, or at least is based
on his choreographic indications) read as follows:

'Under entreakten spelar orkestern Amaranther-ordens stora
marsch [...] Musiken öfvergår till en Quadrille, som dansas af Ama-
ranther-ordens riddare och damer. När Quadrillen slutat, uppspelas
DE FEM SINNENAS GAVOTT
(ord af Sam. Columbus. Musik af G. Düben).
Fem Herdinnor föreställande SYNEN, HÖRSELN, LUKTEN, SMAK-
EN och KÄNSLEN, inkomma på scenen, åtföljda af en Herde.
Denne framräcker till SYNEN en korg, fylld med blommor. Herdin-
nan beundrar blommornas fägring och utsöker åt sig en bukett.
[...] Nu framtager Herden sin flöjt och blåser. Tre af Herdinnorna

spela mandolin och klockspel, omgifvande i åtskilliga grupper HÖR-
SELN.
[...] SYNEN leker med sin bukett och följes tätt i spåren af LUKTEN,
som småningon berusas af blommornas doft, och under en lekfull
strid tillegnar sig buketten.
[...] KÄNSLEN rycker till sig en törnros ur buketten, men sticker sig
på dess taggar. Under den smärta, hon dervid erfar, söka Herden och
Herdinnorna att trösta henne; men Herden allena förmår att lindra
hennes smärta, då han kysser den sårade handen och trycker den till
sitt hjerta.
[...] Under den glädja, som Herdern och Herdinnorna nu visa, fat-
tar SMAKEN en fylld bägare, som hon kredensar och låter gå omkring bland de andra Herdinnorna. När hon slutligen räcker bäg-
aren åt Herden, fatta Herdinnorna tamburiner och afsluta balletten
med en yr och glädtig dans.
När gavotten är slutad, reser sig Kristina från sin plats. Orkestern
uppspelar åter Amaranther-ordens stora marsch, hvarunder Hof-
folket ordnar sig i procession. Riddarne af Amaranther-orden med
deras damer gå sist. [...]'.

According to a later note in his diary on 16.1.1866 Bournonville also planned a Danish staging of *Le Ballet des cinq sens* at
Copenhagen's Royal Theatre. That project, however, was
never carried out.
  Meanwhile, the idea seems to have been recycled by him
in 1868, when he choreographed a very similar allegorical
Dance of the five senses in the second scene of Act I (score no.
2) of his four-act Nordic mythological ballet *The Lay of Thrym*
(*see* 21.2.1868).
  In his diary and in his Swedish *Journal* Bournonville noted
about the 1864 staging of Wijkander's play and its first three
performances:

5.12.1863: 'Collationnering paa Amaranthen.'
30.12.: 'arbeidet paa Repertoiret og componeret paa min Ballet til
Amaranther-Orden'
31.12.: 'arbeidet paa min Composition til Amaranther-Orden'
3.1.1864: 'skrevet'
25.1.: 'Indstuderet Ballet til Amaranther=Orden'
28.1.: 'Indstudering paa Amaranther=Balletten'
29.1.: 'fuldendt min nyeste Composition, der gaaer ret smukt'
30.1.: 'Prøve paa Amaranther=Balletten, som jeg præsenterede for
[O.] Wijkander [...] (å Barntheatern)'
1.2.: 'Amaranther=Ballett (å Barnth.)'
2.2: 'første Sceneri=Repetition paa Amaranthen. Vrøvl med Fru [E.]
Hwasser (Jeg haaber for Fremtiden at slippe for denne Dame.)'
4.2.: 'Amaranther=Balletten'
5.2.: 'Prøve paa Sceneriet til Amaranthen'
8.2.: 'Kl 10 Amaranther Orden (1.e 2' 3.die Akten) Kl 1. Intermediet'
9.2.: 'Prøve paa Amaranthen [...] (3.e 4.e & 5.e Akten) [...] Amaran-
ther-Balletten (Barntheatern)'
12.2.: 'Kl 10 Amaranther Orden (Gen Rep) Kl 1. Intermediet [...]
gjorde megen Lykke. Undgaaet Conflikt med de frigide og egois-
tiske engelske Söstre [i.e. A. and C. Healey] – Jeg udelod Dandserne
af Marschen, men jeg vil uden Vrede og Scandale herefter lade disse
utaknemmelige Pigebørn seile deres egen Sö'
13.2.: 'Prøve paa Amaranther-Orden, der lover at blive kjedelig formedelst Hovedrollens forkeerte Opfatning'
15.2.: 'Amaranther-Orden (Gen Rep.)'
17.2.: 'Amaranther=Orden (utan Intermediet)'
18.2.: 'Amaranther=Orden (Gen Rep)'
19.2.: 'Amaranther=Orden (ultima Gen Rep.) [...] der gik meget
smukt'
20.2.: 'I Dr. Theatern 1.ste Forestilling af Amaranther=Orden, der
gik særdeles smukt fra alle Sider, ogsaa mit Intermedium med de fem
Sandser, men det Hele optages temmelig koldt'
23.2.: 'Amarnther=Orden gik for anden Gang med aldeles udsolgt
Huus'

25.2.: 'Amaranther=Orden der formedelst Fru [J. G.] Sundbergs Upasselighed gik uden Ballet, dog med aldeles udsolgt Huus'.

Le Ballet des cinq sens was an integral part of an intermezzo that was set to music composed and arranged by H. Berens. According to Bournonville's manuscript mise-en-scène this intermezzo was divided into four sections and performed at the opening of Act V as follows:

(1) 'March en rond des Chevaliers & Dames' (also described as 'Marsch til Introduction').
(2) 'Chör till Instiftelsen af Amaranth Orden beledsagad af dans'.
(3) 'Ballet des cinq sens' (also entitled 'Ballet (De fem sinner.)').
(4) 'Marche finale' (also described as 'derpå repeteras marchen som slutar Intermediet.').

The same four numbers are described in the orchestral score as follows:

(1) 'No. 1 Amaranther Ordens Marsch' (44 bars in 4/4 time, without any indication of tempo).
(2) 'No. 2. Chör 'Var vilkommen!' (61 bars in 2/4 time, *Andante*).
(3) 'No. 3 Chör och Dans/1.ste Kupletten'. This number consists of nine sections entitled: 'Gavotte, 1.ste variation'/'2.dra Kupletten'/ '2,dra Variation'/'3.dje Kupletten Chör'/'3.dje Variation'/'4.de Kupletten'/'4.de Variation'/'Finale'. According to the poster the so-called 'Gavotte' (which was sung by a chorus as a couplet between each of the five solo variations in Bournonville's *Le Ballet des cinq sens*) was set to text by S. Columbus (reading: «Lustwin dansar en gavott med de fen sinnena»). Moreover, in the same source the tune of the 'Gavotte' is said to be based on a (not yet identified) work from the 17th century, composed by A. Düben.
(4) 'No. 4 Amarather Ordens Marsch' (set to the same music as no. 1, but this time playing for 70 bars with meas. nos. 11–22 repeated three times).

The Order of the Amaranth received 15 performances during Bournonville's engagement in Stockholm, the last of which was given on 9.6.1864 (one performance on 24.2.1864 was given without the ballet).

Autograph sources:

Recommendation note. Ms. Autograph. Brown ink. 2 pp. (21,2 × 13,3 cm)
[…]Amaranther = Orden […]
Signed and dated: 'ce 29.e Octbr 1863.'
[SSdt; KTA, E2A Ink. breve 1863/64, 29.10.1863

Manuscript mise-en-scène. Ms. Autograph. Black ink and pencil. 1 vol. 18 pp. (22,8 × 18,2 cm)
Amaranther – Orden./Skådespel i fem Akter. (5.de Akten i två tablåu.)/af/Förf till Lucidor. [Historical play in four acts by O. Wijkander, premièred at Stockholm's Royal Theatre (Operahuset) on 27.3.1854]/Sceneri.
Signed and dated: 'd. 27.e Decbr 1863.'
[DKKk; NKS 3285 4° 5 læg 6

Choreographic note. Ms. Autograph. Brown ink. 7 pp. (22,8 × 18,2 cm)
Ballet des cinq sens./composé pour la comedie de/l'Ordre de l'Amaranthe/par/August Bournonville./(Notes chorégraphiques –)/(Musique de Mr Behrens) [i.e. H. Berens]
Signed and dated: 'Stockholm ce 3 Janvier 1864.' [According to the diary choreographed on 30.12. and 31.12.1863]
[DKKk; NKS 3285 4° 5 læg 6

Production note. Ms. Autograph. Black ink. 1 p. (35,5 × 22,8 cm)

Amaranther Orden./Personal – Lista./ (NB Bipersonerna.)
Signed and dated: 'd 3.die Februar 1864.'
[DKKk; NKS 3285 4° 5 læg 6

Musical sources:

Orchestral score. Ms. Autograph (by H. Berens). Black ink. 1 vol. 80 pp. (32,9 × 24 cm)
Amaranther Orden./Musiken til Intermeden med bibehållande/af Amaranther Ordens-Högtids-Marsch, (Andanten vid Receptionen jemte en Gavotte af Düben.)/Componerad/af/Herrn: Berens./ 1864.
Signed and dated (on the front cover): 'Hernn: Berens./1864.'
[SSkma; KT Tal-Pjeser med Musik A 30

Répétiteur's copy. Ms. Copy. 1 vol. 11 pp. (34,1 × 24,4 cm)
Amaranther Orden/Repetiteur.
Unsigned and undated [1864]
[SSkma; KT Tal-Pjeser med Musik A 30
This répétiteur's copy contains the complete music for *Le Ballet des cinq sens* performed in Act V (score no. 3) of *The Order of the Amaranth.*

Parts. Ms. Copy. 17 vol. + 6 vol.
vl I, vl II, vla, vlc, cb, fl, ob, cl 1/2, fag 1/2, cor 1/2, tr 1/2, timp, gr cassa. On stage: vl I, vl II, vla, vlc, arpa, org.
Unsigned and undated [1864]
[SSkma; KT Tal-Pjeser med Musik A 30

Printed sources:

Printed text book. 1 vol. 88 pp. (16,6 × 10,8 cm)
Amaranther-Orden./Skådespel/i/Fem Akter./Svenskt Original/af /Forf. till 'Lucidor'
Stockholm, Joh. Beckman, 1864.
[DKKk; 192, – 239 8°

30.3.1864
La Favorite (Leonora) **(Stockholm's Royal Theatre, Stora Theatern).**
The 1864 Swedish restaging of G. Donizetti's four-act opera (originally premièred at the Paris Opéra on 2.12.1840, and first performed in Stockholm on 9.3.1850) was mounted especially for the début of the Swedish singer, L. Skougaard Severini, who played the rôle of *Fernando*. The staging also represents the first and only time *La Favorite* was mounted with Bournonville's mise-en-scène.

According to the poster, Donizetti's ballet divertissements in Act II (originally choreographed by P. J. W. Pettersson in 1850) seem to have been omitted this year.

In his diary and in his Swedish *Journal* Bournonville noted about the staging:

25.2., 26.2., and 27.2.1864: 'Leonora (sångr)'
1.3.: 'skrevet […] Instruction paa Leonora […] (sångr)'
2.3.: 'Leonora (Instruction Barnth:)'
4.3. and 5.3.: 'Leonora (sångr)'
7.3.: 'Leonora (sång Chör Rep salen)'
8.3.: 'Prøve paa La Favorite […] (sceneri vid piano) […] ([F.] Arlberg har ført sig op som en Slyngel)'
12.3.: 'Leonora (Gen Rep vid piano)'
16.3. and 18.3.: 'Leonora (Gen Rep:)'
28.3.: 'Leonora (sångr)'
29.3.: 'Leonora'
30.3.: 'Leonora (de svaraste Nummer.) […] I Operaen Leonora til Skougaards [i.e. L. Skougaard Severini] Debüt. Hans stemme er tynd, men uddannet i en god Skole. Intonationen er reen og Sangen ikke uden et vist dramatisk Udtryk, forresten uheldig af Been, Gestus

og Opfatning. <u>Han tiltalte ikke</u>. Arlberg sang smukt og gjorde megen Lykke'.

La Favorite received 3 performances during Bournonville's engagement in Stockholm, the last of which was given on 3.4.1864 (Acts II and III were given separately on 7.6.1864).

Autograph sources:

Manuscript mise-en-scène. Ms. Autograph. Brown ink. 9 pp. (22,8 × 17,9 cm)
Leonora (La Favorite)./Opera i fyra Akter af Donizetti./<u>Sceneri</u>
Signed and dated: 'Stockholm d. 1.de Mars 1864.'
[DKKk; NKS 3285 4° 5 læg 17

Musical sources:

Printed orchestral score with manuscript insertions. 2 vol. Act I-II 324 pp., Act III-IV 232 pp. (30,2 × 24 cm)
LA FAVORITE/OPERA EN QUATRE ACTES
s. l., s. a. [c.1850–1864]
[SSkma; KT Operor L 2
This printed orchestral score (of which the title page is missing) dates from the 1850 Stockholm première of Donizetti's *La Favorite* and was used for all performances of it there during Bournonville's lifetime.

No répétiteur's copy for *La Favorite* has yet been traced in SSkma.

Parts. Ms. Copy. 40 vol.
4 vl I, 4 vl II, 2 vla, 4 vlc e cb, fl picc, fl 1/2, ob 1/2, cor inlg, cl 1/2 fag 1/2, cor 1/2/3/4, tr, cnt 1/2, trb 1/2/3, oph, gr cassa, cassa, piatti, tri, arpa.
Unsigned and undated [c.1850–1864]
[SSkma; KT Operor L 2
This set of parts dates from the 1850 Stockholm première of Donizetti's opera and was used for all performances of it there during Bournonville's lifetime.

5.4.1864
Le Marquis de Villemer. Projected staging at Stockholm's Royal Theatre.
According to a note in Bournonville's diary, on this day he read G. Sand's four-act comedy (originally premièred at the Théâtre de l'Odéon in Paris on 29.2.1864). On the same day he made the following comments about its projected staging at Stockholm's Royal Theatre:

'læst George Sands nye Comedie <u>Le Marquis de Villemer</u>. Meget Talent, endeel Unatur, daarlig Vrøvl og efter min Mening liden Anvendelse paa vor Scene'.

G. Sand's comedy was never mounted in Stockholm.

16.4.1864
Montjoye (Stockholm's Royal Theatre, Dramatiska Theatern).
On 27.11.1863 Bournonville wrote an extensive recommendation note to the theatre management of Stockholm's Royal Theatre in which he expressed his opinion about the projected Stockholm staging of O. Feuillet's five-act comedy (originally premièred at the Théâtre Gymnase in Paris on 24.10.1863). Moreover, he carefully indicated the exact number of cuts and changes he felt necessary before a staging of this work could be accepted. These notes read as follows:

'<u>Montjoie</u> (Comédie par O. Feuillet)
Le mérite de cette comédie de mœurs est incontestable, il s'agit seulement pour nous de deux question principales:
<u>1.°</u> Comment faire digérer au public suèdois les points scabreux de l'action?
<u>2.°</u> Quels seraient les artistes capables de donner l'éclat nécessaire aux caractères si habilement dessinés par l'auteur?
'Quant à la première question, je serais d'avis d'exclure entièrement le personnage de <u>la marquise</u>, dont l'existence est suffisamment prouvée par la présence du mari ridicule; – en outre que les deux scènes avec Montjoie ne servent qu'à rendre leur liaison aussi abjecte que ridicule (pour un homme de 50 ans.)
'Quelques modifications dans le rôle du vieux veuf <u>Lajaunnaye</u> pourraient ne pas nuire & le dévergondage du jeune <u>Roland</u> demanderaient une transcription spirituelle.
En général quelquesunes des tirades de morales, ou d'invectives oratoires pourraient subir une abréviation solutaire.

==========

<u>Malheureusement</u>, dans les preuves de talent donné par nos premièrs acteurs, je ne vois que la faculté de rendre <u>la moitié</u> du rôle de Montjoie i.e. <u>Hedin</u> pour la première & <u>Schwartz</u> pour la dernière partie.
Cépendant si nous voulons appoyer sur le côté froid, égoiste & raisonnence, joint aux pointes satiriques & plaisantes, <u>Hedin</u> me parait préférable.
La marquise disparaissante – <u>M.me Hedin</u> conviendrait dans le rôle d'Henrietta.

<u>Cecile</u>	<u>Mme [H.] Kinmansson</u>
<u>Sorel</u>	[A. W. J.] <u>Elmlund</u>
<u>Roland</u>	[G.] <u>Fredriksson</u>
<u>Saladin</u>	[C. G.] <u>Sundberg</u>
<u>Tiberge</u>	[R. G.] <u>Broman</u>
<u>Le Marquis</u>	<u>Almløf</u> [i.e. K. Almlöf]
<u>Lajaunnaye</u>	[J.] <u>Jolin</u>
<u>Le capitaine de pompiers</u>	<u>Swensson</u> [i.e. W. C. A. Svenson]
<u>La rosière</u>	M.e [E. M.] Grabow
<u>L'huisier</u>	Mr [A. F.] Dörum

Bien traduite & avec une mise-en-scène soignée sous tous les rapports – Un succés me parait plus que possible'.

According to Bournonville's manuscript mise-en-scène the staging included a so-called '<u>tablå och kort entracte</u> (Musik)', which was performed in Act IV after scene 10. It consisted of three music numbers (played by an orchestra seated on the stage) which are named in the conductor's part as follows:

(1) 'Lantlig Marsch' (34 bars in 4/4 time, by a not yet identified composer).
(2) 'Marseljäsen' (34 bars, identical with the French national anthem *La Marseillaise*).
(3) 'Geschwind-Marsch' (41 bars in 4/4 time, composed by a not yet identified composer).

Moreover, the staging reused the same décor (although slightly modified) as that used for Bournonville's earlier stagings of P. Dumanoir's three-act comedy *La Maison sans enfants* (Acts I and III, *see* 2.1.1864), and C. Andersen's two-act comedy *Rosa and Rosita* (Act II, *see* 26.3.1863).

In his diary and in his Swedish *Journal* he noted about the performance:

19.3.1864: 'Collationnering paa Montjoie'
21.3.: 'Collationn: <u>Montjoie</u> (5' A.)'
23.3.: 'Decorationsmøde paa <u>Montjoie</u>'
29.3.: 'Instruction Montjoie'
30.3.: 'Første Prøve paa <u>Montjoye</u> [...] (1.e och 2.dra Akten.)'
31.3.: 'Montjoye (1.e och 2.dra Akten.)'

2.4.: 'Montjoÿe (3', 4' 5.te Akten)'
4.4.: Montjoÿe (1' 2' 3' & 4' Akterne)'
6.4.: Montjoÿe (4.e & 5.e Akterne) inställd genom sjukdom'
8.4., 11.4., and 13.4.,: 'Montjoÿe (Gen Rep:)'
14.4.: 'Montjoÿe (Minnesrepetition)'
15.4.: 'Om Eftermiddagen Generalprøve paa Montjoye, der lover at gaae fortræffeligt'
16.4.: 'I dr theatern 1.ste Gang Montjoye Comedie i 5 Aktern af Oc-tave Feuillet. Den gik særdeles godt for fuldt Huus og livligt Bifald. Det bliver formodentlig et Kassestykke'.

Montjoye received 11 performances during Bournonville's engagement in Stockholm, the last of which was given on 27.5.1864.

Autograph sources:

Recommendation note. Ms. Autograph. Brown ink. 2 pp. (21,1 × 13,4 cm)
[…] Monjoie [*sic*]
Signed and dated: 'ce 27 Novbr 1863.'
[SSdt; KTA, E2A Ink. breve 1863/64, 27.11.1863

Manuscript mise-en-scène. Ms. Autograph. Black ink and pencil. 15 pp. (22,8 × 18 cm)
Montjoye./Komedi i fem Akter af Octave Feuillet/Sceneri
Signed and dated: 'Stockholm d 21.de Mars 1864.'
[DKKk; NKS 3285 4° 5 læg 19

Musical sources:

Parts. Ms. Copy. 7 vol.
conductor's part, fl picc-fl, cl 1/2, fag, cor, tr.
Unsigned and undated [c.1864]
[SSkma; KT Dramat. teat. 12
This set of parts represents the only musical material that is still pre-served in SSkma for *Montjoie*.

23.4.1864
Shakespeare's Apotheosis (Shakspeares Apotheos) **(Stockholm's Royal Theatre, Stora Theatern).**
This series of three tableaux was choreographed and staged by Bournonville as an epilogue to W. Shakespeare's five-act tragedy *Hamlet, Prince of Denmark*, which was performed on this day to mark the tercentenary of the birth of the great English poet. The tableaux were set to original music by J. A. Söderman and included a 'Marcia solennis' (49 meas. in 4/4 time) and a 'Hymn' (61 meas. in 4/4 time). On the poster the tableaux are described as follows:

a) Skaldens bildstod, omgifven af Tragediens och Komediens Sång-gudinnor samt Genier'
b) Kring bildstoden uppträda hufvudpersoner ur följande af hans Dramatiska arbeten: »Romeo och Julie«, »Othello«, »Hamlet«, »Macbeth«, »Konung Lear«, »Köpmannen i Vendig«, »Konung Richard II«, »Konung Richard III«, »Muntra Fruarna i Windsor«, och »En Midsommarnattsdröm«.
c) Ryktet, förkunnande hans lof öfver jorden'.

In his diary and in his Swedish *Journal* Bournonville noted about the performance:

11.4.1864: 'Decorationsmøde paa [W.] Shakespeares Apotheose'
20.4.: 'Arbeider til Shakespeares Apotheose. – Eftermiddag Ditto […] (Barnth.)'
21.4.: 'Eftermiddagsprøve paa Shakespeares Apotheose'
22.4.: 'besørget adskilligt til Apotheosen, der blev repeteret efter Forestillingen af Barberen [i.e. G. Rossini's *Almaviva o sia l'inutile*

precauzione/Il Barbiere di Siviglia] og gav et meget tilfredsstillende Resultat'
23.4.: 'i begge Theatrene Sekularfest for Shakespeares Fødselsdag 1564. Det begyndte Kl 1/2 7. Illumination Hamlet, [F.] Kuhlaus Ou-verture til W. Sh. og derpaa min Composition Shakespeares Apo-theose der gik ypperligt og tog sig fortreffeligt ud. – Bifaldet moderato, som ved Alt, hvad der her angaaer en Sag eller Idée og ikke en enkelt Person […] Ak hvilke Tider for Kunsten!'.

The tableaux seem to have been created following the same model as the *Apotheosis* mounted by Bournonville at Copen-hagen's Royal Theatre six years earlier for a performance of C. J. Boye's and F. Kuhlau's four-act romantic play *William Shakespeare* (*see* 10.2.1858).

Musical sources:

Orchestral score. Ms. Autograph. Black ink. 1 vol. 31 pp (25,5 × 16,2cm)
Schackespeares [*sic*] / Apotheos / Partitur/ […] / Fest Musik / till / Schackespeares / Apotheos / komponeras af August Söderman / April 1864.
Signed and dated: 'April 1864.'
[SSkma; KT Epiloger 10

No répétiteur's copy for *Shakespeare's Apotheosis* has yet been traced in SSkma.

Parts. Ms. Copy. 13 vol.
cor 1/2/3/4, cnt 1/2/3/4, trb 1/2/3/4, timp.
Unsigned and undated [1864]
[SSkma; KT Epiloger 10

26.4.1864
Le Roman d'Elvire (Drottning Elviras Saga) **(Stockholm's Royal Theatre, Stora Theatern).**
Four years before the 1864 Stockholm première of A. Tho-mas's three-act comic opera (first performed at l'Opéra Comique in Paris on 4.4.1860) Bournonville had attended a performance of this work in Paris on 25.5.1860, and noted about it in his diary on that day:

'Det Hele meget smukt'.

His later plan for a Swedish staging of this opera is men-tioned for the first time in a recommendation note that he wrote to the theatre management at Stockholm's Royal Theatre on 16.10.1863. It reads as follows:

'Aussitôt nous métterons en scène une autre nouveauté – Le roman d'Elvire […] avec les ressources eclartantes que nous possedons, car l'ancien repertoire se trouvera comlettement impossible par l'ab-sence de nos deux Primedonne'.

In his diary and in his Swedish *Journal* he stated about the production, which was the last major work he mounted in Stockholm and the only opera by Thomas ever staged with his mise-en-scène and choreography:

21.1.1864: 'Collationnering å sangpartierne (Roman d'Elvire)'
20.2.: 'Collationnering En Riddarsaga.'
27.2.: 'skrevet Sceneriet til En Riddarsaga'
29.2.: 'Møde for Decorationerne til En Riddarsaga'
10.3.: 'Eftermiddag: 1.ste Indstudering paa Riddarsagan […] (Dia-log.)'
12.3.: 'Eftermiddags=Instruction paa En Riddarsaga […] (Dialog Barnth:)'

14.3.: 'Riddarsagan (Dialog)'

17.3.: 'Efterm: Drt. Elviras Saga Instruction […] (sångr.)'

18.3.: 'Dr Elv- Saga (sångr.)'

22.3.: 'Riddarsagan (sångr.) […] Eftermiddagsprøve paa Riddarsagan, der nu hedder Drottning Elviras Saga […] (Dialog)'

31.3.: 'Eftermiddagsprøve paa Elviras Saga […] (Barnth.)'

1.4.: 'Efterm: Prøve paa Elviras Saga […] (vid piano Barnth.)'

2.4.: '(Eftermiddags Instruktion paa Elviras Saga)'

4.4.: 'Dr Elviras Saga (Musik=Collationnering.)'

5.4.: 'Dr Elviras Saga (sångr.) […] Musik=Collationnering, Elviras Saga.

6.4.: ' Dr Elviras Saga (sångr.) […] Eftermiddags Instruktion paa Elviras Saga […] (Barntheatern)'

7.4.: 'Elviras Saga sång. […] Ballet=Indstudering til Elviras Saga […] (Barntheatern) […] Elviras Saga (vid piano å theatern)'

8.4.: 'Repetition paa Dandsen […] til Elviras Saga'

9.4.: 'Eftermiddagsprøve paa Elvira […] (Rep salen med Chör)'

12.4.: 'Prøve paa Elviras Saga […] (vid piano)'

13.4.: 'Eftermiddagsprøve paa Elviras saga […] (3.die Akt vid piano å Barnth.)'

14.4.: 'Generalprøve paa de to første Akter af Elviras Saga'

15.4.: 'Prøve paa Elviras Saga (2' & 3' Akt) […] (3.die Akten Gen Rep.)'

16.4.: 'Arrangementer for min Beneficeforestilling'

18.4.: 'Prøve paa Elviras Saga […] (med Orchester)'

21.4.: 'Stor Prøve paa Elviras Saga […] (Gen Rep.)'

23.4.: 'Generalprøve paa Elviras Saga'

25.4.: 'Elviras Saga (sidste Gen Rep.)'

26.4.: 'I Operaen Drottning Elviras Saga, til min Benefice. Jeg havde næsten udsolgt Huus, den kongelige Families Nærværelse. Alt gik udmærket godt og jeg blev til Slutning fremkaldt, som Beneficient. Hermed haaber jeg at have afsluttet med Det kgl. svenske Theater, hvor jeg har havt gode Aar og megen Tilfredsstillelse, men hvor mine Bestræbelser dog altfor ofte ere blevne modarbeidede. – Jeg trakterede Personalet og modtog mange venlige Bevidnelser'.

The staging also included an (unnamed) *Dance*, choreographed by Bournonville and performed by a corps de ballet in the Act I finale (score no. 8) during the chorus, entitled «La joyeuse nuit, oui tout nous séduit» («Här i festligt lag vi hylla nöjets lag»).

The first performance was given as part of a special farewell charity performance for Boumonville, and *Le Roman d'Elvire* reached a total of 10 performances in Stockholm, the last of which took place on 17.4.1865.

Autograph sources:

Recommendation note (included in a letter to E. F. O. L. von Stedingk). Ms. Autograph. Brown ink. 2 pp. (26,8 × 21,3 cm)
[…] à Monsieur/Mr le Baron E de Stedingk./[…]/Aussitôt nous métterons en scène une autre nouveauté – Le roman d'Elvire […]
Signed and dated: 'Stockholm ce 16 Octobre 1863'
[SSdt; KTA, E2A Ink. breve 1862/63, 16.10.1862
Due to a misreading of the date of this letter it has erroneously been placed among the correspondence of the 1862–63 season and is listed under the date of 16.10.1862.

Manuscript mise-en-scène. Ms. Autograph. Brown ink. 15 pp. (23 × 18,1 cm)
En Riddarsaga/Opera – comique i tre Akter ([A.] Dumas & [A. de] Leuven)/Musiken af Ambroise Thomas./Sceneri.
Signed and dated: 'Stockholm d. 27 Februar 1864.'
[DKKk; NKS 3285 4° 5 læg 22

Musical sources:

Printed orchestral score with manuscript insertions. 2 vol. Act I 188 pp., Act II 288 pp. (32,7 × 25,3 cm)
LE/ROMAN/D'ELVIRE,/Opéra comique en 3 actes

Paris, G. Brandus et S. Dufour, pl. no. B. et D. 10,300 (0-8) [1860] [SSkma; Operetter D 20
This French printed orchestral score was used for all performances of *Le Roman d'Elvire* in Stockholm during the 1863–64 and 1864–65 seasons. The music for the (unnamed) *Dance* in the finale of Act I (score no. 8) is included on pp. 142–188.

Répétiteur's copy. Ms. Copy. 1 vol. 16 pp. (33,2 × 24 cm)
Drottning Eliviras/Saga/Repetiteur.
Unsigned and undated [1864]
[SSkma; Operetter D 20
This répétiteur's copy contains the complete music for what is here entitled 'No. 8 Final/Ballet och Chör'. It also includes Bournonville's autographed choreographic numbers ('1–14', written with black ink) which most probably refer to his separate (not yet traced) notation of the (unnamed) *Dance* in the Act I finale.

Parts. Ms. Copy. 32 vol.
3 vl I, 3 vl II, 2 vla, 4 vlc e cb, fl 1/2, ob 1/2, cl 1/2, fag 1/2, cor 1/2/3/4, tr 1/2, trb 1/2/3, timp, gr cassa, piatti.
Unsigned and undated [1864]
[SSkma; Operetter D 20

7.5.1864

N. N.'s Memorial Feast for Shakespeare 1864. (N. Ns Minnefest öfver Shakespeare 1864.) (uncredited) performed at **Lacroix's Saloon, Stockholm.**

This performance was arranged by a Stockholm artists' society named 'N. N.' and given to celebrate the tercentenary of W. Shakespeare's birth. As was the case with the so-called *Shakespeare's Apotheosis*, created for the performance of Shakespeare's five-act tragedy *Hamlet, Prince of Denmark* at Stockholm's Royal Theatre on 23.4.1864, Bournonville on this day arranged a new series of five tableaux and a final apotheosis for this privately arranged celebration of the great English poet. In the printed programme the new tableaux are presented with no mention of Bournonville's name, and are described follows:

'Tablåer:
a) *Shakespeare* inför Drotting Elisabeth (framställer idéen till ett af sine lustspel).
b) *Macbeth*. IV akten, 1:sta scenen.
c) *Coriolanus*. V akten, 3:dje scenen.
d) *Richard den Tredje*. I akten, 2 scenen.
e) *Hamlet*. III akten, 4:de scenen.
Apotheos:
a) Tablå'.

According to the same source, the music was composed by an anonymous composer named 'A.'.

In his diary Bournonville noted about the performance:

'Kl. 7 i selskabet N N (Lacroixs Salon) Shakespearesfest for et pragtfult Auditorium af Damer og Herrer. Tale, Affhandlinger, Ode med Musik, mine Tableauer ganske ÿpperlige og en Cantate af [L.] Norman. Det Hele udmærket smukt men lidt for langt'.

No musical sources for this new series of Shakespearean tableaux have yet been traced in Stockholm.

Printed sources:

Printed programme. 1 p. (21,8 × 13,6 cm)
N. N.s/MINNE FEST ÖFVER SHAKESPEARE/1864./PROGRAM./ […]/ANDRA AFDELINGEN./[…]/Tablåer:/[…]/Apotheos:
s. l., s. a. [Stockholm, 7.5.1864]
[DKKk; Danske Afdeling, Småtryk (Personalhistorie: Bournonville]

13.5.1864
***Hothouse Flowers (Drivhusplanter)* (the Casino Theatre).**
According to a note Bournonville's diary (on 30.7.1863) and
two letters written to him by the Danish author, H. P. Holst,
on 23.7. and 1.8.1863 (now in DKKk, call nos. NKS 3258 A
4°, V, facs. 5, no. 456, and facs. 6, no. 475) Bournonville's
earlier Stockholm mise-en-scène for F. Hedberg's four-act
comedy (*see* 17.5.1862) clearly seems to have been reused by
Holst when he mounted *Blommor i drifbänk* in Copenhagen
in his own Danish translation. Thus, in his 1863 Stockholm
diary Bournonville noted of the then planned Copenhagen
staging opf Hedberg's comedy:

30.7.1863: 'afleveret Sceneri og Bøger hos H. P. Holst'.

Moreover, Holst's letter to Bournonville on 23.7.1863 reads:

'Efter hvad jeg hører er det din Hensigt at komme hertil i din Som-
merferie. Jeg tillader mig – i denne Forudsætning – at besvære Dig
med en lille Commission, som Du endelig maa besørge for mig: [F.]
Hedbergs 'blommor i drifbänk' vil komme til Opførelse her strax i
begyndelsen af næste Saison […] En Afskrift af dit Scenearrangement vil jeg ogsaa indstændig bede Dig om at modtage, da det vil
lette mig Arbeidet ikke lidt'.

Hothouse Flowers received 6 performances at the Casino Theatre, the last of which was given on 20.6.1864.

    No autographed sources by Bournonville relating explic-
itly to the 1864 Copenhagen mise-en-scène of *Hothouse Flowers* have yet been traced. This seems to indicate that it was his
earlier 1862 Stockholm's mise-en-scène of comedy which
would have been employed by Holst in Copenhagen (now in
DKKk, call no. NKS 3285 4° 4 læg 2).

20.6.1864
***The Deportees (De Deporterade)* (Stockholm's Royal Theatre,
Dramatiska Theatern).**
When attending the Danish première of H. Hertz's three-act
play at Copenhagen's Royal Theatre some ten years before
his own Stockholm staging of it, Bournonville noted about
this work in his diary on 27.2.1853:

'Seet De Deporterede af Hertz, i mine Tanker et maadeligt Product.
[F.] Høedt meget charactersitisk.'.

On 15.9.1863 he began working on the Swedish mise-en-
scène of Hertz's play, and on 21.10.1863 he mentioned his
plan for a Stockholm première of *The Deportees* in a recommendation note that he wrote to the theatre management of
Stockholm's Royal Theatre.

    About the play's Swedish staging and première, which was
the last Bournonville directed in Stockholm, he noted in his
diary and in his *Journal*:

15.9.1863: 'De Deporterade (Collationnering)'
20.5.1864: 'De Deporterade (sceneri)'
14.6., 15.6., 16.6., and 18.6.: 'De Deporterade (Gen Rep.)'
19.6.: 'De Deporterade (Minnesrepetition.)'
20.6.: 'De Deporterade (Gen Rep.) […] De Deporterede første
Gang for meget daarligt Huus, men gik særdeles godt'.

The Deportees was given only once during Bournonville's engagement in Stockholm.

Autograph sources:

Recommendation note. Ms. Autograph. Brown ink. 1 p. (21,2 × 13,4
cm)
[…] Comme je me charge des pièces suivantes/De Deporterade.
[…]
Signed and dated: 'ce 21 Octobre 1863.'
[SSdt; KTA, E2A Ink. breve 1863/64, 21.10.1863

19.9.1864
***Souvenir de Taglioni, Pas de deux, composed by Mr. Court Ballet
Master Bournonville (componeret af Hr. Hofballetmester
Bournonville)* performed by A. and C. Healey.**
This dance was originally created for and premièred by the
Healey sisters at Stockholm's Royal Theatre (Dramatiska
Theatern) on 20.1.1864. It was danced by them 5 times in
Copenhagen, the last time on 13.3.1865. Bournonville did
not attend any of these performances. No separate musical
sources for it have yet been traced in Copenhagen.

1865

4.2.1865
La Sylphide (Sylphiden).
This performance represents the third restaging in Copenhagen of Bournonville's and H. S. v. Løvenskjold's Danish
version of F. Taglioni's two-act romantic ballet *La Sylphide* (*see*
28.11.1836). It was mounted by L. Gade and arranged especially for the English dancer, C. Healey, who played the title
rôle for the first and only time this year.

    According to autographed choreographic notes and a
note written in his diary on 13.8.1864 (reading: 'Noteret til
nogle Repetiteurpartier for L. Gade'), Bournonville made a
number of minor musical cuts and also rechoreographed
several of the sections danced by the soloists and the corps
de ballet during the divertissements in Act II (score nos. 2–
4). These changes appear to have followed closely Bournonville's previous Stockholm version (*see* 1.4.1862), but were all
carried out by Gade, since Bournonville did not take any personal part in the actual rehearsals of the ballet this year, nor
did he attend its first performance on 4.2.1865.

    The 1865 production was performed twice, the last time
on 6.2.1865.

    The musical material employed this year was (apart from a
new répétiteur's copy) the same as that used for the previous
1849 and 1856 stagings (now in DKKk, call nos. C II, 117 d,
MA ms 2762 (1–2), and KTB 275).

Autograph sources:

Musical instruction. Ms. Autograph. Ink. 2 pp. (format unknown)
Forandringer i 2.den Akt af Sylphiden.
Signed and dated: 'Fredensborg d 13.e August 1864.'
[USNYp; Dance Collection, call nos. *ZBD (microfilm), and
(S)*MGZMD 30 (photostat copy)

Choreographic note. Ms. Autograph. Ink. 3 pp. (format unknown)
Sylphiden 2.den Akt./No. 2/[…]/No. 3/[…]/No. 4
Unsigned and undated [Written according to Bournonville's diary
most probably on 13.8.1864]

[USNYp; Dance Collection, call nos. *ZBD (microfilm), and (S)*MGZMD 30 (photostat copy)

Choreographic note. Ms. Autograph. Ink. 1 p. (format unknown)
Sylphiderne/2.den Akt.
Unsigned and undated [Written according to Bournonville's diary most probably on 13.8.1864]
[USNYp; Dance Collection, call nos. *ZBD (microfilm), and (S)*MGZMD 30 (photostat copy)

Musical sources:

Répétiteur's copy. Ms. Copy. Brown and black ink. 1 vol. 104 pp. (33 × 25,2 cm)
B./275./Sylfiden./Signalparti./[...]/Repetiteur Parti/til/'Sylfiden.'
Unsigned and undated [1865]
[DKKk; MA ms 2970 b (KTB 275)
This répétiteur's copy clearly dates from Bournonville's 1865 re-staging of *La Sylphide*, since it contains his autographed choreographic numbers ('1–6' written with brown ink) for those sections in the Act II divertissement which he revised this year. The volume also contains several other notes (mainly written with blue ink) which describe the dramatic action and the pantomime throughout the ballet. The répétiteur's copy was used for all later productions at Copenhagen's Royal Theatre between 1865 and well into the next century before it was transformed into the stage manager's record for the changes of sets and décors during performances (the so-called 'Signalparti').

26.2.1865
The Danes in China (De Danske i China).
This divertissement is based on excerpts from Act I of Bournonville's two-act romantic ballet *The Isle of Phantasy* (*see* 28.10.1838). Similar divertissements had been mounted by him on three earlier occasions (*see* 17.9.1839, 28.1.1842, and 27.2.1843), but each time with different dance contents. The 1865 version (which was staged exclusively by L. Gade) included a new set of three dances as follows:

(1) *Chinese* [Dance] (*Chinesisk*) performed A. Fredstrup.
(2) *Las Hermanas de Sevilla* (*see* 4.6.1851) performed by Juliette Price, P. Fredstrup, and L. Stillmann.
(3) *The English Sailor (Den Engelske Matros)* performed by H. Scharff.

On the fifth and final performance of *The Danes in China* on 3.12.1865 Bournonville's and C. C. Møller's Spanish dance *Las Hermanas de Sevilla* was replaced by I. P. E. Hartmann's so-called *Russian* [Dance] (*Russisk*), which originally was part of Act I (score no. 8) of *The Isle of Phantasy.*

5.6.1865
Polka militaire performed by H. Scharff, W. Price, Juliette Price, and S. Price (Christiania's Theatre, Oslo).
This performance represents the last staging in Norway of Bournonville's *Polka militaire* (*see* 1.11.1842). It was mounted this year as part of a summer tour to Norway arranged by four of the leading dancers of Copenhagen's Royal Danish Ballet. The dance was given 4 times in Christiania, the last time on 30.6.1865. Bournonville did not participate in this summer tour. The musical material employed for the 1865 performances was most probably the same as that used for the two earlier summer tours to Norway in 1847 and 1852 (now in NOum, call no. Ms. 216, Eske 24 a, and in DKKk, call nos. MA ms 2628, and KTB 1027).

7.6.1865
'Bolero' (Spanish National Dance) ('Bolero' (spansk Nationaldands)) composed by Bournonville and performed by H. Scharff, W. Price, Juliette Price, and S. Price. (Christiania's Theatre, Oslo)
This dance is almost certainly identical with the much earlier *El Bolero (arranged for four persons)* (*see* 6.7.1840), which in turn had been incorporated in Act II (score no. 11) of Bournonville's two-act idyllic ballet *The Toreador* when this ballet was premièred in Copenhagen on 27.11.1840. *'Bolero'* was given twice in Christiania, the last time on 26.6.1865. No musical sources for it dating from the 1865 performances in Norway have yet been traced in NOum. It is not possible to identify the dance any further.

7.6.1865
'Norwegian Spring Dance' ('Norsk Springdands') performed by W. Price and Juliette Price (Christiania's Theatre, Oslo).
This dance is identical with the *Norwegian Spring Dance* in Bournonville's one-act ballet *Old Memories, or A Magic Lantern* (*see* 18.12.1848). It was performed once during the 1865 Christiania summer season. No separate musical sources dating from this performance have yet been traced in Norway. This seems to indicate that it was performed using the original Copenhagen musical material for *Old Memories, or A Magic Lantern* (now in DKKk, call nos. C II, 114 k, MA ms 2904 (5), and KTB 291).

9.6.1865
'Pas de deux' and 'Balabile' (from the ballet The Flower Festival) ('Pas de deux' og 'Balabile' (af Balletten Blomsterfesten)) performed by H. Scharff, W. Price, Juliette Price, and S. Price (Christiania's Theatre, Oslo).
This work is a divertissement version for two couples (perhaps arranged by Bournonville himself?) of selected excerpts from his one-act ballet *The Flower Festival in Genzano* (*see* 19.12.1858). It was mounted especially for the 1865 Norwegian summer tour of four of the leading dancers of Copenhagen's Royal Danish Ballet. The divertissement, which appears to be identical with an earlier, similar arrangement of two excerpts from this ballet (performed at Stockholm's Mindre Theatern on 1.6. and 3.6.1860) was given twice in Christiania, the last time on 28.6.1865. Only on the poster for the second and last performance was the *'Balabile'* included in the title.

No musical sources dating from the 1865 performances in Norway of these dances have yet been traced in NOum.

9.6.1865
'The Sailor's Return' (Scene with Dance) ('Matrosens Hjemkomst' (Scene med Dands)) performed by W. Price and S. Price (Christiania's Theatre, Oslo).
This performance represents the last time Bournonville's divertissement *'The Sailor's Return'* (*see* 9.6.1852) was mounted outside Denmark. It received 3 performances during the 1865 Christiania summer tour, the last of which was given on 28.6.1865. The musical material employed this year was most probably the same as that used for the 1852 Norwegian première of *The Sailor's Return* (now in NOum, call no.

MS. 216, Eske 24 b, and DKKk, call nos. MA ms 2670, MA ms 2671, and KTB 337).

11.6.1865

'Tarantella' (from the ballet Napoli) ('Tarantella' (af Balletten Napoli)) **performed by H. Scharff, W. Price, J. Price, and S. Price (Christiania's Theatre, Oslo).**

This dance is an adapted divertissement version for only two couples of the *Tarantella* in Act III (score no. 3) of Bournonville's three-act romantic ballet *Napoli or The Fisherman and His Bride* (*see* 29.3.1842). It was most likely arranged especially by Bournonville for the 1865 Norwegian summer tour of four of his leading pupils, and was performed three times by them in Christiania (the last time on 3.7.1865). The musical material employed for the 1865 performances of this dance was most probably the same as that used for the previous première in Norway on 2.7.1852 of Bournonville's divertissement, entitled *'Italian Genre Picture' Divertissement with Tarantellas* (now in NOum, call no. Ms. 216, Eske 24 a, and DKKk, call no. KTB 292).

14.6.1865

'Fragment of the ballet La Somnambule' ('Fragment af Balletten Søvngængersken') **performed by H. Scharff, W. Price, Juliette Price, and S. Price (Christiania's Theatre, Oslo).**

This divertissement was most likely arranged personally by Bournonville and seems (according to its casting) to have consisted of a mime scene and the *Pas de quatre* from Act I (score nos. 7 and 7 B) in Bournonville's 1829 Copenhagen version of J. Aumer's three-act pantomimic ballet *La Somnambule, ou l'Arrivée d'un nouveau seigneur* (*see* 21.9.1829). It was mounted especially for the 1865 Norwegian summer tour of four of Bournonville's most talented pupils and was performed twice by them in Christiania, the last time on 25.6.1865. No musical sources dating from the 1865 performances in Norway of this work have yet been traced in NOum.

16.6.1865

'La Ventana' **performed by Juliette and S. Price (Christiania's Theatre, Oslo).**

This performance represents the second and last time Bournonville's 1854 version of his Spanish mirror-dance *La Ventana* (*see* 19.6.1854) was mounted outside Denmark in his lifetime. It received 3 performances in Christiania, the last of which was given on 3.7.1865.

Musical sources:

Orchestral score. Ms. Copy. Black ink. 1 vol. 41 pp. (24,4 × 33,9 cm)
No II/La Ventana/NB: De Steder som staae imellem { } skulde egentlig/udføres af 2 Flöiter og Guitar paa Scenen.
Unsigned and undated [c.1865]
[NOum; Ms. 216, Eske 24 b.
This orchestral score contains the complete music for H. C. Lumbye's original 1854 version of *La Ventana*.

No répétiteur's copy and set of parts with the original 1854 version of *La Ventana* have yet been traced in Norway. This seems to indicate that the divertissement was most probably performed in Norway in 1865 with the 1854 Copenhagen répétiteur's copy and set of parts (now in DKKk, call nos. MA ms 2997 and KTB 300).

18.6.1865

'La Seguedille' (Spanish National Dance) (spansk Nationaldans) **performed by H. Scharff, W. Price, Juliette Price, and S. Price (Christiania's Theatre, Oslo).**

This dance is explicitly described on the poster as a work 'composed' by Bournonville. It is beyond doubt an adapted version (perhaps arranged personally by Bournonville) for two couples of his so-called *La Seguedilla (after Taglioni.)*, which was originally part of his second and final version of *La Ventana, Ballet Divertissement* (*see* 6.10.1856). The new 1865 version of this dance was arranged especially for the Norwegian summer tour of four of his most talented pupils and was performed three times by them in Christiania, the last time on 28.6.1865. No separate musical sources dating from the 1865 performances in Norway of this dance have yet been traced. This seems to indicate that *'La Seguedille' (Spanish National Dance)* was rehearsed and performed in Christiania with the original 1856 Copenhagen orchestral score, répétiteur's copy and set of parts for it (now in DKKk, call nos. MA ms 1127, MA ms 2997, and KTB 300).

10.9.1865

Il Trovatore (Troubadouren).

The 1865 Copenhagen première of G. Verdi's four-act lyrical drama *Il Trovatore* (premièred at the Teatro Apollo in Rome on 19.1.1853) was originally projected by Bournonville on 30.10.1857. It represents the first and only time he mounted a work by Verdi at Copenhagen's Royal Theatre (*see also* his earlier Stockholm production of *Ernani* on 20.11.1862).

Besides creating the general mise-en-scène and inserting a completely new ballet divertissement in Act III, Bournonville also gave personal stage instructions to his daughter, the alto Charlotte Bournonville, who this year performed the rôle of *Azucena* for the first time.

The new, incorporated divertissement in Act III consisted of three dance numbers entitled as follows:

(1) *Spanish National Dance (Spansk Nationaldans).*
(2) *Gipsy Dance (Zigeunerdans).*
(3) *Gallop (Galopp)*

According to the orchestral score this divertissement was set to music composed by A. F. Schwartz (the so-called 'Zigeunerdans') and by H. C. Lumbye (the final 'Galopp').

The music for the opening number (in the orchestral score named 'Spansk Nationaldans') had many years earlier served as the accompaniment for a dance arranged by Bournonville's pupil, S. Lund, entitled *The Girls from Xeres (Flickorna från Xeres)*. It was premièred as a separate divertissement at Stockholm's Royal Theatre on 29.10.1858, but was later also incorporated in the Stockholm première of Verdi's *Il Trovatore* on 31.5.1860 (*see* 20.11.1862). Thus, on the original 1860 poster for Verdi's lyrical drama this dance is entitled 'Spansk dans' and described as being performed by three women. It employed the exact same popular Spanish tune to which the famous Spanish ballerina of the time, Pepita de Oliva (stage name for Josefa Lopez-Ortega) had performed her immensely popular *El Jaleo de Xeres* at the Casino Theatre in Copenhagen in the spring of 1858. That dance, in turn, was published in Copenhagen in a version for piano by C. G.

Iversen & Solem (a copy of which is now in DKKk, call no. U 30). Later the exact same music was included in A. P. Bergreen's musical anthology, entitled *Folke-Sange og Melodier* (published in Copenhagen by C. A. Reitzel, 1866, *Syvende Bind*, nr. 32, pp. 192–195).

In Lund's ballet for the 1860 Stockholm production of Verdi's *Il Trovatore* this Spanish *Jaleo* tune was followed by a so-called *Gipsy Dance* (on the poster entitled 'Zigeunerdans'), which was performed by four couples and set to a score by A. F. Schwartz. It was the music for this dance which was reused as the second number in Bournonville's 1865 Act III divertissement for Verdi's lyrical drama when it was premièred in Copenhagen.

Because Lund's original versions of both the so-called 'Spansk Nationaldands' and the 'Zigeunerdands' were explicitly credited on the Stockholm posters as works 'arranged' (*arrangeradt*) by him, it is reasonable to assume that the choreography for these dances would also have served as the model for the similar numbers in Bournonville's 1865 divertissement for *Il Trovatore* in Copenhagen. This theory is further supported by the fact that (according to a note in Bournonville's Swedish *Journal* on 29.12.1863) Bournonville also rehearsed in Stockholm what he then described as 'Balletterne till <u>Trubaduren</u>' – in spite of the fact that no immediate performance of Verdi's lyrical drama was planned during that period (*Il Trovatore* was not performed during that season until 4.3.1864). Bournonville's Stockholm rehearsal of Lund's divertissement may thus have resulted from his explicit wish to learn its choreography before bringing it with him to Copenhagen. Moreover, according to several other notes in his diary he clearly seems to have asked A. F. Schwartz to send him the original music for Lund's dances during the summer of 1865. This is clear from the diary in which he noted about the 1865 Copenhagen staging and première of Verdi's lyrical drama:

5.8.1865: 'Brev til [...] Musiker [A. F.] Schwartz i Stockholm'
6.8.: 'Charlotte [Bournonville] gjennemgaaet sin Rolle i Trubadouren med H [S.] Paulli'
8.8.: '(Musiken fra Stockholm)'
9.8.: 'Brev fra [...] [E.] Lehmann'
10.8.: 'Svar til Lehmann'
13.8.: 'Lehmann hos os for nogle Dage'
14.8.: 'Jeg componerede lidt paa Dandsen til Trubaduren'
15.8.: 'Brev til <u>L. Gade</u> med Liste til Trubaduren'
17.8.: 'Skrevet choreographiske Noter til Trubaduren'
18.8.: 'componeret til Trubaduren'
22.8.: 'arbeidet og componeret'
23.8.: 'fuldendt mine Noter til Trubaduren'
24.8.: 'Instruerede Charlotte'
25.8.: 'skrevet og componeret [...] selv indstuderet Solopartierne til Troubadouren, <u>1.ste</u> <u>Prøve</u> [...] Instruction til Charlotte'
26.8.: 'fuldendt Indstuderingen af Trubaduren'
28.8.: 'Prøve paa [...] <u>Trubaduren</u>'
29.8.: 'Eftermiddagsprøve paa <u>Trubaduren</u> (Charlotte og [R. L.] Jastrau)'
30.8.: 'Prøve paa Dandsen og Scener af <u>Trubaduren</u>'
2.9.: 'Instruction paa <u>Trubaduren</u>'
5.9.: 'Prøve paa [...] Dandsen til Trubaduren'
7.9.: 'set og hørt lidt paa Trubaduren'
8.9.: 'Generalprøve paa <u>Trubaduren</u>. Charlotte i Costume og fortræffelig. Min Dands gjorde megen Lykke'
9.9.: 'Generalprøve i Costume paa Trubaduren'
10.9.: 'I Theatret, hvor man gav <u>Trubaduren</u> for første Gang [...] Alt

gik udmærket godt og Charlotte udførte sin Rolle fortræffeligt og høstede meget Bifald. – Min Dands gjorde overordentlig Lykke. Jeg takkede Gud af mit inderste Hjerte og vi glædede os magelöst'.

During the following years Bournonville's divertissement from *Il Trovatore* was also mounted by himself as a separate divertissement on two occasions (*see* 25.1.1867 and 29.4. 1877), thereby becoming one of his most frequently performed opera-ballets ever.

Finally, three months after the 1865 Copenhagen première of *Il Trovatore* Bournonville attended a performance of Verdi's French version of this work at the Paris Opéra on 3.12.1865. On that day he noted about it and Act III (choreographed by L. Petipa):

'Udførelsen langt under Kbhvn og Stockholm. Chorene derimod vare ganske fortræffelige (Soldatersangene langsommere end hos os) – Balletten var høist ubetydelig og som sædvanlig absorberet af Nøgenheden'.

Il Trovatore received 27 performances in Copenhagen during Bournonville's lifetime, the last of which was given on 22.2. 1878.

Autograph sources:

Production note. Ms. Autograph. Black ink. 2 pp. (21,5 × 13,6 cm)
<u>Dands til Operaen</u>/<u>Trubaduren</u>/<u>3.die Akt.</u>
Signed and dated: 'Fredensborg den 15.e August 1865.'
[DKKkt; F.M. (Opera)

Choreographic note. Ms. Autograph. Brown ink. 4 pp. (20,6 × 16,8 cm)
Troubadouren, 3.die Akt.
Signed and dated: 'Fredensborg den 23.de August 1865.'
[Private collection (Copenhagen)

Musical sources:

Orchestral score. Ms. Copy. Black ink. 2 vol. Act I-II 538 pp. of which three are blank, Act III–IV 460 pp. of which four are blank (32,7 × 24,2 cm with minor variants)
Troubadouren/Partitur/1ste og 2den Act/[...]/1/1/Il Trovatore/ del/Maestro Cav.e G.e Verdi/Preludio ed Introduzione/Atto 1.mo / [...]/Troubadouren/Partitur/3die og 4de Act.
Unsigned and undated [c.1865]
[DKKk, MA ms 1995 (KTA 752)
This orchestral score is an Italian manuscript copy of Verdi's 1853 Rome version of *Il Trovatore* which includes S. Cammarano's original Italian text and H. P. Holst's 1865 Danish translation (inserted with brown ink). A conductor's part (for solo violin) containing the complete music of the incorporated Act III ballet is inserted as pp. '44a– 44j' between the opening Act III chorus («Or co dadi, ma fra poco»/ «Tærningspil nu korter Tiden») and the following *Scena e Terzetto* («In braccio al mio rival»/«Hun i min Fjendes Vold!», score no. 9). The score was used for all performances of *Il Trovatore* in Copenhagen during Bournonville's lifetime.

Orchestral score (Act III divertissement). Ms. Autograph (by A. F. Schwartz) and copy. Brown ink. 1 vol. 64 pp. of which six are blank (34,3 × 24,9 cm)
752a/ Ballet Partitur/til/Troubadouren/<u>Bruges ikke</u>/[...]/Spansk Nationaldans/[...]/Zigeunardans/M: af:/A.f. Schwartz/[...]/Galopp. Tempo vivo. H. C. Lumbye.
Signed (on p. 21): 'A.f. Schwartz', undated [c.1858–1865]
[DKKkt; KTA 752 a
This orchestral score is a copy written in Stockholm by A. F. Schwartz. It contains the complete music for Bournonville's 1865 divertisse-

ment in Act III of Verdi's *Il Trovatore* and was used for all performances of it in Copenhagen throughout Bournonville's lifetime. The attribution of the final 'Galopp' to H. C. Lumbye is given by a pencilled note written by an unknown hand on p. 47. The fact that the music for this number is copied in Schwartz's hand clearly indicates that this gallop (for which no autographed sources by Lumbye have yet been traced) was already known in Stockholm in 1865. The attribution to Lumbye was at a much later stage confirmed by A. Grandjean, who also credited the gallop to Lumbye in his printed piano score for Bournonville's complete divertissement in *Il Trovatore*, published by W. Hansen in Copenhagen in 1901 (pl. no. 12878, now in DKKk, call no. U 6 (Verdi)). Both of Schwartz's original scores were slightly changed by Bournonville in Copenhagen in that he omitted the first 24 bars of the so-called '*Zigeunardands*'. Instead he inserted a repeat of the *Allegro* section (53 bars) from the opening '*Spansk Nationaldands*' in this place. Moreover, the Copenhagen score contains an introduction to Lumbye's 'Gallop' (*meno*, 32 bars in 2/4 time) which, however, was clearly omitted before the first performance of this divertissement. Finally, the 'Gallop' was drastically shortened by Bournonville through his omission of a middle-section of 94 bars (meas. nos. 53–148). This cut also seems to have been made before the first performance of the divertissement. The score for Lumbye's 'Gallop' represents the only known full orchestral source for this dance which has yet come to light.

Répétiteur's copy (Act III divertissement, incomplete). Ms. Copy. Brown ink. 8 pp. (34,7 × 25,5 cm)
Troubadouren/<u>Zigeunerdands.</u> [erased]
Unsigned and undated [1865]
[DKKk; MA ms 3092 (KTA 752 a (1))
This (incomplete) répétiteur's copy contains the music for (1) A. F. Schwartz's 'Zigeunerdands', (2) the *meno* introduction to H. C. Lumbye's 'Gallop', and (3) the first 49 measures of the same gallop. It also includes Bournonville's pencilled autographed notes indicating his many musical changes and his casting of each section.

Répétiteur's copy (Act III divertissement, fragment). Ms. Copy. Brown ink. 4 pp. (35 × 26,2 cm)
[Untitled]
Unsigned and undated [1865]
[DKKk; MA ms 2706 (KTA 752 a (2))
This fragment of the original 1865 répétiteur's copy for Bournonville's Act III ballet in Verdi's *Il Trovatore* contains the part of H. C. Lumbye's final 'Gallop' which is omitted in the previous (incomplete) répétiteur's copy.

Répétiteur's copy (Act III divertissement, incomplete). Ms. Copy. Brown ink. 1 vol. 16 pp. of which one is blank (33 × 25,3 cm)
2/A. 752 a/Dansedivertissement/af./<u>Troubadouren</u>.
Unsigned and undated [1865]
[DKKk; MA ms 3093 (KTA 752 a (3))
This (incomplete) répétiteur's copy contains the complete music for Bournonville's definitive version of the Act III divertissement in *Il Trovatore*, except for its first 76 measures. It also includes Bournonville's autographed choreographic numbers (written with brown ink) which seem to refer to his separate choreographic notation of the divertissement that he wrote (according to his diary) on 23.8.1865.

Parts (only the opera). Ms. Copy. 37 + 2 vol.
4 vl I, 4 vl II, 2 vla, 2 vlc, 2 cb, fl picc e I, fl II, ob 1/2, cl 1/2, fag 1/2, cor 1/2/3/4, tr 1/2, trb 1/2/3, tuba, timp, gr cassa, piatti, tri, arpa. On stage: cor, glock. 172 vocal parts.
Unsigned and undated [1865]
[DKKk; KTA 752
This set of parts was used for all performances of Verdi's *Il Trovatore* in Copenhagen during Bournonville's lifetime. The music for the Act III divertissement, however, is not included in these parts.

No separate set of parts for Bournonville's divertissement in Act III of *Il Trovatore* has yet been traced.

Other sources:

Costume drawing by E. Lehmann. Pencil and water colours (23,2 × 15,7 cm)
Zigeuner (Troubadouren)/Hrr. Scharff./(Solodands)
Unsigned and undated [c.1865]
[DKKkt; Kostumetegninger (Lehmann)]
This drawing shows the costume worn by the leading male soloist in Bournonville's Act III divertissement in *Il Trovatore* (performed by H. Scharff).

Costume drawing by E. Lehmann. Pencil and water colours (23,3 × 15,8 cm)
Troubadouren.
Unsigned and undated [c.1865]
[DKKkt; Kostumetegninger (Lehmann)]
This drawing shows the costume worn by the leading female soloist in Bournonville's Act III divertissement in *Il Trovatore* (performed by Juliette Price).

Costume drawing by E. Lehmann. Pencil and water colours (23 × 15,5 cm)
Zigeunersker./Troubadouren/[…]/Troubadouren.
Unsigned and undated [c.1865]
[DKKkt; Kostumetegninger (Lehmann)]
This drawing shows two costumes worn by the gipsy women in Bournonville's Act III divertissement in *Il Trovatore*.

15.9.1865

The Conservatoire, or A Proposal of Marriage through the Newspaper (Conservatoriet, eller Et Avisfrieri).

This performance represents Bournonville's first restaging in Copenhagen of his two-act ballet-vaudeville *Conservatoriet, or A Proposal of Marriage through the Newspaper* (see 6.5.1849). It was mounted this year in a slightly revised version, which was notated by Bournonville in a separate notebook. For these notes he added choreographic numbers that refer to his similar numbers written into the (not yet traced) répétiteur's copy from the ballet's 1849 première (a microfilm of which is now in USNYp, Dance Collection, call no. *ZBD-74). According to Bournonville's autographed notes in the same répétiteur's copy (which was clearly reused for the 1865 production) the difference between the 1849 and 1865 productions consisted mainly of a series of minor musical cuts as follows:

(1) Act I, score no. 3 (the *Pas d'Ecole*): In this dance Bournonville cancelled several repeats and made three music cuts of 8, 29, and 8 bars respectively.
(2) Act I, score no 4 (the *Pas de trois*): Bournonville here omitted 21 bars in the opening *Adagio* movement, and also cancelled two sections of 15 and 35 bars each in the *Rondo*. Moreover, in the *Allegretto* movement (later changed to *Andante* and performed as a solo variation by *Victorine*) he made a minor cut of 16 measures.
(3) Act I, score no 5 (scene 4): In this number Bournonville made two minor cuts of 10 and 15 bars each.
(4) Act II, score no. 7 (scene 1): Bournonville here omitted two sections of 56 and 3 bars respectively.
(5) Act II, score no. 9 (scene 7): Bournonville here omitted a section of 16 bars.
(6) Act II, score no. 9 (scene 9): In this scene Bournonville omitted a section playing for 24 bars.

Bournonville's musical cuts in the *Pas d'Ecole* and *Pas de trois* of Act I have been followed in all later performances of this ballet from 1865 to the present day.

In his diary he noted about the rehearsals and the first performance of his revised 1865 production of this ballet:

19.6.1865: 'Begyndt mit Balletarbeide med Conservatoriet'
24.6.: 'Noteret Conservatoriet'
18.7.: 'skrevet paa Conservatoriet'
19.7.: 'skrevet Balletnoter'
26.8.: 'Eftermiddagsprøve paa Conservatoriet'
28.8.: 'Prøve paa Conservatoriet'
2.9.: 'Jeg besørgede en Prøve paa Conservatoriet'
5.9. and 6.9.: 'Prøve paa Conservatoriet'
8.9.: 'en Times Prøve paa Conservatoriet'
9.9.: 'lille Prøve paa Conservatoriet'
11.9.: 'Prøve paa Conservatoriet indtil Kl 1½'
12.9.: 'Generalprøve paa Conservatoriet. Eftermiddagsprøve for at remplacere den lille [A.] Scholl med [B.] Schnell'
13.9.: 'Prøve paa Conservatoriet'
15.9.: '(Prøve remplaceret i Nødstilfælde Juliettes Rolle i Conservatoriet.) […] Conservatoriet første Gang efter den ný Indstudering, gik udmærket godt og gjorde megen Lýkke'
16.9.: 'Doubleringsprøve paa Conservatoriet'
21.9.: 'S. Price upasselig og 2½ Times Prøve for at indstudere Victorines Rolle til Fru [E.] Gade […] Conservatoriet, der gik meget godt og vandt Bifald'.

The 1865 staging received 5 performances, the last of which was given on 12.12.1865. The musical material employed this year was the same as that used since the 1849 première (now in DKKk, call nos. MA ms 1550, KTB 264, and in USNYp (Dance Collection, call no. *ZBD-74, microfilm).

Autograph sources:

Choreographic note. Ms. Autograph. Brown ink. 1 vol. 25 pp. (20 × 13,3 cm)
Conservatoriet./Ballet i 2 Akter/Notes chorégraphiques:
Unsigned and undated [Written according to the diary on 19.6., 24.6., 18.7., and 19.7.1865]
[DKKk; NKS 3285 4° 2 A–E
This manuscript is included on pp. '1r.–13r.' in a notebook that originally seems to have served as a diary for Bournonville's wife, Helene. It contains a nearly complete notation of *The Conservatoire, or A Proposal of Marriage through the Newspaper* and also includes his autographed choreographic numbers which refer to similar numbers written into the 1849 répétiteur's copy for this ballet-vaudeville. Moreover, p. '13v' contains an incomplete notation of the 1865 version of his three-act romantic ballet *The Kermesse in Brüges, or The Three Gifts* (see 19.11.1865), while pp. '15v.–26r.' include his notes for his two later revised versions of his Norwegian ballet in three tableaux *The Mountain Hut, or Twenty Years* (see 9.10.1865 and 27.3.1877). The remaining pages in this notebook are all blank.

25.9.1865
Norma.
This performance represents Bournonville's fourth and last staging in Copenhagen of V. Bellini's two-act lyrical tragedy (see 20.10.1848), which this year was given in a four-act version. This seems to represent the major difference from his three previous stagings of this work in Copenhagen. In his diary he noted about the performance:

19.9.1865: 'Prøve […] paa Norma 1 – 2½'
25.9.: 'I Theatret Norma med Fru Michaeli [i.e. L. Michaëli] ganske fortræffelig. Operaen gik i det Hele godt og vandt storartet Bifald'.

The 1865 production received 8 performances during Bournonville's lifetime, the last of which was given on 27.9.1866.

The musical material employed this year was the same as that used for all of Bournonville's previous stagings of this work.

12.10.1865
La Muette de Portici (Den Stumme i Portici).
For the 1865 Copenhagen restaging of D.-F.-E. Auber's five-act opera (see 23.9.1834) Bournonville gave personal stage instructions to the dancer, J. Petersen, who this year played the mime rôle of *Fenella* for the first time. The production differed from Bournonville's previous production (see 12.2. 1862) by his omission of the Act I *Guarache* and the *Pas de deux* (set to music by M. E. Caraffa) in the same act. Consequently the Act I *Bolero* and the Act III *Tarantella* were the only dances performed in this staging. In his diary he noted about the production:

2.10.1865: 'jeg begýndte at indstudere Fenellas Partie til Johanne Petersen'
3.10.: 'Indstudering af Fenella og Prøve med de andre Roller'
4.10.: 'Prøvet Fenellas Rolle […] Claveer og Sceneprøve paa Den Stumme'
5.10: 'Generalprøve paa Den Stumme. Johanne Petersen særdeles god som Fenella. [J. L.] Nyrop meldt sýg altsaa ingen Masaniello til imorgen!'
9.10.: 'Eftermiddagsprøve paa Den Stumme'
12.10.: 'I Theatret Den Stumme med Johanne Petersen som Fenella. Nyrop var herlig som Masaniello. Udstýret og Arrangementet var meget tarveligt'.

The 1865 production received 14 performances, the last of which was given on 16.4.1869 (a special charity performance with the overture and Act II was given on 27.11.1872).

The musical material employed this year was the same as that used for the previous 1862 staging (now in DKKkt and in DKKk with the call nos. KTA 273, and MA ms 3055–3056 respectively).

9.10.1865
The Mountain Hut, or Twenty Years (Fjeldstuen eller: Tyve Aar).
This performance represents Bournonville's first, revised restaging of his Norwegian ballet in three tableaux *The Mountain Hut, or Twenty Years* (see 13.5.1859). It was this year divided into two acts, as a result of which completely new score numbers were given to what was originally the music for the second and third tableaux. According to Bournonville's notes in the 1859 répétiteur's copy (which was clearly reused for this restaging) the revised 1865 production differed from the original version by several musical changes and cuts as follows:

(1) Act I, score nos. 4 and 5 (originally the first tableau, scenes 6 and 7): For these numbers Bournonville made A. Winding revise several musical passages, and also omitted three sections of 15, 8, and 13 bars respectively.
(2) Act I, score no. 6 (originally the first tableau, scene 7): This number was drastically shortened by Bournonville by his omission of several sections totalling 74 bars.
(3) Act I, score no. 7 (the *Minuet*) and no. 8 (the *Reel*): The music for these two dances was shortened by Bournonville by his omission of four repeats totalling 48 bars.
(4) Act II, score no. 1 (originally the second tableau, scene 1): Bournonville here omitted a section of 8 bars which, however, was reinstated by him at a later stage (most likely in the last restaging on 27.3.1877).

(5) Act II, score no. 3 (originally the second tableau, scene 2): Bournonville here omitted a section of 13 bars and shortened the whole number drastically by arranging a new ending which played for only 21 bars instead of the original 90 measures.

(6) Act II, score no. 4 (originally the second tableau, scene 4): Bournonville here omitted a section of 9 bars.

(7) Act II, score no. 5, scene 6 (originally the third tableau, scene 1): In this number Bournonville revised and shortened the music to play for only 32 measures.

(8) Act II, score no. 6, scene 7 (originally the third tableau, scenes 2 and 3): Bournonville here omitted three sections of 8, 14, and 16 bars respectively.

(9) Act II, score no. 7, scene 8 (originally the third tableau, scene 4 and the beginning of scene 5): This number was drastically changed by Bournonville's omission of 41 measures, and by his insertion of a partially new transition between scenes 4 and 5 of 27 bars instead of the original 18 measures.

(10) Act II, score no. 8, scene 9 (originally the third tableau, scene 5): In order to allow for the omission of the music for what in 1859 accompanied scenes 6 and 7, Bournonville arranged a partially new ending for this number so that it continued directly into what in 1865 became scene 9 (originally scene 8).

(11) Act II, score nos. 9–10, scene 9 (originally the third tableau, scene 8): In these numbers Bournonville omitted a repeat of 9 bars, cancelled a section of 8 measures, and excluded yet another repeat of 10 bars.

(12) Act II, score no. 13, scene 10 (originally the third tableau, scene 9): Bournonville here made Winding arrange a new, slightly revised version of the opening 6 bars.

(13) Act II, score no. 14, scene 11 (originally the third tableau, scene 10): Bournonville here omitted two sections of 20 and 10 bars each, and also inserted a repeat of 2 bars.

In his diary Bournonville noted about the 1865 staging and its first two performances:

21.7.1865: 'skrevet og arrangeret paa Fjeldstuen'
9.8.: 'arbeidet paa Noteringen af Fjeldstuen'
28.8.: 'Breve til Emil Hartmann'
29.8.: 'Prøve paa [...] Fjeldstuen'
31.8., 4.9., 8.9., and 18.9.: 'Prøve paa Fjeldstuen'
19.9.: 'Prøve paa Fjeldstuen fra 10-1 [...] Fjeldstuen 5–7'
20.9.: 'Eftermiddagsprøve paa Fjeldstuen'
22.9.: 'Prøve paa [...] Fjeldstuen'
23.9.: 'Prøve paa Fjeldstuen fra 10.–1.'
25.9.: 'Generalprøve med Repetition paa Fjeldstuen'
28.9.: 'Tidlig op, omskrevet Programmet til Fjeldstuen og bragt det til Trykkeriet [...] Prøve Kl 10½ paa Dandsene til [...] Fjeldstuen'
2.10.: 'Forhindringer ved Theatret formedelst M.e [L.] Stillmanns Moders dødelige Sygdom – Vi prøvede 1.ste Akt af Fjeldstuen'
8.10.: 'Prøve paa Fjeldstuen'
9.10.: 'Prøve paa Fjeldstuen [...] I Theatret [...] Fjeldstuen der gik ypperligt for brilliant Huus og stort Bifald'
11.10.: 'I Theatret Fjeldstuen for maadeligt Huus men gik udmærket og gjorde Lykke'.

The 1865 production received 5 performances, the last of which was given on 21.2.1866.

The orchestral score, the répétiteur's copy, and the set of parts employed for this restaging were the same as those used since the 1859 première of this work (now in DKKk, call nos. C II, 122 m, MA ms 2977, and KTB 281).

Autograph sources:

Choreographic notes. Ms. Autograph. Brown and black ink. 1 vol. 22 pp. (20 × 13,3 cm)
Fjeldstuen./Ballet i to Akter/(NB Anden Akt delt i tvende Tableauer)

Unsigned and undated [Written according to the diary on 21.7. and 9.8.1865, and rewritten on 11.12., 13.12., 19.12., 20.12.1876, and 5.1.1877]
[DKKk; NKS 3285 4° 2 A–E]
This autographed set of choreographic notations for Bournonville's 1865 and 1877 versions of *The Mountain Hut, or Twenty Years* are included on pp. '15v.26r.' in a notebook that originally seems to have served as a diary for his wife, Helene. Moreover, the notes dating from 1865 contain Bournonville's autographed choreographic numbers which refer to similar numbers inserted in the 1859 répétiteur's copy for *The Mountain Hut, or Twenty Years*. Finally, the same notebook includes Bournonville's nearly complete notation of his two-act ballet-vaudeville *The Conservatoire, or A Proposal of Marriage through the Newspaper* (see 15.9.1865) and his incomplete notation of the three-act romantic ballet *The Kermesse in Brüges, or The Three Gifts* (see 19.11.1865).

Choreographic note. Ms. Autograph. Black ink. 1 p. (21,3 × 13,4 cm)
Danse – sauvage d'Asta.
Unsigned and undated [1865?]
[DKKk; NKS 3285 4° 2 A–E]
This manuscript includes a complete description of the solo (or *Danse sauvage*) performed by *Asta* in Act I (second tableau, score no. 12). Moreover, Bournonville's choreographic numbers inserted in this manuscript clearly refer to his similar autographed numbers written into the original 1859 répétiteur's copy for *The Mountain Hut, or Twenty Years*, which was reused for the 1865 production. Hence the suggested dating (1865) of his choreographic notation for this dance.

Printed sources:

Printed scenario. 1 vol. 15 pp. (19 × 12,7 cm)
Fjeldstuen eller Tyve Aar./Ballet i to Akter/af/August Bournonville./Musiken af August Vinding [*sic*] og Emil Hartmann.
Kjøbenhavn, J. H. Schubothe/Biano Luno/F. S. Muhle, 1865
[DKKk; 17, – 175 8°

19.11.1865
The Kermesse in Brüges, or The Three Gifts (Kermessen i Brügge eller: De tre Gaver).
This performance represents Bournonville's first restaging in Copenhagen of his three-act romantic ballet *The Kermesse in Brüges, or The Three Gifts* (see 4.4.1851). It was given this year with new costumes (drawn by E. Lehmann), in a thoroughly revised version that included several new incorporated dances to borrowed music. These dances were:

(1) A revised version of the Act I *Pas de deux* (performed by *Carelis* and *Eleonora*) that included large portions of additional music, borrowed from Act I (score no. 7) of Paulli's and Bournonville's short-lived three-act Hungarian ballet *In The Carpathians* (see 4.3.1857). This incorporated music served as the accompaniment to what today is still the second solo variations in the Act I *Pas de deux* (performed by *Eleonora* and *Carelis* respectively) and the beginning of the Coda.
(2) After the revised 1865 *Pas de deux* in Act I came the *Slowanka*, also borrowed from Bournonville's and Paulli's *In The Carpathians* (see 4.3.1857). It was incorporated in Act I as score no. '2[A]' and has ever since been performed as an integral number of this act.
(3) According to an orchestral score fragment (*see* Musical sources) a completely new *entr'acte* seems to have been incorporated this year in Act II of *The Kermesse in Brüges, or The Three Gifts* (between score nos. 9 and 10).
(4) According to the poster a so-called 'Jægerdands' was incorporated in 1865 in Act II, where it was listed as score no. '11'. It was set to music completely identical with that of the so-called 'Pas des piqueurs' (or *Vexeldands*) in Act III (score no. 29) of *In the Carpathians*. In that ballet it was originally performed by F. Hoppe and Juliette

Price, who were joined by a group of four men (*Les piqueurs*). In the 1865 version of *The Kermesse in Brüges, or The Three Gifts* this so-called 'Jægerdands' was performed by F. Hoppe and S. Price as a *Pas de deux* at *Madame van Everdingen*'s. It seems to have replaced the original 1851 *Pas de quatre* in that scene.

In his diary Bournonville noted about the revised 1865 production and its first performance:

26.9.1865: 'Componeret til Kermessen hele Formiddagen hjemme'
27.9.: 'Prøve fra Kl 10 til 1½, indstuderet 3 forskjellige Pas til <u>Kermessen</u>'
28.9.: 'Prøve Kl 10½ paa Dandsene til Kermessen'
29.9.: 'componeret og indstuderet Dands til Kermessen'
30.9.: 'Prøve paa Dandsene til Kermessen'
6.10.: 'Indstudering paa Kermessen, skrevet [...] Eftermiddagsprøve paa Kermessen'
10.10.: 'skrevet, stor Indstudering paa Kermessen'
11.10.: 'Prøve paa Kermessen'
12.10.: 'skrevet [...] Prøve paa Kermessen fra 10–1'
13.10.: 'Stor Prøve og Indstudering'
14.10.: 'Indstudering'
16.10.: 'componeret, prøvet og givet Pantomime Lection'
17.10.: 'skrevet, Stor Prøve og Indstudering paa Theatret, færdig med <u>Kermessen</u>'
18.10.: 'Prøve paa <u>Kermessen</u> heelt igjennem med det bedste Udfald'
23.10.: 'Prøve paa Kermessen'
24.10.: 'Presentation af Kermessen, der gik ganske fortræffeligt'
28.10.: 'Besøg paa Malersalen i Anledning af Kermessen'
30.10.: 'Decorationsprøve paa Kermessen'
14.11.: 'Stor Arrangementsprøve paa Kermessen, arbeidet paa Theatret til Kl 3'
15.11.: 'Generalprøve paa Kermessen <u>1.e og 2.e Akt:</u>'
16.11.: 'Prøve Kl 10 og med Orchester Kl 11'
17.11.: 'Generalprøve paa Kermessen'
18.11.: 'prøvet adskilligt af Kermessen'
19.11.: 'Kermessen i Brügge. 1.ste Gang paanÿ indstuderet. Den gik udmærket godt og med stormende Bifald. Det var en stor Succés og jeg takkede Gud der under mig saa meget Held'.

The 1865 production received 10 performances, the last of which was given on 27.1.1867.

Autograph sources:

Production note. Ms. Autograph. Brown ink. 4 pp. (36,6 × 22,8 cm)
<u>Costumer til Balletten/Kermessen i Brügge.</u>
Signed and dated: 'd. 7.de October 1865.'
[DKKkt; F.M. (Ballet)

Production note. Ms. Autograph. Brown ink. 4 pp. (21,4 × 13,3 cm)
<u>Personale i Balletten/Kermessen i Brügge.</u>
Unsigned and undated [c. autumn 1865]
[DKKkt; F.M. (Ballet)

Choreographic note (incomplete). Ms. Autograph. Brown ink. 1 p. (20 × 13,3 cm)
<u>Kermessen i Brügge.</u>/Ballet i 3 Akter./(NB 2.den Akt er deelt i tvende Tableauer.)
Unsigned and undated [c. autumn 1865]
[DKKk; NKS 3285 4° 2 A–E
This (incomplete) 1865 notation of *The Kermesse in Brüges, or The Three Gifts* is included on p. '13v.' in a notebook that originally seems to have served as a diary for Bournonville's wife, Helene. Moreover, the same volume contains Bournonville's nearly complete notation of his two-act ballet-vaudeville *The Conservatoire, or A Proposal of Marriage through the Newspaper* (*see* 15.9.1865), and his 1865 and 1877 notations of his Norwegian ballet in three tableaux *The Mountain*

Hut, or Twenty Years (*see* 9.10.1865 and 27.3.1877). Bournonville's 1865 notes for *The Kermesse in Brüges, or The Three Gifts* only include the ballet's new, revised title, according to which the second act was now divided into two tableaux.

Musical sources:

The orchestral score and the set of parts employed for the 1865 restaging of *The Kermesse in Brüges, or The Three Gifts* are now in DKKk (call nos. MA ms 1551, and KTB 271).

Orchestral score (fragment). Ms. Autograph (by H. S. Paulli). Brown ink. 8 pp. (27 × 37,9 cm)
No. 10 A. Mellemakt.
Unsigned and undated [c.1865]
[DKKk; MA ms 2762 (4) (KTB 271)
According to a note on the last page of this orchestral score fragment (reading: 'attacca No. <u>10 B</u>. Pag. 144') it was originally part of Paulli's autographed orchestral score for *The Kermesse in Brüges, or The Three Gifts*, in which it was performed as a musical *entr'acte* in Act II (incorporated between score nos. 9 and 10). The fact that the fragment is unpaginated clearly indicates that it was not part of Paulli's original 1851 score, but was composed for a later restaging of the ballet (most likely that on 19.11.1865). Later it seems to have been omitted from the ballet. This probably happened in connection with Bournonville's second and last restaging of it on 8.12.1872. This theory is supported by two pencilled notes on p. 66 in the 1865 répétiteur's copy (reading: 'Forandring' and 'Mellemact.') of which the latter is crossed out.
The manuscript was found in the music archive of Copenhagen's Royal Theatre in 1989 and was transferred to DKKk at a later stage.

Orchestral score (fragment). Ms. Autograph (by V. C. Holm) and copy. Black ink. 18 pp. (26,2 × 35,5 cm with variants)
No. 29 [changed to:] <u>12 b</u>/Allegretto.
Unsigned and undated [1857]
[DKKkt; MA ms 2762 (5) (KTB 271)
This fragment was discovered at DKKkt in 1989 among those autographed orchestral score fragments which had either been incorporated or later taken out of Paulli's autographed score for *The Kermesse in Brüges, or The Three Gifts*. It is entitled 'No. 29' and paginated '395–412' and contains Paulli's music for what originally was the 'Pas des piqueurs' (or *Vexeldands*) in Act III (score no. 29) of his and Bournonville's three-act Hungarian ballet *In the Carpathians* (*see* 4.3.1857). According to the 1865 répétiteur's copy for *The Kermesse in Brüges, or The Three Gifts* it was interpolated in Act II of this ballet on 19.11.1865. It was listed there as score no. '11' and was performed (according to the poster) by F. Hoppe and S. Price as a *Pas de deux*, also named 'Jægerdands'.
At Bournonville's last restaging of *The Kermesse in Brüges, or The Three Gifts* on 8.12.1872 the same music served as the accompaniment for yet another *Pas de deux*, which was also performed in the second act, but was then listed as score no. '11½'. This is clear from Bournonville's autographed notes for this dance, written on p. 79 in the 1865 répétiteur's copy. They read: '<u>Kermessen i Brügge</u> <u>Pas de deux</u> (Herr <u>E Hansen</u> og <u>Frk Westberg.</u>)'.
At the much later production of *The Kermesse in Brüges, or The Three Gifts* on 7.11.1909 (mounted by H. Beck) the incorporated music from *In the Carpathians* was omitted from the ballet. Instead Beck interpolated V. C. Holm's 1873 score for yet another Bournonville *Pas de deux*, which was then performed as score no. '12 b'. That dance is identical with the *Pas de deux* which Bournonville had choreographed for D. Krum and M. Westberg in 1873, premièred as an incorporated divertissement in Act I of D.-F.-E. Auber's five-act opera *La Muette de Portici* (*see* 2.9.1873). Since 1909 to this day it has always been performed as an integral part of Act II in *The Kermesse in Brüges, or The Three Gifts*.

Répétiteur's copy. Ms. Autographs (by H. S. Paulli and V. C. Holm) and copy. Black ink. 1 vol. 146 pp. (33,9 × 25,5 cm with minor variants)

Bruges ikke/B. 271/<u>1908</u>/Kermessen i Brygge/Repetiteurpartie./
2.den Udgaven/<u>1851.</u>)/<u>1865.</u>)/B/Bournonville.
Unsigned and dated (on the front cover): '<u>1865.</u>)'
[DKKk; MA ms 2966 b (KTB 271 (2))
This répétiteur's copy dates from the 1865 revised restaging of *The Kermesse in Brüges, or The Three Gifts.* It contains Bournonville's autographed choreographic numbers (written with brown ink) throughout the volume. They seem to refer to a separate (not yet traced) notation of the complete ballet, which he perhaps wrote in connection with either the 1865 production, or for the later, revised restaging of it on 8.12.1872. Moreover, the volume also contains Bournonville's sporadic autographed notes which describe the mime in Act II (score no. 8). Furthermore, his similarly autographed notes in the same act (score no. 9) describe in fine detail the mime scene between *Eleonora* and *Carelis* and the choreography danced by *Eleonora* during her enforced solo variation to the accompaniment of the magic viola da gamba (played by *Carelis*). These notes were most likely written in connection with Bournonville's later incorporation of this scene into his ballet epilogue, entitled *Farewell to the Old Theatre (Farvel til det gamle Theater)*, premièred on 1.6.1874. Finally, in the music for the Act III finale (score no. 19) Bournonville's detailed autographed notes about the mime and the choreography in the ballet's final 61 bars are included.

The music for the revised Act I *Pas de deux* (score no. '2b', performed by *Eleonora* and *Carelis*) in this volume is partly Paulli's autograph, while some of the sections of the music for the so-called 'Jægerdands' in Act II (score no. '11') are written in V. C. Holm's hand.

Other sources:

Costume drawing by E. Lehmann. Pencil and water colours (12 × 22 cm)
Juliette Price/Kermessen
Unsigned and undated [c.1865]
[SSm; Daniel Fryklunds samling no. 268 (F 1335 a)
This drawing shows the costume worn by *Eleonora* in *The Kermesse in Brüges, or The Three Gifts* (performed by Juliette Price).

Costume drawing by E. Lehmann. Pencil and water colours (12 × 22 cm)
<u>Kermessen</u>/Carelis/Scharff
Unsigned and undated [c.1865]
[SSm; Daniel Fryklunds samling no. 270 (F 1335 d)
This drawing shows the costume worn by *Carelis* in *The Kermesse in Brüges, or The Three Gifts* (performed by H. Scharff).

Costume drawing by E. Lehmann. Pencil and water colours (22,1 × 12 cm)
Kermessen.
Unsigned and undated [c.1865]
[DKKkt; Kostumetegninger (Lehmann)
This drawing shows the costume worn by *Geert* in Act I of *The Kermesse in Brüges, or The Three Gifts* (performed by E. Stramboe).

Costume drawing by E. Lehmann. Pencil and water colours (21,2 × 12 cm)
<u>Kermessen.</u>/Petersen
Unsigned and undated [c.1865]
[DKKkt; Kostumetegninger (Lehmann)
This drawing shows the costume worn by *Marchen* in *The Kermesse in Brüges, or The Three Gifts* (performed by J. Petersen).

Costume drawing by E. Lehmann. Pencil and water colours (20,8 × 12 cm)
<u>Kermessen.</u>/Stillmann
Unsigned and undated [c.1865]
[DKKkt; Kostumetegninger (Lehmann)
This drawing shows the costume worn by *Johanna* in *The Kermesse in Brüges, or The Three Gifts* (performed by L. Stillmann).

Costume drawing by E. Lehmann. Pencil and water colours (14,2 × 17,6 cm)
Lense/L. Hansen/Kermessen
Unsigned and undated [c.1865]
[DKKkt; Kostumetegninger (Lehmann)
This drawing shows the costumes worn by the two commedia dell' arte characters. *Pulcinello* and *Bajasso.* in Act I (and/or III?) of *The Kermesse in Brüges, or The Three Gifts* (performed by A. F. Lense and L. Hansen respectively).

Costume drawing by E. Lehmann. Pencil and water colours (22,5 × 12, 1 cm)
<u>Kermessen</u>/Borgere
Unsigned and undated [c.1865]
[DKKkt; Kostumetegninger (Lehmann)
This drawing shows the costume worn by the burghers in Act I (and/ or III?) of *The Kermesse in Brüges, or The Three Gifts.*

Costume drawing by E. Lehmann. Pencil and water colours (18,9 × 12 cm)
<u>Kermessen</u>/Klyver
Unsigned and undated [c.1865]
[DKKkt; Kostumetegninger (Lehmann)
This drawing shows the costume worn by the *Jester* in Act I (and/or III?) of *The Kermesse in Brüges, or The Three Gifts* (performed by J. T. Klüver).

Costume drawing by E. Lehmann. Pencil and water colours (22,2 × 12,3 cm)
Kermessen/Adelsmænd/Dhrr Andersen/Steendrup/Carpentier/ Busch
Unsigned and undated [c.1865]
[DKKkt; Kostumetegninger (Lehmann)
This drawing shows the costume worn by the noblemen in *The Kermesse in Brüges, or The Three Gifts* (performed by R. C. A. Andersen, N. P. Stendrup, C. Carpentier, and F. Busch).

Costume drawing by E. Lehmann. Pencil and water colours (21,7 × 12 cm)
Kermessen./Geert/Stramboe
Unsigned and undated [c.1865]
[DKKkt; Kostumetegninger (Lehmann)
This drawing shows the costume worn by *Geert* in Act II of *The Kermesse in Brüges, or The Three Gifts* (performed by E. Stramboe).

Costume drawing by E. Lehmann. Pencil and water colours (12 × 23 cm)
(Kermessen)/Hr Hoppe./nÿe
Unsigned and undated [c.1865]
[SSm; Daniel Fryklunds samling no. 271 (F 1335 c)
This drawing shows the costume worn by F. Hoppe in the incorporated *Pas de deux* (also entitled 'Jægerdands') in Act II, score no. '11' of *The Kermesse in Brüges, or The Three Gifts.*

Costume drawing by E. Lehmann. Pencil and water colours (12 × 22 cm)
<u>Kermessen</u>/Sophie Price.
Unsigned and undated [c.1865]
[SSm; Daniel Fryklunds samling no. 269 (F 1335 b)
This drawing shows the costume worn by S. Price in the incorporated *Pas de deux* (also entitled 'Jægerdands') in Act II, score no. '11' of *The Kermesse in Brüges, or The Three Gifts.*

Costume drawing by E. Lehmann. Pencil and water colours (22,6 × 12,1 cm)
<u>Kermessen</u>/4 Jægere/Klyver/Walbom/Iversen/Hansen
Unsigned and undated [c.1865]
[DKKkt; Kostumetegninger (Lehmann)
This drawing shows the costume worn by the so-called 'piqueurs' who acompanied F. Hoppe and S. Price in the incorporated *Pas de*

deux (also entitled 'Jægerdands') in Act II, score no. '11' of *The Kermesse in Brüges, or The Three Gifts* (performed by J. T. Klüver, A. Walbom, O. Iversen, and E. Hansen).

Costume drawing by E. Lehmann. Pencil and water colours (22,2 × 12,2 cm)
Dhrr. Hansen og Krum
Unsigned and undated [c.1865]
[DKKkt; Kostumetegninger (Lehmann)
This drawing shows the costume worn by D. Krum and E. Hansen in the *Polonaise* in Act II (score no. 12) of *The Kermesse in Brüges, or The Three Gifts*.

Costume drawing by E. Lehmann. Pencil and water colours (19,6 × 12 cm)
Kermessen/Nielsen
Unsigned and undated [c.1865]
[DKKkt; Kostumetegninger (Lehmann)
This drawing shows the costume of the negro page-boy in Acts II and III of *The Kermesse in Brüges, or The Three Gifts* (performed by a not yet identified child, named Nielsen).

23.11.1865
Pas de trois (uncredited) performed by H. Scharff, E. Gade, and J. Petersen.
According to a note in Bournonville's diary on 20.11.1865 (reading: 'bivaanet en lille Prøve paa Pas de trois af 'Soldat og Bonde') this (uncredited) dance is clearly identical with the *Pas de trois* from his much earlier pantomimic idyll *Soldier and Peasant*, score no. 7 (*see* 13.10.1829). In the rehearsal book of A. Fredstrup all three rehearsals of this dance (held between 18.11. and 23.11.1865) are listed as having been directed by L. Gade. The *Pas de trois* was given twice during the 1865–66 season, the last time on 25.11.1865. Bournonville did not attend any of these performances because of a trip to Paris this autumn, on which he embarked on the very same day as this performance. No separate musical sources for this dance have yet been traced. This clearly indicates that it must have been rehearsed and performed this year using the original 1829 musical material for *Soldier and Peasant* (now in DKKk, call nos. C II, 115, MA ms 3021, and KTB 1026 (originally KTB 286)).

1866

16.1.1866
Paul et Virginie (Divertissement) (Paul og Virginie (Divertissement). Projected restaging in Copenhagen for the 1866–67 season.
In Bournonville's travel diary from his trip to Paris in November and December 1865 (now in DKKk, call no. NKS 747 8°, vol. 29, p. 24r) a note after the date of 16.1.1866 reads as follows:

'Planer for
Theatersaisonen 1866–67.
Paul og Virginie (Divertissement)
Debut for Betty Schnell og Krom.'

This clearly indicates that a restaging of his one-act divertissement *Paul et Virginie* (*see* 19.6.1854) was planned for the débuts of his pupils B. Schnell and D. Krum in the 1866–67 season. However, for unknown reasons this project was never

carried out, and Bournonville's divertissement version of *Paul et Virginie* was given for the last time in Copenhagen on 17.4.1857.

16.1.1866
La Sylphide (Sylphiden). Projected restaging in Copenhagen for the 1866–67 season.
This projected restaging of Bournonville's two-act romantic ballet *La Sylphide* (*see* 28.11.1836) is mentioned in his 1866 Parisian travel diary under the date 16.1.1866. It was part of his projected repertory plan for the 1866–67 season and was intended to be staged for the début of M. Price. She performed this ballet for the first time on 26.4.1867, when she made her début in the title rôle together with H. Scharff (playing *James*).

16.1.1866
The Five Senses (De fem Sandser). Projected divertissement for the 1866–67 season(?).
This projected divertissement to music by H. Berens, is mentioned in Bournonville's 1866 Parisian travel diary under the date 16.1.1866. It was part of a his projected repertory plan for the 1866–67 season and is described as a divertissement performed by five women (S. Price, M. Price, J. Petersen, L. Cetti, and B. Schnell) and a man (E. Hansen). The divertissement is almost certainly identical with Bournonville's earlier intermezzo, entitled *Le Ballet des cinq sens*, first performed in Act V of O. Wijkander's historical five-act play *The Order of the Amaranth (Amarather-Orden)* at Stockholm's Royal Theatre (Dramatiska Theatern) on 20.2.1864.

The 1866 projected divertissement was never mounted in Copenhagen, but Bournonville's idea for a separate allegorical ballet on this theme was in part carried out two years later, when he included a so-called *Dance of the Five Senses* in Act I (scene 2, score no. 2) of his four-act Nordic mythological ballet *The Lay of Thrym* (*see* 21.2.1868).

16.1.1866
L'Africaine. Projected staging in Copenhagen for the 1866–67 season(?).
In his diary for the years 1865–66 (vol. 29, *see* Additional Sources) Bournonville included three pencilled drawings after the date of 16.1.1866. They show the scenery for Acts I, II, and III of G. Meyerbeer's five-act opera *L'Africaine* (premièred at the Paris Opéra on 28.4.1865) and were most probably made after attending a performance of it at the Paris Opéra on 29.11.1865. Moreover, on the same day he made an extensive and most interesting description of this opera assessing the performance, the décor, and the Act III ballet divertissement (choreographed by A. Saint-Léon) as follows:

'i Operaen, hvor vi hørte og saae L'Africaine, Opera i 5 Akter af [E.] Scribe og [G.] Meyerbeer. Kedeligt Sujet, storartet Musik med mange skjønne Effecter, men som ikke kunde fattes ved den første Audition. [J.-B.] Faure som Nelusco sang og spillede med megen Kraft, [E.] Naudin udførte Vasco de Gamas Tenor partie meget smukt, uden mindste Genialitet. Mme [M.-C.] Saxe har en ganske overordentlig Stemme (mezzo soprano) og vistnok en god Skole, men hun skriger for gevaltig og hendes Ydre er intet mindre end erotisk. Det er et Mellemting af en Kokkepige og den hohlenbokliske Venus. [J.-B.] Belval er ogsaa en dygtig Bassanger og [L.-H.]

Obin som Offerpræst gjorde god Virkning. – Decorationerne vare pompøse. En Rundsal i byzantinsk Stiil. – Et Fængsel. – Skibet, hvis Maskiner kun var ganske maadelig. En Troneplads ved Templet i Afrika hvor Alt lige indtil Costumer og Dandse var anlagt efter Hindustans Mønstre. Som Saadanne var Dandsene af St. Léon [i.e. A. Saint-Léon] ret characteristiske og gjorde ved de store Masser en slaaende Virkning. Sidste Akt havde to Tableauer, en tropisk Skov, hvori en superb Duett imellem Selika og Inès (M.lle [M.] Battu), dernæst en Klippedecoration med et stort Piletræ paa Spidsen af en Forbjerg. Hertil var et særdeles pikant Forspil af Strenge-Instrumenter paa G. Strængen. Det gjorde stor Effect og blev Bis'eret. Det Hele varede til Kl 12".

Bournonville's three drawings of A. Rubé's, P. Chaperon's, C. Cambon's, and J. Thierry's décors for the first three acts of Meyerbeer's opera may perhaps have been made with the purpose of a future staging of this work in Copenhagen. That project, however, was never carried out, and *L'Africaine* has to this day never been performed in Denmark.

Autograph sources:

3 drawings inserted in Bournonville's diary (on p. '45r') after the date 16.1.1866. Ms. Autograph. Pencil. 1 p. (13 × 8 cm)
l'Africaine 1.e Akt/[drawing]/2.' Akt (Fængsel)/[drawing]/3.die Akt/[drawing]
Unsigned and undated [Drawn most probably in Paris between 29.11.1865 and 16.1.1866]
[DKKk; NKS 747, 8°, kapsel 5, vol. 29

23.1.1866
Napoli or The Fisherman and His Bride (Napoli eller Fiskeren og hans Brud).
This restaging of Bournonville's three-act romantic ballet *Napoli or The Fisherman and His Bride* (see 29.3.1842) was mounted with J. Petersen playing the rôle of *Teresina* for the first time. As the result of a serious injury suffered by Juliette Price during a performance of *The Kermesse in Brüges, or The Three Gifts* on 22.11.1865, this leading Bournonville ballerina retired definitively from the stage in 1866. Consequently, Petersen learned the rôle of *Teresina* during only four rehearsals under Bournonville's personal direction, in spite of the fact that he was no longer under contract with the Royal Theatre. In his diary he noted about these rehearsals:

12.1.1866: 'Instruction til Johanne Petersen paa Teresina i Napoli'
13.1.: 'Prøve paa Napoli'
15.1.: 'Prøve paa Napoli i tre Timer'
16.1.: 'Prøve og Præsentation af Napoli (Johanne Petersen)'.

Bournonville did not attend Petersen's first performance.

The musical material employed this year was the same as that used since the 1842 première of this ballet (now in DKKk, call nos. C II, 114 k and KTB 292).

The 1866 restaging of *Napoli or The Fisherman and His Bride* received 11 performances, the last of which was given on 11.6.1868.

25.1.1866
The Wedding at Ulfåsa (Brylluppet paa Ulfbjerg).
Although Bournonville did not personally take any part in the actual staging of the Copenhagen première of F. Hedberg's four-act historical play *Bröllopet på Ulfåsa* (first performed at Stockholm's Royal Theatre, Stora Theatern, on

1.4.1865), he clearly seems to have been instrumental in this Danish production. This theory is confirmed by a series of notes in his diary reading as follows:

13.5.1865: 'Læst [F.] Hedbergs ny Skuespil Brölloppet på Ulfåsa med stor Fornøielse, afsendt Stykket til Etatsraad [R.] Kranold med Brev'
5.6.: 'Brev fra Kranold om Hedbergs Stykkes Antagelse – jeg skrev strax til Hedberg'
16.3.1866: 'I Theatret og seet Brylluppet paa Ulfsbjerg (Ulfåsa) der fornøiede mig ganske overordentlig og blev meget godt spillet. – Ved Hjemkomsten fik jeg et hjerteligt Brev fra [T.] Overskou'
18.3.: 'skrevet til Hedberg'
28.3.: 'Brev fra Hedberg'.

The Wedding at Ulfåsa (which was translated into Danish by H. P. Holst and mounted by T. Overskou) received 62 performances in Copenhagen, the last of which was given 29.11. 1877.

19.3.1866
Gioacchino.
For the 1866 Copenhagen restaging of H. P. Holst's four-act drama with music by H. Rung (see 12.10.1844) Bournonville took part (according to his diary) in the rehearsals of the *Tarantella* in Act IV (score no. 14), although it was mounted this year under the general direction of L. Gade. According to the same source he attended only the third performance of *Gioacchino* on 25.3.1866. The 1866 restaging of *Gioacchino* received 5 performances, the last of which was given on 14.4. 1865.

Musical sources:

The orchestral score and the set of parts employed for the 1866 restaging were the same as those used for the 1844 première of *Gioacchino* (now in DKKk, call nos. C II, 119 k, and KTA 388).

Répétiteur's copy. Ms. Copy. Black ink. 1 vol. 4 pp. (33,8 × 24,9 cm)
2. Gioacchino./[...]/3./Repetiteurpartie/til/Gioacchino/[...]/Tarantella
Unsigned and undated [1866]
[DKKk; MA ms 2919 (2) (KTA 388 (2))
This répétiteur's copy dates from the 1866 Copenhagen restaging of *Gioacchino* and contains the music for the Act IV *Tarantella* (score no. 14). Moreover, according to pencilled notes this dance seems to have been shortened in 1866 with the omission of three repeats of 8, 8, and 16 bars respectively, and the cancellation of a section of 4 bars at the end of the dance. The répétiteur's copy is included (on pp. 15–18) in a volume that also contains the répétiteur's copies for five other operas and plays, mounted at Copenhagen's Royal Theatre between 1864 and 1868.

11.4.1866
Pontemolle (An Artists' Party in Rome) (Pontemolle (Et Kunstnergilde i Rom)).
This ballet-vaudeville in two tableaux represents Bournonville's last work in the Italian sphere, and depicts the life of a colony of Danish artists in Rome. According to his diary, Bournonville originally intended to commission the music from I. P. E. Hartmann, N. W. Gade, H. S. Paulli, E. Helsted, H. C. Lumbye, and J. Glæser, but that plan was abandoned at an early stage as a result of several practical difficulties. Instead the score was composed and arranged by four other composers as follows:

(1) The 1st tableau, Introduction and score nos. 1–7: Composed by V. C. Holm.

(2) The 2nd tableau, score no. 8, and no. 9 (in the orchestral score entitled 'Optogsmarsch'): Composed by A. F. Lincke.

(3) The 2nd tableau, score no. 10 (*Pas de deux and Saltarello*, in the orchestral score entitled 'Polonaise' and 'Saltarello'): Composed by V. C. Holm.

(4) The 2nd tableau, score no. 11 (entitled *Ancient Rome*) and score no. 12 (*The Age of Art*): Composed by A. F. Lincke.

(5) The 2nd tableau, score no. 13 (entitled *Roccoco Quadrille*): Composed and arranged by L. W. T. Carlsen. The music employed by Carlsen for the three dances in this number (according to the orchestral score named 'Andante pastorale', 'Chaconne', and 'Contredanse ancienne' respectively) seems to have been based on three (not yet identified) French dances dating from the 18th century. This is clear from Bournonville's separate choreographic notes for these three dances.

(6) The 2nd tableau, score no. 14 (entitled *Pulcinello*): Composed and arranged by A. F. Lincke. Lincke's musical arrangement for this solo character dance is based on the well-known tune in 6/8 time, entitled 'Carneval de Venise'. It is based on a Neapolitan folk tune, named 'La Ricciolella', and had become famous thanks to N. Paganini's virtuosic variations of it for solo violin. Bournonville had earlier used this melody on two different occasions, namely for a *Pas de deux*, danced by himself and A. Krætzmer in P. Larcher's ballet *Le Carnaval de Venise, ou Constance à l'Epreuve* (*see* 20.12.1832), and for his and J. F. Fröhlich's romantic ballet in six tableaux *Raphael* (*see* 30.5.1845).

(7) The 2nd tableau, score no. 15 (entitled *Old Age and Folly (mimetic waltz)*): Composed by F. X. Neruda.

(8) The 2nd tableau, score no. 16 (the *Finale*): Composed by A. F. Lincke.

Pontemolle was restaged for the last time by Bournonville in a slightly revised version at Copenhagen's new Royal Theatre on 21.10.1875.

In his diary he noted about the creation and the 1866 première of the ballet:

24.2.1866: 'Brev til [R.] Kranold'
26.2.: 'Conciperet mit Program til <u>Pontemolle</u> [...] skrevet til Kranold med min Plan'
27.2.: 'beskjæftiget med mit Program. Brev til Theatermaler [C. F.] Christensen'
28.2.: 'Svar fra Kranold [...] Hele Dagen beskjæftiget med Reenskrivningen af Pontemolle'
1.3.: 'copieret og forkortet mit Program'
2.3.: 'til Kranold, hvor mit Program blev læst med stor Fornøielse og hvor jeg fik Chocolade. Honoraret blev aftalt (300 rd. strax og 20 rd. for de første 15 Gange.). Jeg kjørte [...] til Malersalen, hvor jeg aftalte det fornødne med Christensen. Jeg gik til [I. P. E.] <u>Hartmann</u> for at formane ham til i Forening med [N. W.] <u>Gade</u> at componere Musiken til Pontemolle, men allene kunde han ikke paatage sig det herlige Arbeide og <u>Gade</u> var stærkt arrangeret med sit nye Oratorium. – Dog skulde jeg høre nærmere iaften. Jeg spiste Middag hos [H. S.] Paullis. Holger [Paulli] var stærkt forkjølet, [E.] Helsted er stadig sÿg; [H. C.] Lumbÿ[e]i Breslau. J. <u>Glæser</u> udenlands og paa den Maade saare knap Tid paa Composition til min Ballet! Jeg fik fat paa [A. F.] Lincke og satte ham Stevne til imorgen tidlig, derpaa gik jeg Kl 6 til Hartmann, der definitivt undslog sig for Arbeidet. – jeg lod [J.] Thiele læse mit Program [...] Jeg talte med [V. C.] <u>Holm</u> og [F. X.] <u>Neruda</u>, der vare villige til at hjælpe mig med Musiken. Jeg drak The hos Thieles og gik hjem tilsengs temmelig forkjølet'
3.3.: 'Tidlig op, arbeidet med <u>Lincke</u>; derpaa truffet Aftale om Decorationerne og Costumerne, arbeidet med Holm'
4.3.: 'Brev til Kranold i Anledning af Gallaforestillingens Sammensætning'
7.3.: 'modtaget Musik af Holm og Lincke, arbeidet med Neruda og [L. W. T.] Carlsen'

8.3.: 'Hele Dagen hjemme og tilbragt Dagen med at componere Dandse til Pontemolle'
9.3.: 'skrevet og componeret. – 3 Dandse færdige'
12.3.: 'arbeidede med Neruda og Lincke'
13.3.: 'besøgt Holm og Neruda om Musik, været paa Theatret og forberedt mine Prøver [...] arbeidet med <u>Lincke</u>'
14.3.: 'hos Holm og paa Theatret. 1.ste Indstudering <u>Pas de deux</u> og <u>Kunstperioden</u> [...] arbeidet og componeret hjemme'
15.3.: 'Skrevet. <u>2.den Indst!</u> 'Det antike Rom' [...] indst. <u>Pulcinello</u>'
16.3.: 'Skrevet. <u>3.die Indst.</u> Roccoco=Quadrille m m, componeret hjemme'
17.3.: 'Skrevet og componeret. <u>4.e Indst.</u> De tre første Pantomimescener [...] Eftermiddagsprøve med Genierne'
18.3.: 'Paa Theatret, skrevet Costumelister'
19.3.: 'Stor Repetition paa det Lærte, der gestalter sig smukt [...] hjem og componeret'
20.3.: 'Skrevet og arrangeret [...] <u>5.te Indstudering</u> (Valsen) der anstrængte mig betydeligt'
21.3.: 'Besluttet at holde mig hjemme for at faae Bugt med min Forkjølelse. I den Anledning skrevet til [L.] Gade og Holm, der Begge besøgte mig, læst skrevet og componeret'
22.3.: 'Jeg befandt mig noget bedre, og holdt min <u>6.e Indstuderingsprøve</u>. Alt gestalter sig vel'
23.3.: '7.de Instuderingsprøve, Finalen til 2.den Akt færdig og meget heldig'
24.3.: '8.e Indstudering, samlet 2.den Akt'
26.3.: 'Stor Arrangementprøve paa 2.den Akt af Balletten [...] besørget Musik fra Holm, componeret den sidste Scene af 1.ste Akt'
27.3.: 'Tidlig Prøve (Kl 10) paa Balletten, der nu ved 9.e Indstudering staaer fuldkommen færdig og som det kan mærkes paa Alle vellykket'
28.3.: 'Theaterprøve paa 2.den Akt af Pontemolle, der gik ypperligt'
3.4.: 'Besørget mit Program hos Bogtrykkeren. Repetition paa 1.ste Akt af min Ballet og Correcturprøve paa Musiken til 2.den Akt'
4.4.: 'Theaterprøve paa 1.ste Akt af Pontemolle'
5.4.: 'Theaterprøve med Repetiteur og Militairmusik paa Balletten'
6.4.: 'Theaterprøve paa Balletten [...] Prøvet Costumer'
7.4.: 'Theaterprøve paa 2.den Akt af Balletten, der gik udmærket [...] prøvet Costumer paa Theatret'
8.4.: 'afleveret Programmer hos Etatsr. Kranold, besøgt <u>Thiele</u>, der vedvarende er syg'
9.4.: 'Theaterprøve med Orchester paa 1.ste Akt af Balletten'
10.4.: 'Hele Dagen beskjæftiget med min Ballet, der blev prøvet med fuld Belysning i Costume og gjorde overordentlig Lÿkke'
1.4.: 'leveret Programmer til Adm: [C. L. C.] Irminger, Grevinde Dannesjold og Overhofmarskallen [i.e. V. T. Oxholm] [...] Festforestilling i Anledning af hans Majestæts Kongens [i.e. Christian IX] Fødselsdag. Jublende Modtagelse, glimrende Forsamling. Man gav [...] for første Gang min nÿ Ballet <u>Pontemolle</u>, der gik fortræffeligt og gjorde stormende Lÿkke. Jeg takkede Gud af mit inderste Hjerte!'.

The 1866 production received 25 performances in the old Royal Theatre building (the last of which was given on 27.4. 1872), and the ballet reached a total of 38 performances during Bournonville's lifetime (the last given on 21.11.1879).

Autograph sources:

Manuscript scenario (included in a letter to R. Kranold). Ms. Autograph. Brown ink. 3 pp. (26,8 × 21,2 cm)
[...] Da jeg endnu ikke ganske kan binde mig til Detaillerne vil jeg blot i Korthed skizzere det løse Omrids [...]/<u>Første Akt</u> [...] <u>2.den Akt</u> [...] <u>Personerne</u> [...]
Signed and dated: 'Fredensborg d. 26' Februar 1866.'
[DKKk; NKS 3258 4° VII 9

Manuscript scenario. Ms. Autograph. Brown ink. 1 vol. 14 pp. (22,7 × 18,3 cm)

Pontemolle./Ballet i to Tableauer/af/August Bournonville./<u>1866.</u>
Signed and dated: 'Fredensborg d. 28.de Februar 1866.' [Written
according to the diary between 26.2. and 28.2.1866]
[DKKk; NKS 3285 4° 3 L-P

Production note. Ms. Autograph (partially in another's hand). Black
ink. 3 pp. (33,9 × 21 cm)
<u>Pontemolle./Ballet i 2 Tableauer/Costumer.</u>
Signed and dated: 'Kjøbenhavn d. 3.e Martz 1866.'
[DKKkt; F.M. (Ballet, læg P)

Choreographic note. Ms. Autograph. Brown ink. 4 pp. (21,3 × 17
cm)
<u>Pontemolle./Pas de deux (Scharff & Joh: Petersen.)/[...]/Saltarel-
lo./[...]/Quadrille Roccoco./[...]/Chaconne./[...]/Contredanse.</u>
Unsigned and undated [Written according to the diary between 8.3.
and 14.3.1866]
[DKKt; Brevregistrant: Bournonville
Bournonville's autographed choreographic numbers in this manu-
script refer to similar numbers inserted in V. C. Holm's and L. W. T.
Carlsen's musical drafts for the same dances (now in DKKk, call no.
MA ms 2707 (nos. 2 and 5).

Production note. Ms. Autograph (partially in another's hand). Black
ink. 2 pp. (21,2 × 13,8 cm)
<u>Kunstnere.</u>
Unsigned and undated [According to the diary probably written on
18.3.1866]
[DKKkt; F.M. (Ballet, læg P)

Musical sources:

Musical drafts. Ms. Autographs (by V. C. Holm, A. F. Lincke, L. W. T.
Carlsen, and F. Neruda). 12 + 10 + 8 + 2 + 12 + 8 + 2 pp. of which two
are stitched together (35 × 25,7 cm with variants)
Ponte molle/No. 1/[...]/<u>No. 3.</u> Pas de deux (Fabriccio og Camilla.)/[...]/<u>No. 4.</u>/(Gladiatorer og Blomsterpiger)/[...]/<u>No. 5.</u>
Adagio/[...]/<u>No. 5.</u> Roccoco Quadrille./Ponte molle/[...]/Ponte
molle/Tempo di Vals/[...]/Maestoso
Unsigned and undated [Written according to Bournonville's diary
between 3.3. and 22.3 1866]
[DKKk; MA ms 2707 (1–7) (KTB 280)
These musical drafts contain the music for what at the 1866 première
of *Pontemolle (An Artists' Party in Rome)* became:
(1) V. C. Holm: 1st tableau, score nos. 1–3, and 2nd tableau, score
no. 10 (the '<u>Pas de deux</u>' and 'Saltarello').
(2) A. F. Lincke: 2nd tableau, score no. 11 (the dance scene named
'Gladiatorer og Blomsterpiger') and no. 12 (entitled '<u>Adagio</u>').
(3) L. W. T. Carlsen: 2nd tableau, score no. 13 (the '<u>Roccoco-Qua-
drille</u>', 'Chaconne', and 'Contredanse ancienne').
(4) F. X. Neruda: 2nd tableau, score no. 15 (entitled 'Tempo di
Vals').
(5) A. F. Lincke: 2nd tableau, score no. 14 (named 'Maestoso').
From the same drafts it seems as if Bournonville originally intended
to have Neruda's waltz in the 2nd tableau (score no. 15) performed
before Lincke's 'Pulcinello' dance in the same tableau (score no.
14). This is clear from Bournonville's original pagination of these
drafts (written with brown ink). The musical drafts also contain his
autographed choreographic numbers (written with brown ink and
pencil) which clearly refer to his separate choreographic notations
(written between 8.3. and 14.3.1866, *see above*) and some other (not
yet traced) separate notations of this ballet.

Musical drafts (fragment). Ms. Autograph (by A. F. Lincke). Black
ink. 2 pp. (34 × 24,5 cm)
[Untitled]/[...]/<u>her</u> som Sandheden
Unsigned and undated [Written according to Bournonville's diary
before 22.3.1866]
[DKKk; MA ms 2674 (KTB 280)
This musical fragment contains Lincke's drafts for the last 81 bars of

the finale in *Pontemolle (An Artists' Party in Rome)* (2nd tableau, score
no. 16). Moreover, it includes Bournonville's autographed choreographic numbers ('10–15') which seem to refer to a separate (not yet
traced) choreographic notation of this ballet that he may also have
written in 1866. The drafts originally contained a pencilled pagination reading '25–26', which was changed at a later stage to '5–6'.

Orchestral score. Ms. Autographs (by V. C. Holm, A. F. Lincke, L. W.
T. Carlsen, and F. X. Neruda). Brown and black ink. 1 vol. 360 pp. of
which eight are blank (35 × 29,5 cm with variants)
Pontemolle/Ballet i 2 Acter/280/Partitur
Signed and dated (on p. 140): 'Den 6te April 1866 WCHolm', (p.
329) '<u>Franz Neruda</u>, März 1866. – ', (p. 360) 'Den 28.e Marts 1866.
Andr. Fred. Lincke.'
[DKKk; C II, 114 m (KTB 280)
This orchestral score was used for all performances of *Pontemolle (An
Artists' Party in Rome)* during Bournonville's lifetime.

Répétiteur's copy. Ms. Copy. Brown and black ink. 1 vol. 84 pp. (32,5
× 24,5 cm)
B. 280/'Pontemolle.'/No. 2. A. [erased]
Unsigned and undated [1866]
[DKKk; MA ms 2974 (KTB 280(1))
This répétiteur's copy contains Bournonville's autographed choreographic numbers (written with black ink) for the entire first tableau,
and for score nos. 8, 15, and 16 of the second tableau. They seem to
refer to a later (not yet traced) separate notation of this ballet, which
he most probably made in preparation for its slightly revised restaging on 21.10.1875.

Parts. Ms. Copy. 37 + 16 vol.
4 vl I, 4 vl II, 2 vla, 4 vlc e cb, fl 1/2, ob 1/2, cl 1/2, fag 1/2, cor 1/2/
3/4, tr 1/2, trb 1/2/3, timp, gr cassa, cassa, piatti, tri, arpa. On stage:
fl, cl 1/2/3/4, cor 1/2, tr 1/2/3, trb 1/2/3, tuba, gr cassa, piatti e tri.
Unsigned and undated [1866]
[DKKk; KTB 280
This set of parts was used for all performances of *Pontemolle (An Artists' Party in Rome)* in Copenhagen during Bournonville's lifetime.

Other sources:

Costume drawing by E. Lehmann. Pencil and water colours (21 × 12
cm)
Kunstnerdragter/i Rom./Pontemolle.
Unsigned and undated [c.1866]
[SSm; Daniel Fryklunds samling no. 273 (F 1334 b)
This drawing shows the costumes worn by three of the Danish artists
in *Pontemolle (An Artists' Party in Rome)* (first and second tableaux).

Costume drawing by E. Lehmann. Pencil and water colours (21,2 ×
11,8 cm)
7 Blomsterpiger
Unsigned and undated [c.1866]
[DKKkt; Kostumetegninger (Lehmann)
This drawing shows the costume worn by the seven *Flower Maidens*
appearing in the allegorical scene depicting the time of 'Ancient
Rome' in the second tableau of *Pontemolle (An Artists' Party in Rome)*
(scene 2, score no. 11).

Costume drawing by E. Lehmann. Pencil and water colours (20,5 ×
12,2 cm)
Damer fra den Rafaelske Tid/efter denne Tegning i <u>Percé</u>.
Unsigned and undated [c.1866]
[DKKkt; Kostumetegninger (Lehmann)
This drawing shows the costume worn by the women in the scene
which depicted 'The Age of Art' (i.e. the 16th century) in the second
tableau of *Pontemolle (An Artists' Party in Rome)* (scene 2, score no. 12).

Costume drawing by E. Lehmann. Pencil and water colours (20,8 ×
12,3 cm)

samme Tegning. Rødbrun
Unsigned and undated [c.18]
[DKKkt; Kostumetegninger (Lehmann)
This drawing shows the costume worn by the women in the scene depicting 'The Age of Art' in the second tableau of *Pontemolle (An Artists' Party in Rome)* (scene 2, score no. 12).

Costume drawing by E. Lehmann. Pencil and water colours (20 × 13,5 cm)
Hyrde og Hyrdinder/som disse Rosa
Unsigned and undated [c.1866]
[DKKkt; Kostumetegninger (Lehmann)
This drawing shows a figure dressed in a shepherd's costume in the rococo style while holding a shepherd's crook entwined with flower garlands. According to pencilled notes on the reverse (which include the names of the four female dancers, H. Thygesen, J. Hansen, P. Fredstrup and L. Stillmann), it clearly refers to the costume worn by these four dancers during the so-called *Roccoco Quadrille* in the second tableau of *Pontemolle (An Artists' Party in Rome)* (scene 2, score no. 13).

Costume drawing by E. Lehmann. Pencil and water colours (11,5 × 21,5 cm)
Paoluccio/Hr Hoppensach./Pontemolle.
Unsigned and undated [c.1866]
[SSm; Daniel Fryklunds samling no. 272 (F 1334 a)
This drawing shows the costume worn by the character *Paoluccio* (performed by F. Hoppensach) in the allegorical dance *Old Age and Folly (mimetic waltz)* in the second tableau of *Pontemolle (An Artists' Party in Rome)* (scene 2, score no. 15).

Printed sources:

Printed scenario. 1 vol. 12 pp. (20 × 12,6 cm)
Pontemolle./Et Kunstnergilde i Rom.)/Vaudeville=Ballet i to Tableauer/af/August Bournonville./Musiken componeret og arrangeret, 1ste Akt af W. Holm, 2den Akt til=/deels af C. Lincke./Decorationerne malede af C. F. Christensen./Costumerne anordnede af Edw. Lehmann.
Kjøbenhavn, J. H. Schubothe/Bianco Luno/F. S. Muhle, 1866.
[DKKk, 17, – 175 8°

7.9.1866

Two *Quadrilles (Quadriller)* choreographed for a royal ball in 'Appartementssalen' at Copenhagen's Christiansborg Palace.

This set of *Quadrilles* was choreographed for a royal ball given on the occasion of the 49th birthday of Queen Louise Wilhelmine Friederike Caroline Auguste Julie of Denmark. It consisted of a *Quadrille* performed by ladies only, and a *Russian National Quadrille (Russisk National-Quadrille)* danced by a group of children consisting of eight couples from Bournonville's dance students at the Royal Theatre's ballet school mixed with children from private families. They held *carte-de-visite* photographs of the Danish Princess Dagmar in their hands, and were headed by four boys dressed as trumpeters.

On the day before the first rehearsal (3.9.1866) Bournonville noted in his diary: 'modtaget Musik af Lincke'. This clearly indicates A. F. Lincke as the composer and/or organiser of the score for these quadrilles. Moreover, according to a printed piano score (entitled *RUSSISK MAZURKA. Udført af Børn under Balletmester Bournonvilles Ledelse ved Hoffesten paa Chrisitansborg den 7. september*) the music for the *Russian National-Quadrille* was partially based on a composition by the Russian composer, C. Massaloff. It had been published by C.

F. E. Horneman in 1866 as part of his musical anthology *Musikalske Nyheder* (6. Aarg., nr. 12, pp. 70-71, now in DKKk, call no. D 2). However, Massaloff's music (which was originally entitled *Polka Mazurka*) had already been known in Copenhagen since 1863–1864 when it was printed in a slightly different piano version by C. F. E. Hornemann and J. E. Erslev in their musical anthology, named *Musikalsk Museum* (18 Aarg., 10. hefte, p. 73, now in DKKk, call no. D 2). An interesting and highly detailed description of Bournonville's quadrilles to this music is included in *Illustreret Tidende* (16.9.1866, no. 364, p. 419) and reads as follows:

'[…] I 'Appartementssalen' havde Kongen [i.e. Christian IX] og Dronningen [i.e. Queeen Louise Wilhelmine Friederike Caroline Auguste Julie], Kronprindsen [i.e. den later Frederik VIII] og Prindsesse Dagmar [the later Czarina of Russia, known as Maria Feodorovna], Landgreven [i.e. Wilhelm of Hesse-Cassel] og Prindsesse Auguste, samt flere af Kongehusets Familie fra Tydskland taget Plads langs Vinduerne, midtfor det af [A. F.] Lincke ledede Orchester. I begge Ender af salen stode Damer og Herrer, hvis Rækker Ceremonimestrene og Marechallerne af og til maatte søge at bevære tilbage til Fordeel for de Arrangements, der skulde finde Sted midt paa Gulvet. Det var først en Quadrille, udført af lutter Damer, derpaa en Idyl, begge componerede af Hofballetmester Bournonville. Fra det tilstødende Værelse kom da en Dobbeltrække Børn, deels af det kongelige Theaters Ballet personale, deels af private Familier, De vare iførte Dragter fra Store=Rusland, og Musiken spillede russiske Motiver. Med sine Smaamusikanter i Spidsen bevæger den lille Flok sig høitideligt fremad, indtil de midt for den kongelige Familie begynder en lille Idyl: under Dandsens Slyngninger synes 'damerne' – eller, om man vil, de russiske Kvinder – at ville vige for deres Elskere, indtil disse fremdrage smaa Photographier i Visitkortformat, fremstillende Hds. Kgl. Høihed Prindsese Dagmar, bestemt til engang i Fremtiden at være alle Russeres Selvherskerinde. Synet af Visitkortene mildner Hjerterne, de ømme Følelser vaagne atter under Indtrukket af deres Thronfølgers Forlovede, og et Varsel er givet for den Lykke, som den vordende Czarinde vil udbrede over sine Undersaatter.

Man behøver kun at kjende en Smule til det Talent, hvormed Bournonville formaaer at lade Dandsende, og ikke mindst dandsende Børn, præsentere sig, for at forstaae, at denne lille Scene kunde tage sig godt ud, endskjøndt det for Uindviede ikke var saa ganske let, strax at forstaae Betydningen af de photographiske Visitkort, ligesom maaskee den symbolske Idee selv turde være af tvivlsom Værdi fra et æsthetisk Standpunkt. Imidlertid – Kritiken behøver jo ikke her at tale, og Udførelsen tog sig saa nydelig ud, saa at de smaa konstnere maatte frem paany og gjentage deres Dands, som senere afløstes af mere almindelige Balglæder'.

According to Bournonville's diary the *Russian National Quadrille* was later also performed to the musical accompaniment of two violins (played by 'Lincke and accomp: Egense') for a special performance at the Bernstorff Castle on 9.9.1866.

Finally, the *Russian National Quadrille* is almost certainly identical with the similar *Russian National Quadrille (Russisk National-Quadrille)* given as part of a divertissement that Bournonville mounted at the the Court Theatre on 26.12.1866.

In his diary he noted about the creation of the two quadrilles, the first performance at the Christiansborg Palace, and the later performance of the *Russian National Quadrille* at the Bernstorff Castle:

28.8.1866: 'Brev fra Hofmarskal [C. L.] Løvenskjold i Anledning af Dronningens Fødselsdag d. 7' Sept.'

29.8.: 'Afsted til Kbhvn, truffet Hofmarskal Løvenskjold paa Christiansborg og foreløbig aftalt adskilligt'

31.8.: 'talt med Hofmarechal Løvenskjold og truffet forskjellige Arrangement for Hoffesten d. 7.e Sept.'

1.9.: 'componeret en Dame-Quadrille til Hoffesten'

2.9.: 'componeret en russisk Quadrille til Hoffesten'

3.9.: 'talte […] med Hofmarskallen, derpaa til [G.] Brodersen og til Costumiererne […] modtaget Musik af [A. F.] Lincke […] Logis i [Hotel] Kronprindsen, hvor jeg skrev og ordnede mine Affairer'

4.9.: 'reenskrevet mine Quadriller, besørget adskilligt. Prøve med Damerne Kl 12 hos Brodersen. Kl 3 med Børnene, der vare meget behagelige'

5.9.: 'Prøve hos Brodersen fra 12 til 5½. Begge Quadrillerne færdige med smukt Resultat'

6.9.: 'Prøve paa Quadrillerne fra 11–2.'

7.9.: 'Generalprøve paa Quadrillerne oppe i Appartementsalen […] Ballet aabnedes Kl 10 med en Polonaise og derpaa Quadrillerne, der gjorde overordentlig Lykke, navnlig den russiske Børnequadrille. Majestæterne og Prindsesse Dagmar overøste mig med Naade og Bifald […] Det Hele var Kongeligt og Splendid og Stemningen udmærket'

8.9.: 'Bud fra Hofmarskallen om den russiske Dands til Bernstorff imorgen Kl 12.'

9.9.: 'afsted til Bernstorff Kl 9½ to Vogne med Brodersen, Lincke med Accomp: Egense med Kone og 7 Balletbørn. Vi fik Frokost paa Slottet og Kl 12 opførtes den russiske Quadrille for den hele kongelige Familie, Enkedronningen, Provst Bojesen og Hoffolk. Dandsen blev Da Capoet og den mageløste Venlighed vistes imod os Alle. Kongen forærede mig en ligeså kostbar som smagfuld Ring. Det Hele gjorde et ÿndigt Indtryk og med Hensÿn til Prindsesse <u>Dagmar</u> et rörende'.

No autographs by Bournonville or manuscript musical sources dating from the first performance of this set of dances have yet been traced.

10.10.–21.11.1866
Twelve dance lessons in social dance.

According to several notes in his diary Bournonville gave a series of twelve private dance lessons in social dance at the Copenhagen residence of the judge, G. C. V. Obelitz, in Lille Kjøbmagergade no. 60s. These lessons, which took place mainly on Wednesday afternoons, lasted for about two hours each.

12.10.1866
Pas de deux (uncredited) performed by D. Krum and J. Petersen.

This (uncredited) *Pas de deux* was created for the début of Bournonville's last 'thoroughbred' pupil, the sixteen-year-old D. Krum, a dancer whom he later characterised in his memoirs *My Theatre Life* (p. 368):

'as far as technical perfection is concerned [D. Krum is a] first-rate choreographic artist, capable of appearing with bravura on any of the greatest stages of Europe'.

According to the répétiteur's copy for this *Pas de deux* it is musically (and probably also choreographically) a slightly revised version (arranged by V. C. Holm?) of the much earlier F major *Pas de deux* in Act I of Bournonville's 1834 Copenhagen version of L. Milon's two-act pantomimic ballet *Nina, ou La Folle par amour* (first danced by F. Hoppe and L. Grahn on 30.9.1834). This is clear from the fact that only two of the six movements of this dance (the *Moderato* in 4/4 time,

and the final *Polacca* in 2/4 time) are set to music completely different from that of the original 1834 *Pas de deux* in F major.

According to the rehearsal book of A. Fredstrup, Bournonville personally directed the only two rehearsals held of this dance, on 9.10. and 11.10.1866. The *Pas de deux* was given three times by Krum and Petersen, the last time on 31.10.1866.

Musical sources:

No separate orchestral score and set of parts dating from the 1866 staging of this dance have yet been traced. This seems to indicate that the original orchestral score and parts for the 1834 F major *Pas de deux* in Act I of *Nina, ou La Folle par amour* (now in DKKk, call nos. MA ms 2949 and KTB 221) were most likely reused for this performance.

Répétiteur's copy. Ms. Copy. Brown ink. 1 vol. 12 pp. of which one is blank (34 × 25,5 cm)
[…]/Pas de deux af Bournonville/86/[..]/Répétiteurpartie/til/ Pas de deux/af/A. Bournonville
Unsigned and undated [1866]
[DKKk; MA ms 2905 (3)]
This répétiteur's copy clearly dates from Bournonville's 1866 revised staging of the F major *Pas de deux* from Act I of *Nina, ou La Folle par amour*. This is clear from pencilled notes (on p. 16) indicating the names of D. Krum and J. Petersen. The volume also includes Bournonville's autographed choreographic numbers (written with brown ink) which seem to refer to a separate (not yet traced) notation of this dance made the same year. The music is written on pp. 15–26 in a volume that also contains the répétiteur's copies for two other dances, choreographed by Bournonville and F. Hoppe and premièred at Copenhagen's Royal Theatre in 1868.

21.10.1866
The Toreador (Toréadoren).

This performance represents Bournonville's second restaging in Copenhagen of his two-act idyllic ballet *The Toreador* (*see* 27.11.1840). It was mounted with H. Scharff and L. Stillmann playing the leading rôles as *Alonzo* and *Maria*. The 1866 production differed from the previous restaging of this ballet from 21.10.1850 by Bournonville's incorporation in Act II of the so-called *La Seguedilla (after Taglioni.)* from his Spanish Ballet Divertissement, entitled *La Ventana* (*see* 6.10. 1856). It was this year performed by J. Petersen (who played *Céleste*) and E. Hansen, accompanied by a small corps de ballet.

Moreover, according to a musical insertion, which is H. S. Paulli's autograph and is interpolated as pp. '16–20' in the original répétiteur's copy for *The Toreador*), Bournonville seems to have revised the mimic monologue of *Alonzo* in Act I (score no. 4) in connection with this production.

In his diary he noted about the performance:

1.10.1866: 'begyndt mit Theaterarbeide med Indstudering til Toreadoren fra 10½ til 1'
2.10.: 'Prøve fra 5–6½ paa Toreadoren'
3.10.: 'Eftermiddagsprøve paa <u>Toreadoren</u>'
4.10., 5.10., 6.10., 8.10., 11.10. and 16.10.: 'Prøve paa <u>Toréadoren</u>'
17.10.: 'Prøve paa <u>Toreadoren</u> (Theatret)'
19.10.: 'Generalprøve paa <u>Toréadoren</u> der lover godt.'
21.10.: '<u>Toréadoren</u> (nÿ indstuderet) særdeles godt og med levende Bifald heelt igjennem'.

The 1866 restaging of *The Toreador* received 4 performances, the last of which was given on 9.1.1867.

The musical material employed this year was the same as that used since the 1840 première of this ballet (now in DKKk, call nos. C II, 114 k, MA ms 2965, and KTB 1046 (originally KTB 269)).

Autograph sources:

Production note. Ms. Autograph. Black ink. 1 p. (22,6 × 17,8 cm)
Coryphære [*sic*] i Toreadoren.
Unsigned and undated [October 1866]
[DKKkt; F.M. (Ballet)

8.11.1866
A projected *Dance (Dands)* for the ball at the Casino Theatre on 9.11.1866 given on the occasion of the nuptials of Danish Princess Dagmar and the Russian Prince Alexander (later Czar Alexander III).
In his diary Bournonville noted rather sarcastically on 8.11. 1866 about his plan for this dance, which he intended to choreograph for a royal ball, but in which he was not successful:

'mislykket Plan med en Dands til Casinoballet Imorgen. Storartet Confusion hos Comitéen'.

The ball was given in the main auditorium of the Casino Theatre on 9.11.1866. Bournonville did not attend the ball because, as he puts it in his diary:

'Stort Bal i Casino, som jeg var eventualiten [*sic*] indbuden til, men som man glemte at sende mig Billet til'.

21.11.1866
Waldemar.
This performance represents Bournonville's third, revised version of his four-act romantic ballet *Waldemar* (*see* 28.10. 1835). According to his autographed notes in the 1853 répétiteur's copy for *Waldemar* it differed from his previous three-act version by his reinstating of most of the earlier music cuts, thereby returing the ballet to its original 1835 four-act version. Other significant changes in 1866 were a completely new set of costumes for the leading rôles (all drawn by E. Lehmann) and a number of minor choreographic changes, for instance the *Pas de deux* in Act II (score no. '17'), which was performed this year as a *Pas de six* by the characters *Axel Hvide* (E. Hansen) and *Astrid*, accompanied by a group of four Ladies-in-Waiting. Moreover, the ballet was in 1866 mounted with partially new décor, painted by C. F. Christensen. Finally, the dances in *Waldemar* were this year listed and named in the printed scenario for the first time. They were as follows:

In Act I:
(1) A *Circle dance (Runddands)* (score no. 4), performed by two couples (E. Stramboe, F. Hoppensach, H. Thygesen, E. V. A. Møller) together with the corps de ballet.
(2) A *Pas de cinq* (score no. 5), performed by H. Scharff, A. Fredstrup, P. Fredstrup, L. Stillmann, and J. Petersen.

In Act II:
(3) A *Pas de six* (score no. '17'), danced by E. Hansen (in the rôle of

Axel Hvide) B. Schnell (as *Astrid*) together with four women (S. Price, E. Gade, C. Larsen and E. V. A. Møller) dressed as Ladies-in-Waiting. In the earlier 1835 and 1853 versions this dance was originally listed as score no. '18' and performed as a *Pas de deux* by the characters *Waldemar* and *Astrid*.
(4) A *Shield dance (Vaabendands)* (score no. '19'), danced by a group of halberdiers.
(5) A *Torch Dance (Fakkeldance)* (score no. '20 a'), danced by the three Kings, the Knights, the Ladies, the Esquires, and the Halberdiers.

In his diary Bournonville noted about the 1866 production and its reception:

25.4.1866: 'Brev til […] Theatermaler [C. F.] Christensen'
28.4.: 'arbeidet paa Modificationerne til Waldemar'
4.5.: 'talt med Theatermaler Christensen om Decorationerne til *Waldemar*'
5.6.: 'Brev fra […] Theatermaler Christensen. Svar til denne'
24.6.: 'Brev fra Theatermaler Christensen'
26.6.: 'Modtaget Theatermaler Prof. Christensen med Frue, der tilbragte hele Dagen med os. Der arbeidedes lidt paa Balletten Waldemar'
24.8.: 'til [F.] Hoppes Skole, hvor jeg bemærkede Betty Schnell, der skal være Astrid i Waldemar'
27.8.:'Begyndt paa Arrangementerne til Waldemar'
30.8.: 'skrevet og componeret'
18.9. and 19.9.: 'componeret paa Valdemar'
20.9. and 21.9.: componeret'
22.9.: 'componeret og choregrapheret'
24.9. and 25.9.: 'componeret'
27.9.: 'Componeret og sluttet Valdemars Choregraphie'
4.10.: 'besøgt Malersalen i Anledning af Valdemar'
8.10.: 'Eftermiddagsprøve paa Valdemar'
9.10.: 'Indstudering paa Valdemar […] Eftermiddagsprøve paa Valdemar'
10.10.: 'Prøve […] paa Rollerne til Waldemar'
13.10.: 'Indstudering paa Valdemar […] Costumemøde'
15.10. and 16.10.: 'Prøve paa Valdemar'
17.10.: 'Valdemar Indstudering'
18.10.: 'Prøve paa Valdemar'
19.10.: 'Costumemøde'
22.10.: 'Prøve paa Valdemar […] Aftenprøve paa Valdemar'
23.10.: 'Prøve paa Valdemar (ubehageligheder med Edv. Stramboe) […] Anmeldelse til Theater-Intendenten om Stramboes Opførsel'
24.10.: 'Prøve paa Waldemar […] Musikprøve paa Waldemar og fundet [J. F.] Frøhlichs Composition endnu fortræffeligere end nogensinde'
25.10.: 'Prøve paa W.'
26.10.: 'Costumemøde'
27.10.: 'Prøve paa Valdemar […] skrevet paa Programmet til Valdemar'
29.10.: 'Prøve paa Valdemar (Fakkeldandsen)'
30.10.: 'Prøve paa Valdemar (Repetition)'
31.10.: 'Stor Prøve paa Valdemar for [F.] Høedt og Juliette Price (Schnell gjorde sine Ting fortræffeligt.)'
1.11.: 'Prøve paa et Par Dandse, skrevet paa Programmet til Valdemar'
2.11.: 'Stor Arrangementsprøve paa Valdemar'
3.11.: 'Prøve paa Valdemar'
6.11.: 'stor Arrangementsprøve paa Valdemar'
7.11.: 'Aftenprøve paa Valdemars 4.e Akt'
9.11.: 'stor Prøve paa Valdemar'
10.11.: 'Prøve paa Valdemar'
12.11.: 'Partiel Prøve paa Valdemar (3.die Akt)'
14.11.: 'Decorationsprøve paa Valdemar til Kl 12'
15.11.: 'stor Prøve paa Valdemar (med Violin)'
16.11.: '1.ste Generalprøve paa Valdemar. Den gik udmærket godt'
18.11.: 'Costumeprøve for Betty Schnell'
19.11.: 'Generalprøve pa Valdemar, der gjorde et storartet Indtryk […] modtaget Honorar for den nye Udgave af Balletten'

21.11.: 'I Theatret hvor <u>Valdemars</u> nÿe Indstudering gik for første Gang med stor Bravour, baade for Personalets og Publicums Side. <u>Betty Schnell</u> vandt megen Sympathie og <u>W. Price</u> udførte Titelrollen med stort Held, et uforudset Tilfælde havde nær forstemt hans sidste Scene, da Aaget slog ham paa Hovedet og foraarsagede et ikke ringe Blodtab, men han beholdt Contenacen og viste derved sjelden Holdning. Det var en stor Glæde for mig og vistnok en Fordeel for Balletten og Theatret i det Hele. Jeg takkede Gud af mit inderste Hjerte'
24.11.: '(glimrende Artikel i 'Den Berlingske' om min Ballet.)'.

The 1866 version of *Waldemar* received 45 performances, the last of which was given on 12.1.1871.

The musical material employed this year was the same as that used for the previous 1835 and 1853 productions (now in DKkk, call nos. C II, 107, MA ms 2993, MA ms 2994, and KTB 297).

Autograph sources:

Production note. Ms. Autograph. Brown ink. 4 pp. (22,4 × 17,6 cm)
Valdemar/Ballet i tre Akter/af/August Bournonville/Hovedpersonerne.
Signed and dated: 'Fredensborg i September 1866.'
[DKKkt; F.M. (Ballet)

Production note. Ms. Autograph. Black ink. 1 p. (33,9 × 20,9 cm)
Valdemar/Ballet i fire Akter af A. Bournonville./Musiken af F. Fröhlich./Personerne
Unsigned and undated [Autumn 1866]
[DKKkt; F.M. (Ballet)

Other sources:

Costume drawing by E. Lehmann. Pencil and water colours (19,9 × 12,1 cm)
Svend./[...]//Valdemar
Unsigned and undated [c.1866]
[DKKkt; Kostumetegninger (Lehmann)
This drawing shows the costume worn by *Svend Eriksøn* in Act I(?) of *Waldemar* (performed by L. Gade).

Costume drawing by E. Lehmann. Pencil and water colours (19,9 × 12 cm)
Knud/Hr. Brodersen/[...]/Valdemar
Unsigned and undated [c.1866]
[DKKkt; Kostumetegninger (Lehmann)
This drawing shows the costume worn by *Knud Magnussøn* in *Waldemar* (performed by G. Brodersen).

Costume drawing by E. Lehmann. Pencil and water colours (12 × 20 cm)
Valdemar./W. Price./Valdemar
Unsigned and undated [c.1866]
[SSm; Daniel Fryklunds samling no. 280 (F 1322 d)
This drawing shows the costume worn by *Waldemar* in Acts I–III(?) of the ballet of that name (performed by W. Price).

Costume drawing by E. Lehmann. Pencil and water colours (12 × 22 cm)
Astrid (Frk. Schnell/Fru Hennings) Valdemar
Unsigned and undated [c.1866]
[SSm; Daniel Fryklunds samling no. 282 (F 1322 a)
This drawing shows the costume worn by *Astrid* in Act I(?) of *Waldemar* (performed by B. Schnell).

Costume drawing by E. Lehmann. Pencil and water colours (12 × 20 cm)
Svend/Valdemar.

Unsigned and undated [c.1866]
[SSm; Daniel Fryklunds samling no. 279 (F 1322 c)
This drawing shows the costume worn by *Svend Eriksøn* in Acts II–IV(?) of *Waldemar* (performed by L. Gade).

Costume drawing by E. Lehmann. Pencil and water colours (21, 7 × 12,3 cm)
2/[...]/Valdemar
Unsigned and undated [c.1866]
[DKKkt; Kostumetegninger (Lehmann)
This drawing most probably shows the costume worn by *Astrid* in Acts II–III(?) of *Waldemar* (performed by B. Schnell).

Costume drawing by E. Lehmann. Pencil and water colours (12 × 20 cm)
Valdemar/i/Rustning/Valdemar.
Unsigned and undated [c.1866]
[SSm; Daniel Fryklunds samling no. 281 (F 1322 e)
This drawing shows the costume worn by *Waldemar* in Act IV of the ballet of that name (performed by W. Price).

Costume drawing by E. Lehmann. Pencil and water colours (12 × 22 cm)
Astrid 3/Valdemar./Schnell
Unsigned and undated [c.1866]
[SSm; Daniel Fryklunds samling no. 283 (F 1322 b)
This drawing shows the costume worn by *Astrid* wearing full armour, disguised as an esquire in Act IV of *Waldemar* (performed by B. Schnell).

Costume drawing by E. Lehmann. Pencil and water colours (22,1 × 12,3 cm)
Drabanter (Valdemar)
Unsigned and undated [c.1866]
[DKKkt; Kostumetegninger (Lehmann)
This drawing shows the costumes worn by the halberdiers in *Waldemar*.

Printed sources:

Printed scenario. 1 vol. 16 pp. (20 × 12,9 cm)
Valdemar./Ballet i fire Akter/af/Bournonville./Musiken af Fr. Fröhlich./Decorationerne af Christensen./[...]/paany indstuderet, sat i Scene og opført i Novbr. 1866.
Kjøbenhavn, J. H. Schubothe/Bianco Luno/F. S. Muhle, 1866.
[DKKk; 17, – 172 8°

28.11.1866
Pas de deux (uncredited) performed by D. Krum and S. Price.

This (uncredited) dance is most likely identical with the similar (uncredited) *Pas de deux*, performed by D. Krum and J. Petersen on 12.10.1866. That dance, in turn, is a musical arrangement (by V. C. Holm?) of the much earlier F major *Pas de deux* from Act I of Bournonville's 1834 Copenhagen version of L. Milon's pantomimic ballet *Nina, ou La Folle par amour* (see 30.9.1834). According to Bournonville's diary the *Pas de deux* was rehearsed twice by him on 24.11. and 26.11. 1866, and is described after its first performance as:

'Pas de deux af Krum og S. Price [...] (Krum var meget heldig og dÿgtig)'.

The *Pas de deux* was performed twice by Krum and S. Price, the last time on 14.3.1867. It is not possible to identify the dance any further.

26.12.1866

A Divertissement, Pas de trois gracieux and Russian National Quadrille (Et Elev-Divertissement, Pas de trois gracieux og russisk National-Quadrille) (the Court Theatre).

This set of three dances was created for a special charity performance (given for the actor, A. Price), and was performed by a group of students from the Royal Theatre's ballet school. At its first performance only the last of the three dances (the *Russian National Quadrille*) was performed. This quadrille is most probably identical with Bournonville's similar dance of that name, created only three months earlier for a royal ball at the Christiansborg Palace (*see* 7.9.1866). In his diary he noted about the creation of the divertissement and its reported first performance:

26.11.1866: 'Indstudering paa Elev-Dandse'
28.11.: 'Indstudering paa Dandsene'
30.11.: 'Prøve paa Dandsene'
8.12.: 'holdt Prøve paa de to nye Dandse'
28.12.: 'Brev fra Charlotte [Bournonville]med Efterretning om det Bifald, som mit Elev Divertissement havde gjort ved [A.] Prices Forestilling iforgaars'.

The divertissement received 3 performances at the Court Theatre, the last of which was given on 5.1.1867.

No separate musical sources dating from these performances have yet been traced.

1867

25.1.1867

Divertissement from 'Il Trovatore' (Gipsy Dance) (Divertissement af 'Troubadouren' (Zigeunerdands)).

This performance represents the first time Bournonville's Act III divertissement from G. Verdi's four-act lyrical drama *Il Trovatore* (*see* 10.9.1865) was performed separately. It was mounted this year by L. Gade. Bournonville only attended its second performance on 5.3.1867, about which he noted in his diary:

'Divertissement Troubaduren der gik meget smukt og med stærkt Bifald'.

The 1867 staging received 18 performances, the last of which was given on 4.3.1876.

The musical material employed this year was the same as that used since the 1865 première of the divertissement in Verdi's lyrical drama (now in DKKkt and in DKKk with the call nos. KTA 752 a, and MA ms 3092–3093 respectively).

31.1.1867

A projected *Divertissement* for the celebration of the silver-wedding of Denmark's King Christian IX and Queen Louise.

On this day Bournonville noted in his diary:

'Undfanget idéen til et Divertissement for Sølvbryllupsfesten'.

The project, which was planned for the celebration of the Royal silver-wedding on 26.5.1867, was never carried out. In-stead a gala performance of Bournonville's four-act romantic ballet *Waldemar* (*see* 28.10.1835) was given on 29.5.1867.

20.2.1867

***»The Sailor's Return«, Divertissement (»Matrosens Hjemkomst«, Divertissement)* performed by W. Price and S. Price (the Court Theatre).**

This performance represents the last restaging of *The Sailor's Return* (*see* 9.6.1852) in Copenhagen. It was given once this year as part of a special charity performance for the actor, R. L. Jastrau, and the dancer, W. Price. Bournonville did not attend the performance. The musical material employed this year was most likely the same as that used for the previous performance of this divertissement at the Court Theatre on 11.6.1855 (now in DKKk, call. nos. MA ms 2670, MA ms 2671, and KTB 337 a).

14.3.1867

***Pas de deux* (uncredited) performed by D. Krum and S. Price.**

This (uncredited) dance is most likely identical with the similar (uncredited) *Pas de deux*, performed by the same two dancers on 28.11.1866, which in turn, is almost certainly identical with the even earlier (uncredited) *Pas de deux*, mounted by Bournonville for the début of Krum on 12.10.1866. The *Pas de deux* was given once in 1867. It is not possible to identify the dance any further.

17.3.1867

***'Episode in Hyde Park', Divertissement for children ('Episode i Hÿdepark' Divertissement for Børn)* (the Court Theatre).**

This divertissement was created for a special charity performance (arranged by Bournonville in collaboration with the actor, A. Price) in order to collect funds for Queen Louise's orphanage in Rigensgade in Copenhagen. Bournonville, who was a leading board member of the fund-raising committee for this institution, had earlier arranged and directed the opening ceremony of the orphanage, when it was inaugurated in 1866.

'Episode in Hyde Park', which was performed by a selected group of dance students from the Royal Theatre's ballet school, was set to a score composed and arranged by A. F. Lincke. In the opening movement of his score Lincke incorporated T. A. Arne's melody for *Rule Brittania* («When Britain first at Heav'n's command»). This hymn was originally composed for the masque 'Alfred' (first performed at Cliefden (Cliveden)House on 1.8.1740), but after admiral Nelson's victory in the battle of the Nile in 1798 it was elevated almost to the status of a national anthem.

The same melody had earlier been employed by H. S. Paulli in his music for Act III (score no. 17) of Bournonville's three-act ballet *Zulma, or The Crystal Palace* (*see* 14.4.1852). As in the third act of *Zulma, or The Crystal Palace* the action in this divertissement also takes place in Hyde Park in London. Moreover, in his score for *'Episode in Hyde Park'* Lincke employed the very same motifs from C. E. Horn's 1825 melody to R. Herrick's song «Cherry Ripe», which Paulli had used before him in his score for *Zulma, or The Crystal Palace* (Act III, score no. 17). Together these facts seem to indicate that the plot in Bournonville's 1867 divertissement (for which no printed scenario has yet been traced) might have been based on, or at least was drawn from scenes in Act III of *Zulma, or The Crystal Palace*.

In his diary he noted about *'Episode in Hyde Park'*:

22.2.1867: 'Aftalt med Adolf Price en Aftenunderholdning til bedste for Asylet'
24.2.: 'Brev til [G.] Brodersen og A. Price – om en Børnequadrille'
26.2.: 'Brev fra A. Price'
27.2.: 'Brev fra Brodersen [...] Svar'
28.2.: 'Skrevet og ordnet Sager for Asylet og Centralcomitéen'
5.3.: 'Aftale med [A. F.] Lincke [...] Søndags Forestillingen for Asylet udsat formedelst Prices Mathed!. Aftenprøve med Børnene til den lille Ballet, En Episode i Hyde park'
6.3.: 'Componeret og indstuderet med Børnene'
8.3.: 'Børne-Divertissementet færdigt'
11.3: 'prøvet Børneballetten'
12.3: 'prøvet Dandsene til paa Søndag'
16.3.: 'Prøve paa Hoftheatret'
17.3.: 'Aftenunderholdning for Asylet. Lidt over halvt Huus. Billetter 277r uheldige Følger af A. Prices Udsættelseslÿst – Dandsen gik udmærket smukt'
24.3.: 'Regnskab fra Adolf Price hvorved vor hele Indtægt beløber sig til 102r 3sk'.

'Episode in Hyde Park' was given only once at the Court Theatre.

Musical sources:

Orchestral score. Ms. Autograph (by A. F. Lincke). Black ink. 36 pp. (26,3 × 35 cm)
'Episode i Hÿdepark' Divertissement for Börn af A. Bournonville
Signed and dated: 'Den 14 Marts 1867. Andr. Fred. Lincke.'
[DKKk; C II, 105, Efterslæt 3

No répétiteur's copy for *'Episode in Hyde Park'* has yet been traced.

Parts. Ms. Copy. 14 vol.
vl I, vl II, vla, vlc, cb, fl, cl 1/2, cor 1/2, tr 1/2, trb, timp.
Unsigned and undated [1867]
[DKKk; C II, 105, Efterslæt 3

29.3.1867
Mary Stuart in Scotland (*Maria Stuart i Skotland*)
(Christiania's Theatre, Oslo).

For the world première of B. Björnson's five-act drama (with music by R. Nordraak, composed in 1865) Bournonville choreographed a set of four quadrilles in the renaissance style which was named 'Purpose (Dands)'. It was performed at the raising of the curtain in Act I (score no. 1), took place during a ball at the castle of Edinburgh, and was performed by a cast of eight couples (including *Lord Stuart* and *Mary Stuart*, the *Earl of Lathington* and the *Countess of Argyle*, the *Earl of Morton* and an unnamed lady, the *Earl of Bothwell* and an unnamed lady, and four couples of surnumeraries). This dance, which was accompanied by a small orchestra seated on the stage, clearly seems to have been been created at the personal request of Björnson. Thus, in an undated letter to Bournonville received on 9.3.1867 (now in NOum) the great Norwegian poet explicitly asked the Danish ballet-master's advice about the dances for the Christiania première of his drama:

'Min afdøde Fætter Rikard Nordraak har komponeret Musik til min Maria Stuart i Skotland, og deriblandt en 'Purpose', hvorom jeg kun ved, hvad [J.] Knox siger 'den Dands hvori der hviskes'. I Musiken er et sted saaledes mig mærkelig med sin historiske Farve og sin erotiske Tone. Men kunne nu ikke Du, da vi heroppe ikke har et Menneske som forstaaer Dands, sige os fatteligt og uden Benyttelse af termini technici, som vi maaske ikke vilde forstaa – hvorledes vi skulde bære os ad'.

Bournonville immediately replied by writing a detailed description of the requested dance on 11.3.1867. It was mailed to Christiania the same day together with an interesting note to Björnson (now in the Theatre Collection of the University of Oslo Library) which reads:

'Høistærede Herr Bjørnson!
Jeg føler mig særdeles smigret ved den mig udviiste Tillid, men frygter for at jeg ikke tilfredsstillende kan svare til den, deels fordi den Laconisme, der er af saa poetisk Virkning paa selve Scenen ikke saa vel lader sig anvende ved dens ofte altfor omstændige Detailer. Jeg troer imidlertid at have forstaaet Deres Mening saa temmelig, men om De, Høistærede kan hitte Rede i de Forklaringer, som jeg maaa give en vis Bredde, og hvori termini technici ligesaalidt kunne undgaaes, som Stole og Borde i et Ameublement, er en anden Sag, og dersom Theatret ikke eier et eneste Medlem, der forstaaer sig en Smule paa Sammensætningen af en Dands, vil det falde meget vanskeligt, at faae denne lille scene arrangeret paa en nogenlunde behagelig Maade.
    Jeg har, som De vil see, markeret med A. B. C. og D. de forskjellige Momenter i hvert Numer, og for at tydeliggjøre de chorégraphiske Noter, medfølger en veiledende Forklaring.
Trinene ere holdte i størst mulige Simpelhed deels med Hensÿn til Tid og Costume men fornemmelig til de Kræfter, der staae til Deres Theaters Raadighed
    Det skulde være mig kjært om dette originale Experiment kunde lykkes os, ialfald har det forskaffet mig den Ære og Glæde at knytte en skriftlig Forbindelse med en Mand, til hvis Beundrere jeg tør medregne mig, og hvis personlige Bekjendtskab jeg af Hjertet længes efter'.

The dating of Nordraak's autograped score proves that his music for the *Purpose* was actually composed and completed in Copenhagen on 10.2.1865. This seems to indicate that Bournonville most probably already had a copy Nordraak's music at his disposal when he choreographed this dance.

In Christiania it was mounted from Bournonville's notes by a (not yet identified) Norwegian teacher of social dances, named Moe. On the first Christiania poster for *Mary Stuart in Scotland* no indications about Bournonville's dance are included, nor is his name mentioned. Moreover, Bournonville himself never included this work in his list of stagings of operas and plays, written c.1872 (*see* Additional Sources), nor in the printed survey of his works in his memoirs *My Theatre Life* (p. 408).

In his diary he noted about the rather unusual creation of this dance and its reported reception in the Norwegian capital:

9.3.1867: 'Brev fra Bjørnstjerne Bjørnson'
10.3.: 'Skrevet choreographiske Noter til Bjørnsons Marie Stuart'
11.3.: 'expederet Noter og Brev til Bjørnson'
7.4.: 'Brev fra Bjørnstjerne Björnson om hvormeget min lille Composition har bidraget til at give Stemning i hans Marie Stuart. Paa samme Tid fik jeg et Besøg af den Dandselærer, der har sat min Choregraphie en
scene, han hedder Moe og syntes at være en vakker Mand. Han blev hos os til Frokost og Middag'.

Björnson's letter to Bournonville from 1.4.1867 (now in DKKk) reads:

'Deres Dands er saaledes lykkedes, at den i ikke ringe Grad stemmer op den Melodi, hvorpaa Stykket gaar og siden hvifter over den hele Handling med et hvidt Slør fra hendes faa lykkelige Dager. Jeg takker Dem paa min, paa Skuespillernes Vegne; det er i Sandhed genialt at trænge saaledes ind i Musiken og Stykkets Aand...'.

Bournonville did not meet with Björnson until nearly five months later in Copenhagen. At that time he described their first encounter on 9.12.1867 as follows:

'Middag paa Bakkehuset hos Geheimeraad [C. C.] Hall, hvor jeg traf (...) Digteren [B.] Bjørnson der var særdeles behagelig'.

The *Purpose* in Act I of *Mary Stuart in Scotland* was mounted the same year in Copenhagen by L. Gade, who also staged it from Bounonville's choreographic notes when Björnson's drama was given its Danish première at the Royal Theatre on 2.9.1867.

Mary Stuart in Scotland received 44 performances in Christiania during Bournonville's lifetime, the last of which was given on 29.5.1879.

Autograph sources:

Choreographic note. Ms. Autograph. Ink. 1 p. (format unknown)
Man forudsætter at der kan samles <u>otte dandsende Par</u> [...]
Unsigned and undated [Written according to the diary on 10.3. 1867]
[USNYp; Dance Collection, call nos. *ZBD-7 (microfilm), and (S)*MGZMD 30 (photostat copy)

Other sources:

Choreographic note. Ms. Copy. Black ink. 2 pp. (17,7 × 10,8 cm)
<u>Forklaring over de choreografiske Noter.</u>
Unsigned and undated [1867]
[Oslo; Universitetsbiblioteket, Teaterhistorisk Samling (National-theatrets Arkiv, Christiania Theater regi-bøker)
This choreographic note is clearly a copy of Bournonville's original instructions, written as an accompanying note for his original notation of the choreography for the dances in Act I of *Mary Stuart in Scotland* (*see above*). It was most probably copied by the Norwegian dance teacher, named 'Moe', who mounted Bournonville's dances in the 1867 Christiania première of Björnson's drama.

Choreographic note. Ms. Copy. Black ink. 4 pp. (17,7 × 10,7 cm)
<u>Dands til Maria Stuart i Skotland</u>
Unsigned and undated [1867]
[Oslo; Universitetsbiblioteket, Teaterhistorisk Samling (National-theatrets Arkiv, Christiania Theater regi-bøker)
This choreographic note is clearly a copy of Bournonville's original (not yet traced) notation of the choreography for his dances in Act I of *Mary Stuart in Scotland* (*see above*). It was probably copied by the Norwegian dance teacher, named 'Moe', who mounted Bournon-ville's dances in the 1867 Christiania première of Björnson's drama.

Choreographic note. Ms. Copy (by J. Isachsen?). Black ink. 4 pp. (17,3 × 10,4 cm)
Purpose/i/<u>Maria Stuart.</u>/arrangeret/af/Janny Isachsen
Unsigned and undated [c.1867]
[Oslo; Universitetsbiblioteket, Teaterhistorisk Samling (TS Ark/Chr. Th.s repert./M. 683 c)
This manuscript follows closely Bournonville's original choreography for the dances in Act I (score no. 1) of Bjørnson's *Mary Stuart in Scotland* and was (according to its title page) copied by J. Isachsen.

She was the wife of the original director of Björnson's drama, A. H. Isachsen. The note seems to have been written before or soon after the 1867 Christiania première of *Mary Stuart in Scotland*, and was perhaps used for a later staging of it in Norway. Another possibility is that J. Isachsen may have assisted her husband in the original 1867 staging of this drama and for that purpose made her own copy of Bournonville's written choreography.

Musical sources:

Musical draft/piano score. Ms. Autograph. Black and red ink. 3. pp. (35 × 26,5 cm)
Maria Stuart i Skotland/No. 1.a. 1ste Akt. introduction, Purpose (Dans)
Signed and dated (on p. 3): 'Kjøbenhavn 10de Febr. 1865. Søgade No. 20. 1.ste Sal Tilhøire. Richard Nordraak'
[NBo; hGf III Nordraak]

Musical draft/orchestral score. Ms. Autograph. Black ink and pencil. 12 pp. (35 × 26,5 cm)
[Without title]
Unsigned and dated (on p. 1): '12/2 [18]65'
[NBo; hGf III Nordraak]
According to Dan Schjelderup-Ebbe's article *Et Nyfunnet Orkester-partitur med Rikard Nordraaks Musikk til Bjørnstjerne Bjørnsons drama 'Maria Stuart i Skotland'* (in *Studia Musicologica Norvegica*, vol. 1, 1968, pp. 101–131) Nordraak's full autographed orchestral score for the later Copenhagen staging of *Mary Stuart in Scotland* (*see* 2.9.1867) also served for the drama's world première at Christiania's Theatre on 29.3.1867. It is now in DKKk (call no. C II, 118 f (KTA 757)) while two photographic copies of it are today preserved in NOum (call nos. Mus ms a 18:779, and Mus ms mikrofilm 5085:449).

No répétiteur's copy with Nordraak's music for *Mary Stuart in Scotland* has yet been traced in Norway. However, a printed piano score including nearly all of Nordraak's music for Bjørnson's drama was published shortly after Nordraak's death by E. Grieg in Christiania (according to *Berlingske Tidende* around 18.9.1867. (Nordraak had died suddenly in Berlin in 1866 at the age of twenty-four). A copy of this score is now in DKKk (C. Warmuth, Christiania, call no. D 6 (mu 6805. 2213)).

Parts (incomplete). Ms. Copy. 1 vol.
vl II
Unsigned and undated [1867]
[NOum; Mus ms 960:741]
This part for the second violin appears to be the only musical material that has survived from the original 1867 Norwegian première of *Mary Stuart in Scotland*.

26.4.1867
La Sylphide (Sylphiden).
The 1867 Copenhagen restaging of Bournonville's two-act romantic ballet *La Sylphide* (*see* 28.11.1836) was orginally projected by him on 16.1.1866, and represents the fourth restaging of it in Denmark during his own lifetime. According to the rehearsal book of A. Fredstrup it was initially rehearsed by Bournonville on 23.11. and 29.11.1866, but was later mounted exclusively by L. Gade. The staging was arranged especially for the début of M. Price in the title-rôle. According to a note in Bournonville's diary on 28.11.1866 (reading: 'componeret paa Sylphiden') he seems to have revised parts of the choreography especially for this ballerina. About her début he noted in the diary on the opening night:

'Som Sylphiden var Mathilde Price nydelig men bestemt <u>uden</u> Talent'.

Price danced the rôle 5 times in 1867 (the last time on 25.10. 1867). After her last but one performance Bournonville again noted about her on 3.9.1867:

'Sylphiden for særdeles godt Huus. M. Price høist ubetydelig'.

The musical material employed this year was the same as that used for the 1865 restaging (now in DKKk, call nos. C II, 117 d, MA ms 2970 b, and KTB 275).

29.5.1867
Gurre, Romance with Chorus (Romance med Chor) recited by J. C. Hansen with a chorus of mixed voices.

The 1867 Copenhagen restaging of H. C. Andersen's poem with music by H. Rung (*see* 28.3.1842) represents the last time it was mounted with Bournonville's mise-en-scène. It was given this year as part of a gala performance for the celebration of the silver-wedding of Denmark's King Christian IX and Queen Louise. In his diary Bournonville noted about the performance:

27.5. and 28.5.1867: 'Prøve paa Gurre'
29.5.: 'Forberedelser til Galaforestillingen i Det kgl Theater. Der gaves[…] Gurre'.

Gurre was performed 3 times in the 1867–68 season, the last time on 29.11.1867.

The musical material employed this year was the same as that used at its 1842 première (now in DKKk, call no. C II, 157).

29.5.1867
Waldemar.

This staging represents the 99th performance of Bournonville's four-act romantic ballet *Waldemar* (*see* 28.10.1835). It was mounted as part of a gala performance celebrating the silver-wedding of Denmark's King Christian IX and Queen Louise. For this occasion Bournonville wrote a new, revised libretto in French, entitled 'Analyse du Ballet' which includes a new foreword, named 'Augment historique'. According to this scenario Bournonville originally found his first inspiration for the plot of this ballet in the Icelandic sagas, in particular the so-called *Knytlinga-Saga*. Moreover, the 1867 scenario includes a list of the ballet's complete dances which this year were:

In Act I:
(1) A *Ronde des paysans*, performed by the corps de ballet.
(2) A *Pas de cinq*, performed by H. Scharff, E. Hansen, P. Fredstrup, L. Stillmann, and J. Petersen.

In Act II:
(3) A *Pas du ménéstrel*, performed by E. Hansen (as *Axel Hvide*), B. Schnell (as *Astrid*) together with M. Price, E. Gade, C. Larsen, and E. V. A. Møller. This dance was originally a *Pas de deux* performed only by the characters *Waldemar* and *Astrid*.
(4) A *Pas d'armes*, performed by a group of men from the corps de ballet.
(5) A *Danse des flambeaux*, performed by the entire cast.

In Act IV:
(6) An *Apparitions célestes*, performed by women of the corps de ballet.

In his diary Bournonville noted about the performance:

15.5.1867: 'Brev fra Hofmarskal [C. L.] Lövenskjold'
16.5.: 'Brev til Hofmarskallen […] componeret og redigeret Valdemars Program paa Fransk'
18.5.: 'reenskrevet det franske Program'
20.5.: 'talt med Hofmarskal Lövenskjold, der frembragte mig adskillige Indvendinger med Hensyn til Galaforestillingen og Valdemar'
21.5.: 'Besøg hos [N. C. L.] Abrahams, der corrigerer min franske Analyse til Valdemar'
23.5.: 'Correctur fra B. Luno'
24.5.: 'Svar til […] Luno'
28.5.: 'Prøve paa […] Valdemar'
29.5.: 'Forberedelser til Galaforestillingen i Det kgl Theater. Der gaves Sang af [H. P.] Holst; Gurre og Valdemar, der gik ypperligt. Alt var udsolgt til dobbelte Priser. Kongen [i.e. Christian IX] og Dronningen (i.e. Queen Louise], de kongelige Børn (Storfyrsten af Rusland [i.e. the later Czar Alexander III] med Gemalinde [i.e. the Danish-born Princess Dagmar) og Kong Georg [I] af Grækenland) bleve festligt modtagne, flere Huse paa Torvet vare illuminerede og det Hele var smukt og høitideligt'.

The musical material employed in 1867 was the same as that used for the previous 1835, 1853, and 1866 productions (now in DKkk, call nos. C II, 107, MA ms 2993, MA ms 2994, and KTB 297).

Autograph sources:

Manuscript scenario. Ms. Autograph. Brown ink. 1 vol. 6 pp. (20,7 × 16,8 cm)
Valdemar/Ballet-pantomime en 4 Actes/par/Auguste Bournonville /[…] /La 99.me représentation donnée à l'occasion de/l'auguste fête du Jubilé de 25 ans de mariage de/ L.L. M.M. le Roi Christian IX et la Reine/Louise de Danemark le 29 Mai 1867.
Signed and dated: ' le 29 Mai 1867.' [Written according to the diary on 16.5. and 18.5.1867]
[DKKk; Abrahams'ske Autografsaml. 4° Nr. 17, Nr. 268

Printed sources:

Printed scenario. 1 vol. 5 pp. (22,8 × 14,3 cm)
Valdemar./Ballet-pantomime en 4 Actes,/par/Auguste Bournonville./Musique de Fr. Frøhlich./[…]/La 99.me représentation donnée à l'occasion de l'auguste fête du Jubilé de/25 ans de mariage de L. L. M. M. le Roi Christian IX et la Reine/Louise de Danemark le 29 Mai 1867.
Copenhaque/Bianco Luno par F. S. Muhle, 1867.
[DKKk; 17, – 172 8°

6.6.–20.8.1867
Forty-five private dance lessons to B. Schnell, A. Scholl, D. Krum, and J. T. Klüver.

According to several notes in his diary, Bournonville gave two series of private dance lessons (22 and 23 lessons each) to four of his most talented pupils. They took place at his private residence in Fredensborg during the dancers' summer holiday and lasted about two hours each. The lessons were concluded with two separate presentations by his pupils on 2.7. and 27.7.1867 for Bournonville's family and personal friends in Fredensborg. About these presentations the first is described in his diary as follows:

'20.e Lection med Presentation for [H. S.] Paullis og min Familie, glimrende Resultat navnlig for Anna Scholl, der lover at blive noget ganske overordentligt'.

2.9.1867

Mary Stuart in Scotland (Marie Stuart i Skotland).

At the Copenhagen première of B. Björnson's five-act drama to music by R. Nordraak, Bournonville's earlier set of four quadrilles in Act I, score no. 1 (originally created for the Norwegian première of this drama on 29.3.1867) were re-mounted by L. Gade. He clearly staged these dances from Bournonville's original, but not yet traced choreographic notations.

According to A. Fredstrup's rehearsal book, 11 rehearsals of the four quadrilles were held under Gade's personal direction between 16.8. and 31.8.1867.

As with the Norwegian première, the Copenhagen poster does not give any information about the dances in Act I, nor does it mention Bournonville's name. Moreover, Bournonville himself does not include this work in his list of his stagings of operas and plays, written c.1872 (*see* Additional Sources), nor in the printed survey of his works in his memoirs *My Theatre Life* (p. 408).

In his diary he noted about the Copenhagen staging and première of Björnson's drama:

6.7.1867: 'Brev [...] tilligemend en Anmodning til <u>Herr Moe</u> om Choregraphien til Maria Stuart'
18.7.: 'forefundet Brev fra <u>Moe</u>'
26.8.: 'seet Prøven paa min Dands til Maria Stuart i Skotland' .
2.9.: 'i Theatret, hvor man gav den 1.ste Forestilling af Maria Stuart i Skotland af <u>Bjørnstjerne Bjørnson</u>. Jeg saae 3 Akter deraf og det interesserede mig særdeles. Spillet var i mange Henseender tilfredsstillende, men dog over vore Kræfter'
5.9.: 'Seet 1.ste 4.e og 5.e Akt af Maria Stuart i Skotland. Mange poetiske og dramatiske Skjønheder, men det Hele noget manieret og stykkets Composition mangelfuld. Forfatteren var i Theatret men han saae ikke mig'.

Mary Stuart in Scotland received 13 performances in Copenhagen during Bournonville's lifetime, the last of which was given on 17.9.1868.

Musical sources:

Orchestral score. Ms. Autographs (by R. Nordraak and E. Grieg). Brown and black ink. 1 vol. 44 pp. of which five are blank + 4 pp. of which three are blank + a manuscript with text (26,1 × 33,8 cm with variants)
757/757/Marie Stuart/i/Skotland/Partitur./[...]/Partitur/til/ Maria Stuart i Skotland,/af Bjørnstjerne Bjørnson./Musiken,/af/ Rikard Nordraak.
[DKKk; C II, 118 f (KTA 757)]
This orchestral score for *Mary Stuart in Scotland* is, in parts, Nordraak's autograph. It contains his complete music for Björnson's drama and was used for all performances of it in Copenhagen during Bournonville's lifetime. A metronome marking on p. 2 indicates the exact tempo of the four quadrilles in the opening scene of Act I (score no. 1) with a crochet being equal to '60'.
According to D. Schjelderup-Ebbe's article *Et Nyfunnet Orkesterpartitur med Rikard Nordraaks Musikk til Bjørnstjerne Bjørnsons drama 'Maria Stuart i Skotland'* (in *Studia Musicologica Norvegica*, vol. 1, 1968, pp. 101–131) this score also served for the drama's earlier première at Christiania's Theatre (*see* 29.3.1867). According to the same source (p. 117) it was sent to Copenhagen by Björnson on 20.5.1857. He addressed it to the Danish actress, Johanne Luise Heiberg (who mounted the drama in Copenhagen) together with a note reading: 'De kan kaste et Øje deri, før De vil have den Godhed at sende Hr. Intendanten det til Udskrivning'.

Répétiteur's copy. Ms. Copy. Brown ink. 1 vol. Black ink. 4 pp. of which one is blank (33,9 × 24,9 cm)
[...]/6. Maria Stuart./96./[...]/L. Gade/Repetiteurparti/til/Maria Stuart.
Unsigned and undated [1867]
[DKKk; MA ms 2919 (7) (KTA 757)]
This répétiteur's copy contains Nordraak's complete music for the set of four quadrilles performed in the opening scene of Act I (score no. 1) of Björnson's *Mary Stuart in Scotland*. The volume also includes Bournonville's pencilled notes which clearly refer to his separate (not yet traced) autographed choreographic notation of these dances. The répétiteur's copy is included on pp. 49–52 in a volume that also contains the répétiteur's copies for five other operas and plays, mounted at Copenhagen's Royal Theatre between 1864 and 1868.

Parts. Ms. Copy. 28 + 10 vol.
3 vl I, 3 vl II, 2 vla, 3 vlc e cb, fl 1/2, ob, cl 1/2, fag 1/2, cor 1/2, tr 1/ 2, trb 1/2/3, timp, gr cassa, arpa. On stage: vl I, vl II, vla, vlc e cb, fl, cl 1/2, fag, cor 1/2. 24 vocal parts.
Unsigned and undated [1867]
[DKKk; KTA 757]

14.9.1867

Die Lustigen Weiber von Windsor (De lystige Koner i Windsor).

The 1867 Copenhagen première of O. Nicolai's three-act fantastic comic opera (first performed at Berlin's Königlichen Theater on 9.3.1849) was originally projected by Bournonville on 30.10.1857. It included his choreography for three dance scenes in Act III as follows:

(1) A 'Chor und Elfentanz' (also entitled «Ihr Elfen weiss und roth» /«i Maanens Skin vi dandse maa») in Act III, score no. 14. This dance scene, which is performed by a group of elves, is described in the répétiteur's copy (p. 1) as follows: '(Dands af Alfer, kun Grupperinger; Halvdelen af det qvindelige Balletpersonale)'.
(2) A divertissement in Act III, score no. 15 (also entitled 'Mückentanz'). This scene is described in the répétiteur's copy (p. 10) as follows: 'No. 15 Myggedands, Pas de quatre avec Chor de ballet. Fire Solodanserinner [*sic*], forestillende Mygge, luftigt klædt, med Vinger paa Skuldrene og lange Sølvpile i Hænderne. Ved de antydede Mærker (*) stikker den ved Tal betegnede Danserinde Falstaff med sin Piil. Den anden Halvdeel af det qvindelige Balletpersonale, ligeledes forstillende Mygge dandser omkring Falstaff og ved de anförte Mærker stikke de ham. Den förste Halvdeel (Alferne) deeltager i Dandsen ved Grupperinger'.
(3) A 'Chor und allgemeiner Tanz' (also entitled «Fasst ihn, Geister»/«Hurtig, hurtig fat ham tag») in Act III (score no. 16). The dance, performed by the entire corps de ballet during this chorus, is described in the répétiteur's copy (p. 14) as follows: 'En Mængde Masker og Aander, Gnomer, Kobolde, Salamandere etc. – Den mandlige Deel af Balletpersonalet storme ind og omkredse Falstaff med vilde Spring. Salamanderne brende ham af og til, Koboldene rykke i ham. Alferne og Myggene blande dem ogsaa i Dandsen; de sidste stikke ham af og til'.

In his diary Bournonville noted about his staging and the Copenhagen première of Nicolai's opera:

9.7.1867: 'componeret paa Dandsen til <u>De muntre Koner i Windsor</u>'
10.7.: 'componeret'
12.7.: 'reenskrevet de choregraphiske Noter til De muntre Koner i Windsor'
19.8.: 'spillet Violin og overtænkt min Dands til De muntre Koner'
27.8. '1.ste Indstudering paa Dandsen til 'De muntre Koner''
28.8.: '2.den Indstudering paa De muntre Koner'
29.8.: '3.die Indst. paa <u>De muntre Koner</u>. Dandsen færdig'
31.8.: 'Prøve paa Dandsen til 'De muntre Koner''

2.9.: 'Prøve paa De lўstige Koner […] der gaaer meget godt'
3.9.: 'Prøve paa Dandsen til 'De lўstige Koner paa Theatret''
5.9.: 'Prøve paa Dandsen til 'De muntre Koner''
9.9.: 'Prøve paa […] 'De muntre Koner' (paa Theatret)'
12.9.: 'Prøve […] Kl. 1 paa De muntre Koner'
13.9.: 'Generalprøve paa De muntre Koner'
14.9.: ' I Theatret 1,ste Forestilling af 'De muntre Koner i Windsor' der gik ret smukt, men kun gjorde tarvelig Lўkke, hvorimod mit Divertissement fik stærkt Bifald'
19.9.: ''De muntre Koner' for tyndt Huus'
24.9.: ''De lystige Koner' for maadeligt Huus'.

Die Lustigen Weiber von Windsor, which is not included in Bournonville's handwritten list of his stagings of operas and plays, written c.1872 (*see* Additional Sources), reached a total of only 3 performances in Copenhagen, the last of which was given on 24.9.1867.

Musical sources:

Orchestral score (incomplete). Ms. Copy. Black ink and pencil. 2 vol. Act II 292 pp., Act III 228 pp. of which three are blank (28 × 34,5 cm with minor variants)
759 P./DIE/lustigen Weiber/VON WINDSOR/von/OTTO NICO-LAI./PARTITUR./AKT. II./Act III.
Unsigned and undated [c.1867]
[DKKk; MA ms 1275 (KTA 759)
This (incomplete) German manuscript copy of the orchestral score for Nicolai's *Die Lustigen Weiber von Windsor* (of which the volume of Act I is missing) dates from its 1867 Copenhagen première. The music for the three dance scenes in Act III (score nos. 14–16) is included on pp. '709–814'.

Répétiteur's copy. Ms. Brown ink. 1 vol. 20 pp. (33,8 × 25,7 cm)
A. 759/20/De lystige Koner i Windsor./Divertissement i 3.die Akt./af/Bournonville/58./1867../[…]/ Repetiteurparti/til/De muntre Koner fra Windsor
Unsigned and dated (on the front cover): '1867.'
[DKKk; MA ms 3094 (KTA 759)
This répétiteur's copy contains the music for the three dance scenes in Act III of *Die Lustigen Weiber von Windsor* (score nos. 14–16). It also includes Bournonville's pencilled autographed choreographic numbers ('1–18', '1–7', and '1–17') which most probably refer to his separate (not yet traced) choreographic notations of the same scenes, written (according to the diary) between 9.7.and 12.7.1867.

Parts. Ms. Copy. 35 vol.
4 vl I, 3 vl II, 2 vla, 4 vlc e cb, fl 1/2, ob 1/2, cl 1/2, fag 1/2, cor 1/2/3/4, tr 1/2, trb 1/2/3, timp, gr cassa, piatti, tri, arpa. 20 vocal parts.
Unsigned and undated [1867]
[DKKk; KTA 759
This set of parts dates from the 1867 Copenhagen première of *Die Lustigen Weiber von Windsor* and was used for all performances of it there during Bournonville's lifetime.

20.9.1867
A Folk Tale (Et Folkesagn).
The 1867 Copenhagen production of Bournonville's three-act romantic ballet *A Folk Tale* (*see* 20.3.1854) represents Bournonville's first throughly revised staging of this work with B. Schnell playing the rôle of *Hilda* for the first time. The major changes from his previous 1854 and 1857 productions seem to be a revised version of I. P. E. Hartmann's gallop for the trolls in Act II (score no. 13), which now played for only 153 bars. Moreover, a new and considerably extended version of N. W. Gade's Act III divertissement (score no. 20) was included. Being originally performed as a *Pas de*

quatre (danced by a gipsy man and three gipsy women) this dance was transformed into a *Pas de sept* for three men and four women (all gipsies), with completely new choreography. According to the interpolated music sections in the orchestral score for this dance, the new, additional music was apparently orchestrated and (in parts) perhaps even composed by V. C. Holm.

In his diary Bournonville noted about the revised 1867 production of *A Folk Tale*:

21.7.1867: 'Breve til Juliette Price, Betty Schnell og Fru [E.] Gade i Anledning af en Alterneringsplan for Hildas Rolle i Et Folkesagn'
26.7.: 'Besøgt Prof [N. W.] Gade'
5.8.: 'Brev til Gade'
10.8.: 'talt med Gade'
12.8.: 'Brev til Gade'
15.8: 'componeret og reenskrevet en pas de sept til 'Et Folkesagn''
17.8.: 'talt med [L.] Gade og [G.] Brodersen'
27.8.: 'Eftermiddagsprøve paa Et Folkesagn'
28.8.: 'Lille Prøve paa Et Folkesagn'
30.8.: 'Prøve paa Et Folkesagn'
2.9.: 'Prøve paa […] Et Folkesagn, der gaaer meget godt'
3.9.: 'Prøve paa 'Et Folkesagn''
4.9.: 'Prøve paa Et Folkesagn (Schnell)'
5.9.: 'Eftermiddagsprøve paa 'Et Folkesagn''
6.9.: 'Eftermiddagsprøve paa Et Folkesagn. Hildas Rolle færdig indstuderet'
7.9.: 'Prøve paa Et Folkesagn. Hildas Rolle meget heldig'
9.9.: 'Eftermiddagsprøve paa Et Folkesagn (M Price)'
10.9.: 'Prøve paa Et Folkesagn, indstuderet en stor nў pas de sept'
11.9.: 'skrevet 6 Breve til Redactionerne i Anledning af 'Et Folkesagn''
12.9.: 'Prøve Kl 10 paa Et Folkesagn'
13.9.: 'Prøve paa Et Folkesagn'
14.9.: 'Theaterprøve paa 'Et Folkesagn''
16.9.: 'Prøve paa 'Et Folkesagn''
18.9.: 'Generalprøve paa Et Folkesagn'
20.9.: 'Et Folkesagn, der gik særdeles smukt og gjorde megen Lykke. Huset var ikke saa fuldt som vi kunde ønske det. Veiret var for deiligt'.

The 1867 production of *A Folk Tale* received 12 performances, the last of which was given on 8.4.1869.

Autograph sources:

Production note. Ms. Autograph. Brown ink. 3 pp. (22,9 × 17,9 cm)
Personliste til Balletten 'Et Folkesagn'./(Paanў indstuderet i September 1867.)
Signed and dated: 'Fredensborg d 21.e Juli 1867.'
[DKKt; F.M. (Ballet)

Choreographic note. Ms. Autograph. Brown ink. 4 pp. (20,7 × 16,8 cm)
Et Folkesagn (3.die Akts Slutning.)/Pas de sept. (Tempo alla Polacca)
Signed and dated: 'Fredensborg den 15.e August 1867.'
[Private collection (Copenhagen)

Musical sources:

The orchestral score, the two répétiteur's copies, and the set of parts used for the 1867 production of *A Folk Tale* are now in DKKk (call nos. C II, 108, MA ms 2968, and KTB 274).

Répétiteur's copy (*Pas de sept*). Ms. Copy. Black ink. 14 pp. 33,6 × 24,5 cm with minor variants)
Pas de sept/Et Folkesagn./3.die Akt./nyt arrangeret 1867.

Unsigned and dated (on p. 1): '1867.'
[DKKk; MA ms 2969 (KTB 274 (2))]
This répétiteur's copy contains the complete music for Bournonville's new, extended version of the Act III divertissement (score no. 20) in *A Folk Tale*. It also includes his autographed choreographic numbers (written with brown ink) which clearly refer to the similar numbers included in his separate notation of this dance dated 15.8. 1867.

Other sources:

Drawing of the accessories by E. Lehmann. Pencil and water colours (23,9 × 18,8 cm)
[Untitled]
Unsigned and undated [c. late 1860s?]
[DKKkt; Kostumetegninger (Lehmann)]
This drawing shows the diadem worn by Hilda in Act II of *A Folk Tale*. It most probably dates from the 1867 restaging of this ballet.

16.10.–3.12.1867
Twelve dance lessons in social dance.
According to a series of notes in his diary, Bournonville gave a series of twelve private dance lessons in social dance for a group of young girls at the Copenhagen residence in Lille Kjøbmagergade no. 60s of the judge, G. C. V. Obelitz. These lessons, which took place on Tuesday and Saturday afternoons, lasted for about two hours each.

18.10.1867
Pas de trois (uncredited) performed by B. Schnell, E. Poulsen, and A. Scholl.
According to a note in Bournonville's diary this (uncredited) *Pas de trois* is identical with his *Pas des trois cousines* (*see* 20.5.1848 and 8.9.1849). The 1867 performance represents Bournonville's third staging of this dance at Copenhagen's Royal Theatre. For the same occasion he made a complete notation of its choreography. In his diary he noted about the performance:

17.10.1867: 'Prøve paa pas de trois'
18.10.: 'Imellem Stykkerne dandsede [B.] Schnell, [A.] Scholl og [E.] Poulsen le pas des trois cousines og vandt meget Bifald'.

The dance received 4 performances during the 1867–68 season, the last of which was given on 20.11.1867.

Autograph sources:

Chorographic note. Ms. Autograph. Brown ink. 1 p. cut into two pieces (17,4 × 12 cm and 18,6 × 12 cm).
Scholl. Schnell – Poulsen.
Unsigned and undated [c. October 1867]
[DKKk; Utilg. 828 (Harald Landers Arkiv, Supplement, Kapsel 189, 1994/78)
This manuscript contains Bournonville's autographed choreographic notes and numbers ('1–7' and '1–10'), the latter most probably referring to similar numbers written into the (not yet traced) répétiteur's copy from the 1867 restaging of *Pas des trois cousines*.

Chorographic note. Ms. Autograph. Brown ink. 1 p. (36 × 12 cm).
Allegretto:/1°: Schnell & Poulsen ensemble/[...]/2. Scholl seule./ [...]/3.' Schnell seule./[...]/4. Poulsen seule/[...]
Unsigned and undated [c. October 1867]
[DKKk; Utilg. 828 (Harald Landers Arkiv, Supplement, Kapsel 189, 1994/78)
This manuscript contains Bournonville's autographed chorographic notes and set of numbers ('1–4'). They most likely refer to similar numbers in the (not yet traced) répétiteur's copy employed for this restaging of *Pas des trois cousines*.

Musical sources:

Orchestral score. Ms. Copy. Black ink. 1 vol. 44 pp. of which two are blank (34 × 26 cm)
318./Pas de trois cousines/Partitur/Paulli/[...]/Pas de trois cousines./Paulli.
Unsigned and undated [c.1867]
[DKKk; C II, 119 (KTB 318)
This orchestral score is clearly a copy of the original (not yet traced) score for *Pas des trois cousines*, and seems to date from Bournonville's 1867 restaging of it.

No répétiteur's copy dating from the 1867 restaging of *Pas des trois cousines* has yet been traced.

Parts (incomplete). Ms. Copy. 27 vol.
2 vl I, 3 vl II, 2 vla, 3 vlc e cb, fl picc, fl I, ob 1/2, cl 1/2, fag 1/2cor 1/ 2, tr 1/2, Atrb, Ttrb, Btrb, timp, gr cassa e piatti.
Unsigned and undated [c.1867]
[DKKk; KTB 318]
This (incomplete) set of parts clearly relates to the manuscript copy of the orchestral score for *Pas des trois cousines*, dating from c.1867 (*see above*).

5.11.1867
The Elf Maiden (Elverpigen).
For the 1867 première of E. Hartmann's three-act opera (with text by T. Overskou) Bournonville created the mise-en-scène and the dance and mime scenes in Act I (scene 5) and Act II (scene 7).

The dance scene in Act I (score no. 12) seems, in its general concept, to hold a close affinity with that of the *Elf maidens' dance* in Act I (score no. 5) of Bournonville's three-act romantic ballet *A Folk Tale* (*see* 20.3.1854). That ballet had been restaged in a new and thoroughly revised version only two months before the première of Hartmann's opera (*see* 20.9.1867). In *The Elf Maiden*, the Act I dance scene is performed by a corps de ballet of elf maidens during the chorus, entitled «Naar Aftnens Klokker ringe de Mennesker til Ro os Alfer Budskab de bringe nu har vi Magt til at tumle os fro». It is followed by two similar scenes (a so-called *Melodrama*, and a chorus named «Ellers uden Maal of Fred, skal du vanke om paa Jord, ja uden Tanke Maal of Fred!»), during which the same corps de ballet of elf maidens performs different groupings while miming the contents of the text sung by the chorus. Finally, in Act II (score no. 24) yet another similar dance scene is performed by the elf maidens during the chorus, entitled «Kom Hr. Ridder Kom Hr. Ridder Kom Hr. Ridder og følg med os».

In his diary Bournonville noted about the rehearsals of Hartmann's opera and its first two performances:

23.4.1867: 'Brev fra Emil Hartmann og Svar til [H. S.] Paulli'
17.10.: 'Anmodning om at sætte [T.] Overskous og Hartmanns Opera Elverpigen i Scene'
18.10.: 'Jeg læste Elverpigen [...] Conference med Overskou'
19.10.: 'Costumemøde paa Elverpigen [...] Decorationsskue paa Elverpigen'
21.10: 'Bivaanet en stor Quartettprøve med sang og Chor paa Elverpigen [...] Eftermiddags-Instruction paa Elverpigen'
22.10.: 'Jeg skrev og componerede til Elverpigen'

23.10.: 'Prøve og Indstudering paa Elverpigens Dandse'
24.10.: 'Indstuderet Ellepigedandsen [...] Eftermiddagsprøve med Fru [J. E.] Liebe'
25.10: 'Kl 12 Arrangementsprøve paa Elverpigen [...] Eftermiddagsprøve paa Elverpigen'
26.10.: 'Stor Arrangementsprøve paa Elverpigen'
28.10.: 'Theaterprøve paa to Akter af Elverpigen'
30.10.: 'Prøve paa [...] 3.e Akt af Elverpigen'
31.10.: 'stor Theaterprøve paa Elverpigen'
2.11.: 'Theaterprøve paa Elverpigen'
4.11.: 'Generalprøve paa Elverpigen, der gik udmærket smukt'
5.11.: 'I Theatret 1.ste Forestilling af Elverpigen, der gik særdeles godt og vistnok behagede, men dog kun vandt et lunket Bifald. Vort saakaldte musikalske Publicum er just ikke opmuntrende for de indenlandske Talenter'
8.11.: 'I Theatret 'Elverpigen' halvt Huus og en flou Stemning som Følge af en ublid og forhastet Critik'.

The Elf Maiden reached a total of 5 performances, the last of which was given on 25.1.1868.

Autograph sources:

Manuscript mise-en-scène. Ms. Autograph. Black ink. 1 vol. 14 p. (21,6 × 17 cm)
Scene = Arrangement/til Operaen/Elverpigen./1867.
Unsigned and dated: '1867.' [Written according to the diary on 22.10.1867]
[SSm; Daniel Fryklunds samling no. 124

Musical sources:

Music drafts. Ms. Autographs (by E. Hartmann and I. P. E. Hartmann). Black ink, pencil, and blue crayon. 406 pp. of which thirteen are blank (35 × 29,7 cm with minor variants)
[Untitled]
Unsigned and undated [1867]
[DKKk; Emil Hartmanns Samling, kapsel nr. 12-14 (1929–30.997)
These musical drafts contain E. Hartmann's first fragmentary versions of the orchestral score for Act I (score nos. 2–3, 5, 12–18 and 19, the *Finale*), Act II (the *Introduction* and score nos. 20–25 and 26–27), and Act III (score nos. 31–34 and no. 36, the *Finale*). The fact that nearly all of the draft for score no. 19 (the Act I *Finale*) is I. P. E. Hartmann's autograph indicates that most of this number was orchestrated and perhaps even composed by him. The complete set of drafts were originally E. Hartmann's private property, but were donated to DKKk by his heirs on 13.11.1929.

Orchestral score (the overture). Ms. Autograph (by E. Hartmann). Black ink. 1 vol. 40 pp. (34,7 × 29,2 cm)
756/[...]/Elverpigen/Ouverture
Signed (on p. 1): 'Emil Hartmann', undated [1867]
[DKKk; C II, 112 d (KTA 756)

Orchestral score (the opera). Ms. Autograph (by E. Hartmann) and copy. Black ink. 3 vol. Act I 344 pp., Act II 248 pp. of which one is blank, Act III 198 pp. of which five are blank (34,8 × 29 cm with minor variants)
Elverpigen/1.ste Act/[...]/Elverpigen. romantisk Opera i 3 Acter af Th Overskou./[...]/2.den Act/[...]/3.die Act
Signed (in vol. I on p. 1): 'Emil Hartmann', undated [1867]
[DKKk; C II, 112 d (KTA 756)
This orchestral score is E. Hartmann's autograph except for most of the music for Act II (the *Introduction*, score nos. 20–26, and parts of no. 27) which is in a copyist's hand. The music for the two dance scenes mounted by Bournonville in Acts I and II is included in vol. I (on pp. 189–226), and in vol. II (on pp. 75–87).

Répétiteur's copy. Ms. Copy. Brown ink. 1 vol. Black ink. 4 pp. of which one is blank (33,9 × 24,9 cm)

[...]/4. Elverpigen./[...]/Repetiteurpartie/til/Elverpigen
Unsigned and undated [1867]
[DKKk; MA ms 2919 (4) (KTA 756 (1))
This répétiteur's copy contains the music for the chorus in Act I (score no. 12) during which a dance scene is performed by a corps de ballet of elf maidens. It also includes Bournonville's autographed choreographic notes (written with brown ink) which describe in general terms the choreography and the mime. Moreover, his autographed choreographic numbers ('1–10') are inserted in this volume. They seem to refer to his separate (not yet traced) notation of this scene, written (according to his diary) on 22.10.1867.

The répétiteur's copy is included on pp. 23–26 in a volume that also contains the répétiteur's copies for five other operas and plays, mounted at Copenhagen's Royal Theatre between 1864 and 1868.

Répétiteur's copy. Ms. Copy. Brown ink. 1 vol. Black ink. 6 pp. of which one is blank (33,9 × 24,9 cm)
[...]/4. Elverpigen./[...]/Repetiteurparti/til/Elverpigen
Unsigned and undated [1867]
[DKKk; MA ms 2919 (5) (KTA 756 (2))
This répétiteur's copy contains the music for the chorus in Act I (score no. 12) during which a dance scene is performed by a corps de ballet of elf maidens. It also includes the music for the chorus in Act II (score no. 24) during which a similar dance of elf maidens is performed. The first number includes Bournonville's autographed choreographic notes (written with brown ink) which describe the choreography and the mime in more general terms. Moreover, his autographed choreographic numbers ('11–15') are inserted in the music for this scene and seem to refer to his separate (not yet traced) notation of it, written (according to his diary) on 22.10.1867. The second number, too, includes his autographed choreographic numbers ('1–5') which seem to refer to a separate choreographic notation of this dance.

The répétiteur's copy is included on pp. 27–32 in a volume that also contains the répétiteur's copies for five other operas and plays, mounted at Copenhagen's Royal Theatre between 1864 and 1868.

Parts. Ms. Copy. 38 + 2 vol.
4 vl I, 3 vl II, 2 vla, 4 vlc e cb, fl picc, fl 1/2, ob 1/2, cl 1/2, fag 1/2, cor 1/2/3/4, tr 1/2, trb 1/2/3, tuba, timp, gr cassa, tamb, tri, arpa, org.
On stage: vl I e II, vl III. 56 vocal parts.
Unsigned and undated [1867]
[DKKk; KTA 756

29.11.1867
Pas de trois (uncredited) performed by E. Hansen, S. Price, and E. Gade.
This (uncredited) dance is perhaps the same as the similarly uncredited *Pas de trois*, performed by H. Scharff, E. Gade, and J. Petersen on 23.11.1865. That dance, in turn, is identical with the *Pas de trois* (score no. 7) from Bournonville's one-act pantomimic idyll *Soldier and Peasant* (*see* 13.10.1829). The *Pas de trois* was rehearsed under Bournonville's personal direction (on 26.11. and 28.11.1867) and was attended by him at its one and only performance this year on 29.11.1867. It is not possible to identify the dance any further.

29.11.1867
Las Hermanas de Sevilla, Spanish Dance (Spansk Dands) performed by J. Petersen, M. Price, and L. Cetti.
This performance represents Bournonville's first restaging at Copenhagen's Royal Theatre of his and C. C. Møller's Spanish *Pas de trois* divertissement from 4.6.1851. According to his diary he personally directed two rehearsals of it on 26.11. and 28.11.1867, and attended the first of two performances during this season (the second given on 30.4.1868).

The musical material employed this year was the same as that used since the 1851 première at Copenhagen's Royal Theatre (now in DKKk, call nos. C II, 118, and KTB 239).

4.12.1867
Late is not too late (Seent er ikke forsilde).
Although Bournonville did not personally take part in the Copenhagen première of H. H. Nyegaard's one-act comedy, he was clearly instrumental in its staging. This theory is confirmed by a series of notes in his diary that read:

23.7.1867: 'Modtaget Procurator [H. H.] Nyegaard i Anledning af en Vaudeville hvorom jeg skrev til Justitsr: [F. J. G.] Berner'
29.7.: 'Brev til Procurator Nygaard om hans Vaudeville'
4.12.: 'Seet 1.ste Forestilling af et lille versificeret Stykke af Ny[e]gaard 'Seent er ikke forsilde' – ikke <u>saa</u> slet som det var udskreget -'.

Late is not too late reached only one performance.

1868

21.2.1868
The Lay of Thrym (Thrymsqviden).
The earliest trace of this ballet appears to date from Bournonville's Parisian sojourn in November and December 1865, when he noted in his diary on 9.12.1865:

'<u>kjøbt musikalske Bøger</u> som Materiale til et fremtidigt mythologisk Arbeide'.

Among the books he purchased in Paris on this day were (according to his dairy of his travel expenses, *see* Additional Sources) H. Berlioz's book from 1859, entitled *Les Grotesques de la musique* (Paris, 1859). This seems to have provided Bournonville with his first incitement to start working on this, his second full-length ballet within the sphere of Nordic mythology. Another, more evident source of inspiration might (according to notes in his diary) have been A. Hertz's new, abridged 1867 Danish translation of R. Wagner's *Oper und Drama*, a book that Bournonville read for the first time in the original 1852 German edition well before the creation of his first four-act Nordic mythological ballet *The Valkyrie* (*see* 13.9.1861). Finally, Bournonville appears to have found his perhaps most important inspiration for *The Lay of Thrym* in F. L. Liebenberg's 1862 edition of A. Oehlenschläger's cyclus of poems, entitled *Nordens Guder* (Kjøbenhavn, Selskabet til Udgivelse af Oehlenschlägers Skrifter, vol. 29, 1862). This is clear from his personal copy of the then most recent edition of Oehlenschläger's complete writings, in which he inserted numerous pencilled notes and choreographic numbers which emphasise those sections of Oehlenschläger's poems and Liebenberg's critical commentary that seem to have formed the basis for Bournonville's own ideas on how to construct the ballet's programme.

Moreover, at least one of the dance divertissements in *The Lay of Thrym* seems to have been based on an earlier work by Bournonville, namely the so-called *Dance of the five senses* in the second scene of Act I (score no. 2). This dance, which is performed by the five foster daughters of the prophetess *Vola*, is conceived in the exactly same way as Bournonville's intermezzo from four years earlier, named *Le Ballet des cinq sens* and premièred as an integral part in Act V of O. Wijkander's historical five-act play at Stockholm's Royal Theatre (Dramatiska Theatern) on 20.2.1864.

After 7.10.1868 *The Lay of Thrym* was performed without its original recited prologue by H. P. Holst, named *The Norns (Nornerne)*. On 17.9.1871 the ballet was restaged with partially new choreography created especially for the Swedish ballerina, M. Westberg, who that year took over the rôle of *Sigyn* from its original interpreter, B. Schnell. The entire ballet was mounted for the last time by Bournonville on 29.3. 1874, but then with only minor if any changes from his previous 1871 version.

In his diary he noted about the long and rather troubled creation of this bulging balletic vision, on which he worked nearly every single day during a period of 13 months:

9.12.1865: '<u>kjøbt musikalske Bøger</u> som Materiale til et fremtidigt mythologisk Arbeide'
6.2., 12.2., and 13.2.1866: 'læst i [H.] Berlioz [i.e. *Les grotesques de la musique*]'
4.1.1867: 'læst [A.] Hertz's Oversættelse af Wagners Opera og Drama'
5.1.: 'begyndt paa et Balletprogram til <u>Thrymsqviden</u> om det vil lykkes mig'
7.1.: 'Arbeidet den største Deel af Dagen paa min nordiske mythologiske Ballet, som jeg gjorde Udkastet færdigt til, uden at tage nogen Bestemmelse om Navnet'
8.1.: 'skrevet paa <u>Thrymskviden</u>'
10.1.: 'Fortsat mit store Balletprogram'
11.1.: 'tilbragt Størstedelen af Dagen med Thrymsqviden'
13.1.: 'tilbragt Aftenen med mit Program'
14.1.: 'fortsat mit Manuscript, der nærmer sig en heldig Fuldendelse'
15.1.: 'Fuldendt den sidste Scene af <u>Thrymsqviden</u> eller <u>Ragnaroksmythen i Billeder</u>'
29.1.: 'arbeidet pa Decorationslister til <u>Thrymsqviden</u>'
31.1.: 'arbeidet paa Decorationsplaner til <u>Thrymsqviden</u>'
1.2.: 'fuldendt Decorationsplanen og begyndt paa Costumet'
21.2: 'talt med Theaterbestyrelsen og bleven anmodet om et større Arbeide, tænkt paa Thrymsqviden, talt derom til [I. P. E.] Hartmann [...] leveret mit Program til [F. J. G.] Berner'
27.2.: 'reenskrevet paa mit Program'
28.2.: 'reenskrevet paa min Ballet'
2.3: 'fuldendt Reenskrivningen af <u>Thrymsqviden</u> til Brug for <u>Hartmann</u> i det Tilfælde at Balletten bliver antaget'
5.3.: 'Conference med Berner [...] talt med Hartmann'
6.3.: 'besøgt H. P. Holst, der [...] fik mit Program at see'
20.3.: 'Brev til Prof. Hartmann med Udkast til de fem første Scener af Thrymsqviden'
3.4.: 'Brev fra [F.] <u>Ahlgrensson</u>'
8.4.: 'Brev til <u>Ahlgrensson</u> om Decorationerne'
9.4.: 'Brev fra Theaterbestyrelsen om Antagelse af <u>Thrymsqviden</u> og Statens Tilskud foreløbig bevilget af Folkethinget!'
10.4.: 'Arbeidet med [L.] Gade og [A.] Fredstrup i Anledning af <u>Thrymsqviden</u> [...] Conference med Berner [...] arbeidet med Hartmann'
11.4.: 'Conference med Theatermaler [C. F.] Christensen angaaende Balletten og Ahlgrenssons Komme'
13.4.: 'Brev til <u>Ahlgrensson</u>'
15.4.: 'sendt afsted til <u>Gade</u> [...] Udkast til fem Figurer af <u>Thrymsqviden</u> nemlig <u>Loke</u>, <u>Thor</u>, <u>Freyr</u>, <u>Brage</u> og <u>Thrym</u>. – Brev fra <u>Ahlgrensson</u>'
19.4.: '<u>Brev fra Gade</u>'
20.4.: 'Brev fra <u>Ahlgrensson</u>'
27.4.: 'arbeidet med Hartmann, der satte mig Stevne til paa Fredensborg Mandagen d. 6.te Maj: -'

30.4.: 'arbeidet paa Musik-Programmet til <u>Thrymsqviden</u>'
3.5.: 'Skrevet'
4.5.: 'arbeidet paa Thrŷmsqviden'
5.5.: 'Brev fra <u>Hartmann</u>'
6.5.: 'Brev til Gade, Hartmann […] Reenskrevet to Akter af Thrŷms-qviden'
8.5.: 'Brev fra Gade'
9.5.: 'Brev fra Ahlgrensson'
10.5.: 'Arbeidet med <u>Hartmann</u>'
13.5.: 'spillet paa Hartmanns Musik, der er lidt vanskelig'
14.5. and 15.5.: 'skrevet og componeret'
16.5.: 'Brev til Gade'
18.5.: 'Telegram fra <u>Gade</u>, der melder <u>Ahlgrensson</u>'s Ankomst'
19.5.: 'Besøg af den svenske Theatermaler <u>Ahlgrensson</u> ledsaget af Gade. Kl 1. De spiste Middag hos os og tilbragte Aftenen. Augusta [Bournonville] spillede saa yndigt for os'
20.5.: 'Presenteret Ahlgrensson for Christensen og ladet ham see Theatret. Conference med Berner, arbeidet med Hartmann og spist der med Ahlgrensson'
21.5.: 'Arbeidet med Prof Christensen […] <u>Ahlgrensson</u> malet ÿpperlige Modeller til Balletten'
22.5.: 'Ahlgrensson flyttet op til mig i No. 9-10, og malet ÿpperlige Ting […] Udsøgt Materialer af Gammelt til Decorationerne af Thrymsqviden […] Middag hos Prof Christensen med <u>Ahlgrensson</u>, Gade og [G.] <u>Brodersen</u>'
23.5.: 'Brev til <u>Gade</u> og <u>H. P. Holst</u> […] Brev fra Christensen'
24.5.: 'Svar til <u>Christensen</u> […] componeret'
25.5.: 'Brev til Christensen med Besked om Tæpperne: $725 \pi - 1600$ [kvadrat] Alen, der ankom Kl 1. […] skrevet og componeret'
30.5.: 'fulgt <u>Ahlgrensson</u> ombord'
4.6.: 'Brev fra Ahlgrensson. Telegram tilbage'
5.6.: 'componeret'
6.6.: 'arbeidet paa Balletten […] Brev fra […] [E.] <u>Lehmann</u> med Tegninger til <u>Thrŷmsqviden</u>'
7.6.: 'Telegramsvar fra Ahlgrensson'
8.6.: '(Brev til Ahlgrensson) […] componeret'
9.6.: 'skrevet og componeret […] componeret'
10.6.: 'Modtaget Lehmann og arbeidet med ham'
11.6.: 'componeret'
15.6.: 'componeret, sendt Musik og Noter til Hartmann'
16.6.: 'Brev fra Ahlgrensson om Forretninger, som jeg strax med-delte Justitsraad <u>Berner</u>. Brev fra <u>Gade</u>'
17.6.: 'componeret […] Jeg skrev til Ahlgrensson om vore Affairer'
20.6.: 'Brev fra Justitsraad Berner med betÿdelig Skuffelse'
21.6.: 'Brev til <u>Berner</u> og til <u>Ahlgrensson</u> […] Brev fra […] Lehmann med Tegninger'
22.6.: 'Brev til <u>Lehmann</u> […] componeret'
25.6.: 'componeret'
26.6.: 'Brev fra Ahlgrensson […] skrevet og componeret'
27.6.: 'arbeidet med Hartmann, conference med <u>Berner</u>'
2.7.: 'modtaget Musik fra Hartmann […] Brev fra <u>Gade</u>'
3.7.: 'componeret […] Brev fra Prof. Christensen'
4.7.: 'componeret og noteret'
5.7.: 'besøgt […] Hartmann'
6.7.: 'stort Brev med Malernes – Overslag (Christensen)'
7.7.: 'skrevet og modificeret Overslag […] reenskrevet Overslaget og afsendt det med Brev til Berner'
8.7.: 'Skrevet og componeret den største Deel af Dagen, begÿndt 2.den Akt'
10.7.: 'componeret'
11.7.: 'arbeidet med Hartmann, Conference med Justitsr. Berner, Theatermalerne og Maskinmesteren'
14.7.: 'Brev til <u>Ahlgrensson</u>'
15.7.: 'Brev fra Prof Christensen'
16.7.: 'noteret Musik […] Brev og Tegninger fra <u>Lehmann</u>'
18.7.: 'arbeidet med Hartmann, mødt Ahlgrensson og [P. F.] Lind-ström, ankommen igaar Eftermiddags, Conference hos Intendanten [i.e. F. J. G. Berner] med Theatermalere og Maskinmester […] Forefundet Brev fra […] <u>Ahlgrensson</u>'
20.7.: 'componeret […] Brev fra Ahlgrensson'

22.7.: 'componeret'
24.7.: 'Brev fra Ahlgrensson om Hindringer og Besvær, talt med Hof-marskallen […] besørget adskilligt for Theatermalerne'
25.7.: 'været paa Atelieret paa Slottet, søgt for Ahlgrensson og bort-tryddet alle Hindringer'
26.7.: 'Conference med Berner […] Forgjæves hos Hartmann der var tilalters […] Brev fra Hartmann'
27.7.: 'Musik fra <u>Hartmann</u>'
29.7.: 'componeret paa Brudedandsen til <u>Thrymsqviden</u>'
30.7.: 'skrevet og componeret meget'
31.7.: 'skrevet og componeret […] fortsat min Choregraphie'
1.8.: 'talt med <u>Ahlgrénsson</u> og <u>H. P. Holst</u>, arbeidet med Hartmann'
2.8.: 'skrevet Choregraphie'
7.8.: '(Musik fra Hartmann.)'
8.8.: 'componeret'
9.8.: 'Jeg componerede og skrev meget'
10.8.: 'talt med Gade og Ahlgrensson, arbeidet med <u>Hartmann</u>, Con-ference med Berner'
12.8.: 'Brev til Gade […] reenskreet min Composition'
17.8.: 'talt med Gade og Brodersen, arbeidet med <u>Hartmann</u>, besøgt Ahlgrensson paa hans <u>Atelier</u>'
20.8.: 'Musik fra Hartmann, overværet Prøven paa Lindströms Mas-kine (Slangen til Thrymsqviden (Lokes Forvandling)'
22.8.: 'skrevet Brev til Hofmarschall [E. W. af] Edholm i Stockholm om <u>Lindström</u> og <u>Ahlgrensson</u>'
30.8.: 'arbeidet med Hartmann'
2.9.: 'talt med Theatermaler Christensen'
4.9.: 'Besøg paa Malersalen, arbeidet med Hartmann'
7.9.: 'componeret'
8.9.: 'Ahlgrensson og en anden Svensk Theatermaler Lindström hos os til Middag'
10.9.: 'skrevet og componeret'
11.9.: 'Modtaget Brev fra Berner om Udsættelse af Thrÿmskviden. Conference i den Anledning'
12.9.: '(Med Berner paa Ahlgrenssons Malersal) […] componeret'
13.9.: 'besøgt Malersalen […] Middag hos & arbeidet med Hart-mann'
14.9.: 'Besøg og Tractemente paa Ahlgrenssons Malersal'
15.9.: 'Farvel til Ahlgrensson'
16.9.: 'componeret'
17.9.: '1.ste Indstudering paa <u>Thrymsqviden</u> (Det var en god Begÿn-delse, der lover godt.)'
19.9.: '2.den Indstudering paa <u>Thrÿmsqviden</u> […] Costumeprøve i Theatret'
21.9.: '3.die Indstudering paa Thrymsqviden (Søstrenes Dands fær-dig)'
23.9.: 'Prøve Kl 11 paa Thrymsqviden (4' Indstudering)'
24.9.: 'skrevet og componeret. Prøve Kl $10^{1/2}$ (5.te Indstudering)'
25.9.: 'skrevet og componeret. Prøve (6.e Indstudering)'
26.9.: 'skrevet og componeret. <u>Repetition</u> paa Thrÿmsqviden. Møde med Hartmann […] componeret'
27.9.: 'arbeidet med Hartmann'
28.9.: 'Prøve og 7.e Indstudering paa Thrymsqviden (Hartmann, Berner og Fru [J.] Eckardt tilstede og meget henrykte)'
29.9.: 'skrevet og componeret'
30.9.: 'skrevet og componeret […] 8.de Indstudering paa <u>Thrÿms-qviden</u>'
1.10.: 'tidlig paa Theatret, componeret og stor Indstudering (9.de) […] componeret'
2.10.: 'componeret […] Prøve og 10.e Indstudering […] arbeidet med <u>Hartmann</u>'
3.10.: 'skrevet og componeret'
4.10.: 'Prøve og <u>11.e Indstudering</u>'
5.10.: 'Prøve og 12.e Indstudering […] Hele Aftenen hjemme, com-poneret'
6.10.: 'componeret'
7.10.: 'arbeidet med Lehmann paa Costumeringen. Prøve og (13.de Indstudering)'
8.10.: 'componeret og prøvet (14.e Indst.) <u>2.den Akt</u> færdig'
9.10.: 'componeret' […] hjem og componeret'

10.10.: 'Brev fra Ahlgrensson, componeret og holdt en lille [...] Indstudering paa <u>Thrymsqviden</u>'

11.10.: 'Skrevet og componeret. Prøve Kl 0 til 1½ og fuldendt Jettescenerne til 1.ste Akt, altsaa begge Akter færdige (15.de Indstudering). Skrevet en Erklæring i Anledning af Berners Spørgsmaal om Ballettens Udsættelse til næste Saison [...] componeret'

12.10.: 'Prøve og 16.e Indstudering 3.die Akt paabegÿndt [...] Aftenen hjemme for at componere'

13.10.: 'skrevet til Berner og Hartmann. Svar fra Theaterbestyrelsen og Bestemmelse om Thrÿmsqvidens Opførelse i <u>denne</u> Saison'

15.10.: 'componeret'

16.10.: 'Costumemøde hos [J. A.] Pätges. Prøve fra 10½ til 1/2. Viist de to förste Akter for Chefen og Intendanten til deres store Tilfredshed'

17.10.: 'Costumemøde [...] 17.e Indstudering paa Thrymsqviden'

18.10.: 'skrev og gik paa min Prøve <u>18.de Indstudering</u>'

19.10.: 'Prøve Kl 11 og 19.de Indstudering'

20.10.: '<u>Brev til Ahlgrensson</u> [...] skrevet og componeret'

21.10.: 'arrangeret, regleret Alfernes Dands til 3.e Akt af Thrymskviden'

22.10.: 'Repetition paa flere vigtige Steder i <u>Thrymsqviden</u>'

30.10.: 'Freÿas Indstudering til <u>Fru Eckardt</u>'

31.10.: 'Indstudering paa Freÿa'

1.11.: 'Prøve paa [...] <u>Thrÿmsqviden</u> med <u>Fru Eckardt</u>, fortræffelig! Brev fra Ahlgrensson [...] Indstudering til [G.] Döcker <u>EgÏr</u>'

4.11.: 'Arbeidet med Hartmann, der neppe bliver færdig til den bestemte Tid'

5.11.: 'Tidlig paa Theatret for at arrangere om Reqvisiter til Thrymskviden. Prøve paa samme Ballet med <u>Fru Eckardt</u> og <u>Döcker</u>'

6.11.: 'lille Prøve med <u>W. Holst</u> og <u>Döcker</u>'

7.11.: 'Paa Theatret componeret og indstuderet Skjolddandsen (20.e Indstudering) [...] seet til Hartmann'

8.11.: 'Tidlig paa Theatret, confereret med Fÿrværkeren og Theatermaleren. Stor Repetition paa Thrÿmsqviden. De tre første Akter fuldt færdige'

9.11.: 'skrevet og componeret. Ingen Prøve men Choregrapheret de første Scener af 4.e Akt'

10.11.: 'Brev til Ahlgrensson'

11.11.: 'Prøve Kl 10 paa <u>Thrÿmsqviden</u> 21.e Indstudering (4.e Akt) [...] Hørt <u>H P Holst</u> læse sit Forspil til min Ballet <u>Nornerne</u> som jeg fandt udmærket skrevet og poetisk [...] componeret'

12.11.: 'Prøve paa Thrymsqviden (22.e Indstudering 4.e Akt)'

15.11.: 'skrevet paa Maskinreglement for Thrÿmsqviden'

16.11.: 'Prøve paa Thrÿmsqviden (Repetition) [...] arbeidet med <u>Hartmann</u> [...] Brev fra <u>Ahlgrensson</u> der gav mig meget at tænke paa'

17.11.: 'talt med Snedker Nielsen om Balletten'

18.11.: 'Componeret en stor Scene til 4.e Akt. Conference med Justitsraad <u>Berner</u>, componeret endvidere til 4.e Akt'

19.11.: 'tidlig paa Theatret, Prøve paa 4.e Akt af Thrymsqviden (23.e Indstudering)'

21.11.: 'Prøve paa Thrÿmsqviden <u>4.e Akt</u>'

22.11.: 'Brev til <u>Ahlgrensson</u>'

23.11.: 'Prøve paa <u>Thrÿmsqviden</u> (Bestyrelsen tilstede og henrÿkt over det Præsterede)'

25.11.: 'skrevet paa Fortalen til Thrÿmsqviden, arbeidet med <u>Hartmann</u>'

27.11.: 'Theaterprøve paa 1.ste Akt af Thrÿmsqviden [...] skrevet paa mit Balletprogram'

28.11.: 'Prøve paa adskillige Dandse'

1.12.: 'reenskrevet paa mit Program'

2.12.: 'Lille Prøve med Ildaanderne og <u>Betty Schnell</u> [...] fuldendt Reenskrivningen af mit Program'

3.12.: 'Prøve med Ildaanderne'

4.12.: 'Prøve paa Dandsene til Thrymsqviden [...] arbeidet med Hartmann'

5.12.: 'Prøve paa alle fire Akter af Thrymsqviden. Helene og Charlotte [Bournonville] vare tilstede og særdeles fornöiede'

6.12.: 'Optegnelse af Theaterforretninger'

7.12.: 'Prøve med Maskiner paa 1.ste Akt af Thrymsqviden, besørget et Par Costumer'

11.12.: 'Jeg tager til Fredensborg for at blive der indtil Musiken er færdig for da at sætte Balletten i Scene'

12.12.: 'componeret til Gimle=Scenen og skrevet til Hartmann med Sendelse af Musiken'

13.12.: '<u>Brev til Ahlgrensson</u>'

14.12.: 'Brev og Lister til <u>Gade</u>'

20.12.: 'Brev fra Gade'

26.12.: 'modtaget <u>Gade</u>, der bragte mig Brev og Correctur fra H P Holst'

27.12.: 'skrevet Svar med Correcturen til Holst'

3.1.1868: '<u>Brev fra Gade</u>'

6.1.: 'Brev fra <u>Gade</u> og Svar til ham og Hartmann'

8.1.: 'mødt Gade [..] Prøve paa Theatret særdeles tilfredstillende, besøgt H P Holst [...] Møde med Hartmann [...] Prøve med Maskiner og den elektriske Sol – strålende Resultat!'

9.1.: 'Brev til <u>Hartmann</u> og <u>Gade</u>'

12.1.: 'skrevet til <u>Ahlgrensson</u>'

17.1.: 'Brev fra Gade og Svar tilbage'

21.1.: 'skrevet og componeret'

22.1.: 'componeret'

24.1.: '<u>Svar</u> paa et <u>Brev fra Gade</u> modtaget igaar Morges'

28.1.: 'Prøve paa hele Balletten fra 11 til 1. Statistprøve paa Skjolddandsen 1½ – 3 [...] Indstudering med [J. F. S.] <u>Dorph-Petersen</u> Kl 5–5½'

29.1.: 'Telegram til Ahlgrensson. Prøve og 23.e Indstudering paa Thrÿmsqviden (Gimle). Prøve paa Skjolddandsen med Statister [...] Besøg hos Hartmann og paa Malersalen, Eftermiddagsprøve Kl 6 med Dorph-Petersen og Costumeprøve Kl 8.'

31.1.: 'Theaterprøve paa Gimle [...] Behageligt Telegram fra Ahlgrensson'

1.2.: 'paa Theatret Prøve paa 3.die Akt af Balletten, der gik udmærket smukt'

2.2.: 'besøgt [...] Hartmann'

4.2.: ' 'Prøve med doubleringer og Dandse [...] prøvet Costume'

5.2.: 'Prøve paa Gimle og Indstudering med Jetterne. Ahlgrensson og Lindström ankomne <u>Gade</u> sÿg! [...] arbeidet med <u>Ahlg.</u> og Lindström, besørget adskilligt for dem'

6.2.: 'besøgt Gade flere Gange. Bedring. <u>Doublering</u> paa Theatret arrangeret Nornerne, besørget adskilligt for mine Svenske'

7.2.: 'Prøve paa 1.ste Akt og derpaa stor Musikprøve paa <u>1 og 2.den Akt</u>. Middag hos <u>Gade</u>, der endnu var Patient. Costumeprøve paa Theatret, endeel Besvær med Opstillingen [A. P.] <u>Wedén</u> særdeles brav'

8.2.: 'Tidlig paa Theatret, hvor jeg prøvede Grupperingerne til 2.den Akt, derpaa Doubleringen og endelig Indstudering med <u>Joh. Wiehe</u> [...] besørget adskilligt paa Theatret, hvor Ahl: og L: arbeidede hele Natten'

9.2.: 'forberedt en Frokost, som jeg gav til de tre Svenske [...] Vi havde det fiint og behageligt [...] Indstudering med <u>Joh Wiehe</u>'

10.2.: 'stor Prøve paa 1.ste 3.die Akt og <u>Gimle</u> med Orchester. Alt gik udmærket [...] Indstudering med <u>Joh. Wiehe</u>'

11.2.: 'tidlig paa Theatret, prøvet med <u>Nornerne</u> og indstuderet Rollen færdig med Joh Wiehe [...] besørget adskilligt Balletten angaaende [...] Musikprøve paa 4.de Akt efter Theatret – hjem Kl 11½'

12.2.: 'Paa Theatret Arrangement paa 4.e Akt [...] Prøve med den elektriske Sol'

13.2.: 'prøvet <u>Nornerne</u> [...] Costumeprøve'

14.2.: 'Tidlig paa Theatret, prøvet Nornerne og 3 Akter af Thrymsqviden – meget tilfredsstillende – fra 11. – 3.'

15.2.: 'Prøve paa 4.de Akt først med Repetiteur og derpaa med Orchester, prøvet <u>Nornerne</u>'

16.2.: 'holdt Decorationsprøve [...] Costumeprøve'

17.2.: 'tidlig paa Theatret. Prøve paa de tre første Akter af Balletten [...] Costümeprøve [...] Prøve paa Decorationerne og Solen til Gimle'

18.2.: 'Modtaget Programmer til Balletten og 70.r i Honorar, hvoraf det Halve tilfaldt Holst. Ingen Prøve men Forberedelser til imorgen. Dog gjennemgik vi 4.de Akt med sammenstyrtningen ÿpperlig. Sendt Programmer til De Kongelige og Honoratiores [...] Forært Fru Eckardt et Armbaand i Anledning af hendes Freÿa'

19.2.: 'Frokost hos Hartmann. Prøve paa forskjellige Smaating […] stor Generalprøve i Costume og med alle Decorationer. De tre første Akter og Thrÿms Hall gik ypperligt men den midterste Deel af 4.e Akt gik lidt hulter til bulter og trænger til en yderligere Prøve. Det Hele vil nok tage sig ud!'
20.2.: 'Prøve paa flere Momenter i 4.e Akt […] Efter Theatret en vigtig Decorations og Belysningsprøve der varede til Kl 2 og gav et fortrinligt Resultat'
21.2.: 'Alting klart til Balletten […] om Aftenen 1.ste Forestilling af Thrÿmsqviden der gik for udsolgt Huus til forhøiede og fordoblede Priser. Udførelsen var i enhver Henseende mønsterværdig og Bifaldet storartet. Scenen var fuldkommen med Hjerte opfyldt af Taknemlighed mod den Almægtige, der har styrket og opholdt mig til dette Værks lykkelige Fuldførelse. Ahlgrensson bevertede Maskinfolkene. Jeg drak The hos [H. S.] Paulli, hvor Helene var og havde stor Glæde af hendes yndige Deltagelse'
25.2.: 'læst Anmeldelse om Balletten i Folkets Avis, særdeles behagelig i Modsætning til Fædrelandet og Dagstelegrafen, der skulle være meget ublide – men som jeg ikke agter at læse'.

For the first performance of *The Lay of Thrym* in the following season (13.9.1868) Bournonville seems to have made some minor adjustments in the choreography, or he may have renotated it for this occasion. This is clear from notes in his diary reading:

17.7.1868: 'choregrapheret paa Thrÿmsqvidens Partie'
24.7.: 'skrevet til Copist [C. J.] Hansen, skrevet Choregraphie'
25.7.: 'fuldendt min Choregraphie'.

The 1868 production received 32 performances (the last given on 1.5.1869) and the ballet reached a total of 43 performances during Bournonville's lifetime, the last of which took place on 22.5.1874.

Autograph sources:

Manuscript scenario. Ms. Autograph. Brown ink. 1 vol. 23 pp. (22,8 × 18,2 cm)
Thrÿmsqviden./eller/Ragnaroksmÿthen i Billeder./Ballet i 4 Akter af Aug: Bournonville/1867./
Signed and dated: 'Fredensborg den 10.de Januar 1867.' [Written according to the diary between 5.1. and 10.1.1867]
[DKKk; NKS 4183 4°

Manuscript scenario. Ms. Autograph. Brown ink. 1 vol. 29 pp. (22,8 × 17,9 cm)
Thrÿmsqviden./eller/Ragnaroks = Mÿthen i Billeder./Ballet i 4 Akter af A. Bournonville/1867./Første Original=/Manuscript.
Signed and dated: 'Fredensborg den 10.de Januar 1867./[…]/Fredensborg den 15.de Januar 1867.'
[DKKk; NKS 3285 4° 3 R–U

Musical instruction. Ms. Autograph. Brown ink. 4 pp. (21,8 × 13,9 cm)
[Act I:] 6.te Scene/[…]/7.de Scene/[…]/8.de Scene (Finale)/[…]/9.de Scene
Unsigned and dated: 'd. 3.e Maj 1867.' [Written according to the diary between 30.4. and 3.5.1867]
[DKKk; NKS 4183 4°

Musical instruction. Ms. Autograph. Brown ink. 2 pp. (17,9 × 11,5 cm)
2.den Akt (Thrÿmsqviden.)/1.ste Scene./[…]/2.den scène/[…]/3.die Scene/[…]/4.de Scene [incomplete]
Unsigned and undated [Written according to the diary between 30.4. and 15.6.1867]
[DKKk; NKS 4183 4°

Musical instruction. Ms. Autograph. Brown ink. 1 p. (20,9 × 13,6 cm)
Udkast til Brudedandsen/i/2.den Akts 3.die Scene.
Unsigned and undated [Written according to the diary between 30.4. and 15.6.1867]
[DKKk; NKS 4183 4°

Musical instruction. Ms. Autograph. Black ink. 1 p. (20,8 × 13,5 cm)
[Act II:] 4.de Scene. (Finale)
Unsigned and undated [Written according to the diary between 30.4. and 15.6.1867]
[DKKk; NKS 4183 4°

Manuscript mise-en-scène (incomplete). Ms. Autograph. Ink. 2 pp. (format unknown)
Acte 2.me Scène 1.ier (Allegretto)/[…]/Scène 2.me (Allegro Agitato)/[…]/Scène 3.me
Unsigned and undated [Written according to the diary most probably on 8.7.1867]
[USNYp; Dance Collection, call nos. *ZBD-71 (microfilm), and (S)*MGZMD 30 (photostat copy)

Musical instruction. Ms. Autograph. Brown ink. 4 pp. (20,9 × 13,5 cm)
Tredie Akt.
Unsigned and dated: 'd. 1.e August 1867.'
[DKKk; NKS 4183 4°

Production note (included in a letter to F. Ahlgrensson). Ms. Autograph. Brown ink. 2 pp. (20,9 × 13,4 cm)
[…]Thrÿmsqviden/[…]/Erindring [om] de gjenstande, der endnu fattes til Completteringen af den Deel, som De har overtaget. […]
Signed and dated: 'Kjöbenhavn den 13.e September/1867.'
[SSk; Robert Haglunds Autografsaml.

Musical instruction (included in a letter to I. P. E. Hartmann). Ms. Autograph. Brown ink. 4 pp. (20,9 × 13,5 cm)
[…] Musiken til 4.de Akt. […]
Signed and dated: 'Kjöbenhavn den 13.e October 1867'
[DKKk; NKS 4183 4°

Production note. Ms. Autograph (partially in another's hand). Black ink. 1 p. (22,8 × 18,3 cm)
Alfer.
Unsigned and undated [Written according to the diary on 21.10.1867]
[DKKkt; F.M. (Ballet)

Production note. Ms. Autograph. Brown ink. 3 pp. (21,3 × 14 cm)
Plan til Maskineriet/i/Balletten Thrymskviden'
Unsigned and undated [Writen according to the diary on 15.11.1867]
[Private collection (Copenhagen)
This note indicates the stage machinery needed for all four acts of *The Lay of Thrym.*

Production note. Ms. Autograph. Brown ink. 2 pp. (21,4 × 13,4 cm)
Thrymskviden./4.de Akt. (3.die 4.e og 5.te Scene.)/[…]/6.te Scene. (Ragnarok.)/Ahlgrensson./[…]/Den sidste Kamp:/[…]/1.ste Tableau./[…]/2.det Tableau/[…]/3.die Tableau/[…]/(Christensen.)
Unsigned and undated [Written according to the diary between 9.11. and 21.11.1867]
[DKKk; NKS 3285 4° 2 R–U

Musical instruction (included in a letter to I. P. E. Hartmann). Ms. Autograph. Black ink. 1 p. (22,6 × 17,9 cm)
[…] jeg tager mig den Frihed af foreslaae/følgende Modification:/Pag 7. i 6/4 Takt: Beder jeg [word erased] sættes paa dette Sted en Tone høiere […]
Signed and dated: ' d. 21.e Novbr 1867'
[DKKk; NKS 4183 4°
This note includes Bournonville's suggestions to Hartmann about

some minor musical changes in the composer's first draft for *The Lay of Thrym* (Act IV, score no. 34, p. 25). Hartmann's corrections are included on p. 30 in the same drafts together with his pencilled autographed note to Bournonville reading: 'Jeg haaber, det er saaledes,/ De mener./Deres ærb./I.P.E. Hartmann'. However, in the definitive répétiteur's copy for *The Lay of Thrym* (p. 124) these changes are not included.

Manuscript scenario. Ms Autograph. Brown ink. 4 pp. (22,5 × 18 cm)
<u>Forord.</u>
Unsigned and undated [Written according to the diary on 25.11. 1867]
[DKKk; NKS 3285 4° 2 R–U

Manuscript mise-en-scène. Ms. Autograph. Brown ink and pencil. 3 pp. (20,6 × 16,7 cm)
<u>Thrymsqviden</u>/(Slutnings=Tableau)/<u>Noter efter Repétiteur-Partiet.</u>
Unsigned and undated [Written according to the diary on 12.12. 1868]
[Private collection (Copenhagen)
This manuscript mise-en-scène contains Bournonville's pencilled autographed drawings and stage diagrams which describe the scene in *Gimle*. It is divided into eight numbered sections, each of which refers to similar numbers written underneath the music in the répétiteur's copy. The manuscript ends with a description of an (unnumbered) tableau, named '<u>Slutnings-Gruppe</u>'.

Production note. Ms. autograph. Brown ink. 4 pp. (20,6 × 16,7 cm)
Personale og Costumer/til./<u>Slutningstableauet i Thrymsqviden.</u>
Signed and dated: 'Fredensborg d. 14.e Decbr 1867'
[Private collection (Copenhagen)
This note indicates the total number of persons needed for the final scene (named 'Gimle') counting 'Summa <u>81 Personer</u>'.

Production note. Ms. Autograph (partially in another's hand). Black ink. 1 p. (34 × 21 cm)
<u>Personerne</u>
Unsigned and undated [Written according to the diary most probably on 14.12.1867]
[DKKkt; F.M. (Ballet)

Production note. Ms. Autograph. Black ink. 1 p. (34 × 21 cm)
<u>Thrymskviden.</u>/Belysning for Herr Ahlgrenssons Decoration/<u>2.den Akt Egïrs Borg.</u>
Unsigned and undated [1867–1868]
[DKKkt; F.M. (Ballet)

Musical sources:

Musical draft. Ms. Autograph (by I. P.E. Hartmann). Brown ink and pencil. 4 pp. (34,5 × 26 cm)
[Untitled]
Unsigned and undated [Written according to Bournonville's diary most probably in the period between 30.4. and 29.7.1867]
[DKKk; I. P. E. Hartmanns samling, kapsel 'Voksende Samling I, Ms' (1944–45.56)
This manuscript fragment contains Hartmann's first draft (for piano) of the music for what at the première of *The Lay of Thrym* became the divertissement in Act II (scene 4, score nos. 21–22), also entitled *The Bridal Dance (Brudedandsen)*. The manuscript was originally Hartmann's private property, but was donated to DKKk on 15.3.1944 by the singing teacher, P. Winding (a relative of Hartmann's pupil, the composer, A. Winding).

Musical draft. Ms. Autograph (by I. P.E. Hartmann). Black ink. 36 pp. of which four are blank (35,5 × 26,3 cm with several variants)
[Untitled]
Unsigned and undated [Written according to Bournonville's diary most probably in the period between 30.4. and 8.10.1867]

[DKKk; I. P. E. Hartmanns samling, kapsel 'Sulamith – Thrymsqviden'
These five manuscript fragments contain Hartmann's first drafts (for two violins) of the music for what at the première of *The Lay of Thrym* became: (1) Act II, score nos. 15–17, (2) Act IV, score no. 31 (scene 2), (3) Act IV, score nos. 31–32, (4) Act IV, score nos. 32–34, and (5) Act IV, score no. 36 (entitled 'Gimle./(Slutningscene)'). The fragments also contain numerous autographed notes and choreographic numbers by Bournonville (written with brown ink and pencil). They describe his early indications about the ballet's dramatic action and mime, also including his wishes for several minor musical changes. Thus, a pencilled autographed note by Hartmann to Bournonville (on p. 30) reads: 'Jeg haaber, det er saaledes,/ De mener./Deres ærb./IPE Hartmann'. It refers to Bournonville's wish for a minor musical change in Act IV (score no. 34) as indicated in his letter to Hartmann, dated 'd. 21.e Novbr 1867'.

Musical draft. Ms. Autograph (by I. P.E. Hartmann). Black ink. 4 pp. of which one is blank (34,5 × 26 cm)
Gimle/Moderato
Unsigned and undated [Written according to Bournonville's diary most probably in the period between 9.11. and 12.12.1867]
[DKKk; MA ms 2705 (KTB 299)
This manuscript fragment contains Hartmann's first draft (for piano) of the music for what at the première of *The Lay of Thrym* became the final tableau in Act IV, score no. 36 (also named 'Gimle').

Orchestral score. Ms. Autograph (by I. P. E. Hartmann). Black ink. 2 vol. Act I–II 302 pp. of which six are blank. Act III–IV 198 pp. of which six are blank (34,2 × 29 cm)
Indledningsmusik/til/'Nornerne',/Forspil til Balletten 'Thrymsqviden'/[…]/Thrymsqviden./1.ste Act/[…]/Thrymsqviden./3.die Act.
Signed and dated (vol. I, p. '9'): 'I:P:E: Hartmann/15/2 68.', (vol. II, p. '494') 'I:P:E: Hartmann/28 Jan. 1868.'
[DKKk; C II, 114 (KTB 299) (1907–8, Nr. 265)
This autographed orchestral score contains Hartmann's introductory music (57 bars in 3/4 time) for the recited prologue by H. P. Holst, entitled *The Norns*, and the complete music for *The Lay of Thrym*. Pencilled notes in vol. I (p. '9') indicate the duration of the introductory music for *The Norns* to $2\frac{1}{2}$ minutes. Similar notes in vol. II (pp. '442' and '460') indicate the duration of score no. 33 in Act IV (the so-called 'Mellemspil') to between $1\frac{1}{2}$ and 2 minutes, while score no. 34 in the same act is described as to play for $2\frac{1}{2}$ minutes. The score was employed for all performances of *The Lay of Thrym* until H. Beck's revised restaging of it on 13.1.1901. For that production a completely new score was made (now in DKKk, call no. C II, 114) while Hartmann's autographed score was transferred to DKKk the same year.

Orchestral score (*The Norns*). Ms. Autograph (by I. P. E. Hartmann). Brown ink. 1 vol. 18 pp. of which one is blank (34,5 × 29,6 cm)
763/Nornerne/Partitur/763/[…]/'Nornerne', Forspil til Balletten /'Thrymsqviden'
Unsigned and undated [1868]
[DKKk; C II, 114 (KTA 763)
This autographed orchestral score contains Hartmann's complete music for the recited prologue, entitled *The Norns*, except for the introductory music, which is included only in the previous orchestral score for *The Lay of Thrym* (vol. I).

Répétiteur's copy. Ms. Copy. Black ink. 1 vol. 134 pp. of which three are blank (33x 25,6 cm with minor variants)
B. 299/3/[…]/187 b./Repetiteurparti/til Balletten/<u>Thrymsqviden.</u>/af,/Aug: Bournonville./<u>1867</u>./K.S./ventre Side af Scenen/ D.S.(højre Side.
Unsigned and dated (on p. 1): '<u>1867</u>.'
[DKKk; MA ms 2996 (KTB 299)
This répétiteur's copy contains Bournonville's autographed notes (written with brown ink) which describe the complete dramatic action, the mime, several stage diagrams, and most of the choreogra-

phy for *The Lay of Thrym*. Moreover, his autographed choreographic numbers (also written with brown ink) are included for the entire ballet. They seem to refer to his later (not yet traced) complete notation of this work, perhaps written in preparation for his restaging of it on 17.9.1871. This theory is supported by the fact that some of the choreographic numbers included for the so-called *Bridal Dance (Brudedandsen)* in Act II, score nos. 21 and 22 (pp. 59 and 64–65) clearly refer to similar numbers in Bournonville's notation of his revised choreography for the two brief solo variations in this divertissement performed by the character *Sigyn*. According to his diary these notes were most likely written between 22.7. and 13.8.1871. They are now in SSm (call no. Daniel Fryklunds samling no. 148).

No répétiteur's copy for Hartmann's and H. P. Holst's recited prologue *The Norns* has yet been traced.

Parts (*The Lay of Thrym*). Ms. Copy. 37 vol.
4 vl I, 4 vl II, 2 vla, 4 vlc e cb, fl 1/2, ob 1/2, cl 1/2, fag 1/2, cor 1/2/ 3/4, tr 1/2/3, trb 1/2, tuba, timp, gr cassa, piatti, tri, arpa.
Unsigned and undated [1868]
[DKKk; KTB 299

Parts (*The Norns*, incomplete). Ms. Copy. 10 vol.
vl I, vl II, vla, vlc e cb, fl, trb 1/2, tuba, arpa, org. 45 vocal parts.
Unsigned and undated [1868]
[DKKk; KTA 763

Other sources:

Sketch by C. F. Christensen for the back curtain of Act III. Pencil (30 × 45,1 cm)
21 Alen/Thrymsqviden.
Unsigned and undated [1868]
[DKKt; C. F. Christensens dekorationsudkast

Costume drawing by E. Lehmann. Pencil and water colours (12 × 20 cm)
Thrym./Gade/Bruun Tunik/Gade.
Unsigned and undated [c.1868]
[SSm; Daniel Fryklunds samling no. 277 (F 1333 d)
This drawing shows the costume worn by *Thrym* in Acts I and IV of *The Lay of Thrym* (performed by L. Gade). A pencilled note on the reverse reads: 'Ørenringe 1½' '.

Costume drawing by E. Lehmann. Pencil and water colours (20,1 × 11,7 cm)
Loke/[...]/Scharff
Unsigned and undated [c.1868]
[DKKkt; Kostumetegninger (Lehmann)
This drawing shows the costume worn by *Asa-Loke* in *The Lay of Thrym* (performed by H. Scharff).

Costume drawing by E. Lehmann. Pencil and water colours (12 × 18 cm)
Vola 'Thrymskviden'/Jfr. P. Fredstrup.
Unsigned and undated [c.1868]
[SSm; Daniel Fryklunds samling no. 278 (F 1333 d)
This drawing shows the costume worn by *Vola* in Acts I and IV of *The Lay of Thrym* (performed by P. Fredstrup).

Costume drawing by E. Lehmann. Pencil and water colours (19,8 × 12,1 cm)
De 5 Søstre (A. Synet)
Unsigned and undated [c.1868]
[DKKkt; Kostumetegninger (Lehmann)
This drawing shows the costume worn by the five young foster daughters of the prophetess *Vola* who perform the allegorical *Dance of the five senses* in the second scene of Act I (score no. 2) in *The Lay of Thrym*. The drawing shows the dancer who symbolised sight.

Costume drawing by E. Lehmann. Pencil and water colours (12 × 20 cm)
Thor./Thrymskviden/W. Price.
Unsigned and undated [c.1868]
[SSm; Daniel Fryklunds samling no. 274 (F 1333 b)
This drawing shows the costume worn by *Thor* in *The Lay of Thrym* (performed by W. Price).

Drawing of accessories by E. Lehmann. Pencil and water colours (24,1 × 17,7 cm)
[Untitled]
Unsigned and undated [c.1868]
[DKKkt; Kostumetegninger (Lehmann)
This drawing shows the hammer of *Thor* in *The Lay of Thrym*.

Costume drawing by E. Lehmann. Pencil and water colours (19,7 × 11,9 cm)
Freŷr.
Unsigned and undated [c.1868]
[DKKkt; Kostumetegninger (Lehmann)
This drawing shows the costume worn by *Freir* in *The Lay of Thrym* (performed by D. Krum).

Costume drawing by E. Lehmann. Pencil and water colours (20,5 × 12,3 cm)
Gerda/[...]/Jfr. Petersen
Unsigned and undated [c.1868]
[DKKkt; Kostumetegninger (Lehmann)
This drawing shows the costume worn by *Gerda* in *The Lay of Thrym* (performed by J. Petersen).

Costume drawing by E. Lehmann. Pencil and water colours (20,6 × 12,5 cm)
Ildaander
Unsigned and undated [c.1868]
[DKKkt; Kostumetegninger (Lehmann)
This drawing most probably shows the costume worn by the two fire spirits *Thjasse* and *Finn* in Acts I and IV of *The Lay of Thrym* (performed by E. Stramboe and F. Hoppensach respectively).

Costume drawing by E. Lehmann. Pencil and water colours (20 × 11,6 cm)
Odin./[...]/Holst
Unsigned and undated [c.1868]
[DKKkt; Kostumetegninger (Lehmann)
This drawing shows the costume worn by *Odin* in Acts II and III of *The Lay of Thrym* (performed by the actor W. C. Holst).

Costume drawing by E. Lehmann. Pencil and water colours (20,2 × 12 cm)
Thyr./[...]/Brodersen.
Unsigned and undated [c.1868]
[DKKkt; Kostumetegninger (Lehmann)
This drawing shows the costume worn by *Tyr* in Act II and IV of *The Lay of Thrym* (performed by G. Brodersen).

Costume drawing by E. Lehmann. Pencil and water colours (19,7 × 11,8 cm)
Brage
Unsigned and undated [c.1868]
[DKKkt; Kostumetegninger (Lehmann)
This drawing shows the costume worn by *Brage* in Act II of *The Lay of Thrym* (performed by L. Ring).

Costume drawing by E. Lehmann. Pencil and water colours (20,5 × 12 cm)
Egir./[...]/Döcker
Unsigned and undated [c.1868]
[DKKkt; Kostumetegninger (Lehmann)
This drawing shows the costume of *Ægir* in Act II of *The Lay of Thrym* (performed by the singer G. Döcker).

Costume drawing by E. Lehmann. Pencil and water colours (12 × 19 cm)
Thor. (Forklædning).
Unsigned and undated [c.1868]
[SSm; Daniel Fryklunds samling no. 275 (F 1333 c)]
This drawing shows the costume worn by *Thor* disguised as the bride of *Thrym* in Act IV, scene 2 (score no. 31) of *The Lay of Thrym* (performed by W. Price).

Drawing of accessories by E. Lehmann. Pencil and water colours (18,7 × 24 cm)
[Untitled]
Unsigned and undated [c.1868]
[DKKkt; Kostumetegninger (Lehmann)]
This drawing shows the diadem worn by *Thor* in the travesty scene in Act IV of *The Lay of Thrym* (scene 2, score no. 31).

Drawing of accessories by E. Lehmann. Pencil and water colours (18,6 × 24 cm)
[Untitled]
Unsigned and undated [c.1868]
[DKKkt; Kostumetegninger (Lehmann)]
This drawing shows the belt worn by *Thor* in the travesty scene in Act IV of *The Lay of Thrym* (scene 2, score no. 31).

Costume drawing by E. Lehmann. Pencil and water colours (12 × 19 cm)
Loke. (Forklædning)./Thrymskviden.
Unsigned and undated [c.1868]
[SSm; Daniel Fryklunds samling no. 276 (F 1333 a)]
This drawing shows the costume worn by *Asa-Loke* disguised as the bridesmaid of the bride of *Thrym* in Act IV, scene 2 (score no. 31) of *The Lay of Thrym* (performed by W. Scharff).

Costume drawing by E. Lehmann. Pencil and water colours (19,7 × 12 cm)
Baldur. […]/Dorft Petersen
Unsigned and undated [c.1868]
[DKKkt; Kostumetegninger (Lehmann)]
This drawing shows the costume worn by *Baldur* in the final tableau of *The Lay of Thrym* (performed by J. F. S. Dorph-Petersen).

Printed sources:

Printed scenario. 1 vol. 48 pp.
Thrymsqviden,/Ballet i 4 Akter/af/Aug. Bournonville./Med et Forspil:/Nornerne/af/H. P. Holst.
Kjøbenhavn, J. H. Schubothe/Græbes Bogtrykkeri [1868]
[DKKk; 17, – 175 8°]
This scenario, by far the most extensive of all Bournonville scenarios, contains his extensive foreword, the complete text for H. P. Holst's recited prologue *The Norns*, and a complete description of the ballet's action. A second edition containing a slightly different title page was published in 1868 by J. H. Schubothe/Bianco Luno/F. S. Muhle. It is now in DKKk (call no. 17, – 175 8°).

23.8.1868
Seguedilla, Changing Dance in Spanish style (Vexeldands i spansk Stil) (the Court Theatre).
In the summer of 1868 Bournonville gave 36 dance and mime lessons at his private residence in Fredensborg to the dancers, B. Schnell and A. Scholl. As a result of their rapid progress during this period he decided also to choreograph a Spanish national dance for them. According to his diary he originally planned to have the music for it written by H. C. Lumbye, but this project was for unknown reasons abandoned, and the score was finally composed and arranged by H. S. Paulli.

The 1868 *Seguedilla* was performed for the first time as a separate divertissement at a special charity performance at the Court Theatre. Bournonville did not attend this performance, but on 1.9.1868 he restaged the dance at Copenhagen's Royal Theatre as part of the opening performance of the 1868–69 season. In his diary he noted about the dance and its reported première at the Court Theatre:

6.7.1868: 'Brev til [H. H.] Nyegaard om Fru [A.] Scholls Benefice'
14.7.1868: '17.de Lection i Dands, begÿndt en spansk Pas de deux […] Brev til [H. C.] Lumbÿ[e]'
18.7.: 'Brev med […] Undskyldning fra Lumbÿ[e]'
21.7.: 'Spadseret med [H. S.] Paullis'
22.7.: 'Paulli paatager sig at componere Musiken til en lille spansk Dands'
24.7.: 'Jeg arrangerede den spanske Dands efter Paullis Musik'
25.7.: '24.de Lection og indstuderet den spanske Dands'
8.8.: 'Bev fra [G.] Brodersen og Fru Scholl Alt om Aftenunderholdningen. Brev til Overhofmarschalen [i.e. Løvenskjold] i samme Anledning'
9.8.: 'Brev til […] Fru Scholl med Musiken til Seguidilla'en'
13.8.: 'skrevet Invitationer og Cataloger'
14..8.: 'forstsat Inventariet'
16.8: 'expederet 6 Breve med Programmer til Broberg, Holmblad, [M.] Salomonsen, Fru [H. S.] Paulli, [M. H. or A.] Bing og Suhr'
18.8.: 'været paa Brodersens Skole og seet Pigebørnene Prøve og Dandse fortræffeligt […] modtaget 10.r fra Bing til Scholls Aftenunderholdning'
19.8.: 'skrevet til Fru Consulinde [E.] Hage for Scholl […] sendt Bings 10.r ned til Brodersen'
23.8.: 'Brev fra Brodersen om Gaarsforestillingens heldige Udfald'
24.8.: 'Brev fra Fru Scholl med Taksigelse'.

No musical sources dating from the first and only performance of this dance at the Court Theatre have yet been traced. However, a complete set of musical material dating from its later première at the Royal Theatre is now in DKKk (*see* the following entry).

1.9.1868
Seguedilla, Changing Dance in Spanish style (Vexeldands i spansk Stil).
This performance represents the first time Bournonville's 1868 *Seguedilla* (*see* 23.8.1868) was performed at Copenhagen's Royal Theatre. He attended only the third performance of this dance on 16.9.1868 and noted about it in his diary on the same day:

'jeg skyndte mig hen at see Seguidilla'en, der gik meget smukt og med meget Bifald'.

The *Seguedilla* received 12 performances at Copenhagen's Royal Theatre during Bournonville's lifetime, the last of which was given on 21.12.1869.

Musical sources:

Orchestral score. Ms. Autograph (by H. S. Paulli). Brown ink. 18 pp. of which one is blank (29,8 × 35,8 cm with minor variants)
B. 250/Tempo di Bolero.
Unsigned and undated [Written according to Bournonville's diary during the summer of 1868]
[DKKk; MA ms 2607 (KTB 250)]

Répétiteur's copy. Ms. Copy. Brown ink. 1 vol. 4 pp. (34 × 25,5 cm)
B. 250 Seguidilla / […] /B. 250 /Repetieurparti / til / Seguidilla (Paulli)

Unsigned and undated [1868]
[DKKk; MA ms 2905 (1) (KTB 250)
This répétiteur's copy is included on pp. 1–4 in a volume that also contains the répétiteur's copies for two other dances by F. Hoppe and Bournonville respectively (premièred at Copenhagen's Royal Theatre in 1868 and 1866).

Parts. Ms. Copy. 22 vol.
2 vl I, 2 vl II, vla, 2 vlc e cb, fl 1/2, ob 1/2, cl 1/2, fag 1/2, cor 1/2, cnt 1/2, trb, timp, tri.
Unsigned and undated [1868]
[DKKk; KTB 250

4.9.1868
La Dame blanche (Den hvide Dame).
For the 1868 Copenhagen restaging of F.-A. Boyeldieu's three-act comic opera (*see* 1.10.1850) Bournonville gave personal stage instructions to the singer, H. E. Christophersen, who this year performed the rôle of *Georg* for the first time. In his diary he noted about the production, which represents the last but one time he was involved in a staging of this opera:

28.8.1868: 'Brev fra [L.] Gade, der bebudede mig Sangeren [H. E.] Christoffersens Komme Kl 9½ for at gjennemgaae sin Rolle i Den hvide Dame, han blev hos os til Middag og reiste med Kl. 4 Toget'
29.8.: 'bivaanet første Akt af Den hvide Dame Theaterprøve'.

The staging received 11 performances, the last of which was given on 22.3.1870.

The musical material employed this year was the same as that used for the previous production of *La Dame blanche* on 17.11.1858 (now in DKKk, call nos. U 6, MA ms 3047, and KTA 246).

16.9.1868
Pas de deux (uncredited) performed by D. Krum and A. Scholl.
This (uncredited) dance is most probably the same as the two earlier, similarly uncredited *Pas de deux*, performed on 12.10.1866 (by Krum and J. Petersen) and on 14.3.1867 (by Krum and S. Price). According to A. Fredstrup's rehearsal book, Bournonville directed only one rehearsal of this dance on the day of its first performance. Moreover, he attended only one performance of it, on 29.9.1868, noting about it in his diary:

'seet [A.] Scholl og [D.] Krum, der dandsede smukt og gjorde megen Lykke i deres pas de deux'.

The 1868 *Pas de deux* seems (according to the posters) to have reached a total of 12 performances with Krum and Scholl, the last of which took place on 17.1.1871. It is not possible to identify the dance any further.

2.10.1868
La Somnambule, ou l'Arrivée d'un nouveau seigneur (Søvngjængersken).
This production represents Bournonville's third and last complete restaging in Copenhagen of his Danish version of J. Aumer's three-act pantomimic ballet *La Somnambule, ou l'Arrivée d'un nouveau seigneur* (*see* 21.9.1829). It was mounted especially for the début of his pupil, B. Schnell, who this year

played the rôle of *Thérèse* for the first time. The ballet was mounted in a thoroughly revised version which (according to Bournonville's diary) included completely new rechoreographed dances in the opening scenes of the first and third acts. Moreover, according to Bournonville's pencilled autographed notes in the 1829 and 1868 répétiteur's copies for this ballet, he seems to have made several other musical cuts and changes this year (seemingly with the help of V. C. Holm and H. S. Paulli). These changes were the following:

(1) Act I (the *Introduction*): According to the 1868 répétiteur's copy the ballet's original introduction seems this year to have been completely omitted, the ballet apparently beginning with score no. 1.
(2) Act I, score no. 2: Bournonville here omitted a minor section of 15 bars.
(3) Act I, score no. 5: Bournonville here completely cancelled the brief *Pas de trois* (*Allegretto* in 2/4 time, 87 meas.) which was originally performed by the characters *Edmond*, *Thérère*, and *Gertrude*.
(4) Act I, score no. 7 (the *Contredanse/Divertissement*): Bournonville here made two cuts of 8 and 103 bars respectively.
(5) Act I, score no. 7 B (the *Pas de quatre*): In this rechoreographed dance Bournonville omitted a repeat of 8 measures and cancelled two other sections of 8 and 7 bars.
(6) Act I, score no. 7 C (the *Finale/Pas de six*): In this rechoreographed dance Bournonville seems to have omitted a section of 16 bars which was replaced with a new large musical insertion of 84 bars. This is clear from his autographed pencilled note on p. 26 in the 1829 répétiteur's copy for *La Somnambule, ou l'Arrivée d'un nouveau seigneur*, which also served for his preparations of the new 1868 répétiteur's copy. This note reads: 'Nyt Indlæg.' The orchestral score fragments containing the music of this new insertion (now in DKKk, call no. C I, 259 f (b)) are all H. S. Paulli's autograph. This indicates that this insertion was most probably composed by him in 1868.
(7) Act II, score no. 11 (the *Finale*): Bournonville here omitted two sections of 7 and 37 bars each.
(8) Act III, score nos. 12–13: Bournonville here completely omitted the original music for the first two numbers of Act III. Instead he incorporated two other, slightly abridged versions of the music for the two dances in opening scene of Act III (score nos. 28–29) in his much earlier three-act romantic ballet *Faust* (*see* 25.4.1832 and 8.12.1849). This is clear from his pencilled autographed notes on p. 45 in the 1829 répétiteur's copy for *La Somnambule, ou l'Arrivée d'un nouveau seigneur*, which read: 'aldeles forandret/med en ny 1.ste Scene/ Indlæg af Balletten Faust 3.die Akt'.
(9) Act III, score nos. 14–20: Bournonville here made a series of ten musical cuts counting a total of 253 bars.

In his diary he noted about his revision, the rehearsals, and the reception of the 1868 production of *La Somnambule, ou l'Arrivée d'un nouveau seigneur*:

3.9.1868: 'arrangeret og copieret Musik til Søvngængersken'
5.9.: 'besørget Musik til [V. C.] Holm'
9.9.: 'omredigeret Søvngængersken i Cladde'
12.9.: 'Prøve og Indstudering paa Søvngængersken. [B.] Schnell fortræffelig'
13.9.: 'reenskrevet paa Søvngængersken'
14.9.: 'Skrevet Søvngængersken færdig'
15.9.: 'Prøve med Moderens Rolle i Søvngængersken'
17.9.: 'Prøve og Indstudering paa Søvngængersken'
18.9.: 'Op Kl 5½, componeret og skrevet Costumelister. Costume-Møde Kl 9½. 'Prøve og Indstudering paa Søvngængersken'
19.9.: 'skrevet og componeret'
21.9.: 'Jeg prøvede og indstuderede paa Søvngængersken'
22.9.: 'Prøve og Indstudering paa Søvngængersken. [G.] Carey og hans Døttre [i.e. Fanny and Léopoldine Carey] vare tilstede. Schnell aldeles fortræffelig'
23.9.: 'componeret, Prøve paa Søvngængersken, indstuderet Dandse'

24.9.: 'Indstudering af en nỹ Begyndelse til Søvngængerskens 1.ste Akt […] Eftermiddagsprøve med Rollerne til Søvngængersken'
25.9.: 'Indstudering paa Søvngængersken'
26.9.: 'Prøve paa Søvngængersken og Præsentation for Directionen'
28.9.: 'Arrangementsprøve paa Søvngængersken […] Eftermiddagsprøve paa Dandsene til Balletten'
29.9.: 'Orchesterprøve paa to Akter af Søvngængersken, temmelig ufuldkommen. Forestillingen udsat to Dage formedelst Mangel paa Tid og Rum til de nødvendige Prøver'
30.9.: 'Theaterprøve paa 3.die Akt af Søvngængersken […] meget tilfredsstillende […] Honorar fra [J. H.] Schubothe'
1.10.: 'Afsendt Programmer til Hoffet […] Generalprøve paa Søvngængersken […] Costumeprøve paa Søvngængersken'
2.10.: '1.ste Gang Den nỹ Indstudering af Søvngængersken, der gik udmærket godt og for fuldt Huus. Schnell præsterede berømmeligt og vandt meget Bifald endskjøndt Publicum i de to første Akter var lunken til at applaudere'.

The 1868 production of *La Somnambule, ou l'Arrivée d'un nouveau seigneur* received 6 performances, the last of which was given on 19.12.1868.

Autograph sources:

Musical instruction. Ms. Autograph. Ink. 1 p. (format unknown)
Sövngængersken.
Unsigned and undated [Written according to the diary most probably between 3.9. and 5.9.1868]
[USNYp; Dance Collection, call nos. *ZBD-71 (microfilm), and (S)*MGZMD 30 (photostat copy)
This note indicates all the major musical changes made by Bournonville for the 1868 restaging of *La Somnambule, ou l'Arrivée d'un nouveau seigneur*. The note also includes the names of the principal dancers who performed the 1868 production.

Manuscript scenario. Ms. Autograph. Ink. 12 pp. (format unknown)
Søvngængersken/Ballet i tre Akter af Scribe og Aumer/[…] Omredigeret og paanỹ indstuderet i Oktober 1868.
Unsigned and undated [Written according to the diary between 9.9. and 14.9.1868]
[USNYp; Dance Collection, call nos. *ZBD-71 (microfilm), and (S)*MGZMD 30 (photostat copy)

Production note. Ms Autograph. Brown ink. 1 p. (35,9 × 22,5 cm)
Søvngængersken/Ballet i 3 Akter af Scribe og Aumer/paanỹ sat i scene af H. Hofb. Bournonville/Musiken arrangeret af Herold.
Unsigned and undated [Written according to the diary most probably on 18.9.1868]
[DKKkt; F.M. (Ballet, læg S)

Production note. Ms. Autograph. Black ink. 1 p. (36 × 22,8 cm)
Søvngængersken/Personale i 1.ste Akt.
Unsigned and undated [Written according to the diary most probably on 18.9.1868]
[DKKkt; F.M. (Ballet, læg S)

Choreographic note (incomplete). Ms. Autograph. Ink, 2 pp. (format unknown)
La Somnambule (Ballet)/Acte 3.me
Unsigned and undated [Written according to the diary most probably between 18.9.and 23.9.1868]
[USNYp; Dance Collection, call nos. *ZBD-71 (microfilm), and (S)*MGZMD 30 (photostat copy)
This (incomplete) note describes most of Bournonville's revised choreography for the two new, interpolated dances in the opening scene of Act III (score nos. 12 and 13) of his 1868 production of *La Somnambule, ou l'Arrivée d'un nouveau seigneur*. The note also includes Bournonville's autographed choreographic numbers which clearly refer to his similar numbers written underneath the music in the 1868 répétiteur's copy for this ballet (pp. 78–85).

Choreographic note. Ms Autograph. Black ink. 1 p. (11,4 × 17,9 cm)
Arrivée du cortège.
Unsigned and undated [1868?]
[DKKk; NKS 3285 4° 3 R-U

Musical sources:

The orchestral score and the set of parts employed for the 1868 production were the same as those used since the 1829 Copenhagen première of *La Somnambule, ou l'Arrivée d'un nouveau seigneur* (now in DKKk, call nos. C I, 259 f, and KTB 287).

Répétiteur's copy. Ms. Copy. Brown and black ink. 1 vol. 132 pp. (33,1 × 25,5 cm)
B. 287/'Søvngængersken.'/Musik: Herold/8 B./[…]/Repetiteur = Parti/til/Balletten/Sövngængersken.
Unsigned and undated [1867]
[DKKk; MA ms 2985 (KTB 287 (2))
This répétiteur's copy dates from the 1868 staging of *La Somnambule, ou l'Arrivée d'un nouveau seigneur*. This is clear from Bournonville's autographed choreogaphic notes (written with black ink on pp. 44–47), which describe the new, extended version of the Act I *Pas de six* (score no. 7C). In these notes Bournonville explicitly mentions the names of those dancers who performed this divertissement at the première of the 1868 version. Moreover, in the music for score nos. 7, 7B, and 7C (pp. 28–49) Bournonville's autographed choreographic numbers are included (written with black ink). They clearly refer to his later notations of these three dances when they were mounted as a separate divertissement on 17.2.1875. Furthermore, the volume contains Bournonville's pencilled autographed choreographic numbers for the two new, interpolated dances in the opening scene of Act III, which employed music borrowed from his much earlier three-act romantic ballet *Faust*. These choreographic numbers seem to refer to Bournonville's separate (not yet traced) choreographic notation of these dances, which he may have written (according to his diary) during September 1868. Finally, his autographed notes on pp. 130–131 (written with black ink) describe the mime and the dramatic action in the ballet's final scene.

Printed sources:

Printed scenario. 1 vol. 16 pp. (20,2 × 12,6 cm)
Søvngængersken./Ballet i tre Akter af Scribe og Aumer./Indrette for den danske Scene/Af/August Bournonville./Musiken arrangeret af Herold./[…]/omredigeret og paany indstuderet i October 1868.
Kjøbenhavn, J. H. Schubothe/Bianco Luno/F. S. Muhle, 1868
[DKKk; 17, – 171 8°
This scenario differs from the contents of the original 1829 scenario in that the action is here divided into sixteen separate scenes. Moreover, several passages of the text are completely different from those for the same scenes in the 1829 version.

10.10.1868
Les Diamants de la Couronne (Kronjuvelerne).
The 1868 Copenhagen restaging of D.-F.-E. Auber's three-act comic opera from 1841 (first performed in Denmark on 17.2.1843) represents the second and last time this work was mounted by Bournonville. Seven years earlier he had staged Auber's opera for the first time at Stockholm's Royal Theatre (Operahuset) on 18.11.1861. In his diary he noted about the 1868 Copenhagen production and the three performances it received:

22.5.1868: 'Decorationsmøde paa Kronjuvelerne'
25.5.: 'Decorationsmøde & Oplæsning paa Kronjuvelerne (veltilfreds)'
7.7.: 'ordnet Costumevæsenet til Kronjuvelerne'

8.7.: 'skrevet og fortsat mit Costumeforslag [...] afsendt mit Costumeforslag til [F. J. G.] Berner'
13.7.: 'arbeidet paa Scene-Arrangementet til Kronjuvelerne'
15.7.: 'skrevet paa Kronjuvelerne'
16.7.: 'Skrevet og arrangeret Sceneri'
17.7.: 'fuldendt Sceneriet til Kronjuvelerne'
19.7.: 'Arbeidet lidt med [C. F.] Christensen og modtaget Forretningsbrev fra Berner'
5.8.: 'skrevet til Berner med Tilbagesending af Costumeforslaget'
8.8.: 'modtaget Frk. A. Andersen som tilbragte Dagen hos os og gjennemgik sin Rolle til Kronjuvelerne'
18.8.: 'Oplæsning og Correctur paa Kronjuvelerne'
29.8.: 'Instruction med [R. L.] Jastrau paa Kronjuvelerne'
1.9.: ' Instruction paa Kronjuvelerne'
5.9.: 'Instruction paa Kronjuvelerne med Jastrau, Frk Andersen og Charlotte [Bournonville]'
11.9.: 'Instruction paa Kronjuvelerne [...] Eftermiddagsprøve paa Kronjuvelerne'
12.9.: 'Instruction paa Kronjuvelrne'
16.9.: 'Overværet Syngeskolen paa 1.ste Akt af Kronjuvelerne og instrueret den samme Akt'
17.9.: 'Instruction paa Kronjuvelerne fra 5–7'
19.9.: 'Kl 11 Prøve og Instruction paa Kronjuvelerne [...] Eftermiddagsprøve paa Texten til Kr.'
22.9.: 'Eftermiddagsprøve paa Kronjuvelerne'
23.9.: 'Eftermiddagsprøve paa Kronjuvelerne. Det Meste af Indstuderingen færdig'
25.9. and 26.9.: 'Arrangement paa Kronjuvelerne'
29.9.: 'Eftermiddagsprøve paa Kronjuvelerne'
3.10.: 'Prøve med Quartett paa Kronjuvelerne, alle tre Akter'
5.10.: 'Prøve med Orhcester paa Kronjuvelerne (1.e og 2.den Akt)'
6.10.: 'Theaterprøve paa Kronjuvelerne (3.de Akt)'
8.10.: 'Generalprøve i Costume paa Kronjuvelrne, der gik meget smukt'
9.10.: 'Sidste Theaterprøve paa Kronjuvelerne'
10.10.: 'I Theatret 1.ste Forestilling af Kronjuvelerne's nye Indstudering. Alt gik mønsterværdigt og afvæbnede for endeel den ufordeelagtige Stemning, som Bladene gjennem en mindre Coulissecabale havde tilveiebragt i Publicum. Huset var godt besat og Bifaldet skjønt i Begyndelsen sparsomt tiltog med hver Akt. Aftenen syntes at være underholdende. Charlotte var meget heldig og talentfuld som Donna Diana'
11.10.: 'I Theatret Kronjuvelerne for lidt over halvt Huus. Det gik udmærket godt men Bifaldet omtrent som første Gang. – Det kan ikke nægtes at vor lyriske scene er uheldig stillet ligeoverfor den onde Villie indenfor Coulisserne og den indskrænkede musikalske Sands i Publicum'
16.10.: 'I Theatret Kronjuvelerne for 3.die Gang og meget daarligt Huus. Aviserne Bestræbelser for at degoutere Publicum har seiret men Personalet præsterede alligevel udmærket og Folk ikke blot morede sig men applauderede paa flere Steder saavel til Slutning uden mindste Opposition'.

Autograph sources:

Production note. Ms. Autograph. Brown ink. 4 pp. (27,3 × 21,5 cm)
Forslag til Costumeringen i Syngestykket/Kronjuvelerne.
Signed and dated: 'Fredensborg d. 8.e Juli 1868.'
[DKKkt; Brevregistrant (July 8, 1868)

Manuscript mise-en-scène. Ms. Autograph. Brown ink. 1 vol. 21 pp. (19,2 × 16,3 cm)
Kronjuvelerne./Syngestykke i 3 Akter af Scribe og Saint-Georges./Musiken af Auber./Scene = Arrangement af A Bournonville./1868.
Signed and dated: 'Fredensborg den 17 Juli 1868.'
[SSm; Daniel Fryklunds samling no. 132

Manuscript mise-en-scène (incomplete). Ms. Autograph. Black ink. 4 pp. (22,9 × 17,8 cm)
Chor = Arrangement/til/Kronjuvelerne/1.ste akt./2.den scène./[...]/2.den akt. (3.die Scene)/3.die Akt./10.e Scene

Unsigned and undated [Written according to the diary between 13.7. and 17.7.1868]
[SSm; Daniel Fryklunds samling no. 132

Manuscript mise-en-scène (incomplete). Ms. Autograph. Ink. 1 p. (format unknown)
(stærk Belÿsning)/[Choreographic diagram]/Tjenerne flytter Bordet og Stolene og lader Folket komme ind fra K. S./'Drabanterne defilere gjennem Collonaden og stille sig bagom Tronen./'Folket stiller sig paa begge Sider af Prosceniet/' Naar Dronningen træder frem følger Damer og/Herrer med ind og Tjenestefolket stiller sig i/Baggrunden./'Forbauselse over Henriques Knæfald/'Forundring over Dronningens Valg/'Jubel og Hyldning ved Tronbestigningen/'Dyb Compliment ved Dækkets Fald
Unsigned and undated [Written according to the diary between 13.7. and 17.7.1868]
[USNYp; Dance Collection, call nos. *ZBD-71 (microfilm), and (S)*MGZMD 30 (photostat copy)

Musical sources:

Printed orchestral score with manuscript insertions. 3 vol. Act I 192 pp. of which two are blank, Act II 138 pp., Act III 118 pp. of which one is blank (31 × 24 cm)
Les Diamans de la Couronne/Opéra Comique en trois Actes/[...]/Musique/DE/D. F. E. Auber
Paris, E. Troupenas & C.ie, pl. no. T 1041 [1841]
[DKKk; U 6 (KTA 374)]
This printed orchestral score includes T. Overskou's Danish translation (written with black ink) next to the original French text. It was used for all performances of Auber's opera in Copenhagen during Bournonville's lifetime

No répétiteur's copy for *Les Diamants de la Couronne* has been traced.

Parts. Ms. Copy. 33 vol.
4 vl I, 3 vl II, 2 vla, 4 vlc e cb, fl 1/2, ob 1/2, cl 1/2, fag 1/2, cor 1/2/3/4, tr 1/2, trb 1/2/3, timp, gr cassa, piatti e tri. 54 vocal parts.
Unsigned and undated [1843]
[DKKk; KTA 374]
This set of parts dates from the Copenhagen première of *Les Diamants de la Couronne* on 17.2.1843, and was used for all performances of it there during Bournonville's lifetime.

4.11.1868
Hans Heiling.
The 1868 Copenhagen restaging of H. Marschner's three-act romantic opera from 1833 (*see* 20.2.1858) represents the second and last time it was mounted with Bournonville's mise-en-scène in Denmark. According to his diary it was staged this year with only minor if any changes from his previous 1858 production. However, for the 1868 restaging, Bournonville also gave personal stage instructions to the two leading singers, A. D. Pfeil and N. J. Simonsen, who made their débuts this year in the rôles of *The Queen* and *Hans Heiling*.

Finally, four years later he directed two more rehearsals of this opera (on 4.11. and 6.11.1872) prior to a performance of it on 9.11.1872, and in 1874 he supervised a stage rehearsal of it (on 4.2.1874) in preparation of a performance on 13.2.1874. They represent the last times Bournonville worked on Marschner's opera.

In his diary he noted about the 1868 restaging:

21.10.1868: 'Arrangement paa Hans Heiling'
24.10. and 27.10.: 'Instruction paa Hans Heiling'
28.10.: 'Prøve paa Hans Heiling'
30.10. and 1.11.: 'Theaterprøve paa Hans Heiling'
3.11.: 'Generalprøve paa Hans Heiling'

4.11.: 'I Theatret <u>Hans Heiling</u> der gik særdeles smukt med to Debutanter. <u>Frk</u> [A. D.] <u>Pfeil</u> som Dronningen og <u>N.</u> [J.] <u>Simonsen</u> som <u>Heiling</u>. De høstede fortjent Bifald'.

The 1868 production of *Hans Heiling* received 40 performances during Bournonville's lifetime, the last of which was given on 19.11.1879.

The musical material employed this year was the same as that used for the previous 1858 production (now in DKKk, call nos. C I, 275, and KTA 320).

13.11.1868
Pas de deux (uncredited) performed by E. Hansen and L. Cetti.

This (uncredited) dance was (according to notes in Bournonville's diary) mounted especially for the début of his pupil, L. Cetti. It seems to have been based on a much earlier work, originally choreographed by F. Hoppe and set to music by the Italian composer, A. Mussi. This theory is supported by the fact that the répétiteur's copy for the 1868 *Pas de deux* is musically completely identical with the music in the 1844 set of parts for Hoppe's *Pas de deux*. That dance had originally been interpolated as a divertissement in Act II of Bournonville's three-act romantic ballet *Faust* (*see* 30.4. 1844).

According to the rehearsal book of A. Fredstrup, the (uncredited) 1868 *Pas de deux* was given 5 rehearsals between 2.11. and 12.11.1868, all of which were directed by either Bournonville or Hoppe.

In his diary Bournonville noted about the dance:

2.11.1868: 'Overværet [F.] Hoppes pas de deux for E. Hansen og Vicca [i.e. Ludovica] Cetti'
5.11.: 'skrevet til tre Redactioner om <u>Ludovica Cettis</u> Debut'
13.11.: 'I Theatret [...] Pas de deux af Hoppe, udført af E. Hansen og <u>Ludovica Cetti</u>, der gjorde megen Lўkke'.

The *Pas de deux* received 5 performances by Hansen and Cetti, the last of which was given on 23.3.1869. However, according to the posters it also seems to have been performed by D. Krum and Cetti two more times on 7.10. and 8.11.1869.

Musical sources:

No orchestral score and set of parts dating from the 1868 performances of this (uncredited) *Pas de deux* have yet been traced. This seems to indicate that the original set of parts for Hoppe's 1844 *Pas de deux* in Bournonville's ballet *Faust* was reused in 1868 (now in DKKk, call no. KTB 231).

Répétiteur's copy. Ms. Copy. Brown ink. 1 vol. 10 pp. (34 × 25,5 cm)
[...] Pas de deux af Hoppe./[...]/Repetiteurpartie/til/Pas de deux comp. af Hrr/Solodandser Hoppe 1868.
Unsigned and dated '1868'
[DKKk; MA ms 2905 (2) (KTB 231?)]
This répétiteur's copy is included on pp. 5–14 in a volume that also contains the répétiteur's copies for two other Bournonville dances, which were premièred at Copenhagen's Royal Theatre in 1868 and 1866 respectively.

15.11.1868
The Masquerade (Maskeraden).
For the 1868 Copenhagen restaging of L. Holberg's three-act comedy (*see* 12.12.1849 and 11.2.1859) Bournonville's

intermedium between Acts I and II was mounted by L. Gade. While Gade followed closely the original sequence of the dances as in Bournonville's previous 1859 staging, the music was this year presented in a reorchestrated version that seems to have been arranged by Fr. Rung, and included a new prelude (or *Forspil*) to Holberg's comedy. This seems to represent the only significant change from the previous staging. The poster for the 1868 production gives no credit at all to Bournonville for the choreography of the intermedium. The staging received 21 performances during his lifetime, the last of which took place on 17.10.1876.

Musical sources:

Orchestral score. Ms. Autograph (by Fr. Rung?) and copy. Black ink. 1 vol. 54 pp. of which one is blank (33,5 × 25,6 cm with minor variants)
3258/Maskaraden./Partitur./[...]/Forspil/til/Maskeraden/af/Fr. Rung./[...]/Partitur/til/Maskeraden.
Unsigned and undated [1868]
[DKKk, C II, 119 (KTB 258)]
This orchestal score clearly dates from L. Gade's and Fr. Rung's revised and (seemingly) reorchestrated 1868 staging of the intermedium in Holberg's comedy *The Masquerade*. Moreover, it includes Rung's new, additional prelude (pp. 1–16) and the complete score for Bournonville's 1859 intermedium (pp. 17–54). Notes (written with blue crayon) indicate a later change in the sequence of its dances. Finally, according to pencilled notes on p. 17 some four (not yet identified) excerpts from symphonies by J. Haydn appear to have been interpolated as *entr'acte* music in Act I, before Bournonville's intermedium. It is not clear whether these musical insertions were made for the 1868 restaging or for a later production of Holberg's comedy.

Répétiteur's copy. Ms. Copy. Black ink. 1 vol. 16 pp. (33,9 × 25,3 cm with minor variants)
B. 258 / Repetiteurparti / til / Paulli: / Maskeraden. / (Hanedans) / [...]/Repetiteurparti/til/
Maskeraden
Unsigned and undated [1868]
[DKKk; MA ms 2959 (KTB 258 (3))]
This répétiteur's copy contains the complete music for Bournonville's 1859 intermedium between Acts I and II of Holberg's *The Masquerade* and clearly dates from L. Gade's revised 1868 restaging of it. Pencilled notes indicate a later change in the sequence of its dances.

No set of parts dating from the 1868 restaging of Bournonville's intermedium in *The Masquerade* has yet been traced.

23.11.1868
Guillaume Tell (Wilhelm Tell).
The 1868 Copenhagen restaging of G. Rossini's four-act opera (premièred at the Paris Opéra on 3.8.1829, and first performed in Copenhagen on 4.9.1842) was originally projected by Bournonville on 30.10.1857 (*see also* 2.8.1842). It represents the first time this work was mounted with his mise-en-scène, and was premièred only a week after the news of Rossini's death in Paris on 14.11.1868 had reached him.

The poster gives no credit to Bournonville for the staging, nor does it provide any information about the choreography apart from stating: 'Med tilhørende Dands'. This seems to indicate that Bournonville mounted the Act III *Pas de trois* (which this year was danced by H. Scharff, S. Price, and J. Petersen) with the exact same choreography as that in the previous staging of Rossini's opera on 18.1.1863. That production had been mounted by the French choreographer and ballet-master, G. Carey.

Guillaume Tell was staged one more time in Copenhagen by Bournonville on 16.11.1873, but that year with the Act III *Pas de trois* performed by E. Hansen, M. Westberg, and J. Petersen. Finally, on 21.11.1875 the *Pas de trois* was mounted for the last time by Bournonville. According to a separate autographed choreographic note, that year he revised the solo variations especially for A. Scholl, who had replaced J. Petersen in this dance.

In his diary Bournonville noted about the 1868 production of *Guillaume Tell*:

5.11., 9.11., and 13.11.1868: 'Instruction paa W. Tell'
15.11. 'Efterretning om at [G.] Rossini døde igaar i Paris 76 Aar gammel +++ '
19.11.: 'Salsprøve paa Wilhelm Tell, Eftermiddagsprøve paa Dandsen til samme Opera'
20.11.: 'Generalprøve paa W. Tell'
21.11.: 'Prøve paa forskjellige Dandse til [...] Wilhelm Tell'
23.11: 'Wilhelm Tell, som gik meget smukt, men for temmelig tyndt besat Huus! Operaen har kun daarlige Chaaer iaar!'.

The 1868 staging of *Guillaume Tell* was given only one performance.

Musical sources:

Printed orchestral score including several manuscript insertions. 3 vol. Act I 320 pp. of which two are blank, Act II 182 pp. of which two are blank, Act III–IV 372 pp. (30,5 × 22 cm with several variants)
Wilhelm Tell/Partitur/1ste Akt/[...]/2den Akt/[...]/3die og 4de Akt
Paris, s. l. [E. Troupenas], pl. no. 347 [1829]
[DKKkt; KTA 375
This printed French orchestral score (of which the title page is missing) was used for all performances of *Guillaume Tell* in Copenhagen since its première there on 4.9.1842 throughout Bournonville's lifetime.

Répétiteur's copy. Ms. Copy. Black ink. 1 vol. 14 pp. pf which one is blank (34 × 25,5 cm)
1. Wilhelm Tell. A 375/ [...] / Repetiteurpartie / til / Wilhelm Tell/ Tredie Act/No. 11. Pas de trois og Chor.
Unsigned and undated [1863]
[DKKk MA ms 2911 (1) (KTA 375)
This répétiteur's copy contains the complete music for the *Pas de trois* in Act III of *Guillaume Tell* (score no. 11). It also includes Bournonville's autographed choreographic notes (written with brown ink) which most probably were made for the 1868 restaging of Rossini's opera. However, the répétiteur's copy itself dates (according to the names of the dancers written underneath the music) from the earlier staging of the opera on 18.1.1863. That year the Act III *Pas de trois* was mounted by the French dancer and ballet-master, G. Carey, and performed by H. Scharff, S. Price and J. Rostock. This is clear from Carey's autographed notes (written with brown ink on on p. 1) in which he explicitly mentions the name of 'Jf [Sophie] Price'. According to other later pencilled notes (which include the names of the dancers, E. Hansen, A. Scholl, and M. Westberg) the répétiteur's copy was also used for all later restagings of Rossini's opera during Bournonville's lifetime. Moreover, on p. 10 Bournonville's pencilled autographed choreographic numbers ('1–5') are inserted underneath the music for the female solo variation in 2/4 time (*Allegretto*). They clearly refer to similar numbers in his separate notation of this variation that he seems to have made for his last, revised staging of *Guillaume Tell* on 21.11.1875.
The répétiteur's copy is included on pp. 1–14 of a volume that also contains the répétiteur's copies for three other operas and plays, mounted at Copenhagen's Royal Theatre between 1859 and 1861.

Parts. Ms. Copy. 37 + 11 vol.
4 vl I, 4 vl II, 2 vla, 3 vlc, 2 cb, fl 1/2, ob 1/2, cl 1/2, fag 1/2, cor 1/2/3/4, tr 1/2, trb 1/2/3, timp, gr cassa, tri, arpa 1/2. On stage: conductor's part, 10 cor 1/2/3/4. 98 (partially printed) vocal parts.
Unsigned and undated [1842]
[DKKk; KTA 375
This set of parts dates from the 1842 Copenhagen première of Rossini's opera and was used for all performances of it there during Bournonville's lifetime.

1.12.1868
An Idea for the Royal Wedding (En Idée til Formælingen).
Projected work.
In his diary Bournonville mentions on this day an idea that came to him regarding the planned public celebration during the following year of the nuptials of the Danish Crown Prince (later King Frederik VIII) and the Swedish Princess Louise Josephine Eugenie:

30.11.1868: 'Talt med Kronprindsen [i.e. Christian Frederik Wilhelm Carl, Crown Prince of Denmark]'
1.12.: 'Skrevet til [...] Stockholm angaaende en Idée til Formælingen'.

Although Bournonville was personally involved in the organisation of the later feast in the Rosenborg Gardens on 11.8.1869 in honour of the nuptials of the Danish Crown Prince and the Swedish Princess Louise Josephine Eugenie, this original idea does not seem to have been carried out on that occasion.

5.12.1868
Le Maçon (Muurmesteren).
The 1868 Copenhagen restaging of D.-F.-E. Auber's three-act comic opera from 1825 (*see* 7.12.1847) represents the second and last time this work was mounted by Bournonville. In his diary he noted about the production, which (according to his two manuscript mises-en-scène) was mounted with a partially revised mise-en-scène in Act II:

26.11.1868: 'Decorationsprøve til Muurmesteren [...] skrevet og arrangeret'
27.11.: 'Instruction paa Muurmesteren'
28.11.: 'Instructionsprøve paa Muurmesteren'
29.11.: 'Costumemøde'
1.12.: 'Salsrepetition paa Muurmesteren'
2.12.: 'Theaterprøve med Orchester paa Muurmesteren (lille Alteration med [P. L. N.] Schramm i Anledning af hans Kaadhed)'
3.12.: 'fuldstændig Prøve paa Muurmesteren'
4.12.: 'Prøve (Generalprøve) paa Muurmesteren [...] Det Hele gaaer meget smukt'
5.12.: 'I Theatret Muurmesteren (paany indstuderet) gik særdeles smukt og Charlotte [Bournonville] var udmærket'.

The 1868 production of *Le Maçon* received 7 performances during Bournonville's lifetime, the last of which was given on 19.9.1869.

The musical material employed this year was the same as that used for the previous 1847 production (now in DKKk, call nos. U 6, and KTA 247).

Autograph sources:

Manuscript mise-en-scène. Ms. Autograph. Brown ink. 4 pp. (22,7 × 18 cm)
Muurmesteren/2.den Akt.

Unsigned and undated [Written according to Bournonville's diary probably on 26.11.1868]
[SSm; Daniel Fryklunds samling no. 137

Manuscript mise-en-scène. Ms. Autograph. Black ink. 4 pp. (17,6 × 11,4 cm)
Muurmesteren/2.den Akt.
Unsigned and undated [Written according to Bournonville's diary probably on 26.11.1868]
[SSm; Daniel Fryklunds samling no. 137

5.12.1868
La Ventana.

This performance represents Bournonville's last restaging of his second and final version of the Spanish Ballet Divertissement *La Ventana* (*see* 6.10.1856). According to his diary it was mounted this year with partially new choreography, arranged for his pupil, B. Schnell, who played the rôle of *The Señorita* for the first time in this production. In his diary Bournonville noted about her performance:

10.11.1868: 'Prøve paa La Ventana'
11.11.: 'lille Prøve paa La Ventana med Understøttelse af Juliette Price'
13.11., 14.11., 17.11., 23.11., and 25.11.: 'Prøve paa La Ventana'
2.12.: 'Theaterprøve med Orchester paa La Ventana'
4.12.: 'Prøve (Generalprøve) paa […] La Ventana; foretaget en lille Forandring til Bedste for [B.] Schnells Udholdenhed. Det hele gaaer meget smukt. Arrangeret med [V. C.] Holm og [C. J.] Hansen'
5.12.: 'componeret et lille Stÿkke til La Ventana […] I Theatret […] La Ventana ligeledes med nÿ Besætning gjorde megen Lÿkke, og Schnell behagede overordentlig. [F. J. G.] Berner tilkjendte hende en Gratification'.

The 1868 production of *La Ventana* received 7 performances, the last of which was given on 31.5.1869.

The musical material employed this year was the same as that used since the 1856 première of *La Ventana* (now in DKKk, call nos. MA ms 1127, MA ms 2997, KTB 300, and KTB 1055).

1869

1.1.1869
The Festival in Albano (Festen i Albano).

This performance represents Bournonville's third and last restaging in Copenhagen of his one-act idyllic ballet *The Festival in Albano* (*see* 28.10.1839). According to Bournonville's autographed choreographic notes, it was this year mounted in a thoroughly revised version that included three re-choreographed dances for the corps de ballet, entitled *Ballabile*, *Flower Dance (Blomsterdands)*, and *Saltarello*.

Moreover, the original *Pas de deux* (score nos. 8–9) seems (according to the poster) to have been renamed *Amor and Hymen* and performed by two women (B. Schnell and L. Cetti). They danced it to a musically slightly different arrangement of I. P. E. Hartmann's original 1839 score for this dance. Thus, the new 1869 version of this dance omitted the repeat of the opening *Adagio* movement and also cancelled 24 bars in the *Coda*.

Finally, instead of the ballet's original series of five allegorical tableaux (score no. 12), which depicted some of B.

Thorvaldsen's most famous sculptural works, Schnell and Cetti here performed another allegorical figurative dance while dressed as *Amor and Hymen*.

In his diary Bournonville noted about the staging:

8.12.1868: 'arrangeret paa Festen i Albano'
9.12.: 'Prøve […] paa Festen i Albano'
14.12.: 'skrevet og componeret'
15.12.: 'Prøve først paa Festen i Albano […] Aftensprøve paa Dandsene til Festen i Albano'
16.12.: 'Prøve paa […] Festen i Albano […] skrevet, componeret'
17.12.: 'componeret og omskrevet Programmet til Festen i Albano'
19.12.: 'skrevet […] componeret'
21.12. and 23.12: 'Prøve 10–11 paa Festen i Albano (Indstudering)'
22.12. and 24.12.: 'Prøve og Indstudering paa Festen i Albano'
28.12.: 'Prøve paa Festen i Albano'
29.12.: 'Arrangementsprøve paa Albano'
30.12.: 'Prøve paa Albano'
31.12.: 'Generalprøve paa Albano'
1.1.1869: 'Festen i Albano der gik udmærket godt og gjorde stormende Lÿkke'.

Of the 100th performance of *The Festival in Albano* on 9.2. 1869 Bournonville noted:

'Festen i Albano for 100.de Gang. Saltarelloen vandt stærkt Bifald men mig vistes der ingen særskildt Opmærksomhed'.

The 1869 production received 9 performances during Bournonville's lifetime, the last of which was given on 12.11.1870.

Autograph sources:

Choreographic note. Ms. Autograph. Ink. 1 p. (format unknown)
Blomsterdands
Unsigned and undated [Written according to the diary probably between 14.12. and 19.12.1868]
[USNYp; Dance Collection, call nos. *ZBD-71 (microfilm), and (S)*MGZMD 30 (photostat copy)

Choreographic note. Ms. Autograph. Ink. 1 p. (format unknown)
Saltarello.
Unsigned and undated [Written according to the diary most probably between 14.12. and 19.12.1868]
[USNYp; Dance Collection, call nos. *ZBD-71 (microfilm), and (S)*MGZMD 30 (photostat copy)

Choreographic note. Ms Autograph. Ink. 1 vol. 8 pp. (format unknown)
Festen i Albano. 1.ste Scene/[…]/2.den scène/[…]/3.die Scene/ […]/4.de Scene/[…]/5.te Scene/[…]/6.de Scene/[…]/Ballabile./[…]/Coda
Unsigned and undated [Written according to the diary most probably between 14.12. and 19.12.1868]
[USNYp; Dance Collection, call nos. *ZBD-71 (microfilm), and (S)*MGZMD 30 (photostat copy)

Choreographic note. Ms. Autograph. Ink. 7 pp. (format unknown)
Festen i Albano/Blomsterdands. / […] /Saltarello/ […] /Scene/ […]/Scene/[…]/Final. (Danse avec flambeaux)
Unsigned and dated: 'd. 19 Decbr 1868.'
[USNYp; Dance Collection, call nos. *ZBD-71 (microfilm), and (S)*MGZMD 30 (photostat copy)

Choreographic note. Ms. Autograph. Ink. 3 pp. (format unknown)
[Seven untitled drawings including choreographic diagrams]
Unsigned and undated [c. December 1868]
[USNYp; Dance Collection, call nos. *ZBD-71 (microfilm), and (S)*MGZMD 30 (photostat copy)

This manuscript contains 7 numbered drawing and choreographic diagrams that describe the groupings and the movements on stage of the corps de ballet during the so-called *Flower Dance (Blomsterdands)* in the revised 1869 staging of *The Festival in Albano*.

Production note. Ms. Autograph. Ink. 1 p. (format unknown)
1./Silvia & Antonio/2.
Unsigned and undated [c. December 1868]
[USNYp; Dance Collection, call nos. *ZBD-71 (microfilm), and (S)*MGZMD 30 (photostat copy)

Manuscript scenario. Ms. Autograph. Ink. 1 vol. 10 pp. (format unknown)
Festen i Albano./Ballet = Divertissement i een Akt. (*)/af/August Bournonville./Musiken af Fr: Fröhlich./(Decorationen af Professor Christensen)/Opført første gang den 28' October 1839./Paany indstuderet og sat i scene/d. 1.ste Januar 1869./(*) Da den lille Handling ikke tilfredsstiller [changed to:] svarer til de Fordringer/der nu omstunder og hertillands stilles til en Ballet/bÿdes den nÿ Indstudering af dette Arbeide [changed to:] Genrebillede som/et Ballet=Divertissement.
Unsigned and dated: 'd. 1.ste Januar 1869.' [Written according to the diary on 17.12.1869]
[USNYp; Dance Collection (microfilm).]

Musical sources:

The orchestral score and the set of parts employed in 1869 were the same as those used since the 1839 première (now in DKKk, call nos. C II, 107 and KTB 282).

Répétiteur's copy. Ms. Copy. Black and brown ink. 1 vol. 76 pp. (32,2 × 25,2 cm)
B. 282/Festen i Albano./(2.den Udgave)/1839./1869./[…]/Festen i Albano./Idÿllisk Ballet i 1 Act af,/A: Bournonville/Musikken afJ: F: Fröhlich./Repetiteurparti
Unsigned and dated (on the front cover): '1839./1869.'
[DKKk; MA ms 2979 (KTB 282)
This répétiteur's copy dates from the 1839 première of *The Festival in Albano*, but was also used for all later stagings of this ballet during Bournonville's lifetime. It contains four revised musical insertions (score nos. 8–11), of which that for score no. 11 dates from Bournonville's 1869 choreographic revision, while the insertions for nos. 8–10 date from E. Hansen's later restaging of the ballet on 1.6.1882.

Moreover, score no. 2 contains Bournonville's autographed notes (written with brown ink) which most probably date from his first restaging of this ballet on 14.1.1858. They describe the mime and the dramatic action in rather general terms. Other pencilled choreographic notes by an unknown hand (which almost certainly date from 1839) describe the original series of *tableaux vivants* (score no. 12) in which five of B. Thorvalden's most popular sculptural works were depicted.

Finally, in score nos. 1–7 and 11–12 Bournonville's autographed choreographic numbers (written with black ink) are inserted. They refer to his similar numbers in the nearly complete separate notation of the ballet, that he wrote (according to his diary) in December 1868 in preparation for the 1869 production.

Printed sources:

Printed scenario. 1 vol. 8 pp. (20 × 12,6 cm)
Festen i Albano./Ballet i een Act/af/August Bournonville,/Musiken af Frøhlich./Decorationen af Christensen./[…]/Paany sat i Scene/i Januar 1869.
Kjøbenhavn, J. H. Schubothe/Bianco Luno/F. S. Muhle. 1869.
[DKKk; 17, – 173, 8°
This printed scenario differs from the 1839 edition by being divided into eight separate scenes. Moreover, it contains several minor variants from the earlier version in the description of the ballet's dramatic action.

4.1.1869
La Juive (Jødinden).
The 1869 Copenhagen restaging of J.-F. Halévy's five-act opera was originally projected by Bournonville on 30.10.1857 (*see also* 21.10.1855). It represents the first time *La Juive* was mounted in Denmark with his complete mise-en-scène and choreography, and included four dance scenes as follows:

(1) A *Waltz* in Act I (score no. 6), performed by a corps de ballet of townspeople. According to the 1869 répétiteur's copy for this dance the *Waltz* was drastically shortened this year by several musical cuts, thereby playing for a total of 155 bars instead of its original 281 measures.
(2) A *Processional March* in Act I (score no. 7), performed at the beginning of the *Finale* and during the chorus, entitled «Noël Noël Noel tous là bas, tous là bas le cortège s'avance» («O Fryd o Fryd of Fryd, see kun hist, see kun hist Keisertoget sig bølger»).
(3) A *Pantomime scene* and a *Ballet Divertissement* in Act III (score no. 14).
(4) A *Processional March* in Act V (score no. 21).

In the printed Danish libretto for *La Juive* (now in DKKk, call no. 55,– 3 8°, vol. 5, no. 99, p. 5) the Act I *Waltz* is described as follows:

'Nogle, som Vinen allerede har begyndt at gjøre Virkning paa, give sige [*sic*] til at dandse, hele Sværmen følger deres Exempel; Fruentimmerne blande sig i Dandsen, og hele Massen danner et livfuldt Billede af en Folkelystighed.'

The 1869 poster gives no credit to Bournonville for the staging and for the choreography, nor does it contain any specific information about the opera's dances except for stating: 'Med tilhørende Dands'.

The 1869 production, which was mounted for the début of the singer, A. D. Pfeil (as *Rachel*), was restaged the following year by Bournonville with only minor if any changes (*see* 29.10.1870).

In his diary he noted about the 1869 performance:

12.12.1868: 'Instruction paa Jødinden'
15.12.: 'Prøve paa […] Jødinden'
21.12.: 'Theaterprøve paa Jødinden 1.e og 2.den Akt. 11–1'
22.12.: 'lille Prøve paa paa Jødinden'
23.12.: 'Prøve […] fra 11-1 paa de tre sidste Akter af Jødinden'
27.12.: 'Prøve og Arrangement paa Jødinden'
28.12.: 'Prøve paa […] tre Akter af Jødinden'
2.1.1869: 'Generalprøve paa Jødinden fra 11½ til 3½'
4.1.: 'I Theatret Jødinden, der gik meget smukt og hvori Frøken [A. D.] Pfeil udfoldede et betydeligt Talent som Rachel og gjorde fortjent Lÿkke'.

The 1869 production of *La Juive* is not included in Bournonville's handwritten list of his stagings of operas and plays, written c.1872 (*see* Additional Sources). It reached a total of 12 performances during his lifetime, the last of which was given on 13.2.1873.

Musical sources:

Printed orchestral score. 3 vol. Act I 219 pp. of which three are blank, Act II–III 300 pp. of which one is blank, Act IV–V 168 pp. of which one is blank (31,2 × 24,1 cm)
LA JUIVE/Opéra en cinq actes/[…]/Musique de /F. HALEVY.
Paris, M. Schlesinger, pl. no. 2000 [1835]
[DKKk; U 6 (KTA 345)

This French orchestral score contains T. Overskou's Danish translation written (with brown ink) next to the opera's original French text. It was used for all performances of Halévy's opera in Copenhagen throughout Bournonville's lifetime. The music for the Act I *Waltz* is included in vol. I (pp. '115–147'), while that for the Act III *Pantomime scene* and the *Ballet Divertissement* is included in vol. II (pp. '383–436').

Répétiteur's copy. Ms. Copy. Brown ink. 1 vol. 40 pp. (32,8 × 25,2 cm)
Dandsen i Jödinden. – /62. A/[...]/Repetiteur = Partie/til/Dandsene/i/Operaen Jödinden/componeret/af/Halevỹ. -
Unsigned and undated [1838]
[DKKk; MA ms 3074 (KTA 345 (1))
This répétiteur's copy clearly dates from the Copenhagen première of *La Juive* on 25.5.1838. It contains the complete music for the *Waltz* in Act I (score no. 6) as well as that for the *Pantomime scene* and the *Ballet Divertissement* in Act III (score no. 14). Several pencilled notes indicate many musical cuts in these numbers, most of which might have been made for Bournonville's 1869 restaging of this opera.

Répétiteur's copy. Ms. Copy. Brown ink. 1 vol. 4 pp. (33,3 × 25,2 cm)
Noget af Repetiteur Partiet/til/Jödinden
Unsigned and undated [c.1838]
[DKKk; MA ms 3075 (KTA 345 (2))
This répétiteur's copy seems to date from the period immediately after the 1838 Copenhagen première of *La Juive*. It contains two separate movements of the Act III *Ballet Divertissement* (score no. 14) and was most probably written for a restaging of Halévy's opera in the late 1830s or early 1840s.

Répétiteur's copy. Ms. Copy. Black ink. 8 pp. (32,8 × 25,2 cm)
62./Repetiteurpartie/til/Jödinden
Unsigned and undated [1869]
[DKKk; MA ms 3076 (KTA 345 (3))
This répétiteur's copy clearly dates from the 1869 restaging of *La Juive* since it contains only the music for the new, abridged version of the *Waltz* in Act I (score no. 6).

Parts. Ms. Copy. 47 + 7 vol.
4 vl I, 4 vl II, 2 vla, 4 vlc e cb, fl picc, fl 1/2, ob 1/2, cor ingl, cl 1/2, fag 1/2, cor 1/2/3/4, tr 1/2/3/4/5/6, trb 1/2/3/4/5/6, oph, tuba, timp, gr cassa, piatti, tri, arpa. On stage: tr 1/2, gr cassa e piatti e tri, gong, glock, anvil, org. 108 (partially printed) vocal parts.
Unsigned and undated [1838]
[DKKk; KTA 345
This set of parts dates from the 1838 Copenhagen première of *La Juive* and was used for all performances of it there during Bournonville's lifetime.

5.1.1869
Dances for the Royal Ball (Hofballet) given at Christiansborg's Palace in honour of The Prince and Princess of Wales.
In his diary Bournonville noted about his direction of the dances at this royal ball:

26.12.1868: 'paa Christiansborg i Anledning af Hofballet d. 5. Januar'
31.12.: 'Udrettet adskilligt for Hofballet'
5.1.1869: 'Prøve [...] paa Musiken til Hofballet [...] og om Aftenen med L. Gade paa Christiansborg Slot hvor man samledes Kl. 9. Polonaisen begyndte Kl. 10., der blev dandset 4 Francaiser og flere Walse samt Cotillon efter Taffelet. Festen holdtes til Ære for Prindsen [i.e. the later King Edward VII] og Prindsessen af Wales [i.e. the later Queen Alexandra]. Hun var magelös yndig og saavel Hds Kgl. Höihed som Majestæterne [i.e. King Christian IX and Queen Louise] vare yderst naadige imod mig. Jeg fungerede som Bal-Inspecteur og bidrog endeel til Festens ypperlige Gang og Udfald. Kl 2½ var Ballet forbi og vi souperede med Marskallerne. Jeg kom hjem Kl. 3½'
8.1.: 'besørget adskillige Æreindrer paa Amalienborg'
15.1.: 'Modtaget 100 r fra Hoffet'.

No programme and/or musical sources for the dances given at this ball have yet been traced.

7.1.1869
Pas de deux (uncredited) performed by D. Krum and A. Scholl.
This (uncredited) dance is most likely identical with the earlier, similarly uncredited *Pas de deux* performed by the same two dancers on 16.9.1868, which in turn is probably the same as the even earlier (uncredited) *Pas de deux*, performed on 12.10.1866 (by Krum and J. Petersen) and on 14.3.1867 (by Krum and S. Price). In his diary Bournonville noted about his involvement in this dance:

6.1.1869: 'Prøve paa Pas de deux'
7.1.: 'set pas de deux af [A.] Scholl og [D.] Krum'.

The 1869 *Pas de deux* seems (according to the posters) to have been performed at least 6 times by Krum and Scholl, the last of which took place on 17.1.1871 (*see also* 27.4.1874). It is not possible to identify the dance any further.

27.1.1869
Die Zauberflöte (Tryllefløiten).
The 1869 Copenhagen restaging of W. A. Mozart's two-act opera (premièred at Freihaus-Theater auf der Wieden in Vienna on 30.9.1791, and first performed in Copenhagen on 30.1.1826) was originally projected by Bournonville on 30.10.1857. It represents the first and only time this opera was mounted with his complete mise-en-scène and choreography. In 1869 the opera had been out of the Copenhagen repertory for exactly 27 years, the previous performance having been given there on 26.1.1842.

Prior to his 1869 staging Bournonville had written a note to the theatre management of Copenhagen's Royal Theatre on 13.5.1868, in which he included some critical remarks about the new Danish translation made that year by his personal friend, the Danish poet H. P. Holst. Holst's translation was based on an earlier French version that Bournonville himself had seen performed at the Théâtre Lyrique in Paris on 30.11.1865 and then described in his diary as:

'La flute enchantée af Mozart med noget forandret text. Udførelsen var fortræffelig og Deltagelsen stor. M.me [M.] Miolan Carvalho som Pamina var udmærket, er en virkelig Kunstnerinde og hendes Foredrag af Pamina vidner om stor musikalsk Sands, hendes Spil ligner M.lle [M.] Favarts. 1. Troy som Papageno udførtes fortræffeligt, en mægtigt Basbaryton, 2. Michot som Tamino var en virkelig Savoyard höit regnet en Rideknægt med en dygtig Tenorstemme uden mindste Dannelse. 3. Depassio – Sarastro detonerede den hele Tid og havde Grød i Halsen. 4. [H.] Lutz Monostratos var meget brav og hans tvungne Dands meget comisk. No. 1 og 4 særdeles gode. Resten middelmaadig, derimod Orchestret ypperligt. Jeg maa ikke forglemme Christine Nilsson som Nattens Dronning reen og klangfuld Stemme, höi Sopran og en elskværdig Fremtræden, stor Yndest hos Publicum'.

In his 1868 note to the Copenhagen theatre management Bournonville characterised Holst's translation of the dialogues between *Tamino* and *Pamina* as 'Hastværksarbeide'. Consequently, he asked that a new and more 'propert udarbeidet Manuscript' should be made before he would accept responsibility for staging this opera.

In his diary he noted about his preparations and the first performance of the 1869 restaging, which was mounted with new décor and costumes by F. Ahlgrensson and E. Lehmann respectively:

12.5.1868: 'Lang Conference med [F. J. G.] Berner og [H. S.] Paulli'
13.5.: 'læst og skrevet med Hensyn til Oversættelsen af Tryllefløiten […] afsendt Librettoen til Tryllefløiten tilligemed Brev til Berner'
30.5.: 'Oplæsning paa Tryllefløiten'
2.7.: 'skrevet og udarbeidet Scenariet til Tryllefløiten'
5.7.: 'sendt et Decorations-Forslag (Trylleflöiten) med Brev til Justitsraad Berner'
19.7.: 'faaet Forretningsbrev fra Berner'
5.8.: 'skrevet til Berner med Tilbagesending af Costumeforslaget, og arrangeret 1.ste Akt til Tryllefløiten […] Brev til [F.] Ahlgrensson'
6.8.: 'skrevet paa Scene=Arrangementet'
7.8.: 'fuldendt Sceneriet til Tryllefløiten'
19.8.: 'reenskrevet mit Scenarium til Tryllefløiten'
20.8.: 'arbeidet paa Tryllefløiten'
22.8.: 'skrevet Sceneri'
26.8.: 'reenskrevet paa Sceneriet til Tryllefløiten'
12.10.: 'Oplæsning paa Tryllefløiten'
15.10.: 'Costumemøde med Lehmann'
12.12.: 'Arbeidet med Lehmann for Costumet til Tryllefløiten'
6.1. and 7.1.1869: 'Prøve paa […] Texten til Tryllefløiten'
8.1.: 'componeret'
9.1.: 'Indstuderet 3 Dandsenumre til Tryllefløiten og prøvet 1.ste Akt med Pianoforte''
10.1.: 'Prøve paa Tryllefløiten (Instruction)'
11.1.: 'repeteret Dandsene til Tryllefløiten og gjennemgaaet adskillige scener af samme'
12.1.: 'lang Instructionsprøve paa Tryllefløiten'
14.1.: 'Arrangementprøve paa Tryllefløiten 1.ste og. 2.de Akt.'
15.1.: 'Instruction paa 4.de Akt af Tryllefløiten'
16.1.: 'Prøve paa […] 3–4 Akt af Tryllefløiten paa Theatret […] Eftermiddagsprøve med [P. L. N.] Schramm (Papageno)'
18.1.: 'Skrevet Reqvisiter til Tryllefløiten'
19.1.: 'meget lang Theaterprøve paa Tryllefløiten'
20.1.: 'Theaterprøve. [L. J. P.] Erhard-Hansen tog Plads for [J. T. J.] Liebe, der har et daarligt Been. Eftermiddags-Instruction med Erh. Hansen'
21.1.: 'Instruction'
22.1.: 'Instruction paa Tryllefløiten'
23.1.: 'Theaterprøve paa Tryllefløiten'
25.1.: 'Aftenen paa Costumeprøve […] og Decorationsprøve til Kl 12.'
26.1.: 'Generalprøve paa Tryllefløiten'
27.1.: 'I Theatret i Anledning af Mozarts Fødselsdag. Tryllefløiten med dens ny Text efter det franske. Forestillingen gik særdeles godt for fuldt Huus og levende Bifald'.

The 1869 production of *Die Zauberflöte* reached a total of 34 performances during Bournonville's lifetime, the last of which was given on 20.10.1879.

Autograph sources:

Production note. Ms. Autograph. Brown ink. 1 p. (21,3 × 13,7 cm)
Bemærkninger ved Oversættelsen/af/Den franske Bearbeidelse/af/Mozarts Trylleflöite.
Signed and dated: 'Fredensborg den 13.de Mai 1868.'
[DKKkt; Brevregistrant (March 13, 1868)

Production note. Ms. Autograph. Brown ink. 3 pp. (26,8 × 21,6 cm)
Forslag til Decorationsvæsenet i Trylleflöiten
Signed and dated: 'Fredensborg den 5.e Juli 1868.'
[SSm; Daniel Fryklunds samling no. 150 a

Manuscript mise-en-scène. Ms. Autograph. Brown ink. 1 vol. 17 pp. (22 × 17,2 cm)

Trylleflöiten/Opera i 4 Akter./Musik af Mozart til en omarbeidet fransk Text/Scene = Arrangement./af/August Bournonville/1868.
Signed and dated: 'Fredensborg d. 7.de August 1868.' [Written according to the diary on 6.8. and 7.8.1868]
[SSm; Daniel Fryklunds samling no. 150 b

Manuscript mise-en-scène (incomplete). Ms. Autograph. Brown ink. 1 vol. 26 pp. (20,4 × 16,3 cm)
Trylleflöiten/Opera med dialog/i 4 Akter./Musik af Mozart, Texten fransk bearbeidet./Scene = Arrangement af A. Bournonville./1868.
Signed and dated: 'Fredensborg d. 7.de August/reenskrevet den 27 D.o/1868.' [Written according to the diary between 6.8. and 26.8. 1868]
[SSm; Daniel Fryklunds samling no. 150 c

Choreographic note. Ms. Autograph. Brown ink. 2 pp. (21,1 × 13,4 cm)
Trylleflöiten 1.e Akt 1.ste Scene./[…]/Sang/[…]/2.den Akt (10.e Scene)
Unsigned and undated [Written according to the diary most probably on 8.1.1869]
[SSm; Daniel Fryklunds samling no. 150 d

Musical sources:

Printed orchestral score. 1 vol. 366 pp. of which two are blank (30.9.x 24.1 cm)
IL FLAUTO MAGICO/Dramma per musica
Bonn, N. Simrock, pl. no. 1092 [1814]
[DKKkt; KTA 227
This orchestral score was used for all performances of *Die Zauberflöte* in Copenhagen since its première there on 30.1.1826 and throughout Bournonville's lifetime.

Répétiteur's copy. Ms. Copy. Brown ink. 1 vol. 10 pp. of which one is blank (34 × 25,6 cm)
[…]/Trÿlleføiten [*sic*]/[…]/85./[…]/Repetiteurpartie/til/'Trylleflöiten'
Unsigned and undated [1869]
[DKKk; MA ms 2913 (3) (KTA 227)
This répétiteur's copy clearly dates from the 1869 restaging of *Die Zauberflöte*. It contains the music for the dance scenes Act I (scene 1) and Act II (scene 10) as mounted by Bournonville. Moreover, his autographed pencilled choreographic numbers ('1–16' and '1–14') are included in the music for both of these numbers. They refer to his two separate choreographic notations of the same scenes which he most probably wrote on 8.1.1869. The répétiteur's copy is included (on pp. 21–30) in a volume that also contains the répétiteur's copies for four other operas and plays, mounted at Copenhagen's Royal Theatre between 1869 and 1871.

Parts (incomplete). Ms. Copy. 30 vol.
4 vl I, 4 vl II, vla, 4 vlc e cb, fl 1/2, ob 1/2, cl 1/2, fag 1/2, cor 1/2, tr 1/2, trb 1/2/3, timp. 144 (partially printed) vocal parts. 30 text books.
Unsigned and undated [1826]
[DKKk; KTA 227
This (incomplete) set of parts dates from the Copenhagen première of Mozart's opera on 30.1.1826 and was used for all performances of it there during Bournonville's lifetime.

5.2.1869

Bellman or the Polish Dance at Grönalund *(Bellman eller: Polskdandsen paa Grønalund)*.

This 1869 Copenhagen restaging of Bournonville's one-act vaudeville-ballet *Bellman or the Polish Dance at Grönalund (see 3.6.1844)* represents the last time this work was mounted in his lifetime. According to Paulli's original orchestral score (pp. 35–38) and notes in Bournonville's diary, it seems to have been staged this year with a few interpolated music sections (composed and arranged by V. C. Holm) and performed with partially new choreography. In his diary Bournonville noted about the performance:

3.1.1869: 'skrevet og noteret til Bellmann'
4.1.: 'Noteret paa Bellmann […] Prøve og nÿ Indstudering paa Bellmann'
5.1. and 6.1.: 'Prøve paa Bellmann'
11.1.: 'skrevet og componeret. Indstuderet Amor og Bacchus Scenen i Bellmann'
15.1., 18.1., 27.1., 29.1., and 1.2.: 'Prøve paa Bellmann'
4.2.: 'Generalprøve paa Bellmann'
5.2.: 'I Theatret […] <u>Bellmann</u>, fuldt Huus og stort Bifald'.

The 1869 production received 11 performances during Bournonville's lifetime, the last of which was given on 3.11. 1876.

The musical material employed this year was the same as that used since the 1844 première (now in DKKk, call nos. C II, 127 and KTB 293).

21.2.1869
Der Freischütz (Jægerbruden).
The 1869 restaging of C. M. v. Weber's three-act romantic opera was originally projected by Bournonville on 30.10. 1857 (*see also* 4.5.1858). It represents the first and only time this work was mounted with his complete mise-en-scène and under his general supervision. In his diary he noted about the performance:

8.2.1869: 'Decorationsprøve paa Jægerbruden'
9.2.: 'Prøve paa […] Jægerbruden'
11.2.: 'Costumemøde'
12.2.: 'Prøve paa 2 Akter af Jægerbruden'
13.2.: 'Prøve paa 3.e Akt af Jægerbruden'
15.2.: 'Prøve paa <u>Jægerbruden</u> med Orchester'
16.2.: 'Prøve paa <u>Jægerbruden</u> med lille Orchester'
17.2.: 'Sceneprøve Kl 2 paa Jægerbruden'
18.2.: 'Prøve paa <u>Jægerbruden</u>'
19.2.: 'Decorationsprøve'
20.2.: 'Generalprøve paa Jægerbruden'
21.2.: 'I Theatret <u>Jægerbruden</u>, der gik særdeles smukt og gjorde megen Lykke. Huset var saagodtsom udsolgt'.

The staging is not included in Bournonville's handwritten list of his mises-en-scène of operas and plays, written c.1872 (*see* Additional Sources), nor in the printed survey of his works in his memoirs *My Theatre Life* (p. 408).

The 1869 production received 32 performances during Bournonville's lifetime, the last of which was given on 1.11. 1879.

The musical material employed this year was the same as that used for the previous 1858 restaging of Weber's opera (now in DKKk, call nos. C I, 342 and KTA 213).

Autograph sources:

Manuscript mise-en-scène (incomplete). Ms. Autograph. Black ink. 5 pp. (22,7 × 17,9 cm)
<u>Jægerbruden.</u> (Scene = Arrangement) / <u>1.te Akt 1.e Scene</u> / […] / <u>2.den Akt/</u>[…]/<u>3.die Akt.</u>
Unsigned and undated [c. February 1869]
[SSm; Daniel Fryklunds samling no. 129

28.2.1869
The Prophecies of Love, Ballet Divertissement, composed and revised anew (Kjærligheds Spaadomme, Ballet Divertissement, componeret og nyt omarbeidet).
This new, extended version of Bournonville's original *Pas de trois* divertissement, entitled *The Prophecies of Love* (*see* 4.6. 1851), was performed by a cast of three couples that included the three suitors of the maidens from the original 1851 production. In his diary Bournonville noted about the new version:

14.2.1869: 'Jeg traf Aftale med Paulli om Musiken til det nÿe Divertissement'
16.2.: 'begÿndt paa Omarbeidelsen af <u>Kjærligheds Spaadomme</u>'
17.2.: 'componeret og indstuderet paa <u>Kjærligheds Spaadomme</u>'
18.2.: 'Aftenprøve og Indstudering paa <u>Kjærligheds Spaadomme</u>, der blev fuldført med de nÿe Tilsætninger'
22.2.: 'skrevet og prøvet <u>Kjærligheds Spaadomme</u>'
23.2.: 'Prøve paa <u>Kjærl. Spd.</u>'
24.2.: 'Prøve paa <u>Kjærligheds Spaadomme</u> der gaaer udmærket'
25.2.: 'Prøve paa <u>Kjærligheds Spaadomme</u>'
26.2.: 'Costumeprøve i Theatret'
28.2.: 'I Theatret. 1.ste forestilling af […] min nÿ Omarbeidelse af Divertissementet <u>Kjærligheds Spaadomme</u>. Forestillingen var altfor silde ude og Dandsen kom først til at begÿnde Kl 10^1/$_2$. Den gik i det Hele godt og med Bifald'.

The new music added by Paulli to the 1869 version consisted of four numbers (an *Allegro agitato* in 3/4 time, an *Allegretto grazioso* in 3/4 time, an *Allegretto* in 2/4 time, and a *Polka*), and seem to have been composed by him for this occasion.

The new version of *The Prophecies of Love* received 4 performances, the last of which was given on 11.4.1869. The musical material employed this year was a revised version of that used for the original 1851 version (now in DKKk, call nos. MA ms 2668, and KTB 1003).

20.3.1869
Youth and Folly, or Trick upon Trick (Ungdom og Galskab eller List over List).
The 1869 Copenhagen restaging of E. Dupuy's two-act singspiel (first performed on 19.5.1806) was originally projected by Bournonville on 30.10.1857. It represents the first and only time this work was mounted with his mise-en-scène, which consisted mainly of his arrangements for a new set of décors. The production is not included in Bournonville's handwritten list of his mises-en-scène of operas and plays, written c.1872 (*see* Additional Sources), nor in the printed survey of his works in his memoirs *My Theatre Life* (p. 408). In his diary he noted about the performance:

10.3., 16.3., and 18.3.1869: 'Prøve paa <u>Ungdom og Galskab</u>'
20.3.: 'I Theatret <u>Ungdom og Galskab</u> (hvortil jeg havde arrangeret, bedre Decorationer), der var brilliant Huus og megen Munterhed'.

The 1869 production of *Youth and Folly* reached a total of 40 performances during Bournonville's lifetime, the last of which was given on 23.11.1879.

Musical sources:

Orchestral score. Ms. Copy. Black ink. 2 vol. Act I 302 pp., Act II 258 pp. (24,1 × 32 cm with minor variants)
153./<u>Ungdom og Galskab./Partitur./I./</u>[…]/II.

Unsigned and undated [1806]
[DKKk; C II, 106 k (KTA 153)
This orchestral score was used for all performances of Dupuy's sing-spiel since its 1806 Copenhagen première and throughout Bournonville's lifetime.

No repétiteur's copy for *Youth and Folly* has yet been traced.

Parts. Ms. Copy. 30 vol.
4 vl I, 4 vl II, 2 vla, 5 vlc e cb, fl picc, fl 1/2, ob 1/2, cl 1/2, fag 1/2, cor 1/2, tr 1/2, timp, arpa. 9 vocal parts.
Unsigned and undated [1806]
[DKKk; KTA 153
This set of parts was used for all performances of Dupuy's singspiel since its 1806 Copenhagen première and throughout Bournonville's lifetime.

31.3.1869
A Quadrille (En Quadrille) performed by twelve ladies at the home of C. F. Tietgen.
Between 18.2. and 30 3.1869 Bournonville gave a series of twelve private lessons in ballroom dances at the home of the titular councillor of state, C. F. Tietgen. These lessons were concluded with a presentation by his pupils on 31.3.1869, during which a group of twelve young women performed this *Quadrille*. It was choreographed especially for them on 24.3.1869, and was semingly notated by Bournonville on the same day. In his diary he noted about the first and last 1869 lessons:

18.2.1869: '1.ste Lection hos Etats: Tietgen fra 3–5'
24.3.: '11. Lection hos Tietgens, hvor jeg lavede en lille Quadrille'
30.3.: '12.e Lection hos Tietgens'
31.3.: 'Presentation hos Tietgen, mine 12 Elever hædrede sig og mig'.

The presentation was followed by a dinner at Tietgen's home on the following evening, at which all twelve women were present. They are named on this day in Bournonville's diary as follows:

'Tietgens Pleidatter, to Morgenstjerner, tre Fenger, Ibsen, Plenge, Obelitz, to Fabricius, og Pastor Rørdams datter'.

During the same period Bournonville also gave another series of twelve similar lessons in social dance between 13.2. and 2.4.1869. They took place at the Copenhagen residence of Count U. Bernstorff at Amaliegade no. 34. According to his diary these two series of lessons took place on Monday and Wednesday afternoons respectively, with each lesson lasting for about two hours.

No musical source for the *Quadrille* performed at the home of Tietgen on 31.3.1869 has yet been traced.

Autograph sources:

Choreographic note. Ms. Autograph. 2 pp. (format unknown)
Quadrille pour 12 Personnes/[...]/Polonaise./[...]/Contredanse.
Unsigned and undated [Written according to the diary most probably on 24.3.1869]
[USNYp; Dance Collection, call nos. *ZBD-71 (microfilm), and (S)*MGZMD 30 (photostat copy)
This so-called 'Quadrille pour 12 Personnes' consists of two dances, entitled 'Polonaise' and a 'Contredanse'. It is almost certainly identical with the *Quadrille* that he choreographed for his twelve private female dance students on 24.3.1869. This theory is confirmed by the

fact that nowhere in his notation does Bournonville refer to any cavaliers taking part in this dance.

7.4.1869
Les Huguenots (Hugenotterne).
The 1869 Copenhagen restaging of G. Meyerbeer's five-act opera from 1836 was originally projected by Bournonville on 30.10.1857 (*see also* 28.2.1844). It represents the first time this opera was mounted in Copenhagen with his own complete mise-en-scène.

However, the opera's dances in Acts III and V were this year the same as those choreographed two years earlier by L. Gade for the previous Copenhagen restaging of *Les Huguenots* on 7.4.1867. In 1866 Bournonville had already been approached by the management of the Royal Theatre with a proposal to give him sole responsibility for the then planned 1867 restaging of Meyerbeer's opera. This offer, however, was declined by Bournonville, although it seems that he gave several points of choreographic advice to L. Gade, who that year mounted the opera's dances. Thus, in his 1867 diary Bournonville stated about that production:

9.12.1866: 'Mødt hos Justitsraad [F. J. G.] Berner, der talte til mig on Huguenotternes Scenearrangement'
18.12.: 'talt med Justitsraad Berner angaaende Huguenoterne som jeg ikke ønskede at blande mig i'
22.2.1867: 'arbeidet med [L.] Gade til Hugenotterne'
9.4.: 'i Theatret hvor jeg saae Huguenotterne, der hvad Orchester, Chor og Ballet angik udførtes særdeles godt. – Besætningen i det Hele uinteressant'.

Moreover, the theory that L. Gade's 1867 dances for *Les Huguenots* were actually choreographed under Bournonville's personal supervision is further confirmed by the fact that Bournonville also directed a later rehearsal of these dances on 3.10.1867 prior to a performance of Meyerbeer's opera on 14.10.1867.

About his own involvement in the later 1869 restaging of *Les Huguenots* he noted:

26.3.1869: 'skrevet og componeret'
30.3.: 'Instruction paa Hugenotterne'
31.3.: 'bivaanet Claveerprøve paa Hugenottern'
1.4.: 'Arrangement paa tre Akter af Hugunotterne'
2.4.: 'Theaterprøve paa Hugenotterne med Arrangement'
3.4.: 'Stor Prøve og Arrangement paa Hugenotterne'
4.4.: 'Theaterprøve paa 4.de Akt af Hugenotterne'
5.4.: 'Generalprøve paa Hugenotterne'
7.4.: 'I Theatret Hugenotterne til Indtægt for Chorets Pensionsfond. Operaen gik i det Hele smukt, frøken Pfeil gjorde Lykke, men Huset var kun ²/₃ besat! Det var forbi Kl 10³/₄'.

The 1869 production of Meyerbeer's opera received 9 performances, the last of which was given on 27.10.1871 (Acts I and II were given separately three times on 10.3., 12.3., and 13.3.1878).

The musical material employed this year was the same as that used since the 1844 Copenhagen première of this work (now in DKkk, call nos. U 6, MA ms 2908 (2), and KTA 385).

24.4.1869
Little Kirsten (Liden Kirsten).
This performance represents Bournonville's second and last complete restaging of I. P. E. Hartmann's two-act romantic

opera (*see* 6.1.1848 and 29.10.1858). The production appears to have been mounted with some minor choreographic changes from his previous 1858 staging. This theory is based on Bournonville's autographed choreographic numbers, written in the original répétiteur's copy for the music of score nos. 2 and 9 (now in DKkk, call no. MA ms 3085). They seem to refer to a (not yet traced) separate notation of these dances. In his diary he noted about the performance:

20.3.1869: 'confereret med Hartmann om Liden Kirsten'
8.4.: 'Indstudering af tre Dandsestykker til <u>Liden Kirsten</u>'
9.4.: 'Prøve og Instruction paa <u>Liden Kirsten</u>'
13.4.: 'Arrangement paa Liden Kirsten'.

Bournonville was not present at the opening night, but attended the opera's fifth performance on 21.5.1869, about which he noted in his diary:

'Liden Kirsten for fuldt Huus'.

The 1869 production of *Little Kirsten* received 41 performances during Bournonville's lifetime, the last of which was given on 15.2.1877.

The musical material employed this year was the same as that used for the previous 1858 staging (now in DKKk, call nos. C II, 7 c (I. P. E. Hartmanns samling), MA ms 3085, and KTA 396).

25.4.1869
The Wedding Festival in Hardanger (Brudefærden i Hardanger).
This performance represents the last restaging in Copenhagen of Bournonville's two-act Norwegian ballet *The Wedding Festival in Hardanger* (*see* 4.3.1853) during his lifetime. It was mainly carried out by L. Gade and seems to have been mounted with only minor if any changes from the original 1852 version. In his diary Bournonville noted about his own, very limited involvement in this restaging:

28.1., 29.1., 4.3., and 13.4.1869: 'Prøve paa <u>Brudefærden</u>'
24.4.: 'Bivaanet Generalprøve paa Brudefærden'.

Bournonville did not attend the opening night, but after he received a letter from the theatre management on 26.4.1869 he noted about its successful reception in his diary:

'Brev fra [F. J. G.] Berner om det Bifald Brudefærden havde vundet igaar Aftes'.

The 1869 production of *The Wedding Festival in Hardanger* received 15 performances during Bournonville's lifetime, the last of which was given on 31.5.1872.

The musical material employed this year was the same as that used since the 1853 première (now in DKKk, call nos. C II, 119, MA ms 2963, and KTB 266).

17.6.–6.8.1869
Thirty-seven dance lessons to A. Scholl, D. Krum, and A. Forsberg.
According to a series of notes in his diary Bournonville gave a series of private dance lessons to two of his most talented Danish pupils and the Swedish ballerina, A. Forsberg. These lessons, which took place at his private residence in Fredensborg during the summer holiday, lasted about two hours each. On 7.8.1869 he noted about Forsberg in his diary:

'Fulgt Amanda Forsberg til Helsingør Dampskib. Hun begiver sig nu tilbage til Stockholm og efterlader intet Savn tvertimod et "otrevligt Intryck".'

11.8.1869
The feast in the Rosenborg Gardens given in honour of the nuptials of the Danish Crown Prince Frederik and the Swedish Princess Louise Josephine Eugenie.
In his diary Bournonville noted about his involvement in the preparations and the organisation of this public feast, arranged for the celebration of the nuptials of the Danish Crown Prince (later King Frederik VIII) and the Swedish Princess Louise Josephine Eugenie:

25.6.1869: 'Brev fra Geheimeraad [C. J. C.] <u>Bræstrup</u> om Folkefesten i Rosenborghave'
27.6.: 'Skrevet til Geheimeraad Bræstrup med Forslag til Festen'
1.7.: 'Møde i Communalbestyrelsen om Formælingsfesten'
11.7.: 'Besøg af Geheimeraad Bræstrup'
15.7.: 'Brev fra Geheim: Bræstrup'
17.7.: 'Kl 2 i Communalbestyrelsen'
23.7.: 'jeg fik endnu et Brev fra Geheimeraad Bræstrup'
26.7.: 'Møde i Communaludvalget [...] besøgt Excerceerpladsen, hvor Danmark Statuen bliver opreist'
27.7.: 'Møde hos Geheimeraad Bræstrup paa Raadhuset [...] modtaget en stor Deel Anmodninger om Billetter'
28.7.: 'Dagen helliget Glæden over Kronprindsens Formæling med den svenske Kronprindsesse Lovisa i Stockholm'
29.7.: 'Brev til Geheim: Bræstrup i Anledning af Sangen til Danmark, som [F.] Paludan-Müller og [N. W.] Gade skulle levere'
31.7.: 'To Breve fra Bræstrup [...] Besøgt Prof Gade'
2.8.: 'Comitémøde i Rosenborghave [...] talt med [...] N. Gade' [...] Brev til Conferentsraad [C.] <u>Hauch</u> i Anledning af den Orden, hvori Sangene skulle udføres'
4.8.: 'Brev fra <u>Hauch</u> ordnet Sagen angaaende Første=Retten med <u>Gade</u>. Brev til Chor-Regisseur <u>Hanne</u> og Tømmermester Kayser'
8.8.: 'Brev fra [...] <u>Bræstrup</u>'
9.8.: 'modtaget og uddeelt Billetter, tilstede ved comiteen i Rosenborghave [...] sendt Billetter til Fredensborg [...] Overværet en Sangprøve ved Borgerdydskolen paa Chrhavn [...] det regnede meget stærkt til stor Bedrøvelse baade for Fest- og Høstfolkene'
10.8.: 'overværet en Generalprøve af circa 900 sangere de samlede Sangforeninger under [A. W.] Lanzkys Anførsel. Det tog sig brilliant ud'
11.8.: 'Morgenstunden skjøn, men allerede Kl 10 begyndte Bygerne som kun med korte Ophold vedvarede indtil Kl 9 om Aftenen og forstyrrede os i paa en sørgelig Maade den hele store Folkefest, hvorpaa der var anvendt saa megen Flid, Smag og Penge! Dagen hengik i Uvished om Festen skulde finde Sted, men endelig besluttedes den efter at de høie Herskaber vare adspurgte. Kl 6 mødte jeg i Rosenborghave og da var det tarveligt Opinclude svejr men fra Kl 7½ indtil 9 faldt der forfærdelige Byger. Alt strømmede i Vand og Gangene vare opblødte. Ikke desto mindre opretholdt Modet og Humeuret sig i en mærkværdig Grad baade for de Medvirkende og Publicum, og da den kgl Familie havde hørt den første Tale og Sang klaredes det lidt og Concerten paa Excerceerpladsen gik udmærket godt og saavel Statuen som Folkemassen tog sig ypperligt ud. – Enthousiasmen og Jubelen var betydelig. Kl 10 spiste de Indbudne med de Kongelige i det store Telt hvor der var en særdeles fiin Souper og derpaa et vellykket Fyrværkeri. Derpaa tog Herskabet til Festen vedvarede indtil Kl 1, endnu lidt stænket af Regnen. Helene [Bournonville] var med mig og vi mødte flere interessante Bekjendte blandt andre General Hatzelius, Baron [E. F. O. L. von] Stedingk m.

fl. Veiret og den mangelfulde Belÿsning gjode Festen stort Afbræk, men det der blev tilbage af den var endnu betÿdeligt nok til at gjøre den storslaaet og folkelig'.

According to an undated letter, written by N. W. Gade (seemingly on 12.8.1869) to his wife, M. Gade (first published in 1892 in D. Gade's book *Niels W. Gade*), two of the five songs and dance numbers composed for this public feast were performed on a stage erected next to the main fountain in the Rosenborg Gardens. They were:

(1) A choral song for mixed voices, entitled 'Hilsen' («Hil Eder, Hil!») and set to music by I. P. E. Hartmann and text by C. Ploug.
(2) A so-called 'Fakkeldands' by H. C. Lumbye, played by a full orchestra.

The three remaining songs were all performed on a stage erected on 'Excerceerpladsen' in the vicinity of an allegorical statue representing 'Danmark'. These songs were:

(3) A 'Velkomstsang' for mixed voices («I Sommer-solens fulde Glands») set to music by H. Rung and text by a certain 'O. B.' [perhaps identical with C. Hauch?].
(4) A choral song for mixed voices and a brass ensemble, entitled 'Ved Danmarksstøtten' («Hæv i Dæmringens Stund her dit Blik») and set to music by N. W. Gade and text by F. Paludan-Müller.
(5) Several Danish national sungs, performed by a gigantic chorus of 800 male singers.

Musical sources:

Orchestral score. Ms. Autograph. Black ink and pencil. 12 pp. (34,8 × 25,5 cm)
Fakkeldands./componeret i Anledning af Kronprinds Frederiks/og Prindsesse Lovisas Formæling.
Signed and dated: 'af H: C: Lumbÿe/April 1869.'
[DKKk; MA ms 2575 (mu 9405.2702)
This autographed orchestral score was previously in the music archive of Denmark's Broadcasting (Danmarks Radio) where it was catalogued with the call no. '342'. It was purchased by DKKk on 27.5.1994.

Orchestral score. Ms. Copy. Brown ink. 4 pp. (29 × 35,8 cm with minor variants)
Fakkeldands af Lumbye
Unsigned and undated [c.1869]
[DKKK, C II, 34 (mu 6501.2601)
This orchestral score almost certainly dates from soon after the first performance of this dance in the Rosenborg Gardens on 11.8.1869. It was most likely used for public concerts in Copenhagen. The manuscript was donated to DKKk on 26.1.1965 by the music antiquarian, D. Fog.

No répétiteur'c copy for Lumbye's *Fakkeldands* has yet been traced.

Parts. Ms. Copy. 35 vol.
4 vl I, 4 vl II, 3 vla, 3 vlc, 3 cb, fl picc, fl, ob 1/2, cl 1/2, fag 1/2, cor 1/2, tr 1/2, trb 1/2/3, tuba, gr cassa, cassa.
Unsigned and undated [1869 and later]
[DKKk; Tivolis musikarkiv no. 1120 (mu 9405.1400)
This set of parts was used when Lumbye's 'Fakkeldands' was played for the first time at a public concert in the Tivoli Gardens on 28.7.1869. Notes written in several of the parts indicate that the music lasts for approximately 6 minutes. Another complete set of parts for this dance (dating from the 1940s) now exists in the music archive of the Tivoli Gardens (call no. 1120).

Printed piano-vocal score. 1 vol. 15 pp. (32,9 × 25,8 cm)
FEST-SANGE / VED / INDTOGET OG FESTEN I ROSENBORG HAVE/d. 10. og 11. August 1869.

Copenhagen, C. E. Horneman & J. Erslev, pl. no. 723 [August 1869]
This piano-vocal score contains the complete music and text for (1) H. Rung's song, entitled 'Velkomstsang', (2) I. P. E. Hartmann's choral song, named 'Hilsen', and (3) N. W. Gade's choral song, entitled 'Ved Danmarksstøtten'.
[DKKk; Archive of the N.W. Gade Edition

12.8.1869

***A Court Ball* given in honour of the nuptials of the Danish Crown Prince and the Swedish Princess Louise Josephine Eugenie (Christiansborg Palace).**

In his diary Bournonville noted about his participation in the organisation of this royal court ball given to celebrate the nuptials of the Danish Crown Prince (later King Frederik VIII) with the Swedish Princess Louise Josephine Eugenie:

24.4.1869: 'Brev fra Overhofmarschallen angaaende Formælings-høitinden'
28.4.: 'Samtale med […] Overhofmarchallen angaaende Formælingsfesten'
18.6.: 'Brev fra Overhofmarskallen'
23.6.: 'Brev til Overhofmarskall Oxholm'
29.6.: 'talt med Overhofmarskallen om Festballet'
13.7.: 'talt med Ahlgrensson'
19.7.: 'Brev til […] Overhofmarschallen'
22.7.: 'Brev fra Overhofmarschallen besvaret til Greve Holck'
27.7.: 'arrangeret med [F.] Ahlgrensson og Blikkenslager Meyer en Globus til Hofballet […] mødt med [L.] Gade paa Slottet for at tage Riddersalen m m i Øiesyn'
12.8.: 'Kl 8½ til Hofballet der var yderst splendid (2300 Indbudne) Dandsen gik temmelig slet. I Cotillonen benÿttedes en Reduction af min Idée med Globen og Amor midt iblandt Bouquetterne. Den gjorde alligevel en slags Virkning, men det er ikke mere muligt at udføre noget smukt ved vore Hofballer. – De kongelige vare særdels naadige imod mig – Det Hele var forbi Kl 2 og jeg skyndte mig hjem'.

No programme and/or musical sources for this royal court ball have yet been traced.

1.9.1869

The Valkyrie (Valkyrien).

For a gala performance given on this day as part of the celebrations for the nuptials of the Crown Prince (later King Frederik VIII) and the Swedish Princess Louise Josephine Eugenie, Bournonville's four-act Nordic mythological ballet *The Valkyrie* (see 13.9.1861) was given in a new production. It was mounted and directed mainly by his assistant, L. Gade, with B. Schnell playing the leading rôle of *Svava* for the first time. For the same production, which was given with partially new décors by F. Ahlgrensson, Bournonville wrote a new, revised version in French of the ballet's scenario. In his diary he noted about the production and its reception:

24.3.1869: 'Indstudering paa Valkyrien ([B.] Schnell)'
27.3. and 30.3.: 'Indstudering paa Valkyrien'
2.4.: 'Indstudering paa Valkyrien med[G.] Döcker'
12.4.: 'Prøve paa Valkyrien 1.e og 2.den Akt'
28.4.: 'Prøve paa Valkyrien'
3.5.: 'Brev fra […] [F. J. G.] Berner der meldte at Valkyrien skulde gaae til Festforestillingen i August eller September?'
4.5.: 'Brev til Just. Berner om Festforestillingen'
12.5.: 'Valkyrien blev prøvet og gik fortræffeligt'
13.6.: 'modtaget […] [F.] Ahlgrensson med hvem jeg arbeidede for […] Valkyrien'
31.7.: 'skrevet og udarbeidet en fransk Analyse af Valkyrien'
1.8.: 'reenskrevet den franske Analyse'
17.8.: 'jeg besørgede en Prøve paa Valkyrien'

19.8. and 20.8.: 'Prøve paa 'Valkyrien''
21.8.: 'Brev til [L.] Gade'
25.8.: 'Kl 7 Theaterprøve paa Valkyrien der gik meget smukt, takket være Gades Omsorg'
26.8.: 'Prøve paa Dandsene Kl 11'
28.8.: '1.ste Generalprøve paa Valkyrien, der gik særdeles smukt'
30.8.: 'besørget Programmer til Den Kgl Familie og til Kongressens Medlemmer [...] Generalprøve [...] Kl 7 paa Valkyrien der paa [nær] nogle Ubehændigheder fra Belysningens Side gik udmærket godt. Schnell var meget indtagende og tilfredstillende. Prøven overværedes af Døvstumme=Institutets Elever. Deres Lærerinde Caroline Matthiesen forærte mig en deilig Bouquet, som jeg atter presenterede Juliette Price, der ogsaa ved denne Leilighed har viist en yndig Character'
1.9.: 'lille Prøve paa Valkyrien [...] I Theatret Festforestilling i Anledning af Formælingen [...] Valkyrien, der gik fortræffeligt'
2.9.: 'megen Tilfredshed hos de fremmede over min Ballet'
3.9.: 'Til Taffel paa Christiansborg i Riddersalen [...] der var meget behageligt og overalt høstede jeg Roes for min Ballet'.

The 1869 production of *The Valkyrie* received 7 performances, the last of which was given on 29.12.1870.

The musical material employed in 1869 was the same as that used since the 1861 première of this ballet (now in DKKk, call no. C II, 114, MA ms 2995, and KTB 298).

Printed sources:

Printed scenario. 1 vol. 4 pp. (22 × 14,5 cm)
LA VALKYRIE./BALLET D'ACTION EN QUATRE ACTES/PAR/ AUGUSTE BOURNONVILLE.
Copenhagen, Bianco Luno par F. S. Muhle, 1869
[DKKk; 17, – 175 8°

30.9.1869

The Pascha's Daughter (Paschaens Datter).

For the première of P. Heise's four-act singspiel (to a libretto by H. Hertz) Bournonville created both the general mise-en-scène and two dances. According to his autographed choreographic notes the dances were:

(1) An (unnamed) *Dance* in Act I (score no. 1), performed by a corps de ballet of Hindus (eight couples) during the opening chorus, entitled «Det er Dandserne, de brömte, der fra Indien drog herhen».
(2) An (unnamed) *Dance* in Act IV (score no. 17), performed by a group of odalisques (twelve women) during the opening chorus «Under Klokkespillets Klang, til de muntre Tambouriner». On p. 220 of the printed libretto for *The Pascha's Daughter* (now in DKKk, call no. 55, – 96 8°) this dance is described as follows: 'En Mængde unge Fruentimmer komme dandsende hen mod Forgrunden enten fra Salens Baggrund eller ind fra Siderne. Nogle af dem ledsage Dandsen med Instrumenter'.

In his diary Bournonville noted about Heise's singspiel, which represents the first time he ever worked together with this composer:

14.5.1868: 'gjennemlæst Texten til Paschaens Datter, der ikke lover noget særdeles!'
15.5.: 'skrevet min Betænkning over Paschaens Datter og sendt Den tilligemed Librettoen paa Post til [F. J. G.] Berner'
10.8.: 'arbeidet paa Scene-Arrangementet til Paschaens Datter og skrevet til Heise'
11.8.: 'skrevet og fortsat Sceneriet til P. D.'
12.8.: 'fuldendt Arrangementet til Paschaens Datter. Besøg af Componisten [P.] Heyse der spiste her tilligemed [H. S.] Paullis'
15.8.: 'Brev til Heyse med Forslag til hans Opera'
18.8.: 'Arbeide med Heyse'
24.9.: 'Besøg hos Heyse, angaaende hans Opera'

25.9.: 'Brev til Prof. [H.] Herz om Paschaens Datter'
22.4.1869: 'arbeidet paa Scene=Arrangementet til Paschaens Datter'
24.4.: 'Oplæsning paa Paschaens Datter en meget kjedelig og fersk Text'
27.4.: 'componeret'
1.5.: 'Skrevet Scene=Arrangement til Paschaens Datter og afsendt Manuscriptet til Justitsraad Berner'
12.5.: 'Jeg mønstrede nogle Decorationer til Paschaens Datter'
13.5.: 'mønstret Decorationer'
17.6.: 'componeret til Paschaens Datter. 1.ste Balletstykke færdigt'
21.6.: 'skrevet og componeret'
22.6.: 'skrevet'
31.8.: 'componeret'
2.9.: 'Indstudering paa Dandsen til Paschaens Datter'
4.9.: 'Indstudering paa Paschaens Datter – Dands om Formiddagen'
6.9.: 'Kl 10 Indstudering paa Dandsen til Paschaens Datter'
7.9.:'Dandseprøve paa Paschaens Datter [...] Kl 6 Instruction paa Paschaens Datter'
8.9.: 'skrevet og componeret [...] Instruction paa Paschaens Datter'
9.9.: 'lille Prøve paa de nye Dandse'
11.9.: 'Instruction paa Paschaens Datter'
14.9.: 'stor Arrangementprøve paa Paschaens Datter'
17.9.: 'Prøve paa 1.ste og 2 Akt af Paschaen'
18.9.: 'Prøve paa 2.' og 3.e Akt af Paschaen'
20.9.: 'Fuldstændig Prøve paa Paschaens Datter Vrøvl med [J. L.] Nyrop'
21.9.: 'Decorationsprøve til Fordeling af Operaens 3.die Akt'
22.9.: 'forberedet Generalprøven til iaften. Den blev aflyst formedelst [P. L. N.] Schramms Upasselighed'
26.9.: 'Prøve paa Paschaens Datter fra 11 til 1½ [...] Costumeprøve med Nyrop'
27.9.: '1.ste Generalprøve Kl 11 paa Paschaens Datter'
29.9.: 'Generalprøve paa Paschaens Datter'
30.9.: 'Første Forestilling af Paschaens Datter udsolgt Huus og meget Bifald. Alt gik særdeles smukt og Dandsene tog sig glimrende ud'.

The Pascha's Daughter received 10 performances, the last of which was given on 23.2.1871.

Autograph sources:

Production note. Ms. Autograph. Brown ink. 4 pp. (21,3 × 13,8 cm)
Bemærkninger/ved/Iscenesætningen af Paschaens Datter.
Signed and dated: 'Fredensborg d 15.e Mai 1868.'
[SSm; Daniel Fryklunds samling no. 140 a

Manuscript mise-en-scène. Ms. Autograph. Brown ink. 1 vol. 15 pp. (21,3 × 17 cm)
Paschaens Datter/Opera af Herz og Heyse./Scene = Arrangement/ af/August Bournonville./1868.
Signed and dated: 'Fredensborg d 12.e August 1868.'
[SSm; Daniel Fryklunds samling no. 140 b

Manuscript mise-en-scène. Ms. Autograph. Black ink. 1 vol. 18 pp. (20,3 × 16,4 cm)
Paschaens Datter/Syngestykke i 3 Akter.
Signed and dated: 'Fredensborg d 12.e August 1868./reenskrevet/d 1.ste Mai 1869.'
[SSm; Daniel Fryklunds samling no. 140 c

Production note. Ms. Autograph. Brown ink. 3 pp. (21,3 × 17,3 cm)
Scene = Arrangement til Paschaens Datter/Decorationer. (Bazar)
Unsigned and undated [Written according to the diary probably between 22.4. and 1.5.1869]
[SSm; Daniel Fryklunds samling no. 140 d

Choreographic note. Ms. Autograph. Brown ink. 3 pp. (20,9 × 13,5 cm)
Paschaens Datter./(Dands af Hinduer)
Signed and dated: 'Fredensborg d. 17 Juni 1869'
[DKKk; NKS 3285 4° 3 L–P

Bournonville's choreographic numbers included in this manuscript ('1–20') refer to his similar numbers inserted on pp. 1–9 in the 1869 répétiteur's copy for *The Pascha's Daughter* (now in DKKk, call no. MA ms 2912 (1)).

Choreographic note. Ms. Autograph. Brown ink. 3 pp. (20,9 × 13,5 cm)
Paschaens Datter./(Dands af Odalisker)
Signed and dated: 'Fredensborg ce 22 Juin 1869'
[DKKk; NKS 3285 4° 3 L–P
Bournonville's choreographic numbers included in this manuscript ('1–22') refer to similar numbers inserted on pp. 10–15 in the 1869 répétiteur's copy for *The Pascha's Daughter* (now in DKKk, call no. MA ms 2912 (1)).

Production note. Ms. Autograph. Brown ink. 1 p. (21,4 × 14,1 cm)
Særskildte Bemærkninger.
Unsigned and undated [c.1869]
[SSm; Daniel Fryklunds samling no. 140 e

Musical sources:

Orchestral score. Ms. Autograph (by P. Heise). Brown and black ink. 3 vol. Act I 310 pp. of which two are blank, Act II 254 pp. of which one is blank, Act III 272 pp. of which one is blank (35 × 26 cm with minor variants)
Paschaens Datter./Syngestykke i tre Akter af Prof. H. Hertz,/sat i Musik/af/P. Heise./Partitur./[…]/2.den Act./[…]/Tredie Act
Unsigned and undated [1869]
[DKKk; C II, 114 f (KTA 768)
This autographed orchestral score is divided into three acts. However, at the 1869 première the second part of Act III (score nos. 17–18) was given separately as Act IV. The score was used for all performances of Heise's singspiel during Bournonville's lifetime. The music for the two dance scenes is included in vol. I (pp. '89–123') and vol. III (pp. '686–717').

Répétiteur's copy. Ms. Copy. Black ink. 1 vol. 16 pp. of which one is blank (33,2 × 25,2 cm)
Paschaens Datter./[…]/91/[…]/Repetiteurpartie/til/Paschaens Datter
Unsigned and undated [1869]
[DKKk; MA ms 2912 (1) (KTA 768 (1))
This répétiteur's copy contains the music for the two dance scenes performed in Act I (score no. 1) and Act IV (score no. 17) of *The Pascha's Daughter*. It also includes Bournonville's autographed choreographic numbers ('1–20' and '1–12', written with black ink) which refer to similar numbers in his two separate choreographic notations of these dances (written on 17.6. and 22.6.1869 respectively).
     The répétiteur's copy is included on pp. 1–16 in a volume that also contains the répétiteur's copies for five other operas and plays, mounted at Copenhagen's Royal Theatre between 1815 and 1871.

Répétiteur's copy. Ms. Copy. Black ink. 1 vol. 16 pp. of which one is blank (33,9 × 25,5 cm)
Paschaens Datter./[…]/85./[…]/Repetiteurpartie/til/Paschaens Datter.
Unsigned and undated [c.1871]
[DKKk; MA ms 2913 (2) (KTA 768 (2))
This répétiteur's copy contains the complete music for the two dance scenes performed in Act I (score no. 1) and Act IV (score no. 17) of *The Pascha's Daughter*. It also includes the names of the dancers A. Scholl and B. Schnell. Consequently, it must have served for some later performances of Heise's singspiel, and certainly after the retirement in December 1869 of the dancer, L. Cetti (Schnell took over Cetti's part in Heise's singspiel at its restaging on 8.2.1871).
     The répétiteur's copy is included on pp. 5–20 in a volume that also contains the répétiteur's copies for five other operas and plays, mounted at Copenhagen's Royal Theatre between 1869 and 1871.

Parts. Ms. Copy. 36 vol.
4 vl I, 3 vl II, 2 vla, 4 vlc e cb, fl picc, fl 1/2, ob 1/2, cl 1/2, fag 1/2, cor 1/2/3/4, tr 1/2, trb 1/2/3, timp, gr cassa, piatti, tri, arpa. 60 vocal parts.
Unsigned and undated [1869]
[DKKk; KTA 768

7.10.1869
Pas de deux (uncredited) performed by D. Krum and L. Cetti.
According to Bournonville's diary, this (uncredited) *Pas de deux* was arranged and rehearsed by him during the spring of 1869. It was mounted for the second début of L. Cetti, but was actually not performed by her and Krum before on this day. According to the orchestral score, the *Pas de deux* is a musically (and most likely also choreographically) new arrangement by V. C. Holm and Bournonville of the much earlier F major *Pas de deux*, originally incorporated by Bournonville in Act I of *Nina, ou La Folle par amour* for the débuts of F. Hoppe and L. Grahn (*see* 30.9.1834).
     In his diary Bournonville noted about the only three rehearsals he held of this dance during the early spring of 1869:

12.4.1869: 'Aftenprøve paa en Pas de deux til Cetti og Krum'
15.4.: 'Prøve paa Cettis pas de deux'
16.4.: 'Prøve paa Pas de deux'.

On 7.10.1869 he stated about its first performance:

'I Theatret seet to Dandse af de unge Mennesker, der vare udmærket flinke'.

Cetti, who only performed the *Pas de deux* twice (the last time on 8.11.1869), retired from the stage in December 1869 after being married the same year. Subsequently, A. Scholl seems (according to the posters) to have taken over her part in this dance (*see* 28.1.1870).

Musical sources:

Orchestral score. Ms. Autograph (by V. C. Holm). Brown ink. 20 pp. (26,4 × 35 cm)
Pas de deux
Unsigned and undated [1869]
[DKKk; MA ms 2653 (KTB 251)
In the original handwritten catalogue of the music archive of Copenhagen's Royal Theatre this orchestral score and its accompanying set of parts are both entitled 'Pas de deux (Frk Cetti og Hr Krum)'. Three of the six movements in Holm's score (the *Moderato* in F major, the *Moderato* in A flat major, and the *Allegro* in F major, all in 4/4 time) employ music from Bournonville's much earlier *Pas de deux* in F major from Act I of his Copenhagen production of L. Milon's two-act pantomimic ballet *Nina, our La Folle par amour* (*see* 30.9.1834). The music for the remaining three movements was most probably composed by Holm in 1869.

According to the handwritten catalogue of the music archive of Copenhagen's Royal Theatre, no separate répétiteur's copy for this *Pas de deux* was ever made.

Parts. Ms. Copy. 21 vol.
2 vl I, 2 vl II, vla, 2 vlc e cb, fl picc, fl gr, ob 1/2, cl 1/2, fag 1/2, cor 1/2, tr 1/2, timp, tri.
Unsigned and undated [1869]
[DKKk; KTB 251
A pencilled note in the part for the first violin (no. 1) reads: 'Cetti og Krum'.

6.11.1869

The Toreador (Toréadoren).

This performance represents Bournonville fourth restaging in Copenhagen of his two-act idyllic ballet *The Toreador* (*see* 27.11.1840). It was mounted with H. Scharff and J. Petersen in the leading rôles as *Alonzo* and *Maria*, and with one of Bournonville's youngest pupils, L. Cetti, performing the part of *Céleste* for the first time. To Bournonville's great sorrow the latter retired from the stage only three weeks later as the result of her marriage this year to the Bohemian violoncellist and composer, F. X. Neruda.

The 1869 staging seems to have been mounted without any significant changes from the previous production on 21.10.1866, except the omission of the then interpolated *La Seguedilla*.

In his diary Bournonville noted about the performance:

29.6.1869: '9.e Lection og indstuderet Soloen af Toreadoren'
12.10.: 'Prøvet lidt til Toreadoren'
13.10., 14.10., 25.10., 26.10.: 'Prøve paa Toréadoren'
28.10.: 'Prøve paa Rollerne til Toréadoren'
30.10.: 'Prøve paa Toreadoren'
1.11.: 'Prøve paa Toreadoren (Theatret)'
3.11.: 'Prøve paa Toreadoren'
5.11.: 'Theaterprøve paa Toreadoren. Underretning om at Ludovica Cetti ved sit Giftermaal med Fr. [X.] Neruda skal forlade Theatret ved Maanedens Udgang. Denne Hensynsløshed er i mine Tanker en fornærmelse imod vort samfund og vistnok et skridt som i Tiden vil fortrÿdes'
6.11.: 'Toreadoren gik i nÿ Indstudering for brilliant Huus og med levende Bifald'.

The 1869 staging of *The Toreador* received five performances, the last of which was given on 29.11.1869. The musical material employed this year was the same as that used since the ballet's 1840 première (now in DKKk, call nos. C II, 114 k, MA ms 2965, and KTB 269).

17.12.1869

Jean de Paris (Johan fra Paris).

The 1869 Copenhagen restaging of F.-A. Boyeldieu's two-act comic opera (premièred at l'Opéra Comique in Paris on 4.4.1812, and first performed in Copenhagen on 1.2.1815) was originally projected by Bournonville on 30.10.1857. It represents the first and only time this opera was mounted with his mise-en-scène and choreography, which included two brief dance scenes as follows:

(1) An (unnamed) *Dance* in 3/4 time, performed in Act II (score no. 11) by the townspeople during the chorus, entitled «De monsieur jean de monsieur jean que le festin s'apprête» (score no. 11).
(2) An (unnamed) *Dance* in 3/4 time, performed in Act II (score no. 12) by the character *Pédrigo* (while beating a 'tambour de basque') and a corps de ballet of townspeople (playing the castanets) during the chorus, entitled «Au bruit des castagnettes».

Bournonville's 1869 staging of Boyeldieu's *Jean de Paris* is not included in his handwritten list of his mises-en-scène of operas and plays, written c.1872 (*see* Additional Sources), but is mentioned in the printed survey of his works in his memoirs *My Theatre Life* (p. 409).

In his diary he noted about the performance:

2.11.1869: 'Oplæsning paa Johan fra Paris'

12.11.: 'skrevet [...] besørget Sceneriet til Johan fra Paris'
18.11.: 'Costumemøde paa Johan fra Paris'
4.12.: 'Musikprøve paa Johan fra Paris'
5.12.: 'Decorationsprøve paa Johan fra Paris'
6.12.: 'Arrangement paa Johan fra Paris'
7.12.: 'Arrangementprøve paa Johan fra Paris'
9.12.: 'Prøve paa Johan fra Paris fra 10–2'
10.12., 12.12., and 13.12.: 'Prøve paa Johan fra Paris'
15.12.: 'Generalprøve paa Johan fra Paris'
17.12.: 'I Theatret Johan fra Paris der gik meget smukt, men uden synderlig Effekt'.

The 1869 production received 3 performances, the last of which was given on 10.1.1870.

Autograph sources:

Manuscript mise-en-scène. Ms. Autograph. Brown ink. 4 pp. (22,8 × 18 cm)
Johan fra Paris/1.ste Akt 1.e Scene./[...]/2.den Akt. (Have)
Signed and dated: 'd. 12 Novbr 1869'
[SSm; Daniel Fryklunds samling no. 128

Production note. Ms. Autograph. Brown ink. 2 pp. (21,4 × 13,8 cm)
Forslag til Chorfordeling/i/Johan fra Paris/1.ste Akt 1.ste Scene./ [...]/2.den Akt 5.te Scene.
Signed and dated: 'Kbhvn d. 12 Novbr 1869'
[SSm; Daniel Fryklunds samling no. 128

Musical sources:

Printed orchestral score with manuscript insertions. 1 vol. 316 pp. (32,3 × 25,3 cm)
Jean de Paris./Partitur./[...]/JEAN DE PARIS,/Opéra Comique en deux Actes/[...]/PAR/Adrien Boieldieu.
Paris, Boieldieu jeune, pl. no. 94 [1812]
[DKKk; U 6 (KTA 178]
This printed French orchestral score was used for all performances of *Jean de Paris* in Copenhagen. The music for the two dance scenes in Act II (score nos. 11 and 12) is included on pp. '52–60' and '62–76' respectively.

Répétiteur's copy. Ms. Copy. Black ink. 1 vol. 4 pp. of which one is blank (33,2 × 25,2 cm)
[...]/Johan fra Paris./[...]/91/[...]/Repetiteurparti/til/Johan fra Paris
Unsigned and undated [1869]
[DKKk; MA ms 2912 (3) (KTA 178 (2))
This répétiteur's copy contains the music for the two dance scenes in Act II of *Jean de Paris* (score nos. 11 and 12). It is included on pp. 21–26 in a volume that also contains the répétiteur's copies for five other operas and plays, mounted at Copenhagen's Royal Theatre between 1869 and 1871.

Parts. Ms. Copy. 27 vol.
4 vl I, 3 vl II, 2 vla, 4 vlc e cb, fl 1/2, ob 1/2, cl 1/2, fag 1/2, cor 1/2, clno 1/2, timp, tamb. 48 vocal parts.
Unsigned and undated [1815]
[DKKk; KTA 178
This set of parts dates from the 1815 Copenhagen première of *Jean de Paris* and was used for all performances of it there during Bournonville's lifetime.

19.12.1869

Pas de trois (uncredited) performed by E. Hansen, J. Petersen, and M. Price.

This (uncredited) dance is most probably identical with the *Pas de trois* in Bournonville's final version of his Spanish ballet divertissement *La Ventana* (*see* 6.10.1856). This theory is supported by the fact that when *La Ventana* was restaged at Copenhagen's Royal Theatre on 5.12.1868 the *Pas de trois* was performed by the same cast, except for J. Petersen, who in 1869 seems to have replaced L. Cetti, since the latter had retired from the stage with the end of November 1869. Bournonville did not attend the 1869 performance of this *Pas de trois*. It seems (according to the posters) to have been performed twice this year, the last time on 21.12.1869. It is not possible to identify the dance any further.

29.12.1869
Das Unerreichbare (Det Uopnaaelige).
Although he did not take part in the staging of the Copenhagen première of A. Wilbrandt's one-act comedy (first performed in Berlin at Königliches Schauspielhaus on 24.4. 1869 with the title *Unerreichbar*), Bournonville was clearly instrumental in the first Danish production of this work (translated and mounted by an anonymous director). This theory is confirmed by the fact that he attended two performances of the comedy during his sojourn in Munich in the spring of 1869 and noted about it in his diary at that time:

26.5.1869: 'Kl 6½ gik vi i Theatret, hvortil vi hver Aften have Billetter. Vi saae tre smaae Stykker. 1° Underreichbar af [A.] Wilbrandt smukt spillet navnlig af Herr [B.] Rüthling som Leonhard og af Frl Jenke som Hedwig'
31.5.: 'I Theatret og seet for 2' Gang Unerreichbar ypperligt spillet af Rüthling'
13.8.: 'Breve fra München om Stykket 'Unerreichbar''.

Das Unerreichbare received 6 performances in Copenhagen, the last of which was given on 8.2.1870. Bournonville noted about it on the opening night:

29.12.1869: 'I Theatret 1.ste Forestilling af Det Uopnaaelige [...] Stykket blev optaget med Bifald'.

1870

11.1.1870
Iphigenia in Aulis (Iphigenia i Aulis).
This performance represents Bournonville's second and last staging in Copenhagen of R. Wagner's 1846 revision of C. W. v. Gluck's three-act opera (*see* 27.4.1861). It was mounted with the dances of the spirits in Act II (score no. 17) performed by four women instead of the original cast of six dancers. Moreover, according to Bournonville's autographed choreographic numbers in the répétiteur's copy for this opera (now in DKKk, call no. MA ms 2911 (2)) he seems this year to have made a separate (not yet traced) notation of the choreography for this dance. In his diary he noted about the 1870 restaging:

20.12.1869: 'prøvet paa Iphigenia [...] skrevet'
22.12.: 'prøvet Dands og hele Iphigenia'
23.12.: 'Instruction paa Iphigenia, Costümemøde'
24.12.: 'Arrangement og Prøve paa Iphigenia'
9.1.1870: 'prøve paa Iphigenia'.

Bournonville did not attend the opening night, but saw the opera's first act at its second performance on 17.1.1870.

The 1870 production received 16 performances during Bournonville's lifetime, the last of which was given on 12.11. 1879.

The musical material employed this year was the same as that used since the 1861 Copenhagen première (now in DKKkt and in DKKk with the call nos. KTA 478 and MA ms 2911 (2) respectively).

14.1.1870
Cort Adeler in Venice (Cort Adeler i Venedig).
This three-act ballet with a final tableau is freely based on the life of the fifteenth-century Norwegian born sea-hero, Cort Adeler. It was originally projected by Bournonville on 20.7. 1832, and was then dedicated to B. Thorvaldsen. However, for unknown reasons (probably the difficulty of finding a suitable music composer for the ballet in 1832) that project was soon abandoned, although Bournonville resumed working on it during Denmark's war with Germany in 1848. This is clear from a note in his diary on 20.3.1848 reading:

'Begyndt Programmet til en nỹ Ballet: Cort Adeler'.

The ballet was not carried out until two more decades had passed. It was then mounted to a new, original score by P. Heise. The choice of this composer seems to have resulted from Bournonville's earlier very positive experience in choreographing to Heise's music, when he mounted the dances in 1869 in the four-act singspiel *The Pascha's Daughter* (*see* 30.9.1869). This theory is furthermore supported by the fact that in the second scene in Act III (score no. 20) of *Cort Adeler in Venice*, Bournonville included a series of very similar dances to those made for *The Pascha's Daughter*, which were performed by a group of odalisques from the harem of *Ibrahim Pascha*.

However, according to two letters from I. P. E. Hartmann and E. Hartmann to Bournonville (written on 21.11.1868 and 29.5.1869 respectively, now in DKKk, call nos. NKS 3258 A 4°, IV, facs. 14, no. 261, and facs. 13, no. 252), Bournonville originally planned to commission the score for this ballet from one or both of these composers. In his letter I. P. E. Hartmann politely declined the offer by declaring that he was more inclined to write vocal and symphonic music after having completed the score for Bournonville's four-act Nordic mythological ballet *The Lay of Thrym*. However, he strongly recommended his son for this project, and it was actually Emil Hartmann who later suggested that Bournonville approach P. Heise with regard to this ballet.

According to a correspondence between Heise and Bournonville (now in DKKk, call nos. NKS 3258 4°, V, facs. 2, nos. 392–393), Heise began composing the music during a sojourn in Rome in the spring of 1869 and continued working on it during a visit to Venice on his homeward journey. He then collected several Venetian folk tunes which served as his main musical source of inspiration for this ballet.

Fourteen years before the 1870 première of *Cort Adeler in Venice* Bournonville had himself visited Venice during April 1856. That experience resulted in his projected two-act ballet, entitled *Adriana* the following year (*see* 5.10.1857). Several dramatic situations from this projected ballet (for which the music of the first act was even drafted by N. W. Gade) thus clearly seem to have served Bournonville as the basis for some very similar scenes in Acts I and III (part 2) of *Cort Adeler in Venice.*

However, the main stimulus which induced Bournonville to revert to this 1832 project for *Cort Adeler in Venice* came (according to his own foreword in the ballet's printed scenario) from his renewed reading during the late 1860s of P. B. Mylius' biography *Den vidt=berömte Söe=Helte Herr Cort Sivertsøn Adelers Liv og Levnets Beskrivelse* (first published in Copenhagen by J. C. Grotz in 1740). From this literary source Bournonville arranged a dramatic plot that underlined the religious conflicts between the Protestant admiral *Cort Adeler* and the Catholic republic of Venice. It shows the Nordic sea-hero who is imprisoned by the inquisition for his strong religious beliefs, but in the end wins the city's honour and glory for his guidance of its victorious battle between the Venetian and Turkish fleets in 1654 at the island of Tenedos (i.e. Bozca Ada) in the Aegean Sea.

In his diary Bournonville noted about the ballet's creation andits 1870 première:

15.10.1868: 'Aftenen hjemme (Plan til Cort Adeler)'
18.10.: 'skrevet og componeret'
19.10.: 'componeret [...] Eftermiddag fortsat min Composition og conciperet 1.ste Akt til Cort Adeler'
20.10., 21.10., and 22.10.: 'componeret'
23.10.: 'skrevet og componeret, conciperet Cort Adeler færdig og paabegyndt Reenskrivningen'
24.10.: 'skrevet og componeret [...] reenskrevet paa Cort Adeler [...] fortsat Reenskrivningen'
25.10.: 'skrevet og fuldendt Reenskrivningen af Cort Adeler der synes at være lykkes mig godt'
6.11.: 'Reenskrevet en Copi af min ny Ballet'
7.11.: 'skrevet Copie af Cort Adeler'
16.11.: 'talt med [I. P. E.] Hartmann om Cort Adeler i Venedig'
22.11.: 'Besøg af H. C. Andersen der havde læst mit Program til Cort Adeler med stor Fornøielse. Brev fra Hartmann der anbefaler sin Søn [i.e. E. Hartmann] til Musiken af Balletten'
27.11.: 'skrevet Svar til [...] Hartmann'
11.3.1869: 'Bestemmelse om Cort Adeler, afsendt Manuscript og Brev til [P.] Heise.'
10.4.: 'Brev fra Heise'
20.4.: 'tilbragt den største Deel af Dagen med at ordne og reenskrive Musik=Udkastet til de to første Akter af Cort Adeler tilligemed et lille brev til Heise'
21.4.: 'Udarbeidet et Overslag til Cort Adelers Udstyrelse og sendt det med Brev til Justitsraad [F. J. G.] Berner'
25.4.: 'Brev og Decorationsforslag sendt til Just. Berner'
27.4.: 'componeret'
5.5.: 'skrevet og componeret'
8.6.: 'læst Brev [...] fra Heise'
11.6.: 'mødt Heise og talt med [F.] Ahlgrensson der er engageret for et Aar'
12.6.: 'Besøg og første Arbeidstime med Heise, der spiste hos os til Middag'
13.6.: 'modtaget [...] Ahlgrensson med hvem jeg arbeidede for Cort Adeler'
19.6.: '2.det Mødet med Heise der leverede mig et Par ÿpperlige Numere og er saagodtsom færdig med 1.ste Akt'
21.6.: 'skrevet og componeret'
3.7.: 'Brev fra Ahlgrensson'
10.7.: 'Heise bragt nÿ Musik og arbeidet med mig. Han blev hos os til Middag og reiste Kl 4.'
13.7.: 'talt med Ahlgrensson'
15.7.: 'skrevet til Heise'
17.7.: 'arbeidet med Heise Kl 11.'
21.7.: 'Brev til Heise [...] skrevet og choregrapheret'

23.7.: 'choregrapheret [...] arbeidet med Heise der blev hos os til Middag'
24.7.: 'skrevet til Copist [C. J.] Hansen, skrevet Choregraphie'
25.7.: 'fuldendt min Choregraphie'
29.7.: 'Brev til Heise, rendez-vous til Mandag Kl 11.'
2.8.: '(arbeidet med Heise, der har conciperet hele Musiken til Cort Adeler paa Bataillen nær.)'
3.8. and 4.8.: 'choregraphieret'
12.8.: 'hørt Heises sidste Numer'
5.9.: 'tilbragt Dagen med at componere de første Scener til Cort Adeler'
6.9.: 'hjem og componeret paa Cort Adeler'
9.9.: 'componeret'
10.9.: '(besørget Tilladelse fro Ahlgrensson at besøge Modelkammeret og skrevet til [L.] Gade angaaende Ombytningen af Roller i Cort Adeler'
23.9., 24.9., and 27.9.: 'componeret'
28.9.: 'skrevet og componeret [...] 1.ste Indstudering paa Dandsene til Cort Adeler'
30.9.: 'fuldendt Barcarolen til Cort Adeler'
1.10.: 'repeteret Barcarolen for Heise'
3.10. and 5.10.: 'componeret'
8.10.: 'Skrevet og componeret [...] 3.die Indstudering af Cort Adeler (Slavonisk Dands)'
9.10.: 'Skrevet og componeret [...] 4.de Indstudering (La Gondoliera) og Repetition paa Cort Adeler'
10.10.: 'componeret to Dandse'
11.10.: 'Skrevet og ordnet 5.e Indstudering (Springdandsen) og Repetition af de andre tre Dandse'
12.10.: 'Skrevet [...] 6.e Indstudering (Sarabanden). Decorationsmøde og seet Ahlgrenssons Modeller til Cort Adeler'
27.10.: '7.de Indstudering (Slavindernes Dandse)'
29.10.: 'Mine Øine temmelig daarlige alligevel prøvede jeg Dandsene til Cort Adeler'
31.10.: 'componeret og ordnet'
1.11.: 'Skrevet, 8.de Indstudering 1.e Akt 1.ste Scene'
2.11.: '9.e Indstudering 2.e og 3.e Scene'
3.11.: 'Prøve paa Dandsene til Paschaens Datter [...] skrevet og componeret'
4.11.: 'Skrevet, stor Prøve paa Cort Adeler, fuldført d. 10.de Indstudering af 1. Akt'
5.11.: 'Skrevet og componeret'
6.11.: 'componeret'
7.11.: 'skrevet og componeret'
8.11.: 'Større Indstudering (11.e) begyndt 2.den Akt'
9.11.: '12.de Indstudering paa Cort Adeler'
10.11.: 'skrevet og componeret'. 13 Indstudering og 2.den Akt færdig'
11.11.: 'lille Repetition paa Dandsene til Cort Adeler'
12.11.: 'Repetition paa Ballettens 2 første Akter'
13.11. and 14.11.: 'componeret'
15.11.: 'skrevet og componeret. Repetition af de to første Akter for Directionen og indstuderet Fængselsscenen af 3.de Akt. (14.de Indstudering)'
16.11.: 'Prøve og 15.de Indstudering, 3.e Akts 1.ste Scene fra 10½ til 1½ – hjemme Resten af Dagen skrevet og componeret'
17.11.: 'Prøve paa Cort Adeler 16.e Indstudering 3.die Akt Drømmen og Fængselscenen [...] componeret'
18.11.: '17.de og sidste Indstudering paa Cort Adeler, hvis Composition nu er færdig. Jeg tracterede Personalet med Champagne og Kage i Form af en Reisegilde. Chefen [i.e. F. J. G. Berner] var med og det Hele var særdeles gemytligt'
19.11.. 'Skrevet den hele Formiddag, opgjort Personlister til Cort Adeler'
20.11.: 'Repetition paa Cort Adeler'
22.11.: 'Prøve paa Dandsene til Cort Adeler'
23.11.: 'Prøve paa Dandsene til Cort Adeler [...] skrevet og ordnet Costume og Requisit-Listen'
24.11.: 'Prøve paa Dandsene til Cort Adeler [...] modtaget en udmærket Costumeskizze fra Ahlgrensson'

25.11.: 'Costumemøde'
27.11.: 'Prøve paa <u>Cort Adeler</u>'
1.12.: 'Costümemöde'
6.12.: 'Prøve paa Dandsene til Cort Adeler'
8.12.: 'Prøve paa Cort Adeler'
9.12.: 'skrevet paa mit Program, Costümemøde'
11.12.: 'Arrangement paa 1.ste Akt af Cort Adeler […] Costüme-møde om Aftenen'
13.12.: 'Arrangement paa Cort Adeler […] Costümemøde'
15.12.: 'Arrangement 2.den Akt af Cort Adeler'
16.12.: 'skrevet reen paa mit Program'
18.12.: 'Arrangement paa Cort Adeler (en Time for 3.die Akt.), be-sørget adskilligt og reenskrevet paa Balletprogrammet'
19.12.: 'hele dagen skrevet for at fuldende Omskrivningen af mit Program som jeg agter at dedicere til Admiral Edward Suenson'
20.12.: 'Afleveret mit Manuscript til H. P. Holst'
21.12.: 'stor Arrangementprøve paa Cort Adeler'
23.12.: 'Costumemøde'
26.12.: 'ordnet flere Sager til Balletten'
27.12.: 'Prøve […] paa <u>Cort Adeler</u>'
28.12.: 'Prøve paa Dandsene til Cort Adeler'
30.12.: 'Theaterprøve paa Cort Adeler med Repetiteurs'
31.12.: 'Musikcorrecturprøve paa de to første Akter af Cort Adeler'
1.1.1870: 'Theater prøve paa Cort Adeler med Repetiteur'
5.1.: 'Musikprøve paa tredie Akt af <u>Cort Adeler</u>'
6.1.: '1.ste fuldstændige Prøve paa <u>Cort Adeler</u>'
7.1.: 'Som en forfriskelse […] fik jeg <u>Ahlgrenssons</u> ypperlige Decoration til Slutningstableauet at see opstillet og glædede mig overordentlig derover […] Costumeprøve og efter Skuespillet den oven-nævnte Decoration med fuld Belysning'
8.1.: 'Theaterprøve med Orchester og Comparser paa Balletten, der lover brilliant […] Costumeprøve'
9.1.: 'modtaget Programmer. Decorationsprøve paa 1.ste Akt indtil Kl 1.'
10.1.: 'Skrevet og afsendt Programmer til Admiral [E.] Suenson og [C.] Hauch, samt den kongelige Familie og adskillige Honoratiores. Theaterprøve paa Cort Adeler. Costümeprøve, – besøgt [M. H. or A.] Bing og Fru Kofoed med Programmer'
11.1.: 'Igaar modtog jeg 50 Rdlr i Honorar for Balletprogrammet […] Decorationsprøve om Aftenen indtil Kl 12'
12.1.: 'Hele Dagen beskjæftiget med Balletten […] Generalprøve om Aftenen. Den gik fortræffeligt og lovede brilliant Virkning'
13.1.: 'Størstedelen af Dagen beskjæftiget med Ballettens 1.ste Fore-stilling […] Aftenprøve paa Decorationsforvandlingerne, til Kl 12.'
14.1.: 'Allerede inden Kl 11 vare fem Tavler ude til forhøiede Priser […] Første Forestilling af <u>Cort Adeler i Vendig</u>, der gik i enhver Henseende udmærket og gjorde stor Lykke. Huset var udsolgt men Hoffet var i Casino for at see <u>Ole Lukøie!</u> Tak til Gud for al hans Naade imod mig!'.

Cort Adeler in Venice, which was mounted with costumes and décors by F. Ahlgrensson, reached a total of 16 perform-ances, the last of which was given on 24.9.1870.

However, two years after its première Bournonville noted about this ballet in his diary on 11.5.1872:

'choregrapheret <u>Cort Adeler</u>'.

This is followed by four other statements about his notation of some unnamed choreography between 13.5. and 28.5.1872. Together these notes seem to indicate that he may have made a complete (not yet traced) choreographic notation of *Cort Adeler in Venice* for his own record during May 1872.

Another possibility is that in 1872 he was perhaps working on a revision of this ballet with regard to a planned restaging which he never carried out.

Autograph sources:

Manuscript scenario. Ms. Autograph. Brown ink. 21 pp. (23 × 18,1 cm)
<u>Cort Adeler i Venedig.</u>/Ballet i tre Akter og et Slutningstableau/<u>af.</u>/ August Bournonville/<u>1868.</u>
Signed and dated: 'Kjøbenhavn den 25.de October 1868.' [Written according to the diary between 23.10. and 25.10.1868]
[DKKt; Brevregistrant: Bournonville

Musical instruction. Ms. Autograph. Brown ink. 7 pp. (21 × 13 cm)
<u>Udkast</u>/til den musikalske Bearbeidelse af Balletten/<u>Cort Adeler i Venedig.</u>/<u>Første Akt.</u>/[…]/<u>Anden Akt.</u>
Signed and dated: 'Fredensborg den 20' April 1869.'
[DKKt; Brevregistrant: Bournonville]

Musical instruction. Ms. Autograph. Brown ink. 3 pp. (22,8 × 17,9 cm)
[Act II] <u>5.te Scene.</u> (Finale.)/[…]/<u>3.die Akt.</u>/[…]/<u>Slutningstab-leauet.</u>
Signed and dated: 'Conciperet d. 5.e Mai 1869.'
[DKKt; Brevregistrant: Bournonville]

Production note. Ms. Autograph. Brown ink. 4 pp. (36 × 23 cm)
Personliste til Balletten Cort Adeler.
Signed and dated: 'Kbhvn d. 19' November 1869'
[DKKkt; F.M. (Ballet)]

Production note. Ms. Autograph (partially in another's hand). Black ink. 2 pp. (22,6 × 18,1 cm)
<u>Cort Adeler.</u> (Personer i 1.ste Scene)
Unsigned and undated [Written according to the diary most prob-ably on 19.11.1869]
[DKKkt; F.M. (Ballet)]

Production note. Ms. Autograph. Black ink. 1 p. (18,5 × 17 cm)
<u>Cort Adeler i Venedig.</u>/<u>3.die Akt.</u> (1.ste Afdeling.)
Unsigned and undated [Written according to the diary most prob-ably on 23.11.1869]
[DKKkt; F.M. (Ballet)]

Production note. Ms. Autograph. Black ink. 1 p. (34 × 20,8 cm)
<u>6 Sömænd</u>
Unsigned and undated [Written according to the diary most prob-ably on 23.11.1869]
[DKKkt; F.M. (Ballet)]

Musical sources:

Musical draft/répétiteur's copy (incomplete). Ms. Autograph (by P. Heise). Brown ink and pencil. 1 vol. 32 pp. (34,3 × 26 cm)
HEISE/CORT ADELER I VENEDIG/1STE AKT/REPETITEUR-PARTI./[…]/Cort Adeler i Vendig/1ste Akt./Repetiteur – Parti.
Signed (on p. 1): 'P. Heise', undated [Written according to Bour-nonville's diary most probably between 12.6. and 19.6.1869]
[DKKk; C II, 114 f]
This (incomplete) manuscript contains Heise's first draft (for violin and viola) of the music for Act I of *Cort Adeler in Venice* with the excep-tion of the divertissement performed at the end of scene 5 (score no. 5) named 'La Gondoliera' (*see* the following entry). The manuscript also contains Bournonville's autographed choreographic numbers (written with black and brown ink) throughout the volume. They seem to refer to his separate (not yet traced) notation of the entire act. Moreover, several pencilled autographed notes by Heise de-scribe the dramatic action in each number. The exact place of the missing music for the divertissement entitled 'La Gondoliera' is indi-cated by Heise with a pencilled note (on p. 23) reading: 'Tarantella'.

Musical draft (fragment). Ms. Autograph (by P. Heise). Brown ink and pencil. 4 pp. (34,7 × 26 cm with minor variants)
Prestisimo alla Tarantella

Unsigned and undated [Written according to Bournonville's diary most probably between 12.6. and 19.6.1869]
[DKKk; MA ms 2678 (KTB 296)
This autographed manuscript (fragment) contains Heise's first musical draft (for violin and viola) of what at the 1870 première became the divertissement 'La Gondoliera' in Act I (score no. 5) of *Cort Adeler in Venice*. The manuscript also contains Bournonville's autographed choreographic numbers '1–11' (written with brown ink) which seem to refer to a (not yet traced) separate choreographic notation of this dance.

Orchestral score. Ms. Autograph (by P. Heise). Brown ink and pencil. 1 vol. 496 pp. of which eight are blank (34 × 25,5 cm)
296/Cort Adeler/296/Partitur/[…]/<u>Cort Adeler i Venedig</u>./
Förste Akt.
Signed (on p. 1): 'P: Heise', undated [1869-70]
[DKKk; C II, 114 f (KTB 296)
This autographed orchestral score contains several pencilled corrections and additions by Heise. Moreover, to most of the music for Act III, scene 4 (score no. 27, pp. '455–466') Heise added a song-tune with Danish text that served as an accompaniment for the martial hymn performed during the scene in which the appointment of *Cort Adeler* as admiral of the Venetian fleet is shown. The text for this interpolated song (which is perhaps borrowed from another not yet identified song) reads: «Hil, Hil Clotaldo, hil den Kjække, Hil den Faldnes ædle Sön!, Hil den Skjønne, som vil række ham sin Haand til Sejrens Løn! Hil den skjönne som vil række ham sin Haand til Sejrens Løn, Hil Clotaldo, Hil Clotaldo, Hil den skjönne som vil række ham sin Haand til Sejrens Lön!». This seems to indicate that Bournonville and Heise may have planned the inclusion of a chorus on stage for this scene.

Répétiteur's copy. Ms. Copy. Black ink. 1 vol. 130 pp. (33,8 × 26 cm)
B. 296/Cort Adeler/i/Venedig./<u>1870</u>./20/Bournonville./[…]/
Cort Adeler/i/Venedig./
Unsigned and dated (on the front cover): '<u>1870</u>.'
[DKKk; MA ms 2992 (KTB 296)
The numbers and the titles for each section of this répétiteur's copy are completely different from those contained in Heise's autographed orchestral score for *Cort Adeler in Venice*. The répétiteur's copy includes Bournonville's autographed choreographic numbers (written with brown ink) throughout the music. Moreover, his other autographed notes (written with black ink on p. 127) are included, describing the dramatic action in the ballet's final tableau of Act III (score no. 28). Finally, several notes written by a copyist's hand describe (in general terms) the dramatic action and the mime throughout the ballet.

Parts. Ms. Copy. 36 vol.
4 vl I, 3 vl II, 2 vla, 4 vlc e cb, fl 1/2, ob 1/2, cl 1/2, fag 1/2, cor 1/2/3/4, tr 1/2, trb 1/2/3, tuba, timp, gr cassa, piatti, tri, arpa.
Unsigned and undated [1870]
[DKKk; KTB 296

Other sources:

Costume drawing by F. Ahlgrensson. Pencil and water colours (format unknown)
'Cort Adeler i Venedi.'/<u>Cost</u>./(Hr. W. Price)
Signed: 'A.hg', undated [c.1869–70]
[Nationalmuseet, Stockholm; NMH 200/1892 C 20.819
This drawing shows the costume worn by *Cort Adeler* (performed by W. Price) in the ballet of that name.

Costume drawing by F. Ahlgrensson. Pencil and water colours (format unkown)
Cort Adeler i Venedig./Scarramuccia/(Hr Stramboe).
Signed: 'A.hg.', undated [c.1869–70]
[SSdt; Kostumetegninger (Ahlgrensson)
This drawing shows the costume worn by *Scarramuccia* in Act II of *Cort Adeler in Venice* (performed by E. Stramboe).

Costume drawing by F. Ahlgrensson. Pencil and water colours (format unkown)
'Cort Adeler i Venedig.'/Iseppa/(Frk. Schnell)/3.die Kostyme./
(Frk Petersen)/(Frk Larsen)
Signed: 'A.hg.', undated [c.1869–70]
[SSdt; Kostumetegninger (Ahlgrensson)
This drawing shows the costume worn by *Iseppa*, *Lelia*, and a girl-friend of hers during the divertissement, named 'La Capitana', in Act II, scene 2 (score no. 13) of *Cort Adeler in Venice* (danced by B. Schnell, J. Petersen, and C. Larsen respectively).

Costume drawing by F. Ahlgrensson. Pencil and water colours (format unkown)
'Cort Adeler i Venedi.'/Iseppa. (Frøken Schnell)/3.die Kostyme/
(Frk Petersen)
Signed: 'A.hg', undated [c.1869-70]
[SSdt; Kostumetegninger (Ahlgrensson)
This drawing shows the costume worn by *Iseppa* and *Lelia* in Act III, scene 3 of *Cort Adeler in Venice* (performed by B. Schnell and J. Petersen respectively).

Printed sources:

Printed scenario. 1 vol. 23 pp. including Bournonville's autograph dedication to admiral E. Suenson.
Cort Adeler i Venedig./Ballet i tre Akter og et Slutningstableau/af/
August Bournonville.
Copenhagen, J. H. Schubothe/Bianco Luno/F. S. Muhle, 1870.
[Sold as lot. no. 16 at Bruun Rasmussen's Copenhagen auction (no. 599) on 23.3.1994.
Bournonville's autographed dedication to admiral E. Suenson (written with brown ink in this printed scenario) reads: 'Til/Herr Contradmiral/Edward Suenson/Storkors af Dannebroge og Dbmd./Ridder/af Ærelegionen m m/sender jeg denne lille Digtning/ved hvis Udarbeidelse, jeg ret ofte med/Begeistring og Taknemlighed har tænkt/paa den unge danske Officeer fra/<u>Novarin</u> og paa den tappre Com=/mandeur, der paa <u>Hekla</u> og ved/<u>Helgoland</u> seirrig hævdede Flagets/og Fædrelandets gamle Ære./Med dybeste Ærbødighed/August Bournonville/ Kbhvn d. 9 Januar 1870.' Another copy of this scenario is now in DKKk (call no. 17, – 175 8°).

22.1.1870

A Torch Dance (En Fakkeldands).

This *Torch Dance* was choreographed for an artists' party in Helsingfors (Helsinki). It was set to N. C. Bochsa's and J. F. Fröhlich's music for the so-called *Riberhuus March* in Act II (score no. '17½') of Bournonville's 1853 version of his four-act romantic ballet *Waldermar* (see 28.10.1835 and 19.10.1853). The dance is described in his diary as follows:

22.1.1870: 'paa Opfordring fra Helsingfors choregrapheret En Fakkeldands til Riberhuus=Marschen'
17.7.: 'Behagelig Skrivelse fra Helsingfors' Konstnergilde ved [Z.] Topelius'.

According to Z. Topelius's letter to Bournonville (now in DKKk, call no. NKS 3258, A, 4°, kasse 8, facs. 2, letter no. 335) Bournonville's choreographic notation of this dance arrived too late to the Finnish capital to be mounted for the intended purpose. However, according to the same letter it seems to have been employed on a later occasion and in a similar way to Bournonville's earlier 1867 dances for B. Bjørnson's five-act drama *Mary Stuart in Scotland* (see 29.3.1867). It is not possible to identify the 1870 *Torch Dance* any further.

27.1.1870
Jaleo de Xeres (Pas de deux) **(uncredited) (Casino Theatre, Lille Sal).**
This (uncredited) *Jaleo* divertissement was choreographed for and performed as part of a masked ball given in honour of the members of the Royal Danish Ballet. It was described in *Berlingske Tidende* (28.2.1870) as follows:

'Kl. 9¹/₂ aabnedes den store Sal [...] Divertissementernes temmelig anseelige Række aabnedes i den store Sal med et Pulcinel Divertissement og i den lille Sal med en Jaleo de Xeres (Pas de deux), som midt paa Gulvet udførtes med Smag og Dygtighed af nogle af Ballettens Personale'.

The music for the *Jaleo* was most probably arranged by Bournonville himself from an earlier dance of his (perhaps H. C. Lumbye's *Jaleo*, named *El Capricio* and first performed by A. and C. Healey at the Casino Theatre on 1.12.1858). If this theory is correct then the dance was most probably (re)orchestrated by either Lumbye or B. Dahl, who conducted the two orchestras playing in the great and small auditoriums of the Casino Theatre on this evening.

In his diary Bournonville noted about the dance:

22.1.1870: 'lavet en Jaleo om Eftermiddagen'
23.1.: 'prøvet Jaleoen, besøgt [H. C.] Lumbÿe, [E.] Bøgh og Canno, Comitéemøde i Anledning af Carnevalet'.

It is not possible to identify the dance any further.

27.1.1870
'Bouquet Royal', Divertissement **(the Casino Theatre, Store Sal).**
This divertissement consisted of a series of three sets of national quadrilles. They symbolised the unification of seven nations with three recent marriages in the Danish royal family, namely:

(1) the Danish Princess Alexandra's marriage in 1863 to The Prince of Wales (later King Edward VII).
(2) the Danish Prince Christian Wilhelm Ferdinand Adolf Georg (i.e. King Georg I of The Hellenes) marriage in 1867 to the Grand Duchess Olga of Russia.
(3) the Danish Princess Dagmar's marriage in 1868 to Prince Alexander of Russia (later Czar Alexander III).

The divertissement's four dances were choreographed for and first performed at a masked ball given in honour of the members of the Royal Danish Ballet. These dances were entitled:

(1) *English-Scottish National Quadrille* (National=Quadrille, engelsk=skotsk).
(2) *Russian-Greek National Quadrille* (National=Quadrille, russisk=nygræsk).
(3) *Scandinavian Quadrille* (Scandinavisk Quadrille).
(4) *Finale Gallop* ('Bouquet Royal Galop').

As a result of the divertissement's great success with the audience, the first two quadrilles were also staged (although in slightly revised versions) at the Royal Theatre on 6.2. and 10.2.1870, while the *Scandinavian Quadrille* and the *'Bouquet Royal Galop'* were mounted there as a separate divertissement on 6.2.1870 reaching a total of 37 performances (the last of which was given on 26.9.1878).

The music for *'Bouquet Royal'* was pieced together by Bournonville and orchestrated by B. Dahl and H. C. Lumbye as follows:

(1) The opening *English-Scottish National Quadrille* consists of the overture for D.-F.-E. Auber's three-act comic opera from 1826 *La Dame blanche.*
(2) The following *Russian-Greek National Quadrille* was pieced together by Bournonville from popular Russian and Greek folk songs and dances, and was orchestrated by B. Dahl. According to a printed piano score of this dance (published by C. F. E. Hornemann and J. E. Erslev in Copenhagen in 1870, pl. no. 732, now in DKKk, call no. D 24) the quadrille included free arrangements of two Russian folk songs, entitled «Ved den lille Flod» and «Jeg vil gaa til Flodens Bredde», a Greek folk song named «Bladrige Rosers skjønne Krands», another (unnamed) Greek folk dance, and a final *Polka* (composed by B. Dahl). Bournonville's main musical sources for these Russian and Greek folk songs and dances were almost certainly the eighth and ninth volumes of A. P. Berggreen's music anthology, entitled *Folkesange og Melodier* (published by C. A. Reitzel in Copenhagen, 1868–1869, now in DKKk, call no. D 214). This theory is supported by the fact that all of the four tunes employed by Bournonville are included in Berggreen's anthology (in *Russiske Folkesange og Melodier*, vol. 8, nos. 6 b and 8, and in *Nygræske Folkesange og Melodier*, vol. 9, nos. 18 and 22). Moreover, according to the same sources, both of the Greek tunes in *'Bouquet Royal'* originated from the town of Argostólion on the island of Cephalonia.
(3) The *Scandinavian Quadrille* and the *Finale Galop* were both arranged and composed by H. C. Lumbye. He incorporated H. E. Krøyer's melody from c.1820 to A. Oehlenschläger's Danish national hymn «Det er et yndigt Land». It is followed by an excerpt from E. Du Puy's music to N. T. Bruun's song, named «Sankt Hansdag er Glædens og Midsommersfest». This song had many years earlier been incorporated in Act III (score no. 2) of E. Helsted's score to Bournonville's three-act romantic ballet *Kirsten Piil* (*see* 26.2.1845). Next follows Lumbye's arrangement of a Swedish folk song, named *Ack, Värmeland, du sköna*, after which follow two numbers by Helsted, namely his 1848 musical arrangement of the so-called *Norwegian Spring Dance* in Bournonville's one-act ballet *Old Memories, or A Magical Lantern* (*see* 18.12.1848) and his *Polska* from Act I (score no. 9) of *Kirsten Piil.*
(4) The divertissement concludes with Lumbye's new *Bouquet Royal Galop*, composed especially for this occasion.

In his diary Bournonville noted about the creation and the première of this divertissement:

29.11.1869: 'componeret'
30.11.: 'Brev og Program med Forslag til Just: [F. J. G.] Berner, componeret paa Quadrillerne til Carnevallet d. 27. Jan.'
4.12.: 'arrangeret Musik til den russisk græske Quadrille'
17.12.: 'været paa Casino for at undersøge Terrainet'
24.12.: 'Deilig Musik fra [H. C.] Lumbÿe'
25.12.: 'componeret paa mine Carnevals=Quadriller'
26.12.: 'Skrevet og componeret'
1.1.1870: 'Aftenen hjemme componeret paa mine Quadriller'
11.1.: 'Indstudering paa Quadrillerne til Carnevalet'
15.1.: 'Indstudering paa Quadrillerne'
17.1.: 'indstuderet Quadrillerne, Costumemöde paa Samme'
18.1.: 'Dagen mest beskjæftiget med Billetterne til Carnevalet'
19.1.: 'Indstuderet Quadrillerne færdig, beskjæftiget mig med Carnevalet'
20.1.: 'besørget adskilligt for Carnevalet'
21.1.: 'Prøve paa Quadrillerne, der arte sig godt,. Besørget adskilligt, jevnet Sagerne med Lumbÿ[e] og [B.] Dahl, uddeelt Fribilletter'
23.1.: 'besøgt Lumbÿ[e], [E.] Bøgh og Canno, Comitéemøde i Anledning af Carnevalet'
24.1.: 'Meget beskjæftiget med Carnevalet prøvet Quadrillerne og beseet Casinos Localer'
25.1.: 'Prøve paa Quadrillerne i Casino'

26.1.: 'Hele Dagen beskjæftiget med Carnevalet'

27.1.: 'Hele dagen beskjæftiget med Carnevalet [...] i <u>Casino</u> hvor vort Carnaval gik udmærket smukt og mine Quadriller saavel som den hele øvrige Anordning gjorde megen Lykke. Besøget var talrigt og elegant, dog vil vort Overskud neppe blive betydelig da Udgifterne ere enorme. Regnskabet vil vise os Resultatet. Ballet varede indtil Kl 4½ men jeg gik hjem med min Familie <u>Kl 3.</u>'

28.1.: 'læst adskillige rosende Anmeldelser om vort Carneval'.

A more detailed description of the four quadrilles is included in a letter that Bournonville sent to his daughter, Augusta Tuxen, on 4.2.1870 (now in DKKk, call no. NKS 3258, B, 4°, kasse 6, facs. 9, letter no. 166). It reads:

'Kjærnen af Theaterpræstationerne dannedes af mine tre Quadriller. hvori Amor spillede Prologus. Han kommer nemlig ind i Skoven nærved Bernstorff Slot og fortæller Sylphiderne om de Skjønheder, der beboer det og de Besøg, der ville komme: engelske Matroser og skotske Soldater med deres Piger komme dandsende og midt i denne Kreds kommer Amor forklædt som <u>Sailor Boy</u> med det engelske Flag. De løfter ham paa deres Skuldre og dandse afsted til Slottet. – 2.den Quadrille viser Russere omkring en Blomstervase paa Piedestal. De udføre deres Nationaldandse, der vexle med Nŷgrækernes langsomme Trin. En større Livlighed bringes tilveie derved at Grækerne faa russiske Piger at dandse med. Der skiftes Damer og en Polka forener begger Nationer. Amor springer frem af Blomstervasen og udstrøer Bouquetter til de dandsende, der omringe ham i en begeistret Gruppe. Endelig kommer den skandinaviske Quadrille, der aabnes af sjællandske Bønder omkring en Majstang og Amagere, der kommer til i en bekjendt Valsemelodie. – Man hører Svenskerne. Det er Dafolk og Wermlänningere, der til Melodien 'Går man det tilmötes så kommer det emot, och så man vinner mer än halfva vägen' – fraterniserer med danskerne. Nordmændene med deres Jenter dandse ind i en norsk Halling og Svenskerne opfordres til at deeltage, hvilket de ogsaa gjør med en mer comisk Tyngde. Nu kommer Punschebollen frem og en berusende Galoppade af Lumbŷe forener dem Alle. – Amor og Sylpher med de tre Nationers Flag blande sig i Vrimlen og det Hele slutter med en Gruppe omkring den blomsterhængte Maistang.'

Berlingske Tidende reported about the performance on 28.2. 1870:

'Den af Hofballetmester Bournonville til Carnevalet componerede Bouquet royal udførtes paa Theatret af hele Balletpersonalet. Den bestod af tre Afdelinger: en engelsk-skotsk, en russisk-nygræsk og en skandinavisk Quadrille. Det er en Selvfølge, at alle disse Dandse vare arrangerede med fuldendt Smag og bleve udførte med Liv og Ynde, men forrest i Rækken maa dog nævnes den sidste Afdeling, den skandinaviske Quadrille, som virkelig var et lille Mesterstykke baade i Henseende til Composition og Udførelse'.

The divertissement is included in Bournonville's handwritten list of his divertissements, written c.1872 (*see* Additional Sources), and in the published survey of his works in his memoirs *My Theatre Life* (p. 408), but there with the title *Scandinavian Quadrille*.

The *'Bouquet Royal'* was performed once at the Casino Theatre.

Autograph sources:

Production note. Ms. Autograph. Black ink. 3 pp. (23 × 18,2 cm)

<u>Dame = Costumer til Quadrillerne.</u>/<u>Engelsk = Skotsk.</u>/[...]/<u>Russisk – nygræsk.</u>/[...]/<u>Skandinavisk = Quadrille.</u>

Signed and dated: 'd. 16 Januar 1870'

[DKKt; Brevregistrant: Bournonville

Musical sources:

No autographed orchestral scores for the *English-Scottish National Quadrille*, the *Russian-Greek National Quadrille*, and the *Scandinavian Quadrille* have yet been traced. However, a later manuscript copy orchestral score for the *Scandinavian Quadrille* dating from its first separate performance at the Royal Theatre on 6.2.1870 is now in DKKk (call no. MA ms 2662).

Orchestral score (the *Finale Galop*). Ms. Autograph (by H. C. Lumbye) and copy. Brown and black ink. 1 vol. 12 pp. (26 × 34,5 cm)

H. C. <u>Lumbye</u>:/Bouquet Royal Galop./[...]/621A/Bouquet Royal Galop.

Signed and dated (on p. 1): 'af H: C. Lumbye d. 14 Januar 1870, (on p. 12) 'Fra Side 5–12 afskrevet i September 1944/Eskjær <u>Hemme</u>' [DKKk; C II, 34 (1944-45.65a.)

Pages 1–4 of this orchestral score are Lumbye's autograph and represent the oldest still preserved musical source for this dance. The score was originally part of the music archive of the Tivoli Gardens, but was transferred to DKKk in 1944.

Orchestral score (the *Finale Galop*, fragment). Ms. Copy. Brown ink and pencil. 4 pp. (35, × 26,2 cm)

Bouquet Royal Galop. H. C. Lumbye.

Unsigned and undated (late 19th century)

[DKKk; MA ms 2726

This fragment of the orchestral score for Lumbye's *Finale Galop* in *'Bouquet Royal'* seems to date from a later performance of this dance, or from a musical concert of it.

No répétiteur's copy for *'Bouquet Royal'* which dates from its 1870 première at the Casino Theatre has yet been traced. However, a répétiteur's copy for it, which appears to date from the later performances at the Royal Theatre, is now in DKKk (call no. MA ms 2907 (2–5)).

No set of parts for the *English-Scottish National Quadrille* and the *Russian-Greek National Quadrille* have yet been traced.

Parts (the *Scandinavian Quadrille* and the *Bouquet Royal Galop*). Ms. Copy. 31 vol.

vl I (conductor's part), 3 vl I, 3 vl II, 2 vla, 2 vlc e cb, 2 cb, fl picc, fl, ob 1/2, cl 1/2 fag 1/2, cor 1/2, tr 1/2, trb 1/2/3, gr cassa e piatti, cassa, timp.

Unsigned and undated [1870 and later]

[DKKk; Tivolis musikarkiv no. 1124 (mu 9405.1400)

These parts for the *Scandinavian Quadrille* and the *Bouquet Royal Galop* were used when Lumbye's music was played in two public concerts at the Tivoli Gardens on 15.5. and 18.5.1870 respectively. The same parts may perhaps have been used for the première of these dances at the Casino Theatre on 27.1.1870.

27.1.1870

Il Dissoluto Punito, ossia il Don Giovanni (Don Juan).

This performance represents Bournonville's second and last complete restaging of W. A. Mozart's two-act opera from 1787 (*see* 3.4.1848 and 14.3.1858). It seems to have been mounted this year with only minor if any changes from his previous 1858 production. The 1870 staging is not included in Bournonville's handwritten list of his stagings of operas and plays, written c.1872 (*see* Additional Sources). In his diary he noted about the production:

8.10.1869: 'Conference om D. Juan, besørget adskilligt'

15.1.1870: 'Costumemøde paa Don Juan'

19.1.: 'Don Juan prøvedes'

22.1.: 'Prøve paa Don Juan'

25.1.: 'Generalprøve paa <u>Don Juan</u>'

27.1.: 'I Theatret <u>Don Juan</u> nyt indstuderet i Anledning af [W. A.] Mozarts Fødselsdag'.

The 1870 staging reached a total of 41 performances during Bournonville's lifetime, the last of which was given on 7.11. 1879.

Autograph sources:

Production note. Ms. Autograph. Black ink. 2 pp. (21,5 × 13,6 cm) <u>Don Juan</u> (Opera)
Signed and dated: 'Kbhvn den 8.e October 1869'
[SSm; Daniel Fryklunds samling no. 123

Musical sources:

No orchestral score dating from the 1870 restaging of Mozart's opera has yet been traced.

Répétiteur's copy. Ms. Copy. Black ink. 1 vol. 8 pp. of which one is blank (33,7 × 25,6 cm)
<u>Dandse/til</u>:/ [...] /<u>Don Juan</u> /81./<u>1858.</u>./Bournonville./ [...] / Repetiteurparti/til/Don Juan
Unsigned and un dated [c.1870]
[DKKk; MA ms 2910 (5) (KTA 155 (2))
According to the style of this manuscript it clearly dates from the 1870 restaging of Mozart's opera. It contains the complete dance music in the Act I finale (scene 20) and is included on pp. 33–35 in a volume that also contains the répétiteur's copies for three other operas and singspiels, mounted at Copenhagen's Royal Theatre between December 1857 and March 1858.

The set of parts used for the 1870 restaging of *Don Juan* is now in DKKk (call no. KTA 155).

28.1.1870
Pas de deux (uncredited) performed by D. Krum and A. Scholl.
This (uncredited) dance is almost certainly identical with the similarly uncredited *Pas de deux*, performed by D. Krum and L. Cetti on 7.10.1869. That dance, in turn, is a musically (and perhaps also choreographically) revised version of Bournonville's much earlier *Pas de deux* in Act I of *Nina, ou La Folle par amour* (*see* 30.9.1834). L. Cetti had retired from the stage in the late November of 1869 as the result of her marriage the same year. Subsequently A. Scholl seems to have taken over her part in this dance. The 1870 *Pas de deux* seems (according to the posters) to have been performed 4 times by Krum and Scholl, the last time on 27.5.1870. It is not possible to identify the dance any further.

6.2.1870
English-Scottish National Quadrille (National=Quadrille, engelsk=skotsk).
This dance is a slightly revised version of Bournonville's earlier quadrille of that name, originally created for his divertissement *'Bouquet Royal'* and first performed at the the Casino Theatre on 27.1.1870. In his diary he noted about the rehearsals and the reception of this second, revised version:

31.1.1870: 'Prøve paa den modificerede Engelsk-Skotske Quadrille'
1.2.: 'Prøve paa Quadrillen'
4.2. and 5.2.: 'Prøve paa Quadrillerne'
6.2.: 'I Theatret gik mine Quadriler (engelsk og skandinavisk), der gjorde megen Lykke'.

The dance was given once at the Royal Theatre.

Musical sources:

No orchestral score and set of parts for the *English-Scottish National Quadrille* in *'Bouquet Royal'* have yet been traced.

Répétiteur's copy. Ms. Copy. Brown ink. 1 vol. 6 pp. (33,9 × 25 cm with minor variants)
[...]/Bouquet = Royal/?/(<u>Engelsk.</u> <u>Skotsk.</u>)/ [...] /Bournonville./ 90/1870./ [...] /Bouquet = Royal./(Engelsk = Skotsk Quadrille.)/ Ouverture/til/Den hvide Dame/Violino
Unsigned and dated [on the front cover]: '1870.'
[DKKk; MA ms 2907 (2) (originally without number)
This répétiteur's copy must certainly date from the first performance of the *English-Scottish National Quadrille* at the Royal Theatre on 6.2.1870, since it was originally part of the music archive of that theatre. It contains Bournonville's autographed choreographic numbers '1–30' (written with brown ink) which seem to refer to his separate (not yet traced) notation of this dance. Other pencilled notes indicate that the allegorical figure of *Cupido* ('Amor') is included among the cast of this dance.
    The music is written on pp. 17–22 in a volume that also contains the répétiteur's copies for six other Bournonville dances, mounted at Copenhagen's Royal Theatre in 1870.

6.2.1870
Scandinavian Quadrille (Scandinavisk Quadrille).
This dance is identical with the quadrille of that name, originally part of Bournonville's divertissement *'Bouquet Royal'*, first performed at the the Casino Theatre on 27.1.1870. In his diary he noted about its performance at the Royal Theatre on the opening night:

'I Theatret gik mine to Quadriller (engelsk og skadinavisk) og gjorde megen Lykke, den sidste endog enthousiastisk'.

The *Scandinavian Quadrille* was given at the Royal Theatre together with the *'Bouquet Royal Galop'*, and was by far the most popular of the four dances from the *'Bouquet Royal'* divertissement, reaching a total of 37 performances during Bournonville's lifetime (the last of which was given on 26.9. 1878).

Musical sources:

Orchestral score. Ms. Copy. Black ink. 1 vol. 60 pp. (34 × 25,5 cm)
301 /Skand: Quadrille./Partitur/ [...] /Partitur/til/Skandinavisk Quadrille/[...]/Bouquet Royal Galop./af H. C. Lumbÿe.
Unsigned and undated [1870]
[DKKk; MA ms 2662 (KTB 1045, but originally KTB 301)
This manuscript copy of the full orchestral score for the *Scandinavian Quadrille* clearly dates from the first time it was performed at Copenhagen's Royal Theatre, since it was originally part of the music archive of that theatre. It contains the scores for both the *Scandinavian Quadrille* and Lumbye's *Finale Galop*. A pencilled metronome marking indicates the tempo of the gallop with a crotchet being equal to '144'.

Répétiteur's copy. Ms. Copy. Brown ink. 1 vol. 6 pp. (33,9 × 25 cm with minor variants)
[...]/Bouquet = Royal/?/[...]/<u>Skandinavisk Quadrille.</u>/Bournonville./90/1870./[...]/Skandinavisk Quadrille./[...]/<u>Galop</u>
Unsigned and dated [on the front cover]: '1870.'
[DKKk; MA ms 2907 (4) (KTB 1045 (1), but originally KTB 301 (1))
This répétiteur's copy dates beyond doubt from the first performance the *Scandinavian Quadrille* and Lumbye's *Finale Gallop* at the Royal Theatre on 6.2.1870, since it was originally part of the music

archive of that theatre. It contains two sets of choreographic numbers ('1–28' and '1–14', written with brown ink) which most probably refer to two separate (not yet traced) notations of these dances by Bournonville. Other pencilled notes (reading: 'Börnene 2 Gang frem') indicate that a group of children took part in the performing of the gallop.

The répétiteur's copy is included on pp. 29–34 in a volume that also contains the répétiteur's copies for five other Bournonville dances, mounted at Copenhagen's Royal Theatre in 1870.

Parts. Ms. Copy. 29 vol.
4 vl I, 2 vl II, 2 vla, 3 vlc e cb, fl picc, fl gr, ob 1/2, cl 1/2, fag 1/2, cor 1/2, tr 1/2, trb 1/2/3, timp, gr cassa, tri.
Unsigned and undated [1870]
[DKKk; KTB 1045 (originally KTB 301)

10.2.1870
Russian-Greek National Quadrille (National=Quadrille, (russisk=nygræsk)).

This dance is identical with the quadrille of that name, originally part of Bournonville's divertissement *'Bouquet Royal'*, premièred at the the Casino Theatre on 27.1.1870. In his diary Bournonville noted about the rehearsals and the reception of the dance on the opening night:

8.2.1870: 'Prøve paa Quadrillerne'
10.2.: 'Prøve paa Quadrillerne [...] I Theatret den russisk nygræske og skandinaviske Quadrille, der Begge gjorde megen Lykke'.

The quadrille was performed only once at the Royal Theatre.

Musical sources:

No orchestral score and set of parts for the *Russian-Greek National Quadrille* in *'Bouquet Royal'* have been traced.

Répétiteur's copy. Ms. Copy. Brown ink and pencil. 1 vol. 6 pp. (33,9 × 25 cm with minor variants)
[...] /Bouquet = Royal/?/ [...] /(Russisk. Nygræsk.)/ [...] /Bournonville./90/1870./ [...] /Bouquet = Royal./No. 2./Russisk, nygræsk Quadrille:/af/August Bournonville./Musiken arrangeret af Bald: Dahl./1870.
Unsigned and dated (on the front cover and the title page): '1870.'
[DKKk; MA ms 2907 (3) (originally without number)
This répétiteur's copy certainly dates from the first separate performance of the *Russian-Greek National Quadrille* at the Royal Theatre on 10.2.1870, since it was originally part of the music archive of that theatre. It contains Bournonville's autographed choreographic numbers ('1–12', '1–6', and '1–14', all written with brown ink). They seem to refer to his separate (not yet traced) notation of this dance.

The répétiteur's copy is included on pp. 23–28 in a volume that also contains the répétiteur's copies for six other Bournonville dances, mounted at Copenhagen's Royal Theatre in 1870.

2.3.–28.4.1870
Twenty-four dance lessons in social dance.

According to a series of notes in his diary Bournonville gave a series of 24 private dance lessons in social dance for a group of children at the Copenhagen residence of the Russian envoy to Denmark, Baron A. P. von Mohrenheim, at Kongens Nytorv no. 4. These lessons, which took place mainly on Tuesday, Thursday, and Saturday afternoons, each lasted for about two hours, and were concluded with a presentation on 30.4.1870, that is described as follows:

'Presentation for Ministeren, stor Forekommenhed og Betaling 72 r.'.

29.3.1870
A Plan for a Vaudeville (Planen til en Vaudeville). **Projected work.**

On this day Bournonville noted in his diary about a projected vaudeville that he wanted to commission from the Danish writer, H. H. Nyegaard, as part of the repertory for a summer tour in 1870:

'conciperet Planen til en Vaudeville for Reisen'.

The tour, which he planned together with a selected group of actors, singers, and dancers from Copenhagen's Royal Theatre, was meant to visit ten cities at Funen and in Jutland. However, it was not carried out because of some unexpected troubles in obtaining permission to perform in the town of Flensborg in the southern part of Jutland. This town had been lost to Germany in Denmark's 1864 war with Prussia.

About his preparative work for this projected summer tour Bournonville noted in his diary:

27.2.1870: 'Confererede med [R. L.] Jastrau angaaende Jyllands-reisen'
20.3.: 'besørget Forretningsbrev til Herr Nathan i Aalborg'
21.3.: 'skrevet 10 Breve til de respective Stæder, hvor der skal gæstes'
25.3.: 'Modtaget Svar fra Aarhus, Aalborg, Odense, Svendborg og Fredericia [...] Svar fra Randers'
26.3.: 'arbeidet paa vor Reiseplan'
28.3.: 'Møde med de i Jyllandsreisen interesserede Medlemmer'
3.4.: 'Svar fra Haderslev og Viborg'
8.4.: 'Brev fra Steenstrup i Aarhus [...] talt med [H. H.] Ny[e]gaard om en Vaudeville til vor Reise'
9.4.: 'Besøg af Herr Nathan fra Aalborg'
12.4.: 'Brev fra Flensborg, der indbefatter Betingelser om en Ansøgning til Overpræsidiet, som jeg paa ingen Maade gaaer ind paa'
15.4.: 'Møde med Reiseselskabet Jastrau, [G. J. F.] Döcker, [W.] Price, Fru [L.] Stillmann og [E.] Lembcke for at aftale det Nærmere. Reisen blev opgivet, fornemmelig fordi Ansøgningen til Carl [T. A.] v. [Scheel-] Plessen blev anseet for en Umulighed [...] besørget 11 Afsigelsesbreve til Provindserne'.

It is not possible to identify the projected vaudeville any further.

10.4.1870
Pas de trois **(uncredited) performed by E. Hansen, J. Petersen, and M. Price.**

This (uncredited) dance is almost certainly identical with the earlier similarly uncredited *Pas de trois*, performed by the same dancers on 19.12.1869. That dance, in turn, is perhaps identical with the *Pas de trois* from Bournonville's Spanish ballet divertissement *La Ventana* (see 6.10.1856). The 1870 *Pas de trois* seems (according to the posters) to have been performed twice, the last time on 6.9.1870. It is not possible to identify the dance any further.

30.4.1870
Lohengrin.

The 1870 Copenhagen première of R. Wagner's three-act opera *Lohengrin* (first performed at Hof-Theater in Weimar on 28.8.1850) represents the first time a work by this composer was ever mounted in Denmark. It also represents the first of three operas by Wagner mounted in Copenhagen with Bournonville's mise-en-scène and choreography under the musical direction of H. S. Paulli.

According to a note in Bournonville's diary (on 30.5. 1869) and pencilled autographed notes by Paulli (inserted in the printed orchestral score), *Lohengrin* was performed in Denmark with several musical cuts, most of which appear in the second act. They were as follows:

(1) Act I, scene 2 (score nos. 2–3): Bournonville and Paulli here made two minor cuts of 11 and 40 measures each.
(2) Act I, scene 3 (score no. 7): In this number a large cut of 67 bars was made.
(3) Act II, scenes 1–2 (score no. 8): Nine cuts were made in this number, counting a total of 268 bars.
(4) Act II, scene 3 (score no. 10): In this scene six minor cuts were made counting a total of 158 bars.
(5) Act II, scene 4 (score no. 12): Three minor cuts were made in this number counting a total of 92 measures.
(6) Act II, scene 5 (score no. 14): In the final number of Act II a minor cut of 32 bars was made.
(7) Act III, scene 2 (score no. 17): This number was shortened by five minor cuts for a total of 154 bars.
(8) Act III, scene 3 (score no. 20): In the Act III finale two cuts were made, the first of 150 bars and the second of only 11 bars.

In his diary Bournonville noted about his many preparations in Copenhagen and abroad for the Danish première of Wagner's opera:

16.4.1869: 'Conference og Fornyelse af min Contract'
19.4.: 'læst Lohengrin og sendt min Betænkning derom til Justitsraad [F. J. G.] Berner'
24.4.: 'Conference med Berner og [H. S.] Paulli, Reiseproject med Hensyn til Lohengrin'
29.4.: 'Brev til [...] General=Intendenten for de kongelige Theatre i Berlin Herr [B.] v. Hülsen'
6.5.: 'Brev fra Herr v. Hülsen i Berlin. Ingen Lohengrin dér formedelst [A.] Niemanns Bortreise'
7.5.1869: 'Skrevet til Richard Wagner i München angaaende Lohengrin'
14.5.': 'Brev [...] fra Richard Wagner Luzern om Lohengrin, der er ansat i München til d. 28.de Mai!! Jeg skrev strax til Berner sendte ham Hülsens og Wagners Breve tilligemend formen til et Telegram til Baron [K. F. von] Perfall München'
15.5.: 'studeret og optegnet Bayerns Historie med Hensyn til min eventuelle Reise til München'
16.5.: 'Telegram fra München fra Baron Perfall at Lohengrin skal gaae d. 30. Mai'
17.5.: 'Tidlig op, og skrevet til Berner og Paulli [...] Brev fra Berner med curiøse Udflugter. Svar tilbage med Udkast til et Telegram til Regien for Berliner-Operaen'
18.5.: 'Brev [...] fra Berner med adskillige Omstændigheder, der formodentlig ville kuldkaste den hele Plan med Lohengrin. Jeg skrev i den Anledning et Brev til [N. W.] Gade'
20.5.: 'tilbragt Dagen [...] med Forberedelser til en eventuel Udenlandsreise'
21.5.: 'Brev og Resolution om Reisen til München, 150.rd i Reise-Godtgjørelse Paulli følger med'
22.5.: 'Conference med [F.] Ahlgrensson [...] Afsted i Selskab med Paulli med Jernbanen'
25.5.: 'endelig Kl 3½ i München'
26.5.: 'Vi besøgte endelig Theatret, hvor vi bleve modtagne med stor Forekommenhed af Intendant Secretair Stähle der førte os op i en Loge, hvor vi overværede Prøven paa Lohengrin 3.die Akt og fandt den særdeles interessant. Fräulein [M.] Mallinger som Else og en meget god Tenorist (som vi i begyndelsen antage for [A.] Niemann men som hedder [H.] Vogl) udførte Lohengrin. Orchestret henved 80 Medlemmer anførte af H. v. Bülow til hvem vi overleverede et Brev fra [N. W.] Gade, og som var en meget venlig Mand, yderst forekommende imod os. Ligeledes fandt vi udmærket Velvillie hos den

gamle Regisseur Siegel [..] Vi besøgte Malersalen hvor vi gjorde Bekjendtskab med Theatermaler [S.] Quaglio og hans Hjælper Jahn Begge meget talentfulde og venlige unge Mænd'
27.5.: 'jeg skrev sex Sider til Helene [Bournonville]'
28.5.: 'Efter Middag aflagde Paulli og jeg Visit hos [H.] v. Bülow og gik derfra op paa Malersalen hos Quaglio og Döll, der med stor Forekommenhed viste os alle deres Skizzer og Modeller [...] skrevet et Brev til General-Intendant v. Hülsen i Berlin'
29.5.: 'til Theatret, hvor vi med sædvanlig Velvillie bleve anviste Pladser for at høre den partielle Prøve paa Lohengrin, der var meget interessant, men havde saa mange Omgjørelser at jeg undrede mig at den kunde gaae imorgen [...] derpaa arbeidede jeg i fire Timer paa Regiet til Lohengrin og fik det færdigt'
30.5.: 'begyndt et langt Brev til Helene, beseet Decorationernes Opstilling til Lohengrin [...] en galla til Forestillingen i Operaen, hvor der var udsolgt Huus til Lohengrin. Jeg fulgte dette storslaaede Værk med spændt Interesse og fik den Overbevisning at det med betydelige Forkortninger vil gjøre Lykke og Epoke paa vor danske Scene. Udførelsen var mesterlig: Vogl som Lohengrin, [A.] Kindermann som Friederich og navnlig Frl. Mallinger som Elsa vare fortræffelige. Chor og Orchester præsterede mønsterværdigt. Det Hele varede fra Kl 6 ½ til 11¼ med temmelig lange Mellemakter'
31.5.: 'fuldendt mine otte Sider til Helene [...] derpaa expederede jeg Brev til Berner, og skrev to franske Breve til Baron Perfall og Richard Wagner'
3.6.: 'Jeg fik Brev fra Theatersecretair Ullrich i Berlin'
8.6.: 'skrevet til Berner'
11.6.: 'Conference med Berner'
13.8.: 'Brev fra München om [...] Stoffer til Harnisk'
16.8.: 'Brev fra Herr v. Stehle München'
19.8.: 'Afsendt 15 Thaler til Herr v. Stehle'
10.9.: 'Brev til v. Stehle i München'
17.9.: 'Brev fra v. Stehle'
22.12.: '(Brev til v. Stehle)'
30.12.: 'Telegram til Stehle i München'.

About the actual staging, the première and the second performance of *Lohengrin* in Copenhagen he noted:

30.1.1870: 'Optegnet Arrangementet til Lohengrin'
3.2.: 'Costümemøde paa Lohengrin'
5.2.: 'Decorationsmøde paa Lohengrin'
16.2.: 'Costümemøde paa Lohengrin'
19.2.: 'Forsøg paa en Claveerprøve paa Lohengrin, men ucomplet'
20.2.: 'Decorationsmøde paa Lohengrin'
22.2.: 'Overværet Sangprøven paa Lohengrin'
11.3.: 'Skuldet begyndt paa Instructionen til Lohengrin, men atter Upasseligheder ([P. L. N.] Schramm)'
16.3.: '1.ste Instruktionsprøve paa Lohengrin. Besøg hos Edw. Lehmann'
17.3.: '2.den Instructionsprøve paa Lohengrin'
18.3.: 'Instruction paa Lohengrin (3.die)'
19.3.: '4.de Instruction paa Lohengrin'
21.3.: '5.te Instruction paa Lohengrin'
22.3.: 'Repetition paa Lohengrin'
25.3.: '6.de Instructionsprøve paa Lohengrin'
27.3.: '7.de Instructionprøve paa Lohengrin [...] skrevet Scene-Arrangement'
28.3.: 'Arrangement paa Lohengrin, der udsættes, sandsynligviis til d. 28.e April'
30.3.: 'Prøve Kl. 10 paa 1.ste Akt af Lohengrin – Arrangement'
1.4. and 2.4.: 'Arrangementprøve paa Lohengrin'
5.4.: 'fuldstændig Prøve paa 2 Akter af Lohengrin'
7.4.: 'Arrangement af 3.die Akt af Lohengrin'
9.4.: 'Theaterprøve med Orchester paa 2.' og 3.die Akt af Lohengrin'
11.4.: 'Theaterprøve med Orchester paa 1.ste og 2' Akt af Lohengrin'
13.4.: 'Theaterprøve paa 2.' og 3.die Akt af Lohengrin'
16.4.: 'Kl 6 fuldstændig Prøve paa Lohengrin, der gik ret respectablet dog uden de behørige Decorationer'

19.4.: 'fuldstændig Prøve paa Lohengrin […] Costumeprøve Kl 7.'
21.4.: 'Prøve paa <u>Lohengrin</u>'
22.4.: 'Prøvet Decorationer til Lohengrin'
23.4.: 'prøvet 2.den Akt af Lohengrin'
26.4.: 'en Slags Generalprøve paa <u>Lohengrin</u>, som blev opsat til Lördag'
28.4.: 'Generalprøve paa Lohengrin, nogenlunde fuldstændigt'
30.4.: 'Første Forestilling af <u>Lohengrin</u>, der gik fortræffeligt og syntes at gjøre et stort Indtryk paa vort Publicum. [R. L.] Jastrau og Frk. [A. D.] Pfeil præsterede fortrinligt'
2.5.: 'afsendte <u>Brev til Richard Wagner</u> i Luzern […) i Theatret 2.den Forestilling af Lohengrin som gik udmærket og interesserer heelt igjennem'
27.5.: 'Brev fra […] <u>Richard Wagner</u> til Svar paa min Lykønskning'
1.6.: 'skrevet […] et Brev til Richard Wagner'.

Lohengrin reached a total of 27 performances during Bournonville's lifetime, the last of which was given on 1.11.1873.

Autograph sources:

Manuscript mise-en-scène. Ms. Autograph (partially in another's hand). Brown ink and pencil. 1 vol. 9 pp. (22,7 × 18 cm)
Lohengrin./Mise-en-scène par Auguste Bournonville./[…]/<u>1.ste Scene</u> […]
Unsigned and undated [Written according to the diary either in Munich on 29.5.1869, or in Copenhagen on 30.1.1870, or on 27.3.1870]
[SSm; Daniel Fryklunds samling no. 133

Musical sources:

Printed orchestral score. 1 vol. 404 pp. of which four are blank (36 × 29,5 cm with minor variants)
LOHENGRIN/Romantische Oper in drei Akten/von/RICHARD WAGNER.
Leipzig, Breitkopf & Härtel [1852]
[DKKk; U 6 (KTA 773) (mu 9208.3183)]
This German printed orchestral score was used for all performances of Wagner's opera in Copenhagen during Bournonville's lifetime.

No répétiteur's copy for *Lohengrin* has yet been traced.

Parts. Ms. Copy. 41 + 23 vol.
5 vl I, 4 vl II, 2 vla, 4 vlc e cb, fl picc, fl 1/2, ob 1/2, cl 1/2, fag 1/2, cor 1/2/3/4, cor in F 1/2, tr 1/2/3, trb 1/2/3, tuba, timp, tamb, glock e tri, org. On stage: fl 1/2, ob 1/2, cl 1/2/3, fag 1/2, cor 1/2, 11 tr, arpa. 15 vocal parts.
Unsigned and undated [1870]
[DKKk; KTA 773
This set of parts dates from the 1870 Copenhagen première of *Lohengrin* and was used for all performances of it there during Bournonville's lifetime.

2.6.1870
Napoli or The Fisherman and His Bride (Napoli eller Fiskeren og hans Brud).
This performance represents Bournonville's third complete restaging in Copenhagen of his three-act romantic ballet *Napoli or The Fisherman and His Bride* (*see* 29.3.1842). It was mounted for a special charity performance arranged in order to collect funds for the private pension fund of the Royal Danish Ballet, of which Bournonville was the founding member. The production, in which B. Schnell played the rôle of *Teresina* for the first time, was mounted with partially new costumes (drawn by E. Lehmann), but seems otherwise to have been staged with only minor if any changes from Bournonville's previous production on 23.1.1866.

In his diary he noted about the performance:

31.1.1870: 'Brev fra C Hauch og Bevilling til en Sommerforestilling for Ballettens Pensionskasse'
8.4.: '1.ste Indstudering paa <u>Napoli</u> (Teresinas Rolle Betty Schnell)'
11.4.: 'Eftermiddagsprøve paa <u>Napoli</u>'
12.4.: 'Prøve paa <u>Napoli</u>'
22.4.:'erfaret af Dr. Kjær at Betty Schnells Sundhed ikke giver nogen udsigt for hendes Fremtid som Dandserinde'
25.4.: 'Prøve paa Dandsene til Napoli'
30.4.: 'Prøve paa Napoli'
2.5.: 'udrettede adskilligt for vor Beneficeforestilling'
14.5. and 21.5.: 'Prøve paa Napoli'
24.5.: 'skrevet til Berlingske, Dagbladet, Folkets Avis og Dagens Nyheder om vor Pensionsforestilling'
30.5.: 'Stor Arrangementprøve paa Napoli'
31.5.: 'Prøve paa Dandsene og 2.den Akt af Napoli […] Hermed sluttede Saisonen. Nu have vi blot vor Forestilling tilbage – Gud give Held dertil!'
1.6.: 'Generalprøve paa Napoli'
2.6.: 'Forestilling i Theatret til Fordeel for Ballettens private Pensionskasse <u>Alt udsolgt</u> og et betydeligt Udbytte […] <u>Napoli</u>, der vakte sin gamle Begeistring. – <u>Betty Schnell</u> fortræffelig som Teresina. Udførelsen i det Hele ypperlig og levende Deeltagelse fra Publicums Side […] En meget lykkelig Dag!'.

The 1870 staging of *Napoli* received 4 performances, the last of which was given on 16.1.1871.

The musical material employed this year was the same as that used since the 1842 première of this ballet (now in DKKk, call nos. C II, 114 k, and KTB 292).

Manuscript sources:

Costume drawing by E. Lehmann. Pencil and water colours (19,5 × 15,8 cm)
Emilie Bryde/i/'Napoli'. 1870. -
Unsigned and dated: '1870. -'
[DKKt; Lehmann tegninger
This drawing shows the costume worn by E. Bryde in the *Pas de six* in Act III (score no. 2) of *Napoli or The Fisherman and His Bride*. The drawing is interesting in that it seems to indicate that it was Lehmann's designs from 1870 which are used in today's performances of the Act III *Pas de six.*

28.6.1870
Grand pas de deux (uncredited) performed by A. and C. Healey (the Tivoli Gardens, Theatret).
An advertisement in the so-called *Tivoli=Avis* on 24.6.1870 reads:

'Søstrene Healey […] optræde første gang Mandag den 27.de Juni i en Dands af 'Blomsterfesten'.'

This seems to indicate that this (uncredited) dance was an adaptation for two women of Bournonville's earlier *Pas de deux*, originally performed by W. Scharff (as *Paolo*) and J. Price (as *Rosa*) in his one-act ballet *The Flower Festival in Genzano* (*see* 19.12.1858). This theory is confirmed by the fact that in 1860 he had already made a very similar arrangement of this *Pas de deux*, which was performed by the Healey sisters at Stockholm's Royal Theatre (*see* 26.4.1860). The 1870 *Grand pas de deux* was given 17 performances by the Healeys in the Tivoli Gardens, the last of which took place on 4.8.1870. Bournonville did not attend any of these performances. During the following seasons in Tivoli, the French ballerinas, L. and F. Carey, took over the *Grand Pas de deux*, which they performed 19 times between 14.5.–1.9.1871 and

9.5.–30.8.1872. No musical sources for the 1870 *Grand Pas de deux* have yet been traced.

13.7.1870

Polketta Pas de deux (uncredited) performed by A. and C. Healey (the Tivoli Gardens, Theatret).

This performance represents the first time Bournonville's and H. C. Lumbye's *Polketta* (*see* 31.10.1858) was performed in the Tivoli Gardens. It was given there 10 times until 18.8. 1870, and has since that day never been performed in Denmark. Lumbye's score for it, however, was for many more years among the most popular concert-pieces in the repertory of the Tivoli Garden orchestra. Bournonville, whose name is not included on any of the 1870 Tivoli posters for this dance, did not attend any of its performances given this year. No musical sources dating from the 1870 Tivoli performances have yet been traced. However, a later orchestral score and set of parts, which were most probably copied from the original musical material for this dance, are now in the music archive of the Tivoli Gardens (call no. no. 1114).

25.7.1870

'The Bacchantes' (Pas de deux) (*'Bacchantinderne' (Pas de deux)*) (uncredited) performed by A. and C. Healey (the Tivoli Gardens, Theatret).

This (uncredited) dance is named 'Les Bacchantes' in Bournonville's handwritten list of his works, written c.1872 (*see* Additional Sources). It was set to music by G. and H. C. Lumbye, the latter being responsible only for the coda movement, which is identical with his much earlier *Bacchus Gallop* (first played in public at the Casino Theatre on 24.2.1854). In the so-called *Tivoli=Avis* from 25.7.1870, the dance is named and described as follows:

'Bacchantinderne' (Pas de deux) componeret for Søstrene Healey, Musikken componeret og arrangeret af Georg Lumbye. Decorationen malet af Ahlgrenson'.

However, no credit whatsoever is given to Bournonville for the choreography. Moreover, since 25.8.1870 the posters gave credits for the music as follows:

'Musiken af Hr. Georg Lumbye'.

'The Bacchantes' received 8 performances by the Healeys during the 1870 Tivoli season, the last of which was given on 25.8.1870. The dance was also performed in the 1872 and 1873 Tivoli seasons, but then by the French ballerinas, L. and F. Carey, who danced it 13 times between 13.7. and 14.9. 1872 and 7 times between 23.7. and 6.9.1873. During these periods the posters again credited the music solely to G. Lumbye, and still with no mention of Bournonville's name

In his diary Bournonville noted about the creation of this dance and the only two performances he attended of it:

30.4.1870: 'Brev fra Christine Healey'
1.5.: 'Svar til Healey'
7.5.: 'componeret og arrangeret en pas de deux for Søstrene Healey'
18.5.: 'Brev fra Healeys'
12.6.: 'Brev fra Healeys der kommer til Tivoli!'
13.6.: 'Brev […] til H. C. Lumbye angaaende Musik til Healeyernes Dands'
19.6.: 'Besøg af G. Lumby[e]'

25.6.: '(Modtaget Musik fra Lumbÿ[e])'
27.6.: 'Brev fra Chr. Healey der er ankommen til Kbhvn med Søster [Agnes]'
29.6.: 'Brev fra Healeys' der kommer imorgen […] componeret paa en nÿ Dands Bacchantinderne'
30.6.: 'modtaget Søstrene Healey der spiste til Middag med os og tog afsted igjen Kl 4 ¼.
1.7.: 'hentet Søstrene Healey og ført dem til [G.] Brodersens Locale, hvor jeg gav dem Lection og indstuderede dem en nÿ Pas de deux Bacchantinderne kaldet, til Musik af Lumbye (Fader og Søn) […] talt med Directeur [R. U. B.] Olsen i Tivoli'
5.7.: 'gav Lection og Prøve til Søstrene Healey, der forbausede mig ved Bibeholdelsen af Deres gode Skole og fortrinlige Egenskaber […] En Time i Tivoli, hvor jeg saa adskillige Kunster, der nu gjøre et sørgmodigt Indtrÿk paa mig'
9.7.: 'Brev fra Agnes Healey'
10.7.: 'Svar til Agnes Healey'
15.7.. ''(Miss Healey marquerede en Lection, vi talte med Brodersen)'
18.7.: 'Brev fra og til Healeys'
19.7.: 'modtaget Healeys […] der blive hos os Natten over'
20.7.: 'Farvel til Søstrene Healey'
26.7.: 'Brev fra Chr. Healey om deres Dands, der gik for første Gang iaftes.'
27.7.: 'Svar til Chr. Healey'
13.8.: 'om Aftenen i Tivoli, hvor der var Concert og Healeyerne dandsede '
25.8.: 'været paa Tivoli med Mathilde [Bournonville]. Nyt Vrøvl med Healeys og Directeuren [i.e. R. U. B. Olsen] for Tivoli'.

In a letter to Bournonville (dated 26.7.1870) C. Healey reported about the first performance of the dance:

'The scene looked beautiful & was applauded, the music also sounded beautiful, & we looked beautiful (but not in Miss Ryge's dresses). We danced well, were much applauded & called on again, & so all was well, but I will tell you how unfortunate & disappointed we have been about our costumes. On Saturday night we tried them on & everybody laughed at the scarves, Miss Ryge did not carry out our ideas & so the dress was nothing & scarves. Of course we would not wear such costumes & asked permission to put the dance off till we could get another costume, but the Directors would not hear of it as the dance was announced in all the papers, but at the same time they said we could not wear the scarves, & the dress was abominable, down in the front, up behind, would not meet in the waist, body no shape, etc.'

'The Bacchantes' represents the last dance Bournonville ever choreographed for the Healey sisters, although a later work, described as 'Grand Sylphide dance', seems to have been planned for them in 1870. This is clear from a letter from A. Healey to Bournonville, dated 'Sep.t. 1.st [1870]' (now in DKKk, call no. NKS 3258 A 4°, læg 15, letter no. 280).

Many years after the last performance of *'The Bacchantes'* G. Lumbye's music was still among the most popular concert-pieces in the repertory of the Tivoli Gardens orchestra and was regularly played there well into the following century.

Musical sources:

No autographed orchestral score for G. Lumbye's music for *'The Bacchantes'* has yet been traced. However, a later manuscript copy, which was most probably copied either from G. Lumbye's original 1870 score, or from the original set of parts for this dance, is now in the music archive of the Tivoli Gardens (call no. no. 1122).

Orchestral score (the *Bacchus Gallop*). Ms. Copy. Brown ink. 1 vol. 8 pp. of which one is blank (29,4 × 34,4 cm with minor variants)
H. C. Lumbye:/Bacchus Galop./[…]/Bacchus Galop

Signed and dated (by the copyist on p. 1): 'H: C: Lumbye/den 28 December 1853'
[DKKk, C II, 34]
This orchestral score contains the complete music for H. C. Lumbye's original 1853 version of the *Bacchus Gallop*. The dating of the manuscript clearly indicates that it was composed three weeks before it was played in public for the first time as part of a concert in the Casino Theatre on 28.2.1854.

Orchestral score (the *Bacchus Gallop*). Ms. Copy. Brown ink. 1 vol. 5 pp. (25,6 × 34,4 cm with minor variants)
50/C II 34./Partitur./No. 1./Parforce-/Galop/m/flere/[...]/Bacchus = Galop.
Signed (by the copyist on p. '1'): 'af H. C. Lumbye', undated [c.1850s or 1860s.]
[DKKk, C II, 34 (see 'Parforce-Galop').]
This orchestral score contains the complete music for H. C. Lumbye's original 1853 version of the *Bacchus Gallop*. It is included on pp. 49–53 in a volume that also contains a series of manuscript orchestral scores for eleven other dances by Lumbye.

No répétiteur's copy for *'The Bacchantes'* has yet been traced.

Parts. Ms. Copy. 30 vol.
vl I (conductor's part), 4 vlI, 3 vl II, 2 vla, 2 vlc, 2 cb, fl 1/2, ob, cl 1/2, fag 1/2, cor 1/2, tr 1/2, trb 1/2, 2 gr cassa, cassa.
Unsigned and undated [1870]
[Copenhagen, Music Archive of the Tivoli Gardens (call no. 1122)]
This set of parts dates from the 1870 Tivoli Gardens première of *'The Bacchantes'* and was used for all performances of it there during Bournonville's lifetime. According to pencilled notes in several of the parts the dance played for 7 minutes.

Parts. Ms. Copy. 17. vol.
2 vl I, vl II, fl 1/2, ob, cl 1/2, fag, cor 1/2, tr 1/2, trb, tuba, gr cassa, cassa.
Unsigned and undated [c.1854 and later]
[DKKk; Tivolis musikarkiv no. 1955 (mu 9405.1400)]
This set of parts for Lumbye's original 1853 version of his *Bacchus Galop* most probably dates from the first time it was played in public at a concert in the Casino Theatre on 24.2.1854. It differs from the same gallop music in Bournonville's *'The Bacchantes'* in that the 1853 version plays for 168 bars, while the 1870 version is shortened by an omission of a section of 39 measures, thus playing for only 129 bars.

1.8.1870
Plan for a repertory of operas and ballets for the 1870–71 season (*Udkast til en Virksomhedsplan for Opera og Ballet i Theater=Saisonen 1870–71*).
On this and the previous day Bournonville wrote a list of the operas and ballets he intended to mount during the 1870–71 season. Apart from the already current repertory this plan included nine new works and/or restagings as follows:

Operas:
Stratonice.
The projected 1870 Copenhagen première af E.-H. Méhul's one-act comic opera (first performed at the Comédie-Italienne in Paris on 3.5.1792) was never carried out, and *Stratonice* has to this day not been performed in Denmark. In his remarks for the projected Copenhagen staging Bournonville noted: 'Stratonice af Méhul [...] ville vistnok faae en respectabel Udførelse, men dertil kun opnaae en succés d'estime, der i finantiel Henseende ikke vil lønne Anstrængelserne og Tiden, der anvendes paa [...] Indstudering'.

Les Deux Journées, ou Le Porteur d'eau (De to Dage eller Flygtningene).
Bournonville had earlier mounted L. Cherubini's three-act opera from 1800, when it was restaged with his own mise-en-scène at Copenhagen's Royal Theatre on 30.10.1860. His projected 1870 restaging of it was carried out the following year on 15.9.1871, but not by

him. Having attended its first performance that year he described it in his dairy as: 'hørt 1.ste akt af De to Dage, svag Forestilling'.

Les Dragons de Villars (Villars Dragoner).
Bournonville had earlier mounted L. A. Maillart's three-act comic opera from 1856, when it was given its Swedish première at Stockholm's Royal Theatre (Operahuset) on 4.5.1863. His projected 1870 Copenhagen première was carried out on 19.10.1870, when *Les Dragons de Villars* was staged with his completely new mise-en-scène and choreography. In his remarks about the projected Copenhagen staging Bournonville noted about this work: 'Villars Dragoner, med en fortrinlig Text og en i første Grad iørefaldende Musik, vil gjøre Lykke og trække fuldt Huus, under den udtrykkelige Betingelse at den qvindelige Hovedrolle udføres med Genialitet'.

Der Templer und Die Jüdin (Tempelherren og Jødinden).
In 30.10.1857 Bournonville had already proposed a restaging at Copenhagen's Royal Theatre of H. Marschner's three-act opera from 1829. His 1870 projected restaging was carried out by him during the following year, when *Der Templer und Die Jüdin* was mounted on 16.4.1871 with Bournonville's mise-en-scène and choreography for the first and only time. In his remarks for the projected 1870 production he noted about Marschner's opera: 'Tempelherren &c vil blive en fortræffelig Acquisition forudsat at der med de tvende Hovedroller foretages saadanne Modificationer at de med Lethed kunne udføres af [J. L.] Nyrop og Frk [A. D.]Pfeil. De musikalske Autoriteter maa heri nærmest tage Hensyn til Theatrets Tarv og dertil udelade de ganske faa Sangrepliker, der udføres af Den sorte Ridder, som da maatte besættes med Herr W. Wiehe. Saaledes vil denne dramatiske Opera opnaae en frugtbringende Succès'.

Fernand Cortez, ou la Conquête du Mexique (Fernando Cortez eller Mexikos Indtagelse).
G. Spontini's three-act opera from 1808 was first performed in Copenhagen (in Danish) at the Royal Theatre on 29.1.1827, with the opera's dances then choreographed by P. Funck. Bournonville's projected 1870 restaging of this work was never carried out, and the opera has not been performed in Denmark since 19.4.1827 to this day. In his remarks for his projected 1870 restaging Bournonville assessed Spontini's opera as follows: 'Skulde imidlertid Tempelherren støde paa uforudseete Vanskeligheder vilde jeg foreslaae Gjenoptagelsen af [G. Spontinis Fernand Cortes, der naturligviis maatte have en revideret Oversættelse med alle de franske Recitativer. Da Hovedrollen ikke udkræver en fiin Sanger men derimod stærkt dramatisk Foredrag troer jeg at ogsaa her vilde [J. L.] Nyrop, saavel ved sit Spil som ved sin hele Personlighed være af fortrinlig Virkning. [N. J.] Simonsen som Telasco og Frøken [S.] Rung som Amazili. [P. L. N.] Schramm som Montezuma, [H. E.] Christoffersen som Alvar og [C.] Ferslew som Gusman, vilde medHeld complettere Udførelsen af dette Mesterværk, der har det fortrin, at stemme ikke saa lidt med Tidens Bevægelse'.

Ballets:
The Conservatoire, or A Proposal of Marriage through the Newspaper (Conservatoriet, eller Et Avisfrieri).
The projected 1870 restaging of his two-act ballet-vaudeville (*see* 6.5.1849) was carried out only two months later on 28.9.1870, when it was mounted for the third time by Bournonville at Copenhagen's Royal Theatre.

The Kermesse in Brüges, or The Three Gifts (Kermessen i Brügge eller: De tre Gaver).
The projected 1870 restaging of his three-act romantic ballet (*see* 4.4.1851) was not carried out until 8.12.1872, when it was mounted for the third and last time by him, but then in a slightly revised version.

Divertissements:
A major Ballet Divertissement (Et større Balletdivertissement (nærmere Aftale)).
This (unnamed) projected ballet divertissement is most probably

identical with Bournonville's later divertissement, entitled *A Fairy Tale in Pictures (Et Eventyr i Billeder)*, and premièred on 26.12.1871. Another possible identification of this work is his even later ballet divertissement, named *The Mandarin's Daughters (Mandarinens Døttre)*, premièred on 23.4.1873.

A minor Ballet Divertissement of older dances (Et mindre Balletdivertissement af sammenbragte Dandse).
This (unnamed) projected divertissement of older dances is most probably identical with the so-called *Dance Divertissement (Divertissement af Dands)* that was mounted only three months later on 31.10. 1870 and is partially based on excerpts from Bournonville's much earlier three-act Hungarian ballet *In the Carpathians* (*see* 4.3.1857).

In his diary he noted about the preparations for the 1870–71 repertory plan:

31.7.1870: 'udarbeidet et Forslag til Operaens og Ballettens Virksomhed i næste Sæson'
1.8.: 'Conference med [F. J. G.] Berner'.

Autograph sources:

Production note. Ms. Autograph. Brown ink. 3 pp. (23 × 18,5 cm)
Udkast/til en Virksomhedsplan for Opera og Ballet/i/Theater= saisonen 1870 71.
Signed and dated: 'Kbhvn den 1.ste August 1870.' [Written according to the diary on 31.7.1870]
[SSm; Daniel Fryklunds samling no. 103

4.8.–20.8.1870
Eleven private dance lessons to A. Scholl.
According to a series of notes in his diary Bournonville gave 11 private dance lessons to one of his youngest and most talented pupils, A. Scholl. These lessons, which took place at his private residence in Fredensborg during the dancers' summer holiday, lasted for about two hours each.

5.8.1870
Pas de deux gracieux (uncredited) performed by A. and C. Healey (the Tivoli Gardens, Theatret).
This (uncredited) dance is almost certainly identical with the similarly uncredited *Pas de deux gracieux*, first performed by the Healey sisters at Copenhagen's Casino Theatre on 17.11.1858 to a score arranged by C. J. Malmqvist. The dance (which in the so-called *Tivoli=Avis* from 5.8. and 6.8.1870 is named 'Pas gracieux') was performed 8 times in the Tivoli Gardens, the last time on 13.8.1870. Bournonville, whose name is not mentioned on any of the posters for these performances, attended (according to his diary) only one performance of *Pas de deux gracieux* on 13.8.1870, but made no specific remarks about it then except from stating on the following day:

'Besøg af [G.] Brodersen i Anledning af Vrøvl fra [A. and C.] Healey's om deres Costumer, besørget adskilligt'.

No musical sources for this dance have yet been traced.

19.8.1870
Echo from the Ballroom (Echo fra Balsalen (Pas de deux)) (uncredited) performed by A. and C. Healey (the Tivoli Gardens, Theatret).
This (uncredited) dance is identical with the similarly uncredited dance of that name, first performed by the Healey sisters at Copenhagen's Folketheatret on 28.2.1861. During the 1870 summer season it was given 4 times by them in the Tivoli Gardens, the last time on 23.8.1870. None of the posters for these performances give credits either to Bournonville or to H. C. Lumbye. Bournonville did not attend any of the 1870 performances of this dance.

Musical sources:

Orchestral score. Ms. Copy. 1 vol. Black ink. 47 pp. (34,5 × 26,9)
„Ekko fra Balsalen'/H. C. Lumbye
Signed: 'Harald Nielsen' and dated: 'Aalborg i Januar 1941.'
[The Tivoli Gardens (Copenhagen), Musikarkivet no. 1111
This orchestral score dates from 1941, but was almost certainly copied directly from H. C. Lumbye's original autographed score, which seems to have been destroyed in the 1944 World War II bombing of the Tivoli Gardens.

No répétiteur's copy for *Echo from the Ballroom* that dates from 1870 has yet been traced.

Parts. Ms. Copy. 35 vol.
5 vl I, 4 vl II, 3 vla, 2 vlc, 2 cb, fl picc, fl, ob 1/2, cl 1/2, fag 1/2, cor 1/2, tr 1/2, trb 1/2/3, timp, timp e gr cassa e glock, gr cassa, cassa e tri e glock, piano (a partially printed piano score serving as the conductor's part).
Unsigned and undated [c. 1941]
[The Tivoli Gardens (Copenhagen), Musikarkivet no. 1111
These parts were most probably written in 1941 at about the same time when the orchestral score was copied. Notes written into most of the parts indicate that the music played for between 7½ and 8 minutes.

28.9.1870
The Conservatoire, or A Proposal of Marriage through the Newspaper (Conservatoriet, eller Et Avisfrieri).
The 1870 Copenhagen restaging of Bournonville's two-act ballet-vaudeville *The Conservatoire, or A Proposal of Marriage through the Newspaper* (*see* 6.5.1849) was first suggested by Bournonville to the theatre management on 1.8.1870. It represents his third staging of this work in Copenhagen and was mounted for the début of his pupil, A. Scholl, who played the rôle of *Victorine*. According to Bournonville's diary the staging seems otherwise to have been mounted with only minor if any changes from his previous, revised production on 15.9.1865.

In his diary he noted about the performance:

29.8.1870: 'Prøve paa Conservatoriet'
30.8., 1.9., and 3.9.: 'Prøve paa Dandsene til […] Conservatoriet'
5.9.: 'Prøve paa Conservatoriet'
6.9.: 'Prøve paa […] Scenerne af Conservatoriet'
7.9., 8.9., 9.9., 14.9., 15.9., 16.9. and 21.9.: 'Prøve paa Conservatoriet'
22.9.: 'skrevet til Dagbladet og Dagens Nyheder i Anledning af [A.] Scholls Debut i Conservatoriet'
23.9.: 'Theaterprøve paa Conservatoriet'
26.9.: 'Generalprøve paa Conservatoriet'
28.9.: 'gaaet i Theatret, hvor man gav Conservatoriet, der gik udmærket smukt og med stort Bifald. Anna Scholl havde egentlig en glimrende Debut'.

The 1870 staging of *The Conservatoire* received 8 performances, the last of which was given on 2.1.1871.

The musical material employed this year was the same as that used since the 1849 premièreof this work (now in DKKk, call nos. MA ms 1550, and KTB 264, and in USNYp, Dance Collection, call no. *ZBD-74 (microfilm).

19.10.1870

Les Dragons de Villars (Villars Dragoner).

Bournonville had earlier mounted L. Maillart's three-act comic opera from 1856 when it was given its Swedish première at Stockholm's Royal Theatre (Operahuset) on 4.5.1863. The 1870 Copenhagen première was first suggested by him to the Copenhagen theatre management on 1.8.1870. This represents the second and last time this opera was mounted with Bournonville's mise-en-scène and choreography, which included an (unnamed) *Dance* performed by a group of dragoons and young girls in the Act I finale, score no. 6, during the so-called 'Chanson des soldats' («Pour séduire une fillette, faut-il un air de musette»).

In his diary he noted about the rehearsals and the Danish première of Maillart's opera:

15.8.1870: 'Oplæsning paa <u>Villars Dragoner</u>'
18.8.: 'Opskrevet Decorationerne til <u>Villars Dragoner</u> og sendt det til Berner'
27.8.: 'bivaanet Syngeprøven paa Villars Dragoner'
28.8.: 'skrevet Scene-Arrangement til Villars Dragoner'
29.8.: 'Instruction paa Villars Dragoner'
31.8.: 'skrevet Scene=Arrangement'
2.9.: 'skrevet'
5.9. and 6.9.: 'Instruction paa <u>Villars Dragoner</u>'
7.9.: 'Decorationsprøve paa <u>Villars Dragoner</u>'
9.9.: 'Eftermiddagsprøve paa <u>Villars Dragoner</u>'
10.9.: 'componeret Dragondandsen'
13.9. and 20.9.: 'Instruction paa <u>Villars Dragoner</u>'
22.9.: 'Prøve med Instruction paa <u>Villars Dragoner</u>'
29.9.: 'Prøve og Instruction paa Villars Dragoner'
3.10.: 'Arrangementprøve paa Villars Dragoner'
4.10.: 'Arrangement paa <u>V. D.</u> (2.den Akt)'
6.10.: 'Musikprøve paa Villars Dragoner'
8.10.: 'Theaterprøve paa Villars Dragoner (1.e og 2.' Akt)'
9.10.: 'Theaterprøve paa 3.die Akt af Villars Dragoner'
10.10.: 'fuldstændig Prøve paa Villars Dragoner'
12.10.: 'Theaterprøve fuldstændig paa Villars Dragoner [...] Costumeprøve om Aftenen'
15.10.: 'Prøve paa [...] Villars Dragoner'
18.10.: 'Generalprøve paa Villars Dragoner'
19.10.: 'I Theatret <u>Villars Dragoner</u> for første Gang, gik særdeles godt og gjorde Lykke mod forventet Opposition!'.

Les Dragons de Villars reached a total of 13 performances (the last given on 15.12.1871), after which it went out of the Copenhagen repertory.

Autograph sources:

Manuscript mise-en-scène. Ms. Autograph. Brown ink. 1 vol. 12 pp. (22,6 × 18,2 cm)
<u>Villars Dragoner.</u>/(Syngestykke i tre Akter. Musiken af Maillard.)/ <u>Scene = Arrangement.</u>
Signed and dated: 'Kjöbenhavn d. 2.d[en] September 1870' [Written according to the diary between 28.8. and 2.9.1870]
[DKKk; NKS 3285 4° 3 V–Z

Musical sources:

Printed orchestral score with manuscript insertions. 1 vol. 558 pp. of which four are blank (33,6 × 26,2 cm).
774/[...]/Als manuscript gedruckt/LES/DRAGONS de VILLARS/ Opéra comique en 3 Actes/[...]/Musique de/AIMÉ MAILLART Paris, G. Brandus, Dufour et C.ie, pl. no. B. et C.ie 9744 (1–16) [1856]
[DKKk; U 6 (KTA 774)
This orchestral score was used for all performances of *Les Dragons de Villars* in Copenhagen. The music for the dance scene in the Act I finale is included on pp. '223–258'.

Répétiteur's copy. Ms. Copy. Black ink. 1 vol. 8 pp. (33,9 × 25,5 cm)
[...]/Villars Dragoner/[...]/85./[...]/Repetiteurparti/til/Villars Dragoner.
Unsigned and undated [1870]
[DKKk; MA ms 2913 (4) (KTA 774)
This répétiteur's copy contains the music for the (unnamed) *Dance*, performed during the finale of Act I (score no. 6) in Maillart's *Les Dragons de Villars*. The volume also includes Bournonville's autographed choreographic numbers ('1–8' written with brown ink. They seem to refer to his separate (not yet traced) notation of this dance, which (according to his diary) he most probably wrote on 10.9.1870. The répétiteur's copy is included on pp. 31–38 in a volume that also contains the répétiteur's copies for five other operas and plays, mounted at Copenhagen's Royal Theatre between 1869 and 1871.

Parts. Ms. Copy. 32 vol.
3 vl I, 3 vl II, 2 vla, 3 vlc e cb, fl 1/2, ob 1/2, cl 1/2, fag 1/2, cor 1/2/ 3/4, tr 1/2, trb 1/2/3, timp, gr cassa, piatti, tri. 50 vocal parts.
Unsigned and undated [1870]
[DKKk; KTA 774

29.10.1870

La Juive (Jødinden).

The 1870 Copenhagen restaging of J.-F. Halévy's five-act opera (*see* 21.10.1855 and 4.1.1869) represents the second and last time it was mounted under Bournonville's personal direction in Denmark. In his diary he noted about the production, which was performed with only minor if any changes from his previous 1869 staging:

18.10.1870: 'Instruction paa <u>Jødinden</u>'
21.10: 'Prøve paa <u>Jødinden</u> i Salen'
23.10.: 'Sceneprøve paa Jødinden'
24.10.: 'Prøve paa Jødinden <u>3.e</u> – <u>4.e</u> og <u>5.e</u> Akt'
26.10.: 'Prøve [...] fuldstændig paa Jødinden'
28.10: 'Prøve paa [...] Jødinden'.

Bournonville was not present at the opening night, but saw the opera's first three acts on 7.11.1870 about which he stated:

'Jeg hørte tre Akter af Jødinden, der gik for tyndt besat Huus'.

The 1870 staging of *La Juive* received 8 performances during Bournonville's lifetime, the last of which was given on 13.2. 1873.

The musical material employed this year was the same as that used for the previous 1869 staging (now in DKKk, call nos. U 6, MA ms 3074–3076, and KTA 345).

31.10.1870

Dance Divertissement (Divertissement af Dands).

This work is almost certainly identical with the divertissement that was proposed by Bournonville to the management of Copenhagen's Royal Theatre on 1.8.1870 as part of his *Plan for a repertory of operas and ballets for the 1870–71 season (Udkast til en Virksomhedsplan for Opera og Ballet i Theater= Saisonen 1870–71).* It consisted of three dances as follows:

(1) A *Pas de trois* performed by E. Hansen, S. Price, and A. Scholl.
(2) A *Czardas* performed by H. Scharff, W. Price, J. T. Klüver, L. Stillmann, J. Petersen, and C. Larsen.

(3) A *Frischka* performed by the same six dancers as the *Czardas*.

The music for the *Pas de trois* was rearranged by V. C. Holm from a much earlier score by J. Mayseder, which had originally been used by Bournonville for the *Pas de deux* he incorporated in Act II of F. Hérold's three-act comic opera *Le Pré aux clercs* on 28.10.1834. Holm slightly rearranged this score in 1870 by altering Mayseder's introduction and reinstating a solo variation which had earlier been omitted, but was now played immediately before Mayseder's original Coda movement.

The music for the two Hungarian dances was (according to the répétiteur's copy) also pieced together by Holm. They consisted of slightly revised musical and choreographic arrangements of two similar dances from Act I (score no. 6) and Act III (score no. 30) in Bournonville's and H. S. Paulli's three-act Hungarian ballet *In the Carpathians* (*see* 4.3.1857). A few years later these two dances were also given as separate divertissements at Copenhagen's Royal Theatre on 1.3.1872.

In his diary Bournonville noted about the creation and the première of his 1870 *Dance Divertissement*:

26.9.1870: 'skrevet og conciperet Musik Anordninger til den nӳ Ballet'
4.10.: 'componeret'
7.10.: 'ordnet og componeret Dandse'
8.10.: 'skrevet og componeret'
9.10.: 'componeret'
10.10.: 'skrevet og componeret'
11.10: 'indstuderet en nӳ pas de trois'
13.10.: 'Prøve paa den nӳ pas de trois […] Aftenen hjemme og componeret en ungarsk Dands'
15.10.: 'Prøve paa Dandse'
19.10: 'Indstudering paa den ungarske Dands'
21.10.: 'fuldendt Indstuderingen af Divertissementet'
22.10., 25.10., 26.10. and 28.10.: 'Prøve paa Divertissementet'
29.10.: 'Prøve med Orchester paa Divertissementet'
31.10: 'I theatret hvor mit nye Divertissement opførtes for første Gang med meget Bifald. [A.] Scholl udmærkede sig særdeles'.

The divertissement received 9 performances during Bournonville's lifetime, the last of which was given on 11.4.1872.

Autograph sources:

Choreographic note. Ms. Autograph. Ink. 3 pp. (format unknown)
Czardas./[…]/Frischka.
Unsigned and undated [Written according to the diary between 4.10. and 13.10.1870]
[USNYp; Dance Collection, call nos. *ZBD-71 (microfilm), and (S)*MGZMD 30 (photostat copy)

Musical sources:

The orchestral score used in 1870 for the *Pas de trois* in Bournonville's and Holm's *Dance Divertissement* is now in DKKk (call no. C I, 38 g (KTB 311 a, originally KTB 270)).

Répétiteur's copy. Ms. Autograph (by V. C. Holm) and copy. Black ink. 1 vol. 16 pp. of which one is blank (33,7 × 25,6 cm)
167/Divertissement./B. 270/(Pas de trois. Czardas, og Frischka.)/[…]/Pas de deux [changed to:] trois danses af Emil Hansen/[…]/Maestoso/[…]/Czardas/[…]/Frischka
Unsigned and undated [1870]
[DKKk; MA ms 2907 (1) (KTB 311 a, but originally KTB 270 and a partial re-use of MA ms 2971 (KTB 276)).
This répétiteur's copy contains the complete music for Bournon-

ville's 1870 *Dance Divertissement*. The music for the *Czardas* and *Frischka* is V. C. Holm's autograph. The volume also contains Bournonville's autographed choreographic numbers for all three dances ('1–17', '1–12', and '1–18', written with black ink). They refer to his (partially traced) choreographic notation of the 1870 *Dance Divertissement*, which (according to his diary) was made between 4.10. and 13.10.1870.

The music for the divertissement is included on pp. 1–16 in a volume that also contains the répétiteur's copies for three other Bournonville dances mounted at Copenhagen's Royal Theatre in 1870.

Parts (*Pas de trois*). Ms. Copy. 33 vol.
3 vl I, 3 vl II, 2 vla, 3 vlc e cb, fl picc, fl 1/2, ob 1/2, cl 1/2, fag 1/2, cor 1/2/3/4, tr 1/2, trb 1/2/3, timp, gr cassa, piatti, tri.
Unsigned and undated [1834 and 1870]
[DKKk; KTA 311 a (originally KTB 270)
This set of parts dates from the 1834 première of Bournonville's incorporated *Pas de deux* in Act II of Hérold's three-act comic opera *Le Pré aux clercs*. It also includes several later musical insertions and changes which were made by V. C. Holm in 1870 when Mayseder's music was reused by Bournonville for his *Pas de trois* in his *Dance Divertissement*. They clearly indicate that it was the original 1834 set of parts which was reused for this dance in 1870.

Apart from the répétiteur's copy no separate musical sources for the *Czardas* and the *Frischka* dating from 1870 have yet been traced. This seems to incidate that these dances were performed in 1870 with the original musical material for the two similar dances in Acts I and III of *In The Carpathians* (now in DKKk, call nos. C II, 119, and KTB 276).

8.11.1870

Act II of 'Orphée et Euridice' for Alto, Chorus and Orchestra (2den Akt af 'Orpheus og Eurydice' for Alt solo, Chor og Orchester) performed by J. A. Zinck with the chorus and the orchestra of *Musikforeningen* conducted by N. W. Gade (the Casino Theatre, Mindre Sal).

For this concert performance of Act II of C. W. v. Gluck's three-act heroic drama from 1774 Bournonville's Danish translation of the French text was employed (*see* 10.2.1846). Bournonville attended this concert himself, which according to a note in his diary (reading: 'Concert i Musikforeningen, afstumpet ved Fru Zincks Upasselighed') was reduced because of a sudden illness of the alto, J. A. Zinck, who performed the part of *Orphée*. Moreover, according to the same diary Bournonville had received a letter from J. A. Zinck on 20.7.1869 to which he replied on the following day ('Svar med Manuscript tilbage til Zinck). This (not yet traced) letter seems to have contained a copy of his original 1846 translation of Gluck's drama.

The 1870 concert of excerpts from Act II of *Orphée et Euridice* was repeated on 31.1.1871 and represents the last time that Bournonville's Danish translation was performed during his lifetime.

The orchestral score and the set of parts employed in 1870 and 1871 were the same as those used for the earlier concert of excerpts from Act II of Gluck's drama given by *Musikforeningen* on 25.5.1859. This material is now in DKKk (call nos. C I, 245 (Musikforeningens Archiv, no. 153 b, 1944–45.367), and Mf. 153 b).

Printed sources:

Printed programme. 1 vol. 12 pp. of which one is blank (21,6 × 13,5 cm)
MUSIKFORENINGENS/CONCERT FOR ALLE MEDLEMMER/Tirsdagen den 8. November 1870./[…]/2. Gluck, W. C. 2den Akt af

«Orpheus og Eurydice» for Alt solo, Chor og Orchester (comp. 1762).
[Copenhagen], Bianco Luno/F. S. Muhle [1870]
[DKKk; Musikforeningens Arkiv, kapsel 70 (1870-71)
Bournonville's (uncredited) 1846 Danish translation of the text for Act II of Gluck's *Orphée et Euridice* is included in this printed programme on pp. 2–4. A similar programme for the repeated concert on 31.1.1871 is now in DKKk with the same call number.

30.11.1870
The Elves (Alferne).
For the 1870 Copenhagen restaging of J. L. Heiberg's one-act fairy-play from 1835 (*see* 26.10.1860) Bournonville appears (according to his autographed pencilled notes in the 1870 répétiteur's copy for this play) to have made a separate choreographic notation of one of its two (unnamed) *Dance scenes* (score nos. 1 and 4). Both of these dances were in 1870 mounted by his assistant, L. Gade. The 1870 restaging is not included in Bournonville's handwritten list of his stagings of operas and plays, written c.1872 (*see* Additional Sources), nor in the printed survey of his works in his memoirs *My Theatre Life* (p. 408).

In his diary he noted about the second performance of *The Elves*, which he saw on 5.12.1870:

'I Theatret og seet Alferne, der gaaer smukt men for middelmaadigt Huus.'

The 1870 restaging of *The Elves* received 27 performances during Bournonville's lifetime, the last of which was given on 18.3.1879.

Musical sources:

The orchestral score, the conductor's part, and the set of parts employed for the 1870 restaging of *The Elves* were the same as those used for the previous 1860 staging of this work (now in DKKk, call nos. C II, 125, and KTA 313).

Répétiteur's copy. Ms. Copy. Brown ink. 1 vol. 8 pp. of which one is blank (34,3 × 25,7 cm)
Alferne./A 313/[...]/47/[...]/47./Repetiteurparti/til/Alferne
Unsigned and undated [1870]
[DKKk; MA ms 3070 (1) (KTA 313 (1))
This répétiteur's copy contains the complete music for the two (unnamed) *Dance scenes* in *The Elves* (score nos. 1 and 4). It was used for all performances of J. L. Heiberg's play given since 1870 and throughout the last century. The volume also contains Bournonville's pencilled autographed choreographic numbers ('1–8') for the (unnamed) *Dance scene* in 3/8 time (score no. 1). They seem to refer to a separate (not yet traced) choreographic notation of this dance, which he most probably wrote as an *aide-mémoire* for L. Gade, who mounted the dances in Heiberg's play in 1870.

The music for these dances is included on pp. 2–8 in a volume that also contains the much later répétiteur's copy for another play, restaged at Copenhagen's Royal Theatre in 1890.

7.12.1870
The Wedding Festival in Hardanger (Brudefærden i Hardanger).
This performance represents the last restaging in Copenhagen of Bournonville's two-act Norwegian ballet *The Wedding Festival in Hardanger* (*see* 4.3.1853) during his own lifetime. It was mounted especially for the début of A. Scholl as *Ragnhild*. Otherwise the ballet seems (according to Bournonville's diary) to have been mounted with only minor if any

changes from L. Gade's previous 1869 staging. In his diary Bournonville noted about the rehearsals and Scholl's début:

3.11.1870: 'Indstudering af Ragnhilds Rolle i Brudefærden til [A.] Scholl'
5.11.: 'Indstudering paa Brudefærden i Hardanger'
22.11.: 'Prøve paa Brudefærden'
6.12.: 'Prøve paa Brudefærden i Hardanger'
7.12.. 'I Theatret Brudefærden der gik smukt med Scholl som Ragn–hild'

The 1870 production of *The Wedding Festival in Hardanger* received 4 performances during Bournonville's lifetime, the last of which was given on 31.5.1872.

The musical material employed this year was the same as that used for the previous 1869 staging (now in DKKk, call nos. C II, 119, MA ms 2963, and KTB 266).

17.12.1870
Fidelio, oder Die ehelich Liebe (Fidelio).
The 1870 Copenhagen restaging of L. v. Beethoven's two-act singspiel from 1805 (*see* 30.10.1857 and 18.12.1858) represents the second and last time *Fidelio* was mounted with Bournonville's mise-en-scène. It was restaged this year to celebrate the centenary of Beethoven's birth, and seems to have been performed with only minor if any changes from Bournonville's previous 1858 production. In his diary he noted about the performance:

14.11.1870: 'Oplæsning paa Fidelio'
22.11.: 'Decorationsskue paa Fidelio'
26.11.: 'Eftermiddag Instruction paa Fidelio'
3.12.: 'Prøve og Arrangement paa Fidelio (1.e Akt)'
7.12.: 'Theaterprøve paa Fidelio'
14.12.: 'Generalprøve paa Fidelio'
16.12.: 'Prøve paa Fidelio'
17.12.: 'I Theatret Fidelio i Anledning af [L. v.] Beethovens Fødsels-dag 100 Aar. Operaen gik i det Hele godt og for udsolgt Huus'.

The 1870 production of *Fidelio* received 6 performances during Bournonville's lifetime, the last of which was given on 27.2.1871.

The musical material employed this year was the same as that used for the previous 1858 staging (now in DKKk, call no. KTA 231).

1871

9.1.1871
Pas de deux (uncredited) performed by D. Krum and A. Scholl.
This (uncredited) dance is almost certainly identical with the similarly uncredited *Pas de deux* that was performed by the same dancers on 28.1.1870. That dance, in turn, is a musically (and probably also choreographically) revised version of Bournonville's much earlier F major *Pas de deux* in Act I of his Copenhagen version of L. Milon's two-act pantomimic ballet *Nina, ou La Folle par amour* (*see* 30.9.1834). The 1871 *Pas de deux* seems (according to the posters) to have been performed twice by Krum and Scholl in 1871, the last time on 17.1.1871. It is not possible to identify the dance any further.

22.1.1871

Le Cheval de bronze (Broncehesten).

The 1871 Copenhagen restaging of D.-F.-E. Auber's three-act fairy opera (premièred at l'Opéra Comique in Paris on 23.3. 1835, first performed in Copenhagen on 29.1.1836) was originally projected by Bournonville on 30.10.1857. It represents the first and only time *Le Cheval de bronze* was mounted with his mise-en-scène and choreography. Bournonville knew this work well from 1838 when he had incorporated several excerpts of Auber's music into his own two-act romantic ballet *The Isle of Phantasy, or 'From the Shore of China'* (*see* 28.10.1838). Moreover, a few years after the 1871 restaging of *Le Cheval de bronze* he again returned to Auber's music, when he asked V. C. Holm to incorporate many of the exact same excerpts in his score for the one-act Chinese ballet divertissement *The Mandarin's Daugthers* (*see* 23.4.1873).

In his diary he noted about the 1871 performance of Auber's opera:

27.12.1870: 'ordnet Scenerne til Prindsen af China'
28.12.: 'skrevet Scenearrangementet færdigt'
30.12.: 'skrevet og componeret'
4.1.1871: 'Oplæsning paa Prindsen af China'
11.1.: 'Instruction paa <u>Prindsen af China</u>'
12.1.: 'Costumemöde, Arrangement paa Prindsen af China'
14.1.: 'fuldstændig Prøve paa <u>Prindsen af China</u>'
17.1.: 'Theaterprøve paa <u>Prindsen af China</u>'
19.1.: 'Decorations og Maskineri=Prøve paa <u>Broncehesten</u>'
20.1.: 'Generalprøve paa Broncehesten'
22.1.: 'I Theatret 1.ste Forestilling af den nÿ indstuderede Trylleopera <u>Broncehesten</u>, der gik udmærket godt og for fuldt Huus. – [J. L.] Phister fortræffelig i sin gamle Rolle'
26.1.: 'I Theatret <u>Broncehesten</u>, der gik særdeles smukt men for maadeligt Huus. Bladene have ærligt arbeidet paa at nedsætte Stÿkket. Folk morede sig ÿpperligt'.

Bournonville's 1871 production of *Le Cheval de bronze* received 3 performances (the last of which was given on 6.2. 1871), after which it went out of the Copenhagen repertory.

Autograph sources:

Manuscript mise-en-scène. Ms. Autograph. Brown ink. 1 vol. 10 pp. (22,7 × 18,2 cm)
<u>Prindsen af China.</u>/(Opera=Comique i tre Akter)/<u>Scene = Arrangement.</u>
Signed and dated: 'Kbhvn. Januar 1871' [Written according to Bournonville's diary most probably between 27.12. and 28.12.1870]
[DKKk; NKS 3285 4° 3 L–P

Manuscript mise-en-scène. Ms. Autograph. Black ink. 2 pp. (21 × 13,4 cm)
<u>Chor = Arrangement</u>/i/<u>Prindsen af China</u>
Unsigned and undated [December 1870–January 1871]
[SSm; Daniel Fryklunds samling no. 143

Musical sources:

Printed orchestral score. 2 vol. Act I 238 pp. of which one is blank, Act II–III 270 pp. (33,1 × 25,4 cm)
<u>Prindsen af China.</u>/<u>Act I.</u>/[…]/Le/Cheval de Bronze/Opera féerie en trois Actes/[…]/Musique de/D. F. E. AUBER/[…]/<u>Prindsen af China.</u>/<u>Act II.den og III.die</u>
Paris, Dépôt Central de Musique et de Librairie, pl. no. T. 8. [1835]
[DKKk; U 6 (KTA 319)
This French printed orchestral score dates from the 1836 Copenhagen première of Auber's fairy opera and was used for all perform-ances of it there during Bournonville's lifetime. It contains C. F. Güntelberg's original Danish translation, written (with black ink) next to the opera's French text.

No répétiteur's copy for *Le Cheval de bronze* has yet been traced.

Parts. Ms. Copy. 34 vol.
3 vl I, 3 vl II, 2 vla, 3 vlc e cb, fl 1/2, ob 1/2, cl 1/2, fag 1/2, cor 1/2/ 3/4, tr 1/2, trb 1/2/3, timp, gr cassa, piatti, tri, gong, arpa. 53 vocal parts.
Unsigned and undated [1836]
[DKKk; KTA 319
This set of parts dates from the 1836 Copenhagen première of Auber's fairy opera and was used for all performances of it there during Bournonville's lifetime.

31.1.1871

Act II of 'Orphée et Euridice' for Alto, Chorus and Orchestra (2den Akt af 'Orpheus og Eurydice' for Alt solo, Chor og Orchester) **performed by J. A. Zinck with the chorus and orchestra of** *Musikforeningen* **conducted by N. W. Gade (the Casino Theatre, Mindre Sal).**

This concert performance of Act II of C. W. v. Gluck's three-act heroic drama from 1774 is a repeat of the concert given only two months earlier at the same theatre and by the same artists (*see* 8.11.1870). It represents the last time Bournonville's 1846 Danish translation of this opera's French text (*see* 10.2.1846) was employed during his own lifetime. Bournonville did not attend the 1871 concert.

31.1.–30.3.1871

Twelve dance lessons in social dance.

According to a series of notes in his diary Bournonville gave 12 private dance lessons in social dance this year at the Copenhagen residence of the Baron Stampe at Amaliegade no. 7/3. These lessons, which took place mainly on Monday and Tuesday afternoons, lasted for about two hours each.

1.2.–1.4.1871

Twenty dance lessons in social dances.

According to a series of notes in his diary, Bournonville gave 20 private dance lessons in social dance this year at the Copenhagen residence of the Russian envoy to Denmark, Baron A. P. von Mohrenheim, at Kongens Nytorv no. 4. These lessons, which took place mainly on Wednesday and Friday afternoons, lasted for about two hours each.

19.2.1871

The King's Corps of Volunteers on Amager, (Episode from 1808) (Livjægerne paa Amager, (Episode fra 1808)).

Bournonville's first inspiration for this one-act ballet-vaudeville seems (according to his diary) to stem from early January 1866, when he was asked to write a biography of the legendary French singer, composer, and member of the so-called 'King's Corps of Volunteers', E. Dupuy. This task was fulfilled on 21.1.1866. During the following year Bournonville met with and later visited a childhood girlfriend, named Ane Jensdatter, at her farm on the isle of Amager. Together these experiences seem to represent the main impulses that led to his later creation of this ballet in 1870. Other sources of inspiration were (according to his memoirs *My Theatre Life*, p. 368) the many popular paintings of J. Exner, which depicted folk scenes of the large colony of Dutch farmers on the isle of Amager.

The ballet was set to a score divided into 16 numbers. It was composed and arranged by V. C. Holm, but also included a *Finale Gallop* (score no. 16) composed especially for this ballet by H. C. Lumbye. In his score Holm incorporated several musical borrowings from the works of Dupuy and other composers in order to add specific local colours to the ballet's setting and to help the audience interpret its many and rather long mime scenes. These musical borrowings are identified as follows:

(1) Scene 1 (score no. 1): For the opening scene, in which the Amager children are seen playing blind man's buff, Holm incorporated a tune (by an anonymous composer) that originally accompanied P. A. Heiberg's poem from 1794, entitled *Lanterna Magica* («Komme hvo, som komme kan»). The exact same tune also accompanies a popular Danish children's song, named «I en Kælder sort som Kul».
(2) Scene 3 (score no. 2): In this number Holm interpolated the tune of the so-called *Drikkevise* («Hvis et godt Raad I følge kan») in E. Dupuy's score for N. T. Bruun's two-act singspiel *Youth and Folly* (*Ungdom og Galskab*), premièred at Copenhagen's Royal Theatre on 19.5. 1806. It was originally sung in Act II (score no. 11) by the characters *Rose* and *Poul*.
(3) Scene 4 (score no. 3): Holm here incorporated the leading melody in Dupuy's vocal quartet for male voices, entitled «Harmonie! Douce harmonie viens consoler mon cœur». It was originally part of his collection of six quartets, named *Six Quatrours pour Deux Tenors et Deux Basses*, first published in Stockholm by C. Müller in the early 19th century (a copy is now in DKKk, call no. D 240).
(4) Scene 6 (score no. 5): For this scene Holm interpolated H. O. C. Zinck's 1801 tune for W. H. F. Abrahamson's song, entitled«Vi alle Dig elske, livsalige Fred». After 1820 this tune was also used as accompaniment for N. F. S. Grundtvig's song, named «Langt højere Bjerge saa vide paa Jord».
(5) Scene 8 (score no. 7): Holm here employed the melody for a song that was composed and first performed by Dupuy in E. T. A. Hoffmann's and E.-H. Méhul's one-act comedy *Le Trésor supposé, ou Le Danger d'écouter aux portes (Skatten eller Staa ikke paa Lur)* at its Copenhagen première on 17.5.1804. Dupuy's song was incorporated there in scene IX (score no. 5) and performed with a text reading: 'Det hedder en Acquisition, jeg viser jeg min Profession fra Grunden har studeret. Det Land, hvor man et sligt Talent med haanligt Blik har Ryggen vendt maa være upoleret'. The same tune later also served as accompaniment for another song by N. T. Bruun, entitled «Skænk i Dit Glas til bredfuldt Maal».
(6) Scene 9 (score no. 8): For this scene Holm employed Dupuy's music for the romance, named «Jeg er endnu i Livets Vaar», first sung by the character *Vilhelmine* in Act I (score no. 3) of Dupuy's and N. T. Bruun's two-act singspiel *Youth and Folly*.
(7) Scene 11 (score no. 10): According to a letter from Bournonville to R. Watt, dated 17.2.1871 (now in DKKk, call no. NBD, 2 Rk.) Holm seems in this number to have incorporated a (not yet identified) march by Dupuy, that is described by Bournonville as '<u>Livjæger-marschen</u>'.
(8) *Polonaise* (score no. 11): In his score for the *Polonaise* (also named 'De gamles Dands' and performed by twelve couples) Holm employed excerpts from a song by Dupuy, entitled «Falderi, falderala, røde Rose!». It was originally sung by the characters *Johan* and *Rose* in Act II (score no. 8) in his and N. T. Bruun's singspiel *Youth and Folly*.
(9) For the so-called *Tøndebaands-Dands* (performed during the same number by the entire corps de ballet) Holm reused the exact same tune which H. S. Paulli had employed before him in the score for Bournonville's much earlier divertissement, entitled *Echo on Sunday* (*see* 20.3.1849). That tune was originally used by J. F. Fröhlich in his score for the actress J. L. Heiberg's one-act vaudeville named *A Sunday on Amager (En Søndag paa Amager)*, premièred at Copenhagen's Royal Theatre on 5.3.1848. However, the same tune was already known and had been published in Copenhagen in 1787, when it had

been included in N. Schiørring's music anthology, entitled *Blandinger for Sang og Claveer. No. 2* (Kiøbenhavn, Steins Skrifter, p. 8). In that volume it is named *Amager=Dands* (a copy is now in DKKk, call no. D 2).
(10) *Militair-Polka* (score no. 12): In his music for this dance (performed by *Louise* disguised as a vivandière, *Edmond*, and three other couples) Holm employed the tunes of two (not yet identified) songs by Dupuy. This is clear from Bournonville's letter to R. Watt (dated 17.2.1871) in which they are described as: '<u>To Viser</u> sammensmeltede i en Polka'.
(11) *Pas de trois* (score no. 13): For this divertissement (performed by *Emil* disguised as *Prince Carnival*, and *Else* and *Trine* representing the *Goddesses of Folly*) Holm employed nearly all of Dupuy's so-called *Polonoise*. It was first published in Copenhagen in 1800–01 by S. Sønnichsen as part of the music anthology *Apollo* (3.die Aargang, 7de Hefte, pp. 4–6, now in DKKk, call no. D 2, BoxA 7.2006). This dance was republished in 1803 in a slightly revised version, entitled *Polonoise for Klaveer eller Fortepiano No. 1.* (a copy of which is now in DKKk, call no. D 24). Dupuy's *Polonoise* is followed by several solo variations (all presumably composed by Holm), and the *Pas de trois* concludes with an *Allegro* movement in 6/8 time, which is Holm's free arrangement of the final movement in the *Terzet* («Nu ingen Kiv og Klage, leve Enghed!») of Act II (score no. 9) in Dupuy's and N. T. Bruun's *Youth and Folly* (originally sung by the characters *Vilhelmine, Grøndal*, and *Johan*).
(12) *Molinaski* (score no. 14): In his score for this dance for the corps de ballet Holm borrowed (according to Bournonville's letter to R. Watt, dated 17.2.1871) a theme from a (not yet identified) so-called '<u>Rondo</u>' by Dupuy. It is followed by the *Reel* (performed by three couples) which was seemingly composed by Holm.
(13) *En Quadrille af holbergske Figurer* (score no. 15): In his score for this masked quadrille (which depicts the main characters from the comedies of L. Holberg) Holm interpolated the complete music of a dance, entitled '*La Folie*'. It was orginally part of P. Larcher's 1823 Copenhagen production of L. Milon's two-act pantomimic ballet *Le Carneval de Venise, ou La Constance à l'épreuve (Carnevalet i Venedig eller Kjærlighed paa Prøve)*. That ballet was set to a score by L.-L. L. de Persuis' and R. Kreutzer, and had originally been performed at the Paris Opéra on 22.2.1816. Holm's borrowed musical excerpt from Milon's ballet is followed by a *Tempo di marcia* (in 4/4 time) and the so-called '<u>Valse de la Capricieuse</u>', both of which are presumably composed by himself.

In his diary Bournonville noted about the series of events that led to the creation of this ballet and its 1871 première:

10.1.1866: 'Brev fra Consul Efverløv [i.e. F. A. Everlöf] om [E.] Dupuy?'
21.1.: 'skrevet Svar til Everlöf om Dupuy
23.1.: 'Brev fra Everlöf med Taksigelse'
15.10.1867: 'Tour med Helene og Charlotte [Bournonville] til Kastrup paa Amager for at besøge min gamle Veninde <u>Ane Jensdatter</u> Sognefogdens Kone'
20.10.: 'Jeg havde min gamle Amagerveninde <u>Ane Jensdatter</u> Sognefogdens Kone i Theatret'
11.9.1870: 'begyndt paa et Program til en Ballet kaldet `Livjægerne paa Amager´'
12.9.: 'componeret lidt paa den nŷ Ballet'
13.9.: 'fuldendt Programmet til 'Livjægerne paa Amager''
19.9.: 'skrevet og fuldendt Reenskrivningen af Livjægerne paa Amager'
26.9.: 'skrevet og conciperet Musik-Anordningen til den nŷ Ballet'
1.11.: 'arbeidet med [V. C.] Holm'
2.11.: 'Arbeidet paa min ny Ballet'
4.11.: 'componeret og skrevet'
7.11.: 'arbeidet med Holm'
12.11.: 'Middag hos Capelmusikus Holm'
16.11. and 18.11.: '(arbeidet med Holm)'
22.11.: 'componeret paa min ny Ballet'
25.11.: 'arbeidet med Holm, componeret'

27.11.: 'componeret'

30.11. and 6.12.: 'arbeidet med Holm'

7.12.: 'skrevet og componeret'

8.12.: '1.ste Indstudering paa min nÿ Ballet 'Livjægerne paa Amager', skrevet og componeret'

9.12.: '2.den Indstudering'

11.12.: 'arbeidet med Holm'

12.12.: '3.die Indstudering. Decorationsprøve'

13.12.: 'arbeidet med [E.] Lehmann […] skrevet og componeret'

15.12.: '4.de Indstudering paa Livjægerne, Costumemøde, arbeidet med Holm'

17.12.: 'Repetition paa Scener af den nÿ Ballet'

19.12.: 'arbeidet med Holm'

20.12.: '5.te Indstudering […] skrevet Costumelister til den nÿ Ballet'

21.12.: 'Repetition af Scenerne i den ny Ballet […] arbeidet med Holm, skrevet og componeret'

22.12.: 'Repetition paa den ny Ballet'

25.12.: 'modtagen Lehmann, der blev hos os hele Dagen […] Lehmann reiste med Aftentoget'

26.12.: 'componeret en Dands til den nÿ Ballet'

30.12.: 'skrevet og componeret'

31.12.: 'Modtaget Musik fra Holm og Componeret Tøndebaandsdandsen […] Brev fra […] Lehmann'

3.1.1871: '6.te Indstudering paa den nÿ Ballet'

4.1.: 'Prøve paa 1.ste Dands til den nÿ Ballet'

5.1.: 'Prøve og Repetition paa den nÿ Ballet, arbeidet med Holm […] skrevet og componeret'

6.1.: '7.de Indstudering (Polka)'

7.1.: '(.de Indstudering (Reelen)'

8.1.: 'Aftenen hjemme componeret'

9.1.: 'arbeidet med Holm'

10.1.: '9.de Indstudering og Repetition paa den nÿ Ballet […] Costumemøde'

13.1.: 'arbeidet med Holm'

14.1. and 15.1.: 'componeret'

16.1.: 'Costümemøde'

17.1.. 'skrevet Annoncer om Personlister til 4 Blade'

18.1.: '10.e Indstudering (pas de trois) Costümemøde paa Balletten'

19.1.: 'stor Prøve og Indstudering (No. 11) paa den nÿ Ballet'

20.1.: 'Aftenen hjemme og componeret'

21.1.: 'Prøve og 12.de Indstudering paa Livjægerne, arbeidet med Holm'

22.1.: 'skrevet Programmet til Balletten rent og færdigt'

23.1.: '13 Indstudering paa Livjægerne. Den Holbergske Quadrille, besøgt [H. C.] Lumbÿ[e] for at anmode ham om en Finale Gallop'

24.1.: 'besørget adskilligt for Balletten […] Aftenprøve paa den Holbergske Quadrille og de dertil hørende Costümer'

25.1.: 'Repetition paa Balletten […] Arbeidet med Lumbÿ[e] der componerer en Finale til mig'

27.1.: 'Prøve paa den nÿ Ballet og Presentation for Directionen der var henrykt over Arbeidet'

28.1.: 'componeret min Finale til H. C. Lumbyes Galop'

30.1.: 'arbeidet med [A. W.] Lanzky paa Finalen til den nÿ Ballet'

31.1.: '14.de Indstudering paa Balletten, Finalen saagodtsom færdig'

1.2.: 'Prøve og Arrangement paa Balletten, sidste Indstudering vellykket! Gud være Lovet!'

3.2.: 'Prøve paa Dandsene til Balletten'

4.2.: 'Arrangement paa Balletten'

6.2. 'Theaterprøve paa Balletten'

7.2.: 'Costümeprøve til Balletten'

8.2.: 'Prøve og remplacering til Balletten'

9.2.: 'holdt Costumeprøve paa den holbergske Quadrille'

10.2.: 'Theaterprøve paa Balletten […] holdt Costumeprøve'

11.2.: 'Prøve paa Pas de trois […] skrevet paa en Artikel, der skal indeholde Barndomsminder fra Amager'

12.2.: 'hjemme og skrevet min Artikel færdig'

13.2.: 'Remplacering til Balletten' […] reenskrevet min Artikel'

14.2.: 'Musikprøve paa Balletten, der er ypperlig instrumenteret […] Costumeprøve Kl. 8'

15.2.: 'holdt fuldstænmdig Prøve paa Livjægerne paa Amager (Carl Price meldt syg!) […] Afsendt min Artikel til [O. H.] Delbanco'

16.2.: 'Costumeprøve'

17.2.: 'stor Prøve med Orchester paa Balletten […] Costumeprøve'

18.2.: 'besørget Programmer til den kongelige Familie og til Velyndere, modtaget Honorar for Programmet […] Generalprøve paa Balletten, der gjorde stormende Lykke – Nu ville vi see, hvad det større Publicum siger'

19.2.: 'modtaget den Illustrede Tidende med min Artikel […] i Theatret […] den første Forestilling af min Ballet Livjægerne paa Amager. Den gik ganske fortræffeligt og blev lønnet af Publicum med storartet Bifald. Jeg takkede Gud for al min Lÿkke og tilbragte Aftenen seent med mine to Døttre og Lehmann'

20.2.: 'I Theatret 2.den Forestilling af Livjægerne for brilliant Huus og endnu livligere Bifald end ved første Aften'

23.2.: 'læst en meget rosende Recension af Balletten i Folkets Avis og sendt den til Helene'

26.2.: 'læst en behagelig Artikel i Illustreret Tidende om den nÿ Ballet'

28.2.: 'I Theatret Livjægerne for fuldt Huus. Helene var henrykt, og den gik ogsaa fortræffeligt'.

The *King's Corps of Volunteers on Amager* received 60 performances during Bournonville's lifetime, the last of which was given on 2.6.1878. According to Bournonville's letter to R. Watt, written on 17.1.1871 (now in DKKk, call no. NBD 2. Rk.), the complete ballet played for nearly an hour.

Autograph sources:

Manuscript scenario. Ms. Autograph. Brown ink. 1 vol. 7 pp. (22,7 × 18,3 cm)

Livjægerne paa Amager/(Episode fra 1808.)/Vaudeville – Ballet i een Akt af A Bournonville/Musiken componeret og arrangeret af W. Holm

Signed and dated: 'Kjøbenhavn d. 12.e September 1870.' [Written according to the diary between 11.9. and 19.9.1870]

[DKKk; NKS 3285 4° 3 L–P

Manuscript scenario. Ms. Autograph. Brown ink. 1 vol. 10 pp. (22,7 × 18,3 cm)

Livjægerne paa Amager/(Episode fra 1808.)/Vaudeville = Ballet i een Akt/af/August Bournonville/1870.

Signed and dated: 'Kjøbenhavn den 12.de September 1870.' [Written according to the diary between 11.9. and 19.9.1870]

[DKKk; NKS 3285 4° 3 L–P

Production note. Ms. Autograph (partially in another's hand). Brown ink. 1 p. (22,7 × 18,3 cm)

Costumer til Balletten Livjægerne/paa Amager./(Damer)/Bipersoner.

Signed and dated: 'Kjøbenhavn d. 20.e Decbr 1870.'

[DKKkt; F.M. (Ballet)

Production note. Ms. Autograph. Brown ink. 1 p. (22,7 × 18,3 cm)

Costumer/til/Balletten Livjægerne paa Amager. (Damer)/Hovedpersonerne.

Unsigned and undated [Written according to the diary on 20.12. 1870]

[DKKkt; F.M. (Ballet)

Production note. Ms. Autograph (partially in another's hand). Black ink. 1 p. (22,7 × 18,3 cm)

Costumer/til/Balletten Livjægerne paa Amager. (Herrer)/Hovedpersonerne.

Unsigned and undated [Written according to the diary on 20.12. 1870]

[DKKkt; F.M. (Ballet)

Production note. Ms. Autograph (partially in another's hand). Brown ink. 1 p. (22,7 × 18,3 cm)
Dame – Costümer til <u>Livjægerne paa Amager</u>
Unsigned and undated [Written according to the diary on 20.12.1870]
[DKKkt; F.M. (Ballet)

Production note. Ms. Autograph (partially in another's hand). Black ink. 2 pp. (22,7 × 18,3 cm)
Costumer til Balletten. (Herrer.)/<u>Livjægerne paa Amager.</u>/<u>Bipersoner</u>
Signed and dated: 'Kjøbenhavn den 21.e Decbr 1870.'
[DKKkt; F.M. (Ballet)

Choreographic note. Ms. Autograph. Brown ink. 1 p. (20,8 × 13,4 cm)
<u>Töndebaands – Dands.</u>/[…]/<u>Polonaise fra K S</u>/[…]/<u>Töndebaands – Dandsen</u>/[…]/<u>Polonaisen gjentages.</u>/[…]/<u>Rondo.</u>
Unsigned and undated [Written according to the diary most probably on 31.12.1870]
[DKKk; NKS 3285 4° 3 L–P

Production note. Ms. Autograph. Black ink. 3 pp. (22,7 × 18,2 cm)
<u>Livjægerne paa Amager.</u>/<u>Forklædninger.</u>
Signed and dated: 'Kjøbenhavn den 9.e Januar 1871.
[DKKkt; F.M. (Ballet)

Production note. Ms. Autograph. Black ink. 1 p. (21 × 13,5 cm)
<u>Livjægerne paa Amager</u>/(Episode fra 1808.)/Vaudeville = Ballet af <u>Hofb. Bournonville</u>/Musiken: arrang. og comp. af <u>W. Holm.</u>/<u>Personerne</u>
Unsigned and undated [Written according to the diary most probably on 17.1.1871]
[DKKkt; F.M. (Ballet)

Choreographic note. Ms. Autograph. Black ink. 3 pp. (20,8 × 13,6 cm)
<u>Holbergs – Quadrille.</u>/[…]/<u>Valse de la Capricieuse.</u>/[…]/<u>La Capricieuse</u>/[…]/<u>Groupe générale.</u>
Unsigned and undated [c. January 1871]
[DKKk; NKS 3285 4° 2 A–E

Production note. Ms. Autograph (partially in another's hand). Brown ink. 1 p. (19 × 13,9 cm)
Requisiter til den holbergske/<u>Quadrille -</u>
Unsigned and undated [c. January 1871]
[DKKkt; F.M. (Ballet)

Production note. Ms. Autograph. Black ink. 1 p. (21,7 × 13,9 cm)
<u>Kl 10½.</u>/<u>Finale</u>/til/<u>Livjægerne paa Amager.</u>
Unsigned and undated [c. January 1871]
[DKKkt; F.M. (Ballet)

Musical sources:

Orchestral score. Ms. Autograph (by V. C. Holm) and copy (by A. W. Lanzky?). Black ink. 1 vol. 260 pp. (24,9 × 34 cm with variants).
302./<u>Livjægerne paa Amager./Partitur</u>/[…]/Livjægerne paa Amager (Episode fra 1808)/Vaudeville = Ballet/i een Akt/af/August Bournonville/Musiken componeret og arrangeret/af/V. C. Holm/1871
Signed and dated (on p. 10): 'V. C. Holm den 17 Februar 1871.', (p. 242) 'V C Holm Den 12.te Februar 1871.'
[DKKk; MA ms 776 (KTB 302)
This orchestral score is V. C. Holm's autograph except for Lumbye's *Finale Gallop* (score no. 16), which is in a copyist's hand (according to Bournonville's diary most likely that of A. W. Lanzky). No autographed score for Lumbye's gallop has yet been traced.

The original 1871 répétiteur's copy for *The King's Corps of Volunteers on Amager* has not yet been traced since it disappeared from the music archive of Copenhagen's Royal Theatre in 1975.

Répétiteur's copy. Ms. Copy (by P. Grønfeldt). Black ink. 1 vol. 52 pp of which two are blank (32,7 × 33,4 cm)
Grønfeldt/Le Carnaval de Wenise/par/Monsieur Larcher./Violino 1.mo/Repetiteur Partie/1823
Signed and dated (on the front cover): 'Grønfeldt/1823'
[DKKk; MA ms 3019 (KTB 1009, originally KTB 195)
Bournonville's autographed notes and choreographic numbers ('1–16') for the so-called 'En Quadrille af holbergske Figurer' (score no. 15) are inserted in this volume (with brown ink) on pp. 20–23. They clearly refer to his separate 1871 choreographic notation of this dance (now in DKKk, call no. NKS 3285 4° 2 A–E).

Parts. Ms. Copy. 35 vol.
4 vl I, 3 vl II, 2 vla, 2 vlc, 2 cb, fl 1/2, ob 1/2, cl 1/2, fag 1/2, cor 1/2/3/4, tr 1/2, trb 1/2/3, tuba, timp, gr cassa, piatti, tri.
Unsigned and undated [1871]
[DKKk; KTB 302
This set of parts was used for all performances of *The King's Corps of Volunteers on Amager* during Bournonville's lifetime.

Other sources:

Sketch by V. Güllich(?) of the décor. Pencil and water colours (16,8 × 31 cm)
[Untitled]
Unsigned and undated [1871?]
[DKKt; V. Güllichs dekorationsudkast (20)

Costume drawing by E. Lehmann. Pencil and water colours (19,8 × 12 cm)
'Livjægerne paa Amager'/Tegn. af Edv Lehmann:
Unsigned and undated [c.1871]
[SSm; Daniel Fryklunds samling [without number] (F 1329)
This drawing shows the costume of a soldier in the *King's Corps of Volunteers on Amager* (most likely that worn by the character *Edouard*, performed by W. Price).

Costume drawing by E. Lehmann. Pencil (12,1 × 20,6 cm)
[Untitled]
Unsigned and undated [c.1871]
[DKKkt; Kostumetegninger (Lehmann)
This drawing shows the costumes of four women, who played the rôles as guests from Copenhagen in *The King's Corps of Volunteers on Amager*.

Costume drawing by E. Lehmann. Pencil and water colours (20,9 × 12 cm)
<u>Husarmarkedtendersker</u>/Dam Stillmann, Gade, Larsen, Price
Unsigned and undated [c.1871]
[DKKkt; Kostumetegninger (Lehmann)
This drawing shows the costume worn by the four women, who (dressed as vivandières or 'Markedstendersker') performed the *Polka militaire* (score no. 12) in *The King's Corps of Volunteers on Amager* (performed by L. Stillmann as *Louise*, E. Gade, M. Price, and C. Larsen).

Costume drawing by E. Lehmann. Pencil and water colours (20,8 × 11,9 cm)
Prinds Carneval
Unsigned and undated [c.1871]
[DKKkt; Kostumetegninger (Lehmann)
This drawing shows the costume worn by *Prince Carnival* in the *Pas de trois* (score no. 13) of *The King's Corps of Volunteers on Amager* (performed by D. Krum).

Costume drawing by E. Lehmann. Pencil and water colours (20,8 × 12,1 cm)
Daarskabsgudinder/dam Petersen – Scholl
Unsigned and undated [c.1871]

[DKKkt; Kostumetegninger (Lehmann)
This drawing shows the costume worn by the *Goddesses of Folly* in the *Pas de trois* (score no. 13) of *The King's Corps of Volunteers on Amager* (performed by J. Petersen and A. Scholl).

Printed sources:

Printed scenario. 1 vol. 12 pp. (20,2 × 12,8 cm)
Livjægerne paa Amager./(Episode fra 1808.)/Vaudeville=Ballet i een Akt/af/August Bournonville./Musiken arrangeret og componeret af W. Holm./Decorationerne af V. Güllich./Costumerne tegnede af Edv. Lehmann.
Kjøbenhavn, J. H. Schubothe/Bianco Luno/F. S. Muhle, 1871.
[DKKk; 17, – 175 8°

4.3.1871
La Ventana, Ballet Divertissement (Balletdivertissement).
This restaging of Bournonville's second and final version of *La Ventana* (*see* 6.10.1856) represents the last time it was mounted by him. It was staged especially for the début of A. Scholl, who played *The Señorita*, partnered by D. Krum as *The Señor*. In his diary Bournonville noted about the production, which was clearly given without any significant changes from his previous 1868 staging:

21.2.1871: 'begyndt at indstudere La Ventana til Anna Scholl'
23.2.: 'Indstudering paa La Ventana, Scholl fortræffelig'
24.2.: 'Anna Scholl og [D.] Krum resp: udnævnte til Dandserinde og Danser, hun med Feu af 3.e Classe [...] Prøve Kl 6 paa La Ventana'
2.3. and 3.3.: 'Prøve paa La Ventana'
4.3.: 'I Theatret [...] La Ventana med Anna Scholl, der udmærkede sig og blev meget applauderet'.

The 1871 production of *La Ventana* received 37 performances during Bournonville's lifetime, the last of which was given on 16.5.1879.

The musical material employed this year was the same as that used since the 1856 première of the divertissement (now in DKKk, call nos. MA ms 1127, MA ms 2997, KTB 300, and KTB 1055).

3.4.1871
A Folk Tale (Et Folkesagn).
This performance represents Bournonville's second restaging of his three-act romantic ballet *A Folk Tale* (*see* 20.3.1854). It was mounted for M. Price, who this year played *Hilda* for the first time. The production differed from the previous 1867 staging by some minor choreographic changes made by Bournonville in the two solo variations for *Hilda* in Act II (score no. 12). These modifications seem to represent the only significant differences from the previous production.

In his diary Bournonville noted about the staging and its second performance that he attended:

10.11.1870: 'Indstudering af Hildas Rolle i 'Et Folkesagn' til M. Price'
11.11.: 'Indstudering paa 'Et Folkesagn'
14.11., 26.11., 30.11., 1.12., 14.12., 16.12., 19.12., and 21.12.: 'Prøve paa 'Et Folkesagn''
4.1.1871: 'Prøve paa Et Folkesagn'
17.3.: 'Theaterprøve paa Et Folkesagn'
23.3.: 'Prøve paa Dandsene til Et Folkesagn'
1.4.: 'Theaterprøve paa Et Folkesagn'
13.4.: 'I Theatret Et Folkesagn, der gik smukt med sin tildeels nÿe Besætning'.

The 1871 production of *A Folk Tale* received 9 performances, the last of which was given on 28.5.1872.

The musical material employed this year was the same as that used for the 1867 production (now in DKKk, call nos. C II, 108, MA ms 2968–2969, and KTB 274).

Autograph sources:

Choreographic note. Ms. Autograph. Brown ink. 1 pp. (20,9 × 13,5 cm)
Et Folkesagn. (Hildas Solo 2.d[en] Akt)
Unsigned and undated [Bournonville's autographed notes on the reverse side of this sheet indicate beyond doubt that it was written during the late March 1871]
[DKKt; Brevregistrant: Bournonville
This manuscript describes Bournonville's revised choreography for the two solo variations of *Hilda* in Act II (score no. 12) of *A Folk Tale*, made for M. Price prior to the restaging of this ballet on 3.4.1871. Moreover, the note contains Bournonville's autographed choreographic numbers ('1–7' and '1–4' written with brown ink) which clearly refer to his similar numbers inserted on pp. 51–55 in the original 1854 répétiteur's copy for *A Folk Tale* (now in DKKk, call no. MA ms 2968 (KTB 274 (1)).

16.4.1871
Der Templer und die Jüdin (Tempelherren og Jødinden).
The 1871 Copenhagen restaging of H. Marschner's three-act romantic opera (premièred at Städtisches Theater in Leipzig on 22.12.1829, and first performed in Copenhagen in a four-act version on 21.4.1834) was originally projected by Bournonville on 30.10.1857 and reproposed by him on 1.8.1870. It represents the first and only time *Der Templer und Die Jüdin* was mounted with his mise-en-scène and choreography. The staging included two (unnamed) *Dances*, performed by a group of 28 persons during the chorus in the opening scene of Act IV, score nos. '13' and '14', entitled «Schlinget frohe Tänze, windet Blumenkränze» (i.e. Act III, score no. 14 in the 1829 German version). Both of these dances are repeated, in part, after the romance, named «Wer ist der Ritter hochgeehrt» (sung by *Ivanhoe*, *Rowena*, and *Cedric*). In Bournonville's staging they were performed by a ballerina, three soloists, and three groups of eight persons each (two standard-bearers, two page-boys, and four young girls).

The 1871 production is not mentioned in Bournonville's handwritten list of his stagings of operas and plays, written c.1872 (*see* Additional Sources), but is included in the published survey of his works in his memoirs *My Theatre Life* (p. 410).

In his diary he noted about the performance:

21.2.1871: 'skrevet paa Scene=Arrangementet til Tempelherren og Jødinden'
26.2.: 'skrevet Scene=Arrangement til Tempelherren og Jødinden'
2.3.: 'Costumemøde paa Tempelherren'
4.3.: 'Decorationsprøve paa Tempelherren'
9.3.: 'componeret paa Dandsen til Tempelherren og Jødinden'
10.3.: 'Oplæsning paa Tempelherren'
13.3.: 'componeret Dands til Tempelherren og Jødinden'
14.3.: 'Indstudering paa Dandsen til Tempelherren'
21.3.: Prøve og Indstudering paa Dands og Scener til Tempelherren og Jødinden'
23.3.: 'Prøve paa Dandsene til Tempelherren og Jødinden'
24.3.: 'Prøve paa Remplacering og 1.ste og 2.den Akt af Tempelherren og Jødinden'
30.3.: Theaterprøve paa 1.ste og 2.den Akt'

31.3.: 'Theaterprøve'
12.4.: 'fuldstændig Prøve'
14.4: 'Generalprøve paa Tempelherren og Jødinden, der hvad Udførelse angaaer ikke lover meget'.

Bournonville was not present on the opening night, but attended the sixth performance on 12.5.1871 about which he noted in his diary:

'hørt et par Akter af Tempelherren og Jødinden'.

Moreover, during the following season he directed two brief rehearsals of the opera's dances on 4.9. and 6.9.1871 prior to a performance of it on 7.9.1871. They represent the last times he ever worked on Marschner's opera.

The 1871 staging received 10 performances (the last of which was given on 24.11.1871) after which *Der Templer und die Jüdin* went out of the Copenhagen repertory.

Autograph sources:

Manuscript mise-en-scène. Ms. Autograph. Black ink. 8 pp. (22,8 × 18 cm)
Scene = Arrangement til Tempelherren og/Jødinden Opera i tre Akter af Marschner.
Signed and dated: 'Kbhvn d. 25.de Februar 1871.' [Written according to the diary between 21.2 and 26.2.1871]
[SSm; Daniel Fryklunds samling no. 147

Choreographic note. Ms. Autograph. Brown ink. 2 pp. (23 × 18,3 cm)
Dands til Tempelherren og Jødinden./4.de Akt 1.ste Scene
Unsigned and undated [Written according to the diary on 10.3.1871]
[DKKkt; F.M. (Ballet)

Production note. Ms. Autograph. Black ink. 1 p. (18,4 × 11,4 cm)
Tempelherren og Jødinden/4.de Akt
Unsigned and undated [c. March 1871]
[DKKkt; F.M. (Ballet)

Musical sources:

Orchestral score. Ms. Copy (including several later manuscript insertions, partly by a copyist and partly by H. S. Paulli). Black and brown ink. 3 vol. Act I 344 pp. of which five are blank, Act II 348 pp. of which one is blank, Act III 240 pp. of which one is blank (25 × 34,5 cm with several variants)
Tempelherren og Jødinden/Partitur/1.ste Akt/[…]/Der Templer und die Jüdin/Grosse romantische Oper in 3 Aufzügen/nach W. Scotts Ivanho, frei bearbeitet/von/Wilhelm August Wohlbrück/Music/von/Heinrich Marschner/[…]/Tempelherren og Jødinden/Partitur./2.den Akt./[…]/Tempelherren og Jødinden/Partitur/3.die Akt.
Unsigned and undated [c.1834]
[DKKk; C I, 275 (KTA 306)
This German manuscript orchestral score dates from the 1834 Copenhagen première of Marschner's opera. It contains T. Overskou's and A. Hertz's Danish translations of text and recitatives dating from 1834 and 1871 respectively. It is written (with brown ink) next to Wohlbrück's original German text. The music for the two (unnamed) *Dances* in Act IV, score nos. '13 and 14' (i.e. Act III, score no. 14 in the original 1829 version) is included in vol. III, pp. 1–23 and 37–43.

Répétiteur's copy. Ms. Copy. Brown ink. 1 vol. 6 pp. of which one is blank (32,2 × 24,6 cm)
Repetiteur Parti/til/A. 306/Tempelherren og Jödinden/No. 39/

Marschner/43/ […] /Repetiteur Parti/til/Syngestykket/Tempelherren og Jödinden/af/Marschner/3.die Akt
Unsigned and undated [1834]
[DKKk; MA ms 3069 (KTA 306)
This répétiteur's copy dates from the 1834 Copenhagen première of Marschner's opera, and contains the complete music for the two (unnamed) *Dances* in Act IV, score nos. '13' and '14' (i.e. Act III, score no. 14 in the original 1829 version). Moreover, it includes Bournonville's autographed choreographic numbers ('1–11' and '1–3', written with black ink) which clearly refer to the separate notation of the Act III dances, which he wrote (according to his diary) on 10.3.1871.

Parts. Ms. Copy. 35 + 8 vol.
4 vl I, 3 vl II, 2 vla, 4 vlc e cb, fl picc, fl 1/2, ob 1/2, cl 1/2, fag 1/2, cor 1/2/3/4/5, tr 1/2, trb 1/2/3, timp, tamb, arpa. On stage: fl, cl 1/2, fag 1/2, cor, tr 1/2. 55 vocal parts.
Unsigned and undated [1834]
[DKKk; KTA 306
This set of parts dates from the 1834 Copenhagen première of Marschner's opera and was used for all performances of it there during Bournonville's lifetime.

Other sources:

Manuscript libretto. Ms. Copy. Brown ink. 12 pp. of which four are blank (21,6 × 17,2 cm)
Indlagte Recitativer/i/Tempelherren og Jødinden/istedetfor den hidtil benyttede Dialog. –
Unsigned and undated [c.1871]
[DKKk; NKS 3285 4°, kapsel 9, læg 2
This libretto, which was part of Bournonville's private archive, contains the new Danish translations of the recitatives performed in Act I (scene 3) and Act II (scenes 1, 2, 5 and 6) of Marschner's *Der Templer und die Jüdin*. They replaced the earlier Danish texts, which had been employed in all previous stagings of this opera since its 1834 Copenhagen première.

17.4.1871
The Dannebrog or The Dream of King Volmer (Dannebrog eller Kong Volmers Drøm). **Projected staging.**

The original manuscript for this tragedy (written by a certain 'Capt. Pengel') was, according to Bournonville's diary, sent to him unsolicited. In an accompanying letter the author requested his opinion with regard to a possible staging of this work at Copenhagen's Royal Theatre. In his diary Bournonville noted about the manuscript and his reply:

16.4.1871: 'Brev og Manuscript til Gjennemlæsning fra Capt. Pengel […] læst den ovennævnte Folketragedie'
17.4.: 'gjennemlæst Capt. Pengels Tragedie Dannebrog eller Kong Volmers Drøm som jeg ikke fandt anvendelig for Scenen, hvorfor jeg skrev ham til og erklærede mig incompetent'.

The tragedy was never mounted in Copenhagen, neither at the Royal Theatre nor at any of the private theatres.

30.4.1871
Iphigenia in Aulis (Ifigenia i Aulis) (**Stockholm's Royal Theatre, Stora Theatern**).

During a sojourn in Stockholm in the spring of 1871 Bournonville gave (according to his diary) personal stage instructions to the singer, F. Stenhammer, who performed the title-rôle in R. Wagner's 1846 revision of C. W. v. Gluck's three-act opera during the 1870–71 season at Stockholm's Royal Theater (*see also* 27.4.1861). In his diary he noted about this session with Stenhammer:

29.4.1871: 'hørt lidt af Prøven til <u>Iphigenia</u>'
30.4.: 'instrueret Fru Stenhammer til Iphigenia'.

Stenhammer performed in the opera for the last time during this season on 31.5.1871.

14.5.1871
Le Papillon (Sommerfuglen) (uncredited) performed by
M. Gérard (Tivoli Gardens, Theatret).

This solo dance was created for a French ballerina, M. Gérard, who was engaged at the Tivoli Gardens during the 1870 and 1871 seasons. There she often shared the evening ballet performances with Bournonville's two other private pupils, the English sisters A. and C. Healey. Moreover, during the autumn and winter of 1870–71 Gérard was admitted as a guest student in Bournonville's daily ballet classes at the Royal Theatre.

Bournonville had probably seen Gérard performing in Tivoli for the first time on 13.8.1870. Thus, according to a note in his diary, he attended a performance on that day in the Tivoli Gardens in which the Healey sisters danced his so-called *Pas de deux gracieux* (*see* 5.8.1870). On the same evening Gérard performed her extraordinarily successful gallop, entitled *Fransk Storm=Marche*. It was set to a score composed and arranged by B. Dahl, who employed the French national anthem *La Marseillaise* in his music. Gérard's gallop was created as an expression of moral support to the besieged population of Paris in the Franco-Prussian war.

Gérard (who performed her gallop for the first time in the Tivoli Gardens on 7.8.1870) may then have caught Bournonville's attention and full sympathy. Thus, in his diary he noted about his allowing her to take part in his daily ballet classes and also stated about the solo dance that he choreographed for her later:

20.9.1870: 'Conference med <u>Justr</u> [F. J. G.] <u>Berner</u> angaaende Optagelsen paa min Dandse=Lection af <u>Mlle</u> [M.] <u>Gérard</u>, hvis Moder og Søster ere i det beleirede Paris'
21.9.: 'Møde med Mlle Gerard hos <u>Balduin Dahl</u>'
27.9.: '1ste Lection paa Theatret. <u>Mlle Marie Gérard</u> deeltog deri'
15.3.1871: 'arrangeret Musik til <u>Mlle Gérard</u> og leveret den til <u>B. Dahl</u>'
29.3.: 'prøvet <u>Le Papillon</u> for Mlle Gérard'
21.4.: 'Brev til <u>Balduin Dahl</u>'.

Bournonville attended only one performance of the *Le Papillon*, about which he noted on 22.5.1871:

'paa Tivoli hvor vi saa Mlle Gérard [..] dandse'.

According to his diary the music for this solo dance seems have been arranged by himself, and was most probably orchestrated by B. Dahl. *Le Papillon* received 28 performances in the Tivoli Gardens between 14.5. and 1.10.1871. It was listed in the so-called *Tivoli=Program* without any mention of either Bournonville's name or that of the music composer. No musical sources for *Le Papillon* have yet been traced.

14.5.1871
Grand pas de deux (uncredited) performed by F. and
L. Carey (the Tivoli Gardens, Theatret).

This (uncredited) dance is almost certainly identical with the earlier similarly uncredited *Grand pas de deux* performed by the Healey sisters in the Tivoli Gardens during the previous season (*see* 28.6.1870). That dance, in turn, was most likely an adaptation for two women of Bournonville's much earlier *Pas de deux* from his one-act ballet *The Flower Festival in Genzano* (*see* 19.12.1858). During the 1871 and 1872 Tivoli seasons the *Grand Pas de deux* was performed 19 times by the Carey sisters, the last time on 30.8.1872. Bournonville attended one of these performances on 1.9.1871. On that day a special 'Flower Festival' ('Blomsterfest') was celebrated in the Tivoli Gardens and was described in his diary as follows:

'Vi gik i Tivoli hvor der var Blomsterfest [...] jeg saae endnu Carey-erne dandse meget smukt'.

No musical sources for this dance have yet been traced.

18.5.1871
L'Aragonaise (uncredited) performed by M. Gérard (the
Tivoli Gardens, Theatret).

In Bournonville's handwritten list of his works, written c.1872 (*see* Additional Sources), this (uncredited) Spanish solo dance is named '*l'Arragonnaise*'. According to a note in his diary on 15.3.1871 the music for it appears to have been arranged by himself from selected Spanish dance tunes, and was (according to the same source) most likely orchestrated by B. Dahl. In his diary he noted about the creation of the dance:

15.3.1871: 'arrangeret Musik til <u>Mlle</u> [M.] <u>Gérard</u> og leveret den til <u>B. Dahl</u>'
4.4.: 'componeret en spansk Dands til Mlle Gérard (Rondo arragonnaise)'
13.4.: 'Indstudering til Mlle Gérard (l'Arragonnaise)'
14.4.: 'fuldendt den besværlige Indstudering af l'Arragonnaise'.

According to the same source, Bournonville attended only one performance of the dance on 1.9.1871, but made no specific remarks about it. *L'Arragonaise* reached a total of 17 performances in the Tivoli Gardens between 18.5. and 26.9.1871. During this period it was always presented in the so-called *Tivoli=Program* with no credit to Bournonville and the music composer. No musical sources for this solo dance have yet been traced.

2.6.1871
*Two Tableaux (To Tableauer) Mozartiana. The Sally from
Classens Have (1807) (Udfaldet i Classens Have (1807)).*

This series of two tableaux was created for a charity performance arranged to collect funds for the Royal Danish Ballet's private pension fund, of which Bournonville was the founding member. The first tableau, entitled *Mozartiana*, was, according to the printed scenario, a somewhat revised version of Bournonville's earlier series of four similar apotheotic tableaux with this title (originally premièred at Stockholm's Royal Theatre on 7.3.1862).

Moreover, according to the 1871 scenario the first of the four tableaux was set to the overture and selected excerpts from W. A. Mozart's four-act comic opera from 1786 *Die Hochzeit des Figaro*. It was followed by three apotheotic tableaux showing scenes from Mozart's operas *Die Zauberflöte*, *La Clemenza di Tito*, and *Il Dissoluto Punito, ossia il Don Gio-*

vanni. They were set to the accompaniment of the chorus «O Isis, und Osiris, welche Wonne!», sung by the priests in Act II, score no. 18, of *Die Zauberflöte*.

According to a printed piano score, which contains the music for the second tableau and is entitled 'Udfaldet i Classens Have' (published in Copenhagen in 1871 by C. F. E. Hornemann and J. E. Erslev, pl. no. 796, now in DKKk, call no. D 6), this tableau was arranged after a picture by C. W. Eckersberg depicting the sally from Classens Have at the northern outskirts of Copenhagen on 31.8.1807. In that historic battle the Danish army had repelled the occupying British forces.

In the musical arrangement for this tableau V. C. Holm incorporated two melodies, the first of which was originally a song, entitled «I Freden blev min Isse graae», borrowed from J. A. P. Schultz's score to T. Thaarup's one-act singspiel *The Harvest Festival (Høstgildet)* from 16.9.1790. The second tune, too, originally accompanied a song, named «Til Værn for den Gamle, den Svage, for Barnet og Qvinden og Brud». It was first performed as part of F. L. Kunzen's score to T. Thaarup's one-act singspiel *The Homecoming (Hiemkomsten)* from 30.1.1802. Later this tune also served as an accompaniment for a song by E. de Falsen, entitled «Til Vaaben, see Fjenderne komme!». The two borrowed song tunes were interpolated by Holm as the opening and concluding movements of his score for *The Sally from Classens Have*. They framed an *Allegro piu mosso* section of 35 measures (presumably composed by Holm), which served to illustrate the combat scene between the Danish and the British armies.

In his diary Bournonville noted about the creation and the première of his two 1871 tableaux:

13.5.1871: 'Skrevet og ordnet til Pensionskassens Forestilling Tableauerne Mozartiana og Classens Have, Besøg hos H. P. Holst, Conference med [F. J. G.] Berner'
15.5.: 'Brev til [L.] Gade og til [V. C.] Holm'
19.5.: 'Breve fra Gade, Holm'
22.5.: 'besørget adskilligt, Frokost hos W. [i.e. V. C.] Holm og arbeidet med ham. Paa Theatret, stillet Grupper til vor Forestilling d. 2.den Juni. Ordnet Decorationerne dertil'
23.5.: 'et par Ord til Gade og Programmet til Tableauerne'
1.6.: 'stillet Decorationer til Tableauerne [...] Generalprøve paa Tableauerne'
2.6.: 'beskjæftiget mig med Forestillingen til Indtægt for vor Pensionskasse. – Stor Indtægt og Tilstrømning [...] Udsolgt for det Meeste til forhøiede Priser. Vi gav Mozartiana, <u>Valgerda</u>, [Udfaldet i] <u>Classens Have</u> og Livjægerne [i.e. *The King's Corps of Volunteers on Amager*]. Alt gik udmærket og gjorde megen Lykke'.

The tableaux were performed only once.

Autograph sources:

Manuscript scenario. Ms. Autograph. Black ink. 2 pp. (22,7 × 18 cm)
<u>Tableauer</u>/fremstillede ved Forestillingen i Det kongelige Theater/<u>Fredagen den 2. Juni 1871.</u>/[...] <u>Mozartiana!</u>/[...]/<u>II.</u>/<u>Udfaldet i</u> <u>Classens Have</u>
Unsigned and undated [Written according to the diary on 13.5. 1871]
[Private collection (Copenhagen)]
The text in this autographed manuscript is almost identical with that in the printed scenario.

Manuscript scenario. Ms. Autograph (included in a letter to R. Watt). Black ink. 1 p. (21 × 13,5 cm)

[..] den Forestilling der gives d. 2.den Juni [...] bestaae af følgende Sager/[...] <u>Mozartiana!</u>/[...]/<u>Udfaldet i Classens Have</u> (1807)/ [...]
Signed and dated: 'Kbhvn d. 22.de Mai 1871'
[DKKk; NBD III, 227, 22.5.1871

Musical sources:

No separate musical sources for *Mozartiana* have yet been traced.

Orchestral score (*The Sally from Classens Have*). Ms. Autograph (by V. C. Holm). Brown ink. 20 pp. of which one is blank (26,2 × 34,7 cm)
Clasens [*sic*] Have,/Tableau/af/Aug. Bournonville
Unsigned and undated [1871]
[DKKk; MA ms 2759 (1) (KTB 338)

No répétiteur's copy for *The Sally from Classens Have* has yet been traced.

Parts (*The Sally from Classens Have*). Ms. Copy. 32 vol.
4 vl I, 3 vl II, 2 vla, 3 vlc e cb, fl 1/2, ob 1/2, cl 1/2, fag 1/2, cor 1/2/ 3/4, tr 1/2, Atrb, Ttrb, Btrb, timp, gr cassa e piatti, tri.
Unsigned and undated [1871]
[DKKk; MA ms 2759 (2–33) (KTB 338)

Printed sources:

Printed scenario. 1 vol. 3 pp. (20,5 × 13,5 cm)
TABLEAUER/FREMSTILLEDE VED FORESTILLINGEN/I/DET KONGELIGE THEATER/Fredagen den 2den Juni 1871./til Fordeel for Ballettens private Pensionskasse./[...]/I./MOZARTIANA./[...] / II./UDFALDET/I/CLASSENS HAVE/under Kjøbenhavns Beleiring (1807)./(Tableau efter C. V. Eckersbergs bekjendte Billede). Kjøbenhavn, M. W. Volkersen [1871]
[DKKt; Balletprogrammer: Bournonville.

8.6.1871
Oberon, or The Elf King's Oath (Oberon). **Projected Danish restaging.**
According to a note in his diary and a manuscript mise-en-scène, on this day Bournonville seems to have resumed working on a projected restaging of C. M. v. Weber's three-act romantic fairy-play at Copenhagen's Royal Theatre:

8.6.1871: 'Brev til [F. J. G.] Berner med indlagt til [G. F.] Törner og et Udkast til Iscenesætningen af Oberon'.

The project had first been planned by him on 30.10.1857, and was reproposed to the Copenhagen theatre management on 6.10.1859. However, it was for unknown reasons never carried out, and *Oberon, or The Elf King's Oath* was not staged in Copenhagen until 18.12.1886 (for the celebration of the centenary of Weber's birth).

Autograph sources:

Production note. Ms. Autograph. Brown ink. 3 pp. (20,8 × 13,6 cm)
<u>Oberon</u>/Lyrisk Tryllespil i 3 Akter til Musik/af C. M. v. Weber./ Texten omskreven/efter den engelske Original og indrettet/for <u>Théâtre = Lyrique</u> af franske Forfattere./[...]/<u>Decorationerne</u>/[...] /<u>Personerne</u>
Signed and dated: 'Fredensborg d 8.e Juni/1871.'
[SSm; Daniel Fryklunds samling no. 139 f

8.7.–18.8.1871
Thirty private dance lessons to M. Westberg.
According to a series of notes in his diary Bournonville gave

30 private dance lessons to the Swedish ballerina, M. Westberg, who made her Copenhagen début in the title-rôle of his two-act romantic ballet *La Sylphide* on 6.9.1871 and was permanently engaged at the Royal Theatre from July 1872. These lessons, which took place at Bournonville's private residence in Fredensborg, lasted for about two hours each.

4.9.–16.9.1871
Twelve private dance lessons to 'Mlle Pira'.
According to a series of notes in his diary Bournonville gave 12 private dance lessons to the Swedish dancer, G. C. Pira (M. Stedingk). These lessons, which took place at the Royal Theatre mainly during the afternoons, lasted for about two hours each.

6.9.1871
La Sylphide (Sylphiden).
This performance represents the fifth and last restaging in Copenhagen of Bournonville's two-act romantic ballet *La Sylphide* (*see* 28.11.1836) during his lifetime. It was mounted for the Copenhagen début of the Swedish ballerina, M. Westberg, in the title-rôle. According to his diary, Bournonville gave 30 private dance lessons to this ballerina at his private residence in Fredensborg between 8.7. and 18.8.1871, during which she learned the ballet. According to the same source the 1871 production was mounted by Bournonville with only minor if any changes from the previous 1867 staging. In his diary he also noted about the rehearsals and the ballet's first two performances:

18.7.1871: '8.e Lection (Den største Deel af Sylphiden lært)'
21.7.: 'd. 10.e Lection i hvilken vi gjennemgik hele Sylphidens Rolle'
31.7.: '18.de Lection [...] Presentation Sylphiden'
23.8.: 'Presentation af Vestberg [i.e. M. Westberg]'
24.8.: 'Eftermiddagsprøve paa Sylphiden 1.ste Akt'
25.8. and 26.8.: 'Prøve paa Sylphiden'
28.8.: 'Prøve paa Sylphiden til 1½ [...] Eftermiddagsprøve paa Sylphiden 2.den Akt'
29.8.: 'Prøve paa Sylphiden'
31.8.: 'Fuldstændig Prøve paa Sylphiden, der gik særdeles smukt'
4.9.: 'tidlig Genralprøve paa Sylphiden, der gik særdeles smukt'
6.9.: 'I Theatret [...] Sylphiden til Marie Westberg's Debut, der gik særdeles smukt og med fortjent Bifald. Huset var brilliant besat, men Varmen utaalelig'
8.9.: 'I Theatret Sylphiden der gik meget smukt – Westberg endnu bedre end første Gang'.

The 1871 production of *La Sylphide* received only 3 performances during Bournonville's lifetime, the last of which was given on 12.9.1871.

The musical material employed this year was the same as that used for the previous 1867 staging (now in DKKk, call nos. C II, 117 d, MA ms 2970 b, and KTB 275).

Autograph sources:

Production note. Ms. Autograph. Black ink. 2 pp. (21,4 × 17,3 cm)
Personliste/til/Balletten Sylphiden.
Signed and dated: 'Fredensborg d. 9.e August 1871.'
[DKKkt; F.M. (Ballet)

17.9.1871
The Lay of Thrym (Thrymsqviden).
This, Bournonville's first restaging of his four-act Nordic

mythological ballet *The Lay of Thrym* (*see* 21.2.1868) was mounted for the Swedish ballerina, M. Westberg. She took over the leading rôle of *Sigyn* from its original interpreter, B. Schnell, since the latter had retired as a dancer in 1871 to become an actress. According to Bournonville's autographed choreographic notes, the 1871 production was mounted with partially revised choreography in the two solo dances of *Sigyn*, performed during the so-called *Bridal Dance* in Act II (scene 4, score no. 21).

In his diary Bournonville noted about the staging and the first two performances:

15.7.1871: 'skrevet til [...] [L.] Gade [F.J.G.] Berner og Betty Schnell [...] i Anledning af Thrÿmsqviden'
18.7.: 'Besøg af Gade [....] Brev fra Berner'
19.7.: 'Brev fra Betty Schnell'
22.7.: 'Om Eftermiddagen 11.te Lection og begÿndt paa Sigyn, skrevet'
25.7.: '13.de Lection [...] forstsat Sigyn'
30.7.: 'Brev fra Berner om Slangen i Thrymsqviden'
1.8.: 'afsted til Kbhvn med Mlle Vestberg [i.e. M. Westberg] [...] holdt en Memoreringsprøve paa Thrymsqviden assisteret af Betty Schnell, [H.] Scharff, Gade og [A.] Fredstrup – Alle venlige og vakkre imod den nÿe Kamerat'
6.8.: 'skrevet til Agnes Dehn for at bede hende overtage Freyas Partie, som Fru [J.] Eckardt har afgivet'
8.8.: 'Svar fra Agnes Dehn, invilligende'
13.8.: 'skrevet [...] choregraferet'
23.8.: 'Presentation af Vestberg [i.e. M. Westberg] og Prøve paa Thrymsqviden indtil Kl 1½'
24.8.: 'Prøve paa Thrÿmsqviden (2' og 3.e Akt.)'
30.8.: 'bivaanet Musikprøve paa Thrymsqviden'
1.9.: '(Gade holdt min Prøve paa Thrymsqviden)'
5.9.: 'Prøve paa Thrÿmsqviden'
7.9.: 'prøvede meget paa Thrÿmsqviden'
9.9.: 'Theaterprøve paa Thrÿmsqviden'
11.9.: 'Prøve paa Thrymsqviden'
13.9.: 'Prøve paa [...] Rollerne til Thrÿmsqviden'
14.9.: 'Theaterprøve med Orchester paa Nornerne og Thrÿmsqviden'
15.9.: 'Prøve paa Enkeltheder af Thrymsqviden'
16.9.: 'Generalprøve paa Nornerne og Thrymsqviden. Alt gik fortrinligt og [M.] Westberg præsterede berömmeligt'
17.9.: 'I Theatret Nornerne og Thrÿmsqviden. Balletten gik udmærket godt og Marie Westberg feirede en sand Triumph i Sigyns Partie, som hun spillede og dandsede særdeles godt'
18.9.: 'I Theatret Thrymsqviden for godt Huus og livligt Bifald. Balletten gik smukt, dog mindre godt end 1.ste Gang'.

About the fifth performance on 12.10.1871 he stated:

'I Theatret Thrymsqviden, der gik for brilliant Huus men for det dvaskeste Publicum i Verden'.

The 1871 production of *The Lay of Thrym* received 5 performances, the last of which was given on 12.10.1871.

The musical material employed this year was the same as that used since the 1868 première (now in DKKk, call nos. C II, 114, MA ms 2996, KTB 299, and KTA 763).

Autograph sources:

Production note. Ms. Autograph (partially in another's hand). Black ink. 3 pp. (21,4 × 17,3 cm)
Personliste/til/Balletten Thrÿmskviden
Signed and dated: 'Fredensborg d. 9' August 1871.'
[DKKkt; F.M. (Ballet)

Choreographic note. Ms. Autograph. Brown ink. 1 p. (21,3 × 13,5 cm)

Sigyns Solo. (Marie Westberg)./Brudedandsen./[...]/2.de Solo
Unsigned and undated [Written according to the diary most probably between 22.7. and 13.8.1871]
[SSm; Daniel Fryklunds samling no. 148
This manuscript contains Bournonville's revised choreography for the part of *Sigyn* in *The Bridal Dance* of *The Lay of Thrym* (Act II, scene 4, score no. 21). It also includes his autographed choreographic numbers ('9–13' and '19–22') which refer to similar numbers inserted underneath the music on pp. 59 and 64–65 in the 1868 répétiteur's copy (now in DKKk, call no. MA ms 2996 (KTB 299)).

8.10.1871
Le Dieu et la bayadère, ou La Courtisane amoureuse (Brama og Bayadèren).
This performance represents Bournonville's second and last complete restaging of D.-F.-E. Auber's two-act opera-ballet at Copenhagen's Royal Theatre (*see* 7.2.1841 and 6.10.1859). It was mounted with the Swedish ballerina, M. Westberg, dancing the rôle of *Zoloé* for the first time, in (according to Bournonville's diary) a new choreography that he had created especially for her. Moreover, an undated choreographic note contains Bournonville's revised choreographic version for the part of *Fatmé* in the Act II *Pas de deux* (score no. 10) and indicates that this dance was rearranged for A. Flammé (perhaps the understudy of A. Scholl?). This note seems to have been written at about the same time as the 1871 staging. Flammé, however, never came to perform the rôle of *Fatmé* on stage.

In his diary Bournonville noted about the 1871 production:

25.8.1871: 'Decorationsprøve paa Brama'
30.8.: 'indstuderet [A.] Scholls Dands til Brama og Bayadèren'
31.8.: 'Scholl Indstudering'
17.9.: 'componeret til Brama'
18.9.: 'componeret og arrangeret til Brama'
19.9.: 'Eftermiddagsprøve og Indstudering paa Brama og Bayadèren 5 til 8'
20.9.: 'Indstudering og Prøve paa Brama'
22.9.: 'Prøve paa Brama'
24.9.: 'prøvet to Timer med Indstudering paa Brama'
25.9.: 'Prøve paa Brama'
26.9.: 'Indstuderinger fuldendt paa Brama'
27.9.: 'Prøve paa Brama'
28.9.: 'Prøve paa Dandsen til Brama og Bayadèren'
2.10.: 'Prøve paa Dands til Brama fra Kl 2 indtil 10'
3.10.: 'Prøve paa Brama'
4.10.: 'Arrangements og Orchesterprøve fuldstændig paa Brama'
5.10.: 'fuldstændig Prøve paa Brama ([M.] Westberg udmærkede sig)'
6.10.: 'prøvet Costumer til Brama'
7.10.: 'Generalprøve paa Brama og Bayaderen'
8.10.: 'I Theatret Brama og Bayadèren for brilliant Huus og livligt Bifald. Westberg havde en virkelig Succès og dandsede med stor Bravour. Charlotte [Bournonville] sang særdeles smukt og blev paaskjønnet'.

The 1871 staging of *Le Dieu et la bayadère* received 9 performances during Bournonville's lifetime, the last of which was given on 12.1.1873.

Autograph sources:

Production note. Ms. Autograph. Black ink. 1 p. (21,8 × 14 cm)
Brama og Bayaderen/(Slutningsgruppe –)/Indiske Guddomme.

Unsigned and undated [c. August–September 1871]
[DKKkt; F.M. (Ballet)

Production note. Ms. Autograph. Brown ink. 2 pp. (21,2 × 13,4 cm)
Requisiter til Maaltidet/i/2,den Act af Brama./[...]/Slutnings-gruppe/i/Brama og Bayaderen.
Unsigned and undated [c. August–September 1871]
[DKKkt; F.M. (Ballet)

Choreographic note. Ms. Autograph. Brown ink. 1 p. (22,8 × 18,3 cm)
Brama og Bayaderen (2' Akt)/Pas de deux./Fatmé (modificeret for Flammé. Doubleante.)
Unsigned and undated [Written according to the diary most probably on 17.9. and/or 18.9.1871]
[DKKk; MA (Box)
This manuscript contains Bournonville's revised choreography for the part of *Fatmé* in the Act II *Pas de deux* of *Le Dieu et la bayadère* (score no. 10). It also includes his choreographic numbers ('1–6') which refer to similar numbers written underneath the music on pp. 39–40 in the 1847 répétiteur's copy (now in DKKk, call no. MA ms 3064 (KTA 301 (2)). Several other choreographic numbers in the same répétiteur's copy seem to refer to another (not yet traced) separate notation of the opera's dances which Bournonville most probably made for the 1871 production of Auber's opera-ballet.

Musical sources:

The orchestral score and the set of parts employed this year were the same as those used for the previous 1859 staging of *Le Dieu et la bayadère* (now in DKKk, call nos. U 6, and KTA 301 respectively).

Répétiteur's copy. Ms. Copy. Black ink. 1 vol. 24 pp. (33,2 × 25,2 cm)
Brama og Bayaderen/[...]/91/[...]/Repetiteurpartie/til/Brama og Bayaderen.
Unsigned and undated [1871]
[DKKk; MA ms 2912 (5) (KTA 301 (3))
This répétiteur's copy contains the complete music for the two dance scenes in Act I (score no. 5) and Act II (score no. 10) of *Le Dieu et la bayadère*. The répétiteur's copy dates almost certainly dates from the 1871 restaging and is included on pp. 39–62 in a volume that also contains the répétiteur's copies for five other operas and plays, mounted at Copenhagen's Royal Theatre between 1815 and 1871.

22.10.1871
Les Huguenots (Hugenotterne).
This performance represents Bournonville's second and last complete staging of Meyerbeer's five-act opera from 1836 (*see* 28.2.1844 and 7.4.1869). According to the poster it differed from his previous 1869 staging by having the opera's dances in Acts III and V this year choreographed by L. Gade. In his diary Bournonville noted about the performance:

13.10.1871: 'Theaterprøve paa Hugenotterne'
17.10.: 'Sceneprøve paa Hugenotterne'
18.10.: 'Theaterprøve paa 3.e og 5.e Akt af Hugenotterne'
19.10.: 'Fuldstændig Prøve paa Hugenotterne'
21.10.: 'Generalprøve paa Hugenotterne'
22.10.: 'hørte de to sidste Akter af Hugenotterne, der gik ganske fortrinligt med [F. P. B.] Hartmann som Marcel'.

The 1871 production of *Les Huguenots* received 5 performances during Bournonville's lifetime, the last of which was given on 27.11.1871 (Acts I and II were performed separately three times between 10.3. and 13.3.1878).

The musical material employed this year was the same as that used for the previous 1869 production (now in DKKk, call nos. U 6, MA ms 2908 (2), and KTA 385).

26.12.1871

A Fairy Tale in Pictures (Et Eventyr i Billeder).

The idea of creating a three-act ballet, with the second act freely based on H. C. Andersen's fairy tale from 1838, *The Steadfast Tin Soldier*, seems to have come to Bournonville some time before, on 1.8.1870. On that day he wrote a repertory plan for the 1870–71 season which included what he then described as: 'Et større Balletdivertissement (nærmere Aftale)'.

The ballet's music, which is divided into 18 numbers, was composed and arranged by V. C. Holm. In order to help the audience interpret the ballet's rather long mimic sequences and the dramatic action, Holm incorporated, at Bournonville's personal request, several musical borrowings. They are identified as follows:

(1) Act I, scene 1 (score no. 1): In the ballet's opening scene Holm interpolated the tune of an anonymous composer which originally accompanied J. Baggesen's song from 1785, entitled «Der var en Tid da jeg var meget lille». It is followed by an excerpt of 56 measures, borrowed from the so-called *Allegro a la Rondo* in Act III of C. Schall's score to V. Galeotti's four-act tragic ballet *Bluebeard (Rolf Blaaskiæg)*, premièred on 13.12.1808. Next come two excerpts (entitled *dolce*, 34 bars, and *Allegretto*, 24 bars), both of which were borrowed from another score by Schall, namely Galeotti's two-act comic ballet *The Mountaineers, or The Children and the Mirror (Biergbeboerne eller Børnene og Speilet)* from 23.9.1802. This is followed by a third excerpt by Schall (an *Allegro* of 33 bars) borrowed from the score of Act I (1. Optog) in Galeotti's three-act pantomimic tragedy *Lagertha* (premièred on 30.1.1801).

(2) Act I, scenes 2–3 (score nos. 2–4): During these three scenes a series of eight *tableaux vivants* are shown depicting situations from some of the most popular of H. C. Andersen's fairy tales. This series is set to I. P. E. Hartmann's melody from 1838 to C. Winther's 1826 poem «Flyv Fugl! flyv over Furresøens Vove». This illustrated the first tableau showing Andersen's fairy tale *Storkene* (1839). Next follows C. E. F. Weyse's melody for A. Oehlenschläger's text «Tommeliden var sig saa spæd en Mand». This romance was originally part of Weyse's score for Act II (score no. 10) of his four-act singspiel *The Cavern of Ludlam (Ludlams Hule)*, premièred on 30.1.1816. In Bournonville's ballet it accompanied the tableau representing Andersen's 1835 fairy tale *Tommelise*. For the following tableau (depicting the 1844 fairy tale *Nattergalen*) Holm interpolated Schall's melody for P. A. Heiberg's song «Fra Chinas Kyst til Østersøens Grændser», which was originally part of his two-act singspiel *The China Travellers (China-farerne)* from 2.3.1792. It is followed by a section in 6/8 time (presumably composed by Holm) illustrating the tableau showing Andersen's 1837 fairy tale *Den lille Havfrue*.

In the following tableau (depicting the 1844 tale *Den grimme Ælling*) Holm interpolated the tune of a Swedish folksong, entitled 'Hönsgummans visa' («Hanar och Höner och kycklingar små»). It is followed by yet another Swedish tune, originating from the region of Westergöthland and entitled 'Sorgens makt' («Liten Kjerstin och hennes moder»). This tune served as an accompaniment for the tableau in which a scene from Andersen's 1842 fairy tale *Svinedrengen* is shown. Both of these Swedish tunes were published by J. N. Ahl-ström in 1856 in his collection, entitled *300 Nordiska Folkvisor* (Stockholm, P. A. Huldberg, pp. 14 and 35).

Next follows a tableau representing Andersen's 1842 fairy tale *Ole Lukøie*. It was set to the melody of M. Hauser's *Wiegenlied* for violin and piano (op. 11), which had been published by C. C. Lose & Olsen in Copenhagen during the early 1840s (a copy of which is now in DKKk, call no. U 68). Finally, the series of eight tableaux concludes with a scene showing Andersen's 1844 fairy tale *Engelen*, for which Holm employed an excerpt of 24 bars, entitled *Larghetto*. It was borrowed from Act II (2. Optog) of Schall's score for Galeotti's 1801 ballet *Lagertha*, in which it accompanied the scene where the cer-

emony of marriage between the characters *Regnar* and *Thora* takes place.

(3) Act I, scene 5 (score no. 7): According to Bournonville's musical instructions to Holm the music for this scene employed two (not yet identified) French songs, named 'Le Petit Tambour français' and 'Quel plaisir d'être soldat' respectively.

(4) Act II, scene 1 (score no. 10): For this number Holm borrowed a motif from Act II (score no. 3) of G. Rossini's three-act opera *Le Siège de Corinthe* (first performed at the Paris Opéra on 9.10.1826). In Rossini's opera the motif was originally part of the *Allegro moderato* section in the aria, entitled «Chef d'un peuple», sung by the character *Mahomet*.

(5) Act II, scene 3 (score no. 12): Holm here incorporated an excerpt of 12 bars that he borrowed from Act I of G. Rossini's two-act heroic melodrama *Tancredi* (premièred in Venice at Teatro La Fenice on 6.2.1813). In that work it was part of the cavatina entitled «Tu, che accendi questo cuore», sung by *Tancredi*. In Bournonville's ballet the excerpt accompanied the mime scene during which the dancer, *Montplaisir* declares his love for the ballerina *Rosalie*.

(6) Act II, scene 10 (score no. 16): In this scene Holm incorporated an excerpt of 18 bars that he borrowed from Act II (score no. 19) of L. Persuis's and N. Dalayrac's score for L. Milon's two-act ballet *Nina, ou La Folle par amour* (premièred at the Paris Opéra on 23.11.1813). It is followed by two other excerpts (of 34 and 7 bars respectively) which were borrowed from Schall's overture to Galeotti's 1801 ballet *Lagertha*. In Bournonville's ballet these excerpts served as an accompaniment for the scene in which the soldier *Oscar* rescues the ballerina *Rosalie* from a sudden outbreak of fire at the Drury Lane theatre in London.

(7) Act III, scene 1 (score no. 17): For this number Holm borrowed the two melodies by M. Hauser and C. Schall which also accompanied the *tableaux vivants* in Act I scenes 2–3 (score nos. 3–4) showing scenes from H. C. Andersen's fairy tales *Ole Lukøie* and *Engelen*.

(8) Act III, scene 2 (score no. 18): For the ballet's final scene Holm incorporated the same tune to J. Baggensen's song «Der var en Tid da jeg var meget lille» which he had employed earlier for the opening scene of Act I.

Two years after the 1871 première of *A Fairy Tale in Pictures* Bournonville mounted an abridged divertissement version of the first act, which was premièred on 19.3.1873.

In his diary he noted about the ballet's creation and reception in 1871:

5.4.1871: 'begyndt paa et Program til en mindre Ballet – Et Børne-Eventyr – Gud veed om jeg faaer rigtig Skik derpaa'
15.4.: 'conciperet en nÿ Ballet i to Akter, Et Børne-Eventÿr'
16.4.: 'Fuldendt mit Program (der behagede mine Nærmeste meget)'
15.5.: 'Brev til […] [V. C.] Holm'
19.5.: 'Brev fra […] Holm'
22.5.: 'Frokost hos W. [i.e. V. C.] Holm og arbeidet med ham'
24.5.: 'copieret mit nÿ Balletprogram'
14.6.: 'Brev og Program fra Holm'
15.6.: 'Skrevet Musikprogram til <u>Holm</u> tilligemed et Par Linier i et Brev'
19.6.: 'arbeidet med <u>Holm</u>'
27.6.: 'componeret paa min Ballet'
14.7.: 'Brev til Holm med Programmet til Balletten'
30.8.: '(arbeidet med Holm paa Et Eventyr)'
31.8.: 'budt [H. C.] Andersen Velkommen fra Norge'
12.9.: 'arbeidet med Holm'
23.9.: 'arrangeret Decorationsvæsenet til Et Eventyr'
6.10.: 'componeret 1.ste Scene af min nÿ Ballet (Et Eventyr)'
8.10. and 9.10.: 'componeret'
10.10.: '1.ste Indstudering med Børnene til min nÿ Ballet'
11.10.: '2.den Indstudering med Børnene'
12.10.: '3.die Indstudering paa <u>Et Eventyr</u>'
14.10.: '<u>4.de Indstudering paa Et Eventyr</u>'

16.10.: 'skrevet og componeret [...] 5.te Indstudering paa Et Eventyr'

17.10.: 'Repetition paa Et Eventyr [...] componeret'

18.10.: 'componeret'

22.10.: '(Møde med Theatermaler [V.] Güllich.)'

23.10.: '6.te Indstudering paa <u>Et Eventyr</u>'

24.10.: 'componeret'

25.10.: 'componeret og sluttet 1.ste Akt af min nÿ Ballet'

26.10.: '7.de Indstudering'

27.10.: 'Arbeidet med Holm'

28.10.: 'Repetition paa 1.ste Akt af Balletten, der gik særdeles smukt'

30.10.: 'skrevet og componeret [...] Aftenen hjemme, componeret'

31.10.: 'Eftermiddagen hjemme og componeret. (NB Igaar Costumemøde og Idag Decorationsmøde paa min nÿ Ballet'

1.11.: '9.de Indstudering paa Balletten. 2.den Akt begyndt [...] skrevet, arbeidet med Holm Aftenen hjemme, componeret'

2.11.: 'componeret'

3.11.: '11.e Indstudering'

4.11.: 'tidlig Prøve og 12.e Indstudering (pas de deux færdig)'

5.11.: 'Decorationsprøve til <u>Et Eventyr</u>'

6.11.: 'arbeidet med Holm, Repetition paa Dandsen til `Et Eventyr´'

8.11.: 'arbeidet med Holm'

9.11.: '13.e Indstudering paa Et Eventyr. [...] Aftenen hjemme, Jeg modtog den sørgelige Efterretning at [H.] <u>Scharff</u> ved at dandse i Divertissement af Troubadouren havde sprængt sin venstre Knæskal og formodentlig neppe kommer til at dandse mere, om han end bliver cureret! Det er et betydeligt Tab for Balletten og smerter mig dybt!'

10.11.: 'Dispositioner for at remplacere Scharff. Repetition paa Et Eventyr [...] Eftermiddag arbeidet med Holm'

12.11.: 'componeret og skrevet'

13.11.: 'arbeidet med Holm, 14.de Indstudering'

14.11.: 'Repetition paa Et Eventyr [...] arbeidet med Holm, skrevet og componeret'

15.11.: '16.e Indstudering. Møde med Maler og Maskinmester'

17.11.: 'componeret paa Skolen, 17.e Indstudering'

18.11.: 'Repetition paa Et Eventyr [...] arbeidet med Holm, skrevet'

19.11.: 'skrevet paa Balletprogrammet'

20.11.: 'reenskrevet mit Program, som jeg leverede til [J. H.] Schubothe'

21.11.: '18.e Indstudering, componeret'

22.11.: 'skrevet og componeret, 19.e Indstudering og Prøve for W. Price. Eftermiddagsprøve med Børnene til Finalen'

23.11.: 'Prøve og <u>20.e Indstudering</u>. Balletten fra min side fuldført'

25.11.: 'Repetition paa [...] hele den nÿ Ballet'

27.11.: 'Presentation af min nÿ Ballet og stor Succès'

29.11.: 'skrevet'

30.11.: 'Besøg [..] paa Malersalen'

2.12.: '1.ste Theater-Arrangementsprøve paa Et Eventyr'

4.12.: 'Theaterprøve paa endeel af Balletten'

5.12.: 'Repetition paa 2.den Akt af Balletten'

6.12.: 'Costumeprøve'

9.12.: 'Theaterprøve paa 2.den Akt af Et Eventyr [...] lille Costumeprøve'

10.12..: 'Besøg hos H. C. Andersen'

12.12.: 'Theaterprøve paa Et Eventyr i Billeder'

13.12..: 'Prøve paa [...] Et Eventyr'

14.12.: 'Prøve paa adskillige Remplacements til [...] Et Eventyr'

15.12.: 'Melding om [D.] Krum, der har et daarligt Been! nÿ Modgang for Balletten. Prøve og Indstudering til [A.] <u>Walbom</u> da [E.] Hansen ikke vovede at remplacere Krum'

16.12.: 'Costumeprøve til stor Tilfredshed'

18.12.: 'Theaterprøve og Correcturprøve paa Balletten'

20.12.: 'Theaterprøve med Orchester paa Balletten, gik i det Hele godt – ude Kl 2½! [...] Costümeprøve'

21.12.: 'Theaterprøve og stillet Slutningsgruppen til Balletten [...] modtog mine Balletprogrammer og 25r. i Honorar'

22.12.: 'Repetition paa Dandsene Kl 10½ og fuldstændig Prøve Kl 11 paa Balletten [...] Om Aftenen skulde der have været Decorationsprøve paa Balletten, men Güllich har forsömt sig utilladeligt og vi maatte udsætte Generalprøven indtil Søndagen d. 24.e til stor Ubehagelighed for Mange'

23.12.: 'uddelt Programmer og besørget endeel paa Theatret [...] Efter Forestillingen af *Tartuffe* prøvede vi Decorationer og Maskiner, vi bleve færdige henved Kl 1. – Jeg laae længe inden jeg kunde falde i Søvn men jeg var glad og rolig for Udfaldet'

24.12.: 'Kl 10 paa Theatret, hvor vi holdt en god Generalprøve Kl 12. Alt gik udmærket og gjorde megen Lykke'

26.12.: 'I Theatret [...] 1.ste Forestilling af <u>Et Eventyr i Billeder</u>. Balletten gik i enhver Henseende udmærket og blev modtaget med overordentlig Bifald. Det var en virkelig Succès for udsolgt Huus og et livligt Publicum [...] i Forening [...] feirede vi denne glade Aften og takkede Gud for al den Lykke, han har forundt os'

28.12.: 'Læsning af nogle temmelig fornemme og affejende Anmeldelser af min Ballet, der som sædvanlig af Critiken betragtes fra Vrangsiden [...] Et Eventyr i Billeder for 2.den Gang med særdeles livligt Bifald og for brilliant Huus; Udførelsen fortrinlig'.

A Fairy Tale in Pictures received 14 performances during Bournonville's lifetime, the last of which was given on 18.1. 1873.

Autograph sources:

Manuscript scenario. Ms. Autograph. Black ink. 1 vol. 12 pp. (22,7 × 18 cm)
<u>Et Börne = Eventÿr</u>/<u>Ballet i to Akter.</u>/ af / August Bournonville / (Motivet efter H. C. Andersens 'Tinsoldaten') /1871.
Signed and dated: 'Fredensborg d. 15.e April 1871'
[DKKk; NKS 3285 4° 2 A–E]

Musical instructions. Ms. Autograph. 5 sheets. 9 pp. (21,7 × 13,5 cm/ 21 × 13,2 cm/21,1 × 13,6 cm/21,7 × 13,5 cm/22,3 × 13 cm)
<u>Et Eventyr.</u>/Ballet i to Akter af A. Bournonville./Musiken arrangeret og componeret/af/<u>W. Holm.</u>
Unsigned and undated [Written according to the diary for the main part on 15.6.1871]
[DKKk; NKS 3285 4° 2 A–E]
While four of these five sheets are undated, the last is dated '12.e September 1871.' It describes Bournonville's wishes for some late musical changes in what became the ballet's final two scenes of Act II (score nos. 6 and 7).

Production note. Ms. Autograph. Black ink. 1 p. (21 × 13,5 cm)
<u>Rollebesætning</u>/<u>Et Eventÿr i Billeder</u>/Ballet i to Akter af A Bournonville (Motivet af/H. C. Andersens 'Tinsoldat') Musiken comp og arrang:/af W Holm, Decorationerne af W. Güllich.
Signed and dated: 'Kbhvn den 29.e Novbr 1871.'
[DKKk; NBD III, 231, 29.11.1871]

Production note. Ms. Autograph. Black ink. 2 pp. (22,3 × 14,3 cm)
<u>Belysning</u>/i/<u>Balletten Et Eventyr i Billeder</u>
Signed and dated: 'd 17.e December 1871.'
[DKKkt; Brevregistrant (December 17, 1871)]

Production note. Ms. Autograph. Black ink. 1 p. (22,8 × 18,3 cm)
<u>Et Eventyr i Billeder.</u>/Ballet i tre Akter af Herr Hofballetmester Bournonville/(Motivet af H. C Andersens: 'Tinsoldaten') [erased]
Unsigned and undated [c. late 1871]
[DKKkt; F.M. (Ballet)]

Production note. Ms. Autograph. Brown ink. 1 p. (21,8 × 13,8 cm)
<u>Dhrr</u> [L.] Ring – <u>Fru</u> [E.] <u>Gade</u>
Unsigned and undated [c. late 1871]
[DKKkt; F.M. (Ballet)]

Musical sources:

Orchestral score. Ms. Autograph (by V. C. Holm). Brown ink. 1 vol. 322 pp. of which four are blank. (25,5 × 34,2 cm)

303/Et Eventyr/i/Billeder/1871/ [...] /Et Eventỹr i Billeder/Ballet/i 3 Acter/af/August Bournonville/Musikken componeret og arrangeret/af/Vilhelm Holm
Signed and dated (on p. 148): 'Den 4.de December 1871. VCHolm', (p. 329) 'V C Holm/Den 17 December/1871.'
[DKKk; C II, 114 m (KTB 303)]

Répétiteur's copy. Ms. Copy. Black ink. 1 vol. 122 pp. of which one is blank (34,1 × 25,3 cm)
B. 303/Balletten/Et Eventỹr i Billeder/(Ballet i tre Akter.)/Bournonville/1871./[...]/Et Eventyr/i/Billeder.
Unsigned and dated (on the front cover): '1871.'
[DKKk; MA ms 2998 (KTB 303)]
This répétiteur's copy contains several pencilled notes (written by an unknown hand) which describe (in rather general terms) the dramatic action of each scene. Other choreographic numbers (written with brown ink by an unknown hand) seem to refer to a separate choreographic notation of the complete ballet which (according to his diary) Bournonville appears to have made between October and December 1871.

Parts. Ms. Copy. 35 vol.
3 vl I, 3 vl II, 2 vla, 3 vlc e cb, fl 1/2, ob 1/2, cl 1/2, fag 1/2, cor 1/2/3/4, tr 1/2, trb 1/2/3, tuba, timp, gr cassa, piatti, tri, glock, arpa.
Unsigned and undated [1871]
[DKKk; KTB 1036 (originally KTB 303)]

Other sources:

Costume drawing by E. Lehmann. Pencil and water colours (18,9 × 12,4 cm)
Fru Stillmann (Eventyr i Billeder)
Unsigned and undated [c.1871]
[DKKkt; Kostumetegninger (Lehmann)]
This drawing shows the costume worn by the *Fairy* in Act I, scene 3 of *A Fairy Tale in Pictures* (performed by L. Stillmann).

Costume drawing by E. Lehmann. Pencil and water colours (18,8 × 12,4 cm)
[Untitled]
Unsigned and undated [c.1871]
[DKKkt; Kostumetegninger (Lehmann)]
This drawing almost certainly shows the costumes worn by the vivandières ('Markedtendersker') in the *Waltz* in Act I, scene 5 (score no. 8) of *A Fairy Tale in Pictures*.

Printed sources:

Printed scenario. 1 vol. 16 pp. (19,9 × 12,5 cm)
Et Eventyr i Billeder./Ballet i tre Akter/af/August Bournonville./(Motivet af H. C. Andersens 'Tinsoldat'.)/Musikken componeret og arrangeret af W. Holm/Decorationerne af W. Güllich.
Kjøbenhavn, J. H. Schubothe/Bianco Luno/F. S. Muhle, 1871.
[DKKk; 17, -175 8°]

1872

4.1.1872
A Quadrille (En Quadrille).
In the three-month period between 9.11.1871 and 1.2.1872 Bournonville gave 12 private lessons in social dances at the Copenhagen residence of J. C. F. v. Wedel-Heinen (the Lord-in-Waiting at the court of the Queen Dowager, Caroline Amalie), at Dronningens Tværgade no. 5. These lessons, which were taught on Thursday afternoons, concluded with a performance by Bournonville's pupil of a *Quadrille* that he

had choreographed for this occasion on 4.1.1872. It was performed at a soirée on 15.2.1871. In his diary he noted about the lessons and the *Quadrille*:

9.11.1871: '1.ste Lection hos Kmhr. [J. C. F. v.] Wedel Heinen' [...]
4.1.1872: 'componeret en Quadrille til Wedel-Heinens [...] 8.de Lection hos W. H.'
1.2.: 'sidste Lection hos Wedel-Heinen'
15.2: 'Presentation af mine Elever hos W. Heinen'.

No musical sources for this *Quadrille* have yet been traced. It is not possible to identify the dance any further.

13.2.–12.4.1872
Sixteen dance lessons in social dance.
According to a series of notes in his diary Bournonville gave 16 private dance lessons in social dance this year at the Copenhagen residence of the Russian envoy to Denmark, Baron A. P. von Mohrenheim, at Kongens Nytorv no. 4. These lessons, which took place mainly on Tuesday and Wednesday afternoons, each lasted for about two hours.

14.2.1872
Amanda.
Although Bournonville does not include the 1872 Copenhagen restaging of H. Hertz's four-act romantic comedy (first performed on 20.4.1844) in the printed survey of his stagings of operas and plays in his memoirs *My Theatre Life*, he clearly seems to have given personal stage instructions to the dancer-actress, B. Schnell, who this year played the title-rôle. This theory is confirmed by a note in his diary on 13.2.1872 reading: 'Prøve paa Dandsen til imorgen'.

According to Hertz's printed text book (now in DKKk, call no. 55, – 96 8°, vol. 2, pp. 139–331) the (unnamed) *Dance scene* performed by Schnell in this comedy is included in Act III, scene 6, and is described by Hertz (on p. 260) as follows:

'Amanda (udfører, nynnede dertil, nogle Tacter af en gammeldags Folkedands, men standser med et krænket Udtryk, da hun mærker [...] Spot og Latter)'.

The 1872 restaging of *Amanda* received 7 performances (the last of which was given on 12.3.1872), after which the comedy went out of the repertory. Bournonville attended only the last of these performances, but made no specific remarks about it in his diary. No musical sources for the dance scene in Act III have yet been traced.

1.3.1872
Czardas and Frischka (Hungarian National Dances) (Czardas og Frischka (ungarske Nationaldandse)).
This set of Hungarian dances was performed by three couples, and is almost certainly identical with the two similar dances that were originally part of Bournonville's so-called *Dance Divertissement* from 31.10.1870. The *Czardas and Frischka* were performed only once in 1872. Bournonville did not attend this performance. No separate musical sources for these dances dating from the 1872 performance have yet been traced. This seems to indicate that they were rehearsed and performed using the earlier musical material for Bournonville's *Dance Divertissement* (now in DKKk, call nos. C II, 119, MA ms 2907 (1), and KTB 276).

12.3.1872

Idea for a Prologue to The Restless (Idée til et Forspil [til] Den Stuneslöse). **Projected prologue.**

Bournonville's idea of adding this recited prologue to the planned 200th performance on 3.5.1872 of L. Holberg's three-act comedy from 1750 *The Restless (Den Stundesløse)* was for unknown reasons never carried out. The autographed manuscript scenario for it was originally send to 'Velbaarne Herr Erik Boëgh, dansk Digter', whom Bournonville asked in an accompanying letter to write the text of the prologue, while he clearly intended to create the mise-en-scène himself. In his diary he noted about the project:

11.3.1872: 'Aftale med Erik Bögh om et Følgestykke til Jubilæet for Holbergs Stundesløse 200.e Gang, arbeidet paa Planen'
18.3.: 'færdigskrevet Planen til Et Enaktsstykke og bragt det til Erik Bögh'
24.3.: 'Conference med Erik Bögh om Forspillet'.

Autograph sources:

Manuscript scenario. Ms. Autograph. Black ink. 4 pp. (22,7 × 17,9 cm)
Idée til et Forspil/anvendeligt ved den 200.de Forestilling af Holberg's/Den Stundesløse.
Signed and dated: 'Kbhvn d. 12.e Martz 1872.' [Written according to the diary on 11.3.1872]
[DKKk; NKS 3285 4° 3 R-U

23.3.1872

Die Meistersinger von Nürnberg (Mestersangerne i Nürnberg).
This performance represents the Copenhagen première of R. Wagner's three-act opera (first performed at Königlich Hof- und Nationaltheater in Munich on 21.6.1868). It was mounted with Bournonville's mise-en-scène and choreography, which included a so-called *Tanz der Lehrbuben* in Act III. This dance (a lively waltz movement of 151 bars) was performed by a group of apprentices and young peasant girls in scene 5 (score no. 35). In the orchestral score (p. '468') the girls who perform this scene are described as: 'Ein bunter Kahn mit jungen Mädchen in reicher bäurischer Tracht kommt an', while the scene itself is described in the same score (p. '470') as:

'(Das Charakteristische des folgenden Tanzes, mit welchem die LEHRBUBEN und MÄDCHEN zunächst nach dem Vordergrund kommen, besteht darin, dass die LEHRBUBEN die MÄDCHEN scheinbar nur am Platz bringen wollen; sowie die GESELLEN zugreifen wollen, ziehen die BUBEN die MÄDCHEN aber immer wieder zurück, als ob sie sie anderswo unterbringen wollten, wobei sie meistens den ganzen Kreis, wie wählend, ausmessen, und somit die scheinbare Absicht auszuführen anmuthig und lustig verzögern.).'

A note in Bournonville's diary on 1.4.1872 (reading: 'Sceneprøve paa Forkortelser til Mestersangerne') clearly indicates that Wagner's opera was performed with several musical cuts after its third performance (on 27.3.1872). According to other pencilled autographed notes by the conductor (H. S. Paulli) in the printed orchestral score these cuts were:

(1) Act I, scene 2 (score no. 3): In this scene Paulli made one minor cut of 11 bars.
(2) Act I, scene 2 (score no. 4): Here Paulli made a musical cut of 77 measures.

(3) Act I, scene 3 (score no. 6): An omission of 43 bars was made in this number.
(4) Act I, scene 3 (score no. 7): In this number Paulli made a large cut of 122 bars.
(5) Act II, scene 5 (score no. 17): Here a minor musical cut of 30 bars was made.
(6) Act II, scene 6 (score no. 19): 53 bars were omitted in this number.
(7) Act II, scene 6 (score no. 20): In this number Paulli made two musical cuts of 88 and 34 bars each.
(8) Act III, scene 2 (score no. 25): Paulli here made three musical cuts of 15, 41, and 48 bars respectively.
(9) Act III, scene 2 (score no. 26): In this number two musical cuts of 5 and 58 bars were made.
(10) Act III, scene 3 (score no. 29): Two omissions of 53 and 71 bars each were made in this scene.
(11) Act III, scene 4 (score no. 31): An omission of 57 measures was made in this scene.
(12) Act III, scene 5 (score no. 36): One musical cut of 34 bars was made in this number.
(13) Act III, scene 5 (score no. 37): This number was shortened by a minor musical cut of 17 bars.
(14) Act III, scene 5 (score no. 39): In the Act III finale Paulli made a large omission of 71 bars before the so-called 'Schlussgesanges'.

In his diary Bournonville noted about the rehearsals, the staging and the opera's three first performances in Copenhagen:

11.12.1871: 'begyndt paa Sceneriet til Mestersangerne'
29.12.: 'skrevet Sceneri til Mestersangerne'
31.12.: 'skrevet Sceneri'
3.1.1872: 'hørt 1.ste Akt af [R.] Wagners Mestersangerne (paa Syngeskolen) forfærdeligt!'
4.1.: 'paa Theatret, hvor jeg besørgede Costumelister til Mestersangerne'
17.1.: 'overværet Chorprøven paa Mestersangerne'
30.1.: 'overværet Sangprøve paa Mestersangerne'
1.2.: 'holdt den første Instructionsprøve paa Mestersangerne'
2.2.: '2' Instruction paa Mestersangerne'
3.2.: '3.die Instruction paa Mestersangerne'
7.2.: '4.de Instruction paa Mestersangerne'
9.2.: '1.ste Akt af Mestersangerne paa Theatret fra 12–2'
10.2.: '5.te Instruction paa Mestersangerne'
12.2.: 'Costumemøde paa Mestersangerne'
14.2.: 'overværet Musik og Sangprøven paa Mestersangerne (mildest talt saare vanskeligt.)'
15.2.: 'Musikprøve paa 2' Akt af Mestersangerne'
16.2.: '3.die Sitzprobe paa Mestersangerne [...] 6.te Instructionsprøve'
17.2.: 'skrevet og componeret Dands og Optog til Mestersangerne'
19.2.: 'Prøve paa 1.ste Akt af Mestersangerne paa Theatret og med Orchester'
20.2.: 'Theaterprøve paa 1.ste Akt af Mestersangerne'
21.2.: '7.de Instruction paa Mestersangerne'
22.2.: 'Costumemøde [...] Arrangement paa Finalen af 2.den Akt af Mestersangerne'
24.2.: 'Theaterprøve paa 2.den Akt af Mestersangerne'
25.2.: 'skrevet og componeret'
26.2.: 'Theaterprøve paa Mestersangerne 1.ste og 2' Akt'
27.2.: 'indstudering paa Dandsen til Mestersangerne' [...] fuldendt Scenearrangementet til Mestersangerne'
28.2.: 'Instruction paa Mestersangerne, 3.e akt'
29.2.: 'repeteret Dandsen til Mestersangerne og 9.de Indstudering'
1.3.: 'skrevet og arrangeret Optogene til 3.die Akts 2' Afdeling af Mestersangerne'
4.3.: 'Arrangement og Theaterprøve paa Mestersangerne (3.e Akt)'
6.3.: 'Theaterprøve paa Mestersangerne 2.' og 3' Akt.'
7.3.: 'Prøve paa[..] 1.ste Akt af Mestersangerne'
8.3.: 'Prøve paa 2' og 3' Akt af Mestersangerne'

9.3.: 'Prøve paa 1.ste akt af Mestersangerne'
10.3.: 'Prøve paa 2.den og 3.die akt af Mestersangerne'
12.3.: 'Fuldstændig Prøve paa Mestersangerne fra 10½ til 3½. Costumeprøve Kl 7 […] og Decorationen til 2' Akt belyst'
13.3. 'Generalprøve paa Mestersangerne (spiller 4 Timer), den gik i det Hele smukt og mit Scenearrangement tog sig godt ud'
15.3.: 'Forestillingen til iaften Mestersangerne gaaet overstyr formedelst [P. L. N.] Schramms Upasselighed, – stor Skuffelse'
21.3.: 'fuldstændig Prøve paa Mestersangerne'
23.3.: 'I Theatret 1.ste Forestilling af Mestersangerne, der gik særdeles godt, men gjorde kun egentlig Lykke i 3.die Akt […] Operaen var forbi lidt over elleve og vil neppe interessere vort Publicum, hvilket er en Lykke, da det Wagnerske Musiksystem tiltrods for hans ubestridelige Dygtighed er en storartet Misforstaaelse af den dramatiske Tonekunst'
25.3.: 'I Theatret 2.den Forestilling af Mestersangerne, der gik særdeles godt og vandt Bifald af det talrige Publicum'
27.3.: 'I Theatret 3.e Forestilling af Mestersangerne der gik meget godt og for godt Huus, dog uden særdeles Tilstrømning'.

Die Meistersinger von Nürnberg received 11 performances in Copenhagen during Bournonville's lifetime, the last of which was given on 11.10.1872.

Musical sources:

Printed orchestral score. 2 vol. Act I–II 318 pp. of which two are blank, Act III 260 pp. (34 × 26,5 cm)
Mestersangerne./1.ste og 2.den Akt./Partitur/[…]/55/DIE/Meistersinger von Nürnberg/von/Richard Wagner./[…]/Mestersangerne./3.die Akt./Partitur.
Mainz, B. Schott's Söhnen, pl. no. 18469 [1868]
[DKKk; U 6 (KTA 777) (mu 9208.3181)
This printed orchestral score was used for all performances of Wagner's opera in Copenhagen during Bournonville's lifetime. An autographed inscription by the editor (written with brown ink on the reverse of the title page) reads: 'mit Aufführungsrecht für das Hof=/theater in Copenhagen/Mainz dem 12 April 1871/B Schotts Söhne'. A. Hertz's 1871 Danish translation is written (with black ink) next to the original German text.
    The music for the so-called *Tanz der Lehrbuben* in Act III, scene 5 (score no. 35) is included in the second volume on pp. '470–476'. A metronome marking (written with blue crayon on p. '470') indicates the exact tempo of this dance with a dotted minim being equal to '63'.

Répétiteur's copy. Ms. Copy. Brown ink. 1 vol. 10 pp. of which one is blank (33,8 × 25,6 cm)
Repetiteurparti/[….]/Mestersangerne/[…]/83./[…]/Repetiteurparti/til/Mestersangerne
Unsigned and undated [1871]
[DKKk; MA ms 2915 (7) (KTA 777)
This répétiteur's copy contains Bournonville's autographed choreographic numbers ('1–9', written with black ink) in the music for the so-called *Tanz der Lehrbuben* in Act III, scene 5 (score no. 35). They seem to refer to his separate (not yet traced) notation of this dance, which (according to his diary) was written on 17.2.1872. Other pencilled notes describing the dramatic action during the same dance seem to date from a later restaging of the opera.
    The répétiteur's copy is included (on pp. 31–40) in a volume that also contains the répétiteur's copies for six other operas and plays, mounted at Copenhagen's Royal Theatre between 1856 and 1874.

Parts. Ms. Copy. 43 + 12 vol.
6 vl I, 5 vl II, 3 vla, 4 vlc e cb, fl picc, fl 1/2, ob 1/2, cl 1/2, fag 1/2, cor 1/2/3/4, tr 1/2/3, trb 1/2/3, tuba, timp, gr gassa, piatti, tri, arpa. On stage: cor 1/2, tr 1/2/3/4/5/6/7/8, glock, org. 80 vocal parts.
Unsigned and undated [1871]
[DKKk; KTA 777
This set of parts dates from the 1871 Copenhagen première of *Die*

Meistersinger von Nürnberg and was used for all performances of it there during Bournonville's lifetime.

30.4.1872
Die Hochzeit des Figaro (Figaros Bryllup).

This performance represents Bournonville's third and last complete staging of W. A. Mozart's four-act comic opera from 1786 at Copenhagen's Royal Theatre (*see* 7.1.1844). According to his diary it was mounted with partially revised choreography in the third act, and with a number of minor changes from his two previous productions on 21.5.1858 and 7.10.1860. In his diary Bournonville noted about the performance:

5.4.1872: 'Instruction paa Figaro'
6.4.: 'Componeret Dands til Figaro […] indstuderet en nÿ Dands til Figaro'
8.4.: 'Decorationsmøde og Instruction paa Figaro'
10.4.: 'lille Prøve paa Dandsen til Divertissementet'
12.4. and 16.4.: 'Instruction paa Figaro'
19.4.: 'Theaterprøve paa Figaro'
20.4.: 'Theaterprøve med Orchester paa Figaro'
27.4.: 'Prøve paa Figaro'
29.4.: 'Generalprøve paa Figaro'
30.4.: 'I Theatret Figaros Brÿllup, nÿt indstuderet og gik udmærket saavel fra Personalets som fra Publicums Side'.

The 1872 production of *Die Hochzeit des Figaro* received 10 performances during Bournonville's lifetime, the last of which was given on 22.5.1875.
    The musical material employed this year was the same as that used since the 1844 staging (now in DKKk, call nos. C I, 280, MA ms 3042, and KTA 215).

Autograph sources:

Choreographic note. Ms. Autograph. Ink. 2 pp. (format unknown)
Figaros Bryllup./3.die Akt/(Corps de Ballets)/[…]/Fandango (uforandret)/(2.me Corps de Ballets)
Signed and dated: 'Ce 6 Avril 1872'
[USNYp; Dance Collection, call nos. *ZBD-71 (microfilm), and (S)*MGZMD 30 (photostat copy)
Bournonville's choreographic numbers ('1–5') included in this manuscript seem to refer to his similar numbers written (with black ink) next to the music in the répétiteur's copy for *Die Hochzeit des Figaro* (now in DKKk, call no. MA ms 3042 (KTA 215)). This theory is supported by the fact that for neither of his two previous stagings of Mozart's opera did Bournonville give any indications in his diary about any notations made for this work.

4.6.1872
Waldemar and *Dawn, Prologue to the ballet Waldemar (Dæmring, Forspil til Balletten Waldemar).*

For this, Bournonville's fourth restaging of his four-act national romantic ballet *Waldemar* (*see* 28.10.1835), a new recited prologue with text by C. Andersen and music by E. Hartmann was performed by the singers, P. L. N. Schramm and A. D. Pfeil, accompanied by a chorus of mixed voices and surrounded by a corps de ballet of elf-maidens. The ballet was mounted this year as part of a special charity programme given for the Royal Danish Ballet's private pension fund, of which Bournonville was the founding member. The cast included three actors in the leading parts, namely B. Schnell (who had retired from the ballet to become an actress in 1870) in her old rôle as *Astrid* (now as a mimed part), P. W. Jerndorff playing *Knud Magnussøn*, and A. W. Wiehe performing *Axel Hvide*. In his diary Bournonville noted about the performance:

22.3.1872: 'Indstudering af Knuds Rolle i Waldemar til [P. W.] Jerndorff'
25.3.: 'Prøve og Indstudering for W. Wiehe som Axel Hvide'
26.3.: 'Indstudering paa Valdemar Wiehe og Jerndorff'
27.3.: 'lille Prøve paa Børnescenerne i Valdemar'
2.4. and 3.4.: 'Prøve paa Valdemar'
5.4.: 'Brev til Carl Andersen om et Forspil til d. 4 Juni'
8.4.: 'Talt med Emil Hartmann om Forspillet'
11.4. and 15.5.: 'Prøve paa Valdemar'
11.5.: 'Skrevet til […] E Hartmann'
13.5.: 'skrevet og choregrapheret. Brev fra <u>E Hartmann</u>'
14.5.: 'componeret'
16.5.: 'skrevet Annoncer til Balletforestillingen'
17.5.: 'Brev fra Carl Andersen, componeret Alfegrupper til "Dæmring" Forspil til Valdemar'
21.5. and 22.5.: 'choreographeret'
25.5.: 'Prøve paa Valdemar'
27.5: 'Indstudering af Alfegrupperne til 'Dæmring''
28.5.: 'choregrapheret'
31.5.: 'Prøve paa `Dæmring´'
1.6.: 'Prøve paa Dæmring og Valdemar'
3.6.: 'Generalprøve paa `Dæmring´ og Balletten Valdemar'
4.6.: 'Prøve paa <u>Dæmring</u> […] I Theatret Forestilling til Indtægt for Pensionskassen, fuldt Huus og levende Bifald. Det Hele gik udmærket. <u>Betty Schnell</u> som Astrid var Gjenstanden for en virkelig Ovation, ligesaavel W. Wiehe som Axel Hvide, der var sand Begeistring hos Publicum – Indtægten gik over <u>1300rd.</u>'.

The 1872 production of *Waldemar* received 13 performances, the last of which was given on 14.2.1874.

Autograph sources:

Production note. Ms. Autograph. Black ink. 1 p. (21,8 × 14 cm)
<u>Valdemar.</u>/Sædvanlig Besætning med Undtagelse af:
Unsigned and undated [1872?]
[DKKkt; F.M. (Ballet)

Musical sources:

The orchestral score, the répétiteur's copy and the set of parts employed this year were the same as those used for the previous 1867 staging of *Waldemar* (now in DKKk, call nos. C II, 107, MA ms 2993, MA ms 2994, and KTB 297).

Piano vocal score (the prologue *Dawn*). Ms. Copy. Brown ink. 28 pp. of which one is blank (26,1 × 34,7 cm)
779 a/'Danmark' [changed with blue crayon to] Dæmring/Lyrisk Forspil til Balletten/'Valdemar'/Texten af/Carl Andersen/Musiken af/Emil Hartmann.
Unsigned and undated [1872]
[DKKk; MA ms 2746 (1) (KTA 779 a)

Piano vocal score (the chorus of the prologue *Dawn*). Ms. Copy. Black ink. 16 pp. (26,1 × 34,7 cm)
779 a/Chorudtog/til/Dæmring
Unsigned and undated [1872]
[DKKk; MA ms 2746 (2) (KTA 779 a)

Parts (the prologue *Dawn*). Ms. Copy. 39 + 44 vol.
4 vl I, 3 vl II, 2 vla, 4 vlc e cb, fl picc, fl 1/2, ob 1/2, cl 1/2, fag 1/2, cor 1/2/3/4, tr 1/2, trb 1/2/3, tuba, timp, gr cassa, piatti, tri, arpa 1/2, org. 44 vocal parts.
Unsigned and undated [1872]
[DKKk; KTA 779 a

11.6.–20.8.1872
Forty-eight private dance lessons to **E. Schousgaard, A. Scholl, and M. Westberg.**
According to his diary Bournonville gave a series of 48 private dance lessons to three of his most talented pupils during the 1872 summer holiday. These lessons, which all took place at his private residence in Fredensborg, lasted for about two hours each.

13.7.1872
The Bacchantes, pas de deux (Bacchantinderne, pas de deux) **(uncredited) performed by F. and L. Carey (the Tivoli Gardens, Theatret).**
This (uncredited) dance is almost certainly identical with Bournonville's earlier dance of that name, choreographed for the English ballerinas, A. and C. Healey, and first performed by them in the Tivoli Gardens on 25.7.1870. The 1872 *Tivoli=Program* describes the dance as 'Bacchantinderne, pas de deux, Musiken af Georg Lumbye, dandses af Frkne. Carey', but does not credit to Bournonville for the choreography. The dance was performed 13 times by the Careys in 1872 (between 13.7. and 14.9.1872), and 7 times during the following Tivoli season (between 23.7. and 6.9. 1873). Bournonville did not attend any of these performances. The musical material employed in these seasons was most probably the same as that used for the 1870 Tivoli première of the *'The Bacchantes'* (*see* 25.7.1870).

11.9.1872
The Flower Festival in Genzano (Blomsterfesten i Genzano).
This performance represents the second time the complete version of Bournonville's one-act ballet *The Flower Festival in Genzano* (*see* 19.12.1858) was mounted by him in Copenhagen. According to his diary it was staged with partially revised choreography and was performed with the Swedish ballerina, M. Westberg as *Rosa*, and D. Krum as *Paolo*. In his diary Bournonville noted about the production:

2.5.1872: 'arbeidet paa Choregraphien til Blomsterfesten'
3.5.: 'Choregrapheret til Blomsterfesten'
6.5.: 'skrevet Choreographie'
7.5.: 'choregrapheret'
8.5.: 'componeret'
10.5.: 'skrevet Choregraphie'
13.5.: 'skrevet og choregrapheret'
14.5.: 'componeret'
21.5.: 'skrevet, choregrapheret'
22.5.: 'choregrapheret'
23.5.: 'skrevet og choregrapheret'
28.5.: 'choregrapheret'
26.7.: '<u>32'</u> Lection […] begyndt paa Blomsterfesten'
24.8.: 'studeret Dandsene til Blomsterfesten'
26.8.: 'Prøve paa Blomsterfesten […] Pantomimeprøve paa Blomsterfesten'
27.8.: 'Prøve paa Dandse til […] Blomstefesten'
28.8.: 'Indstudering paa Blomsterfesten'
30.8.: 'Prøve og Indstudering pa Blomsterfesten'
5.9.: 'Eftermiddagsprøve paa <u>Blomsterfesten</u>'
6.9. and 7.9.: 'Prøve paa Blomsterfesten'
9.9.: 'Partiel Prøve, Arrangement, Musikprøve og fuldstændig Prøve paa Blomsterfesten, der lover fortrinligt'
10.9.: 'Partiel Prøve […] og Generalprøve paa Blomsterfesten der gik udmærket […] prøvede Costumer for [M.] Westberg og [D.] Krum'

11.9.: 'I Theatret <u>Blomsterfesten i Genzano</u> (1.ste Gang nÿindstuderet) Balletten gik udmærket smukt og med livligt Bifald'.

The 1872 production of *The Flower Festival in Genzano* received 10 performances, the last of which was given on 10.2. 1874.

The musical material employed this year was most probably the same as that used since the 1858 première of this ballet (now in DKKk, call nos. C I, 114 k, and KTB 267).

10.10.1872
Pas de trois composed by Mr. Court Ballet Master Bournonville (Pas de trois componeret af Hr. Hofballetmester Bournonville) performed by E. Hansen, M. Westberg, and A. Scholl.
This *Pas de trois* was performed to a slightly revised version of H. S. Paulli's much earlier score for Bournonville's so-called *Changing Dance (Vexeldands)* in Act I, score no. 2 of his three-act ballet *Abdallah* (*see* 28.3.1855). It was choreographed for three of his most talented pupils, who had come to his private residence in Fredensborg to take dance lessons with him during the summer holiday of 1872. The male part of the 1872 *Pas de trois* was originally choreographed for D. Krum, but was actually premièred by E. Hansen, with Krum dancing only once, at its sixth and last performance on 26.11.1872. According to Bournonville's choreographic notes for it, the male solo variation and the Coda movement both contain close affinities with the original choreography to the same music as notated by Bournonville in the 1855 répétiteur's copy for *Abdallah* (now in DKKk, call no. MA ms 2967 (KTB 273)). In his diary he noted about the new *Pas de trois* and its première:

7.6.1872: '[H. S.] Paulli ankommen'
8.6.: 'begyndt at componere en pas de trois for [M.] Westberg, [D.] Krum og <u>Anna Scholl</u>'
10.6.: 'Skrevet og componeret en Pas de trois færdig til Westberg, Scholl og Krum'
15.7.: 'begyndt Indstuderingen af en Pas de trois for Krum, Westberg og Scholl'
16.7.: 'fortsættelse af Pas de trois'
18.7.: 'fuldendt Indstuderingen af Pas de trois'
4.10.: 'Eftermiddagsprøve paa Doublering af Krums Partie i den nÿ Pas de trois'
5.10: 'lille Prøve paa <u>Pas de trois</u>'
7.10.: 'Prøve paa pas de trois'
9.10.: 'Prøve med Orchester paa <u>Pas de trois</u> ([E.] Hansen, Westberg og Scholl)'
10.10.: 'I Theatret 1ste gang den nÿ <u>pas de trois</u> gik smukt, men for et lunkent Publicum. Huset var brilliant besat'.

The *Pas de trois* reached a total of 6 performances during Bournonville's lifetime, the last of which was given on 26.11. 1872.

Autograph sources:

Choreographic note. Ms. Autograph. Brown ink. 4 pp. (22,7 × 17,9 cm)
<u>Pas de trois.</u>/pour/M.lle Westberg – - Mr Krum & M.lle Scholl./Musique tirée du Ballet d'"Abdallah"/par/<u>H. Paulli.</u> -/(Notes chorégraphiques.)
Signed and dated: 'Fredensborg d. 10.de Juni 1872.'
[DKKk; Utilg. 828 (Harald Landers Arkiv, Supplement, Kapsel 189, 1994/78)

Next to the choreography in this manuscript are inserted Bournonville's autographed choreographic numbers. They refer to his similar numbers written underneath the music in the 1855 répétiteur's copy for *Abdallah* (pp. 6–20).

Musical sources:

No separate orchestral score for this dance has yet been traced. This seems to indicate that Paulli's original autographed score for *Abdallah* (now in DKKk, call no. C II, 119 (KTB 273)) also was used for the 1872 performances of this *Pas de trois*.

The original répétiteur's copy for *Abdallah* (now in DKKk, call no. MA ms 2967 (KTB 273)) was also used for rehearsing this *Pas de trois*. This is clear from Bournonville's autographed choreographic numbers and choreographic notes written underneath the music (on pp. 6–20). They refer to his similar numbers included in the separate choreographic notation of his 1872 *Pas de trois* that he wrote on 10.6.1872.

Parts. Ms. Copy. 31 vol.
3 vl I, 3 vl II, 2 vla, 3 vlc e cb, fl picc e II, fl I, ob 1/2, cl 1/2, fag 1/2, cor 1/2/3/4, tr 1/2, trb 1/2/3, timp, gr cassa, piatti e tri.
Unsigned and undated [1872]
[DKKk; KTB 273 a

16.10.1872–26.4.1873
Fifty dance lessons in social dance.
According to a series of notes in his diary Bournonville gave 50 private dance lessons in social dance during the winter of 1873–74. They were taught at the residence of L. Castenskjold (the Lord-in-Waiting of Denmark's Queen Louise), at Copenhagen's Christiansborg Palace. These lessons, which took place mainly on Wednesday and Saturday afternoons, lasted for about two hours each and were concluded with a presentation of Bournonville's pupils on 30.4.1873. It is described in his diary as follows:

'Præsentation af Eleverne hos [L.] Castenskjolds overværet af H. M. Dronningen [i.e. Queen Louise Wilhelmine Friederike Caroline Auguste Julie], Kronprindsessen [i.e. Louise Josephine Eugenie] og Prindsesse Thyra [Amelie Caroline Charlotte Anne]'.

22.11.1872
L'Elisire d'Amore (Elskovsdrikken).
The 1872 Copenhagen restaging of G. Donizetti's two-act comic opera from 1832 (*see* 28.11.1859) represents the second and last time this work was mounted under Bournonville's general direction. In his diary he noted about the staging, which seems to have been mounted with only minor if any changes from his previous production:

15.11.1872: 'Instructionsprøve paa Elskovsdrikken'
17.11. and 19.11.: 'Theaterprøve paa Elskovsdrikken'
21.11.: 'Generalprøve paa Elskovsdrikken'
22.11.: 'I Theatret Elskovsdrikken [...] Alt gik meget smukt'.

The 1872 production received 11 performances during Bournonville's lifetime, the last of which was given on 30.10. 1877.

The musical material employed this year was the same as that used for the 1859 staging (now in DKKk, call nos. C I, 256 n, and KTA 464).

4.12.1872

Pas de deux (uncredited) performed by D. Krum and
A. Scholl.

According to a note in Bournonville's diary on this day
(reading: 'seet [...] Pas de deux af den Stumme') this (uncredited) dance is identical with his and M. E. Caraffa's
much earlier *Pas de deux*, first incorporated for F. Hoppe and
L. Grahn in Act I of D.-F.-E. Auber's five-act opera *La Muette
de Portici* (*see* 23.9.1834). The 1872 performances represent
the last time that the 1834 version of this dance was given at
the Royal Theatre. According to his diary, Bournonville directed all three rehearsals held of this dance on 25.11.,
26.11., and 2.12.1872. The *Pas de deux* received 3 performances by Krum and Scholl in 1872, the last of which was
given on 18.12.1872.

Musical sources:

The orchestral score employed for this *Pas de deux* in 1872 was most
probably the same as that used since the 1834 première of it in Act I
of *La Muette de Portici* (now in DKKk, call no. MA ms 2603 (KTB
209)).

Répétiteur's copy. Ms. Copy. Brown ink. 4 pp. (34,8 × 26,1 cm)
[...]/Pas de deux af 'Den Stumme.' ect. [*sic*]
Unsigned and undated [c.1872]
[DKKk; MA ms 2699 (KTB 1030, originally KTB 209)
This répétiteur's copy represents the earliest preserved, separate
répétiteur's copy of Caraffa's music for the *Pas de deux* that was originally performed in Act I of *La Muette de Portici* on 23.9.1834. It almost
certainly dates from Bournonville's final 1872 restaging of it. The
volume also contains several pencilled notes (written by an unknown
hand) that indicate who performed which sections throughout the
dance. Moreover, the manuscript includes a fragment (p. 1) containing the music of the final 23 bars from another (not yet identified)
dance.

Parts (incomplete). Ms. Copy. 20 vol.
vl I, vl II, vla, vlc e cb, fl 1/2, ob 1/2, cl 1/2, fag 1/2, cor 1/2/3/4, tr
1/2, Atrb, Ttrb.
Unsigned and undated [c.1872]
[DKKk; KTB 1030 (originally KTB 209)
This set of parts is bound together with the music for seven other
dances (most of which were choreographed by Bournonville). It
represents the earliest preserved set of parts for Bournonville's and
Caraffa's 1834 *Pas de deux* in Act II of *La Muette de Portici*, and was most
probably prepared for Bournonville's last restaging of this dance in
1872.

4.12.1872

Las Hermanas de Sevilla (uncredited) performed by
M. Westberg, J. Petersen, and M. Price.

This performance represents Bournonville's second and last
restaging at Copenhagen's Royal Theatre of his and C. C.
Møller's Spanish dance *Las Hermanas de Sevilla, Spanish
Dance* (*see* 4.6.1851). According to his diary, Bournonville directed all three rehearsals held of it on 25.11., 30.11., and
2.12.1872, and noted about its first performance:

'Las Hermanas, der gik meget godt'.

The 1872 restaging received 3 performances (the last of
which was given on 18.12.1872) after which *Las Hermanas de
Sevilla* went out of the repertory.

Musical sources:

The orchestral score and the set of parts employed this year were
most probably the same as those used since the 1851 première of this
divertissement (now in DKKk, call nos. C II, 118, and KTB 239).

Répétiteur's copy. Ms. Copy. Brown ink. 4 pp. of which one is blank
(34,7 × 26 cm)
Las Hermanas
Unsigned and undated [c.1872]
[DKKk; MA ms 2629 (KTB 239)
This répétiteur's copy represents the earliest still preserved copy of
C. C. Møller's 1851 music for *Las Hermanas de Sevilla*. It almost cer-
tainly dates from Bournonville's 1872 restaging of this dance.

8.12.1872

*The Kermesse in Brüges, or The Three Gifts (Kermessen i Brügge
eller: De tre Gaver).*

This performance, which represents Bournonville's second
and last restaging in Copenhagen of his three-act romantic
ballet *The Kermesse in Brüges, or The Three Gifts* (*see* 4.4.1851
and 19.11.1865), had first been proposed by him to the theatre management on 31.8.1870. According to the ballet's orchestral score and Bournonville's autographed notes in the
1865 répétiteur's copy (which was reused this year), the 1872
production included a new, thoroughly revised version of
the Act I *Pas de deux* (score no. 2). It was performed by D.
Krum (playing *Carelis*) and A. Scholl (as *Eleonora*).

Moreover, a choreographically new version of the *Pas de
deux* in Act II that had been incorporated since 1865 (score
no. 11, also named 'Jægerdands') was this year revised by
Bournonville for E. Hansen and M. Westberg. This new version was listed as score no. '11½' and is musically nearly
identical with the 1865 'Jægerdands', the score of which had
originally been borrowed from Act III (score no. 29) of
Paulli's and Bournonville's short-lived Hungarian ballet *In
the Carpathians* (*see* 4.3.1857). These new versions of the *Pas
de deux* in Acts I and II seem to represent the only significant
changes made by Bournonville in the 1872 restaging of *The
Kermesse in Brüges, or The Three Gifts*.

In his diary he noted about this production:

19.1.1872: 'componeret en ny pas de deux'
20.1.: 'indstuderet en pas de deux af Kermessen til [D.] Krum og [A.]
Scholl'
24.1.: 'componeret til Kermessen'
25.1.: 'Indstudering paa Kermessen'
26.1.: 'Prøve paa Kermessen'
6.2.: 'lille Prøve pa Dandsen til Kermessen'
16.11.: 'arbeidet paa Choreographeringen af Kermessen'
17.11.: 'skrevet paa Kermessen'
18.11.: 'skrevet [...] 1.ste Indstudering paa Kermessen. – Eftermiddagsprøve paa den Samme'
19.11.: 'Prøve paa Kermessen' [...] Eftermiddagsprøve paa Kermessen'
20.11.: 'Prøve paa Kermessen'
21.11.: 'Prøve paa pas de deux af Kermessen [...] skrevet og componeret'
22.11.: 'Tidlig op og arbeidet paa Kermessen [...] Indstudering paa
2.den Akt'
23.11.: 'componeret [...] Prøve paa Kermessen'
25.11.: 'indstuderet pas de deux til E Hansen og [M.] Westberg,
medens [L.] Gade lod repetere det øvrige af Kermessen'
26.11.: 'Prøve [...] paa sidste Scene af Kermessen'

28.11.: 'Prøve paa Dandsene og Finalen af Kermessen, der lover godt […] leveret Annoncer og Personlister til fire Dagblade'
29.11.: 'tidlig Prøve paa Kermessen'
30.11.: 'Presentation af Prøven paa Kermessen'
2.12.: 'Decorationsprøve paa Kermessen'
5.12.: 'stor Arrangementsprøve paa Kermessen'
6.12.: 'fuldstændig Prøve paa Kermessen, skrevet, Costumeprøve'
7.12.: 'Generalprøve paa Kermessen'
8.12.: 'I Theatret <u>Kermessen</u> der gik udmærket, for brilliant Huus og gjorde megen Lÿkke'.

The 1872 staging received 25 performances during Bournonville's lifetime, the last of which was given on 22.10.1879.

The musical material employed this year was the same as that employed for the previous 1865 production (now in DKKk, call nos. MA ms 1551, MA ms 2762 (5), MA ms 2966 b, and KTB 271).

Autograph sources:

Production note. Ms. Autograph (partially in another's hand). Brown ink. 3 pp. (35,9 × 22,6 cm)
<u>Kermessen i Brügge</u>/<u>1.ste Akt</u>/<u>Almue.</u>
Signed and dated: 'Kbhvn d. 18' Novbr 1872.'
[DKKkt; F.M. (Ballet)

Production note. Ms. Autograph. Black ink. 1 p. (27,7 × 21,7 cm)
<u>Bryggernes Optog -</u>
Unsigned and undated [c. November 1872]
[DKKkt; F.M. (Ballet)

1873

19.1.1873

Robert le Diable (Robert af Normandiet).

The 1873 Copenhagen restaging of G. Meyerbeer's five-act grand opera from 1831 was originally projected by Bournonville on 30.10.1857 (*see also* 15.12.1841 and 18.1.1848). It represents the first and only time this work was mounted in Copenhagen with his complete mise-en-scène and choreography. The so-called 'Ballet of the Nuns' in Act III (score no. 16) was for this occasion notated anew by Bournonville, who this year also seems to have made a number of minor choreographic changes in the choreography of his previous 1848 staging. In his diary he noted about the new production and its first two performances:

2.10.1872: 'skrevet og studeret paa Dandsen til Robert'
3.10.: 'Componeret Dandsen til Robert'
7.10.: 'Prøve paa […] Robert'
10.10.: 'Indstudering paa Dandsen til Robert'
1.11.: 'Costumemøde paa Robert'
10.12.: Prøve paa Robert'
13.12.: 'Eftermiddagsprøve paa 1.e og 3.e Akt af Robert'
14.12.: 'Prøve paa Dandsen til […] Robert'
15.12. and 16.12.: 'Instructionsprøve paa Robert'
17.12.: 'Prøve paa 3.e Akt af Robert […] skrevet, læst og componeret'
18.12.: 'Regieforretninger […] Instructionsprøve paa Robert 4' og 5' Akt'
19.12.: 'Arrangement paa 1. ste og 2.' Akt af Robert'
20.12.: 'Arrangementsprøve paa Robert <u>3.e</u> og <u>4.e</u> Akt (min Gravscene gik udmærket smukt)'
30.12.: 'Prøve paa Gravscenen i Robert'

2.1.1873: 'Prøve paa de to første Akter af Robert […] skrevet og componeret'
3.1.: 'Prøve paa Robert 3.e og 4.e Akt med Orchester […] componeret'
4.1.: 'componeret og holdt Aftenprøve paa Robert'
5.1.: 'skrevet og componeret'
8.1.: 'lille Prøve med [M.] Westberg'
9.1.: 'Prøve paa Robert 1.e – 2.' og 4.e Akt'
10.1.: 'Prøve pa 3.de og 5.te Akt af Robert'
13.1.: 'Prøve paa hele Robert (Westberg dandsede overordentlig)'
15.1.: 'Prøve paa hele Robert'
17.1.' Generalprøve pa Robert, der gik særdeles smukt'
19.1.: 'I Theatret Robert af Normandiet, der gik udmærket godt, og for brilliant Huus (Westberg udførte sit Partie fortræffeligt)'
21.1.: 'overværet 2' Forestilling af Robert der gik meget smukt, for brilliant Huus men et dvask Publicum'.

The 1873 production of *Robert le Diable* received 5 performances during Bournonville's lifetime, the last of which was given on 6.3.1873.

Autograph sources:

Manuscript mise-en-scène. Ms. Autograph. Brown ink. 4 pp. (22,5 × 18 cm)
<u>Scene = Arrangement.</u>/<u>til</u>/<u>Robert af Normandiet.</u>
Unsigned and undated [Written according to Bournonville's diary most probably between December 1872 and January 1873]
[SSm; Daniel Fryklunds samling no. 145

Production note. Ms. Autograph (partially in another's hand). Black ink. 2 pp. (35,5 × 21,8 cm)
<u>Robert af Normandiet.</u>/<u>Bipersonerne</u>/(1ste Akt.)
Unsigned and undated [c. December 1872]
[DKKkt; F.M. (Ballet)

Musical sources:

The orchestral score and the set of parts employed in 1873 were the same as those used for Bournonville's previous 1848 staging of Meyerbeer's opera (now in DKKk, call nos. U 6 and KTA 303).

Répétiteur's copy. Ms. Copy by an unknown hand. Brown ink. 1 vol. 20 pp. of which one is blank (33,6 × 24,9 cm with minor variants)
168/Repetiteurpartier/til/1. Robert af Normandiet/ […] /89/[…]/Repetiteurparti/til/ Robert af Normandiet
Unsigned and undated [1863]
[DKKk; MA ms 2920 (1) (KTA 303 (2))
This répétiteur's copy dates from the previous restaging in Copenhagen of Meyerbeer's opera on 8.11.1863 (then mounted by the French dancer and choreographer, G. Carey). This date can be deduced from the fact that the music is included in a volume which also contains the répétiteur's copies for two other works, entitled *A Night in the Mountains (En Nat mellem Fjeldene)* and 'Divertissement Dansant' (by G. Carey). They were premièred at Copenhagen's Royal Theatre on 11.4.1863, and 7.11.1862 respectively. The répétiteur's copy was clearly reused by Bournonville for his 1873 restaging of *Robert af Normandiet* since it contains his autographed choreographic numbers and notes (written with brown ink) which describe nearly all of the choreography for the Act III divertissement. According to his diary these notes were written between 2.10.1872 and 5.1.1873 and include the name of the ballerina who performed the part of the abbess *Hélène* in 1873, the Swedish ballerina M. Westberg.

Another, later répétiteur's copy for Meyerbeer's opera, which clearly dates from the last restaging of it in Copenhagen on 28.2.1893, is now in DKKk (call no. MA ms 3066 (KTA 303 (3)). That production was mounted by Bournonville's successor, E. Hansen, whose autographed pencilled signature is written on the title-page. It also contains Hansen's complete 1893 transcription of Bournonville's choreographic notes for the 1873 production of *Robert af Nor-*

mandiet. Moreover, Hansen also inserted several pencilled notes which explain in further detail Bournonville's technical terms. These notes prove beyond doubt that Bournonville's 1873 choreography was restaged with only minor if any changes by Hansen in 1893.

Printed piano vocal score. 1 vol. 370 pp. (27 × 19 cm)
ROBERT LE DIABLE/Opéra en 5 actes par G Meyerbeer./Robert der Teufel/OPER IN 5 ACTEN VON SCRIBE/Deutsch von Th. Hell/Music von G. MEYERBEER./Volständiger Clavierauszug/mit deutschem und französischem Text/VON G. PIXIS.
Berlin, Schlesinger (Rob. Lienau), pl. no. S. 6656 [c.1873]
[DKKk; KTA 303 (Instruktørpartier)]
This German printed piano vocal score was used by Bournonville when he mounted Meyerbeer's opera for the last time in Copenhagen in 1873. It contains several pencilled notes indicating the musical cuts and omissions made that year throughout the entire opera.

29.1.1873
The Valkyrie (Valkyrien).
This performance represents the second and last restaging of Bournonville's four-act Nordic mythological ballet *The Valkyrie* (*see* 13.9.1861) and was mounted under his personal direction. It was staged this year for the Swedish ballerina, M. Westberg, who played the rôle of *Svava* for the first time (partnered by D. Krum as *Helge*). In his diary Bournonville noted about the performance, which otherwise seems to have been staged with only minor if any changes from his previous 1869 production:

21.10.1872: 'studeret Valkyriens Noter'
22.10.: 'nÿ Indstudering paa Valkyrien'
23.10.: 'Prøve paa Valkyrien'
25.10.: 'Indstudering paa Valkyrien'
26.10.: 'Prøve paa Valkyrien'
29.10.: 'Prøve paa Valkyrien med [D.] Krum'
30.10. and 31.10.: 'Prøve paa Valkyrien'
1.11.: 'Prøve paa Valkyrien med Bistand af Juliette Price'
2.11., 5.11., 12.11. and 14.11.: 'Prøve paa Valkyrien'
21.12.: 'Prøve paa Valkyrien'
23.12.: 'Prøve Kl 10 paa […] Scener af Valkyrien'
28.12.: 'Prøve med [M.] Westberg paa Valkyrien'
11.1.1873: 'Prøve paa […] flere Sager af Valkyrien'
16.1., 20.1. and 21.1.: 'Prøve paa Valkyrien'
23.1.: 'Arrangement paa Valkyrien'
24.1.: 'Sceneprøve paa Valkyrien. Musikprøve paa Samme'
25.1.: 'Theaterprøve med Repetiteur paa Valkyrien'
26.1.: 'Decorationsprøve paa Valkyrien'
27.1.: 'fuldstændig Prøve paa Valkyrien'
28.1.: 'Generalprøve paa Valkyrien ([A.] Scholl atter sygemeldt)'
29.1.: 'lille Prøve paa Dandsene til iaften […] I Theatret Valkyrien. 1.ste Gang i sin nye Indstudering, gik i det Hele udmærket godt, Westberg gjorde fuldkommen fyldest og Krum var meget brav. Huset var med Hensyn til […] Uden Abbonnement godt besat (800r.) og Bifaldet paa flere Steder meget varmt'.

The 1873 restaging received 7 performances, the last of which was given on 15.4.1873. The musical material employed this year was the same as that used since the 1861 première (now in DKKk, call nos. C II, 114, MA ms 2995, and KTB 298).

8.2.1873
Le Petit Chaperon rouge (Den lille Rødhætte).
In his diary Bournonville stated about this, his second and last complete staging of F.-A. Boyeldieu's three-act fairy opera in Copenhagen (*see also* the three previous productions on 1.12.1852, 25.1.1855, and 20.12.1860):

7.1.1873: 'Oplæsning paa Rødhætten'
18.1.: 'skrevet'
20.1., 21.1., and 29.1.: 'Instruction paa Rødhætten'
30.1.: 'Theaterprøve paa 2.' og 3.e Akt af Rødhætten'
31.1.: 'Instruction paa Rødhætten'
1.2.: 'Theaterprøve paa Rødhætten […] Aftenen hjemme, componeret'
2.2.: 'Instuderingsprøve paa Dandsene til Rødhætten'
4.2. and 5.2.: 'Theaterprøve paa Rødhætten'
7.2.: 'Generalprøve paa Rødhætten'
8.2.: 'I Theatret Den lille Rødhætte der gik særdeles smukt og for brilliant Huus'.

According to Bournonville's two autographed manuscript mises-en-scène, written for the 1873 production, the opera was mounted with a completely new mise-en-scène, while the dances in Act I (score no. 7) and Act II (score no. 12) seem to have been restaged with only minor if any changes from the previous 1860 production.

The 1873 staging received 13 performances during Bournonville's lifetime (the last given on 18.3.1874) after which the opera went out of the Copenhagen repertory.

The musical material employed this year was the same as that used since the 1852 production (now in DKKk, call nos. U 6, MA ms 2902 (17), and KTA 198).

Autograph sources:

Manuscript mise-en-scène. Ms. Autograph. Black ink. 1 vol. 10 pp. (20,3 × 16,4 cm)
Den lille Rödhætte/ […] /(Scene = Arrangement)/1.ste Akt (1.e Scene)
Signed and dated: 'Kbhvn d. 18.e Januar 1873'
[SSm; Daniel Fryklunds samling no. 140 c

Manuscript mise-en-scène. Ms. Autograph. Black ink. 5 pp. (21,8 × 13,2 cm)
Den lille Rödhætte/1.ste Akt 1.ste Scene.
Unsigned and undated [c. January 1873]
[SSm; Daniel Fryklunds samling no. 122

Manuscript mise-en-scène. Ms. Autograph. Black ink. 1 p. (21,8 × 17,8 cm)
Den lille Rødhætte/(Chor Arrangement)/1.ste Akt (1.e Scene)
Unsigned and undated [c. January 1873]
[SSm; Daniel Fryklunds samling no. 122

15.3.1873
Napoli or The Fisherman and His Bride (Napoli eller Fiskeren og hans Brud).
This performance represents Bournonville's fourth complete restaging in Copenhagen of his three-act romantic ballet *Napoli or The Fisherman and His Bride* (*see* 29.3.1842). The leading rôles of *Gennaro* and *Teresina* were this year played by W. Price and M. Westberg for the first time. In his diary Bournonville noted about the staging, which otherwise seems to have been mounted with only minor if any changes from his previous production from 2.6.1870:

21.2.1873: 'Indstudering paa Napoli til [M.] Westberg'
24.2. and 25.2.: 'Indstudering paa Napoli'
26.2.: 'Indstudering paa Napoli og Prøve paa 2.den Akt af samme'

27.2.: 'Prøve paa Napoli'
1.3.: 'Prøve paa […] 1.ste Akt af Napoli'
3.3.: 'Prøve paa Scener af Napoli'
4.3.: 'Prøve paa Dandsene til Napoli'
5.3. and 6.3.: 'Prøve paa Napoli'
7.3.: 'Arrangementsprøve paa Napoli'
8.3.: 'Prøve paa de vigtigste Punkter af Napoli og 2.' Akt nede paa Scenen med Repetiteur'
9.3.: 'Repetition paa de to nye Hovedroller i Napoli'
10.3.: 'Theaterprøve paa Napoli hvis Opførelse er udsat til Lørdag'
12.3.: 'Sceneprøve paa Napoli'
13.3.: 'Generalprøve paa Napoli, gik udmærket baade for Westberg og W. Price'
15.3.: 'I Theatret Napoli for fuldt Huus og begeistret Bifald. W. Price og Marie Westberg udførte Hovedrollerne med stor Bravour og fik hver en Gratification paa 50r. tilsagt af Intendanten Justitsraad [F. J. G.] Berner'.

Moreover, on 20.4.1873 Bournonville wrote a (not yet traced) scenario in French of this ballet for a special gala performance given on that day in honour of the visiting Japanese Prince Ivakura. About that performance Bournonville noted in his diary:

'skrevet en fransk Analyse af Napoli til Veiledning for det Japanesiske Gesandtskab og sendt den til Kmhr Sick […] i Theatret, hvor Napoli gik for fuldt Huus og den Japanesiske Ambassade, anført af Prinds Ivakura'.

The 1873 restaging of *Napoli or The Fisherman and His Bride* received 15 performances, the last of which was given on 7.3. 1874.

The musical material employed this year was the same as that used since the ballet's 1842 première (now in DKKk, call nos. C II, 114 k, and KTB 292).

Autograph sources:

Production note. Ms. Autograph. Brown ink. 2 pp. (22,7 × 17,9 cm)
Napoli./Personliste. (1.e Akt)
Unsigned and undated [c. February-March 1873]
[DKKkt; F.M. (Ballet)]

16.3.1873
Faust.
The original 1859 version of C. Gounod's five-act opera was first performed in Denmark on 21.12.1864 with choreography by L. Gade. However, Bournonville had already mounted this opera two years earlier when it was given its Swedish première at Stockholm's Royal Theatre (Operahuset) on 5.6.1862. For the 1873 Copenhagen restaging he gave personal stage instructions to the singer, A. D. Erhard-Hansen, who this year played *Margarethe* for the first time. Apart from these instructions he seems only to have supervised the staging of the opera's dances, which this year were most probably mounted by Gade with minor if any changes from his previous 1864 production. This is clear from Bournonville's diary in which he noted about his involvement in the staging:

26.2.1873: 'Instructionsprøve med Fru Erhardt-Hansen [i.e. A. D. Erhard-Hansen] til Faust'
28.2.: 'Prøve paa 1.ste Akt af Faust'
11.3.: 'Sceneprøve paa Faust'
12.3.: 'Prøve paa Faust'
14.3. 'Generalprøve paa Faust'

16.3.: 'I Theatret Faust der gik særdeles smukt og for fuldt Huus. Fru Erhard-Hansen var meget god som Margarethe og gjorde fortjent Lykke'.

The 1873 production of *Faust* received 32 performances during Bournonville's lifetime, the last of which was given on 17.11.1879.

Musical sources:

Printed orchestral score with later manucript insertions. 2 vol. Act I–III 308 pp. of which one is blank, Act IV–V 246 pp. of which three are blank (27 × 18,1 cm)
Faust/Opéra en cinq actes/[…]/Musique de/CH. GOUNOD
Paris, Choudens, Exemplaire N. 81 [1859–1863 and later]
[DKKkt, KTA 479]
This printed French orchestral score was used for all performances of Gounod's *Faust* in Copenhagen during Bournonville's lifetime. The authorisation for performing the opera is given with an inscription by Choudens on p. 2 and is dated '1863'. A pencilled autographed note by H. S. Paulli (written in the second vol. on p. '501') reads: 'Her kommer Indlægget'. It refers to his addition of an orchestral section in the so-called 'Scène de la Prison' of Act V, score no. 30 (*see* the following entry).

Orchestral score (Act V, fragment). Ms. Copy (by H. S. Paulli). Brown ink. 4 pp. (34,5 × 25,9 with minor variants)
Faust. 479/[…]/Partitur til Faust. 5.te Akt.
Unsigned and undated [c.1864 or later?]
[DKKk; MA ms 2648 (KTA 479)]
This orchestral score fragment is H. S. Paulli's autograph, and contains his addition in Gounod's *Faust* of an orchestral section before the *Mouvement de la valse* in the so-called 'Scène de la Prison' of Act V (score no. 30). Thus, a pencilled autographed note by Paulli (on p. 1) reads as follows: 'Slutnings Takter/i Partituret Pag. 501/her begynder det nye Indlæg som følger efter Slutningstakterne Pag. 501 i Partituret'.

Répétiteur's copy. Ms. Copy. Brown ink. 1 vol. 14 pp. of which one is blank (33,6 × 25,7 cm)
1. Faust./[…]/96/[…]/Repetiteurparti/til Faust/L. Gade./[…]/Faust/2/Repetiteurpartie
Unsigned and undated [1864]
[DKKk; MA ms 2919 (1) (KTA 479)]
This répétiteur's copy contains the complete music for the dance scenes in Act I, score no. 9 (entitled 'Valse et Chœur', «Ainsi que la brise légère»), and in Act V, score nos. 28 and 29 (entitled 'Scène et Chœur' and 'Chant bachique' respectively). The répétiteur's copy clearly dates from the 1864 Copenhagen première of *Faust*, for which all dances were choreographed and mounted by L. Gade, whose autographed signature is added on the title-page (written with black ink).
The répétiteur's copy is included (on pp. 1–14) in a volume that also contains the répétiteur's copies for five other operas and plays, mounted at Copenhagen's Royal Theatre between 1866 and 1868.

Parts. Ms. Copy. 49 vol.
8 vl I, 7 vl II, 4 vla, 4 vlc, 3 cb, fl 1/2, ob 1/2, cor ingl, cl 1/2, fag 1/2, cor 1/2/3/4, tr 1/2, trb 1/2/3, timp e tri, gr cassa, tamb rul, piatti, org. 81 vocal parts.
Unsigned and undated [1864]
[DKKk; KTA 479]
This set of parts dates from the 1864 Copenhagen première of Gounod's *Faust* and was used for all performances of it there during Bournonville's lifetime.

19.3.1873
Ballet Divertissement of 'A Fairy Tale in Pictures' (Act I)
(Balletdivertissement af 'Et Eventyr i Billeder' (1.ste Act)).
This work is a divertissement version of the dances from Act

I of Bournonville's three-act ballet *A Fairy Tale in Pictures* (*see* 26.12.1871). In his diary Bournonville noted about its first and only performance:

19.3.1873: 'Prøve Kl 10 paa Et Eventȳr i Billeder (1.ste Akt) […] i det kgl. Theater hvor Eventyrets 1.ste Akt gik som Balletdivertissement, meget smukt'.

The musical material employed this year was the same as that used for the first act in *A Fairy Tale in Pictures* (now in DKKk, call nos. C II, 114 m, MA ms 2998, and KTB 1036 (originally KTB 303)).

7.4.1873
The Corsican (Korsikaneren).
In his diary Bournonville noted about the mise-en-scène that he created for the première of E. Hartmann's two-act singspiel with a text based on V. de Saint-Georges' 1833 opera libretto *Ludovic* and translated into Danish by A. Hertz:

22.2.1873: 'Oplæsning paa Corsikaneren'
10.3.: 'skrevet og componeret'
11.3.: 'Skrevet Scene-Arrangement til Korsikaneren'
12.3.: 'skrevet og fuldendt Scene-Arrangem: til Korsikaneren'
18.3.: 'Scene-Arrangement Korsikaneren'
19.3.: 'Arrangementprøve ved Claveer paa Korsikaneren'
20.3.: 'Instructionsprøve paa Korsikaneren'
21.3.: 'Theaterprøve paa Korsikaneren'
24.3.: 'Prøve paa […] Korsikaneren'
27.3. and 29.3.: 'Theaterprøve paa Korsikaneren'
31.3.: 'Textprøve paa Korsikaneren'
3.4.: 'Prøve paa Corsikaneren'
6.4.: 'Generalprøve paa Corsikaneren'
7.4.: 'I Theatret […] 1.ste Forestilling af <u>Corsicaneren</u> (Ludovic) til Musik af Emil Hartmann (fuldt Huus og iiskold Modtagelse!)'.

The Corsican reached a total of 4 performances, the last of which took place on 19.4.1873.

Autograph sources:

Manuscript mise-en-scène. Ms. Autograph. Brown ink. 1 vol. 10 pp. (22,5 × 14,1 cm)
Korsikaneren./Scene = Arrangement
Signed and dated: 'Kbhvn d. 12' Martz 1873' [Written according to the diary between 10.3. and 12.3.1873]
[SSm; Daniel Fryklunds samling no. 131

Production note. Ms. Autograph. Brown ink. 2 pp. (22,5 × 14,1 cm)
<u>Dame – Costumet</u>/<u>til</u>/<u>Korsikaneren.</u>/<u>Francesca</u> (en ung Enke)/ […]/<u>Bianca</u>/[…]/<u>Choret</u>
Signed and dated: 'd. 25.e Martz 1873'
[SSm; Daniel Fryklunds samling no. 131

Musical sources:

Orchestral score. Ms. Autograph (by E. Hartmann). Black ink. 2 vol. Act I 264 pp. of which one is blank, Act II 136 pp. (34,1 × 25,7 cm)
<u>Korsikaneren</u>/Partitur./1.ste Act/[…]/Korsikaneren./[…]/2.den Act
Signed and dated (in vol I, p. 1): 'Emil Hartmann', (p. 263) 'Ende/ paa 1.ste Act/Februar 1872'
[DKKk; C II, 112 d (KTA 782)

Orchestral score. Ms. Copy. Brown ink. 1 vol. 412 pp. (33,7 × 25,5 cm)
<u>Korsikaneren</u>/Opera/[…]/No. 1./Allegretto
Unsigned and undated [c.1873 or later]

[DKKk; Emil Hartmanns Samling, no. 23 (1929-30.1006)
This orchestral manuscript copy was originally E. Hartmann's private copy, but was donated to DKKk by his heirs on 13.11.1929. The original title page and the whole of the overture (pp. '1–44') are missing.

No répétiteur's copy for *The Corsican* has yet been traced.

Parts. Ms. Copy. 38 vol.
4 vl I, 3 vl II, 2 vla, 4 vlc e cb, fl picc, fl 1/2, ob 1/2, cl 1/2/3, fag 1/ 2, cor 1/2/3/4, tr 1/2, trb 1/2/3, tuba, timp, gr cassa, piatti, tri e gong, arpa. 50 vocal parts.
Unsigned and undated [1873]
[DKKk; KTA 782]

23.4.1873
The Mandarin's Daughters (Mandarinens Døttre).
According to a letter written to Bournonville on 16.9.1872 by the chief librarian of Copenhagen's Royal Library, C. Brosbøll (now in DKKk, call no. NKS 3258 A 4°, II, 12, no. 558), Bournonville seems to have borrowed nine major literary works about Chinese history and culture (published between 1766 and 1860) as part of his preparations for this one-act ballet divertissement, which is set in the exotic sphere of 16th-century China.

The music was composed and arranged by V. C. Holm, who divided the score into six action-packed numbers, followed by a large dance divertissement (the so-called *Ballet of the Chessmen*), and a *Finale*. Moreover, Holm incorporated several musical borrowings to add a more distinctive 'far-eastern' flavour to the ballet's exotic setting. These musical borrowings are identified as follows:

(1) Score no. 1: Holm here incorporated several musical excerpts borrowed from the opening chorus «Clochets de la Pagode» from Act I (score no. 1) of D.-F.-E. Auber's three-act fairy opera *Le Cheval de bronze* (premièred in Paris at l'Opéra Comique on 23.3.1835, and first performed in Copenhagen on 29.1.1836).
(2) Score no. 3: In this scene (which depicts the arrival of the prince, *Yang-Tchoong*, and his imperial suite) Holm interpolated five excerpts that were borrowed from Act I (score no. 3) of H. S. Paulli's 1852 music arrangement for Bournonville's three-act ballet *Zulma, or The Crystal Palace* (*see* 14.4.1852). In that ballet the same music accompanied the scene during which a series of sacred temple dances are performed. One of these five excerpts (an *Allegro* movement in 6/8 time) was, in turn, borrowed by Paulli from an even earlier score by I. P. E. Hartmann, namely his three-act opera *The Raven* (*see* 29.10.1832). In this opera it originally accompanied a *Pas de cinq* (also choreographed by Bournonville) that was performed during the final chorus in Act II, entitled «Under Sang og glade Dandse for Kong Millo og hans Brud». The fact that Holm made such extensive use of Paulli's music from *Zulma, or The Crystal Palace* seems to indicate that Bournonville's 1873 choreography for this scene was perhaps very close to that in his earlier ballet.
(3) Score no. 4: For this scene (during which the Mandarin's three daughters and *Ping-Sin* are being presented for the prince, *Yang-Tchoong*) Holm incorporated three large musical excerpts (an *Allegro* in 2/4 time, a *Tempo di marcia* in 4/4, and an *Adagio cantabile* in 4/4). They were all borrowed from Paulli's earlier score for Bournonville's three-act Persian ballet *Abdallah* (*see* 28.3.1855). In that ballet the music accompanied the scene in Act II (score no. 9) in which *Abdallah* lights his magic lamp and suddenly sees himself surrounded by a group of odalisques and harem women, from among whom he can choose his bride. Holm's extensive reuse of Paulli's music from this ballet seems to indicate that Bournonville's 1873 choreography for this scene might, at least in parts, have been based on the earlier choreography in *Abdallah* to the exact same music.

(4) For the ballet's *Finale* Holm incorporated the complete music of the overture in Auber's 1835 fairy opera *Le Cheval de bronze*.

The choreographic highlight in the *The Mandarin's Daughters* was the dance scene, entitled *The Ballet of the Chessmen (Schackbrikkernes Dands)*. The idea for this scene seems to have been based, at least in part, on a similar divertissement named *Les Échecs*, originally created by the French choreographer, J. Mazilier, for Act III of F. Hérold's five-act opera *La Magicienne* (premièred at the Paris Opéra 17.3.1858).

In his diary Bournonville noted about the creation and the première of *The Mandarin's Daughters*:

28.10.1872: 'conciperet og reenskrevet Programmet til et chinesisk Ballet-divertissement kaldet Frieri og Schakspil'
29.10.: 'sendt mit Program til [F. J. G.] Berner […] Brev fra Berner med Bifald over mit nÿ Divertissement samt Overenskomst om Honnorar'
2.1., 3.1., 4.1., and 5.1.1873: 'componeret'
11.2.: 'Størstedelen af Dagen spadseret med Componisten til mit nÿe Divertissement'
12.2.: '1.ste Indstudering paa det nye Divertissement […] componeret'
13.2.: '2.' Indstudering'
14.2.: 'Componeret […] arbeidet med [V. C.] Holm'
17.2.: '3.e Indstudering paa det nÿ Divertissement, skrevet og componeret'
19.2.: 'Skrevet og componeret […] 4.de Indstudering paa Divertissementet'
21.2.: 'Prøve paa det Nÿe'
27.2.: 'Prøve paa […] Divertissementet'
10.3.: 'skrevet og componeret'
13.3.: 'componeret'
17.3.: '4.e Indstudering paa Divertissementet'
19.3.: 'Indstudering af Schakspillet, der sÿnes at lykkes'
20.3.: 'Skrevet og componeret […] lille Indstudering paa det nÿ Divertissement […] Costumemøde i Theatret'
21.3.: 'Indstudering paa Divertissementet'
22.3.: 'Indstudering paa Mandarinens Døttre'
23.3.: 'skrevet og componeret'
24.3.: 'Prøve paa Mandarinens Døttre [..] componeret Finalen'
25.3.: 'Indstudering paa Finalen til Mandarinens Döttre'
27.3.: 'fuldendt Indstuderingen af Mandarinens Döttre'
28.3.: 'Prøve paa […] Det nÿe'
1.4.: 'Prøve paa Mandarinens Døttre'
2.4.: 'complet Prøve paa Mandarinens Døttre'
4.4.: 'Prøve paa Mandarinens Døttre'
5.4.: 'Prøve paa Mandarinens Døttre og Presentation for Bestÿrelsen, Costumemøde'
9.4.: 'Prøve paa Mandarinens Døttre'
15.4.: 'Musikprøve Kl 11, og Arrangementprøve paa Mandarinens Döttre 12–1.'
16.4.: 'Theaterprøve paa Mandarinens Døttre, der lover godt'
18.4.: 'Remplaceringsprøve paa det Nÿe […] Costümeprøve'
19.4.: 'Theaterprøve paa Mandarinens Døttre […] Costumeprøve'
22.4.: 'Generalprøve paa Mandarinens Døttre, der gik meget smukt'
23.4.: 'Jeg prøvede adskillige Reqvisiter til iaften [..] I Theatret hvor man […] gav Mandarinens Døttre for føste Gang og for et saa dvask Publicum, som jeg endnu ikke har oplevet her i mit Fødeland. Balletten gik i det Hele ypperligt og var efter vore Forhold glimrende udstyret men med Undtagelse af en ringe Applaus og af den Morskab som Skakspillet voldte – mødte mit smukke Arbeide en nedtrykkende Kulde. Ak! var det ikke for det daglige Bröds Skyld og for adskillige Byrder, skulde jeg gjerne hermed afslutte min møisommelige Theaterbane'.

The Mandarin's Daughters received 14 performances, the last of which was given on 26.10.1875.

Autograph sources:

Production note. Ms. Autograph (included in a letter to *Dagens Nyheder*). Brown ink. 2 pp. (21 × 13,5 cm)
[…] Rollebesætningen i mit nÿ Ballet-Divertissement/Mandarinens Döttre./Musiken arrang: og comp: af W Holm/Decorationerne af V. Güllich./Personerne
Signed and dated: 'Kbhvn d' 29 Martz 1873.'
[DKKk; NBD III, 233, 29.3.1873

Musical sources:

Orchestral score. Ms. Autograph (by V. C. Holm) and copy (by 'I. I.'). Brown and black ink. 1 vol. 172 pp. of which two are blank (25,5 × 34,5 cm)
304/Mandarinens Döttre/Partitur/V. Holm
Signed and dated (on p. 15): 'V C Holm d. 13 [changed to: '12'] April 1873.', (p. 112) 'V C Holm 3 April 1873', (p. 172) 'I.–I.'.
[DKKk; C II, 114 m (KTB 304)
Most of the music for the *Finale* (which is that of D.-F.-E. Auber's overture to *Le Cheval de bronze*) is here written by a copyist, whose signature is included on p. 172 and reads: 'I.–I.'.

Répétiteur's copy. Ms. Copy. Brown ink. 1 vol. 64 pp. of which one is blank (33,2 × 25,3 cm)
B 304/Mandarinens Döttre/(Ballet = Divertissement.)/34 A./1873. / […] /Mandarinens Döttre/Ballet = Divertissement,/af,/August Bournonville./1873.
Unsigned and dated (on the front cover and the title page): '1873.'
[DKKk; MA ms 2999 (KTB 304 (1))
This répétiteur's copy contains several choreographic numbers written (with brown ink, and by an unknown hand) underneath the music throughout the ballet. They seem to refer to a separate (not yet traced) notation of the complete ballet. Other notes (written on pp. 45–46) describe in rather general terms the choreographic evolution of *The Ballet of the Chessmen*.

Répétiteur's copy. Ms. Copy (by A. Grandjean) and print. Black ink. 1 vol. 49 pp. (34,1 × 26,2 cm)
B. 304/Mandarinens Døttre/Repetiteur Parti/34 B./[…]/Mandarinens Döttre./Ballet-divertissement/af/Aug. Bournonville/Musiken/af/V. Holm/1873./Claver Udtog ved Axel Grandjean.
Signed and dated (on the title page): '1873./Axel Grandjean'
[DKKk; MA ms 3000 (KTA 304 (2))
This piano score was arranged and prepared by A. Grandjean. It seems to date from a later, projected restaging of *The Mandarin's Daughters* at about the turn of the century. Pages 31–33 are printed music pasted into Granjean's manuscript score. They were originally part of a printed piano score (first published in 1873 by C. F. E. Hornemann and J. E. Erslev in their musical anthology *Musikalsk Museum*, 27. Aargang, 11 Hefte) and contain Holm's music for the numbers, entitled 'Bryllupsfest' (score no. 6) and 'Schackbrikkernes Dands'.

Parts. Ms. Copy. 30 vol.
3 vl I, 3 vl II, 2 vla, 3 vlc e cb, fl 1/2, ob 1/2, cl 1/2, fag 1/2, cor 1/2, tr 1/2, trb 1/2/3, timp, gr cassa, tri, arpa.
Unsigned and undated [1873]
[DKKk, KTB 304

Other sources:

Sketch by V. Güllich of the décor. Pencil and water colours (33,5 × 52,5 cm)
[Untitled]
Unsigned and undated [1875]
[DKKt; V. Güllichs dekorationsudkast (89/180)

Costume drawing by E. Lehmann. Pencil and water colours (20,7 × 10,5 cm)
[Untitled]

Unsigned and undated [c.1873]
[DKKkt; Kostumetegninger (Lehmann)]
This drawing shows the costume worn by the *Pawn* in *The Ballet of the Chessmen* in *The Mandarin's Daughters.*

Costume drawing by E. Lehmann. Pencil and water colours (20,5 × 11,4 cm)
[Untitled]
Unsigned and undated [c.1873]
[DKKkt; Kostumetegninger (Lehmann)]
This drawing shows the costume worn by the *Kingpin* in *The Ballet of the Chessmen* in *The Mandarin's Daughters.*

Costume drawing by E. Lehmann. Pencil and water colours (20,6 × 8 cm)
[Untitled]
Unsigned and undated [c.1873]
[DKKkt; Kostumetegninger (Lehmann)]
This drawing shows the costume worn by the *Queenpin* in *The Ballet of the Chessmen* in *The Mandarin's Daughters.*

Costume drawing by E. Lehmann. Pencil and water colours (20,7 × 9,3 cm)
[Untitled]
Unsigned and undated [c.1873]
[DKKkt; Kostumetegninger (Lehmann)]
This drawing shows the costume worn by the *Knight* in *The Ballet of the Chessmen* in *The Mandarin's Daughters.*

Costume drawing by E. Lehmann. Pencil and water colours (20,7 × 9,4 cm)
[Untitled]
Unsigned and undated [c.1873]
[DKKkt; Kostumetegninger (Lehmann)]
This drawing shows the costume worn by the *Bishop* in *The Ballet of the Chessmen* in *The Mandarin's Daughters.*

Costume drawing by E. Lehmann. Pencil and water colours (22 × 17,7 cm)
[Untitled]
Unsigned and undated [c.1873]
[DKKkt; Kostumetegninger (Lehmann)]
This drawing shows several different types of Chinese hats used in *The Mandarin's Daughters.*

Printed sources:

Printed scenario. 1 vol. 7 pp. (19,8 × 12,8 cm)
Mandarinens Døttre./Ballet=Divertissement/af/August Bournonville./Musiken arrangeret og komponeret af W. Holm./Dekorationen af W. Güllich.
Kjøbenhavn, J. H. Schubothe/Bianco Luno, 1873
[DKKk; 17, – 175 8°]

21.5.1873
Pas de trois (uncredited) performed by M. Westberg, A. Scholl, and C. Schousgaard.
According to a series of notes in Bournonville's diary this (uncredited) dance is identical with his much earlier *Pas des trois cousines* (*see* 20.5.1848 and 8.9.1849). It had been taught by him personally to the same three dancers less than a month before on 28.4.1873. The 1873 performance represents Bournonville's fourth staging at Copenhagen's Royal Theatre of this dance and was (according to the rehearsal book of A. Fredstrup) taught to two different casts this year at six rehearsals held between 5.5 and 17.5.1873.

In his diary Bournonville noted about his own involvement in the staging, for which he made a new, slightly revised choreographic notation:

25.4.1873: 'skrevet [...] Indstudering paa Pas des trois cousines'
28.4.: 'fuldendt Indstuderingen af Pas des trois Cousines til [M.] Westberg, [A.] Scholl og [C.] Schousgaard.'
7.5.: 'prøvet Pas de trois'
14.5.: 'repeteret Pas de trois'.

Bournonville did not attend the first performance. The 1873 restaging received 3 performances, the last of which was given on 4.9.1873. The musical material employed this year was the same as that used for Bournonville's previous staging of this dance on 18.10.1867 (now in DKKk, call nos. C II, 119, and KTB 318).

Autograph sources:

Choreographic note. Ms. Autograph. Black ink. 1 p. (25,4 × 11,9 cm)
Pas des trois cousines/1. Scholl & Skousgaard/[...]/Westberg/[...]
Unsigned and undated [Written according to the diary most probably on 25.4.1873]
[DKKk; Utilg. 828 (Harald Landers Arkiv, Supplement, Kapsel 189, 1994/78)]
This manuscript contains Bournonville's revised choreographic notes for the opening movement of his *Pas des trois cousines*. It also includes his choreographic numbers ('1–9', written with black ink) which most likely refer to similar numbers inserted into the (not yet traced) original répétiteur's copy for this dance.

3.6.1873
Holbergiana, Apotheotic Tableau (apotheotisk Tableau).
This tableau was first performed at a charity performance given for the private pension fund of the Royal Danish Ballet, of which Bournonville was the founding member. In his diary he noted about his main sources of inspiration for this work, the creation of the tableau, and its first and only performance:

20.10.1870: 'Besøgt [T.] Stein og seet hans [L.] Holberg-Statue'
23.11.: 'Besøgt Billedhugger Stein'
2.12.: 'componeret en Apotheose for Holberg'
5.4.1873: 'Skrevet et Brev til Theaterbestyrelsen angaende vor aarlige Pensionsforestilling'
24.5.: 'Brev fra [L.] Gade, der meldte [J. L.] Nyrops Sygdom og Omvæltning i vor Pensionsforestilling. Brev til [F. J. G.] Berner'
26.5.: 'Tidlig op og afsted til Kbhvn, arrangeret vor Forestilling med et Tableau, Holbergs Apotheose'
28.5.: 'arrangeret mit Tableau til Holbergiana'
31.5.: 'Prøve i Costume paa Holbergiana,'
3.6.: 'Forestilling for Pensionskassen (lidt mindre besat end de forrige Aar, formedelst den stærke Varme og Hoffets Fraværelse) Ialt med Overbetaling 921r. 2 sk. Holbergiana gjorde megen Lykke'.

No musical sources for this work have yet been traced. However, according to the poster the music employed was by J. Haydn, and most probably consisted of a movement from one of his symphonies.

Autograph sources:

Production note. Ms. Autograph (included a letter to *Dagens Nyheder*). Brown ink. 1 p. (21 × 13,5 cm).
[...] Indholdet af den Forestilling, der skal gives [...] den 3.e Juni [...] Holbergiana/apotheotisk Tableau comp: af Bournonville/til Musik af Haydn./[...]

Signed and dated: 'Kjøbenhavn den 28' Maj 1873.'
[DKKk; NBD III, 234, 28.5.1873

3.6.1873
Act I of *Le Dieu et la bayadère, ou La Courtisane amoureuse (Brama og Bayadèren)*.

This separate performance Act I of D.-F.-E. Auber's two-act opera-ballet (*see also* 7.2.1841 and 8.10.1871) seems to have been mounted with revised choreography for the dancing bayadère, *Zoloé* (performed by M. Westberg). This theory is supported by the fact that (according to the poster) the staging differed from Bournonville's previous production of this opera on 8.10.1871 by completely omitting the rôle of the second dancing bayadère, *Fatmé*. The 1873 version was arranged for a special charity performance given for the private pension fund of the Royal Danish Ballet, of which Bournonville was the founding member. In his diary he noted about the performance:

24.5.1873: 'Brev fra [L.] Gade, der meldte [J. L.] Nyrops Sygdom og Omvæltning i vor Pensionsforestilling. Brev til [F. J. G.] Berner'
26.5.: 'Tidlig op og afsted til Kbhvn, arrangeret vor Forestilling med 1.ste Akt af Brama'
31.5.: 'Prøve i Costume paa […] 1.ste Akt af Brama'
3.6.: 'Brama […] lønnedes med levende Bifald'.

The 1873 staging of Act I of *Le Dieu et La Bayadère* was only given once. The musical material employed this year was the same as that used for the previous production on 8.10.1871 (now in DKKk, call nos. U 6, MA ms 2912 (5), and KTA 301).

2.9.1873
New *Pas de deux* in Act I of *La Muette de Portici* performed by D. Krum and M. Westberg and a corps de ballet of eight women.

This dance, which was set to a new score by V. C. Holm, replaced Bournonville's much earlier *Pas de deux* (to music by M. E. Caraffa), which he had incorporated for F. Hoppe and L. Grahn in Act I of D.-F.-E. Auber's five-act opera on 23.9. 1834. In his diary he noted about the creation and the première of this completely new *Pas de deux* in *La Muette de Portici*:

14.5.1873: 'componeret Dands til <u>Den Stumme</u>'
15.8.: 'Talt med [D.] Krum, A. Scholl og [M.] Westberg, der Alle forberede sig paa Saisonens Komme'
17.8.: 'Besøg af W. [i.e. V. C.] Holm, anlagt en pas de deux for Krum og Westberg'
22.8.: 'componeret paa en nÿ pas de deux til Krum og Westberg'
23.8.: 'Indstudering af Pas de deux'
24.8.: 'componeret'
25.8.: 'Indstudering paa Dandse'
26.8.: 'Prøve paa Dandsen'
1.9.: 'Prøve paa Dandse'
2.9.: 'Krum og Westberg dandsede deres nÿ Pas de deux med stor Bravour'.

Bournonville's choreography for the second male solo variation was replaced six years later by a new male solo variation. It, too, was set to music by Holm, but was choreographed by the French ballet-master and teacher, G. Carey. He arranged the solo especially for H. Beck, who made his début as a soloist in this dance on 28.11.1879, partnering M. Westberg.

Bournonville's original 1873 version of the *Pas de deux*

reached a total of 19 performances in Auber's opera, the last of which was given on 2.6.1878.

Autograph sources:

Choreographic note. Ms. Autograph. Ink. 4 pp. (format unknown)
<u>Pas de deux</u> (Krum & Westberg)/(Ballet)/[…]/<u>Adagio.</u>/[…]/<u>Alle</u><u>gretto.</u>/Solo de Westberg)/[…]/(Solo de Krum)/(<u>Ballet</u>.) <u>5</u>
<u>Damer</u>/[…]/<u>Solo de M.lle Westberg</u>/[…]/(Solo de Krum)/<u>Coda</u>
(Ballet.)
Signed and dated: 'Fredensborg ce 24 Août 1873'
[USNYp; Dance Collection, call nos. *ZBD-71 (microfilm), and (S)*MGZMD 30 (photostat copy)

Musical sources:

Orchestral score. Ms. Autographs (by V. C. Holm and A. Grandjean). Black ink. 1 vol. 32 pp. + 4 pp. with added introductory music (25 × 34 cm with several variants)
<u>316.</u>/Pas de deux./(V. C. Holm)./(Indlagt i 'den Stumme i Portici' for /Frk Westberg og Hr. Hans Beck)./[…]/<u>Pas de deux</u>
Signed and dated (on p. 32): 'V C Holm den 28 August 1873'
[DKKk; C II, 114 m (KTB 316)
The first two pages in this score (pp. i–ii) contain the new introductory music that was added, it seems, when the *Pas de deux* was incorporated by H. Beck in Act II of *The Kermesse in Brüges, or The Three Gifts* on 7.11.1909. They are A. Grandjean's autograph. The following page (p. iv) contains Holm's new autographed *Allegro* introduction (four measures in 6/8 time) which seems to date from when the dance was mounted as a separate divertissement in a slightly revised version arranged for the début of H. Beck (*see* 28.11.1879).

The original 1873 répétiteur's copy for Holm's and Bournonville's *Pas de deux* in *La Muette de Portici* has not yet been traced. However, a slightly revised répétiteur's copy (dating from the restaging of this dance on 28.11.1879) is now in DKKk (call no. MA ms 2641 (1)). It contains several choreographic numbers (written by an unknown hand), which clearly refer to the similar numbers included in Bournonville's autographed choreographic notation of this dance (written on 24.8.1873).

Parts. Ms. Copy. 34 vol.
4 vl I, 3 vl II, 2 vla, 4 vlc e cb, fl 1/2, ob 1/2, cl 1/2, fag 1/2, cor 1/2/ 3/4, tr 1/2, trb 1/2/3, tuba, timp, gr cassa, tri.
Unsigned and undated [1873]
[DKKk; KTB 209 A (originally KTB 316)
This set of parts dates from the 1873 première of Holm's and Bournonville's new *Pas de deux* in *La Muette de Portici*. It was also used when this dance was mounted in a slightly revised version for the début of H. Beck on 28.11.1879.

2.9.1873
La Muette de Portici (Den stumme i Portici).

This performance represents Bournonville's last complete staging in Copenhagen of D.-F.-E. Auber's five-act opera (*see* 23.9.1834 and 22.10.1847). Originally he had planned a completely new mise-en-scène for the fourth act, but this idea was abandoned at an early stage in the rehearsals because of some unexpected troubles with the singer, J. L. Nyrop, who played *Masaniello*. Thus, in his diary Bournonville noted about the performance:

14.5.1873: 'componeret Dands til <u>Den Stumme</u>'
24.5.: 'Brev fra [L.] Gade, der meldte J. L.] Nyrops Sÿgdom og omvæltning i vor Pensionsforestilling'
22.8.: 'Arrangement paa 1.ste Akt af Den Stumme
23.8.: 'Arrangement paa 3.e og 5.e Akt af Den Stumme'
25.8.: 'Indstudering paa Dandse og Arrangement til Den Stumme'

26.8.: 'Prøve paa Dandsen og 4 Akter af <u>Den Stumme</u> (Vrøvl med Nyrop)'
28.8.: 'Sceneprøve paa Den Stumme (ladet min Composition gaae ud og 4.de Akt bliver som Nyrop er vant til)'
29.8.: 'Theaterprøve paa <u>Den Stumme</u>'
30.8.: 'Generalprøve paa Den Stumme'
2.9.: 'I Theatret, hvor man gav Den Stumme i Portici for fuldt Huus […] Operaen gik smukt i sin Helhed'.

The 1873 staging of *La Muette de Portici* received 18 performances during Bournonville's lifetime, the last of which was given on 7.5.1877.

The musical material employed this year was the same as that used for the previous productions on 22.10.1847 and 12.10.1865. (now in DKKkt and in DKKk, call nos. KTA 273, and MA ms 3055–3056 respectively).

25.9.1873
Le Postillon du Lonjumeau (Postillonen i Lonjumeau).
A. Adam's three-act comic opera (premièred at l'Opéra Comique in Paris on 13.10.1836) was given its first Copenhagen performance on 28.10.1837. It included an incorporated *Pas de trois* in Act I, which was set to music by M. E. Caraffa and choreographed by Bournonville.

The 1873 Copenhagen restaging of Adam's opera was originally projected by Bournonville on 30.10.1857 and represents the first and only time this opera was mounted with his own, complete mise-en-scène. However, it was this year performed without any incorporated dance divertissements. Thus, the 1873 production only included the opera's usual dance scene in Act I (score no. 1), which consists of a *Wedding Dance* performed by a corps de ballet of eight couples during the opening chorus, entitled «Le joli mariage enfin ils sont unis». In his diary Bournonville noted about the production:

4.9.1873: 'arrangeret Postillonen i Lonjumeau'
12.9. and 13.9.: 'Instruction paa Postillonen'
15.9.: 'Instruction paa Postillonen (vrøvl med [H. E.] Christoffersen)'
17.9.: 'Theaterprøve paa Postillonen med Arrangement'
18.9.: 'Prøve paa […] 1.ste Akt af Postillonen'
19.9.: 'Prøve paa […] alle tre Akter af Postillonen'
20.9.: 'Prøve paa 2.e og 3.e Akt af Postillonen'
22.9.: 'fuldstændig Prøve paa Postillonen'
24.9.: 'Generalprøve paa Postillonen'
25.9.: 'i Theatret 1.ste Forestilling af Reprisen af Postillonen i Lonjumeau, der gik meget smukt og med Bifald'.

The 1873 restaging of *Le Postillon du Lonjumeau* received 30 performances during Bournonville's lifetime, the last of which was given on 19.2.1879.

Autograph sources:

Manuscript mise-en-scène. Ms. Autograph. Brown ink and pencil. 1 vol. 8 pp. (22,7 × 18 cm)
<u>Postillonen i Longjumeau.</u> [*sic*] / (Scene = Arrangement.)
Signed and dated: 'Fredensborg den 4.e September 1873'
[SSm; Daniel Fryklunds samling no. 142

Choreographic note. Ms. Autograph. Black ink. 1 p. (23,1 × 18,3 cm)
<u>Dands til Postillonen i Longjumeau.</u> [*sic*]
Unsigned and undated [c. early September 1873]
[SSm; Daniel Fryklunds samling no. 142
This choreographic manuscript describes the *Wedding Dance* per-

formed by a corps de ballet of eight couples during the opening chorus of Act I (score no. 1), entitled «Le joli mariage enfin ils sont unis».

Production note. Ms. Autograph. Black ink. 1 p. (11 × 18,4 cm)
<u>Dands i Postillonen.</u>
Unsigned and undated [c. September 1873]
[DKKkt; F.M. (Ballet)

Musical sources:

Printed orchestral score. 1 vol. 443 pp. + 6 manuscript pp. (H. S. Paulli's autograph) including a musical insertion in Act III replacing the original score no. 11 (34,5 × 26,5 cm with minor variants)
LE Postillon de Lonjumeau, / Opéra Comique en trois actes / […] / PAR / ADOLPHE ADAM.
Paris, J. Delahante, pl. no. 1294 [1836]
[DKKk; U6 (KTA 338)
This French printed orchestral score contains several manuscript insertions including T. Overskou's 1837 Danish translation of the opera's French text. Moreover, an autographed musical insertion by H. S. Paulli (6 pp.) is incorporated in Act III immediately before score no. 11. The score was used for all performances of *Le Postillon de Lonjumeau* given in Copenhagen between 28.10.1837 and 19.2.1879. The music for the *Wedding Dance* in Act I is included on pp. '5–48'. A pencilled metronome marking indicates the exact tempo of this dance with a dotted crochet being equal to '96'.

Répétiteur's copy. Ms. Copy. Brown ink and pencil. 1 vol. 4 pp. (33,8 × 25,6 cm)
<u>Repetiteurparti/</u> [….] /<u>Postillonen i Lonjumeau/</u> […] /83./ […] / Repetiteurparti/til/Postillonen i Lonjumeau
Unsigned and undated [1873]
[DKKk; MA ms 2915 (2) (KTA 338)
This répétiteur's copy contains Bournonville's autographed notes and choreographic numbers ('1–7', written with black ink) underneath the music for the *Wedding Dance* in Act I (score no. 1) of *Le Postillon de Lonjumeau*. His numbers clearly refer to the similar numbers in his separate choreographic notation of this dance, which (according to his diary) was most likely written in September 1873. The répétiteur's copy is included (on pp. 11–14) in a volume that also contains the répétiteur's copy for six other operas and plays, mounted at Copenhagen's Royal Theatre between 1856 and 1874.

Parts. Ms. Copy. 35 vol.
4 vl I, 4 vl II, 2 vla, 4 vlc e cb, fl I, fl II e picc, ob 1/2, cl 1/2, fag 1/2, cor 1/2/3/4, tr 1/2, trb 1/2/3, timp, gr cassa, piatti, tri. 55 vocal parts.
Unsigned and undated [1837]
[DKKk; KTA 338
This set of parts was used for all performances of *Le Postillon de Lonjumeau* in Copenhagen since its première there on 28.10.1837 up to its last performance on 19.2.1879.

4.11.–19.12.1873
Fourteen dance lessons in social dance.
According to a series of notes in his diary Bournonville gave 14 private dance lessons in social dance at the Copenhagen residence of the widow of the Lord-in-Waiting, F. Lowzow, at Frederiksholm Kanal no. 6/1. These lessons, which took place mainly on Tuesday, Friday, and Saturday afternoons, lasted for about two hours each.

16.11.1873
Guillaume Tell (Wilhelm Tell).
This performance represents Bournonville's second and last complete staging of G. Rossini's four-act opera in Copenhagen (*see* 23.11.1868). It was mounted with only minor if any

changes from the previous 1868 production, with the Act III *Pas de trois* performed this year by E. Hansen, M. Westberg, and J. Petersen. In his diary Bournonville noted about the performance:

1.11. and 3.11.1873: 'Instruction paa Wilhelm Tell'
5.11.: 'Theaterprøve paa W. Tell'
6.11.: 'Prøve paa Dandsen til Wilhelm Tell'
7.11.: 'Prøve paa 3.e og 4.e Akt af Wilhelm Tell'
8.11.: 'Prøve paa Wilhelm Tell'
10.11.: 'Arrangement af Dandsen til Wilhelm Tell'
11.11.: 'Theaterprøve paa W. Tell'
12.11.: 'lille Prøve paa Dandsen til W. Tell'
13.11.: 'Generalprøve paa W. Tell, der lover en brilliant Forestilling'
15.11.: 'sidste Prøve paa W. Tell'
16.11.: 'I Theatret Wilhelm Tell for udsolgt Huus og i det Hele fortræffelig udført'.

The 1873 restaging of *Guillaume Tell* received 10 performances, the last of which was given on 7.2.1874.

The musical material employed this year was the same as that used for the previous production on 23.11.1868 (now in DKKt and in DKKk, call nos. KTA 375, and MA ms 2911 (1) respectively).

28.11.1873
The Toreador (Toréadoren).
This performance represents Bournonville's fifth and last restaging of his two-act idyllic ballet *The Toreador* (*see* 27.11.1840). It was mounted with a partially new cast (including M. Westberg as *Céleste*), but was otherwise performed with only minor if any changes from the previous 1869 production. This is clear from Bournonville's diary in which he noted about the staging:

8.10.1873: 'lille Prøve paa Toreadoren ([M.] Westberg upasselig)'
15.10.: 'lille Prøve pa Toreadoren'
16.10.: 'Prøve paa [...] Toréadoren'
18.10.: 'Eftermiddagsprøve paa Toreadoren 2.' Akt'
20.10., 21.10., and 22.10.: 'Indstudering paa Toreadoren'
23.10.: 'Prøve paa Toreadoren færdig indstuderet'
25.10.: 'partiel Prøve paa Toreadoren'
28.10.: 'Prøve paa Toreadoren'
17.11. and 18.11.: 'lille Prøve paa Toreadoren'
21.11.: 'Prøve paa Toreadoren'
24.11.: 'Theaterprøve med Orchester paa Toreadoren'
28.11.: 'I Theatret 1.ste Forestiling af den nÿ indstuderede Toreadoren der gik udmærket, for fuldt Huus of stort Bifald'.

The 1873 production of *The Toreador* received 17 performances during Bournonville's lifetime, the last of which was given on 27.3.1876.

The musical material employed this year was (apart from a new répétiteur's copy made especially for this production) the same as that used for the previous production on 6.11.1869 (now in DKKk, call nos. C II, 114 k and KTB 269).

Musical sources:

Répétiteur's copy. Ms. Copy. Brown and black ink. 1 vol. 114 pp. (33,2 × 25,2 cm)
B.269/'Toreadoren.'/[...]/Repetiteurparti/til Balletten/Torèadoren.
Unsigned and undated [1873]
[DKKk; MA ms 2965 b (KTB 269 (2))
This répétiteur's copy dates from the last restaging of *The Toreador* in

Bournonville's lifetime on 28.11.1873. This is clear from notes (written by the répétiteur himself) which include the name of M. Westberg. She performed the rôle of *Céleste* for the first time in the 1873 production. The volume also includes other notes (written by the music copyist) describing the mime and the dramatic action throughout the ballet.

28.12.1873
La Fiancée (Bruden).
The 1873 Copenhagen restaging of D.-F.-E. Auber's three-act comic opera (*see* 20.11.1853 and 7.10.1858) represents the fourth and last time this work was staged under Bournonville's direction in Copenhagen. It was mounted this year with new costumes and a completely new mise-en-scène and partially revised choreography. This is clear from Bournonville's detailed 1873 production notes for Auber's opera and from his diary, in which he noted about the staging:

19.11.1873: 'Oplæsning paa Bruden'
24.11.: 'skrevet og lavet Sceneri til Bruden'
25.11.: 'Decorationsprøve for Bruden'
30.11.: 'skrevet et Forslag til Costümet i Bruden'
5.12.: 'Costümemøde paa Bruden'
12.12.: 'Bivaanet Sangprøve paa Bruden'
13.12.: 'Aftenen hjemme'
15.12.: 'Indstudering paa Dandsen til Bruden, læst og skrevet'
16.12.: 'Theaterprøve ved Claveer paa Bruden'
18.12.: 'Prøve ved Claveer paa Bruden'
20.12. and 22.12.: 'fuldstændig Prøve paa Bruden'
24.12.: 'Theaterprøve paa Bruden'
27.12.: 'Generalprøve paa Bruden (Costümevrøvl)'
28.12.: 'I Theatret 1.ste Forestilling af den nÿ Indstudering af Bruden, der gik særdeles smukt og med meget Bifald, Charlotte (Bournonville) fortrinlig som Modehandlerinden'.

The 1873 production of *La Fiancée* received 6 performances during Bournonville's lifetime (the last of which was given on 19.1.1874) after which the opera went out of the Copenhagen repertory.

The musical material employed this year was the same as that used for the previous production on 7.10.1858 (now in DKKk, call nos. U 6, MA ms 3059, and KTA 281).

Autograph sources:

Manuscript mise-en-scène. Ms. Autograph. Brown ink. 8 pp. (22,7 × 18,2 cm)
Bruden (Scene = Arrangement.)/(Første Akt.)/Decoration
Signed and dated: 'Kbhvn den 24.e November 1873.'
[SSm; Daniel Fryklunds samling no. 119

Production note. Ms. Autograph. Black ink. 1 p. (33,9 × 20,7 cm)
Bruden/Chor og Bipersonerne.
Unsigned and undated [Written according to the diary on 30.11.1873]
[DKKkt; F.M. (Ballet)

Choreographic note. Ms. Autograph. Brown ink. 3 pp. (20,8 × 16,9 cm)
Bruden 2de Akt./(Quadrille.)/[...]/Tyrolienne./[...]/1.ste Vers./[...]/2' Vers/[...]/3.de Vers.
Unsigned and dated: 'd. 13 Decbr 1873.'
[DKKk; MA (Box)
Bournonville's autographed choreographic numbers included in this manuscript ('1–16' and '1–12') refer to his similar numbers written underneath the music in the répétiteur's copy for *La Fiancée* (now in DKKk, call no. MA ms 3059 (KTA 281)).

1874

10.1.–1.4.1874
Twenty dance lessons in social dance.
According to his diary Bournonville gave a series of 20 private dance lessons in social dance at the Copenhagen residence of Count C. C. S. Danneskjold, at Norgesgade no. 68/1. These lessons, which took place on Wednesday afternoons, lasted for about two hours each.

17.1.–7.4.1874
Twenty dance lessons in social dance.
According to a series of notes in his diary Bournonville gave 20 private dance lessons in social dance this year at the Copenhagen residence of the Russian envoy to Denmark, A. P. von Mohrenheim, at Kongens Nytorv no. 4. These lessons, which took place mainly on Tuesday afternoons, lasted for about two hours each.

24.1.1874
Pas de trois (uncredited) performed by M. Westberg, A. Scholl, and C. Schousgaard.
According to a note in Bournonville's diary on this day (reading: 'seet Pas des trois cousines, der gik […] paany indstuderet') this (uncredited) dance is identical with his much earlier *Pas des trois cousines* (*see* 20.5.1848 and 8.9.1849). The 1874 performances (which were rehearsed by Bournonville on 6.1., 19.1., and 23.1.1874) represent the fifth and last staging of this dance during his lifetime. It seems to have been mounted with only minor if any changes from his previous staging on 21.5.1873, and received 3 performances, the last of which was given on 27.2.1874. The musical material employed was the same as that used for Bournonville's previous 1873 staging (now in DKKk, call nos. C II, 119, and KTB 318).

3.2.1874
Il Matrimonio Segreto (Det hemmelige Ægteskab).
The 1874 Copenhagen restaging of D. Cimarosa's two-act comic opera (*see* 24.1.1860) represents the second and last time this work was mounted by Bournonville. It was this year performed in a three-act version with a completely new mise-en-scène. In his diary Bournonville noted about the production:

16.1.1874: 'hørt paa Syngeprøve af Det hemmelige Ægteskab'
19.1.: 'componeret Scene-Arrangement til Det hemmelige Ægteskab'
24.1. and 26.1.: 'Instruction paa Det hemmelige Ægteskab'
27.1.: 'Prøve med Orchester paa 1' og 2' Akt af Det hemmelige Ægteskab'
28.1.: 'Theaterprøve paa 'Det hemmelige Ægteskab''
29.1.: 'Theaterprøve paa alle tre Akter af 'Det hemmelige Ægteskab''
30.1.: 'heel Prøve paa Det hemmelige Ægteskab'
31.1.: 'Prøve paa […] Det hemmelige Ægteskab'
2.2.: 'Generalprøve paa Det hemmelige Ægteskab'
3.2.: 'Iste Forestilling af Det hemmelige Ægteskab ny indstuderet gik udmærket og gjorde megen Lykke. Charlotte (Bournonville) fortræffelig som Fridolina'.

The 1874 production received 6 performances during Bournonville's lifetime (the last of which was given on 7.12.1874)

after when it went out of the Copenhagen repertory. The musical material employed this year was the same as that used for the previous 1860 production (now in DKKk, call nos. C I, 231, and KTA 116).

Autograph sources:

Manuscript mise-en-scène. Ms. Autograph. Black ink. 12 pp. (20,7 × 16,9 cm)
Det hemmelige Ægteskab./Scene = Arrangement)/<u>Decoration:</u>
Signed and dated: 'Kjøbenhavn d. 19.de Januar 1874.'
[SSm; Daniel Fryklunds samling no. 121

6.2.–12.3.1874
Sixteen dance lessons in social dance.
According to a series of notes in his diary Bournonville gave 16 private dance lessons in social dance at the Copenhagen residence of the consul, F. H. Bloch, at Badstuestræde no. 2/s. These lessons, which took place mainly on Monday and Friday afternoons, lasted for about two hours each.

5.3.1874
The Sleeping-Draught (Sovedrikken).
The 1874 Copenhagen restaging of C. E. F. Weyse's four-act singspiel from 1809 was mounted for a special performance celebrating the centenary of the composer's birth. It represents the first and only time *The Sleeping-Draught* was staged with Bournonville's own, complete mise-en-scène (*see also* 30.10.1857 and 15.1.1858). In his diary he noted about the performance:

21.2.1874: 'Instruction paa Sovedrikken'
23.2.: 'Theaterprøve paa […] de to første Akter af Sovedrikken'
24.2.: 'Theaterprøve paa […] 3.e og 4.e Akt af Sovedrikken'
26.2. and 3.3.: 'Theaterprøve paa Sovedrikken'
4.3.: 'Generalprøve paa Sovedrikken'
5.3.: 'I Theatret festforestilling i Anledning af 100.e Aarsdagen for [C. E. F.] Weyses Fødsel (1774) Sovedrikken […] gik fortræffeligt og gjorde megen Lykke'.

The 1874 restaging received 9 performances during Bournonville's lifetime, the last of which was given on 30.5.1874. The musical material employed this year was the same as that used for the previous production on 15.1.1858 (now in DKKk, call nos. C II, 123 (KTA 150).

5.3.1874
In Memory of Weyse, Epilogue with Tableaux (Weyses Minde, Efterspil med Tableauer).
This pantomimic epilogue with six tableaux was created for the celebration of the centenary for the birth of the Danish composer, C. E. F. Weyse. It opened with a scene from one of the composer's most popular works, the one-act operetta *A Fairy Tale in the Rosenborg Gardens (Et Eventyr i Rosenborg Have).* It was originally premièred at Copenhagen's Royal Theatre on 26.5.1827 and had reached its one-hundreth performance in 1869.

After a selected series of mime scenes showing situations from this operetta, Bournonville added an allegorical scene in which the five muses *Euterpe, Polyhymnia, Thalia, Melpomene,* and *Terpsichore* pay homage to Weyse, whose bust was erected in the middle of a temple in the Rosenborg Gardens. The epilogue ended with a series of *tableaux vivants* showing scenes from five of Weyse's most popular operas and singspiels, followed by a final tableau in which Saint Cecilia is seen playing the organ high above the composer's bust. This epilogue (which was divided into 6 scenes and 13 music numbers) was set to a score composed and arranged by V. C. Holm. He incorporated several musical borrowings from the works of Weyse as follows:

(1) Scene 1 (score no. 1): For this number Holm employed the entire overture from Weyse's and J. L. Heiberg's one-act 1827 operetta *A Fairy Tale in the Rosenborg Gardens*.

(2) Scene 2 (score no. 2): In this scene Holm employed Weyse's romance from 1838 (to text by J. L. Heiberg), entitled «Solen sank bag grönne Lund». It was first published in Copenhagen by C. C. Lose & Olsen in 1840, and had also been incorporated in 1866 in J. L. Heiberg's three-act play from 1819 *The Prophecy of Tycho Brahe (Tycho Brahes Spaadom)*.

(3) Scene 2 (score no. 3): In this number Holm interpolated an *Allegretto* in 6/8 time, which he borrowed from the duet, entitled «Hold op, hold op mig at fixere». It was originally part of Weyse's and J. L. Heiberg's 1827 operetta *A Fairy Tale in the Rosenborg Gardens*, in which it was listed as score no. 6.

(4) Scene 3 (score no. 4): Holm here incorporated an excerpt from the music of the chorus, named «Til Værket afsted med vingede Fod». It was originally sung by the elf maidens in Act I (score no. 8) of Weyse's and C. J. Boye's lyrical-romantic drama in three-act *Floribella* (premièred at Copenhagen's Royal Theatre on 12.12.1824). This excerpt is followed by Weyse's melody for C. J. Boye's patriotic song «Der er et Land, dets Sted er höit mod Norden», composed in 1826 and first performed at a private charity performance given at the Court Theatre on 8.1.1826.

(5) Scene 4 (score no. 5): For this scene (in which *Terpsichore* enters the stage and performs a solo variation in front of Weyse's bust) Holm incorporated an *Andantino quasi allegretto* in 6/8 time. It was borrowed from the ballet music in the finale of Act I (score no. 15 c) of Weyse's and H. C. Andersen's three-act romantic singspiel from 1836 *The Feast at Kenilworth (Festen paa Kenilworth)*.

(6) Scene 5 (score no. 6): In the music for the first of the five *tableaux vivants* (showing a scene from Weyse's and H. C. Andersen's singspiel *The Feast at Kenilworth*) Holm incorporated an excerpt of the music from the duet, entitled «Du, Kjærlighed, gjör Hiertet glad». It was originally performed by the characters *Leicester* and *Emmy* in Act I (score no. 7) of *The Feast at Kenilworth*.

(7) Scene 5 (score no. 7): For this number (a *Gipsy Dance* performed by E. Hansen and A. Scholl) Holm employed Weyse's complete music for the *Gipsy Dance (Zigeunerdands)* in the Act I finale (score no. 15 b) of *The Feast at Kenilworth*. It was originally choreographed by P. Funck at the 1827 Copenhagen première of this singspiel.

(8) Scene 5 (score no. 8): For the second *tableau vivant* (which depicted a scene from Weyse's and C. J. Boye's lyrical-romantic drama *Floribella*) Holm employed a large excerpt of Weyse's music from the chorus, entitled «Knitrer, Flammer, höit med Brag». It was originally sung by the elf maidens as an *entr'acte* between Acts II and III of *Floribella*. During the final part of this excerpt a *Solo* for *Terpsichore* (danced by M. Westberg) was performed amidst the dances of two other elf-maidens.

(9) Scene 5 (score no. 9): For the third *tableau vivant* (which showed a scene from Weyse's and A. Oehlenschläger's four-act opera from 1816 *The Cavern of Ludlam (Ludlams Hule)*) Holm incorporated the music for the canzonetta, entitled «Vil du være stærk og frie». It was originally sung by the character *George* in Act II (score no. 15) of this opera.

(10) Scene 5 (score no. 10): In this number a *Scottish Reel (Skotsk Reel)* was performed by two women (I. Berthelsen and V. Monti). It was set to Weyse's so-called 'Taffelmusik' in his score for W. Shakespeare's five-act tragedy *Macbeth* (premièred at Copenhagen's Royal Theatre on 15.11.1817).

(11) Scene 5 (score no. 11): For the fourth *tableau vivant* (showing a scene from Weyse's and W. Shakespeare's five-act tragedy *Macbeth*

from 15.11.1817) Holm employed most of Weyse's music for the so-called 'Hexe-Sabbat' («Tudse, Du som Dag og Nat», score no. 4) in Shakespeare's tragedy. During the same number an (unnamed) *Dance* was performed by nine elf-maidens.

(12) Scene 5 (score no. 12): For the fifth *tableau vivant* (in which a scene from Weyse's and A. Oehlenschläger's three-act singspiel *Faruk* is seen) Holm incorporated a large instrumental excerpt from the terzet, entitled «Risler alle Bölger smaa». It was originally part of Act I (score no. 3) of Weyse's singspiel. Thus, at the première of *Faruk* on 30.1.1812 the terzet was accompanied by an (unnamed) *Dance*, originally choreographed by V. Galeotti, but rechoreographed by Bournonville's father, Antoine Bournonville, in 1817.

According to pencilled notes in Holm's autographed orchestral score (p. 111) the sixth and final tableau (score no. 13), in which Saint Cecilia is seen playing an organ high above the bust of Weyse, was omitted at a later stage.

In his diary Bournonville noted about his creation and the première of this work:

1.2.1874: 'Componeret <u>Weyses Minde</u> Efterspil til 100 Aars Dag for hans Fødsel (5.de Marts 1874.) […] W. [i.e. V. C.] Holm og hans Frue […] hos os til Middag'
2.2.: 'componeret til Weyses Minde'
3.2.: 'arbeidet med Holm'
4.2.: 'skrevet Regien til Weyses Minde'
6.2.: 'componeret paa Weyses Minde'
7.2.: '1.ste Indstudering paa Weyses Minde'
8.2.: 'kjørt ud til Holm og arbeidet sammen med ham paa Weyses Minde […] Decorationsmøde paa Weyses Minde'
9.2.: 'skrevet og componeret […] Indstudering paa Weyses Minde'
10.2.: 'Repetition paa Weyses Minde, componeret'
11.2.: 'skrevet og componeret […] indstuderet tvende Dandse til Weyses Minde […] skrevet og componeret'
12.2.: 'Indstudering paa Weyses Minde'
13.2.: 'Repetition paa Weyses Minde'
14.2., 15.2., and 16.2.: 'componeret'
17.2.: 'fuldendt Indstuderingen paa Weyses Minde'
18.2.: 'heel Repetition paa Weyses Minde, der vil vare 25 Minuter […] hjemme reenskrevet <u>Weyses Minde</u>'
19.2.: 'Skrevet og ordnet Lister til Balletten'
20.2.: 'Repetition af Dandsene i Weyses Minde […] Meget Besvær for at skaffe Costumetegninger'
23.2. and 24.2.: 'Theaterprøve paa Weÿses Minde'
28.2.: 'Decorationsprøve paa Weyses Minde'
2.3.: 'Musik og fuldstændig Prøve paa <u>Weyses Minde</u>'
4.3.: 'Generalprøve paa […] Weyses Minde'
5.3.: 'Besørget Programmerne […] I Theatret Festforestilling i Anledning af 100.de Aarsdagen for [C. E. F.] Weyses Fødsel (1774) Sovedrikken og mit Efterspil gik fortræffeligt og gjorde megen Lykke'.

In Memory of Weyse reached a total of 9 performances, the last of which was given on 30.5.1874.

Autograph sources:

Production note. Ms. Autograph. Ink. 1 p. (format unknown)
<u>Belysnings – Signaler</u>/til/<u>Weyses Minde</u>
Signed and dated: 'd 19.e Februar 1874'
[USNYp; Dance Collection, call nos. *ZBD-71 (microfilm), and (S)*MGZMD 30 (photostat copy)

Musical sources:

Orchestral score. Ms. Autograph (by V. C. Holm). Brown ink. 1 vol. 128 pp. of which two are blank (34,1 × 25,7 cm)
305/V. Holm/305/Weyses Minde/Partitur./[..]/Weyses Minde
Unsigend and undated [1874]

[DKKk; C II, 114 m (KTB 305)

Répétiteur's copy. Ms. Copy. Brown ink. 1 vol. 36 pp. (33,7×25,4 cm)
B. 305/Weÿses Minde!/mimisk=lyrisk Efterspil til Sovedrikken/d. 5
Martz 1774: d 5.e Martz 1874./W. Holm/Bournonville./30/Weyses
Minde/Efterspil med Tableauer/af/August Bournonville/Musiken
efter Weyses Compositioner/arrangeret af/W Holm./1874.
Unsigned and danted (on the title page): '1874.'
[DKKk; MA ms 3001 (KTA 305)
This répétiteur's copy contains several choreographic numbers writ-
ten (with brown ink) by an unknown hand. They are inserted only in
those parts of the epilogue which were actually danced, and seem to
refer to a separate (not yet traced) choreographic notation, which
Bournonville most likely made during early February 1874.

Parts. Ms. Copy. 31 + 9 vol.
3 vl I, 3 vl II, 2 vla, 3 vlc e cb, fl 1/2, ob 1/2, cl 1/2, fag 1/2, cor 1/2,
tr 1/2, trb 1/2/3, tuba, timp, gr cassa, tri, arpa. On stage: vl I, vl II,
vla, vlc e cb, cor 1/2, tr 1/2, org e piano.
Unsigned and undated [1874]
[DKKk; KTB 305

10.3.1874

**A *Procession of Personalities from the time of Christian IV (Optog
af Personligheder fra Christian IV Tid)*, a *Quadrille Noble
(Polonaise, Contredanse)*, a *Quadrille Hongrois (Entrée,
Mazurque, Frischka)*, and a *Quadrille Italien (Entrée, Valse
figurée, Tarentelle)* performed by members of the Royal
Danish family and the nobility at a masked ball at the
Amalienborg Palace.**

In his diary Bournonville noted about this series of dances
created for a masked ball at the Royal Palace in Copenhagen:

19.2.1874: 'Møde hos Overmarskallen i Anledning af et forestaaende
Maskebal [...] og derpaa Audients hos Hd M. Dronningen [i.e.
Queen Louise Wilhelmine Friederike Caroline Auguste Julie of Den-
mark] i samme Anledning for at componere to Quadriller'
21.2.: 'Møde hos Dronningen om Quadrillerne'
22.2.: 'Skrevet og componeret, Conference hos Scavenius i Anledning af Hofmaskeraden'
24.2.: 'skrevet og componeret'
25.2.: 'componeret [...] 1.ste Indstudering af Quadrille noble hos
Scavenius'
26.2.: 'Kl. 7 paa Amalienborg, hvor jeg indstuderede 1.e og 2.n Deel
af en italiensk Quadrille H.M. Kongen [i.e. King Christian IX]
dandsede selv med'
27.2.: '2' Indstudering hos Scavenius'
1.3.: 'componeret [...] talt med Kronprindsessen [i.e. Princess Louise Josephine Eugenie], Grevinde Frijs og Overhofmarskalinden i
Anledning af Anordning og Prøver'
2.3.: ' Indstudering hos Kmhr [O.] Sehested-Juul [...] Indstudering
hos Kronprindsessen og efter lidt Hvile, Italiensk Quadrille hos
Kongen. – En meget fortjent Dag!'
3.3.: 'Prøve og Indstudering ved Hoffet. Den ungarske Quadrille'
4.3.: 'Skrevet og componeret [...] Indstudering med Prindsesse
Thyra'
5.3.: 'Arrangement af Optog hos Grev [Frederik Julius Krag-Juel-
Vind-] Frijs'
6.3.: 'Prøve paa noble Quadrille Kl 3 paa Amalienborg, – og Kl 7½
ved Hoffet paa de to andre Quadriller'
7.3.: 'besørget adskilligt til Hoffesten'
9.3.: 'to Prøver paa Optog og Quadriller paa Amalienborg [...] Indbudt til Taffel hos Kronprindsen [i.e. the later King Frederik VIII]
hvor der vare særdeles behageligt. Vi prøvede den ungarske og italienske Quadrille og der blev dandset efter Theen. Man fik mig med
i Cotillonen og jeg dandsede vexelviis med Kronprindsessen og
Prindsesse Thyra'

10.3.: 'besørget adskilligt til Hoffesten. Kl 8½ til Amalienborg hvor
jeg dirigerede Optoget og de tre Quadriller ved det brilliante
Maskebal og høstede stor Ære derfor. Kongen vilde drikke et Glas
med mig og takkede mig med de varmeste Ønsker. Det hele var i høi
Grad vellykket, jeg tog hjem efter Soupéen Kl 1½, men Ballet varede
indtil Kl 5 med stor Livlighed og Glæde'
11.3.: 'bivaanet og grupperet Photographien af Chr. IV Optog ved
Grev Frijs'.

No musical sources for this set of dances have yet been
traced.

Autograph sources:

Choreographic note. Ms. Autograph. Black ink. 1 p. (22,7×18,3 cm)
Quadrille hongrois/[...]/Quadrille Italien
Signed and dated: '21. février 1874.'
[DKKk; NKS 3285 4° 1 læg B 8

Choreographic note. Ms. Autograph. Black ink. 3 pp. (22,7 × 18,3
cm)
Quadrille – noble./[...]/Contredanse.
Unsigned and undated [c. February 1874]
[DKKk; NKS 3285 4° 1 læg B 8

Choreographic note. Ms. Autograph. Black ink. 1 p. (21,7×13,8 cm)
Quadrille noble. (Polonaise)/[...]/Contredanse.
Unsigned and undated [February 1874]
[DKKk; NKS 3285 4° 1 læg B 8

Choreographic note. Ms. Autograph. Black ink. 2 pp. (22,7 × 18,3
cm)
Quadrille hongrois./(Czardas)/[...]/Mazurka./[...]/Frischka.
Unsigned and undated [c. February 1874]
[DKKK; NKS 3285 4° 1 læg B 8

Choreographic note. Ms. Autograph. Black ink. 1 p. (33,9×11,2 cm)
Ungarsk Quadrille./Czardas/[...]/Mazurka./[...]/Frischka.
Unsigned and undated [c. February 1874]
[DKKk; NKS 3285 4° 1 læg B 8

Choreographic note. Ms. Autograph. Black ink. 2 pp. (21,7 × 14,1
cm)
Quadrille hongrois (Czardas)/[...]/Mazurque/[...]/Frischka.
Unsigned and undated [c. February 1874]
[DKKk; NKS 3285 4° 1 læg B 8

Choreographic note. Ms. Autograph. Black ink. 2 pp. (22,7 × 18,3
cm)
Quadrille italien (No. 1 Entrée)/ [...] /No. 2 (Valse)/ [...] /No. 3
(Tarentelle.)
Unsigned and undated [c. February 1874]
[DKKk; NKS 3285 4° 1 læg B 8

Choreographic note. Ms. Autograph. Black ink. 2 pp. (20,9 × 13,4
cm)
Italiensk – Quadrille/ [...]/2.e figure. (Valse)/ [...] /3.me figure.
(Tarentelle.)
Unsigned and undated [c. February 1874]
[DKKK; NKS 3285 4° 1 læg B 8

Choreographic note. Ms. Autograph. Black ink. 2 pp. (22,6 × 18,2
cm)
Quadrille italien./[...]/Tarentelle.
Unsigned and undated [c. February 1874]
[DKKk; NKS 3285 4° 1 læg B 8

Production note. Ms. Autograph. Black ink. 1 p. (22,8 × 17,9 cm)
Personer/No. 1/[...]No. 9./[...]/Christian/Grev Frijs Frijsenborg/
Prinsesse Thyra.

Unsigned and undated [c. February 1874]
[DKKk; Danske Afdeling, Småtryk (Personalhistorie: Bournonville)
This production note seems to be Bournonville's first draft for the procession, entitled 'Personligheder fra Christian IV Tid', which opened the royal masked ball on 10.3.1874.

Printed sources:

Printed synopsis. 1 p. (32,4 × 23,5 cm)
OPTOG AF PERSONLIGHEDER/FRA/CHRISTIAN IV TID.
Privately printed, s. l., s. a. [c. 10.3.1874]
[DKKk; Danske Afdeling, Småtryk (Personalhistorie: Bournonville)

29.3.1874
The Lay of Thrym (Thrymsqviden).
This restaging represents the last time Bournonville's four-act Nordic mythological ballet *The Lay of Thrym* (*see* 21.2. 1868) was mounted by himself, and the first time the rôle of *Loke* was played by D. Krum. According to his diary the 1874 staging seems to have been given with only minor choreographic changes from the previous staging on 17.9.1871:

1.12.1873: 'skrevet og studeret Choregraphien til Thrymsqviden
[…] Prøve paa 1.ste Scene og sandsernes Dands af Thrymsqviden'
2.12.: 'skrevet og componeret […] Prøve paa Thrymsqviden'
3.12., 5.12., and 6.12.: 'Prøve paa Thrymsqviden'
8.12.: 'Repetition paa Thrymsqviden'
11.12. and 12.12.: 'Prøve paa Thrymsqviden'
13.12.: 'Prøve paa Brudedandsen til Thrymsqviden'
15.12.: 'Prøve paa Thrymsqviden'
19.12.: 'Indstudering paa Thrymsqviden'
23.12.: 'Prøve paa Thrymsqviden'
2.1.1874: 'lille Prøve paa Thrymsqviden'
3.1.: 'Prøve paa Thrymsqviden'
6.1.: 'Indstudering til Fru [E.] Poulsen som Freÿa'
7.1.: 'Prøve paa […] Drømmen til Thrymsqviden'
8.1.: 'Indstudering med Freya til Thrymsqviden'
9.1.: 'Prøve paa Thrymsqviden'
10.1.: 'Prøve paa Thrymsqviden 2' og 3' Akt'
12.1., 13.1., 15.1., 19.1., 22.1., and 3.2.: 'Prøve paa Thrymsqviden'
14.3.: 'Musikprøve paa Thrymsqviden'
16.3. and 17.3.: 'Prøve paa Thrymsqviden'
18.3.: 'Theaterprøve paa Thrymsqviden (Arrangement)'
20.3.: 'Theaterprøve med Orchester paa Thrymsqviden'
25.3.: 'partiel Prøve paa Thrymsqviden […] Kl 6. Theaterprøve paaa Nornerne og Thrymsqviden fortræffelig fra Ballettens Side, men kummerlig fra Maskineriets, færdig Kl 10½.'
28.3.: 'Generalprøve paa Thrymsqviden'
29.3.: 'I Theatret Nornerne og Thrymsqviden for fuldt Huus og livligt Bifald, Balletten gik overordentlig godt og navnlig [D.] Krum tilfredsstillede meget som Loke'.

The 1874 production received 6 performances during Bournonville's lifetime, the last of which was given on 22.5.1874. The musical material employed this year was the same as that used since the 1868 première of this ballet (now in DKKk, call nos. C II, 114, MA ms 2996, KTB 299, and KTA 763).

27.4.1874
Pas de deux (uncredited) performed by D. Krum and A. Scholl.
This (uncredited) dance is most likely identical with the earlier, similarly uncredited *Pas de deux* performed by the same dancers on 7.1.1869. That dance, in turn, is probably identical with two even earlier (uncredited) *Pas de deux*, performed on 12.10.1866 (by Krum and J. Petersen) and on 14.3.1867 (by Krum and S. Price).

Another possible identification of this dance is the (uncredited) *Pas de deux*, performed by Krum and Scholl on 4.12.1872, which in turn is identical with the even earlier Bournonville *Pas de deux* to music by M. E. Caraffa, that was first incorporated in Act I of D.-F.-E. Auber's five-act opera *La Muette de Portici* (*see* 23.9.1834).

According to the rehearsal book of A. Fredstrup the *Pas de deux* was given three rehearsals on 24.4., 25.4., and 27.4. 1874, all of which were held under the personal supervision of L. Gade. Bournonville did not attend the first and only performance of this dance in 1874 because of his four-week journey to Russia on which he embarked on 15.4.1874.

It is not possible to identify the dance any further.

28.4.1874
Iphigénie en Tauride (Iphigenia paa Tauris).
The 1874 Copenhagen première of C. W. v. Gluck's four-act lyrical tragedy (first performed at the Paris Opéra on 18.5. 1779) was mounted with Bournonville's mise-en-scène and choreography. It included two dance scenes as follows:

(1) A so-called 'Schytternes Dands' in Act II, scene 4 (score nos. 8–10), performed by a corps de ballet of twelve men dressed as Scythian warriors.
(2) A *Pantomime scene* in Act II, scene 5 (score nos. 14–15), performed by a group of Furies (nine women) during the recitative and aria of *Oreste*, and in the succeeding chorus of the Furies, entitled «Vengeons et la Nature». («Vi straffe dine Synder, vi tjene Guders Vrede»). This pantomimic dance scene is described in the printed French orchestral score as follows: 'Les Euménides sortent du fond du Théâtre, et entourent Oréste; les unes executent autour de lui un ballet Pantomime de terreur, les autres lui parlent. Oreste est sans connaissance pendant tout=cette scene'.

In his diary Bournonville noted about his staging (which was performed to A. Hertz's Danish translation of N. F. Guillard's original French text):

6.12.1872: 'Repertoiremøde, skrevet og læst […] indleveret en Betænkning om [C. W. v.] Glucks Iphigenia i Tauris'
20.1.1874: 'læst Texten til Iphigenia i Tauris […] skrevet '
12.3.: 'Componeret til Iphigenia i Tauris, skrevet og ordnet. Indstuderet Skytterne og Furierne til ovennævnte Opera'
13.3.: 'Repetition paa Iphigenia i Tauris […] Aftenen hjemme, fuldendt Scene-Arrangementet til Iphigenia i Tauris'
15.3.: 'componeret'
16.3.: 'Instruction paa Orestes Rolle i Iphigenia paa Tauris'
27.3.: 'skrevet og componeret'
29.3: 'arbeidet paa Iphigenia'
31.3.: 'Scenearrangement til Iphigenia paa Tauris'
4.4.: 'Indstudering paa Iphigenia'
7.4.: 'Instruction paa Iphigenia'
9.4.: 'Arrangementprøve paa Iphigenia i Tauris'
10.4.: 'Prøve paa Iphigenia'
14.4.: 'prøvet 3.e og 4.e Akt af If. i Tauris'.

Bournonville did not attend the first performance because of his departure for Russia on 15.4.1874. However, later the same year he did see the first two acts when *Iphigénie en Tauride* was given its sixth performance on 6.11.1874. He then noted in his diary:

'hørt de to første Akter af Iphigenia paa Tauris, der gik temmelig kjedeligt formedelst Fru [A. D.] Erh[ard-] Hansens store Utydelighed'.

Iphigénie en Tauride reached a total of 8 performances (the last of which was given on 1.12.1875), after which it went out of the Copenhagen repertory.

Autograph sources:

Recommendation note (included in a letter to F. J. G. Berner). Ms. Autograph. Black ink. 1 p. (27,9 × 21, 8 cm)
[…]/Efter paany at have gjort mig bekjendt med Texten til Glucks berømte Opera <u>Iphigenia i Tauris</u> […]
Unsigned and undated [Written according to the diary on either 6.12.1872 or 21.1.1874]
[DKKkt; Brevregistrant (ad January 21, 1874)

Manuscript mise-en-scène. Ms. Autograph. 2 pp. (27,9 × 21, 8 cm)
[…]/Scene=Arrangement til Operaen/<u>Iphigenia i Tauris.</u>
Signed and dated: 'Kjøbenhavn d. 21.e Januar 1874' [Written according to the diary most probably on 20.1. and 21.1.1874]
[DKKkt; Brevregistrant (January 21, 1874)

Choreographic note. Ms. Autograph. Ink. 2 pp. (format unknown)
<u>Schytternes Dands.</u>/[…]/<u>4.de Scene.</u>/[…]/<u>Dands af vilde Schytter</u>.
Unsigned and undated [Written according to the diary on 12.3.1874]
[USNYp; Dance Collection, call nos. *ZBD-71 (microfilm), and (S)*MGZMD 30 (photostat copy)
Bournonville's choreographic numbers ('1–12') in this manuscript clearly refer to his similar numbers written underneath the music in the répétiteur's copy for *Iphigénie en Tauride* (pp. 1–2).

Pantomimic note. Ms. Autograph. Black ink. 2 pp. (20,9 × 13,5 cm)
<u>Iphigenia paa Tauris</u>/(2.den Akt 5.te Scene) <u>Lento.</u>/[…]/<u>Chor og Pantomime</u> (Animato)
Unsigned and undated [Written according to the diary most probably in mid-March 1874]
[SSm; Daniel Fryklunds samling no. 127
Bournonville's choreographic numbers ('1–19') in this manuscript clearly refer to his similar numbers written underneath the music in the répétiteur's copy for *Iphigénie en Tauride* (pp. 3–5).

Musical sources:

Printed orchestral score. 1 vol. 216 pp. of which three are blank (31,9 × 25,7 cm)
IPHIGENIE/EN TAURIDE/[…]/PAR/M. LE CH.ER GLUCK.
Paris, Deslauriers [1879]
[DKKk; U 6 (KTA 783)
This printed French orchestral score was used for all performances of Gluck's opera in Copenhagen during Bournonville's lifetime. It contains several pencilled autographed notes by H. S. Paulli. According to these notes, the opera was performed with only two minor cuts in Act III (score no. 22) and Act V (score 28) of 13 and 19 bars respectively. Moreover, the end of Act IV was slightly changed by Paulli. The music for the two dance scenes in Act II is included in this volme on pp. '62–66' and '84–100' respectively.

Répétiteur's copy. Ms. Copy. Brown ink. 1 vol. 10 pp. of which one is blank (33,8 × 25,6 cm)
<u>Repetiteurparti</u>/[….]/<u>Iphigenia paa Tauris</u>/[…]/83./[…]/<u>Repetiteurparti/til/Iphigenia paa Tauris</u>
Unsigned and undated [1874]
[DKKk; MA ms 2915 (1) (KTA 783)
This répétiteur's copy contains the music for Act II (score nos. 8–10, 14–15, and 18) and Act IV (score no. 28). It also includes Bournonville's autographed choreographic numbers ('1–12', written with black ink) for the so-called 'Schytternes Dands' in Act II, scene 4 (score nos. 8–10) and his numbers ('1–19') for the *Pantomime scene* of the Furies in Act II, scene 5 (score nos. 14–15). All of these numbers refer to his two separate choreographic and mimic descriptions of the same scenes, which he most likely wrote during mid-March 1874.

The répétiteur's copy is included (on pp. 1–10) in a volume that also contains the répétiteur's copy for six other operas and plays, mounted at Copenhagen's Royal Theatre between 1856 and 1874.

Parts. Ms. Copy. 35 vol.
5 vl I, 5 vl II, 3 vla, 4 vlc e cb, fl 1/2, ob 1/2, cl 1/2, fag 1/2, cor 1/2, tr 1/2, trb 1/2/3, timp, gr cassa, piatti e tri. 52 vocal parts.
Unsigned and undated [1874]
[DKKk; KTA 783]

Other sources:

Costume drawing by E. Lehmann. Pencil and water colours (15 × 20 cm)
Arcona./<u>Scyther</u>
Unsigned and undated [c.1874]
[SSm; Daniel Fryklunds samling no. 255 (F 1328)
This drawing shows two costumes worn by the so-called 'vilde Scytter' in Act II, scene 4 (score nos. 8 and 9) of Bournonville's 1874 Copenhagen staging of Gluck's *Iphigénie en Tauride*. The drawing was erroneously identified by D. Fryklund in 1929 as showing two costumes from Bournonville's four-act national historical ballet *Arcona* (*see* 7.5.1875), hence the reference to this ballet in the title.

1.6.1874
A Folk Tale (Et Folkesagn).
This performance represents the third restaging of Bournonville's three-act romantic ballet *A Folk Tale* (*see* 20.3.1854) during his own lifetime. It was mounted for a special charity performance arranged in order to collects funds for the private pension fund of the Royal Danish Ballet, of which Bournonville was the founding member. According to his diary the production (in which M. Westberg played *Hilda* for the first time) was performed with only minor if any changes from Bournonville's previous staging on 3.4.1871.

In his diary he noted about the rehearsals and the first two performances:

23.3. and 24.4.1874: 'Indstudering paa Et Folkesagn'
4.4.: 'Indstudering til Frk [M.] Westberg'
7.4.: 'Repetition paa […] Et Folkesagn'
8.4., 9.4., and 10.4.: 'Prøve paa […] Et Folkesagn'
20.5.: 'Prøve paa <u>Et Folkesagn</u>'
23.5.: 'Theater- og Orchesterprøve paa <u>Et Folkesagn</u>'
29.5.: 'Prøve paa Et Folkesagn'
1.6.: 'I Theatret […] Vi gav 'Et Folkesagn' med Marie Westberg som Hilda, – gik ganske fortræffeligt'
1.11.: 'fulgt H. C. Andersen i Theatret, Et Folkesagn for fuldt Huus og livligt Bifald, gik ypperligt, <u>Westberg</u> ret paa sin Hylde'.

The 1874 production of *A Folk Tale* received 13 performances, the last of which was given on 24.1.1876. After 1.11. 1874 the ballet was performed with a partially new décor in Act II (by F. Ahlgrensson) arranged especially for the performances in the new Royal Theatre building.

The musical material employed this year was the same as that used for the previous 1871 production (now in DKKk, call nos. C II, 108, MA ms 2968, MA ms 2969, and KTB 274).

Other sources:

Sketch by F. Ahlgrensson of the décor for Act II. Water colours (20,3 × 30,1 cm)
[Untitled]
Unsigned and undated [1874]
[DKKkt; Ahlgrensson, Et Folkesagn, 2 (Nr. 12)

1.6.1874

Farewell to the Old Theatre, Ballet Epilogue (Farvel til det gamle Theater, Ballet=Epilog).

This ballet epilogue represents the last work Bournonville created for Copenhagen's old Royal Theatre building. It was mounted as part of a special charity performance given to collect funds for the private pension fund of the Royal Danish Ballet, of which Bournonville was the founding member. The work involved the participation of a large number of actors and dancers, and consisted of a series of selected excerpts from 14 Bournonville ballets. These had originally been created for the old Royal Theatre between 1829 and 1871 and represented those of his works which he intended to tranfer to the stage of new Royal Theatre building (inaugurated on 15.10.1874). According to the répétiteur's copy and the orchestral score, the excerpts were performed as a continuous (although not strictly chronological) potpourri, and contained the following scenes from 14 works:

(1) *La Somnambule, ou l'Arrivée d'un nouveau seigneur* (*see* 21.9.1829): The sleep-walking scene of *Thérèse* (Act II, scene 2, score no. 11).
(2) *Soldier and Peasant* (*see* 13.10.1829): The mime scene showing the homecoming of *Victor* (Score no. 4).
(3) *The Tyroleans* (*see* 6.3.1835): The scene in which *Fritz* dances with his bride (Score no. 4).
(4) *Faust* (*see* 25.4.1832): The scene in which *Mephistofeles* tempts *Martha* (Act II, score no. 17).
(5) *La Sylphide* (*see* 28.11.1836): Dances and groupings by the corps de ballet of sylphs (Act II, score nos. 4–5).
(6) *Waldemar* (*see* 28.10.1835): The ballet's final tableau to the accompaniment of the Danish song «Danmarks deiligst Vang og Vænge» (Act IV, score no. 32).
(7) *The Wedding Festival in Hardanger* (*see* 4.3.1853): The *Spring Dance* (Act II, scene 4, score no. 16).
(8) *Bellman or the Polish Dance at Grönalund* (*see* 3.6.1844): The scene in which *Bellman* teases *Ulla Wiinblad* with his songs to the accompaniment of the tune from C. M. Bellman's *Epistler*, no. 84, entitled «Hvila vid denna källa» (scene 2, score no. 2).
(9) *The Toreador* (*see* 27.11.1840): The *El Jaleo de Xeres* (Act I, score no. 6).
(10) *The Conservatoire, or A Proposal of Marriage through the Newspaper* (*see* 6.5.1849): The mime scene in which *Dufour* makes his proposal of marriage to the disguised *Eliza* (Act II, scene 3, score no. 9).
(11) *Napoli or The Fisherman and His Bride* (*see* 29.3.1842): The scene with *Gennaro* and *Teresina* reunited in the blue grotto to the accompaniment of the Neapolitan folk song «Te voglio bene assaje» (Act II, score no. 3).
(12) *The King's Corps of Volunteers on Amager* (*see* 19.2.1871): The *Reel* performed by a group of sailors and girls from Amager (Scene 11, score no. 14).
(13) *The Kermesse in Brüges, or The Three Gifts* (*see* 4.4.1851): The enforced dance of *Elenora* to the accompaniment of the magic viola da gamba played by *Carelis* (Act II, score no. 9).
(14) *The Valkyrie* (*see* 13.9.1861): The scene in which the viking *Bjørn* allows himself to be disarmed and entwined with garlands by the Greek women and dances off with them in a bacchantic chain (Act III, scene 5, score no. 24).

After this initial set of 14 excerpts (pieced together by V. C. Holm) followed a second set of more march-like processions divided into three sections. It showed the principal characters from all of the most important operas, plays and ballets in the current repertory of Copenhagen's Royal Theatre during this period. As a musical accompaniment for this set of processions Holm incorporated nearly all of I. P. E. Hart-

mann's triumphal march from the last scene in Act IV (score no. 35) of Bournonville's four-act Nordic mythological ballet *The Valkyrie* (*see* 13.9.1861).

In his diary Bournonville noted about the creation, the rehearsals, and the first and only performance of this ballet epilogue:

17.3.1874: 'Læst, skrevet og studeret [...] Eftermiddagen og Aftenen hjemme; componeret et nyt Efterspil 'Farvel til det gamle Theater.''
26.3.: 'Indstudering paa en mimisk Epilog, <u>Farvel til det gamle Theater</u>'
29.3: 'arbeidet paa [...] Farvel'
30.3. and 31.3.: 'Indstudering til <u>Farvel</u>'
1.4.: 'Prøve og Indstudering paa 'Farvel''
3.4.: 'skrevet '
7.4.: 'Repetition paa Farvel'
8.4.: 'Prøve paa Farvel'
11.4.: 'Indstudering paa Farvel (Introduction)'
22.5.: 'Bryderi og Løben omkring for at samle Personale til 'Favel'. Vrøvl med [F. W.] Hultmann, Fru [J. W.] Sødring og E Poulsen, Prøve og Indstudering paa 'Farvel'
24.5.: 'skrevet og redigeret Programmet til 'Farvel''
26.5.: 'Arrangement paa `Farvel´'
30.5.: 'Generalprøve paa `Farvel´'
31.5.: 'besørget Billetter til Forestillingen imorgen, hvis Indtægt lover at blive glimrende'
1.6.: 'I Theatret udsolgt Huus til dobbelte af forhøiede Priser til Indtægt for Ballettens Pensionskasse [...] Vi gav [...] tilsidst 'Farvel til det gamle Theater', der gjorde stormende Lykke og fandt et varmt og enthusiastisk Publicum, der gik ypperligt ind paa Idéen'.

Autograph sources:

Manuscript scenario. Ms. Autograph. Black ink. 3 pp. (22,5 × 17,8 cm)
<u>Farvel til det gamle Theater</u>/(Ballet = Epilog af August Bournonville)/fremstillet [changed to:] <u>opført</u> d 1.ste Juni 1874: ved Forestillingen/til Indtægt for Ballettens private Pensionsfond
Signed and dated: 'Kbhvn den 3.e April 1874:' [Written according to the diary between 17.3. and 3.4 1874]
[DKKk; NKS 3285 4° 2 F

Choreographic note. Ms. Autograph. Black ink. 4 pp. (21,2 × 13,9 cm)
<u>Søvngængersken</u> (J. Petersen)/[...]/<u>Soldat og Bonde</u> ([D.] Krum [S.] Rung)/[...]/<u>Tyrolerne</u> ([C. O. N.] Lauenberg, [A.] Flammé)/[...]/<u>Faust.</u> (L Hanne Fru [J.] Hansen)/[...]/<u>Les sylphides</u> ([A.] Scholl) & 8 danseuses/[...]/<u>Valdemar</u>/[...]/<u>Brudefærden</u>/[...]/<u>Bellman</u>/[...]/<u>Toreadoren</u>/[...]/<u>Conservatoriet</u>/[...]/<u>Napoli</u>/[...]/<u>Livjægerne</u>/[...]/<u>Kermessen</u>/[...]/<u>Valkyrien</u>.
Unsigned and undated [Written c. March–April 1874]
[Private collection (Copenhagen)
Bournonville's numerous autographed choreographic numbers included in this manuscript refer to similar numbers inserted in the répétiteur's copy for this work.

Mimic and choreographic note. Ms. Autograph. Ink. 2 pp. (format unknown)
<u>Farvel til det gamle Theater</u>/[...]/<u>1.ste Scene</u>
Unsigned and undated [Written c. March–April 1874]
[USNYp; Dance Collection, call nos. *ZBD-71 (microfilm), and (S)*MGZMD 30 (photostat copy)

Production note. Ms. Autograph. Black ink. 2 pp. (21 × 13,6 cm)
<u>Personliste</u>/til/Ballet-Epilogen – <u>Farvel til det gamle</u>/<u>Theater!</u>
Unsigned and undated [Written c. March-April 1874]
[Private collection (Copenhagen)

Musical sources:

Orchestral score/conductor's part (incomplete). Ms. Autograph (by V. C. Holm). 1 vol. Black ink and pencil. 24 pp. of which one is blank (34,7 × 26,1 cm)
Farvel!
Unsigned and undated [1874]
[DKKk; KTB 1032 (originally without number)
This (incomplete) score contains all the music for *Farewell to the Old Theatre* except for its final two numbers, which were borrowed from Bournonville's four-act ballet *The Valkyrie*. According to Holm's autographed pencilled notes on p. 23, these numbers were performed using I. P. E. Hartmann's original score for that ballet (now in DKKk, call no. C II, 114 (KTB 298)).

Répétiteur's copy. Ms. Autograph (by V. C. Holm). 1 vol. Black and brown ink. 30 pp. of which two are blank (33,8 × 25,5 cm with variants)
Farvel/til/Det gamle Theater/Bournonville/d.1.ste Juni 1874./26
Unsigned and dated (on the front cover): 'd. 1.ste Juni 1874.'
[DKKk; MA ms 3025 (KTB 1032, but originally without number)
This répétiteur's copy contains Bournonville's autographed choreographic numbers (written with black ink) throughout the volume. They refer to his separate choreographic notes for this work, written c. March–April 1874.

Parts. Ms. Copy. 34 vol.
3 vl I, 3 vl II, 2 vla, 3 vlc e cb, fl picc, fl 1/2, ob 1/2, cl 1/2, fag 1/2, cor 1/2/3/4, tr 1/2, Atrb, Ttrb, Btrb, tuba, timp, gr cassa, tri, arpa.
Unsigned and undated [1874]
[DKKk; KTB 1032 (originally without number)

Printed sources:

Printed scenario. 1 vol. 4 pp. (19,8 × 12,5 cm)
'Farvel til det gamle Theater!'/Ballet=Epilog i 1 Akt med Tableauer og Optog/[...]/af August Bournonville./Musiken arrangeret af W. Holm. Decorationerne af F. Ahlgrensson.
Kjøbenhavn, J. H. Schubothe/Bianco Luno, 1874.
[DKKk; 17, – 175 8°

27.8.1874
A Divertissement (et Divertissement). **Projected work.**
This projected work was clearly conceived during Bournonville's sojourn in Paris in the summer of 1874. This is clear from notes in his diary which read as follows:

27.8.1874: 'Læst og skrevet (anlagt et Divertissement)'
29.8.: 'hjem og componeret paa Divertissementet, skrevet i den Anledning om Musik til [P. C.] Johansson i St. Petersbourg'.

They seem to indicate that Bournonville was planning this divertissement for the inaugural performance at the new Royal Theatre building in Copenhagen on 15.10.1874. This theory is also supported by the reply from P. C. Johansson to Bournonville, dated 25.9.1874 (now in DKKk, call no. NKS 3258 4°). In this, Johansson acknowledges his receipt of Bournonville's letter from Paris, in which Bournonville had asked this old pupil of his to provide him with copies of some unspecified 'Russian ballet music' from the music archive of the Imperial Theatre in St. Petersburg. Moreover, according to Johansson's letter it seems that it was Bournonville's clear intention to make use of this Russian music in Copenhagen before October 1874.

Another possible identification of this projected 1874 divertissement is that it may represent Bournonville's earliest draft for what two years later became his two-act Russian ballet *From Siberia to Moscow* (*see* 7.12.1876). An indication which supports this assumption is found in his notes in his 1874 travel diary from his sojourn in Paris. Thus, on 11.8.1874 and during the following days Bournonville repeatedly visited the reading-room of the main library in Paris, where he studied what he described as 'a German translation of the Slavonic poems by Talvy' (i.e. T. A. L. Talvj). This book may thus represent Bournonville's first source of inspiration for this 1874 projected divertissement, which later was perhaps transformed into his 1876 ballet *From Siberia to Moscow*.

It is not possible to identify the divertissement any further.

15.10.1874
Tableau (Holberg.). Tableau (Oehlenschläger.).
This set of two tableaux was created for the inaugural performance at the new Royal Theatre building in Copenhagen. According to Bournonville's diary they were conceived during a sojourn in Paris in the late summer of 1874. Thus, on 7.8.1874 he noted about them while still in the French capital:

'Skrevet og componeret Tableauer til Indvielsen af Kbhvns ny Theater'.

In the same diary he noted about their later rehearsals in Copenhagen and the inauguration of the new theatre:

15.9.: 'skrevet og componeret'
21.9.: 'besøgt [...] [T.] Steins Atelier, Aftale om [L.] Holbergs Billede'
10.10.: 'Indstudering af Tableauerne'
14.10.: 'forberedt Alt til de to Tableauer, Holberg, Øehlenschläger [*sic*] og prøvet dem fra Kl 7–9'
15.10.: 'Forberedelser til Forestillingen [...] Festforestilling til det nÿ Theaters Indvielse [...] Mit Tableau (Holberg) [...] og til Slutning mit Tableau (Øehlenschläger). Stor Applaus og høitidelig Stemning. Sang og Ovation for Kongen [i.e. King Christian IX] og den kongelige Familie, forbi Kl 11'.

The tableaux, for which no musical sources have yet been traced, were performed 3 times, the last time on 17.10.1874.

Autograph sources:

Manuscript mise-en-scène. Ms. Autograph. Black ink. 2 pp. (22,5 × 17,8 cm)
Tableau./tilegnet Holberg ved Indvielsen af den nÿ Theaterbygning/comp. af A Bournonville:/Decoration/[...]/Tableau/tilegnet Øehlenschläger ved Indvielsen af den nÿ/Theaterbygning/Decoration.
Signed and dated: 'Paris den 7.e August 1874.'
[Private collection (Copenhagen)
This manuscript mise-en-scène contains a complete description of the décor and the characters from the plays and dramas of L. Holberg and A. Oehlenschläger shown in these tableaux.

Mauscript mise-en-scène. Ms. Autograph. Brown ink. 4 pp. (22,6 × 17,8 cm)
Holbergs Apotheose./ [...] /Decorations-Opstilling (til Holberg)/ [...]/Øehlenschlägers Apotheose/(Opstilling og Gruppering.)
Signed and dated: 'Kjøbenhavn d. 16.e September 1874.'
[Private collection (Copenhagen)
This mise-en-scène contains a complete description of the décor and the characters from most of the plays and dramas of L. Holberg and A. Oehlenschläger shown in these tableaux.

7.11.1874

Pas de deux (uncredited) performed by D. Krum and M. Westberg.

This (uncredited) dance is almost certainly identical with Bournonville's and V. C. Holm's earlier *Pas de deux*, created for Act I of D.-F.-E. Auber's five-act opera *La Muette de Portici* and first performed by the same dancers and a corps de ballet of eight women on 2.9.1873. According to his diary Bournonville personally directed the two rehearsals held of this dance on 6.11. and 7.11.1874, but did not attend the opening night because of his departure on a trip to Berlin on that day. The *Pas de deux* was (according to the posters) performed four times by Krum and Westberg in 1874, the last time on 21.12.1874. It is not possible to identify the dance any further.

4.12.1874

The Conservatoire, or A Proposal of Marriage through the Newspaper (Conservatoriet, eller Et Avisfrieri).

This performance represents Bournonville's fourth and last staging in Copenhagen of his two-act ballet-vaudeville *The Conservatoire, or A Proposal of Marriage through the Newspaper* (*see* 6.5.1849). It seems to have been mounted this year with only minor if any changes from his two previous productions on 15.9.1865 and 28.9.1870. This is clear from his 1874 diary in which he noted about this performance:

23.11.1874: 'Indstudering paa Balletten Conservatoriet'
24.11., 25.11., and 26.11.: 'Indstudering paa Conservatoriet'
29.11.: 'holdt en lille Indstudering paa Conservatoriet'
30.11: '3½ Times Prøve og Indstudering paa Conservatoriet'
1.12: 'Theaterprøve paa Conservatoriet'
2.12.: 'Sygemelding fra <u>Anna Scholl</u>. Arbeide den hele formiddag med remplacering ved <u>Johanne Petersen</u> [...] Aftenprøve paa <u>Conservatoriet</u>'
3.12.: 'Repetition paa Conservatoriet'
4.12.: 'besøgt den syge Anna Scholl [...] Conservatoriet for udsolgt Huus og meget Bifald, gik i det Hele smukt. Folk morede sig godt'.

The 1874 staging received 21 performances during Bournonville's lifetime, the last of which was given on 24.3.1879.

The musical material employed this year was the same as that used for the previous 1870 production (now in DKKk, call nos. MA ms 1550 and KTB 264, and in USNYp, Dance Collection, call no. *ZBD-74 (microfilm)).

20.12.1874

Pas de trois (uncredited) performed by E. Hansen, J. Petersen, and C. Schousgaard.

According to a note in the rehearsal book of A. Fredstrup on this day (reading: 'opført La Ventana (2. Afd.)'), this (uncredited) dance is clearly identical with the *Pas de trois* in Bournonville's second and final version of his Spanish ballet divertissement *La Ventana* (*see* 6.10.1856). The 1874 staging represents the first time this dance was ever given as a separate divertissement at Copenhagen's Royal Theatre. Bournonville, who attended the second performance of it on 5.1.1875, noted that day in his diary:

'seet Dandsen af <u>La Ventana</u>, der gik særdeles smukt'.

The *Pas de trois* received 4 performances as a separate diver-

tissement in Bournonville's lifetime, the last of which was given on 4.3.1875.

The musical material employed this year was most probably the same as that used since the 1856 première of *La Ventana* (now in DKKk, call nos. MA ms 1127, MA ms 2997, KTB 300, and KTB 1055).

20.12.1874

Seguedilla (uncredited) performed by D. Krum, J. T. Klüver, C. Iversen, A. Scholl, E. Gade, and C. Larsen.

According to a note in the rehearsal book of A. Fredstrup on this day (reading: 'opført La Ventana (2. Afd.)') this (uncredited) dance is clearly identical with *La Seguedilla (after Taglioni)* in Bournonville's second and final version of his Spanish ballet divertissement *La Ventana* (*see* 6.10.1856). The 1874 staging represents the first time this dance was ever given as a separate divertissement at Copenhagen's Royal Theatre. Bournonville, who attended the second performance of it on 5.1.1875, noted that day in his diary:

'seet Dandsen af <u>La Ventana</u>, der gik særdeles smukt'.

The *Seguedilla* received 4 performances as a separate divertissement during Bournonville's lifetime, the last of which was given on 4.3.1875.

The musical material employed this year was most probably the same as that used since the 1856 première of *La Ventana* (now in DKKk, call nos. MA ms 1127, MA ms 2997, KTB 300, and KTB 1055).

1875

1.1.1875

The Flower Festival in Genzano (Section II) (Blomsterfesten i Genzano, (2den Afdeling)).

According to some of the musical material for this abridged divertissement version of Bournonville's one-act ballet *The Flower Festival in Genzano* (*see* 19.12.1858), it consisted of the ballet's opening mime scene (score no. 3) followed by a shortened version of the second section (score nos. 11–13 and the *Finale*). It was arranged and mounted personally by Bournonville, and received 16 performances during his own lifetime, the last of which was given on 29.5.1879. In his diary he noted about the rehearsals and the first two performances:

28.12.1874: 'Prøve paa Dandsen til Blomsterfesten og Decorations-Skue'
30.12.: 'Prøve paa Blomsterfesten'
31.12.: 'Theaterprøve paa Blomsterfesten (2' Afdeling)'
1.1.1875: 'Kl 9 i Theatret hvor man gav [...] 2' Afdeling af Blomsterfesten der gjorde megen Lykke'
2.1.: 'I Theatret Blomsterfestens 2' Afdeling, der gik endnu smukkere end igaar'.

The musical material employed this year was most likely the same as that used for the previous production of the entire ballet on 11.9.1872 (now in DKKk, call nos. C I, 114 k, and KTB 267). Moreover, a later répétiteur's copy dating from the restaging of the same divertissement version on 2.3.1884 is now in DKKkt (call no. KTB 267 3. B 2).

11.1.1875

La Dame blanche (Den hvide Dame).
This performance represents the first time F.-A. Boyeldieu's three-act comic opera (*see* 1.10.1850) was performed in Copenhagen's new Royal Theatre building, and the last time that it was mounted under Bournonville's personal direction. In his diary he noted about the production:

16.12.1874: 'Textprøve paa <u>Den hvide Dame</u> og om Aftenen Theaterprøve ved Claveer paa samme Opera'
19.12.: 'Prøve paa Dandse [...] til Den hvide Dame'
21.12. and 26.12.: 'Prøve paa Den hvide Dame'
27.12.: 'Forandring i Theatret formedelst [H. E.] Christoffersens Upasselighed. Istedetfor <u>Den hvide Dame</u> gaaer En Kone der springer ud af Vinduet'
7.1. and 8.1.1875: 'Theaterprøve paa [...] Den hvide Dame'
11.1.: 'I Theatret endelig <u>Den hvide Dame</u>, der gik udmærket smukt'.

The production, which seems to have been mounted with only minor if any changes from Bournonville's previous staging on 4.9.1868, received 18 performances during his lifetime, the last of which was given on 5.2.1878.

The musical material employed this year was the same as that used for the 1868 production (now in DKKk, call nos. U 6, MA ms 3047, and KTA 246).

9.2.1875

Pas de deux (uncredited) performed by D. Krum and M. Westberg.
This (uncredited) dance is almost certainly identical with Bournonville's and V. C. Holm's new *Pas de deux* created as an incorporated divertissement in Act I of D.-F.-E. Auber's five-act opera *La Muette de Portici* and first performed by the same two dancers and a corps de ballet of eight women on 2.9.1873. According to the rehearsal book of A. Fredstrup, only one rehearsal was held of the dance under Bournonville's personal direction on 9.2.1875. It is described in his diary as follows:

'Pas de deux Hr Krum Frk Westberg med 8 Balletdandserinder'.

Bournonville attended the performance that same evening, but made no specific remarks about it in his diary. The *Pas de deux* was performed only once by Krum and Westberg in 1875. It is not possible to identify the dance any further.

17.2.1875

Divertissement of the ballet La Somnambule (Divertissement af Balletten Søvngængersken).
According to Bournonville's choreographic notes in the 1868 répétiteur's copy for his Copenhagen version of J. Aumer's three-act pantomimic ballet *La Somnambule, ou l'Arrivée d'un nouveau seigneur* (now in DKKk, call no. MA ms 2985) this divertissement version was based on selected and partially rechoreographed excerpts from score nos. 7, 7 B, and 7 C of Act I (*see* 21.9.1829 and 2.10.1868). The divertissement was arranged and mounted especially for the début of Bournonville's pupil, A. Flammé, who performed the rôle of *Thérèse* partnered by D. Krum (as *Edmond*) and joined by a corps de ballet of four men and six women. In his diary Bournonville noted about the staging:

10.2.1875: 'Indstudering med [A.] Flammé paa Søvngængersken'
11.2.: 'Indstudering paa Divertissement'
12.2.: 'indstuderet Corps de Ballets til Divertissementet'
13.2. and 15.2.: 'Prøve paa Divertissementet'
16.2.: 'Theater- og Orchesterprøve paa Divertissement af Søvngængersken'
17.2.: 'Orchesterprøve paa Divertissementet. I Theatret [...] Debut for Athalia Flammé, der dandsede smukt og gjorde megen Lÿkke'.

The divertissement received 8 performances during Bournonville's lifetime, the last of which was given on 1.3.1876.

The musical material employed for it was the same as that used for the previous complete 1868 staging of *La Somnambule, ou l'Arrivée d'un nouveau seigneur* (now in DKKk, call nos. C I, 259 f, C I, 259 f (b), MA ms 2985, and KTB 287).

Autograph sources:

Choreographic note. Ms. Autograph. Ink. 1 p. (format unknown)
<u>Divertissement af Søvngængersken</u>/efter de to Scener.
Unsigned and undated [c. February 1875]
[USNYp; Dance Collection, call nos. *ZBD-71 (microfilm), and (S)*MGZMD 30 (photostat copy)
This choreographic note describes the choreography of the opening movement for the corps de ballet (i.e. the *Contredanse*) in Bournonville's 1875 divertissement version of *La Somnambule, ou l'Arrivée d'un nouveau seigneur*. It also includes his autographed choreographic numbers ('1–11') which refer to similar numbers written underneath the music in the 1868 répétiteur's copy for this ballet (score no. 7, pp. 28–35).

Choreographic note. Ms. Autograph. Ink. 2 pp. (format unknown)
Finale
Unsigned, dated 'Ce 12 fevrier 1875'
[USNYp; Dance Collection, call nos. *ZBD-71 (microfilm), and (S)*MGZMD 30 (photostat copy)
This choreographic note describes the choreography of the concluding movement in Bournonville's 1875 divertissement version of *La Somnambule, ou l'Arrivée d'un nouveau seigneur*. It also includes his autographed choreographic numbers ('1–16') which refer to similar numbers written underneath the music in the 1868 répétiteur's copy for this ballet (score no. 7 C, pp. 44–49).

Production note. Ms. Autograph, Black ink. 1 p. (14 × 21,1 cm)
<u>Divertissement af Balletten Søvngængersken</u>/arrangeret af Hof Balletmester Bournonville.
Unsigned and undated [c. February 1875]
DKKkt; F.M. (Ballet, læg S)

Production note. Ms. Autograph. Black ink. 1 p. (21,5 × 17,7 cm)
<u>Divertissement af Balletten Søvngængersken.</u>
Unsigned and undated [c. February 1875]
[DKKkt; F.M. (Ballet, læg S)

17.3.1875

Tannhäuser und der Sängerkrieg auf der Wartburg (Tannhäuser og Sangerkrigen paa Wartburg).
The 1875 Copenhagen première of R. Wagner's three-act opera (first performed at Königlich Sächsisches Hoftheater in Dresden on 19.10.1845) was mounted with Bournonville's general mise-en-scène and with his choreography for the opening scene of Act I (score no. 1). The latter is described in the printed orchestral score (p. '40') as follows:

'Die Bühne stellt das Innere des Venusberges dar. Weite Grotte, welche sich im Hintergrunde durch eine Biegung nach rechts wie unabsehbar dahin zieht. Im fernsten sichtbaren Hintergrunde dehnt sich ein bläulicher See aus; in ihm erblickt man die badenden Gestalten von Najaden; auf seinen erhöheten Ufer=Vorsprüngen sind Sirenen gelagert. Im äussersten Vordergrunde links liegt Venus auf einem Lager ausgestreckt, vor ihr halb knieend Tannhäuser, das Haupt in ihrem Schoose. Die ganze Grotte ist durch rosiges Licht erleuchtet, den Mittelgrund nimmt eine Gruppe tanzender Nymfen ein; auf etwas erhöhten Vorsprüngen an den Seiten der Grotte sind liebende Paare gelagert, von denen sich einzelne nach und nach in den Tanz der Nymfen mischen'.

According to autographed pencilled notes by H. S. Paulli in the opera's printed orchestral score and Bournonville's autographed notes in the répétiteur's copy, only three musical cuts were made in this opera at its Copenhagen premiére. They were as follows:

(1) In the *Dance scene*, performed by the bacchantes during the opening scene of Act I (score no. 1), Paulli and Bournonville made a minor omission of 16 bars.
(2) At the end of Act II, score no. 16 (i.e. *Der Sängerkrieg*) Paulli made a musical cut of 63 measures.
(3) At the end of the so-called 'Chor der jungen Pilger' («Heil! Heil! Der Gnade Wunder Heil») in Act II (score no. 24) Paulli omitted a section of 12 bars.

In his diary Bournonville noted about the rehearsals and the Copenhagen première of Wagner's opera:

3.9.1860: 'Om Eftermiddagen læst Tannhäuser af [R.] Wagner'
12.5.1868: 'lang Conference med [F. J. G.] Berner og [H. S.] Paulli'
21.5.: 'Gjennemlæst Partituret til Wagners Tannhaüser som jeg mod-tog fra Erslew [i.e. J. E. Erslev]'
23.5.: 'Brev til […] Justitsraad Berner angaaende Tannhaüser'
10.1.1875: 'Costumemøde paa Tannhäuser'
12.1.: 'Decorationsprøve paa Tannhäuser'
20.1.: 'componeret Dandsen til Tannhäuser'
28.1.: 'ordnet Lister til Tannhäuser'
29.1.: 'Indstudering paa Dandsen til Tannhäuser efter en diabolsk Musik'
1.2.: '1.ste Theaterprøve paa Tannhäuser 1.e Akts 1.ste Afdeling'
4.2.: 'Overværet Musikprøve paa de to første Akter af Tannhäuser'
14.2.: 'Costumemøde paa Tannhäuser'
15.2.: 'Resten af Dagen hjemme skrevet'
16.2.: 'Decorationsprøve paa Tannhäuser, besørget adskilligt'
17.2.: 'Instruction paa 1.e og 2' Akt af Tannhäuser'
19.2.: 'Repetition paa Dandsen til Tannhäuser'
22.2.: 'Prøve paa Tannhäuser 1.e Akt'
23.2.: 'Prøve paa 2' Akt af Tannhäuser'
28.2.: 'Theaterprøve med Orchester paa 1.ste og 2' Akt af Tann-häuser'
1.3: 'Theaterprøve paa 3.die Akt af Tannhäuser'
5.3. and 6.3.: 'Prøve paa […] 3.die Akt af Tannhäuser'
8.3.: 'Decorationsprøve til Tannhäuser'
9.3.: 'stor og fuldstændig Theaterprøve paa Tannhäuser'
10.3.: 'fuldstændig Prøve paa Tannhäuser'
12.3.: 'Theaterprøve paa Tannhäuser'
15.3.: 'Generalprøve i Costume paa Tannhäuser (gik smukt)'
17.3.: 'Slutnings=Arrangement paa Tannhäuser […] I Theatret 1.ste Forestilling af Tannhäuser, der i det Hele gik særdeles smukt og vandt Bifald endskjøndt mod Formodning Huset ikke var fuldt besat'.

As a result of a later change in the décor for Act III, Bour-nonville revised his mise-en-scène for this act prior to a per-formance of the opera on 3.9.1875. About this change he noted in his diary on 26.8.1875:

'Prøve paa Dandsene til […] Tannhäuser. – Arrangement paa 3.die Akt af Tannhäuser med den nÿ Decoration'.

Tannhäuser und der Sängerkrieg auf der Wartburg received 21 performances in Copenhagen during Bournonville's life-time, the last of which was given on 5.4.1879.

Autograph sources:

Manuscript mise-en-scène. Ms. Autograph. Brown ink. 5 pp. (21,1 × 17,2 cm)
Tannhäuser / (Scene = Arangement)
Signed and dated: 'Kbhvn den 16 Februar 1875.' [Written according to the diary most probably on 15.2. and 16.2.1875]
[SSm; Daniel Fryklunds samling no. 146

Production note. Ms. Autograph (partially in another's hand). Black ink, red pen, and pencil. 3 pp. (22,7 × 18,3 cm)
1.ste Akts 1.ste Scene./[…]/1.ste Akt 3.die Scene./[…]/Tannhäu-ser/1.ste Akts 4.e Scene./[…]/2.den Akt (4.e Scene)/[…]/3.die Akt.
Unsigned and undated [Written according to the diary most prob-ably on 28.1.1875]
[SSm; Daniel Fryklunds samling no. 146

Musical sources:

Printed orchestral score. 1 vol. 328 pp. of which two are blank (32,3 × 25,5 cm)
784. / Tannhäuser. / Partitur. / […] / Tannhäuser/und/Der Sänger-krieg auf Wartburg/VON/RICHARD WAGNER.
Berlin/Dresden, C. F. Meser, pl. no. H. M. 670 [c.1875]
[DKKk; U 6 (KTA 784) (mu 9208.3184)
This German printed orchestral score contains A. Hertz's Danish translation written (with brown ink) next to the original German text. The music for the *Dance scene* in Act I, scene 1 (score no. 1) is included on pp. '40–54'.

Répétiteur's copy. Ms. Copy. Brown ink. 1 vol. 12 pp. of which one is blank (34,1 × 25,5 cm)
Repetiteurpartier/til/1, Tannhäuser/ […] /84./ […] /Repetiteur-parti/til/Tannhäuser
Unsigned and undated [1874]
[DKKk; MA ms 2916 (1) (KTA 784)
This répétiteur's copy contains the complete music for the *Dance scene* in Act I, scene 1 (score no. 1) in ???. It also includes Bournon-ville's autographed choreographic numbers ('1–24', written with black ink) which seem to refer to his separate (not yet traced) nota-tion of this scene, written (according to his diary) on 20.1.1875. The répétiteur's copy is included on pp. 1–11 in a volume that also con-tains the répétiteur's copies for five other operas, plays, and occa-sional works, mounted at Copenhagen's Royal Theatre between 1875 and 1878.

Parts. Ms. Copy. 44 + 16 vol.
5 vl I, 5 vl II, 3 vla, 3 vlc, 3 cb, fl picc, fl 1/2, ob 1/2, cl 1/2/3, fag 1/2, cor 1/2/3/4, tr 1/2/3, trb 1/2/3, tuba, timp, gr cassa, piatti e tri, arpa. On stage: vla 1/2, vlc 1/2, cor ingl, cor 1/2/3/4, tr 1/2/3, trb 1/2/3, tuba. 17 vocal parts.
Unsigned and undated [1875]
[DKKk; KTA 784
This set of parts (for which the choral parts are missing) was used for all performances of *Tannhäuser* in Copenhagen during Bournon-ville's lifetime.

27.3.1875
A Quadrille performed by sixteen couples at a masked ball given for the artists of Copenhagen's Royal Theatre in the foyer of that theatre.

For a costume ball arranged on this day by the artists of the Royal Theatre, Bournonville choreographed this *Quadrille*, which was performed by 16 couples, with the women dressed as valkyries. The dance, which according to Bournonville's diary seem to have been set to music by B. Dahl, consisted of the following three movements:

(1) Quadrille af Valkyrier.
(2) Valse.
(3) Galoppade. [*sic*]

In his diary Bournonville noted about the *Quadrille* which was performed only once:

28.1.1875: 'Aftale med Balduin Dahl'
18.3.: 'componeret en Quadrille til Aftenselskabet'
22.3.: 'Indstudering paa en Quadrille til Aftenselskabet (16 Par)'
24.3.: 'Prøve paa Quadrillen'
27.3.: 'Generalprøve paa Quadrillen hos [G.] Brodersen, der tracterede Selskabet gentilt [...] forberedet mig til Festen paa Theatret. – Kl 8$^{1}/_{2}$ samledes vi, omtrent 90 i Tallet af alle Theatrets Brancher, drak The i Foyéeren og spiste til Aften i Concertsalen; Kl 12 begyndte Dandsene som fortsattes indtil Kl. – Jeg gik ved Cotillonen Kl 3, og kom først tilsengs Kl 4. – Alt var i høieste Grad vellykket'.

No musical sources for Bournonville's 1874 *Quadrille* have yet been traced.

Autograph sources:

Choreographic note. Ms. Autograph. Brown ink. 2 pp. (21,2 × 12,6 cm)
Quadrille af Valkyrier./ [...] /(16 Par)/ [...] /Valse./ [...] /Galoppade. [*sic*]
Unsigned and undated [Written according to the diary on 18.3. 1875]
[DKKk; NKS 3285 4° 3 V–Z
This manuscript contains Bournonville's choreographic numbers ('1–16', '1–2', and '1–7') which seem to refer to similar numbers in the (not yet traced) music score for his 1874 *Quadrille*.

7.5.1875
Arcona.

This four-act ballet was deliberately created as Bournonville's first major work for Copenhagen's new Royal Theatre building, inaugurated only seven months previously, on 15.10.1874. It represents Bournonville's last full-length ballet within the national-historical sphere, and depicted the crusade of King Valdemar the Great of Denmark in 1168–69 against the Wendish pirates, and his Christianizing of the Slavs of Rügen.

The score was composed by I. P. E. Hartmann except for two dances in the third scene of Act I, which were arranged and composed by V. C. Holm and C. C. Møller as follows:

(1) *The Proposal Dance (Frierdandsen)* in Act I, scene 3 (score nos. 4–5): For the opening section of this divertissement Holm employed J. F. Fröhlich's much earlier score for a similar dance of that name. It was originally performed in Act II (score no. 9) of Bournonville's four-act national-historical ballet *The Childhood of Erik Menved (see* 12.1.1843). In *Arcona* this music was rearranged and reorchestrated by Holm, who also added a 'Reel', a 'Tempo di Marcia', and a 'Galop' (all presumably composed by himself).
(2) *The Weavers Dance (Væverdandsen)* in Act I, scene 3 (score no. 6): The music for this dance was composed and arranged by C. C. Möller. He employed the tune of an old folk song, entitled «Nu væve vi Vadmel, nu slaae vi det sammen», deriving from the isle of Als in the region of Southern Jutland. This is clear from Møller's printed piano score for this dance, which was published by W. Hansen in Copenha-

gen in 1875 (a copy is now in DKKk, call no. D 6). According to a letter from Bournonville to G. Rosenkilde (dated 21.1.1875, now in DKKt, call no. Brevregistrant: Bournonville) the choreography of *The Weavers Dance* was based on an authentic folk dance from Als. Bournonville himself had seen this dance performed by the local peasants as part of the festivities there at the wedding of his son, E. Bournonville, to D. Ahlmann on 23.6.1873. Thus, in his letter to Rosenkilde the *Weavers Dance* is described as follows: 'Det Vink, De var saa god at give mig for et Par Aar siden i Anledning af den nationale Væverdands har jeg i sandhed havt Nytte af, navnlig ved at see samme Dands udført med tilhørende Sang, ved min Søns Bryllup paa Als hos Proprietair [N.] Ahlmann; kort efter modtog jeg af Herr Musikdirektør C. C. Møller en Bearbeidelse af Musiken, som jeg har lagt til Grund for en munter Bondedands i min nÿ Ballet Arcona, hvor De vil komme til at see Væverdandsen arrangeret for Scenen og som jeg troer, af en ret god Virkning'.

Moreover, in Act II, scene 4 (score no. 14) Hartmann incorporated most of the music for his much earlier *Processional March (Optog)* in score no. 9 of his one-act singspiel *Little Kirsten (see* 6.1.1848).

In his diary Bournonville noted about the long and rather troublesome creation of *Arcona*, which represents the most extensively notated work among his full-length ballets:

2.5.1873: 'Paabegyndt Programmet til en nÿ stor Ballet Arcona, om Gud vil, bestemt til at opføres paa det ny Theater med Musik af [I. P. E.] Hartmann?'
3.5.: 'Dagen beskjæftiget med min nÿ store Ballet, hvoraf jeg skrev 2' og 3' Akt færdig'
4.5.: 'fuldendt Concepten til Balletten Arcona, og takket den Almægtige for hans Naade mod min Aand og mod mit Legeme'
5.5.: 'reenskrevet min ny Ballet'
6.5.: 'afsendt mit Program til [F. J. G.] Berner'
8.5.: 'forelæst min Ballet'
14.5.: 'Conference med Berner. Besøg hos [E.] Lehmann'
18.5.: 'Brev fra [...] samt mit Program antaget fra Berner. Brev til Hartmann med Manuscriptet'
30.5.: 'Conference med Prof. Hartmann om Balletten Arcona'
19.6.: 'Brev fra Hartmann'
1.7.: 'været to Gange paa Stationen for at modtage Prof. Hartmann, der kom Kl 1, og arbeidede sammen med mig, samt bragte mig de tre første Numre af Arcona. Han blev hos os til Middag tilsammen med [H. S.] Paulli og Frue. Han rejste Kl 4$^{1}/_{4}$'
6.8.: 'Brev fra Hartmann, Svar tilbage med Musik=Program'
11.9.: 'arbeidet med Hartmann'
14.9.: 'Lehmann hos os'
18.9., 8.10., and 19.10.: 'arbeidet med Hartmann'
23.10.: 'begyndt Compositionen af Arcona efter Hartmanns Musik'
24.10.: 'componeret'
27.10.: 'arbeidet med Hartmann'
29.10., 30.10., and 31.10.: 'componeret'
1.11.: 'skrevet, arbeidet med Hartmann'
2.11. and 3.11.: 'componeret'
10.11.: 'componeret paa Arcona'
22.11.: 'componeret paa min store Ballet og confereret med Hartmann'
16.12.: 'arbeidet med Hartmann'
3.1., 6.1., and 8.1.1874: 'skrevet og componeret'
10.1.: 'componeret'
11.1.: 'arbeidet med Hartmann, der har leveret smukke Sager til 3.die Akt af Arcona'
8.2.: 'arbeidet med Hartmann'
13.4.: 'Arbeidet med Hartmann'
23.5.: 'besøgt Hartmann'
11.8.: 'Arbeidet paa Besætningen i Arcona'
5.10.: 'skrevet til Hartmann'
16.10.: 'skrevet og componeret paa Theatret'
21.10.: 'Morgentour ud til [V. C.] Holms [...] skrevet paa Theatret'

22.10.: 'studeret paa min store nÿ Ballet'

23.10.: 'componeret [...] 1.ste Indstudering paa Arcona (Absalon og Saxo)'

24.10.: '2.den Indstudering (Börnenes Dands)'

26.10.: 'Repetition paa det Lærte'

27.10.: 'skrevet og componeret'

28.10.: 'componeret'

29.10.: 'Skrivelse til Chefen angaaende Decorationer, Beslutning at reise til Berlin og tydsk Brev til [P.] Gropius [...] componeret'

30.10.: 'I Theatret skrevet og componeret'

1.11.: 'componeret Dandse til Arcona'

2.11.: 'componeret'

3.11.: 'Indstudering paa Frierdandsen til Arcona, Brev fra Gropius [...] Conference angaaende min forestaaende Reise til Berlin'

4.11.: 'Indstudering paa Væverdandsen til Arcona'

5.11.: 'componeret en Dands til Arcona [...] skrevet Brev til Professor Gropius [...] Repetition til Arcona'

9.11.: 'til Gropius (Georgenstrasse 37-38) med hvem jeg arbeidede paa det Behageligste'

10.11.: 'arbeidet med Gropius, der allerede havde en Model til Grathe Hede færdig, besluttet at reise endnu iaften'

13.11.: 'Indstudering paa Narrens Dands til Arcona, Decorationsmøde med [V.] Güllich angaaende Arcona'

14.11. and 15.11.: 'skrevet og componeret'

16.11.: 'Indstudering paa Arcona (Herrernes og Jomfruernes Dands) [...] arbeidet med Hartmann'

17.11.: 'componeret [...] componeret paa 3.die Akt af Arcona og fortsat dette Arbeide hjemme hele Eftermidagen'

18.11.: 'componeret [...] lagt Text under Hartmanns Musik til Arcona og bragt ham 3.die Akt'

19.11.: 'Skrevet og componeret'

20.11.: 'arbeidet med [F.] Ahlgrensson, Brev fra Gropius besvaret strax'

21.11.: 'Conference med Chefen og Ahlgrensson om Decorationerne til Arcona'

23.11.: 'arbeidet med Hartmann. Resten af Aftenen hjemme, Lehmann besøgte os med Tegninger til Arcona'

24.11.: 'Brev fra Gropius og Svar tilbage [...] componeret'

28.11.: 'componeret'

1.12.: 'skrevet Personlister til Arcona'

4.12.: 'skrevet og componeret'

5.12.: 'Repetition paa Arcona [...] udarbeidet Costumeringen til Arcona'

6.12.: 'arbeidet paa Theatret'

7.12.: 'Indstudering paa Dandsen til 3.die Akt af Arcona'

9.12.: 'Kl 5½ Indstudering paa 3.e Akts Dands i Arcona'

10.12.: 'componeret til Arcona'

11.12.: 'componeret'

12.12.: 'Indstudering paa Dands til 1.ste Akt af Arcona, skrevet og componeret'

14.12.: 'componeret'

15.12.: 'Prøve med Indstudering paa Offringen i 3.e Akt af Arcona, componeret, Besøg af Hartmann'

16.12.: 'Repetition paa Offerdandsen'

17.12.: 'Indstudering paa 3.die Akt [...] arbeidet med Hartmann og componeret paa Theatret'

18.12.: 'Indstudering paa 3.die Akt'

20.12.: 'Møde paa Theatret i Anledning af Costumerne til Arcona [...] componeret, skrevet og arbeidet med Hartmann'

22.12.: 'Prøve og Indstudering fra 10. til 12., færdig med Mazurka'en som er den ottende Dands og Finale til 3.die Akt. Costumemøde for Damedragterne til Arcona'

23.12.: 'Repetition paa Alt hvad der er lært til Arcona'

25.12.: 'componeret'

28.12.: 'skrevet og componeret'

30.12: 'Indstudering paa 2' Akt af Arcona (Absalon, Esbern, Fru Inge og Huldfried) Betty Schnell fortræffelig'

31.12.: 'arbeidet med Hartmann'

2.1.1875: 'Repetition paa 3.e Akt af Arcona [...] Møde hos [A. C. P.] Linde i Anledning af Decorationer til Arcona'

4.1.: 'Indstudering paa 2' Akt af Arcona, componeret'

5.1.: 'stor Indstudering paa 2' Akt af Arcona'

8.1.: 'arbeidet med Hartmann'

9.1.: 'componeret [...] Indstudering paa 2' Akt af Arcona'

12.1.: 'Repetition paa alt det Lærte af Arcona'

13.1.: 'Tidlig op og Kl 9 paa Theatret, hvor jeg componerede tre Scener til 4.e Akt af Arcona [...] Indstudering paa bemeldte Scener, der lover godt'

14.1.: 'componeret paa 4.e Akt'

15.1.: 'Indstudering paa 4.e Akt [...] arbeidet med Hartmann'

16.1.: 'Repetition paa 4.e og 3.e Akt af Arcona [...] skrevet og componeret'

18.1.: 'arbeidet paa Personlisterne til Arcona'

19.1.: 'Skrevet, componeret, repeteret 3.die Akt og fuldendt den første Afdeling af 4.e Akt. – reenskrevet Personlisterne til Balletten'

23.1.: 'besøgt Theatermaler-Atelierne'

25.1.: 'Prøve paa Arcona 2' og 3' Akt med Complettering'

26.1.: 'Prøve paa 4.e Akt af Arcona'

30.1.: 'Prøve paa Arcona hvoraf jeg præsenterede 3.e og 4.e Akt for Chefen og Hartmann m: fl.'

5.2.: 'Prøve paa og 2' Akt af Arcona'

6.2.: 'begyndt Reenskrivningen af mit Balletprogram'

18.2.: 'Program til Hartmann'

19.2.: 'Ahlgrenssons tvende Decorationer fortræffelige'

20.2.: 'arbeidet med Hartmann'

22.2.: 'Møde angaaende Decorationer'

26.2.: 'reenskrevet paa mit Balletprogram'

27.2.: 'reenskrevet paa mit Program'

1.3.: 'Skrevet og fuldendt mit Program'

2.3.: 'Prøve paa Arconas 4.de Akt med Assistance [...] Møde med Ahlgrensson hos Linde om Decorationen til 3' Akt! [...] Modtaget den sidste Scene Musik af Hartmann'

3.2.: 'Indstudering paa Tableauerne til Arcona'

4.2.: 'læst Correctur'

5.2.: 'Oprørt over Ahlgrenssons hensynsløse Opførsel, da han istedetfor at begynde paa min Ballet, er i fuldt Arbeide med Decorationer til Christiania Theater, opsagde jeg ham aldeles og vil vente indtil Güllich kan blive færdig med alle fem Decorationer'

7.3.: 'Stor Uforskammethed og Tølperagtighed af Ahlgrensson'

9.3.: 'Conference i Anledning af Ahlgrenssons Uforskammethed'

11.3.: 'stor Repetition paa Arcona'

13.3.: 'componeret paa den sidste Scene af Arcona'

15.3.: 'udarbeidet Lister m m til Balletten Arcona'

16.3.: 'componeret og indstuderet Slutning-Scenen til Balletten Arcona'

18.3.: 'Repetition paa 4' Akt af Arcona [...] Brev fra Gropius'

19.3.: 'Skrevet Svar til Gropius'

20.3.: 'Stor Arrangementsprøve paa 1.ste Akt af Arcona'

23.3.: 'Arrangementprøve paa 1.ste Akt af Arcona'

24.3.: 'Costumemøde fra 6 til 8½'

30.3.: 'Arrangement paa 2' Akt af Arcona'

1.4.: 'Arrangementsprøve paa Arconas 2' Akt'

3.4.: 'Arrangementsprøve paa 2' Akt af Arcona [...] Besøg hos [...] Hartmann'

5.4.: 'Modtaget Honorar for Programmet til Arcona'

7.4.: 'Repetition 3' og 4.e Akt af Arcona. Musik-prøve paa 2' Akten'

8.4.: 'Brev fra Gropius'

9.4.: 'Arrangement paa 1.ste 2' og 3.die Akt af Arcona'

11.4.: 'Musikprøve'

12.4.: 'Svar til Gropius – Arrangementprøve i en Time'

14.4.: 'Prøve paa Dandsene til Arcona'

15.4.: 'Musikprøve paa 1.ste Akt af Arcona'

16.4.: ' fuldstændig Prøve paa 1.ste og 2' Akt med Orchester'

17.4.: 'Arrangement og Prøve paa 3.e og 1.ste Afdeling af 4.e Akt'

18.4.: 'Prøve paa Decorationerne til 1.ste Akt af Arcona'

19.4.: 'fuldstændig Prøve paa de tre første Akter af Arcona'

20.4.: 'Prøve paa Dandsene til Arcona [...] Costumeprøve i Theatret'

21.4.: 'Arrangement paa 4.de Akt. Det Hele færdigt [...] Costumeprøve i Theatret'

22.4.: 'fuldstændig Prøve paa tre Akter af Arcona, som gik udmærket smukt'

24.4.: 'Musikprøve paa 4.e Akt'
25.4.: 'fuldstændig Prøve paa 4.de Akt af Arcona'
26.4.: 'Ubehagelig Anmeldelse <u>forud</u> af min Ballet i De flyvende Blade, – Straf for min Troskyldhed!'
27.4.: 'fuldstændig Prøve paa alle 4 Akter'
28.4.: 'Theaterprøve med Orchester paa Arcona […] Audients hos Enkedronningen [i.e. Queen Caroline Amalie of Denmark], der var yderst naadig og modtog mit Program. – Costumeprøve for Mændene til Balletten'
29.4.: 'Costumeprøve for Damerne […] Decorationsprøve paa 1.ste og 2' Akt varede til Kl 1^1/$_4$, hjem og tilsengs Kl 1^3/$_4$.!'
1.5.: 'nærmere Bestemmelse med Hensyn til Arconas første Forestilling, udsat til Fredagen d. 7' Maj formedelst Decorationernes Forsinkelse'
2.5.: 'Theaterprøve paa 3' og 4.e Akt <u>med</u> Decorationer'
3.5.: 'Theaterprøve og Correctur paa Balletten'
4.5.: 'Decorations og Belysningsprøve paa Arcona fra Kl 11 til 1.'
5.5.: 'Stor Generalprøve i Costume og fuldkommen som en udmærket Forestilling […] det gik i enhver Henseende fortrinligt'
7.5.: 'Hele Dagen sysselsat med Aftenens Begivenhed […] Første Forestilling af Balletten Arcona for fuldt Huus og et skjønsomt Publicum, der fulgte Handling og Dands med levende Bifald. Udførelsen var udmærket i enhver Henseende og jeg takker Gud for den Lykke hans Godhed har undt mig at fuldføre dette betydelige Værk med et saa afgjort Held'.

A later projected staging of *Arcona* at Vienna's Hof-Operntheater was suggested to Bournonville only a fortnight after the Copenhagen première. This project, however, was firmly turned down by him on 20.5.1875, and described on the same day in his diary as follows:

'Modtaget Breve fra Wien med Tilbud om at give <u>Arcona</u> paa Operatheatret dersteds (Silas, [C.] Telle) besvaret Begge undskyldende formedelst Sujettets Umulighed'.

Arcona reached a total of 14 performances in Copenhagen, the last of which was given on 15.2.1876.

Autograph sources:

Manuscript scenario. Ms. Autograph. Brown ink. 1 vol. 17 pp. (20,8 × 17,1 cm)
<u>Arcona!</u>/Ballet i fire Akter/<u>af</u>/August Bournonville. (Concept.)/<u>1873.</u>
Signed and dated: 'Fredensborg den 4.de Maj 1873.' [Written according to the diary between 2.5. and 5.5.1873]
[DKKk; NKS 3285 4° 2 A–E

Manuscript scenario. Ms. Autograph. Brown ink. 1 vol. 14 pp. (20,8 × 17,1 cm)
<u>Arcona!</u>/<u>Ballet i fire Akter.</u>/af./August Bournonville./1873.
Signed and dated: 'Fredensborg den 4.de Maj 1873.' [Written according to the diary between 2.5. and 5.5.1873]
[DKKk; NKS 3285 4° 2 A–E

Manuscript mise-en-scène (including three drawings). Ms. Autograph. Black ink. 1 p. (20,6 × 17 cm)
<u>Arcona.</u> (1.ste Akt 1.ste Scene)/<u>Saxe-Lange</u> seer i sin historiske Begeistring/<u>Tre Grupper fra Oldtiden.</u>
Unsigned and undated [Written according to the diary most probably on 23.10.1873]
[Private collection (Copenhagen)
This manuscript mise-en-scène describes in words and diagrams the three tableaux performed in the opening scene of Act I.

Manuscript mise-en-scène. Ms. Autograph. Ink. 13 pp. (format unknown)
<u>Arcona.</u>/1.ste Akt 1.ste Scene/[…]/<u>Anden Akt.</u>

Unsigned and undated [Written according to the diary between 23.10.1873 and December 1874]
[USNYp; Dance Collection, call nos. *ZBD-71 (microfilm), and (S)*MGZMD 30 (photostat copy)

Manuscript mise-en-scène. Ms. Autograph. Ink. 1 p. (format unknown)
1. <u>Forspil Dækket gaae op.</u> [= Act I, scene 3]
Unsigned and undated [Written according to the diary between 23.10.1873 and December 1874]
[USNYp; Dance Collection, call nos. *ZBD-71 (microfilm), and (S)*MGZMD 30 (photostat copy)

Manuscript mise-en-scène. Ms. Autograph. Ink. 4 pp. (format unknown)
<u>Arcona</u> (1.ste Akt 3.e Scene)/[…]/<u>Anden Akt/</u>[…]/<u>3.die Scene</u>
Unsigned and undated [Written according to the diary between 23.10.1873 and December 1874]
[USNYp; Dance Collection, call nos. *ZBD-71 (microfilm), and (S)*MGZMD 30 (photostat copy)

Manuscript mise-en-scène. Ms. Autograph. Ink. 2 pp. (format unknown)
<u>Arcona.</u> 1.de [*sic*] Akt (Finale) [= Act I, scene 6]
Unsigned and undated [Written according to the diary between 23.10.1873 and December 1874]
[USNYp; Dance Collection, call nos. *ZBD-71 (microfilm), and (S)*MGZMD 30 (photostat copy)

Manuscript mise-en-scène. Ms. Autograph. Ink. 2 pp. (format unknown)
<u>Arcona</u> 2° Akt (Finale) [= Act II, scene 7-9]
Unsigned and undated [Written according to the diary between 23.10.1873 and December 1874]
[USNYp; Dance Collection, call nos. *ZBD-71 (microfilm), and (S)*MGZMD 30 (photostat copy)

Manuscript mise-en-scène. Ms. Autograph. Ink. 3 pp. (format unknown)
<u>Arcona.</u> (3.de Akt)/<u>1.ste Scene</u>/[…]/<u>2.d. Scene</u>/[…]/<u>Offring.</u> [= Act III, scene 1-2]
Unsigned and undated [Written according to the diary between 23.10.1873 and December 1874]
[USNYp; Dance Collection, call nos. *ZBD-71 (microfilm), and (S)*MGZMD 30 (photostat copy)

Manuscript mise-en-scène. Ms. Autograph. Ink. 5 pp. (format unknown)
<u>Arcona.</u> (4.de Akt)/1.ste Scene (Forspil) Poco Andante./[…]/<u>6 Scene</u> [= Act IV, scene 1-6]
Unsigned and undated [Written according to the diary between 23.10.1873 and December 1874]
[USNYp; Dance Collection, call nos. *ZBD-71 (microfilm), and (S)*MGZMD 30 (photostat copy)

Choreographic note. Ms. Autograph. Ink. 3 pp. (format unknown)
<u>Frierdandsen.</u> [= Act I, scene 3]
Unsigned and undated [Written according to the diary most probably on 1.11. and 2.11.1874]]
[USNYp; Dance Collection, call nos. *ZBD-71 (microfilm), and (S)*MGZMD 30 (photostat copy)

Choreographic note. Ms. Autograph. Ink. 2 pp. (format unknown)
<u>Krum Solo</u> (Tempo di Marcia)/[…]/<u>Galoppe</u> [= Act I, scene 3 'Frierdandsen']
Unsigned and undated [Written according to the diary most probably on 1.11. and 2.11.1874]
[USNYp; Dance Collection, call nos. *ZBD-71 (microfilm), and (S)*MGZMD 30 (photostat copy)

Choreographic note. Ms. Autograph. Ink. 1 p. (format unknown)
Væverdandsen. [= Act I, scene 3]
Unsigned and undated [Written according to the diary most probably on 1.11. and 2.11.1874]
[USNYp; Dance Collection, call nos. *ZBD-71 (microfilm), and (S)*MGZMD 30 (photostat copy)

Choreographic note. Ms. Autograph. Ink. 2 pp. (format unknown)
Efter Væverdandsen. /(1.e Akt 4.e scene) [= Act I, scene 4]
Unsigned and undated [Written according to the diary most probably on 1.11. and 2.11.1874]
[USNYp; Dance Collection, call nos. *ZBD-71 (microfilm), and (S)*MGZMD 30 (photostat copy)

Choreographic note. Ms. Autograph. Ink. 2 pp. (format unknown)
Arcona. 2.d[en] Akt/No. 9 [= 'Jomfruernes Brudedands' in Act II, scene 3]
Unsigned and undated [Written according to the diary most probably on 14.11. and 15.11.1874]
[USNYp; Dance Collection, call nos. *ZBD-71 (microfilm), and (S)*MGZMD 30 (photostat copy)

Choreographic note. Ms. Autograph. Ink. 2 pp. (format unknown)
Arcona (3.die Akt)/Dands af Blomsterbesmÿkkede Piger. […]/Allegro [= Act III, scene 2 'Offringsdandsen']
Unsigned and undated [Written according to the diary most probably between late November and mid-December 1874]
[USNYp; Dance Collection, call nos. *ZBD-71 (microfilm), and (S)*MGZMD 30 (photostat copy)

Choreographic note. Ms. Autograph. Ink. 1 p. (format unknown)
fortsættelse af Pigernes Dands. [=Act III, scene 2 'Offringsdandsen']
Unsigned and undated [Written according to the diary most probably between late November and mid-December 1874]
[USNYp; Dance Collection, call nos. *ZBD-71 (microfilm), and (S)*MGZMD 30 (photostat copy)

Choreographic note. Ms. Autograph. Ink. 3 pp. (format unknown)
Arcona (3.die Akts Finale)/[…]/Mazurka. [= Act III, scene 6 'Finale']
Unsigned and undated [Written according to the diary most probably between late November and mid-December 1874]
[USNYp; Dance Collection, call nos. *ZBD-71 (microfilm), and (S)*MGZMD 30 (photostat copy)

Mimic and choreographic note. Ms. Autograph Ink. 7 pp. (format unknown)
Arcona (3.die Akt)/(1.ste scene)/[…]/4.de Scene (B) [= Act III, scene 1–5]
Unsigned and undated [Written according to the diary between 28.11. and 9.12.1874]
[USNYp; Dance Collection, call nos. *ZBD-71 (microfilm), and (S)*MGZMD 30 (photostat copy)

Production note. Ms. Autograph. Black ink. 2 pp. (13,6 × 21,5 cm)
Rollerne i følgende Orden
Unsigned and undated [Written according to the diary most probably on either 1.12.1874 or 15.3.1875]
[DKKkt; F.M. (Ballet)

Production note. Ms. Autograph. Ink. 4 pp. (format unknown)
Forslag/til Costümeringen i Balletten Arcona./Det mandlige Personale
Unsigned and undated [Written according to the diary on 5.12. 1874]
[USNYp; Dance Collection, call nos. *ZBD-71 (microfilm), and (S)*MGZMD 30 (photostat copy)

Production note. Ms. Autograph. Ink. 2 pp. (format unknown)
fortsættelse af Forslag/til Costümeringen i Balletten Arcona.

Signed and dated: 'Kbhvn d 6 Decbr 1874.'
[USNYp; Dance Collection, call nos. *ZBD-71 (microfilm), and (S)*MGZMD 30 (photostat copy)

Mimic note. Ms. Autograph. Ink. 3 pp. (format unknown)
Arcona (4.e Akt)/forvandling til Svantevits Tempel. [= Act IV, scene 8–10]
Unsigned and undated [Written according to the diary between 13.1. and mid-March 1875]
[USNYp; Dance Collection, call nos. *ZBD-71 (microfilm), and (S)*MGZMD 30 (photostat copy)

Mimic note. Ms. Autograph. Ink. 4 pp. (format unknown)
Arcona (4.e Akt)/(Finale) [= Act IV, scene 8–10]
Unsigned and undated [Written according to the diary between 13.1. and mid-March 1875]
[USNYp; Dance Collection, call nos. *ZBD-71 (microfilm), and (S)*MGZMD 30 (photostat copy)

Production note. Ms. Autograph. Black ink. 2 pp. (21,1 × 18 cm)
Arcona/Ballet i 4 Acter af Hofballetmester Bournonville/Musiken af Professor J. P. E. Hartmann./Decorationerne af Theatermaler Güllich./-/Personerne.
Unsigned and undated [Written according to the diary on 18.1. and 19.1.1875]
[DKKkt; F.M. (Ballet)

Production note. Ms. Autograph. Black ink. 4 pp (36,6 × 22,7 cm)
Bipersonale/til/Balletten Arcona.
Signed and dated: 'Kjøbenhavn den 19' Januar 1875.'
[DKKkt; F.M. (Ballet)

Manuscript scenario. Ms. Autograph. Black ink. 22 pp. (22,7 × 18 cm)
Arcona.!/Ballet i 4 Akter./af/August Bournonville/Musiken af J. P. E Hartmann (Decorationerne af W. Güllich.)/1875.
Signed and dated: 'Conciperet den 4.e Maj 1873/Reenskrevet den 1.e Martz 1875.' [Written according to the diary between 6.2. and 1.3.1875]
[DKKk; Arthur Palsbos Håndskriftssaml., Ea Sp 147
On the second title page (which was cancelled at a later stage) the décor is credited to 'F. Ahlgrensson og W. Güllich'.

Production note. Ms. Autograph. Ink. 4 pp. (format unknown)
Arcona/(1.ste Akt)/Arrangement
Unsigned and undated [Written according to the diary most probably in late March 1875]
[USNYp; Dance Collection, call nos. *ZBD-71 (microfilm), and (S)*MGZMD 30 (photostat copy)

Production note. Ms. Autograph. Black ink. 1 p. (34, 1 × 21,1 cm)
Til Prøven paa Tableauerne
Unsigned and undated [Written according to the diary most probably in mid-April 1875]
[DKKkt; F.M. (Ballet)

Production note. Ms. Autograph. Black ink. 1 p. (21 × 17 cm)
Bemærkninger/ved/Chorets damers Omklædninger i Balletten/Arcona.
Signed and dated: 'd 27.de April 1875.'
[SSm; Daniel Fryklunds samling no. 117

Musical sources:

Musical drafts. Ms. Autograph (by I. P. E. Hartmann). Pencil and black ink. 14 pp. (26,4 × 34,6 cm)
[Untitled]
Unsigned and undated [c.1873–75]
[DKKk; I. P. E. Hartmanns Samling (Arkona. Skitse)
These musical drafts contain several melodies that are also included

in Hartmann's final score for Acts I and II of *Arcona*. Many of them are here referred to by Hartmann as being originally part of a (not yet identified) collection of songs, named 'Historiske Sange'. This seems to indicate that Hartmann's score for this ballet was based on several old Danish songs and folk tunes.

Musical drafts. Ms. Autograph (by I. P. E. Hartmann). Brown and black ink and pencil. 2 vol. Act I–II 96 pp. of which four are blank, Act III–IV 70 pp. of which two are blank (33,2 × 25,4 cm with several variants)
[Untitled]
Signed and dated (in vol. I, p. 3): '21/6 [18]73.', (p. 84) '22/11 [18]73', (in vol II, p. 46) '26/3/[18]74.', (p. 70) '17/4 [1875]/ IPEHartmann'.
[DKKk; I. P. E. Hartmanns Samling (Arkona. Skitse)
These musical drafts contain Hartmann's first piano version of the complete music for *Arcona*.

Musical drafts. Ms. Autograph (by I. P. E. Hartmann). Brown and black ink and pencil. 34 pp. of which five are blank (33,2 × 25,4 cm)
I. P. E. Hartmann: 'Arkona'./[...]/Skizzer af Arkona. Hartmanns Manuskript/[...]/3.die Acts Finale/omcomponeret/[...]/Arcona Fjerde Act op. 72.
Unsigned and dated (on p. 9): 'Søllerød/2/12 [18]74.'
[DKKk; C II, 114 (1959–60.159)
These musical drafts contain Hartmann's first piano version of what in 1875 became the music for the Act III finale (score no. 26), and Act IV (score nos. 27–31 B) in *Arcona*. The manuscript was purchased by DKKk on 29.8.1959 from the Copenhagen music publisher K. Larsen.

Orchestral score. Ms. Autograph (by I. P. E. Hartmann). Black ink and pencil. 2 vol. Act I–II 304 pp. of which six are blank, Act III–IV 278 pp. of which five are blank (34 × 25,5 cm)
Arcona/1ste og 2den Act/Partitur/[...]/3die [erased] – 4 Act
Signed and dated (in vol. I, p. 35): 'IPEHartmann/14/4 [18]75.', (p. 38) 'Novbr: 1873.', (p. 304) '2/11 [18]74.', vol. II, p. 278) '21 April/ 1875/I:P:E:Hartmann'.
[DKKk; C II, 114 (KTB 306)
Hartmann's autographed note in vol. I (written with black ink on p. 73) reads: 'NB Herefter følger 3 Dandse med/indlagt Musik'. It indicates the exact places where *The Proposal Dance* (set to music by J. F. Fröhlich, rearranged by V. C. Holm), and *The Weavers Dance* (arranged by C. C. Møller) were incorporated in Act I of *Arcona*.

Orchestral score (insertions in Act I, score nos. 4–6). Ms. Autograph (by V. C. Holm). Black and brown ink, and pencil. 1 vol. 58 pp. of which one is blank (33,9 × 25,5 cm)
306/Arcona/Arcona/Partitur/Indlæg i 1ste Act./comp af Holm og C. C. Møller/No. 4/[...]/No. 5/[...]/No. 6
Unsigned and undated [1875]
[DKKk; C II, 114 m (KTB 306)
This orchestral score contains the music for *The Proposal Dance* and *The Weavers Dance* in Act I (score nos. 4–5, and no. 6) of *Arcona*. The score is V. C. Holm's autograph throughout, and the music for *The Weavers Dance* (which was arranged by C. C. Møller) is only partially orchestrated.

Répétiteur's copy. Ms. Copy and autographs (by V. C. Holm). Black ink. 1 vol. 138 pp. of which five are blank (33,7 × 25,3 cm)
B. 306/Arcona./Ballet i 4 Akter./1875/39./[...]/Repetiteurparti./ til/Arcona/Ballet i 4 akter,/af/August Bournonville./Musiken af J. P: E: Hartmann.
Unsigned and dated (on the front cover): '1875'
[DKKk; MA ms 3002 (KTB 306)
The music for *The Proposal Dance* in Act I (score nos. 4–5, pp. 9–15) is here V. C. Holm's autograph. The répétiteur's copy contains numerous autographed notes by Bournonville (written with black ink) which describe large parts of the pantomime, the dramatic action and the choreography throughout the ballet. Moreover, his autographed choreographic numbers are inserted throughout the vol-

ume. They refer to the similar numbers included in his eleven separate mimic and choreographic notations for this ballet, written between 1.11.874 and mid-March 1875. The score numbers added to each section in this volume are either incomplete or completely different from those given to the same sections in Hartmann's autographed orchestral score.

Parts. Ms. Copy. 41 + 10 vol.
4 vl I, 3 vl II, 2 vla, 4 vlc e cb, fl picc, fl 1/2, ob 1/2, cl 1/2, fag 1/2, cor 1/2/3/4, tr 1/2/3/4, trb 1/2/3, tuba, timp, gr cassa, tamb rul, tamb, piatti, gong, arpa. On stage: cl 1/2, cor 1/2, tr 1/2, Tcor 1/2, tuba, org.
Unsigned and undated [1875]
[DKKk; KTB 306

Other sources:

Sketch by V. Güllich of the décor for Act I. Pencil and water colours (42,3 × 57,5 cm)
[Untitled]
Signed and dated: 'V/G [18]75.'
[DKKt; V. Güllichs dekorationsudkast (89/141)
This sketch was (according to notes written on the reverse of the frame) originally donated by Güllich as a personal gift to Bournonville in 1875. In 1928 it was donated to DKKkt by Bournonville's granddaughter, Helene Kiær (b. Irminger).

Sketch by V. Güllich of the décor for Act II. Pencil and water colours (45 × 62,8 cm)
[Untitled]
Signed and dated: 'V/G [18]75.'
[DKKt; V. Güllichs dekorationsudkast (89/138)
This sketch was (according to notes written on the reverse of the frame) originally donated by Güllich as a personal gift to Bournonville in 1875. In 1928 it was donated to DKKkt by Bournonville's granddaughter, H. Kiær (b. Irminger).

Sketch by V. Güllich of the décor for Act III. Pencil and water colours (38,5 × 67,2 cm)
[Untitled]
Signed and dated: 'V/G [18]75.'
[DKKt; V. Güllichs dekorationsudkast (89/140)

Sketch by V. Güllich of the décor for Act IV. Pencil and water colours (36,5 × 52 cm)
[Untitled]
Signed and dated: 'V/G [18]75.'
[DKKt; V. Güllichs dekorationsudkast (89/137)

Costume drawing by E. Lehmann. Pencil and water colours (23,4 × 14 cm)
[Untitled]
Unsigned and undated [c.1875]
[DKKkt; Kostumetegninger (Lehmann)
This drawing shows the costumes worn by a priest from the temple of *Svantevit* in Act III of *Arcona* (performed by C. Carpentier).

Costume drawing by E. Lehmann. Pencil and water colours (22,3 × 13 cm)
[Untitled]
Unsigned and undated [c.1875]
[DKKkt; Kostumetegninger (Lehmann)
This drawing shows the costume worn by a *Jester* in the so-called *Jester Dance (Narredandsen)* in Act II, scene 5 of *Arcona* (performed by J. T. Klüver).

Costume drawing by E. Lehmann. Pencil and water colours (22,5 × 16 cm)
[Untitled]
Unsigned and undated [c.1875]
[DKKkt; Kostumetegninger (Lehmann)

This drawing shows the costume worn by a *Jester* in the so-called *Jester Dance (Narredandsen)* in Act II, scene 5 of *Arcona* (performed by A. F. Lense).

Costume drawing by E. Lehmann. Pencil and water colours (23,3 × 13 cm)
[Untitled]
Unsigned and undated [c.1875]
[DKKkt; Kostumetegninger (Lehmann)]
This drawing shows the costume worn by a *Jester* in the so-called *Jester Dance (Narredandsen)* in Act II, scene 5 of *Arcona* (performed by C. O. N. Lauenberg).

Costume drawing by E. Lehmann. Pencil and water colours (18 × 10,2 cm)
[Untitled]
Unsigned and undated [c.1875]
[DKKkt; Kostumetegninger (Lehmann)]
This drawing shows the costume worn by a *Jester* in the so-called *Jester Dance (Narredandsen)* in Act II, scene 5 of *Arcona* (performed by C. Christensen).

Costume drawing by E. Lehmann. Pencil and water colours (23,3 × 12,4 cm)
[Untitled]
Unsigned and undated [c.1875]
[DKKkt; Kostumetegninger (Lehmann)]
This drawing shows the costume worn by an archer in Act IV(?) of *Arcona.*

Costume drawing by E. Lehmann. Pencil and water colours (25,6 × 15,5 cm)
[Untitled]
Unsigned and undated [c.1875]
[DKKkt; Kostumetegninger (Lehmann)]
This drawing shows the costume worn by a warrior (holding a lance) in Act IV(?) of *Arcona.*

Costume drawing by E. Lehmann. Pencil and water colours (23,5 × 13,7 cm)
[Untitled]
Unsigned and undated [c.1875]
[DKKkt; Kostumetegninger (Lehmann)]
This drawing shows the costume worn by a viking warrior in Act IV(?) of *Arcona.*

Costume drawing by E. Lehmann. Pencil and water colours (19,7 × 12 cm)
[Untitled]
Unsigned and undated [c.1875]
[DKKkt; Kostumetegninger (Lehmann)]
This drawing shows the costumes worn by two slavs in Act IV (?) of *Arcona.*

Printed sources:

Printed scenario. 1 vol. 16 pp. (20.9 × 13,5 cm)
Arcona./Ballet i 4 Akter/af/August Bournonville./Musiken af I. P. E. Hartmann./Decorationerne af W. Güllich.
Kjøbenhavn, J. H. Schubothe/Bianco Luno, 1875.
[DKKk; 17, – 175 8°
In an identical copy of this printed scenario (now in SSm, call no. Daniel Fryklunds Samling no. 152) Bournonville inserted two (un-dated) notes that read as follows: 'NB. Det bemærkes at Frierdands-en og Væverdandsen/ere indlagte Musiknumere (altsaa ikke af Hartmanns Composition)/[...]/Anm: Forholdet imellem Absalon og Saxo,/imellem Esbern og Hulfried, samt/imellem Tvillingbrød-rene og deres Moder,/Fru Inge, er historisk, saavelsom Vendernes/Hærgninger, Svantevitsdyrkelsen og de/danskes Indtagelse af [erased] Arconas Indtagelse/af de danske. Resten er fuldstændig Digt/og lempet efter Ballettens Fordringer./August Bournonville'.

1.6.1875
Famous Men from Denmark's Past (Hemicycle of tableaux vivants) (Berømte Mænd fra Danmarks Fortid (Hemicyclus i levende Tableauer).
This series of *tableaux vivants* is described in Bournonville's memoirs *My Theatre Life* (p. 408) as:

'Apotheosis for a series of famous Danes' (Apotheose for en Cyclus af berømte Danske)'.

According to the poster it showed nine great personalities in Danish national history from the ecclesiastical, the scientific, the military, the naval, and the literary fields. They were:

(1) Bishop Absalon, (2) Saxo Grammaticus, (3) Esbern Snare, (4) Daniel Rantzau, (5) Tycho Brahe, (6) Ole Rømer, (7) Niels Juul, (8) Peder Tordenskjold, and (9) Ludvig Holberg.

The tableaux were created for a special charity performance given in order to raise funds for the private pension fund of the Royal Danish Ballet, of which Bournonville was the founding member.
In his diary he noted about the tableaux, which were per-formed only once:

14.5.1875: 'Besørget endeel paa Theatret med Hensyn til vor Pen-sionsforestilling'
21.5.: 'skrevet og expederet Breve og Annoncer til Kmhr [C. L.] Løv-enskjold og fem forskjellige Blade i Anledning af vor forestaaende Pensionsforestilling'
29.5.1875: 'stillet Grupperne til Hemicyclen for berømte Mænd fra Danmarks Fortid'
31.5.: 'Generalprøve paa Hemicyclen og Operetten til vor Pensions-forestilling'
1.6.: 'I Theatret til Indtægt for vor Pensionsfond: – Berømte Mænd fra Danmarks Fortid [...] Alt gik fortræffeligt og med stort Bifald men Huset skjøndt ret godt besat, var ikke saa fuldt, som vi havde kunnet ønske det. Aarsagen var næstefter det smukke Sommerveir tvende paafølgende Beneficeforestillinger af O. Poulsen og Ch. Hansen d. 2.e og 5. Juni.'
2.6.: 'erfaret at vor Brutto-Indtægt var 2830 Kr. [...] saa vi kunne vente at see de 30,000 Rdlr completterede i denne Sommer'.

According to Bournonville's autographed manuscript mise-en-scène for this work, the tableaux were accompanied by J. F. Fröhlich's overture for his and Bournonville's four-act ro-mantic ballet *Waldemar* (*see* 28.10.1835).

Autograph sources:

Manuscript mise-en-scène. Ms. Autograph. Ink. 2 pp. (format un-known)
Ouverture til Balletten Valdemar/Berømte Mænd fra Danmarks Fortid/(Hemicyclus i levende Tableaux.)
Signed and dated: 'Kbhvn d 14.e Maj 1875'
[USNYp; Dance Collection, call nos. *ZBD-71 (microfilm), and (S)*MGZMD 30 (photostat copy)

Manuscript mise-en-scène. Ms. Autograph. Ink. 1 p. (format un-known)
[A drawing of the décor for the nine tableaux, entitled *Famous Men from Denmark's Past*]
Unsigned and undated [Written according to the diary most pro-bably on 14.5.1875]
[USNYp; Dance Collection, call nos. *ZBD-71 (microfilm), and (S)*MGZMD 30 (photostat copy)
This drawing includes Bournonville's autographed choreographic

numbers ('1–4') which refer to similar numbers in his separate manuscript mise-en-scène for this work (*see* the previous entry).

10.9.1875

Napoli or The Fisherman and His Bride (Napoli eller Fiskeren og hans Brud).

This performance represents the fifth and last restaging in Copenhagen of Bournonville's three-act romantic ballet *Napoli or The Fisherman and His Bride* (*see* 29.3.1842) during his lifetime. It also marks the first time this ballet was performed in the new Royal Theatre building. The production was mounted with completely new décors, painted by the German scene painter, P. Gropius (Act II), and by V. Güllich (Acts I and III). According to Bournonville's autographed production notes for this staging he seems to have made a number of changes in the casting of the tritons and naiads in Act II, and some minor choreographic changes in the Act III *Pas de six*. They were most likely caused by the larger and much improved stage area of the new Royal Theatre.

In his diary he noted about the 1875 production and its two first performances:

13.11.1874: ' Decorationsmøde med [V.] Güllich angaaende […] Napoli'
24.5.1875: 'Conference med [A. C. P.] Linde og [F. J. G.] Berner samt [P.] Gropius om fremtidige Arbeider'
1.7.: 'Skizze med Brev fra Gropius'
2.7.: 'Svar til Gropius angaaende Skizzen, som jeg først modtog igaar samt Brev til Berner om denne Sag'
6.7.: 'Brev til Berner med Sendelse af Skizzerne fra Gropius'
15.7.: 'Brev fra Gropius'
23.7.: 'Brev fra [L.] Cetti med Gropius' Skizzer'
1.8.: 'skrevet […] Om Eftermiddagen afsendt breve til […] [L.] Gade og Justitsr. Berner'
18.8.: 'Prøve paa Napoli. 2' Akt'
26.8. and 30.8.: 'Prøve paa Dandsene til Napoli'
1.9.: 'Sceneprøve paa Napoli'
2.9.: 'Prøve paa Dandsene med Remplacement til Napoli'
3.9.: 'partiel Prøve paa Napoli'
6.9.: 'Theaterprøve Kl 10 paa 1.ste og 2' Akt af Napoli'
8.9.: 'Eftermiddag Kl 6 Arrangement paa Napoli 3' Akt og Kl 7½ Generalprøve paa samme, der varede til Kl 10½!'
9.9.: 'partiel Prøve paa Napoli'
10.9.: 'I Theatret […] Napoli, der nÿt udstyret med Decorationer af Gropius og Güllich gik med stor Bravour og for fuldt Huus'
15.9.: 'I Theatret […] Napoli, der gik for godt Huus (1300 rdlr) og Kongehusets Nærværelse men for et iskoldt Publicum, hvis fornemme Taushed oprørte mig'.

The production received 25 performances during Bournonville's lifetime, the last of which was given on 5.11.1879.

The musical material employed this year was the same as that used since the 1842 première of this ballet (now in DKKk, call nos. C II, 114 k, and KTB 292).

Autograph sources:

Production note. Ms. Autograph. Brown ink. 1 p. (20,9 × 13,4 cm)
Napoli (2.d[en] Akt.)/Tritoner./[…]/Nayader/[…]/Pas de six
Signed and dated: 'd 1.ste August 1875'
[Private collection (Copenhagen)

Other sources:

Sketch by V. Güllich (after P. Gropis?) of the décor for Act II. Pencil (22,4 × 31 cm)

[Untitled]
Unsigned and undated [1875?]
[DKKt; V. Güllichs dekorationsudkast (89/188)
This pencilled sketch is curious in that it shows the blue grotto in mirror image to what was actually seen on stage.

21.10.1875

Pontemolle (An Artists' Party in Rome) (Pontemolle, (Et Kunstnergilde i Rom)).

This performance represents the second and last time Bournonville's ballet-vaudeville in two tableaux *Pontemolle (An Artists' Party in Rome)* (*see* 11.4.1866) was staged by him. It was performed this year for the first time in the new Royal Theatre and seems to have been mounted in a slightly revised version. Thus, according to the 1866 répétiteur's copy (which was reused for the 1875 production) Bournonville inserted several choreographic numbers (written with black ink) in the music for the entire first tableau and score nos. 8, 15, and 16 of the second. They most probably refer to similar numbers in a separate (not yet traced) notation of the ballet that he may have been written prior to this production. Moreover, Bournonville's autographed indications of two musical cuts (16 and 40 bars each) in F. X. Neruda's so-called *Old Age and Folly (mimetic waltz)* in the second tableau (score no. 15) are included in the same répétiteur's copy (on pp. 71–73). These changes seem to represent the main differences from the original 1866 version of this ballet.

In his diary Bournonville noted about the new production:

14.9.1875: 'Prøve paa 1.ste Akt af Pontemolle'
24.9. and 18.10.: 'Prøve paa Pontemolle'
20.10.: 'Theaterprøve paa Pontemolle med Orchester'
21.10.: 'I Theatret […] Pontemolle der gik udmæket godt og med livligt Bifald fra det kun halvt besatte Huus'.

The 1875 staging received 13 performances during Bournonville's lifetime, the last of which was given on 21.11.1879.

The musical sources employed this year were the same as those used for the 1866 première (now in DKKk, call nos. C II, 114 m, MA ms 2974, and KTB 280).

31.10.1875

From the Last Century (Fra det forrige Aarhundrede).

This ballet divertissement was created on the occasion of the unveiling of T. Stein's statue of the great 18th-century Danish writer, L. Holberg, erected in front of Copenhagen's new Royal Theatre building. The action takes place in the gardens of the Royal Fredensborg Castle during the summer of 1747. It depicts a scene of entertainment arranged in honour of King Frederik V, who a only a few months earlier had granted Holberg permission to open a theatre in Copenhagen, which later became the first public stage of the Royal Theatre.

The music for this divertissement is divided into 8 scenes and 10 music numbers, and was composed and arranged by V. C. Holm. He incorporated (at Bournonville's direct request) several musical borrowings in order to add a true historical flavour to the score. These borrowings are identified as follows:

(1) Scene 1 (score no. 1): Holm here incorporated J. F. Fröhlich's

complete music for the opening scene in the second tableau (score no. 4) of Bournonville's much earlier Itlaian ballet in six tableaux, entitled *Raphael* (*see* 30.5.1845).

(2) Scene 2 (score no. 2): In this scene Holm incorporated another, slightly revised excerpt borrowed from Fröhlich's music for the second tableau (score no. 5) of Bournonville's ballet *Raphael*.

(3) Scene 4 (score no. 4): Holm here incorporated yet another excerpt from Fröhlich's 1845 score to *Raphael*, but this time from the opening scene of the first tableau (score no. 1). In *From the Last Century* it served as an accompaniment for an allegorical 'Ballet i Roccostil', and during which *Juno, Minerva,* and *Venus* enter to perform a *Pas de trois* to compete for the prize of the golden apple from *Prince Paris*.

(4) Scene 5 (score no. 5): In his score for this number Holm employed a theme from E. Helsted's earlier musical arrangement of score no. 2 in Bournonville's one-act ballet *Old Memories, or A Magic Lantern* (*see* 18.12.1848). The theme, however, was originally borrowed by Helsted from the *Musset* and the *Second Air de ballet* in Act IV (scene 2) of C. W. v. Gluck's five-act lyrical tragedy *Armide* (premièred at the Paris Opéra on 23.9.1777). In *From the Last Century* it accompanied an allegorical *Pas de deux* performed by *Prince Paris* (D. Krum) and *Venus* (A. Scholl).

(5) Scene 6 (score no. 7): Holm here interpolated the complete overture for J.-J. Rousseau's intermedium *Le Devin de village* (premièred at Fontainebleau on 18.10.1752). It served as an accompaniment for a *Clog Dance (Træskodands)* and was performed by a group of dancers dressed as peasants from the Danish island of Zealand.

(6) Scene 6 (score no. 8): In this number Holm incorporated an excerpt from E. Helsted's score of the *Waltz* in Act I (score no. 3) of Bournonville's three-act romantic ballet *Kirsten Piil* (*see* 26.2.1845). It served as an accompaniment for a so-called 'Polskdands' and was performed by the same group of peasants who danced the *Clog Dance* that precedes it.

(7) Scene 7 (score no. 9): Holm here interpolated a revised version of the music for the 'Menuetto' (score no. 5) in Bournonville's intermedium for L. Holberg's three-act comedy *The Masquerade* (*see* 12.12. 1849). It served as an accompaniment for the scene in which a procession, entitled 'Holbergs Optog', moves across the stage while showing the main characters in the most popular of Holberg's comedies.

In his diary Bournonville noted about the rehearsals and the première of this ballet divertissement:

21.9.1875: 'modtaget Anmodning om et Divertissement til Holbergiana'

23.9.: 'conciperet et Efterspil til Holbergs Comedie i Anledning af Statuens Afsløring'

24.9.: 'arbeidet paa min nÿ Composition'

25.9.: 'arbeidet paa Musikarrangementet med [V. C.] Holm, skrevet og Decorations Conference'

26.9.: 'skrevet og arrangeret paa min nÿ Composition'

27.9.: 'efter Frokosten arbeidede jeg paa Personlisterne til min nÿ Ballet'

28.9. and 29.9.: 'componeret'

30.9.: '1.ste Indstudering paa 'Fra det forrige Aarhundrede', componeret videre'

1.10.: 'componeret og indstuderet paa Det Nÿe til [D.] Krum og [A.] Scholl, Eftermiddagsprøve og 2.den Indstudering'

2.10.: 'arbeidet med Holm'

4.10.: 'Repetition paa det nÿe Festdivertissement, Costümemøde'

5.10.: 'arbeidet med Holm, Costumemøde, componeret'

6.10.: '3.die Indstudering, Træskodandsen'

7.10.: 'Repetition paa det Nÿe'

8.10.: '4.de Indstudering til Fru [A. F.] Nyrop, [C. G. L.] Meyer og Chorets Assistance'

11.10.: 'componeret'

12.10.: '6.e Indstudering' […] reenskrevet mit Program'

13.10.: 'Repetition paa det Lærte af Divertissementet'

14.10.: 'componeret en Finale'

22.10.: 'Prøve paa mit nÿ Balletdivertissement og den sidste Indstudering, Finalen færdig. – Holberg-Statuen opstillet idag og skal afsløres <u>Søndagen d. 31' October</u>'

26.10.: 'Arrangementprøve paa Theatret paa Balletdivertissementet'

27.10.: 'Arrangementprøve paa Det Nÿe'

28.10.: 'Theaterprøve paa Det Nÿe'

29.10.: 'Theaterprøve med Orchester paa Det Nÿe, der gik udmærket smukt og tiltalte meget'

30.10.: 'Generalprøve paa 'Fra det forrige Aarhundrede'

31.10.: 'Morgentour med Billetter til Holbergstatuens Afsløring der skete med stor Høitidelighed Kl 12. – Sang af H. P. Holst og [H. S.] Paulli, Tale af [C.] Ploug. […] I Theatret […] min ny Ballet, Alt gik fortræffeligt og Stemningen var i høieste Grad animeret'.

From the Last Century reached a total of 7 performances, the last of which was given on 15.5.1876.

Autograph sources:

Manuscript scenario. Ms. Autograph. Black ink. 3 pp. (22,6 × 18 cm)
<u>Efterspil/I Anledning af Holbergs Billedstøttes Afsløring./d.</u> [space left open] <u>October 1875./Ballet = Divertissement af August Bournonville.</u>
Signed and dated: 'Kbhvn d. 23.de September 1875.'
[DKKt; Brevregistrant: Bournonville

Musical instructions. Ms. Autograph. Black and brown ink. 3 pp. (21,4 × 13,8 cm and 21 × 13,3 cm)
<u>Musik = Arrangement/til/Det holbergske Efterspil</u>
Unsigned and undated [Written according to the diary most probably on 25.9.1875]
[DKKt; Brevregistrant: Bournonville

Manuscript scenario. Ms. Autograph. Black ink. 1 vol. 9 pp. (21 × 16,9 cm)
<u>Fra det forrige Aarhundrede.</u> / Balletdivertissement, / af. / <u>August Bournonville.</u>/Musiken arrangeret af W Holm./(opfört første Gang i Anledning af Holberg – Statuens/Afslöring.)
Unsigned and dated: '(Den [space left open] .de November 1875.)'
[Written according to the diary most probably on 12.10.1875]
[DKKk; NKS 3285 4° 2 F

Musical sources:

Orchestral score. Ms. Autograph (by V. C. Holm). Brown and black ink, and pencil. 1 vol. 186 pp. of which three are blank (34 × 25,3 cm)
Fra det forrige Aarhundrede/Ballet i 1 Act/af A. Bournonville/Musiken arr af Holm/Partitur
Signed and dated (on p. 185): 'D. 25 Octbr 1875/V C Holm'
[DKKk; C II, 114 m (KTB 309)

Répétiteur's copy. Ms. Copy. Brown ink. 1 vol. 44 pp. of which one is blank (33,9 × 25,5 cm)
B. 309/Fra det forrige Aarhundrede/(opført 1.ste Gang ved Holbergfesten d. 31' October..)/1875./24/[…]/Fra det forrige/Aarhundrede./Ballet af August Bournonville/October 1875.
Unsigned and dated (on the title page): 'October 1875.'
[DKKk; MA ms 3003 (KTB 309)
This répétiteur's copy contains numerous choreographic numbers written (with brown ink) by an unknown hand throughout the music. They most probably refer to a separate (not yet traced) choreographic notation of the entire divertissement, which Bournonville (according to his diary) may have written during late September and/or early October 1875.

Parts. Ms. Copy. 32 vol.
4 vl I, 3 vl II, 2 vla, 3 vlc e cb, fl 1/2, ob 1/2, cl 1/2, fag 1/2, cor 1/2/ 3/4, tr 1/2, trb 1/2/3, timp, gr cassa, tri.
Unsigned and undated [1875]
[DKKk; KTB 309

21.11.1875
Guillaume Tell (Wilhelm Tell).
The 1875 Copenhagen restaging of G. Rossini's four-act opera (*see* 23.11.1868) represents the last time Bournonville worked on a staging of this work. It was this year performed with slightly revised choreography in the solo variation of the Act III *Pas de trois* (arranged especially for A. Scholl). Moreover, the staging was mounted with completely new décors painted by F. Ahlgrensson. In his diary Bournonville noted about the performance, which was the first production of *Guillaume Tell* in the new Royal Theatre building:

2.11.1875: 'Skrevet [...] Indstudering til Pas de deux [*sic*]'
16.11.: 'Prøve paa Dandsen til Wilhelm Tell'
20.11.: 'bivaanet en Deel af Generalprøven paa Wilhelm Tell'
21.11.: 'I Theatret <u>Wilhelm Tell</u>, der gik meget smukt. Nÿe Decorationer af [F.] Ahlgrensson, særdeles effectfulde'.

The 1875 production received 17 performances during Bournonville's lifetime, the last of which was given on 23.5.1879.

The musical material employed this year was the same as that used for the previous production on 16.11.1873 (now in DKKkt and in DKKk, call nos. KTA 375, and MA ms 2911 (1) respectively).

Autograph sources:

Choreographic note. Ms. Autograph. Ink. 1 p. (format unknown)
<u>Solo de M.lle Scholl</u>/ (de remplacement dans Guillaume Tell.)
Unsigned and undated [Written according to the diary most probably on 2.11.1875]
[USNYp; Dance Collection, call nos. *ZBD-71 (microfilm), and (S)*MGZMD 30 (photostat copy)
Bournonville's autographed choreographic numbers ('1–5') included in this manuscript refer to his similar pencilled numbers inserted underneath the music (on p. 6) in the répétiteur's copy for *Guillaume Tell* (now in DKKk, call no. MA ms 2911 (1) (KTA 375)).

1876

4.1.–1.2.1876
Eight dance lessons in social dance to the children of the Princess of Wales.
According to his diary Bournonville gave a series of 8 dance lessons in social dance to the three children of the Princess of Wales (the Danish-born Princess Alexandra): Prince Edward, Prince George (later King George V), and Princess Louise. These lessons, which were taught at the Amalienborg Palace, took place mainly on Tuesday and Friday afternoons and lasted for about two hours each. In his diary Bournonville noted about the lessons:

31.12.1875: 'Kaldet til Hd. M. Dronningen [i.e. Queen Louise Wilhelmine Friederike Caroline Auguste Julie of Denmark] indfandt jeg mig paa Amalienborg, hvor jeg traf sammen med hele den kgl Familie og Prindsessen af Wales [i.e. the later Queen Alexandra of Great Britain and Ireland], hvis Børn jeg skal informere i Dands'
4.1.1876: 'Første Lection til Prindsessen af Wales' Børn [Albert Victor Christian] <u>Edward</u>, <u>George</u> [Frederik Ernest Albert], <u>Louise Victoria</u> [Alexandra Dagmar] [...] Hele den kongelige Familie var nærværende og Undervisningen gik smukt'
1.2.: '8.de og sidste Lection til de engelske Prindsebørn, lavet min

Anbefaling for Healeyerne til Prindsessen af Wales; mageløs Venlighed af den hele kgl Familie og en smuk Brystnaal i Present tilligemed Prindsens [i.e. the later King Edward VII of Great Britain and Ireland] og Prindsessens af Wales Portraiter i stort Format. – Brev fra General Knolley for at tilbyde mig Honorar, som jeg frabad mig'.

4.2.1876
La Fille du régiment (Regimentets Datter).
In his diary Bournonville stated about this, his second and last restaging of G. Donizetti's two-act comic opera (sung in Danish) at Copenhagen's Royal Theatre (*see also* 10.1.1849 and 20.10.1859):

31.1.1876: 'Skandale med [P. L. N.] Schramm, der meldte sig sÿg fra Prøven paa Regimentets Datter og alligevel vil synge i Iphigenia imorgen!'
4.2.: 'I Theatret Regimentets Datter til Fru [H.] Willmanns Debut, der gjorde megen Lykke'.

The 1876 restaging, which seems to have been mounted with only minor if any changes from the previous 1859 production, received 7 performances during Bournonville's lifetime, the last of which was given on 6.6.1879.

The musical material employed this year was the same as that used for the previous 1859 production (now in DKKkt and in DKKk, call no. KTA 300).

8.4.1876
Tableaux created on the occasion of King Christian IX's birthday (Tableauer til Kongens Fødselsdag) **(Christiansborg Palace).**
At the personal request of Queen Louise, Bournonville arranged this series of 10 tableaux for a ball celebrating the forty-seventh birthday of Denmark's King Christian IX. They were performed by 53 persons who formed the letters of the monarch name while marching through different groupings of positional anagrams, with each group representing one of the following ten characters: 'C-H-R-I-S-T-I-A-N-IX'. In his diary Bournonville noted about the rehearsals and the performing of these tableaux:

29.3.1876: 'Audients og Conference hos hds M. Dronningen [i.e. Queen Louise Wilhelmine Friederike Caroline Auguste Julie of Denmark] i Anledning af nogle projecterede Tableauer til Kongens [i.e. King Chrsitian IX] Fødselsdag'
30.3.: 'Arrangeret Lister til de omtalte Tableauer'
31.3.: 'Møde paa Christiansborg i Anledning af Tableauerne'
1.4.: 'Brev til <u>Frk Oxholm</u> om Tableauerne [...] Svar fra Frk. Oxholm'
4.4.: 'Møde paa Christiansborg, hvor Dronningen var tilstede'
5.4.: 'Arrangement af Tableauer paa Christiansborg'
7.4.: 'to Gange oppe paa Slottet for Tableauerne. – Kl 6 igjen derop til Generalprøve paa Tableauerne. Musiken først, derpaa Kl 8 begyndte det Hele [...] Det gik meget smukt og Dronningen var særdeles virksom. Det Hele varede to timer, men vil imorgen kun medtage 1½ Time'
8.4.: 'Flagning og Høitidelighed i Byen i Anledning af Kongens Fødselsdag, componeret og ordnet. Kl 7½ undfundet mig paa Christiansborg-Slot, hvor der var Galla-Selskab til Tableauerne, der efter Dronningens Opfindelse i 10 Afdelinger fremstilte Anagrammet <u>Christian</u>. 53 Personer vare deri præsenterede og <u>Simonna</u> med Fru <u>Havkins</u> sang 4 Gange. Det Hele gik udmærket godt og behagede særdeles. Jeg gik lidt over 10'.

No musical sources for this series of tableaux have yet been traced.

10.5.1876

The Bewitched (Den Bjergtagne/Den Bergtagna).

The Copenhagen première of I. Hallström's four-act roman-tic opera to text by F. Hedberg (first performed in a five-act version at Stockholm's Royal Theatre on 20.5.1874) was staged with Bournonville's mise-en-scène and choreography. According to several conductor's notes in the Copenhagen orchestral score, it was performed in Denmark in a rather abridged version with several large musical cuts (particularly in Act III). As a result of these cuts and the joining of Acts IV and V into one act, the numbering of each section in the Danish score is completely different from that of the original Stockholm version.

The Copenhagen production included several dance scenes which were as follows:

(1) A *Minuet* in Act I (score no. 2), performed by the corps de ballet during the chorus, entitled «Så dansa vi nu med lusteligt sinn».
(2) A so-called 'Trollpolska' in Act I (score no. 6), performed by a group of gnomes and dwarves during the song of the *King of the Mountain*, named «Neckan sin harpa slår, dansen i skogen går lus-tigt»i ful galopp'.
(3) Two (unnamed) *Dance scenes* in Act II, score nos. 11–12, per-formed by a corps de ballet of trolls. Of these the latter takes place during the chorus of the mountain spirits, named «Guldet flammer i bergets kammar».
(4) An (unnamed) *Dance* in Act III (score no. 14, originally no. 18 (1)), performed by a corps de ballet (16 couples of gnomes and elf maidens) during the chorus, entitled «Glädtiga sångers muntra ljud».
(5) A *Pas de cinq* divertissement in Act III (score no. 14, originally no. 18 (2)), performed by a man and four women (D. Krum, A. Scholl, J. Petersen, E. Schousgaard, and A. Flammé) and sur-rounded by 12 couples of gnomes and elf maidens.
(6) A *Processional March ('Bergandarnes Intåg')* in the Act III finale (score no. 14, originally no. 18 (3)), performed the spirits of the mountain.

Bournonville had earlier heard excerpts of Hallström's op-era at two concerts in Copenhagen in 1874. Moreover, he attended a performance of the complete opera the same year at Stockholm's Royal Theatre (Stora Theatern) where it was mounted with choreography by Théodore (stage name for T. I. Marckhl).

In his diary he thus noted about his preparations for Copenhagen staging of this already well-known work and its first two performances in Denmark:

24.9.1874: 'Samtale med […] Componisten [I.] Hallström om denne Sidstes Opera `Den Bergtagna´ […] Bivaanet en Sangprøve paa ovennævnte Opera, Musiken interessant […] Hört Hallstrøms [i.e. I. Hallström] Opera Den Bergtagna foredraget med en udmær-ket Sopran'
9.6.1875: 'Den Bergtagna, der interesserede mig særdeles og hvori [C. O.] Arnoldsson og M.lle [W. A.] Riego udmærkede sig baade ved sang og Spil'
10.6.: 'talt med Theatermaler [C.] Jan[s]son og Maskinmester [P. F.] Lindström'
11.6.: 'Formiddagen hos Hallström hvor vi forhandlede endeel om Den Bergtagne'
12.6.: 'Besøg af Hallström […] Middag med Hallstrøm (vi trakte-rede)'
21.6.: 'Skrevet, ordnet og lavet Scene-Arrangement til Den Bjerg-tagne'
25.6.: 'Skrevet'
26.11.: 'skrevet Decorations=Arrangement for Den Bjergtagne'
12.1.1876: 'Arbeidet paa Dandsen til Den Bjergtagne'

13.1.: 'componeret'
19.1.: 'componeret til Den Bjergtagne'
20.1.: 'Componeret paa den Bjergtagne'
21.1.: 'componeret'
22.1.: 'Indstudering af Dands til Den Bjergtagne'
26.1. and 28.1.: 'Indstudering paa Dandsen til Den Bjergtagne'
29.1.: 'fuldendt den større Dands til Den Bjergtagne'
1.2.: 'Prøve paa den nÿ Dands'
9.2.: 'givet [E.] Lehmann Anvisning til Tegninger for Den Bjerg-tagne'
11.2.: 'componeret til Den Bjergtagne'
12.2.: 'Indstudering til Den Bjergtagne'
14.2.: 'Prøve paa Dandsene til Den Bjergtagne […] skrevet og com-poneret'
18.2.: 'modtaget Tegninger af Lehmann […] Prøve paa Dands'
8.3.: 'modtaget Costumer af Lehmann til Den Bjergtagne'
11.3.: 'componeret paa Dandsen til Den Bjergtagne'
12.3.: 'Costumemøde paa Den Bjergtagne'
13.3.: 'Prøve paa Dandsene til Den Bjergtagne, componeret'
14.3.: 'Indstudering af Dands til Den Bjergtagne'
15.3.: 'Prøve paa Dandsene til Den Bjergtagne, som jeg præsenter-ede for [H. S.] Paulli og de Rollehavende'
17.3.: 'Bryderier angaaende Decorationerne til "Den Bjergtagne"'
19.3.: 'Decorationsmøde paa Theatret'
21.3.: 'Brev til Bestyrelsen med Reservation i Anledning af Decora-tionerne til Den Bjergtagne'
28.3.: 'Prøve paa Dandsen til Den Bjergtagne'
29.3.: 'Indstudering af Dands til 1.ste Akt af Den Bjergtagne'
1.4.: 'Indstudering paa Dands til Den Bjergtagne'
4.4. and 6.4.: 'Instruction paa Den Bjergtagne'
7.4.: 'stor Arrangement paa 1.e og 2' Akt af Den Bjergtagne'
10.4.: 'Instruction paa 3.e Akt af Den Bjergtagne'
12.4.: 'Besøg hos Fru Bäckström hvis Mand og Ivar Hallström jeg mødte. – Sangprøve for Componisten paa Den Bjergtagne'
14.4.: 'seet den Pragtfulde men besværlige Decoration til Den Bjerg-tagnes 3.die Akt'
18.4.: 'Prøve i Salen paa 1.ste Akt af Den Bjergtagne'
19.4.: 'hele Formiddagen sysselsat med Theaterprøve paa 3.die Akt af Den Bjergtagne'
20.4.: 'Theaterprøve paa 2' Akt af Den Bjergtagne'
21.4.: 'Instruction paa 4.e Akt af Den Bjergtagne'
22.4. and 26.4.: 'Theaterprøve paa 1.ste og 2' Akt af Den Bjergtagne'
27.4. and 29.4.: 'Theaterprøve paa 3.e og 4.e Akt af Den Bjergtagne'
1.5.: 'Theaterprøve paa Den Bjergtagne heelt igjennem (atter op-sat)'
3.5.: 'holdt Costumeprøve til Den Bjergtagne'
5.5.: 'fuldstændig Prøve med ufuldstændige Decorationer paa Den Bjergtagne'
6.5.: 'Costümeprøve paa Theatret'
8.5.: 'Generalprøve paa 'Den Bjergtagne' der gaaer smukt og hvori min Dands og Scene-Arrangement tager sig godt ud'
10.5.: 'I Theatret 1.ste Forestilling af Den Bjergtagne der gik i enhver Henseende mønsterværdigt men blev i Begyndelsen temmelig koldt modtaget, senere ved og efter Balletten livlig Applaus; i det Hele vellykket'
13.5.: 'I Theatret Den Bjergtagne for fuldt Huus, men et koldt Pub-licum, der først fik Liv ved Dandsene'.

About the fifth performance on 29.5.1876 he stated:

'I Theatret Den Bjergtagne i Nærværelse af Componisten, der var særdeles tilfreds, Alt gik udmærket smukt'.

Hallström's opera reached a total of 7 performances in Copenhagen, the last of which was given on 13.9.1876.

Autograph sources:

Manuscript mise-en-scène. Ms. Autograph. Brown ink. 8 pp. (21,4 × 17,5 and 22,7 × 17,9 and 20.9 × 17,1 cm)

Scene = Arrangement./til/Operaen Den Bjergtagne./Text af Hedberg. Musik af Hallström./Kjøbenhavn/ 1875.
Signed and dated: 'Fredensborg d 25.e Juni 1875.' [Written according to the diary between 21.6. and 25.6.1875]
[SSm; Daniel Fryklunds samling no. 120

Manuscript mise-en-scène. Ms. Autograph. Black ink. 8 pp. (22,3 × 17,8 cm)
Den Bjergtagne/Arrangement for Choret.
Unsigned and undated [Written according to the diary most probably on 26.11.1875]
[SSm; Daniel Fryklunds samling no. 120

Choreographic note. Ms. Autograph. Black ink. 5 pp. (20,6 × 16,8 and 22,4 × 17,8 cm)
Den Bjergtagne/1.ste Akt./[...]/Trollpolska./[...]/(2.e Akt. 4.de Scene)/[...]/5.te Scene
Unsigned and undated [Written according to the diary most probably between late March and early April 1876]
[SSm; Daniel Fryklunds samling no. 120
This manuscript contains Bournonville's choreography for the *Minuet* in Act I (score no. 2) of *The Bewitched*, and the so-called 'Trollpolska' in the same act (score no. 6). Moreover, it includes Bournonville's two sets of choreographic numbers ('1–5' and '1–8') which refer to his similar numbers written underneath the music (on pp. 3–9) in the répétiteur's copy for Hallström's opera (now in DKKk, call no. MA ms 3095 (KTA 789 (1)). Furthermore, the manuscript contains his notes describing the complete choreography for the two (unnamed) *Dance scenes* in Act II (score nos. 11–12), to which Bournonville also added choreographic numbers ('1–20') that refer to similar numbers inserted in the second répétiteur's copy for *The Bewitched* (now in DKKk, call no. MA ms 3096 (KTA 789 (2)).

Choreographic note. Ms. Autograph. Ink. 2 pp. (format unknown)
Den Bjergtagne/(Dands i 3.die Akt.)
Unsigned and undated [Written according to the diary most probably between 12.1. and 21.1.1876]
[USNYp; Dance Collection, call nos. *ZBD-71 (microfilm), and (S)*MGZMD 30 (photostat copy)
This manuscript contains Bournonville's first, general choreographic survey of the complete dances in Act III of Hallström's opera.

Choreographic note. Ms. Autograph. Ink. 2 pp. (format unknown)
Den Bjergtagne (3.die Akt.)/(Chor og Dands)
Unsigned and undated [Written according to the diary most probably between 12.1. and 21.1.1876]
[USNYp; Dance Collection, call nos. *ZBD-71 (microfilm), and (S)*MGZMD 30 (photostat copy)
This manuscript contains Bournonville's choreography performed by the corps de ballet of gnomes and elf maidens in Act III, score no. 14 (originally no. 18 (1)) during the chorus, entitled «Glädtiga sångers muntra ljud». The manuscript also includes his autographed choreographic numbers ('1–9') which refer to similar numbers written underneath the music (on pp. 10–13) in the répétiteur's copy for Hallström's opera (now in DKKk, call no. MA ms 3095 (KTA 789 (1)).

Choreographic note. Ms. Autograph. Ink. 4 pp. (format unknown)
Den Bjergtagne/Pas de cinq/&/Corps de Ballets./[...]/Andante grazioso./[...]/Allegretto 6/8./[...]/Maestoso./[...]/Allegro – Presto/[...]/Moderato 3/4/[...]/Coda
Unsigned and undated [Written according to the diary most probably between 12.1. and 21.1.1876]
[USNYp; Dance Collection, call nos. *ZBD-71 (microfilm), and (S)*MGZMD 30 (photostat copy)
This (undated) manuscript contains Bournonville's first version of the choreography for the *Pas de cinq* divertissement in Act III, score no. 14 (originally no. 18 (2)) of *The Bewitched*. The manuscript also includes his autographed choreographic numbers ('1–8' and '1–28') that correspond to his similar numbers written underneath the

music (on pp. 14–23) in the répétiteur's copy for Hallström's opera (now in DKKk, call no. MA ms 3095 (KTA 789 (1)).

Choreographic note. Ms. Autograph. Ink. 6 pp. (format unknown)
Den Bjergtagne/Andante grazioso/[...]/Allegretto 6/8/[...]Krum & Petersen (& D S)/[...]/Maestoso./[...]/ Moderato 3/4/[...]/ Coda
Signed and dated: 'ce 19 Janvier 1876.'
[USNYp; Dance Collection, call nos. *ZBD-71 (microfilm), and (S)*MGZMD 30 (photostat copy)
This manuscript contains Bournonville's definitive version of the choreography for the *Pas de cinq* divertissement in Act III, score no. 14 (originally no. 18 (2)) of *The Bewitched*. It also includes his autographed choreographic numbers ('1–8' and '1–28') which correspond to his similar numbers written underneath the music (on pp. 14–23) in the répétiteur's copy for Hallström's opera (now in DKKk, call no. MA ms 3095 (KTA 789 (1)).

Musical sources:

Orchestral score. Ms. Copy. Black ink. 3 vol. Act I 240 pp. of which two are blank, Act II–III 420 pp. of which one is blank, Act IV 262 pp. of which three are blank (43,8 × 28,3 cm)
Den Bjergtagne/Hallström/Partitur./1.ste Act/[...]/2.den og 3.die Act/[...]/4.de act
Unsigned and undated [1876]
[DKKk; C I, 259 d fol. (KTA 789)
This orchestral score is a copy of the Swedish score that omits F. Hedberg's original text and includes only A. Hertz's 1876 Danish translation.

Répétiteur's copy. Ms. Copy (by V. C. Holm). Brown ink. 1 vol. 32 pp. of which two are blank (34 × 26 cm)
A. 789./Den Bjergtagne/(/Repetiteurparti)/54/[...]/Den Bjergtagne/(Repetiteurparti)
Unsigned and undated [1876]
[DKKk; MA ms 3095 (KTA 789 (1))
This répétiteur's copy contains the complete music for the dances in Acts I and III of Hallström's opera. It also includes Bournonville's autograph choreographic numbers (written with black ink) which refer to the similar numbers in his separate notations of these dances, written (according to his diary) most likely between mid-January and early April 1876.

Répétiteur's copy. Ms. Copy (by V. C. Holm). Brown ink. 8 pp. (35 × 25,5 cm)
2.den Act. (4de Scene)
Unsigned and undated [1876]
[DKKk; MA ms 3096 (KTA 789 (2))
This répétiteur's copy contains the music for the two (unnamed) *Dance scenes* in Act II (score nos. 11–12) of Hallström's opera. The volume also includes Bournonville's autographed choreographic notes and numbers (written with black ink). They refer to similar numbers in his separate notations of these scenes, written (according to his diary) most likely between late March and early April 1876.

Parts. Ms. Copy. 37 vol.
4 vl I, 3 vl II, 2 vla, 4 vlc e cb, fl picc, fl 1/2, ob 1/2, cl 1/2, fag 1/2, cor 1/2/3/4, tr 1/2, trb 1/2/3, tuba, timp, gr cassa, piatti, tri, arpa. 61 vocal parts.
Unsigned and undated [1876]
[DKKk; KTA 789

5.9.1876
The Valkyrie (Valkyrien).
This peformance represents Bournonville's third and last restaging of his four-act nordic mythological ballet *The Valkyrie* (*see* 13.9.1861). It also marks the first time this ballet was performed in the new Royal Theatre building. Apart from par-

tially new décors by the German scene painter, P. Gropius, the ballet seems this year to have been mounted with only minor if any changes from Bournonville's previous 1873 production. This is clear from his diary, in which he stated about the performance:

3.11.1875: 'Prøve paa <u>Valkyrien</u> 1.ste Akt'
6.11.: 'Prøve paa 1.ste Akt af Valkyrien'
8.11.: 'Prøve paa Valkyrien 2' Akt'
19.11.: 'Prøve og nÿ Indstudering paa Valkÿrien'
22.11.: 'Prøve paa 3' Akt af Valkyrien'
23.11.: 'lille Prøve paa Valkyrien'
25.11.: 'Prøve paa 3.die Akt af Valkyrien'
4.12.: 'Skrevet Plan til Valkyriens Decorationer'
6.12.: 'Prøve paa 3.e Akt af Valkyrien'
7.12.: 'Prøve paa Valkyrien'
10.12.: 'Prøve paa 4'e Akt af Valkyrien'
11.12.: 'Prøve paa Valkyrien, <u>4.e Akt</u>'
14.12.: 'Prøve paa 3' og 4' Akt af Valkyrien'
18.12.: 'Prøve paa 1.ste og 2' Akt af Valkyrien'
11.4.1876: 'Repetition af 3.die Akt af Valkyrien'
24.4.: 'Prøve paa Valkÿriens 1.ste og 2' Akt'
18.5.: 'Prøve paa Valkyrien'
24.5.: 'lille Prøve paa Valkyrien'
27.5.: 'Prøve paa Dandsene til Valkyrien'
18.8.: 'Kl 5 – Prøve paa Theatret paa Valkyriens 1' og 2' Akt'
19.8.: 'Prøve paa [...] 3.e Akt af Valkyrien [...] Eftermiddagsprøve paa Valkyriens 3.die Akt'
22.8.: 'Prøve paa Valkyriens 4.e Akt'
24.8.: 'Theaterprøve med Orchester paa 1.ste og 2' Akt af Valkyrien'
25.8.: 'Decorationsprøve paa Valkyrien fra 6 til 9.'
26.8.: 'Aftenprøve paa 3.e og 4.e Akt af Valkyrien'
29.8.: 'Theaterprøve paa 3.e og 4. Akt af Valkyrien'
31.8.: 'Generalprøve i Costume paa Valkyrien, som gik særdeles godt fra Ballettens Side, men yderst slet fra Maskineriets'
2.9.: 'Prøve paa Dandsene til [...] Valkyrien'
4.9.: 'Prøve paa Valkyrien med Maskiner og Statister'
5.9.: 'I Theatret <u>Valkyrien</u> for fuldt Huus, gik udmærket smukt'

About the second performance on 11.9.1875 he noted:

'i Theatret <u>Valkyrien</u> for udsolgt Huus, gik udmærket fra alle Sider med Undtagelse af vort jammerlige Maskineri og vort søvnige fornemme Publicum'.

The 1876 production of *The Valkyrie* received 8 performances during Bournonville's lifetime, the last of which was given on 28.1.1879.

The musical material employed this year was the same as that used for the previous production on 29.1.1873 (now in DKKk, call nos. C II, 114, MA ms 2995, and KTB 298)).

Autograph sources:

Production note. Ms. Autograph. Black ink. 3 pp. (20,9 × 17 cm)
<u>Plan til Decorationerne</u>/i/<u>Balletten Valkyrien</u>
Unsigned and undated [Written according to the diary on 4.12. 1875]
[DKKk; Utilg. 828 (Harald Landers Arkiv, Kapsel 182)
This manuscript describes Bournonville's new arrangement of the décors for *The Valkyrie* when it was mounted for the first time in the new Royal Theatre building with mixed sets of older and new décors. Among these was the old scenery, created in 1874 by the German scene painter, P. Gropius, for Act IV of Bournonville's four-act national historical ballet *Waldemar*. It depicted Grathe Heath, but was not actually used in *Waldemar* until its last restaging during Bournonville's lifetime on 1.6.1877. In *The Valkyrie* Gropius' 1874 scenery of Grathe Heath was employed for the final scene in Act IV, where it served as décor for the scene depicting the battle at Braavalla Heath.

Other sources:

Sketch by V. Güllich of the décor for Act II. Pencil and water colours (45,8 × 72 cm with sight 35,2 × 62,3 cm)
[Untitled]
Signed: 'SVG', undated [1876? or 1894?]
[DKKt; V. Güllichs dekorationsudkast (89/142)

7.12.1876
From Siberia to Moscow (Fra Sibirien til Moscow).
This two-act ballet, which is set to a score composed and arranged by C. C. Møller, represents the last full-length ballet Bournonville created for Copenhagen's Royal Theatre (*see also* 27.8.1874). According to his memoirs *My Theatre Life* (p. 399), its plot was inspired from his recollection earlier the same year of a much earlier meeting and conversation he had in Stockholm in 1863 with the well-known Russian politician and republican, M. Bakunin, who died in exile in 1876. Bournonville's first meeting with this flamboyant personality, who clearly became the model for the character *Smirnoff* in this ballet, is described in his diary on 20.9.1863 as follows:

'i Selskab med [...] den russiske Revolutions Apostel <u>Bakunin</u>, en mærkværdig Mand med en tilsyneladende stor Overbevisning og med en sjelden Veltalenhed i det franske Sprog'.

The news of Bakunin's death in 1876 thus seems to have spurred Bournonville with the idea of portraying a Russian nobleman (*Smirnoff*), who, taken with the ideas of the first French revolution, has incurred the disfavour of the Czar, but in the end is forgiven by him.

Moreover, during a sojourn in Paris in 1874 Bournonville read (according to his travel diary) a drama by a certain H. Chrysafulli, entitled *L'Exil*, the plot of which had originally been suggested to its author by Bournonville's long-time friend, the Danish merchant in Paris, A. Bing. This drama (about which Bournonville also wrote an extensive review) clearly formed the basis for most of the dramatic action in his own ballet *From Siberia to Moscow*.

Among the ballet's many dances the allegorical divertissement in Act II (score no. 22) stands out. It represented five of Europe's biggest rivers, and seems to have been based (at least partially) on a very similar divertissement that Bournonville had seen performed in St Petersburg in 1874 as part of M. Petipa's and C. Pugni's three-act ballet *La Fille du Pharaon*. Thus, the Russian solo dance representing the river *La Newa* (danced by the daughter of *Smirnoff*, *Nathalia*) was most likely based on the exact same choreography and music as that of the divertissement with that name in M. Petipa's *La Fille du Pharaon*. This theory is supported by a note in Bournonville's diary on 30.4.1874, in which he stated after having seen this dance in St Petersburg:

'Om Aftenen i Det store Theater, <u>La Fille de Pharaon</u>. [...] Mlle [M.] <u>Madaeva</u> henrivende og passende i en lille russisk Dands (som Neva-floden)'.

Moreover, in his (unpublished) foreword to his first manuscript scenario for *From Siberia to Moscow* (dated 23.2.1876) Bournonville noted about this divertissement:

'for at undgaae Beskyldning for Plagiat, maa jeg herved erklære at den oprindelige Idee til <u>Flodernes – Repræsentation</u>, ikke tilhører mig, men er af [A.] Saint Léon [*sic*] anvendt i hans Fille de Pharaon dog under en anden Form og til et Motiv, der er høist forskjelligt fra det, der i min Composition danner Festens Kjærne.'

In his arrangement of the music for Act I (score no. 3) C. C. Møller employed A. Warlamoff's tune for the Russian folk song, entitled *Krasnyj Sarafan* («Ne sēj ty mne matuška»), and in the ballet's final scene of Act II (score no. 23) he interpolated A. L'vov's melody from 1833 to W. A. Schukowskij's Russian national hymn «Bozhe, tsarya khrani» («God save the Czar»).

According to an undated letter from Bournonville to Queen Olga of Greece (now in DKKk, call no. NKS 3258 B 4°, VII, 9) the costumes (which were all drawn by E. Lehmann) were based on a not yet identified collection of Russian national costumes, described by Bournonville as: 'recueil de Costumes, dont Votre Majesté a daigné me faire cadeau à l'intention de mon ballet nouveau'.

In his diary he noted about the ballet's creation and its first two performances:

20.2.1876: 'jeg conciperede Udkastet til en nÿ Ballet Nathalia eller De Forviiste'
22.2.: 'reenskrevet Udkastet til min nÿ Ballet'
23.2.: 'fuldført Programmet til Nathalia'
24.2.: 'Indleveret mit Balletprogram med Brev til Conf [A. C. P.] Linde'
5.3.: 'truffet Aftale med Musikdirecteur [C. C.] Møller om Composition til min nÿ Ballet'
8.3.: 'arbeidet 1.ste Gang med C C Møller der skal componere Musiken til min nÿ Ballet'
13.3.: '1.ste Møde med C C Møller, der leverede mig fire Numre meget smukke til min nÿ Ballet'
15.3.: 'componeret'
16.3.: 'Ubehagelig Efterretning om W. Prices Knæskade der vil standse Repertoiret i længere Tid'
20.3.: '2.det Møde med Møller for Musiken til Nathalia'
24.3.: 'besørget adskilligt'
27.3.: 'Arbeidet med Møller (4.e Gang)'
3.4.: 'Musikmøde med C C Møller, der har fuldendt 1.ste Akt af Balletten Nathalia'
8.4.: 'componeret og ordnet'
14.5.: 'Arrangeret Personlister til min nÿ Ballet'
22.5.: 'Begyndt at componere paa min nÿ Ballet Nathalia'
9.6., 13.6., 14.6., and 15.6.: 'skrevet og componeret'
2.7.: 'Besøg af [E.] Lehmann'
19.7.: 'skrevet og componeret'
20.7. 'componeret 1.ste Akt af den nÿ Ballet færdig'
21.7.: 'componeret to Dandse til 2' Akt'
22.7.: 'componeret en Dands til den nÿ Ballet'
25.7.: 'componeret en Dands til Balletten'
27.7.: 'skrevet og componeret'
29.7.: 'componeret'
30.7.: 'componeret og skrevet'
13.8.: 'Brev til C C Møller'
15.8.: 'modtaget Musik af [C. C.] Möller'
25.8.: 'skrevet og componeret'
9.9.: 'Brev til […] [F.] Hildebrand (Petersborg) [..] skrevet og componeret'
12.9.: 'Første Indstudering paa min nÿ Ballet "Fra Sibirien"'
13.9.: 'componeret'
14.9.: '2.den Indstudering paa min nÿ Ballet'
16.9.: '3.die Indstudering'
20.9.: 'Repetition paa det Lærte af den nÿ Ballet'
21.9.: '4.de Indstudering […] componeret i Theaterværelset'
22.9.: '5.te Indstudering, skrevet og componeret'
25.9.: 'Repetition paa den nÿ Ballet'

27.9.: '6.te Indstudering'
28.9.: 'Repetition paa den nÿ Ballet'
29.9.: 'componeret'
30.9.: '7.e Indstudering Guadalqvivir i 2' Akt'
1.10.: 'componeret Forslag til Costumerne'
3.10.: '8.e Indstudering […] Brev til Hildebrand i St Petersborg'
5.10.: 'Prøve paa den nÿ Ballet (Farandolen)'
6.10.: 'Repetition paa den nÿ Ballet […] Besøg i Kongens Haandbibliothek'
8.10.: 'componeret paa Theatret'
9.10.: '9.de Indstudering, modtaget et Billedværk fra Kongens Haandbibliothek'
10.10.: 'Repetition paa Themsen, componeret, skrevet Costumering og arbeidet med Lehmann'
11.10.: '10.de Indstudering (Rhône)'
12.10.: 'componeret'
13.10.: 'Brev til Kmhr [M. E.] Fallesen om min nÿ Ballet […] skrevet Personlister til Balletten'
14.10.: 'Skrevet og expederet Requisitlister til den nÿ Ballet […] repeteret Dandsene til den nÿ Ballet […] Aftenen hjemme, skrevet og componeret'
15.10.: 'Aftenen hjemme læst og componeret'
16.10.: '11.e Indstudering (Vestberg [i.e. M. Westberg] Neva)'
17.10.: '12.e Indstudering (Undinerne)'
18.10.: '12' [*sic*] Indstudering (Westberg)'
19.10.: 'Repetition paa alt det Lærte af den ny Ballet, componeret'
20.10.: 'Prøve og 14.e Indstudering'
23.10.: 'Repetition paa det Nÿe'
24.10.: 'skrevet den Hele Aften paa Regien til min nÿ Ballet'
25.10.: '15.e Indstudering, componeret'
26.10.: 'reenskrevet paa Theatret Programmet til min nÿ Ballet 'Fra Sibirien til Moskow'. Ubehageligt Repertoiremøde […] fuldendt Reenskrivningen af Balletten'
27.10.: 'leveret mit Program til Boghandelen'
28.10.. 'Repetition paa ' Akt'
29.10.: 'Costümemøde paa Theatret'
30.10.: '16.e Indstudering (Finalen af 1.e Akt)'
1.11.: '17.de Indstudering(Polonaisen)'
6.11.: 'Prøve Kl 10½ paa hele Balletten. Costumemøde for Damedragterne'
8.11.: 'Om Aftenen Costümeprøve'
10.11.: 'Stort Arrangement paa Theatret af 2.den Akt til Balletten, skrevet og læst, fyldt Møllers Claveerudtog'
11.11.: 'Arrangement paa 1.ste Akt af Balletten'
13.11.: 'Costumeprøve'
14.11.: 'Theater-Arrangement paa 2' Akt'
17.11.: 'Repetition paa den nÿ Ballet'
18.11.: 'præsenteret Balletten (paa Salen) for Chefen [i.e. M. E. Fallesen] og [F. J. G.] Berner. Den gik udmærket'
20.11.: 'Theaterprøve paa Balletten med Repetiteurs'
23.11.: 'Costümemøde paa Theatret'
24.11.: 'noteret i Møllers Claveerudtog af Balletten'
25.11.: 'skrevet og noteret paa Theatret'
27.11.: 'partiel Prøve paa Rollerne i den nÿ Ballet. Musikprøve paa Samme, meget heldig'
28.11.: 'Costumeprøve'
29.11.: 'Fuldstændig Prøve paa min nÿ Ballet […] Costumeprøve'
30.11.: 'Repertoiremøde og deri en skarp Udtalelse til Chefen i Anledning af Søndagsprojectet med de to Forestillinger'
4.12.: 'fuldstændig Prøve paa Balletten, der gik særdeles smukt. Modtaget Programmer og sendt dem til Hoffet. Costumeprøve paa Theatret'
5.12.: 'Costumeprøve'
6.12. 'besørget Alting til Generalprøven paa Balletten Fra Sibirien til Moskow, der gik i enhver Hensende fortræffeligt'
7.12.: 'I Theatret hvor Fra Sibirien til Moskow opførtes for første Gang, gik i enhver Henseende fortræffeligt og blev modtaget med livligt Bifald. Der blev stor Glæde i Hjemmet over denne succès og jeg takkede Gud af mit inderste Hjerte!'
8.12.: 'modtaget mange Lykønskninger i Anledning af Balletten […]

I Theatret 2' Forestilling af Balletten der gik ligesaa smukt som igaar og med livligt Bifald men desværre kun for et mindre velbesat Huus. Denne Vinter er i finantiel Henseende ikke heldig med sine Nyheder […] Man maa trøste sig med at have gjort sit Bedste, og regne det mindre talrige Besøg til de slette Conjunkturer i Pengeverdenen'.

From Siberia to Moscow received 27 performances during Bournonville's lifetime, the last of which was given on 29.9. 1879.

Autograph sources:

Manuscript scenario. Ms. Autograph. Black ink. 1 vol. 10 pp. (22,9 × 18,3 cm)
Nathalia eller De Forviiste/Ballet i to Akter./af/August Bournonville/1876.
Signed and dated: 'Kjøbenhavn den 23.e Februar 1876' [Written according to the diary between 20.2. and 23.2.1876]
[DKKk; NKS 3285 4° 3 L–P]
This manuscript scenario includes an autographed foreword by Bournonville, which was never included in the printed scenario for *From Siberia to Moscow*.

Manuscript scenario. Ms. Autograph. Black ink. 1 vol. 8 pp. (22,9 × 18,3 cm)
Nathalia eller De Forviiste/Ballet i to Akter./af/August Bournonville
Signed and dated: 'Kjøbenhavn den 23.e Februar 1876' [Written according to the diary between 20.2. and 23.2.1876]
[DKKk; NKS 3285 4° 3 L–P]

Production note. Ms. Autograph. Black ink. 3 pp. (35,8 × 22,8 cm)
Forslag (Det qvindelige Personale)/til/Costumeringen i Balletten 'Fra Sibirien'
Signed and dated: 'Kjøbenhavn den 25.de October 1876' [Written according to the diary on 24.10. and 25.10.1876]
[DKKkt; F.M. (Ballet)]

Musical sources:

Orchestral score. Ms. Autograph (by C. C. Møller). Black ink. 1 vol. 306 pp. of which three are blank (29,3 × 35 cm with minor variants)
Fra Sibirien til Moskau/Partitur/[…]/Fra Sibirien/Nathalia eller De Forviiste. [erased]/Ballet i 2 Akter./af/Kongl: Hofballetmester A. Bournonville./Musiken/af/C. C. Møller.
Unsigned and dated (by C. C. Møller on p. 306): 'Kjøbenhavn d 19.de Juli 1876./d 8.de Novmbr 1876.'
[DKKk; C II, 118 (KTB 311)]

Répétiteur's copy. Ms. Copy. Brown ink. 1 vol. 68 pp. of which three are blank (33,9 × 25,7 cm)
B 311/Fra Sibirien/til/Moskow/No. 19 [erased]/[…]/Fra Sibirien/til Moskow./Repetiteur Parti
Unsigned and undated [1876]
[DKKk; MA ms 3004 (KTB 311 (1))]
This répétiteur's copy contains several choreographic numbers written (with brown ink, by an unknown hand) throughout the volume. They seem to refer to similar numbers included in a separate (not yet traced) choreographic notation of this ballet, which Bournonville (according to his diary) most likely wrote between mid-March and mid-October 1876. Moreover, in the printed piano score of *From Siberia to Moscow*, published by W. Hansen in Copenhagen in 1877 (pl. no. 3379, now in DKKk, call no. D 6) Bournonville's extensive annotations concerning the mime and the dramatic action are included. According to his diary they were written between 10.11. and 25.11. 1876.

Parts. Ms. Copy. 40 vol.
4 vl I, 4 vl II, 2 vla, 4 vlc e cb, fl picc, fl 1/2, ob 1/2, cl 1/2, fag 1/2, cor 1/2/3/4, tr 1/2, cnt, trb 1/2/3/4, tuba, timp, gr cassa e tamb rul, piatti, tri, arpa.

Unsigned and undated [1876]
[DKKk; KTB 1035 (originally KTB 311)]

Other sources:

Sketch by V. Güllich for the décor of Act I. Pencil and water colours (37,5 × 61 cm with sight 36 × 60 cm)
[Untitled]
Signed: 'V/G', undated [1876]
[DKKt; V. Güllichs dekorationsudkast (89/154)]

Costume drawing by E. Lehmann. Pencil and water colours (23,7 × 15,6 cm)
Ivanoff.
Unsigned and undated [c.1876]
[DKKkt; Kostumetegninger (Lehmann)]
This drawing shows the costume worn by *Iwanoff* in Act I(?) of *From Siberia to Moscow* (performed by D. Krum).

Costume drawing by E. Lehmann. Pencil and water colours (23,6 × 15,9 cm)
Viingaardsfolk.
Unsigned and undated [c.1876]
[DKKkt; Kostumetegninger (Lehmann)]
This drawing shows the costumes worn by the men who performed the divertissement representing the river Rhine in Act II of *From Siberia to Moscow*.

Costume drawing by E. Lehmann. Pencil and water colours (23,6 × 15,9 cm)
[Untitled]
Unsigned and undated [c.1876]
[DKKkt; Kostumetegninger (Lehmann)]
This drawing shows the costumes of the women who performed the divertissement representing the river Rhine in Act II of *From Siberia to Moscow*.

Costume drawing by E. Lehmann. Pencil and water colours (16 × 24 cm)
Nathalia./'Fra Sibirien til Moskov'
Unsigned and undated [c.1876]
[SSm; Daniel Fryklunds samling no. 264 (F 1332 b)]
This drawing shows the costume worn by *Nathalia* in Act I of *From Siberia to Moscow* (performed by M. Westberg).

Costume drawing by E. Lehmann. Pencil and water colours (16 × 24 cm)
Nathalia – (Newa floden)/'Fra Sibirien til Moscov'
Unsigned and undated [c.1876]
[SSm; Daniel Fryklunds samling no. 265 (F 1332 a)]
This drawing shows the costume worn by *Nathalia* in the divertissement representing the river Neva in Act II of *From Siberia to Moscow* (performed by M. Westberg).

Costume drawing by E. Lehmann. Pencil and water colours (16 × 24 cm)
Petroff/Gade
Unsigned and undated [c.1876]
[SSm; Daniel Fryklunds samling no. 266 (F 1332 c)]
This drawing shows the costume worn by *Petroff* in Act I of *From Siberia to Moscow* (performed by L. Gade).

Printed sources:

Printed scenario. 1 vol. 14 pp.
Fra Sibirien til Moskow./Ballet i to Akter/af/August Bournonville./Musiken af C. C. Møller./Decorationerne af W. Güllich og Fr. Ahlgrensson.
Kjøbehanv, J. H. Schubothe/Bianco Luno, 1876
[DKKk; 17, – 176 8°

1877

30.1.–12.4.1877
Twenty-two dance lessons in social dance.
According to several notes in his diary Bournonville gave a series of 22 private dance lessons in social dance at the Copenhagen residence of Count A. L. Schack-Brockenhuus, at Norgesgade no. 26/3. These lessons, which took place mainly on Tuesday and Friday afternoons, lasted for about two hours each, and represent the last series of private dance lessons Bournonville ever gave. About the final lesson (given on 12.4.1877) he stated in his diary:

'Sidste Lection hos Grev [A. L.] Brockenhuus-Schack og modtaget et meget godt Honorar (200 Kroner)'.

7.2.1877
A Danish translation of the French text for Fidès' aria («Donnez donnez pour une pauvre âme») in Le Prophète (Oversættelse af Tiggerarien af Profeten) **performed by Charlotte Bournonville (the Casino Theatre, Mindre Sal).**
According to a note in his diary on 23.1.1877 (reading: 'oversat Tiggerarien af Profeten til Brug for Charlotte') Bournonville made a Danish translation of E. Scribe's French text for the aria of *Fides* (entitled 'Complainte de la mendiante') in Act IV, score no. 22 of G. Meyerbeer's five-act opera *Le Prophète* (*see also* 10.3.1858). This translation was made especially for his daughter, the alto C. Bournonville, who performed it at the Casino Theatre as part of a concert given by the Copenhagen association of merchant officials, named *Foreningen af Handelsbetjente af 5.te Juni 1864*. The aria, which was one of Charlotte Bournonville's most popular star turns, was included in nearly all of her concerts given in Denmark and abroad (Sweden, Germany, France) during the 1850s, 1860s, and 1870s.

Bournonville attended the 1877 concert and noted about it in his diary:

'Concert i Casino's mindre Sal for Charlotte [Bournonville] og [R. L.] Jastrau i compagni. Der var et talrigt og skjønsomt Publicum og saavel Sangen, som violinspiller [C. F.] Hilmer og Pianisten [F.] Schousboe udmærkede sig ved smukke Numere'.

According to pencilled notes written by an unknown hand (on pp. 220–223) in C. Bournonville's private copy of the printed piano vocal score for *Le Prophète* (now in DKKk, call no. U 6, mu 7908.2304), Bournonville's 1877 Danish translation of the aria of *Fides* appears to read as follows:

'En Skjæbne! En Skjæbne forlöser en Synder,
oplader ham, oplader ham Guds Moders Skjød
En Skjæbne! En Skjæbne! En Moder forkynder
sin Qval, sin Nød, min Gud, sin bittre Nød!
O, giv en Skjærv o ædle Herre giv, o giv
Saa beder han i Frelsens Navn
o, fri min Tvang og skjænk mig Trøst,
da skal fromt en Messe tone og bringe ham til Naadens Kyst,
og bringe ham til Naadens Kyst,
og bringe min arme Søn til Naadens Kyst,
ak ak ak Barmhjertighed Barmhjertighed
Hvor koldt! Hvor koldt! Min Fred –! I Gravens Skjød er Fred
men ak, naar jeg er stedt til Ro

Hvo da her beder for ham? hvo da her beder for ham,
for ham, for ham, hvo beder da, hvo beder da?
Vedbeder ham Frelsens Krone,
o fri min Tvang og skjænk mig Trøst,
da skal fromt en Messe tone og bringe ham til Naadens Kyst,
og bringe ham til Naadens Kyst
og bringe min arme Søn til Naadens Kyst,
ak ak ak Barmhjertighed, ak ak ak Barmhjertighed'.

2.3.1877
A Shield Dance and a Tableau vivant, entitled Episode from the Middle-Age: The Crusaders (Skjolddands og En Episode fra Middelalderen: Korsfarerne) **performed by D. Krum and a group of non-comissioned officers in the Danish army (the Court Theatre).**
According to Bournonville's diary this *Shield Dance* and *Tableau vivant* were choreographed by D. Krum, but based on an idea by Bournonville. They were created for a special charity performance given by the association of non-comissioned officers in the Danish army, named *Underofficeersforeningen af 1870*. They received 5 performances at the Court Theatre, the last of which was given on 5.3.1877. On each evening Krum's dances were followed by a orchestral concert, conducted by B. Dahl, who most likely also wrote and/or arranged the music for these dances. Bournonville, who supervised the final stage rehearsal of the performance, attended its second performance on 3.3.1877 and noted about it in his diary:

1.3.1877: 'Generalprøve paa Underofficerernes Bazar og Vaabenøvelser'
3.3.: 'Om Aftenen […] til Hoftheatret og overværet Underofficerernes Bazar, hvor vi tog Lodder, saae Skjolddandsen og den lille krigeriske Episode Korsfarerne, hvortil jeg havde givet Ideen, og [D.] Krum Udførelsen. Det gik med stor Præcision, forbi og hjem Kl 11'.

No musical sources for the 1877 *Shield Dance* and *Tableau vivant* have yet been traced.

27.3.1877
The Mountain Hut, or Twenty Years (Fjeldstuen eller: Tyve Aar).
This performance represents Bournonville's second and last restaging of his Norwegian ballet *The Mountain Hut, or Twenty Years* (*see* 13.5.1859). It was mounted in a thoroughly revised version that included several rechoreographed sections, arranged especially for A. Flammé, who played *Asta* for the first time this year. These choreographic changes occured mainly in the ballet's second act, in which (according to the 1877 répétiteur's copy) a brief *entr'acte* (or 'Mellemscene') of 28 measures was inserted between what originally were the second and third tableaux. Moreover, according to the same source and Bournonville's separate 1877 choreographic notation of the entire ballet, many other minor musical cuts and changes were made in Act II.

Thus, in his diary he noted about the revised 1877 version and its first three performances:

6.5.1876: 'lille Indstudering med [A.] Flammé paa Fjeldstuen'
9.5.: 'Prøve [,…] med Flammé som Bjergpigen'
11.12.: 'Paa Theatret, skrevet og componeret paa Fjeldstuen'
12.12.: 'Prøve paa 2' Akt af Fjeldstuen'
13.12.: 'componeret paa Fjeldstuen'

14.12.: 'Prøve og Indstudering paa Fjeldstuen', 2' Akt (Bjergscenen færdig)'

15.12.: 'Indstudering og Prøve paa Scener af Fjeldstuen 1.ste Akt'

16.12.: 'arbeidet paa Scenerne til Fjeldstuen'

18.12.: 'Indstudering paa Fjeldstuen'

19.12. and 20.12.: 'Indstudering paa Fjeldstuen, skrevet og componeret paa Samme'

21.12.: 'Indstudering paa Fjeldstuen'

22.12.: 'Repetition paa tvende Scener af Fjeldstuen'

27.12., 28.12., and 29.12: 'Indstudering paa Fjeldstuen'

30.12.: 'Repetition paa 2' og 1' Akt af Fjeldstuen'

3.1.1877: 'Repetition paa 1.ste Akt af Fjeldstuen samt 2.den Akt første Afdeling'

4.1.: 'skrevet og componeret, Indstudering paa 2' Akt af Fjeldstuen'

5.1.: 'Arbeidet 4 Timer paa Compositionen til Fjeldstuens 2' Akt'

6.1.: 'Indstudering paa 2.den Akt af Fjeldstuen'

8.1.: 'sidste Indstudering paa Fjeldstuen, der lover godt'

11.1.: 'Prøve paa Flammés Dands i Fjeldstuen'

12.1.: 'Prøve paa begge Akter af Fjeldstuen (ubehageligt og dumt Brev fra [G.] Brodersen)'

13.1.: '(Flammé ubehagelig) Musikaftale med Emil Hartmann'

20.1.: 'Repetition paa Fjeldstuen'

25.1.: 'Repetition paa 2' Akt af Fjeldstuen'

30.1.: 'Repetition paa Scener af Fjeldstuen'

31.1.: 'Præsentation af Fjeldstuen hvori navnlig Flammé udmærkede sig'

19.2.: 'Decorationsprøve til Fjeldstuen'

16.3.: 'Prøve paa Fjeldstuen'

17.3.: 'Musikprøve paa Fjeldstuen'

19.3.: 'Theaterprøve paa Fjeldstuen'

20.3.: 'fuldstændig Prøve paa Fjeldstuen der gik meget smukt'

23.3.: 'Repetition paa Rollerne til Fjeldstuen'

26.3.: 'Generalprøve paa Fjeldstuen der gik udmærket'

27.3.: 'I Theatret […] Fjeldstuen, der gjorde megen Lÿkke. Flammé havde deri sin anden Début og udførte sin Rolle med Bravour […] Huset var udsolgt'

5.4.: 'Fjeldstuen for tyndt besat Huus'

13.4.: 'Fjeldstuen der gik meget smukt, men for tyndt besat Huus'.

The 1877 production of *The Mountain Hut, or Twenty Years* received 9 performances during Bournonville's lifetime, the last of which was given on 13.5.1878.

Autograph sources:

Choreographic notes. Ms. Autograph. Brown and black ink. 1 vol. 22 pp. (20 × 13,3 cm)

Fjeldstuen./Ballet i to Akter/(NB Anden Akt deelt i tvende Tableauer)

Unsigned and undated [Written according to the diary on 21.7. and 9.8.1865, and rewritten on 11.12., 13.12., 19.12., 20.12.1876, and 5.1.1877]

[DKKk; NKS 3285 4° 2 A–E

The two notations of the 1865 and 1877 revised versions of *The Mountain Hut, or Twenty Years* are both included in a notebook (on pp. '15v.–26r.') that originally seems to have served as H. Bournonville's diary. Moreover, the notes dating from 1877 include Bournonville's autographed choreographic numbers, which clearly refer to his similar numbers, written underneath the music in the 1877 répétiteur's copy for this ballet. Finally, the volume also includes Bournonville's almost complete notation of his two-act ballet-vaudeville *The Conservatoire, or A Proposal of Marriage through the Newspaper* (*see* 15.9.1865), and his incomplete notation of his three-act romantic ballet *The Kermesse in Brüges, or The Three Gifts* (*see* 19.11.1865).

Production note. Ms. Autograph. Brown ink. 1 p. (23 × 14,5 cm)

Vuggedandsen. (Fjeldstuen)

Unsigned and undated [Written according to the diary most probably in December 1877]

[DKKt; F.M. (Ballet, læg F)

Musical sources:

The orchestral score and set of parts used for the 1877 restaging of *The Mountain Hut, or Twenty Years* are now in DKKk (call nos. C II, 122 m, and KTB 281).

Orchestral score. Ms. Autograph (by E. Hartmann). Brown ink. 6 pp. of which two are blank (34,3 × 26 cm)

Fjeldstuen 2den [Akt]/No. 5 b [changed to:] a

Signed (on p. 1): 'Emil Hartmann', undated [1877]

[DKKk; C II, 122 m (KTB 281), ad vol II, p. 77

This autographed orchestral score contains the new *entr'acte* music composed by E. Hartmann for the 1877 restaging of *The Mountain Hut, or Twenty Years*. It was interpolated between what in the original 1859 version were the second and third tableaux.

Répétiteur's copy. Ms Copy. Black ink. 1 vol. 130 pp. of which three are blank (33,7 × 25,7 cm)

B. 281/17 B./Fjeldstuen./(Aug. Winding)/Rep/1859:/1877:/[…]/Fjeldstuen./Ballet af August Bournonville./Musik: Aug. Winding.

Unsigned and dated (on the front cover): '1877:'

[DKKk; MA ms 2978 (KTB 281 (2))

This répétiteur's copy contains the complete music of the revised 1877 version of *The Mountain Hut*. As a result of the many musical cuts, changes, and additions made this year the music is here given new score numbers (Act I, score nos. 1–12, Act II, score nos. 1–4, 5 A, 5 B, 6–14) which are completely different from those in the 1859 and the 1865 versions. The music for Act I (score nos. 1–7) includes choreographic numbers (written with red ink). They were most probably written by L. Gade, and seem to refer to Bournonville's 1877 separate notation of this ballet (made, according to his diary, on 11.12., 13.12., 19.12., 20.12.1876, and 5.1.1877).

Printed sources:

Printed scenario. 1 vol. 15 pp. (19 × 12,7 cm)

Fjeldstuen eller Tyve Aar./Ballet i to Akter/af/August Bournonville./Musiken af August Vinding og Emil Hartmann./[…]/(Paany instuderet i Marts 1877).

Kjøbenhavn, J. H. Schubothe/Græbes Bogtrykkeri. [1877]

[DKKt; Balletprogrammer (Bournonville)

29.4.1877

Divertissement from 'Il Trovatore' (Gipsy Dance)
(Divertissement af 'Troubadouren' (Zigeunerdands)).

This performance represents the second and last separate restaging of Bournonville's divertissement from Act III of G. Verdi's four-act lyrical drama *Il Trovatore* (*see* 10.9.1865 and 25.1.1867). The leading rôle of the gipsy woman was this year performed by M. Westberg for the first time. The divertissement seems otherwise to have been mounted with only minor if any changes from Bournonville's previous 1867 staging. In his diary he noted about it:

28.4.1877: 'Prøve paa Dandsen til Troubadouren'

29.4.: 'Dandsen af Troubadouren. – Alt gik med livlig Applaus'

The 1877 restaging received 8 performances during Bournonville's lifetime, the last of which was given on 6.9.1878.

Musical sources:

The orchestral score employed in 1877 was the same as that used since the 1865 première of Bournonville's divertissement in Verdi's *Il Trovatore* (now in DKKt, call no. KTA 752 a).

Répétiteur's copy. Ms Copy. Brown ink. 12 pp. of which two are blank (34 × 25,8 cm)

Dands til Op. 'Troubadouren.'
Unsigned and undated [1877]
[DKKk; MA ms 2691 (KTA 752 a (4))
This répétiteur's copy contains the complete music for Bournonville's 1865 divertissement in Act III of *Il Trovatore*. It also includes
several notes written (with pencil and brown ink) by an unknown
hand. They provide exact information about who performed which
section, also including a specific note describing the solo variation
performed by M. Westberg, hence the dating of this volume to 1877.

No separate set of parts for Bournonville's Act III divertissement in
Il Trovatore has yet been traced.

1.5.1877

The Flower Festival in Genzano (Blomsterfesten i Genzano).

This performance represents the last, complete restaging of
Bournonville's one-act Italian ballet *The Flower Festival in Genzano* (*see* 19.12.1858) during his lifetime. According to the
(incomplete) set of parts for it, the ballet seems this year to
have been mounted in a slightly revised version that included several minor musical cuts in score nos. 2, 6, 8, and
13 (the *Saltarello*, at the ballet's première listed as score no.
14). According to the same source the so-called *Flower Dance*
(in 1858 listed as score no. 13 and performed before the *Saltarello*) appears to have been omitted this year.

Moreover, for the 1877 production Bournonville made a
nearly complete notation of the ballet, which describes in
fine detail the dramatic action and the mime, and also indicates (although in more general terms) the choreography.
According to its title page this manuscript was intended as
an *aide-mémoire* for future producers of the ballet, primarily
L. Gade who restaged the ballet's *Section II* ('2. Afd.') only six
months later on 11.9.1877.

In his diary Bournonville noted about his own, revised
1877 production of the complete ballet:

10.3.1877: 'Prøve med ny Indstudering paa Blomsterfesten i Genzano'
11.3.: 'Prøve paa Blomsterfesten'
13.3.: 'Prøve paa 1.ste Akt af 'Blomsterfesten' færdig indstuderet'
31.3.: 'Skrevet'
10.4.: 'Repetition paa Blomsterfesten'
18.4.: 'Prøve paa hele Blomsterfesten'
26.4.: 'jeg indregistrede Balletmusiken'
27.4.: 'Arrangementprøve paa Blomsterfesten'
30.4.: 'Theaterprøve paa Blomsterfesten, der gik ganske udmærket;
afleveret Musik og Repetiteurpartier til [L.] Gade og [D.] Krum'
1.5.: 'I Theatret [...] Blomsterfesten, der gik udmærket smukt'.

The staging received 3 performances during Bournonville's
lifetime, the last of which was given on 18.5.1877.

Autograph sources:

Choreographic note. Ms. Autograph. Brown ink. 1 vol. 12 pp. (22,8
× 18,2 cm)
Blomsterfesten i Genzano/Ballet i 1 Akt/af/August Bournonville/
(Choreographiske Noter til Memorering.)
Signed and dated: 'Kjøbenhavn d. 31.e Martz 1877'
[Private collection (Copenhagen)
This manuscript contains Bournonville's notation of the complete
mime and most of the choreography for *The Flower Festival in Genzano*
except for the *Pas de six*, the *Pas de deux*, the *Flower Dance* (*Blomster-
dands*) and the *Saltarello*, which are described only in general terms.
The dramatic action is here divided into nine scenes and two final
Changements (described as 'Osteri Stue' and 'Gaden i Genzano').

Moreover, Bournonville's autographed choreographic numbers are
inserted for each scene. They most likely refer to similar numbers
written into the original (not yet traced) répétiteur's copy from the
ballet's 1858 première. These numbers are as follows: Scene 1: nos.
'1–16'; Scene 2: nos. '1–15'; Scene 3: nos. '1–10'; Scene 4: nos. '1–3';
Scene 5: nos. '1–5'; Scene 6: nos. '1–12'; Scene 7: nos. '1–5'; Scene 8:
nos. '1–5'; Scene 9: nos. '1–20'; <u>Changement</u> (Osteri-Stue) nos. '1–
4'.

Finally, the four dances performed after the last *Changement* are
here described as follows:
'1. <u>Allegro non troppo</u>. Alle komme fra Kirken, løbe rundt og stille
sig til begge Sider med de tre dandsende Par i Midten.
<u>Pas de six</u>
2. de tre Damer, <u>3</u> De tre Herrer, <u>4.</u> To damer vexle, 5 En Dame <u>Solo</u>,
<u>6</u> Herrerne omkring Damerne, <u>7.</u> Ensemble, 8. <u>To Herrer</u>, <u>9</u> – <u>10.</u> og
<u>11</u> Herrerne vexelviis..., <u>12 og 13</u> Herrerne vexelviis, <u>14</u> – 15 – 16:
Ensemble og Slutning.
<u>Pas de deux</u>
1. Pigerne med Tambouriner Gruppe og Placement [a dotted ob-
lique line indicating the position of six female dancers]
2. – 3. Soloer af Paolo og Rosa. – – <u>Allo</u> non troppo. – Ballet. -
Adagio og Gruppe.
Solo af <u>Paolo</u>. – af Rosa. – - Ballet – <u>Paolo</u>. <u>Rosa</u>. Ballet
og Finale.
<u>Blomsterdands.</u>
<u>fulgt af</u>
<u>Saltarello…</u>'.

Musical sources:

The orchestral score employed this year was the same as that used
since the 1858 première of *The Flower Festival in Genzano* (now in
DKKk, call no. C II, 114 k (KTB 267)).

No répétiteur's copy dating from the 1877 restaging of *The Flower
Festival in Genzano* has yet been traced.

Part for the second violin (fragment). Ms. Copy. 2 pp.
vl II
Unsigned and undated [c.1877]
[DKKk; MA ms 2765 (5) (KTB 267)
This fragment of the part for the second violin contains the music for
score nos. 6–8 in *The Flower Festival in Genzano*. According to the style
of it, the part seems to date from the 1877 restaging of this ballet.

Parts (incomplete). Ms. Copy. 2 vol.
cl I, tr I.
Unsigned and undated [c.1877]
[DKKk; MA ms 2784 (1–2) (KTB 267)
According to the style of these manuscript parts they seem to date
from the 1877 restaging of *The Flower Festival in Genzano*. They are
written and bound together with two similar parts for the first clarinet and the first trumpet in Bournonville's Spanish ballet divertissement *La Ventana*, which were most probably made for a performance
of this work on 9.1.1877.

19.5.1877

Tableau for the Overture to The Elves' Hill (Ouverturen til Elverhöj: Illustration: Kong Christian IV paa Trefoldigheden).
Projected tableau.

This projected tableau was planned by Bournonville as a cur-
tain-raiser for the annual charity performance, given for the
private pension fund of the Royal Danish Ballet on 1.6.1877.
For unknown reasons it was not carried out, and instead F.
Kuhlau's 1828 overture to J. L. Heiberg's national fairy-play
The Elves' Hill was given as a separate concert number.

Autograph sources:

Production note. Ms. Autograph. Brown ink. 2 pp. (21,6 × 13,6 cm)
Ouverturen til Elverhöj:/Illustration/Kong Christian IV paa Trefol-
dighed.
Signed and dated: 'Fredensborg d. 19. Maj 1877'
[DKKk; NKS 3285 4 ° 2 A–E

1.6.1877
Waldemar.
This performance represents Bournonville's fifth and last restaging in Copenhagen of his four-act national historical ballet *Waldemar* (*see* 28.10.1835). It also represents the first time
this work was performed in the new Royal Theatre building.
Moreover, it was the last full-length ballet Bournonville
mounted before his definitive retirement from the theatre at
the end of the 1876–77 season.

In his choreographic advice and suggestions to Krum he
The ballet was given this year as part of a special charity
performance arranged for the private pension fund of the
Royal Danish Ballet, of which Bournonville was the founding
member. It differed from his previous staging in the old
Royal Theatre (*see* 4.6.1872) by the omission of the prologue, entitled *Dawn.* Moreover, the ballet was now performed with a partially new cast (including several actors
and singers in the mime rôles) and with a new décor for the
scene of Act IV showing *Grathe Heath*, which was painted by
the German scenographer, P. Gropius.

In his diary Bournonville noted about the production:

3.11.1874: 'Brev fra [P.] Gropius. Conference angaaende min forestaaende Reise til Berlin'
5.11.: 'skrevet Brev til Professor Gropius'
9.11.: 'til Gropius (Georgenstraße 37–38) med hvem jeg arbeidede
paa det behageligste'
10.11.: 'arbeidet med Gropius, der allerede havde en Model til
Grathe-Hede færdig, besluttet at reise endnu iaften'
11.4.1877: 'Indstudering paa Axel Hvides Rolle til N. [J.] Simonsen,
ordnet Musikalier'
12.4.: 'Prøve paa de to første Akter af Valdemar'
16.4.: 'Prøve paa […] 3.e Akt af Valdemar'
19.4.: 'Prøve paa Dands og Roller til Valdemar'
20.4.: 'Prøve paa Dandsene til Valdemar'
26.4.: 'Paa Theatret, hvor [L.] Gade prøvede Valdemar, og jeg ind-
registrerede Balletmusiken'
30.4.: 'Skrevet […] afleveret Musik og Repetiteurpartier til Gade og
[D.] Krum'
2.5.: 'Costume-Revision til Valdemar'
29.5.: 'paa Theatret, hvor vi prøvede 4.e Akt af Waldemar med Statister &c.'
30.5.: 'Partiel Prøve Kl 10½ og Theaterprøve med Orchester Kl 12'
31.5.: 'Generalprøve paa Valdemar Kl. 12'
1.6.: 'I Theatret til Forestillingen for Pensionsfonden. Udsolgt
Huus! […] Valdemar der gik med stort Bifald'.

The 1877 staging received 13 performances in Bournonville's lifetime, and on 27.11.1879 (only three days before
Bournonville's sudden death on 30.11.1879) it reached its
150th performance.

The musical material employed this year was the same as
that used for the previous 1872 production (now in DKKk,
call nos. C II, 107, MA ms 2993, MA ms 2994, and KTB 297).

Autograph sources:

Production note. Ms. Autograph. Brown ink. 1 p. (22,7 × 13,9 cm)

Shakespeares – S∫n./[…]/I Balletten Valdemar/[…]/vil Fru [B.]
Hennings/optræde i [changed to:] som Astrid […]
Unsigned and undated [c. May 1877]
[DKKk; NKS 3285 4° 3 V–Z

Other sources:

Sketch by V. Güllich for the back curtain in Act I(?). Pencil and water
colours (sight 35,5 × 48 cm)
[Untitled]
Signed: 'V G', undated [1877?]
[DKKt; V. Güllichs dekorationsudkast (permanent udstilling)

Sketch by V. Güllich of the décor used in Act II. Pencil and water
colours (sight 41 × 50 cm)
[Untitled]
Signed: 'V G', undated [1874]
[DKKt; V. Güllichs dekorationsudkast (permanent udstilling)
This sketch was originally made for Act II of I. P. E. Hartmann's two-
act romantic opera *Little Kirsten* when it was mounted as the inaugu-
ral performance of the new Royal Theatre building on 11.10.1874.
Since 1.7.1877 the same décor was reused for Act II of *Waldemar.*

3.11.1877
A Folk Tale (Et Folkesagn).
This performance represents the fourth and last restaging of
Bournonville's three-act romantic ballet *A Folk Tale* (*see* 20.3.
1854) during his own lifetime. It was mounted exclusively by
L. Gade and was performed A. Flammé in the rôle of *Birthe*,
and Bournonville's daughter, the opera singer C. Bournon-
ville, playing the mimic part as the nurse *Cathrine.*

Bournonville, who attended the ballet's fourth performances on 4.12.1877, noted about it on the same evening in
his diary:

'i Theatret, hvor jeg saae 2' og 3.die Akt af Et Folkesagn, der gik
udmærket godt fra alle Sider, kun var [A.] Flammé ikke rigtig indstuderet og instrueret'.

The 1877 restaging received 5 performances during Bournonville's lifetime, the last of which was given on 11.1.1878.

The musical material employed this year was the same as
that used for the previous production of this ballet on
1.6.1874 (now in DKKk, call nos. C II, 108, MA ms 2968–
2969, and KTB 274).

1878

23.1.1878
The Bacchic Feast (Bacchusfesten).
This one-act ballet divertissement was choreographed by
Bournonville's pupil, D. Krum, from a scenario suggested to
him by Bournonville. This is clear from a letter written by
Bournonville to Krum on 17.10.1877 in which a detailed sce-
nario together with several other other suggestions for the
contents and the staging of this divertissement are included.
This proves beyond doubt that Bournonville should be con-
sidered as the true originator of *The Bacchic Feast.*

In his choreographic advice and suggestions to Krum he
stated as follows:

'Jeg kan ikke andet end gratulere Dem til den Idee at fremstille en

Bachusfest, der er i stand til at give et Billede, der ikke før er seet paa vor Scene […] Kjære Krum, maa jeg fremsætte nogle Bemærkninger, der […] maa blive en dyb Hemmelighed for enhver Anden en Dem selv og til Nød Deres Musikcomponist. Først og fremmest skal de ikke lade trykke noget Program, da ellers Divertissementet bliver bedømt som en Ballet med Handling (Saaledes vil De f. Ex. ikke finde noget Program, hverken til Gratiernes Hyldning, Kjærligheds Spaadomme eller La Ventana) […] See nu her, kjære Ven, hvorledes det forekommer mig at De bør gribe Sagen an:
En eneste sydlandsk Decoration med Viinranker i Guirlander fra Kolonne til Kolonne og et antikt Bacchusbillede (Marmorstatue paa Piedestal) i Midten. Nogle unge Piger og Karle have sluttet et nedplukke Druerne, der frembæres i store Kurve. Den gamle Ejer af Viinbjerget, Fader til en af Pigerne, byder dem at pryde Statuen med Epheu og Viinløv og idet de bringe Guden deres Takoffer, opføres der muntre Dandse, hvori den unge Elsker, viser sig ustadig, og straffes af sin Kjæreste og af hendes Fader; Han slaaer det Hele hen i Spög og aftaler noget Hemmeligt med sine Kamerater: De bortfjerner sig leende. – Pigerne dandse til Ære for Viinguden. Et Optog nærmer sig med alle bacchanalske Symboler og en tyk gammel Mand forklædt som Silenus. – Den gamle Viin bæres frem i Læderflasker og saavel Gamle som Unge bringe Bacchus deres Hyldning. – Der opföres Lege, som f: Ex Kaplöb, Bueskydning, Diskuskastning som slutter med Dands. – Man hörer Hyrdefløiten og en Satyr kommer dandsende ind, blæser, drikke og gjækkes med Pigerne, der slutte med at afrive hans Skjæg og Øren. Karlene løfte ham i Veiret og aftrække hans forlorne Bukkebeen og nu staaer den unge Elsker triumferende for den glade Forsamling, han knæler for sin Elskede, faaer Faderens Velsignelse og dandser en alvorsfuld Pas de deux, og derpaa følger en Finale i al den Yppighed som Genren tillader'.

The divertissement was set to a score by A. Grandjean, and reached a total of 22 performances, the last of which was given on 1.9.1885.

Bournonville, who attended the opening night, noted about it in his diary:

'Til Slutning gik for første Gang [D.] Krums Divertissement Bachusfesten, der fornøiede mig særdeles, blev smukt udført, og nød fortjent Bifald. – Jeg haaber ved denne hæderlige Debut at see min Spaadom opfyldt nemlig i Krum at see en brav efterfølger'.

Autograph sources:

Manuscript scenario. Ms. Autograph (included in a letter to D. Krum). Brown ink. 4 pp. (20,8 × 13,3 cm)
[…]/En eneste sydlandsk Decoration med Viinranker/[…]
Signed and dated: 'Fredensborg den 17.de October 1877.'
[DKKk; NBD III, 236, 17.10.1877

Musical sources:

Orchestral score. Ms. Autograph (by A. Grandjean). Brown ink. 1 vol. 222 pp. of which two are blank (34 × 25,7 cm)
312/Bacchusfesten/Partitur/[…]/Bacchusfesten/Balletdivertissement i 1 Act/af/D Krum/Musiken componeret/af/Axel Grandjean/op. 16./1877./Partitur
Signed and dated (on p. 221): 'A Grandjean/30 November 1877./op 16.'
[DKKk; C II, 110 (KTB 312)

Répétiteur's copy. Ms. Copy. Black ink. 1 vol. 72 pp. of which three are blank (33,9 × 25,8 cm)
B. 312/Bacchusfesten./Krum/1878./43A/[…]/Bacchusfesten./Balletdivertissement.
Unsigned and dated (on the title page): 'Januar 1878.'
[DKKk; MA ms 3006 (KTB 312)
This répétiteur's copy contains several choreographic numbers written (with black ink) by an unknown hand. They most probably refer

to similar numbers in a separate (not yet traced) notation of the entire ballet, which Krum most likely wrote during late 1877.

Parts. Ms. Copy. 34 vol.
4 vl I, 4 vl II, 2 vla, 4 vlc e cb, fl 1/2, ob 1/2, cl 1/2, fag 1/2, cor 1/2, tr 1/2, trb 1/2/3, tuba, timp, gr cassa, tri, arpa.
Unsigned and undated [1877]
[DKKk; KTB 312

9.3.1878
The Valiant Soldier, a suite of five tableaux in memory of Faber (Den tappre Landsoldat. Suite af fem Tableauer til Fabers Minde) (Folketheatret).
This series of five *tableaux vivants* was created for a special charity performance arranged to collect funds for the erection of a monument to the Danish poet and playwright, P. Faber, who had died in 1877. The tableaux were performed to a score composed and arranged by C. C. Møller. He repeatedly employed J. O. E. Hornemann's 1848 melody for Faber's imesely popular patriotic song, entitled *Den tappre Landsoldat* («Dengang jeg drog af sted»). The same tune had many years before been employed in the scores for two other works by Bournonville, namely the solo dance 'Echo de Dannemark' (see 26.9.1849), and the divertissement *The Irresistibles* (see 3.2.1850).

On the poster for the second performance on 10.3.1878 Bournonville's five tableaux are described as follows:

1.ste Tableau: Soldatens Afsked fra sin Pige og sine Forældre («Dengang jeg drog afsted»)
2.det Tableau: Fanen («Om Dannebrog jeg veed»)
3.die Tableau: Angrebet («Vi byde Fjenden Trods»)
4.de Tableau: Den saarede (Tapperhedens Løn tilkjendes den brave Landsoldat)
5. Tableau: Seir og Fred («Sit Løfte han holdt») Folket jubler den hjemvendende Kriger imøde. Danmark rækker ham sin Krands.

In his diary Bournonville noted about the performance:

27.2.1878: 'Besøg af Leuit. Hartvigson, Formand for den kjøbenhavnske Afdeling af Vaabenbrødrene for at anmode mig om en Illustration til P. Faber's 'Tappre Landsoldat'. Endskjøndt jeg ganske havde renonceret paa Compositioner gik jeg dog ind paa dette Forlangende og udarbeidede strax et Program, som jeg bragte til Folketheatrets Directeur R. Watt'
1.3.: 'skrevet Regien til Den tappre Landsoldat og et Brev til Directeur R. Watt'
5.3.: 'conference med R. Watt og Udvalg af Personale'
7.3.: 'Prøve og Opstilling af Tabelauerne til Den tappre Landsoldat der lover godt'
8.3.: 'Kl 9 gik jeg […] hen i Folketheatret hvor jeg efter Forestillingen holdt Generalprøve i Costüme paa Tableauerne, der gjorde stormende Lykke'
9.3.: 'I Folketheatret til Vaabenbrødrenes Forestilling for et Mindesmærke til P. Faber […] til Slutning mine Tableauer, der gjorde stormende Lykke. Hele den kongelige Familie var tilstede'.

The tableaux reached a total of 9 performances, the last of which was given on 17.3.1878.

Autograph sources:

Manuscript mise-en-scène. Ms. Autograph (partially in another's hand). Brown ink. 1 p. (22,7 × 18 cm)
Den tappre Landsoldat./Suite af fem Tableauer til Minde om P: Faber/(comp: af Hofballetmester A. Bournonville. Musiken arrang: af C. C. Møller.)/1.ste Tableau/[…]/5.te Tableau.

Unsigned and undated [Written according to the diary most probably on 27.2.1878]
[DKKk; NBD 2. Rk. (Breve fra Bournonville til Robert Watt)

Manuscript mise-en-scène. Ms. Autograph. Brown ink. 3 pp. (22,7 × 18,1 cm)
Den tappre Landsoldat./Suite af fem Tableauer til Fabers Minde./componeret af August Bournonville./Musiken arrangeret af C. C. Møller.
Signed and dated: 'Kjøbenhavn d. 27.e Februar 1878.'
[DKKk; NKS 3285 4° 2 R–U

Production note (included in a letter to R. Watt). Ms. Autograph. Brown ink. 2 pp. (22,7 × 18 cm)
Den tappre Landsoldat.!/(Suite af fem Tableauer til Minde om Faber)/comp af Bournonville. Musiken arrang: af C. C. Möller./Regie/1.ste Tableau/[…]/5.te Tableau
Unsigned and dated: 'Kbhvn d. 1.ste Martz 1878.'
[DKKk; NBD 2. Rk. (Breve fra Bournonville til Robert Watt)

Musical sources:

Orchestral score. Ms. Autograph (by C. C. Møller). Black ink. 1 vol. 38 pp. (25,1 × 33,9 cm)
Den tappre Landsoldat/Suite i fem Tableaux/af/Hofballetmester A. Bournonville/Musiken af/C. C. Möller
Signed and dated (on p. 38): 'd. 5/3 [18]78. Vesterbro'
[DKKk; Folketheatrets Music Arkiv no. 293 (kasse 104, mu 7307. 2000.293)

No répétiteur's copy for *The Valiant Soldier* has yet been traced.

Parts. Ms. Copy. 14 vol.
vl I, vl II, vla, vlc e cb, fl, cl 1/2, cor 1/2, tr 1/2, trb, timp, tamb.
Unsigned and undated [1878]
[DKKk; Folketheatrets Music Arkiv no. 293 (kasse 104, mu 7307. 2000.293)

1879

30.3.1879
A Midsummer Night's Dream (En Skjærsommernatsdrøm).
According to a note in his diary on 30.8.1878 (reading: 'Brev og Sceneri (Midsommernatsdrømmen) til [L.] Gade') Bournonville wrote a complete mise-en-scène on that day for the planned 1879 Copenhagen première of W. Shakespeare's five-act play from c.1595–96 (set to F. Mendelssohn-Bartholdy's music op. 61 from 1842). This 1878 mise-en-scène (which is actually based on an even earlier Swedish production of Shakespeare's play) was clearly written as an *aide-mémoire* for L. Gade, who had taken over Bournonville's responsibilities at Copenhagen's Royal Theatre since the 1877–78 season, and mounted the first Danish production of Shakespeare's play. Bournonville's written mise-en-scène, therefore, proves beyond doubt that although he was no longer under contract with Copenhagen's Royal Theatre he must be considered as the true originator of the staging of the Danish première of *A Midsummer Night's Dream.*

Moreover, on 18.2.1879 he received a letter from Gade about which he noted in the diary:

'Brev fra [L.] Gade […] med Anmodning om Raad til en indlagt burlesk Dands i Shakespear [*sic*] Sommernatsdröm'.

After replying on the following day he stated:

'Skrevet udførlig til Gade i Anledning af den projekterede Grotesk-dands'

Shakespeare's play would have been known to Bournonville from his earlier engagement as managing director of Stockholm's Royal Theatre between 1861–64. There he had attended a restaging of *En Midsommernatsdröm* at Stockholm's Royal Theatre (Operahuset) on 6.11.1862. On that occasion the play's four dance scenes were all choreographed and mounted by his own pupil, S. Lund, who served as ballet-master in Stockholm between 1856 and 1862.

Furthermore, on 9.11.1874 Bournonville attended a performance of *Ein Sommernachtstraum* at Berlin's Hofoper about which he had noted in his diary:

'En Midsommernatsdrøm. Damerne [C.] Meyer og [M.] Kessler særdeles gode som Hermia og Helena, Haandværkerne farceagtige. Frk. Wienrich som Puk nydelig. Resten temmelig ubetydelig og saavel Alfedandsen som Sceneriet langt under den Stockholmske Udførelse (Costumet burgundisk)'.

Finally, after having attended the seventh performance of the 1879 Copenhagen production he noted rather sarcastically in his diary on 20.4.1879:

'i Theatret, hvor man gav 'Skjærsommernatsdrøm' med [F.] Mendelsohns [*sic*] fortræffelige Musik og ganske udmærkede Decorationer. Hvad Stykket og Spillet angaaer, tænkte jeg paa Eventyret om Keiserens nye Klæder da Navnet [W.] Shakespeare maatte dække alt det geniale Nonsens, der i dette phantastiske Stykke blive leveret og man maatte gjelde for dum dersom man ikke deelte den almindelige Beundring. – Der var anvendt meget paa Udstyrelsen og Dandserinderne vare ganske efter Udlandets Mode – Begrebet vil snart følge efter!'

A Midsummer Night's Dream received 23 performances in Copenhagen during Bournonville's lifetime, and the 1879 production as such reached a total of 56 performances in Copenhagen, the last of which took place on 22.3.1886.

Autograph sources:

Manuscript mise-en-scène. Ms. Autograph. Brown ink. 2 pp. (26,7 × 21,2 cm)
En Midsommernatsdröm/(saaledes som Stykket er sat i Scene paa Det kgl. Theater i Stockholm)
Signed and dated: 'Fredensborg d. 30.de August 1878.'
[SSm; Daniel Frylunds samling no. 125

Musical sources:

Printed orchestral score with manuscript insertions. 1 vol. 184 pp. of which three are blank (30 × 23,1 cm)
bruges ikke/En Sommernatsdröm/Bruges ikke/Partitur/802/Mendelssohn/ […] /Felix Mendelssohn/Bartholdy's/Sämtliche Werke./Ein/Sommernachtstraum/von/ Shakespeare./Op. 61.
Leipzig & Berlin, C. F. Peters, pl. no. 6059 6056 [c.1874–1879]
[DKKt; KTA 802
This printed orchestral score was used for all performances of *A Midsummer Night's Dream* during Bournonville's lifetime. The music for the so-called 'Melodram' (score no. 6) is here a manuscript insertion, and is musically slightly shortened.

Répétiteur's copy. Ms. Copy. Brown ink. 1 vol. 38 pp. (34,3 × 25,8 cm)

Repetiteurpartier/[...]/3, Sommernatsdrømmen./[...]/L Gade./
Repetiteurparti/til/En Sommernatsdröm.
Unsigned and undated [1879]
[DKKk; MA ms 2918 (3) (KTA 802 (1))
This répétiteur's copy contains the complete music for the four
dance scenes in Shakespeare's play, which were as follows:
(1) A so-called 'Alfemarsch' in Act II (score no. 2).
(2) An (unnamed) *Dance* in Act II (score no. 3), performed during
the 'Vise med Chor' («Slange hist med Braadens Kløft!»).
(3) A 'Grotesk dands' in Act V (score no. 11), performed by the
boors.
(4) An (unnamed) *Dance* in Act V (score no. 12), performed during
the final chorus, entitled «Om de halvudslukte Flammer».
The music is included on pp. 17–38 in a volume that also contains
the répétiteur's copies for five other operas and plays, mounted at
Copenhagen's Royal Theatre between 1878 and 1879.

Parts. Ms. Copy. 59 vol.
7 vl I, 6 vl II, 4 vla, 8 vlc e cb, 2 fl I, 2 fl II, 2 ob I, 2 ob II, 2 cl I, 2 cl II,
2 fag I, 2 fag II, cor 1/2/3/4, 2 tr I, 2 tr II, tr III, trb 1/2/3, oph, tuba,
timp 1/2, gr cassa, piatti e tri.
Unsigned and undated [1879]
[DKKk; KTA 802
This set of parts was used for all performances of *A Midsummer Night's
Dream* in Copenhagen during Bournonville's lifetime.

5.5.1879
A Shakespearian Apotheosis (en Shakespearesk Apotheose).
Projected tableau.
Since 1870 Bournonville had (according to his diary)
planned and written a Shakespearian tableau for the annual
charity performance given for the Royal Danish Ballet's private pension fund at the end of each season. According to
his autographed manuscript scenario it was entitled 'Shakespeares Syn: Allegorisk Tableau' and is described as follows:

'Den store Digter, omsvævet af phantastiske Væsener fra hans 'sommernatsdröm', skuer i Aanden sine udödelige Mesterværker, ud-
bredte til Verdens fjerneste Egne og tilhørende den seneste Efterslægt'.

However, the project was not carried out, and the charity
performance this year (given on 30.8.1879) consisted of
some minor musical concert numbers and a regular performance of Bournonville's four-act romantic ballet *Waldemar* (*see* 28.10.1835). In the latter B. Hennings made her return to the stage (as an actress) in the mimic parts of the rôle
of *Astrid*.

In his diary Bournonville noted about the projected tableau:

5.5.1879: 'Brev fra [L.] Gade om Pensionsforestillingen, Svar tilbage
og udarbeidet Projektet til en Shakespearesk Apotheose'
6.5.: 'Afsendt Projektet til Apotheose med Brev til Gade'.

Moreover, in a letter to L. Gade, dated 6.5.1879 (now in
DKKk, call no. NKS 3258 B 4°) he described the project in
further detail as follows:

'[...] skjøndt jeg just ikke føler mig rigtig disponeret til nye Compositioner vil jeg gribe din Idee om en Apotheose for [W.] Shakespeare
og om Du synes saa stille vi den som Ouverture til vor Forestilling og
behøve saaledes ikke at uleilige Nogen med et lille nyt Stykke. Nu
skal Du sige mig Din Mening om Planen, nemlig Kuhlau's Ouverture
til William Shakespeare Usynligt Chor til Tableauet – og Valdemar.
Jeg sætter mig strax til at arbeide paa den omtalte Apotheose som jeg

skal give Dig Tegning og Regie paa saanart jeg erholder din Bestemmelse og saa kommer jeg til Byen Fredagen før Pintsen for at stille
Figurerne saa vi uden Besværlighed kunne gae vor Forestilling
imøde til den 3' Juni uden for store Forventlinger men ved godt
Haab'.

Autograph sources:

Manuscript scenario. Ms. Autograph. Brown ink. 1 pp. (21,4 × 13,7
cm)
Det kongelige Theater./Den aarlige Forestilling til Indtægt for Bal-
lettens private Pensionskasse/[...]/Shakespeares Syn:
Unsigned and undated [Written according to the diary on 5.5.1879]
[DKKk; NKS 3285 4°, kapsel 7, læg 16

14.11.1879
A Memorial Wreath to Denmark's Great Poet. Suite of Tableaux
(Mindets Krands for Danmarks store Digter. Suite af Tableauer)
(Folketheatret).
This series of four *tableaux vivants* was created for a special
charity performance marking the centenary of the birth of
the Great Danish poet, A. Oehlenschläger. It represents the
last theatrical work created and mounted by Bournonville.
The tableaux, which (according to the poster) were performed to a score arranged by C. C. Møller, were introduced
with a prologue, written by S. Schandorph and recited by the
actress, E. F. M. Holst. Each of the following tableaux was
introduced by an allegorical figure, who represented the
work of Oehlenschläger depicted in the tableau.

On the poster the complete suite of tableaux is described
as follows:

1.ste Tableau: Hakon Jarl med Offerhornet. Motto: Gak til høie
Guder Giv dem det Bedste!
2det Tableau: Palnatoke, efter at have skudt Æblet af Sønnens
Hoved, truer Kong Harald.
3die Tableau: Axel og Valborg forenes i Døden ved Klangen af Vil-
helms Harpe.
4de Tableau: Nordens Guder skue ned paa Oehlenschlægers Billede, der bekrandses af Danmarks, Norge og Sverig.
Personerne: Danmarks Genius. – En Skjald fra Vikingetiden. – En
Minnesanger. – En dansk Kunstner.

In his diary Bournonville noted about his creation and the
first performance of these tableaux:

5.11.1879: 'Brev fra [...] R Watt om en Idee til Øehlenschlägers[i.e.
A. Oehlenschläger] 100 Aars Fest [...] svaret R Watt med en Plan'
7.11.: 'Et elskeligt Brev fra R Watt; Udarbeidet Programmet til Øehlenschlägers 100' Aarsfest og afsendt det pr Express. Brev til R. W.
senere'
8.11.: 'redigeret Programmet til Mindets Krands for Øehlenschläger'
12.11.: 'Prøve paa Folketheatret Kl 1. Tableauerne love godt'
13.11.: 'Prøve Kl 1 paa Tableauerne, hvortil [L.] Gade havde
besørget alle Requisiter [...] Generalprøve paa Tableauerne Kl 10–
11½'
14.11.: '(Øehlenschlägers Hundredaarsfest) [...] stor Høitidelighed
[...] Middag hos Charlotte [Bournonville] og med hende i Folketheatret hvor jeg ogsaa havde skaffet Billet til [J. L.] Phister. Fest-
forestillingen bestod af Festouverture af C. C. Møller, Prolog af R
Kaufmann fremsagt af [J. H. S.] Abrahams (Sang), Feriegæsterne,
Ouverture til Correggio af [I. P. E.] Hartmann og endelig Mindets
Krands Suite af Tableauer af mig, med en declameret Introduction
(Danmarks Genier) af [S.] Schandorph. – Det Hele gik med sand
Begeistring'.

The tableaux received 3 performances, the last of which was given on 16.11.1879. According to the handwritten catalogue for the music archive of Copenhagen's Folketheatret (now in DKKk) the musical material employed for these tableaux was originally listed with the call no. '296' and entitled 'Øehlenschlægerfesten'. This material, however, is no longer preserved.

Autograph sources:

Manuscript mise-en-scène (included in a letter to R. Watt). Ms. Autograph. Brown ink. 2 pp. (20,4 × 13,8 cm)
[...]Folketheatret [kan] med Fordeel (om kun med/Tableauer) illustrere hans storartede og ældste/nordiske Digtninge i fire Billeder [...]
Signed and dated: 'Fredensborg den 5' November 1879.'
[DKKk; NBD 2. Rk. (Breve fra Bournonville til Robert Watt)

Manuscript mise-en-scène. Ms. Autograph. Brown ink (including pencilled drawings). 3 pp. (27,5 × 21,6 cm)
Tableauer./Fremstillede paa Folketheatret ved Hundredaarsfesten/for/Oehlenschlägers Fødsel./[...]/Til Underretning for Herr Balletdirigent/L. Gade/ fra hans gamle Ven og Mester/ [...] /Dette Blad kan rives særskildt af til fornøden Underretning for Musikdirecteuren/og Iscenesætningen.'
Signed and dated: 'Fredensborg den 7.e November 1879'
[DKKk; NKS 3285 4° 3 R–U

28.11.1879
Pas de deux (uncredited) performed by H. Beck and M. Westberg.

This (uncredited) dance is partially based on Bournonville's and V. C. Holm's earlier *Pas de deux*, incorporated six years earlier in Act I of D.-F.-E. Auber's five-act opera *La Muette de Portici* (*see* 2.9.1873) and first performed by D. Krum and M. Westberg together with a corps de ballet of eight women. In 1879 it was mounted in a slightly revised version arranged especially for the début of H. Beck. According to Beck's memoirs *Fra Livet og Dansen* (p. 44) it contained a new male solo variation inserted immediately before the Coda movement where it replaced Bournonville's second male solo variation. This new solo was choreographed by Beck's teacher, the French ballet-master G. Carey, and set to new music composed by V. C. Holm. Moreover, according to Holm's autographed orchestral score the revised 1879 version of this *Pas de deux* contained a new *Allegro* introduction of four bars (in 6/8 time), which clearly must have been added to the score this year.

In his diary Bournonville noted about the 1879 version of this dance and Beck's début, which represents the last performance Bournonville attended in the Royal Theatre before his sudden death from a stroke two days later on 30.11. 1879:

'Efter Opførelsen af Tartuffe og efter et Besøg af L. Gade, saae jeg Hans Beck debutere som Solodandser i en Pas de deux, og var særdeles tilfreds med hans brillante Udførelse, Lethed og Vigueur samt et fordeelagtigt Ydre. Vestberg [i.e. M. Westberg] dandsede smukt og Polka Militaire gik med Liv'.

According to *Berlingske Tidende* (1.12.1879) Bournonville made the following comments about Beck's performance on his way out of the theatre:

'det var Synd, at dette unge Menneske [i.e. H. Beck] ikke kom til at vise sig første Gang i noget større og bedre Nummer. Havde jeg endnu virket her – enfin – saa havde jeg lavet noget nyt for ham'.

Musical sources:

V. C. Holm's autographed orchestral score for the revised 1879 version of this *Pas de deux* is now in DKKk (call no. C II, 114 m (KTB 316)).

Repétiteur's copy. Ms. Autograph (by A. Grandjean) and copy. Black and brown ink. 1 vol. 12 pp. of which one is blank (34,3 × 25,6 cm with several variants)
No. 87/Pas de deux/af/Bournonville/nr. 88/Frøken Westberg,/Hans Beck/1879.
Unsigned and dated (on the front cover): '1879.'
[DKKk; MA ms 2641 (1) (KTB 316)
This répétiteur's copy contains a new musical introduction which is A. Grandjean's autograph. It is entitled 'Overgang til denne indlagte Pas de deux' and seems to have been added when the revised 1879 *Pas de deux* was incorporated by H. Beck in Act II of his restaging of Bournonville's three-act romantic ballet *The Kermesse in Brüges, or The Three Gifts* on 7.11.1909. Moreover, the répétiteur's copy includes several choreographic numbers written with brown ink by an unknown hand. They most probably refer to a separate (not yet traced) choreographic notation of this dance.

The parts employed for the revised 1879 restaging of this *Pas de deux* were the same as those used for the 1873 première (now in DKKk, call no. KTB 209 A (originally KTB 316)).

Parts (incomplete). Ms. Copy. 2 vol.
vl I, vlc e cb.
Unsigned and undated [1879 and later]
[DKKk; MA ms 2641 (3) (KTB 316)
These two separate parts contain the 1879 version of Holm's music for Bournonville's *Pas de deux* in *La Muette de Portici*. They also include the later musical changes that were made when this dance was incorporated by H. Beck on 7.11.1909 as a divertissement in Act II of *The Kermesse in Brüges, or The Three Gifts*.

Unidentified and unverified works

Bournonville's participation in royal celebrations in his capacity as court choreographer (1840–1846).
For the following seven royal festivities and court balls (all of which took place at Copenhagen's Christiansborg Palace) Bournonville is known to have taken part in his capacity as royal court choreographer and ballet-master:

22.4.1840
15.4.1842
20.3.1843
16.11.1844
10.5.1846
1.11.1846
29.11.1846

It has not been possible to verify whether he choreographed any specific dances for these occasions or not.

An unidentified dance, dating seemingly from the early 1860s.
According to Bournonville's autographed choreographic note for this dance (entitled 'Grande chaîne'), it seems to relate to a Swedish opera or play mounted by him during his

tenure with Stockholm's Royal Theatre between 1861 and 1864. This theory is supported by the clear Nordic character of the choreography, which includes the Norwegian so-called 'Pas de Halling'. Moreover, the dance is described as a long chain of people moving in circles around two larges stones ('pierres') placed at centre stage. Finally, the initials for what appears to be two (not yet identified) singers or actors are included (reading: 'B.' and 'Hj.'). It is not possible to identify the dance any further.

Autograph sources:

Choreographic note. Ms. Autograph. Brown ink. 1 p. (17,9 × 11,1 cm)
<u>1</u>.e Grande chaîne – autour des pierres.
Unsigned and undated [c. early 1860s?]
[DKKk; NKS 3285 4° 3 R–U

Additional Sources

Bournonville's handwritten lists of his works
(in chronological order)

Ms. Autograph. Brown ink. 2 pp. (18,3 × 12 cm)
Compositioner/af,/<u>Auguste Bournonville</u>
Unsigned and undated [c.1829]
[DKKk; NKS 3285 4° 1 B 6
According to the works included in this list of Bournonville's early projected works it must have been written some time around 1829.

Ms. Autograph. Brown ink. 1 p. (34,7 × 20,9 cm)
<u>Pas de Danse.</u>
Unsigned and undated [c.1837]
[DKKt; Brevregistrant (Hoppe)
According to the works included in this list of 17 individual *pas* and dances by Bournonville and other choreographers it must have been written some time around 1837.

Ms. Autograph. Brown ink. 2 pp. (21,3 × 17,3 cm)
Compositioner og Arrangements (x [indicating] fremmede Forfattere.)/af/<u>Aug. Bournonville.</u>/[...]/<u>særskildte Pas og Scene Arrangements.</u> × [indicating works] tildeels efter Andre.
Unsigned and undated [c.1851]
[DKKk; NKS 3285 4° 1 B 6
According to the works included this list it must have been written some time around 1851.

Production note. Ms. Autograph. Brown ink. 4 pp. (26,6 × 21,3 cm)
<u>Opera Repertoire:</u>
Unsigned and dated (by an unknown hand): '30/10 1857'
[The State Archive (Copenhagen); Det kgl. Teaters Arkiv, Gruppe E, pakke 288

Production note. Ms. Autograph. Brown ink. 4 pp. (26,6 × 21,3 cm)
<u>Operaernes Besætning,</u>/<u>Indstudering og Opførelse.</u>
Signed and dated: 'Kbhvn d L» October 1857.'
[The State Archive (Copenhagen); Det kgl. Teaters Arkiv, Gruppe E, pakke 288

Production note. Ms. Autograph. Brown ink. 2 pp. (26,9 × 21,4 cm)
<u>Plan til Operaens Virksomhed/i Martz, April og Mai 1859.</u>
Unsigned and undated [c.1859]
[SSm; Daniel Fryklunds samling no. 101

Production note. Ms. Autograph. Brown ink. 3 pp. (22,7 × 18,1 cm)
Udkast./til en Virksomhedsplan for Opera og Ballet./i/Theater = Saisonen 1870–71.
Signed and dated: 'Kbhvn den 1.de August 1870.'
[SSm; Daniel Fryklunds samling no. 103

Ms. Autograph. Brown ink. 1 p. (35,4 × 22,1 cm)
Balletter. Divertissements. Arrangements. Dandse.
Unsigned and undated [c.1872]
[DKKk; NKS 3285 4° 1 B 6
Since Bournonville's restaging of W. A. Mozart's *Die Hochzeit des Figaro (Figaros Bryllup)* on 30.4.1872 is included as the last work in this chronological list it must have been written soon after this production.

Bournonville's holographs about his choreography and technical terms *(in chronological order)*

Book manuscript (incomplete). Ms. Autograph. Brown ink. 38 pp. of which four are blank (26,6 × 22,2 cm)
<u>Etudes Chorégraphiques</u>/par/<u>Auguste Bournonville.</u>/<u>Première Partie.</u>
Signed and dated [on p. 35]: 'Copenhaque le 30 Janvier 1848'.
[DKKk; NKS 3285 4°, Kapsel 1, læg C 6
This manuscript contains Bournonville's general reflections on the art of dance and his descriptions of some of its leading artists from J.-G. Noverre up to his own time. It gives clear testimony that he had already begun working on his *Etudes chorégraphiques* in 1848, although the contents of this manuscript were never included in his two later published works with this title (*Etudes chorégraphiques*, 1855 and 1861). The manuscript has remained unpublished to this day.

Choreographic note. Ms. Autograph. Black ink. 3 pp. (36,8 × 22,6 cm with variants)
<u>Chorégraphie.</u>/<u>Signes pour marquer les directions differentes/</u>[...]/<u>Noms surannés, impropres ou ridicules/</u>[...]/<u>Abreviation d'Enchaînements.</u>/Temps modernes, consacrés par le talent d'un executant/ou par le caractère d'un pas.
Unsigned and undated [c.1848–1855]
[DKKk; NKS 3285 4°, Kapsel 1, læg C 1
This manuscript is interesting in that Bournonville's descriptions of the meaning of several of his stenochoreographic signs here are the exact opposite (in terms of directions and turns) to those explanations given for the same symbols in his later so-called *Vocabulaire de danse* from 1855. Moreover, the manuscript contains several valuable descriptions of combinations of steps with which many of the leading dancers of the pre-Romantic and Romantic ballet distinguished themselves. These steps were invented and/or performed by such prominent artists as A. Vestris, L. Duport, Ferdinand (stage name for Jean La Brunières de Médicis), Albert (stage name for François Decombe), A. Paul, L.-F. Gosselin, J. Perrot, M. Taglioni, C. Grisi, and F. Elssler.

Choreographic note. Ms. Autograph. Brown ink. 4 pp. of which two are blank (36,8 × 22,6 cm)
<u>Chorégraphie.</u>/<u>Système = Général</u> [erasures]/<u>des cinq variantes de tous les mouvements de la Danse.</u>
Unsigned and undated [c.1848–1855]
[DKKk; NKS 3285 4°, Kapsel 1, læg C 1

Choreographic note. Ms. Autograph. Brown ink. 1 vol. 59 pp. (16,9 × 10,7 cm)
<u>Notes</u>/<u>Chorégraphiques</u>/<u>1855.</u>/[...]/<u>Explication</u>/des/<u>Signes chorégraphiques</u> / <u>employés</u> / par /<u>Auguste Bournonville</u> / [...]/ Titelblad./<u>Etudes chorégraphiques</u>/dediées aux/Artistes de la Danse/par:/Auguste Bournonville.
Signed and dated (on the front cover): '<u>1855.</u>'
[DKKk; Utilg. 828 (Harald Landers Arkiv, kapsel 182)
This manuscript seems to represent Bournonville's earliest draft for his later so-called *Vocabulaire de danse* and the first 1855 edition of his *Etudes chorégraphiques* (*see* the following entries). The manuscript holds his later additions and corrections (written with black ink) which seems to have been made in 1855–56. The volume was donated by Bournonville to L. Gade, who, in turn, handed it over to H. Beck in 1894. Both of their autographed owners' signatures are written on the title page. Later H. Lander came into possession of the manuscript, and in 1989 his widow, L. Lander, donated it to DKKk.

Choreographic note. Ms. Autograph. Brown ink. 30 pp. (pp. '21–50') in a volume of 90 pp. (22,1 × 17 cm)
Chapitre 2:me/Vocabulaire de Danse/avec/Les signes d'abréviation.
Unsigned and undated [1855]
[DKKk; NKS 3285 4°, Kapsel 1, læg C 7
This manuscript represents Bournonville's final version for his second chapter, entitled *Vocabulaire de danse* which he intended to publish in the first 1855 edition of *Etudes chorégraphiques*. However, for unknown reasons it was never included in this volume and the manuscript was not published until 1990 (*see* K. A. Jürgensen, *The Bournonville Heritage*, pp. 160–165).

Choreographic note. Ms. Autograph. Brown ink. 21 pp. (pp. '51–70') in a volume of 90 pp. (22,1 × 17 cm)
x./Système du nombre 'Cinq'/adapté/aux/Elémens et Genres de la danse./x. Chapitre 3:me
Unsigned and dated (on p. '70'): 'Copenhague ce 7. mars 1855.'
[DKKk; NKS 3285 4°, Kapsel 1, læg C 7
This manuscript represents Bournonville's final version for his third chapter, entitled *Système du nombre 'cinq'* which he intended to publish in the first 1855 edition of *Etudes chorégraphiques*. However, for unknown reasons it was never included in this volume, and the manuscript has remained unpublished to this day.

Choreographic note. Ms. Autograph. Black ink. 24 pp. (23,4 × 17,6 cm)
Nomenclature/par/ordre alphabétique/à/mon élève et digne collègue/Ferdinand Hoppe/1861.
Unsigned and dated (on the title page): '1861.'
[Private collection (Copenhagen)]
This manuscript about Bournonville's technical terms and steno-choreographic signs was clearly made as a personal gift to his pupil and colleague, F. Hoppe. It seems to have been written soon before Bournonville's departure in the late summer of 1861 for his three-year engagement at the Royal Theatre in Stockholm. The manuscript was most probably intended as an *aide-mémoire* for Hoppe, who in 1861 seems to have taken over responsibility for rehearsing Bournonville's ballets during his three-year absence.

Choreographic note. Ms. Autograph. Brown ink. 2 pp. (32,8 × 25,5 cm)
Forklaring paa Flere choreographiske Tegn.
Signed and dated: 'Fredensborg d. 25 Juli 1869.'
[SSm; Daniel Fryklunds samling no. 99

Choreographic note. Ms. Autograph. Brown ink. 1 p. (32,8 × 25,5 cm)
Tegn og Forkortelser.
Unsigned and undated [Written most probably on the same day as the previous manuscript (i. e. 25.6.1869)]
[SSm; Daniel Fryklunds samling no. 99 A

Bournonville's diaries
(in chronological order)

No indications about diaries written prior to 2.5.1820 have yet been found.

1820

Diary and travel expenses. Ms. Autograph. Brown and black ink. 223 pp. (various sizes)
Journal/for/Antoine Auguste Bournonville/Fra den 2.den Maÿ [til] den 13 December/1820.
Signed and dated.
[DKKk; NKS 747 8°, kapsel 8
This diary covers Bournonville's travel to and sojourn in Paris (from 2.5. to 6.11.1820), and his return to Copenhagen (from 7.11. to

12.12.1820). For its contents *see* August Bournonville: *Lettres à la maison de son enfance vol. 1II* (ed. S. K. Jacobsen & N. Schiørring; Copenhagen, Munksgaard, 1970).

1820–1824

According to his 1879 diary Bournonville's diaries from the years 1820–1824 existed until 11.5.1879 when he personally destroyed them. In his diary he stated about his reason for this decision:

8.5.1879: 'Gjennemset min Journal for 1820 (min første Reise og Ophold i Paris med min Fader)'
11.5.: 'Gjennemlæst Aargangene af min Journal fra d. 13 Decbr 1820 til 31' Martz 1824, efter at den i over 50 Aar har ligge forseglet; men da den indeholdt Meddelelser, deels om ulykkelige Familiebegivenheder, om gammelt Theatervrøvl, og mine egne ungdommelige Sværmerier, samt paa Flere Sider led af en latterlig Omstændelighed og daarlig Orthographie fandt jeg det ikke tjenligt at overantvorde [*sic*] den til min Efterslægt, men idet jeg beholdt Dagbogen fra Paris 1820: ofrede jeg hele Resten til Ilden'.

1824–1834

No diaries are preserved from the period between 1.4.1824 and 20.5.1834 (for these years *see* August Bournonville: *Lettres à la maison de son enfance vol. I*, ed. S. K. Jacobsen & N. Schiørring; Copenhagen, Munksgaard, 1969).

Diary and travel expenses. Ms. Autograph. Brown and black ink. 23 pp. (various sizes)
Noter og Erindringer/Paris./1834
Signed and dated.
[DKKk; NKS 747 8°, kapsel 8
This diary covers Bournonville's sojourn in Paris from 21.5. to 5.8. 1834.

1834–1836

No diaries are preserved for the period between 6.8.1834 and 17.4. 1836.

Diary. Ms. Autograph. Brown and black ink. 11 pp. (21,5 × 13 cm)
Dagbog. -/paa/Reisen.
Unsigned and dated: 'Berlin 1836'
[DKKk; NKS 747 8°, kapsel 8
This diary covers Bournonville's travel to and sojourn in Berlin (from 18.4. and 26.4.1836).

1836–1838

No diaries are preserved for the period between 27.4.1836 and 5.7. 1838.

Diary. Ms. Autograph. Brown ink. 8 pp. (19 × 11,6 cm)
Theater-Bemærkninger/London/[..] Paris
Unsigned and dated.
[DKKk; NKS 747 8°, kapsel 8
This diary covers Bournonville's sojourns in London (from 6.7. to 12.7.1838) and Paris (from 18.7. to 13.8.1838).

1838–1845

No diaries are preserved from Bournonville's stay in Denmark between 14.8.1838 and 6.4.1841.

Diary and travel expenses. Ms. Autograph. Brown and black ink. 65 pp. (various sizes)
Journal og Regnskaber/fra Reisen til og fra Ialien/1841.
Unsigned and dated: '1841.'
[DKKk; NKS 747 8°, kapsel 8

This diary covers Bournonville's sojourns in Paris (from 7.4. to 10.5. 1841), Naples (from 20.5. to 10.7.1841), Rome (from 12.7. to 28.7. 1841), Florence (from 2.8. to 13.8.1841), and his travel to and sojourn in Milan (from 14.8. to 3.9.1841).

No diaries are preserved from Bournonville's stays in Denmark and abroad (Hamburg) between 4.9.1841 and 9.8.1843.

Diary (fragment). Ms. Autograph. Brown ink. 2 pp. (16,1 × 10 cm)
Kiel./Tirsd. d. 10/August.
Unsigned and undated [1843]
[DKKk; NKS 747 8°, kapsel 1, vol. 1
This fragment covers Bournonville's travel from Kiel to Fredensborg (from 10.8. to 13.8.1843).

No diaries are preserved from Bournonville's stay in Denmark between 13.8.1843 and 30.11.1845.

1845–1848

Diary. Ms. Autograph. Brown ink. 1 vol. 88 pp. (16,3 × 10,4 cm)
Journal/fra/1.ste Decbr 1845 til d. 27 Sept 1848.
Unsigned and dated [1845–1848]
[DKKk; NKS 747 8°, kapsel 1, vol. 1
This volume covers Bournonville's stay in Denmark between 1.12. 1845 and 28.3.1846 (and from 30.8.1847 to 27.9.1848).

No diaries are preserved for Bournonville's stay in Denmark between 29.3. and 29.4.1846.

Diary. Ms. Autograph. Brown ink. 28 pp. (16,3 × 9,9 cm)
Onsd: d. 15.de Julii 1846.
Unsigned and dated [1846]
[DKKk; NKS 747 8°, kapsel 1, vol. 2
This diary is inserted in a copy of J. H. Schultz's printed 'Skriv- og Reise-Calender for det Aar efter Christi Fødsel 1846'. It covers Bournonville's travel to and sojourn in Paris (from 30.4. to 21.6.1847), his travel to and stay in London (from 22.6. to 26.6.1846), and his travel back to and sojourn in Paris (from 27.6. to 31.7.1846). The twelve periods written in this volume are inserted in the following order:
(1) 15.7.–23.7.1846, (2) 15.6.–21.6.1846, (3) 22.6.–26.6.1846, (4) 27.6.1846–29.6.1846, (5) 30.6.–6.7.1846, (7) 7.7.–14.7.1846, (8) 30.4.1846, (9) 1.5.–28.5.1846, (10) 29.5.–4.6.1846, (11) 5.6.–14.6. 1846, (12) 24.7.–6.8.1846.

No diaries are preserved from Bournonville's stay in Denmark between 7.8.1846 and 18.5.1847.

Diary (projected). Ms. Autograph. Brown ink. 13 pp. (16,3 × 9,9 cm)
Erindringer paa Reisen.
Unsigned and dated [1847]
[DKKk; NKS 747 8°, kapsel 1, vol. 3
This (projected) diary is inserted in a copy of J. H. Schultz's printed 'Skriv- og Reise-Calender for det Aar efter Christi Fødsel 1847'. It contains Bournonville's advice to his wife, Helene, who accompanied their daughter, Augusta, on a trip to Paris in the summer of 1847.

Diary and travel expenses. Ms. Autograph. Brown and black ink. 49 pp. (16,1 × 9,9 cm)
Udlæg til Stockholms=Reisen
Unsigned and dated [1846]
[DKKk; NKS 747 8°, kapsel 1, vol. 4
This diary is inserted in a copy of J. H. Schultz's printed 'Skriv- og Reise-Calender for det Aar efter Christi Fødsel 1847'. It covers Bournonville's travels to and sojourns in Stockholm (from 19.5.– 1.7.1847), and Paris (from 2.7. to 14.8.1847), and his return to Copenhagen (from 15.8. to 20.8.1847). The travel expenses are listed at the beginning of the volume and the diary is inserted at the end.

No diaries are preserved from Bournonville's stay in Denmark between 21.8. and 29.8.1847, but his notes covering the period between 30.8.1847 and 27.9.1848 are written into the 1845 volume.

1848–1849

Diary. Ms. Autograph. Brown and black ink. 1 vol. 58 pp. (16,8 × 11 cm)
Journal/fra/d: 28 Sept. 1848 til d. 20. August 1849.
Unsigned and dated [1848]
[DKKk; NKS 747 8°, kapsel 1, vol. 5
This volume covers Bournonville's stay in Denmark between 28.9. 1848 and 20.8.1849.

Diary. Ms. Autograph. Brown and black ink. 1 vol. pp. (16,8 × 11 cm)
Scene= [erased]/Journal./=Arrangement. [erased]/fra d. 21.e August 1849 til/d. 1.ste Januar 1850./Sept 1848. [erased]
Unsigned and dated [1848–1849]
[DKKk; NKS 747 8°, kapsel 1, vol. 6
This volume served originally as a notebook for Bournonville's opera mises-en-scène written in September 1848, two of which ('Dronningens Livgarde' and 'Brÿluppet ved Como=Söen') are still included on the first 15 pages. The diary covers Bournonville's stay in Denmark between 21.8. and 31.12.1849.

1850–1851

Diary. Ms. Autograph. Brown ink. 1 vol. 91 pp. (16,8 × 10,7 cm)
Journal/d. 1.ste Januar 1850. til 31 Marts/1851.
Unsigned and dated [1850–1851]
This volume covers Bournonville's stay in Denmark from 1.1.1850 to 31.3.1850.
[DKKk; NKS 747 8°, kapsel 2, vol. 7

Daily expenses. 1 vol. 0 pp. (17 × 11,5 cm)
Udgivter og Indtægter./for/1850–51.
Unsigned and dated [1850–1851]
[DKKk; NKS 747 8°, kapsel 2, vol. 9
The contents of this (empty) volume seems to have already been missing when it was donated to Copenhagen's Royal Library by the heirs of Charlotte Bournonville in 1911.

1851–1852

Diary. Ms. Autograph. Brown ink. 1 vol. 86 pp. (17,1 × 10,9 cm)
Journal./fra 1.ste April 1851. til d. 1.ste Juni/1852./sluttet i Christiania.
Unsigned and dated [1851–1852]
[DKKk; NKS 747 8°, kapsel 2, vol. 8
This volume covers Bournonville's stay in Denmark from 1.4.1851 to 4.5.1852, and his travel to and sojourn in Christiania (Oslo) from 5.5. to 31.5.1852.

Diary. Ms. Autograph. Brown ink. 1 vol. 60 pp. (16,6 × 10,8 cm)
Journal./for/Bournonville./d. 1.ste Junii til 31 Decbr 1852./1852.
Unsigned and dated [1852]
[DKKk; NKS 747 8°, kapsel 2, vol. 10
This volume covers Bournonville's sojourn in Norway (from 1.6. to 15.8.1852), and his return to and stay in Denmark (from 16.8. to 31.12.1852).

1853–1854

Diary. Ms. Autograph. Brown ink. 1 vol. 60 pp. (16,6 × 10,8 cm)
Journal./d. 1.ste Januar 1853. til/d. 14.de Julii 1854.
Unsigned and dated [1853–1854]
[DKKk; NKS 747 8°, kapsel 2, vol. 11
This volume covers Bournonville's stay in Denmark (from 1.1.1853 to 9.4.1854), his travels to and sojourns in Vienna (from 10.4.– 1.5.1854) and Berlin (1.5.–2.5.1854), the return to and stay in Den-

mark (from 3.5. to 17.6.1854), and his second travel to and sojourn in Vienna (from 18.6. to 14.7.1854).

1854–1856

Daily expenses. 1 vol. 0 pp. (17,3 × 11 cm)
Sommerlyst./Fredensborg./1854-55-56
Unsigned and dated [1854–1856]
[DKKk; NKS 747 8°, kapsel 2, vol. 12
The contents of this (empty) volume seem to have been already missing when it was donated to Copenhagen's Royal Library by the heirs of Charlotte Bournonville in 1911.

Diary. Ms. Autograph. Brown ink. 1 vol. 144 pp. (17,5 × 11,3 cm)
Journal/d. 15 Julii 1854. – 30 Sept. 1855.
Unsigned and dated [1854–1855]
[DKKk; NKS 747 8°, kapsel 3, vol. 13
This volume covers Bournonville's sojourn in Vienna (from 15.7. to 7.8.1854), his travel to and stay in Denmark (from 8.8.1854 to 30.6.1855), and his return to and sojourn in Vienna (from 1.7.–30.9. 1855).

Travel expenses and income. Ms. Autograph. Black and brown ink. 1 vol. 29 pp. (16,6 × 10,9 cm)
Regnskabs-Bog./for/Augst Bournonville./d. 26.de Junii 1855.
Unsigned and dated [1855]
[DKKk; NKS 747 8°, kapsel 2, vol. 14
This volume covers the period between 26.6. and 30.9.1855.

Diary. Ms. Autograph. Brown and blue ink. 1 vol. 154 pp. (16,7 × 11 cm)
Journal/d. 1.ste October 1855. – 1 Oct. 1856.
Unsigned and dated [1855–1856]
[DKKk; NKS 747 8°, kapsel 3, vol. 15
This volume covers Bournonville's sojourn in Vienna (from 1.10. 1855 to 31.3.1856), his travels to and sojourns in Milan (from 1.4. to 15.4.1856), and Paris (from 16.4. to 27.4.1856), and his return to and stay in Denmark (from 28.4. to 30.9.1856).

Diary. Ms. Autograph. Brown ink. 89 pp. (23,2 × 14,4 cm)
Reise=Route./fra/Wien til Mayland/over/Triest og Venedig:
Unsigned and dated '1.ste April 1856/[…]/14.e April'
[DKKk; NKS 747 8°, kapsel 8
This diary covers Bournonville's travel from Vienna to Milan between 1.4. and 14.4.1856

Daily expenses. Ms. Autograph. Brown ink. 1 vol. 55 pp. (17,4 × 11 cm)
Journal/for/Udgivter og Indtægter./1855–56
Unsigned and dated [1855–1856]
[DKKk; NKS 747 8°, kapsel 3, vol. 16
This volume covers the time between July 1855 and 31.12.1856.

1856–1857

Diary. Ms. Autograph. Brown and blue ink. 1 vol. 151 pp. (17,2 × 11 cm)
Journal/d. 1.ste October 1856. – 31 Oct. 1857.
Unsigned and dated [1856–1857]
[DKKk; NKS 747 8°, kapsel 3, vol. 17
This volume covers Bournonville's stay in Denmark (from 1.10.1856 to 1.4.1857), his travel to and sojourn in Stockholm (from 2.4. to 27.6.1857), and his return to and stay in Denmark (from 28.6. to 31.10.1857).

1857–1858

Diary. Ms. Autograph. Brown, blue and black ink. 1 vol. 156 pp. (16,8 × 10,8 cm)
Journal,/d. 1.ste Novbr 1857 til d. 31 Decbr 1858.
Unsigned and dated [1857–1858]

[DKKk; NKS 747 8°, kapsel 3, vol. 18
This volume covers Bournonville's stay in Denmark (from 1.11. to 1.4.1858), his travel to and sojourn in Stockholm (from 2.4. to 21.6. 1858), and his return to and stay in Denmark (from 22.6. to 31.12. 1858).

1859–1860

Diary. Ms. Autograph. Brown and black ink. 1 vol. 150 pp. (16,8 × 11 cm)
Journal,/den 1.ste Januar 1859. til/d. 30 April 1860.
Unsigned and dated [1859–1860]
[DKKk; NKS 747 8°, kapsel 4, vol. 19
This volume covers Bournonville's stay in Denmark (from 1.1.1859 to 28.4.1860), and his travel to and sojourn in Hamburg (from 29.4. to 30.4.1860).

1860–1861

Daily expenses and income. Ms. Autograph. Brown and black ink. 1 vol. 90 pp. (17 × 11,3 cm)
Journal./for/ Indtægter og Udgivter d. 1.ste Januar 1860 til 31 Decbr/1861.
Unsigned and dated [1860–1861]
[DKKk; NKS 747 8°, kapsel 4, vol. 20
This volume covers the period between 1.1.1860 and 31.12.1861.

Diary. Ms. Autograph. Brown and black ink. 1 vol. 154 pp. (16,8 × 11,2 cm)
Journal,/1.ste Mai 1860. til den/23.de October, -/1861.
Unsigned and dated [1860–1861]
[DKKk; NKS 747 8°, kapsel 4, vol. 21
This volume covers Bournonville's travels to and sojourns in London (from 1.5. to 10.5.1860) and Paris (from 11.5. to 27.5.1860), his return to and stay in Denmark (from 28.5.1860 to 15.5.1861), his travel to and sojourn in Stockholm (from 16.5. to 29.5.1860), his return to and stay in Denmark (from 30.5. to 9.10.1861), and his second travel to and sojourn in Stockholm (from 10.10. to 23.10. 1861).

Diary and travel expenses. Ms. Autograph. Black and brown ink, and pencil. 1 vol. 102 pp. (14 × 9,3 cm)
London./[…]/Journal/Paa Reisen til London og Paris./1860.
Unsigned and dated [1860–1861]
[DKKk; NKS 747 8°, kapsel 4, vol. 22
This diary covers Bournonville's travels to and sojourns in Hamburg and London (from 29.4. to 10.5.1860), his travel to and sojourn in Paris (from 11.5. to 27.5.1860), his return to and stay in Denmark (from 28.5. to 4.8.1860, and from 13.5. to 15.5.1861), his travel to and sojourn in Stockholm (from 16.5. to 27.5.1861), his return to and stay in Denmark (from 28.5. to 31.5.1861), and his second travel to and sojourn in Stockholm (from 9.10. to 15.10.1861). The volume also contains lists of addresses in Stockholm, plans for a repertory and the rehearsals at Stockholm's Royal Theatre between October and December 1861, a speech given in Swedish by Bournonville on his first day as managing director of Stockholm's Royal Theatre, and his lists of travel expenses for the years of 1860 and 1861.

1861–1862

Diary. Ms. Autograph. Brown and black ink. 1 vol. 121 pp. (16,8 × 11 cm)
Journal./Fire Opera – Scene [erased]/d. 24.e October 1861.. til/ Mises en Scènes [erased]/d. 1.ste Novbr/1861 [erased]/1862.
Unsigned and dated [1861–1862]
[DKKk; NKS 747 8°, kapsel 4, vol. 23
Originally this volume contained Bournonville's manuscript mises-en-scènes (written in 1861) for four operas, but was later transformed into his diary. It begins with his 'Obervations critiques sur la mise en scène & sur l'execution' of six works seen in Stockholm between 20.5. and 25.5.1861. These notes are followed by his diary

covering the sojourn in Stockholm (from 24.10.1861 to 10.6.1862), the travel to and stay in Denmark (from 11.6. to 20.8.1862), and his return to and sojourn in Stockholm (from 22.8. to 31.10.1862).

1862–1864

Daily expenses and income. Ms. Autograph. Brown and black ink. 1 vol. 60 pp. (16,5 × 11,3 cm)
1862/Journal.
Unsigned and dated [1862]
[DKKk; NKS 747 8°, kapsel 4, vol. 24
This volume covers the period between 1.1.1862 and 1.7.1864.

Diary. Ms. Autograph. Brown and black ink. 1 vol. 152 pp. (16,7 × 11,3 cm)
Journal./d 1.ste Novbr 1862. til/d 29.e Febr: 1864 incl
Unsigned and dated [1862–1864]
[DKKk; NKS 747 8°, kapsel 4, vol. 25
This volume covers Bournonville's sojourn in Stockholm (from 1.11.1862 to 22.6.1863), his travel to and stay in Denmark (from 23.6. to 14.8.1863), and his return to and sojourn in Stockholm (from 15.8.1863 to 29.2.1864).

1864–1865

Diary. Ms. Autograph. Brown and black ink. 1 vol. 108 pp. (16,3 × 11 cm)
Journal/fra d. 1.ste Martz 1864./til/d. 31.e Maj 1865 [written on a label pasted on the original title of the volume that read: 'Opera./ Scene=Instruction/1857.–58.']
Unsigned and dated [1864–1865]
[DKKk; NKS 747 8°, kapsel 5, vol. 26
This volume originally contained Bournonville's manuscript mises-en-scènes (written in 1857–1858) for two operas, G. Donizetti's *Lucia di Lammermoor* and A. Lortzing's *Czaar und Zimmermann*, but was at a later stage transformed into his diary. It covers his sojourn in Stockholm (from 1.3. to 21.6.1864), and his travel to and stay in Denmark (from 22.6.1864 to 31.5.1865).

Daily expenses and income. Ms. Autograph. Brown and black ink. 1 vol. 53 pp. (16,9 × 11,1 cm)
Journal./for/Udgivter og Indtægter/1864:
Unsigned and dated [1864–1865]
[DKKk; NKS 747 8°, kapsel 5, vol. 27
This volume covers Bournonville's stay in Denmark (from 23.6.1864 to 20.11.1864), his travel to and sojourn in Paris (from 20.11. to 18.12.1865), and his return to and stay in Denmark (from 19.12. to 30.12.1865).

Diary. Ms. Autograph. Brown and black ink. 1 vol. 62 pp. (16,7 × 11,5 cm)
Journal./d. 1.ste Juni 1865, til d. 31 Decb/1865.
Unsigned and dated [1865]
[DKKk; NKS 747 8°, kapsel 5, vol. 28
This volume covers Bournonville's stay in Denmark (from 1.6. to 19.11.1865), his travel to and sojourn in Paris (from 20.11. to 15.12.1865), and his return to and stay in Denmark (from 16.12. to 31.12.1865).

Diary and travel expenses. Ms. Autograph. Brown and black ink, and pencil. 1 vol. 60 pp. (12,9 × 8,2 cm)
Mandagen d. 20.e November./1865.
Unsigned and dated [1865–1866]
[DKKk; NKS 747 8°, kapsel 5, vol. 29
This volume covers Bournonville's travel to and sojourn in Paris (from 20.11. to 15.12.1865), and his return to and stay in Denmark (from 16.12.1865 to 16.1.1866). The volume, moreover, contains Bournonville's travel expenses for 1865 and 1866, his plan for a ballet repertory in Copenhagen for the 1866–67 season, his three pencilled drawings of the décors for Meyerbeer's opera *L'Africaine* seen in Paris, and a list of names and addresses in Paris. Finally, the vol-

ume contains fragments of Helene Bournonville's diary covering the days of 22.4., 23.4., and 2.5.1880.

1866–1867

Diary. Ms. Autograph. Brown and black ink, and pencil. 1 vol. 157 pp. (16,5 × 11,1 cm)
Journal/fra d. 1.ste Januar 1866/til/d. 31.e Juli 1867.
Unsigned and dated [1866–1867]
[DKKk; NKS 747 8°, kapsel 5, vol. 30
This volume covers Bournonville's stay in Denmark between 1.1. 1866 and 3.7.1867.

Daily expenses and income. Ms. Autograph. Brown and black ink. 1 vol. 90 pp. (16,6 × 11 cm)
Journal/for/Indtægter og Udgivter/1866.–67:
Unsigned and dated [1866–1867]
[DKKk; NKS 747 8°, kapsel 5, vol. 31
This volume covers Bournonville's stay in Denmark between 1.1. 1866 and 31.12.1867.

1867–1869

Diary. Ms. Autograph. Brown and black ink. 1 vol. 152 pp. (16,4 × 11,1 cm)
Journal/fra d. 1.ste August 1867./til/d. 1.ste Martz 1869
Unsigned and dated [1867–1869]
[DKKk; NKS 747 8°, kapsel 6, vol. 32
This volume covers Bournonville's stay in Denmark between 1.8. 1867 and 28.2.1869.

1869–1870

Diary. Ms. Autograph. Brown and black ink. 1 vol. 156 pp. (16,9 × 11 cm)
Journal./fra/1.ste Martz 1869 til d. 1.ste Juli 1870.
Unsigned and dated [1869–1870]
[DKKk; NKS 747 8°, kapsel 6, vol. 33
This volume covers Bournonville's stay in Denmark (from 1.3. to 21.5.1867), his travel to and sojourn in Munich (from 22.5. to 4.6. 1869), and his return to and stay in Denmark (from 5.6.1869 to 30.6. 1870).

Daily expenses and income. Ms. Autograph. Brown and black ink. 1 vol. 59 pp. (16,6 × 11,1 cm)
Journal/for/Indtægter og Udgivter/1.ste Aug: 1869.
Unsigned and dated [1869–1870]
[DKKk; NKS 747 8°, kapsel 6, vol. 34
This volume covers Bournonville's stay in Denmark betwen 1.8.1869 and 30.12.1870.

1870–1872

Diary. Ms. Autograph. Brown and black ink. 1 vol. 192 pp. (16,6 × 10,9 cm)
Journal./fra/d. 1.ste Juli 1870 til 1.ste Mai/1872:
Unsigned and dated [1870–1872]
[DKKk; NKS 747 8°, kapsel 6, vol. 35
This volume covers Bournonville's stay in Denmark (from 1.7. to 24.4.1870), his travel to and sojourn in Stockholm (from 25.4. to 9.5.1870), and his return to and stay in Denmark (from 10.5.1870 to 30.4.1872).

1872–1879

Diary. Ms. Autograph. Brown and black ink. 1 vol. 282 pp. (16,6 × 10,7 cm)
Journal/begyndt d. 1.ste Mai 1872./sluttet den 31' October 1874.
Unsigned and dated [1872–1874]
[DKKk; NKS 747 8°, kapsel 6, vol. 36

This volume covers Bournonville's stay in Denmark (from 1.5.1872 to 14.4.1874), his travel to and sojourns in St Petersburg and Moscow (from 15.4. to 13.5.1874), the return to and stay in Denmark (from 14.5. to 3.6.1874), his travels to and sojourns in Vienna (from 4.6. to 10.6.1874), Venice (from 11.6. to 14.6.1874), Milan (from 15.6 to 18.6.1874), Florence (from 19.6. to 25.6.1874), Rome (from 26.6 to 11.7.1874), Naples (from 12.7. to 24.7.1874), and Paris (from 25.7. to 9.9.1874), and his return to and stay in Denmark (from 10.9. to 31.10.1874).

Diary and travel expenses. Ms. Autograph. Brown, blue, and black ink, and pencil. 1 vol. 120 pp. (16,5 × 10,7 cm)
[…]/Onsdagen d. 15.e April 1874/[…]
Unsigned and dated [1874]
[DKKk; NKS 747 8°, kapsel 7, vol. 37]
This volume covers Bournonville's travel to and sojourns in St Petersburg and Moscow (from 15.4. to 13.5.1874), his return to and stay in Denmark (from 14.5. to 3.6.1874), his travels to and sojourns in Vienna (from 4.6. to 10.6.1874), Venice (from 11.6. to 14.6.1874), Milan (from 15.6 to 18.6.1874), Florence (from 19.6. to 25.6.1874), Rome (from 26.6 to 11.7.1874), Naples (from 12.7. to 24.7.1874), and Paris (from 25.7. to 9.9.1874), and his return to and stay in Denmark (from 10.9. to 31.10.1874). The volume, moreover, contains Bournonville's travel expenses and a survey of the travel routes during the above-mentioned voyages.

Daily expenses and income. Ms. Autograph. Brown and black ink. 1 vol. 96 pp. (16,9 × 11 cm)
Journal/for/Indtægter og Udgivter/fra 1.ste Januar 1873 til 31 Decbr/1875.
Unsigned and dated [1873–1875]
[DKKk; NKS 747 8°, kapsel 7, vol. 38]
This volume covers Bournonville's stay in Denmark (from 1.1.1873 to 6.11.1874), his travel to and sojourn in Berlin (from 7.11. to 10.11.1874), the return to and stay in Denmark (from 11.11.1874 to 4.6.1875), his travel to and sojourn in Stockholm (from 5.6. to 14.6. 1875), and his return to and stay in Denmark (from 15.6.1875 to 30.12.1875).

Diary. Ms. Autograph. Brown and black ink. 1 vol. 281 pp. (16,6 × 10,9 cm)
Journal./fra d. 1.ste Novbr 1874. til/den 31.de Maj 1877:
Signed and dated [1874–1877]
[DKKk; NKS 747 8°, kapsel 7, vol. 39]
This volume covers Bournonville's stay in Denmark (from 1.11. to 6.11.1874), his travel to and sojourn in Berlin (from 7.11 to 10.11. 1874), the return to and stay in Denmark (from 11.11.1874 to 4.6. 1875), his travel to and sojourn in Stockholm (from 5.6. to 14.6. 1875), and his return to and stay in Denmark (from 15.6.1875 to 31.5.1877).

Daily expenses and income. Ms. Autograph. Brown, black, and blue ink. 1 vol. 145 pp. + 4 pp. on separate sheets (16,8 × 11,1 cm)
Journal/for/Indtægter og Udgifter/d. 1.ste Januar 1876.
Unsigned and dated [1875–1879]
[DKKk; NKS 747 8°, kapsel 7, vol. 40]
This volume covers Bournonville's stay in Denmark from 5.11.1875 to the day of his death on 30.11.1879.

Diary. Ms. Autograph. Brown and black ink. 1 vol. 242 pp. (17 × 11,3 cm)
Journal/fra d: 1.ste Juni 1877./[added with pencil by Charlotte Bournonville:] Faders sidste Dagbog/1879/til den 30.te November 1879
Unsigned and dated [1877–1879]
[DKKk; NKS 747 8°, kapsel 7, vol. 41]
This volume covers Bournonville's stay in Denmark from 1.6.1877 to his death on 30.11.1879.

Handwritten rehearsal books of H. C. J. Fredstrup and A. Fredstrup

Rehearsal book. Ms. Autograph (by H. C. J. Fredstrup). Brown ink. 1 vol. 155 pp. including an index of works (33,1 × 21,4 cm)
[…]/Balletregissør – Protocol/1817–1833 [sic]
Unsigned and undated [1817–1837]
[The State Archive (Copenhagen); Det kgl. Teaters Arkiv, Gruppe I, no. 515
This volume describes the casting and lists the rehearsals of dances in operas, singspiels, and plays at Copenhagen's Royal Theatre between 17.11.1817 and 10.4.1837.

Rehearsal book. Ms. Autograph (by H. C. J. Fredstrup). Brown ink.1 vol. 182 pp. (33,2 × 21,2 cm)
Balletregissør H. C. J. Fredstrups regiejournal 1823–42
Unsigned and dated (on p. 1): 'Denne Protocol autoriseres herved/ til Brug for Regisseuren ved Dandseprøverne/[…]/Den 18.de August 1823.'
[DKKkt; Fredstrup's protokol
This volume contains a list of the ballet rehearsals held at Copenhagen's Royal Theatre between 13.8.1823 and 20.5.1842.

Rehearsal book. Ms. Autograph (by H. C. J. Fredstrup and A. Fredstrup). Brown ink. 1 vol. 182 pp. of which 104 are blank (33,2 × 21,4 cm)
Prøve =/Journal/[…]/Fortegnelse over de med Balletpersonalet holdte Prøver
Unsigned and dated (on p. 1): 'Denne Protocol autoriseres hermed til Brug/for Regisseuren ved Dandseprøverne/[…]/d. 31' August 1842.'
[The State Archive (Copenhagen); Det kgl. Teaters Arkiv, Gruppe I, no. 518
This volume contains a list of the ballet rehearsals held at Copenhagen's Royal Theatre between 20.8.1842 and 28.3.1855.

Rehearsal book. Ms. Autograph (by A. Fredstrup and others). Brown ink. 1 vol. 420 pp. of which six are blank (38,8 × 24,3 cm)
Prøve Journal./[…]/Fortegnelse/over de med Balletpersonalet/ holdte Prøver.
Unsigned and dated (on p. 1): 'September 1855.'
[The State Archive (Copenhagen); Det kgl. Teaters Arkiv, Gruppe I, no. 519
This volume contains a list of all ballet rehearsals held at Copenhagen's Royal Theatre between 7.9.1855 and 2.6.1880.

Handwritten performing journals of Copenhagen's Royal Theatre

Journal of the daily performances given at Copenhagen's Royal Theatre. Ms. Autograph (by unknown hands). Brown and black ink. 5 vols. (37,4 × 24,3 cm)
JOURNAL
[DKKkt; Det kgl. Teater's Journal
This set of five volumes contains a complete list of the daily performances at Copenhagen's Royal Theatre between 1.9.1825 and 2.6. 1880. Several entries are accompanied by notes and commentaries that describe in further detail the reception of each performance, particular incidents occurred, etc.

Handwritten repertory books of F. Hoppe

Repertory book. Ms. Autograph (by F. Hoppe). Black ink. 3 pp. (17,3 × 10,8 cm)
Erindrings=Liste. -/over de/Balletter Stÿkker og Pas de deux/hvori jeg haver dandset./Kjöbenhavn den 16. September 1836./F: Hoppe.
Signed and dated [1836–1837]

[Private collection (Copenhagen)
This manuscript contains a survey of the repertory in which F. Hoppe performed at Copenhagen's Royal Theatre between 12.9. 1836 and 25.2.1837.

Repertory book. Ms. Autograph (by F. Hoppe). Black ink. 1 vol. 77 pp. (18,9 × 11,8 cm)
Fortegnelse. –/over de/Aftener jeg har gjort Tjeneste./12/9.42. Mandag. –
Signed and dated '12/9.[18]42.'
[Private collection (Copenhagen)
This volume contains a complete survey of the repertory in which F. Hoppe performed at Copenhagen's Royal Theatre between 4.9. 1842 and 3.6.1858.

Handwritten catalogues of the music archive of Copenhagen's Royal Theatre

Music catalogue. Ms. Autograph (by an unknown hand). Brown and black ink. 1 vol. 45 pp. (36 × 21 cm with minor variants)
Alphabetisk/Fortegnelse/over/Balletter/i/det Kongelige Theaters Musikarchiv.
Unsigned and undated [c. mid-1860s–April 1986]
[DKKkt; Musikarkivet
This volume contains an alphabetical list of the ballets performed at Copenhagen's Royal Theatre between the late eighteenth century and April 1986. To each entry is added a survey of the musical material (orchestral score, répétiteur's copy, and parts) and the original call number. A photocopy of the catalogue is now in DKKk (Musikafdelingen).

Music catalogue. Ms. Autograph (by an unknown hand). Brown and black ink. 1 vol. 25 pp. (36 × 21 cm with minor variants)
Register/over Det kongl. Theaters Balletmusik/[...]/Componister og aArrangeurer af/Balletmusik for Det kongl. Theater
Unsigned and undated [c. mid-1860s–April 1986]
[DKKkt; Musikarkivet
This volume contains a list of the ballets given at Copenhagen's Royal Theatre between the late eighteenth century and April 1986. The catalogue is arranged in numerical order after the call number of the musical material for each work. Moreover, an alphabetical list of the music composers is added at the end of the catalogue with the titles of their respective works given after each composer. A photocopy of the catalogue is now in DKKk (Musikafdelingen).

Music catalogue. Ms. Autograph (by an unknown hand). Black and brown ink, and pencil. 1 vol. 48 pp. of which twelve are blank (33,5 × 22,6 cm)
Alphabetisk/Fortegnelse/over/Operaer og Syngestÿkker/Dramaer og Skuespil med Sang/samt Vaudeviller som forefindes/i/det Kongelige Theaters Musikarchiv.
Unsigned and undated [c. mid-1860s and later]
[DKKk; Musikafdelingen
This volume contains a (not strictly) alphabetical list of the operas, singspiels, plays, and vaudevilles performed at Copenhagen's Royal Theatre between the late eighteenth century and April 1986. To each title is added the original call number of the musical material which for the main part is now preserved in DKKk.

Music catalogue. Ms. Autograph (by an unknown hand). Brown and black ink. 1 vol. 30 pp. (36 × 21 cm with minor variants)
Register/over Det kongl. Theaters Balletmusik/[...]/Componister og Arrangeurer af/Balletmusik for Det kongl. Theater
Unsigned and undated [c. mid-1860s–c. May 1983]
[DKKkt; Musikarkivet
This volume contains a list of the operas and plays given at Copenhagen's Royal Theatre between the late eighteenth century and May 1983. The catalogue is arranged in numerical order after the call number of the musical material for each work. Moreover, to each entry is added a survey of the musical material, including orchestral scores, prompt's books, vocal scores, piano vocal scores, vocal parts, parts, and music played by an orchestra seated on the stage. A photocopy of the catalogue is now in DKKk (Musikafdelingen).

Music catalogue. Ms. Autograph (by an unknown hand). Brown and black ink. 1 vol. 183 pp. of which 46 are blank (33 × 21,2 cm with minor variants)
Fortegnelse/over/Det Kongelige Theaters/Musikaliesamling/af Operaer Sÿngestÿlkker Skuespil med Sang/samt Vaudeviller./Første Afdeling/[...]/Anden Afdeling/[...]/Tredie Afdeling/[...]/Alphabetisk Componistfortegnelse/[...]/Fortegnelse over [...] Doubletter/[...]/Fortegnelse over den af F. Valentin skænkede Samling Klaver Udtog.
Unsigned and dated (on p. 1): 'den 1.ste mai 1864.'
[DKKk; Musikafdelingen
This volume contains a (not strictly) alphabetical list of the operas, singspiels, plays, and vaudevilles performed at Copenhagen's Royal Theatre between the late eighteenth century and throughout the nineteenth century. To each title is added a survey of the musical material for it and the original call number. The catalogue is divided into three sections, the first of which includes orchestral scores, prompt's books, vocal scores and piano vocal scores. The second section lists conductor's parts, vocal parts, orchestral parts, and parts for the music which is played by an orchestra seated on the stage. The third section includes the musical material for individual arias, duets, terzetts, chorus, cantatas, and music arranged and composed for occasional works. Furthermore, an alphabetical list of the music composers is added to the catalogue and includes the titles of the respective works listed after each composer's name. Finally, two alphabetical lists of all dublicates of musical material (mainly full scores and piano vocal scores) are included, the latter consisting of a collection of piano vocal scores donated to the Royal Theatre by F. Valentin in the 1930s.

Handwritten catalogues of the music archive of Stockholm's Royal Theatre and Dramatiska Theatern

Music catalogue. Ms. Autograph (by A. F. Schwartz) and print. Black and brown ink. 1 vol. 453 pp. (28,6 × 19,7 cm) CATHALOG/öfver/Kongl. Theaterns/Musikalier./1.a Bandet./[Upprättad år 1841 af Bibliothekarien A. F. Schwartz
Unsigned and dated: '1841'
[SSkma; A. F. Schwartz's kataloger öfver Kungliga Theaterns musikarkiv
This partly printed, partly handwritten catalogue describes the music material in the music archive of Stockholm's Royal Theatre for operas, operettas, plays, pantomimic ballets, ballet divertissements, individual *pas* and dances, prologues, and epilogues (all now in SSkma). Nearly all entries are accompanied by a handwritten musical incipit. The last entries date from the late 1890s.

Music catalogue. Ms. Autograph (by an unknown hand). Black ink. 64 pp. (in various sizes)
Kungl. Theaterns Dram. Musik-bibliotek
Unsigned and undated [late 19th century]
[SSkma; Dramatiska Theaterns musik katalog
This catalogue contains a list of the musical material employed for vaudevilles and plays at Stockholm's Mindra Theatern and Kungliga Theatern (Dramatiska Theatern) between c.1844 and c.1888.

Tailor's handwritten records and inventories of the costumes at Copenhagen's Royal Theatre

Tailor's record. Ms. Autograph (by an unknown hand). Brown and black ink. 1 vol. 145 pp. (34 × 22 cm)
Protokol over Garderobe-/Anskaffelser/(ført systematisk)/1833–35

Unsigned and dated: 'Tilgang fra 1 September =/= 1833 =/= til d. 31.te Mai 1835
[DKKkt; G. 11.
This volume contains the tailor's record of the acquisitions and expenses of the costume department at Copenhagen's Royal Theatre during the period between 1.9.1833 and 31.5.1835.

Tailor's record. Ms. Autograph (by an unknown hand). Brown and black ink. 1 vol. 383 pp. (34 × 22 cm)
Protokol over Garderobe-/Anskaffelser/(ført systematisk)/1835–36
Unsigned and undated [1835–1836]
[DKKkt; G. 12.
This volume contains the tailor's record of the acquisitions made at Copenhagen's Royal Theatre during the 1835–36 season.

Tailor's record. Ms. Autograph (by an unknown hand). Brown and black ink. 1 vol. 126 pp. (33,5 × 21,5 cm)
Fortegnelse/over/alt det Arbeide som er Forfærdiget/paa/det kongelige Theaters Skræddersale/fra 1.ste... til 1. sept 1844 [sic]
Unsigned and undated [1835–1845]
[DKKkt; G. 13.
This volume contains the tailor's record of the costumes made at Copenhagen's Royal Theatre between 1.9.1835 and 1.9.1845.

Tailor's record. Ms. Autograph (by an unknown hand). Brown and black ink. 1 vol. 262 pp. (34,7 × 21,8 cm)
Protokol over/skrædderarbeide/1845–74(?)
Unsigned and undated [1845–1874]
[DKKkt; G. 14.
This volume contains the tailor's record of the costumes made at Copenhagen's Royal Theatre between 1.9.1845 and the 1873–74 season.

Stage director's handwritten records and inventories of the décor and props at Copenhagen's Royal Theatre

Stage director's record. Ms. Autograph (by an unknown hand). Black and brown ink. 1 vol. 359 pp. (34,2 × 21 cm)
Ballet 0
Unsigned and undated [1823–1872]
[DKKkt; Ballet 0
This volume describes the *régie* and the props employed for all ballets given at Copenhagen's Royal Theatre between 22.12.1823 (*The Carnival in Venice*) and 22.9.1872 (Bournonville's last but one restaging of his 1835 ballet *Waldemar*).

Stage director's record. Ms. Autograph (by an unknown hand). Brown ink. 1 vol. 419 pp. including an index of works and 335 blank pp. (35 × 17,9 cm)
[...]/'Ballet-Regie'/[c.1860]
Unsigned and undated [early 1860s]
[The State Archive (Copenhagen); Det kgl. Teaters Arkiv, Gruppe I, no. 516
This volume describes the *régie*, the sets, the props, and the lighting of eighteen Bournonville ballets in the repertory of Copenhagen's Royal Theatre during the early 1860s. Among these the oldest is *Soldier and Peasant* (from 13.10.1829) and the latest *The Valkyrie* (from 13.9.1861).

Stage director's record. Ms. Autograph (by an unknown hand). Black and brown ink. 1 vol. 96 pp. (35,4 × 22,6 cm)
Regiebog A./over/Balletter, Divertissementer/og/Dandse. Paabegyndt Anno 1868. -
Unsigned and undated [1868–1871]
[DKKkt; Ballet 1
This volume describes the *régie* and the props employed for all ballets given at Copenhagen's Royal Theatre between 21.2.1868 (*The*

Lay of Thrym) and 19.2.1871 (*The King's Corps of Volunteers on Amager*).

Stage director's record. Ms. Autograph (by an unknown hand). Black and brown ink. 1 vol. 127 pp. (34,4 × 22,6 cm)
Regiebog B./over/Balletter, Divertissementer/og/Dandse. Paabegyndt Anno 1871
Unsigned and undated [1871–1885]
[DKKkt; Ballet 2
This volume describes the *régie* and the props employed for all ballets given at Copenhagen's Royal Theatre between 2.9.1871 (Bournonville's last restaging of *La Sylphide*) and 1885.

Stage director's record. Ms. Autograph (by an unknown hand). Brown ink. 1 vol. 84 pp. including an index of works (31,8 × 20,6 cm)
Maskinmester-Protokol/for Balletten/Påbegyndt sæs. 1824/25 [sic]
Unsigned and undated [1821–1854]
[DKKkt; M 1
This volume describes the stage plans for all ballets given at Copenhagen's Royal Theatre between 4.12.1821 (P. Larcher's *Rustic Love*) and 20.3.1854 (the première of Bournonville's *A Folk Tale*).

Stage director's record. Ms. Autograph (by an unknown hand). Brown ink. 1 vol. 259 pp. including an index of works (33,2 × 20,6 cm)
Maskinmester-Protokol/for Syngestykker og Operaer/Påbegyndt sæs. 1824/25
Unsigned and undated [c.1824 – c.1856]
[DKKkt; M 2
This volume describes the stage plans for all operas and singspiels given at Copenhagen's Royal Theatre between c.1824 and c.1856.

Stage director's record. Ms. Autograph (by an unknown hand). Black ink. 1 vol. 311 pp. including an index of sets of props and 22 blank pp. (33,2 × 20,6 cm)
Maskinmester-Protokol/(Alle Kunstarter)
Unsigned and undated [c.1855 – c.1866]
[DKKkt; M 5
This volume describes the stage plans for all ballets, operas, singspiels, and plays given at Copenhagen's Royal Theatre between c.1855 and c.1866, including all Bournonville ballets between *Abdallah* (28.3.1855) and *Pontemolle* (11.4.1866).

Stage director's record. Ms. Autograph (by an unknown hand). Black ink. 1 vol. 186 pp. including an index of works (22,3 × 17,8 cm)
Maskinmester-Protokol/1866 –
Unsigned and undated [1866 – c.1868]
[DKKkt; M 6
This volume describes the stage plans for all works given at Copenhagen's Royal Theatre between 1866 and c.1868, including all Bournonville ballets in this period beginning with his restaging of *Waldemar* on 21.11.1866 and ending with the première of *The Lay of Thrym* on 21.2.1868.

Stage director's record. Ms. Autograph (by an unknown hand). Brown ink. 1 vol. 460 pp. including an index of works (15,8 × 10 cm)
Maskinmester-bog
Unsigned and undated [1876 – c.1894]
[DKKkt; M 11 (lille Maskinmester-bog)
This volume describes the stage plans for all works given at Copenhagen's Royal Theatre between 1876 and c.1894, including Bournonville last ballet *From Siberia to Moscow* from 7.12.1876 and the restagings of ten of his ballets during the 1880s and 1890s under the supervision of L. Gade, E. Hansen, and H. Beck.

For several other stage director's records and lists of sets and props dating from Bournonville's lifetime, now for the most part in private collections, *see* K. A. Jürgensen, *The Bournonville Heritage*, pp. 182–183.

Select Bibliography

The Select Bibliography contains mainly literature, including surveys and/or specific descriptions of Bournonville's oeuvre, or reference books used frequently in my compilation of his complete works. For more general Bournonville literature see the General Bibliography in the Volume I.

Anker, Øyvind: *Christiania Theater's Repertoire 1827–99* (Oslo, Gyldendal Norsk Forlag, 1956).

Aschengreen, Erik: *Bournonville, August* in *International Dictionary of Ballet*, vol. 1, pp. 188-192 (Detroit, St James Press, 1993).

Aschengreen, Erik, Marianne Hallar & Jørgen Heiner (eds): *Perspektiv på Bournonville* (Copenhagen, Nyt Nordisk Forlag Arnold Busck, 1980).

Aumont, Arthur & Edgar Collin: *Det danske Nationaltheater, 1748–1899. En Statistisk Fremstilling*, vol. I–III (Copenhagen, Alfred G. Hassings Forlag, 1899).

Bournonville, August: *Lettres à la maison de son enfance*, vol. I–III, edited by Kragh-Jacobsen, Svend, and Schiørring, Nils (Copenhagen, Munksgaard, 1969-1978).

Bournonville, August: *The ballet poems of August Bournonville: the complete scenarios*, trans. Patricia N. McAndrew (*Dance Chronicle* vols. 3–5, New York, 1979–83).

Bournonville, August: *My Theatre Life*, trans. from the Danish by Patricia N. McAndrew (Middletown, Conn., Wesleyan University Press, 1979).

Dahlgren, Fredrik August: *Anteckningar om Stockholms Theatrar* (Stockholm, P. A. Nordstedt & Sönner, 1866).

Derkert, Kerstin: *Repertoaren på Mindre teatern under Edvard Stjernströms cheftid 1854–63* (Stockholm, Akademielitteratur, 1979).

Fog, Dan: *The Royal Danish Ballet 1760–1958 and August Bournonville, A chronological catalogue of the Ballets and the Ballet-Divertissements performed at the Royal Theatre of Copenhagen and A Catalogue of August Bournonville's works – With a musical bibliography* (Copenhagen, Dan Fog Music Publisher, 1961).

Fridericia, Allan: *August Bournonville Balletmesteren som genspejlede et århundredes idealer og konflikter* (Copenhagen, Rhodos, 1979).

Gademan, Göran: *Realismen på Operan, Regi, spelstil och iscensättningsprinciper på Kungliga Teatern 1860–82* (Stockholm, THEATRON-serien, 1996).

Guest, Ivor: *The Romantic Ballet in Paris* (2nd ed., Dance Books, London, 1980).

Guest, Ivor: *The Ballet of the Second Empire 1847–1858* (London, A & C Black, 1955).

Guest, Ivor: *The Ballet of the Second Empire 1858–1870* (London, A & C Black, 1953).

Hadamowsky, Franz: *Die Wiener Hoftheater (Staatstheater)* (Vienna, Verlag Brüder Hollinek, 1975).

Jürgensen, Knud Arne: *The Bournonville Ballets – A Photographic Record 1844–1933* (London, Dance Books, 1987)

Jürgensen, Knud Arne: *The Verdi Ballets* (Parma, Istituto Nazionale di Studi Verdiani, 1995).

Jürgensen, Knud Arne & Ann Hutchinson Guest: *The Bournonville Heritage – A Choreographic Record 1829–1875*, vol. I–II (London, Dance Books, 1990).

Jürgensen, Knud Arne & Vivi Flindt: *Bournonville Ballet Technique Fifty Enchaînements*, vol. I–II + video (London, Dance Books, 1992).

Kronlund, Dag: *'Musiken Låten Ljuda, Mina Vänner!' Musiken i talpjäserna på Kungliga teatern vid 1800-talets mitt* (Täby, Akademitryck, 1989).

Lajarte, Théodore de: *Bibliothèque musical du Théâtre de l'Opéra, Catalogue historique, chronologique, anecdotique*, vol. I–II (Paris, Librairie des Bibliophiles, 1878, reprint by Georg Olms Verlag, Hildesheim, 1969).

McAndrew, Patricia: *A Chronology of Bournonville's stage works: Ballets and divertissements, individual dances, and stagings of operas and plays* (*Dance Chronicle*, vol. 3, no. 2, New York, 1979).

Overskou, Th.: *Den danske Skueplads, i dens Historie, fra de første Spor af danske Skuespil indtil vor Tid*, vol. I–VII (Copenhagen, Forlagt af Samfundet til den danske Literaturs Fremme, 1854–1876).

Raab, Riki: *Biographischer Index des Wiener Opernballetts von 1631 bis zur Gegenwart* (Wien, Verlag Brüder Hollinek, 1994).

Strömbeck K. G., Hofsten, Sune, and Ralf, Klaus: *Kungliga Teatern Repertoar 1773–1973, Opera, operett, sångspel. Balett* (Stockholm, Skrifter från Operan 1, 1974).

Svanberg, Johannes: *Kungl. Teatrarne under ett halft sekel 1860–1910, I–II* (Stockholm, Nordisk Familjeboks Tryckeri, 1917).

Winter, Marian Hannah: *The Pre-Romantic Ballet* (New York, Dance Horizons, 1974).

List of Names

The List of Names identifies all the names that appear in this volume. Full Christian names are given whenever possible and followed (in parentheses) by birth name and/or married name together with the years of birth and death. When years of birth and death have not been traced the year when the person is mentioned in the chronology of Bournonville's works has been added (–in parentheses–).

Abbreviations
b., birthname, *m.,* married name

Am., American; *Arg.,* Argentine; *Aus.,* Austrian; *Bel.,* Belgian; *Boh.,* Bohemian; *Da.,* Danish; *Eng.,* English; *Finn.,* Finnish; *Fl.,* Flemish; *Fr.,* French; *Ger.,* German; *Gr.,* Greek; *Hun.,* Hungarian; *Ir.,* Irish; *It.,* Italian; *Mor.,* Moravian; *Nor.,* Norwegian; *Pol.,* Polish; *Ru.,* Russian; *Sc.,* Scottish; *Sp.,* Spanish; *Sw.,* Swedish; *Tur.,* Turkish; *Ty.,* Tyrolean.

Åberg, Gulli (or Gurli) Johanna Carolina (1843–1922), Sw. actress

Abrahams, Johannes Henrik Severin (1843–1900), Da. actor and later director at Copenhagen's Folketheatret

Abrahams, Nicolai Christian Levin (1798–1870), Da. writer and translator

Abrahamson, Werner Hans Friedrich (1744–1812), Da. music historian and composer

Absalon (1128–1201), Da. archbishop and founder of Copenhagen

Adam, Adolphe Charles (1803–1856), Fr. composer

Adeler, Cort Sivertsen (1622–1677), Nor.-Da. admiral and sea-hero

Ahlgrensson, Fritz August (1838–1902), Sw. scene painter

Ahlmann, Nicolai (1809–1890), Da. farmer and politician, father of Bournonville's daughter-in-law, Doris Ahlmann

Ahlmann, Doris (m. Bournonville, 1848–1927/1928), Bournonville's daughter-in-law

Ahlström, Jacob Niklas (1805–1857), Sw. music historian and composer

Albert (stage name for François Decombe, 1787–1865), Fr. dancer and choreographer

Alexander II (1855–1881), Czar, Emperor and Autocrat of all the Russias

Alexander III (1845–1894), Czar, Emperor and Autocrat of all the Russias

Alexandra Caroline Marie Charlotte Louise Julie, (1844–1925) Da. Princess, later Princess of Wales, and Queen of Great Britain and Ireland

Allenbom(?), P. (–1858–), Sw. costumier(?) at Stockholm's Royal Theatre

Almlöf, Carl Anders Knut (1829–1899). Sw. actor and translator

Almlöf, Nils Wilhelm (1799–1875), Sw. actor

Ambrosiani, Charles Jean (late 18th–early 19th century), Sw.-It. dancer

Anacreon, (c.582–c.485 BC), Gr. poet

Anatole, Constance Hippolyte (b. Gosselin, 1794 –?), Fr. ballerina

Andersen, Anna Henriette (1839–1899), Da. singer

Andersen, Carl (1828–1883), Da. writer

Andersen, Clara (1826–1895), Da. writer

Andersen, H. (–1854–), Da. craftsman

Andersen, Hans Christian (1805–1875), Da. writer

Andersen, Reinhard C. A. (1829–?), Da. dancer

André, Johan Anton (1775–1842), Ger. music publisher

Andrée, Fredrika (m. Stenhammer, 1836–1880), Sw. singer

Antier-Chevrillon, Benjamin (1787–1870), Fr. writer

Arlberg, Geord Efraim Fritz (1830–1896), Sw. actor and regisseur

Arne, Thomas Augustine (1710–1778), Eng. composer

Arnoldson (or Arnoldsson), Carl Oscar (1830–1881), Sw. singer-actor

Arrhenius, Sofia Carolina Elisabeth Augusta (1838 –?), Sw. ballerina

Auber, Daniel-François-Esprit (1782–1871), Fr. composer

Audinot, Nicolas-Médard (1732–1801), Fr. writer

Augier, Guillaume Victor Emile (1820–1889), Fr. writer

Auguste Sophie Friederike Marie Caroline Julie, Princess of Hesse-Cassel (1823–1873)

Aumer, Jean–Pierre (1774–1833), Fr. choreographer

Balfe, (b. Balph), Michael William (1808–1870), Ir. composer

Backman, Alexis (1794–?), Sw. writer and theatre director

Baggesen, Jens (1764–1826), Da. writer

Bakunin, Mikhail Aleksandrovich (1814–1876), Ru. writer and politician

Barba, J.-N. (19th century), Fr. publisher

Barbier, Paul Jules, (1825–1901), Fr. writer

Barrière, Théodore (1825–1877), Fr. writer

Baseg (or Basegg, or Baßeg), Eleonora (or Eleonore, 1812–1874), Aus. ballerina

Battu, Marie (1838–1888), Fr. singer

Bauditz, Ferdinand Carl Adolph von (1811–1866), Da. commandor

Bauer (–1851–), Ty. musician

Bauer, Charlotte A. (b. Weyle, 1800 –1882), Da. ballerina

Bay, David Vilhelm Rudolph (1791–1856), Da. composer

Bayard, Jean François Alfred (1796–1853), Fr. writer

Bayly, Thomas Haynes (1797–1839), Eng. poet and song writer

Beau, Joseph (or Giuseppe, 1818–1903), It.-Aus. dancer and mime

Beaulieu, (late 18th century), Fr. dancer

Beaumarchais, Pierre Augustin Caron de (1732–1799), Fr. writer

Beck, Hans (1861–1952), Da. dancer and ballet-master

Beckman, Frans Herrman (1825–?), Sw. dancer and mime

Beckman, Johan (–1864–), Sw. publisher

Beethoven, Ludwig van (1770–1827), Ger. composer

Behrendt, Nicolai (1826–1889), Da. composer

Behrens, Hans Conrad Friedrich Wilhelm Behrend (1835–1898), Sw. singer

Bellini, Vincenzo (1801–1835), It. composer

Bellman, Carl Michael (1740–1795), Sw. poet and song writer

Belval, Jules-Bernard (1819–1876), Fr. singer

Benincori, Ange-Marie (1779–1821), Fr. composer

Benoist, François (1794–1878), Fr. composer

Bentzen, Maria (b. Hinch, c.1800 –?), Da. ballerina

Berens, Johan Herman (1826–1880), Ger.-Sw. composer and conductor

Berg, Fredrik Niklas (–1861–), Sw. translator

Berggreen, Andreas Peter (1801–1880), Da. music historian

Bergnehr, Vilhelmine Leocadie Theresia (m. Fossum, later Gerlach, 1827–1919), Sw.-Da. singer

Berling frères (i.e. Johan Carl Ernst Berling, 1812–1871), Da. publisher

Berlioz, Louis Hector (1803–1869), Fr. composer

Berner, Freund Jakob Gottlob (1823–1914), Da. director of Copenhagen's Royal Theatre

Bernstorff, U. (–1869–), Da. count

Berton, Henri (1767–1844), Fr. composer

Berwald, Franz Adolf (1796–1868), Sw. composer

Berwald, Johan Fredrik (1787–1861). Sw. composer and conductor

Beskow, Bernhard von (1796–1868), Sw. writer

Bias, Fanny (1789–1825), Fr. ballerina

Bigottini, Emilie (1784–1858), Fr. ballerina

Bille, Carl Steen Andersen (1828–1898), Da. newspaper editor

Bille, Steen Andersen (1797–1883), Da. admiral and commodore

Bills (or Bils), Bianca (m. Wulff, ?–1863), Da. ballerina

Bing, Alfred (–1876–), Da. merchant in Paris and friend of Bournonville

Bing, Meyer Herman (1807–1883), Da merchant and friend of Bournonville

Birch-Pfeiffer, Charlotte (b. Pfeiffer, 1800–1868), Ger. actress and play writer

Bishop, Anna (b. Riviere, 1810–1884), Eng. singer

Bishop, Henry Rowley (1786–1855), Eng. composer

Bissen, Herman Vilhelm (1798–1868), Da. sculptor

Bjerregaard-Jensen, Bernhard (1888–?), Da. composer and music editor

Björnson (or Bjørnson), Björnstierne (1832–1910), Nor. writer

Blache, Fréderic-Auguste (1791–?), Fr. dancer and choreographer

Blache, Jean Baptiste (1765–1834), Fr. dancer and choreographer

Bloch, Anton (1862–1936), Da. tenor-violinist and music copyist

Bloch, F. H. (–1874–), Da. consul

Blunck, Ditlev (or Detlev) Conrad (1798–1854), Da. painter

Bocha, Robert Nicolas Charles (1789–1856), Fr. harpist and composer

Bock, Bertha Carolina Mathilda (m. Tammelin, 1836–1915), Sw. actress

Bodenhoff, Gotthold Ernst Emil (1852–1934), Da. writer and editor

Bøgh (or Bögh or Boëgh), Erik (1822–1899), Da. composer and writer

Bohlin, W. (–1862–), Sw. writer

Boieldieu jeune (i.e. François-Adrien Boyeldieu, 1775–1834) Fr. music publisher

Boisen, Peter Outzen (1815–1862), Da. priest and music editor

Bojesen (–1866–), Da. priest

Bomholt, C. F. (–1858–), Da musician(?)

Borgaard, Carl (or Karl) Peter (1801–1868), Da. writer and director of Christiania's Theatre (Oslo)

Börjesson, Johan (1790–1866), Sw. writer

Borri, Pasquale (1820/1823–1884), It. dancer and choreographer

Borup, Nielsine (1824–1864), Da. ballerina

Bourgeois (also Anicet-Bourgeois), Auguste Anicet (b. Auguste Anicet, 1806–1871), Fr. writer

Bournonville, Antoine Théodore (Bournonville's father, 1760–1843)

Bournonville, Charlotte Helene Frederikke (Bournonville's second daughter, 1832–1911)

Bournonville, Edmond Mozart August (Bournonville's third son, 1846–1904)

Bournonville, Helene Frederikke (Bournonville's wife, b. Håkansson, 1809–1895)

Bournonville, Louise Antoinette Augusta (Bournonville's first daughter, m. Tuxen, 1831–1906)

Bournonville, Margaretha Therese (or Theresia) Augusta (Bournonville's fourth daughter, m. Irminger, 1840–1913)

Bournonville, Mathilde (Bournonville's third daughter, 1835–1890)

Bournonville, Wilhelmine (Bournonville's adopted daughter, 1833–1908)

Boyce, William (1711–1779), Eng. composer

Boye (or Boije), Birgitte Cathrine (1742–1824), Da. writer

Boye (or Boije), Caspar Johannes (1791–1853) Da. writer

Boyeldieu (or Boieldieu/Boïeldieu), François-Adrien (1775–1834), Fr. composer

Brahe, Tycho (or Tyge, 1546–1601), Da. astronomer

Bræstrup, Christian Jacob Cosmos (1789–1870), Da. government councellor

Brandus & Cie (i.e. Gemmy Brandus, 1823–1873), Fr. music publisher

Bredal, Ivar Frederik (1800–1864), Da. composer and conductor

Breitkopf, Bernhard Theodor (1749–c.1820), Ger. music publisher

Briol, Giovanni (?–1851), It. dancer and choreographer

Brioschi, Carlo (1826–1895) It. scene painter at Vienna's Kärnthnerthor Theatre

Brix (–1859–), Da. friend of Bournonville

Broberg (–1859–1868–), Da. friend of Bournonville

Broman, Robert Gustaf (1815–1874), Sw. actor

Brodersen, Georg Nicolai (1819–1908), Da. dancer

Brosbøll, Carl (pen name for Carit Etlar, 1816–1900), Da. writer

Brugnoli, Amalia (c.1808–1892), It. ballerina

Brun, Michael Walleen (pen name for B. W. Michael, 1819–1891) Da. writer

Brünnich, Boas (late 18th and early 19th century), Da. publisher

Bruun (–1849–), Da. carpenter

Bruun (–1851–1852–), Da. priest

Bruun, C. (–1842–), Da. ballerina

Bruun, Christian (–1848–), Da. friend of Bournonville

Bruun, Enkefru (–1860–), Da. friend of Bournonville

Bruun, Niels Thorup (1778–1823), Da. writer

Bryde, Emilie Henriette (m. Poulsen, 1846–1909), Da. ballerina

Bull, Christian Grönlund (1816–1873), Da. music editor

Bülow, Hans von (1830–1894), Ger. composer and conductor

Bülow, Frederik Rubeck Henrik (1791–1858), Da. major

Busch, Ferdinand J. C. (1824–?), Da. dancer

Calderon de la Barca Henao y Riaño, Don Pedro (1601–1687), Sp. writer

Cambon, Charles–Antoine (1802–1875), Fr. scene painter

Cammarano, Salvatore (1801–1852), It. writer

Camprubì, Mariano (–1839–1840–), Sp. dancer

Canno (–1870–), unidentified person apparently working at Copenhagen's Casino Theatre

Cantiran de Boirie, Eugène (1783–1837), Fr. writer

Capendu, Ernest (1826–1868), Fr. writer

Caraffa, Michele Enrico (1787–1812), It. composer

Carey, Fanny (–1870–1871–1872–), Fr.(?) ballerina

Carey, Isidore Camile Gustave (1812–1881), Fr.-Sw.(?) dancer, choreographer, and ballet-master

Carey, Léopoldine (–1870–1871–1872–), Fr.(?) ballerina

Carl XII, King of Sweden (1682–1718)

Carl XV Ludvig Eugen, King of Sweden and Norway (1826–1872)

Carl Frederik Christian, Crown Prince of Denmark (later King Frederik VII, 1808–1863)

Carl Johan XIV, King of Sweden and Norway (formerly Jean Baptiste Bernadotte, 1763–1844)

Carlini, Luigi (early 19th century), It. composer active at Naples' Teatro San Carlo between 1820–1823

Carlsen, Lauritz Wilhelm Theodor (1820–1889), Da. composer and répétiteur

Carmouche, Pierre Frédéric Adolphe (1797–1868), Fr. writer

Caroline Amalie, Queen of Denmark (1796–1881)

Caroline Charlotte Marianne, Crown Princess of Denmark (1821–1876)

Carpentier, Charles Jean Edouard (1834–1913), Da. dancer

Castelli, Ignaz Franz (1781–1862), Ger. poet and translator

Castenskjold, L. (–1872–1873–), Da. Lord-in-Waiting of Queen Louise of Denmark

Cetti, Ludovica Camilla (m. Neruda, 1848–1935), Da. ballerina

Champnes, Mr. (–1852–), Eng. actor-singer

Chaperon, Philippe (1823–1907), Fr. scene painter

Cherubini, Maria Luigi (1760–1842), It. composer

Chodowiecki, Daniel Nikolaus (1726–1801), Ger. painter

Chopin, Fryderyk Franciszek (1810–1849), Pol. composer

Choudens, Antoine de (1825–1888), Fr. music publisher

Christensen (–1854–), Da. saddler

Christensen, Charlotte (1945–), Da. art historian

Christensen, Christian Ferdinand (1805–1883), Da. scene painter

Christensen, Christian Johannes (1861–1928), Da. dancer

Christensen, Harald Constantin (1823–1892), Da. managing director of Copenhagen's Royal Theatre

Christensen, N. (19th century), Da. publisher

Christian I, King of Denmark (1426–1481)

Christian II, King of Denmark (1481–1559)

Christian III, King of Denmark (1503–1559)

Christian IV, King of Denmark (1557–1648)

Christian V, King of Denmark (1646–1699)

Christian VIII, King of Denmark (1786–1848)

Christian IX, King of Denmark (1818–1906)

Christian Frederik Wilhelm Carl, Crown Prince of Denmark (later King Frederik VIII, 1843–1912)

Christophersen (also Christoffersen), Harald Edvard (1838–1919), Da. singer

Chrysafulli, Henry (–1876–), Fr.(?) writer

Cimarosa, Domenico (1749–1801), It. composer

Clausen (–1859–), Da. theatre agent

Clausen (or Claussen), Henrik Nikolaj (1793–1877), Da. professor

Clotilde, M.me (l9th century), Fr. ballerina

Colbjørnsdatter, Anna (c.1665–1736), Nor. wife of a priest in Norderhov

Cole, John (1774–1855), Eng. composer

Colin (or Collin), Jonas (1776–1861), Da. writer and member of the direction of Copenhagen's Royal Theatre

Collin, Edgar (1836–1906), Da. writer

Columbus, Samuel (1642–1679), Sw. writer and translator

Comberousse (also Decomberousse), Alexis-Barbe-Benoît de (1793–1862), Fr. writer

Coralli, Jean (b. Peracini, Jean Coralli, 1779–1854), Fr. dancer and choreographer

Cornet, Julius (c.1793–1860), Aus. director of Vienna's Kärnthnerthor Theatre

Cotelle, Alexandre (?–1858), Fr. music publisher

Croce, Ferdinando (or Ferdinand) (–1854), It. dancer in Vienna

Curmi (or Curmy), A. (–1849–), It. composer

Dagmar Marie Sophie Frederikke, Princess of Denmark, took the name of Maria Feodorovna when she married the later Czar Alexander III of Russia (1847–1928)

Dahl, Christian Florus Balduin (1834–1891), Da. composer and conductor

Dahl, Emma (b. Sessi, also known as Freyse-Sessi, 1819–1896), It.-Da. singer

Dahl, Johan Fjeldsted (1807–1877), Nor. writer and publisher

Dahlén, Carl (1770–1851), Sw. dancer

Dahlgren, Conrad Theodor (1821–?), Sw. dancer

Dahlgren, Fredrik August (1816–1895), Sw. writer and translator

Dahlqvist, Carl Georg (1807–1873), Sw. actor

Dalayrac (or d'Alayrac), Nicolas (1753–1809), Fr. composer

D'Almaine & Co. (1830s), Eng. music publisher

Damse, Józef (1788–1852), Pol. composer

Danneskjold, Christian Conrad Sophus (1836–1908), Da. count

Danneskjold, Grevinde (–1866–), Da. countess

Danske, Holger (12th century), Da. hero and legendary figure

Dauberval, Jean (b. Bercher, 1742–1806), Fr. choreographer and ballet-master

Decourcelle, Adrien (1821–1892), Fr. writer

Dehn, Agnes Nathalie (m. Gjørling, 1851–1920), Da. actress

Dela Gardie (or Delagardie), Jacob Gustaf (1768–1842), Sw. count

Delahante, Julius (?–1866), Fr. music publisher

Deland, Hedvig Lovisa Charlotta (1807–1864), Sw. actress

Deland, Louis Joseph Marie (1772–1823), Sw. dancer and ballet-master

Deland, Pierre Joseph (1805–1862), Sw. actor

Delbanco, Otto Herman (1821–1890), Da. music publisher

Della Maria, Domenico (1768–1800), It. composer

Depassio (–1869–) Fr. singer at Théâtre Lyrique in Paris

Deshayes, André-Jean-Jacques François (1777–1846), Fr. choreographer

Desvergers (pen name for Armand Chapeau, 19th century), Fr. writer

Devrient, Philip Eduard (1801–1877), Ger. actor and writer

Didelot, Charles-Louis (1767–1837), Fr. choreographer and ballet-master

Dietrich (or Dittrich), Caroline Schanerz (–1854–1856–), Aus. ballerina

Dinaux (pen name for Beudin, Jacques Félix, 1796–1880, and Goubaux, Prosper Parfait, 1795–1859), Fr. writers

Distefano, Girolamo (–1854–), It. dancer at Vienna's Kärntherthor Theatre

Dittersdorf, Carl Ditters von (1739–1799), Ger. composer

Döcker, Gerhard Julius Frederik (1832–1905), Da. singer

Döll (–1870–), Ger. scene painter at Munich's Hoftheater

Donizetti, Gaetano (1798–1848), It composer

Dorph, Niels Vinding (1783–1858), Da. professor and member of the direction of Copenhagen's Royal Theatre

Dorph–Petersen, Jens Frederik Siegfred (1845–1927), Da. actor

Dörum, August Fredrik (1841–1880), Sw. actor

Drake (–1861–), Sw. costumier at Stockholm's Royal Theatre

Dreylich (or Dreilich), Gottlieb (–1855–), Aus. stage manager at Vienna's Kärnthnerthor Theatre (engaged from 1.4.1855 to 31.12.1883)

Drewes, Frederik Christian (1805–1879), Da. bugler

Drewsen, Adolph (1803–1885), Da. judge and friend of Bournonville

Drinnenberg, J. (–1863–), Ger.(?) composer

Dübeck, Richard (1811–1877), Sw. composer

Düben, Andreas (c.1597–1662), Ger.-Sw. composer

Düben, Gustaf (c.1628–1690) Sw. composer

Duchesne de Belleroust(?) (–1855–), Fr. friend of Bournonville

Dufour, Selim François (1799–1872), Fr. music publisher

Dumanoir, Philippe François Pinel (1808–1865), Fr. writer

Dumas, Alexandre (the elder, 1802–1870), Fr. writer

Dupuy (or Du Puy), Jean Baptiste Edouard Louis Camille (1770/1773–1822), Fr. singer-actor, composer

Duval, Alexandre (pen name for Pineu, Alexandre Vincent, 1767–1842), Fr. writer

Eckardt, Josephine Hortensia Nancy Adelaide (b. Thorberg, 1839–1906), Da. actress

Eckardt, Lauritz Andreas (1829–1889), Da. actor-singer

Eckersberg, Christoffer Wilhelm (1783–1853), Da. painter

Edberg, Carolina Gustafva (1835–?), Sw. ballerina

Edholm, Erik Wilhelm af (1817–1897), Sw. master of ceremony at the Royal Swedish Court

Edward Albert Victor Christian, Prince (1864–1892)

Edward VII, King of Great Britain and Ireland, Emperor of India (1841–1910)

Egense (–1866–) Da. répétiteur

Egense, Johanne Emilie Margrethe (m. Liebe, 1831–1881), Da. ballerina, later actress-singer

Ek, Hedvig Elisabeth Charlotta (1817–?), Sw. ballerina

Elmlund, Axel Wilhelm Julius (1838–1901), Sw. actor

Elsner, Johann Gottfried (1784–1869), Ger. writer

Elssler, Fanny (or Franziska), 1810–1884), Aus. ballerina

Elssler, Therese (m. morganatic as Freifrau von Barmin, 1809–1878), Aus. ballerina

Engel, Louis (–1856–), Aus. composer

Ennery (or Dennery), Adolphe D' (pen name for Eugène Philippe, 1811–1899), Fr. writer

Erhard-Hansen, Anna Doris (b. Pfeil, 1847–1917), Da. singer

Erhard-Hansen, Ludvig Jørgen Peter (1839–1915), Da. singer

Ernst, Heinrich Wilhelm (1814–1865), Mor. violinist

Erslev, Jacob Emil (1817–1882), Da. music publisher

Everlöf, Frans Anton (1799–1883), Sw. consul and writer

Ewald, Johannes (1743–1781), Da. writer

Exner, Julius (1825–1910), Da. painter

Eydrup (or Eidrup), Christiane Frederikke Marie Nielsen (1832–?), Da. ballerina

Faaborg, Rasmus Christian (1811–1857), Da. actor

Faber, Peter Kristjan Frederik (1810–1877), Da. writer

Fallesen, Morten Edvard (1817–1894), Da. director of Copenhagen's Royal Theatre

Falsen, Enevold de (1755–1808), Da. writer

Faure, Jean-Baptiste (1830–1914), Fr. singer

Favart, Marie (b. Pierette Ignace Pingaud, 1833–1908) Fr. actress

Ferdinand (stage name for Jean La Brunière de Médicis, 1791–1837), Fr. dancer

Ferslew, Christian Lunov Laasby (1817–1883), Da. singer

Fessy, Alexandre-Charles (1804–1856), Fr. composer

Feuillet, Octave (1812–1890), Fr. writer

Fitzjames, Louise (1809–?), Fr. ballerina

Fjeldsted, Caroline Wilhelmine (m. Kellermann, 1821–1881), Da. ballerina

Flammé, Athalia Anna Henriette (m. Reumert, 1859–1952), Da. ballerina

Flotow, Friedrich von (1812–1883), Ger. composer

Fog, Dan (1919–), Da. antiquarian and music seller

Forchhammer, Johan Georg (1794–1865), Da. professor

Foroni, Jacopo Giovanni Battista (1825–1858), It. conductor

Forsberg (or Forssberg), Amanda (–1863–1869–), Sw. ballerina

Forsberg, Fredrik Wilhelm (1800–1863), Sw. stage engineer at Stockholm's Royal Theatre

Förster, Emanuel Aloys (1748–1823), Aus. composer

Fossum, Vilhelmine Leocadie Theresia (b. Bergnehr, later m. Gerlach, 1827–1919), Da. singer

Franceschini, Girolamo (1820–1859), It.-Aus. costumier at Vienna's Kärnthner-thor Theatre

Frappart (or Frappard, born Ruault), Louis (1832–1921), Fr.-Aus. dancer

Frederik I, King of Denmark (1471–1533)

Frederik II, King of Denmark (1534–1588)

Frederik III, King of Denmark (1609–1670)

Frederik IV, King of Denmark (1671–1730)

Frederik V, King of Denmark (1723–1766)

Frederik VI, King of Denmark (1768–1839)

Frederik VII, King of Denmark (1808–1863)

Frederik VIII, King of Denmark (1843–1912)

Frederik Carl Christian, Crown Prince of Denmark (*see* Frederik VII)

Frederik Ferdinand, Hereditary Prince of Denmark (1792–1863)

Fredriksson (or Fredrikson), Johan Gustaf (1832–1921), Sw. actor

Fredstrup, Hans Carl Jørgen (1784–1859), Da. dancer and régisseur at Copenhagen's Royal Theatre

Fredstrup, Julie Annette Charlotte (1812–1906), Da. ballerina

Fredstrup, Petrine Georgine Caroline (1827–1881), Da. ballerina

Fredstrup, Thor Bjarke Axel (1830–1894), Da. dancer and régisseur at Copenhagen's Royal Theatre

Fridericia, Allan (1921–1991), Da. dance historian

Friebel, Carolina Desideria (b. Granberg, 1818–?), Sw. ballerina

Friedrich Wilhelm of Hesse-Cassel (also Frederik Wilhelm af Hessen), Elector of Hesse and regent of the electorate (1802–1875)

Friedrich William IV, King of Prussia, (1795–1861)

Frijs (–1874–), Da. Countess

Frijs, Frederik Julius Krag-Juel-Vind- (1821–1885), Da. Count

Fröhlich (or Frøhlich), Johannes (or Johann) Frederik (1806–1860), Da. composer

Funck, Frederik Christian (1783–1866), Da. violoncellist

Funck, Peter Ferdinand (1788–1859), Da. concert-master

Funck, Poul Erik (1790–1837), Da. dancer and choreographer

Funck, Pouline Augusta (m. Fallesen, 1826–1879), Da. ballerina

Funck, Wilhelm Erik (1824–?), Da. dancer

Füssel, Gotthilf Andreas (1809–1865), Da. dancer and mime

Füssel, Gustav Adolph (1815–1884), Da. dancer and mime

Gabrielli (or Gabrieli), Luigi (or Ludovico) (–1842–1856), Aus.-It. dancer and choreographer at Vienna's Kärnthner-thor Theatre

Gade, Dagmar (1863–1951), daughter and biographer of N. W. Gade

Gade, Elise Sophie (b. Garlieb, 1831–1906), Da. ballerina

Gade, Ludvig Harald (1823–1897), Da. dancer

Gade, Niels Wilhelm (1817–1890), Da. composer

Galeotti, Vincenzo (b. Tomaselli, 1733–1816), It.-Da. dancer, choreographer, and ballet-master

Gallenberg, Robert Wenzel von (1783–1839), Aus. composer

Gardel, Maximilien-Léopold-Philippe-Joseph (Gardel aîné, 1741–1787), Fr. dancer, choreographer, and ballet-master

Gardel, Pierre-Gabriel (1758–1840), Fr. dancer, choreographer, and ballet-master

Garlieb, Elise Sophie (m. Gade, 1831–1906), Da. ballerina

Garrick, David (1716–1779), Eng. actor and writer

Gassmann (or Gaszmann), Florian Leopold (1729–1774), Ger. composer

Gaudelius, Carl (–1863–), Ger. artistic director at Rotterdam's opera, leader of a touring Ger. opera company

Gautier, Théophile (1811–1872), Fr. writer

Gaveaux, Pierre (1760–1825), Fr. music publisher

Geijer, Erik Gustaf (1783–1847), Sw. professor and composer

Gelhaar, Wilhelmina Charlotta (1837–1923), Sw. singer

Gentzen, Johannes (–1842–1843–1846–), Ger. bugler

George I, King of the Hellenes, formerly Prince Christian Wilhelm Ferdinand Adolf Georg of Denmark (1845–1913)

George Frederick Ernest Albert, Prince (the later King George V of Great Britain and Ireland, 1867–1936)

Gérard, Marie (–1871–), Fr. ballerina

Gether, Enkefru (–1860–), Da. friend of Bournonvile

Gide, Casimir (1804–1868), Fr. composer

Giebelhausen, Signe (b. Winsløw, 1811–1879), Da.-Nor. actress

Gillberg, Johanna Gustafva (m. Sundberg, 1828–1910), Sw. ballerina

Gjødesen (–1849–), Da. dance student at Copenhagen's Royal Theatre

Gjørling, August (–1839–), Da. répéti-teur(?)

Gläser (or Glaëser), Franz Joseph (1798–1861), Boh.-Da. composer

Gläser, P. (–1857–), Aus. impressario

Glæser (or Gläser or Glaëser), Joseph August Eduard Friedrich (1835–1891), Da. composer

Gluck, Christoph Willibald von (1714–1787), Boh.-Aus. composer

Goethe, Johann Wolfgang von (1749–1832), Ger. writer

Gold, Fritz Georg Pius (1845–?), Da. dancer

Goldschmidt, Meïr Aron (1819–1887), Da. writer

Golinelli, Giovanni (or Johann, or Johan) Baptiste (1809–1884), It. dancer and choreographer at Vienna's Kärnthner-thor Theatre

Gosselin, Géneviève, ainée (?–1817), Fr. ballerina

Gottschalk, Louis Moreau (1829–1869), Am. composer

Gounod, Charles François (1818–1893), Fr. composer

Gozlan, Léon (1803–1866), Fr. writer

Grabow, Emma Mathilda (1852–1940), Sw. singer

Græbe, Johan Christian Frederik (1805–1883), Da. publisher

Grahn, Lucina (called Lucile) Alexia (m. Young, 1819–1907), Da. ballerina

Gram, Hans (1685–1748), Da. translator

Grammaticus, Saxo (mid-12th–early 13th century), Da. historian and author of Denmark's early national history (the so-called *Gesta Danorum*)

Grandjean, Axel Carl William (1847–1932), Da. composer

Grieg, Edvard (1843–1907), Nor. composer

Griffenfeldt, Peder Schumacher (1635–1699), Chancellor of Denmark during the reign of King Christian V

Grisi, Carlotta (1819–1899), It. ballerina

Grønfeldt, Peter (1765–1824), Da. répéti-teur

Gropius, Paul (1821–1888), Ger. scene painter at Berlin's Königlichen Theater

Grotz (or Groth), Johan Christoffer (–1870–), Da. publisher (active 1730s–1740s)

Grundtvig, Nicolai Frederik Severin (1783–1872), Da. priest and writer

Guerra, Antonio (1810–1846), It. dancer

Guillard, Nicolas François (1752–1814), Fr. writer

Guillou, Joseph (1781/1786–1853), Fr. flutist and composer

Güllich (or Gyllich), Valdemar (1836–1895), Da. scene painter

Gundersen (–1854–), Da. friend of Bournonville

Güntelberg, Christian Carl Herman Frederik (1791–1842), Da. translator

Gustaf III, King of Sweden (1746–1792)

Gyrowetz, Adalbert (1763–1850), Boh.-Aus. composer

Haack, Lovise D. (b. Höier, 1804 –?), Da. ballerina

Habeneck, François-Antoine (1781–1849), Fr. composer

Hagberg, Carl August (1810–1864), Sw. translator

Hagberg, Jacob Theodor (1825–1893), Sw. writer

Hage, Emmy (b. Tutein, 1832–1894), Da. friend of Bournonville

Hagemann (–1851–), Da. Commander

Hagen, Carl Harald (1816–1871), Da. actor

Halévy, Jacques-François-Fromenthal-Elie (1799–1862), Fr. composer

Hall, Carl Christian (1812–1888), Da. politician

Hallberg, D.lle (–1858–), Sw. ballerina

Hallström, Ivar Christian (1826–1901), Sw. composer

Halm, Friedrich (pen name for Eligius Freiherr Münch=Bellinghausen, 1806–1866), Pol. writer

Hammer, Hansine (m. Thygesen, 1831–?), Da. ballerina

Hammer, Jfr. (–1860–), Da. singer

Hammerich, Peter Frederik Adolf (1809–1877), Da. priest and writer

Hammerich, Martin Johannes (1811–1881), Da. writer

Hanne, L. (–1869–1874–), Da. regisseur at Copenhagen's Royal Theatre

Hans (or Johannes), King of Denmark (1455–1513)

Hansen, Anna Jeanette (b. Tardini, 1845–1918), Da. ballerina

Hansen, B. (–1860–), Da. actress

Hansen, cand. (–1859–), Da. graduate

Hansen, Carl Christian Constantin (1804–1880), Da. painter

Hansen, Christian Frederik (1756–1845), Da. architect

Hansen, Christian Julius (1814–1875), Da. music copyist

Hansen, Hans Emil (1843–1927), Da. dancer, choreographer, and ballet-master

Hansen, Jens A. (–1854–), Da. organizer

Hansen, Jens Wilhelm (1821–1904), Da. music publisher

Hansen, Jørgen Christian (1812–1880), Da. singer

Hansen, Ludvig Wonsel (1850–1919), Da. dancer

Hansen, Marie Charlotte (m. Wiehe-Béreny, 1865–1947), Da. ballerina, later actress

Hansen, Nicolai (1855–1932), Da. composer

Hansen, Styrmand (–1849–), Da. navigator

Harris, Augustus Glossop (–1861–), Eng. writer

Hart, John Thomas (1805–1874), Eng. music publisher and dealer

Härtel, Gottfried Christoph (1763–1827), Ger. music publisher

Hartkopff (–1861–), Da. agent(?)

Hartman, Victor Laurentius (1839–1898), Sw. actor

Hartmann, August Wilhelm (1775–1850), Da. precentor and composer

Hartmann, Frantz Paul Bernhard (1841–1916), Da. singer

Hartmann, Johan Ernst (1726–1793), Da. composer

Hartmann, Iohan Peter Emilius (1805–1900), Da. composer

Hartmann, Wilhelm Emilius Zinn (1836–1898), Da. composer

Hartvigson (–1878–), Da. lieutenant

Hatzelius (–1869–), Sw.(?) general

Hauch, Carsten (1790–1872), Da. writer and government councellor

Hauser, Miska (or Michael, 1822–1887), Boh. violinist and composer

Havkins, Fru (–1876–), Da. musician

Haydn, Franz Joseph (1732–1809), Aus. composer

Healey, Agnes Isabella (1840–1883), Eng. ballerina

Healey, Christine Mary (c.1836/1837–1921), Eng. ballerina

Hedberg, Frans Theodor (1828–1909), Sw. writer

Hedin, Zelma Carolina Esolinda (b. Bergnéhr, also m. Kinmansson, later Bergmansson, 1827–1874), Sw. actress

Heiberg, Johan Ludvig (1791–1860), Da. writer and director of Copenhagen's Royal Theatre

Heiberg, Johanne Louise (b. Pätges, 1812–1890), Da. actress

Heiberg, Peter Andreas (1758–1841), Da. writer

Heise, Peter Arnold (1830–1879), Da. composer

Hell, Theodor (pen name for Karl Gottfried Theodor Winkler, 1775–1856), Ger. poet

Hellmesberger, Georg (1800–1873), Aus. composer

Helms, Johannes (–1860–), Da. song writer and poet

Helsted, Edvard (or Edouard, or Eduard) Mads Ebbe (1816–1900), Da. composer

Hennings, Betty Mathilde (b. Schnell, 1850–1939), Da. actress

Henriques, Martin Rubin (1825–1912), Da. stockbroker and friend of Bournonville

Henriques, Thérèse (b. Abrahamsen, 1833–1882), Da. wife of M. R. Henriques

Henry, Louis-Xavier-Stanislas (1784–1836), Fr.-It. choreographer and ballet-master

Herbès, François d' (1805–1877), Fr. scene painter

Herder, Johann Gottfried (1744–1803), Ger. music historian

Hérold, Louis-Joseph-Ferdinand (1791–1833), Fr. composer

Herr, C. (–1852–), Nor. bassoonist

Herrick, Robert (1591–1640), Eng. poet and songwriter

Hertz, Adolf (1824–1882), Da. writer and translator

Hertz, Henrik (1797–1870), Da. writer

Hildebrand, Frantz (1842–1898), Da. violinist in St. Petersburg

Hindenburg (–1851–), Da. lieutenant and corps commander

Hirsch. Abraham (1815–1900), Sw. music publisher

Hjerta (or Hierta), Lars Johan (1801–1872), Sw. newspaper editor, and publisher

Hjorth (or Hjort), Jenny Gustafva Petronella (m. Lind, 1835–?), Sw. ballerina

Høedt, Frederik Ludvig (1820–1885), Da. actor

Hoffmann, Ernst Theodor Amadeus (1776–1822), Ger. writer

Hofmann, Emilie (–1855–), Aus. singer

Högfeldt, Johan Fredrik Isidor (–1862–), Sw. regisseur at Stockholm's Dramiska Theatern

Hoguet, François-Michel (or Michel-François, 1793–1871), Fr. choreographer

Holberg, Ludvig (1684–1754), Da. Baron and writer

Holck (–1869–), Da. Count

Holm, Augusta (1827–?), Da. singer-actress

Holm, Bertha (1832–1888), Aus. singer

Holm, Vilhelm Christian (1820–1886), Da. répétiteur and composer

Holmblad (–1868–), Da. friend of Bournonville

Holmström, Carl Ferdinand Alexander (1820–1858), Sw. copyist and writer

Holst, Elisabeth Frederikke Margrethe (b. Heger, 1811–1891), Da. actress

Holst, Hans Peter (1811–1893), Da. writer

Holst, Wilhelm Conrad (1807–1898), Da. actor

Holstein, Frederik Conrad von (1771–1853), Da. director of Copenhagen's Royal Theatre

Holtei, Karl Edward von (1798–1880), Ger. writer and translator

Hoppe, Johan Ferdinand (1815–1890), Da. dancer

Hoppensach, Frederik Ferdinand (1817–1878), Da. dancer and mime

Hörberg (–1857–1858–), Sw. publisher

Horn, Charles Edward (1786–1849), Eng. composer

Horneman, Christian Frederik Emil (1840–1906), Da. music publisher and composer

Horneman, Johan Ole Emil (1809–1870), Da. music publisher and composer

Hostrup, Jens Christian (1818–1892), Da. writer

Huguet (18th–19th century), Fr. music publisher

Huldberg, P. A. (–1871–), Sw. music publisher

Hülsen, Botho von (1815–1886), Ger. managing director at Berlin's Königlichen Theater

Hultmann, Fritz Wilhelm (1820–1894), Da. actor

Hus (or Huss), Pietro (c.1770–?), Fr.-It. choreographer and ballet-master

Hvasser (or Hwasser), Ebba Charlotta Elisa (b. Jacobsson, 1831–1894), Sw. actress

Hvasser (or Hwasser), Daniel (1817–1871), Sw. director at Stockholm's Royal Theatre

Hyltén-Cavallius, Gunnar Olof (1818–1889), Sw. director at Stockholm's Royal Theatre

Ingemann, Bernhard Severin (1789–1862), Da. writer

Ipsen, Alfred (1852–1922), Da. writer

Irgens (19th century), Da. publisher

Irminger, Carl Ludvig Christian (1802–1888) Da. admiral

Irminger, Eskil (1950–), Da. great-great-great grandson of Bournonville

Isachsen, Andreas H. (–1867–), Nor. theatre director

Isachsen, Janny (–1867–), Nor. ballerina(?)

Isouard, Nicolo (1775–1818), Fr. composer

Ivakura Tòmomi, Prince of Japan and governmental envoy to Europe (1825–1883)

Iversen, Christian Gellert (1817–1881), Da. publisher

Iversen, Carl Oscar (1849–1920), Da. dancer

Jacobson, Johan Jacob Georges Preben (1832–1897), Da. naval officer and friend of Bournonville

Jahn (–1870–), Ger. scene painter at Munich's Hoftheater

Janet, Pierre-Honoré (early 19th century), Fr. music publisher

Jansson, Christian (–1876–), Sw. scene painter

Jastrau, Richard Leopold (or Louis, 1828–1902), Da. singer

Jenke (–1869–), Ger. actress at Munich's Hoftheater

Jensdatter, Ane (–1871–), Da. friend of Bournonville

Jensen, Christian (–1859–), Da musician

Jerndorff, Peter William (1842–1926), Da. actor

Jessen, Tycho (1799–1857), Da commandor

Johansson, Pehr Christian (1817–1903), Sw. dancer and teacher

Jolin, Johan Christofer (1818–1884), Sw. actor and writer

Jørgensen (Jörgensen), Peter Nikolaj (?–1850), Da. publisher

Joséphine Maximilienne Eugénie Napoléone, Queen of Sweden and Norway (1807–1876)

Josephson (or Josephsson), Ludvig Oscar (1832–1899), Sw. actor and director

Juel, Laura (or Lauritse) Thora Margrethe Lovise (m. Frederiksen, 1837–1902), Da. ballerina

Julia (stage name for Julia de Varennes, 1805–1849), Fr. ballerina

Julie, Louise Wilhelmine Friederike Caroline Auguste, Princess of Denmark (later Queen Louise of Denmark, 1817–1898)

Jungberg, Carl Gustaf (–1862–), Sw. translator

Jürgensen, Knud Arne (1952–), Da. music and ballet historian

Just (–1851–), Da. commander

Juul, Christian (1813–1854), Da. writer

Juul (or Juel), Niels (1628–1697), Da. admiral

Kalliwoda, Johann Wenzeslaus (1801–1866), Boh. composer

Kaufmann, Richard (1846–1894), Da. writer

Kayser (–1869–), Da. carpenter

Keck, Philip Ludvig (1790–1848), Da. composer

Kellermann (or Kjellermann), Caroline Wilhelmine (b. Fjeldsted, 1821–1881), Da. ballerina

Kessler, Marie (m. Kahle, 1844–1896), Ger. actress

Kiær, Helene (b. Irminger, 1867–1935), Bournonville's granddaughter

Kierulf (or Kjerulf), Halfdan (1815–1868), Nor. composer

Kind, Johann Friedrich (1768–1843), Ger. poet

Kindermann, August (1817–1891), Ger. singer

King, Giovannina (1821–?), It. ballerina

Kinmansson, Helfrid (b. Torsslow, 1831–1906), Sw. actress

Kittendorff, Johan Adolf (1820–1902), Da. lithographer

Kjær, Dr. (–1870–), Da. physician

Kjellberg, Wilhelm (1810–1864), Sw. regisseur and later managing director at Stockholm's Royal Theatre

Kjerulf, Fru (–1853–), Nor. singer

Klefberg, Hilda Amalia (1845–1912), Sw. actress

Klüver, Johannes Theodor (1845–1917), Da. dancer

Knolley (–1876–), Eng. general

Knudsen, Hans Peter (1819–1854), Da. actor

Kock, Lavrids Olufsen (1634–1691), Da. poet

Kofoed, Fru (–1870–), Da. friend of Bournonville

Kotzebue, August Friedrich Ferdinand von (1761–1819), Ger. writer

Knapton, Philip (1788–1833), Eng. composer

Knox, John (1514–1572), Scottish reformer and writer

Krætzmer, Andrea Marie (b. Møller, 1811–1889), Da. ballerina

Kranold, Rudolph Heinrich Carl Conrad (1819–1889), Da. director of Copenhagen's Royal Theatre

Kreutzer, Rodolphe (1766–1831), Fr. composer

Kröyer, Hans Ernst (1798–1879), Da. composer and Royal precantor

Krum, Jacob Daniel (1850–1887), Da. dancer

Küchler, Albert (1803–1886), Da. painter

Kuhlau, Daniel Frederik Rudolph (1786–1832), Ger.-Da. composer

Kunzen, Friedrich Ludwig Aemilius (1761–1817), Ger.-Da. composer

Kurpinski, Karol (1785–1857), Pol. composer

Labarre, Théodore (1805–1870), Fr. composer

Laborde, Henri (–1860–), Fr. dance teacher at the court of Napoleon III

Lacour (–1851–), Da. friend of Bournonville

Lacroix, Emilie (1805 –?), Fr. ballerina

Lafont, Charles Aimable Gaspard (1809–1864), Fr. writer

Lagerbjelke, Gustaf, Count (1777–1837), Sw. theatre director of Stockholm's Royal Theatre

Lagus (pen name for Josef Julius Wecksell, 1838–1907), Finn.-Sw. writer

Lander, Harald (b. Stevnsborg, Alfred Bernhardt, 1904–1971), Da. dancer, choreographer, and ballet-master

Lane, Edward Williams (1801–1876), Eng. orientalist and editor of Arabian tales in London (1845)

Lange, Hans Wilhelm (1815–1873), Da. director of Copenhagen's Versterbroe's Theatre

Langlé, Aylic (pen name fpr Marie-Ange-Ferdinand Langlois, 1829–1870), Fr. writer

Lanner, Katherina (or Katti, or Kathi, 1829–1908), Aus. ballerina

Lanzký̆ (or Lanzky), Axel Waldemar (1825–1885), Da. music teacher and conductor

Larcher, Elisabeth Eva (1800–1882), Da. ballerina

Larcher, Frederikke Nicoline (b. Lange, 1812–1892), Da. actress

Larcher, Kmd. (–1847–), Da. friend of Bournonville

Larcher, Pierre Joseph (1801–1847), Da. dancer and choreographer

Larsen, Christiane (or Christine) (1838–?), Da. ballerina

Larsen, Knud (–1875–), Da. music publisher (1950s)

Lassen, Gothilf Ferdinand (1803–1860), Da. financial officer at Copenhagen's Royal Theatre

Lasson, Fru (–1853–), Da. singer

Lauenberg, Christian Olaf Nicolai (1853–1902), Da. dancer

Le Brun (or Lebrun), Louis-Sebastian (1764–1813), Fr. composer

Lee, George Alexander (1802–1851), Eng. composer

Lefèbvre, François (c.1803–?), Fr. dancer and choreographer

Lefèbvre, François-Charlemagne (1775–1839), Fr. composer, music copyist and librarian at the Paris Opéra

Legouvé, Gabriel Jean Baptiste Ernest Wilfried (1807–1903), Fr. writer

Lehmann, Caroline (1828–1879), Da. singer

Lehmann, Otto Ludvig Edvard (1815–1892), Da. painter and costume designer

Lembcke, Christian Ludvig Edvard (1815–1897), Da. poet

Lense, Adolph Frederik Johannes (1849–after 1913), Da. dancer

Leonhardt, Andreas (1800–1866), Aus. composer

Leroux, Pauline (1809–1891), Fr. ballerina

Leuven, Adolphe de (b. Ribbing, 1800–1884), Fr. writer and theatre director

Levasseur, Allegrini (–1854–), Aus.-It. ballerina in Vienna

Levetzau, Joachim Godske (1782–1859), Da. director at Copenhagen's Royal Theatre

Levÿsohn, M. C. (1821–1879), Da. merchant

Liebe, Johanne Emilie (b. Egense, 1831–1881), Da. actress-singer

Liebe, Johannes Theodor Julius (1823–1893), Da. singer

Liebenberg, Frederik Ludvig (1810–1894), Da. literary historian and editor of A. Oehlenschläger's complete writings

Liebmann, Axel (–1861–), Da. physician and amateur composer (1940)

Lienau, Emil Robert (1838–1920), Ger. music publisher

Lincke, Andreas Frederik (1819–1874), Da. composer

Linde, Andreas Conrad Putscher (1814–1888), Da. director at Copenhagen's Royal Theatre

Lindeman, Ludvig Mathias (1812–1887), Nor. composer

Lindmark, Carl Otto (1830–1901), Sw. regisseur

Lindorff, W. (–1853–), Nor. music publisher

Lindqvist, Zelma Axeline (1851–1895), Sw. actress

Lindström, Peter Fredrik (1840–1893), Sw. stage engineer

Lise (–1852–), unidentified Da. dancer

Loose (or Lose), Carl Christian (1787–1835), Da music publisher

López y Planes, Vincente (1784–1856), Arg. poet

Lortzing, Gustav Albert (1801–1851), Ger. composer

Louise Charlotte, Princess of Denmark, later Countess (1789–1864)

Louise (b. Lovisa) Josephine Eugenie, Swedish Princess (later Queen Louise of Denmark, 1851–1926)

Louise Victoria Alexandra Dagmar, Princess (1867–1931)

Louise Wilhelmina Frederika Alexandra Anna, Queen of Sweden and Norway (1828–1871)

Louise Wilhelmine Friederike Caroline Auguste Julie, Queen of Denmark (1817–1898)

Løvenskjold (or Lövenskjold), Carl Ludvig (1822–1898), Da. master of ceremonies at the Royal Danish Court

Løvenskjold (or Lövenskjold), Herman Severin von (1815–1870), Da. composer

Lowzow, F. (–1873–), Da. Lord-in-Waiting

Lumbye, Carl Christian (1841–1911), Da. composer

Lumbye, Georg August (1843–1922), Da. composer

Lumbye (or Lumbÿe), Hans Christian (1810–1874), Da. composer

Lumbye, Th. (–1858–), Da. journalist and grandson of H. C. Lumbye (1930)

Lund, Helga Rinda (m. Petersen, 1820–?), Da. ballerina

Lund, Hilda Maria (b. Lindh, 1840–?), Sw. ballerina

Lund, Josephine Amalie (m. Zinck, 1833–1919), Da. singer

Lund, Sigurd Harald (1823–1906), Da. dancer and later ballet-master in Stockholm

Lund, Troels (1802–1867), Da. scene painter

Lundin, Claës Johan (1825–1908), Sw. translator

Lundquist, Abraham (1817–1892), Sw. music publisher

Lundquist. Ernst Gustaf (1851–1938), Sw. translator

Luno, Christian Peter Bianco (1795–1852), Da. publisher

Lüttichau (–1859–), Da. friend of Bournonville

Lutz, Henri (–1869–), Fr. singer at Théâtre Lyrique in Paris

L'vov, Aleksej Fyodorovich (1798–1870), Ru. composer

Madaeva, Matilda Natalia (–1876–), Ru. ballerina

Madvig, Johan Nicolai (1804–1886), Da. politician

Magnus (–1854–), Da. friend of Bournonville

Maillart, Louis Aimé (1817–1871), Fr. composer

Malling, Peter Tidemand (1807–1878), Nor. music publisher

Mallinger, Mathilde (m. Schimmelpfennig, 1847–1920), Ger. singer at Munich's Hoftheater

Malmqvist, Carl Julius (1819–1859), Da. composer

Mannerhjerta, Ulrik Emanuel (1775–1849), Sw. costumier at Stockholm's Royal Theatre

Manzoni, Alessandro (1785–1873), It. writer

Maria [Jacob] (c.1818–?), Fr. ballerina

Marie Sophie Frederikke, Queen of Denmark (1767–1852)

Marivaux, Pierre Carlet de Chamblain de (1688–1763), Fr. writer

Marschner, Heinrich (1795–1861), Ger. composer

Marsollier (des Vivetières), Benoît Joseph (1750–1817), Fr. writer

Marstrand, Wilhelm (1810–1873), Da. painter

Martin, Théodore (1814–1870), Fr. choreographer and ballet-master at Stockholm's Royal Theatre

Massaloff, Constantin (–1866–), Ru. composer

Matthiesen, Caroline (–1869–), Da. teacher

Maximilien (–1840–1843–), Fr.(?) dancer

Mayseder, Joseph (1789–1863), Aus. composer

Mazilier, Joseph (b. Giulio Mazarini(?), 1797–1868), Fr. dancer, choreographer and ballet-master

Mazurier, Charles Ernest (1798–1828), Fr. dancer

Mehemed Ali Pascha (b. Karl Detroit, 1827–1878), Ger.-Tur. commandor and Prince of Egypt

Méhul, Etienne-Henri (1763–1817), Fr. composer

Meilhac, Henri (1831–1897), Fr. writer

Meister (–1851–), Ty. musician

Melbÿ (or Melbÿe, or Melbye), Daniel Herman Anton (1818–1875), Da. painter

Mélesville's (pen name for Duveyrier, Anne Honoré Joseph, 1787–1865), Fr. writer

Melle (19th century), Ger. publisher

Mendelssohn-Bartholdy, Felix (1809–1847), Ger. composer

Ménestrel, M. (mid-19th century), Fr. music publisher

Mercadante, Giuseppe Saverio Raffaele (1795–1870), It. composer

Meser, Carl (or Karl) Friedrich (late 19th century), Ger. music publisher

Meyer (–1869–), Da. plumber

Meyer, Carl Gustav Lauenbach (1839–?), Da. singer-actor

Meyer, Clara (m. Schmidt, 1848–1922), Ger. actress

Meyer, Eduard (–1849–), Da. publisher

Meyer, Philip Joel (1826–1861), Ger. writer

Meyerbeer, Giacomo (b. Jakob Liebmann Meyer Beer, 1791–1864), Ger. composer

Meza, Christian Julius de (1792–1865), Da. general

Michaëli, Lovisa Charlotta Helena (b. Michal, 1830–1875), Sw. actress-singer

Michot (–1869–), Fr. singer at Théâtre Lyrique in Paris

Mikel, J. (pseudonym for Joseph Meykiechel(?), ?–1892?), Fr.(?) composer

Millerceck (or Millersheck, or Millerschek, or Millercek), Anna (1837–1891), Aus. ballerina

Millière, Antoine (early 19th century), Fr. dancer

Milon, Louis Jacques (1766–1849), Fr. choreographer

Miolan-Carvalho, Marie (1827–1895), Fr. singer

Moe (–1867–), Nor. dance teacher

Mohrenheim, Arthur Pavlovitsj von (1824–1906), Ru. baron and envoy to Denmark

Moja, Angelo (–1851–), It. scene painter at Turin's Teatro Regio

Molander, Johan Harald (1858–1900), Sw. translator

Molière, Jean Baptiste (b. Poquelin, 1622–1673), Fr. actor and writer

Möller, M. (–1851–), Da. naval captain

Møller, Capt. (–1860–), Da. naval captain

Møller (or Möller), Carl Christian (1823–1893), Da. composer

Møller, Einar (–1861–), Da. music antiquarian (1942)

Møller, Elvilda Victoria Antonia (m. Scharff, 1846–1934), Da. ballerina

Møller, Nanna (b. Fredstrup, 1820–1897), Da. ballerina

Møller, S. C. (1806–?), Da. ballerina

Monies, David (1812–1894), Da. painter

Montessu, Pauline (b. Paul, 1805–1877), Fr. ballerina

Monvel, Jean Marie Boutet (1745–1812), Fr. writer

Moore, Thomas (1779–1852), Ir. poet and composer

Mozart, Johann Chrysostomus Wolfgang Amadeus (1756–1791), Aus. composer

Muhle, Frederik Sigfred (1829–?), Da. bogtrykker

Müller, C. (–1871–), Sw. music publisher, (early 19th century)

Müller, Charles (1828–1907), Ger.-Aus. dancer

Müller (or Miller), E. L. (?–1811), Fr. composer

Müller, Frederik Gotthold von (1795–1882), Da. general

Münster (or Mynster), Jacob Peter (1775–1854), Da. bishop

Musset, Louis Charles Alfred de (1810–1857), Fr. writer

Mussi, Antonio (–1844–1868–), It. composer

Muth-Rasmussen, Paul Diderich (1806–1855), Da. composer

Mylius, Peder Benzon (1689–1745), Da. writer

Napoléon Bonaparte I (1769–1821), French emperor

Napoléon, nephew of Napoléon Bonaparte I, later Napoléon III (Charles Louis Napoléon Bonaparte, 1808–1873), Fr. Prince

Nathan, Adolph (1814–1885), Da. composer

Naudin, Emilio (1823–1890), It. singer at the Paris Opéra

Naumann, Johann Gottlieb (also Giovanni Amadeo and/or Johann Amadeus, 1741–1801), Ger. composer

Nehm, Lauritz Christian Waldemar (1830–1899), Da. actor

Neiiendam, Klaus (1938–), Da. theatre historian

Nelson, Horatio (1758–1805), Eng. admiral

Nelson, Sydney (1800–1862), Eng. composer

Neruda, Franz Xaver (1843–1915), Boh. violoncellist and composer

Nestler, F. H. (19th century), Ger. publisher

Nicolai, Carl Otto Ehrenfried (1809–1849), Ger. composer

Nicolle, Henri (1819–?), Fr. writer

Nielsen (–1865–), Da. child dancer

Nielsen (–1868–), Da. carpenter

Nielsen, Augusta Wilhelmine (m. Afzelius, 1822–1902), Da. ballerina

Nielsen, Ida (1815–1889), Da. writer

Nielsen, Nicolai Peter (1795–1860), Da. actor

Niemann, Albert (1831–1917), Ger. singer at Berlin's Königlichen Theater

Nilsson, Christine (1843–1921), Sw. singer at Théatre Lyrique in Paris

Nissen (–1836–), Da. publisher

Noblet, Félicité (m. Dupont, 1807–1877), Fr. ballerina

Noblet, Lise (1801–1852), Fr. ballerina

Norberg, Maria Charlotta (m. Törner, 1824–1892), Sw. ballerina

Norbý, Jf. (–1853–), Nor. singer

Nordraak, Rikard (1842–1866), Nor. composer

Nordström (–1838–1839–), Sw. publisher

Norman, Fredrik Wilhelm Ludvig (1831–1885), Sw. composer

Norrby, Georg (1816–1898), Sw. actor

Noverre, Jean-Georges (1727–1810), Fr. choreographer and ballet-master

Nyegaard, Hans Haagen (1824–1893), Da. writer

Nyerup, Rasmus (1759–1829), Da. literary historian

Nyrop, Agnes Flemmine (b. Lange, 1841–1903), Da. actress

Nyrop (or Nyrup), Jens Larsen (1831–1904), Da. singer

Obelitz, Gerhard Christian Vilhelm (1817–1881), Da. judge

Obin, Louis-Henri (1820–1895), Fr. singer at the Paris Opéra

Oehlenschläger (also Øehlenschlæger), Adam Gottlob (1779–1850), Da. writer and poet

Ohlsson, Gustaf Robert (1841–1888), Sw. actor

Olga, Grand Duchess of Russia and sometime Queen Regent of Greece (1851–1926)

Olsen, Peter Wilhelm (1791–1859), Da. music publisher

Olsen, Rasmus Ulrik Bernhardt (1836–1922), Da. managing director of The Tivoli Gardens

Onslow, Georg (1784–1852), Ger. composer

Oscar Fredrik of East Götland, Swedish Crown Prince (the later King Oscar II of Sweden and Norway, 1829–1907)

Østergaard, Vilhelm (1852–1928), Da. writer

Østgaard, Nicolai Ramm (1812–1873), Nor. writer

Overskou, Thomas (1798–1873), Da. actor, writer, translator, and theatre historian

Oxholm, Frk. Georgine (–1876–), Da. daughter of Valdemar Oxholm

Oxholm, Valdemar Tully (1805–1876), Da. master of ceremony at the Royal Danish Court

Pacini (or Paccini), Giovanni (1796–1867), It. composer

Pacius, Friedrich (or Fredrik, 1809–1891), Ger.-Finn. composer

Pætges (or Pätges), Johan Anton (1807–1883), Da. actor and later financial officer at Copenhagen's Royal Theatre

Paganini, Niccolò (1782–1840), It. violinist and composer

Paisiello, Giovanni (1740–1816), It. composer

Paludan-Müller, Frederik (1809–1876), Da. writer

Panseron, Auguste Mathieu (1796–1859), Fr. composer

Parera, Blas (1777–after 1830) Arg. composer

Paul, Antoine (dit l'Aërien, 1798–1871), Fr. dancer

Paulli, Holger Simon (1810–1891), Da. composer

Paulli, Just Henrik Voltelen (1809–1865), Da. priest

Paulsson (or Paulson), Erika Amalia (1836–?), Sw. ballerina

Paxton, Sir Joseph (1801–1865), Eng. architect

Payne, John Howard (1791–1852), Am. actor and writer

Pengel (–1871–), Da. naval captain and writer

Pepita de Oliva (stage name for Josefa Lopez-Ortega, 1830–1872), Sp. ballerina

Perceval, Amélie (early 19th century), Fr. ballerina

Perfall, Karl Freiherr von (1824–1907), Ger. Baron and managing director at Munich's Hoftheater

Perrot, Jules Joseph (1810–1892), Fr. choreographer and ballet-master

Persuis, Louis-Luc (1769–1819), Fr. choreographer

Peters, Carl Friedrich (1779–1827), Ger. music publisher

Petersen, Johanne (1844–1933), Da. ballerina

Petersen, Peter (1810–1892), Da. medallist

Petipa, Lucien (1815–1898), Fr. dancer and choreographer

Petit, Anatole (early 19th century), Fr. dancer and choreographer

Petit, Baptiste (?–1827), Fr. dancer and teacher

Pettersson, Per Johan Wilhelm (1814–1854), Sw. dancer and choreographer

Pfeil, Anna Doris (m. Erhard-Hansen, 1847–1917), Da. singer

Phister, Joachim Ludvig (1807–1896), Da. actor

Pichler, A. (–1854–1856–), Aus. publisher

Piil, Kirsten (14th century), Da. legendary figure

Pio. V. (–1860–), Da. publisher

Pira, Gustava Charlotte (m. Stedingk. –1871–), Sw. ballerina

Pitrot (or Pitreau, or Pittrò), Domenico (or Dominik) (1837–1891), Fr. dancer in Vienna

Pixis, Johann Peter G. (1788–1874), Ger. pianist and composer

Planché, James Robinson (1796–1880), Eng. poet and writer

Plantade, Charles-Henri (1764–1839), Fr. composer

Plenge, Carl I. (1817–1905), Da. music publisher

Plessen, Carl Theodor August von Scheel– (1811–1892), Da. count and councellor of state

Pleyel, Ignaz Joseph (1757–1831), Fr. music publisher

Ploug, Carl (1813–1894), Da. writer

Pocchini, (or Pochini) Carolina (or Carlotta, or Carila, b. Ranieri Pochini, m. Borri, 1836–1901), It. ballerina

Poirson, Paul (–1863–), Fr. writer

Ponsard, Francis (or François, 1814–1867), Fr. writer

Poujol, Alphonse-André-Vérand (c.1800–?), Fr. writer

Poulsen, Emilie Henriette (b. Bryde, 1846–1909), Da. ballerina

Poulsen, Olaf Rye (1849–1923), Da. actor

Pracht, A. (–1861–), Da. music copyist

Praxiteles (c.370–330 BC), Greek sculptor

Prechtler, Johann Otto (1813–1881), Aus. writer

Price, Adolf James Julius (1833–1893), Da. dancer

Price, Adolph Frederik (or Friedrich) Waldemar (1837–1908), Da. dancer-mime

Price, Carl Nicolai Andreas (1839–1909), Da. dancer and later actor

Price, Flora Mathilde (b. Levin, 1813–1863), Da. ballerina

Price, Hanne Amalia Nicoline (m. Hagen, 1831–1892), Da. ballerina and later actress

Price, Hanne Sophie (1833–1905), Da. ballerina

Price, James (1801–1865), Da. dancer-actor-mime

Price, Johan Adolph (1807–1890), Da. dancer-actor-mime

Price, Juliette Elisa Christiane (1831–1906), Da. ballerina

Price, Mathilde Juliane Engeline (1847–1937), Da. ballerina, later painter

Price, Rosa (or Rosetta) Caroline (1809–1887), Da. ballerina

Price, Theodor (–1849–), Da. child dancer

Printzlau, Frederik Ferdinand (1814–1859), Da. translator

Prüme, François Humbert (1816–1849), Bel. violinist

Pugni, Cesare (1802–1870), It. composer

Purcell, Henry (1659–1695), Eng. composer

Quaglio, Simon (1795–1878), Ger. scene painter at Munich's Hoftheater

Qvist, Jørgen Didrik (1789–1866), Da. book dealer

Ræder (or Räder), Jacob (1798–1853), Da corps commander

Rahbek, Knud Lyhne (1760–1830), Da. writer

Ramstén (or Ramsten), Aurora Olivia (1844–1875), Sw. actress

Randel, Andreas (1806–1864), Sw. composer

Rantzau, Adelaide Ida Rosaline (m. Brun, 1825–1909), Da. singer

Rantzau, Daniel (1529–1569), Da. commander

Rasmussen, Poul Edvard (1776–1860), Da. composer

Rasmussen, Th. (–1859–), Da. actor

Rauch, Peter Ferdinand (1817–1871), Da. violoncellist

Raymond, Josef Ritter von (1801–1873), Aus. government councellor

Reber, Napoléon-Henri (1807–1880), Fr. composer

Recke, Adolph Fredrik von der (1820–1867), Da. writer and artistic director of the Tivoli Gardens

Rée (or Rhé), Immanuel (1825–1859), Da. music publisher and editor

Reisinger (or Reissinger, or Reißinger), Edouard (or Edward, 1822–1886), Aus. dancer

Reisinger (or Reissinger), Johann Nepomuk (1849–1914), Aus. dancer

Reitzel, Christian Andreas (1789–1853), Da. publisher

Rewentlov, Cont.ssa (–1857–), Da. Lady, daughter of Count Rewentlov

Ricci (Ferdinando or Luigi, 1805–1859), It. conductor/concert-master and composer in Vienna

Ricci, Pia (–1855–), Aus. ballerina

Ricordi, Giovanni (1785–1853), It. music publisher

Riego, Wilhelmime Amalia (1850–1926), Sw. singer

Rimestad, Christian Vilhelm (1816–1879), Da. editor and politician

Ring, Ludvig Christian Julius (1818–?), Da. dancer

Roberg, Paul Emil Richard (1821–1859), Sw. scene painter at Stockholm's Royal Theatre

Rode, Jacques Pierre (1774–1830), Fr. composer

Rogert, Ditlev Ludvig (1742–1813), Da. judge and amateur composer

Roll, Eveline (–1855–1856–), Aus. ballerina

Romani, Felice (1788–1865), It. composer

Rømer, Ole (1644–1710), Da. astronomer

Roqueplan, Nestor (1804–1870), Fr. director at the Paris Opéra

Rosa, Salvatore (1615–1673), It. painter

Rosenkilde, Anna Kristine (b. Paaske, 1825–1885), Da. actress

Rosenkilde, Christen Niemann (1786–1861), Da. actor

Rosenkilde, G. (1814–1891), Da. judge and friend of Bournonville

Rossini, Gioacchino Antonio (1792–1868), It. composer

Rostock, Julie (m. Carpentier, 1832–1902), Da. ballerina

Rothe, Harald (1819–1882), Da. naval captain

Rouget d'Isle, Claude Joseph (1760–1836), Fr. composer

Rousseau, Jean-Jacques (1712–1778), Fr. writer

Rubé, Auguste Alfred (1815–1899), Fr. scene painter at the Paris Opéra

Rudolph, Johann Joseph Rainer, Archduke of Austria (1788–1831)

Rung, Frederik (1854–1914), Da. composer

Rung, Henrik (1807–1871), Da. composer

Rung, Sophie Helene Henriette (m. Keller, 1850–1929), Da. singer

Rüthling, Bernhard (1834–1881), Ger. actor at Munich's Hoftheater

Ryge (or Rÿge, or Rüge), Charlotte Betzy Rosalia (b. Anthon, 1794–1860), Da. costumier at Copenhagen's Royal Theatre

Ryge, Miss (–1870–), Da. costumier at The Tivoli Gardens

Sacco, Raffaele (–1842–), It. poet

Sahlertz, Ludvig Ferdinand (1812–1886), Da. actor

Saint-Georges, Jules-Henry Vernoy de (1799–1875), Fr. writer

Saint-Léon, Arthur (1821–1870), Fr. choreographer and ballet-master

Saint Louin, Catharina (–1858–), Ir. ballerina

Saint-Romain, Angelica (or Angélique) Mées, c.1805–?), Fr. ballerina

Saint-Victor, Jacques Benjamin Maximilien Bins comte de (1772–1858), Fr. writer

Sallÿ (or Sally), N. H. C. V. (–1854–), Da. councellor of justice

Saloman, Siegfried (1816–1899), Da.-Sw. composer

Salomon, Amsel Isaac Gottschalck (1802–1878), Da. publisher

Salomon, Sallÿ B. (1815–1886), Da. publisher

Salomonsen, Moritz (1804–1871), Da. merchant, later consul-general, and personal friend of Bournonville

Samengo, Paolo (or Paul, 1799–1879), Aus.-It. dancer and choreographer

Sand, George (pen name for Armandine Lucile Aurore Dupin, marchioness Dudevant, 1804–1876), Fr. writer

Sandberg, Anna Helena Mathilda (m. Kinmanson, 1842–1909), Sw. actress

Sandstedt, Georg Victor (1828–1895), Sw. actor

Sandström, Gustaf (1826–1875), Sw. singer

Sardou, Victorien (1831–1908), Fr. writer

Saxe (or Sass, or Sasse), Marie-Constance (1814–1907), Fr. singer at the Paris Opéra

Scavenius (–1857–), Da. dance pupil of Bournonville

Scavenius (–1874–), Da. nobleman

Schack, Hans Egede (1820–1859), Da. writer

Schack-Brockenhuus, A. L. (–1877–), Da. Count

Schall, Anna Margaretha (b. Schleüter, 1775–1852), Da. ballerina

Schall, Claus (1757–1835), Da. composer

Schandorff, Sophus (1836–1901), Da. writer

Scharff, Harald Anton (1836–1912), Da. dancer

Scheel-Plessen, Wulff Count (1809–1876), Da. envoy to Sweden

Schellenberger, Venantius (or Venantzius) Johan Baptiste (c.1803–1864), Aus. dancer and mime at Vienna's Kärnthner-thor Theater

Schepellern (or Schepelern), Christian August (1794–1870), Da. commandor

Schiörring, Niels (1743–1798), Da. music historian and composer

Schjelderup-Ebbe, Dan (1926–), Nor. music historian

Schleisner, Christian Andreas (1810–1882), Da. painter

Schlesinger, Maurice (1798–1871), Fr.-Ger. music publisher

Schmidt, Hermann (–1855–), Aus. composer

Schmidt-Phiseldeck, Thora (1858–?), Da. teacher and distant relative of Bournonville

Schneider (–1846–), Da. publisher

Schneitzhoeffer, Jean-Madeleine (1785–1852), Fr. composer

Schnell, Betty Mathilde (m. Hennings, 1850–1939), Da. ballerina, later actress

Schnötzinger, Anton Johann (1816–1865), Aus. dancer and mime

Scholl, Anna Regine (m. Tychsen, 1853–1896), Da. ballerina

Schonenberger, Georges (1808–1856), Fr. music publisher

Schott, Bernhard (1748–1809), Ger. music publisher

Schousboe, August Frederik Alexander Fritz (1857–1898), Da. pianist and composer

Schousgaard, Charlotte Elisabeth (m. Dahl, 1854–1953), Da. ballerina

Schouw (or Schou), Sophie Amalie (b. Clausen, 1788–1864), Da. actress

Schramm (or Schram), Peter Ludvig Nicolaj (1819–1895), Da. singer

Schrøder-Devrient, Wilhelmine (1804–1860), Ger. singer

Schubert, F. L. (–1860–), Ger. music historian

Schubothe, Johan Henrich (1761–1828), Da. publisher

Schück, Martin (1819–1872), Sw. translator

Schukowskij, Wassilij Andrejewitsch (1783–1852), Ru. poet

Schultz (–1849–), Da. commandor

Schultz, Jens Hostrup (b. Jens Niels Nicolai Hostrup, 1782–1849), Da. publisher

Schultz, Johan Abraham Peter (1747–1800), Da. composer

Schultz, W. (–1863–), Sw. publisher

Schütz, Carl Mathias Theodor (1814–1890), Da. priest, composer, and collector of Danish folk songs

Schwartz, Adolf Fredrik (1800–1881), Sw. composer

Schwartz, Adolf Theodor (1822–?), Sw. actor

Schyberg, Svante (or Sven) Gustaf (1796–1874), Sw. director at Stockholm's Royal Theatre

Scott, Sir Walter (1771–1832), Sc. writer

Scribe, Augustin Eugène (1791–1861), Fr. writer

Sehested, G. (–1854–), Da. Lord-in-Waiting

Sehested-Juul, Ove (1830–1882), Da. Lord-in-Waiting

Selinder, Anders (1806–1874), Sw. dancer, choreographer, and ballet-master

Serral, Dolores (–1839–1840–), Spanish dancer

Shakespeare, William (1564–1616), Eng. writer

Sick, Julius Frederik (–1873–), Da. Lord-in-Waiting

Siegel (–1870–), Ger. regisseur at Munich's Hoftheater

Signol, Alphonse (–1834–1835–1836–), Fr. writer

Silas (–1875–), Aus. theatre director(?)

Simonna (–1876–), Da. singer(?)

Simonsen, Cathrine (or Catharina) Elisabeth (b. Ryssländer, 1816–1849), Da. singer

Simonsen, Niels (1807–1885), Da. painter

Simonsen, Niels Juel (1846–1906), Da. singer

Simony, Carl Frederik (1806–1872), Da. minister of culture

Simrock, Nicolaus (1751–1832), Ger. music publisher

Skjöldebrand, Anders Fredrik (1757–1834), Sw. writer

Skougaard Severini, Lorentz (b. Severin Skougaard, 1837–1885), Nor. singer

Snare, Esbern (c.1127–1204), Da. hero

Söderman (or Södermann), Johan August (1832–1876), Sw. composer and concert-master

Sødring, Julie Weber (b. Rosenkilde, 1823–1894), Da. actress

Søeborg, Carl (1775–1852), Da. actor and song writer

Solem (–1865–), Da. music publisher

Sommer, Mogens (1829–1901), Da. professor

Sonne, Jørgen Valentin (1801–1890), Da. painter

Sophie Wilhelmine Marianne Henriette, Princess of Nassau (1836–1913)

Sor, Joseph Fernando Macari (1778–1839), Sp. composer

Spandst(?) (–1854–), Da. speaker

Spina, Carl Anton (–1856–), Aus. music publisher

Spontini, Gaspare Luigi Pacifico (1774–1851), It. composer

Stähle (or Stehle), C. von (–1870–), Ger. secretary at Munich's Hoftheater

Stage, Johan Adolf Gottlob (1791–1845), Da. actor

Stage, Ulrica Augusta (b. Kofoed, 1816–1894), Da. actress

Stampe (–1871–), Da. baron

Stampe, C. (–1840–1857–), Da. baroness

Stampe, Christian (–1857–), Da. dance pupil of Bournonville

Stedingk, Eugène Fredrik Oscar Ludvig von (1825–1871), Sw. baron and director at Stockholm's Royal Theatre

Steenberg, Julius August (1830–1911), Da. singer

Stein, Theobald (1829–1901), Da. sculptor

Steiner, Siegmund Anton & Co. (19th century), Aus. music publisher

Stenderup, N. H. (–1860–), Da. publisher

Stendrup, Niels Peter (1833–1870), Da. dancer

Stenhammar, Fredrika (b. Andrée, 1836–1880), Sw. singer

Stenhammar, Oscar Fredrik (1834–1884), Sw. singer

Stephanini (or Stefanini), Ippolito (–1884), It. scene painter at Milan's Teatro alla Scala

Stillmann, Laura Henriette Jasmine (b. Stramboe, 1830–1914), Da. ballerina and mime

Stjernström, Lovisa Elisabeth (b. Granberg, 1812–1907), Sw. writer and translator

Stramboe, Edvard Julius Lorentz (1825–1895), Da. dancer

Stramboe, Johan Adolph Frederik (1801–1850), Da. dancer and mime

Stramboe, Laura Henriette Jasmine (m. Stillmann, 1830–1914), Da. ballerina and mime

Stramboe, Sophie Maria Frederikke (b. Svanemann, 1803–1865), Da. ballerina

Strandberg, Carl Wilhelm August (1818–1877), Sw. writer and translator

Strauss, Johann Baptist, the elder (1804–1849), Aus. composer

Strauss, Johann Baptist, the younger (1825–1899), Aus. composer

Strebinger Matthias (or Mathias, 1807–1874), Aus. composer

Suell, Eva (b. Håkansson, 1803–1884), sister of Helene Bournonville

Suenson, Edward (or Edouard, 1805–1887), Da. admiral

Suhr (–1868–), Da. friend of Bournonville

Sulestad, Jfr. (–1853–), Nor. aspirant actress

Sundberg, Carl Gustaf (1817–1898), Sw. actor

Sundberg, Johanna Gustafva (b. Gillberg, 1828–1910), Sw. ballerina

Svendsen, Jfr. (–1853–), Nor. aspirant actress

Svenson (or Swensson), Wilhelm Carl Arnold (1803–1876), Sw. actor and writer

Swartz, Edvard Mauritz (1826–1897), Sw. actor

Taglioni, Amalia (or Amalie) (b. Galster, 1801–1881), Ger. ballerina

Taglioni, Filippo (1777–1871), It. choreographer

Taglioni, Luisa (or Luigia, 1823–1893), It. ballerina

Taglioni, Marie the elder (1804–1884), Sw.-It. ballerina

Taglioni, Marie the younger (1833–1891), Ger. ballerina

Taglioni, Paul (or Paolo, 1808–1884), Sw.-It. dancer and choreographer

Taglioni, Salvatore (1789–1868), It. choreographer and ballet-master

Talvj (or Talvy), Therese Albertine Luise (b. von Jacob, m. Robinson, 1797–1870), Ger. writer

Tardini, Anna Jeanette (m. Hansen, 1845–1918), Da. ballerina

Taylor, Tom (1817–1880). Eng. writer

Tegner, J. (or I.) W. (1815–1893), Da. lithographer

Telle, Carl (1826–1895), Aus. choreographer and ballet-master

Teniers, David, the younger (1610–1690), Fl. painter

Tetens, (–1851–), Da. chief administrative officer

Thaarup, Thomas (1749–1821), Da. writer

Théaulon de Lambert, Marie Emanuel Guillaume Marguérite (1787–1841), Fr. writer

Theodore (stage name for Marckhl, Theodor Ignaz, 1825– ?), Aus.-Sw. dancer, choreographer, and ballet-master

Thiele, Just (1823–1876), Da. publisher

Thiele, Just Mathias (1795–1874), Da. writer

Thierry, Joseph François Désiré (1812–1866), Fr. scene painter at the Paris Opéra

Thomas, Ambroise (1811–1896), Fr. composer

Thomsen, Amanda Flora Mathilde (m. Fallesen, 1832–1900), Da. writer and actress

Thorberg, Juliette (1845–1863), Da. ballerina

Thorup, Christian (–1849–), Da. property man at Copenhagen's Royal Theatre

Thorvaldsen, Bertel (1768/70–1844), Da. sculptor

Thræn, Johan Peter (1765–1830), Da. composer

Thygesen, Hansine (b. Hammer, 1831–?), Da. ballerina

Thyra Amelie Caroline Charlotte Anne, Danish Princess (1853–1923)

Thyselius. Johan Erik August (1864–1924), Sw. translator

Tichatscheck, Joseph Aloys (1807–1886), Boh. singer

Tietgen, Carl Frederik (1829–1901), Da. titular councillor of state

Tillisch, Frederik Ferdinand von (1801–1899), Da. director at Copenhagen's Royal Theatre

Titus, Antoine Danché (also known under the stage name Alexandre, c.1800–?), Fr. choreographer and ballet-master in Berlin and St. Peterburg

Topelius, Zachris (or Zacharias, 1818–1898), Sw. professor and writer

Tordenskjold, Peter (or Peder) Wessel (1691–1720), Da.-Nor. sea-hero

Törner, Gustaf Fredrik (1821–1898), Sw. official of Stockholm's Royal Theatre

Törner, Maria Charlotta (b. Norberg, 1824–1892), Sw. ballerina

Torp, Oberst (–1851–), Da. commander

Torrente, G. (–1842–1845–), It. composer

Trentsensky, Mathias (1790–1868), Aus. music publisher

Troupenas, Eugène-Théodore (1799–1860), Fr. music publisher

Troy (–1869–), Fr. singer at Théâtre Lyrique in Paris

Tveskjæg, Svend (?–1014), Da. medieval King

Uhr, Conrad Rudolf af (1819–?), Sw. composer

Ullrich (–1870–), Ger. secretary and later managing director at Berlin's Königlichen Theater

Unna (–1860–), Da. consul

Vaccai (or Vaccaj), Niccolo (1791–1849), It. composer

Valdemar the Great, King of Denmark (1131–1182)

Vanderburch, Emile Louis (1794–1862), Fr. writer

Vaque-Moulin, Elise (early 19th century), Fr. ballerina

Védel-Sainte-Claire, Josephine G. (m. Carey, early 19th century), Fr. ballerina

Venua, Frédéric-Marc-Antoine (1788–c.1863), Fr. composer

Verdi, Giuseppe (1813–1901), It. composer

Vestris, Armand (1795–1825), Fr. choreographer

Vestris, Auguste (b. Marie–Jean–Augustin Allard, 1760–1843), Fr. dancer, choreographer and teacher

Vestris, Lucia (b. Lucy Elisabeth Bartolozzi, 1787–1856), It. actress-singer

Vett, Major (–1851–), Da. major

Vibe, Andreas (1801–1860), Nor. writer and translator

Vienna, Lorenzo (1830–?), It. dancer and choreographer at Vienna's Kärnthnerthor Theatre

Vieweg (mid-19th century), Aus. music publisher

Villeneuve, Théodore Ferdinand Vallou de (1801–1858), Fr. writer

Visby, Carl Holger (1801–1871), Da. priest and school-master

Vogl, Heinrich (1845–1900), Ger. singer at Munich's Hoftheater

Vogler, Georg Joseph (1749–1814), Ger. composer

Waage Petersen (or Waagepetersen) (–1851–), Da. merchant

Wagner, Wilhelm Richard (1813–1883), Ger. composer

Wailly, Augustin Jules de (also known under the pen name Devormc, 1800–?), Fr. writer

Walbom, Arnold Alfred Constantin (1851–1898), Da. dancer

Wallich (or Wallick), Arnold (b. Aron) N. Wulff (1779–1845), Da. scene painter

Walter (–1851–), Da. lieutenant and corps commander

Waltz, Johan Rudolph (1811–1853), Da. actor

Warlamoff, Alexandr Jegorovich (1801–1848), Ru. composer

Warmuth, Carl (1811–1892), Nor. music publisher

Watt, Robert (1837–1894), Da. newspaper editor and director at Copenhagen's Folketheatret

Watz, Paulina Albertina (1823–1849), Sw. ballerina

Weber, Carl Maria von (1786–1826), Ger. composer

Weber, J. J. (–1861–), Ger. publisher

Wecksell, Josef Julius (1838–1907), Finn.-Sw. writer

Wedel-Heinen, Julius Christian Frederik von (1814–1887), Da. Lord-in-Waiting at the court of the Queen Dowager, Caroline Amalie

Weden (or Wedén, or Wedden, or Weddén), Andreas Peter (1809–1888), Da. stage engineer at Copenhagen's Royal Theatre

Welhaven, Johann Sebastian Cammermeyer (1807–1873), Nor. poet

Wennbom, Per Adolf (1803–1863), Sw. actor

Werning, Marie Cathrine the elder (m. d'Abis, 1798–1871), Da. ballerina

Werning, Marie Cathrine the younger (m. von Kohl, 1822–1900), Da. ballerina

Westberg, Maria Charlotte (1853–1893), Sw. ballerina

Westerdahl, Fanny Amalia (m. Hjortsberg, 1817–1873), Sw. actress

Westermarck (or Westermark), August Felix (1834–1894), Sw. actor

Westphal, Frederik (or Frits) Bernhard (1804–1844), Da. costumier at Copenhagen's Royal Theatre

Westrell, E. (–1862–), Sw. publisher

Wexschall, Caroline (b. Damm, c.1816–1848), Da. wife of F. T. Wexschall

Wexschall, Frederik Thorkildsen (1798–1845), Da. violinist

Weyse, Christoph Ernst Friedrich (1774–1842), Da. composer

Wiegand (or Wigandt), Manna Wilhelmina Henrietta (1833–?), Sw. ballerina

Wiehe, Anton Wilhelm (1827–1884), Da. actor

Wiehe, Johan Henrik (1830–1877), Da. singer

Wieland, Christoph Martin (1733–1813), Ger. writer and poet

Wienrich (–1879–), Ger. actress at Berlin's Königlichen Theater

Wijkander, Carl Oscar (1826–1899), Sw. writer

Wilbrandt, Adolf (1837–1911), Ger. writer

Wildauer, Mathilde (1820–1878), Aus. singer, and actress

Wilhelm of Hesse-Cassel (Wilhelm af Hessen), Landgrave and sometime Governor of Copenhagen (1787–1867)

Willman, Hedvig Charlotta Constantina (b. Harling, 1841–1887), Sw. singer

Willman, Per Anders Johan (1834–1898), Sw. actor-singer

Wilster (–1851–), Da. lieutenant and corps commander

Winding (or Vinding), August Henrik (1835–1899), Da. composer

Winding, P. (–1868–), Da. singing teacher and a relative of A. Winding (c.1944)

Winther, Christian (1796–1876), Da. poet

Winkler, Josef (1822–1898), Aus. dancer and mime

Wintherhalter, Franz-Xaver (1805–1873), Ger. painter

Wohlbrück, Wilhelm August (1794/1796–1861), Ger. writer and actor

Wolff (or Wolf), Pius Alexander (1784–1828), Ger. writer

Zinck, August Georg Ludvig (1831–1885), Da. singer

Zinck, Hardenack Otto Conrad (1746–1832), Da. composer

Zinck, Johan Wilhelm Ludvig (1776–1851), Da. composer

Zinck, Josephine Amalie (b. Lund, 1833–1919), Da. singer

Zrza, Christiane Eleonore (1797–1862), Da. singer

Zytphen, J. F. von (–1857–), Da. baron

Index of Works

The index of works is arranged into the following nine main groups of works according to genre:

1. Ballets
2. Divertissements, tableaux, intermezzi, mimic prologues and epilogues.
3. Individual rôles, *pas*, and dances.
4. Operas, operettas, singspiels, vaudevilles, plays, intermediums, ballades, romances and recited prologues and epilogues.
5. Translations into Danish of French texts for operas, vaudevilles, and plays.
6. Dances and tableaux choreographed and taught for Royal festivities, court balls, and masked balls.
7. Drama lessons, social or theatrical dances choreographed for and taught at private lessons.
8. Organisation of and dances choreographed for major public and social events.
9. Unidentified and unverified works.

All titles are given in English, followed (in parentheses) by the Danish titles with which they were first performed in Denmark. The only exception to this rule are works that were originally premièred with titles in languages other than English or Danish. These works (mainly foreign operas and plays) are listed with their original titles, followed (in parentheses) by the Danish title under which they were first mounted by Bournonville. Works that were originally premièred in Swedish are, though, listed with English titles, followed (in parentheses) by their original Swedish titles.

Ballets

The name of the choreographer of the works in this group is added (in parentheses) if different from Bournonville. Similarly, the date of the first performance is added (in parentheses) to those works for which an immediate identification could be rendered difficult by the presence of other revised versions of the same work, or by completely different works with almost identical titles.

Abdallah, 176
Adriana, 204
[*Aladin*], 7
Alfred le Grand (J. Aumer), 10
Alphonse et Leonore ou L'Amant peintre (A. Petit), 14
Annitta, or The Vintage in the mountains of Albano (Annitta eller Viinhösten i Albanerbjergene), 118
Arcona, 407
Arrivo del Gran Signore, L' (L. Henry), 17
Astolphe et Joconde, ou Les coureurs d'aventures (J. Aumer), 26, 38
At the Shore of China (Vid Chinas Kust) (S. Lund after A. Bournonville, 19.1.1860), 46, 243
Autumn, The (Efteraaret), 7
Bellman or the Polish Dance at Grönalund (Bellman eller Polskdandsen paa Grönalund) (3.6.1844), 87, 134, 346
Bellman, or the Polish Dance at Grönalund (Bellman, eller Polskan på Grönalund) (11.6.1847, 21.4.1858), 106, 217
Bluebeard (Rolf Blaaskjæg) (V. Galeotti), 32, 121, 380
Carita (P. Borri), 181
Carnaval de Venise, Le, ou Constance à l'Epreuve, (L. Milon), 22, 371
Carnaval de Venise, Le, ou Constance à

l'Epreuve, (Carnavalet i Venedig eller Kjærlighed paa Prøve) (P. Larcher/L. Milon), 22, 317, 371
Castello di Kenilworth, Il (P. Hus/G. Gioja), 68
Cendrillon (Albert), 8, 10, 26, 38, 41
Childhood of Erik Menved, The (Erik Menveds Barndom), 79
Clari, ou La Promesse de mariage (L. Milon), 8, 12
Conservatoire, The, or A Proposal of Marriage through the Newspaper, (Conservatoriet, eller Et Avisfrieri) (6.5.1849), 126, 310, 365–6, 404
Conservatoire, The, or A Proposal of Marriage through the Newspaper, (Conservatoriet, eller Ett Frieri i Tidningarne) (26.5.1857), 200
Cort Adeler in Venice (Cort Adeler i Venedig) (20.7.1832 and 14.1.1870), 21, 354
Devin du village, Le (Landsbye Spaamanden), 5
Diable à quatre, Le (J. Mazilier), 103
Diable amoureux, Le (J. Mazilier), 70
Diable boiteux, Le (J. Coralli), 43
Don Quixote (P. Taglioni/G. Golinelli), 176
Don Quixote at Camacho's Wedding (Don Quixote ved Camachos Bryllup), 38, 121
Fairy Tale in Pictures, A (Et Eventyr i Billeder), 380
Far from Denmark, or: A Costume Ball on Board (Fjernt fra Danmark eller: et Costumebal ombord), 245
Faust, 20, 75, 86, 105, 133, 183, 239
Faust, Romantic Pantomimic Ballet revised into one act (Romantisk Pantomime-Ballett, sammandragen i 1 Akt) (9.6.1847), 105
Fest in Albano, Das (Festen i Albano) (15.7.1854, 6.2.1855), 174, 176
Festival in Albano, The (Festen i Albano), 55, 84, 199, 213, 272, 343
Fee und der Ritter, Die (Arm. Vestris), 13
Fille du pharaon, La (M. Petipa), 418

Fille mal gardée, La (J. Dauberval/J. Aumer), 19, 20
Five projected stagings of French ballets in Copenhagen (18.4.1829), 8
Flore et Zéphire (Ch.-L. Didelot), 9, 13–14, 17
Flower Festival in Genzano, The (Blomsterfesten i Genzano), 225, 385, 404, 423
Folk Tale, A (Et Folkesagn), 166, 201, 328, 374, 401, 424
Four Seasons, The, or Cupid's Journey, A Ballet Cycle, (De fire Aarstider eller Amors Reise. Ballet-Cyclus), 96
From Siberia to Moscow (Fra Sibirien til Moscow), 418
Gazelle von Bassora, Die (Abdallah), 181
Gipsy, La (J. Mazilier), 75
Giselle, ou Les Wilis (J. Coralli and J. Perrot), 76
Grotta Azzurra, La (F. Lefèbvre), 148
Habor and Signe (Habor og Signe), 5
Homecoming, The (Hemkomsten), 41
Idol in Ceylon, The (Afguden paa Ceylon) (V. Galeotti), 32
In the Carpathians (I Karpatherne), 196, 240
Isle of Phantasy, or 'From the Shore of China', The (Phantasiens Øe eller 'Fra Chinas Kyst'), 45, 121
Istituto delle Fanciulle, L' (G. Briol), 68
Jolie Fille de Gand, La (Albert), 77–8, 106–7
Jovita, ou les Boucaniers (J. Mazilier), 181
Kermesse in Brüges, The, or The Three Gifts (Kermessen i Brügge eller: De tre Gaver) (4.4.1851), 143, 312, 365, 387
Kermesse in Brüges, The, or The Three Gifts, (La Kermesse de Brüges ou Les trois dons) (16.4.1854), 170
Kermesse in Brüges, The, or The Three Gifts, (Kermessen i Brügge eller De tre gåfvorna) (30.12.1858), 227
King's Corps of Volunteers on Amager, The,

(Episode from 1808), (Livjægerne paa Amager, (Episode fra 1808)), 370

Kirsten Piil (26.2.1845), 89, 121

Kirsten Piil or Two Midsummer Festivals (Kirsten Piil eller to Midsommerfeste), 90

Lagertha (V. Galeotti), 32, 121, 380

Lay of Thrym, The (Thrymsqviden), 331, 378, 400

Little Pixie, The (Den lille Nisse), 74

Lucas et Laurette (L. Milon), 13

Lydie (J. Aumer), 8, 10

Macbeth (Arm. Vestris), 11, 15

Marco Visconti (S. Taglioni), 67

Mars et Vénus ou Les Filets de Vulcain (J. B. Blache), 126

Mohicans, Les (A. Guerra), 47

Mother's Birthday (Moders Födselsdag), 59

Mountaineers, The, or The Children and the Mirror (Bjergbeboerne, eller Börnene og Speilet) (V. Galeotti), 32, 163, 380

Mountain Hut, The, or Twenty Years (Fjeldstuen eller Tyve Aar), 232, 311, 421

Napoli, oder: Der Fischer und seine Braut (Napoli eller Fiskeren og hans Brud) (27.6.1843 and 31.1.1856), 80, 187

Napoli, or The Fisherman and His Bride (Napoli eller Fiskeren og hans Brud) (29.3.1842), 72, 92, 201, 241, 316, 363, 389, 413

New Penelope, The, or The Spring Festival in Athens (Den nye Penelope, eller Foraarsfesten i Athen), 100

Nina, ou La Folle par amour (L. Milon), 8, 26, 380

Nina, ou La Folle par amour (Nina, eller Den vanvittige af Kjærlighed) (30.9.1834), 26, 124

Night at Norderhov, The (Natten paa Norderhoug), 6

Noces de Gamache, Les (L. Milon), 38

Old Memories, or A Magic Lantern (Gamle Minder eller En Laterna magica), 121

Oresteia, The, tragic Ballet in 3 parts (unperformed) (Orestias, Tragisk Ballet i 3 Dele (Uopfört.)), 88

Orgie, L' (J. Coralli), 40

Pages du Duc de Vendôme, Les (J. Aumer), 8, 14

Pages du Duc de Vendôme, Les (Hertugen af Vendômes Pager) (3.9.1830), 14

Paul et Virginie (P. Gardel), 8, 15

Paul et Virginie (Paul og Virginie) (29.10.1830), 15

Peasant Wedding, The, or The Corsairs (Bondbrölloppet eller Corsarerne) (L. J. M. Deland), 126

Polichinel without knowing it (Polichinel uden at vide af det), 6

Pontemolle (An Artists' Party in Rome) (Pontemolle, (Et Kunstnergilde i Rom)), 316, 413

Praxiteles, 7

Prize, The (Gevinsten), 5

Psyche, 136

Raphael (Rafael), 91

Révolte au sérail, La (F. Taglioni), 28

Robert und Bertrand (F.-M. Hoguet/P. Taglioni), 176, 181

Romeo and Giulietta (Romeo og Giulietta) (V. Galeotti/A. Bournonville), 24, 32

Rosiera, La (G. Casati and A. Saint-Léon), 110

Rosière, La (M. Gardel), 110, 126

Rosière de Salency, La (J.-G. Noverre), 110

Servante justifiée, La (P. Gardel), 8

Sicilien, Le, ou l'Amour peintre (A. Petit), 14, 16

Soldier and Peasant (Soldat og Bonde), 12, 63, 115, 139, 259

Somnambule, La, ou l'Arrivée d'un nouveau seigneur (J. Aumer), 10

Somnambule, La, ou l'Arrivée d'un nouveau seigneur (Sövngjængersken) (21.9.1829), 10, 204, 255, 338

Somnambule, La, ou l'Arrivée d'un nouveau seigneur (Sövngængersken) (14.8.1840), 63

Spring, The (Foraaret), 5

Summer, The (Sommeren), 6

Sylphide, La (F. Taglioni), 35

Sylphide, La (Sylphiden), 35, 131, 194, 201, 273, 278, 306, 315, 325, 378

Talisman, The (Talismanen), 6

Telemaco nell'Isola di Calipso (P. Gardel), 10

Thea, oder Die belebten Blumen (P. Taglioni), 182

Therese, die Nachtwandlerin (La Somnambule, ou l'Arrivée d'un nouveau seigneur/ Sövngjængersken) (31.7.1843), 82

Toreador, The (Toréadoren), 64, 81, 92, 104, 140, 320, 353, 396

Toreador, Der (Toréadoren) (15.7.1854), 174

Toreador (spanische Stierbekämpfer) und die Tänzerin, Der (Toréadoren) (10.7.1843), 81

Tyroleans, The (Tyrolerne) (6.3.1835), 29, 51, 55, 84

Tyroleans, The, or: The Mischievous Boy (Tyrolerne, eller: Den Skälmaktige Gossen) (8.6.1839), 51

Valkyrie, The (Valkyrien), 260, 350, 389, 417

'Valkyrierne' (13.9.1861) 260

Verwandelten Weiber, Die (Le Diable à quatre) (J. Mazilier/P. Taglioni, 6.10.1856), 191

Veteran, The, or The Hospitable House (Veteranen eller Det gjæstfrie Tag), 23

Victor's Wedding, or The Ancestral House (Victors Bryllup eller Fædrene=Arnen), 17

Waldemar, 32, 44, 164, 211, 321, 326, 384, 424

Wedding Festival in Hardanger, The (Brudefärden i Hardanger) (22.6.1857 and 1.11.1861), 202, 266

Wedding Festival in Hardanger, The (Brudefärden i Hardanger), 160, 349, 369

Weiberkur, Die (J. Mazilier/P. Taglioni, 6.10.1856), 192

Wesele w Ojcowie, 75

Whims of Cupid, The (Amor's skämt) (S. Lund from V. Galeotti), 46, 257

Whims of Cupid and the Ballet-master, The (Amors og Balletmesterens Luner), 121

White Rose, The, or The Summer in Bretagne (Den hvide Rose eller Sommeren i Bretagne), 110

Zémire et Azore (A. Deshayes), 16

Zephyr and Flora (Zephyr og Flora) (P. Funck), 14, 17

Zulma, or The Crystal Palace (Zulma eller: Krystalpaladset), 150

Divertissements, tableaux, intermezzi, mimic prologues and epilogues

The name of the choreographer of the works in this group is added (in parentheses) if different from Bournonville. Similarly, the date of the first performance is added (in parentheses) to those works for which an immediate identification could be rendered difficult by the presence of other revised versions of the same work, or by completely different works with almost identical titles.

Acclaim to the Graces (Gratziernes Hyldning) (25.2.1827), 8

Acclaim to the Graces, New Divertissement (Gratiernes Hyldning, nyt Divertissement) (1.9.1829), 9

Apotheosis (Apotheose) in *William Shakespeare. Epilogue and Apotheosis (Efterspil: Oberon og Titannia [...] Apotheose: Britannia bekrandser Shakspeare* [sic]*, der staaer omringet af sine Digterværker.')* (Act IV finale), 215

Apparitions célestes in *Waldemar* (Act IV, 29.5.1867), 326

Bacchic Feast, The (Bacchusfesten) (D. Krum after Bournonville, 23.1.1878), 424

Ballet des cinq sens, Le in *The Order of the Amaranth (Amarather-Orden)* (Act V, score no. 3), 301

'Ballet des cinq sens' ('Ballet (De fem sinner)') in *The Order of the Amaranth (Amarather-Orden)* (Act V, score no. 3), 302

Ballet Divertissement, A (Ett Ballet= Divertissement) (12.9.1863), 290

Ballet Divertissement of 'A Fairy Tale in Pictures' (Act I) (Balletdivertissement af 'Et Eventyr i Billeder' (1.ste Act)) (19.3.1873), 390

Ballet of the Chessmen, The (Schackbrikkernes Dands) in *The Mandarin's Daughters (Mandarinens Döttre),* 391

'Ballet of the Nuns' in *Robert le Diable (Robert af Normandiet)* (Act III, score no. 16), 114, 388

Battle at Bravalla Heath, The (Slaget paa Bravalla Hede) in *The Valkyrie (Valkyrien)* (Act IV, score no. 33), 260

Battle at Stiklestad, The (Slaget ved Stiklestad) in *St. Olave (Olaf den Hellige)* (Act V, score no. 4), 43

'Bouquet Royal', Divertissement (27.1.1870), 358

Children's Party, New Divertissement, A (En Börnefest, nyt Divertissement) (23.10.1844), 88

Dance Divertissement (Divertissement af Dands) (6.10.1840), 64

Dance Divertissement (Divertissement af Dands) (31.10.1870), 367

Danes in China, The (De Danske i China) (17.9.1839, 28.1.1842, 27.2.1843, 26.2.1865), 55, 71, 80, 307

Divertissement (uncredited, 14.7.1843), 81

Divertissement, A (et Divertissement) (27.8.1874), 403

Divertissement, A (Et Elev-Divertissement) (26.12.1866), 323

Divertissement (Ballet) in *The Elves (Alferne)* (Score no. 4), 254

Divertissement (Ballet) in *Les Huguenots (Hugenotterne)* (Act V, score no. 23), 85

'Divertissement Dansant' (G. Carey, 19.1.1873), 388

Divertissement from 'The Isle of Phantasy' (Divertissement af 'Phantasiens Øe') (3.9.1839), 55

Divertissement from *The Isle of Phantasy* (31.7.1843), 82

'Divertissement from The Toreador' ('Divertissement af Toréadoren') (11.6.1852), 154

Divertissement from 'Il Trovatore' (Gipsy Dance) (Divertissement af 'Troubadouren' (Zigeunerdands)) (25.1.1867 and 29.4.1877), 323, 422

Divertissement in *Gustave III, ou Le Bal masqué* (uncredited, 5.7.1843), 81

Divertissement of the ballet La Somnambule (Divertissement af Balletten Søvngængersken) (17.2.1875), 405

Divertissement (The motif from Gardel's Paul et Virginie) (Divertissement (Motivet fra Gardel's Paul og Virginie)) (19.6.1854), 172

'Drømmebilleder' in *An Episode (En Episode)* (2.9.1852), 158

Earnest Maiden, The, A Pastoral Picture in the form of a Ballet (Den alvorlige Pige, Landligt Billede i Balletform) (15.10.1856), 193

Earnest Maiden, The, Ballet Divertissement (Den alvorlige Pige, Balletdivertissement) (23.11.1856), 194

Échecs, Les in *La Magicienne* (J. Mazilier, 23.4.1873), 392

Echo from the Ballroom (Echo fra Balsalen (Pas de deux)) (uncredited, 19.8.1870), 366

Echo from the Ballroom, Character Dance (Echo fra Balsalen, Characteerdands) (uncredited, 28.2.1861), 258

Echo from the Ballroom, New Pas de deux (Echo från Balsalen, Ny Pas de deux) (uncredited, 3.10.1862), 279

Epilogue (Efterspil) in *William Shakespeare. Epilogue and Apotheosis (Efterspil: Oberon og Titannia [...] Apotheose: Britannia bekrandser Shakspeare [sic], der staaer omringet af sine Digterværker.')* (Act IV, score no. 8), 215

'Episode in Hyde Park', Divertissement for children ('Episode i Hÿdepark' Divertissement for Børn) (17.3.1867), 323

Famous Men from Denmark's Past (Hemicycle of tableaux vivants) (Berømte Mænd fra Danmarks Fortid (Hemicyclus i levende Tableauer) (1.6.1875), 412

Farewell to the Old Theatre, Ballet Epilogue (Farvel til det gamle Theater, Ballet=Epilog), 402

Fatherland's Muses, The (Fædrelandets Muser), 58

Feast of the Muses, The (Musernes Fest), 6

Fisher Girls, The, Hornpipe and Reel (Fiskerpigerne, Hornpipe og Reel) (uncredited, 21.11.1858), 223

Five Senses, The (De fem Sandser) (16.1.1866), 315

Flower Festival in Genzano, The (Section II) (Blomsterfesten i Genzano, (2den Afdeling)) (1.1.1875), 404

Flower Maids of Florence, The (De florentinske Blomsterpiger), Pas de trois (8.6.1850), 137, 140

'Flower Maids of Florence, The', Character dance ('De florentinske Blomsterpiger' Characteerdands) (12.7.1852), 156

'Fragment of the ballet La Somnambule' ('Fragment af Balletten Søvngængersken') (14.6.1865), 308

Forward! National Divertissement in four Tableaux (Framåt! National-Divertissement i 4 tablåer) (7.11.1862), 280

From the Last Century (Fra det forrige Aarhundrede), 121, 413

Gallery of ten Danish Kings of the House of Oldenburg, depicted in tableaux vivants, arranged by Mr Ballet-master Bournonville, A (Gallerie af 10 danske Konger af den oldenborgske Stamme, fremstillede i levende Tableauer, arrangerede af Hr. Balletmester Bournonville) (13.5.1840), 59

Hertha's Offering (Herthas Offer), 42

Holbergiana in *From the Last Century (Fra det forrige Aarhundrede)*, 134

Holbergiana, Apotheotic Tableau (apotheotisk Tableau) (3.6.1873), 393

Holmen's Old Guard, Divertissement (Holmens faste Stok, Divertissement) (9.6.1849), 129

Improvisatoren paa Molo/Lÿrisk = Genremalerie, 75

In Memory of Schall, Prologue (Schalls Minde, Forspil), 31

In Memory of Wexschall, Prologue (with Tableau) (Wexschalls Minde, Prolog (med Tableau)) (uncredited, 10.2.1846), 94

In Memory of Weyse, Epilogue with Tableaux (Weyses Minde, Efterspil med Tableauer) (5.3.1874), 397

Intermedium in *The Masquerade (Maskeraden)* (12.12.1849, 11.2.1859), 133, 230

Intermezzo in *The Order of the Amaranth (Amarather-Orden)* (20.2.1864), 301

Irresistibles, The (De Uimodstaaelige), 135

'Italian Genre Picture', Divertissement with Tarantella ('Italiensk Genrebillede' Divertissement med Tarantella) (2.7.1852), 156

Italian Genre Pictures and Tarantella (Italienske Genrebilder och Tarantella) (5.6.1860), 251

Kirsten Piil's Dream in *Kirsten Piil* (Act III, score no. 2), 90

'Kongens Hjemkomst', 98

Major Ballet Divertissement, A (Et større Balletdivertissement (nærmere Aftale)) (1.8.1870), 365

Mandarin's Daughters, The (Mandarinens Døttre), 391

Maritana, Divertissement in the form of a Carnival scene (Divertissement i Form af en Carnevals=Scene), 101, 102

Masaniello (Neapolitan Tableau) (Masaniello (Neapolitansk Tableau)), 75

Masquerade Divertissement of Dance, A (Ett Maskerad-Divertissement af Dans) (A. Selinder), 50

Matrosens Hjemkomst (27.12.1856), 195

Memorial Wreath to Denmark's Great Poet, Suite of Tableaux, A (Mindets Krands for Danmarks store Digter. Suite af Tableauer) (14.11.1879), 427

Minor Ballet Divertissement of older dances, A

(Et mindre Balletdivertissement af sammenbragte Dandse) (1.8.1870), 366

Mozartiana, Four Apotheotic Tableaux (fyre apotheotiska Tablåer) (7.3.1862), 272

Muses de la patrie, Les (Fædrelandets Muser), 58

New Divertissement (Nyt Divertissement) (1.11.1842), 77

New Divertissement (after Holberg's indications) as an intermezzo in The Healing Spring, A (Intermedium, Et nyt Divertissement (efter Holbergs Opgave) i Kildereisen) (22.5.1859), 237

New Divertissement as an intermezzo in The Healing Spring, A (Intermedium i Kildereisen) (30.5.1840), 60

N. N.'s Memorial Feast for Shakespeare 1864. (N. Ns Minnefest öfver Shakespeare 1864.) (uncredited, 7.5.1864), 305

Ny Række af Thorvaldsenske Billeder in *The Festival in Albano (Festen i Albano)* (8.1.1844), 84

Pantomime scene in *William Shakespeare. Epilogue and Apotheosis (Efterspil: Oberon og Titannia [...] Apotheose: Britannia bekrandser Shakspeare [sic], der staaer omringet af sine Digterværker.')* (Act I, score no. 3), 215

'Pas de deux' and 'Balabile' (from the ballet The Flower Festival) ('Pas de deux' og 'Balabile' (af Balletten Blomsterfesten)) (9.6.1865), 307

Pas de deux and Balabile from the ballet The Flower Festival in Genzano (Pas de deux et Balabile ur Balletten Blomsterfesten i Genzano) (1.6.1860), 250

Patineurs, Les in *Le Prophète (Profeten)* (Act III, 18.4.1863), 288

Paul et Virginie, Dance Divertissement after Gardel and A. Bournonville, mounted by Ballet-master S. Lund (Paul och Virginie, Divertissement af Dans, efter Gardel och A. Bournonville, uppsatt af Hr Balletmästaren S. Lund) (7.2.1858), 214

Paul et Virginie, Divertissement (The motif from Gardel) (Paul og Virginie, Divertissement (Motivet efter Gardel) (21.1.1855), 176

Paul et Virginie (Divertissement) (16.1.1866), 315

Pitman's Dream, The, Hungarian Ballet Divertissement in 1 Act (Excerpt from the Ballet In The Carpathians) (Bjergmandens Drøm, Ungarsk Balletdivertissement i 1 Act (Uddrag af Balletten I Karpatherne) (6.11.1859), 240

Projected Divertissement for the celebration of the silver-wedding of Denmark's King Christian IX and Queen Louise (31.1.1867), 323

Projected Intermezzo for The Healing Spring, A (Kildereisen), 60

Polichinel-vampire (F. A. Blache), 6

Prophecies of Love, The, Tyrolean Scene and Dance (Kjærligheds Spaadomme, Tyroler Scene og Dands) (4.6.1851 and 21.9.1851), 147, 149

'Prophecies of Love, The', Tyrolean Scene and Dance ('Kjærligheds Spaadomme' Tyroler-Scene og Dands) (7.6.1852), 152

Prophecies of Love, The, Tyrolean Scene and Dance (Kärleks Spådomar, Scen och Tyrolienne) (10.5.1858), 219

Prophecies of Love, The, Ballet Divertissement, composed and revised anew (Kjærligheds Spaadomme, Ballet Divertissement, componeret og nyt omarbeidet) (28.2.1869), 347

Sailor and His Bride, The (Matrosen og hans Brud) (R. Price), 153

Sailor's Return, The (Matrosens Hjemkomst) (1.6.1860), 251

Sailor's Return, The, Dance Divertissement arranged by Mr. Ballet Master Sigurd Lund (Sjömannens hemkomst, Divertissement af Dans arrangeradt af Herr Ballettmästaren Sigurd Lund) (27.12.1856), 195

Sailor's Return, The, Divertissement (Matrosens Hjemkomst, Divertissement) (11.6.1855), 180

»Sailor's Return, The«, Divertissement (»Matrosens Hjemkomst«, Divertissement) (20.2.1867), 323

'Sailor's Return, The', Scene and English Character Dance ('Matrosens Hjemkomst', Scene og engelsk Characteerdands) (9.6.1852, 7.9.1857), 153, 203

Sailor's Return, The, Scene and Dance (Matrosens Hjemkomst, Scene og Dands) (23.9.1855), 183

'Sailor's Return, The' (Scene with Dance) ('Matrosens Hjemkomst' (Scene med Dands)) (9.6.1865), 307

Scene and Pas de deux from the opera Le Dieu et La Bayadère (Scène och Pas de deux ur Operan Brama och Bayadéren) (5.6.1860), 251

Scene and Pas de quatre from the Ballet La Somnambule (Scene och Pas de quatre utur Balletten Sömngångerskan (uncredited, 10.7.1839), 54

'Scene and Pas de quatre from La Somnambule' ('Scene og Pas de quatre af Sövngængersken') (18.6.1852), 155

'Scene and Pas de trois from The Conservatoire' ('Scene og Pas de trois af Conservatoriet') (22.6.1852), 155

Scene and Pas de trois from The Return (Scen och Pas de trois från Hemkomsten) (23.4.1860), 249

Scene and Solo from the Ballet La Sylphide (Scene och Solo utur Balletten Sylphiden) (uncredited, 15.7.1839), 54

Scene from the Ballet La Sylphide (Scen utur Balletten Sylphiden/ Scène de la Sylphide) (uncredited, 14.6.1839), 52

'Scene og Pas de deux af Balletten Toreadoren' (9.1.1842), 71

Scene, Pas de deux and Gallopade from the ballet 'The Isle of Phantasy' (Scene, Pas de deux och Gallopade utur Balletten 'Phantasiens Ö') (5.7.1839), 53

Scene, Pas de deux, and Gallopade from the ballet 'The Isle of Phantasy' (Scene, Pas de deux og Galopade af Balletten 'Phantasiens Øe') (10.11.1839), 57

Scene, Pas de deux, and Galop (from the ballet The Isle of Phantasy) (Scene, Pas de deux & Galop (utur Balletten: l'Isle des Fantasies [sic])) (2.6.1839), 50

Scene, Solo and Pas de deux, in two sections, from the ballet 'La Sylphide' (Scène, Solo och

Pas de deux I två afdelningar, ur Balletten 'Sylphiden')) (12.6.1860), 252

Scenes and Pas de quatre from the ballet 'La Somnambule' (Scèner och Pas de quatre ur Balletten 'Sömngångerskan') (uncredited, 16.6.1860), 252

Section II of 'The Flower Festival in Genzano ' (Andra Afdelingen af 'Blomsterfesten i Genzano') (26.4.1860), 252

Section II ('2. Afd.') of The Flower Festival in Genzano (Blomsterfesten i Genzano) (1.5.1877), 423

Shakespeare's Apotheosis (Shakspeares Apotheos) (23.4.1864), 304

Shakespearean Apotheosis, A (en Shakespearesk Apotheose) (5.5.1879), 427

Shield Dance and a Tableau vivant, entitled Episode from the Middle-Age: The Crusaders, A (Skjolddands og En Episode fra Middel-alderen: Korsfarerne) (D. Krum after Bournonville, 2.3.1877), 421

Soldier and Peasant (Soldat og Bonde) (12.8.1840), 63

'Spring and Hertha, The', Divertissement ('Vaaren og Hertha', Divertissement), 62

Sylphide, La, Romantic Ballet in 3 Parts, arranged by Ballet Master Bournonville (Sylphiden, romantisk Ballet i 3 Afdelinger, arrangeret af Hr. Balletmester Bournonville) (31.7.1840), 62

'Tableauerne' (12.10.1846), 99

Tableau for The Overture to The Elves' Hill (Ouverturen til Elverhöj: Illustration: Kong Christian IV paa Trefoldigheden) (19.5.1877), 423

Tableau (Holberg.). Tableau (Oehlenschläger.). (15.10.1874), 403

Tableau mounted for the anniversary of the Battle at Fridericia (Fest-Forestilling til Minde om Fredericia-Slaget) (6.7.1850), 138

Tableau with Dance (Tableau med Dands) (12.10.1846), 98

Tableau with Song and Dance (Tableau med Sang og Dands) (uncredited, 1.3.1859), 230

Tableaux and a March in Le Petit Chaperon rouge (Den lille Rødhætte) (Act II, score no. 12), 159

Tableaux vivants: a. Sacrifice to Hygæa b. The wounded Warrior (a. Offer til Hygæa, b. Den saarede Kriger) (31.3.1846), 96

Terpsichore (5.10.1860), 253

Troubadour, The (Troubadouren) (28.2.1824), 6

Two Tableaux, a. Sacrifice to Hygæa, b. The wounded Warrior, arranged by Ballet Master Bournonville (2 Tableaux, a. Offer til Hygæa, b. Den saarede Kriger, arrangerede af Hr. Balletmester Bournonville) (4.6.1846), 96

Two Tableaux entitled 'The Storming at Vestervold' ('Stormen paa Vestervold') and 'The Blessing of Peace' ('Fredens Velsignelse'), staged on the occasion of the bicentenary of the Storming of Copenhagen (Borgerfesten ved To=Hundrede =Aars Jubilæet for Stormen paa Kjøbenhavn) (10.2.1859), 229

Two Tableaux (To Tableauer) Mozartiana. The

Sally from Classens Have (1807) (Udfaldet i Classens Have (1807)) (2.6.1871), 376

Valiant Soldier, The, a suite of five tableaux in memory of Faber (Den tappre Landsoldat. Suite af fem Tableauer til Fabers Minde) (9.3.1878), 425

'Ventana, La' (16.6.1865), 308

Ventana, La, Ballet Divertissement (Ballet-divertissement) (6.10.1856), 191, 203, 343, 374

Ventana, La, (Mirror Dance) (Spegeldans) (16.6.1860), 252

Ventana, La, Spanish Character Dance (La Ventana, spansk Characteerdands) (26.12.1854), 175

Ventana, La, Spanish Solo (new), (spansk Solo (ny)) (19.6.1854), 173

Ventana, La (The Window) (fönstret.) Ballet-Divertissement (7.12.1858), 225

Ventana, La (The Window) (La Ventana, (Fönstret.)), Ballet-Divertissement in 2 Tableaux (i 2 Tablåer) (15.6.1858), 220

Individual rôles, *pas*, and dances

The name of the choreographer of the works in this group is added (in parentheses) if different from Bournonville. Similarly, the date of the first performance is added (in parentheses) to those works for which an immediate identification could be rendered difficult by the presence of other revised versions of the same work, or by completely different works with almost identical titles.

Adolphe in *Adolphe et Clara, ou les deux Prisonniers (Adolph og Clara eller De to Arrestanter)*, 21

'af Galai=Slaverne' in *The Masquerade (Maskeraden)* (12.12.1849), 134

Age of Art, The in *Pontemolle (An Artists' Party in Rome) (Pontemolle, (Et Kunstnergilde i Rom))* (2nd tableau, score no. 12), 317

'Alfemarsch' in *A Midsummer Night's Dream (En Skjærsommernatsdrøm)* (Act II, score no. 2), 427

Amager=Dands (20.3.1849), 125

Amor and Hymen [Figurative dance] in *The Festival in Albano (Festen i Albano)* (Score no. 12, 1.1.1869), 343

Amor and Hymen [Pas de deux] in *The Festival in Albano (Festen i Albano)* (Score nos. 8–9, 1.1.1869), 343

Ancient Rome in *Pontemolle (An Artists' Party in Rome) (Pontemolle, (Et Kunstnergilde i Rom))* (2nd tableau, score no. 11), 317

'Andante pastorale' in *Pontemolle (An Artists' Party in Rome) (Pontemolle, (Et Kunstner-gilde i Rom))* (2nd tableau, score no. 13), 317

Aragonaise, L' (uncredited, 18.5.1871), 376

'Arragonnaise, l' ' (18.5.1871), 376

'Bacchantes, Les' (25.7.1870), 364

'Bacchantes, The', (Pas de deux), ('Bacchantinderne' (Pas de deux)) (uncredited, 25.7.1870), 364

Bacchantes, The, pas de deux (Bacchantinderne, pas de deux) (uncredited, 13.7.1872), 385

Bacchantic Waltz (Bachantisk Vals) in

Divertissement from 'The Isle of Phantasy' (*Divertissement af 'Phantasiens Øe'*), 55

'Bacchantinderne' (Pas de deux) (uncredited, 25.7.1870), 364

Ballabile in *The Festival in Albano (Festen i Albano* (1.1.1869), 343

Ballabile in *Napoli or The Fisher and His Bride (Napoli eller Fiskeren og hans Brud* (Act I, score no. 5), 72

Ballabile in *Napoli, oder: Der Fischer und seine Braut (Napoli eller Fiskeren og hans Brud)* (31.1.1856), 187

'Ballet' in *Hermann von Unna* (V. Galeotti), 31

'Ballet of the Nuns' in *Robert le Diable* (F. Taglioni/Bournonville), 114, 388

'Ballet no. 3' in Act I of *La Vestale* (P. Gardel), 16

Ballet Performance, A (En Ballet=Forestilling) (11.8.1843), 82

Ballet Performance, A (Forestillingen i Helsingør) (16.12.1846), 99

Battle at Braavalla Heath in *The Valkyrie (Valkyrien)*, 260

Battle at Stiklestad, The in *St. Olave (Olaf den Hellige)*, 43

'Begyndelsen af Fandango i C Mol som Introduction: –/Pas de deux. Bournonville og Jf. Grahn' in *Don Quixote at Camacho's Wedding (Don Quixote ved Camachos Bryllup)*, 38

'Beltedands' in *The New Penelope, or The Spring Festival in Athens (Den nye Penelope, eller Foraarsfesten i Athen)* (Act II, score no. 9), 100, 137

'Blomsterdandsen' (12.10.1846), 99

Bolero, El (arranged for four persons) (El Bolero (arrangeret for 4 Personer)) (6.7.1840), 61

Boléro (uncredited) in *Le Domino noir (Eventyret paa Maskeraden eller Den sorte Domino)*, 47

Boléro from *La Muette de Portici* in *Don Quixote at Camacho's Wedding (Don Quixote ved Camachos Bryllup)*, 38

Bolero in *Maritana, Divertissement in form of a Carnival scene (Divertissement i Form af en Carnevals=Scene)*, 101

Bolero in *La Muette de Portici (Den Stumme i Portici)* (Act I), 25, 140, 269

Boléro in *La Muette de Portici* (J. Aumer), 15, 38

Bolero in *Les Pages du Duc de Vendôme (Hertugen af Vendômes Pager)*, 14

Boléro in *The Toreador (Toréadoren)* (Act II, score no. 11), 65

Bolero à quatre in *'Divertissement from The Toreador' ('Divertissement af Toréadoren')* (11.6.1852), 154

'Bolero' (Spanish National Dance) ('Bolero' (spansk Nationaldands)) (7.6.1865), 307

'Börnecomedie' in *Don Quixote at Camacho's Wedding (Don Quixote ved Camachos Bryllup)*, 38

'Bord Dands' in *The Wedding Festival in Hardanger (Brudefærden i Hardanger)* (Act II, score no. 12), 161

Bouquet Royal Galop in *'Bouquet Royal', Divertissement*, 358

Boys' Dance (Drengedands) in *The New Penelope, or The Spring Festival in Athens*

(Den nye Penelope, eller Foraarsfesten i Athen) (Act II, score no. 11), 100

Bridal Dance, The (Brudedandsen) in *The Lay of Thrym (Thrymsqviden)* (Act II, scene 4, score nos. 21–22), 335, 378

Bridal Waltz (Brudevals) in *A Folk Tale (Et Folkesagn)* (Act III, score no. 20), 167

Cachucha, La (F. Elssler/L. Grahn), 43, 127

Can Can in *The Conservatoire, or A Proposal of Marriage through the Newspaper (Conservatoriet, eller Ett Frieri i Tidningarne)* (Act II, score no. 7), 201

La canzonetta in *Napoli, oder: Der Fischer und seine Braut (Napoli eller Fiskeren og hans Brud)* (31.1.1856), 187

'Capricio, El', arranged by A. Bournonville (arrangerad af A. Bournonville) (30.4.1860), 250

Capricio, El, Jaleo (uncredited, 1.12.1858), 224

Castilliana in *Gustave III, ou Le Bal Masqué* (uncredited, 5.7.1843), 81

'Chaconne' in *Daniel Hjort* (Act V?), 299

'Chaconne' in *Pontemolle (An Artists' Party in Rome) (Pontemolle, (Et Kunstnergilde i Rom))* (2nd tableau, score no. 13), 317

Changing Dance (Vexeldands) in *Abdallah* (Act I, score no. 2), 177

'Chant bachique' in *Faust* (Act V, score no. 29, 16.3.1873), 390

'Chiaconne' in *The Masquerade (Maskeraden)* (12.12.1849), 133

Chinese [Dance] *(Chinesisk)* in *The Danes in China (De Danske i China)* (28.1.1842, 27.2.1843, 26.2.1865), 71, 80, 307

Chinese Dance in *The Isle of Phantasy (Phantasiens Øe)*, 45

Chinese Dance (Chinesisk Dands) in *Gustav III (Gustav den Tredie)*, 124

Choeur dansé in *Robert le Diable (Robert af Normandiet)* (Act II, score no. 7), 114

Choeur dansé in *Robert le Diable (Robert af Normandiet)* (Act III, Finale), 114

'Choeur et Ballet' in *Oberon; or The Elf King's oath (Oberon)* (Act III, score no. 21), 219

'Chör och Ballet' in *Faust* (C. Gounod, Act V, score no. 28), 277

'Chor und allgemeiner Tanz' in *Die Lustigen Weiber von Windsor (De lystigen Koner i Windsor)* (Act III, score no. 16), 327

'Chor und Elfentanz' in *Die Lustigen Weiber von Windsor (De lystige Koner i Windsor)* (Act III, score no. 14), 327

'Ciaccona' in *Don Quixote at Camacho's Wedding (Don Quixote ved Camachos Bryllup)*, 38

Ciacconne in *Don Quixote at Camacho's Wedding (Don Quixote ved Camachos Bryllup)*, 39

Ciacconne in *Old Memories, or A Magic Lantern (Gamle Minder eller En Laterna magica)*, 121

Circle Dance in *Undine* (Act II, score no. 7), 76

Circle Dance (Kredsdands) in *Little Kirsten (Liden Kirsten)* (Score no. 12), 113

Circle Dance (Ringdans) in *The Slanderer (Smädeskrifvaren, eller: Vänner och Ovänner)* (Act I, scene 4), 275

Circle Dance (Ringdands) in *William Shake-*

speare. Epilogue and Apotheosis (Efterspil: Oberon og Titannia [...] Apotheose: Britannia bekrandser Shakspeare [sic]*, der staaer omringet af sine Digterværker.')* (Act I, score no. 1), 215

Circle Dance (En Runddands) in *A Cup of Welcome (Ett Hemkomstöl)* (22.6.1857), 202

Circle Dance (Runddands) in *La Dame Blanche (Den hvide Dame)* (Act I, score no. 1), 139, 223

Circle Dance (Runddands) in *Waldemar* (Act I, score no. 4, 21.11.1866), 321

Clog Dance in *Soldier and Peasant (Soldat og Bonde)* (Score no. 8), 12

Clog Dance ('Tanz mit Holzschuhen') in *Czaar und Zimmermann (Czaren og Tømmermanden)* (Act III finale, score no. 16), 98, 212

Clog Dance (Træskodands) in *From the Last Century (Fra det forrige Aarhundrede)* (Scene 6, score no. 7), 414

Cock's Dance (Hanedands) in *The Masquerade (Maskeraden)* (12.12.1849), 133

'Cont Dands Træns' in *The Masquerade (Maskeraden)* (12.12.1849), 134

Contradands in *Kirsten Piil* (Act II, score no. 7), 90

'Contradands' in *The Masquerade (Maskeraden)* (12.12.1849), 134

'Contra-ça-ira!' in *The Masquerade (Maskeraden)* (11.2.1859), 230

Contredands in *The Mulatto (Mulatten)*, 115

'Contredands' in *Victor's Wedding, or The Ancestral House (Victors Bryllup eller Fædrene=Arnen)*, 18

Contredanse in *Le Domino Noir (Eventyret paa Maskeraden eller Den sorte Domino)*, 47

Contredanse in *La Somnambule, ou l'Arrivée d'un nouveau seigneur* (J. Aumer), 10

Contredanse (or Quadrille) in *La Fiancée (Bruden)*, 165

'Contredanse ancienne' in *Pontemolle (An Artists' Party in Rome) (Pontemolle, (Et Kunstnergilde i Rom))* (2nd tableau, score no. 13), 317

Contredanse/Divertissement in *La Somnambule, ou l'Arrivée d'un nouveau seigneur (Sövngjængersken)* (Act I, score no. 7, 2.10.1868), 338

Cracovienne, La (uncredited, 9.11.1855 and 15.10.1856), 185, 193

Cracovienne, La, Polish National Dance after Fanny Elssler (Polsk Nationaldands efter Fanny Elssler) (J. Mazilier/F. Elssler/A. Bournonville, 10.6.1842), 75

Cracovienne, La, Polish National Dance, (Polsk Nationaldands) (uncredited, 25.6.1847), 108

Czardas in *Dance Divertissement (Divertissement af Dands)* (31.10.1870), 367

Czardas and Frischka (Hungarian National Dances) (Czardas og Frischka (ungarske Nationaldandse)) (1.3.1872), 382

Dance from the Act I finale of *La Fille du regiment* (10.11.1860), 256

Dance (Dands) in *Hagbarth and Signe (Hagbarth og Signe)* (Act III, 20.9.1849), 131

Dance of the Bridal Maids from *La Fiancée* (10.11.1860), 256

Dance of the Five Senses in *The Lay of Thrym (Thrymsqviden)* (Act I, scene 2, score no. 2), 331

Dance of the Priestesses of Lesbos in *Iphigenia in Aulis (Iphigenia i Aulis)* (Act II, score no. 17), 259

Dance of the Valkyries (Valkyriernes Dands) in *The Valkyrie (Valkyrien)* (Act I, score no. 1), 262

Dance of the Witches in *Macbeth (Hexenes Dands i Macbeth)* (uncredited, 10.1.1860), 241

Dance (Slutnings-Sang og Dands) in *A New Divertissement* (after Holberg's indications) as an intermezzo in *The Healing Spring (Intermedium, Et nyt Divertissement (efter Holbergs Opgave) i Kildereisen)* (22.5.1859), 237

Dance (unnamed) in *The Bewitched (Den Bjergtagne/Den Bergtagna)* (Act III (score no. 14, originally no. 18 (1)), 416

Dance (unnamed) in *I Capuleti ed i Montecchi (Familierne Montecchi og Capulet)* (Act II, score no. 6), 244

Dance (unnamed) in *Cyprianus* (Finale, score no. 13), 241

Dance (unnamed) in *Czaar und Zimmermann (Czaren og Tømmermanden)* (Act II, score no. 11), 98, 212

Dance (unnamed) in *La Dame Blanche (Den hvide Dame)*
(Act III, score no. 12), 139
(Act III finale, score no. 14), 139

Dance (unnamed) in *Das Diamantkreuz (Diamantkorset)*
(Act II, scene 5, score nos. 9 a–c), 101
(Act II, score no. 9 e), 101

Dance (unnamed) in *Les Dragons de Villars (Villars' Dragoner)* (Act I finale, score no. 6, 4.5.1863 and 19.10.1870), 289

Dance (unnamed) in *Faruk* (Act I, score no. 3, 5.3.1874), 398

Dance (unnamed) in *Fra-Diavolo, ou l'Hôtellerie de Terracine (Fra Diavolo eller Værtshuset i Terracina)* (Act III, score no. 13), 212

Dance (unnamed) in *Hagbarth and Signe (Hagbarth og Signe)* (Act III, 20.9.1849),131

Dance (unnamed) in *In Memory of Weyse, Epilogue with Tableaux (Weyses Minde, Efterspil med Tableauer)* (Scene 5, score no. 11), 398

Dance (unnamed) in *Jean de Paris (Johan fra Paris)*
(Act II, score no. 11), 353
(Act II, score no. 12), 353

Dance (unnamed) in *Lucia di Lammermoor (Lucia af Lammermoor)* (Act III, score no. 9), 210

Dance (unnamed) in *A Midsummer Night's Dream (En Skjærsommernatsdrøm)*
(Act II, score no. 3), 427
(Act V, score no. 12), 427

Dance (unnamed) in *Nina, ou La Folle par amour (Nina, eller Den Vanvittige af Kjærlighed)* (Act I, score no. 10), 27

Dance (unnamed) in *The Pascha's Daughter (Paschaens Datter)*
(Act I, score no. 1), 351
(Act IV, score no. 17), 351

Dance (unnamed) in *Le Petit Chaperon rouge (Den lille Rødhætte)* (Act I, score no. 7), 159

Dance (unnamed) in *Preciosa*
(Act I, score no. 4), 146
(Act III, score no. 10), 146

Dance (unnamed) in *Princess Isabella, or Three Nights at the Court (Prindsesse Isabella eller Tre Aftener ved Hoffet)* (Act II, score no. 4), 13

Dance (unnamed) in *I Puritani di Scozia/I Puritani ed i Cavalieri (Puritanerne)* (Act I, scene 2, score no. 1), 291

Dance (unnamed) in *Le Roman d'Elvire (Drottning Elviras Saga)* (Act I finale, score no. 8), 305

Dance (unnamed) in *Undine* (between Act III and IV), 76

Dance (unnamed) in *William Shakespeare. Epilogue and Apotheosis (Efterspil: Oberon og Titannia […] Apotheose: Britannia bekrandser Shakspeare [sic], der staaer omringet af sine Digterværker.')* (Act IV, score no. 6), 215

Dance scene in *Tannhäuser und der Sängerkrieg auf der Wartburg (Tannhäuser og Sangerkrigen paa Wartburg)* (Act I, scene 1, score no. 1), 406

Dance scene (unnamed) in *Amanda* (Act III, scene 6), 382

Dance scene (unnamed) in *The Elves (Alferne)* (Score no. 1), 254, 369

Dance scene (unnamed) in *Little Kirsten (Liden Kirsten)* (Score no. 6), 113

Dance scenes (unnamed) in *The Bewitched (Den Bjergtagne/Den Bergtagna)* (Act II, score nos. 11–12), 416

Dances in *The Guerilla Band (Guerillabanden)*, 24

Dances (unnamed) in *Der Templer und Die Jüdin (Tempelherren og Jødinden)* (Act III, score nos. 13 and 14), 374

'Dands af Regnar og Thora' in *Lagertha* (V. Galeotti), 121

'Dans' in *Le Médecin malgré lui (Läkaren mot sin Vilja)*
(Act I finale, scene 7), 297
(Act II finale, scene 12), 297

Dans af Demoner' in *Faust* (C. Gounod, Act V, score no. 29), 277

Danse in *Cendrillon (Cendrillon eller Den lille grønne Sko)* (Act II, score no. 7), 190

'Danse/Corps de Ballet/Pas de deux/pas de troix/Corps de ballet' in *Romeo and Giulietta (Romeo og Giulietta)* (V. Galeotti/A. Bournonville), 24

'Danse des battoirs' in *The White Rose, or The Summer in Bretagne (Den hvide Rose eller Sommeren i Bretagne)* (Score no. 4), 110

Danse des flambeaux in *Waldemar* (Act II, 29.5.1867), 326

'Danse du barbier' in *The Wedding Festival in Hardanger (Brudefärden i Hardanger)* (Act II, score no. 13, 22.6.1857), 202

Danse générale in *Cendrillon (Cendrillon eller Den lille grønne Sko)* (Act III, scene 10, score no. 16), 190

'Danse rustique' in *Don Quixote at Camacho's Wedding (Don Quixote ved Camachos Bryllup)*, 39

'Danse rustique' in *Waldemar*, 34

Danse sauvage in *The Mountain Hut, or Twenty Years (Fjeldstuen eller Tyve Aar)* (Third tableau, scene 8, score no. 12), 233

'Dansmusik ur Faust' (9.6.1847), 105

'Devin de Village, Le/All° brillante' in *The Homecoming (Hemkomsten)*, 371

'Ditto [i.e. Pas de Cinq] af Ravnen' in *The Raven (Ravnen eller Broderprøven)*, 22

'Echo de Dannemark', *Pas Seul*, arranged by Aug. Bournonville (*Pas Solo, arrangerad af Aug.Bournonville*) (26.9.1849), 131

Echo of Sunday, Dance from Amager (Søndags= Echo. Amagerdands) (20.3.1849), 125

Edmond in A. Selinder's production of J. Aumer's *La Somnambule, ou l'Arrivée d'un nouveau seigneur (Sömngångersken i Provence)* (14.6.1839), 53

'Einlage Balett/Napoli/Zweiter Akt/[…]/La Najade' in *Napoli, oder: Der Fischer und seine Braut (Napoli eller Fiskeren og hans Brud)* (31.1.1856), 187

Elf maidens' dance in *A Folk Tale (Et Folkesagn)* (Act I, score no. 5), 169

'Engelsk dands' in *The Masquerade (Maskeraden)* (12.12.1849), 133

English Sailor, The, (Den Engelska Matrosen) (25.6.1847), 107

English Sailor, The, (Den Engelske Matros) in *The Danes in China (De Danske i China)* (28.1.1842, 27.2.1843, 26.2.1865), 71, 80, 307

English Sailor, The, Scene and Hornpipe (Den Engelska Matrosen, Scene och Hornpipe (uncredited, 10.7.1839), 54

English Sailor, The (Scene and Hornpipe) (Den Engelska Matrosen, (Scen och Hornpipe)/Le Matelot Anglais (Scène & Hornpipe)) (uncredited, 14.6.1839), 53

'English Sailor, The', Scene and Hornpipe ('Den Engelske Matros', Scene og Hornpipe (uncredited, 14.8.1840), 63

English Sailor's Dance in *The Isle of Phantasy (Phantasiens Øe)* (Act I, score no. 10), 45

English-Scottish National Quadrille (National= Quadrille, engelsk=skotsk) (6.2.1870), 360

English-Scottish National Quadrille (National= Quadrille, engelsk=skotsk) in *'Bouquet Royal'*, *Divertissement* (27.1.1870), 358

Eskimo Dance in *Far from Denmark, or: A Costume Ball on Board (Fjernt fra Danmark eller: et Costumebal ombord)* (Act II), 249

Fandango in *Don César de Bazan (Don Cæsar de Bazan)* (P. Larcher/Bournonville), 120

Fandango in *Far from Denmark, or: A Costume Ball on Board (Fjernt fra Danmark eller: et Costumebal ombord)* (Act II), 247

Fandango in *Die Hochzeit des Figaro (Figaros Bryllup)* (Act III, score no. 25), 84

Fandango (uforandret) in *Die Hochzeit des Figaro (Figaros Bryllup)* (30.4.1872), 384

Fandango in *Le Nozze di Figaro* (25.5.1842), 74

Festive Dance (Festdands) in *Zulma, or The Crystal Palace (Zulma eller: Krystalpaladset)* (Act I, score no. 13), 150

Final (Danse avec flambeaux) in *The Festival in Albano (Festen i Albano)* (1.1.1869), 249

'Finale' in *Arcona* (Act III, scene 6), 410

Finale in *The Childhood of Erik Menved (Erik Menveds Barndom)* (Act III, score no. 23), 79

Finale in *The Conservatoire, or A Proposal of Marriage through the Newspaper (Conservatoriet, eller Et Avisfrieri)* (Score no. 12), 127, 200

Finale in *The Flower Festival in Genzano (Section II) (Blomsterfesten i Genzano, (2den Afdeling))* (1.1.1875), 404

Finale in *A Folk Tale (Et Folkesagn)* (Act III, score no. 20), 167

Finale in *The Mandarin's Daughters (Mandarinens Døttre)*, 391

Finale in *Napoli or The Fisher and His Bride (Napoli eller Fiskeren og hans Brud* (Act I, score no. 7), 72

Finale in *Oberon; or The Elf King's oath (Oberon)* (Act II, score no. 15), 219

Finale in *Pontemolle (An Artists' Party in Rome) (Pontemolle, (Et Kunstnergilde i Rom))* (2nd tableau, score no. 16), 317

Finale in *Preciosa* (Act III, score no. 10), 146

Finale in *La Somnambule, ou l'Arrivée d'un nouveau seigneur (Sövngjængersken)* (Act II, score no. 11, 2.10.1868), 338

Finale in *Victor's Wedding, or The Ancestral House (Victors Bryllup eller Fædrene=Arnen)*, 18

Finale in *The White Rose, or The Summer in Bretagne (Den hvide Rose eller Sommeren i Bretagne)*, 110

Finale (uncredited, 18.7.1839), 55

Finale in *Zulma, or The Crystal Palace (Zulma eller: Krystalpaladset)* (Act III, score no. 23), 150

Finale Gallop ('Bouquet Royal Galop') in *'Bouquet Royal', Divertissement* (27.1.1870), 358

Finale Gallop in *Forward! National Divertissement in four Tableaux (Framåt! National-Divertissement i 4 tablåer)* (Score no. 13, 7.11.1862), 281

Finale Gallop in *The King's Corps of Volunteers on Amager, (Episode from 1808) (Livjægerne paa Amager, (Episode fra 1808))* (Score no. 16), 371

Finale Gallop in *Napoli or The Fisher and His Bride (Napoli eller Fiskeren og hans Brud* (Act III, score no. 4), 72

Finaledands in *The New Penelope, or The Spring Festival in Athens (Den nye Penelope eller Foraarsfesten i Athenen)* (Act II, score no. 12), 100

Finale/Pas de six in *La Somnambule, ou l'Arrivée d'un nouveau seigneur (Sövngjængersken)* (Act I, score no. 7 C, 2.10.1868), 338

Flower Dance (Blomsterdands) (20.10.1847), 112

Flower Dance (Blomsterdands) in *The Festival in Albano (Festen i Albano* (1.1.1869), 343

Flower Dance (Blomsterdands) in *The Flower Festival in Genzano (Blomsterfesten i Genzano)* (Scene 12), 423

Flower Festival Pas de deux, 187, 189

'Folie, La' in *Le Carnaval de Venise, ou Constance à l'Epreuve (Carnevalet i Venedig eller Kjærlighed paa Prøve)* (L. Milon/P. Larcher), 371

'Fragment of the ballet La Somnambule' ('Fragment af Balletten Søvngængersken') (14.6.1865), 308

Fransk Storm=Marche (M. Gérard, 14.5.1871), 376

Frischka in *Dance Divertissement (Divertissement af Dands)* (31.10.1870), 368

Frisckha in *In the Carpathians (I Karpatherne)* (Act III, score no. 30), 196

Funeral March in *Richard II (Konung Richard den Andre)* (Act V, score no. 15), 293

Funeral March (Sørge musik) in *Hagbarth and Signe (Hagbarth og Signe)* (Act V, 20.9.1849), 131

Gallop in *Maritana, Divertissement in form of a Carnival scene (Divertissement i Form af en Carnevals=Scene)*, 101

Gallop (Galopp) in *Il Trovatore (Troubadouren)* (Act III, 10.9.1865), 308

Gallopade in *A Children's Party, New Divertissement (En Børnefest, nyt Divertissement)* (23.10.1844), 88

Gallopade in *The Isle of Phantasy (Phantasiens Øe)* (Act I, score no. 4), 45

Gallopade in *The Isle of Phantasy (Phantasiens Øe)* (Act II, score no. 7), 55

Gallopade in *The Tyroleans (Tyrolerne)* (7.2.1842), 71

'Galop' in *Arcona* (Act I, scene 3, score nos. 4–5), 407

Galop militaire (uncredited, 21.1.1859), 229

'Galopp' in *Hothouse Flowers (Blommor i drifbänk)*, 276

Galopin=Finale in *Zulma, or The Crystal Palace (Zulma eller: Krystalpaladset)* (Act III, score no. 23), 150

'Gamles Dands, De' in *The King's Corps of Volunteers on Amager, (Episode from 1808) (Livjægerne paa Amager, (Episode fra 1808))* (Score no. 11), 371

'Gavotta' in *Romeo and Giulietta (Romeo og Giulietta)* (V. Galeotti/A. Bournonville), 24

Gavotte from *The Elves' Hill (Elverhøi)* (23.3.1861), 259

Gipsy Dance (Danse Bohémienne) in *Les Huguenots (Hugenotterne)* (Act III, score no. 14), 85

Gipsy Dance in *In Memory of Weyse, Epilogue with Tableaux (Weyses Minde, Efterspil med Tableauer)* (Scene 5, score no. 7), 398

Gipsy Dance (Zigeunerdands) in *The Feast at Kenilworth (Festen paa Kenilworth)* (Act I finale, score no. 15 b, 5.3.1874), 398

Gipsy Dance (Zigeunerdans) in *Il Trovatore (Troubadouren)* (Act III, 10.9.1865), 308

Gipsy Dance (Zigeuner=Tanz) in *Les Huguenots (Die Hugenotten)* (25.10.1855), 184

Girls from Xeres, The, Spanish National Dance arranged by Mr. Ballet Master S. Lund (Flickorna från Xeres, spansk Nationaldans; arrangeradt af Herr Ballettmästaren Sigurd Lund) (29.10.1858 and 10.9.1865), 222, 308

'Gitana, La' in *Faust* (F. Hoppe, 30.4.1844), 20, 86

'Gladiatorer og Blomsterpiger' in *Pontemolle (An Artists' Party in Rome) (Pontemolle, (Et Kunstnergilde i Rom))* (2nd tableau, score no. 11), 318

'Gondoliera, La' in *Cort Adeler in Venice (Cort Adeler i Venedig)* (Act I, score no. 5), 356

'Grand Ballabile' in *Carita* (P. Borri, 27.7.1855), 181

'Gran Ballabile' in *Robert und Bertrand* (F.-M. Hoguet/P. Taglioni), 176

'Grand Menuet de la Cour!' in *The Masquerade (Maskeraden)* (11.2.1859), 230

Grand pas de deux (uncredited, 28.6.1870), 363

Grand pas de deux (uncredited, 14.5.1871), 376

Grand Pas de deux composed by Mr Ballet Master Bournonville (Stor Pas de deux, Componerad af Hr Ballettmästaren Bournonville) in Robert le Diable (Robert af Normandie) (13.6.1839), 52

Grand Pas de deux from 'Robert le Diable', composed by Bournonville (Grand Pas de deux af 'Robert af Normandiet', componeret af Bournonville) (29.6.1847), 108

Grand Pas de deux from the ballet The Flower Festival (Stor Pas de deux, ur Balletten 'Blomsterfesten') (uncredited, 26.4.1860), 249

Grand Pas de deux from the ballet Waldemar (Stor Pas de deux utur Balletten Waldemar/ Grand Pas de deux du Ballet de Waldemar) (uncredited, 14.6.1839, 18.7.1839), 52, 54

Grand Pas de deux from the ballet Waldemar (Stor 'Pas de deux af Balletten Waldemar') (3.8.1840), 62

Grand Pas de gracieux, (previously danced by the Elssler sisters) (förut dansad af systrarne Elssler) (uncredited, 17.5.1860), 250

Grand solo variation in *Waldemar* (Act I, score no. 10), 33, 164

'Greetings to Jutland', Hussar Dance from the Fair in the Rosenborg Gardens ('Hilsen til Jylland', Husardands fra Rosenborg=Marked) (21.11.1849), 132

'Grotesk dands' in *A Midsummer Night's Dream (En Skjærsommernatsdrøm)* (Act V, score no. 11), 427

'Grupperet Pas de deux, af Fædrelandets Muser, En' (3.11.1840), 64

Guarache in *La Muette de Portici (Den Stumme i Portici)* (Act I), 25, 112, 140, 271

Guarache in *Princess Isabella, or Three Nights at the Court (Prindsesse Isabella eller Tre Aftener ved Hoffet)*, 13

Halling in *The Wedding Festival in Hardanger (Brudefærden i Hardanger)* (Act II, score no. 15), 161, 202

Halling Dance in *The Wedding Festival in Hardanger (Brudefärden i Hardanger)* (Act II, score no. 15, 22.6.1857), 202

'Hamborger=Dands' (8.2.1844), 84

'Hamborgerdands' in *The Tyroleans (Tyrolerne)* (8.2.1844), 84

Hamburg Dance, Pas de deux performed in

costumes of the Vierländers (*Hamborger=Dands, Pas de deux i Vierländer-Costume* (uncredited, 18.12.1844), 84

Hamburg-Dance (Hamborger=Dands) (uncredited, 18.12.1844), 89

'*Hanedands*' in *The Masquerade (Maskeraden)* (12.12.1849), 133

'*Hanedandsen*' in *The Masquerade (Maskeraden)* (11.2.1859), 230

Hermanas de Sevilla, Las (uncredited, 4.12.1872), 387

Hermanas de Sevilla, Las in *The Danes in China (De Danske i China)* (26.2.1865), 307

'*Hermanas de Sevilla, Las*', *Spanish Character Dance (spansk Characteerdands)* (6.7.1852, 25.7.–27.7.1852), 156

Hermanas, Las, Spanish Charactercerdance (Spansk Characters-Dans) (uncredited, 8.12.1852), 283

Hermanas de Sevilla, Las, Spanish Dance (Spansk Dands) (4.6.1851, 2.11.1851, 29.11.1867), 148, 149, 330

Hilda's Dream in *A Folk Tale (Et Folkesagn)* (Act I, score no. 10), 169

Hilda's solo variations in *A Folk Tale (Et Folkesagn)* (Act II, score no. 12, 3.4.1871), 374

'*Holbergs Optog*' in *From the Last Century (Fra det forrige Aarhundrede)* (Scene 7, score no. 9), 414

'*Holmen's Old Guard*', *Dance for Sailor's children* ('*Holmens faste Stok*', *Dands for Matrosbørn*) (20.5.1849), 128, 129

Hornpipe from *The Fishermen (Fiskerne)* (18.12.1848), 121

·*Hornpipe* in *The Isle of Phantasy (Phantasiens Øe)* (Act I, score no. 10), 45

Hungarian Dance (Ungarsk Dands) in *Gustav III (Gustav den Tredie)*, 124

Hungarian hussar solo (Ant. Bournonville), 78

Hussar Dance (16.8.1849–18.8.1849), 129

Indian War Dance in *Far from Denmark, or: A Costume Ball on Board (Fjernt fra Danmark eller: et Costumebal ombord)* (Act II), 249

'*Indlagt Contradands C dur*' in *Faust* (8.12.1849), 133

Jaleo de Xeres, El (uncredited, 29.6.1847), 108

Jaleo de Xeres, El, in '*Divertissement from The Toreador*' ('*Divertissement af Toréadoren*') (11.6.1852), 154

Jaleo de Xerxes, El, in *The Toreador (Toréadoren)* (Act I, score no. 6), 65

Jaleo de Xeres (Pas de deux) (27.1.1870), 358

Jaleo de Xeres, Spanish Dance (Spansk Dans) (uncredited, 16.10.1863), 294

Jaleo de Xeres, El, (Spanish National Dance) (Spansk Nationaldans) (uncredited, 12.6.1839), 51

Jaleo de Xeres, El, (Spanish National Dance) (El Jaleo de Xeras (Spansk Nationaldans)) (uncredited, 8.7.1839), 54

'*Jaleo de Xerxes, El*', 47

Jaleo de Xerxes, El [sic] in *La Muette de Portici (Den Stumme i Portici)* (uncredited, 24.11.1839), 57

Jaleo del Toreador (uncredited, 28.8.1841), 68

Jaleo di Xeres, El, Spanish Dance (spansk Dands) (uncredited, 29.11.1838), 47

Jaleo from the ballet The Toreador (Jaleo af Balletten Toréadoren) (9.1.1842), 71

Jaleo in *Maritana, Divertissement in form of a Carnival scene (Divertissement i Form af en Carnevals=Scene)*, 101

Jester Dance (Narredandsen) in *Arcona* (Act II, scene 5), 411

'*Je suis la Bayadère*' in *The Toreador (Toréadoren)* (Act I, score no. 7), 65

'*Jomfruernes Brudedands*' in *Arcona* (Act II, scene 3), 410

'*Jægerdands*' in *The Kermesse in Brüges, or The Three Gifts (Kermessen i Brügge eller: De tre Gaver)* (Act II, score no. '11', or '11½'), 312

'*Kehraus!*' in *The Masquerade (Maskeraden)* (11.2.1859), 230

'*Kör*' or *Czardas* in *In the Carpathians (I Karpatherne)* (Act III, score no. 27), 196

'*Lampe, La, Pas de 3 Gallenberg 4.me et dernière Edition Mr. Paul &c.*' in *Aladin, ou La Lampe merveilleuse*, 18

'*Maisang med Dands*' in *The Treasure of Claus Rigmand (Claus Rigmands Skat)*, 231

Manchegas in *The Guerilla Band (Guerillabanden)*, 24

March from the Act I finale of *La Fille du regiment* (10.11.1860), 256

March in *The Childhood of Erik Menved (Erik Menveds Barndom)*, 79

March in *Gustaf Wasa* (Act III, scene 3), 285

March in *Hagbarth and Signe (Hagbarth og Signe)* (Act I, 20.9.1849), 131

March (Marsch) in *The Slanderer (Smädeskrifvaren, eller: Vänner och Ovänner)* (Act I, scene 4), 275

March in *Undine* (Act II, score no. 6), 76

Marche funèbre in *The New Penelope, or The Spring Festival in Athens (Den nye Penelope eller Foraarsfesten i Athenen)*, 100

Marche sacrée in *L'Etoile du Nord (Der Nordstern)* (Act II, score no. 13), 185

'*Marcia*' in *Don Quixote at Camacho's Wedding (Don Quixote ved Camachos Bryllup)*, 38

Maritana, (Spanish Gipsy Dance) (Spansk Zigeuner-Dands) (16.12.1846), 99

'*Marsch*' in *Hothouse Flowers (Blommor i drifbänk)* (Act I finale, scene 14), 276

'*Marsch und Eingang des Königs*' in *La Juive (Die Jüdin)* (Act I finale), 184

'*Matrosdans*' (25.6.1847), 107

'*Matrosdands*' in *The Harvest Festival (Høstgildet)* (Ant. Bournonville?), 45

Mazurka (uncredited, 12.8.1840), 63

Mazurka in *Faust* (1842), 20

Mazurka in *Russian National Dance (Russisk Nationaldands)* (1.6.1838), 44

'*Mazurka*', *Russian National Dance* ('*Mazurka*', *russisk Nationaldands*) (31.7.1840), 62

Menuetto in *The Kermesse in Brüges, or The Three Gifts (Kermessen i Brügge eller: De tre Gaver)* (Act II, score no. 12), 144

'*Menuetto*' in *The Masquerade (Maskeraden)* (12.12.1849 and 31.10.1875), 134, 414

'*Menuetto von Tyboe*' in *The Masquerade (Maskeraden)* (12.12.1849), 134

Militaïr Polka (8.8.1847), 109

Militair-Polka in *The King's Corps of Volunteers on Amager, (Episode from 1808) (Livjægerne paa Amager, (Episode fra 1808))* (Score no. 12), 371

'*Military Dance by Bournonville*' ('*Militairdands af Bournonville*') (8.8.1847), 109

Military Polka (Militär-Polka) (12.6.1860), 252 (2.6.1848), 118

'*Military Polka, Character dance in Hungarian style*' ('*Militair Polka*' *Characteerdands i ungarsk Stiil*') (9.6.1852), 154

Minuet (also named '*Dands*') in *The King on Fuurland (Kongen paa Fuurland)*, 195

Minuet from *The Elves' Hill (Elverhøi)* (Act V), 90, 259

Minuet from *Nina, ou La Folle par Amour* (10.11.1860), 255

Minuet in *The Bewitched (Den Bjergtagne/Den Bergtagna)* (Act I, score no. 2), 416

Minuet in *The Mountain Hut, or Twenty Years (Fjeldstuen eller: Tyve Aar)* (Act I, score no. 7), 311

Minuet (Menuet) in *Bellman, or the Polish Dance at Grönalund (Bellman, eller Polskan på Grönalund)* (11.6.1847, 21.4.1858), 106

Minuet (Menuetto) in *Il Dissoluto Punito, ossia il Don Giovanni (Don Juan)* (Act I finale, scene 20), 117, 160

Minuet (Menuet) in *A Folk Tale (Et Folkesagn)* (Act I, score no. 3), 169

Minuet (Menuet) in *Little Kirsten (Liden Kirsten)* (Score no. 9), 113

Minuet (Menuet) in *The Lucky Wheel or The Last Number-Lottery Office (Lykkens Hjul eller Den sidste Tallotteri=Collecteur)* (Act I, score no. 8), 116

Minuet (Menuet) in *Gustav III (Gustav den Tredie)* (Act III, score no. 5), 124 (Act V, score no. '10½'), 124

Minuet (Minuetto) in *Marshal Stig (Marsk Stig)* (Act I, score no. 1), 136

Minuet in *The Treasure of Claus Rigmand (Claus Rigmands Skat)* (Act V), 231

Molinaski in *The King's Corps of Volunteers on Amager, (Episode from 1808) (Livjægerne paa Amager, (Episode fra 1808))* (Score no. 14), 371

'*Mückentanz*' in *Die Lustigen Weiber von Windsor (De lystige Koner i Windsor)* (Act III, score no. 15), 327

Najade, La, in *Napoli, oder: Der Fischer und seine Braut (Napoli eller Fiskeren og hans Brud)* (31.1.1856), 187

New Hamburg-Scottish, Character Dance (Ny Hamborger=Skotsk, Characteerdands) in *The Tyroleans (Tyrolerne)* (8.2.1844), 85

New Jaleo de Xeres 'Le Domino Noir', Music by Auber (Nye Jaleo de Xeres 'Den sorte Domino', Musik af Auber), 57

New Pas de deux arranged by Mr. Ballet Master Bournonville (Ny Pas de deux arrangeret af Hr. Balletmester Bournonville) (14.10.1841), 68

New Pas de deux composed by Mazilier, music by Fessy (Ny Pas de deux, componeret af Mazilier, Musikken af Fessy) (8.9.1842), 76

New Pas de deux composed by Mr. Ballet Master

Bournonville (Ny Pas de deux componeret af Hr. Balletmester Bourmnonville) in Robert le Diable (Robert af Normandiet) (5.12.1841), 70

New Pas de deux composed by Mr. Dance Director Bournonville (Ny Pas de deux, componeret af Hr. Dandsedirecteur Bournonville) (23.9.1834), 25

New Pas de deux in Act I of La Muette de Portici (2.9.1873), 394

New Pas de deux (Ny Pas de deux) in Faust (F. Lefèbvre, 17.10.1842), 77

New Pas de deux (Ny Pas de deux) in The Festival in Albano (Festen i Albano) (F. Lefèbvre, 22.1.1842), 71

New Pas de trois, (Debut.) arranged by Balletmaster Sigurd Lund (En af Herr Ballet- mästaren Sigurd Lund arrangerad ny Pas de Trois, (Debut.)) (16.3.1857), 199

New Scenic Pas de deux (Ny scenisk Pas de deux) in The Tyroleans (Tyrolerne) (F. Lefèbvre, 8.2.1844), 84

New Scenic Pas de deux in Spanish style named: La Sevilliana. (En ny scenisk Pas de deux i spansk Stiil, kaldet: La Sevilliana) in The Danes in China (De Danske i China) (F. Lefèbvre, 28.1.1842), 71

Norwegian Spring Dance (Norsk Springedans) (21.11.1849), 132

Norwegian Spring Dance (Norsk Springedans) (uncredited, 12.3.1850), 136

Norwegian Spring Dance (Norsk Springdands) (9.6.1853), 163

Norwegian Spring Dance (Norsk Spring-Dans) (8.6.1860), 251

'Norwegian Spring Dance' ('Norsk Springdands') (7.6.1865), 307

Norwegian Spring Dance (Norsk Springedans) in Old Memories, or A Magic Lantern (Gamle Minder eller En Laterna magica), 121

Norwegian Spring Dance (Norsk Springdands) in The Whims of Cupid and the Ballet- master Amors og Balletmesterens Luner) (V. Galeotti), 121

No. III/Pas de deux/af Balletten/Faust (29.6.1852), 155

No. 6./Pas de deux/af Balletten/Sövn- gjængersken (18.6.1852), 155

'No. 8 Final/Ballet och Chör' in Le Roman d'Elvire (Drottning Elviras Saga) (26.4.1864), 305

'No. 16 Tanz Tacet/Tanz Zigeuner/La Tarentella/Tanz Musik/Gregorius' in Les Huguenots (Die Hugenotten) (25.10.1855), 185

No. 61./Pas de deux/af/Faust. (9.6.1847), 106

Nuovo passo a due composto dal signor Bournonville in Quadro II of S. Taglioni's historical ballet d'action in eight parts Marco Visconti (26.6.1841), 67

Nuptial March (Bryllupsmarsch) in Undine (Act IV, score no. 9), 76

Nuptial March (Cortège de Noce) in Les Huguenots (Hugenotterne) (Act III, score no. 19), 85

'Nÿ Pas' in Hermann von Unna, 31

'Nye Dands med Tableaux, En', 99

Offrande' in Hertha's Offering (Herthas Offer), 42

'Offringsdandsen' in Arcona (Act III, scene 2), 410

Old Age and Folly (mimetic waltz) in Pontemolle (An Artists' Party in Rome) (Pontemolle, (Et Kunstnergilde i Rom)) (2nd tableau, score no. 15), 317, 413

'Optogsmarsch' in Pontemolle (An Artists' Party in Rome) (Pontemolle, (Et Kunstnergilde i Rom)) (2nd tableau, score nos. 8, and 9), 317

Pantomime scene and Ballet divertissement in La Juive (Die Jüdin)
(Act III, score no. 14), 83
(Act III, score no. 14, 4.1.1869), 344

Pantomime scene in Iphigénie en Tauride (Iphigenia paa Tauris) (Act II, scene 5, score nos. 14–15), 400

Papillon, Le (Sommerfuglen) (uncredited, 14.5.1871), 376

Parisian Polka, Social Dance, (Pariser=Polka, Selskabsdands) (8.2.1845), 89

'Pas af Grækere og Grækerinder' in The New Penelope, or The Spring Festival in Athens (Den nye Penelope, eller Foraarsfesten i Athen) (Act II, score no. 9), 100, 137

Pas de bouquets (composed by Albert, the music by Adam) (componeret af Albert, Musiken af Adam) (1.11.1842), 77

Pas de bouquets from the ballet:'La Jolie Fille de Gand' (ur Balletten 'La jolie fille de Gand') (uncredited, 25.6.1847), 106

Pas de caractère in Die Gazelle von Bassora (Act I, score no. 3), 181

Pas de cinq from Abdallah (Act III, score no. 15), 195

Pas de cinq from the ballet 'Abdallah' arranged by Mr. Ballet Master Sigurd Lund (En af Herr Ballettmästaren S. Lund arragerad Pas de cinq ur balletten 'Abdallah') (12.2.1857), 195

Pas de cinq in A Folk Tale (Et Folkesagn) (Act III, score no. 20), 167

Pas de cinq in The Bewitched (Den Bjergtagne/ Den Bergtagna) (Act III (score no. 14, originally no. 18 (2)), 416

Pas de cinq in La Gioventú di Enrico V (Henrik den Femtes Ungdom), 18

Pas de cinq in Napoli or The Fisher and His Bride (Napoli eller Fiskeren og hans Brud (Act III, score no. 2), 72

Pas de cinq in Paul et Virginie (Paul og Virginie), 16

Pas de cinq in Robert le Diable (Robert af Normandiet) (F. Taglioni), 114

Pas de cinq in Waldemar (Act I, score no. 5), 164, 321, 326

Pas de cinq (uncredited) in The Raven (Ravnen eller Broderprøven), 22

Pas de Clochette in La Clochette ou Le Diable Page, La (Alfen som Page) (P. Funck, 30.10.1857), 208

Pas d'Ecole in The Conservatoire, or A Proposal of Marriage through the Newspaper (Conservatoriet, eller Et Avisfrieri) (Act I, score no. 3), 126, 200, 310

'Pas de Danse' in Waldemar, 32

Pas de debut, arranged by Mr. Court Ballet Master Bournonville (arrangeret af Hr.

Hofballetmester Bournonville) (4.6.1851), 147

Pas de deux (F. Hoppe, 30.10.1857), 208

Pas de deux (uncredited)
(5.6.1835), 31
(7.11.1837), 41
(6.1.1838), 41
(28.2.1840), 57
(27.4.1840), 59
(19.1.1841), 66
(17.12.1842), 78
(22.12.1844), 89
(23.2.1847), 100
(21.9.1849), 131
(24.4.1851), 146
(3.2.1852), 149
(11.9.1852), 159
(29.11.1852), 159
(14.3.1853), 162
(2.6.1855), 179
(11.6.1855), 179
(14.3.1856), 190
(15.10.1856), 193
(18.10.1857), 205
(18.2.1861), 258
(12.10.1866), 320
(28.11.1866), 322
(14.3.1867), 323
(16.9.1868), 338
(13.11.1868), 341
(7.1.1869), 345
(7.10.1869), 352
(28.1.1870), 360
(9.1.1871), 369
(4.12.1872), 387
(27.4.1874), 400
(7.11.1874), 404
(9.2.1875), 405
(28.11.1879), 428

Pas de deux (uncredited) in Le Carnaval de Venise, ou Constance à l'Epreuve (Carna- valet i Venedig eller Kjærlighed paa Prøve) (20.12.1832), 22, 317

Pas de deux (uncredited) in Cendrillon (Cendrillon eller Den lille grønne Sko) (17.12.1837), 41

Pas de deux (uncredited) in Dieu et La Bayadère, ou La Courtisane amoureuse, Le (Liebende Bayadère oder Der Gott und die Bayadere, Die) (20.7.1843), 81

Pas de deux (uncredited) in A Divertissement in Oriental Style (Et Divertissement i Orientalsk stiil) (26.9.1829), 12, 66

Pas de deux (uncredited) in Le Domino Noir (Eventyret paa Maskeraden eller Den sorte Domino) (29.1.1839), 47

Pas de deux (uncredited) in Gustave III, ou Le Bal Masqué (5.7.1843), 81

Pas de deux (uncredited) in Hermann von Unna (17.5.1835), 30

Pas de deux (uncredited) in Jeannot et Colin (Jeannot og Colin eller Fosterbrødrene) (1.9.1829), 8

Pas de deux (uncredited) in Waldemar (27.6.1838), 44

Pas de deux (uncredited) in Zephyr and Flora (Zephyr og Flora) (22.12.1830), 17

Pas de deux in La Belle au Bois dormant (P. Gardel?), 26

Pas de deux in Cendrillon (Cendrillon eller Den

lille grønne Sko) (Act III, scene 10 (score no. 16), 190

Pas de deux in *The Childhood of Erik Menved (Erik Menveds Barndom)* (Act II, score no. 16), 79

Pas de deux in *Don Quixote at Camacho's Wedding (Don Quixote ved Camachos Bryllup)*
(Act I, score no. 4, *Boléro*), 38
(Act I, score no. 5), 38

Pas de deux in *Faust*
(25.4.1832), 20
(8.12.1849), 133

Pas de deux in *Faust* (F. Hoppe, 30.4.1844), 86

Pas de deux in *The Fatherland's Muses (Fædrelandets Muser)* (Score no. 5), 58

Pas de deux in *Das Fest in Albano (Festen i Albano)* (P. Borri, 6.2.1855), 176

Pas de deux in *The Festival in Albano (Festen i Albano)* (F. Lefèbvre, 22.1.1842), 71

Pas de deux in *The Festival in Albano (Festen i Albano)*
(Score no. 9), 71, 174
(Score no. 12, 5.5.1857), 200

Pas de deux in *Flore et Zéphire* (Ch.-L. Didelot), 13–14, 28

Pas de deux in *The Flower Festival in Genzano (Blomsterfesten i Genzano)* (Score no. 12), 423

Pas de deux in *From the Last Century (Fra det forrige Aarhundrede)* (Scene 5, score no. 5), 414

Pas de deux in *Die Gazelle von Bassora (Abdallah)* (P. Borri, Act III, score no. 16), 181

Pas de deux in *Hertha's Offering (Herthas Offer)*
(Score no. 4), 42
(Score no. 5), 42

Pas de deux in *The Isle of Phantasy (Phantasiens Øe)* (Act II), 55

Pas de deux in *Jean*, 32

Pas de deux in *The Kermesse in Brüges, or The Three Gifts (Kermessen i Brügge eller: De tre Gaver)*
(Act I, score no. 2), 145, 171, 312
(Act II, score no. '11', 19.11.1865), 312
(Act II, score no. '11½', 8.12.1872), 387
(Act II, score no. '12 b', 2.9.1873), 394

Pas de deux in *La Muette de Portici (Den Stumme i Portici)*
(Act I, 23.9.1834), 25, 112, 140, 271
(Act I, 2.9.1873), 394

Pas de deux in *Napoli, oder: Der Fischer und seine Braut (Napoli eller Fiskeren og hans Brud)* (L. Vienna, 31.1.1856), 187

Pas de deux in *The New Penelope, or The Spring Festival in Athens (Den nye Penelope, eller Foraarsfesten i Athen)* (Act II, score no. 8), 100

Pas de deux in *Nina, ou La Folle par amour (Nina, eller Den vanvittige af Kjærlighed)*
(Act I, score no. 9 C), 26
(Act I, F major), 26, 124

Pas de deux in *L'Oriflamme* (A. Vestris), 26–7

Pas de deux in *The Peasant Wedding or The Corsairs (Bondbrölloppet eller Corsarerne)* (L. J. M. Deland), 126

Pas de deux in *Le Pré aux clercs (Klerkevænget)*, 28, 29

Pas de deux in *Princess Isabella, or Three Nights at the Court (Prindsesse Isabella eller Tre Aftener ved Hoffet)*, 13

Pas de deux in *La Révolte aux sérail* (F. Taglioni), 28

Pas de deux in *Robert le Diable (Robert af Normandiet)* (Act II), 114

Pas de deux in *Robert und Bertrand* (8.3.1856), 189

'*Pas de deux*' in *Romeo and Giulietta (Romeo og Giulietta)* (V. Galeotti/A. Bournonville), 24

Pas de deux in *Le Rossignol* (A. Vestris), 26, 28

Pas de deux in *La Somnambule, ou l'Arrivée d'un nouveau seigneur (Søvngjængersken)* (Act I, score no. 7 B, 21.9.1829), 10

Pas de deux in *La Sylphide (Sylphiden)*
(31.7.1840), 62
(Act I, 17.9.1862), 278
(Act II, D major), 36

Pas de deux in *Der Toreador (spanische Stierbekämpfer) und die Tänzerin (Toréadoren)* (10.7.1843), 81

Pas de deux in *The Tyroleans*
(score no. 5), 29, 85
(score no. 12), 29, 85

Pas de deux in *La Vestale* (P. Gardel), 30

Pas de deux in *The Veteran or The Hospitable House (Veteranen eller Det gjæstfrie Tag)*, 34

Pas de deux in *Waldemar*
(Act I), 33, 44
(Act II), 33, 164, 321

Pas de deux in *The Whims of Cupid (Amor's skämt)*, 257

Pas de deux in *The White Rose, or The Summer in Bretagne (Den hvide Rose eller Sommeren i Bretagne)*, 110

Pas de deux in *Zampa, ou La Fiancée de Marbre (Zampa eller Marmorbruden)*, 19

Pas de deux af Balletten Faust. (29.6.1852), 155

Pas de deux af Balletten 'Sylphiden. (9.6.1852), 153

'*Pas de deux af Balletten Toreadoren*' (10.7.1843?), 81

'*Pas de deux af den Stumme*' in *La Muette de Portici (Den Stumme i Portici)*, 25

'*Pas de deux af Herr Bournonville og Jfr. Fjeldsted*' (9.5.1843), 80

'*Pas de deux af Hr. Funck og Jfr. Norberg*' (14.3.1847), 101

'*Pas de deux af Prindsesse Isabella*', 41

'*Pas de deux af Robert*', 70

'*Pas de deux* ('*af Robert af Normandie*')' (13.11.1856), 194

Pas de deux, after Taglioni (Pas de deux, efter Taglioni) (uncredited)
(6.7.1840), 61
(10.8.1840), 62

'*Pas de deux af Zampa*', 19

'*Pas de deux* (*à la Taglioni*)', 50

Pas de deux à la Taglioni (6.11.1845), 93

Pas de deux, à la Taglioni (uncredited)
(7.1.1841), 66
(9.11.1850), 141

Pas de deux à la Taglioni arranged by Mr. Ballet Master Bournonville (arrangerad af Herr Balletmästaren Bournonville) (6.11.1845), 93

(26.5.1847), 104

Pas de deux à la Taglioni composed by Mr. Court Ballet Master Bournonville (componeret af Hr. Hofballetmester Bournonville) (13.3.1851), 143
(9.6.1852), 153

Pas de deux (*à la Taglioni*) in *La Sylphide* (uncredited, 27.9.1842), 77

Pas de deux and *Gallopade* in *The Isle of Phantasy (Phantasiens Øe)* (Act II, score no. 7), 69

Pas de deux and *Gallopade* from the ballet *Isle of Phantasy (Pas de deux og Galopade af Balletten 'Phantasiens Øe')* (1.12.1841), 69

Pas de deux and *Polka* composed by A. Bournonville *(Pas de deux och Polka componerad af A. Bournonville)* (4.5.1848), 117

Pas de deux and *Polka* from the ballet '*Le Diable à quatre*' by Mazilier *(Pas de deux og Polka af Balletten 'le diable à quatre' af Mazilier)* (11.5.1847), 103

Pas de deux and *Polka* from the ballet '*Le Diable à quatre*', composed by Mazilier *(Pas de deux og Polka af Balletten 'le diable en [sic] quatre', componeret af Mazilier)* (25.6.1847), 108

Pas de deux and *Polka* from the ballet: '*Le Diable à quatre*' *(Pas de deux og Polka af Balletten: 'le diable à quatre')* (uncredited, 6.6.1851), 148

Pas de deux and *Saltarello* in *Pontemolle (An Artists' Party in Rome) (Pontemolle, (Et Kunstnergilde i Rom))* (2nd tableau, score no. 10), 317

'*Pas de deux arr: af Balletm: Lund*' (13.11.1856), 194

'*Pas de deux, arr: par Bournonville/per [sic] Faust*' (9.6.1847), 106

Pas de deux arranged after Taglioni (En Pas de deux arrangeret efter Taglioni) (4.10.1839), 55

Pas de deux arranged by Ballet Master Bournonville (arrangeret af Balletmester Bournonville) (14.3.1847), 101

Pas de deux, arranged by Mr. Ballet Master Bournonville (arrangered af Herr Ballettmästaren Bournonville) in *Robert le Diable (Robert af Normandie)* (28.6.1847), 108

Pas de deux by Ballet Master Bournonville (Pas de deux, af Balletmästaren Bournonville) (19.6.1839), 53

Pas de deux arranged by Mr Ballet Master Sigurd Lund (En af Herr Balletmästaren Sigurd Lund arrangerad Pas de deux) (13.11.1856), 194

Pas de deux (by Taglioni) (Pas de deux (Af Taglioni)) (F. Taglioni/A. Bournonville) (5.6.1839), 50
(5.7.1839), 53

'*Pas de deux Carnavalet*' in *Le Carnaval de Venise, ou Constance à l'Epreuve (Carnavalet i Venedig eller Kjærlighed paa Prøve)*, 22

Pas de deux composed by Mr. Ballet Master Bournonville (componeret af Hr. Balletmester Bournonville)
(18.11.1834), 29
(3.3.1836), 34
(12.9.1836), 35
(17.9.1836), 35

(21.2.1837), 38
(3.10.1837), 39
(10.10.1837), 39
(12.10.1837), 40
(5.7.1838), 44
(3.9.1838), 45
(15.11.1838), 47
(17.12.1838), 47
(12.3.1839), 49
(15.10.1839), 55
(26.10.1839), 55
(8.11.1839), 57
(30.10.1840), 64
(3.11.1840), 64
(22.11.1840), 64
(1.2.1841), 66
(3.9.1841), 68
(26.10.1841), 69
(9.5.1843), 80
(11.10.1843), 83
(27.12.1850), 142
(7.9.1852), 158
(1.9.1857), 203
(28.10.1860), 254

Pas de deux D dur (Sylphiden)' in *Faust*
(8.12.1849), 133
Pas de deux de la rose in *Flore et Zéphire* (Ch.-L.
Didelot), 14
'Pas de deux de retour' (14.10.1841), 68
'Pas de deux de Waldemar', 52, 54, 62, 67–8
*'Pas de deux en fa/de m° Perrot et Mlle Taglioni/
par m° Schneizhöfer'* in *Le Rossignol* (A.
Vestris), 26
'Pas de deux for Jfr. Norberg' (23.2.1847), 100
*'Pas de deux for Jfr. Verning [sic] og Hr Hoppe i
Nina'* in *Nina, ou La Folle par amour*
(Nina, eller Den vanvittige af Kjærlighed),
27
Pas de deux français in *The Whims of Cupid
(Amor's skämt)* (29.1.1861), 257
'Pas de deux (Frk Cetti og Hr Krum)'
(7.10.1869), 352
*Pas de deux, from the ballet 'The Veteran',
composed by Mr. Ballet Master Bournonville,
(En Pas de deux, af Balletten 'Veteranen',
componeret af Hr. Balletmester Bournonville)*
(27.4.1836), 34
Pas de deux from *The Isle of Phantasy* in *The
Whims of Cupid (Amor's skämt)*
(29.1.1861), 257
*Pas de deux from La Muette de Portici (Pas de
deux ur Den Stumma)* (uncredited,
8.7.1839), 54
*Pas de deux from 'La Muette de Portici' (Pas de
deux af 'Den Stumme i Portici')* (uncredited, 2.5.1849), 126
*Pas de deux from La Muette de Portici (Pas de
deux af den Stumme i Portici)* (uncredited,
20.5.1849), 128
*Pas de deux from La Muette de Portici, composed
by Albert (Pas de deux af den Stumme i
Portici, componeret af Albert)* (2.7.1847),
109
*Pas de deux from La Muette de Portici, composed
by Mr. Ballet Master Bournonville (Pas de
deux, af Den Stumma från Portici,
componerad af Herr Ballettmästaren
Bournonville)* (16.6.1847), 106
*'Pas de deux from La Muette de Portici'
composed by Mr. Bournonville ('Pas de deux*

*af den Stumme i Portici' componeret af Hr
Bournonville)* (15.6.1852), 154
*Pas de deux from 'The New Penelope '(Pas de
deux af 'Den nye Penelope')* (27.5.1847),
104
*Pas de deux from Robert le Diable (Pas de deux
af 'Robert af Normandiet')* (5.12.1841), 70
*'Pas de deux' (from the ballet Faust) composed by
Mr. Bournonville ('Pas de deux (af Balletten
Faust) componeret af Hr Bournonville)*
(29.6.1852), 155
*Pas de deux from the ballet Nina (Pas de deux
utur Balletten Nina)* (uncredited,
12.7.1839), 54
*Pas de deux from the ballet 'La Sylphide' (Pas de
deux af Balletten 'Sylphiden')* (28.10.1843),
83
Pas de deux gracieux (uncredited,
17.11.1858), 223
Pas de deux gracieux (uncredited, 5.8.1870),
366
'Pas de deux Grahns Debut' in *Nina, ou La Folle
par amour (Nina, eller Den vanvittige af
Kjærlighed)*, 26
'Pas de deux i Hermann v: Unna', 30
Pas de deux ('Jægerdands') in *The Kermesse in
Brüges, or The Three Gifts (Kermessen i
Brügge eller: De tre Gaver)* (Act II, score
no. '11', or '11½'), 145, 387
'Pas de deux/Nel Gran Ballo/TELEMACO' (P.
Gardel), 10
*Pas de deux (new) by Mr. Ballet Master
Bournonville (Pas de deux (ny) af Hr.
Balletmester Bournonville)* (19.6.1854),
172
'Pas de deux oriental', 12, 49
'Pas de deux, Polka et Mazurka' in *Le Médecin
malgré lui (Läkaren mot sin Vilja)*
(14.12.1863), 297
'Pas de deux. Retour de Fjeldsted' (11.10.1843),
83
Pas de deux serieux (Passo a due serio)
(uncredited, 29.8.1841), 68
'Pas de deux/La Sylphide/af Mayseder', 36
'Pas de deux/til Faust/af Fædrelandets Muser'
(3.11.1840), 64
'Pas de deux til Herthas Offer', 42
*Pas de Diane (af Balletten 'La Jolie Fille de
Gand' af Albert)*, 77
Pas d'ensemble in *Paul et Virginie (Paul og
Virginie)*, 16
Pas d'ensemble in *The Tyroleans (Tyrolerne)*, 30
'Pas de la Vestale' (P. Gardel/A. Bournon-
ville), 30
'Pas de Polonaise' (uncredited, 18.5.1860),
250
Pas de quatre in *Acclaim to the Graces, New
Divertissement (Gratiernes Hyldning, nyt
Divertissement)* (1.9.1829, 20.9.1847), 10,
111
Pas de quatre in *Aladdin, or The Magic Lantern
(Aladdin eller den forundelige Lampe)*, 49
Pas de quatre in *Das Fest in Albano (Festen i
Albano)* (15.7.1854), 174
Pas de quatre in *A Folk Tale (Et Folkesagn)* Act
III, score no. 20), 167, 169, 210, 328
Pas de quatre in *The Kermesse in Brüges, or The
Three Gifts (Kermessen i Brügge eller: De tre
Gaver)*
(Act II, score no. 12), 144, 177

(Act II, 30.12.1858), 228
Pas de quatre in *Les Mohicans* (A. Guerra), 47
Pas de quatre in *Napoli, oder: Der Fischer und
seine Braut (Napoli eller Fiskeren og hans
Brud)* (L. Gabrielli, 31.1.1856), 187
Pas de quatre in *Napoli or The Fisher and His
Bride (Napoli eller Fiskeren og hans Brud*
(Act III, score no. 2), 72, 156
Pas de quatre in *La Somnambule, ou l'Arrivée
d'un nouveau seigneur (Sövngjængersken)*
(Act I, score no. 7 B, 2.10.1868), 338
Pas de quatre in *Victor's Wedding, or The
Ancestral House (Victors Bryllup eller
Fædrene=Arnen)*, 18
Pas de quatre in *The White Rose, or The Summer
in Bretagne (Den hvide Rose eller Sommeren i
Bretagne)* (Score no. 13), 110
'Pas de quatre af Diamantkorset' (20.3.1847),
101
Pas de sept in *A Folk Tale (Et Folkesagn)* (Act
III, score no. 20), 169, 201, 328
Pas de sept in *Psyche* (Score no. 6), 136
Pas de six in *Astolphe et Joconde, ou Les coureurs
d'aventures* (J. Aumer), 38
Pas de six in *The Childhood of Erik Menved
(Erik Menveds Barndom)*, 80
Pas de six in *Das Diamantkreuz (Diamant-
korset)*, 101
Pas de six in *The Festival in Albano (Festen i
Albano)* (Score no. 7, 5.5.1857,
14.1.1858), 200, 213
Pas de six in *The Flower Festival in Genzano
(Blomsterfesten i Genzano)* (1.5.1877), 423
Pas de six in *Guillaume Tell* (J. Aumer), 29
Pas de six in *Napoli or The Fisher and His Bride
(Napoli eller Fiskeren og hans Brud* (Act III,
score no. 2), 72, 413
Pas de six in *La Somnambule, ou l'Arrivée d'un
nouveau seigneur* (J. Aumer), 10
Pas de six in *La Somnambule, ou l'Arrivée d'un
nouveau seigneur (Sövngjængersken)*, 338
Pas de six in *Waldemar*
(Act I, score no. 5, 19.10.1853), 164, 211
(Act II, score no. '17', 21.11.1866), 321
Pas de soldats in *Guillaume Tell* (J. Aumer),
20
*Pas de solo, after Carlotta Grisi (Pas de solo, efter
Carlotta Grisi)* (17.5.1847), 103
Pas de solo in *The Festival in Albano (Festen i
Albano)* (uncredited, 6.10.1848), 118
Pas de tambourin in *Carita* (P. Borri,
5.9.1855), 181
'Pas de Tambourin' in *La Vestale* (P. Gardel),
16
'Pas de trois' (12.10.1846), 98
Pas de trois (29.5.1854), 171
Pas de trois in *Guillaume Tell (Wilhelm Tell)*
(7.2.1858), 215
Pas de trois (uncredited)
(18.5.1840), 59
(8.4.1848), 117
(4.1.1849), 122
(21.11.1849), 132
(9.2.1851), 142
(14.12.1852), 159
(23.1.1853), 160
(23.1.1854), 166
(13.10.1855), 183
(21.1.1856), 186
(24.10.1860), 254

(28.1.1861), 257

(30.1.1862), 270

(23.11.1865), 315

(18.10.1867), 329

(29.11.1867), 330

(19.12.1869), 353

(10.4.1870), 361

(21.5.1873), 393

(24.1.1874), 397

(20.12.1874), 404

Pas de trois (uncredited) in *The Festival in Albano (Festen i Albano)* (2.6.1841), 67

Pas de trois (uncredited) in *Paul et Virginie, Dance Divertissement after Gardel and A. Bournonville, mounted by Ballet-master S. Lund (Paul och Virginie, Divertissement af Dans, efter Gardel och A. Bournonville, uppsatt af Hr Balletmästaren S. Lund)* (7.2.1858), 215

Pas de trois (uncredited) in *Waldemar* (27.6.1838), 44

Pas de trois in *Aladin, ou La Lampe merveilleuse* (P. Gardel), 7

Pas de trois (Passo a tre) in *L'Arrivo del Gran Signore* (L. Henry), 17

Pas de trois in *Carita* (27.7.1855), 181

Pas de trois in *The Conservatoire, or A Proposal of Marriage through the Newspaper (Conservatoriet, eller Et Avisfrieri)* (Act I, score no. 4), 126, 200, 201, 310 (Act II, score no. 10), 127 (Act II, score no. 9), 201

Pas de trois in *La Dame Blanche (Den hvide Dame)* (Act III, score no. 14), 139

Pas de trois in *Dance Divertissement (Divertissement af Dands)* (31.10.1870), 367

Pas de trois in *Divertissement dansant* (27.7.1855), 181

Pas de trois in *Faust* (1832), 20

Pas de trois in *Die Fee und der Ritter* (Arm. Vestris), 13

Pas de trois in *The Festival in Albano (Festen i Albano)* (score no. 9, 5.5.1857, 14.1.1858), 200, 213 (uncredited, 2.6.1841), 67

Pas de trois in *La Fille mal Gardée* (J. Aumer),

Pas de trois in *From the Last Century (Fra det forrige Aarhundrede)* (Scene 4, score no. 4), 414

Pas de trois in *Guillaume Tell (Wilhelm Tell)*, 76, 346, 396, 415

Pas de trois in *The King's Corps of Volunteers on Amager, (Episode from 1808) (Livjægerne paa Amager, (Episode fra 1808))* (Score no. 13), 371

Pas de trois in *Mars et Vénus ou Les Filets de Vulcain* (J. B. Blache), 126

Pas de trois in *Nina, ou La Folle par amour* (L. Milon), 26

Pas de trois in *Nina, ou La Folle par amour (Nina, eller Den vanvittige af Kjærlighed)*, 26

Pas de trois in *Old Memories, or A Magic Lantern (Gamle Minder eller En Laterna magica)*, 121

Pas de trois in *L'Orgie* (J. Perrot), 40

Pas de trois in *Les Pages du Duc de Vendôme* (J. Aumer), 15

Pas de trois in *Les Pages du Duc de Vendôme (Hertugen af Vendômes Pager)*, 15

Pas de trois in *Le Postillon de Lonjumeau (Postillonen i Lonjumeau)*, 40, 50, 54, 395

Pas de trois in *Preciosa* (Act III, score no. 10), 146

Pas de trois in *Raphael (Rafael)* (Third tableau, score no. 13), 91

Pas de trois in *Robert und Bertrand* (27.7.1855), 181

Pas de trois in *Soldier and Peasant (Soldat of Bonde)*, 12

Pas de trois in *La Somnambule, ou l'Arrivée d'un nouveau seigneur (Sövngjængersken)*, 338

Pas de trois in *La Ventana, Ballet Divertissement (Balletdivertissement)* (6.10.1856), 191

Pas de trois in *Victor's Wedding, or The Ancestral House (Victors Bryllup eller Fædrene=Arnen)*, 191

Pas de trois in *Waldemar* (Act II), 33, 44

Pas de trois/af Balletten/Napoli (2.7.1852), 156

'*Pas de trois af Den nye Penelope*' (8.6.1850), 137

'*Pas de trois af Postillonen*' (28.10.1837), 40, 215

'*Pas de trois af Søvngjængersken*' (8.4.1848), 117

'*Pas de trois arr. af Lund*' (7.2.1858), 215

'*Pas de trois/Cendrillon/2.de Divertissm./Mr. Paul*' in *Cendrillon* (Albert), 10

Pas de trois, composed by Mr. Ballet Master Bournonville (En Pas de trois, componeret af Hr. Balletmester Bournonville) (22.9.1836), 35 (8.9.1849), 130 (17.10.1836), 35 (3.11.1837), 41

Pas de trois composed by Mr. Court Ballet Master Bournonville (componeret af Hr Hofballetmester Bournonville) (26.2.1856), 189 (10.10.1872), 386

'*Pas de trois, dansé dans Cendrillon. Musique: Mozart, arrangée par Schneitzhoeffe[r] [sic]*' (Albert), 38

'*Pas de trois de Coulon*' in *Lydie* (Albert), 10

'*Pas de trois de Mr Paul*' in *La Fille mal Gardée* (J. Aumer), 19

Pas de trois from Le Postillon du Lonjumeau (Pas de trois, utur Postiljonen i Lonjumeau), 54

Pas de trois from Le Postillon de Lonjumeau (Pas de trois utur Postillonen i Lonjumeau) (uncredited, 2.6.1839, 10.7.1839), 50, 54

Pas de trois gracieux (26.12.1866), 323

'*Pas de trois gracieux*' in *The Masquerade (Maskeraden)* (11.2.1859), 230

'*Pas de trois Johansson*', 35

'*Pas de trois (Julius Price)*' (29.5.1854), 171

Pas de trompette in *La Somnambule, ou l'Arrivée d'un nouveau seigneur* (J. Aumer), 11

Pas des jardiniers (11.5.1847), 103

'*Pas des moissonneurs*' in *La Fille mal Gardée* (J. Dauberval/J. Aumer), 20

'*Pas des piqueurs*' or *Vexellands* in *In the Carpathians (I Karpatherne)* (Act III, score no. 29), 196

'*Pas des quatre rosières*' in *The White Rose, or The Summer in Bretagne (Den hvide Rose eller Sommeren i Bretagne)* (Score no. 13), 110

Pas des trois cousines (20.5.1848), 117, 128, 166, 329, 393, 397

'*Pas des trois cousines*' (7.6.1852), 152

Pas des villageois in *La Somnambule, ou l'Arrivée d'un nouveau seigneur* (J. Aumer), 11

Pas du ménéstrel in *Waldemar* (Act II, 29.5.1867), 326

'*Pas-Russe*', 44

Pas seul in *La Jolie Fille de Gand* (Albert), 77

Pas seul de Carlotta (17.5.1847), 103

Pas seul, de Carlotta Grisi/dansé au ballet le diable a quatre (17.5.1847), 104

'*Pas/Solo/v. Carita./in E*' in *Die Gazelle von Bassora (Abdallah)* (5.9.1855), 181

Pas Styrien (27.6.1847), 108

Pas Styrien in *Le Domino Noir (Eventyret paa Maskeraden eller Den sorte Domino)*, 49

'*Pas Styrien/til Den sorte Domino*' in *Le Domino Noir (Eventyret paa Maskeraden eller Den sorte Domino)*, 49

'*Pas/Trois/v. Strebinger*' in *Carita* (27.7.1855), 181

'*Pasdedu/Musica/Del Sig.r Cav:re D. Michele Carafa*' (P. Gardel), 10

Passo nazionale spagnolo detto EL JALEO DEL TOREADOR, composto dal signor Bournonville in G. Briol's two-act comic ballet *L'Istituto delle Fanciulle* (26.6.1841), 67

'*Pastoral – Grupp –*' in *Le Médecin malgré lui (Läkaren mot sin Vilja)* (Act I finale, scene 7), 297

Peasant Dance (Bondedands) in *Little Kirsten (Liden Kirsten)* (Score no. 2), 113

Peasant Dance (Bondedands) in *The Nix (Nøkken)*, 160

Peasant Dance in *A Folk Tale (Et Folkesagn)* (Act I, score no. 2), 169

Performance, A (14.3.1860), 245

'*Pochinelle*' in *The Masquerade (Maskeraden)* (12.12.1849), 133

'*Polacca a Rondo pour Mr. Albert/pas Mr. Albert/Paul et Virginie/par Caraffa*' in *Paul et Virginie* (Albert), 12

'*Polacca a Rondo/Paul et Virginie/par Mr Caraffa*' in *The Homecoming (Hemkomsten)*, 42

Polacca guerriera, Pas de deux, 97

Polichinel (Pulcinello) in *Pontemolle (An Artists' Party in Rome) (Pontemolle, (Et Kunstnergilde i Rom))*, 7, 317

Polka in *The Conservatoire, or A Proposal of Marriage through the Newspaper, The (Conservatoriet, eller Ett Frieri i Tidningarne)* (Act II, score no. 8), 201

Polka in *Gustav III (Gustav den Tredie)*, 124

Polka in *Gustave III, ou Le Bal Masqué* (uncredited, 5.7.1843), 81

Polka in *The Lucky Wheel or The Last Number-Lottery Office (Lykkens Hjul eller Den sidste Tallotteri=Collecteur)*, 116

Polka in *Zulma, or The Crystal Palace (Zulma eller: Krystalpaladset)* (Act III, score no. 23), 150

Polka militaire (Polka, (Militairdands)), 78

Polka militaire (25.6.1847), 107

Polka militaire (5.6.1865), 307

Polka, (Military Dance) (Militairdands) (16.12.1846), 99

Polketta (uncredited, 13.2.1861), 258

Polketta, arranged by A. Bournonville (arranger-ad af A. Bournonville) performed by A. and C. Healey (23.4.1860), 249

Polketta Pas de deux (uncredited) (13.7.1870), 364 (31.10.1858 and 14.12.1863), 222, 297

Polonaise (uncredited) (24.2.1861), 258 (31.3.1859), 231

'*Polonaise*' in *Daniel Hjort* (Act I, scene 11), 299

'*Polonaise*' in *Estrella de Soria* (Act II, scene 9, score no. 21), 275

Polonaise in *The Kermesse in Brüges, or The Three Gifts (Kermessen i Brügge eller: De tre Gaver)* (Act II, score no. 12, 19.11.1865), 315

Polonaise in *The King's Corps of Volunteers on Amager, (Episode from 1808) (Livjægerne paa Amager, (Episode fra 1808))* (Score no. 11), 371

Polonaise in *Kirsten Piil* (Act II, score no. 6), 90

'*Polonaise*' in *Pontemolle (An Artists' Party in Rome) (Pontemolle, (Et Kunstnergilde i Rom))* (2nd tableau, score no. 10), 317

Polonaise in *The Tyroleans (Tyrolerne)*, 30, 85

Polsk Dands in *Bellman, or the Polish Dance at Grönalund (Bellman, eller Polskan på Grönalund)* (11.6.1847), 106,

Polska in *Kirsten Piil* (Act I, score no. 9), 90

'*Polskdands*' in *From the Last Century (Fra det forrige Aarhundrede)* (Scene 6, score no. 8), 414

'*Presto*' in *The Masquerade (Maskeraden)* (12.12.1849), 134

'*Prix de la Danse*' in *La Vestale* (P. Gardel), 30

Procession in *Lucia di Lammermoor (Lucia af Lammermoor)* (Act II finale, score no. 7), 210

Procession in *The Treasure of Claus Rigmand (Claus Rigmands Skat)* (Act V), 231

Processional March ('Bergandarnes Intåg') in *The Bewitched (Den Bjergtagne/Den Bergtagna)* (Act III finale, score no. 14, originally no. 18 (3)), 216

Processional March in *Das Diamantkreuz (Diamantkorset)* (Act I, scene 4, score no. 3), 101

Processional March in *La Juive (Die Jüdin/Jødinden)* (Act I finale, score no. 7), 183 (Act I, score no. 7, 4.1.1869), 344 (Act V, score no. 21), 183 (Act V, score no. 21, 4.1.1869), 344

Processional March (Optog) in *Little Kirsten (Liden Kirsten)* (Score no. 9), 113, 221

Processional March (Optog) in *A New Divertissement (after Holberg's indications) as intermezzo in The Healing Spring (Intermedium, Et nyt Divertissement (efter Holbergs Opgave) i Kildereisen)* (22.5.1859), 237

Projected performance in memory of Adam Oehlenschläger (Idée for en Mindefest for Adam Oehlenschläger) (21.1.1850), 135

Projected series of performances of individual pas and dances at Stockholm's Royal Theatre (May 1840), 59

Proposal Dance, The (Frierdandsen) in *Arcona* (Act I, scene 3, score nos. 4–5), 407

Proposal Dance, The (Frierdandsen) in *The Childhood of Erik Menved (Erik Menveds Barndom)*, 79

Pulcinello in *Pontemolle (An Artists' Party in Rome) (Pontemolle, (Et Kunstnergilde i Rom))* (2nd tableau, score no. 14), 317

'*Purpose*' in *Mary Stuart in Scotland (Maria Stuart i Skotland)* (29.3.1867), 324

Purpose (Dands)' in *Mary Stuart in Scotland (Maria Stuart i Skotland)* (29.3.1867), 324

Quadrille in *Nina, ou La Folle par amour (Nina, eller Den vanvittige af Kjærlighed)*, 27

'*Quadrille af holbergske Figurer, En*' in *The King's Corps of Volunteers on Amager (Livjægerne paa Amager)*, 373

Quadrille af holbergske Figurer, En in *The King's Corps of Volunteers on Amager, (Episode from 1808) (Livjægerne paa Amager, (Episode fra 1808))* (Score no. 15), 371

Quadrille de fête (Fest Quadrille) (22.5.1840), 60

'*Recit de Victor*' in *Soldier and Peasant (Soldat og Bonde)*, 41

Redowa, La (Albert, 17.5.1847), 104

Reel (16.8.–18.8.1849), 129

'*Reel*' in *Arcona* (Act I, scene 3, score no. 4–5), 407

Reel in *A Folk Tale (Et Folkesagn)* (Act I, score no. 2), 169

Reel in *The King's Corps of Volunteers on Amager, (Episode from 1808) (Livjægerne paa Amager, (Episode fra 1808))* (Score no. 14), 371

Reel in *The Mountain Hut, or Twenty Years (Fjeldstuen eller Tyve Aar)* (First tableau/Act I, scene 7/score no. 8), 311

Reel in *A New Divertissement (after Holberg's indications) as intermezzo in The Healing Spring (Intermedium, Et nyt Divertissement (efter Holbergs Opgave) i Kildereisen)* (22.5.1859), 237

Reel in *La Sylphide (Sylphiden)*, 35

'*Riberhus March*' in *Waldemar* (Act II, score no. '17½'), 164

Roccoco Quadrille in *Pontemolle (An Artists' Party in Rome) (Pontemolle, (Et Kunstnergilde i Rom))* (2nd tableau, score no. 13), 317

'*Romanesca, La,*' in *The Kermesse in Brüges, or The Three Gifts (Kermessen i Brügge eller: De tre Gaver)*, 144

'*Romanesca, La, fameux air de danse du seizième siècle*', 144

Ronde des paysans in *Waldemar* (Act I, 29.5.1867), 326

Rosenborg Quadrille (16.8.1849–18.8.1849), 129

Russian [Dance] *(Russisk)* in *The Danes in China (De Danske i China)* (28.1.1842, 27.2.1843, 26.2.1865), 71, 80, 307

Russian Dance in *The Isle of Phantasy (Phantasiens Øe)* (Act I, score no. 8), 45

Russian-Greek National Quadrille (National=Quadrille, (russisk=nygræsk)) (10.2.1870), 361

Russian-Greek National Quadrille (National=Quadrille, russisk=nygræsk) in '*Bouquet Royal*', *Divertissement* (27.1.1870), 358

Russian National Dance (Russisk National-dands) (1.6.1838), 44

Russian National Quadrille (Russisk National-Quadrille) (26.12.1866), 323

Sacred Temple Dance (Hellige Tempeldandse) in *Zulma, or The Crystal Palace (Zulma eller: Krystalpaladset)* (Act I, score no. 3), 150

Saltarello in *The Festival in Albano (Festen i Albano* (1.1.1869), 343

Saltarello in *The Flower Festival in Genzano (Blomsterfesten i Genzano)*, 423

Saltarello in *The Heart on Trial (Hjærtet paa Prøve)* (uncredited, 16.9.1860), 252

'*Saltarello*' in *Pontemolle (An Artists' Party in Rome) (Pontemolle, (Et Kunstnergilde i Rom))* (2nd tableau, score no. 10), 317

Saltarello in *The Wedding at Lake Como (Brylluppet ved Como=Søen)* (Act III, score no. 13), 123

Scandinavian Quadrille (Scandinavisk Quadrille) (6.2.1870), 360

Scandinavian Quadrille (Scandinavisk Quadrille) in '*Bouquet Royal*', *Divertissement* (27.1.1870), 358

'*Scène et Chœur*' in *Faust* (Act V, score no. 28, 16.3.1873), 390

Scène et Ronde Bohémienne in *L'Etoile du Nord (Der Nordstern)* (Act I, score no. 6), 185

'*Scene og Pas de deux af Balletten Toreadoren*' (9.1.1842), 71

'*Schytternes Dands*' in *Iphigénie en Tauride (Iphigenia paa Tauris)* (Act II, scene 4, score nos. 8–10), 400

Scottish Reel (Skotsk Reel) in *In Memory of Weyse, Epilogue with Tableaux (Weyses Minde, Efterspil med Tableauer)* (Scene 5, score no. 10), 398

Seguedilla (uncredited) (20.12.1874), 404 (3.10.1862), 280

Seguidilla, La in *Die verwandelten Weiber (Le Diable à quatre)* (P. Taglioni, 6.10.1856), 191

Seguidilla in *The Guerilla Band (Guerilla-banden)*, 24

Seguedilla, La (after Taglioni) (efter Taglioni) in *La Ventana, Ballet Divertissement (Ballet-divertissement)* (6.10.1856), 192

Seguedilla, Changing Dance in Spanish style (Vexeldands i spansk Stil) (23.8.1868 and 1.9.1868), 337

Seguedilla, La (d'après Taglioni.) (6.10.1856), 192

Seguidille (Spanish Dance) (Spansk Dans) (1.6.1860), 251

'*Seguedille, La*' *(Spanish National Dance) (spansk Nationaldands)* (18.6.1865), 308

'*Serieux [Pas de] 2/Distributions des Prix*' in *La Vestale* (P. Gardel), 30

Series of three performances with a (not yet identified) repertory of individual pas and dances at Malmö's Theatre, A (May 1840), 59

Serieux solo danced by Miss Fjeldsted, composed for her by Ballet Master Albert in Paris

(Serieux solo dandses af Jfr. Fjeldsted, componeret for hende af Balletmester Albert i Paris) (9.1.1844), 84

Shield Dance *(Vaabendands)* in *Waldemar*, 34, 321

Shield Dance *(Vaabendands)* in *Waldemar* (Act II, score no. '19', 21.11.1866), 321

'Skotske Sextour, Den' in *The Masquerade (Maskeraden)* (11.2.1859), 230

Slowanka in *The Kermesse in Brüges, or The Three Gifts (Kermessen i Brügge eller: De tre Gaver)* (Act I, score no. '2[A]'), 312

Slowanka in *In the Carpathians (I Karpatherne)* (Act III, score no. 28), 196

Solo in *'Divertissement from The Toreador' ('Divertissement af Toréadoren')* (11.6.1852), 154

Solo in *The Festival in Albano (Festen i Albano)* (14.1.1858), 213

Solo in *Die Gazelle von Bassora (Abdallah)* (Act II, score no. 9), 181

Solo in *Die Gazelle von Bassora (Abdallah)* (P. Borri, Act III, score no. 16), 181

Solo in *In Memory of Weyse, Epilogue with Tableaux (Weyses Minde, Efterspil med Tableauer)* (Scene 5, score no. 8), 398

Solo in *Napoli, oder: Der Fischer und seine Braut (Napoli eller Fiskeren og hans Brud)* (31.1.1856), 187

Solo in *La Ventana, Ballet Divertissement (Balletdivertissement)* (6.10.1856), 191

Solo *(danced by Carlotta Grisi in the ballet Le Diable à quatre) (dandset af Carlotta Grisi i Balletten Le Diable à quatre)* (17.5.1847), 103

'Solo for Miss Fjeldsted' *('Solo til Jf. Fjeldsted')* (6.10.1848), 118

Solo *(Incorporated) (Solo (indlagt))* in *The Festival in Albano (Festen i Albano)* (uncredited, 17.5.1847), 103

Solo variation in *Undine* (between Act III and IV), 76

'som Pas de deux i Søvngængersken', 40

Souvenir de Taglioni, Pas de deux (uncredited, 20.1.1864), 300

Souvenir de Taglioni, Pas de deux, composed by Mr. Court Ballet Master Bournonville (componeret af Hr. Hofballetmester Bournonville) (19.9.1864), 306

'Souvenir de Taglioni./Pas de deux/pour/Mlles Agnes & Christine Healey' (20.1.1864), 300

'Spanisch' in *Don Quixote* (P. Taglioni/G. Golinelli), 176

Spanish Dance in *Don César de Bazan (Don Cæsar de Bazan)* (P. Larcher/Bournonville), 120

Spanish Dance *(Spansk dans)* in *Il Trovatore (Trubaduren)* (Act III, 20.11.1862), 282

Spanish National Dance *(Spansk Nationaldans)* in *Il Trovatore (Troubadouren)* (Act III, 10.9.1865), 308

Spring Dance in *The Wedding Festival in Hardanger (Brudefärden i Hardanger)* (Act II, score no. 16, 22.6.1857), 202

'Spring Dance' *(after Norwegian motifs) from the ballet 'Old Memories' ('Springdands' (efter norske Motiver) af Balletten 'Gamle Minder')* (22.6.1852), 155

Styrian Dance *(Steirisk Dands)* (uncredited)

('Styrian Dance', 11.6.1865), 83 (1.10.1843, 15.10.1857), 82, 204

Styrian Dance *(Steirisk Dands)* in *Le Domino Noir (Eventyret paa Maskeraden eller Den sorte Domino)* (uncredited, 29.1.1839), 47, 51

Styrian National Dance, The *(den steiriske Nationaldands/Den Steiriske Nationaldands)* (uncredited, 21.10.1839, 29.7.1840), 55, 61

Styrian National Dance, The *(Den Steijermarkska Nationaldansen)* (uncredited, 5.7.1839), 53

'Styrian National Dance' composed by Mr. Bournonville *('Steyrisk Nationaldands' componeret af Hr. Bournonville')* (2.7.1852), 156

Styrian National Dance, The *(Den Steijermarkska Nationaldansen)* in *The Tyroleans, or: The Mischevous Boy* (uncredited, 8.6.1839), 51

Styrian Peasant Dance by Ballet-master Perrot *(Steyersk Bondedands af Balletmester Perrot)* (J. Perrot, 27.6.1847), 108

'Styrians, The, National Pas de deux' *('Steiermarken, Pas de deux National')* (2.5.1847), 102

Sylphides, Les Contredanses nouvelles *(Sylphiderne. Nye Françaiser)*, 40

Tableau in *The New Penelope, or The Spring Festival in Athens (Den nye Penelope eller Foraarsfesten i Athenen)*, 100

Tanz der Lehrbuben in *Die Meistersinger von Nürnberg (Mestersangerne i Nürnberg)* (Act III, scene 5, score no. 35), 383

'Tanz' in *La Juive (Die Jüdin)* (Act I, scene 7), 184

'Tarantella, La' (uncredited, 17.5.1860), 250

'Tarantella' in *Cort Adeler in Venice (Cort Adeler i Venedig)* (Act I, scene 5, score no. 5), 356

Tarantella in *Das Fest in Albano (Festen i Albano)* (15.7.1854), 174

Tarantella in *The Festival in Albano (Festen i Albano)* (Score no. 10), 213

Tarantella in *Gioacchino* (Act IV, score no. 14), 88, 316

Tarantella in *Napoli or The Fisher and His Bride (Napoli eller Fiskeren og hans Brud)* (Act III, score no. 3), 72, 156

Tarantella in *La Muette de Portici (Den Stumme i Portici)* (Act III), 112, 271

Tarantella in *Paul et Virginie* (P. Gardel), 16

Tarantella in *Paul et Virginie (Paul og Virginie)*, 16

Tarantella in *Princess Isabella, or Three Nights at the Court (Prindsesse Isabella eller Tre Aftener ved Hoffet)*, 13

Tarantella in *Le Sicilien ou l'Amour peintre* (A. Petit), 14, 16

Tarantella/af Balletten/Napoli (2.7.1852), 156

'Tarantella' *(from the ballet Napoli (af Balletten Napoli)* (11.6.1865), 308

'Tarantella Napoletana', 96

'Tarantella Neapolitana, La' (uncredited, 2.7.1847), 109

Tarantella Napoletana (uncredited, 12.5.1846 and 2.7.1846), 96, 97

Tarantella Napolitana, Charactercance from The

Festival in Albano *(Characteerdands af Festen i Albano)* (10.8.1840), 63

Tarantella=Napolitana in *Tableau with Song and Dance (Tableau med Sang og Dands)* (uncredited, 1.3.1859), 230

Tarantelle in *Les Pages du Duc de Vendôme (Hertugen af Vendômes Pager)*, 15

'Tempo di marcia' in *Arcona* (Act I, scene 3, score nos. 4–5), 407

Teresina in *Napoli, or The Fisherman and His Bride (Napoli eller Fiskeren og hand Brud)* (12.2.1848), 114

'Terzett' in *Die Fee und der Ritter* (Arm. Vestris), 13

Three performances at Drammen's Theatre (16.7.–22.7.1852), 157

Tøndebaands-Dands in *The King's Corps of Volunteers on Amager, (Episode from 1808) (Livjægerne paa Amager, (Episode fra 1808))* (Score no. 11), 125, 371

Torch Dance *(Fakkeldands)* in *The Childhood of Erik Menved (Erik Menveds Barndom)*, 79

Torch Dance *(Fakkeldands)* in *Little Kirsten (Liden Kirsten)* (Score no. 9), 113

Torch Dance *(Fakkeldands)* in *Waldemar* (Act II), 164 (Act II, score no. '17½', 19.10.1853), 164 (Act II, score no. '20 a', 21.11.1866), 321

'Trollpolska' in *The Bewitched (Den Bjergtagne/Den Bergtagna)* (Act I, score no. 6),

Trolls' Gallop *(Trolde Galop)* in *A Folk Tale (Et Folkesagn)* (Act II, score no. 13), 169

Two performances at Frederikshald's Theatre (25.7.–27.7.1852), 158

Tyrolean Polka composed by Mr. Bournonville *(Tyroler=Polka componeret af Hr. Bournonville)* (15.5.1849), 128

'Tyrolerne (med nÿe Dandse)', 84

Vaabendands in *The New Penelope, or The Spring Festival in Athens (Den nye Penelope eller Foraarsfesten i Athenen)*, 100

'Valhalla Marsch' in *The Valkyrie (Valkyrien)* (Act I, score no. 2), 262

Valse bachique in *The Isle of Phantasy (Phantasiens Øe)*, 45

'Valse de la Capricieuse' in *The King's Corps of Volunteers on Amager, (Episode from 1808) (Livjægerne paa Amager, (Episode fra 1808))* (Score no. 15), 371

'Valse et Chœur' in *Faust* (C. Gounod, Act I, score no. 9), 390, 277

Varsovienne *(Varsoviana)*, 164

'Vierlaender Dands' (25.6.1847), 107

'Vierländerne Hamborger Dands' (24.1.1847), 99

Vierländers, (Hamborger Waltz), The *(Vierländerne, (Hamborger-Vals))* (16.12.1846), 99

Vierländers, Hamburg Dance, The *(Vierländerne, (Hamburger-Dans))* (24.1.1847), 99 (28.5.1847), 104

Vierländers, Scenic Character Dance, The *(Vierländerne, scenisk Charakteerdands)* (uncredited, 25.6.1847), 107

Waltz in *A Fairy Tale in Pictures (Et Eventyr i Billeder)* (Act I, scene 5, score no. 8), 382

Waltz in *L'Etoile du Nord (Der Nordstern)* (Act II, score no. 10), 185

Waltz (or *Tyrolienne*) in *La Fiancée (Bruden)*, 165

Waltz in *La Juive (Die Jüdin/Jødinden)*
(Act I, score no. 6), 183
(Act I, score no. 6, 4.1.1869), 344

Waltz in *Kirsten Piil* (Act I, score no. 3), 90

Waltz (or *Allemande*) in *The Nix (Nøkken)*, 160

Weavers Dance, The (Væverdandsen) in *Arcona*
(Act I, scene 3, score no. 6), 407

Wedding Dance in *Le Postillon du Lonjumeau
(Postillonen i Lonjumeau)* (Act I, score no. 1, 25.9.1873), 395

Zapatéado, El, in *The Toreador (Toréadoren)*
(Act I, score no. 2), 65

'Zémire et Azor/Pas de 4./ferdinand' in *Zémire et Azore* (A. Deshayes), 16

Zigeuner-Tanz in *Die Huguenotten*
(25.10.1855), 185

'2.de Pas à donner/le Pas de Quatre/de Mr Guerra à donner icï' in *Les Mohicans* (A. Guerra), 47

'Zrza's Benefice' (8.2.1845), 89

Operas, operettas, singspiels, vaudevilles, plays, ballades, romances, intermediums, and recited prologues and epilogues

Abu Hassan, 206

Act II of Gluck's opera 'Orphée et Euridice' (2den Act af Glucks Opera Orpheus. (Underverdenen. Elysium.)) (10.2.1846), 95

Act II of 'Orphée et Euridice' for Alto, Chorus and Orchestra (2den Akt af 'Orpheus og Eurydice' for Alt solo, Chor og Orchester) (8.11.1870 and 31.1.1871), 368, 370

Adlers Horst, Des (Ørnens Rede), 206

Adolphe et Clara, ou les deux Prisonniers (Adolph og Clara eller De to Arrestanter), 21

Africaine, L', 315

After Fifty Years (Efter femtio år), 267

Aladin, ou La Lampe merveilleuse, 7

Aladdin, or The Magic Lantern (Aladdin eller den forundelige Lampe), 49

Alcade de la Véga, L' (Alcalden af Vega), 207

Alessandro Stradella (Stradella), 206

Alfred, 150

Aline, Reine de Golconde, 126

Almaviva o sia l'inutile precauzione/Il Barbiere di Siviglia (Barberen i Sevilla), 209, 214

Amor contrastato, L', 126

Amore Artigiano, L'/Liebe unter den Handwerksleuten, Die (De forliebte Haandværksfolk), 206

Anna Bolena, 210

Armide, 121

Artists' Life (Kunstnerliv), 121

At Sunset (I Solnedgången/Naar Solen gaar ned), 273

Avare, L' (Den Girige), 286

Barbiere di Sevilla, Il, 38

Belle au bois dormant, 26

Benefactor's Testament, A, (En Arfs- och Kärleksfråga/En Velgjörers Testamente), 273

Bewitched, The (Den Bjergtagne/Den Bergtagna), 416

Blossom of Happiness, The (Lykkens Blomst), 89

Bohemian Girl, The (Zigeunerinden), 209

Brigands' Castle, The (Røverborgen), 205, 244

Calife de Bagdad, Le (Califen af Bagdad), 207

Capitaine de vaisseau, Le, ou le Salamandre (Fregattkaptenen eller 'Salamandern'), 53

Caprice, The (Capricen), 224

Capuleti ed i Montecchi, I (Familierne Montecchi og Capulet), 111, 125, 209, 244

Carl XII (Karl den tolfte), 293

Cavern of Ludlam, The (Ludlams Hule), 257, 380, 398

Cendrillon (Cendrillon eller Den lille grønne Sko), 39, 41, 190, 207

Chef-d'œuvre inconnu, Le (Törne och Lager), 297

Cheval de Bronze, Le (Prindsen af China/ Broncehesten), 45, 208, 370, 391

Childbed Room, The, (Barselstuen), 120

China Travellers, The (Chinafarerne), 32, 45, 380

Cigüe, La (Giftbägaren), 267

Clari, or The Maid of Milan, 150

Clemenza di Tito, La (Titus), 206, 252

Clochette, La, ou Le Diable Page (Alfen som Page), 208

Colporteur, Le, ou L'Enfant du Bucheron (Skovhuggerens Sön), 207

Comedy of Errors (Förvexlingarne), 268

Comte Ory, Le, 38, 144

Concert à la cour, Le, ou La Débutante (Hof-Concerten eller Debutaninden), 208

Contes de la Reine de Navarre, Les, ou la Revanche de Pavie (En Saga af Drottningen af Navarra/Dronning Marguerites Noveller), 280

Cor, Le, Ballade (16.12.1832), 22

Cora, ou l'Esclavage (Cora eller Slafveriet), 268

Corpus Kirsti (Korp=Kirsti), 295

Correggio, 427

Corsican, The (Korsikaneren), 391

Cup of Welcome, A, (Ett Hemkomstöl), 202

Cyprianus, 240

Czaar und Zimmermann (Czaren og Tømmermanden), 98, 206, 212

Dame Blanche, La (Den Hvide Dame Hvita Frun på Slottet Avenel), 139, 223, 207, 298, 338, 405

Daniel Hjort, 299

Dannebrog, The, or The Dream of King Volmer (Dannebrog eller Kong Volmers Drøm), 375

Dawn, Prologue to the ballet Waldemar (Dæmring, Forspil til Balletten Waldemar), 384

Day Waxes! (Dagen gryr!), 284

Death of Balder, The (Balder's Død), 121

Demoiselle à marier, La, ou La Première Entrevue (Friaran kommer/Första mötet), 296

Deportees, The (De Deporterade), 306

Deux Forçats, Les, ou La meunière du Puy-de-Dôme (De to Galejslaver eller Møllen ved St. Aldervon), 134

Deux Journées, Les, ou Le Porteur d'eau (De to Dage eller Flygtningene/Wattendragaren), 207, 255, 296, 365

Deux Mots, ou Une Nuit dans la forêt (To Ord eller Natten i Skoven), 129

Devin du village, Le, 5, 13, 42, 414

Diamantkreuz, Das (Diamantkorset), 101

Diamants de la couronne, Les (Kronjuvelerna)
(18.11.1861), 266
(10.10.1868), 339

Dido and Aenea, 269

Dieu et la bayadère, Le, ou La Courtisane amoureuse (Brama och Bajaderen), 287

Dieu et la bayadère, Le, ou La Courtisane amoureuse (Brama og Bayadèren), 67, 109, 132, 238, 379

Dieu et la bayadère, Le, ou La Courtisane amoureuse (Brama og Bayadèren) (Act I, 3.6.1873), 394

Dieu et la bayadère, Le, ou La Courtisane amoureuse (Liebende Bayadère oder Der Gott und die Bayadere, Die), 81

Dissoluto Punito, Il, ossia il Don Giovanni (Don Juan), 117, 160, 205, 217, 359

Doktor und Apotheker, Der (Apothekeren og Doktoren), 206

Domino noir, Le (Eventyret paa Maskeraden eller Den sorte Domino/Den sorte Domino), 47, 208, 214, 236

Don César de Bazan, 101, 163

Don César de Bazan (Don Cæsar de Bazan), 120

Donna del Lago, La (Pigen ved Söen), 209

Dragons de Villars, Les (Villars' Dragoner)
(4.5.1863), 289, 365, 367

Earl Hakon (Hakon Jarl), 43

Elf Maiden, The (Elverpigen), 329

Elves, The (Alferne), 254, 369

Elisir d'amore, L', 209, 240, 386

Elisir d'amore, L' (Elskovsdrikken), 209, 240, 386

Elves' Hill, The (Elverhøi), 58, 90, 97, 119

Entführung aus dem Serail, Die (Bortførelsen af Seraillet), 206, 236

'Epilogue' ('Epilog'), 157, 203

Episode, An, (En Episode), 158

Erik and Abel (Erik og Abel), 31

Ernani, 295, 308

Ernani (Hernani), 210

Estrella de Soria, 275

Etoile du Nord, L' (Der Nordstern), 185

Exil' L, 418

Fairy Tale in The Rosenborg Gardens, A, (Et Eventyr i Rosenborg Have), 398

Familie, Eine (En Familj), 286

Family Dispute, A, or The Strange Year (Familietvist eller Det mærkværdige Aar), 167

Faruk, 205, 398

Faust (J. W. v. Goethe), 20

Faust (C. Gounod), 277, 390

Faux Bonhommes, Les (Så kallade Hedersmän), 290

Favorite, La (Leonora), 302

Feast at Kenilworth, The (Festen paa Kenilworth), 205, 398

Feast of May, The (Maigildet), 33

Fechter von Ravenna, Der (Fäktaran från Ravenna), 281

Federigo, 116

Feriegæsterne, 427

Fernand Cortez, ou la Conquête du Mexique, 365

Fernand Cortez, ou la Conquête du Mexique (Fernando Cortez eller Mexikos Indtagelse), 365

Feuerprobe, Die (Ildprøven), 120

Fiancée, La (Bruden), 165, 176, 208, 220, 396

Fidelio, oder Die ehelich Liebe (Fidelio), 206, 225, 369

Figlia del regimento, La (Regimentets Datter), 122

Fille du régiment, La (Regimentets Datter), 209, 214, 238, 415

Fiorella, 43

Fishermen, The (Fiskerne), 121

Flickarnas Ja, 266

Floribella, 398

Fortress of the Arts (Kunstens Dannevirke), 120

Fourberies de Scapin, Les (Scapins Skälm-stycken), 292

Fra-Diavolo, ou l'Hôtellerie de Terracine (Fra Diavolo eller Värdshuset i Terracina), 208, 211, 276

Freischütz, Der (Jægerbruden), 206, 218, 347

Freyschutz, Le, 126

Gamin de Paris, Le (Pariser-Pojken), 288

Ganaches, Les, 283

Gazza Ladra, La, 38

Gioacchino, 88, 316

Gioventú di Enrico V, La (Henrik den Femtes Ungdom), 18

Gipsy, The (Zigeunaren), 273

Giulietta e Romeo, 111

Gorm the Old (Gorm den gamle), 33

Guerilla Band, The (Guerillabanden), 24

Gurre (Evening prospect) (Gurre (Aftenprospect)) (28.3.1842), 71

Gurre, Romance with Chorus (Romance med Chor) (29.5.1867), 326

Gustav III (Gustav den Tredie), 124

Gustave III, ou Le Bal Masqué, 70, 77, 81

Guillaume Tell (Wilhelm Tell), 20, 51, 76, 209, 341, 395, 415

Gustaf Wasa, 285

Hagbarth and Signe (Hagbarth og Signe), 5, 131

Hakon Jarl, 121

Hamlet, Prince of Denmark (Hamlet, Prins af Danmark), 276

Hans Heiling, 206, 216, 294, 340

Harlequin's Invasion, or a Christmas gamble, 150

Harvest Festival, The (Høstgildet), 45, 58, 90

Healing Spring, The (Kildereisen), 60, 237

Heart on Trial, The (Hjærtet paa Prøve), 252

Héléna, 206

Hermann von Unna, 30, 121

Heure de mariage, Une, (En Times Ægteskab), 207

Hochzeit des Figaro, Die (Figaros Bryllyp), 83, 126, 206, 219, 253, 384

Homecoming, The (Hiemkomsten), 41

Homme de rien, Un, (Richard Sheridan), 300

Horace et Lydie, Une ode d'Horace (Horatius och Lydia), 295

Hothouse Flowers (Blommor i drifbänk/ Drivhusplanter), 276, 306

House of Svend Dyring, The (Svend Durings Huus), 141

Huguenots, Les (Die Hugenotten), 85, 184

Huguenots, Les (Hugenotterne), 85, 208, 348, 379

Idea for a Prologue to The Restless (Idée til et Forspil [til] Den Stundesløse), 383

Intrigue aux Fenêtres, L' (Kærlighedsintriguen i Vinduerne), 207

Iphigenia in Aulis (Ifigenia i Aulis) (30.4.1871), 375

Iphigenia in Aulis (Iphigenia i Aulis) (27.4.1861), 259, 354

Iphigénie en Tauride (Iphigenia paa Tauris) (28.4.1874), 400

Jacob von Tyboe, 134

Jean, 32

Jean de Paris (Johan fra Paris), 207, 353

Jeannot et Colin (Jeannot og Colin eller Fosterbrødrene), 8, 207

Jérôme le porteur de chaise (Portechaisebäraren), 266

Jeu de l' Amour et du hasard, Le (Kärlekens Försyn), 284

Jeunesse d'Henry V, La (Henrik den femtes Ungdom), 45

Joconde, ou Les Coureurs d'Aventures (Joconde eller Frierne paa Eventyr), 207

Joseph (Joseph og hans Brødre i Ægypten/Joseph i Egypten), 206, 221, 299

Juive, La (Judinnan/Die Jüdin/Jødinden), 183, 208, 210, 292, 344, 367

King on Fuurland, The (Kongen paa Fuurland), 195

King's Goddaughter, The (Konungens gud-dotter), 283

Late is Not Too Late (Seent er ikke forsilde), 331

Léon, ou Le Château de Monténero (Slottet Montenero), 142, 207

Lestocq (Lestocq eller Stats=Intrigen), 208

Liebende Bayadère oder Der Gott und die Bayadere, Die (Le Dieu et La Bayadère, ou La Courtisane amoureuse), 25, 57, 81, 287

Linda di Chamounix (Linda af Chamounÿ), 210

Liten Demon, En, 268

Little Kirsten (Liden Kirsten), 113, 205, 221, 348

Little Treasure, The (La Joie de la maison/En liten Skatt/Gertrude eller En lille Skat), 268

Lodoiska, 207

Lohengrin, 361

Louise de Lignerolles, 50

Lucia di Lammermoor, 209–11

Lucia di Lammermoor (Lucia af Lammermoor/ Lucie eller Bruden från Lammermoor), 209, 210, 278

Lucrezia Borgia, 209, 214, 232, 238, 253

Ludovic, 214, 231

Luisa Miller, 149

Lulu, 205, 214

Lustigen Weiber von Windsor, Die (De lystige Koner i Windsor), 209, 327

Ma Tante Aurore ou Le Roman impromtu/Ma Tante Aurore (Tante Aurora), 207

Macbeth, 398

Maçon, Le (Muurmesteren), 113, 342

Magicienne, La, 392

Mail Robbers, The (Poströfvarne), 287

Maison sans enfants, La (Ett Barnlöst Hem), 298

Mari à la campagne, Le (Den gifta Mannen i staden och på landet), 249

Mariotta, 205

Marquis de Villemer, Le, 303

Marshal Stig (Marsk Stig), 136

Martha oder Der Markt zu Richmond (Martha eller Markedet i Richmond), 206, 214, 250

Mary Stuart in Scotland (Maria Stuart i Skotland) (29.3.1867), 324 *(2.9.1867)*, 327

Masquerade, The (Maskeraden), 133, 230, 341

Matrimonio Segreto, Il (Det hemmelige Ægte-skab), 243, 397

Médecin malgré lui, Le (Läkaren mot sin Vilja), 297

Meistersinger von Nürnberg, Die (Mestersang-erne i Nürnberg), 383

Midsommernatsdröm, En, 426

Midsummer Night's Dream, A, (En Skjærsommer-natsdrøm), 426

Moïse, 82

Molinara, La, 126

Montjoye, 303

Mosè in Egitto (Moses), 82, 209

Mousquetaires de la Reine, Les (Dronningens Livgarde), 119, 208

Muette de Portici, La (Den Stumma från Portici/ Den Stumme i Portici), 25, 112, 140, 207, 269, 271

Mulatto, The (Mulatten), 115

Night in the Mountains, A, (En Nat mellem Fjeldene), 388

Nix, The (Nøkken), 160

Norma, 119, 209, 214, 245, 311

Norns, The (Nornerne) in *The Lay of Thrym (Thrymsqviden)*, 331, 335

Nouveau Seigneur de village, Le (Den nya Egendomsherrn/Den nye Jordegodseier), 207, 214, 266, 268

Nozze di Figaro, Le, 74

Oberon, or The Elf King's Oath (Oberon), 206, 219, 238, 377

On ne badinez pas avec l'amour (Lek ej med kärleken), 278

Opéra-comique, L' (Operetten), 207

Order of the Amaranth, The (Amarather-Orden), 301

Oriflamme, L', 26–7

Orphée at the tomb of Euridice, Scene for Alto, Chorus and Orchestra (Orpheus ved Eurydices Grav, Scene for Alt solo, Chor og Orchester) (26.1.1860), 243

Orphée et Euridice, 368

Orphée et Euridice (Orpheus), 95

Otello, 205

Otello ossia Il Moro di Venezia (Othello), 209

Papillonne, La (Fjärilsfebern), 279

Pascha's Daughter, The (Paschaens Datter), 351

Paul Pry, 150

Petit Chaperon rouge, Le (Den lille Rødhætte), 159, 176, 207, 256, 389

Philomèle, Romance (25.10.1829), 13

Plan for an opera repertory for the 1857–58 and 1858–59 seasons, 205

Plan for a repertory at Stockholm's Royal Theatre in September 1861 (Repertoire for Stockholms Theater i September 1861) (24.7.1861), 260

Plan for a repertory at Stockholm's Royal Theatre from 28.8. to 15.9.1862 (1.8.1862), 278

Plan for a repertory of operas and ballets for the 1870–71 season (Udkast til en Virksomheds-plan for Opera og Ballet i Theater=Saisonen 1870–71) (1.8.1870), 365

Plan for a repertory of operas in the months of

March, April and May 1859 (Plan til Operaens Virksomhed i Martz, April og Mai 1859) (20.1.1858), 214

Plan for a vaudeville (Planen til en Vaudeville) (29.3.1870), 361

Pluie et le beau temps, La (Regn och Solsken), 270

Postillon de Lonjumeau, Le (Postillonen i Lonjumeau), 40, 50, 54, 208, 395

Pré aux clercs, le (Klerkevænget), 28–9, 208

Preciosa, 146

Preciosa (Préciosa), 271

Princess Isabella, or Three Nights at the Court (Prindsesse Isabella eller Tre Aftener ved Hoffet), 13

Projets de ma tante, Les (Min tants planer), 280

Prophecy of Tycho Brahe, The (Tycho Brahes Spaadom), 398

Prophète, Le, 205, 421

Prophète, Le (Profeten), 217, 288

Puritani di Scozia, I/Puritani ed i Cavalieri, I (Puritanerne), 209, 291

Raven, The (Ravnen eller Broderprøven), 22, 150, 391

Recommendation notes concerning the projected (re)stagings of several plays at Stockholm's Royal Theatre (31.10.1861), 266

Restless, The (Den Stundeslöse), 383

Retour de Pierre, Le, Romance (16.12.1836), 22

Richard II (Konung Richard den Andre), 292

Robert le Diable, 72

Robert le Diable (Robert af Normandie/Robert af Normandiet/Robert der Teufel), 114, 180, 208, 284, 388

Roman d'Elvire, Le (Drottning Elviras Saga), 293, 304

Romeo and Juliet (Romeo og Julie), 149

Rosa and Rosita (Rosa och Rosita/Rosa og Rosita), 288

Rossignol, Le, 26, 28

Rustic Love (Kjærlighed paa Landet), 21

St. Olave's Day (Sanct Olafs Dag), 120

St. Olave, The Battle at Stiklestad (Olaf den Hellige, Slaget ved Stiklestad), 43, 260

Scenes from 'Orphée et Euridice' for Alto, Chorus and Orchestra (Scener af 'Orpheus og Eurydice' for Alt solo, Chor og Orchester) (25.5.1859), 237

Seven Sleepers' Day, The (Syvsoverdag), 61

Siège de Corinthe, Le, 380

Siri Brahe och Johan Gyllenstjerna, 290

Slanderer, The (Smädeskrifvaren, eller: Vänner och Ovänner/Smædeskriveren eller Talentet paa Afvej), 274, 283

Sleeping-Draught, The (Sovedrikken), 45, 121, 205, 213, 397

Sommernachtstraum, Ein, 426

Sonnambula, La (Søvngængersken), 209

Soprano, The (Dramatic motif for a new Italian aria) (Sangerinden, (dramatisk Motiv for en ny Italiensk Arie)), 69

Stratonice, 365

Sunday on Amager, A, (En Søndag paa Amager), 125, 371

Sunset. The final Days of Gustaf I (Solen sjunker. Gustaf I:s sista dagar), 285

Tancredi, 380

Tannhäuser und der Sängerkrieg auf der Wartburg (Tannhäuser og Sangerkrigen paa Wartburg), 405

Tartuffe, 381

Télégramme, Le (Telegrammet), 289

Templer und Die Jüdin, Der (Tempelherren og Jødinden), 206, 365, 374

Ticket of Leave Man, The, 296

Töchter des Cid, Die (Cids döttrar), 270

Tonnelier, Le (Bødkeren), 213

Torkel Knutson, 269

Train du minuit, Le (Goda exempel), 294

Treasure of Claus Rigmand, The (Claus Rigmands Skat), 231

Trésor supposé, ou Le Danger d'écouter aux portes, Le (Skatten eller Staa ikke paa Lur), 206, 371

Trine-Brother of Damascus, The (Trillingbrødrene fra Damask), 49

Trovatore, Il (Troubadouren/Trubaduren), 210, 282, 308

Turco in Italia, Il (Turken i Italien), 104

Undine, 76

Unerreichbare, Das (Det Uopnaaelige), 354

Uthal, 102

Valgerda, 377

Vestale, La, 16, 30

Vida es Sueno, La (Lifvet en Dröm), 290

Voitures versées, Les/Le Séducteur en Voyage, ou LesVoitures versées (De væltede Vogne), 207

Wedding at Lake Como, The (Brylluppet ved Como=Søen), 123, 205

Wedding at Ulfåsa, The (Brylluppet paa Ulfbjerg/Bröllopet på Ulfåsa), 316

Wedding of the Dryad, The, Mythological Poem for Solo voices, Chorus and Orchestra (Dryadens Bryllup, mythologisk Digt for Solostemmer, Chor og Orchester), 239

William Shakespeare. Epilogue and Apotheosis (Efterspil: Oberon og Titannia [...] Apotheose: Britannia bekrandser Shakspeare [sic], der staaer omringet af sine Digterværker.'), 215

Yelva, ou L'Orpheline Russe (Yelva), 31, 269

Youth and Folly, or Trick upon Trick (Ungdom og Galskab eller List over List), 205, 347, 371

Zampa, ou La Fiancée de Marbre (Zampa eller Marmorbruden), 19, 144

Zauberflöte, Die (Trylleføiten), 205, 345

Translations into Danish of French texts for operas, vaudevilles, and plays

Act II of Gluck's opera 'Orphée et Euridice' (2den Act af Glucks Opera Orpheus. (Underverdenen. Elysium.)) (10.2.1846), 95

Act II of 'Orphée et Euridice' for Alto, Chorus and Orchestra (2den Akt af 'Orpheus og Eurydice' for Alt solo, Chor og Orchester) (8.11.1870 and 31.1.1871), 368, 370

Danish translation of the French text for Fidès' aria («Donnez donnez pour une pauvre âme») in Le Prophète (Oversættelse af Tiggerarien af Profeten) (7.2.1877), 421

Orphée at the tomb of Euridice, Scene for Alto, Chorus and Orchestra (Orpheus ved Eurydices Grav, Scene for Alt solo, Chor og Orchester) (26.1.1860), 243

Scenes from 'Orphée et Euridice' for Alto, Chorus and Orchestra (Scener af 'Orpheus og

Eurydice' for Alt solo, Chor og Orchester) (25.5.1859), 237

Dances and tableaux choreographed and taught for Royal festivities, court balls, and masked balls

Bridal Dance (Brudesang og Dands) projected for a ball at Stockholm's Royal Theatre to celebrate the nuptials of the Danish Princess Alexandra, and the Prince of Wales (3.3.1863), 286

Court Ball given in honour of the nuptials of the Danish Crown Prince Frederik and the Swedish Princess Louise Josephine Eugenie (12.8.1869), 350

Dances performed at a soirée given by the Royal Family (9.3.1834), 25

Eight dance lessons in social dances to the three children of the Princess of Wales (4.1.–1.2.1876), 415

Feast-Quadrille in honour of Count Wilhelm of Hessen's and Princess of Denmark, Countess Charlotte's Golden Anniversary (Fest-Quadrille i Anledning af [...] Landgreve Wilhelm af Hessens og [...] Landgrevinde Charlotte, født Prindsesse til Danmarks høie Guldbryllup) (10.11.1860), 255

Military Quadrille for the Royal Masked Ball (En Militair Quadrille for Hof=Masqueraden) (4.3.1862), 272

Idea for the Royal Wedding (En Idée til Formælingen) (1.12.1868), 342

Procession and two Quadrilles choreographed for the Royal Masked Ball given by Prince Frederik Wilhelm of Hessen (Et Optog, en Mousquetair=Quadrille, og en Polka Quadrille ved Maskeraden hos Prinds Frederik Wilhelm af Hessen) (28.2.1854), 166

Procession entitled 'Cortège de Quintin Durwards', and three Quadrilles named 'Mauresques', 'Polkeurs', and 'Rococo' (18.2.1846), 95

Procession of Personalities from the time of Christian IV (Optog af Personligheder fra Christian IV Tid), a Quadrille Noble (Polonaise, Contredanse), a Quadrille Hongrois (Entrée, Mazurque, Frischka), and a Quadrille Italien (Entrée, Valse figurée, Tarentelle) (10.3.1874), 399

Projected Dance (Dands) for the ball at The Casino Theatre on 9.11.1866 given on the occasion of the nuptials of Danish Princess Dagmar and the Russian Prince Alexander (8.11.1866), 321

Quadrille (7.9.1866), 319

Russian National Quadrille (Russisk National-Quadrille) (7.9.1866), 319

Tableaux created on the occasion of King Christian IX's birthday (Tableauer til Kongens Fødselsdag) (8.4.1876), 415

Tableaux vivants. Psyché. (uncredited, 26.11.1845), 93

Tableaux vivants. Représentés au palais royal d'Amalienborg (uncredited, 24.4.1844), 86

Tableaux vivants. Représentés au palais royal d'Amalienborg à l'occasion de la fête de S. A.

R. la Princesse Julie de Danemarck (uncredited, 18.2.1844), 85

Tableaux vivants. Les Saisons (uncredited, 26.11.1845), 94

Two Quadrilles (Quadriller) (7.9.1866), 319

Drama lessons, social or theatrical dances choreographed for and taught at private lessons

Dance lessons in social dance
  12 lessons (10.10.–21.11.1866), 320
  12 lessons (16.10.–3.12.1867), 329
  12 lessons (31.1.–30.3.1871), 370
  14 lessons (4.11.–19.12.1873), 395
  16 lessons (13.2.–12.4.1872), 382
  16 lessons (6.2.–12.3.1874), 397
  20 lessons (1.2.–1.4.1871), 370
  20 lessons (10.1.–1.4.1874), 397
  20 lessons (17.1.–7.4.1874), 397
  22 lessons (30.1.–12.4.1877), 421
  24 lessons (2.3.–28.4.1870), 361
  50 lessons (16.10.1872–26.4.1873), 386
New Quadrille, A (19.3.1854), 166
Quadrille, A, (En Quadrille) (21.2.1848), 115
Quadrille, A, (En Quadrille) (31.3.1869), 348
Quadrille, A, (En Quadrille) (4.1.1872), 382
Quadrille des Lanciers, Le: La Dorset, La Victoria, Les Moulinets, Les Visites, Les Lanciers (16.1.1860), 242
Quadrille noble (Ridder Quadrille) and *Tarantella* (16.2.1857), 196
Quadrille pour 12 Personnes (31.3.1869), 348
Private dance lessons
  11 lessons (4.8.–20.8.1870), 366
  12 lessons to 'Mlle Pira' (4.9.–16.9.1871), 378
  21 dance lessons for the Prince of Denmark (23.3.1861), 259
  30 lessons to M. Westberg (8.7.–18.8.1871), 377

37 lessons (17.6.–6.8.1869), 349
45 lessons (6.6.–20.8.1867), 326
48 lessons (11.6.–20.8.1872), 385
Private drama lessons
  33 lessons for the students of The Norwegian Drama School (14.5.–1.7.1853), 163
  36 lessons and a performance presentation of Bournonville's Swedish drama students (23.6.1857), 202
Two series of drama and dance lessons in Christiania, (Oslo) (11.5.–9.7.1852), 152

Organisation of and dances choreographed for major public and social events

Dances for an artists' carnival (Dandse ne til Kunsterkarnevallet) (10.3.1853), 162
Decoration and the illumination of the main hall in the Royal Shooting Gallery for the celebration of the 50th anniversary since the foundation of the King's Corps of Volunteers (Decorationen og Belysningen af Skydebanen ved Festen for Livjægercorpsets Stiftelsesdag 1801) (25.3.1851), 143
Decoration of a tent erected in the court yard of the Garnison's Hospital for a feast for the wounded soldiers (16.9.1849), 130
Decoration of the barracks for a welcome-feast given for the returning soldiers of the artillery (10.9.1849), 130
Fair in the Rosenborg Gardens on behalf of distressed Jutlanders (Markedet i Rosenborg Have til Fordel for de betrængte Jyder) including a Divertissement of three dances (16.8.1849–18.8.1849), 129
Feast in the Rosenborg Gardens given in honour of the nuptials of the Danish Crown Prince Frederik and the Swedish Princess Louise Josephine Eugenie (11.8.1869), 349
Four tableaux, entitled 'Peace', 'War', 'Victory',

and 'Memory', performed at the Temple of Memory as part of the fair in the Rosenborg Gardens (Fire Tableauer (Freden, Krigen, Seiren og Mindet) fremstillede i Mindets Tempel ved Høstfesten i Rosenborg Have) (30.8.1850–1.9.1850), 138
Masked Ball given on the occasion of the 50th performance of La Sylphide (Sylphiden) (6.1.1846), 94
Organisation of a concert for the charity health organisation 'Hygæa'
  (11.3.1848), 116
  (13.9.1851), 149
  (4.5.1852), 152
Organisation of the banquets and the decoration of the Riding School at Copenhagen's Christiansborg Palace (2.2.1851–20.2.1851), 142
Organisation of the celebrations of the Constitution day at the Hermitage (Grundlovsfesten paa Eremitagen) (5.6.1854), 171
Quadrille, A (27.3.1875), 406
Song and a dance written and choreographed for the celebration of the rentrée of the actress, Johanne Louise Heiberg (5.4.1853), 163
Tarantella for A Students Carnival (Tarentella til Studenternes Karneval) (7.3.1848), 115
Torch Dance, A, (En Fakkeldands) (22.1.1870), 357

Unidentified and unverified works

Bournonville's participation in Royal celebrations in his quality of court choreographer (1840–1846), 428
Unidentified dance, dating seemingly from the early 1860s, 428